CATALOGUE OF BOOKS

ADDED TO THE

LIBRARY OF CONGRESS,

FROM

DECEMBER 1, 1866, TO DECEMBER 1, 1867.

WASHINGTON:
GOVERNMENT PRINTING OFFICE.
1868.

NOTE.

The publication of the present annual catalogue has been delayed by two principal causes: 1. The large extent of the additions to the Library which it was deemed important to include in it; and, 2. The adoption of a full and accurate system of collation in describing the works catalogued.

Up to the year 1867, the annual accessions to the Library of Congress were embraced in pamphlet catalogues of 50 to 200 pages, printed in large type, and distributed near the commencement of each session of Congress. The very large additions embraced in the present volume rendered necessary the use of smaller type, and the adoption of a different form for the catalogue. It has been the purpose of the Librarian to include in it not only all the regular accessions of the past year, but also the chief portion of the books of the Smithsonian Library and of the Force collection, both of which are now incorporated with the Library of Congress. So great is the extent of these collections, (the titles embraced in the Force library alone being estimated at 55,000,) that it has been necessary to reserve for future catalogues the great body of pamphlets in both libraries, together with all the maps, manuscripts, and the larger portion of the *incunabula* of the Force collection.

LIBRARY OF CONGRESS, *March*, 1868.

LIST OF ABBREVIATIONS EMPLOYED.

pp. Pages.
l. Leaves.
p. l. Preliminary leaves.
pl. Plates.
n. p. No place of publication.
unp. Unpaged.
n. d. No date of publication.
anon. Anonymous.
pseudon. Pseudonymous.
ed. Edition.
pam. Pamphlets.
sm. Small.
sq. Square.
obl. Oblong.
fol. Folio. 4°. Quarto. 8°. Octavo. 12°. Duodecimo, etc.

The letter S, affixed to any title, denotes that the work belongs to the library of the Smithsonian Institution.

The books are described as folio, quarto, octavo, duodecimo, etc., according to the apparent size of the volume, and not according to the printer's designations derived from the fold of the sheets.

In the alphabetical arrangement, the prefix *Mc, M'*, or *Mac*, is treated uniformly as a component part of the word, as if spelled *Mac*. Thus, *McLeod* or *M'Leod* precedes *Maclure*. In like manner, the prefixes *New, La, Du*, etc., are treated as component parts of the words to which they belong. Thus *New England* follows *Newell* instead of preceding it, as it would do if the prefix *New* were treated as a separate word.

It is one of the aims of the present catalogue to furnish with the titles a sufficiently full collation of each work. Thus it is made a part of the description to give the number of pages in the case of all works not exceeding two volumes, together with the number of maps and plates, if any, and the name of the publisher. The information thus conveyed will, it is believed, be found of practical value to readers, as conveying at a glance some idea of the extent of each work, while the addition of publishers' names is useful as supplying a guide to the identification of editions. In the case of books printed without date, the actual or approximate date is uniformly supplied, in brackets.

Brackets in any part of a title indicate that the words included in them are not found in the title, but are inserted.

The employment of capital letters in titles has been strictly confined to proper names, and to the initial letter of each sentence. Although this departs from a very general usage in printing the German and some other languages, it secures a uniform and elegant typography. The capitalization of substantives was not practiced in the earlier days of German typography, and high modern authorities (including the new *Wörterbuch* of the brothers Grimm) have abandoned it for a uniform type.

CATALOGUE.

CATALOGUE.

Abbeville (Nicolas Sanson d'). *See* **Sanson** d'Abbeville, (Nicolas).

Abbey (Alonzo J.) The triad; a new collection of vocal music, sacred and secular. 380 pp. Oblong 8°. *New York, H. G. Abbey,* 1866.

Abbot (George, *D. D., Archbishop of Canterbury*). A brief description of the whole world. 6th ed., 187 pp. *index, ms.,* 16 pp.; sm. 4°. *London, John Marriott,* 1624.

——— The same. 332 pp. 18°. *London, William Sheares,* 1634.

——— The same. 5th ed., 340 pp. 24°. *London, Margaret Sheares,* 1664.

Abbott (Jacob). China and the English. [*anon.*] 264 pp. 18°. *New York, Leavitt, Lord & Co.,* 1835.

——— *Editor*). Harper's school history; from the earliest times to the establishment of the American constitution. 12°. *New York, Harpers,* 1856. s.

——— History of king Alfred of England. 16°. *New York, Harpers,* 1849.

——— History of Cyrus the great. 16°. *New York, Harpers,* 1850.

——— History of king Richard the first of England. 16°. *New York, Harpers,* 1857.

——— History of William the conqueror. 16°. *New York, Harpers,* 1849. s.

Abdallatif. *See* **Mowaffak eddin,** etc. s.

Abd-el Kerim Ben Abd-el-jebbar. Voyage de l'Inde à la Mekke, traduit de la version anglais, avec des notes, etc., par L. Langlès. 18°. *Paris,* 1797. s.

Abd-er-rezzak, Kemal eddin. Voyages de la Perse dans l'Inde. Traduit du persan par L. Langlès. 2 v. 18°. *Paris,* 1798. s.

Abdulkurreen *or* Abdoul-Kerym. *See* **Abd-el-Kerim** Ben Abd-el-jebbar. s.

Abdullah. Bahwa ini Kesah-Pŭ-Layar-an Abdullah, ben Abdulkadir, Munshi Deri Singapuri Ka-Kalantan. Tŭrzarong Ulihnya. (English and Malay characters.) 159 pp. 8°. *Singapura, press of Am. mission,* 1838. s.

Abel (Clarke). Narrative of a journey in the interior of China, and of a voyage to and from that country, 1816–17. xvi, 420 pp. 4 maps. 19 pl. 4°. *London, Longman,* 1818.

About (Edmond François Valentin). Lettres d'un bon jeune homme à sa cousine Madeleine. 393 pp. 16°. *Paris, Lévy frères,* 1861.

——— La vieille roche: les vacances de la comtesse. 8°. *Paris, L. Hachette & Co.,* 1865.

——— ——— Le marquis de Lanrose. 8°. *Paris, L. Hachette & Co.,* 1865.

——— Germaine. Translated by Mary L. Booth. 341 pp. 12°. *Boston, Tilton & Co.,* 1860.

——— The man with the broken ear. Translated from the French by Henry Holt. 254 pp. 16°. *New York, Leypoldt & Holt,* 1867.

Abraham (Henry A.) Whom do you worship? A popular treatise on reasonable religion. 44 pp. 12°. *New York,* 1867.

Abreu (Antonio José Alvarez de). Victima real legal; discurso uno juridico-historico-politico sobre que las vacantes mayores y menores de las iglesias de las Indias Occidentales pertenecen à la corona de Castilla y Leon con pleno y absoluto dominio. 2ª ed., 18 p. l. 374 pp., 14 l., sm. fol. *Madrid, A. Ortega,* 1769.

Abreu de Galineo (Juan de). History of the discovery and conquest of the Canary islands. [With] a description of the island and the modern history of the inhabitants. By George Glas. viii, 368 pp. 3 maps. 4°. *London, Dodsley,* 1764.

——— The same. 2 v. xvi, 227 pp; 223 pp. 1 map. 18°. *Dublin, D. Chamberlaine,* 1767.

Abstract of the sufferings of the people called quakers, for the testimony of a good conscience, from 1660 to 1666. [*anon.*] 2 v. xii, 575, xl pp.; xxxii, 522, xlv pp. 8°. *London, Assigns of J. Sowle,* 1733–38.

Acarete *du Biscay.* A relation of Mr. R. M.'s voyage to Buenos Ayres; and from thence by land to Potosi. [Abridged and altered from account of a voyage up the river de la Plata]. v, 117 pp. 1 map. 16°. *London, John Darby,* 1716.

Account of the customs and manners of the Micmakis and Maricheets, savage nations, now depending on the government of Cape-Breton, from a letter written by a French abbot. [With] pieces relative to the savages, to Nova Scotia, and to North America. [*anon*]. viii, 138 pp. *London, S. Hooper & A. Morley,* 1758.

Account of an expedition to the interior of New Holland. [*anon*]. 2d ed. xi, 235 pp. 18°. *London, R. Bentley,* 1849. s.

Account (An) of Jamaica, and its inhabitants. By a gentleman long resident in the West Indies. [*anon*]. 2d ed. 213 pp. 1 pl. 8°. *Kingston, Jamaica,* 1809.

Account of the state prison or penitentiary house in the city of New York. By one of the inspectors of the prison. [*anon*]. 97 pp. 2 pl. 8°. *New York, Isaac Collins & Son,* 1801.

Accounts and papers relating to Mary, queen of Scots. Edited by A. J. Crosby and J. Bruce. xxiii, 134 pp. 1 pl. sm. 4°. *London,* 1867. [*Camden soc. pub. No.* 93.]

Acharius (Erik, *M. D.*) Methodus qua omnes detectos lichenes, secundum organa carpomorpha, ad genera, species et varietates redigere atque observationibus illustrare tentavit. lv, 393 pp. 8 pl. 8°. *Stockholmiæ, Ulrich,* 1803. s.

NOTE: appended,

Supplementum, species quamplures novas descriptas necnon observatas variis complectens, etc. 52 pp.

Acland (*Rev.* Charles). Popular account of the manners and customs of India. vii, 156 pp. 16°. *London, J. Murray,* 1847.

Acland (Henry W.) *and* Ruskin (John). The Oxford museum. 111 pp. 3 pl. 12°. *London, Smith, Elder & Co.,* 1859.

Acosta (José de). Historia natvrale e morale delle Indie. Nouamente tradotta della lingua spagnuola nella italiana da G. P. Galvcci. 23 p. l. 173 pp. sm. 4°. *Venetia, B. Basa,* 1596.

——— De natvra novi orbis libri dvo. Et de promvlgatione evangelii apvd barbaros, siue, de procvranda Indorvm salute, libri sex. 8 p. l. 640 pp. 18°. *Coloniæ Agrippinæ, Mylius,* 1596.

Acrelius (Israel). Beskrifning om de swenska församlingars forna och närwarande tilständ, uti det så kallade Nya Swerige, sedan Nya Nederland, men nu för tiden Pensylvanien, samt nästliggande orter wid alfwen De La Ware, Wäst-Yersey och New-Castle county uti Norra America. 10 p. l. 534 pp. sm. 4°. *Stockholm, Harberg & Hesselberg,* 1759.

Adair (D. L.) New system of bee-keeping; adapted to the habits of the honey-bee, with improved methods of artificial swarming. 74 pp. 8°. *Cincinnati, R. Clarke & Co.,* 1867.

Adair (Robert Alexander Shafto, *F. R. S.*) Ireland and her servile war. 72 pp. 8°. *London, Ridgway,* 1866.

Adams (Arthur), Baikie (William Balfour), *and* Barron (Charles). Manual of natural history for the use of travellers. [With] directions for collecting and preserving. viii, 749 pp. 12°. *London, J. Van Voorst,* 1854. s.

Adams (F. Colburn). Our world; or, the democrat's rule. By Justia, a know-nothing. In 2 v. v. 1. viii, 398 pp. 4 pl. 12°. *London, S. Low, son & Co.,* 1855.

——— The siege of Washington, written expressly for little people. Illustrated by A. W. Waud. 130 pp. 8 pl. sq. 18°. *New York, Dick & Fitzgerald,* 1867.

Adams (H. G.) Cyclopædia of female biography. iv, 788 pp. 1 pl. 16°. *London, Groombridge & Sons,* 1857.

Adams (Henry *and* Arthur). The genera of recent mollusca; arranged according to their organization. 3 v. xl, 484 pp; 661 pp; 138 pl. 8°. *London, J. Van Voorst,* [1853–58.] s.

Adams (John, *President of the U. S.*) Correspondence; originally published in the Boston Patriot, in a series of letters. iv, 572 pp. 8°. *Boston, Everett & Munroe,* 1809.

——— Defence of the constitutions of government of the United States of America. 3d ed. 3 v. 8°. *Philadelphia, William Cobbett,* 1797.

——— Discourses on Davila; a series of papers on political history, published 1790, in the Gazette of the United States. [*anon.*] 248 pp. 8°. *Boston, Russell & Cutler,* 1805.

Adams (John Quincy). The duplicate letters, the fisheries and the Mississippi; documents relating to transactions at the negotiation of Ghent. 2d ed. 223 pp. 8°. *Louisville, S. Penn, Jr.,* 1823.

Adams (Nehemiah). Broadcast. [Religious reflections.] 210 pp. 16°. *Boston, Ticknor & Fields,* 1863.

Adams (Robert). Narrative of R. A., an American sailor, wrecked on the western coast of Africa in 1810, detained three years in slavery by the Arabs of the Great Desert, and [who] resided several months in Tombuctoo. [Ed. by S. Cock]. xxviii, 200 pp. 1 map. 8°. *Boston, Wells and Lilly,* 1817.

Adams (Samuel). *See* **Hunt** (Leigh) *and* **Adams** (S.) Book of the sonnet, etc.

Adams (*Rev.* Seymour Webster). Memoir. [With sermons]. Edited by J. P. Bishop. 237 pp. 16°. *Cleveland, (O.,) Fairbanks, Benedict & Co.,* 1866.

Adams (William T.) The boat club; or, the Bunkers of Rippleton; a tale for boys. By Oliver Optic. *(pseudon).* 16°. *Boston, Brown, Bazin & Co.,* 1855. s.

——— Haste and waste; or, the young pilot of Lake Champlain. A story for young people. By Oliver Optic. [*pseud*]. 313 pp. 4 pl. 16°. *Boston, Lee & Shepard,* 1867.

——— Hope and have; or, Fanny Grant among the Indians. A story for young people. By Oliver Optic. [*pseudon*]. 283 pp. 4 pl. 16°. *Boston, Lee & Shepard,* 1867.

——— Outward bound; or, young America afloat. A story of travel and adventure. By Oliver Optic. [*pseudon*]. 336 pp. 4 pl. 16°. *Boston, Lee & Shepard,* 1867.

——— The starry-flag; or, the young fisherman of Cape Ann. By Oliver Optic. [*pseudon*]. 312 pp. 8 pl. 16°. *Boston, Lee & Shepard,* 1868.

——— Work and win; or, Noddy Newman on a cruise; a story for young people. By Oliver Optic. [*pseudon*]. 16°. *Boston,* 1866.

——— Yankee Middy; or, adventures of a naval officer. [A sequel to the "Tailor Boy]." By Oliver Optic. [*pseudon*]. 16°. *Boston,* 1866.

Adanson (Michel). Voyage to Senegal, the isle of Goree, and the river Gambia. Translated from the French. xiii, 337 pp. 1 map. 12°. *London, J. Nourse,* 1759.

Addison (Henry R.) Traits and stories of Anglo-Indian life. viii, 284 pp. 8 pl. 16°. *London, Smith, Elder & Co.,* 1858.

Addison (Joseph). Dialogues sur l'utilité des anciennes médailles. (*With* **Winckelmann** (J. J.) *and* others. De l'allégorie. v. 2.)

——— Poetical works. 8°. *Edinburgh,* 1793. (**Anderson's** Brit. Poets, v. 7).

Address to farmers. [*anon*]. 64 pp. 16°. *Salem, John Dabney,* 1796.

Addresses of the Philadelphia society for the promotion of national industry. 4th ed. xi, 248 pp. 12°. *Philadelphia, M. Carey & Son,* 1819.

——— The same. 5th ed. xii, 299 pp. 12°. *Philadelphia, J. Maxwell,* 1820.

Adelung (Johann Christoph). Geschichte der menschlichen narrheit, oder lebensbeschreibungen berühmter schwarzkünstler, goldmacher, teufelsbanner, etc. [*anon*]. 8 v. 12°. *Leipzig, Weygand,* 1785. (v. 8 wanting).

Adhelmus *(Saint). See* **Aldhelm.**

Adlard (George). The Sutton-Dudleys of England and the Dudleys of Massachusetts in New England. From the Norman conquest to the present time. xvi, 160 pp. 2 pl. 8°. *New York, C. B. Richardson,* 1862.

Adlzreiter (Johann). Annalium Boicæ gentis partes iii, quibus historia a prima Bojorum origine ad mdcli continetur. Accessere Andreæ Brunneri annalium Boicorum a primis initiis ad annum mcccxi partes iii. Cum praefatione G. G. Leibnitii. Ed. nova. 5 p. l. 296 pp., 26 l., 123 pp, 5 l. fol. *Francofurti ad Mœnum, J. F. Gleditsch & filii,* 1710.

Adresse (Une) illisible. Par Fanjot. [*pseudon*]. 220 pp. 16°. *Paris, Amyot,* 1862.

Adventures of a German toy. [*anon*]. 171 pp. 18°. *Boston, W. V. Spencer,* 1866.

Aegidius Columna, *or,* Romanus. *See* **Colonna** (Egidio).

Ælianus (Claudius). Various histories. Rendered into English by Thomas Stanley. 7 p. l. 314 pp. 14 l. 18°. *London, T. Basset,* 1670.

Aepinus *or* **Höck?** (Fr. Johann). Die geschichte von Meklenburg für jedermann, in einer folge von briefen. [*anon*]. 3 v. 12°. *Neubrandenburg, C. G. Korb,* 1791–93. s.

Aesopus. Esopo volgarizzato per uno da Siena. (Pietro Berti.) Testo di lingua. *Padova, nel Seminario,* 1811. [*Printed on vellum*].

African (The) observer. Edited by Enoch Lewis. [April, 1827, to March, 1828.] V. 1. 8°. *Philadelphia, J. Ashmead & Adam Waldie & Co.,* 1827–28.

Agapetus, *diaconus.* Expositio admonitoria ad Justinianum imperatorem. (*With* **Isocrates.** Paraenesis, ed. 1699.) s.

Agardh (Jakob Georg). Species, genera et ordines algarum. 2 v.; viii, 363 pp.; xii, 1291 pp. 8°. *Lundæ; C. W. K. Gleerup,* 1848—63. s.

CONTENTS.

V. 1. Fucoideae. V. 2. Florideae.

Agassiz (Alexander). Embryology of the starfish. [From v. 5 of **Agassiz.** Nat. hist. of U. S.] 66, ix pp. 8 pl. 4°. [*Boston,* 1865.] s.

Agathias. De imperio et rebvs gestis Jvstiniani imperatoris libri qvinqve. [*Gr. et Lat.*] Interpretatione B. Vvlcanii. Accesserunt epigrammata græca [latine reddita per J. Scaligervm et J. Dovsam]. 388 pp. fol. *Lvgdvni Batavorvm, F. Raphelengius,* 1594.

Agnew (David Hayes, *M. D.*) Practical anatomy. A new arrangement of the London dissector. With additions, illustrations, [etc]. 2d ed. 307 pp. 12°. *Philadelphia, J. B. Lippincott,* 1868.

Agostini (Leonardo). *See* **Paruta** (Filippo) *and* Agostini. Sicilia nvmismatica.

Agrippa von Nettesheim (Heinrich Cornelius). De occvlta philosophia libri tres. 6 p. l. unp., ccclxii pp. fol. [*Coloniæ,*] 1533.

Agustin (Antonio), *and* **Orsini** (Fulvio). De Romanorvm gentibvs et familiis scriptores dvo præstantissimi. 4 p. l. 156 pp. 4°. *Lvgdvni, F. Faber,* 1592.

Agustin de Escudero (J.) *See* **Escudero.**

Ahmed Ibn Mohammed Al-Makkari (Shiháb-ed-din). History of the Mohammedan dynasties in Spain. Trans. by Pascual de Gayangos. 2 v. xxxix, 548, xcv pp.; xii, 544, clxxii pp. 4°. *London, Oriental translation fund,* 1840.

Ahn (F.) Rudiments of the German language: pronouncing, spelling, and translating. Am. ed. 89 pp. 16°. *New York, E. Steiger,* 1867.

Aikin (John, *Surgeon*). Biographical memoirs of medicine in Great Britain, from the revival of literature to the time of Harvey. xi, 338 pp., 6 l. 8°. *London, J. Johnson,* 1780.

Aikin (Lucy). The arts of life. New ed. xi, 228 pp. 18°. *London, Longman,* 1858.

Ailly (Pierre d'). Cōcordātia astronomie cū theologia, cū hystorica narratione, et elucidariū duorum precedentium. sm. 4°. *Venetiis,* 1490. s.

Aimard (Gustave). Curumilla. 336 pp. 16°. *Paris, Amyot,* 1860.

——— La loi de Lynch. 3e éd. 464 pp. 12°. *Paris, Amyot,* 1859.

Airy (George Biddell). Essays on the invasion of Britain by Julius Cæsar, by Plautius, and by Claudius Cæsar; the early military policy of the Romans in Britain; the battle of Hastings. 4°. *London,* 1865. s.

——— Populäre physische astronomie. Aus dem Englischen von K. L. Edlem von Littrow. xxiii, 216 pp., 4 pl. 12°. *Stuttgart, Hoffmann,* 1839. s.

Aitken (William). Science and practice of medicine. From the 4th London ed., with additions, by M. Clymer. 2 v., 955 pp.; xliii, 1114 pp. 8°. *Philadelphia, Lindsay & Blakiston,* 1866.

Aitzema (Leeuw van). Saken van staet en oorlogh, in, ende omtrent de Vereenigde Nederlanden, beginnende met 1621, ende eyndigende met 1669. 7 v. fol. *Graven-Haghe, J. Veely,* 1669--72.

Ajokaersutit illuartut Gudimik pekkorsèjniglo innungnut. [*Esquimaux.* Knowledge of the righteous God. *anon.*] 158 pp. 16°. *Kiöbenhavnime, C. F. Skubartimit,* 1818.

Akenside (Mark). The pleasures of imagination. [With] odes. vi, 116 pp. 16°. *Edinburgh, Ruddiman & Co.,* 1758. [**Select** collection of modern poems].

——— Poetical works. 8°. *Edinburgh,* 1794. [**Anderson's** Brit. poets, v. 9].

Akerly (Samuel). An essay on the geology of the Hudson river, and the adjacent regions. 69 pp. 1 map. 12°. *New York, Goodrich & Co.,* 1820.

Alabama, University of. Catalogue of the library. By W. G. Richardson. 8°. *Tuscaloosa,* 1848. s.

Alauzet (François Isidore). Essai sur les peines et le système pénitentiaire. xviii, 295 pp. 8°. *Paris, imprimerie royale,* 1842. s.

——— Traité général des assurances maritimes, terrestres, mutuelles et sur la vie. 2 v. xi, 496 pp.; 527 pp. *Paris, Cosse,* 1843. s.

Albany (N. Y.) Directory for 1867. 338 pp. 1 map. 8°. *Albany, Sampson, Davenport & Co.,* 1867.

Albèri (Eugenio). Vita di Caterina de' Medici. viii, 473 pp., 19 pl. 8°. *Firenze, Batelli,* 1838.

Albers (Johann Christian). Heliceen nach natürlicher verwandtschaft systematisch geordnet. Zweite ausgabe, besorgt von Eduard von Martens. xviii, 359 pp. 8°. *Leipzig, Engelmann,* 1860. s.

Albert (von Bollstädt). *See* **Albertus** Magnus.

Alberti (Leon Battista). Of statues. Translated from the Italian by John Evelyn. 61—75 pp. [*With* **Evelyn** (J.) Account of architects and architecture. fol. *London,* 1706].

Albertus *Magnus.* Liber de natura locorum. 46 l. sm. 4°. *Argentorati, Matthiæ Schurerii,* 1515.

——— Liber de ad herendo Deo et vltima et superna perfectione hominis ad Deum quātū possibile ē. 9 l. unp. fol. [*Eslingæ, Conrad Fyner.* n. d.; *about* 1473?] (*With* **Chrysostomus,** In Job de paciencia sermones. n. d.)

Albertus *Magnus.* The same. fol. [Eslingæ, Conrad Fyner, n. d.] (*With* **Aquino** (Tommaso d'). Postilla in Job.) s.

Albric, *or* **Albricius.** Libellvs de deorvm imaginibvs. 9 l. unp. Small 4°. *Vienne, H. Victor,* 1510. (*With* **Fiocchi** (A. D.) De Romanorum magistratibus. *Vienne,* 1510.)

Alcedo y Bexarano (Antonio de). Diccionario geográphico-históiico de las Indias Occidentales ó América: es á saber: de los reynos del Perú, Nueva España, Tierra Firme, Chile, y nuevo reyno de Granada. 5 v. 8°. *Madrid, B. Cano,* 1786—89.

Alciati (Andrea). Emblemata: opera et vigiliis Ioannis Thvilii. Acceserunt Federici Morelli corollaria et monita ad eadem emblemata. lxxx; 1001 pp. 4°. *Patauii, P. Frambotti,* 1661.

Alcock (Thomas). Travels in Russia, Persia, Turkey, and Greece, in 1828-9. vi, 227 pp. 1 map. 8°. *London, Clarke & Son,* 1831.

Alcripe (Philippe d'). La nouvelle fabrique des excellens traités de vérité; livre pour inciter les resveurs tristes et mélancoliques à vivre de plaisir. Nouv. éd. Augmentée des nouvelles de la terre de Prestre Jehan. xvi, 220 pp. 16°. *Paris, P. Jannet,* 1853.

Alden (Joseph, *D. D.*) Christian ethics; or, the science of duty. 170 pp. 12°. *New York, Ivison & Co.,* 1866.

——— Text-book of ethics for Bible classes. 92 pp. 16°. *New York, A. D. F. Randolph,* 1867.

——— The young citizen's manual. A textbook on government for common schools. 134 pp. 12°. *New York, Sheldon & Co.,* 1867.

Alden (Timothy, *D. D.*) Account of sundry missions performed among the Senecas and Munsees. 180 pp. 1 pl. 18°. *New York, J. Seymour,* 1827.

Aldhelm (*Saint*). Sancti Aldhelmi ex abbate Malmesburiensi episcopi Schireburnensis opera quae extant omnia e codicibus mss emendavit. Ediit J. A. Giles. xxiii, 392 pp. 8°. *Oxonii, J. H. Parker,* 1844.

Alessandri (Alessandro). Genialivm diervm libri sex. 14 p. l. 175 pp. fol. *Parisiis, C. Guillard,* 1539.

Alexander *ab Alexandro. See* **Alessandri** (Alessandro).

Alexander (*Sir* James Edward). Travels from India to England; comprehending a visit to the Burman empire, and a journey through Persia, Asia Minor, European Turkey, etc., 1825-26. xvi, 301 pp. 2 maps. 21 pl. 4°. *London, Parbury, Allen & Co.,* 1827.

Alexander (*Rev.* John). Jesuitico-quakerism examined, or a confutation of the blasphemous and unreasonable principles of the quakers. 16 p. l., 219 pp., 4 l. sm. 4°. *London, Dorman Newman,* 1680.

Alexander (John Henry). Engineer's reports on topographical survey of Maryland, for 1834-36. 8°. *Annapolis,* 1835. (*With* **Maryland** geology, v. 1.)

——— Report on the manufacture of iron; addressed to the governor of Maryland. 269 pp., 3 pl. 8°. *Annapolis,* 1840. (*With* **Maryland** geology, v. 2.)

Alexander (John Henry). Catena dominica: a series of Sunday idyls. 2d ed. v, 177 pp. 16°. *New York, A. D. F. Randolph,* 1867.

Alexander (*Sir* William). An encouragement to colonies. 2 p. l. 47 pp. 8°. *London, W. Stansby,* 1625.

Algarotti (Francesco). Saggio sopra il commercio. (**Scrittori** class. ital. di econ. pol. v. 1.)

Alger (Horatio, *jr*). Charlie Codman's cruise; a story for boys. 231 pp. 1 pl. 16°. *Boston, Loring,* 1867.

——— Helen Ford. [A tale]. 297 pp. 12°. *Boston, Loring,* 1866.

——— Paul Prescott's charge. A story for boys. 224 pp. 2 pl. 16°. *Boston, Loring,* 1865.

Alger (William Rounseville). The solitudes of nature and of man; or the loneliness of human life. 3d ed. 412 pp. 12°. *Boston, Roberts Bros.,* 1867.

Ali Jelebi. *See* **Diez** (Heinrich Friedrich).

Aliaco *or* Alliaco (Petrus de). *See* **Ailly** (Pierre d').

Alice and her friends. (Prize stories.) 310 pp. 16°. *Boston,* 1866.

Alig (*Rev.* Mathias). Die sieben zeitalter der kirche Jesu Christi auf erden bis zu ihrem triumphe im himmel. Geschichte der ereignisse mit bezug auf der kirche Christi. 398 pp. 1 pl. 8°. *Washington, author,* [1865].

All the year round: conducted by Charles Dickens. July, 1866, to June, 1867. v. 16-17, 8°. *London, Chapman & Hall,* 1867.

Allen (Harrison, *M. D.*) Monograph of the bats of North America. xxiii, 85 pp. 8°. *Washington,* 1864. (Smithsonian miscel. coll. v. 7.)

Allen (J. Adams, *M. D.*) Medical examination for life insurance. 143 pp. 8°. *Chicago,* 1867. *Horton & Leonard.*

Allen (*Rev.* Wilkes). History of Chelmsford, [Mass.] from 1653 to 1820. 192 pp. 8°. *Haverhill, (Mass.) P. N. Green*, 1820.

Allen (William, *D. D., President Bowd. Coll.,*) American biographical and historical dictionary. 2d ed. 8°. *Boston*, 1832. s.

——— Lectures to young men, with the Dudleian lecture delivered at Harvard University. 272 pp. 1 pl. 12°. *Boston*, 1833.

Alletz (Pons Augustin). L'esprit des femmes célèbres du siècle de Louis XIV, et de celui de Louis XV jusqu'à présent. [*anon*]. 2 v. viii, 469 pp. 1 l; 2 p. l. 156 pp. 16°. *Paris, Pissot*, 1768.

Allgemeine deutsche bibliothek. *See* **Nicolai** (C. F.)

Alliaco *or* Aliaco (Petrus de). *See* **Ailly** (Pierre d').

Allin (Abby). Home ballads: a book for New Englanders. 238 pp. 16°. *Boston, Munroe & Co.*, 1851.

Allix (Peter, *D. D.*) The judgment of the ancient Jewish church against the unitarians in the controversy upon the holy trinity and the divinity of our blessed saviour. 2d ed. xx, 371 pp., 5 l. 8°. *Oxford, Clarendon press*, 1821.

Allonville (Armand François, *comte* d'). *See* **Mémoires** d' un homme d' état.

Al-Makkari (Ahmed Ibn Mohammed). *See* **Ahmed Ibn Mohammed.**

Almanach du commerce et de l'industrie. Publié par le Messager franco-américain. 255 pp. 8°. *New York, H. De Mareil*, 1865.

Almanach et directorium français des États-Unis pour 1865–67. 3 v. 12°. *New York, J. D. L. Zender*, 1865–67.

Almanach de Gotha. Annuaire diplomatique et statistique pour l' année 1867. 1116 pp. 32°. *Gotha, J. Perthes*, 1867.

Almanach impérial, pour 1866–67. 2 v. 8°. *Paris, Guyot & Scribe*, 1866–67.

Almeloveen (Theodor Janssen ab). Bibliotheca promissa et latens. 16°. *Gandæ*, 1688. s.

——— The same. Accessiones. *See* **Meelführ.**

Aloysius Gonzaga, (*St*). Opera omnia, partim Italice, partim Latine. Edidit A. Heuser. 116 pp. 1 pl. 24°. *Coloniæ, J. M. Heberle*, 1850.

Alpha (The), or first principle of the human mind; a philosophical inquiry into the nature of truth. [*anon*]. xvi, 362 pp. 8°. *London, Chapman & Hall*, 1851.

Alpino (Prospero). Historiæ Ægypti naturalis pars prima, qua continentur rerum Ægyptiarum libri quatuor: pars secunda, sive de plantis Ægypti liber, et dissertatio de laserpitio, et loto ægyptia. Accedunt Joannis Veslingii paræneses ad rem herbariam et vindiciæ opobalsami. 2 v. 9 p. l. 248 pp. 6 l. 25 pl; 306 pp. 12 l. 72 pl. 4°. *Lugduni Batavorum, G. Potuliet*, 1735. s.

Alsop (Richard), *and* Dwight (Theodore). The echo, with other poems. [*anon*]. xv, 331 pp. 5 l. 7 pl. 8°. *New York, Pasquin Petronius*, 1807.

Althamer (Andreas). Eyn predig von dem teüffel das er alles vnglück in der welt anrichte. 6 l. unp. [n. p.] 1532.

Alvarado (Pedro de). Proceso de residencia contra Pedro de Alvarado y Nuñez de Guzman. Por José Fernando Ramirez. 8°. *Mexico*, 1847. s.

Alvarez (José Justo), *and* **Durán** (Rafael). Itinerarios y derroteros de la republica mexicana. 8°. *Mexico*, 1856. s.

Alvarez y Baena (José Antonio). Hijos de de Madrid, illustres en santidad, dignidades, armas, ciencias y artes; diccionario historico. 4 v. Sm. 4°. *Madrid*, 1789–91. s.

Alvear y Lara (Francisco de). Memoria sobre el proyecto de conduccion a la Habana de las aguas de los Manantiales de vento. 2 l. xii, 149, 47 pp. 2 pl. 4°. *Habana*, 1856.

Alvernia (Petrus de). *See* **Aquino** (Tommaso d'.)

Amat (Felix Torres). Memorias para ayudar a formar un diccionario critico de los escritores catalanes. xliv, 720 pp. 8°. *Barcelona, J. Verdaguer*, 1836. s.

Ambler (A. I.) Jessie Reed, and other poems. 16°. *Philadelphia*, 1867.

Ambrosoli (Francesco). Manuale della letteratura italiana. 2ª ed. 4 v. 12°. *Firenze, G. Barbèra*, 1863–64. s.

Amé (Léon). Étude économique sur les tarifs de douanes. ii, 448 pp. 8°. *Paris, Guillaumin & Cᵉ.*, 1859. s.

——— The same. 2ᵉ éd. vii, 540 pp. 8°. *Paris, Guillaumin et Cᵉ*, 1860. s.

American anecdotes, characters and incidents; revolutionary and miscellaneous. v, 148 pp. *Philadelphia, John Conrad*, 1823.

American anecdotes, original and select. [Attributed to Freeman Hunt]. 2 v. 300; 300 pp. 12°. *Boston, Putnam & Hunt*, 1830.

American annual encyclopædia and register of important events for the year 1866. v. 6. 8°. *New York, D. Appleton & Co.*, 1867.

American antiquarian society. Catalogue of books in the library. 8°. *Worcester, (Mass.,) H. J. Howland*, 1837. s.

American colonization society. Memorial of the semi-centennial anniversary, celebrated at Washington, Jan. 15, 1867. With documents concerning Liberia. 192 pp. 8°. *Washington, Colonization Society,* 1867.

American gazetteer. Il gazzettiere americano; continente un distinto ragguaglio di tutte le parti del nuoo mondo, della loro situazione, clima, terreno, prodotti, stato antico e moderno, mercy manifatture, e commercio. 3 v. xxiii, 217 pp.; 254 pp., 257 pp.; 21 maps, 57 pl. 4°. *Livorno, M. Coltellini,* 1763.

American (The) farmer; a monthly journal devoted to agriculture, horticulture, domestic and rural economy. Illustrated. [1866.] V. 1. 384 pp. 8°. *Rochester, (N. Y)., J. Turner,* 1866.

American (The) historical magazine, January to June, 1836. (V. 1.) 240 pp. 8°. [*New Haven,*] 1836.

American homœopathic review. July, 1865, to Jan., 1866. v. 6. 8°. *New York, J. T. S. Smith & Sons,* 1866.

American (The) Hoyle; or, gentleman's handbook of games. By "Trumps." [*anon.*] 4th ed. 525 pp. 12°. *New York, Dick & Fitzgerald,* [1867].

American institute library; alphabetical and analytical catalogue. 8°. *New York,* 1852.

American (The) journal of horticulture and florist's companion, January to June, 1867. v. 1. viii, 392 pp. 1 pl. 8°. *Boston, J. E. Tilton & Co.,* 1867.

American journal of the medical sciences. Edited by Isaac Hays, *M. D.* January to October, 1867. New series. v. 53–54. 8°. *Philadelphia, H. C. Lea,* 1867.

American (The) kalendar; or, United States register for 1798. [*anon*]. 211 pp. 18°. *London, J. Debrett,* 1798.

American literary gazette and publishers' circular, Nov. 1866 to Nov. 1867. v. 8–9. 8°. *Philadelphia, G. W. Childs,* 1867.

American Lloyd's register of American and foreign shipping. R. T. Hartshorne & J. F. H. King, proprietors. xxxii, 730 pp. 5 pl. *New York, J. W. Pratt & Co.,* 1867.

American Lloyd's universal register of shipping, from June 1, 1867, to May 31, 1868, under the approval of the board of underwriters. Thos. D. Taylor, proprietor. xlii, 693 pp. 8 pl. obl. 8°. *New York, C. Vogt,* 1867.

American (The) magazine and historical chronicle. [Pub. by S. Eliot & J. Blanchard.] 3 v. 8°. *Boston, Rogers & Fowle,* 1744–46.
(*Imp.* v. 1 wants title.)

American (The) magazine and monthly chronicle for the British colonies. Vol. 1, from Oct., 1757, to Oct., 1758, by a society of gentlemen. 654 pp. 8°. *Philadelphia, W. Bradford,* 1757–58.
(*Imp.* pp. wanting at the end.)

American (The) magazine of useful and entertaining knowledge. v. 1–3. Sept., 1834–Sept., 1837. 8°. *Boston, John L. Sibley,* 1834–37.

American poems, selected and original. v. 1. viii, 304 pp. 4 l. 12°. *Litchfield, (Conn.,) Collier & Buel,* [*about* 1793].

American (The) shooter's manual, comprising [matters relating] to the dog, and the use of the gun; also a description of the game of this country. By a gentleman of Philadelphia county. (*anon.*) 251 pp. 8°. *Philadelphia, Carey, Lea & Carey,* 1827.

American sketches; by a native of the United States. xviii, 412 pp. 12°. *London, J. Miller,* 1827.

American (The) statistical association. Collections. v. 1. 596 pp. 8°. *Boston, T. R. Marvin,* 1847.

American (The) weekly messenger, or register of state papers, history and politics. [Sept. 25, 1813, to Sept. 17, 1814.] 2 v. viii, 473; vii, 408 pp. 8°. *Philadelphia, John Conrad,* 1814–15.

Ames (Joseph). Typographical antiquities; being an historical account of printing in England, with an appendix concerning printing in Scotland and Ireland. 4°. *London, W. Faden,* 1749.

——— The same; or, an historical account of the origin and progress of printing in Great Britain and Ireland. Augmented by William Herbert. 3 v. 4°. *London, printed for the editor,* 1785–90.

Amiens. Catalogue méthodique de la bibliothèque communale—belles-lettres. viii, 646 pp. 8°. *Amiens, Duval et Herment,* 1854. s.

Amunategui (Miguel Luis). La dictadura de O'Higgins. iv, 495 pp. 8°. *Santiago, (Chile,) J. Belin i Cª,* 1853.

——— *and* (Gregorio Victor). Biografias de Americanos, [viz: Andres Bello, Simon Rodriguez, Camilo Henriquez, Manuel Salas, José Rodriguez Ballesteros]. 8°. *Santiago, (Chile),* 1854. s.

——— De la instruccion primaria en Chile. xii, 391 pp. 8°. *Santiago, Ferrocarril,* 1856. s.

Amyot, (C. J. B.) *and* Audinet Serville (Jean Guillaume). Histoire naturelle des insectes. Hémiptères. lxxvi, 675 pp. 8°. *Paris, Roret,* 1843. (Plates wanting.)

Anacreon. Odes and epigrams. Translated by F. Fawkes. 8°. *Edinburgh,* [1792–94]. (**Anderson's** British poets, v. 5).

——— Works, translated into English verse, with notes; to which are added odes, fragments and epigrams of Sappho. By [J]. Addison. 11 p. l. 279 pp. 2 pl. 16°. *London, J. Watts,* 1735.

——— *and* Sappho. Les œuvres, traduites de grec en vers françois par [H. B. de R., baron de] Longepierre. 9 p. l. 398 pp. 1 pl. 18°. *Paris, C. Clouzier,* 1692.

——— Sappho, (*and others*). Works; with pieces from ancient authors, and essays on their lives and writings; with the Classic, an introductory poem [by Barnaby Edward Greene]. xxii, 287 pp. 18°. *London, J. Ridley,* 1768.

Ancell (Samuel). Journal of the blockade and siege of Gibraltar, 1779 to 1783. 3d ed. 274 pp. 7 pl. *Edinburgh,* 1786.

Ancona. *See* **Augustinus** *de Ancona.*

Andagoya (Pascual de). Relacion de los sucesos de Pedrarias Dávila en las provincias de Tierra firme ó Castilla del Oro, y delo ocurrido en el descubrimiento de la Mar del Sur y costas del Perú y Nicaragua. (**Navarrette.** Coleccion de los Viages, etc. V. 3, pp. 393–459.)

——— The same. Narrative of the proceedings of Pedrarias Davila in the provinces of Tierra Firme or Castilla del Oro, and of the discovery of the South Sea and the coasts of Peru and Nicaragua. Translated, with notes and introduction, by C. K. Markham. xxix, 88 pp. 1 map. 8°. *London, Hakluyt Society,* 1865.

Andersen (J. A.) A Dane's excursion in Britain. 2 v. in 1. viii, 224 pp; 155 pp, 6 l. 16°. *London, Mathews & Leigh,* 1809.

Anderson (Æneas). Narrative of the British embassy to China, 1792–94. xxiv, 278 pp.; 13 l. 8° *Dublin, William Porter,* 1795.

Anderson (Andreas). A tour in Zealand in 1802, with sketch of the battle of Copenhagen. By a native of Denmark. [*anon*]. 131 pp. 16°. *Philadelphia, Bartram & Reynolds,* 1807.

Anderson (Elbert). Claims on the United States, by the late contractor for the State of New York, for services during the late war. 179, 24 pp. 8°. *New York,* 1824.

Anderson (James, *LL. D.*) Recreations in agriculture, natural history, arts, and miscellaneous literature. 6 v. 8°. *London, T. Bensley,* 1799—1802.

Anderson (John J.) Pictorial school history of the United States; with the declaration of independence, and the constitution of the United States. 363, 38 pp. 12°. *New York, Clark & Maynard,* 1867.

——— Introductory school history of the United States. 16°. *New York, Clark & Maynard,* 1867.

Anderson (Robert, *M. D.*) Select British poets and translations, with prefaces, biographical and critical. 9 v. 8°. *Edinburgh, Mundell & Son,* 1792–94. [*London,* 1810].

CONTENTS.

Addison, v. 7.
Akenside, v. 9.
Anacreon, [Fawkes], v. 5.
Apollonius Rhodius, [Fawkes], v. 5.
Bion, [Fawkes], v. 5.
Blackmore, v. 7.
Blair, v. 8.
Broome, v. 8.
Browne, v. 4.
Carew, v. 3.
Collins, v. 9.
Coluthus, v. 5.
Congreve, v. 7.
Crashaw, v. 4.
Daniel, v. 4.
Davenant, v. 4.
Davies, v. 2.
Donne, v. 4.
Dorset, v. 6.
Drayton, v. 3.
Drummond, v. 4.
Dryden, v. 5.
Duke, v. 6.
Dyer, v. 9.
Fenton, v. 7.
Fletcher, G., v. 4.
Fletcher, P., v. 4.
Garth, v. 7.
Gay, v. 8.
Granville, v. 7.
Halifax, v. 6.
Hall, v. 2.
Hamilton, v. 9.
Hammond, v. 8.
Harte, v. 9.
Hesiod, [Cooke], v. 5.
Hill, v. 8.
Horace, [Francis], v. 1.
Hughes, v. 7.
Jonson, v. 4.
King, v. 6.
Lucretius, [Creech], v. 5
Mallet, v. 9,
Moschus, [Fawkes], v. 5.
Musaeus, [Fawkes], v. 5.
Otway, v. 6.
Ovid, [Garth], v. 1.
Parnell, v. 7.
Pattison, v. 8.
Philips, A., v. 9.
Philips, John, v. 6.
Pitt, v. 8.
Pomfret, v. 6.
Pope, v. 8.
Prior, v. 7.
Rochester, v. 6.
Roscommon, v. 6.
Rowe, v. 7.
Sappho, [Fawkes], v. 5.
Savage, v. 8.
Shakspeare, v. 2.
Sheffield, v. 7.
Shenstone, v. 9.
Smith, v. 6.
Somerville, v. 8.
Spenser, v. 2.
Sprat, v. 6.
Statius, [Lewis], v. 1.
Stepney, v. 6.
Suckling, v. 3.
Sulpicia, [Grainger], v. 5.
Swift, v. 9.
Theocritus, [Fawkes], v. 5.
Thomson, v. 9.
Tibullus, [Grainger], v. 5.
Tickell, v. 8.
Walsh, v. 6.
Watts, v. 9.
West, v. 9.
Yalden, v. 7.

Anderson (*Mr.*) History of life and adventures in Europe and America, compiled from his own papers. 243 pp. 16°. *Glasgow, William Neilson,* 1799.

Andersson (Charles John). The Okavango river; a narrative of travel, exploration, and adventure. 8°. *New York, Harpers,* 1861. s.

Andover Theological Seminary. Catalogue of library. By O. A. Taylor. 8°. *Andover, (Mass.,)* 1838. s.

——— Triennial catalogue [of officers and graduates]. 1867. 229 pp. 8°. *Andover, W. F. Draper,* 1867.

Andral (Gabriel). Précis d'anatomie pathologique. 2 v. 479 pp; 364 pp. 8°. *Bruxelles, Soc. typographique belge,* 1837. s.

Andrea Vivano; or, the Italian poisoner. [*anon*]. 11 pp. 8°. *London*, 1841. [**Hazlitt's** romancist and novelist's lib'y, v. 3].

Andreana. Containing the trial, execution, and various matter connected with the history of Major John André, adjutant general of the British army in America, A. D. 1780. 2 p. l. 67 pp, 2 l. 12 pl. fol. *Philadelphia, H. W. Smith*, 1865.

Andreini (Giovanni Battista). L'Adamo, sacra rapresentatione. 13 p. l. 177 pp. 40 pl. [in text]. 4°. *Milano, G. Bordoni*, 1617.

Andrew (William). Constitution of nature. Theories intended to unfold nature. 100 pp. 8°. *Milwaukee, Jermain & Brightman*, 1863. s.

Andrew (William P.) Memoir on the Euphrates valley route to India; with official correspondence. xvi, 267 pp. 2 maps. 8°. *London, W. H. Allen & Co.* 1857.

Andrews (Charles). Prisoners' memoirs, *or*, Dartmoor prison; a complete history of the captivity of the Americans in England from the commencement of the late war until the treaty of Ghent. [*anon*]. 283 pp. 12°. *New York, author*, 1815.

Andrews (Charles C., *teacher*). History of the New York African free schools, from their establishment in 1787. 148 pp. 16°. *New York, M. Day*, 1830.

Andrews (*Rev.* C. W.) Memoir of *Mrs.* Anne R. Page. 101 pp. 1 pl. 18°. *Philadelphia, Herman Hooker*, 1844.

Andrews (John, *LL. D.*) History of the revolutions of Denmark, with an account of the present state of that kingdom and people. 2 v. viii, 416 pp; 446 pp. 8°. *London, J. Nourse*, 1774.

Anecdotes. The Holy Scriptures. 5th ed. viii, 214 pp. 18°. *London, Rel. tract soc.*, [*about* 1840].

Anecdotes, medical, chemical, and chirurgical; collected, arranged, and transmuted by an adept. [*anon*]. 2 v. xii, 204 pp. 231 pp. 16°. *London, J. Callow*, 1816.

Anecdotes of the family circle. [*anon*]. vi, 244 pp. 2l. 16°. *London, Orr & Smith*, 1836.

Anecdotes of the house of Bedford, from the Norman conquest to the present period. [*anon*]. vii, 284 pp. 8°. *London, J. S. Barr*, [1797].

Anecdotes parisiennes. 24°. *Londres, Law & others*, 1815.

Angela *de Fulginio*. Visionum et instructionum liber. Recensuit J. H. Lammertz. 391 pp. 24°. *Coloniæ, J. M. Heberle & Co.*, 1851.

Angelis (Pedro de). Coleccion de obras y documentos relativos a la historia antigua y moderna de las provincias del Rio de la Plata. Ilustrados con notas y disertaciones. 6 v. fol. *Buenos Aires, Imp. del estado*, 1836–37. s.

——— Memoria sobre el estado de la hacienda publica. 219 pp. 8°. *Buenos Aires*, 1834. s.

Angelus (Johann). Astrolabium planū in tabulis ascendens cum quodā tractatu natiuitatū vtili ac ornato. 174 l. unp. 4°. *Auguste Vindelicorū, Erhardt Ratdolt*, 1488.

Angeville (Adolphe, *comte* d'). La vérité sur la question d'orient et sur M. Thiers. iv, 368 pp. 8°. *Paris, Delloye*, 1841. s.

Angreville (J. E., d'). La flore vallaisanne. viii, 218 pp. 12°. *Genève, M. Mehling*, 1862. s.

Annales des ponts et chaussées. Mémoires et documents relatifs à l'art des constructions et au service de l'ingénieur; lois, etc. concernant l' administration des ponts et chaussées. 108 v. 8°. *Paris, Carilian-Goeury, etc.*, 1831–65.

CONTENTS.

1e série, 1831–40. Mémoires et documents. 20 v.
——— Lois, décrets, etc. 10 v.
——— Tables générales, 1831–1840.
2e série, 1841–50. Mémoires et documents. 20 v.
——— Lois, décrets, etc. 10 v.
——— Tables générales, 1841–1850.
3e série, 1851–60. Mémoirés et documents. 20 v.
——— Lois, décrets, etc. 10 v.
——— Tables générales, 1850–1860.
4e série, 1861–65. Mémoires et documents. v. 1–10.
——— Lois, décrets, etc. v. 1–5.

Annals and magazine of natural history, including zoology, botany, and geology. 3d series, v. 18–19. 8°. *London, Taylor & Francis*, 1866–67.

Annius *Viterbiensis*, *or* Nanni (Giovanni). Cōmentaria super opera diuersorum auctorum de antiquitatibus loquentiū. fol. *Rome, E. Silber*, 1498. s.

Annuaire-almanach du commmerce: ou almanach des 500,000 adresses de Paris, des départments, et des pays étrangers. Pour 1867. 3,600 pp. 8°. *Paris, Didot*, 1867.

Annuaire de l'économie politique et de la statistique pour 1866–67. Par M. Block. V. 23–24. 18°. *Paris, Guillaumin*, 1866–67.

——— Table générale, 1844–67. 18°. *Paris, Guillaumin*, 1867.

Annuaire encyclopédique. 1865–66. 8°. *Paris, bureau de l'encyclopédie du 19e siècle*, 1866.

Annual (The) register. A review of public events for the year 1866. New series. vii. 337, 340 pp. 8°. *London, Rivingtons*, 1867.

Annual of scientific discovery; or, year-book of facts in science and art for 1865, and 1866–67. 2 v. 12°. *Boston, Gould & Lincoln,* 1865–67.

Anquetil (Louis Pierre). A summary of universal history; exhibiting the rise, decline, and revolutions of the different nations of the world from the creation to the present time. Translated from the French. 9 v. 8°. *London, G. & J. Robinson,* 1800.

Anselm (*Saint, Archbishop of Canterbury*). Liber meditationum. Textum recognovit [et] vita s. doctoris exornavit A. Buse. xi, 272 pp. 24°. *Coloniæ, J. M. Heberle & Co.,* 1851.

Ansted (David Thomas). Elementary course of geology, mineralogy, and physical geography. 2d ed. xvi, 606 pp. 12°. *London, J. Van Voorst,* 1856. s.

——— Geological science, including the practice of geology and the elements of physical geography. x, 302 pp. 8°. *London, Orr,* 1855. s.

——— *and* Nicolay (*Rev.* Charles Grenfell). Atlas of physical and historical geography. 6 maps. 4°. *London, J. W. Parker & Son,* (1852). s.

Anstey (Christopher). The patriot; a pindaric address to Lord Buckhorse, with appendix. [*anon.*] 67 pp. sm. 4°. *Cambridge, Fletcher & Hodson,* 1768.

Anstey (John). Pleader's guide, a didactic poem, in two parts. By J. J. S. [*anon.*] 4th ed. xvi, 212 pp. 16°. *London, Cadell & Davies,* 1804.

Antequera (José Maria). Historia de la legislacion española, desde los tiempos mas remotos hasta la época presente. 290 pp. 8°. *Madrid, Martinez y Minnesa,* 1849.

Anthing (Friedrich). History of the campaigns of Count Alexander Suworow-Reymnikski. [*or* Rimninskoi.] Translated from the German. [*anon.*] 112 pp. 8°. *London, J. Davis,* 1813. [**Royal** military chronicle, v. 2.]

Antine *or* Dantine (Maur François d'). *See* **Art** de vérifier les dates.

Antiquités du Bosphore cimmérien, conservées au musée impérial de l'Ermitage: [Par le comte Ouvaroff français et russe.] texte 2 v., avec atlas des planches. fol. *St. Pétersbourg,* 1854. s.

Anton (Jehan d'). *See* **Auton** (Jehan d').

Antoninus *Augustus.* Vetera Romanorum itineraria, cum J. Simleri, etc., notis. Itinerarium hierosolymitanum, et Hieroclis grammatici synecdemus curante Petro Wesselingio. 11 p. l. 762 pp. 28 l. 4°. *Amstelaedami, apud J. Wetstenium & G. Smith,* 1735. s.

Antoninus (Marcus Aurelius). The commentaries. Containing his maxims of science and rules of life. Wrote for his own use, and addressed to himself. Translated from the Greek, by James Thomson, *gent.* xii, 234 pp. 8°. *London, T. Parker,* 1747.

Apelt (Ernst Friedrich). Die epochen der geschichte der menschheit, eine historisch-philosophische skizze. 2 v. 8°. *Jena, Hockhausen,* 1845–46. s.

Aphthonius, *sophista.* Progymnasmata, a R. Agricola, [et] I. M. Catanaeo latinitate donata: cum scholiis R. Lorichii. 2 p. l. 218 l, 5 l. 18°. *Londini, T. Marsh,* 1583.

Apollonius *Rhodius.* The Argonautics. Translated by F. Fawkes. 8°. *Edinburgh,* [1792]. [**Anderson's** British Poets, v. 5].

Apollonius *Tyrius.* The Anglo-saxon version of the story of Apollonius of Tyre, upon which is founded the play of Pericles, attributed to Shakespeare; with a literal translation by Benj. Thorpe. v, 92 pp. 12°. *London, J. & A. Arch,* 1834.

NOTE.—Barth ascribes this work to Symposius, a christian author.

Apophthegmata graeca. Studio et labore Mathæi Gothi. (*With* **Neander** (Michael). Opus aureum.) s.

Appianus *Alexandrinus.* Romanorum libri qui Libicus, Syrius, Parthicus, Mithridaticus inscribuntur. Traductio P. Candidi. 131 l. unp. 4°. *Venetiis, B. Pictor & E. Ratdolt,* 1477.

——— Ciuiliū bellorū libri 1–5. Traductio P. Candidi. 211 l. unp. 4°. *Venetiis, B. Pictor & E. Ratdolt,* 1477. (*With* **Appianus** *Alexandrinus.* Romanorum libri, *Venetiis,* 1477.)

——— Romanorum libri qui Illyrius et Celticus inscribuntur. Traductio P. Candidi. 10 l. unp. 4°. *Venetiis, B. Pictor & E. Ratdolt,* 1477. (*With* **Appianus** *Alexandrinus.* Romanorum libri, *Venetiis,* 1477.)

——— Romanarvm historiarvm celtica, libyca, illyrica, syriaca, parthica, mithridatica, ciuilis, quinque libris distincta. Ex bibliotheca regia. 393 pp. 1 l. fol. *Lvtetiæ, C. Stephanus,* 1581.

Applegarth (Robert). A theological survey of the human understanding. [*anon*]. 3 p. l. 276 pp. 7 l. 8°. *Salisbury, Wallis & Stonehouse,* 1776.

Appletons' (D. & Co.) Hand-book of American travel: southern tour. With maps, etc. By Edward H. Hall. xii, 142 pp., 7 maps. 12°. *New York, D. Appleton & Co.,* 1866.

Appletons' (D. & Co.) Hand-book of American travel: northern tour. With maps, [etc.] By Edward H. Hall. 9th ed. xvi, 318 pp., 11 maps. 12°. *New York, D. Appleton & Co.* 1867.

Appleton (Elizabeth H.) Insurrection at Magellan. Narrative of the imprisonment and escape of Capt. Chas. H. Brown from the Chilian convicts. 228 pp. 1 pl. 12°. *Boston, Geo. C. Rand,* 1854.

Appleton (William S.) Ancestry of Mary Oliver, who lived 1640—1698, and was the wife of Samuel Appleton, of Ipswich. 29 pp. 3 tables. 4°. *Cambridge, (Mass.), J. Wilson & Son,* 1867.

Aprosio (Angelico). La visiera alzata; hecatoste di scrittori, che vaghi d'andare in maschera fuor del tempo di carnouale sono scoperti da Gio. Pietro Giacomo Villani. [*pseudon*]. 90 pp. 18°. *Parma, Vigna,* 1689.

——— Pentecoste d'altri scrittori, che andando in maschera fuor del tempo di carneuale, sono scoperti da Gio. Pietro Giacomo Villani. [*pseudon*]. 45 pp. 18°. *Parma, Vigna,* 1689. (*With* **Aprosio**, La visiera alzata hecatoste di scrittori. *Parma,* 1689.)

Apuleius *Madaurensis* (Lucius). Les metamorphoses, ov l'asne d'or. Nouvellement reveves, corrigées, et mises en meilleur ordre. [Engraved title.] 8 p. l. 382 pp. 16 pl. 12°. *Paris, N. & J. de La Coste,* 1648.

——— Commentaires sur la métamorphose de l'asne d'or de l'Apulée. [*anon.*] 270 pp. 20 l. [*With* **Apuleius**, *Paris,* 1648.]

——— The birth of pleasure, the story of Cupid and Psyche. [Translation.] 110 pp. 16°. *New York, James Porteus,* 1867.

——— Cupid and Psyche; a mythological tale, from the "Golden Ass." From the 2d anonymous London ed. of 1800; with the life of Apuleius, by J. L. Wilson. 88 pp. 3 pl. 8°. *Charleston, (S. C.,) B. B. Hussey,* 1842.

——— L'asino d'oro, traslatato da messer. Agnolo Firenzuola dilatino in lingua toscano. (**Firenzuola**. Opere, v. 3.)

Apuleius *Barbarus.* Herbarium. [Anglo-saxon text, with English translation.] (*With* **Leechdoms**, wortcunning, and starcraft of early England. Ed. by O. Cockayne. V. 1. 8°. *London,* 1864.)

Aquila *Romanus.* *See* **Rutilius Lupus** (P.) De figuris sententiarum.

Aquinas, (*Saint* Thomas). *See* **Aquino.**

Aquino (*Saint* Tommaso d'). Catena aurea [patrum] in quatuor evangelistas. fol. [*Aug. Vind., G. Zainer,* n. d.] s.

Aquino, (*Saint* Tommaso d'). De corpore Cristi. 17 l. unp. sm. 4°. [*Coloniæ, Arnold Therhoern, about* 1480.]

——— De desertione anime a Deo. 2 l. unp. sm. 4°. [*Leydis, per Heynricū Heynrici,* 1484.] (*With* **Aquino**. Tractatus de humanitate Christi. *Leydis,* 1484.)

——— De duobus præceptis charitatis, et decem legis præceptis, ejusdemque de venerabili sacramento altaris. Recognovit C. Martin. vii, 340 pp. 24°. *Coloniæ, J. M. Heberle & Co.,* 1852.

——— Glosa continua sup. quatuor euangelistas. fol. [Basileæ.] 1476. s.

——— In libros meteorologicorvm Aristotelis proeclarissima commentaria, cum duplici textus interpretatione, vna Francisci Vatabli, antiqua altera. 2 l., 270 pp. in 68 l. fol. *H. Scottus, Venitiis;* 1561. (*With* preceding.) s.

——— In qvatvor libros Aristotelis de cvclo et mundo commentāria, quae cum morte praeuentus perficere non potuerit, absoluit Petrus de Aluernia; cvm dvplici textus translatione, antiqua videlicet, et Joannis Argyropili noua diligenter recognitis. 6 p. l., 176 pp. fol. *Venetiis, haeredes H. Scoti,* 1575. s.

——— Postilla in Job. fol. [Eslingæ.] 1474. s.

——— The same. fol. (n. p., *Conrad Fyner.*) 1476. s.

——— Prima pars summe sacre theologie. [v. 1]. fol. *In urbe Venetiarū, B. Locatellus,* 1494. s.

——— Prima pars secunde partis summe theologiæ. fol. *Venetijs, B. Locatellus,* 1495. (*With* preceding.) s.

——— Secūda secūde partis sūme theologie summe [et] id est de ptibus pnīe, et primo de stritione. [v. 2.] fol. [n. d. *or* p.] s.

——— Tertia pars, additiones tertie partis. [v. 3.] fol. *Venetijs, B. de Tridino,* 1486. s.

——— Remediū circa carnalē delectationem. 2 l. unp. sm. 4°. [*Leydis, per Heynricū Heynrici,* 1484.] (*With* **Aquino**. Tractatus de humanitate Christi. *Leydis,* 1484.)

——— Tractatus de humanitate Christi. 97 l. sm. 4°. *Leydis, per Heynricū Heynrici,* 1484.

Arago (Jacques Étienne Victor). Promenade autour du monde, pendant 1817—1820, sur les corvettes l'Uranie et la Physicienne. 2 v. 8°. *Paris,* 1822. s.

Aratus. [Phænomena et diosemeia, cum Theonis scholiis et Eratosthenis catasterismis, etc. [*Græce.*] Accesserunt annotationes in Eratosthenem et hymnos Dionysii: curante J. Fell.] 238 pp. 12°. *Oxonii, e theatro Sheldoniano,* 1672.

Archambault (P. J.). *See* **Violette** (J. H. M.) *and* **Archambault.** Dictionnaire des analyses chimiques.

Archer (*Mrs.* Ann). Authentic and interesting memoirs of Miss Ann Sheldon, [afterwards Mrs. Archer]. 4 v. 16°. *London,* 1790.

Archer's (The) guide. [With] instructions for the use of the bow; [also] a history of the long-bow. By an old toxophilite. [*anon.*] xii, 178 pp. 1 pl. 16°. *London, T. Hurst,* 1833.

Archiac (Étienne Jules Adolphe, *Vicomte* d'). Histoire des progrès de la géologie de 1834 à 1845. 5 v. 8°. *Paris, L. Martinet,* 1847–53. s.

Archilochus. Iambographorum principis reliquiæ. Edidit J. Liebel. Ed. repetita. xvi, 280 pp. 8°. *Lipsiæ, I. C. Sommer,* 1818.

Archimedes. I teoremi sulla sfera, e sul cilindro; quello della misura de cerchio; e le note critiche e geometriche, [da V. Flauti]. 75 pp. 8°. *Napoli,* 1852. (*With* **Euclid.** Elementi di geometria, ed. Napoli, 1852, v. 2.) s.

Archivio storico italiano. Serie III. 1866. V. 4—5. 8°. *Firenze,* 1866.

Arco (Giambattista Gherardo, *Conte* d'). Dell' armonia politico-economica tra la città e il suo territorio; 1, sulla populazione. 2, dell' annona. (v. 30.) Dell' influenza del comercio sopra i talenti e i costumi; Risposta al quesito, se in una stato di terreno fertile, favorir debbasi maggiormente l'estrazione delle materie prime, ovvero quella della manifatture; Del diritto ai transiti. v. 31. (**Scrittori** class. ital. di econ. pol. v. 30—31.)

Arenhold (Silvius Johannes). Conspectus bibliothecæ universalis epistolarvm. [Epistolographi.] 4°. *Hanoveriæ,* 1746. s.

Aretin (Johann Christoph Anton Maria, *Freiherr von*). Beyträge zur geschichte und literatur, vorzüglich aus den Schätzen der Centralbibliothek zu München. [Codices græci MSS. recensiti et notis illustrati ab I. Hardt.] 9 v. 8°. *München,* 1803—07. s.

Arfwedson (Carl David). Colonia Nova Svecia in Americam borealem deducta, historiola. 2 pl. 34 pp. 1 map. 4°. *Upsaliæ,* 1825.

Argens (Jean Baptiste de Boyer, *Marquis* d'). Philosophical visions. Translated from the French. [*anon*]. xxvi, 235 pp. 16°. *London, R. Griffiths,* 1757.

——— *and* **Cochois** (*Mlle* —). New memoirs, a critical inquiry into the nature of friendship and happiness, and essays on other important subjects, by the marquis d'Argens. [With] two novels, Count de Ronancourt and Isabella Mendosa, and thoughts on the art of beautifying the face, by Mlle. Cochois. 2 v. xxii, 261 pp.; 7 l., 274 pp. *London, D. Brown and others,* 1747.

Argensola (Bartolomé Leonardo de). Conqvista de las islas Malvcas. 6 p. l., 407 pp. fol. *Madrid, A. Martin,* 1609.

——— Discovery and conquest of the Molucco and Philippine Islands. 3 p. l., 260 pp., 4 l., 1 map. sm. 4°. *London,* 1708. (*In* **Stevens,** John. New collection of voyages and travels.)

Argensola (Lupercio Leonardo de). Informacion de los sucesos del reino de Aragon, en los años de 1590 y 1591. 8 p. l. 232 pp. 8°. *Madrid, imp. real,* 1808.

Argenville (Antoine Joseph Dézallier d'). *See* **Dézallier d'Argenville.**

Argis (Antoine Gaspard Boucher d'). Principes sur la nullité du mariage, pour cause d'impuissance. Par M*** avocat en parlement. Avec le traité de J. Bouhier, sur les procédures qui sont en usage en France, pour la preuve de l'impuissance de l'homme. Et quelques pièces curieuses sur le même sujet. [*anon.*] xiv, 388 pp., 3 l. 16°. *Londres,* 1756.

Argosy (The); a magazine of tales, travels, essays, and poems. v. 2–4. 8°. *London, Strahan,* 1866–7.

Argüelles (Agustin de). Exámen historico de la reforma constitutional que hicieron las córtes generales y estraordinarias, 1810—1813. 2 v. viii, 479 pp.; vii, 459 pp. 8°. *Londres, Carlos Wood e hijo,* 1835.

Argumentum anti-Normanicum; or, an argument proving from ancient histories and records that William, Duke of Normandy, made no absolute conquest of England by the sword. [*anon*]. 5 p. l. 164 pp. 1 pl. 12°. *London, John Darby,* 1682.

Aristoteles. De animalibvs, interprete Theodoro Gaza. 6 p. l. unp. 106 l. fol. *Venetiis, J. & G. de Gregoriis,* 1492.

——— Commentary illustrating the poetic of Aristotle, by examples from the modern poets. [With] a new and corrected edition of the translation of the poetic. By Henry James Pye. xvi, 564 pp., 5 l. [1 pl. inserted.] 4°. *London, J. Stockdale,* 1792.

——— On fallacies; or the sophistici elenchi. [Gr.] With a translation and notes, by Edward Poste. viii, 252 pp. 8°. *London. Macmillan & Co.,* 1866.

Arizona. Journals of the second and third legislative assembly. December sessions, 1865–66. 258 pp.; 269 pp. 8°. *Prescott*, 1866.

Arlincourt (Victor, *Vicomte* d'). Ipsiboé, translated from the French. 2 v. viii, 284 pp.; 270 pp. 18°. *London, J. Robins & Co.*, 1823.

——— The renegade, translated from the French. 2 v. viii, 256 pp; 272 pp. 18°. *London, J. Robins & Co.*, 1822.

Armstrong (John, *poet and physician*). The art of preserving health; a poem. 59 pp. 16°. *London*, 1756. [**Select** collection of modern poems. 16°. *Edinburgh*, 1758.]

——— The same. 99 pp. 16°. *London, T. Cadell*, 1768.

Armstrong (M. K.) History and resources of Dakota, Montana, and Idaho. 72 pp. 1 map. 16°. *Yankton, (D.T.,) G. W. Kingsbury*, 1866.

Armstrong (Robert, *C. E.*) Chimneys for furnaces, fire-places, and steam boilers. 64 pp. 1 pl. 16°. *London, E. & F. N. Spon*, 1866.

Army and Navy Journal, August, 1866, to August, 1867. v. 4. 4°. *New York, W. F. Church*, 1867.

Arnold (George). Poems, grave and gay. 214 pp. sq. 16°. *Boston, Ticknor & Fields*, 1867.

Arnold (Isaac N.) The history of Abraham Lincoln and the overthrow of slavery. 736 pp. 1 pl. 8°. *Chicago, Clarke & Co.*, 1866.

Arnold (Matthew). Heinrich Heine. 64 pp. 18°. *Philadelphia, F. Leypoldt*, 1863.

Arnoudt (*Rev.* P. J.) Imitation of the sacred heart of Jesus. Translated from the Latin by Rev. J. A. M. Fastre. xxii, 774 pp. 1 pl. 12°. *Cincinnati, J. P. Walsh*, 1865.

Arretinus. *See* **Aretinus.**

Arrianus. Voyage round the Euxine sea; translated and accompanied with a geographical dissertation. Added, discourses: I. On the trade to the East Indies; II. On the distance which the ships of antiquity usually sailed in 24 hours; III. On the measure of the Olympic stadium. [By William Falconer, M. D.] 222 pp. 1 pl. 2 maps. 4°. *Oxford, J. Cooke*, 1805. s.

Art (l') de vérifier les dates des faits historiques, *etc.* [*anon.*] 3e éd., [par Antine, Clément, etc.] 3 v., fol. *Paris, A. Jombert*, 1783–87. s.

Art Journal [of London]. New series. v. 5. Jan.—Dec., 1866. 4°. *London, Virtue*, 1866.

Artaud de Montor (Alexis François, *le chevalier*). Histoire de Dante Alighieri. vi, 635 pp. 3 pl. 8°. *Paris, Adrien le Clerc*, 1841. s.

——— Histoire de la vie et des travaux politiques du comte d'Hauterive, comprenant une partie des actes de la diplomatie française, 1784—1830. 2e éd. vii, 576 pp. 8°. *Paris, A. Le Clerc & Ce.*, 1839. s.

——— Histoire de pape Léon XII. 2 v. xxvii, 449 pp.; 465 pp. 8°. *Paris, A. Le Clerc*, 1843. s.

——— Histoire de pape Pie VIII. xl, 469 pp. 8°. *Paris, A. le Clerc*, 1844. s.

Artedi (Peter). Bibliotheca ichthyologica, seu historia litteraria ichthyologiæ. Emendata et aucta a Iohanne Iulio Walbaum. 3 p. l. 230 pp. 8°. *Grypeswaldiæ, A. F. Roese*, 1788. (**Artedi**, Ichthyologiæ, part I.) s.

——— Philosophia ichthyologica. Emendata et aucta a Iohanne Iulio Walbaum. 3 p. l. 196 pp. 1 pl. 8°. *Grypeswaldiæ, A. F. Roese*, 1789. (**Artedi.** Ichthyologiæ, part II. *With* preceding.) s.

——— Synonymia piscium græca et latina emendata, aucta atque illustrata. Accedit disputatio de veterum scriptorum hippopotamo. Auct. Ioh. Gottl. Schneider. viii, 352 pp., 4 l. 3 pl. 4°. *Lipsiæ*, 1789. s.

Arthur (Robert, *M. D.*) Some suggestions concerning the nature and treatment of decay of the teeth. 70 pp. 12°. *Baltimore, J. Murphy & Co.*, 1867.

——— Treatise on the use of adhesive gold foil. 86 pp. 8°. *Philadelphia, Jones, White & McCurdy*, 1857.

Articles of agreement between the lord proprietary of Maryland and the proprietarys of Pensilvania, &c., touching the limits and boundaries of the two provinces, with the commission constituting certain persons to execute the same. 19 pp. folio. Map. *Philadelphia, B. Franklin*, 1733.

Asbjörnsen (P. Christian). Norske huldreeventyr ag folkesagn. 2en udgave. v. 1. xxx, 301 pp. 12°. *Christiania, P. F. Steensballe*, 1859. s.

Ash (Simeon). *See* **Ball** (*Rev.* John). Letter of many ministers in old England. 1643.

Ash (Thomas). Carolina; or a description of the present state of that country, and the natural excellencies thereof. [*anon.*] 2 p. l. 40 pp. sm. 4°. *London*, 1682.

Ashburner, (W.) *See* **California.** Geological survey.

Ashe (Thomas). The spirit of "The book"; or memoirs of Caroline, princess of Hapsburgh. 2d ed. 3 v. 8°. *London, Allen & Co.*, 1811.

Asher (A.) Bibliographical essay on the collection of voyages and travels edited by Levinus Hulsius and his successors, 1598 to 1660. 118 pp. 4°. *Berlin, A. Asher*, 1839.

Asher (G. M.) A list of the maps and charts of New-Netherland, and of the views of New-Amsterdam. A supplement to his bibliographical essay on New-Netherland. 22, 120 pp., 25 l. 4°. *Amsterdam, F. Müller*, 1855.

Asher (*Rev.* Jeremiah). An autobiography; with details of a visit to England, and some account of the Meeting st. Baptist church, Providence, R. I., and of Shiloh Baptist church, Philadelphia. x, 227 pp. 1 pl. 16°. *Philadelphia, J. Asher*, 1862.

Asheton (William, *D. D.*) The royal apology; or, an answer to the rebel's plea. 2d ed. 4 p. l., 59 pp. *London, Robert Clavel*, 1686.

Ashhurst (John, *Jr., M. D.*) Injuries of the spine, with an analysis of nearly 400 cases. 127 pp. 12°. *Philadelphia, J. B. Lippincott & Co.*, 1867.

Aslak Bolt. Jordebog: fortegnelse over jordegods og andre herligheder tilhörende erkebiskopstolen, i nidaros. Efter originalhaandskriftet udgivet af P. A. Munch. vii, 142 pp. 8°. *Christiania, C. Gröndahl*, 1852. s.

Assigny (Marius d'). *See* **Gaultruche.**

Assurance (The) Magazine. V, 1—2. 8°. *London*, 1850—51. (Institute of Actuaries.)

Asta-Buruaga (Francisco Solano). Diccionario jeografico de la republica de Chile. viii, 421 pp. 12°. *Nueva York, D. Appleton & Co.*, 1867.

Astley (Philip). System of equestrian education, exhibiting the beauties and defects of the horse. 7th ed. xii, 197 pp., 10 pl. 8°. *Dublin, T. Burnside*, 1802.

Astonishing (An) affair. The Rev. Samuel Arnold cast and tried for his cruelty. By Philandros. [*pseudon.*] 168 pp. 1 pl. 18°. *Concord, (N. H.,) Luther Roby*, 1830.

Astrop (Robert Francis). Original poems, interspersed with tales. 132 pp. 16°. *Philadelphia, Carey & Hart*, 1835.

Athenaeum (The); a journal of literature, science, and the fine arts. July, 1866 to June 1867. 2 v. 4°. *London*, 1866-7.

Atheneum (The); or spirit of the English magazines, [1st series.] v. 1—11. 8°. *Boston*, 1817-22. (v. 1 and 8 wanting.)

Athenian sport; or, two thousand paradoxes merrily argued, to amuse and divert the age. By a member of the Athenian Society. [*anon.*] xxxii, 544 pp. 12°. *London, B. Bragg*, 1707.

Atkinson (Edward). On the collection of revenue. 70 pp. 8°. *Boston, A. Williams & Co.*, 1867.

Atkinson (*Rev.* John). Memorials of Methodism in New Jersey, from 1770 to [1790]. Containing sketches of the ministerial laborers, [etc.,] of that period. 2d ed. 435 pp. 1 pl. 12°. *Philadelphia, Perkinpine & Higgins*, 1860.

Atlantic Monthly; a magazine of literature, art, and politics. January to Dec. 1867. v. 19-20. 8°. *Boston, Ticknor & Fields*, 1867.

Atlas de l' archéologie du nord, représentant des échantillons de l'age de bronze et de l'age de fer. 10 pp. 22 pl. 4°. *Copenhague, Thiöle*, 1857.

Attersoll (*Rev.* William). The badges of christianity; or, a treatise of the sacraments fully declared out of the word of God. 11 p. l.; 392 pp., 24 l. sm. 4°. *London, W. Iaggard*, 1606.

Atwater (Caleb). Essay on education. 123 pp. 8°. *Cincinnati, Kendall & Henry*, 1841.

——— Mysteries of Washington city, during several months of the session of the 28th Congress. 218 pp. 18°. *Washington, G. A. Sage*, 1844.

Atwater (Lyman H.) Manual of elementary logic. 244 pp. 12°. *Philadelphia, J. B. Lippincott & Co.*, 1867.

Atwell (*Rev.* B. W.) Principles of elocution and vocal culture; [with] rules for correct reading [etc]. 98 pp. 12°. *Providence, Bangs Williams News Co.*, 1867.

Atwood (D. T., *Architect*). Rules of proportion; compiled and original; and adapted to modern practice. v. 1. 71 pp. 5 pl. 12°. [*New York*], *Author*, 1867.

Atwood (George, *F. R. S.*) Treatise on the rectilinear motion and rotation of bodies. xv, 436 pp. 8 pl. 8°. *Cambridge, (Eng.) J. Archdeacon*, 1784. s.

Aubert (E.) Om mundtlig rettergang og edsvorne. v, 688 pp. 8°. *Christiania, P. T. Malling*, 1849.

Aubeuf (Vertot d'). *See* **Vertot** d'Aubeuf.

Aubigné (Théodore Agrippa d'). Aventures du baron de Fæneste. Nouv. éd. revue et annotée par Prosper Mérimée. xx, 348 pp. 16°. *Paris, P. Jannet*, 1855.

Aubinac (François Hédelin, *abbé* d'). Des satyres, brvtes, monstres, et démons; de levr nature et adoration. 16°. *Paris*, 1627.

Auburn (N. Y.) Boyd's Auburn directory, [with] business directory of Cayuga co., 1867—68. Compiled by A. & W. H. Boyd. 286 pp. 1 map. 12°. *Auburn, A. & W. H. Boyd*, [1867.]

Aucher (Paschal, *D. D.*) A grammar, Armenian and English. [2d ed.] 231 pp. 12°. *Venice, Armenian press*, 1832. s.

Auctores Historiæ Ecclesiasticæ. fol. *Basileæ,* 1523. s.

CONTENTS.

Eusebii Pamphili libri ix. Ruffino interprete.
Ruffini Aquileiensis libri ii.
Item ex Theodoreto, Sozomeo, et Socrate libri xii.
Versi ab Epiphanio scholastico, abbreviati per Cassiodorum.

Audinet-Serville (Jean Guillaume). Histoire naturelle des insectes. Orthoptères. xviii, 776 pp. 14 pl. col. 8°. *Paris, Roret,* 1839. s.

——— *See* **Amyot** *and* **Audinet-Serville.**

Audouin (Jean Victor), *and* **Edwards** (Henri Milne). Recherches pour servir à l'histoire naturelle du littoral de la France. 2 v. 406 pp. 6 maps, &c.; 290 pp. 4 tab. 8 pl. 8°. *Paris, Crochard,* 1832–34. s.

CONTENTS.

V. 1. Voyage à Granville, aux îles Chausey et à Saint Malo.
V. 2. Annélides. Considérations sur l'état actuel des pêches maritimes en France, par M. Milne Edwards.
Mémoire sur la pêche de la morue à Terre neuve, par M. Milne Edwards.

Aughey (*Rev.* John H.) The iron furnace: or slavery and secession. 296 pp. 12°. *Philadelphia, J. S. Claxton,* 1865.

August (E. F.) Vollständige logarithmische und trigonometrische tafeln, &c.· 4^e aufl. x, 225 pp. 18°. *Berlin, Veit & Co.,* 1857. s.

Augusta, Hallowell, and Gardiner directory, for 1867—68. By Langford & Chase. 182, 32 pp. 12°. *Augusta, (Me.,) Pierce Bros.,* 1867.

Augustin (Antonio). *See* **Agustin** (Antonio).

Augustinus (Aurelius, *Saint*). Sermones de tempore. fol. *Basilee,* 1495. s.

——— Sermones de sanctis. fol. *Basilee,* 1495. (*With preceding.*) s.

Augustinus *Triumphus, de Ancona.* Summa de sũma potestate ecclesiastica. 469 l. fol. *Auguste,* [*J. Schussler*], 1473. s.

Ault Dumesnil (—— d'). Dictionnaire historique, géographique, et biographique des croisades, publié par J. P. Migne. cxcv, 1042 pp. 8°. *Paris, J. P. Migne,* 1852.

Auntient lere, containing aphoristical and preceptive passages from the works of eminent English authors of the 16th and 17th centuries. viii, 304 pp. 1 pl. 16°. *London, Longman,* 1812.

Aurifodina; or, adventures in the gold region. By Cantell A. Bigly. [*pseudon.*] 12°. *New York,* 1849. s.

Austria. Notes sur l' élevage du bétail des espèces bovine, ovine et porcine de l'empire d'Autriche. xv, 102 pp. 6 pl. 8°. *Paris, Didot,* 1856. s.

——— Topographisches post lexicon des kronlandes Oesterreich unter der Enns. xii, 305 pp. 8°. *Wien, k. hof-und staatsdruckerei,* 1864.

Austrius *Rubeaquensis* (Sebastian). *See* **Cornelius.** De puerorum morbis.

Authentic biography of Colonel Richard M. Johnson. [*anon.*] 107 pp. 12°. *New York, Henry Mason,* 1833.

Authentic and interesting memoirs of Mrs. Clarke, [with] Wardle's charges relative to the Duke of York, and minutes of evidence. From authentic documents. [*anon.*] 371 pp 8°. *Boston, J. Belcher,* 1809.

Authentic narrative of the Seminole war and miraculous escape of Mrs. Mary Godfrey and her four children, [also] massacre of whites by indians and negroes in Florida. [*anon.*] 24 pp. 8°. *Providence, (R. I.)* 1836.

Authentic (The) records of the court of England, for the last seventy years [1761—1831]. [*anon.*] 395 pp. 8°. *London, J. Phillips,* 1832.

Auton, Autun, Authon, (Jehan d') *or* Danton. Chroniques, avec une notice, et des notes, par P. L. Jacob, bibliophile. [Paul Lacroix.] 4 v. 8°. *Paris, Silvestre,* 1834–5.

Aviler (Augustin Charles d'). Cours d' architecture, qui comprend les ordres de vignole, avec des commentaires, et tout ce qui regarde l' art de bâtir. Nouv. éd. 4°. *Paris, J. Marriette,* 1738. s.

Avogadro (Amedeo). Fisica de corpi ponderabili; ossia trattato della costituzione general de corpi. 4 v. 8°. *Torino, stamperia reale,* 1837–41. s.

Awful calamities, or the shipwrecks of December, 1839, on the coast of Massachusetts. 5th ed. 8°. 24 pp. *Boston,* 1840.

Aydelott (B. P., *D. D.*) Ethics for our country and the times. 214 pp. 12°. *Cincinnati, R. W. Carroll & Co.,* 1866.

Ayora (Gonzalo). Cartas escribialas al rey Don Fernando en el año 1503 desde el Rosellon, sobre el estado de la guerra con los Franceses. Dalas a luz D. G. V. 88 pp. 8°. *Madrid, Sancha,* 1794. s.

Babbage (Charles). Observations on the temple of Serapis at Pozzuoli, near Naples, etc.; with a supplement, Conjectures on the physical condition of the surface of the moon. 42 pp. 8°. *London, author*, 1847. s.

Babbidge (*Rev.* Charles). The claims of congregational churches; a centennial address, being a vindication of the rights of the first church in Pepperell, Mass. 8°. 44 pp. *Boston, Crosby & Nichols*, 1847.

Babié de Bercenay (François), *and* **Beaumont** (L.) Galerie militaire, ou notice historique sur les généraux, les amiraux, etc., qui ont commandé les armées françaises depuis le commencement de la révolution jusqu'à present. 7 v. 16°. *Paris*, 1805. s.

Bachaumont (François le Coigneux de). Œuvres. *See* **Chapelle** (C. E. L.)

Bachiller y Morales (Antonio). Prontuario de agricultura general para el uso de los labradores i haciendados de Cuba. 8°. *Habana*, 1856. s.

Bache (Alexander D.) Discussion of the magnetic and meteorological observations made at Girard College in 1840–45. Third section, comprising parts vii–ix. Vertical force. 70 pp. 4°. [*Washington, Sm. Inst*]. 1863. (*In* Smithsonian contrib. to knowl. v. 14.)

——— The same. Fourth section. Parts x–xii. Dip and total force. 41 pp. 4°. [*Washington, Sm. Inst*]. 1864. (*In* Smithsonian contrib. to knowl. v. 14.)

——— Observations at the magnetic and meteorological observatory at Girard college, 1840–45. 1 v. in 3. 8°. 3,213 pp. atlas, 210 pl., oblong fol. *Washington, Topographical bureau*, 1847. s.

Backer (Augustin et Alois). Bibliothèque des écrivains de la compagnie de Jésus, ou notices bibliographiques. v. 1–7. 8°. *Liége*, 1853–61.

Bacon (Francis, *lord*). Essays, with annotations by Richard Whately. xx, 536 pp. 8°. *New York, C. S. Francis & Co.* 1857. s.

——— Essays, with a sketch of his life and character, [etc.] and portions of the annotations of Archbishop Whately. By J. R. Boyd. 426 pp. 12°. *New York, A. S. Barnes & Co.* 1867.

——— Resuscitatio; or, bringing into public light several pieces of the works, hitherto sleeping, of Francis Bacon, with life. By William Rawley. 12 p. l. 282, 122 pp. 1 pl. fol. *London, W. Lee*, 1657.

CONTENTS.

Advertisement touching the controversies of the church of England.
Advice to the King, touching Mr. Sutton's estate.
Beginning of the history of Great Britain.
Confession of the faith.
Considerations touching the pacification of the church of England.
Considerations touching the plantation in Ireland.
Discourse of the union of England and Scotland.
Fragment of an essay, of fame.
Letter and discourse to Sir H. Savill, touching helps for the intellectual powers.
Letters.
Observations upon a libel, 1592.
Proposition to the King, touching the compiling and amendment of the lawes of England.
Report of Dr. Lopez, his treason.
Speeches.

Bacon (George Washington), *and* **Larkins** (William George). Descriptive handbook of America. viii, 392 pp. 2 pl. 2 maps. 12°. *London, G. W. Bacon & Co.* [1866].

Bacon (Leonard, *D. D.*) Slavery discussed in occasional essays, from 1833 to 1846. 241 pp. 12°. *New York, Baker & Scribner*, 1846.

Baddeley (F. H.) Geognosy of a part of the Saguenay country. 79, 116 pp. [*With* **Quebec**, Lit. & hist. soc. Transactions. v. 1.]

——— The same. Partie géognostique d'une exploration du territoire du Saguenay. 7–66 pp. [*With* **Canada**, Rapport des commissaires pour explorer le Saguenay.]

——— Localities of metallic minerals in the Canadas. 332 to 426 pp. [*With* **Quebec**, lit. & hist. soc. Transactions. v. 2.]

Baden (Gustav Ludvig). Dansk-norsk historisk bibliothek, indeholdende efterretning om de skrifter, som bidrage til dansk-norsk historie kundskab. 7 p. l. 358 pp. 18°. *Odense, S. Heurpel*, 1815. s.

Baden (Jacob). Fuldstændig tydsk og dansk ordbog. Med en fortale om det tydske sprogs, etc. 2 v. xxiv, 1536 pp.; 1224 pp. 8°. *Kjöbenhavn, Gyldendal*, 1787–97. s.

——— [*See* **Amberg** (H. C.) Fuldstændig dansk og tydsk ordbog].

Baden. Amtliche beiträge zur statistik der staats finanzen des grossherzogthums Baden. xi, 392 pp. 4°. *Karlsruhe, C. F. Müller*, 1851. s.

——— Uebersicht der strafrechts pflege im grossherzogthum Baden wahrend das jahr 1829. xiv, 96 pp. 4°. *Carlsruhe, C. F. Müller*, 1830. s.

——— The same for 1830. xii, 131 pp. 4°. *Heidelberg, C. F. Winter*, 1831. (*With* preceding). s

Baer (Friedrich Carl). Essai historique et critique sur l'Atlantique des anciens. 2e éd. 114 pp. 2 maps. 8°. *Avignon, Seguin*, 1835. s.

Baerle (Caspar). Rervm per octennivm in Brasilia et alibi gestarum, sub præfectura illustrissimi comitis I. Mauritü historia. Editio 2[a]. Cui accesserunt Gulielmi Pisonis tractatvs de aëribus et locis in Brasilia. 5 p. l. 644 pp., 10 l. 2 maps. 5 pl. *Clivis, T. Silberling*, 1660.

Baeyer (J. J.) Die küstenvermessung und ihre verbindung mit der Berlinier grundlinie. Ausgeführt von der trigonometrischen abtheilung des generalstabes. xx, 587 pp. 1 map. 2 pl. 4°. *Berlin, F. Dümmler,* 1849.

Baffled schemes. A novel. 159 pp. 8°. [*anon*]. *Boston, Loring,* 1867.

Bagay (V.) Nouvelles tables astronomiques et hydrographiques. 7, xxvi, 615, 125 pp. 5 pl. 4°. *Paris, F. Didot,* 1829. s.

Bagehot (Walter). The English constitution. viii, 348 pp. 12°. *London, Chapman & Hall,* 1867.

Bagster (C. Birch). The progress and prospects of Prince Edward Island. 139, xxxvi pp. 12°. *Charlottetown, J. Ings,* 1861. s.

Bailey (*Rev.* B.) A dictionary, English and Malayalim. viii, 546 pp. 8°. *Cottayany, Church Mission Press,* 1849. s.

Bailey (John C. W.) Series of practical masonry. The secretary's special help; a monitor for the secretary of the lodge. 2d ed. 95 pp. 16°. *Chicago, J. C. W. Bailey,* 1867.

——— The senior deacon's special help; a monitor for the senior deacon of the lodge. 63 pp. 16°. *Chicago, J. C. W. Bailey,* 1866.

——— The worshipful master's special help; a monitor for the master of the lodge. 127 pp. 16°. *Chicago, J. C. W. Bailey,* 1866.

Bailey (J. W.) Notes on fossil fresh water infusoria from Oregon. [*With* **Fremont** (J. C.) exploring expedition to Rocky mountains in 1842, &c., (p. 302). *Ed. Washington,* 1845. s.

Bailey (Loring Woart). Observations on the geology of southern New Brunswick, 1864. 159 pp. 8°. *Frederickton, Assembly,* 1865. s.

Bailey (Samuel). On the received text of Shakespeare's dramatic writings and its improvement. v. 2. vi, 413 pp. 8°. *London, Longmans,* 1866.

Baillie (Joanna). A collection of poems, chiefly manuscript and from living authors. xliv, 330 pp. 8°. *London, Longman,* 1823.

——— Fugitive verses. new ed. viii, 58 pp., 8°. *London, E. Moxon,* 1842.

Baillie (*Captain* William). [Works: a series of prints and etchings, after Rembrandt, Ostade, Teniers, Gerard Dow, Terburg, Poussin, and other old masters]. 2 v. in 1. 60 pl., 53 pl., fol. n. p. *Author,* [1792].

Baillie (William Balfour). Natural history, etc. *See* **Adams**, (Arthur, etc.)

Baird (Spencer Fullerton). The mammals of North America. xxxiv, 764, 55 pp. 87 pl. 4°. *Philadelphia, J. B. Lippincott & Co.,* 1859.

Baird, (Spencer Fullerton.) Mammals, [of Chile] [*With* **Gilliss** (J. M.) U. S. ast. exped. v. 2].

——— Mammals: birds: reptiles. [*With* **Emory** (W. H.) Report on the U. S. and Mexican boundary survey. v. 2, pt. 2]

——— [*Editor.*] Outlines of general zoology. [Reprinted from the Iconographic encyclopædia.] xxi, 502, xvi pp. 8°. Atlas, 4°. *New York, R. Garrigue,* 1851. s.

CONTENTS.

Baird (S. F.) Fishes and Reptiles.
Cassin (John). Birds.
Girard (Charles). Mammals.
Haldeman (S. S.) Invertebrates.
[Atlas wanting].

Baker (Charles). Contributions to publications of the society for the diffusion of useful knowledge, and the central society of education. Privately reprinted. vi, 404 pp. 8°. [*Doncaster, Yorkshire Inst. press.*] 1842. s.

Baker (George M.) Amateur dramas for parlor theatricals, etc. 252 pp. 16°. *Boston, Lee & Shepard,* 1867.

Baker (Lafayette C.) History of the United States' secret service. 704 pp. 17 pl. 8°. *Philadelphia, L. C. Baker,* 1867.

Baker (Sir Richard). Theatrum redivivum; or, the theatre vindicated. In answer to Mr. Pryn's histrio-mastix. 4 p. l. 141 pp 18°. *London, F. Eglesfield,* 1662.

Baker (Thomas). Reflections upon learning, [showing] the insufficiency thereof, in order to evince the usefulness and necessity of revelation. By a gentleman. [*anon*]. 4th ed. 8 p. l. 295 pp. 12°. *London, A. Bosvile,* 1708.

Bakewell (Frederick C.) Great facts: a popular history and description of the most remarkable inventions during the present century. xii, 304 pp. 1 pl. 12°. *London, Houlston & Wright,* 1859. s.

Bakewell (Robert). Introduction to geology, comprising the elements of the science, with an outline of the geology of England and Wales. Edited by Prof. Benjamin Silliman, with an appendix containing an outline of his course of lectures on geology. 1st Am. ed. xx, 400 pp. 7 pl. 8°. *New Haven, H. Howe,* 1829. s.

Balbuena (Bernardo de). El Bernardo, poema heroyco. 3 v. 16°. *Madrid, Sancha,* 1808.

Baldinucci (Filippo). Opere. Con note ed aggiunte. 14 v. 8°. *Milano, Soc. de clas. ital.,* 1808—11. s.

CONTENTS.

V. 1. Cominciamento progresso dell'arte dell'intagliare in rame, colle vite.
V. 2-3. Vocabolario toscano dell'arte del disegno.
V. 4-14. Notizie de'professori del disegno da Cimabue.

Baldwin (Edward). Fables, ancient and modern. 4th ed. 2 v. viii, 206 pp; iv, 219 pp. 18°. *London, Godwin & Co.* 1815.

Baldwin (Thomas). Universal pronouncing gazetteer. 8th ed. 648, 56 pp. 12°. *Philadelphia, E. H. Butler & Co.*, 1849. s.

Ball (John, *editor*). Peaks, passes, and glaciers: a series of excursions by members of the alpine club. 5th ed. xiii, 328 pp. 1 map. 12°. *London, Longman,* 1860. s.

Ball (*Rev.* John). A letter of many ministers in old England, requesting the judgment of their reverend brethren in New England concerning nine positions, written A. D. 1637. Together with their answer thereunto returned, 1639. And the reply made unto the said answer, and sent over, 1640. Published by Simeon Ash and William Rathband. 6 p. l. 90 pp. sm. 4°. *London, Thomas Vnderhill,* 1643.

Ballantyne (Robert Michael). Hudson's Bay; or, every-day life in the wilds of North America, during six years' residence in the territories of the Hudson's Bay company. 3d ed. 16°. *London, T. Nelson & sons,* 1859. s.

Ballier (Gertrude). A week on an iceberg. Narrative of the sufferings of Herman and Gertrude Ballier, who, eloping from England, sailed on the ill-fated ship Monarch of the Sea, which struck an iceberg in mid-ocean and sunk, with over 700 souls. 48 pp. 8°. *Philadelphia, C. W. Alexander,* [1866].

——— The same. Woche auf einem eisberge. Begebenheit der leiden von Hermann und Gertrude Ballier. 48 pp. 8°. *Philadelphia, C. W. Alexander,* [1866].

Baltimore. 1st, 5th, 6th, 8th, 9th, 12th, 17th, 20th, 21st, 23d to 30th, and 32d annual reports of the commissioners of public schools. 18 v. (in 3). 8°. *Baltimore,* 1829—61. s.

Baltimore Bar. Catalogue of the law library of the library company of the Baltimore bar, compiled by S. Campbell Dorry. 143 pp. 8°. *Baltimore, J. D. Toy,* 1860. s.

Baltimore city directory, 1859—60. By W. Eugene Ferslew. 237 pp. 8°. *Baltimore, Sherwood & Co.* 1859. s.

Baltimore library company. Catalogue of books, etc. xxvi, 196 pp. 8°. *Baltimore, Edes & Leakin,* 1809. s.

Baltimore mercantile library. Catalogue, 1851. 338 pp. 8°. *Baltimore, J. W. Woods,* 1851.

Baltus (Jean François). A continuation of the answer to the history of oracles, [of Fontenelle]. Translated from the French. By a priest of the church of England. [*anon*]. lxxxvii, 275 pp. 13 l. 12°. *London, R. Sare,* 1710.

Balzac (Honoré de). Mother and daughter; or, la Marana. iii, 36 pp. 8°. *London,* [1841?] [Hazlitt's romancist and novelist's libr., v. 5.]

Balzac (Jean Louis Guez de). Letters. Translated out of French into English by Sir Richard Baker and others. 4 v. in 1. 8 p. l. 477 pp. 1 pl. 16°. *London, J. Williams,* 1654.

Bampton lectures, 1865. *See* **Mozley** (*Rev.* J. B.)

Bancroft (Aaron, *D. D.*) An essay on the life of George Washington. vii, 552 pp. 1 pl. 8°. *Worcester, Thomas & Sturtevant,* 1807.

——— Life of George Washington. 2 v. 223, 218 pp. 18°. *Boston, T. Bedlington,* 1826.

Bancroft (Edward, *M. D.*) Experimental researches concerning the philosophy of permanent colours; and the best means of producing them, by dyeing, calico printing, etc. 2 v. xlv, 401 pp; 394 pp. 8°. *Philadelphia, T. Dobson,* 1814. s.

Bancroft (George). Joseph Reed; a historical essay. 64 pp. 8°. *New York, W. J. Widdleton,* 1867.

Bandello (Matteo). Romeo and Juliet; or, the lovers of Verona. Translated from the Italian. 18 pp. 8°. *London,* 1841. [Hazlitt's romancist and novelist's libr., v. 3.]

Bandiera (Alessandro M.). Novelle. (**Novelle** de autori senesi. v. 2. 18°. *Milano,* 1815.)

Bandini (Angiolo Maria). Catalogvs codicvm latinorvm et italicorum bibliothecae mediceae lavrentianae. 5 v. fol. *Florentiæ,* 1774–78. s.

Bandini (Salustio Antonio). Discorso economico; con elogio, scritto da G. Gorani. (**Scrittori** class. Ital. di econ. pol., v. 1.)

Bankers' magazine and statistical register. Edited by J. S. Homans. 3d series, July, 1866, to June, 1867, v. 1, complete series, v. 21. 8°. *New York, J. S. Homans,* 1867.

Bankes (John). A short critical review of the political life of Oliver Cromwell. [*anon*]. 4 p. l. 272 pp. 1 pl. 12°. *London, J. Hodges,* 1739.

Banks (Abraham). Medical etiquette. xvi, 104 pp. 16°. *London, C. Fox,* 1839.

Banks (John). Cyrus, the great; or, the tragedy of love. 4 p. l. 57 pp. 2 l. sm. 4°. *London, R. Bentley,* 1696.

——— Destruction of Troy; a tragedy. 4 p. l. 75 pp. 1 l. sm. 4°. *London, C. Blount,* 1679.

——— The innocent usurper; or, death of Lady Jane Grey. A tragedy. 4 p. l. 60 pp. sm. 4°. *London, R Bentley,* 1694.

Banks (John). Mary, queen of Scotland. A tragedy. (orig. ed.). 2 p. l. 70 pp. sm. 4°. [*London, about* 1696]. [imp.; title wanting].

——— The same. The Albion queens. (altered). 3 p. l. 64 pp. sm. 4°. *London, R. Wellington,* [*about* 1696.]

——— The rival kings. A tragedy. 5 p. l. 54 pp. sm. 4°. *London, L. C.,* 1677.

——— The unhappy favorite; or, Earl of Essex. A tragedy. 4 p. l. 73 pp. 2 l. sm. 4°. *London, R. Bentley,* 1682.

——— Vertue betray'd; or, Anna Bullen. A tragedy. 4 p. l. 79 pp. 1 l. Sm. 4°. *London, R. Bentley,* 1682.

Banks (T. C.) Copies and translations of the royal charters by which the territories of Nova Scotia and Canada, with the islands and seas adjacent, were granted, in 1621, 1625, and 1628, to the Right Hon. Sir William Alexander. 3, 62 pp. fol. *London, Ridgway,* 1831.

Bannister (*Rev.* James). A view of the arts and sciences, from the earliest times to the age of Alexander the Great. vii, 124 pp. 12°. *London, J. Bell,* 1785.

Baptist (The) confession of faith, to which is added a short treatise of church discipline. 108 pp. 18°. *Portland, Thomas Baker Wait,* 1794.

Baraga (*Rev.* Frederic). A dictionary of the Otchipwe language; spoken by the Chippewa Indians, as also by the Otawas, Potawatamis, and Algonquins, with little difference. vii, 662 pp. 12°. *Cincinnati, J. A. Hemann,* 1853. s.

Barbachano (Tomas Azmar), *and* **Carbo** (Juan). Memoria sobre la conveniencia y necesidad de eriger constitucionalmente en estado de la confederation mexicana el antiguo distrito de Campeche. 8°. *Mexico,* 1861. s.

Barbarities of the enemy, exposed in a report of the committee of the house of representatives of the United States, appointed to enquire into the spirit and manner in which the war has been waged by the enemy. 192 pp. 16°. *Worcester, Remark Dunnell,* 1814.

Barbault (J.) Les plus beaux monumens de Rome ancienne, dessinés et gravés en 128 planches, avec leur explication. viii, 89 pp. fol. *Rome, Bouchard & Gravier,* 1761.
[Imp., wanting pl. 56.]

Barber (John W.) *and* **Howe** (Henry). All the western states and territories, their history, with geographical descriptions, etc. 704 pp. 8°. *Cincinnati, Henry Howe,* 1867.

Barber (Joseph). War letters of a disbanded volunteer. [*anon*]. 312 pp. 1 pl. 12°. *New York, F. A. Brady,* 1864.

Barberi (J. Philippe). Grammaire des grammaires italiennes, élémentaire, raisonnée, méthodique et analytique; ou cours complet de langue italienne. 2 v. xxxii, 401 pp; 482 pp. 8°. *Paris, Eymery,* 1819. s.

Barbeyrac (Jean). Traité de la morale des pères de l'église. xliv, 334 pp. 4°. *Amsterdam, Pierre de Coup,* 1728.

Barbier (Hippolyte). Biographie du clergé contemporain, par un solitaire. [*pseudon*]. 10 v. 18°. *Paris, A. Appert,* 1840–51.
[V. 10 wanting.]

Barchou de Penhoën (Auguste Théodore Hilaire, *baron*). L'Inde sous la domination anglaise. 2 v. xii, 482 pp; 455 pp. *Paris, Guiraudet et Jouaust,* 1844.

Barclay (John). Argenis, nunc primum illustrata. Archombrotus et Theopompus, sive Argenidis secunda et tertia pars. 2 v. 13 p. l. 637 pp. 7 l; 16 p. l. 624 pp. 8 l. 12°. *Lugd. Batav., Hack,* 1664–69.

Barclay (John). Memoirs of the rise, progress, and persecutions of the people called quakers in the north of Scotland. (Appendix, pp. 191–451, to Jaffray, (Alex.) Diary, etc. 3d ed. 4°. *Aberdeen,* 1856.)

Barclay (Robert). An apology for the quakers; being a full explanation and vindication of their principles and doctrines. 4th ed. 8°. *London,* 1701.

——— The same. 5th English ed. 7 p. l. 574 pp. 11 l. 8°. *London, T. Sowle,* 1703.

Bárdy (Rudolph C.) Das meuchelmörderische haus Hapsburg-Lothringen; oder, der durch die oesterreichische regierung gegen Ludwig Kossuth, den gouverneur von Ungarn, beabsichtige, doch entdeckte und verhinderte meuchelmord. Aus dem ungarischen original übersetzt von Samuel Ludvigh. 198 pp. 16°. *Baltimore, J. W. Müller,* 1851. s.

Baretti (Joseph). Dictionary, Spanish and English, English and Spanish. New ed. 840 pp. 4°. *London, F. Wingrave and others,* 1794.

Barfuss (Friedrich W.). Optik, catoptrik und dioptrik. Ein populäres handbuch. xxiv, 526 pp. 41 pl. 12°. *Weimar, B. F. Voigt,* 1839. s.

Bargagli (Scipione). Novelle. (**Novelle** di autori senesi. v. 2. 18°. *Milano,* 1815.)

Bargrave (John, *D. D.*) Pope Alexander the seventh and the college of cardinals. With catalogue of Dr. Bargrave's museum. xxviii, 144 pp. 1 pl. sm. 4°. *London,* 1867. [Camdem soc. pub. No. 92.]

Barham (*Rev.* Richard Harris). My cousin Nicholas. By Thomas Ingoldsby. [*pseudon.*] New ed. viii, 360 pp. 16°. *London, Routledge & Co.,* 1856.

Baring-Gould (Sabine). Curious myths of the middle ages. 241 pp. 1 pl. 12°. *London, Rivingtons,* 1866.

——— On household stories: appendix, (pp. 298—344 of **Henderson** (William). Notes on the folk lore, etc.)

Barker (Jacob). Incidents in the life of J. Barker, from 1800 to 1855. v, 285 pp. 2 pl. 8°. *Washington,* [*author,*] 1855.

Barker (Robert). The unfortunate shipwright: or cruel captain. A faithful narrative of the unparallel'd sufferings of Robert Barker, in a voyage to the coast of Guinea and Antigua. 40 pp. 2 pl. 12°. *London, author,* [1756?]

Barlæus. *See* **Baerle.**

Barlow (Henry Clark, *M. D.*) Essays on symbolism. x, 144 pp. 12°. *London, Williams & Norgate,* 1866.

Barlow (Joel). The columbiad, a poem. 2 v. xiv, 258; 218 pp. 16°. *Philadelphia, C. & A. Conrad & Co.* 1809.

——— *See* **Watts** (Isaac). Psalms carefully suited to the christian worship. 24°. *Wilmington,* 1797.

Barnard (*Capt.* Charles H.) Narrative of sufferings and adventures in a recent voyage round the world, [with] account of residence for two years on an uninhabited island. 266 pp. 1 map, 6 pl. 8°. *New York, J. P. Callender,* 1836.

Barnard (Daniel Dewey). Speeches and reports in the assembly of New York, 1838. xi, 228 pp. 12°. *Albany, Oliver Steele,* 1838.

Barnard (*Rev.* Frederick A. P., *D. D.*) Proceedings at [his] inauguration as president of Columbia college, Oct. 3, 1864. [Including his inaugural discourse.] 106 pp. 8°. *New York, Hurd & Houghton,* 1865.

Barnard (George). The brunnens of Nassau and the river Lahn. 2 p. l. 28 pl. fol. *London, T. McLean,* [*about* 1850.]

Barnard (Henry). Discourse in commemoration of the life, character, and services of the Rev. Thomas H. Gallaudet, Hartford, Jan. 7, 1852. With appendix on deaf mute instruction and institutions. 8°. *Hartford, (Conn.)* 1852. s.

——— Educational memoirs of teachers, educators, and promoters and benefactors of education, literature, and science. Part I. Teachers and educators. v. 1. U. S. 524 pp. 26 ports. 8°. *New York, F. C. Brownell,* 1859. s.

Barnard (Henry). Practical illustrations of the principles of school architecture. 175 pp. 8°. *Hartford, Case, Tiffany & Co.* 1851. s.

——— *editor.* The American journal of education. v. 1–17. 8°. *Hartford,* 1855–67. s.

Barnard (John, *D. D.*) Theologo-historicus; or the true life of the most reverend divine and excellent historian, Peter Heylyn. [Reprint.] [*With* Heylyn, (Peter) Ecclesia restaurata, etc. v. 1. *Cambridge,* 1849.]

Barnard (*Rev.* John, *of Marblehead*). The imperfection of the creature, and the excellency of the divine commandment. 4 p. l. 248 pp. 8°. *Boston, Rogers & Fowle, and D. Gookin,* 1747.

Barnard (*Rev.* Mordaunt Roger). Sport in Norway, and where to find it. [With] a short account of the vegetable productions of the country; a list of the alpine flora of the Doore fjeld and the Norwegian ferns. xvi, 334 pp. 1 pl. 12°. *London, Chapman & Hall,* 1864.

Barnard (W. D. W. *and* James). Price current of Barnard & Co., [druggists,] importers and jobbers, Saint Louis. 124 pp. 8°. *St. Louis, C. G. Ramsey & Co.* 1859. s.

Barnes (Frederick K. *joint author*). *See* **Watts,** (Isaac, *and others.*) Shipbuilding.

Barnes *or* Berners (Juliana). The gentleman's academie, or, the book of S. Albans: containing three most exact and excellent books. The first of hawking, the second of all the proper terms of hunting, and the last of armorie. All compiled in 1486. And now reduced into method by G. M. [Gervase Markham.] 3 p. l. 95 l. sm. 4°. *London, H. Lownes,* 1595.

Barnet (James). Coast pilot for the lakes on both shores, from Chicago to Buffalo, [etc.] Fourth issue. 8°. *J. Barnet, Chicago,* 1867.

Barns (*Rev.* William). Sermons on the most important subjects in the book of God. 350 pp. 1 pl. 12°. *Philadelphia, J. G. Miller,* 1866.

Barnum (Phineas Taylor). The humbugs of the world. 424 pp. 12°. *New York, Carleton,* 1866.

Barocci *or* Barocius (F.) *See* **Barozzi** (F.)

Baron (*Rev.* Richard). The pillars of priestcraft and orthodoxy shaken. 2 v. xxiii, 349 pp; xi, 340 pp. 18°. *London, R. Griffiths,* 1752.

Barozzi *or* Barocius, (Francesco). Admirandvm illvd geometricvm problema tredecim modis demonstratvm, etc. 269 pp. 5 l. 4°. *Venetiis, J. B. Fantini,* 1586. s.

Barr (*Capt.* James). Correct and authentic narrative of the Indian war in Florida, with a description of Maj. Dade's massacre, [etc.] 32 pp. 18°. *New York, J. Narine,* 1836.

Barra (Justo de la.) Los dos Robinsones ó aventuras de Carlos y Fanny dos niños ingleses abandonados en una isla de América. Relacion imitada del inglés. 2a ed. 3 v. 18°. *Madrid, Marin,* 1792–97.

Barrande (Joachim). Systême silurien du centre de la Bohême. 1e partie; recherches paléontologiques. 2 v. text. Atlas, 2 v. in 3. 4°. *Prague, l'auteur,* 1852–67.

CONTENTS.

v. 1. Crustacés, trilobites, xxx, 936 pp.; atlas, 51 pl.
v. 2. Classe des mollusques, ordre des céphalopodes. xxxiv, 712 pp. atlas, 244 pl. [in 2 v.]

Barreiros *or* Barros (Caspar). Commentarius de Ophyra regione. 42 l. unp. 18°. *Roterodami, Berewout,* 1616. (*With* **Novus** orbis, *Roterodami,* 1616.)

Barrett (Solomon, *jr*). The principles of grammar: a compendious treatise on the languages, English, Latin, and Greek. Revised ed. 204 pp. 12°. *Albany, J. Munsell,* 1848. S.

Barringer (*Mrs.* M. M.) Dixey cookery; or, how I managed my table for twelve years. 121 pp. 12°. *Boston, Loring,* 1867.

Barrington (Daines). The probability of reaching the north pole discussed. 1 p. l. 90 pp. 4°. *London, C. Heydinger,* 1775.

Barrois (J.) Bibliothèque protypographique, ou librairies des fils du roi Jean, Charles V, Jean de Berri, Philippe de Bourgogne et les siens. xl, 346 pp. 1 pl. 4°. *Paris, Treuttel & Würtz,* 1830. S.

Barron (Charles). Natural history, etc. *See* **Adams** (Arthur), etc.

Barron (*Rev.* Richard). *See* **Baron** (*Rev.* R.)

Barros (Caspar). *See* **Barreiros** (Caspar).

Barrow (Isaac). The mathematical works. Edited by W. Whewell. 2 v. in 1, xix, 414 pp; 320 pp. 27 pl. 8°. *Cambridge, university press,* 1860. S.

——— The usefulness of mathematical learning explained and demonstrated, being mathematical lectures at Cambridge. xxxii, 440 pp. 2 pl. 8°. *London, S. Austen,* 1734. S.

Barrow (*Sir* John). Travels in China, containing descriptions, observations, and comparisons at the imperial palace of Yuew-minyuen, and on a journey from Pekin to Canton. 1st Am. ed. 422 pp. 8°. *Philadelphia, W. F. M'Laughlin,* 1805.

Barruel (*abbé* Augustin de). Memoirs illustrating the history of Jacobinism. Translated from the French. [By R. Clifford.] 1st Am. ed. 4 v. 8°. *New York, C. Davis,* 1799.

Barry (*Rev.* Henry Boothby). Cæsar and the Britons. 3 p. l. 174 pp. 8°. *London, Baldwin & Cradock,* 1831.

Barry (Martin, *M. D.*) Zusätze [*With* **Kreber** (G. A. F.) Mikroskopische untersuchungen, 1854.] S.

Barry (P). Shoeburyness and the guns. xiii, 262 pp. 4 pl. 8°. *London, Low,* 1865.

Bartas. *See* **Du Bartas.**

Barth (Carl). *See* **Longhi** (J.) *and* **Barth** (C.) Die kupferstecherei, u. s. w. S.

Barth (Johann August). Pacis annis 1814 et 1815 fœderatis armis restitutæ monumentum, orbis terrarum de fortuna reduce gaudia gentium linguis interpretans principibus piis felicibus augustis, populisque victoribus liberatoribus liberatis dicatum. 50 l. unp. fol. *Vratislaviæ, Barth et Co.,* (*about* 1815?)

Bartholin (Albert). Liber de scriptis Danorum, Norwagorum et Islandorum. *See* **Moller** (Johann), Bibliotheca, etc. S.

Bartholin (Caspar). Enchiridion physicum ex priscis et recentioribus philosophis accurate concinnatum, etc. 6 p. l. 855 pp, 35 l. 24°. *Argentinæ, E. Zetzner,* 1625. S.

——— De studio medico inchoando, continuando, et absolvendo—consilium. [*With* **Conring** (H.) Introductio in universam artem medicam.] ed. 1726. S.

Bartlett (Elisha, *M. D.*) The history, diagnosis, and treatment of the fevers of the United States. 547 pp. 8°. *Philadelphia, Lea & Blanchard,* 1847. S.

Bartlett (John Russell). Dictionary of Americanisms. A glossary of words and phrases regarded as peculiar to the United States. xxvii, 412 pp. 8°. *New York, Bartlett & Welford,* 1848. S.

——— A history of the destruction of his Britnanic majesty's schooner Gaspee in Narragansett bay on the 10th of June, 1772. 140 pp. 8°. *Providence, A. Crawford Greene,* 1861.

Bartlett (Samuel C. *D. D.*) Life and death eternal: a refutation of the theory of annihilation. 390 pp. 12°. *Boston, Am. Tract Soc.* [1866.]

Bartoli (Pietro Santi) *or* Santi-Bartoli (Pietro). Lucernæ veterum sepulchrales iconicæ, ex cavernis romanis subterraneis collectæ, cum observationibus J. Petri Bellorii, [et] studio L. Begeri. 3 v. in 1. 10 p. l. fol. *Coloniæ Marchicæ, U. Liebpert,* 1702. S.

(Imperfect, wanting 3d part, 35 pl.)

CONTENTS.

v. 1. Continens varios ritus, et ludos funebres, etc. 2 l. 16 pp. 37 pl.
v. 2. Cont. gentilium deos. 2 l. 15 pp. 46 pl.
v. 3. Cont. symbola et emblemata, simul cum lucernis sacris veterum christianiarum. 2 l. 12 pp. (Wanting 35 pl).

Bartoli (Pietro Santi) *or* Santi-Bartoli (Pietro). *See* **Bellori** (G. P.), *and* La Chausse, Picturæ antiquæ, etc.

Barton (Benjamin Smith). Memoir concerning the disease of goitre, as it prevails in different parts of North America. viii, 94 pp. 8°. *Philadelphia, author,* 1800. s.

——— Observations on some parts of natural history: [with] an account of several remarkable vestiges, of an ancient date, which have been discovered in different parts of North America. Part I. 8°. 2 p. l. 76 pp. 1 pl. *London, printed for the author,* [1787?]

Bartram (William). Voyage dans les parties sud de l'Amérique septentrionale. Traduit de l'anglois par P. V. Benoist. 2v. 457 pp; 436 pp. 4 pl. 8°. *Paris, Cartaret et Brosson, Maradan,* 1799–1801.

Bartsch (Adam von). Anleitung zur kupferstichkunde. 2 v. in 1. viii, 292 pp.; 296 pp. 11 pl. 8°. *Wien, J. B. Wallishausser,* 1821. s.

——— Catalogue raisonné de toutes les estampes qui forment l'œuvre de Rembrandt, et ceux de ses principaux imitateurs; composé par Gersaint, Helle, Glomy et P. Voer. Nouv. éd. 2 pts. in 2 v. xlii, 302 pp. 4 pl.; 208 pp. 1 pl. 8°. *Vienne, A. Blumauer,* 1797. s.

——— Le peintre graveur. 21 v. 8°. *Vienne, J. V. Degen, P. Merchetti,* 1803–21. s.

CONTENTS.

v. 1–5. Les écoles flamande et hollandaise.
v. 6–11. L'école allemande.
v. 12–13. L'école d'Italie.
v. 14–15. Marc Antoine et son école.
v. 16–21. La suite de l'école d'Italie.

——— Suppléments au peintre-graveur recueillis et publiés par Rudolph Weigel. v. 1. Peintres et dessinateurs néerlandais. viii, 350 pp. 12°. *Leipzig, R. Weigel,* 1843. s.
[No more published.]

Bary (Émile Louis François). Nouveaux problèmes de physique, suivis des questions posées au concours général depuis 1805 jusqu'à ce jour dans les classes des physique et de chimie. xvi, 368 pp., 2 pl. 8°. *Paris, L. Hachette,* 1838. s.

Bascom (*Rev.* H. B.) Methodism and slavery; with other matter in controversy between the north and the south; being a review of the manifesto of the majority in reply to the protest of the minority of the late general conference of the methodist E. church, in the case of Bishop Andrew. 8°. *Frankfort (Ky.),* 1845.

Basilius, Magnus (*Saint*). De poetarum, oratorum, historicorũque ac philosophorũ legendis libris, cum commentariolo Johannis Honorii. 24 l. unp., sm. 4°. *Liptzick, Jac. Thanner,* 1508.

Basire (Isaac, *D. D.*) The history of the English and Scotch presbytery. [*anon*]. 2d ed. 23 p. l. 240 pp. 1 pl. 16°. *Villa Franca,* 1660.

Basnage de Beauval (Jacques). Dissertation historique sur les duels et les ordres de chevalerie. Par Monsieur B...... [*anon*]. 8 p. l. 173 pp. 16°. *Amsterdam, P. Brunel,* 1720.

Basnage de Flottemanville (Samuel). Annales politico-ecclesiastici annorum dcxlv, a Cæsare Augusto ad Phocam usque. 3 v. fol. *Roterodami, R. Leers,* 1706.

Bassanville (Anaïs Lebrun, *comtesse de*). Les salons d'autre fois. Souvenirs intimes. Séries 4. 318 pp. 16°. *Paris, P. Brunet,* 1866.

Bassini (Carlo). Method for the baritone voice. 4°. *New York,* 1858. s.

——— Twenty melodic exercises, in form of solfeggios, for soprano and mezzo-soprano voices. 62 pp. 4°. *New York, Wm. Hall & Son,* 1865.

Bastard de Saulieu (*Madame*). Dernière année du pensionnat; entretiens sur l'histoire sainte, l'histoire profane, et la littérature, entre une institutrice et ses jeunes élèves. xii, 346 pp. 4 pl. 16°. *Paris, L. Tanet,* 1826.

Bateman (C. F.) Noah, and other poems. 170 pp. 12°. *Cincinnati, Moore, Wilstach & Baldwin,* 1865.

Bates (Elisha). The doctrines of friends; or, the principles of the christian religion as held by the society of friends, commonly called quakers. vi, 244 pp. 16°. *London, E. Fry & Son,* 1835.

Bates (Ely). Christian politics. 2d ed. xvi, 445 pp. *London, Longman,* 1806.

Bates (Henry Walter). Naturalist on the river Amazons. 2d ed. xii, 466 pp. 1 map. 12° *London, Murray,* 1864. s.

Batines (Colomb de). Bibliografia dantesca, traduzione italiana. 2 v. in 3. 4°. *Prato, Tipografia aldina ed,* 1845–46.

Batterly (*Rev.* John). Antiquitates rutupinæ. 4 p. l. 92 pp. 1 map, 3 pl. 8°. *Oxoniæ, theatro Sheldoniano,* 1711.

Batuta (Abn Abdallah Mohammed Ebn). Travels in Bengal and China. 129 pp. (*With* **Yule** (Henry), Cathay, etc., v. 2.

Baudier (Michael). The history of the administration of Cardinal Ximenes, translated from French into English, by W[alter] Vaughan. 24 p. l. 150 pp. 1 pl. 16°. *London, John Wilkins,* 1671.

Baudrimont (A.) *and* Martin Saint Ange (Gaspard Joseph). Recherches anatomiques et physiologiques sur le développment du fœtus, et en particulier sur l'évolution embryonnaire des oiseaux et des batraciens. 224 pp. 13 pl. col. 4°. *Paris*, 1850. s.

Baumgartner (Andreas). Anfangsgründe der naturlehre. iv, 263 pp. 8°. *Wien, J. G. Heubner*, 1837. s.

Baumgartner (J.) Die Schweiz in ihren kämpfen und umgestaltungen von 1830 bis 1850. 2 v. 496 pp; 470 pp. 8°. *Zürich, F. Schulthess*, 1853–54.

Baumstark (Edward). Volkswirthschaftliche erläuterungen vorzüglich über David Ricardo's system. 8°. *Leipzig*, 1838. s.

Bavaria. Landes-und volkskunde des königsreichs Bayern. Bearbeitet von einem kreise bayerischer gelehrter. v. 1–3 in 6 v. 8°. *München, J. G. Cotta*, 1860–65. s.

Baxter (Richard). Petition for peace, with the reformation of the liturgy. (Imperfect.) 96 pp. sm. 4°. *London*, 1661.

Baxter (*Rev.* R., *of Richmond, Va.*) The most important tenets of the Roman catholic church fairly explained. 76 pp. 12°. *Washington, Davis & Force*, 1820.

Baxter (Thomas). An illustration of the Egyptian, Grecian, and Roman costume. 16 pp. 41 pl. 8°. *London, W. Miller*, 1810.

Bay (Christian Friderich). Fuldstaendigt dansk og engelsk haand-lexicon. Anden forbedret udgave. 2 p. l. 1031 pp. 12°. *Kjöbenhavn, Sebastian Popp*, 1807.

——— Fuldstaendig engelsk og dansk ordbog. 2 v., 2 p. l. 1235 pp. 8°. *Kjöbenhavn, B. K. Horrebow*, 1806.

Bayfield (H. W.) Geology of Lake Superior. 43 pp. [*With* **Quebec.** Lit. and histor. soc. trans., v. 1.]

Bayley (James Roosevelt, *D. D.*) Brief sketch of the history of the Catholic church of the island of New York. 156 pp. 16°. *New York, Dunigan & Bro.*, 1853.

Bayly (*Mrs.* M.) Workmen and their difficulties. vii, 235 pp. 16°. *New York, R. Carter & Bros.*, 1861.

Bayma (Joseph, *S. J.*) The love of christian perfection. Translated from the Latin. 254 pp. 18°. *Baltimore, J. Murphy & Co.*, 1865.

Bayne (Peter). English puritanism: its character and history. vi, 142 pp. 8°. *London, W. Kent & Co.*, 1862. [*With* **Documents** relating to settlement of the Ch. of England.]

Bazeley (C. W.) New juvenile atlas. 2 pts. 25 maps. 8°. *Philadelphia, B. B. Hopkins*, 1815. [Imperfect; 2 maps wanting.]

Beale (Lionel Smith). How to work with the microscope. xii, 124 pp. 12°. *London, J. Churchill*, 1857. s.

——— The microscope in its application to practical medicine. 2d ed. xix, 390 pp. 1 col. pl. 8°. *London, J. Churchill*, 1858. s.

Beard (Thomas, *D. D.*) The theatre of God's ivdgements; revised and augmented. 3d ed. 7 p. l. 592 pp. 6 l. sm. 4°. *London, A. Islip*, 1631.

Bearzi (Jean Baptiste, *Chevalier* de). Catalogue de livres rares et précieux composant (sa) bibliothèque. 2 v. in 1. xii, 221, 192 pp. 8°. *Paris, E. Tross*, 1855. s.

Beatson (Robert). Political index to the histories of Great Britain and Ireland; or, a complete register of the hereditary honours, public offices, and persons in office, from the earliest periods to the present time. 2d ed. 2 v. vi, 481, 16 pp; vii, 392, 20 pp. 8°. *London, G. G. J. & J. Robinson*, 1788.

Beauchamp (Alphonse de). Histoire de la guerre de la Vendée et des Chouans, depuis son origine jusqu'à la pacification de 1800. 3e éd. 3 v. 1 map, 3 pl. 12°. *Paris, Giguet et Michaud*, 1809.

——— An authentic narrative of the invasions of France in 1814 and 1815, comprising a circumstantial detail of the battle of Waterloo. 2d ed. 2 v. in 1. v, 360 pp; vi, 346, xiv, 52 pp. 8°. *London, H. Colburn*, 1816.

Beauchamp (*Mrs.* Jenny). Maplehurst; or, Campbellism not christianity. With an introduction by A. P. Williams, *D. D.* 214 pp. 16°. *St. Louis, P. M. Pinckard*, 1867.

Beauchamp (Jeroboam). Confession of J. Beauchamp, who was executed at Frankfort, Ky., for the murder of Col. Solomon P. Sharp, late att'y gen'l of Ky; [also] some poetical pieces by [his wife] Mrs. Ann Beauchamp. 100 pp. 8°. *Kentucky, H. T. Goodsell*, [1854.]

Beauford (William). *In* **Vallancey** (C). Collectanea de rebus Hibernicis. v. 1–5. 8°. *Dublin*, 1774–90.

CONTENTS.

Of the origin and language of the Irish; and of the learning of the Druids. 30 pp. [v. 2, No. 7.]
Ancient topography of Ireland. 173 pp., 1 map. [v. 3, No. 11.]
Druidism revived; or, a dissertation on the characters and modes of writing used by the Irish in their pagan state, and after their conversion to christianity. 56 pp., 7 pl. [v. 2., No. 7.]

Beaufort (Louis de). La république romaine, ou plan général de l'ancien gouvernement de Rome. 2 v. 12, xxxvii, 430 pp; 434 pp. 4°. *La Haye, N. van Daalen*, 1766.

Beaumarchais (La Barre de). *See* **La Barre de Beaumarchais** (Antoine de).

Beaumont (Élie de). *See* **Élie de Beaumont.**

Beaumont (Gustave de). Notice sur Alexis de Tocqueville. [*With* **Tocqueville** (A. de). Œuvres complètes. v. 5. *Paris*, 1866].

Beaumont (Jeanne Le Prince de). *See* **Le Prince de Beaumont** (Jeanne).

Beaumont-Vassy (Édouard Ferdinand, *vicomte* de). Histoire des États Européens depuis le congrès de Vienne—Suéde et Norwège—Denmark. 206 pp. 8°. *Paris, Amyot*, 1843. s.

Beaumont de Péréfixe. *See* **Péréfixe.**

Beaunoir (Alexandre Louis Bertrand Robineau, *dit*). Histoire secrète et anecdotique de l'insurrection belgique, ou Vander-Noot; drame historique. Traduit du Flamand de van-Schön-Swaartz, gantois, par M. D. B. [*pseudon*]. 8°. *Bruxelles*, 1790. s.

Beauties and spirit of English tragedy. [*anon*]. iv, 292 pp. 12°. *London, W. Trenter*, 1833.

Beauvais (Remi de). La Magdeleine. xlv, 746 pp. 3 l. 18°. *Tovrnay, Charles Martin*, 1617.

Beauvoir (*Madame* Roger de). Confidences de M'lle Mars. 16°. *Paris, Dondey-Dupré*, 1855.

Beccaria (Cesare). Elementi de economia publica. 2 v. Della riduzione delle misure di lunghezza all'uniformità per lo stato de Milano. (**Scrittori** class. Ital. di econ. pol. v. 11-12).

Beccharia (Antonio). Prooemiū in Dionysii traductionem de situ orbis habitabilis. 17 l. unp. sm. 4°. *Venetiis, F. Renner de Halibrun*, 1478. [*With* **Pomponius** Mela. De situ orbis libri tres. *Venetiis*, 1478].

Beche (*De la*). *See* **De La Beche.**

Bechstein, (Johann Matthäus). Gemeinnützige naturgeschichte Deutschlands nach aller drei reichen. 2e ausg. 4 v. 8°. *Leipzig, S. L. Crusius*, 1801-09. s.

CONTENTS.

v. 1. Vorkenntnisse säugethiere.
v. 2-4. Vögel.

Beck (Lewis C.) Adulterations of various substances used in medicine and the arts, with the means of detecting them. 333 pp. 12°. *New York, S. S. & W. Wood*, 1846. s.

—— Botany of the United States north of Virginia; comprising descriptions of the flowering and fernlike plants hitherto found in those States. 2d ed. xiii, 480 pp. 12°. *New York, Harpers*, 1848. s.

Becker (Carl Ferdinand). Das wort in seiner organischen verwandlung. x, 299 pp. 8°. *Frankfurt a M., J. C. Hermann*, 1833. s.

—— A grammar of the German language. xii, 284 pp. 8 tab. 8°. *London, J. Murray*, 1830. s.

Becker (E. D. H.) Uebersichtliche darstellung der gegenwärtigen landwirthschaftlichen verhältnisse der grossherzogthümer Mecklenburg. 78 pp. 8°. *Rostock, J. M. Oeberg*, 1841. s.

Becker (Ferdinand). Sixty-three etchings after nature, with fifteen etchings after F. Kobel. 54 pl. sm. fol. *Bath*, 1821.

Beckford (Peter). Thoughts upon hunting. In a series of familiar letters to a friend. 3d ed. 6 p. l. 360 pp. 2 pl. sm. 4°. *Sarum, E. Easton*, 1784.

Beckmann (Johann). A history of inventions, discoveries, and origins. Translated from the German, by William Johnston. Carefully revised and enlarged by William Francis and T. W. Griffith, M. D. 5th ed. 2 v. 16°. *London, H. G. Bohn*, 1846.

Becon (Thomas). Prayers and other pieces. Edited by Rev. J. Ayre. iv, 644 pp. 8°. *Cambridge, (Eng.) univ. press.* 1844.
[Parker Society.]

Bécourt (R. de). The grave of human philosophies, ancient and modern, or, the universal system of the Bramins unveiled. Translated from the French by A. Dalmas. ix, 95, xiii pp. 1 pl. 8°. *London, Sherwood*, 1827.

Becquerel (Antoine César). Traité des applications de l'électricité à la thérapeutique médicale et chirurgicale. 2e éd. vii, 550 pp. 8°. *Paris, G. Baillière*, 1860. s.

—— Traité complet du magnétisme. cxi, 547 pp. 18 pl. *Paris, Didot*, 1846. s.

—— *and* (Alexandre Edmond). Éléments de physique terrestre et de météorologie. 2 p. l. 706 pp. 14 pl. 8°. *Paris, Didot*, 1847. s.

—— Traité d'électricité et de magnétisme; leur applications aux sciences physiques, aux arts et à l'industrie. 3 v. 8°. *Paris, Didot*, 1855-56. s.

Bédarride (J.) Les Juifs en France, en Italie, et en Espagne. 3e éd. viii, 611 pp. 8°. *Paris, Lévy*, 1867.

Beddoes (Thomas). Alexander's expedition down the Hydaspes and the Indus to the Indian ocean. [*anon*]. viii, 90 pp. 1 pl. 4°. *London, J. Murray*, 1792.

Beecher (*Rev.* George). Biographical remains. 345 pp. 16°. *New York, Leavitt, Trow & Co.* 1844.

Beecher (Lyman, *D. D.*) A plea for the west. 2d ed. 190 pp. 12°. *Cincinnati, Truman & Smith,* 1835.

Beechey (Frederic William). Narrative of a voyage to the Pacific and Beering's strait, to co-operate with the polar expeditions, in the years 1825–28. 2 v. xxiii, 392 pp; viii, 393–742 pp. 3 maps. 23 pl. *London, H. Colburn & R. Bentley,* 1831.

——— The same. 8°. *Philadelphia,* 1832. s.

Beeckmann (Daniel). Voyage to and from the island of Borneo. 12°. *London,* 1718. s.

Beelen (Jean Théodore). Chrestomathia rabbinica et chaldaica, cum notis grammaticis, historicis, theologicis, glossario et lexico abbreviaturarum. 6 v. in 3. 8°. *Lovanii, Vanlinthout & Vandenzande,* 1841–43. s.

Beer (August). Einleitung in die höhere optik. xiii, 430 pp. 2 pl. 8°. *Braunschweig, Vieweg,* 1853. s.

——— Einleitung in die elektrostatik die lehre vom magnetismus und die elektrodynamik. Herausg. von Julius Plücker. xvi, 518 pp. 8°. *Braunschweig, Vieweg,* 1855. s.

Beer (Wilhelm), *and* **Mädler** (Johann Heinrich). Der mond noch seinen kosmischen und individuellen verhältnissen: oder allgemeine vergleichende selenographie mit besonderer beziehung auf die mappa selenographica. xviii, 412 pp. 5 pl. 4°. *Berlin, S. Schropp & Co.* 1837. s.

Beeton (*Mrs.* Isabella). How to dine: dinners and dining, with bills of fare. v, 138 pp. 16°. *London, Ward, Lock & Tyler,* [1866].

——— How to manage house and servants, and to make the most of your means. 120 pp. 16°. *London, Ward, Lock & Tyler,* 1865.

Beeton (S. O.) Beeton's book of anecdote, jokes, and jests. vii, 279 pp. 8°. *London, S. O. Beeton,* [1866].

——— Shakespeare memorial. [*anon.*] 48 pp. 1 pl. fol. *London, Beeton,* [1864].

Beever (W. Holt). Notes on fields and cattle, from the diary of an amateur farmer, [with] a prize essay on time of entry on farms. xv, 275 pp. 12°. *London, Chapman & Hall,* 1862.

Beger (Lorenz). Regum et imperatorum romanorum numismata, æri a Biæo incisa; Rubenii commentario illustrata; subjectis annotationibus. 10 p. l. 103 pp; 9 l. 12 pp. 68 pl. fol. *Coloniæ Brandenburgicæ, U. Liebpert,* 1700. s.

——— Ulysses Sirenes prætervectus, ex delineatione pighiana, dialogo illustratus. 24 pp. fol. *Coloniæ Brandenburgicæ, U. Liebpert,* 1703. s.

Beharrell (*Rev.* T. G.) Complete alphabetically arranged biblical biography; a full history of bible men and women, etc. 512 pp. 8°. *Indianapolis, Downey & Brously,* 1867.

Behm (E.) Geographisches jahrbücher. Band I. 1866. xi, 600, cix pp. 2 pl. 8°. *Gotha, J. Perthes,* 1866. s.

Beil (T. A.) Technologisches wörterbuch der deutschen, franzöischen, und englischen sprache: Gewērbe, physik, chemie, nautik, bergbau, u. s. w. viii, 678 pp. 8°. *Wiesbaden, C. W. Kreidel,* 1853.

Beke (*Mrs.* Emily). Jacob's flight; or, a pilgrimage to Harran, and thence in the patriarch's footsteps into the promised land. xi, 360 pp. 1 map. 9 pl. 12°. *London, Longmans,* 1865.

Belgium. Discussion de la loi sur l'enseignement supérieur, du 27 Septembre, 1835, et de la loi sur le jury d'examen, du 8 Avril, 1844. xxvi. 1400 pp. 8°. *Bruxelles, T. Lesigne,* 1844. s.

——— Exposé de la situation de la province de la Flandre-orientale, pour 1843. 8°. *Gand,* 1843. s.

Bell (*Sir* Charles). The nervous system of the human body. 230 pp. 9 pl. 8°. *Washington, Register, etc. of medical science,* 1833. s.

Bell (J. *Veterinary surgeon*). Farriery taught on a new and easy plan; a treatise on the diseases and accidents of the horse. By John Hinds. [*pseudon.*] With considerable additions by Thomas M. Smith, and a supplement by J. S. Skinner. 2 v. in 1. xiv, 224 pp; 101 pp. 12°. *Philadelphia, Grigg, Elliot & Co.* 1848. s.

Bell (John, *M. D. of Philadelphia,*) *and* **Stokes** (William). Lectures on the theory and practice of physic. 4th ed. 2 v. 784 pp; 907 pp. 8°. *Philadelphia, E. Barrington and G. D. Haswell,* 1848. s.

Bell (Luther V. *M. D.*) The practical methods of ventilating buildings; with appendix on heating by steam and hot water. 131 pp. 5 pl. 8°. *Boston, Damrell and Moore,* 1848. s.

Bell (Robert, *Editor*). Songs from the dramatists. 2d ed. xii, 268 pp. 16°. *London, Parker and son,* 1855.

Bell (Thomas). *See* **Owen** (R.) Fossil reptilia of the London clay, etc.

Bell (*Rev.* William). Hints to emigrants; in a series of letters from Upper Canada. 236 pp. 1 map. 12°. *Edinburgh, Waugh & Innes,* 1824.

Bellamy (Daniel). Ethic amusements; revised by his son, D. Bellamy. 14 p. l. ix, 260, 86, 14 pp. 72 pl. 4°. *London, W. Faden*, 1768.

CONTENTS.

Comforts of philosophy, from the Latin of Boëtius, by W. Causton, and Mr. Bellamy.
Marriage, a theatrical dialogue by Mr. Bellamy.
Court of Beauty; or judgment of Venus, after Fenelon.
The Projector, in Miltonic verse, by Mr. Holdsworth.
Gratitude, an historical tale.
Damon and Celia; a cantata.
Æsop at Court; or, the labyrinth of Versailles, in French and English, with plates by Bickham.
Ethic tales and fables, by Fenelon.
August: a serenetta.

Bellamy (Joseph, *D. D.*) Theron, Paulinus, and Aspasio, or, letters and dialogues upon the nature of love to God, faith in Christ, assurance of a title to eternal life. 2 p. l. v, 227 pp. 16°. *Boston, S. Kneeland*, 1759.

Bellamy (Thomas, *M. D.*) Noctes Sarniæ; de jecinoris morbis, vel tractatio simul de morbidis urinæ signis. 690 pp. 1 pl. 32°. *Sarnia, W. Hamilton*, 1850.

Bellarmino (Roberto). De ascensione mentis in Deum per scalas rerum creatarum liber singularis. Curavit F. X. Dieringer. xxii, 389 pp. 1 pl. 24°. *Coloniæ, J. M. Heberle*, 1850.

Bellebon et Guérault. *See* **Edmond** (Charles).

Bellemare (Louis de). Scènes de la vie sauvage au Mexique. 3e éd. 347 pp. 12°. *Paris, Charpentier*, 1856.

Bellew (H. W.) Journal of a political mission to Afghanistan in 1857, under Major Lumsden; with an account of the country and people. xv, 480 pp. 8 pl. 8°. *London, Smith, Elder & Co.*, 1862.

Bellicard (Jérôme Charles), *and* **Cochin** (Charles Nicolas). Observations upon the antiquities of the town of Herculaneum, with some reflections on the painting and sculpture of the ancients. 2d ed. 2 p. l. vii, 236 pp, 43 pp. 42 pl. 8°. *London, Wilson & Durham*, 1756.

Belloni (Girolamo). Dissertazione sopra il comercio. (**Scrittori** class. ital. di econ. pol. v. 2).

Bellori (Giovanni Pietro). Le vite de pittori, scultori, ed architetti moderni. xvi, 394 pp. 15 pl. 4°. *Roma, F. Ricciardo e G. Buono*, 1728. [Imp: 1 pl. wanting (F. Fiammingo)]. s.

——— *and* **La Chausse** (Michel Ange de). Picturæ antiquæ cryptarum Romanorum et sepulcri Nasonum descriptæ. Delineatæ a Petro Bartholi. fol. *Romæ*, 1738. s.

Bellot (Joseph René). Journal d'un voyage aux mers polaires, en 1851 et 1852. Précédé d'une notice sur la vie de l'auteur par J. Lemer. lvi, 414 pp. 1 pl. 1 map, fac. sim. 8°. *Paris, Perrotin*, 1854. s.

Belly (Félix). Canal de Nicaragua. *See* **Gamond.**

Belon (Pierre). Les observations de plvsievrs singvlaritez et choses memorables, trovvees en Grèce, Asie, Inde, Égypte, Arabie, et autres pays estranges. xii, 468 pp. 1 pl. sm. fol. *Paris, H. de Marnef*, 1588.

Belsham (*Rev.* Thomas). The epistles of Paul the apostle, translated, with an exposition and notes. 2 v. lvii, 574 pp; 721 pp. 1 map, 1 pl. 4°. *London, R. & A. Taylor*, 1822.

Beltrami (J. C.) La découverte des sources du Mississippi et de la rivière sanglante. v, 327 pp. 8°. *Nouvelle Orleans, Benj. Levy*, 1824.

Bembo (Pietro). Rerum venetarum historiæ libri xii. 19 p. l. 311 l. 4°. *Lutetiæ, M. Vasco*, 1551.

Bénard (—). Cabinet de Paignon Dijonval, etc. *See* **Morel de Vindé** (C. G).

Bénard (—). Éloge de l'enfer, ouvrage critique, historique, et moral. [*anon.*] 2 v. viii, x, 265 pp.; vi, 353 pp., 14 pl. 18°. *La Haye, P. Gosse*, 1759.

Benavente (D. J.) Memoria sobre las primeras campañas en la guerra de la independencia de Chile. viii, 200 pp. 8°. *Santiago*, 1845.

Beneden (P. J. van). Les vers cestoides ou acotyles, considérés sous la rapport de leur classification, de leur anatomie et de leur développement. (Extract). 190 pp., 26 pl. 4°. *Bruxelles, Acad. royale de Belgique*, 1850. s.

——— *See* **Dumortier** (B. C.) *and* **Beneden**, Hist. nat. des polypes composés d'eau douce.

——— *See* **Gervais** (P.) *and* Beneden, note sur la Sépiole.

Benedict (Erastus C.) The beginning of America; a discourse before the New York historical society, 1863. 64 pp. 8°. *New York, J. F. Trow*, 1864.

Benedict (Lewis, *Col. of* 162*d Reg. N. Y. V.*) Memorial. (A record of his services during the civil war). 155 pp., 1 pl. 8°. *Albany, J. Munsell*, 1866.

Benezet (Anthony). Caution and warning to Great Britain and her colonies, in a short representation of the calamitous state of the enslaved negroes in the British dominions. 35 pp. 16°. *Philadelphia, Henry Miller*, 1766.

Benfey (Theodor). Sanskrit-English dictionary. xi, 1145 pp. 8°. *London, Longman,* 1866.

Benga (The) primer and hymns. By the Corisco mission, west coast of Africa. 200 pp. 12°. *New York, Am. Tract Soc.,* (*about* 1850.) s.

Benjamin (Park., *Midshipman U. S. N.*) Shakings. Etchings from the naval academy, engraved by John Andrew. 61 l. obl. 12°. *Boston, Lee & Shepard,* [1867].

Bennet (Henry, 1*st earl of Arlington*). Letters of state to the dukes of Ormond and Buckingham; [277–440 pp. of **Brown** (T.) Miscellanea aulica. *London,* 1702].

Bennett (James Risdon). The causes, nature, diagnosis, and treatment of acute hydrocephalus. vii, 248 pp. 8°. *London, S. Highley,* 1843. s.

Bennett (John). Short-hand explained, being a concise exposition of the art. 46 pp. 12°. *London, Longman,* 1825.

Benoit (Élie). History of the famous edict of Nantes, containing an account of all the persecutions that have been in France during the reign of Lewis the XIII. Translated into English [from the French]. 2 v. 9 p. l., 567 pp., 7 l; xxxv, 561 pp., 1 l. 4°. *London, John Dunton,* 1694.

Benson (Egbert). Names, chiefly of places once held by the Dutch (in) New Netherlands. 2d ed., 127 pp. 12°. *Jamaica,* (N. Y.), *H. C. Sleight,* 1825. s.

Benson (*Rev.* Henry C.) Life among the Choctaw Indians, and sketches of the southwest. 314 pp. 12°. *Cincinnati, Swormstedt & Poe,* 1860.

Bentham (George). Flora Hongkongensis. A description of the flowering plants and ferns of the island of Hong-Kong. ii, 482 pp., 1 map. 8°. *London, L. Reeve,* 1861. s.

——— *and* **Hooker** (Joseph Dalton). Genera plantarum ad exemplaria imprimis in herbariis Kewensibus servata definita. xii, xv, 1040 pp. 8°. *Londini, A. Black, etc.,* 1862—67. s.

Bentley (Richard, *D. D.*) La friponnerie laïque des pretendus esprits forts d'Angleterre: ou remarques de Phileleuthère de Leipsick sur le discours de la liberté de penser [de A. Collins.] Traduites de l'Anglois par N. N. [Armand de la Chapelle.] xxxvi, 581 pp. 16°. *Amsterdam, Wetstein & Smith,* 1738.

Bentley (Samuel). Excerpta historica, or illustrations of English history. xviii, 444 pp. 8°. *London, Richard Bentley,* 1833.

Bentley's Miscellany. July 1866 to June 1867. v. 60–61. 8°. *London, Chapman & Hall,* 1866–67.

Benton (James G.) A course of instruction in ordnance and gunnery. 3d ed. 585 pp. 8°. *New York, D. Van Nostrand,* 1867.

Benzenberg (J. F.) Die sternschnuppen. xxiii, 357 pp. 9 pl. 8°. *Hamburg, Perthes,* 1839. s.

Benzoni (Girolamo), *and* **Lery** (Jean de). Historia Indiæ occidentalis, tomis duobus comprehensa. Prior, res ab Hispanis in India Occidentali hactenus gestas, acerbum illorum in eas gentes dominatum, insigneque in Gallos ad Floridam insulam sæuitiæ exemplum describit. Alter Brasilie (quæ et America dicitur) rerumque in ea obseruatione dignarum a nobis penitus incognita descriptionem continet. 2 v. in 1. x, 6 p. l. 480 pp. 6 l.; 31 p. l. 342 pp. 8 l. 1 pl. 16°. [*Genevae,*] *E. Vignon,* 1586.

——— *and* Martire d' Anghiera, (Pietro). Der newenn weldt vnd indianischen nidergängischen königreichs newe vnd wahrhaffte history. Auss dem latein in das teutsch gebracht durch Nicolaum Königer. 10 p. l., dcii pp. fol. *Basel, S. Henricpetri,* 1582.

Berault (*Rev.* Peter). Treatise clearly shewing God's existence; the certainty of the holy scriptures; and the immortality of our souls. With [logick, or] the key of sciences, and [moral sciences, etc., in English and French.] 6 p. l. 275 pp. 18°. *London, R. Redmayne,* 1700.

Berendt (Georg Carl, *editor*). Die im bernstein befindlichen organischen reste der vorwelt gesammelt, u. s. w. 3 v. in 2. fol. *Berlin, Nicolai,* 1845–56. s.

CONTENTS.

v. 1. Abth. 1. Der bernstein und die in ihm befindlichen pflanzenreste der vorwelt, von H. R. Gœppert und G. C. Berendt. 3 p. l. iv, 125 pp. 7 pl. 1845.

v. 1. Abth. 2. Die im bernstein befindlichen crustaceen, myriapoden, arachniden und apteren der vorwelt, von C. L. Koch und G. C. Berendt. iv, 124 pp. 17 pl. 1854.

v. 2. Abth. 1. Die im bernstein befindlichen hemipteren und orthopteren der vorwelt. Von E. F. Germar und G. C. Berendt. 2 l. pp. 1–40, pl. 1–4.

v. 2. Abth. 2. Die im bernstein befindlichen neuropteren der vorwelt. Von F. J. Pictet-Barabon und H. Hagen. pp. 41–125. pl. 5–8.

Bérenger (Alphonse Marie Marcellin Thomas). Des moyens propres a généraliser en France le système pénitentiaire. 3e éd. 252 pp. 2 pl. 8°. *Paris, Imprimerie royale,* 1837.

Beresford-Hope (Alexander J.) The report of her majesty's commission on the laws of marriage, relative to marriage with a deceased wife's sister, examined in a letter to Sir R. H. Inglis. 183 pp. 8°. *London, J. Ridgway,* 1849.

Bergamo (Jacopo Filippo). Supplementum chronicharum. 1 p. l. unp., 256 l. paged, 12 l. unp. fol. *Venetiis, B. Ricius de Nouaria,* 1492. [*Imperfect; wanting page* 1.]

Bergeron (Pierre). Traicté de la navigation et des voyages de descovverte et conqueste modernes et principalement des François. 5 p. l. 303 pp. 16°. *Jean de Hevqveville et Michel Soly,* 1629. (*With* Bethencourt [J. de] Histoire des Canaries, *Paris*, 1630.)

Bergh (Henry). "Married off." (A Newport sketch). 75 pp. 8 pl. 12°. *New York, Carleton,* 1862.

Berghaus (Heinrich). Allgemeine länder- und völkerkunde, nebst einem abriss der physicalischen erdbeschreibung. 6 v. in 7. 8°. *Stuttgart,* 1837-44. s.

CONTENTS.

v. 1-3. Gründzüge der physikalischen erdbeschreibung.
v. 4-5. Das europäische staatensystem nach seinem geographisch-statistischen hauptverhältnissen.
v. 6. Das amerikanische staatensystem; das mohammedanische staatensystem; die christlichen staaten von Abyssinien, das buddhaistische staatensystem; und die heidenwelt.
v. 7. Register.

——— Landbuch der mark Brandenburg und des margrafthums Nieder-Lausitz in der mitte des 19 jahrhunderts; oder geographisch-historisch-statistische beschreibung der provinz Brandenburg. 3 v. sm. 4°. *Brandenburg,* 1854-56. s.

Bergmann (Leo). Schule des zeichners; insbesondere für ausübende künstler im fache des stahl-und kupferstichs, des lithographie and des holzschnittes. 2e auflage. 8°. *Leipzig,* 1855. s.

——— Zehn tafeln säulen-ordnungen nebst construction der architektonischen glieder. 2e ausg. 4°. *Leipzig,* [1856.]

——— Das buch der arbeit. 2 v. (in 1), vi, 182 pp. 1 pl; vi, 178 pp. 1 pl. 12°. *Leipzig, O. Spamer,* 1854-5. s.

Berlien (Johann Heinrich Ferdinand). Der elephanten-orden und seine ritter. 8°. *Kopenhagen,* 1846. s.

Berlin (*königliche bibliothek*). Index librorum manuscriptorum et impressorum quibus bibliotheca regia aucta est anno 1836 et 1839. 2 v. 4°. *Berolini,* [1837-40.] s.

——— Die handschriften-verzeichnisse der königlichen bibliothek, herausgegeben von Dr. Pertz. v. 1. Verzeichniss der sanskrit handschriften, von Dr. Weber. xxiv, 481 pp. *Berlin, Nicolai,* 1853. (*Wanting* 6 pl.) s.

——— königlichen gewerbe Akademie zu Berlin. Katalog der bibliothek. vii, 371 pp. 1 pl. 8°. *Berlin, A. W. Schade,* 1866. s.

Berling (Edward Wilhelm). Öfwersigt af stadens historia och öpiga markwardigheter. [*anon.*] 12°. *Lund,* 1859. s.

Bermejo (Damian). Descripcion artística del real monasterio de S. Lorenzo del Escorial, y sus preciosidades despues de la invasion de los Franceses. vii, 400 pp. 16°. *Madrid, Roza Sanz,* 1820.

Bernadotte (Charles XIV. *of Sweden*). Recueil des ordres de mouvement, proclamations et bulletins de S. A. R. le prince royal de Suéde, commandant en chef de l'armée combinée du nord de l'Allemagne, 1813-14. 2e éd. 8°. *Stockholm,* 1839. s.

Bernaldez (Andrés). Historia de los reyes catolicos, D. Fernando y Da. Isabel. 2 v. sm. 4°. *Granada,* 1856.

Bernard (Francis, *and others*). Letters to the earl of Hillsborough from governor Bernard, general Gage, and his majesty's council for the province of Massachusetts Bay. 83 pp. fol. *Boston, Edes & Gill,* 1769.

——— The same. [*Imperfect; wanting pp.* 81-83.]

Bernard (Jean Frédéric). Réflexions morales satiriques et comiques sur les mœurs de notre siècle. 2e éd. [*anon.*] 15 p. l. 311 pp. 2 l. 18°. *Amsterdam, J. F. Bernard,* 1713. [*With* **Passe-tems** (le) agréable. *Rotterdam,* 1742.]

Bernard (Pierre Joseph). Œuvres. 8°. *Paris,* 1823.

Bernard (Thomas Dehany). Progress of doctrine in the New Testament. From 2d London ed. with improvements. 358 pp. 12°. *Boston, Gould & Lincoln,* 1867. [Bampton lectures, 1864.]

Bernardus (*Saint*). De verbis Simonis Petri ad Jesū. 40 l. unp. sm. 4°. [n. p. *about* 1480.]

——— Floretus. *See* **Garland** (Jean de).

Bernd (Christian Samuel Theodor). Die hauptstücke der wappenwissenschaft. 2 abtheilungen in 2 v. 8°. *Bonn, E. Weber,* 1841—49. s.

CONTENTS.

v. I. Wappenwesen der Griechen und Römer, und anderer alter völker.
v. II. Die allgemeine wappenwissenchaft.

Berneaud (Arsène Thiébaut de). *See* **Thiébaut de Berneaud.**

Berners (Juliana). *See* **Barnes** (Juliana).

Bernhardi (Carl). Sprachkarte von Deutschland. 4 p. l. 138 pp. 1 map col. 12°. *Kassel, J. J. Bohné,* 1844. s.

——— *See* **Schomburg** (C.) Briefwechsel, u. s. w.

Berni (Francesco). Tvtte le opere, in terza rima, nvovamente con somma diligentia stampate. [Con le terze rime del Molza, del Varchi, del Dolce et d'altri: et dialogo contra i poeti.] 227 l. 16°. (n. p.) 1542.

Berquin (Arnaud). L'ami des enfants. Nouv. éd., précédée d'une notice biographique par J. N. Bouilly. Illustrée de nombreuses vignettes dessinées par MM. G. Staal et Gérard Seguin. xv, 480 pp. 10 pl. 8°. *Paris,* [1858.]

Berquin-Duvallon (—). Schilderung von Louisiana. Aus dem Französischen, zweckmässig abgekürzt. Mit einer einleitung und zusätzen herausgegebenen von Theophil Friedrich Ehrmann. xxviii, 344 pp. 1 map. 8°. *Weimar, Industrie comptoirs,* 1804.

Berry (*Mrs.* Martha E.) Celesta; a girl's book. 257 pp. 3 pl. 16°. *Boston, W. V. Spencer,* 1867.

——— Crooked and straight, or Jotham and Annette at home. 291 pp. 3 pl. 16°. *Boston, W. V. Spencer,* 1867.

Bert, *or* **Bertius** (Pierre). Brevis ac succincta Americæ descriptio, excerpta e tabulis geographicis P. Bertii. 11 l. folio. [*With* **Herrera** (Antonio de). Novvs orbis. *Amstelodami,* 1622.]

——— The same. Description d'Amérique. 229—254 pp. folio. [*With* **Herrera** (Antonio de). Description des Indes Occidentales. Ed. *Amsterdam,* 1622.]

Berthiaud (—). Nouveau manuel complet de l'imprimeur en taille douce. Rédigé par M. Boitard. 320 pp. 3 pl. 18°. *Paris, Roret,* 1837. S.

Berthold (Arnold Adolph). Lehrbuch der zoologie. vi, 591 pp. 8°. *Göttingen, Vandenhoeck,* 1845. S.

Bertie (*Lady* Georgina). Five generations of a loyal house. Part i., containing the lives of Richard Bertie and his son Peregrine, Lord Willoughby. lx, 544 pp. 4 pl. 8°. *London, Rivingtons,* 1845.

Bertius (Petrus). *See* **Bert** (Pierre).

Berton (Jean Michel). Intérêts rivaux de la France et de l'Angleterre en Europe et en Orient. xvi, 366 pp. 8°. *Paris, Paulin,* 1841. S.

Bertrand (François Marie). Chrestomathie hindoustani. *See* **Parie** (T.)

Berzelius (Johann Jacob). Lehrbuch der chemie, aus der schwedischen handschrift des verfassers übersetzt von F. Woehler. 4e aufl. 10 v. 8°. *Dresden, &c., Arnold,* 1835—41. S.

Beschi (C.) A grammar of the high dialec of the Tamil language, termed Shen-Tamil; to which is added an introduction to Tamil poetry. Tr. from the Latin, by Benjamin Guy Babington. v, xii, 117 pp. 4°. *Madras, College press,* 1822. S.

Bessarion (Joannes). In calumniatorē Platonis libri iv. Correctio librorum Platonis de legibus, Georgio Trapezuntio interprete. De natura et arte aduersus eundem Trapezuntiū tractatus. 8 p. l. 112 l. fol. *Venetiis, Aldus,* 1503. S.

Bessel (Friedrich Wilhelm). Untersuchungen über die länge des einfachen secundenpendels. (Extract.) 3 p. l. 254 pp. 2 pl. 4°. *Berlin, k. akad. der wissenschaften,* 1828. S.

——— Tabulae regiomontanae reductionum observationum ab anno 1750 usque ad annum 1850 computatae. lxxxiii, 542 pp. 8°. *Regiomonti Prussorum, Borntraeger,* 1830. S.

Besuchungen des hochheiligsten altarssakramentes. Ein gebet-und-erbauungsbuch. Bearbeitet von F. Willam. 414 pp. 18 pl. 24°. *New York, Benziger Bros.,* 1867.

Betham (Matilda). Biographical dictionary of the celebrated women of every age and country. vi, 852 pp. 1 pl. 8°. *London, B. Crosby & Co.,* 1804.

Betham (*Rev.* William). The baronetage of England, or the history of the English baronets, and such baronets of Scotland as are of English families. 5 v. 52 pl. 4°. *Ipswich, Burrell & Bransby,* 1801—05.

Bethencourt (Jean de). Histoire de la première descovverte et conqueste des Canaries, faites dés l'an 1402. Escrite du temps mesme par Pierre Bontier et Jean le Verrier. Et mise en lumiere par Galien de Bethencourt. 10 p. l. 208 pp. 6 l. 16°. *Paris, Jean de Hevqveville,* 1630.

Béthune (Philippe de). Covnsellor of estate, contayning considerations seruing for the managing of publicke affairs. [*anon.*] Translated from the French by E. G[rimeston.] 16 p. l. 336 pp. sm. 4°. *London, Nicholas Okes,* 1634.

Betta (Edoardo de). Erpetologia delle provincie venete e del Tirolo meridionale. xvi, 365 pp. 1 pl. 8°. *Verona, Vicentini e Franchini,* 1857. S.

——— Ittiologia veronese ad uso popolaree per servire all' introduzione della piscicultura nella provincia. 2a ed. 153 pp. 8°. *Verona, Vicentini e Franchini,* 1862. S.

Beudant (François Sulpice). Voyage minéralogique et géologique en Hongrie, 1818. 4 v. 7 pl. 7 maps. 4°. *Paris, Verdière,* 1822. S.

Beurard (Jean Baptiste). Dictionnaire allemand-français, contenant les termes propres à l' exploitation des mines, à la métallurgie et à la minéralogie. 696 pp. 8°. *Paris, Mongie,* 1819. s.

Bevan (Edward, *M. D.*) The honey bee; its natural history, physiology, and management. xxiv, 447 pp. 12°. *London, Van Voorst,* 1838.

Bevan (Samuel). Sand and canvas; a narrative of adventures in Egypt, with a sojourn among the artists in Rome. xii, 370 pp. 8 pl. 8°. *London, Charles Gilpin,* 1849.

Beverland (Adraan). De stolatæ virginitatis jure lucubratio academica. 6 p. l. 223 pp. 18°. *Lugduni in Batavis, J. Lindan,* 1680.

——— De fornicatione cavenda admonitio, sive adhortatio ad pudicitiam et castitatem. Ed. nova, juxta exemplar Londinense. 109 pp. 18°. [*Hollande*], 1698.

——— Peccatum originale kat' exochen sic nuncupatum philologice elucubratum. v, 146 pp. 18°. *Eleutheropoli,* 1678.

Beverley (Thomas). A scripture-line of time drawn from the lapsed creation to the restitution of all things, discoursed upon Dan. 3, 14. 5 p. l. 93, 190 pp. 4°. [n. p.] 1684.

Bey (Hekekyan), *or* Hekkeyan bey. Treatise on the chronology of Siriadic monuments, demonstrating that the Egyptian dynasties of Manetho are records of astrogeological Nile observations. 8°. *London,* 1863. s.

Beyer (August). Memoriae historico-criticæ librorum rariorum; accedunt Evangeli cosmopolitani notæ ad Menckenii de charlataneria eruditorum declamationes. 8 p. l. 304 pp. 16°. *Dresdæ et Lipsiæ, F. Hekel,* 1734. s.

Beyle (Henri). De l'amour. Par de Stendhal [*pseudon.*] xxiii, 371 pp. 12°. *Paris, Lévy,* 1856.

——— La chartreuse de Parme. Nouv. éd, précédée d'une lettre et d'une étude littéraire sur Beyle, par [H.] de Balzac. lix, 479 pp. 12°. *Paris, A. Delahays,* 1856.

——— Rome, Naples, and Florence in 1817. By the count de Stendhal. [*pseudon.*] xi, 339 pp. 8°. *London, H. Colburn,* 1818.

Bhâgavata (Le) Purâna. Ou histoire poétique de Krichna, traduit et publié par Eugène Burnouf. 3 v. fol. *Paris, Imprimerie royale,* 1840–47. [Collection orientale.]

Bianconi (Giovanni Battista). Cenni intorno all' origini, ed i progressi dell' arte galvanoplastica. (Extract.) 67 pp. 2 pl. 8°. [*Bologna, about* 1842.]

Bianconi (Giovanni Lodovico). Briefe über Celsus. [**Celsus**. Über die arzneiwissenschaft. *Ed.* 1846.] s.

Bible (*Cherokee.*) Translation of Genesis into the Cherokee language. Dinetlvanvhi goweli didalenisgv wosi uwowelanvhi. [By Evan Jones. 4th to 50th chap. In **Cherokee** messenger. 12 nos. 8°. *Cherokee,* 1844–6.] [1–3 chap. in **Bible**, *Cherokee.* Select passages from the holy scriptures. 24°.]

——— Gospel according to Matthew, translated into the Cherokee language. Oedvkanohedv maduuwowelanvhi. 4th ed. 120 pp. 24°. *Park Hill, Mission Press,* 1844.

——— Gospel according to Luke. Dinetlvtanvhi osdv kanohedv lgauwonvhi. [Translated into Cherokee by Evan Jones. *In* **Cherokee** messenger, Nos. 8–12. 8°. *Cherokee*, 1844–46.]

——— Gospel according to John. Osdvkanohedv tsani uwowelanvhi tsoine digaleyvtanohi. 3d ed. 101 pp. 24°. *Park Hill, Mission Press,* 1847. [*With* **Bible**, *Cherokee,* gospel according to Matthew. *Park Hill,* 1844.]

——— Acts of the apostles, translated into the Cherokee language. Getsinvsidv nunadvnelitolvi taline digaleyvtanvhi. 2d ed. 124 pp. 24°. *Park Hill, Mission Press,* 1842. [*With* **Bible**, *Cherokee.* Gospel according to Mathew. *Park Hill,* 1844.]

——— Epistle of Paul, the apostle, to the Ephesians. Translated into Cherokee by Evan Jones and John B. Jones. Quola atsinosidv etlusi anehi widuwowelanelvhi. 24 pp. 24°. *Cherokee, Bapt. Miss. Press,* 1848.

——— First epistle of Paul to the Thessalonians. Igvyiyequola duwowelanelv desaloniga anehi. *In* Cherokee messenger, No. 12. 8°. *Cherokee,* 1844–46.]

——— Epistles of Paul to Timothy, translated into the Cherokee language. Quola tsuwowelanvhi, dimaditsuwowelanelvhi. 28 pp. 24°. [*Park Hill,* 1844. *With* **Bible**, *Cherokee,* gospel according to Matthew. *Park Hill,* 1844.]

——— The general epistle of James. Translated into the Cherokee language. Tsimiuwowelanvhi. 16 pp. 24°. *Park Hill,* 1847. [*With* **Bible**, *Cherokee,* gospel according to Matthew. *Park Hill,* 1844.]

——— Epistles of John translated into the Cherokee language. Tsani tsuwowelanelvhi. tsunandodi. 20 pp. 24°. *Park Hill,* 1840.

——— The same. 3d ed. *Park Hill,* 1848. [*With* **Bible**, *Cherokee,* gospel according to Matthew. *Park Hill,* 1844.]

Bible—continued.

——— (*Cherokee*). General epistle of Jude. Tsuda naniv tsunanelodi tsuwowelanelvhi. [*In* **Cherokee** messenger, No. 11. 8°. *Cherokee*, 1844–46.]

——— Select passages from the holy scriptures. 24 pp. 24°. [n. d.] [*With* **Bible**, *Cherokee*, gospel according to Matthew. *Park Hill*, 1844.]

——— *Choctaw.* Gospel according to Matthew, translated into the Choctaw language. Ubanumpa mahlu vt holissocchi tok. [With alphabet.] 198 pp. 16°. *Boston, Am. Board For. Miss.*, 1842.

——— *English.* Holy bible, conteyning the old testament and the new. Newlie translated out of ye originall tongues and with the former translations diligently compared and revised, by his majesties speciall commandement. fol. *London, Robert Barker*, 1633. S.

——— Complete analysis of the holy bible; containing the old and new testament, collected and systematically arranged by Rev. N. West, D. D. lxiv, 1035 pp. 1 map. 8°. *New York, A. J. Johnson*, 1868.

——— The same. Ezekiel and Daniel; with notes, by H. Cowles, *D. D.* 472 pp. 12°. *New York, D. Appleton & Co.*, 1867.

——— Minor prophets; with notes. By *Rev.* Henry Cowles. 12°. *New York*, 1867.

——— Notes on the epistle of Paul to the Hebrews. [With the authorized English version]. By Joseph Longking. 480 pp. 24°. *New York, Carlton & Porter*, [1867].

——— The same. 720 pp. 16°. *Newburyport, (Ms.) W. B. Allen & Co.* 1815.

——— Commentary on the holy scriptures: critical, doctrinal, and homiletical, with special reference to ministers and students. By J. P. Lange, *D. D.*, and others. Translated from the German by P. Schaff, *D. D.*, [and others.] New Testament. v. 9. Containing the epistles of James, Peter, John, and Jude. [Translated by J. I. Mombert]. 8°. *New York, Scribner*, 1867.

——— Job, Ecclesiastes and Canticles. New translation with introductions and notes. By George R. Noyes. 3d ed. 351 pp. 12°. *Boston, Am. Unit. Assoc.*, 1867.

——— Psalms and Proverbs. New translation, with introductions and notes. By George R. Noyes. 3d ed. 421 pp. 12°. *Boston Am. Unit. Assoc.*, 1867.

——— Prophets. New translation of the Hebrew prophets, with introduction and notes. By George R. Noyes. 3d ed. 2 v. 12°. *Boston, Am. Unit. Assoc.*, 1866.

Bible—continued.

——— The new testament, translated into English, with annotations by the English college in Rhemes. 5th ed., (the first in folio.) xix, 646 pp.; 16 l., 4 pl. fol. [n. p.] 1738.

——— New testament of our lord and saviour Jesus Christ. 232 l. unp. 8°. *Trenton, (N. J.) Isaac Collins*, 1788.

——— A commentary on the New Testament. By Lucius R. Paige. v. 5. I. and II. Corinthians. 383 pp. 12°. *Boston, Univ. Pub. House*, 1867.

——— The apocryphal new testament. xvi, 184 pp. 8°. *New York, H. G. Daggers.*[n. d.]

——— An harmony of the four gospels, with historical and doctrinal notes; by John Chambers. xxiii, 884, 30, 6 pp. 8°. *Retford, E. G. Woodhead*, [*about* 1814.]

——— A harmony of the four gospels, in the English authorized version, arranged according to Greswell's "Harmonia evangelica" in Greek. Intended to accompany Mimpriss's pictorial chart. x, 351 pp. 8°. *London, S. Low*, 1833.

——— Disquisitions and notes on the gospels. Matthew, by J. H. Morrison. 2d ed. 538 pp. 12°. *Boston, Walker, Wise & Co.*, 1861.

——— The epistles of Paul translated, with an exposition and notes by Rev. T. Belsham. 2 v. 4°. *London*, 1822.

——— The second epistle of Peter, the epistles of John and Judas, and the Revelation: translated from the Greek, on the basis of the common English version. [Revised version of the Am. Bible union.] xi, 253 pp. 4°. *New York, Am. Bible union*, 1854.

——— *Esquimaux.* Genesis. Testamentitokamit Mosesim aglegèj siurdleet. Pellesiúnermit Ottomit Fabriciusimit. 202 pp. 16°. *Kiöbenhavnime, C. F. Skubartimit*, 1822.

——— Psalms. Testamentitokamit Davidim wngerutéj. Pellesimit Nielsimit Wolfimit. 238 pp. 16°. *Kiöbenhavnime, C. F. Schubartimit*, 1824. [*With* **Bible**, *Esquimaux*. Testamentitokamit Mosesim. [Genesis.] 16°. *Kiöbenhavnime*, 1822.]

——— Isaiah. Testamentitokamit profetib Esaiasim aglegèj. Pellesimit N. G. Wolfimit. 200 pp. 16°. *Kjöbenhavnime, C. F. Skubartimit*, 1825. (*With* **Bible**, *Esquimaux*. Testamentitokamit Mosesim. [Genesis.] *Kiöbenhavnime*, 1822.

——— Testamente nutak. [New Testament.] [Translated by Otho Fabricius.] 1072 pp. 16°. *Kiöbenhavnime, C. F. Skubartimit*, 1799.

Bible—continued.

——— *Gothic.* The Gothic and Anglo-Saxon gospels in parallel columns, with the versions of Wycliffe and Tyndale; arranged, with preface and notes, by Rev. J. Bosworth, assisted by G. Waring. xxxvi, 584 pp. 1 pl. 8°. *London, J. R. Smith,* 1865.

——— *Greek.* Divinæ scripturæ veteris nouaeq. omnia. 4 p. l. 275 pp. 18°. *Argentorati, V. Cephal,* 1529.

——— Bibliorum codex sinaiticus petropolitanus. Auspiciis Alexandri II. edidit Tischendorf. 4 v. fol. *Petropoli,* 1862. s.

——— *Hawaiian.* Ke karioha hou a ko kakou haku e ola'i a Jesu Kristo. 504 pp. 12°. *Oahu, Misionari i poi,* 1835. s.

——— *Indian, Massachusetts.* Mamvsse wunneetupanatamwe up-biblum God naneeswe nukkone testament kah wonk wusku testament. Ne quosh-Kinnumuk nashpe wuttineumoh Christ noh asoowesit John Eliot. [2d ed.] 575 l. sm. 4°. *Cambridge, Samuel Green,* 1685.

——— The same. Wuskv wuttesta mentum nul-lordumun Jesus Christ nuppoquohwussuaeneumum. [New testament. 2d ed.] 170 l. sm. 4°. *Cambridge, for the corporation in London, for the propagation of the gospel among the Indians in N. E.,* 1680. [*With* the preceding].

——— Psalms and John. [Massachusetts psalter; asuh, Uk-kuttooho-maongash David weche winnaunchemookaonk ne ansukhogup John. Indian and English. Translated by Experience Mayhew.] 212 l. unp. 18°. *Boston, B. Green, for soc. propag. Gospel,* 1709.
[Imperfect: wants title and 13 leaves.]

——— *Latin.* Biblia [sacra.] Interprete Sebastiano Castalione. Una cum eiusdem annotationibus. fol. *Basileæ,* 1551. s.

——— *Mohawk.* The gospel according to St. Mark. St. Mark Raorighwadogeaghty.... Translated by Capt. Joseph Brant, [T'hayendanegea.] [*With* 176 to 341 pp. of the book of common prayer, according to the use of the church of England. In the Mohawk language. 8°. *London,* 1789.]

——— Nene karighyoston tsinihorighhoten ne Saint John. Gospel according to Saint John. 116, 116 pp. 24°. *New York, Am. Bible soc.,* 1818.

——— Ne totyerenhton kahyatonhsera ne royatadogenhti Paul shagohyatonni ne Corinthians. First epistle of Paul the apostle to the Corinthians. Translated by H. A. Hill. 50, 50 pp. 12°. *New York, young men's bible soc.,* 1834.

Bibliographie de la France. *See* **Journal** générale de l'imprimerie.

Bibliophile (Le) belge. Par M. de Reiffenberg. v. 1–9. 8°. *Bruxelles,* 1845–52. s.

Bibliotheca Americana. Catalogue raisonné d'une très-précieuse collection de livres anciens et modernes sur l'Amérique et les Philippines. Classés par ordre alphabétique de noms d'auteurs. Rédigé par Ch. Leclerc. vii, 407 pp. 8°. *Paris, Maisonneuve & Cie.,* 1867.

Bibliotheca politica, or a discourse by way of dialogue whether monarchy be jure divino. [*anon.*] 4 p. l. 64 pp. sm. 4°. *London, Richard Baldwin,* 1691–2.

Bibliotheca (The) sacra. Edited by E. A. Park and S. H. Taylor. Jan. to Oct. 1867. v. 24. 8°. *Boston, Draper & Halliday,* 1867.

Bickham (George). The British monarchy, or a new chorographical description of all the dominions subject to the king of Great Britain, comprehending the British isles, the American colonies, etc. Engraved. 190 pl. fol. *London,* 1748.

Bicknell (Alexander). Doncaster races; or the history of Miss Maitland. 2 v. 272 pp; 275 pp. 16°. *London, C. Stalker,* [1790.]

Bie (Cornelis de). Het gulden cabinet van de schilderconst inhovdende den lof van de vermaerste schilders, architecten, beldthowers ende plaetsnyders, van dese eevw. 4°. *Antwerpen,* 1661. s.

Bienville (J. D. T. de, *M. D.*) La nymphomanie, ou traité de la fureur utérine. Nouv. éd. xxviii, 198 pp. 24°. *Londres,* 1789.

——— The same. Nymphomania, or, a dissertation concerning the furor uterinus. Translated by E. S. Wilmot, M. D. 189, 16 pp. 8°. *J. Bew, London,* 1775.

Biffi (Serafino). Sulla vita scientifica e sulle opere di anatomia e fisiologia comparata del dottor Mauro Rusconi commentario. 167 pp. 1 pl. 8°. *Milano, ed. annali univ. di medicina,* 1853. s.

——— Reminiscenzi di un viaggio in Germania. 4 p. l. 127 pp. 7 tab. 4°. *Milano, G. Chiusi,* 1858. s.

——— Reminiscenzi di un viaggio nel Belgio e nella Francia. 2 p l. 144 pp. 4°. *Milano, G. Chiusi,* 1856. s.

Bigelow (Abijah). Voters' guide, or, the power, duty, and privileges of the constitutional voters in the commonwealth of Massachusetts. 156 pp. 16°. *Leominster, (Mass.) S. & J. Wilder,* 1807.

Bigelow (Jacob, *M. D.*) Modern inquiries; classical, professional, and miscellaneous. xi, 379 pp. 12°. *Boston, Little, Brown & Co.* 1867.
——— Remarks on classical and utilitarian studies, read before the American academy of arts and sciences, Dec. 20, 1866. 57 pp. 12°. *Boston*, 1867.
——— Some account of the White mountains of New Hampshire. [From the New England journal of medicine and surgery, for October, 1816.] 18 pp. 8°. [*Boston*, 1816.]

Bigelow (L. J.) Bench and bar: a complete digest of the wit, humor, asperities, and amenities of the law. 364 pp. 1 pl. 8°. *New York, Harpers*, 1867.

Biggs (James). The history of Don Francisco de Miranda's attempt to effect a revolution in America. In a series of letters. With life of Miranda, and geographical notices of Caraccas. xv, 312 pp. 8°. *London, author*, 1809.

Biglow (William). History of Sherburne, Mass. 1674 to 1830. 80 pp. 8°. *Milford, (Mass.) Ballou & Stacy*, 1830.

Bigly (Cantell A.) [*pseudon.*] *See* **Aurifodina**, etc.

Bigney (M. F.) The forest pilgrims, and other poems. 258 pp. 12°. *New Orleans, J. A. Greesham*, 1867.

Bigorie de Laschamps (F.) Michel de Montaigne. 326 pp. 12°. *Paris, A. Vatou*, 1855.

Bigot de Morogues (Pierre Marie Sébastien). Recherches théoriques et pratiques de la meilleure méthode pour faire fermenter économiquement le vin, le cidre et les autres liqueurs du même genre. 237 pp. 12°. *Paris, Huzard*, 1825.

Bill (a) in the chancery of New Jersey, at the suit of John, earl of Stair, and others, proprietors of the eastern division of New Jersey, against Benjamin Bond and other persons of Elizabeth-town. [With] the publications of the council of prop ietors of east New Jersey concerning the riots. 124, 39 pp. 3 maps. fol. *New York, James Parker*, 1747.

Bill (Ledyard). Pen pictures of the war. Lyrics, incidents, and sketches of the rebellion, [with] a complete historical record. 6th ed. 368 pp. 1 pl. 8°. *New York*, 1866.
——— History of the Bill family. 368 pp. 1 pl. 8°. *New York*, [*author*], 1867.

Billaut (Adam). Le vilebrequin de Mr Adam, menvisier de Nevers, contenant toutes sortes de poësies gallantes, etc. [*pseudon.*] 295 pp. 57 l. 16°. *Paris, G. de Lvnye*, 1663.
[Imp: wanting pp. 133-4.]

Bille (Steen). Bericht über die reise der corvette Galathea um die welt, 1845-47. Aus dem dänischen übersetzt von W. v. Rosen. 2 v. xiv, 464 pp. 7 pl. 1 map; x, 517 pp. 7 pl. 1 map. 8°. *Kopenhagen, C. A. Reitzel*, 1852. s.

Billet (F.) Traité d'optique physique. 2 v. xv, 540 pp. 7 pl; 640 pp. 7 pl. 8°. *Paris, Mallet-Bachelier*, 1858-59. s.

Bilson (Thomas). The trve difference betweene christian svbiection and vnchristian rebellion. 5 p. l. 820 pp. 4°. *Oxford, J. Barnes*, 1585.

Binder (Christian). Württembergische münz- und medaillen-kunde. viii, 628 pp. 8°. *Stuttgart, F. H. Köhler*, 1846. s.

Bindley (Charles). The sportsman's friend in a frost. By Harry Hieover. [*pseudon.*] 4 p. l. 416 pp. 8°. *London, T. C. Newby*, 1857.

Bingham (William). Grammar of the Latin language, with exercises. 388 pp. 12°. *Philadelphia, E. H. Butler & Co.* 1867.

Bingley (*Rev.* William). Biographical conversations on celebrated travellers. x, 360 pp. 16°. *London, J. Sharpe*, 1819.
——— Biographical conversations on the most eminent British characters. xii, 348 pp. 16°. *London, J. Sharpe*, 1818.
——— Biographical conversations on the most eminent voyagers of different nations. xii, 348 pp. 16°. *London, J. Sharpe*, 1818.

Bini, (Gianfrancesco). Le terze rime, 1542. (*With* **Berni** (F.) Tutte le opere, etc).

Binney (Amos). The terrestrial air-breathing mollusks of the United States. Edited by A. A. Gould. 4 v. 4°. *Boston, Little, Brown & Co.* 1851-60. s.

Binney (William G.) Land and fresh water shells of North America. Part ii. Pulmonata, limnophila, and thalassophila. ix, 161 pp. 8°. *Washington*, 1865. (Smithsonian miscel. coll. v. 7).
——— The same. Part iii. Ampullaridae, valvatidae, viviparidae, fresh-water rissoidae, cyclophoridae, truncatellidae, fresh-water neritidae, helicinidae. viii, 120 pp. 8°. *Washington*, 1865. (Smithsonian miscel. coll. v. 7).
——— *See* **Binney** (A.) Terrestrial air-breathing mollusks. Supp. [v. 4.]

Biographical memoirs of Gen. G. Washington, containing a history of the principal events of his life, with extracts from his journals, speeches to Congress, and public addresses. 3d ed. 217 pp. 24°. *Philadelphia, R. Folwell*, 1801.

Biographical memoirs of George Washington. [*anon.*] 160 pp. 24°. *Barnard, [Vt.] Joseph Dix*, 1813.

Biographie moderne, ou galerie historique, civile, militaire, politique, et judiciare. [*anon.*] 2 v. 8°. *Paris, A. Eymery,* 1815.

Bion. Works. Translated [by F. Fawkes]. 18°. *London,* 1760. (*With* Anacreon, etc. Works. Ed. *London,* 1760).

——— The same. Translated by F. Fawkes. 8°. *Edinburgh,* [1792]. [Anderson's British poets, v. 5].

——— The same. (*In* Greek pastoral poets. Done into English by M. J. Chapman. 3d ed. 12°. *London,* 1856).

Biondo (Flavio). Roma instaurata, libri tres. 43 l. unp. fol. *Veronae, per Boninum de Boninis de Ragusia,* 1481.

——— De origine et gestis Venetorum. 14 l. unp. fol. *Veronae, per Boninum de Boninis de Ragusia,* 1481. (*With* preceding).

——— Italia illustrata. 93 l. unp. fol. *Veronae, Boninum de Boninis de Ragusia,* 1482. (*With* preceding).

Biot (Jean Baptiste). Mélanges scientifiques et littéraires. 3 v. 8°. *Paris,* 1858. s.

CONTENTS.

V. 1. Voyages; opérations géodésiques. Études sur Newton. (iv, 472 pp).
V. 2. Critique littéraire et scientifique. Esquisses biographiques. (462 pp).
V. 3. Économie sociale. Voyages de découvertes. (532 pp).

——— La razionale scoperta del pianeta de Le Verrier logicamente presentata; recata italianamente con prefazione e note da Giuseppe Bianchi. xxiii, 238 pp. 16°. *Parma, P. Fiaccadori,* 1854. s.

Birch (Thomas, *D. D.*) An inquiry into the share which king Charles I had, in the transactions of the Earl of Glamorgan, for bringing over a body of Irish rebels, in 1645–46. [*anon.*] 2d ed. viii, 376 pp. 8°. *London, A. Millar,* 1756.

Brigitta (*Saint, of Sweden*). *See* **Brigitta.**

Birkinshaw (Maria Louisa). The chevaliers; a tale. 416 pp. 8°. *London, Simpkin, Marshall & Co.* 1860.

Bischoff (Theodor Ludwig Wilhelm). Entwicklungsgeschichte des hunde-eies. 134 pp. 15 pl. 4°. *Braunschweig, Vieweg,* 1845. s.

——— Entwicklungsgeschichte des kaninchen-eies. 134 pp. 15 pl. 4°. *Braunschweig, Vieweg,* 1842. s.

Bishop (Abraham). Georgia speculations unveiled. In two parts. 144 pp. 8°. *Hartford, Elisha Babcock, and Hudson & Goodwin,* 1797--98.

Bishop (*Rev.* Robert H.) Outline of the history of the church in Kentucky, during a period of forty years [1783--1823]; containing memoirs of Rev. David Rice, [with his two epistles to presbyterians, and a tract in opposition to slavery]. 420 pp. 16°. *Lexington, (Ky.) F. T. Skillman,* 1824.

Bishop's (The) council; with reminiscences of an annual conference of the methodist episcopal church. By an ex-presiding elder. [*anon.*] 338 pp. 12°. *St. Louis, P. M. Pinckard,* 1867.

Bitaubé (Paul Jérémie). Joseph. [Poëme en prose]. 2 v. in 1. 5e éd. 194, 271 pp. 9 pl. 24°. *Paris, Didot,* 1786.

Björnson (Björnstjerne). Arne, a sketch of Norwegian life. Translated from the Norwegian, by A. Plesner and S. Rugeley-Powers. xvi, 202 pp. 12°. *London, A. Strahan,* 1866.

Black (The) book of England; exhibiting the state policy and administration of the united kingdom. xii, 384 pp. 16°. *London, C. Mitchell,* 1847.

Black (The) crook, a most wonderful history. [*anon.*] 148 pp. 6 pl. 8°. *Philadelphia, Barclay & Co.* 1867.

Blackburn (*Rev.* W. M. *editor*). *See* **Kirkpatrick** (*Rev.* Jacob). Kirkpatrick memorial, etc.

Blackburne (Francis). The confessional; or, a full and free inquiry into the right, utility, edification and success, of establishing systematical confessions of faith and doctrine in protestant churches. [*anon.*] 2d ed. xliii, xciii, 410 pp. 8°. *London, S. Bladon,* 1767.

Blackley (*Rev.* Frederick R.) The Greenland minstrel; a poem, with introductory narrative and notes. 16°. *London,* 1839.

Blackmore (*Sir* Richard). Creation; a poem. 8°. *Edinburgh,* 1793.
[Anderson's Brit. poets, v. 7.]

Blackson (Lorenzo D.) The rise and progress of the kingdoms of light and darkness; or the reign of kings Alpha and Abaddon. 288 pp. 13 pl. 12°. *Philadelphia, J. Nicholas,* 1867.

Blackwell (Robert). Original acrostics on some of the southern states and the most eminent men of the southern confederacy, and on other subjects. 24 pp. 16°. *Loudon Co. Va.* 1863.

Blackwood's Edinburgh magazine, July 1866 to June 1867. v. 100–101. 8°. *Edinburgh, W. Blackwood & son,* 1866–67.

Blainville (——— de). Œuvres diverses ud sieur D***. [*anon.*] 8 p. l. 283 pp. 15 l. 1 pl. 18°. *Paris, D. Thierry,* 1683.

Blair (*Rev.* David). A grammar of chemistry. Revised by B. Tucker. 180 pp. 1 pl. 18°. *Philadelphia, D. Hogan,* 1810.

Blair (*Rev.* Robert). The grave; a poem. 8°. *Edinburgh,* 1794.
[Anderson's Brit. poets, v. 8.]

—— The same. Illustrated by twelve etchings [from designs by William Blake]. xiv, 36 pp. 12 pl. 4°. *London, T. Bensley,* 1808. s.

Blake (Alexander V.) American bookseller's complete reference trade list and alphabetical catalogue of books published in the U. S. With an article on the law of copyright by P. T. Washburn. 4°. *Claremont, (N. H.)* 1847.

—— The same. Supplement. 4°. *Claremont, (N. H.)* 1848. s.

Blake (*Rev.* Mortimer). A centurial history of the Mendon association of congregational ministers, with the centennial address delivered at Franklin, Mass. Nov. 19, 1851. 344 pp. 12°. *Boston, Sewall Harding,* 1853.

Blake (William). Designs illustrating The grave; a poem. *See* **Blair** (Robert). s.

Blanc (Jean Joseph Louis). History of the French revolution of 1789. Translated from the French. v. 1. (Introduction and first year). 8°. *Philadelphia, Lea & Blanchard,* 1848. s.
[No more published in English].

Blanchard (Émile). *See* **Cuvier** (G. L. C. F. D.) Règne animal—zoophytes.

Blanchard (P.) *and* **Dauzats** (Adrien). San Juan de Ulùa, ou relation de l'expédition française au Mexique, sous les ordres de la contre-amiral Baudin. Suivi de notes et d'un aperçu sur l'état actuel du Texas par E[ugène] Maissin. xii, 591 pp. 18 pl. 8°. *Paris, Gide,* 1839.

Blanco (Manuel). Flora de Filipinas. lxxviii, 887 pp. 8°. *Manila, C. Lopez,* 1837. s.

Bland (Robert, *M. D.*) Observations on human and comparative parturition. xv, 223 pp. 8°. *London, J. Johnson,* 1794. [*With* **Fowler** (Thomas). Effects of blood-letting, etc. *London,* 1795.]

Blandin (Philippe Frédéric). Traité d'anatomie topographique, ou anatomie des régions du corps humain, etc. 2e éd., xxxii, 680 pp. 1 tab. 8°. *Germer Baillière,* 1834. s.
[Wanting atlas, 20 pl. fol.]

Blane (William). Cynegetica; or, essays on sporting: consisting of observations on hare hunting. With The chase: a poem, by William Somerville. New ed. 292 pp. 8°. [*London,* 1781].

Blaney (*Capt.*) An excursion through the United States and Canada, 1822--23. By an English gentleman. [*anon*]. 2 p. l. 511 pp. 2 maps. 8°. *London, Baldwin, Cradock & Joy,* 1824.

Blanford (H. F.) *See* **Salter**, John William *and* **Blanford**, (H. F.)

Blatchly (A.) Mining and milling in the Reese river region, central and southeast Nevada. 48 pp. 12°. *New York, Slote & Janes,* 1867.

Bledsoe (Albert Taylor, *LL. D.*) Is Davis a traitor; or, was secession a constitutional right, previous to the war of 1861? vi, 264 pp. 12°. *Baltimore, Innes & Co.* 1866.

Bleile (Joseph). Beiträge zur kaltwasserheilkunde. Mit einem anhang, enthaltend Nutzen und gebrauch des kalten badens nach P. J. Ferro; * * * Wirkungen des kalten badens, und trinken nach J. Floyer; Natur und heilkräfte der milch, nach J. Floyer. xxiii, 382 pp. 16°. *Kempten, F. Dannheimer,* 1852.

Blenkarn (John). British timber trees: their rearing and subsequent management, in woods, groves, and plantations. xii, 276 pp. 12°. *London, Routledge,* 1859. s.

Blesensis (Peter). *See* **Pierre** de Blois.

Bloch (Mark Elieser). Ichtyologie, ou histoire naturelle, générale et particulière, des poissons. 12 v. in 6. fol. *Berlin, auteur,* 1785--97. s.

—— Oeconomische naturgeschichte der fische Deutschlands. 3 v. 4°. atlas fol. *Berlin, verfasser,* 1782--84. s.

Blome (Richard). Description of the island of Jamaica, with the other isles and territories of America, to which the English are related. 4 p. l. 192 pp. 1 map. 24°. *London, T. Milbourn,* 1672.

Blondel (François). Histoire du calendrier romain, qui contient son origine et les divers changemens qui luy sont arrivez. 312 pp. 4 l. 4°. *Paris, auteur,* 1699.

Blot (Pierre). Hand-book of practical cookery; containing the whole science and art of preparing human food. 478 pp. 12°. *New York, D. Appleton & Co.* 1867.

Blount (Thomas Pope). Censura celebriorum authorum. Ed. nova. 4 p. l. 1070 pp. 4°. *Genevae, De Tournes,* 1710. s.

Blowe (Daniel). Geographical, commercial, and agricultural view of the United States of America, with account of Canada. 758, xxxvi pp. 2 maps. 8°. *Liverpool, H. Fisher,* (*about* 1820).

Blowe (Daniel). The same. [*anon.*] 746, xvi pp. 1 pl. 1 map, 1 table. 8°. *London, [Liverpool], Edwards & Knibb*, 1820.

Blum (J. Reinhard). Lithurgik, oder mineralien und felsarten nach ihrer ökonomischer hinsicht systematisch abgehandelt. 501 pp. 8°. *Stuttgard, E. Schweizerbart*, 1840. (Naturgeschichte, supplement). s.

——— Lehrbuch der oryktognosie. 2e. aufl. xxii, 706 pp. 8°. *Stuttgard, E. Schweizerbart*, 1345. (Naturgeschichte, v. 2). s.

Blume (Friedrich). Iter italicvm; archive, bibliotheken, und inschriften. 4 v. in 2. 16°. *Berlin, Nicolai*, 1824--30. s.

Blundell (John W. F.) The muscles and their story, from the earliest times. xvi, 304 pp. 1 pl. 16°. *London, Chapman & Hall*, 1864.

Blunt (Edmund M.) American coast pilot. 21st ed. 84, 842 pp. 3 charts. 8°. *New York, G. W. Blunt*, 1867.

——— Stranger's guide to the city of New York. 306 pp. 24°. *New York, E. M. Blunt*, 1817.

Blunt (George W.) The way to avoid the centre of our violent gales. [Also, observations on the hurricanes and storms of the West Indies and the coast of the U.S. By W. C. Redfield.] 31 pp. 1 chart. 8°. *New York, G. W. Blunt*, 1866.

Blunt (*Rev.* John James). The veracity of the gospels, and Acts of the apostles, argued from their undesigned coincidences. 1st Am. ed. 127 pp. 12°. *Boston, Perkins & Marvin*, 1829.

Blyton (Emma). The pleasures of freedom. A poem. 53 pp. 8°. *London, Saunders & Otley*, 1860.

Boaden (James). Memoirs of the life of John Philip Kemble. 2 v. in 1. xxvii, 607 pp. 8°. *Philadelphia, Robert H. Small*, 1825.

Boardman (*Mrs.* M. M.) Haps and mishaps of the Brown family. 319 pp. 4 pl. 16°. *Philadelphia, Perkinpine & Higgins*, [1865].

——— Nellie Gates and the little missionary. 357 pp. 4 pl. 16°. *Philadelphia, Perkinpine & Higgins*, [1867].

——— The mother-in-law. Sequel to Nellie Gates. 402 pp. 4 pl. 16°. *Philadelphia, Perkinpine & Higgins*, [1867].

Böbert (Carl F.) Über serpentengebilde im urgebirge auf Modun. 1838. [*With* **Keilhau** (B. M.) Gæa norvegica, I]. s.

Boccaccio (Giovanni). Decamerone. [Per cura di Ugo Foscolo, con un discorso storico sul testo.] 3 v. 8°. 11 pl. *Londra, W. Pickering*, 1825.

——— The decameron. Translated from the Italian, [by Edward Dubois]. 4 v. 24°. *London, S. Richards*, 1822.

Bochart (Samuel). Hierozoicon, seu de animalibus scripturæ compendium. 2 v. in 1. 10 p. l. 332 pp; 468 pp. 12 l. 4°. *Franequerae, J. Gyselaer*, 1690. s.

Böck (Christian P. Bianco). Übersicht der bisher in Norwegen gefundenen formen der trilobiten-familie. [*With* **Keilhau** (B. M.) Gæa norvegica, I.] s.

Böck (Wilhelm). Syphilisationen studeret ved sygesengen. 211 pp. 8°. *Christiania, Brögger & Christie*, 1854. s.

——— Recherches sur la syphilis, appuyées de tableaux de statistique tirés des archives des hôpitaux de Christiania. 509 pp. 4°. *Christiania, H. J. Jensen*, 1862. s.

Böckh (August). Metrologische untersuchungen über gewichte, münzfüsse und masse des alterthums. xxviii, 481 pp. 8°. *Berlin, Veit & Co.* 1838. s.

——— Untersuchungen über das kosmische system des Platon, mit bezug auf Gruppe's kosmische system der Griechen. vi, 152 pp. 8°. *Berlin, Veit*, 1852. s.

Boddington (*Mrs.*) Sketches in the Pyrenees; with some remarks on Languedoc, Provence, and the Cornice. [*anon*]. 2 v. xii, 440 pp.; xi, 486 pp. 12°. *London, Longman*, 1837.

Bode (Johann Elert). Allgemeine betrachtungen über das weltgebäude. 3e ausg. 16°. *Berlin*, [1807.] s.

——— Anleitung zur kenntniss des gestirnten himmels. 9e aufl. xvi, 662 pp. 5 pl. 8°. *Berlin, Nicolai*, 1823. s.

——— Nachtrag zu J. E. Bode's anleitung, etc. von Jabbo Oltmanns. iv, 168 pp. 8°. *Berlin, Nicolai*, 1833. s.

Bodemann (Eduard). Xylographische und typographische incunabeln der königlichen öffentlichen bibliothek zu Hannover. vi, 130 pp. 41 pl. 4°. *Hannover, Hahn*, 1866. s.

Bodemann (Friedrich Wilhelm). Sammlung liturgischer formulare, aus älteren und neueren agenden. 2 v. in 1. ix, 245, 4 pp; xvii, 238, 58 pp. 8°. *Göttingen, Vandenhoeck & Ruprecht*, 1845–46.

Bodenhamer (William). A practical treatise on the ætiology, pathology, and treatment of the congenital malformations of the rectum and anus. 368 pp. 16 pl. 8°. *New York, S. S. & W. Wood*, 1860. s.

Bodleian library, Oxford. Catalogues of books purchased 1806–1824. [With prices]. fol. [*Oxford*, 1806–24.] s.

Bodleian library, Oxford. Catalogue of the books relating to British topography, and Saxon and northern literature, bequeathed in 1799, by Richard Gough. iv, 459 pp. 4°. *Oxford, Clarendon press*, 1814 s.

——— Catalogue of the printed books and manuscripts bequeathed by Francis Douce. 2 p. l. 311 pp. fol. *Oxford, Univ. press*, 1840. (*With* preceding.) s.

——— Catalogue of the early English poetry and other works illustrating the English drama, collected by Edmond Malone. viii, 52 pp. fol. *Oxford, Univ. press*, 1836. (*With* preceding.) s.

——— Catalogus dissertationum academicarum, 1832. 448 pp. 31 l. fol. *Oxonii*, 1834. s.

——— Catalogus librorum hebraeorum. Digessit M. Steinschneider. cxxxi, 3104, xc pp. 4°. *Berolini, A. Friedlaender*, 1852-60. s.

Boeckh (*See* **Böckh**).

Boehme (Anton Wilhelm). *See* **Böhme**.

Boemius (Johannes). *See* **Böhme** (Johann).

Boerhaave (Hermann). Praelectiones academicae in proprias institutiones rei medicae. Edidit et notas addidit Albertus Haller. 6 v. in 7. 12°. *Gottingae, A. Vandenhoeck*, 1744. s.

CONTENTS.

v. 1. Chylificatio.
v. 2. Arteria, cor, pvlmo, sangvis, glandvla, cerebrum.
v. 3. Lien, hepar, renes, musculi, cutis, nutritio.
v. 4. Sensvs externi, interni, somnvs.
v. 6. Respiratio, loqvela, semen masculinvm.
v. 7. Menstrva, conceptvs.
v. 6. Pathologia, semeiotice, hygiene, therapeutice.

——— Consultationes medicae; sive sylloge epistolarum cum responsis. Adcesserunt ejusdem de calculo libellus, et introductio ad praxin clinicam. 3 v. in 1. 16°. *Gottingae, A. Vandenhoeck*, 1744. s.

Boethius (Anicius M. T. S.) Comforts of philosophy: in five books. From the Latin, by W. Causton and Mr. Bellamy. 150 pp. 4°. [*With* **Bellamy** (Daniel). Ethic amusements, *London*, 1768].

Boettiger (Carl August). *See* **Böttiger** (C. A.)

Bogota. Almanaque de Bogota i guia de forasteros para 1867. Por J. M. Vergara i J. B. Gaitan. 32°. xx, 384 pp. *Bogota, Gaitan*, 1866.

Bohadsch (Johann Baptista). Beschreibung einiger minderkannten seethiere, und ihren eigenschaften. Aus dem lateinischen von Nathanael G. Leske. xii, 160 pp. 12 pl. 4°. *Dresden, Walther*, 1776. s.

Böhme (Anton Wilhelm, *editor*). Propagation of the gospel in the east: being an account of the success of two Danish missionaries in Malabar, etc. 3d ed. 3 pts. 8 pl. lxviii, 369 pp. 16°. *London, J. Downing*, 1718.

Böhme *or* Boemius (Johann). Repertorivm librorvm trivm de omnivm gentivm ritibvs. 6 p. l. unp. 81 l. 4°. *Augustae Vindelicorum*, 1520. s.

Bohnenberger (J. G. F.) Anleitung zur geographischen ortsbestimmung vorzüglich mittels des spiegelsextanten. Neu bearbeitet von Dr. G. A. Jahn. xx, 346 pp. 5 pl. 8°. *Göttingen, Vandenhöck & Ruprecht*, 1852. s.

——— Astronomie. 3 p. l. 710 pp, 8 pl. 8°. *Tübingen, J. G. Cotta*, 1811. s.

Bohun (William). A brief view of ecclesiastical jurisdiction, as it is at this day practiced in England. [*anon.*] 13 pp. 12°. *Boston, Thomas and John Fleet*, 1765.

Boileau de Bouillon (Gilles). La sphère des deux mondes, composée en François, par Darinel, pasteur des Amadis. [*pseudon.*] 4 p. l. unp. 60 l. paged as 57 l. 18 maps. sm. 4°. *Anvers, Jean Richart*, 1555.

Boinvilliers (Édouard). L'état et les chemins de fer en 1865. 40 pp. 8°. *Paris*, 1865. [Ext. de la Revue contemporaine.]

Boisard (J. J. F. M.) Fables. 2 v. in 1. 2e éd. 220 pp; 307 pp. 9 pl. 12°. *Paris, Lacombe*, 1777.

Boiste (Pierre Claude Victoire). Dictionnaire de géographie universelle, ancienne, du moyen age et moderne, comparées; rédigé sur le plan de Vosgien. 3 p. l. 629 pp. 8°. *Paris, Desray*, 1806.

Boitard (Pierre). Guide-manuel de la bonne compagnie, du bon ton, et de la politesse. 478 pp. 16°. *Paris, Passard*, 1851.

——— Nouveau manuel complet d'entomologie, ou histoire naturelle des insectes et des myriapodes. 3 v. 18°. *Paris, Roret*, 1843. s.

Bolanden (Conrad von). Barbarossa; an historical novel of the xii. century. 486 pp. 12°. *Philadelphia, E. Cummiskey*, 1867.

Bolingbroke (*lord*). *See* **St. John** (Henry).

Bolton (Robert, *jr.*) Guide to New Rochelle and its vicinity. [*anon.*] 67 pp. 2 l. 1 pl. 18°. *New York, A. Hanford*, 1842.

Bolts (William). Considerations on India affairs, particularly respecting the present state of Bengal and dependencies. [part 1.] xxxii, 228, 165 pp. 1 map. 4°. *London, J. Almon*, 1772.

Bonaparte (Charles Lucien). American ornithology. [*See* **Wilson** (A.) *and* **Bonaparte.** American ornithology. 4 v. 1831.] s.

——— Observations on the nomenclature of Wilson's ornithology. 128 l. unp. 8°. *Philadelphia, A. Finley*, 1826. s.

Bonaparte (Charles Lucien) *and* **Schlegel** (Hermann). Monographie des Loxiens. xvii, 55 pp. 54 pl. 4°. *Leiden et Düsseldorf, Arnz,* 1850.

Bonaparte (Louis). *See* **Louis**, *King of Holland.*

Bonaparte (Louis Napoléon). *See* **Napoléon** III.

Bonaparte (Napoléon). *See* **Napoléon** I.

Bonar (Horatius, *D. D.*) Hymns of faith and hope. 9th ed. 3 v. 16°. *London, Jas. Nisbet & Co.* 1862–66.

——— Words old and new; or gems from the christian authorship of all ages. 356 pp. 16°. *London, Jas. Nisbet & Co.* 1866.

Bonarelli (*Conte* Guid 'Ubaldo). Filli di Sciro, favola pastorale. 2 v. in 1. xviii, 110 pp; 152 pp. 8°. *Londra, L. Nardini,* 1800.

Bonaventura (Giovanni di Fidanza, *Saint*). Breuiloquiū de scriptura. 68 l. unp. fol. *Nurmberge* [*J. Sensenchmid*], 1472.
[Imperfect; wanting last page of table.]

——— Liber profectuum religiosorum. 169 l. unp. sm. 4°. [*Daventriae, about* 1480].

——— Meditacōes vite dñi ñri ihu Xti. 71 l. unp. fol. *Augustæ, Zeyner de Reutlingen,* 1468.

Bond (John J.) Handy-book of rules and tables for verifying dates of historical events [etc.] giving tables of regnal years of English sovereigns, [etc.] 1066—1866. xxxii, 344 pp. 12°. *London, Bell & Daldy,* 1866.
[Also, calendar card, with preceding].

Bond (J. Wesley). Minnesota and its resources. 364 pp. 2 pl. 1 map. 12°. *New York, Redfield,* 1853. s.

Bond (Thomas E. *M. D.*) A practical treatise on dental medicine. 2d ed. 366 pp. 8°. *Philadelphia, Lindsay & Blakiston,* 1852. s.

Bondy (Pierre Marie Taillepied, *comte* de). Mémoire sur la nécessité de reviser le législation actuelle, concernant les enfans trouvés, abandonnés, et orphelins pauvres. xii, 236 pp. 8°. *Auxerre, Gallot-Fournier,* 1835.

Bonner (James). A new plan for speedily increasing the number of beehives in Scotland, and which may be extended to England, Ireland, America, etc. xviii, 260 pp. 8°. *Edinburgh, W. Creech,* 1795.

Bonneval (Henri, *vicomte* de). Études diplomatiques. viii, 350 pp. 8°. *Paris, Didot,* 1857.

Bonomi (Joseph). Nineveh and its palaces; the discoveries of Botta and Layard, applied to the elucidation of holy writ. xxii, 402 pp. 8°. *London, Ill'd library,* 1852. s.

Bontier (Pierre). Histoire des Canaries. *Paris,* 1530. *See* **Bethencourt** (Jean de).

Book of bubbles; a contribution to the New York fair in aid of the sanitary commission. [*anon.*] iv pp. 68 pl. obl. 18°. *New York, Endicott & Co.* 1864.

Book of psalms in metre. Newly translated, by William Barton. 11 p. l. unp. 407 pp. 18°. *London, Tho. Snowden,* 1692.

Bookseller (The); a handbook of British and foreign literature, [and] Bent's literary advertiser. Jan. to Dec. 1866. [v. 9.] 8°. *London, E. Tucker,* 1867.

Bookworm (The). An illustrated literary and bibliographical review. Jan. to Dec. 1866. 8°. *London,* 1866–67.

Boone (H. H.) Life sketches of the state officers [etc.] of New York in 1867. *See* **Harlow** (S. R.) *and* **Boone** (H. H.)

Boone (*Rev.* Thomas Charles). The book of churches and sects; or the opinions of all denominations of christians differing from the church of England. xxiv, 560 pp. 8°. *London, C. & J. Rivington,* 1826.

Boone (*Rev.* William J. *D. D.*) An essay on the proper rendering of the words elohim and theos into the Chinese language. 69 pp. 8°. *Canton,* 1848.

Booth (James C.) The phonographic instructor. 78 pp. 12°. *Philadelphia, E. H. Butler & Co.* 1849. s.

——— *and* **Morfit** (Campbell). On recent improvements in the chemical arts. 216 pp. 8°. *Washington, Smithsonian Inst.* 1851. s.

Booth (Mary L.) History of the city of New York. Illustrated. 2 v. 892 p. 1 pl. 8°. *New York, W. R. C. Clark,* 1867.

Boothby (*Sir* Brooke). Fables and satires, with a preface on the Esopean fable. 2 v. lxiii, 192 pp; x, 241 pp. 8°. *Edinburgh, Constable & Co.* 1809.

Bordoni (Benedetto). Isolario nel qual si ragiona di tutte l'isole del mondo. 4 p. l. unp. 72 l. 4 maps. fol. *Vinegia, Nicolò d'Aristotile,* 1534.

Borkhausen (Moriz Balthasar). Deutsche fauna, oder kurzgefasste naturgeschichte der thiere Deutschlands. 1er theil; säugethiere und vögel. xxiv, 620 pp. 8°. *Frankfurt am Mayn, Varrentrapp & Wenner,* 1797. s.
[No more published.]

Borring (L. S.) Fransk-dansk og dansk-fransk haand-ordbog. Förste deel, fransk-dansk. 2 v. in 1. 476 pp.; 496 pp. 12°. *Kjöbenhavn, A. Soldan & Cie.* 1841–45. s.

Bory de St. Vincent (Jean Baptiste Marcellin). Traité élémentaire d'erpétologie, ou d'histoire naturelle des reptiles, etc. 3 p. l. 292 pp. 32°. *Paris, Mairet & Fournier*, 1842. s.

——— Iconographie des reptiles, etc. 20 pp. 52 pl. 32°. *Paris. A. Fournier*, 1843. s. [Atlas to the preceding.]

Bosc (Louis Augustin Guillaume). Histoire naturelle des coquilles. 5 v. 18°. *Paris*, 1830. s.

——— Histoire naturelle des vers. 2e éd. 3 v. 18°. *Paris* 1830. s.

Bosquier (Philippe). Tragœdie nouvelle dicte Le petit razoir des ornemens mondains. 1589. Réimpression. 16°. *Mons*, 1863.

Bossange (Hector). Extrait du catalogue général (pp. 273—402, 841—864), sciences naturelles, sciences médicales. 8°. *Paris, H. Bossange*, 1845. s.

——— Liste alphabétique des ouvrages périodiques, journaux religieux, scientifiques, politiques, littéraires et des beaux-arts publiés à Paris. 5e supplément au catalogue général [extrait. pp. 1467—1516]. 8°. *Paris, H. Bossange*, 1853. s.

Bosse (Abraham). De la manière de graver à l'eau forte et au burin, et de la gravûre en manière noire. Nouv. éd. 8°. *Paris*, 1745. s.

Bossi (Giuseppe). Del cenacolo di Leonardo da Vinci libri iv. 4°. *Milano*, 1810. s.

Bosso (Matteo). Dialogi, orationes et epistolæ; [sunt eiusdem recuperationes fesulanae]. 166 l. unp. sm. 4°. *Bononiæ, Bazalerus*, 1493.

Bossu (N. *or* F.) Nouveaux voyages aux Indes Occidentales; une relation des différens peuples qui habitent les environs du grand fleuve Saint-Louis, appellé vulgairement le Missisippi. 2 pts. in 1. xx, 244; 264 pp. 4 pl. 16°. *Paris, Le Jay*, 1768.

Bost (Jean Augustin). History of the Bohemian and Moravian brethren. Translated from the French, and abridged. 2d ed. v, 428 pp. 18°. *London, Rel. Tract Soc.* 1838.

Boston. Annual report of the school committee of Boston for 1858 and 1863. 8°. *Boston*, 1859–64. s.

——— List of persons, copartnerships, and corporations who were taxed on $10,000 and upwards in 1861. 164 pp. 8°. *Boston, J. E. Farwell & Co.* 1862.

——— Railroad jubilee; commemorative of the opening of railroad communication between Boston and Canada, September, 1851. 288 pp. 1 map. 8°. *Boston, J. H. Eastburn*, 1851. s.

Boston. Report of the joint standing committee on Boston harbor for the year 1852. 79 pp. 2 pl. 8°. *Boston, J. H. Eastburn*, 1853.

Boston almanac for 1867. v. 32. 18°. *Boston, G. Coolidge*, 1867.

Boston board of trade. Thirteenth annual report, Jan. 1867. By Lorenzo Sabine, sec'y. 8°. *Boston, J. Wilson & son*, 1867.

Boston (The) directory. 117 pp. 1 map. 16°. *Boston, Manning & Loring*, 1796.

——— The same, for the years 1846–1853, 1855, 1856, 1861, and 1867. 12 v. 8°. *Boston*, 1846--67.

Boston library society. Catalogue of books. x, 335, 73 pp. 8°. *Boston, T. R. Marvin*, 1844. s.

Boston (The) magazine, [Oct. 1783, to Dec. 1786.] v. 1--3. 27 pl. 8°. *Boston, Norman & White*, [1783--86].

Boston (The) medical and surgical journal. v. 1—21, bound in 11 v. 8°. *Boston*, 1829--40. (v. 4--5 wanting).

Boston public library. Catalogue of books. iv, 180 pp. 8°. *Boston, J. Wilson & Son*, 1854. s.

——— Index to the catalogue of books in the Bates hall. First supplement. v, 718 pp. 8°. *Boston, J. E. Farwell & Co.* 1866.

——— Index to the city documents, 1834 to 1865. 21 pp. 8°. [*With* preceding.]

Boston social law library. Catalogue. 3d ed. vi, 281 pp. 8°. *Boston*, 1865.

Bosworth (*Rev.* Joseph). Origin of the English, Germanic, and Scandinavian languages and nations, etc. with a map of European languages. ccviii pp. 1 col. map. 8°. *London, Longman*, 1836. [Title wanting]. s.

——— Gothic and Anglo-Saxon gospels. *See* Bible—*Gothic.*

Bosworth (Newton). The accidents of human life; with hints for their prevention, and removal of their consequences. x, 247 pp. 7 pl. 18°. *New York, S. Wood*, 1814.

——— Hochelaga depicta; the early history and present state of the city and island of Montreal. 284 pp. 2 maps. 16 pl. 12°. *Montreal, William Greig*, 1839.

Botelho de Moraes y Vasconcellos (Francisco). El nuevo mundo, poemma heroyco, con las alegorias de Pedro de Castro. 16 p. l. 476 pp. sm. 4°. *Barcelona, Francisco Barnola*, 1701.

Botfield (Beriah). Stemmata Botevilliana. Memorials of the families of De Boteville, Thynne, and Botfield, in the counties of Salop and Wilts. With appendix. xvi, 204, dxlviii pp. 25 pl. 4°. *Westminster, J. B. Nichols & sons*, 1858. s.

Botta (Vincenzo). Dante as philosopher and patriot. With an analysis of the divina commedia, its plot and its episodes. x, 113 pp. 12°. *New York, Charles Scribner & Co.* 1867.

Böttiger (Carl August). Les furies, d'après les poëtes et les artistes anciens. Traduction de l'Allemand par T. F. Winckler. viii, 126 pp. 4 pl. 8°. *Paris, A. Delalain,* 1802.

Botto (G. D.) Catechismo agrologico, ossia principii di scienza applicata all'agricoltura. 3 p. l. 256 pp. 3 pl. 8°. *Torino, Stamperia reale,* 1846. s.

——— Elementi di fisica generale esperimentale. 432 pp. 8°. *Torino, Stamperia reale,* 1850. s.

Boturini-Benaduci (Lorenzo). Idea de una nueva historia general de la America septentrional. 167 pp. 96. sm. 4°. 20 p. l. 167 pp. 4 l. *Madrid, Juan de Zuñiga,* 1746.

Boubée (Nérée). Cours abrégé de géologie, ou développement du tableau de l'état du globe à ses différens ages. viii, 200 pp. 1 pl. 8°. *Paris, Bulletin d'hist. nat. de France,* 1834. s.

Boucheporn (Félix de). Du principe général de la philosophie naturelle. 468 pp. 8°. *Paris, Carilian-Gocury & V. Dalmont,* 1853.

Bouchet (Jean). Les triumphes de la noble et amovrevse dame, et l'art de honnestement aymer, composé par le trauerseur des voyes perilleuses. Nouuellement imprimé. 12 p. l. unp. cccxc l. paged. 18°. *Paris, Pierre Sergent,* 1545.

Boudin (Jean Christiern Marc François Joseph). Traité de géographie et de statistique médicales et des maladies endémiques. 2 v. lvi, 575 pp. 4 pl; 744 pp. 9 pl. 8°. *Paris, J. B. Baillière,* 1857. s.

Boudrye (*Rev.* Louis N.) Historic records of the fifth New York cavalry, first Ira Harris guard, during the rebellion of 1861–65. Also, accounts of prison life and of the secret service. 2d ed. 358 pp. 11 pl. 12°. *Albany, S. R. Gray,* 1865.

Bougeant (Guillaume Hyacinthe). Voyage merveilleux du prince Fan Férédin dans la Romancie. [*anon.*] 7 p. l. 275 pp. 16°. *Paris, P. G. Le Mercier,* 1735.

Bouhier (Jean). Sur la preuve de l'impuissance de l'homme. *See* **Argis** (A. G. B. d'). Principes, etc.

Bouillet (Marie Nicolas). Dictionnaire universel d'histoire et de géographie. 2e éd. viii, 8, 1924 pp. 8°. *Paris, L. Hachette,* 1843.

Boulard (S.) Traité élémentaire de bibliographie. 2 pts. in 1 v. 140, 131 pp. 8°. *Paris, Boulard,* 1804. s.

Boullenois (Frédéric de). Conseils aux nouveaux éducateurs de vers à soie. xi, 216 pp. 1 pl. 8°. *Paris, Bouchard-Huzard,* 1842. s.

Boulter (Hugh, *D. D. archbishop of Armagh*). Letters to several ministers of state in England, containing an account of the most interesting transactions in Ireland from 1724 to 1738. 2 v. in 1. viii, 288 pp; 198 pp. 7 l. 8°. *Dublin, G. Faulkner & J. Williams,* 1769–70.

Boulton (D'Arcy). Sketch of his majesty's province of Upper Canada. xi, 99 pp. 1 map. 4°. *London, C. Rickaby,* 1805.

Bouquet (The). A selection of poems from the most celebrated authors. [*anon.*] 2 v. 200, 192 pp. 18°. *London, J. Deighton,* 1792.

Bourdon de Sigrais (Claude Guillaume). Histoire des rats, pour servir à l'histoire universelle. [*anon.*] xvi, 140 pp. 6 l. 12°. *Ratopolis,* [*Paris?*] 1738.

Bourget (Jean). History of the royal abbey of Bec, near Rouen in Normandy. Translated from the French [by Dr. A. C. Ducarel]. viii, 140 pp. 12°. *London, J. Nichols,* 1779.

Bourne (Vincent). Miscellaneous poems, consisting of originals and translations. xvi, 352 pp. 4°. *London, W. Ginger,* 1772.

Bourrienne (Louis Antoine Fauvelet de). Life of Napoleon Bonaparte. 669 pp. 8°. *Philadelphia, Carey & Lea,* 1832.

Boutigny (G. H.) Studien über die körper im sphäroidalen zustande, nach der 3e auflage übersetzt von R. Arendt. xii, 301 pp. 8°. *Leipzig, Brockhaus,* 1858. s.

Boutruche (A.) Tableaux synoptiques de l'histoire d'Angleterre, et de l'histoire générale comparées, depuis la première invasion des Romains jusqu'en 1837. 92 pp, 1 map. obl. 4°. *Paris, Daubrée,* 1843.

Boutwell (George S.) Manual of the direct and excise tax system of the United States; including the forms, regulations, decisions, etc. of the commissioner of internal revenue. 4th ed. 8°. *Boston, Little, Brown & Co.* 1864.

——— Speeches and papers relating to the rebellion and the overthrow of slavery. vii, 628 pp. 12°. *Boston, Little, Brown & Co.* 1867.

Bouvet (Joachim). Icon regia monarchæ Sinarvm nunc regnantis, ex Gallico versa. 6 p. l. 128 pp, 1 pl. 18°. 1699. [*With* **Leibnitz** (G. W.) Novissima sinica. *Ultrajecti,* 1699.]

Bouvier (Hannah M.) Familiar astronomy; or, an introduction to the study of the heavens. Illustrated. [Also] a treatise on the globes. 499 pp. 8°. *Philadelphia, Sower, Barnes & Potts,* [1858].

——— The same. [Except parts v. and vi. Treatise on the globes, and history of astronomy]. 283 pp. 8°. *Philadelphia, Sower, Barnes & Potts,* [1858].

Bowden (*Rev.* John). Norway: its people, products, and institutions. xii, 250 pp. 12°. *London, Chapman & Hall,* 1867.

Bowden (Samuel, *M.D.*) Poems on various subjects; with some essays in prose. xxi, 390 pp. 8°. *Bath, T. Baddeley,* 1754.

Bowdich (T. Edward). Analysis of the natural classifications of mammalia, for the use of students and travelers. 115 pp. 16 l. 14 pl. 8°. *Paris, J. Smith,* 1821.

——— Elements of conchology, including the fossil genera and the animals. 2 pts. in 1 v. 75 pp. 6 l; 33 pp. 4 l. 27 pl. 8°. *Paris, J. Smith,* 1822.

Bowditch (Nathaniel Ingersoll). Memoir of Nathaniel Bowditch. [*anon.*] xiii, 158 pp. 12°. *Boston, James Munroe & Co.* 1841.

Bowdoin College. Catalogus senatus academici [etc.] in collegio bowdoinensi, [1867]. 89 pp. 8°. [*Brunsvici*], *J. Griffin,* 1867.

Bowles (John). The retrospect; or, a collection of tracts published at various periods of the war. xl, 387 pp. 8°. *London, T. N. Longman,* 1798.

Bowles (William). Introduzione alla storia naturale e alla geografia fisica di Spagna. Pubblicata e commentata dal Giuseppe Niccola d'Azara, e dopo la seconda ed. spagnuola, etc. tradotta da Francesco Milizia. 2 v. xvi, 330 pp; 358 pp. 8°. *Parma, Stamperia reale,* 1783.

Bowles (*Rev.* William Lisle). Sonnets and other poems. 9th ed. 2 v. vii, 180 pp; 165 pp. 8 pl. 18°. *Bath, R. Cruttwell,* 1803.

Bowman (Hildebrand). *See* **Travels** of H. Bowman, etc.

Bowman (*Rev.* Thomas). The principles of christianity; discourses on our lost state in Adam, our recovery by Jesus Christ, and the necessity of regeneration and sanctification by the holy ghost. 175 pp. 18°. *Boston, Philip Freeman,* 1769.

Boxhorn (Marc Zuer). Arcana imperii detecta: or, divers select cases in government. [Translation of Disquisitiones politicæ. *anon.*] 8 p. l. 366 pp. 8°. *London, J. Knapton,* 1701.

Boyd (Hugh). Miscellaneous works. With account of his life and writings by L. D. Campbell. 2 v. xii, 291, 323 pp; 495 pp. 1 pl. 8°. *London, Cadell & Davies,* 1800.

CONTENTS.

v. 1. Life and writings.
Letters of Democraticus, Freeholder, and Whig.
Abstracts of Chatham's speeches.
Poems.
v. 2. Embassy to Candy.
Indian observer, essays.

Boyd (Robert, *D.D.*) Wee Willie; or, truth sought and found. 324 pp. 18°. *Chicago, Church & Goodman,* 1867.

Boye (Johan). America: om af de gamle kiendt, af de nyere hvorledes opdaget; og i sin natur tildeels hvorledes befundet. 54 pp. 12°. *Kiöbenhavn, J. Rüse,* 1829.

Boyer (*Lieut.* ——). Journal of Wayne's campaign against the northwestern Indians, from July 28 to Nov. 2, 1794. 23 pp. 4°. *Cincinnati, Wm. Dodge,* 1866.

Boyer (Abel). Foreign tales, witty and merry sayings, repartees, etc. from the best authors. In French and English. [*anon.*] 195 pp. 16°. *London, S. Ballard,* 1719.

Boyle (John, *5th earl of Cork and Orrery*). Letters from Italy in 1754–55. xlvi, 267 pp. 16°. *London, B. White,* 1773.

Boyle (Robert). Opera varia. 19 v. [in 1.] 4°. *Genevæ, S. De Tournes,* 1680–88. s.

——— *See* **Grew** (N.) *and* **Boyle** (R.) "Recueil d'expériences," etc.

Boyle (Roger, *1st earl of Orrery*). Collection of state letters, with life by Thomas Morrice. 2 v. xxi, 133, 287 pp; 445 pp. 8°. *Dublin, G. Faulkner,* 1743.

Boynton (Charles Brandon, *D.D.*) The four great powers: England, France, Russia, and America; their policy, resources, and probable future. 520 pp. 8°. *Cincinnati, C. F. Vent & Co.* 1866.

——— The history of the navy during the rebellion. Illustrated. v. 1. 576 pp. 15 pl. 8°. *New York, D. Appleton & Co.* 1867.

Boynton (*Rev.* J.) Sanctification practical; a book for the times. With an introduction by Mrs. Palmer. iv, 142 pp. 18°. *New York, Foster & Palmer,* 1867.

Bracken (Henry, *M. D.*) Farriery improved; or, a compleat treatise upon the art of farriery. 7th ed. 2 v. x, 363 pp. 17 l; xvi, 298 pp. 10 l. 16°. *London, J. Shuckburgh,* 1752.

——— *See* **Burdon** (William). Pocket farrier.

Brackenridge (Henry M.) Voyage to South America, performed by order of the American government, in 1817–18, in the frigate Congress. 2 v. 351 pp; 381 pp. 1 map. 8°. *Baltimore, author,* 1819. s.

Brackenridge (William D.) Living plants and seeds of Chili. [*With* **Gilliss** (J. M.) U. S. astron. exped. v. 2.]

Bradbury (Charles). History of Kennebunkport [Maine], from 1602 to 1837. 301 pp. 12°. *Kennebunk, James K. Remich,* 1837.

Bradbury (Osgood). Isabelle; or, the emigrant's daughter. 100 pp. 8°. *Boston, F. Gleason,* 1848.

Braddon (Lawrence). Essex's innocency and honour vindicated. 4 p. l. 62 pp. sm. 4°. *London, author,* 1690.
[Imperfect; wanting plate.]

Bradford (*Rev.* James). An address delivered Sept'r 5, 1839, the second centennial anniversary of the settlement of Rowley. 114 pp. [*With* **Gage** (Thos.) History of Rowley. *Boston,* 1840.]

Bradley (Abraham). A philosophical retrospect on the general outlines of creation and providence. 194 pp. 2 l. 16°. *Wilkesbarre, (Pa.) Charles Miner,* 1808.

Bradley (*Rev.* James). Miscellaneous works and correspondence. [With memoir of Bradley, by S. P. Rigaud]. cviii, 528, 7 pp. 4°. *Oxford, University press,* 1832.

Bradley (Richard, *F. R. S.*) The virtue and use of coffee, with regard to the plague, and other infectious distempers. 34 pp, 1 pl. 8°. *London, E. Matthews,* 1721.

Bradstreet (*Mrs.* Anne). Several poems compiled with great variety of wit and learning, full of delight. 2d ed. 7 p. l. 255 pp. 24°. *Boston, John Foster,* 1678.

——— Works in prose and verse. Edited by J. H. Ellis. lxxvi, 434 pp, 2 pl. 1 fac. sim. 4°. *Charlestown,* [*Ms.*] *A. E. Cutter,* 1867.

Brady (James T.) Christmas dream. Illustrated by Edward S. Hall. 41 pp. sq. 16°. *New York, Appleton,* 1861.

Brady (Nicholas), *and* **Tate** (Nahum). New version of the psalms of David. 216 pp. 24°. *London,* 1776.

Brady (William). The naval apprentice's kedge anchor: or, young sailor's assistant. 328 pp, 9 pl. 12°. *New York, Frye & Shaw,* 1841.

Braidwood (James). Fire prevention and fire extinction. With a memoir and portrait of the author. vi, 197 pp. 1 pl. 12°. *London, Bell & Daldy,* 1866.

Brainard (John Gardner Calkins). Fugitive tales, No. 1; Fort Braddock letters. 97 pp. 18°. *Washington, Charles Galpin,* 1830.

Braithwaite (Richard). *See* **Brathwait** (Richard).

Braithwaite (William, *M. D.*) On cholera; its pathology and treatment. 27 pp. 16°. *Leeds, D. I. Roebuck,* 1866.

Braithwaite (W. *and* James). The retrospect of medicine. July, 1866, to June, 1867. v. 54–55. 12°. *London, Simpkin, Marshall & Co.* 1866–67.

Branch (William, *jr.*) Life, a poem in three books. xii, 218 pp. 16°. *Richmond, W. W. Gray,* 1819.

Brande (William Thomas) *and* **Cox** (George W.) Dictionary of science, literature, and art. New ed. 3 v. xi, 945 pp; 952 pp; 1,068 pp; 8°. *London, Longman, Green & Co.* 1865–67.

Brandes (Carl). Sir John Franklin, die unternehmungen für seine rettung, und die nordwestliche durchfahrt. viii, 312 pp. 1 map. 2 tables. 8°. *Berlin, Nicolai'schen buchhandlung,* 1854.

Brandon (Raphael *and* **J.** Arthur). Parish churches; being perspective views of English ecclesiastical structures. 2 v. 74 pp.; 75 pp. 161 pl. sm. fol. *London, D. Bogue,* 1851.

Brandt (Johann Friedrich). Beiträge zur nähern kenntniss der säugethiere Russlands. (Extract). 2 p. l. 365 pp. 19 pl. 4°. *St. Petersburg, K. akad. der wissenschaften,* 1855. s.

Brann (*Rev.* Henry A.) Curious questions [in philosophy]. 12°. *Newark, (N. J.)* 1866.

Brannan (William P.) Vagaries of Vandyke Browne. An autobiography in verse. 230 pp. 16°. *Cincinnati, R. W. Carroll & Co.* 1865.

Branson (L.) First book in composition; applying the principles of grammar to the art of composing. 140 pp. 12°. *Raleigh, (N. C.) Branson, Farrar & Co.* 1863.

Brant (*Capt.* Joseph, *or* Thayendanegea). *See* **Bible,** (*Mohawk*).

Brants (A.) Het geslacht der muizen door Linnaeus opgesteld, in familien geslachten en soorten verdeeld. xii, 190 pp. 1 pl. 8°. *Berlin, akad. bockdrukkery,* 1827. s.

Brard (Cyprien Prosper). Élémens pratiques d'exploitation. xi, 363 pp. 32 pl. 18°. *Bruxelles, Hauman, Cattoir et Cie.* 1837.

——— Nouveaux éléments de minéralogie. Éd. revue et augmentée d'un indicateur minéralogique par Drapiez. 2 v. in 3, 672 pp; 332 pp. 1 pl. 16°. *Bruxelles, Hauman & Cie* 1838. s.

Brasbridge (Joseph). The fruits of experience; or, memoir written in his 80th year. 258 pp. 8°. *London, Simpkin & Marshall,* 1824.

Brashears (Noah). Columbia's wreath; or, miscellaneous poems. 2d ed. 120 pp. 12°. *Washington, S. A. Elliot,* 1830.

Brathwait *or* **Braithwaite** (Richard). The English gentleman: containing sundry excellent rules how to demeane himselfe in publike or private affaires. 3d ed. 5 p. l. 262 pp. portrait. fol. *London,* 1641.

——— The English gentlewoman. 3d ed. 6 p.l. pp. 271–417. fol. *London,* 1641. [*With* the preceding].

——— Ladies' love-lecture. 2 p. l. pp. 423–454. fol. *London,* 1641. [*With* the preceding].

——— Turtle's trivmph: a supplement to the "English gentleman." fol. *London,* 1641. [*With* the preceding].

Braun (Alexander). Das individuum der pflanze in seinem verhaltniss zur species. Generationsfolge, generationswechsel und generationstheilung der pflanze. (Extract). 106 pp. 6 pl. 4°. *Berlin, k. akad. der wissenschaften,* 1853. s.

Braun (August Emil). Introduction to the study of art-mythology. Translated by John Grant. 56 pp. 100 pl. 4°. *Gotha, J. Perthes,* 1856. s.

Braun (Carl). Monographie des eaux minérales de Wiesbaden. v, 117 pp. 2 maps. 8°. *Wiesbaden, C. G. Kreidel,* 1852. s.

Braxton (Carter M.) Map of the battle field of Fredericksburg, explained by extracts from official reports; also, Gen. Rob. E. Lee's report of the battle. [*anon.*] 44 pp. 8°. 1 map. *Lynchburg, Virginian,* 1866.

Bray (Charles). On force, its mental and moral correlates; and on that which is supposed to underlie all phenomena; with speculations on spiritualism, [etc]. vii, 164 pp. 8°. *London, Longmans,* [1866].

Bray (Thomas, *D. D.*) Bibliotheca parochialis, etc. or, a scheme of such theological and other heads as seem requisite to be perused .... by the reverend clergy, [with] the books which may be profitably read on each of those points, in order to promote the forming and erecting libraries .... throughout her majesty's dominions. 2d ed. v. 1. 34 p. l. 412 pp. 8°. *London, R. Wilkin,* 1707.

[No more published.]

Brégeaut (L. R.) Nouveau manuel complet théorique et pratique du dessinateur et de l'imprimeur lithographe. Nouv. éd. xxxvi, 304 pp. 3 pl. 18°. *Paris, Roret,* 1839. s.

Brehm (Alfred Edmund). Das leben der vögel. Dargestellt für haus und familie. xx, 707 pp. 27 pl. 8°. *Glogau, C. Flemming,* 1861. s.

——— Ergebnisse einer reise nach Habesch im gefolge des herzogs Ernst II. viii, 440 pp. 8°. *Hamburg, O. Meissner,* 1863. s.

——— Illustrirtes thierleben. Eine allgemeine kunde des thierreichs. Mit abbildungen, ausgeführt unter leitung von R. Kretschmer. v. 1-4. 8°. *Hildburghausen, Bibliographische institut,* 1864–67. s.

CONTENTS.

v. 1–2. Die säugethiere. xl, 696 pp. 15 pl; viii, 901 pp. 19 pl.
v. 3–4. Die vögel. 2 p. l. 970 pp. 30 pl; 2 p. l. 1036 pp. 21 pl.

——— *and* **Rossmässler** (Emil Adolf). Die thiere des waldes geschildert. v. 1. Die wirbelthiere. xiv. 658 pp. 20 pl. 8°. *Leipzig, C. F. Winter,* 1864. s.

Brehm (Christian Ludwig). Die kunst, vögel als bälge zu bereiten, auszustopfen, aufzustellen und aufzubewahren. Nebst einer kurzen anleitung schmetterlinge und käfer zu fangen, zu präpariren, aufzustellen und aufzubewahren. 2e aufl. xii, 145 pp. 16°. *Weimar, B. F. Voigt,* 1860. s.

——— Lehrbuch der naturgeschichte aller europäischen vögel. 2 pts in 1 v. xii, viii, 1047 pp. 1 pl. 8°. *Jena, A. Schmid,* 1823–24. s.

——— Die naturgeschichte und zucht der tauben, oder vollständige beschreibung aller europäischen wilden und zahmen taubenarten und ihrer abänderungen, u. s. w. xii, 177 pp. 8°. *Weimar, B. F. Voigt,* 1857. s.

Brehon laws of Ireland. 24 pp. 8°. [Vallancey, (C.) Collectanea de rebus hibernicis, nos. 4. 5, 10, and v. 5.]

Bremer, (Fredrika). Father and daughter. A portraiture from the life. Translated by Mary Howitt. 348 pp. 12°. *Philadelphia, T. B. Peterson & Bros.* [*about* 1860.]

——— The four sisters. A tale of social and domestic life in Sweden. Translated by Mary Howitt. 393 pp. 12°. *Philadelphia, T. B. Peterson & Bros.* [*about* 1860.]

——— Homes of the new world; impressions of America. Translated by Mary Howitt. 2 v. 12°. *New York, Harper,* 1853. s.

Bremiker (Carl). Logarithmorum sex decimalium nova tabula berolinensis, et numerorum vulgarium ab 1 usque ad 100,000, et functionum trigonometricarum ad decades minutorum secundorum. 82 pp. 263 l. 8°. *Berolini, F. Nicolai,* 1852. s.

Bremser (Johann Gottfried). Über lebende würmer in lebenden menschen. xii, 284 pp. 4 col. pl. 4°. *Wien, C. Schaumberg & Co.* 1819. s.

Bresson (Jacques). Des fonds publics français et étrangers, et des opérations de la bourse de Paris. 8e éd. vii, 279 pp. 12°. *Paris, Béthune et Plon,* 1843. s.

——— Histoire financière de la France. 2e éd. 2 v. 586 pp; 486 pp. 8°. *Paris, F. Locquin,* 1840. s.

Bretagne pittoresque; ou choix du monuments, de costumes, et de scènes. Dessinés et lithographiés par MM. Rouarge et Saint-Germain, avec un texte par Émile Souvestre. 11 l. unp. 10 pl. fol. *Nantes, Mellinet et Baudoux,* [*about* 1840.]

Breton (Nicholas). A poast with a pacquet of letters. [*anon.*] 2 pts. in 1 v. 3 p. l. 90 pp. sm. 4°. *London, T. Fabian,* 1685.

Breton (Raymond). Dictionaire caraibe-françois et françois-caraibe. 2 pts. in 1 v. 8 p. l. 480 pp; 415 pp. 18°. *Avxerre, Gilles Bovqvet,* 1565.

Brett (Thomas). A chronological essay on the sacred history, from the creation of the world to the birth of Christ; being a defence of the computation of the septuagint. 94 pp. 8°. *London, F. Gyles,* 1729.

——— A general history of the world, from the creation to the destruction of Jerusalem by Nebuchadnezzar. xvi, 320 pp. 8°. *London, F. Gyles,* 1732. [*With* **Brett** (Thomas). Chronological essay on sacred history, etc. *London,* 1729.]

Brettes (Martin de). Études sur les appareils électro-magnétiques destinés aux expériences de l'artillerie en Angleterre, Russie, France, Prusse, Belgique, Suède, etc. 388 pp, 6 pl. 8°. *Paris, J. Corréard,* 1854. s.

Breviarium romanum. 698 l. unp. sm. 4°. *Venetijs, J. de Rubeus,* 1474.

Brevint (Daniel, *D. D.*) Saul and Samuel at Endor, or the new ways of salvation and service, which usually temt men to Rome, and detain them there. 8 p. l. 413 pp. 8°. *Oxford,* 1674.

Brevoort (James Carson). Notes on some figures of Japanese fish, taken from recent specimens, by the artists of the U. S. Japan expedition. [Extract, Perry's Japan exp.] 36 pp. 12 pl. col. 4°. *Washington* [*Philadelphia*], 1856. s.

Brewer (E. Cobham). A guide to the scientific knowledge of things familiar. 490 pp. 16°. *New York, C. S. Francis & Co.* 1853. s.

Brewster (Charles W.) Lecture on printing, April 11, 1835. 16 pp. 8°. *Portsmouth,* 1835.

Brewster (*Sir* David). Manuel d'optique, ou traité complet et simplifié de cette science. Trad. par P. Vergnaud. 2 v. iv, 268 pp; ii, 289 pp, 5 pl. 18°. *Paris, Roret,* 1833. s.

Bricknell (*Rev.* William Simcox). The judgment of the bishops upon tractarian theology. viii, 753 pp. 8°. *Oxford, J. Vincent,* 1845.

Bride (The) of Fort Edward, founded on an incident of the revolution. [*anon.*] 174 pp. 16°. *New York, S. Colman,* 1839.

Bridgeport library association. Catalogue of the library, Jan. 1860. 88 pp. 8°. *Bridgeport, (Conn.) Pomeroy & Morse,* 1860. s.

Bridger (Charles). Index to printed pedigrees, contained in county and local histories, the heralds' visitations, and in the more important genealogical collections. 384 pp. 8°. *London, J. R. Smith,* 1867.

Bridges (John Henry). France under Richelieu and Colbert. xi, 201 pp. 12°. *Edinburgh, Hamilton,* 1866.

Bridgman (E. C.) A Chinese chrestomathy in the Canton dialect. xxxvi, 698 pp. 4°. *Macao, S. W. Williams,* 1841. s.

Bridgman (Thomas). Memorials of the dead in Boston, containing exact transcripts of the sepulchral monuments in the king's chapel burial ground. 12°. *Boston,* 1853.

Brief (A) account of the proceedings of the committee, appointed 1795, by the yearly meeting of friends, of Pennsylvania, New Jersey, etc. for promoting the improvement and civilization of the Indian natives. [*anon.*] 48 pp. 8°. *London,* 1806.

Brief (A) account of the proceedings of the committee appointed by the yearly meeting of friends, held in Baltimore for promoting the improvement and civilization of the Indian natives. [*anon.*] 47 pp. 8°. *London,* 1806.

[With the preceding.]

Brief notice of the settlement of Newton, prepared by the committee charged with erecting a monument to its first settlers. 8°. 38 pp. *Boston, C. C. P. Moody,* 1852.

Brief (A) relation of the state of New England, from the beginning of that plantation to 1689. In a letter to a person of quality. [*anon.*] 18 pp. sm. 4°. *London, R. Baldwine,* 1689.

Briganti (Filippo). Esame economico del sistema civile. [Scrittori class. ital. di econ. pol. v. 28–29].

Brigham (Amariah, *M. D.*) Remarks on the influence of mental cultivation and mental excitement upon health, with a preface by James Simpson. 7th ed. 86 pp. 16°. *London, H. Washburne,* 1847. s.

Bright (John). Speeches on the American question. With introduction by F. Moore. xv, 278 pp. 1 pl. 12°. *Boston, Little, Brown & Co.* 1865.

Brightwell (Cecilia Lucy). Memorials of the early lives and doings of great English lawyers. 251 pp. 16°. *London, T. Nelson & sons,* 1866.

Brigitta (*Saint, of Sweden*). Revelationes selectae. Textum cognovit A. Heuser. 351 pp. 1 pl. 24°. *Coloniæ, J. M. Heberle,* 1851.

Brinsley (*Rev.* John). The arraignment of the present schism of new separation in old England. 2 p. l. 75 pp. sm. 4°. *London, Ralph Smith,* 1646.

Briscoe (John). A discourse on the late funds of the million-act, lottery act, and bank of England, with proposals for a national land-bank. 3d ed. iv, 187 pp. 8°. *London, Andrew Bell,* 1696.

Brisson (Mathurin Jacques). Dictionnaire raisonné de physique. 3 v. xvi, 708 pp; 768 pp. Atlas 90 pl. 4°. *Paris, hôtel de Thou,* 1781. s.

——— Observations sur les nouvelles découvertes aërostatiques, et sur la probabilité de pouvoir diriger les ballons; supplément à son dictionnaire, etc. 34 pp. 4°. *Paris, Le Boucher, &c.* 1784. s.
[With the preceding.]

Brisson (Pierre Raymond de). Voyage to the coast of Africa. *See* **Saugnier,** ——— *and* **Brisson.**

Brissot de Warville (Jean Pierre). [Address] to his constituents. Translated from the French. New ed. xl, 121 pp. 8°. *London, J. Stockdale,* 1794.

——— *See* **Clavière** (E.) *and* **Brissot.** De la France et des États-Unis.

Bristed (John). Les États-Unis d'Amérique; ou tableau de l'agriculture, du commerce, des manufactures, des finances, de la politique, de la littérature, des arts, et du caractère moral et religieux du peuple anglo-américain; traduit de l'Anglais. 2 v. 380 pp; 320 pp. 8°. *Paris, A. Eymery,* 1826.

Bristol County [*Mass*]. Directory and gazetteer for 1867–68. Compiled by Dudley & Greenough. 223, 84 pp. 8°. *Boston, Dudley & Greenough,* 1867.

Bristow (Henry William). A glossary of mineralogy. xlvii, 420 pp. 12°. *London, Longman,* 1861. s.

British almanac and companion; or, year-book of general information, for 1866–67. 2 v. 16°. *London, Knight & Co.* 1866–67.

British (The) grammar: an essay towards speaking and writing the English language grammatically, and inditing elegantly. 30, 281 pp. 12°. *Boston, John Norman,* 1784.

British institution, London. An account of all the pictures exhibited in the rooms, from 1813 to 1823, belonging to the nobility and gentry of England. xxxvi, 320 pp. 8°. *London, Priestley & Weale,* 1824. s.

British military biography, from Alfred to Wellington. [*anon.*] x, 638 pp. 1 pl. 18°. *London, Scott & Co.* 1841.

British museum. Catalogue of the specimens of heteropterous-hemiptera in the collection of the British museum. By F. Walker. Part i. Scutata. 240 pp. 8°. *London, Trustees Br. mus.* 1867.

——— Catalogue of the Hebrew books in the library. [Compiled by Joseph Zedner.] viii, 891 pp. 8°. *London, Longman and Co.* 1867.

——— List of specimens of birds in the collection. Part v. Gallinæ. By G. R. Gray. 120 pp. 16°. *London,* 1867.

British (The) quarterly review, Jan. 1866 to Oct. 1867. v. 43–46. 8°. *London, Jackson, Walford & Hodder,* [1866–67].

Broaddus (*Rev.* William F.) Centennial sermon of the Potomac baptist association, of Virginia. 58 pp. 16°. [*Alexandria?*] 1867.

Brocchi (Giovanni Battista). Conchologia fossile subapennina, con osservazioni geologiche sugli Apennini e sul suolo adiacente. 2 v. 56, lxxx, 712 pp. 16 pl. 4°. *Milano, Stamperia reale,* 1814. s.

Broch (Otto T.) Lehrbuch der mechanik. xvi, 700 pp. 3 l, 3 pl. 8°. *Berlin, Veit & Co.* 1854. s.

Brockett (L. P. *M. D.*) Philanthropic results of the war in America. By an American citizen. [*anon.*] 160 pp. 18°. *New York, Sheldon & Co.* 1864.

——— *and* **Vaughan** (*Mrs.* Mary C.) Woman's work in the civil war; a record of heroism, patriotism, and patience. 799 pp. 8°. *Philadelphia, Zeigler, McCurdy & Co.* 1867.

Brockhaus (Friedrich Arnold). Zur erinnerung an das fünfzigjährige jubiläum der firma F. A. Brockhaus in Leipzig, 1856. 67 pp. 9 pl. 4°. *Leipzig, F. A. Brockhaus,* 1857.

Brodie (George). History of the British empire, from the accession of Charles I. to the restoration; with an introduction tracing the progress of society and of the constitution, from feudal times. 4 v. 8°. *Edinburgh, Bell & Bradfute,* 1822.

Broecke (J. C. Van den). *See* **Van den Broecke** (J. C.)

Brogden (J. Ellett). Provincial words and expressions current in Lincolnshire. 241 pp. 16°. *London, R. Hardwicke,* 1866.

Broggia (Carlo Antonio). Trattato de' tributi. Trattato della monete. (Scrittori class. ital. de econ. pol. v. 45–46.)

Brolo. *See* **Lancia di Brolo.**

Brome (James). Travels over England, Scotland, and Wales. 2[d] ed. 6 p. l. 315 pp. 4 l. 12°. *London, R. Gosling,* 1707.

Bromfield (William Arnold, *M. D.*) Flora vectensis: a systematic description of the phænogamous or flowering plants and ferns indigenous to the isle of Wight. Edited by Sir W. J. Hooker and Thomas B. Salter. xxxv, 678 pp. 1 pl. atlas, 1 map. 8°. *London, W. Pamplin,* 1856. s.

——— Letters from Egypt and Syria. xv, 280 pp. 1 pl. 8°. *London,* [*privately printed*], 1856. s.

Bromley (W.) Several years' travels through Portugal, Spain, Italy, Germany, Prussia, Sweden, Denmark, and the United Provinces. [*anon.*] iv, 280 pp. 12°. *London, A. Roper,* 1702.

Bronn (Heinrich Georg). Essai d'une réponse à la question de prix proposée en 1850, par l'académie des sciences, savoir; étudier les lois de la distribution des corps organisés fossiles dans les différents terrains sédimentaires, suivant l'ordre de leur superposition, etc., (Extract). 542 pp. 8 tab. 4°. *Paris, Acad. des sciences,* 1861. s.

——— Handbuch einer geschichte der natur. 4v. (in 5 pts.) 8°. Atlas, 4°. *Stuttgart, E. Schweizerbart,* 1841–49. (Naturgeschichte, v. 13–15). s.

CONTENTS.

v. 1. Einleitung. i. Theil. Kosmisches leben. ii. Th. Tellurisches leben.
v. 2. iii. Th. Organisches leben. Ergebnisse hauptsächlich aus der lebenden welt über entwickelung; verbreitung und untergang der früheren bevölkerungen der erde.
v. 3. Abth. i. iii. Th. Organisches leben. (Fortsetzung)—Index palæontologicus, bearbeitet unter mitwirkung der H. R. Göppert und Herm. v. Meyer: A. Nomenclator palæontologicus.
v. 3. Abth. ii. B. Enumerator palæontologicus. iv. Th. Vernunftleben.

Bronn (Heinrich Georg). Lethæa geognostica, oder abbildungen und beschreibungen der für die gebirgs-formation bezeichnendsten versteinerungen. 2 v. 1346 pp. 8°. Atlas, 4°. *Stuttgart, E. Schweizerbart,* 1835–38. s.

——— Morphologische studien über die gestaltungs-gesetze der naturkörper überhaupt, und der organischen insbesondere. ix, 481 pp. 8°. *Leipzig, C. F. Winter,* 1858. s.

——— Untersuchungen über die entwickelungs-gesetze der organischen welt wahrend der bildungs-zeit unserer erd-oberfläche. x, 502 pp. 8°. *Stuttgart, Schweizerbart,* 1858. s.

Brönsted (Peter Olaf). Reisen und untersuchungen in Griechenland, nebst darstellung und erklärung vieler neuentdeckten denkmäler griechischen styls, u. s. w. 2 v. xx, 318, xxi pp. 62 pl. 4°. *Paris,* [*Didot*], 1826–30. s.

——— The same. Voyages dans la Grèce, accompagnés de recherches archéologiques, et suivis d'un aperçu sur toutes les entreprises scientifiques qui ont eu lieu en Grèce depuis Pausanias. Livr. 1–2. xx, xxii, 314 pp. 62 pl. 4°. *Paris, Didot,* 1826–30. s.
(No more published.)

Brook (Mary). Reasons for the necessity of silent waiting in order to the solemn worship of God. 6th ed. 32 pp. 8°. *Boston, Jacob Johnson & Co.* 1795.

Brookes (L. De Garmo). Modern dancing, with an essay on etiquette. 104 pp. 12°. *New York,* [*author*], 1867.

Brookes (Richard, *M. D.*) A new and accurate system of natural history. 6 v. 132 pl. 12°. *London, Newbery,* 1763.

CONTENTS.

v. 1. Quadrupeds, including amphibious animals, frogs, and lizards.
v. 2. Birds; with the method of bringing up and managing those of the singing kind.
v. 3. Fishes and serpents, including sea turtles, crustaceous and shell fishes.
v. 4. Insects.
v. 5. Waters, earths, stones, fossils, and minerals.
v. 6. Vegetables.

Brooklyn (*L. I.*) Documents and plans, submitted by the water committee to the common council, 1854. 145 pp, 27 pl. 4°. *Brooklyn, Heighway & Co.* 1864.

Brooklyn city directory for 1867 and 1868. Compiled by J. and G. T. Lain. 2 v. 8°. *Brooklyn, J. Lain & Co.* 1866–67.

Brooklyn mercantile library. Catalogue. 3 p. l. 138, 76 pp. 8°. *Brooklyn Mercantile lib. ass.* 1859. s.

Brooklyn water-works and sewers. [By James P. Kirkwood, *C. E.* and others.] xxvi, 160 pp. 60 pl. fol. *New York, D. Van Nostrand,* 1867.

Brooks (J. Tyrwhitt, *M. D.*) Four months among the gold-finders in Alta California. xviii, 207 pp. 1 map. 8°. *London, David Bogue,* 1849.

——— The same. 94 pp. 8°. *New York, D. Appleton & Co.* 1849.

Broome (William). Poetical works. 8°. *Edinburgh,* 1794.
[Anderson's British poets. v. 8.]

Brotuff (Ernst). Chronica und antiquitates des alten stiffts der römischen burg colonia, und stadt Marsburg an der Salah in obern Sachssen. 8 p. l. cvi l. 12 l. fol. *Leipzig, G. Hantzsch,* 1557. s.

Brougham (Henry, *lord*). Political philosophy. New ed. 3 v. 8°. *London, H. G. Bohn,* 1861. s.

Broughton (Thomas Duer). Costume, character, manners, domestic habits, and religious ceremonies of the Mahrattas. 6 p. l. 358 pp. 10 pl. col. 4°. *London, J. Murray,* 1813.

Brown (Charles F.) Artemus Ward in London, and other papers. Illustrated by J. H. Howard. 229 pp. 6 pl. 12°. *New York, G. W. Carleton & Co.* 1867.

Brown (*Mrs.* D. C.) Memoir of Rev. Lemuel Covell, and of his son Rev. Alanson L. Covell. 2 v. in 1. 174; 226 pp. 16°. *Brandon (Vt.)* 1839.

Brown (Edward). Travels and adventures, containing his observations on France and Italy; voyage to the Levant; account of the isle of Malta; journies thro' lower and upper Egypt; [and] brief description of the Abyssinian empire. xvi, 434 pp, 7 l. 8°. *London, Betteswortli & Hitch,* 1739.

Brown (G. W.) Ladies' friend, containing the ceremonials of the adoptive degrees of masonry. 128 pp. 24°. *Ann Arbor (Mich.) A. W. Chase,* 1866.

Brown (*Rev.* Isaac V.) Historical vindication of the abrogation of the plan of union by the Presbyterian church. 325 pp. 8°. *Philadelphia, W. S. & A. Martien,* 1855.

Brown (*Rev.* John, *D. D.*) Dissertation on the rise, union, power, progressions, etc. of poetry and music, [with] The cure of Saul, a sacred ode. 244 pp. 4°. *London, L. Davis & Co. Reymers,* 1763.

——— Essays on the characteristics [of Shaftesbury]. viii, 408 pp. 8°. *London, C. Davis,* 1751.

Brown (*Rev.* J. Newton). Encyclopedia of religious knowledge; or, dictionary of the bible, theology, religious biography, all religions, ecclesiastical history, and missions; with a missionary gazetteer, by Rev. B. B. Edwards. 1,275 pp. 8°. *Brattleboro, Fessenden & Co.* 1836.

Brown (John William). Life of Leonardo da Vinci, with a critical account of his works. xv, 256 pp. 1 pl. 12°. *London, W. Pickering,* 1828. s.

Brown (*Dr.* O. Phelps). Complete herbalist; or, the people their own physicians by the use of nature's remedies; and new system of hygienic principles. 408 pp. 12°. *Jersey City,* 1867.

Brown (Thomas). A collection of all [his] dialogues, with translations and imitations of the odes of Horace, etc. 388 pp. 8°. *London, J. Nutt,* 1704.

Brown (*Capt.* Thomas). The taxidermist's manual; or, the art of collecting, preparing, and preserving objects of natural history. 10th ed. xii, 150 pp. 6 pl. 12°. *London, A. Fullarton & Co.* 1851. s.

Brown (T.) Miscellanea aulica; or, a collection of state treatises never before published. Faithfully collected from their originals. 8 p. l. 440 pp. 8°. *London, J. Hartley,* 1702.

Brown (William Wells). The negro in the American rebellion; his heroism and his fidelity. xvi, 380 pp. 12°. *Boston, Lee & Shepard,* 1867.

Brown university. Triennial catalogue of the library and the members of the Philermenian society. 92 pp. 8°. *Providence, (R. I.)* 1849. s.

Browne (Isaac Hawkins). Poems upon various subjects, Latin and English. 5 p. l. 160 pp. 8°. *London, I. H. Brown,* 1768.

Browne (J. Ross). The land of Thor. 542 pp. 12°. *New York, Harpers,* 1867.

Browne (Patrick, *M. D*). The civil and natural history of Jamaica, in three parts, containing, 1, an accurate description of that island, etc. 2, a history of the natural productions, etc. 3, an account of the nature of climates in general, etc. with a detail of the diseases arising from this source, particularly within the tropics. viii, 506 pp. 2 maps, 50 pl. fol. *London, author,* 1756. s.

Browne (*Rev.* Peter, *bishop of Cork and Ross*). A letter in answer to a book [of John Toland], entituled, "Christianity not mysterious." 188 pp. 8°. *London, R. Clavell,* 1697.

Browne (*Sir* Thomas). Works. Edited by Simon Wilkin. 3 v. 12°. *London, H. G. Bohn,* 1852.

CONTENTS.

v. 1. Four books of vulgar errors.
v. 2. The three last books of vulgar errors, religio medici, and the garden of Cyrus.
v. 3. Urn-burial, christian morals, miscellanies, correspondence, etc.

——— Certain miscellany tracts. 4 p. l. 215 pp. 3 l. 1 pl. 12°. *London, Charles Mearne,* 1684.

——— Hydriotaphia, urne-burial, with the garden of Cyrus. 4 p. l. 73 pp. 1 pl. 4°. *London, H. Brome,* 1658. [*With* his Pseudodoxia epidemica. *London,* 1658].

——— Pseudodoxia epidemica; or, enquiries into very many received tenets and commonly presumed truths. 4th ed. 8 p. l. 468 pp. 8 l. 4°. *London, E. Dod,* 1658.

——— The same. 6th ed. 10 p. l. 440 pp. 6 l. 4°. *London, Nath. Ekins,* 1672.

——— Religio medici, with annotations. Also, observations by Sir Kenelm Digby. 4 p. l. 144 pp. 4°. *London, Andrew Crook,* 1672. [*With* his Pseudodoxia epidemica. *London,* 1672.]

Browne (Thomas Gunter). Hermes unmasked; or, the art of speech, founded on the association of words and ideas. 128 pp. 18°. *London, T. Payne,* 1795.

Browne (William). Britannia's pastorals and other poems. 8°. *Edinburgh,* 1793. [**Anderson's** Brit. poets, v. 4.]

Browne (W. H. *Lieut. R. N.*) Ten colored views taken during the arctic expedition of Sir James C. Ross, with summary of the expeditions in search of Sir John Franklin. 8 pp. 7 pl. fol. *London, Ackermann & Co.* 1850.

Brownell (Charles DeWolf). The Indian races of North and South America. 720 pp. 40 pl. 8°. *New York, H. & S. Scranton,* 1853. [Imperfect; 4 plates wanting.]

Brownell (Henry Howard). The people's book of American history. 2 v. in 1. 8°. *Hartford, L. Stebbins,* 1854. s.

Bruce (D.) Poems, chiefly in the Scottish dialect, originally written under the signature of the Scots-Irishman. xii, 126 pp. 6 l. 12°. *Washington, John Colerick,* 1801.

Bruce (George). Specimen of printing types and ornaments. 113 l. unp. 8°. *New York,* 1827.

——— The same. 180 l. unp. 8°. *New York,* 1828.

——— The same. 124 l. unp. 8°. *New York,* 1848. s.

Brück (R.) Électricité, ou magnétisme du globe terrestre. 295 pp. 8°. *Bruxelles, Delavingue & Callewaert,* 1851. s.

——— The same. 2e partie. 2 v. xv, 298 pp. 2 tab. 6 maps; ix, 542 pp. 2 tab. 8°. *Bruxelles, Delavingue & Callewaert,* 1855–58. s.

Bruen (*Rev.* Mathias). Essays, descriptive and moral, on scenes in Italy, Switzerland, and France. By an American. [*anon.*] xi, 265 pp. 12°. *Edinburgh, Constable,* 1823.

Bruhns (C.) Die astronomische strahlenbrechung in ihrer historischen entwickelung. xiv, 181 pp. 4 pl. 8°. *Leipzig, Voigt & Günther,* 1861. s.

Brunet (Jacques-Charles). Manuel du libraire et de l'amateur de livres; contenant, un nouveau dictionnaire bibliographique, une table en forme de catalogue raisonné. etc. 2e éd. 4 v. 8°. *Paris,* 1814.

Bruni (Leonardo Aretino). *See* **Aretinus.**

Brunius (C. G.) Nordens äldsta metropolitankyrka, eller historisk ock arkitektonisk beskrifning om Lunds domkyrka. 8°. *Lund,* 1854. s.

——— Skånes konsthistoria för medeltiden. viii, 704 pp. 16 pl. 8°. *Lund, G. W. K. Gleerup,* 1850.

Brunner (Andreas). Annalium boicorum libri iii. *See* **Adlzreiter** (Johann). Annalium boicæ gentis partes iii. fol. *Francofurti ad Mœnum,* 1810.

Brünnow (*Dr.* F.) Lehrbuch der sphärischen astronomie, mit einem vorwort von J. F. Encke. xxiv, 591 pp. 1 pl. 8°. *Berlin, F. Dümmler,* 1851. s.

Brunswick-Lüneburg (August *herzog* von). *See* **Mantua,** della.

Bruscambille. [*pseudon.*] *See* **Deslauriers.**

Brush (George T.) Supplements (viii to x). *With* **Dana** (James Dwight). Supplements to mineralogy. s.

Bruzen de La Martinière (Antoine Auguste). Introduction à l'histoire de l'Asie, de l'Afrique, et de l'Amérique. 2 v. xxii, 504 pp. 2 maps. 2 pl. 12°. *Amsterdam, Z. Chatelain,* 1735.

Bryan (James, *M. D.*) Treatise on the anatomy, physiology and diseases of the human ear. 124 pp. 12°. *Philadelphia, author,* 1851. s.

Bryant (Charles S.) History of the great massacre by the Sioux Indians in Minnesota, [in 1862; with] narratives of many who escaped. 504 pp. 6 pl. 12°. *Cincinnati, Rickey & Carroll,* 1864.

Bryant (Jacob). Observations upon the poems of Thomas Rowley: in which the authenticity of those poems is ascertained. 2 v. 2 p. l. 593 pp. 8°. *London, Payne & son,* 1781.

——— A treatise upon the authenticity of the scriptures and the truth of the christian religion. xii, 194 pp. 8°. [*London,*] 1791.

Bryant (William Cullen). Letters of a traveller; in Europe and America. 2d ed. 442 pp. 12°. *New York, G. P. Putnam,* 1850. s.

——— Voices of nature. With illustrations. 91 pp. sq. 18°. *New York, D. Appleton & Co.* 1865.

Bryce (T. A. *LL. D.*) American commercial arithmetic. 341 pp. 8°. *Erie, (Pa.) T. Cook & Co.* 1867.

Brydges (*Sir* Samuel Egerton). Cimelia: seu examen criticum librorum, ex diariis literariis lingua præcipue gallica, 1665–1792, scriptis, selectum. xxxvi, 415, xlvii pp. 8°. *Genevae, G. Fick,* 1823.
(75 copies printed.)

Brydges (Thomas) *See* **Homer.** Burlesque translation. 2 v. 16°. *New York,* 1809.

Buch (Das) der geologie, oder die wunder der erdrinde und der urwelt. Unter benutzung von "Jukes' popular geology" bearbeitet von einem alten geologen. Durchgesehen von C. C. ritter v. Leonhard. 2 v. in 1. viii, 192 pp. 8 col. pl. vi, 160 pp. 10 col. pl. 8°. *Leipzig, O. Spamer,* 1855.

Buchanan (*Rev.* Claudius). Memoir on the expediency of an ecclesiastical establishment for British India. xvii, 126 pp. 4°. *London, Cadell & Davies,* 1805.

Buchanan (George). Opera omnia, curante Thoma Ruddimanno. 2 v. 1 portrait. fol. *Edinburgi, R. Freebairn,* 1515.

CONTENTS.

v. 1. Vita, ab ipso scripta.
Testimonia.
Editionum catalogus.
Rerum scoticarum historia.
De jure regni apud Scotos.
Detectio Mariæ reginæ Scotorum.
Ane admonition to the trew lordis.
v. 2. De metris Buchananæis.
Poemata omnia.
Rudimenta grammatices.
Lodoicus de ratione studii.
De prosodia libellus.
Epistolae.

——— Rerum scoticarum historia: ejusdemque dialogus de jure regni apud Scotos. 12°. *Edinburgi,* 1827. s.

Buchanan (Harrison Gray). Asmodeus; or, legends of New York. Being a complete exposé of the upper ten thousand. 96 pp. 8°. *New York, Munson & Co.* 1848.

Buchanan (James, *British consul*). Sketches of the history, manners and customs of the North American Indians. 2 v. 182 pp; 156 pp. 16°. *New York, Borradaile,* 1825.

Buchanan (Robert). Idyls and legends of Inverburn. 206 pp. 18°. *London, A. Strahan,* 1865.

Büchele (*Dr.* C.) Land und volk der Vereinigten Staaten von Nord Amerika. viii, 622 pp. 8°. *Stuttgart, Halberger,* 1855. s.

Buchon (Jean Alexandre). La Grèce continentale et la Morée. vii, 568 pp. 16°. *Paris, C. Gosselin,* 1843.

Buchschriften (Die) des mittelalters mit besonderer berücksichtigung der deutschen, und zwar vom sechsten jahrhundert bis zur erfindung der buchdruckerkunst historischtechnisch begründet. 45 pp. 23 pl. 8°. *Wien, k. hof und staatsdruckerei,* 1852. [*With* **Hagen** (T.) Urkendenbuch für die geschichte des stiftes Kremsmuenster.] s.

Büchsel (Carl, *D. D.*) My ministerial experiences. ix, 290 pp. 12°. *London, A. Strahan & Co.* 1863.

Buckingham (*Duke* of). *See* **Villiers** (George).

——— *See* **Sheffield** (John).

Buckingham (James Silk). America, historical, statistic, and descriptive. 2 v. 515 pp.; 516 pp. 1 pl. 8°. *New York, Harpers,* 1841. s.

——— National evils and practical remedies, with the plan of a model town. xxx, 512 pp. 2 pl. 8°. *London, P. Jackson,* [1849]. s.

——— Travels in Assyria and Persia. xvi, 545 pp. 1 map. 1 pl. 4°. *London, H. Colburn,* 1829.

Buckingham (Joseph Tinker). Miscellanies selected from the public journals. 2 v. 268, 256 pp. 12°. *Boston, J. T. Buckingham,* 1822–24.

Buckland (William, *D. D.*) Geology and mineralogy considered with reference to natural theology. 2 v. 443 pp; viii, 131 pp. 69 pl. 8°. *Philadelphia, Carey, Lea & Blanchard,* 1837. s.

——— Reliquiæ diluvianae; or observations on the organic remains contained in caves, fissures, and diluvial gravel, and on other geological phenomena, attesting the action of an universal deluge. 2d ed. vii, 803 pp. 1 tab. 27 pl. 4°. *London, J. Murray,* 1824. s.

Buckler (John Chessell). Sixty views of endowed grammar schools, from original drawings. 1 p. l. 60 pl. 4°. *London, Hurst,* 1827. s.

Buckley (S. B.) A preliminary report of the geological and agricultural survey of Texas. [Also] Description of new Texas grasses. 81 pp. 8°. *Austin, J. Walker*, 1866. s.

——— The same. [With **Texas**. Journal H. R. 8°. *Austin*, 1866.]

Buckmaster (J. C.) The elements of mechanical physics. 222 pp. 12°. *Philadelphia, H. C. Baird*, 1865. s.

Buckner (*Rev.* H. F.) *and* **Herrod** (G.) A grammar of the Masköke, or Creek language, etc. 139 pp. 12°. *Marion, (Ala.) So. Baptist Dom. and Ind. mission board*, 1860. s.

Buddeus (Aurelio). Schweizerland. Natur und menschenleben. 2 v. 246 pp; 320 pp. 12°. *Leipzig, Avenarius und Mendelssohn*, 1853.

Budé (Guillaume). De cōtemptu rerum fortuitarum libri tres. 57 l. sm. 4°. [*Parisiis, in officina Ascensiana*, 1526?]

Buder (Christian Gottlieb). Bibliotheca scriptorum rerum germanicarum. *See* **Struve** (Burkhard Gotthelf). Corpvs historiæ Germanicæ. *Jenæ*, 1730. s.

Budge (Julius). Über die bewegung der iris. x, 206 pp. 3 pl. 8°. *Braunschweig, Vieweg*, 1855. s.

Budgell (Eustace). Memoirs of the life of Charles, late Earl of Orrery; and likewise of the family of Boyle. 2d ed. [With] an account of Hon. Robert Boyle. xl, 258, 34 pp. 12°. *London, W. Mears*, 1734.

Budington (William Ives, *D. D.*) History of the first church, Charlestown, [Mass.] 258 pp. 1 pl. 8°. *Boston, Charles Tappan*, 1845.

Buff (*Dr.* Heinrich). Grundzüge der experimental physik, mit rücksicht auf chemie und pharmacie. viii, 676, 53 pp. 6 pl. 8°. *Heidelberg, C. F. Winter*, 1853. s.

——— Lehrbuch der stöchiometrie. 2e aufl. x, 213 pp. 8°. *Nürnberg, J. L. Schrag*, 1842. s.

——— Zur physik der erde. Vorträge für gebildete über den einfluss der schwere und wärme auf die natur der erde. 3 p. l. 521 pp. 8°. *Braunschweig, Vieweg*, 1850. s.

Buffon (George Louis Leclerc, *comte* de). Œuvres complètes, augmentées par F. Cuvier de deux volumes supplémentaires, offrant la description des mammifères et des oiseaux les plus remarquables découverts jusqu'à ce jour. 29 v. 8°. Atlas, 236 pl. large 8°. *Paris, F. D. Pillot*, 1829–32. s.

CONTENTS.

v. 1–2. Théorie de la terre.
v. 3–4. Histoire des minéraux.
v. 5–9. Époques de la nature.
v. 10. Expériences sur végétaux.
v. [10] 11. Histoire des animaux.
v. 11–13. Histoire de l'homme.
v. 14–18. Mammifères.
v. 19–26. Oiseaux.
v. [27.] Table des matières.
Suppl. v. 1–2. Mammifères. Par F. Cuvier.
[Atlas imperfect; wanting pl. 1, 2, 7, 8.]

——— Naturgeschichte der vögel, aus dem französischen übersetzt, mit anmerkungen, zusätzen und vielen kupfern vermehrt durch H. Martini und Bernhard C. Otto. 39 v. 8°. *Berlin, J. Pauli*, 1722—1806. s.

[Wanting v. 19, 33–37, and 2 v. supp.]

——— Natural history abridged. A new edition by Rev. W. Hutton. 2 v. 8°. *London, editor*, 1821. s.

[V. 1 with new title, viz: *G. Virtue*, etc. 1828.]

——— *and* **Daubenton** (Louis Jean Marie). Histoire naturelle générale et particulière. Théorie de la terre, histoire de l'homme et des quadrupèdes. 15 v. 4°. *Paris, Imprimerie royale*, 1749–67. s.

Bugg (Francis). The picture of quakerism drawn to the life. 2 pts. in 1 v. 7 p. l. 123 pp; 6 l. 196 pp. 16°. *London, W. Kettleby and W. Rogers*, 1697.

Buhoup (Jonathan W.) Narrative of the central division, or army of Chihuahua, commanded by brigadier general Wool. 168 pp. 12°. *Pittsburgh, M. P. Morse*, 1847.

Builder (The); an illustrated weekly magazine, for the architect, engineer, archæologist, constructor, and art-lover. Conducted by George Godwin. Jan. to Dec. 1866. [v. 24.] fol. *London*, [*Wyman & sons*, 1866.]

Buisson (A. G. du). *See* **Edmond** (Charles).

Buist (Robert). American flower-garden directory. 4th ed. 339 pp. 12°. *Philadelphia, A. Hart*, 1851.

Bulger (George E.) Leaves from the records of St. Hubert's club; or, reminiscences of sporting expeditions in many lands. viii, 336 pp. 8°. *London, L. Booth*, 1864.

Bulkeley (*Rev.* Peter). The gospel-covenant; or, the covenant of grace opened. 8 p. l. 383 pp. 4 l. 4°. *London, Benjamin Allen*, 1646.

——— The same. 7 p. l. 432 pp. 5 l. 4°. *London, Matthew Simmons*, 1651.

Bullard (*Mrs.* Anna Tuthill Jenkins). Sights and scenes in Europe. 255 pp. 1 map. 12°. *St. Louis, Chambers & Knapp*, 1852. s.

Bullard (*Rev.* Asa). The children's album of pictures and stories. 208 pp. 1 pl. 8°. *Springfield, (Mass.) W. J. Holland & Co.* 1867.

Bulletin du bibliophile. Publié par J. Techener. 2e—10e série, 1836–1851, 1855–56. 17 v. 8°. *Paris, Techener*, 1836–56. s.

Bulletin de la société de géographie; rédigé par MM. Maltebrun, Barbié du Bocage, et C. Maunoir. 5e série. Année 1866. v. 11–12 in 1 v. 544, 527 pp. 5 maps. 8°. *Paris, Soc. de géographie,* 1866.

Bullinger (Edwin W.) Guide to skating; a complete manual of the art. Illustrated. 60 pp. 18°. *New York, Dick & Fitzgerald,* 1862.

Bullions (Peter, *D. D.*) A practical grammar of the English language; with analyses of sentences. Revised ed. x, 336 pp. 12°. *New York, Sheldon & Co.* 1867.

Bullock (William). Virginia impartially examined, and left to publick view, to be considered by all iudicious and honest men. 6 p. l. 66 pp. sm. 4°. *London, John Hammond,* 1649.

Bülow (Adam Heinrich von). Histoire de la campagne de 1800 en Allemagne. *See* **Okouneff** (N. A.) Opérations de la campagne de 1812, en Russie. *Bruxelles,* 1841.

Bulstrode (*Sir* Richard). Memoirs and reflections upon the reign and government of king[s] Charles i and ii. 11 p. l. 439 pp. 8°. *London, N. Mist,* 1721.

Bulstrode (Whitelock). Essays. xviii, 264 pp. 1 pl. 8°. *London, A. Betteswortk & J. Clarke,* 1724.

Bulwer (*Sir* Henry Lytton Earle). An autumn in Greece. 231 pp. 12°. *London, J. Ebers,* 1826.

Bulwer (John, *D. D.*) Anthropometamorphosis: man transformed; or, the artificial changling historically presented, in the mad and cruel gallantry ... and loathsome loveliness of most nations, ... altering their bodies from the mould intended by nature ...; with ... the pedigree of the English gallant. 25 p. l. 559 pp. 15 l. sm. 4°. *London, W. Hunt,* 1653.

Bünau (Heinrich, *graf* von). Catalogus bibliothecæ bvnavianae, [cura M. Francke]. 3 v. in 7. 4°. *Lipsiæ, Fritsch,* 1750–56. s.

Bunsen (Christian Carl Josias). Egypt's place in universal history. An historical investigation. Translated from the German by C. H. Cottrell, with additions by S. Birch. v. 5. 8°. *London, Longmans,* 1867.

Bunsen (Robert). Gasometry, comprising the leading physical and chemical properties of gases. Translated by Henry E. Roscoe. xii, 298 pp. 8°. *London, Walton & Maberly,* 1857. s.

——— Méthodes gasométriques. Traduction par Schneider. x, 320 pp. 8°. *Paris, V. Masson,* 1858. s.

Bunyan (John). The holy war. 252 pp. 2 pl. 16°. *New York, J. H. Turney,* 1832.

——— Translation of [part of] Pilgrim's progress [into the Cherokee language]. Tsunelodi dunigisvsvi. [*In* **Cherokee** messenger. nos. 1–4. 8°. *Cherokee,* 1844–46.]

Buonaparte, sa famille et sa cour: anecdotes secrètes, etc. Par un chambellan forcé a l'être. [*anon.*] 2 v. in 1. xviii, 378 pp. 362 pp. 12°. *Paris, Ménard et Desenne,* 1816.

——— *See* **Napoléon.**

Buonarroti (Filippo). Osservazioni sopra alcuni frammenti di vasi antichi di vetro, ornati di figure trovati ne' cimiteri di Roma. 31 pl. fol. *Firenze,* 1716.

Burchard (C. W. T.) Die landwirthschaftliche buchhaltung, mit besonderer rücksicht auf die wirthschaftsmethode in Mecklenburg und der angrenzenden länden. xvi, 128, 138 pp. 4°. *Rostock, F. Behm's erben,* 1840. s.
[Imperfect; wanting pp. 1–8.]

Burchiello (Domenico). Rime. Comentate dal Doni. 8 p. l. 261, 25 pp. 16°. *Vicenza, Perin,* 1597.

Burdett (Charles). Arthur Martin; or, the mother's trials. 225 pp. 18°. *New York, Harpers,* 1847. s.

Burdett (*Sir* Francis). Speech in the house of commons, [on parliamentary reform]. 16 pp. 8°. *London, R. Carlyle,* 1817. [*With* Sherwin, (W. T.) Political Register. v. 1. *London,* 1817].

Burdick (William). The Massachusetts manual, for 1814–15. v. 1. 219 pp. 12°. *Boston, Charles Callender,* 1814.

——— Oration on the nature and effects of the art of printing, July 5, 1802. 12°. 31 pp. *Boston, Munroe and Francis,* 1802.

Burdon (William). The gentleman's pocket-farrier. With remarks by Henry Bracken. 8 p. l. 82 pp. 3 l. 18°. *Dublin, S. Powell,* 1733.

Bureaud-Riofrey (A. M.) Curabilité de la phthisie et des scrofules appuyée sur des preuves authentiques. 216 pp. 8°. *Paris, Baillière,* 1847. s.

——— Londres et les Anglais des temps modernes. 2 v. 432 pp; 416 pp. 8°. *Paris, Truchy,* 1846. s.

——— Physical education; especially adapted to young ladies. 2d ed. xxii, 574 pp. 1 pl. 8°. *London, Longman,* [1838].

Buret (Antoine Eugène). De la misère des classes laborieuses en Angleterre et en France, avec l'indication des moyens propres à en affranchir les sociétés. 2 v. viii, 432 pp; vii, 492 pp. 8°. *Paris, Paulin,* 1840.

Burette (Théodore). Histoire de France depuis l'établissement des Francs dans la Gaule jusqu' en 1830. [Illustrée.] 2 v. 629, 684 pp. 8°. *Bruxelles, Hauman & Cie,* 1842.

Bürger (Gottfried August). Lenore; or death and the maiden. [Eng. and Ger.] Translated by J. W. Grant. With some original poems. 52 pp. 16°. *London, Murray & Co.* 1865.

——— The same. Translated by Albert Smith. (English and German text). [*With* **Smith** (Albert) Wild oats and dead leaves. pp. 341–359.]

——— The same. Lénore. Traduit de l'Allemand par E. de Labédollière. 20 pp. 1841. [*In* **Pléiade** (La). Ballades, etc.)

Burger (Johann). Agriculture du royaume lombardo-vénetien. Trad. de l'Allemand et annoté par Victor Rendu. viii, 360 pp. 8°. *Paris, Bouchard-Huzard,* 1842. s.

Burgess (*Rev.* Anthony). The doctrine of original sin, asserted and vindicated, in four parts. 17 p. l. 555 pp. 10 l. fol. *London, Thomas Underhill,* 1658.

Burgess (Ebenezer). *See* **Sûrya-Siddhânta.**

Burggraeve (Ad. *M. D. of Ghent*). Les appareils ouatés, ou nouveau système de déligation pour les fractures, les entorses, les luxations, les contusions, les arthropathies, etc. 83, viii pp. 21 pl. fol. *Bruxelles, A. Labroue & Cie.* 1857. s.

——— Études sur André Vésale, précédées d'une notice historique sur sa vie et ses écrits. xxxiii, 16, 439 pp. 1 pl. 8°. *Gand, C. Annoot-Broeckman,* 1841. s.

Burgoyne (*Lieut. Gen.* John). The lord of the manor. Comic opera. [*anon.*] 63 pp. 16°. *Philadelphia, Henry Taylor,* 1791.

Burke (Edmund). Miscellaneous works. 2 v. 588 pp; 622 pp. 8°. *New York, Eastburn, Kirk & Co.* 1813.

CONTENTS.

v. 1. Letters, miscellaneous.
Letters on a regicide peace. pp. 11–76.
Address to the British colonists in North America. pp. 115–123.
Tracts and letters on Ireland, pp. 185–262.
Fragments and notes of speeches in parliament. pp. 263–343.
Abridgment of English history. pp. 355–588.
v. 2. Administration of justice in India. Ninth report. pp. 9–225.
Articles of charge against Warren Hastings. pp. 226–622.

——— Philosophical enquiry into the origin of our ideas of the sublime and beautiful. [*anon.*] ix, 7, 342 pp. 8°. *London, J. Dodsley,* 1770.

Burke (Edmund, *of N. H.*) Report of the commissioner of patents on the subject of steam boiler explosions. 8°. *Washington,* 1849. s.

Burke (*Rev.* John). Chivalry, slavery, and young America. By Sennoia Rubek. [*anagram*]. 183 pp. 8°. *New York, F. A. Brady,* 1866.

——— Stanzas to queen Victoria, and other poems. By Sennoia Rubek. [*anagram*]. 208 pp. 1 pl. 8°. *New York, F. A. Brady,* 1866.

Burke (*Sir* John Bernard). Genealogical and heraldic dictionary of the peerage and baronetage of the British empire. 29th ed. xlviii, 1316 pp. 8°. *London, Harrison,* 1867.

Burke (Peter). The public and domestic life of Edmund Burke. xvi, 315 pp. 2 pl. 12°. *London, Ingram, Cook & Co.* 1853.

Burkitt (Lemuel), *and* **Read** (Jesse). Concise history of the Kehukee baptist association, from its rise to the present time. 319 pp. 16°. *Halifax, N. C. A. Hodge,* 1803.

Burmeister (Hermann Carl Conrad). Erläuterungen zur fauna Brasiliens, enthaltend abbildungen und ausführliche beschreibungen neuer oder ungenügend bekannter thierarten. viii, 115 pp. 32 col. pl. fol. *Berlin, G. Reimer,* 1856. s.

——— Genera quædam insectorum iconibus illustravit et descripsit Burmeister. v. 1. [Rhynchota.] *Berolini,* 40 pl. 8°. *auctor,* 1838–46. s.

[No more published.]

——— Handbuch der entomologie. 5 v. 8°. *Berlin, Reimer, u. s. w.* 1832–55. s.

[Wanting v. i, 1832. iv, 1844–55. (2 pts.) v, 1847.]

——— Reise durch die La Plata staaten, mit besonderer rücksicht auf die physische beschaffenheit und den culturzustand der argentinischen republik. Ausgeführt in den jahren 1857–60. 2 v. vi, 504 pp. 1 pl. 1 map; v, 539 pp. 1 map. 8°. *Halle, H. W. Schmidt,* 1861. s.

——— Systematische uebersicht der thiere Brasiliens, welche während einer reise durch die provinzen von Rio de Janeiro und Minas Geraës gesammelt oder beobachtet wurden. 3 v. 8°. *Berlin, G. Reimer,* 1854–56. s.

CONTENTS.

v. 1. Säugethiere. x. 341 pp.
v. 2–3, Vögel. x, 436 pp; xiv, 466 pp.

——— Zoologischer hand-atlas zum schulgebrauch und selbstunterricht, mit besonderer rücksicht auf seinen "Grundriss," und sein "Lehrbuch der naturgeschichte." 2[e] ausg. besorgt durch C. G. Giebel. 2 p. l. 192 pp. 42 pl. 4°. *Berlin, G. Reimer,* 1860. s.

Burmeister (Hermann Carl Conrad). Zoonomische briefe. Allgemeine darstellung der thierischen organisation. 2 v. viii, 367; x, 470 pp. 8°. *Leipzig, O. Wigand*, 1856. s.

Burn (Andrew, *Maj. Gen. R. N.*) Memoirs, collected from his journals [by O. Gregory and others.] 2 v. xxiii, 287 pp; 248, 55 pp. 1 pl. 12°. *London, Winchester & son*, 1815.

Burn (Jacob Henry). Descriptive catalogue of the London traders', tavern, and coffee-house tokens current in the 17th century. Presented to the corporation library by H. B. H. Beaufoy. xlv, 238 pp. 1 pl. 8°. *London, A. Taylor*, 1853. s.

Burn (John Southerden). History of parish registers in England; also, of the registers of Scotland, Ireland, East and West Indies, etc. 2d ed. viii, 296 pp. 8°. *London, J. R. Smith*, 1862.

Burnell (George R. *C. E.*) Rudiments of hydraulic engineering. v, 184 pp. 16°. *London, J. Weale*, 1852. [*With* **Law** (Henry). Civil engineering. *London*, 1859.]

——— *See* **Law** (Henry).

Burnet (Gilbert, *D. D. bishop of Sarum*). A collection of eighteen papers relating to the affairs of church and state during the reign of king James the second. 3 p. l. 244 pp. sm. 4°. *London, John Starkey & Richard Chiswell*, 1689.

——— Enquiry into the present state of affairs, and in particular, whether we owe allegiance to the king in these circumstances? 16 pp. sm. 4°. *London, John Starkey*, 1689. [*With* his collection of eighteen papers. *London*, 1689.]

——— An essay on the memory of the late queen [Mary, consort to King William III.] 197 pp. 8°. *London, Ric. Chiswell*, 1695.

——— The lawfulness of taking the new oaths asserted. 13 pp. sm. 4°. *London, J. Mills*, 1689. [*With* his collection of eighteen papers. *London*, 1689.]

——— Life and death of Sir Matthew Hale, Kt. 9 p. l. 218 pp. portrait. 16°. *London, W. Shrowsbery*, 1682.

——— A pastoral letter to the clergy of his diocess, concerning the oaths of allegiance and supremacy. 29 pp. sm. 4°. *London, J. Starkey*, 1689. [*With* his collection of eighteen papers. *London*, 1689.]

——— Reflections on a paper, intituled, his majesty's reasons for withdrawing himself from Rochester. 8 pp. sm. 4°. *London, John Starkey*, 1689. [*With* his collection of eighteen papers. *London*, 1689.]

——— A representation of the threatning dangers impending over protestants in Great Britain. 54 pp. sm. 4°. [n. p.] 1689. [*With* his collection of eighteen papers. *London*, 1689].

——— Six papers, (against repealing the test and concerning his citation,) with an apology for the church of England, and an enquiry into the measures of submission to the supream authority. 68 pp. sm. 4°. *London*, 1689.

——— Some letters containing an account of what seem'd most remarkable in travelling thro' Switzerland, Italy, some parts of Germany, etc. in 1685–86. [With] appendix. xxvi, 355 pp. 12°. *London, J. Lacy*, 1724.

Burnet (Thomas, *LL. D. master of Charter house*). The theory of the earth; containing an account of the original of the earth, and of all the changes which it hath already undergone, or is to undergo till the consummation of all things. [From the Latin.] 9 p. l. 327 pp. 2 pl. 8°. *London, W. Kittilby*, 1684. s.

Burnet (William, *Gov. of New York*). An essay on scripture prophecy. [*anon.*] 2 p. l. 167 pp. sm. 4°. [n. p.] 1724.

Burnett (George). Specimens of English prose writers, from the earliest times to the close of the seventeenth century, with sketches, biographical and literary. 2d ed. 3 v. 12°. *London, J. Bumpus*, 1813.

Burnouf (Eugène). Commentaire sur le Lotus de la bonne loi, et mémoires relatifs au buddhisme. (*See* **Saddharma** pundarîka. 4°. *Paris*, 1852.)

——— Commentaire sur le Yaçna, l'un des livres religieux des Parses, attribué à Zoroastre. (*See* **Zendavesta**. 4°. *Paris*, 1833).

——— Introduction à l'histoire du buddhisme indien. Tome 1. 3 p. l. v, 648 pp. 4°. *Paris*, 1844.

[No more published].

——— *See* **Bhâgavata** Purâna.

Burns (Robert). The cotter's Saturday night; a poem. With illustrations, drawn by F. A. Chapman; engraved by J. Filmer. 48 pp. 4 pl. sm. 4°. *New York, C. Scribner & Co.* 1867.

Burroughs (John). Notes on Walt Whitman, as poet and person. 108 pp. 16°. *New-York, Amer. news co.* 1867.

Burroughs (Stephen). Memoirs, [by himself]. 2 v. in 1. 356 pp. 2 l. 18°. *Boston, Charles Gaylord*, 1832.

Burrowes (Thomas H.) Pennsylvania school architecture; a manual of directions and plans for common school houses. 276 pp. 1 pl. 8°. *Harrisburg, A. B. Hamilton*, 1855. s.

Burt (N. C. *D. D.*) National character; a thanksgiving discourse, delivered 1855, in the Franklin street presbyterian church. 28 pp. 8°. *Baltimore, John D. Toy,* 1855.

Burton (John, *D. D.*) The genuineness of Ld. Clarendon's history of the rebellion vindicated. Mr. Oldmixon's slander confuted. 173 pp. 8°. *Oxford, J. Fletcher,* 1744.

——— The present state of the navigation on the Thames considered; and certain regulations proposed. [*anon.*] 2d ed. 54 pp. 4°. *Oxford, D. Prince,* 1767. [*With* the preceding].

Burton (Richard F.) Personal narrative of a pilgrimage to El-medinah and Meccah; with introduction, by Bayard Taylor. 492 pp. 1 map. 12°. *New York, G. P. Putnam & Co.* 1856. s.

Burton, *alias* **Crouch** (Robert, *or* Richard). The history of the kingdoms of Scotland and Ireland. By R. B. 230 pp. 1 pl. 18°. *London, N. Crouch,* 1685.
[Imperfect.]

——— The wars in England, Scotland, and Ireland, during the reign of king Charles I. 10th ed. 18°. *London,* 1737.

Burton (Thomas de, *abbot*). Chronica monasterii de Melsa, ad annum 1396. Accedit continuatio ad annum 1406, a monacho quodam ipsius domus. Edited by E. A. Bond. v. 2. xliii, 394 pp. 8°. *London, Longmans,* 1867.
[Chronicles of Great Britain in the middle ages].

Burton (William). Commentary on Antoninus, his itinerary, or journies of the Roman empire, so far as it concerneth Britain. 11 p. l. 266 pp. 3 l. 1 map. 1 pl. fol. *London, H. & T. Twiford,* 1658.

Burtt (John). Horæ poeticæ, consisting of poems and songs in English and Scotch. 183 pp. 18°. *Bridgeton,* [*N. J.*] *William Schultz,* 1819.

Burty (Philippe). Chefs d'oeuvre des arts industriels. 598 pp. 54 pl. sm. fol. *Paris, Ducrocq,* [1866].

Bury (*Lady* Charlotte Maria). The three great sanctuaries of Tuscany; Valombrosa, Camaldoli, Laverna: a poem, with historical and legendary notices, [and] engravings by Edward Bury. xi, 139 pp. 7 pl. obl. 4°. *London, J. Murray,* 1833.

Bury (T. Talbot). Rudimentary architecture; for the use of beginners. History and description of the styles of architecture in various countries. 4th ed. vii, 201 pp. 16°. *London, J. Weale,* 1857. [*With* **Leeds,** (W. H.) Rudimentary architecture. *London,* 1854].

Busawun (Lal). Memoirs of the Puthan soldier of fortune, the Nuwab Ameer-ood-Doulah Mohummud Ameer Khan, chief of Seronj, Tonk, and other places in Hindostan. [Translated from the Persian by H. T. Prinsep]. xxii, 508 pp. 1 map. 1 pl. 8°. *Calcutta, G. H. Huttmann,* 1832.

Busch (A. L.) Systematisches verzeichniss der in der bibliothek der königl. universitäts sternwarte zu Königsberg enhaltenen bücher. 8°. *Königsberg,* 1852. s.

Busch (Hermann). Decimationvm plavtinarvm pemptas, sive qvintana secvnda. 18 l. unp. sm. 4°. *Coloniæ, apud Helisabet viduam,* 1518.

——— Decimationum plautinarum pemptades, sive quinariæ. 24 l. unp. sm. 4°. *Coloniæ,* [*about* 1518.]

Buschmann (Johann Carl Eduard). Vergleichende grammatik der Indsee-sprachen, u. s. w. [*With* **Humboldt** (C. W. von). Über die Kawi-sprache, v. 3.] s.

Bushnell (Horace, *D.D.*) Christ and his salvation. 3d ed. 456 pp. 12°. *New York, C. Scribner & Co.* 1865.

Busk (George). Monograph of the fossil polyzoa of the crag. 4°. *London,* 1859. [Palæont. soc.] s.

Busk (Hans). Hand-book for Hythe; comprising a familiar explanation of the laws of projectiles, and an introduction to the system of musketry. viii, 184 pp. 9 pl. 18°. *London, Routledge,* 1860.

Busti (Bernardino de'). Secunda pars rosarii. [Compendium sermonum.] 17 p. l. unp. 409 l. sm. 4°. *Venetiis, Georgius de Arriuabenis,* 1498.

Butel-Dumont (George Marie). Histoire et commerce des colonies angloises, dans l'Amérique Septentrionale. [*anon.*] xxiv, 336 pp. 16°. *Londres,* 1755.

Butler (Charles). The book of the Roman Catholic church. 295 pp. 12°. *Baltimore, James Myres,* 1834.

Butler (James). American bravery displayed, in the capture of fourteen hundred vessels of war and commerce, since the declaration of war by the president. 322 pp. 16°. *Carlisle,* (*Pa.*) *George Phillips,* 1816.

Butler (Samuel). *See* **Secret** history of the calves-head club.

——— *See* **Vindication** (A) of the royal martyr.

Butler (William Allen). Nothing to wear: an episode of city life. [*anon.*] 68 pp. 8 pl. 16°. *New York, Rudd & Carleton,* 1857.

Butler (William Allen). Two millions. 93 pp. 16°. *New York, Appleton & Co.* 1858.

Butterworth (*Rev.* John). New concordance to the holy scriptures. First Amer. ed. viii pp. 332 l. 8°. *New York, W. W. Woodward,* 1811.

Butterworth (William). Three years' adventures of a minor. vi, 492 pp. portrait. 8°. *Leeds, Edward Baines,* [*about* 1820].

Buttmann (Philipp Carl). Mythologus, oder gesammelte abhandlungen über die sagen des alterthums. 2 v, 352 pp, 1 map; 378 pp, 1 pl. 8°. *Berlin, Mylius,* 1828–29. s.

Buxton (Thomas Fowell). The African slave trade and its remedy. viii, 582 pp. 1 map. 8°. *London, J. Murray,* 1840.

Buxtorf (Johann, *the father*). De abbreviaturis hebraicis liber; cvi accesservnt operis talmudici brevis recensio et index; item bibliotheca rabbinica. 18°. *Herbornæ Nassaviæ, J. N. Andrea,* 1708. s.

Buys Ballot (C. H. D.) Les changements périodiques de température, dépendants de la nature du soleil et de la lune, mis en rapport avec le pronostic du temps, déduits d'observations néerlandaises de 1727 à 1846. 5 p. l. 123 pp. 10 tab. 4°. *Utrecht, Kemink,* 1847. s.

Byam (William). An exact relation of the most execrable attempts of John Allin, committed on the person of Francis lord Willoughby of Parham, captain general of Guiana, etc. 12 pp. sm. 4°. *London, Richard Lowndes,* 1665.

Byfield (Nathanael). An account of the late revolution in New England. 20 pp. sm. 4°. *London, R. Chiswell,* 1689.

Byford (William H. *M. D.*) Practice of medicine and surgery applied to the diseases and accidents incident to woman. 2d ed. 616 pp. 8°. *Philadelphia, Lindsay & Blakiston,* 1867.

By-Laws, muster-roll, and papers selected from the archives of the first troop Philadelphia city cavalry, from 1774 to 1840. 64 pp. 8°. *Philadelphia, C. Sherman & Co.* 1840.

Byrd (William). History of the dividing line and other tracts. 2 v. xix, 233 pp; 276 pp. 4°. *Richmond, Va.* [*J. Munsell, pr.*] 1866.

CONTENTS.

v. 1. History of the dividing line between Virginia and North Carolina, as run in 1728–29.
v. 2. Journey to the land of Eden and other tracts.

Byrn (M. Lafayette, *M. D.*) The family physician, and household companion; a treatise, in plain language, on health and diseases, with treatment. 377 pp. 11 pl. 8°. *New York, M. L. Byrn,* 1867.

Byrom (John). The universal English shorthand. ix, 92 pp. 8°. *Manchester (Eng.) Joseph Harrop,* 1767.

Byron (George Gordon Noel, *lord*). The corsair. 96 pp. 18°. *Philadelphia, Moses Thomas,* 1814.

——— Don Juan. [canto 1 and 2]. New ed. 2 p. l. 227 pp. 8°. *London, T. Davison,* 1819.

——— The same. 2 v. 2 p. l. 343 pp; 4 p. l. 371 pp. 18°. *London, T. Davison,* 1828.

——— The Giaour, a fragment of a Turkish tale. [1st ed.] 3 p. l. 41 pp. 8°. *London, J. Murray,* 1813.

——— Hours of idleness, a series of poems, original and translated. [1st published ed.] xiii, 187 pp. 16°. *Newark, S. & J. Ridge,* 1807.

——— Lara, a tale. [*anon.* 1st ed.] 4 p. l. 93 pp. 18°. *London, J. Murray,* 1814.

——— Manfred, a dramatic poem. [1st ed.] 80 pp. 8°. *London, J. Murray,* 1817. [*With* the Giaour. ed. of 1813].

——— Marino Faliero, doge of Venice. 179 pp. 18°. *Philadelphia, M. Carey & Sons,* 1821.

——— Poems on his domestic circumstances. 2d ed. 36 pp. 1 pl. 8°. *London, W. Hone,* 1816. [*With* the Giaour. ed. of 1813].

——— The vision of judgment. [*anon.*] 1st ed. 38 pp. 16°. *London, T. M. Rowe,* 1822. [*With* the Giaour. ed. of 1813.]

Bysshe (Edward). The British Parnassus; or, a compleat common-place-book of English poetry. With a dictionary of rhymes. 2 v. 3 p. l. 986 pp. 16°. *London, J. Nutt,* 1714.

Bywater (Abel). The Sheffield dialect. 2d ed. 295 pp. 18°. *London, W. Evans & Co.* 1854.

Cabanis (Pierre Jean Georges). Œuvres complètes; accompagnées d'une notice sur sa vie et ses ouvrages. 5 v. 8°. *Paris, Bossange,* 1823–25. s.

CONTENTS.

v. 1. Révolutions et réforme de la médicine.
Rapport sur l'organisation des écoles de médicine.
Du degré de certitude de la médicine.
v. 2. Journal de la maladie et de la mort de Mirabeau.
Observations sur les affections catarrhales.
Note sur le supplice de la guillotine.
Quelques principes et quelques vues sur les secours publics.
Observations sur les hôpitaux.
Travail sur l'éducation publique.
Note sur un genre particulier d'apoplexies.
v. 3–4. Rapports du physique et du moral de l'homme.
v. 5. Lettre sur les causes premières.
Discours sur Hippocrate.
Éloge de Vicq-d'Azyr.
Notice sur Benjamin Franklin.
Lettre sur les poëmes d'Homère.
Fragments de la traduction de l'Iliade.
Serment d'un médicin.

——— Rapports du physique et du moral de l'homme. 2e éd. 2 v. xliii, 569 pp; 720 pp. 8°. *Paris, Crapelet,* 1805. s.

Cabanis (Pierre Jean Georges) Sketch of the revolutions of medical science, and views relating to its reform. Translated from the French, with notes, by A. Henderson. xii, 421 pp. 8°. *London, J. Johnson,* 1806.

Cabeza de Vaca (Alvaro). *See* **Nuñez Cabeza de Vaca** (Alvaro).

Cabinet (The); or, works of darkness brought to light; a retrospect of the anti-christian conduct of some of the leading characters in the society of friends, towards Elias Hicks. [By L. P. *anon.*] 2d ed. 36 pp. 8°. *Philadelphia, John Mortimer,* 1825.

Cabinet of Momus; a choice selection of humourous poems, from P. Pindar, Freneau, Ladd, Swift, etc. viii, 136 pp. 6 pl. 16°. *Philadelphia, M. Carey,* 1809.

Cabinet de l'éloquence françoise, en forme de dialogue; très utile et nécessaire pour apprendre à bien parler en toutes compagnies, etc. [*anon.*] 47 pp. 18°. *Troyes, Garnier,* [*about* 1695. *With* **La Valliere** (*duchesse* de). Vie, 1695.]

Cabrera. *See* **Cayetano de Cabrera**.

Cadwalader (John). Reply to Gen. Joseph Reed's remarks on a late publication in the Independent gazetteer; with some observations on his address to the people of Pennsylvania. With the letters of Washington, Hamilton, etc. [pp. 15–54 of **Smith** (Horace W.) Nuts for future historians to crack.]

Cæsar (Caius Julius). Commentariorum de bello gallico, libri vii; Hircii additio. Commentariorum de bello ciuli, libri iii. Hirtii de bello alexandrino, africo, hispano, iv-vi. fol. *Venitiis, Bernardinus,* 1498. [*With* **Annius**. Cōmentaria, etc. fol. 1498.] s.

——— Quæ extant, interpretatione et notis illustravit Johannes Godvinus, in usum Delphini. New edition by William Mann. 304 pp. 3 maps. 8°. *Philadelphia, Desilver, Thomas & Co.* 1836.

——— The commentaries of his warres in Gallia, translated into English, with many observations thereupon by Clement Edmonds, with the life of Cæsar and an account of his medalls. 23 p. l. 196 pp. 6 pl. fol. *London, R. Daniel,* 1655.

——— Observations upon Cæsar's commentaries of the civile warres betwixt him and Pompey, by Clement Edmonds, [with the art of our tactick practice]. 142, 10 pp. 6 pl. fol. *London, R. Daniel,* 1655. [*With* **Cæsar** (C. J.) Commentaries of his warres in Gallia. *London,* 1655].

Cæsius (Fredericus). *See* **Hernandez** (F.)

Cail. *See* **Derosne**.

Calamy (Edmund). An abridgment of Mr. Baxter's history of his life and times, with an account of the ministers, etc. who were ejected after the restauration of king Charles ii. [With the reformed liturgy.] 2d ed. 2 v. 12 p. l. 726, 82 pp; 16 p. l. xxxii, 864 pp. 1 pl. 12°. *London, J. Lawrence,* 1713.

——— A continuation of the account of the ministers [etc.] who were ejected and silenced after the restoration in 1660, by or before the act for uniformity. 2 v. lxxii, 1,005, 63 pp. 12°. *London, R. Ford,* 1727.

——— The church and the dissenters compar'd as to persecution, [with remarks upon Dr. Bennett's essay on the thirty-nine articles]. 145 pp. 12°. *London,* 1727. [*With* v. 2 of **Calamy** (E.) Continuation of the account of ministers ejected. ed. 1727].

Calcott (Wellins). A candid disquisition of the principles and practices of the most antient and honourable society of free and accepted masons. [London, 1769; reprinted], xvi, 158 pp. 8°. *New York, J. W. Leonard & Co.* 1855.

Calderini (Carlo, *M. D.*) Prospetto clinico sopra le malattie veneree, e particolarmente sulla cura di esse senza mercurio. 128 pp. 4 tab. 8°. *Milano, Tamburini e Valdoni,* 1835. s.

Caldwell (Charles, *M. D.*) Elements of phrenology. viii, 100 pp. 1 pl. 8°. *Lexington, (Ky.) author,* 1824. s.

Calef (Robert). More wonders of the invisible world; [containing] an account of the sufferings of Margaret Rule, written by the Rev. Mr. C[otton] M[ather]. Several letters to the author and his reply relating to witchcraft, etc. *London, N. Hillar,* 1700. Reprint. 212. 167 pp. sm. 4°. 1866.

[*With* DRAKE (S. G.) Witchcraft delusion in New England, v. 2–3.]

Calendar of letters, despatches, and state papers, relating to the negotiations between England and Spain, preserved in the archives at Simancas and elsewhere. v. 2. Henry viii, 1509–1525. Edited by G. A. Bergenroth. ccxix, 863 pp. 8°. *London, Longmans,* 1866.

Calfhill (James, *D. D.*) Answer to John Martiall's treatise of the cross. Edited by Rev. Richard Gibbings. xii, 418 pp. 8°. *Cambridge, univ. press,* 1846.

[Parker society publications.]

California. Geological survey. J. D. Whitney, state geologist. Geology. v. i. Report of progress, and synopsis of the field-work, from 1860 to 1864. xxvii, 498 pp. 4°. *Philadelphia, Sherman & Co.* 1865. s.

California. Geological survey.—Continued.

CONTENTS.

Ashburner (W.) Tabular statement of the operations of the principal quartz mills running in California in 1861. (app. A.)
Meek (F. B.) Descriptions of fossils from the auriferous slates of California. (app. B.)
Whitney (J. D.) Preface. Geology of the coast range. pt. 1. Geology of the Sierra Nevada. pt. 2.

——— The same. Palæontology. v. i. xx, 243 pp. 32 l. 32 pl. 4°. *Philadelphia, Sherman & Co.* 1864. s.

CONTENTS.

Gabb (William M.) Description of the triassic fossils of California and the adjacent territories. § 2. Description of the cretaceous fossils. § 4.
Meek (F. B.) Description of the carboniferous fossils. §1. Description of the jurassic fossils. § 3.
Whitney (J. D.) Preface.

——— Geographical catalogue of the mollusca found west of the Rocky Mountains, between latitudes 33° and 49° north. By J. G. Cooper. 40 pp. 4°. *San Francisco, Towne & Bacon,* 1867. s.

California and her gold regions, compiled from the best sources. [*anon.*] 70 pp. 16°. *Philadelphia, G. B. Zieber,* 1849.

California gold regions, with a full account of their mineral resources, and sketches of California. 48 pp. 8°. *New York, F. M. Pratt,* [*about* 1850.]

California state library. Catalogue, Jan. 1, 1855. 172 pp. 8°. *Sacramento, B. B. Redding,* 1855. s.

Calliat (Victor), *and* **Lance** (Adolphe). [*editors*]. *See* **Encyclopédie** d'architecture.

Callisen (Adolph Carl Peter). Medicinisches schriftsteller-lexicon der jetzt lebenden aerzte, u. s. w. 33 v. 16°. *Copenhagen und Altona,* 1830–45. s.

CONTENTS.

v. 1–21. A—Z, 1830–35.
v. 22–23. Die anonymischen schriften, mit einschluss der cholera, der homöopathie, und der pharmacopöen, arzneitaxen, und allgemeinen medicinal ordnungen.
v. 23–25. Die zeitschriften, gesellschaftschriften, und die gesammelten schriften mehrerer verfasser. A—Z.
v. 26—33, Nachtrag; enthaltend berichtigungen, ergänzungen, die neuere literatur, und die seit 1830 verstorbenen medicinischen schriftsteller. Mit einigen beiträgen von Choulant, Koberwein, Richter, und A. von Schönberg. A—Z.
v. 33. Die periodischen und gesammelten schriften. A—Z.

Callistratus. *See* **Philostratus.** Quæ svpersvnt omnia. *Lipsiae,* 1709.

Calmberg (Ernst Philipp Ludwig). Katalog der [seiner] hinterlassen bibliothek. 3 p. l. 275 pp. 8°. *Hamburg, Meissner,* 1851. s.

Calmeil (L. F. *M. D.*) De la folie considérée sous le point de vue pathologique, philosoque, historique et judiciaire, depuis la renaissance des sciences en Europe, jusqu' au dixneuvième siècle. 2 v. viii, 534 pp. 8°. *Paris, J. B. Baillière,* 1845.

Calvert (George H.) First years in Europe. 303 pp. 12°. *Boston, W. V. Spencer,* 1866.

Calvert (James). Mission history. *See* **Williams** (Thomas) *and* **Calvert,** (J.) Fiji, etc.

Calvin (Jean). Institvtionvm christianæ religionis libri iv. Praemissa est vita, authore T. Beza. 16 p. l. 544, 54 pp. fol. *Lugduni Batavorum, F. Hack,* 1654. s.

Calvo (Charles). Amérique latine. Recueil historique complet des traités, conventions, capitulations, armistices, questions de limites, et autres actes diplomatiques et politiques de tous les états compris entre le golfe du Mexique et le cap de Horn, depuis l'année 1493, jusqu'à nos jours. 1e période. v. 7–10. 8°. *Paris, Durand,* 1865–66.

——— The same. 2e période. Annales historiques de la révolution de l'Amérique latine, accompagnées de documents à l'appui. De l'année 1808, jusqu'à la reconnaissance de l'indépendence. v. 4–5. 8°. *Paris, Durand,* 1865–67.

Calwer (C. G.) Recensio avium in academici liberi baronis de Mueller ornithologico museo stuttgardiano collectarum. 2 p. l. 77 pp. 8°. *Stuttgardiæ, typis officinæ regiæ,* 1854.

Cambridge (Eng.) University. Calendar for 1867. xxxviii, 614 pp. 1 chart. 12°. *Cambridge, Deighton, Bell & Co.* [1867.]

——— Graduati cantabrigienses: sive catalogus, exhibens nomina eorum quos, ab anno MDCLIX-MDCCCXXIII, gradu quocunque ornavit academia cantabrigiensis. 537, 28 pp. 8°. *Cantabrigiae, J. Smith,* 1823.

——— Mechanical problems, adapted to the course of reading pursued in the university of Cambridge. [*anon.*] vi, 184 pp. 8°. *London, G. B. Whittaker,* 1828. s.

Camden society publications. Nos. 92 and 93. sm. 4°. *London,* 1867.

CONTENTS.

Accounts and papers relating to Mary queen of Scots. Edited by A. J. Crosby and J. Bruce. [No. 93].
Bargrave (John). Pope Alexander the seventh and the college of cardinals, with a catalogue of Dr. Bargrave's museum. Edited by J. C. Robertson. [No. 92].

Camden (William). Britannia, newly translated into English, by Edmund Gibson 17 p. l. cxcv, 1116 pp. 22 l. fol. *London, A. Swalle,* 1695. s.

Camerarius *or* Kammermeister (Philipp). The living librarie, or, meditations and observations historical, natvral, moral, political and poetical. [Translated from] Latin into English by John Molle. 2d ed. 5 p. l. 428 pp. 2 l. fol. *London, A. Islip,* 1625.

Cameron (Charles Hay). Address to parliament on the duties of Great Britain to India in respect of the education of the natives, and their official employment. 175 pp. 8°. *London, Longman, Brown & Co.* 1853.

Campaign (The) of general Moreau, in Germany, in 1796; with the retreat through the Black forest. [*anon.*] 78 pp. 8°. *London, J. Davis,* 1813.
[Royal military chronicle, v. 1].

Campanella (Tomasso). His advice to the king of Spain for attaining the universal monarchy of the world. Translated into English by Ed. Chilmead, with preface by William Prynne. 7 p. l. 232 pp. sm. 4°. *London, Philemon Stephens,* 1659.

Campbell (Albert H.) Report upon the Pacific wagon roads. 125 pp. 6 maps. 8°. *Washington, government press,* 1859. S.

Campbell (*Rev.* Alexander). Debate on christian baptism with Rev. W. L. Maccalla, a presbyterian teacher, October 1823; with animadversions on treatises on the same subject, written by J. Mason, S. Ralston, etc. 420 pp. 16°. *Buffaloe, (Va.) Campbell & Sala,* 1824.

——— Familiar lectures on the pentateuch; delivered [at] Bethany college, 1849–60. Also extracts from his sermons, [and] sketch of [his] life. Edited by W. T. Moore. 379 pp. 1 pl. 12°. *Cincinnati, H. S. Bosworth,* 1867.

——— *and others.* The christian hymn book. 840 pp. 24°. *Cincinnati, H. S. Bosworth,* 1867.

Campbell (A. D.) Dictionary of the Teloogoo language, commonly called the Gentoo, peculiar to the Hindoos of the N. E. provinces of the Indian peninsula. 5 p. l. 601 pp. 4°. *Madras,* 1821. S.

Campbell (E. R.) Scientific reader and key. 2 v. in 1. 12°. *Cincinnati,* 1854. S.

Campbell (Gabriel). New practical course in the German language. part 1. 44 pp. 12°. *Chicago,* 1867.

Campbell (J. Allan). Design book [for funeral monuments], 1867. Containing 91 designs. 33 l. unp. obl. 16°. [*Chicago,*] *J. A. Campbell,* 1867.

Campbell (J. F.) Frost and fire; with sketches taken at home and abroad by a traveller. 2 v. xxxi, 506 pp; xii, 519 pp. 2 maps. 8°. *Edinburgh, Edmonston & Douglas,* 1865.

Campbell (J. L.) Manual of scientific and practical agriculture. 442 pp. 1 pl. col. 12°. *Philadelphia, Lindsay & Blakiston,* 1859. S.

Campbell (Lawrence D.) Life of Hugh Boyd. *See* **Boyd** (Hugh).

Campbell (Mark). Self-instructor in the art of hair work, dressing hair, [etc.] and hair jewelry. 276 pp. incl. 50 pl. 8°. *New York, M. Campbell,* 1867.

Campbell (Thomas). Gertrude of Wyoming; a Pennsylvanian tale. And other poems. 4°. *London, T. Bensley,* 1809.

Campe (Joachim Heinrich). Le nouveau Robinson, pour servir à l'amusement et à l'instruction des enfans. Traduit de l'Allemand. 24°. xiv, 436 pp. *Londres, Darton & Harvey,* 1807.

Campo *or* **Campi** (Antonio). Cremona rappresentata in disegno, col suo contado, et illustrata d'una breve historia et dei ritratti de duchi et duchesse di Milano, e compendio delle lor vite. 2ª ed. 4°. *Milano, Bidelli,* 1645. S.

Camps (William, *M. D.*) Railway accidents or collisions; their effects upon the brain and spinal cord, and other portions of the nervous system. 18 pp. 8°. *London, H. K. Lewis,* 1866.

Canada. Geological survey. Report of progress from commencement to 1863, with maps and sections. 42 pp. 3 l. 10 maps. 8°. *Montreal, Dawson,* 1865.

——— The same. Report of progress from 1863 to 1866. viii, 321 pp. 8°. *Ottawa, G. E. Desbarats,* 1866.

——— Seventh report from the select committee of the house of assembly on grievances. [With] report on the petition of William Forsyth, late proprietor of the Niagara falls pavilion. W. L. Mackenzie, chairman. 5 p. l. 372, 26 pp. 8°. *Toronto, M. Reynolds,* 1835.

Canadas (The) as they now are, comprehending a view of their climate, rivers, lakes, canals, trade, etc. By a late resident. [*anon.*] xv, 116 pp. 16°. *London, James Duncan and others,* 1833.
[Map wanting].

Canadian guide book. [*anon.*] With a map of the province [by E. Staveley]. 154 pp. 16°. *Montreal, Armour & Ramsay,* 1849. S.

Cancellieri (Francesco Girolamo). Dissertazioni epistolari bibliografiche sopra Cristoforo Colombo, e Giovanni Gersen, avtore del libro De imitatione Christi. xi, 415 pp. 8°. *Roma, F. Bovrliè,* 1809. S.

Candid (The) retrospect; or, the American war examined, by whig principles. [*anon.*] 28 pp. 18°. *Charlestown printed, New York re-printed,* 1780.

Candolle (Alphonse de). Géographie botanique raisonnée. 2 v. xxxii, 1,365 pp. 2 maps; 8°. *Paris, V. Masson,* 1855. s.

Candolle (Augustin Pyramus de). Mémoires et souvenirs; écrits par lui-même et publiés par son fils. xvi, 599 pp. 8°. *Genève, J. Cherbuliez,* 1862. s.

Candy (Thomas *and* George). *See* **Molesworth** (J. T.) *and* **Candy.**

Canina (Luigi). L'architettura antica descritta e dimostrata coi monumenti. 3 v. fol. *Roma, Canini,* 1830–44. s.

CONTENTS.

v. 1. L'architettura egiziana. vii pp. 197 pl. 1839–44.
v. 2. L'architettura greca. vii pp. 168 pl. 1830–40.
v. 3. L'architettura romana. viii pp. 250 pl. 1830–40.

Canning (George). *See* **Poetry** of the Antijacobin.

Cantù (Cesare). Storia di cento anni (1750–1850). 4ª ed. 5 v. 16°. *Torino,* 1863–64. s.

Cantù (Ignazio). L' Italia scientifica contemporanea; notizie sugli Italiani ascritti ai cinque primi congressi. 6 p. l. 320, 172 pp. 8°. *Milano, Stella,* 1844. s.

Cap (Paul Antoine). Camille Montagne, botaniste. viii, 98 pp. 1 portrait. 8°. *Paris, J. B. Baillière,* 1866. s.

Capefigue (Jean Baptiste Honoré Raymond). Agnès Sorel et la chevalerie. xi, 227 pp. 16°. *Paris, Amyot,* 1860.

——— Aspasie et le siècle de Périclès. xvi, 216 pp. 16°. *Paris, Amyot,* 1862.

——— Les bacchantes et les jeunes patriciens sous les Césars. xxiii, 178 pp. 16°. *Paris, Amyot,* 1864.

——— La belle Corisande et les galanteries du Béarnais. 2 p. l, viii, 214 pp. 1 pl. 16°. *Paris, Amyot,* 1864.

——— La comtesse de Parabère et le palais royal sous la régence. 2 p. l. vii, 204 pp. portrait. 16°. *Paris, Amyot,* 1863.

——— Les cours d'amour, les comtesses et chatelaines de Provence. 2 p. l. vii, 204 pp. 1 pl. 8°. *Paris, Amyot,* 1863.

——— Les déesses de la liberté. 8, 260 pp. 1 pl. 16°. *Paris, Amyot,* 1862.

——— Diane de Poitiers. v, 305 pp. 16°. *Paris, Amyot,* 1860.

——— La duchesse de Portsmouth et la cour galante des Stuarts. 2 p. l. xxiv, 199 pp. portrait. 16°. *Paris, Amyot,* 1861.

——— Gabrielle d'Estrées, et la politique de Henri iv. xx, 278 pp. 16°. *Paris, Amyot,* 1859.

——— Les héroines de la ligue, et des mignons de Henri iii. 2 p. l. viii, 233 pp. 1 pl. 16°. *Paris, Amyot,* 1864.

——— Madame la comtesse Du Barry. 2 p. l. vii, 276 pp. 16°. *Paris, Amyot,* 1858.

——— Madame la marquise de Pompadour. 2 p. l. iii, 296 pp. 18°. *Paris, Amyot,* 1858.

——— Mademoiselle de la Vallière, et les favorites des trois ages de Louis xiv. xi, 276 pp. 16°. *Paris, Amyot,* 1859.

——— Ninon de Lenclos, et les précieuses de la Place royale. 2 p. l. viii, 218 pp. 1 pl. 16°. *Paris, Amyot,* 1864.

Capel (Arthur, *1st earl of Essex*). Letters written [by the] lord lieutenant of Ireland, 1675, [with] historical account of his life. xvi, 428 pp. 4°. *London, J. Dodsley,* 1770.

Capmany y Montpalau (Antonio de). Memorias historicas sobre la marina, comercio, y artes de la antigua ciudad de Barcelona. 4 v. 4°. *Madrid, Ant. de Sancha,* 1779–92.

Capodieci (Giuseppe Maria). Antichi monumenti di Siracusa. 2ª ed. 2 v. 304 pp. 1 pl. 1 map; 376 pp. 1 pl. 1 map. 4°. *Siracusa, F. M. Pulejo,* 1816. s.

Capper (James). Observations on the passage to India, through Egypt, and across the great desert. xx, 110 pp. 2 maps. 4°. *London, W. Faden,* 1783.

Capucins (Les) sans barbe, histoire napolitaine. [*anon.*] 64 pp. 18°. [n. p.] 1761.

Caquets (Les) de l'accouchée. [*anon.*] Nouv. éd. revue sur les pièces originales, et annotée par Édouard Fournier; avec une introduction par Le Roux de Lincy. xlvii, 298 pp. 16°. *Paris, P. Jannet,* 1855.

Caracci. *See* **Carracci.**

Caraccioli, (Domenico, *marchese di Villamaina*). Riflessioni sull' economia e l'estrazione de frumenti della Sicilia fatte in occasione della carestia dell' indizione iii, 1784–5. (Scrittori class. ital. di econ. pol. v. 40.)

Caraccioli (Louis Antoine). De la gayeté. Nouvelle éd. [*anon.*] x. 221 pp. 16°. *Liége, J. F. Bassompierre & J. Van den Berghen,* 1763.

——— Le livre à la mode. Nouvelle éd. [*anon.*] xxxviii, 88 pp. 18°. [*Paris*]. *Les libraires,* 1759.

——— *See* **Clement** xiv. Lettere.

Caraccioli (Roberto). Quadragesimale de peccatis. 191 l. 4°. *Venetiis, A. de Toresanis de Asula,* 1488.

——— Sermones quadragesimales de aduētu, de timore judiciorum Dei, cū q̄busdā aliis annexis. 336 l, 2 l. unp. 4°. *Venetiis, J. de Forliuio,* 1490. [*With* the preceding.]

Caraccioli (Roberto). Sermones de laudibus sanctorum. 219 l. unp. fol. *Auguste, A. Sorg.*

Caracciolo (Henrietta). The mysteries of the Neapolitan convents; with a sketch of the early life of the authoress. Translated from 4th Italian ed. by J. S. Redfield. With an introduction by J. Dowling. 484 pp. 1 pl. 12°. *Hartford, A. S. Hale & Co.* 1867.

Caradoc (of Lhancarvan). The history of Wales, written originally in British, englished by Dr. Powell, and augmented by W. Wynne; with a description of Wales, by Sir John Price. 21 p. l. xlii, 396 pp, viii l. unp. 8°. *London, T. Evans,* 1774.

Carayon (Auguste). Bibliographie historique de la compagnie de Jésus, ou catalogue des ouvrages relatifs à l'histoire des jésuites, depuis leur origine jusqu'à nos jours. viii, 612 pp. 4°. *Paris, Durand,* 1864.

Carbo (Juan). *See* **Barbachano** (T. A.) *and* **Carbo** (J.) Memoria, etc.

Care (Henry). The history of popery: with alterations and additions, [and a supplement carrying on the history to the end of the council of Trent]. By several gentlemen. [*anon.*] 2 v. 3 p. l. 481 pp, 6 l; 3 p. l. 676 pp. 5 l. 2 pl. 4°. *London, J. Oswald,* 1735–36.

Carew (George, *earl of Totness*). Calendar of the Carew Mss. preserved in the archiepiscopal library at Lambeth, 1515–1574. Edited by J. S. Brewer and W. Bullen. cxix, 572 pp. 8°. *London, Longmans,* 1867.

Carew (Richard). Survey of Cornwall; [with] notes of its history and antiquities by Thomas Tonkin. Published by Francis Lord de Dunstanville, [and] journal of the parliament of tinners, held at Truro, 1710. xxxix, 459 pp. 1 pl. 4°. *London, T. Bensley,* 1811.

Carew (Thomas). Poetical works. 8°. *Edinburgh,* 1793.
[Anderson's Brit. poets, v. 3.]

Carey (George Saville). The balnea: or an impartial description of all the popular watering places in England. 2d ed. xii, 275 pp. 12°. *London, W. West,* 1799.

Carey (Mathew). Address before the Philadelphia society for promoting agriculture, July 20th, 1824. 4th ed. 108 pp. 24°. *Philadelphia, R. A. Skerrett,* 1824.

Carey (William, *D. D.*) Dictionary of the Mahratta language. vii, 652 pp. 8°. *Serampore,* 1810. s.

——— (*and others*). Memoir relative to the progress of the translations of the sacred scriptures, in the year 1815, into the various languages of India; with the present and past of "to be" in 34 languages. 38 pp. 8°. *Serampore,* 1816.

Carey. *See* **Cary.**

Carléer (Léon Henri Marie). Examen des principales classifications adoptées par les zoologistes. [Extract.] 284 pp. 1 pl. 8°. *Bruxelles, T. Lesigne,* 1861. s.

Carleton (*Capt.* George, *pseud.*] *See* **Defoe** (Daniel).

Carlier (Auguste). Marriage in the United States. Translated from the French by B. J. Jeffries. 3d ed. xvi, 179 pp. 16°. *Boston, De Vries, Ibarra & Co.* 1867.

Carlisle (Nicholas). Concise description of the endowed grammar schools in England and Wales. 2 v. xliv, 856 pp; 883 pp. 8°. *London, Baldwin, Cradock & Joy,* 1818.

Carlisle (*Pa.*) Charter and ordinances of the borough of Carlisle, with incidents of its early history, and a notice of its present condition. 64 pp. 2 maps. 8°. *Carlisle,* 1841.

Carlyle (Thomas). History of Friederich ii of Prussia, called Frederick the great. 7 v. sq. 18°. *Leipzig, B. Tauchnitz,* 1858–62.

——— Passages selected from [his] writings; with a biographical memoir, by Thomas Ballantyne. xii, 351 pp. 12°. *London, Chapman & Hall,* 1855.

Carmoly (Éliacin, *M. D.*) History of the Jewish physicians. From the French, with notes. [With notes on surgery.] By John R. W. Dunbar. 94 pp. 8°. *Baltimore, J. Murphy,* [*about* 1845]. s.

Carnell (P. P.) A treatise on family wine making; from the various fruits of this country. 160 pp. 8°. *London, Sherwood & Co.* 1814.

Carnot (Lazare Nicolas Marguerite, *comte*). Réflexions sur la métaphysique du calcul infinitésimal. 4e éd. 160 pp. 1 pl. 8°. *Paris, Mallet-Bachelier,* 1860.

——— An exposition of [his] political conduct since July 1, 1814. Translated by Henry Wheaton. 72 pp. 18°. *New York, Van Winkle & Wiley,* 1815.

Carnot (Lazare Hippolyte). Mémoires sur Carnot, par son fils. 2 v. 592 pp; 640 pp. 1 pl. 8°. *Paris, Pagnerre,* 1861–63.

Caro (Ramon Martinez). Verdadera idea de la primera campaña de Tejas y sucesos ocurridos despues de la accion de San Jacinto. vii, 162 pp. 8°. *Mexico, S. Perez,* 1837.

Carolina. [Charter, fundamental constitutions, etc]. Nos. 1–14. 67 pp. sm. 4°. *London,* 1705.
[Title wanting.]

Carpenter (F. B.) Inner life of Abraham Lincoln. 24th ed. 359 pp. 16°. *New York, Hurd & Houghton,* 1867.
[Same as his "Six months at the white house"].

Carpenter (Philip P.) Lectures on mollusca; or, shell-fish and their allies. 8°. *Washington,* 1861. s.

——— Report on the present state of our knowledge with regard to the mollusca of the west coast of North America. [Extract]. iv, pp. 159—368 4 pl. 8°. *London, Taylor & Francis,* 1857. s.

Carr (George P.) The contest; a poem. 115 pp. sq. 18°. *Chicago, P. L. Hanscom,* 1866.

Carr (John). Early times in middle Tennessee. 248 pp. 18°. *Nashville, E. Carr,* 1857.

Carra (Jean Louis). Mémoires historiques et authentiques sur la bastille. 3 v. in 1. 8°. *Paris, Buisson,* 1789.

Carracci (Annibale). Aedium farnesiarum tabulæ ab Annibale Caraccio depictæ, a Carolo Cæsio æri insculptæ, atque a Lucio Philarchæo explicationibus illustratæ. 6 p. l. lxxiv pp. 35 pl. fol. *Romæ, V. Monaldini,* 1753.

Carrera (Pietro). A treatise on the game of chess. Translated from the Italian, with notes, by W. Lewis. 3 p. l. 300 pp. 8°. *London, J. M. Richardson, & R. Triphook,* 1822.

Carrey (Émile). L'Amazone. Les révoltés du Para. 337 pp. 16°. *Paris, Lévy,* 1857.

Carriere (Moriz). Die kunst im zusammenhang der culturentwickelung und die ideale der menschheit. v. 1–2. 8°. *Leipzig, F. A. Brockhaus,* 1863–66. s.

CONTENTS.

v. 1. Die anfänge der cultur und das orientalische alterthum in religion, dichtung und kunst. xxi, 569 pp.
v. 2. Hellas und Rom in religion und weisheit, dichtung und kunst. xvi, 612 pp.

Carrington (H. E.) The Plymouth and Devonport guide. 4th ed. viii, 316 pp. 7 pl. 18°. *Devonport (Eng.) W. Byers,* 1837. s.

Carrington (Richard Christopher). Observations of the spots on the sun from Nov. 9, 1853, to March 24, 1861, made at Redhill. 248 pp. 166 pl. 4°. *London, Williams & Norgate,* 1863. s.

Carruthers (William). The [British] diatomaceæ. [*With* **Gray** (J. E.) Handbook of British waterweeds. 1864]. s.

Cartari (Vincenzo). Le vere e nove imagini degli dei delli antichi. Ridotte da Lorenzo Pignoria, [con] annotationi. Con le allegorie sopra le imagini di Cesare Malfatti. 16 p. l. 576 pp. 2 l, lxiii pp. sm. 4°. *Padoua, P. P. Tozzi,* 1615.

Cartée (Cornelius S.) A school atlas of physical geography. 3 p. l. 13 col. maps. 8°. *Boston, Hickling, Swan & Brown,* 1856. s.

Carter (Charles L.) Treatise on general pathology and its relation to practical medicine. 149 pp. 8°. *St. Louis, G. Knapp & Co.* 1867.

Cartier (Jacques). Trois voyages au Canada 1534–40. 77 pp. 8°. *Québec, William Cowan et fils,* 1843. [*With* **Voyages** de découverte au Canada, 1534 et 1542. *Québec,* 1840].

——— Voyage de Jacques Cartier av Canada en 1534 [avec] documents inédits sur Jacques Cartier et le Canada. Nouv. éd. vii, 71, 53 pp. 2 maps. 12°. *Paris, Tross,* 1865.

Cartier de Saint Philip (—). Le je ne sçai quoi, ou mélanges curieux historiques et critiques de bons môts et pensées choisies. Par Mr. C. D. S. P. [*anon.*] 2 v. in 1. v, 310 pp; 4 p. l. 270 pp, 3 l. 16°. *La Haye,* 1724.

Cartouche (Louis Dominique). Histoire de la vie, et du procès de. *See* **Histoire.**

Carus (Carl Gustav). Traité élémentaire d'anatomie comparée, suivi de recherches d'anatomie philosophique ou transcendante. Trad. de l'Allemand, sur la 2e éd. par A. J. L. Jourdan. 3 v. 8°. Atlas, 31 pl. 4°. *Paris, J. B. Baillière,* 1835. s.

——— The same. 808 pp. 8°. Atlas, 31 pl. 4°. *Bruxelles, Soc. typog. belge,* 1836–37. s.

Carus (Julius Victor). System der thierischen morphologie. xii, 506 pp. 8°. *Leipzig, W. Engelmann,* 1853. s.

Carvajal (Bernardo de). Oratio super præstanda solenni obedientia sanctissimo Alexandro papæ vi, ex parte christianissimorum dominorum Fernandi et Helisabe regis et reginæ Hispaniæ: habita Romæ in consistorio publico, xix Iunii, m.cccc.xciii. 8 l. unp. sm. 4°. [*Romæ, Besicken, aut Silber,* 1493.]

Carve (Thomas). Itinerarium, cum historia facti Butleri, Gordon, Lesly et aliorum. Nova ed. xx, 432 pp. 1 pl. sm. 4°. *Londini, B. Quaritch,* 1859.

Carver (*Capt.* Jonathan). Travels through the interior parts of North America, in 1766–68. 10 p. l. 543 pp. 4 pl. 8°. *London,* 1778.

——— The same. 22, xvi, 543 pp. 2 maps. 6 pl. 8°. *London, C. Dilly,* 1781.

——— The same. Three years' travels through the interior parts of North America for more than five thousand miles, with appendix. xx, ix, 360 pp. 8°. *Philadelphia, Key & Simpson,* 1796.

Carver (*Capt.* Jonathan). Voyage dans les parties intérieures de l'Amérique Septentrionale, pendant les années 1766-68. Traduit sur la 3e éd. angloise, par M. de C——. 23, xxviii, 451 pp. 1 map. 8°. *Paris, Pissot,* 1784.

—— The same. Aventures chez les sauvages de l'Amérique Septentrionale. 5e éd. 236 pp. 2 pl. 16°. *Tours, Mame et Cie,* 1852.

Cary (Alice). The bishop's son; a novel. 416 pp. 12°. *New York, G. W. Carleton & Co.* 1867.

—— A lover's diary. With illustrations. ix, 240 pp. sq. 16°. *Boston, Ticknor & Fields,* 1868.

—— Snow-berries: a book for young folks. With illustrations. x, 206 pp. 6 pl. sq. 16°. *Boston, Ticknor & Fields,* 1867.

Cary (Phœbe). Poems of faith, hope, and love. v, 249 pp. 16°. *New York, Hurd & Houghton,* 1868.

Cary (*Rev.* Samuel). *See* **Freeman** (James, *D.D.*) and **Cary** (*Rev.* S.) Funeral sermons. *Boston,* 1820.

Cary. *See* **Carey.**

Casa (Giovanni della.) Le terze rime, 1542. [*With* **Berni** (F.) Tutte le opere.]

Casanova de Seingalt (Jacques). Memoirs. From the French by A. Tolliab. 6 v. sq. 18°. *Brunswick, H. Neuhoff & Co.* 1863.

Casaregi (Giovanni Bartolommeo). Sonette e canzoni. *See* **Salvini** (Salvino.)

Case (The) of the planters of tobacco in Virginia, as represented by themselves; signed by the president of the council and speaker of the house of burgesses. [With] a vindication of the said representation. [*anon.*] 64 pp. 8°. *London, J. Roberts,* 1733.

Case (The) of protestant dissenters in Carolina, shewing how a law to prevent occasional conformity there has ended in the total subversion of the constitution in church and state. [To which are appended, documents respecting Carolina, in 14 nos]. 42, 67 pp. sm. 4°. *London,* 1706.

CONTENTS.

No. 1. First charter of Carolina. March 24, 1663.
2. Fundamental constitutions of Carolina, March 1, 1669.
3 Fundamental constitutions of Carolina, agreed on Apr. 11, 1689.
4. The present state of affairs in Carolina. By John Ash, gent.
5. Representation and address of several of the members of this present assembly for Colleton county, etc. to his excellency John Granvill, esq. palatine.
6. Act requiring all hereafter chosen members of the house of assembly to take the oaths and subscribe the declaration appointed by this act, to conform to the church of England, etc.
7. Address, May 10, 1704, of the dissenters to his excellency John Granville.
8. Letter of Mrs. Blake, widow of the late governor, to the lords proprietors, May 16, 1704.
9. Petition of the committee of the Pennsylvania company, and other merchants trading to Carolina.
10. Act for the establishment of religious worship in this province according to the church of England, etc. Nov. 4, 1704.
11-14. [Papers respecting the persecution of Rev. Edward Marston, rector of church of St. Philip, in Charleston, S. C.]

Casgrain (H. R.) Un contemporain.—F. X. Garneau. 135 pp. 1 portrait. 18°. *Québec, J. N. Duquet,* 1866.

Casiri (Michael). Bibliotheca arabico-hispana escurialensis, sive librorum omnium mss. quos arabice bibliotheca cœnobii escurialensis complectitur recensio et explanatio. 2 v. 8 p. l. xxiv, 544 pp; 3 p. l. 352 pp. 108 l. fol. *Matriti, A. P. de Soto,* 1760-70.

Caspari (C. P.) Ungedruckte, unbeachtete und wenig beachtete quellen zur geschichte des taufsymbols und der glaubensregel. v. 1. ix, 248 pp. 8°. *Christiania, P. T. Malling,* 1866. s.

Caspipina (Tamoc, *pseudon.*) Letters. *See* **Duché** (Jacob.)

Casseday (Ben.) History of Louisville, [Ky.] from its earliest settlement to 1852. 255 pp. 1 map. 16°. *Louisville, Hull and brother,* 1852.

Cassin (John). Birds. [*With* **Baird** (Spencer F.) Outlines of zoology.] s.

—— Birds of Chili. [*With* **Gilliss** (J. M.) U. S. astronomical exped. v. 2.]

Castalione (Sebastiano). *See* **Bible,** *Latin.* fol. *Basileæ,* 1551.

Castell (*Rev.* William). A petition of W. C. exhibited to the high covrt of parliament now assembled, for the propagating of the gospel in America and the West Indies. 19 pp. sm. 4°. [n. p.] 1641. [*With* **Higginson** (*Rev.* Francis). New England's plantation, 1641.]

—— A short discoverie of the coasts and continent of America, from the equinoctiall northward, and of the adjacent isles. [With] the author's petition to parliament, for the propagation of the gospel in America; ordinance of parliament for the better government of English plantations there, and Sir Benjamin Rudyer's speech in parliament concerning America. 12 p. l. 48, 54 pp. sm. 4°. *London,* 1644.

—— The same. [Imperfect; pp. 17-25 supplied in ms.] *London,* 1644.

Castelman (Richard). Voyage, etc. with description of Philadelphia. [*With* **Chetwood** (W. R.) Voyages of Capt. Rob't Boyle].

Castelnau (François L. de Laporte, *comte* de), *and* **Brullé** (Auguste). Monographie du genre diaperis. 90 pp. 1 pl. 8°. *Paris, Thuau*, 1831. s.

——— [Two manuscript catalogues of his insects. 4°. n. p. 1822--26]. s.

Castéra (Jean Henri). Les baisers de Zizi, poème. 2e éd. [*anon.*] 93 pp. 24°. *Paris, Royez*, 1786.

Castiglione (Baldassare). Il libro del cortegiano. 7, 215 pp. 18°. *Venetia, Aldo et A. d'Asola*, 1533.

Castiglioni (Cesare). Risposta al tema pubblicato dalla società medico-chirurgica di Bologna, 15 Maggio, 1842. [Arteritis. Extract]. 209 pp. 4°. *Bologna, Soc. medico-chirurgica*, 1844.

Castillioneus (Johannes), *or*, **Castiglione** (G. M. M. Salvimeni di). (*See* **Newton** (J.) Arithmetica universalis, commentarius).

Castle builders; or, the history of William Stephens; with a vision of a child left in a wood to be fed by ravens. [*anon.*] 2d ed. xv, 320 pp. 12°. *London, E. Cabe and others*, 1759.

Castleman (Harry). [*pseudon*]. *See* **Frank** on the lower Mississippi.

Castleman (*Rev.* T. T.) Plain sermons for servants. 438 pp. 12°. *New York, Stanford & Delisser*, 1858.

Castrucci (Giuseppe Emmanuele). Viaggio da Lima ad alcune tribù barbare del Perù e lungo il fiume delle Amazzoni. xvi, 115 pp. 2 l. 9 pl. 8°. *Genova, Ponthenier*, 1854.

Catalogue (A) of books printed in England since the dreadful fire of London in 1666, to the end of Michaelmas term, 1695, with an abstract of the general bills of mortality since 1660. [With a catalogue of books printed 1696-99. *anon.*] 127 pp. 79 l. fol. *London, R. Clavel*, 1696--[99?]

Catalogue of a costly and choice collection of rare, curious, and valuable books on the history of America. 62 pp. 8°. *New York, Bangs*, 1853.
[With prices at sale].

Catalogue of friends' books. [*anon.*] 238 pp. 12°. *London, J. Sowle*, 1708.

Catcott (*Rev.* Alexander). Treatise on the deluge. 2d ed. enlarged. viii pp. 4 l. 423 pp. 1 pl. 8°. *London, E. Allen*, 1768.

Catechism on the foundations of the christian faith; [with] the conversation of Mr. de Fenelon with Mr. de Ramsey on the existence of God, and the worship which is due to him. [*anon.*] 113, 55 pp. 12°. *New York*, 1811.

Catesby (Mark). *See* **Edwards** (G.) *and* **Catesby**. Sammlung verschiedener vögel.

Catlin (George). Last rambles amongst the Indians of the Rocky mountains and the Andes. x, 361 pp. 8 pl. 16°. *New York, D. Appleton & Co.* 1867.

——— Life amongst the Indians. A book for youth. xii, 339 pp. 8 pl. 16°. *New York, D. Appleton & Co.* 1867.

Cato (Dionysius). Cathonem glosatū et moralisatum. 69 l. unp. sm. 4°. [n. p. or d.]

——— Moralissimus Cato cū elegantissimo cōmento Roberti de Euremodio. 41 l. sm. 4°. *Argētine*, 1487.

Cato (Marcus Portius). (*With* **Libri** de re rustica.)

Catskill association, formed for the purpose of improving the town of Catskill, New York, December 28, 1836. [*anon.*] 47 pp. 1 map. 16°. *New York, Mitchell & Turner*, 1837.

Catton (Charles, *jr.*) Animals, drawn from nature, and engraved in aqua-tinta. [Re-published from the London ed. of 1787.] 36 l. unp. 36 pl. fol. *New Haven, H. Howe*, 1825.

Catullus (Caius Valerius). Opera, ex recensione Isaaci Vossii, cum ejusdem notis ac observationibus. Ed. 2a. 3 p. l. 332 pp. 12 pl. 4°. *Lugduni Batavorum, D. à Gaesbeeck, etc.* 1691. s.

——— Poems, in English verse: [translated by George Frederick Nott] with the Latin text revised, and classical notes. 2 v. in 1. xxxvi, 221, 4 pp. 1 l.; 236 pp. 1 l. 2 pl. 8°. *London, J. Johnson*, 1795. [*pp.* 173–6 *of v.* 2 *in mss.*]

Caualli (Louis). Verzeichniss der ornitologischen sammlung. 2 p. l. 30 pp. 1 col. pl. 4°. *Darmstadt, J. J. Schmidt*, 1829.

Caulkins (Frances Manwaring). History of Norwich, Conn. [2d ed. 8°. *Hartford*,] *author*, 1867.

Caumont (Arcisse de). Abécédaire ou rudiment d'archéologie. [L'architecture du moyen-age.] iv, 416 pp. 8°. *Caen, Harde*, 1850. s.

Causton (H. Kent Staple). Howard papers: with a biographical pedigree and criticism. 690 pp. 8°. *London, Causton & son*, [1863.]

Cavalcanti (Bartolommeo). La retorica in vii libri. 16 p. l. unp. 563 pp. 4°. *Vinegia, G. Giolito da' Ferrari*, 1560.

Cavelier (Jean). Relation du voyage entrepris par La Salle, pour découvrir dans le golfe du Mexique l'embouchure du fleuve Missisipy. 54 pp. 16°. *Manate, J. M. Shea*, 1858.

——— Account of La Salle's voyage to the mouth of the Mississippi, etc. Translated into English. (pp. 13–42 of **Shea** (J. S.) Early voyages. 4°. *Albany*, 1861.)

Cavendish (Georgiana, *duchess of Devonshire*). The passage of S. Gotthard, a poem. pp. 79–92. [*With* **Sketch** of a journey through Switzerland. [*anon.*] *Berne*, 1816.]

Cavendish (Margaret, *duchess of Newcastle*). Poems and phancies. 2d ed. 12 p. l. 299 pp. sm. fol. *London, W. Wilson*, 1664.

——— True relation of the birth, breeding, and life of Margaret Cavendish, duchess of Newcastle. Written by herself. With preface by Sir E. Brydges. 5 p. l. 9, 36 pp. portrait. 8°. *Lee Priory, Kent, Johnson and Walker*, 1814.

Cayetano de Cabrera y Quintero (——). Escudo de armas de Mexico: celestial proteccion de esta nobilissima ciudad, de la Nueva-España, y de casi todo el nuevo mundo, Maria santissima, en su portentosa imagen del mexicano Guadalupe, milagrosamente apparecida en el palacio arzobispal el año de 1531. Y jurado su principal patrona el passado de 1737, en la angustia que ocasionà la pestilencia. 18 p. l. 522 pp. 12 l. fol. *Mexico, Viuda de Joseph Bernardo de Hogal*, 1747.

Cazeaux (Paulin). Theoretical and practical treatise on midwifery, including the diseases of pregnancy and parturition. Translated from the second French ed. etc. by Robert P. Thomas. 765 pp. 2 pl. 8°. *Philadelphia, Lindsay & Blakiston*, 1850. s.

Cean-Bermudez (Jean Agustin). Memorias para la vida de Gaspar Melchor de Jovellanos, y noticias de sus obras. 4 p. l. 395 pp. 16°. *Madrid*, 1814.

Cebes. Tabla de Cebes. [*With* **Veen**, (O. van). Theatro moral de la vida humana. 1701.]

Cedrenus (Georgius). Compendivm historiarvm. Ex versione Gvillelmi Xylandri: accedvnt notae Iacobi Goar et Caroli Annibalis Fabroti; glossarium item Ioannis Scylitzæ curopalatæ, (Gr. et Lat.) 2 v. 33 p. l. 868, 60 pp. 26 l. *Parisiis, S. Cramoisy*, 1647. s.

Cellarius (Christoph). Breviarium antiquitatum romanorum, accurante H. Freyero. xii, 192 pp. 16°. *Augustæ Taurinorum, Typ. regia*, 1742. s.

——— Notitia orbis antiqvi, sive geographia, etc. Ed. alt. 2 v. 1088 pp. 135 l. 20 maps, 1 pl; 990 pp. 40 l. 4°. *Lipsiae, Gleditsch*, 1731–32.

Celsus (Aurelius Cornelius). Medicinae libri viii. xcii. 4 l. unp. fol. *Venetiis, P. Pinzi*, 1497.

——— The same. De medicina libri octo, cum notis integris Joannis Cæsarii, Roberti Constantini, Josephi Scaligeri, Isaaci Casanboni, Johannis Baptistæ Morgagni, ac locis parallelis, cura et studio Th. J. ab Almeloveen. Accedunt J. Rhodii vita C. Celsi, etc. itemque loci aliquot Hippocratis et Celsi ab Henrico Stephano παραλληλως concinnati. ed. 2ª. 38 p. l. 749 pp. 12°. *Basileae, J. R. Thurneisen*, 1748. s.

——— The same. Ex rec. L. Targae. 2 v. 678 pp; 463 pp. 4°. *Lugduni Batavorum, S. & J. Luchtmans*, 1785.

——— Über die arzneiwissenschaft, in acht büchern, übersetzt und erklärt von Eduard Scheller [Nebst Bianconi's briefe über Celsus.] 2 v. 304 pp; 423 pp. 8°. *Braunschweig, Vieweg*, 1846. s.

Cent (Les) nouvelles nouvelles; publiées d' après le seul manuscrit connu, avec introduction et notes par Thomas Wright. 2 v. xliii, 303 pp; 323 pp. 16°. *Paris, Jannet*, 1857–8.

Centenary (The) singer: a collection of hymns and tunes popular during the last one hundred years; compiled for the [M. E.] Sunday school union. vi, 419 pp. 16°. *New York, Carlton & Porter*, 1867.

Cerisier (Antoine Marie). Tafereel der algemeene geschiedenissen van de veréénigde Nederlanden, [tot 1752] gevolgd naar 't Fransch. 10 v. 8°. *Utrecht, B. Wild*, 1787. s.

Cervantes Saavedra (Miguel de.) The history of the valorous and witty knight-errant, Don Quixote, of the Mancha. Translated out of the Spanish by Thomas Shelton, etc. 2 pts. in 1 v. 8 p. l. 273 l. fol. *London, R. Scot, and R. Hodgkinson*, 1672-75.

——— The same. History of the most renowned Don Quixote of Mancha, and his trusty squire Sancho Pancha. [*anon.*] Now made English. By J[ohn] P[hilips]. With plates. fol. *London*, 1687.

——— The same. The history of the valorous and witty knight-errant Don Quixote of the Mancha. Translated into English by Thomas Shelton, and printed from the 4° ed. of 1620. 4 v. 16°. *London, R. Knaplock, etc.* 1725.

——— The wit and wisdom of Don Quixote. v, 161 pp. 16°. *New York, D. Appleton & Co.* 1867.

Cesena (Amédée Gayet, *dit* de). Les Césars et les Napoléons. 8°. *Paris, Amyot*, 1856.

Cevallos (Pedro Ordoñez de). *See* **Ordoñez.**

Chabrier (J. *chevalier*). Essai sur le vol des insectes, et observations sur quelques parties de la mécanique des mouvemens progressifs de l'homme et des animaux vertébrés. iv, 328 pp. 14 pl. 4°. *Paris, A. Belin*, 1823. s.

——— Idées nouvelles sur le système solaire. viii, 64 pp. 4°. [*With* the preceding.]

Chadbourne (Paul A. *M. D.*) Lectures on natural theology, delivered before the Lowell institute, Boston. 320 pp. 12°. *New York, G. P. Putnam & son*, 1867.

Chaillot (P. *jeune*). Manuel du libraire, du bibliothécaire, et de l'homme de lettres. Par un libraire. [*anon.*] 18°. *Paris, Chaillot*, 1829. s.

Chaix (Paul). Histoire de l'Amérique Méridionale au 16e siècle, comprenant les découvertes et conquêtes des Espagnols et des Portugais. Première partie. Pérou. 2 v. xvi, 344 pp. 2 maps; 348 pp. 3 maps. 16°. *Genève, J. Cherbuliez*, 1853. s.

Chalmers (Alexander). The projector; a periodical paper, originally published in monthly numbers, Jan. 1802 to Nov. 1809. 3 v. 8°. *London, Longman, Hurst & Co.* 1815.

Chalmot (J. A. de). Biographisch woordenboek der Nederlanden. A-Dre. 8 v. 8°. *Amsterdam, J. Allart*, 1798-1800.

Chamberlain (N. B. & D. *dealers*). A catalogue of pneumatic instruments, etc. 2 p. l. 63, xiv pp. 8°. *Boston, B. Perkins*, 1844. s.

Chamberlain (N. H.) The autobiography of a New England farm-house. 365 pp. 12°. *New York, Carleton*, 1865.

Chamberlayne (Edward). L'état présent de la Grande Bretagne et de l'Irlande. Traduit de l'Anglois; rev. et augm. par H. Scheurleer. 3 v. 16°. *La Haye, H. Scheurleer*, 1728. s.

Chambers (John). Harmony of the four gospels. *See* **Bible**, *English*, gospels.

Chambers (William *and* Robert). Treasury of knowledge. Edited by D. M. Reese. 3 v. in 1. 12°. *New York, A. S. Barnes & Co.*, 1849. s.

——— Chambers' journal of popular literature, science, and arts. 1866. 8°. *Edinburgh, W. & R. Chambers*, [1866].

Chambray. *See* **Fréart de Chambray** (Roland).

Champfleury (Jules Fleury, *dit*). Histoire des faïences patriotiques sous la révolution. 2e éd. xii, 404 pp. 28 pl. 16°. *Paris, Dentu*, 1867.

Champion (Maurice). Les inondations en France depuis le vie siècle jusqu'à nos jours. 6 v. 8°. *Paris, Dalmont et Dunod*, 1858–64.

Champlain (Samuel de). Voyages et descovvertvres faites en la Novvelle France, depuis l'année 1615, iusques à la fin de l'année 1618. 7 p. l. unp. 158 pp. 4 pl. 16°. *Paris, Clavde Collet*, 1620.

——— Les voyages de la Novvelle France occidentale dicte Canada, 1603–29. Auec vn traitté des qualitez requises à vn bon nauigateur. Ensemble ce qui s'est passé en ladite Nouuelle France en l'année 1631. 16, 310, 8, 54 pp. 4°. *Paris, Lovis Sevestre*, 1632.

Champollion-Figeac (Jean Jacques). Nouvelles recherches sur la ville gauloise d'Uxellodunum. 116 pp. 7 pl. 4°. *Paris, impr. royale*, 1820. s.

——— Texte historique et descriptif. *See* **Pfnor** (Rodolphe.) Monographie du palais de Fontainebleau.

Chancourtois (E. B. de.) *See* **Edmond** (Charles).

Chandler (Henry C. & Co.) Illinois directory. (*See* **Illinois**).

Chandler (Richard, *D. D.*) The life of William Waynflete, bishop of Winchester. xvi, 428 pp. 5 pl. 8°. *London, White & Cochrane*, 1811.

Chandler (Samuel, *D. D.*) The history of persecution, viz: amongst the heathens; under the christian emperors; under the papacy and inquisition; amongst protestants. xcii, 468 pp. 9 pl. 8°. *London, J. Gray*, 1736.

——— A vindication of the antiquity and authority of Daniel's prophecies, and their application to Jesus Christ. xxiv, 220 pp. 8°. *London, J. Gray*. (*With* his Reflections on the conduct of the modern deists, 1727.)

——— A vindication of the history of the old testament, in answer to Thomas Morgan. xxxi, 610 pp. 8°. *London, J. Noon*, 1741.

Chandler (Thomas Bradbury, *D. D.*) An appeal to the public, in behalf of the church of England in America. xi, 127 pp. 8°. *New York, James Parker*, 1767.

——— Life of Samuel Johnson, D. D. the first president of King's college, in New York. 3 p. l. 208 pp. 12°. *New York, T. & J. Swords*, 1805.

Channing (William Ellery, *D. D.*) Works. 17th ed. 6 v. in 3. 12°. *Boston, Am. unit. assoc.* 1867.

——— A selection from [his] works. v, 480 pp. 12°. *Boston, Am. unit. assoc.* 1855.

Chanvalon (Jean Baptiste Thibault de). Voyage à la Martinique, contenant diverses observations sur la physique, l'histoire naturelle, l'agriculture, les mœurs, et les usages de cette isle, faites en 1751, et dans les années suivantes. viii, 192 pp. 40 l. 1 map. 4°. *Paris, J. B. Bauche*, 1763. s.

Chapelle (Claude Emmanuel Lhuillier) *and* Bachaumont, (F. le C. de). Œuvres. Nouv. éd. revue et corrigée sur l'éd. de 1732. Précédée d'une notice par Tenant de Latour. 285 pp. 16°. *Paris, P. Jannet,* 1854.

Chapin (Stephen). The duty of living for the good of posterity; sermon at North Yarmouth, Dec. 22, 1820, in commemoration of the close of the 2d century from the forefathers. 48 pp. 8°. *Portland, Thomas Todd & Co.* 1821.

Chapin (S. R.) Stray leaves. 78 pp. sq. 16°. [*Boston,* 1867].

Chapman (*Rev.* Frederick W.) The Chapman family; or, the descendants of Robert Chapman, one of the first settlers of Saybrook, Conn. 414 pp. 10 pl. 8°. *Hartford, Case, Tiffany & Co.* 1854. s.

Chapman (John *M. D.*) Diarrhoea and cholera, their nature, origin, and treatment, through the agency of the nervous system. 2d ed. xix, 248 pp. 8°. *London, Trübner & Co.* 1866.

Chapman (Maria Weston). Right and wrong in Massachusetts. 177 pp. 16°. *Boston, Dow & Jackson,* 1839.

Chappe d'Auteroche (Jean). Voyage en Sibérie; contenant la description du Kamtchatka, par Kracheninnikow, traduit du Russe. 2 v. in 3. xxxii, 767 pp. 36 pl; xvi, 632 pp. 17 pl. 4°. *Paris, Debure,* 1768. s.

Chapter (The) and council manual; a ritual of the master, [etc.] degrees [of masonry]. [Also] a monitorial ritual for the order of high priesthood, compiled by Wm. Hacker. 192 pp. 1 pl. 24°. *Cincinnati, J. Ernst & Co.* 1867.

Chapuy (Nicolas Marie Joseph) *and* **Ramée** (Daniel). Le moyen age monumental et archéologique; vues, details et plans des monuments les plus remarquables de l'Europe, depuis le 6e jusq'au 16e siècle, lithographiés. Avec un résumé et des notices spéciales par D. Ramée. 5 pts. in 2 v. 444 pl. fol. *Paris, Hauser,* 1843. s.

Characteristics of men of genius; a series of biographical, historical, and critical essays, chiefly from the North American Review. Selected [by John Chapman]. 2 v. xix, 316 pp. 12°. *London, Chapman,* 1847.

CONTENTS.

v. 1. Gregory VII, [by J. H. Perkins]; Loyola, [by J. H. Perkins]; Pascal, [by F. Bowen]; Dante, [by S. G. Brown]; Petrarch, [by G. W. Greene]; Milton, [by R. W. Emerson]; Shelley, [from The Dial]; Byron, [by E. P. Whipple].

v. 2. Walter Scott, [by W. H. Prescott]; Wordsworth, [by E. P. Whipple]; Poets of Germany, [by J. M. Mackie]; Goethe, [from The Dial]; Michael Angelo, [by R. W. Emerson]; Canova, [from The Dial]; Machiavelli, [by G. W. Greene]; Louis IX, [by J. H. Perkins]; Peter the Great, [by J. L. Motley].

Charito Aphrodisiensis. De Chærea et Callirrhoe. J. P. d'Orville publicavit, animadversionesque adjecit. J. J. Reiskius vertit. 2 v. xx, 168, 233 pp; 788 pp. 28 l. 4°. *Amstelodami, P. Mortier,* 1750.

Charles xiv [Jean Baptiste Jules Bernadotte], (*of Sweden*). Choix de discours tenus en 1843, á l'occasion du jubilé de [son] règne. (Par Atel Eure, J. C. Soderberg et le prof. Hvasser). 140 pp. 8°. *Stockholm,* 1843. s.

Charles (*Mrs.* Elizabeth). Winifred Bertram, and the world she lived in. [*anon.*] 476 pp. 12°. *London, Nelson & sons,* 1866.

Charleston (*S. C.*) Apprentices' library society. Catalogue of the books. 336 pp. 12°. *Charleston, (S. C.) B. B. Hussey,* 1840. s.

Charlestown (The) directory, containing the names of the inhabitants for the year 1834. 76 pp. 1 map. 18°. *Charlestown,* [*Mass.*] *A. Quimby,* 1834.

Charlevoix (Pierre François Xavier de). Letters to the dutchess of Lesdiguières, giving an account of a voyage to Canada, and travels through Louisiana to the gulf of Mexico. Translated from the French. xiv, 384 pp. 12°. *London, R. Goadby,* 1763.

——— Geschichte von Paraguay. 2 v. 4 p. l. 332 pp; 370 pp. 1 map. 12°. *Wien,* 1830. s.

Charley Chalk; or, the career of an artist; being sketches from real life. [*anon.*] 310 pp. 8°. *London, G. Berger,* 1841.

[Hazlitt's romancist and novelist's library, v. 6].

Charma (Antoine). [Reponses aux] questions de philosophie contenues dans le programme adopté pour l'examen du baccalauréat ès lettres. 3e éd. 225 pp. 16°. *Paris, L. Hachette,* 1841. s.

Charnay (Désiré). *See* **Cités** et ruines américaines, etc. photographiées.

Charpentier (Toussaint de). Orthoptera descripta et depicta. iv, 54 l. unp. 60 pl. col. 4°. *Lipsiæ, Leopold Voss,* 1841--45. s.

Chartier (Jean). Chronique de Charles vii, roi de France. 3 v. 16°. *Paris, P. Jannet,* 1858.

Chartrouse (*baron de*). *See* **Meiffren-Laugier** (*baron* de Chartrouse).

Chase (A. W. *M. D.*) Recepte, oder belehrung für jedermann. In's deutsche übersetzt von C. F. Spring. 282 pp. 12°. *Ann Arbor, (Mich.)* 1865.

Chase (Enoch). Merchants' tables of advance on British sterling, with other calculations. 60 l. unp. sm. 4°. *Boston, Josiah Loring,* 1822.

Chase (Ezra B.) Teachings of patriots and statesmen, on slavery. 495 pp. 1 pl. 12°. *Philadelphia, J. W. Bradley*, 1860.

Chase (Stephen). A treatise on algebra. 335 pp. 12°. *New York, D. Appleton & Co.* 1849. s.

Chase (William S.) 1848, a year of revolutions. With an appendix containing the revolutionary events of 1849, [and] a brief survey of the causes of the third French revolution. 285 pp. 4 pl. 16°. *Hartford, Robins & Co.* 1850.

Chasles (Victor Euphémion Philarète). *See* **Roche** (Antonin).

Chassant (L. Alphonse). Dictionnaire des abréviations latines et françaises usitées dans les inscriptions lapidaires et métalliques, les manuscrits, et les chartes du moyen age. 3e éd. iii, 170 pp. 16°. *Paris, A. Aubry*, 1866.

Chassériau (Frédéric Victor Charles). Vie de l'amiral Duperré, ancien ministre de la marine et des colonies, etc. vii, 531 pp. 8°. *Paris, Imprimerie nationale*, 1848. s.

Chatelet (*duc* de). *See* **Desoteux de Cormatin** (Pierre Marie Felicité, *baron*).

Chatelain (Henri Abraham). Atlas historique, ou introduction à l'histoire, à la chronologie, et à la géographie, ancienne et moderne. [*anon.*] Avec dissertations par Mr. Gueudeville [et] H. P. de Limiers. 7 v. fol. *Amsterdam, Honoré & Chatelain*, 1705–20.

Chatrian (Alexandre). *See* **Erckmann** (Émile) *and* **Chatrian**.

Chaudoir (*baron* Max de). Mémoire sur la famille des carabiques. Supplément à la faune des carabiques de la Russie. (Extract.) 3 v. in 1. 8°. *Moscou, Soc. imp. des naturalistes*, 1848–50. s.

Chaudon (Esprit Joseph). Dictionnaire interprète-manuel des noms latins de la géographie ancienne et moderne. [*anon.*] viii, 444 pp. 8°. *Paris, Lucombe*, 1777. s.

Chaudon (Louis Mayeul). Nouveau dictionaire historique, ou histoire abrégée de tous les hommes, etc. 7e éd. 9 v. 8°. *Caen, G. Leroy*, 1789.

Chaumonot (Pierre Joseph Marie). Copie d'un écrit à son confesseur. pp. 45–66.
[*With* Suite de la vie de Chaumonot. 1858.]

——— Sa vie. Écrite par lui-même, 1688. sm. 4°. *Nouvelle York, J. M. Shea*, 1858.

Chauncy (Charles, *D. D.*) A letter to a friend, containing remarks on certain passages in a sermon of [John Ewer] the bishop of Landaff, before the society for the propagation of the gospel in foreign parts. 56 pp. 8°. *Boston, Thomas Leverett*, 1767.

Chauncy (Charles, *D. D.*) The validity of presbyterian ordination asserted and maintained: discourse at the anniversary Dudleian lecture, Harvard college; with an appendix giving an account of the epistles ascribed to Ignatius. 118 pp. 8°. *Boston, R. Draper*, 1762.

Chaussard (Pierre Jean Baptiste, *dit* Publicola). Fêtes et courtisanes de la Grèce. Supplément aux voyages d'Anacharsis et d'Anténor. [*anon.*] 2e éd. v. 1—3. 8°. *Paris, Barba*, 1803.

Chautard (Léon). Escapes from Cayenne. 63 pp. 8°. *Salem, (Ms.) Observer office*, 1857.

Chauvenet (William). Binomial theory and logarithms. 92 pp. 8°. *Philadelphia, Perkins & Purves*, 1843. s.

——— A treatise on plane and spherical trigonometry. 256 pp. 8°. *Philadelphia, H. Perkins*, 1850. s.

Chayer (Christophe). Les doux et paisibles délassemens de l'amour. [*anon.*] viii, 117 pp. 16°. *Au temple de Vénus*, 1770.

Checkley (*Rev.* John). Speech upon his tryal at Boston, for publishing [Charles Leslie's] short and easy method with the deists. 40 pp. 8°. *London, J. Wilford*, 1730.
[*With* LESLIE (*Rev.* C.) Short method with the deists. *London*, 1723.]

Cheever (George Barrell, *D. D.*) The elements of national greatness, an address before the New England society of the city of New York, Dec. 22, 1842. 40 pp. 8°. *New York, J. S. Taylor & Co.* 1843.

Cheever (*Rev.* Henry T.) Autobiography and memorials of Captain Obadiah Congar. 18°. *New York*, 1851. s.

——— Island world of the Pacific; being travel through the Sandwich Islands and other parts of Polynesia. 406 pp. 12°. *New York, Harpers*, 1851. s.

Chénier (Louis Chauveur de). Present state of the empire of Morocco; history of the dynasties since Edris, etc. 2 v. vi, 377 pp; 427 pp. 1 map. 8°. *London, G. G. J. & J. Robinson*, 1788.

Chénier (Marie André de). Poésies. Précédées d'une notice par H. de Latouche, suivies de notes et jugements extraits des ouvrages de Chateaubriand, etc. Nouv. éd. xlv, 312 pp. 1 portrait. 16°. *Paris, Charpentier*, 1841.

Chenevix (Richard). Phrenology article of Foreign quarterly review. With notes by J. G. Spurzheim. 4, 112 pp. 12°. *Boston, Marsh, Capen & Lyon*, 1833.
[*With* SPURZHEIM (J. G.) Examination of objections, etc. 1833.]

Chenu (Jean Charles), **Des Murs** (Parfait O.) *and* **Verreaux** (Jules). Leçons élémentaires sur l'histoire naturelle des oiseaux. 2 v. 3 p. l. 384 pp; 380 pp. 12°. *Paris, V. Masson et fils*, 1862. s.

Cherokee hymns. Compiled from several authors. Tsalagi dikanogisdi hilosgi iyanidv tsunowelanvhi. 69 pp. 24°. *Park Hill*, 1844.
[*With* BIBLE, *Cherokee*. Gospel according to Matthew. *Park Hill*, 1844.]

Cherokee messenger. Tsalagi atsinvsidv. 12 nos. August, 1844, to May, 1846. [Edited by Evan Jones.] 192 pp. 8°. *Cherokee, Bapt. miss. press*, 1844–46.

Chéruel (A.) Dictionnaire historique des institutions, moeurs, et coutumes de la France. 2e éd. 2 v. lxxvi, 1271 pp. 12°. *Paris, Hachette*, 1865.

——— Mémoires sur la vie publique et privée de [Nicolas] Fouquet, surintendant de finances, d'après ses lettres et des pièces inédite, 2 v. 2 p. l. xv, 519 pp.; 2 p. l, 563 pp. 16°. *Paris, Charpentier*, 1862.

Chesebrough (*Rev.* A. S.) Home work; or, parochial christianization. 235 pp. 16°. *Boston, Am. Tract Soc.* [1867.]

Chesterfield (*4th earl of*). *See* **Stanhope** (Philip Dormer).

Chetwood (William Rufus). The voyages and adventures of Captain Robert Boyle, in several parts of the world. [*anon.*] With the adventures of Richard Castelman, gent. and a description of the city of Philadelphia, and the country of Pennsylvania. [*anon.*] 3 p. l. 317 pp. 16°. *Wolverhampton, Geo. Wilson*, 1744.

——— The voyages, travels, and adventures of William Owen Gwin Vaughan, with the history of his brother, Jonathan Vaughan. 2d ed. 2 v. vi, 282 pp; 276 pp. 3 pl. 12°. *London, T. Lownds*, 1760.

Chevalier (C. *l'abbé*) *and* **Charlot** (G.) Études sur la Touraine; hydrographie, géologie, agronomie, statistique. iv, 391 pp. 3 pl. 1 map. 8°. *Tours, Guilland-Verger*, 1858. s.

Chevalier (E.) *See* **Darondeau** (B.) *and* **Chevalier.**

Chevalier (Michel). Essais de politique industrielle: Souvenirs de voyage, France, République d'Andorre, Belgique, Allemagne. 451 pp. 8°. *Paris, C. Gosselin*, 1843. s.

Chevalier (Charles). *See* **Fau** (J.) *and* **Chevalier,** Nouveau manuel complet du physicien-préparateur.

Chevé (Émile). Le dernier mot de la science officiale. Examen des leçons de lecture musicale de M. F. Halévy. 160 pp. 8°. *Paris, auteur*, 1857. s.

Chevreau (Urbain). Histoire du monde. 2 v. in 1. 6 p. l. 702, 84 pp.; 628, 92 pp. 4°. *Paris, Martin & Boudot*, 1686.

Chevreul (Michel Eugène). De la loi du contraste simultané des couleurs, et de l'assortiment des objets coloriés, etc. xv, 735 pp. 2 tab. 8°. *Paris, Pitois, Levrault & Cie*, 1839. s.

Chevrolat (Auguste). Coléoptères du Mexique. vii pp. 207 l. unp. 12°. *Strasbourg, G. Silberman*, 1833–35. s.

Cheyne (Andrew). Description of islands in the western Pacific ocean, north and south of the equator, with sailing directions, vocabularies of their languages, etc. vii, 198 pp. 8°. *London, J. D Potter*, 1852. s.

Cheyne (George). Philosophical principles of religion, natural and revealed. 4th ed. 2 pts. in 1 v. 15 p. l. 353 pp; 12 p. l. 189 pp. 12°. *London, G. Strahan*, 1733–34.

Chiaie (Stefano delle). Compendio di elmintografia umana. xiv, 180 pp. 6 pl. 8°. *Napoli, Fibreno*, 1833. [Imperfect.] s.

Chicago. Hall & Smith's Chicago city directory for 1853–54. 2d annual ed. xii, 254 pp. 12°. *Chicago, R. Fergus*, 1853. s.

Chicago illustrated. (Issued in parts.) Parts 1–13. obl. 4°. *Chicago, Jevne & Almini*, 1866–67.

Chicago young men's association. Catalogue of the library. 8°. *Chicago, (Ill.)* 1856. s.

Child (A. B. *M. D.*) Christ and the people. 203 pp. 16°. *Boston, W. White & Co.* 1866.

Child (David Lee). Review of a report to the house of representatives of the commonwealth of Massachusetts, on the case of William Vans. With observations upon the dispensing power of the legislature, and upon a decision of the supreme judicial court, nullifying the said power. 97, 11 pp. 8°. *Boston*, 1833.

Child (G. Chaplin, *M. D.*) The great architect: Benedicite; illustrations of the power, wisdom and goodness of God, as manifested in his works. 2 v. in 1. 376 pp. 12°. *New York*, 1867.

Child (John). New England's Jonas cast up at London. 22 pp. sm. 4°. *London*, 1647.

Child (*Mrs.* Lydia Maria). Autumnal leaves: tales and sketches in prose and rhyme. 365 pp. 16°. *New York, Francis & Co.* 1857.

Child (*Mrs.* Lydia Maria). Looking toward sunset. From sources new and old, original and selected. ix, 455 pp. 12°. *Boston, Ticknor & Fields,* 1865.

——— A romance of the republic. 442 pp. 12°. *Boston, Ticknor & Fields,* 1867.

Childs (C. G. *engraver*). Views in Philadelphia and its environs. 38 p. l. unp. 25 pl. sm. fol. *Philadelphia, C. G. Childs,* 1827–30.

Chili. Curso de lectura por el método de enseñanza mútua: mandado imprimir por el supremo gobierno de Chile. 256 pp. 8°. *Santiago, Imprenta del estado,* 1841. s.

——— Estadistico comercial correspondiente al año de 1844. 4°. *Santiago,* 1845. s.

——— Estadistico comercial correspondiente al segundo trimestre del año 1850. 4°. *Valparaiso,* 1850. s.

Chipman (Samuel). Report of an examination of poor-houses, jails, etc. in the state of New York, and in the counties of Berkshire, Mass. Litchfield, Conn. and Bennington, Vt. etc. 69 pp. 12°. *Albany, N. Y. S. temp. soc.* 1834.

Chladni (Ernst Florens Friedrich). Die akustik. Neue ausg. xxvi, 242 pp. 12 pl. 4°. *Leipzig, Breitkopf & Härtel,* 1830. s.
[Imperfect: wanting pl. 2, 9, 10, 12].

Choiseul-Stainville (Claude Antoine Gabriel de). Histoire du procès des naufragés de Calais. Extraits de ses mémoires inédits. (**Mémoires** des contemporains. 4e livraison. 8°. *Paris,* 1824).

Chomel (Auguste François). Elements of general pathology. Translated from the French by F. E. Oliver and W. W. Morland. 3d ed. xix, 458 pp. 8°. *Boston, Ticknor & Co.* 1848. s.

Choulant (*Dr.* Ludwig). Die vorwelt der organischen wesen auf der erde. 1 p. l. 90 pp. 16°. *Dresden, P. G. Kilscher,* 1830. s.
[*With* HOLL (F.) Handbuch der petrefactenkunde.]

Christ (Johann Friedrich). Mvsei richteriani dactyliotheca gemmas scalptas opere antiqvo plerasque complexa. 9 p. l. unp. 34 pp. 1 pl. fol. *Lipsiæ, B. C. Breitkopf,* 1743.
[*With* HEBENSTREIT (J. E.) Musevm richterianum.]

Christian (The) examiner. Jan. to Nov. 1867. v. 82–83. New [6th] series, v. 3–4. 8°. *New York, J. Miller,* 1867.

Christian (The) history, containing accounts of the revival and propagation of religion in Great Britain and America, for the year 1743[–4. Edited by Thomas Prince, jr.] vi, 416 pp. 8°. *Boston, T. Prince, jr.* 1744.

Christie (Robert). A brief review of the political state of Lower Canada, with memoirs of the administrations of the colonial government of Lower Canada, by Sir Gordon Drummond, and Sir John Coape Sherbrooke. 92 pp. 8°. *New York, W. A. Mercein,* 1818.

Christison (Robert). A dispensatory, or commentary on the pharmacopœias of Great Britain (and the United States). Revised by R. E. Griffith. 2d ed. 1008 pp. 8°. *Philadelphia, Lea & Blanchard,* 1848. s.

Christy (David). Letters on geology, originally addressed to Dr. John Locke, giving an outline of the geology of the west and southwest, with an essay on the erratic rocks of North America. 68 pp. 2 l. 11 pp. 6 pl. 8°. *Rossville, (Ohio,) J. M. Christy,* 1848.

Chronica de Mailros. [*anon.*] fol. *Oxoniæ,* 1684.
[GALE (Thomas), and FELL (John). Rerum anglicarum scriptores veteres. *Oxoniæ,* 1684–91. v. 1.]

Chronicles (The) of the kings of England, from William the conqueror to 1795, in imitation of the holy writings. By Nathan Ben Saddi. [*pseudon?*] 196 pp. 18°. *Worcester, Isaiah Thomas,* 1795.

Chronicles (The) of Cooperstown. [*anon.*] 100 pp. 12°. *Cooperstown, H. & E. Phinney,* 1838.

Chronicles of the great rebellion against the United States of America; a concise [chronological] record and digest of events, April 23, 1860—Oct. 31, 1865. 136 pp. 8°. *Philadelphia, A. Winch,* 1867.

Chronicum Scotorum. A chronicle of Irish affairs from the earliest times to A. D. 1135; with a supplement containing the events from 1141 to 1150. Edited, with a translation, by Wm. M. Hennessy. lvii, 419 pp. 1 fac sim. 8°. *London, Longmans,* 1866.
[Chronicles of Great Britain in the middle ages.]

Chronological account of remarkable occurrences from the commencement of the French revolution to Dec. 1815. Extracted from the Belfast News letter. xi, 324 pp. 12°. *Belfast, Mackay,* 1816.

Chronologist (The) of the present war; a faithful series of the events which have occurred in Europe, etc. from the commencement of the French revolution, to the end of the year 1796. 2d ed. xi, 348 pp. 16°. *London, G. C. & J. Robinson,* 1797.

——— The same. Continued to 1798. 144 pp. 16°. *London, Robinson,* 1799.

Chrysostomus (Johannes, *St.*) In Job de paciencia sermones. 21 l. unp. fol. [*Eslingæ, Conrad Fyner? about* 1473.]

Chrysostomus (Johannes *St.*) Sermones de paciencia beati Job. fol. *Esslingæ, Conrad Fyner*, n. d.

[*With* Aquino (*Saint* Thomas d'), Postilla in Job. 1474.]

——— Traductio librorum super Matheum e Greca in Latinum edita a Georgio Trapezoncio. fol. [*Argentorati, Joh. Mentelin.* n. d.] s.

Church (A) of Christ vindicated. [*anon.* Result of the council at Eastham.] 56 pp. 18°. *Boston*, 1721.

[Imperfect: title wanting.]

Church (Benjamin). The entertaining history of king Philip's war; also of expeditions more lately made against the common enemy, and Indian rebels, with some account of Col. Benjamin Church. 2d ed. iv. 198 pp. 1 pl. 12°. *Newport (R. I.) S. Southwick*, 1772.

——— The same. History of king Philips' war, part 1; with introduction and notes by Henry M. Dexter. sm. 4°. *Boston, J. K. Wiggin*, 1865.

[Library of New England history, No. 2.]

——— [History of king Philip's war, part 2.] The history of the eastern expeditions of 1689–1704, against the Indians and French. With introduction and notes by H. M. Dexter. xxxii, 203 pp. 1 map. sm. 4°. *Boston, J. K. Wiggin & Lunt*, 1867.

[Library of New England history, No. 3.]

Church (*Mrs.* Ross, *born* Florence Marryat). Forever and ever: a drama of life. 3 v. 12°. *London, R. Bentley*, 1866.

Churchill (Fleetwood). On the diseases of pregnancy and childbed, with notes by D. F. Condie. 663 pp. 8°. *Philadelphia, Blanchard & Lea*, 1852. s.

——— On the theory and practice of midwifery. With notes, etc. by D. Francis Condie. New Am. from last Dublin ed. 510 pp. 8°. *Philadelphia, Blanchard & Lea*, 1851. s.

Churchman (John). An account of [his] gospel labors and christian experiences, [with] a short memorial of Joseph White. vii, 351 pp. 8°. *London, J. Phillips*, 1781.

Ciampi, (Sebastiano). Bibliografia critica delle antiche reciproche corrispondenze politiche, ecclesiastiche, scientifiche, letterarie, artistiche dell' Italia colla Russia, colla Polonia, ed altre parte settentrionali. 3 v. 8°. *Firenze, L. Allegrini & Co.* 1834–43.

Cicero (Marcus Tullius). Opera omnia ex recensione Io. Avgvsti Ernesti. [ed. 3ª.] 5 v. (in 8.) 8°. *Halis Saxonvm, orphanotropheum*, 1774–76. s.

——— Orationes quædam selectæ, cum interpretatione et notis quas in usum serenissimi Delphini edidit P. Carolus Merouille. xxviii, 433 pp. 8°. *Philadelphiæ, Desilver, Thomas & Co.* 1836. s.

——— Select orations, translated into English; with the original Latin. By William Duncan. New ed. 3 p. l. 671 pp. 8°. *New York, E. Duyckinck*, 1811.

——— Orator, Brutus, topica de optimo genere oratorum, cum annotationibus Caroli Beieri. Denuo recensuit Io. Casp. Orellius. Præmittitur epistola critica, etc. cxxii, 469 pp. 8°. *Turici, Orelli, Fuesslin & socii*, 1830. s.

——— Brutus; or, history of famous orators: also, his orator. Translated by E. Jones. vi, 412 pp. 8°. *London, B. White*, 1776.

——— Cato major, or discourses on old age, [translated by James Logan.] With notes by Benjamin Franklin. 2 p. l. 163 pp. 8°. *London, Fielding & Walker*, 1778.

——— Cato and Lælius; or, essays on old age and friendship. With remarks by William Melmoth. New ed. 2 v. 4 p. l. 318 pp; 3 p. l. 343 pp. 8°. *London, J. Dodsley*, 1785.

——— Two last pleadings against Verres; translated, and illustrated with notes, by C. Kelsall. With remarks on the state of modern Sicily. xi, 368 pp. 4 pl. 8°. *London, White, Cochrane & Co.* 1812.

——— I frammenti de' sei libri della republica. Volgarizzati dal principe Pietro Odescalchi. xxiii, 194 pp. 1 pl. 8°. *Roma, Salviucci*, 1826. s.

——— Livres académiques; traduits et éclaircis par M. de Castillon. 2 v. in 1. 8 p. l. 311 pp; lxii, 288 pp. 22 l. 8°. *Berlin, C. J. Decker*, 1779. s.

CONTENTS.

v. 1. Discours préliminaire: 1. Histoire des académiques de Cicéron. 2. Ébauche d'une partie de la philosophie ancienne. 3. Traduction d'une partie du livre vii de Sextus Empiricus contre les mathématiciens et contre les logiciens. Les académiques, ou des moyens de juger du vrai, par Pierre Valence. v. 2. Lettres de Cicéron, avec des notes, etc.

——— Locvtioni dell' epistole scielte da Aldo Manutio, vtilissime al comporre nell'una, e l'altra lingua. 24 p. l. 367 pp. 32 l. 18°. *Venetia*, 1575.

Cicognara (Leopoldo, *conte*). Memorie spettanti alla storia della calcographia. 262 pp. 8°. Atlas, 18 pl. fol. *Prato, Giachetti*, 1831. s.

——— Storia della scultura dal suo risorgimento in Italia fino al secolo di Canova. Ed. 2ª. 7 v. 8°. Atlas, fol. *Prato, Giachetti*, 1824. s.

Cieza de Leon (Pedro de). Chronica del gran regno del Perv. Parte prima. Tradotta nella italiana per Agostino di Cravaliz. 11 p. l. 219 pp. 16°. *Venetia, Francesco Lorenzini,* 1560.

——— Seventeen years' travels through Peru, Cartagena, and Popayan. 4 p. l. 244 pp. 6 l. 1 map, 1 pl. sm. 4°. *London,* 1709.
[Stevens (John). Voyages and travels. Imperfect; wanting pp. 118–121.]

Cincinnati. Ohio school library. Catalogue of books and papers in the library and reading room. viii, 114 pp. 8°. *Cincinnati, C. F. Bradley & Co.* 1856. s.

——— Williams' directory, June, 1867. 8°. *Cincinnati,* 1867.

Cincinnati commercial (daily), Jan. 1861, to June, 1867. 13 v. fol. *Cincinnati,* 1861–67.

Cincinnati mercantile library association. Catalogue of the young men's mercantile library. 260 pp. 8°. *Cincinnati, M. L. association,* 1846. s.

Cist (Charles). Cincinnati miscellany, from Oct. 1, 1844, to April 1, 1846. 2 v. 272 pp; 364, iv pp. 8°. *Cincinnati, Caleb Clark,* 1845–46.

Cités et ruines américaines, Mitla, Palenqué, Izamal, Chichen-itza, Uxmal, recueillies et photographiées par Désiré Charnay. Avec un texte par M. Viollet-Le-Duc; suivi du voyage et des documents de l'auteur. Texte, 543 pp. 8°. Atlas, 49 planches photog. fol. *Paris, Morel,* 1863.

Civil (The) engineer and architect's journal, 1866. v. 29. 4°. *London, W. Kent & Co.* [1866].

Civilization, or the Indian chief and British pastor. [*anon.*] 335, 301, 259 pp. 12°. *London, T. Egerton,* 1818.

Clapp (A. *M. D.*) A synopsis, or systematic catalogue of the medicinal plants of the United States. (Extract.) 222 pp. 8°. *Philadelphia Am. medical assoc.* 1852. s.

Clapp (*Rev.* Thomas). A letter to the Rev. Mr. Edwards, of North-Hampton, expostulating with him for his injurious reflections in his late letter to a friend. 11 pp. sm. 4°. *Boston, T. Fleet,* 1745.

Clarendon (Edward Hyde, 1st *earl* of). *See* **Hyde.**

Clark (Alexander, *A.M.*) School-day dialogues. 352 pp. 12°. *Philadelphia, J. W. Daughaday & Co.* 1867.

Clark (Christopher). A shock to shakerism; or, a serious refutation of the idolatrous divinity of Ann Lee. 12°. *Richmond,* (*Va.*) 1812.

Clark (George Edward). Seven years of a sailor's life. By Yankee Ned. 358 pp. 9 pl. 12°. *Boston, Adams & Co.* [1867].

Clark (John, *F. S. A.*) A letter to the right hon. Charles Jenkinson on the late mutinies in the highland regiments. By the translator of the Caledonian bards. [*anon.*] 31 pp. 8°. *Edinburgh, C. Elliot,* 1780.

Clark (*Rev.* Jonas). The fate of bloodthirsty oppressors, and God's tender care of his distressed people. Sermon preached at Lexington, Apr. 19, 1776, to commemorate the commencement of hostilities between Great Britain and America, in that town. 39 pp. 8°. *Boston, Powars & Willis,* 1776.

Clark (Rufus W. *D. D.*) Heroes of Albany. A memorial of the patriot-martyrs of the city and county of Albany, 1861–65. With brief histories of the Albany regiments. 870 pp. 9 pl. 8°. *Albany, S. R. Gray,* 1866.

Clark (W.) Concise history of England, to queen Victoria. Edited, with additions, by J. C. Moffat. Revised ed. 12°. *Cincinnati, Moore & Anderson,* 1853. s.

Clark (William). A history of the British marine testaceous mollusca. lx, 536 pp. 8°. *London, J. Van Voorst,* 1855. s.

Clarke (*Rev.* Edward). Letters concerning the Spanish nation, written at Madrid, 1760–61. 4 p. l. xlix, 354 pp. 4°. *London, Becket & De Hondt,* 1763.

Clarke (James). Catechism of the rudiments of music for teachers of the piano-forte. 93 pp. 24°. *Boston, O. Ditson & Co.* [1867].

Clarke (*Rev.* James Freeman). The christian doctrine of forgiveness of sin; an essay. 2d ed. 166 pp. 16°. *Boston, Am. Unit. assoc.* 1867.

——— The christian doctrine of prayer; an essay. 6th ed. xviii, 313 pp. 16°. *Boston, Am. Unit. assoc.* 1867.

——— Orthodoxy; its truths and errors. xi, 512 pp. 12°. *Boston, Amer. Unit. assoc.* 1866.

Clarke (John, *of Philadelphia*). A treatise on the mulberry tree and silkworm, and on the production and manufacture of silk. 363 pp. 12°. *Philadelphia, Thomas, Cowperthwait & Co.* 1839.

Clarke (*Rev.* Richard). Jesus the Nazarene, addressed to Jews, deists, and believers. xvi, 610 pp. 8°. *London, R. Clarke,* [1795?]

——— A series of letters, essays, dissertations, and discourses, on various subjects. v. 1. v, 358 pp. 8°. *London, Raithby,* [1795.]
[No more published.]

Clarke (*Rev.* Samuel, *the father*). The marrow of ecclesiastical history, in two parts: the first, containing the life of Christ, of the fathers, school men, first reformers, and modern divines; the second, the lives of christian emperors, kings, and sovereign princes, [with] the lives of inferiour christians. 3d ed. 11 p. l. 504 pp; 4 l. 116, 104 pp. 1 pl. fol. *London, W. Birch,* 1675.

——— Lives and deaths of most of those eminent persons who, by their virtue and valor, obtained the sirnames of magni, or the great. 2d ed. 303 pp. 1 pl. fol. *London, W. Birch,* 1675. [*With* the preceding].

Clarke (Samuel, *D. D. the son*). Reply to Dr. Waterland's defense of his queries, [relating to Dr. Clarke's scheme of the Holy Trinity.] By a clergyman in the country [*anon.*] xvi, 534 pp. 12°. *London, J. Knapton,* 1722.

Clarke (*Rev.* W. B.) Researches in the southern gold fields of New South Wales. ix, 305 pp. 1 col. map. 8°. *Sydney, Reading & Wellbank,* 1860. s.

Clarkson (*Rev.* Thomas). An essay on the impolicy of the African slave trade. 2 parts in 1 v. 2 p. l. 79, 134 pp. 8°. *Philadelphia, F. Bailey,* 1788.

——— The history of the rise, progress, and accomplishment of the abolition of the African slave trade, by the British parliament. Abridged by Evan Lewis. 348 pp. 16°. *Wilmington, (Del.) R. Porter,* 1816.

Classified mercantile directory for the cities of New York and Brooklyn. 124 pp. 1 map. 18°. *New York, J. Disturnell,* 1837. [*With* **New York** as it is, in 1837.]

Clater (Francis). Every man his own farrier; with a treatise on diseases of dogs, by Francis Clater and son. 24th ed. xii, 411 pp. 8°. *London, Baldwin, Cradock and Joy,* 1823.

Claudianus (Claudius). Opus de raptu Proserpinæ, commentariis, et italica versione versibus tradita, illustratum a N. Biffio. Ed. 2ª. 4 p. l. 648 pp. fol. *Lucæ, A. Baldelli,* 1751.

——— Translations from Claudian, by Rev. Henry Howard. 251 pp. 12°. *London, John Murray,* 1823.

Clausius (R.) Abhandlungen über die mechanische wärmetheorie. 2 v. xviii, 361 pp; xii, 351 pp. 8°. *Braunschweig, Vieweg,* 1864--67. s.

Clausson (Niels Christian). Undersögelse, om Amerikas opdagelse har mere skadet eller gavnet det menneskelige kjön. 160 pp. 12°. *Kiöbenhavn, L. C. Simmelkicer,* 1785.

Clavers (*Mrs.* Mary, *pseudon*). *See* **Kirkland** (*Mrs.* Caroline M. Stansbury).

Clavière (Étienne) *and* **Brissot de Warville** (Jean Pierre). De la France et des États Unis; ou de l'importance de la révolution de l'Amérique pour le bonheur de la France. Nouv. éd. xxiii, 448 pp. 12°. [n. p. *about* 1787].

Clavigero (Francisco Saverio). The history of Mexico, collected from Spanish and Mexican historians, from manuscripts, and ancient paintings of the Indians. Translated by Charles Cullen. 2 v. xxxii pp. 2 l. 476 pp; 2 p. l. 463 pp. 1 map. 26 pl. 4°. *London, G. G. J. & J. Robinson,* 1787.

Clayton (Robert, *bishop of Clogher*). The chronology of the Hebrew bible vindicated. 3 p. l. 493 pp. 2 maps. 4°. *London, J. Brindley,* 1747.

Clebsch (A.) Theorie der elasticität fester körper. xi, 424 pp. 8°. *Leipzig, B. G. Teubner,* 1862. s.

Cleland (John). Specimen of an etimological vocabulary; or, essay by means of the analitic method to reileve the ancient Celtiç; with additions. [*anon.*] xvi, 231, xvii, 46 pp. 12°. *London, L. Davis,* 1748--49.

Clemens (F. A.) Grundriss der naturlehre, etc. 2 v. vi, 110 pp. 2 pl; vii, 183 pp. 4 pl. 8°. *Königsberg, Vornträger,* 1839. s.

Clemens (Samuel). The celebrated jumping frog of Calaveras county, and other sketches. By Mark Twain. [*pseudon*]. Edited by John Paul. 198 pp. 16°. *New York, C. H. Webb,* 1867.

Clement XIV, *pope, or* Ganganelli (Giovanni Vincenzo Antonio). Lettere. Nuova ed. da Romualdo. 2 v. x, 360 pp; viii, 304 pp. 1 pl. 16°. *Londra, G. F. Dove,* 1829.
Note.—By Luigi Antonio Caraccioli.

Clene maydenhod. (From a ms. written about A. D. 1370.) A supplement to "Hali meidenhed." 7 pp. 8°. *London, N. Trübner & Co.* 1867. [Early English text society, No. 25.]

Clergyman's (The) companion in visiting the sick. [*anon.*] 9th ed. 6 p. l. 228 pp. 12°. *London, Wilde and others,* 1764.

Clerical guide (The), or ecclesiastical directory, containing a complete register of the present prelates and other dignitaries of the church of England. 2d ed. xxxix, 299 pp. 8°. *London, F. C. & J. Rivington,* 1822.

Clermont (Thomas, *Lord*). A guide to the quadrupeds and reptiles of Europe. viii, 277 pp. 12°. *London, J. Van Voorst,* 1859. s.

Cleveland city directory, 1857-58. 343 pp. 1 map. 8°. *New York, W. H. Boyd*, 1857. [Imperfect; title wanting.]

Cleveland (Charles Dexter). English literature of the nineteenth century. 2d ed. 798 pp. 12°. *Philadelphia, J. A. Bancroft & Co.* 1867.

Cleveland (Henry). Alexander H. Stephens in public and private; with his letters and speeches before, during, and since the war. 838 pp. 4 pl. 4 fac. sim. 8°. *Philadelphia, National pub. co.* [1866].

Clifford (Jeronimy). The case and replication of [his] legal representatives, to the information of the directors of the society of Surinam. 478 pp. 8°. *London, C. Say*, 1763.

Climbers (The). [A tale. *anon.*] 263 pp. 5 pl. sq. 16°. *New York, Am. tract soc.* [1866].

Clinton (De Witt). An introductory discourse before the literary and philosophical society of New York. [With copious notes.] 160 pp. 4°. *New York*, 1815.

Clive (I. H.) Mavor abbreviated by the application of a new principle to his system of stenography. Illustrated by fifteen copper plates. 3d ed. 96 pp. 12°. *London, Baldwin, Cradock & Joy*, 1821.

Cloppenburg (Jan Everhardts). Le miroir de la cruell et horrible tyrannie espagnole perpetrée au Pays Bas par le duc de Albe et aultres. 4 p. l. unp. 87 l. sm. 4°. *Amsterdam, Jan E. Cloppenburg*, 1620.

Clotilde de Vallon Chalys (Marguerite Éléonore, *madame* de Surville). [*pseudon.*] *See* **Surville** (Joseph Étienne, *marquis de*).

Clulow (William Benton). Aphorisms and reflections; a miscellany of thought and opinion. 522 pp. 12°. *London, J. Murray*, 1843.

Clusa (Jacobus de), *or*, Jacob de Junterbuk. Tractatus peroptimus de animabus exutis a corporibus. 26 l. unp. sm. 4°. [*Esslingæ, Conrad Fyner? about* 1475].

Coates (George). Herd book; containing the pedigrees of improved short-horned cattle. 16 v. 8°. *London and Doncaster*, 1843-65.

CONTENTS.

v. 1—3 in 1, cows.
v. 1—4 in 2, bulls.
v. 5 in 2, cows.
v 6—16. Continued by H. Strafford.

Cobb (J. H.) A manual containing information respecting the growth of the mulberry tree, with suitable directions for the culture of silk. 4th ed. 162 pp. 3 pl. 16°. *Boston, Weeks, Jordan & Co.* 1839.

Cobb (Sylvanus, *D. D.*) Autobiography of the first forty-one years of [his] life. [With] a memoir of his son, S. Cobb, jr. 552 pp. 1 pl. 12°. *Boston, Univ. pub. house*, 1867.

Cobbett (James Paul). A grammar of the Italian language. xvi, 392 pp. 12°. *London, author*, 1830. s.

Cobbett (*Rev.* Thomas). A practical discourse of prayer. 7 p. l. unp. 551 pp. 18°. *London, Joseph Cranford*, 1654.

Cobbett (William). The bloody buoy, thrown out as a warning to the political pilots of America; [being] acts of the French revolution. 3d ed. [*anon.*] x, 217 pp. 1 pl. 12°. *Philadelphia, P. M. Davis*, 1823.

Cobbold (Thomas Spencer). Entozoa; an introduction to the study of helminthology, with reference more particularly to the internal parasites of man. xxvi, 480 pp. 21 col. pl. 8°. *London, Groombridge*, 1864.

——— On the present state of our knowledge respecting [human] entozoa. [Extract]. 9 pp. 8°. *London, B. Clowes*, 1865. s.

Coccius (Adolf). Ueber die ernährungsweise der hornhaut und die serum führenden gefässe im menschlichen körper. viii, 177 pp. 1 pl. 8°. *Leipzig, J. Müller*, 1852. s.

Cochin (Charles Nicolas). Antiquities of Herculaneum. *See* **Bellicard** (Jérôme Charles).

Cochois (*M'lle.*) Isabella Mendosa; and, Count de Romancourt. Two novels. *See* **Argens** (J. B. de Boyer, *marquis* d') and **Cochois**.

Cochrane (Archibald, *9th earl of Dundonald*). Account of the qualities and uses of coal tar and coal varnish, with certificates from shipmasters and others. [*anon.*] 43 pp. 12°. *London, T. & G. Wilkie*, 1785.

Cochrane (Richard, *and* John). A comprehensive system of practical geometry, with observations on drawing, etc. 265 pp. 1 pl. 8°. *Baltimore, R. Cochrane*, 1857. s.

Cockeram (Henry). English dictionarie; or, an interpreter of hard English words. 10th ed. 114 l. unp. 24°. *London, W. Bentley*, 1651.

Cockings (George). The American war; a poem. [*anon.*] 2 p. l. 181 pp. 1 pl. 8°. *London, W. Richardson*, 1781.

——— The same. The war; an heroic poem. xvi, 190 pp. 12°. *London*, 1762. [Imperfect.]

Cocteau (J. Théodore). Études sur les scincoïdes. [1re liv.] 3 p. l. 33 pp. 4 pl. 4°. *Paris, auteur*, 1836. s.
[No more published].

Codex sinaiticus. *See* **Bible**, *Greek*. Bibliorum codex, etc. 4 v. 4°.

Codman (John). Ten months in Brazil; with incidents of voyages and travels, etc. 208 pp. 6 pl. 12°. *Boston, Lee & Shepard*, 1867.

Coetlogon (Dennis de). *See* **De Coetlogon.**

Coffey (W. A.) Inside out; or, an interior view of the New York state prison. By one who knows. [*anon.*] 251 pp. 12°. *New York, printed for the author*, 1823.

Coffin (Alexander, *jr.*) The death of general Montgomery, or the storming of Quebec. 69 pp. 18°. *New York*, 1814.

Coggeshall (George). Voyages to various parts of the world, 1799--1844. 8°. *New York, Appletons*, 1851.

——— The same. 2d series, 1802--1841. 335 pp. Portrait. 8°. *New York, Appletons*, 1852. s.

Coggeshall (William T.) The signs of the times; a history of the spirit-rappings in Cincinnati and other places. 144 pp. 16°. *Cincinnati, Bagley and Freeman*, 1851.

Cohen (Félix). Étude sur les impots et sur les budgets des principaux états de l'Europe. xiii, 650 pp. 8°. *Paris, Guillaumin et Cie.* [1865].

Cohen (J. Solis, *M. D.*) Inhalation; its therapeutics and practice. A treatise on the inhalation of gases, [etc. with] description of the apparatus employed, [etc.] Illustrated. 305 pp. 8°. *Philadelphia, Lindsay & Blakiston*, 1867.

Cohn (Albert). Shakespeare in Germany in the sixteenth and seventeenth centuries: account of English actors in Germany and the Netherlands, and of the plays performed by them during the same period. With two plates of facsimiles. 5 p. l. cxxxvii, 422 pp. 4°. *London, Asher & Co.* 1865.

Coicy (*M'de* de). Les femmes comme il convient de les voir, ou apperçu de ce que les femmes ont été, etc. [*anon.*] 2 v. in 1. 146, 113 pp. 18°. *Paris, Bacot*, 1785.

Coin (The) act, by way of dialogue [on genuine religion]. By J. C. [*anon.*] 24 pp. 12°. *London, Vallance & Simmons*, 1775.

Colburn (Dana P.) The first book of arithmetic. 16°. *Philadelphia, B. Cowperthwait & Co.* 1856. s.

Colburn (Warren). An introduction to algebra. 276 pp. 8°. *Boston, Hilliard, Gray, Little, and Wilkins*, 1828.

Colburn's new monthly magazine. *See* "**New** monthly magazine."

Colburn's united service magazine, and naval and military journal, Sept. 1866, to Aug. 1867. 3 v. 8°. *London, Hurst & Blackett*, [1866–67].

Colby (Albert). Life of Christ and his apostles, from the writings of Dr. Adam Clarke, Rev. R. W. Clark, etc. 355 pp. 12°. *Baltimore, A. Colby*, 1867.

——— True christian religion. 52 pp. 12°. *Baltimore, A. Colby*, 1867.
[*With* the preceding].

Colby (*Rev.* John). Life, experience, and travels, written by himself. 12°. 2 v. in 1. 248, 64 pp. 1 pl. *Lowell, N. Thurston & A. Watson*, 1838.

Colden (Cadwallader). The history of the five Indian nations of Canada, which are dependent on the province of New York in America. 3d ed. 2 v. xii. pp. 2 l. 260 pp; 2 p. l. 251 pp. 1 map. 16°. *London, L. Davis*, 1755.

——— The same. Reprinted exactly from Bradford's New York edition, [1727]. With an introduction and notes by John G. Shea. xl, xviii, 141 pp. portrait. 8°. *New York, T. H. Morrell*, 1866.

Cole (John). The American war, an ode. 123 pp. 8°. [*Hull, Eng.*, 1779?]

——— Miscellany of poems, odes, and songs. 112, vi. pp. 8°. *Hull, Eng.*, 1791.
[*With* the preceding].

Cole (Miriam). A rosary for lent; or devotional readings, original and compiled. [*anon.*] 360 pp. 12°. *New York, G. W. Carleton & Co.* 1867.

Colebrooke (Henry Thomas). Grammar of the Sanscrit language. v. 1. xxii, 368 pp, 2 l. fol. *Calcutta*, 1805.

Coleman (Seth, *M. D.*) Memoirs, journal, and letters, with a sermon at his funeral by Rev. Nathan Perkins. 288 pp. 16°. *New Haven, Flagg & Gray*, 1817.

Colenso (John William, *bishop of Natal*). Natal sermons: a series of discourses. viii, 373 pp. 12°. *London, Trübner & Co.*, 1866.

Coleridge (Hartley). Essays and marginalia. Edited by his brother, Derwent. 2 v. xii, 376; iv, 359 pp. portrait. 16°. *London, Ed. Moxon*, 1851.

Coleridge (Samuel Taylor). Biographia literaria; or, my literary life and opinions. 2 v. in 1. 183 pp; 196 pp. 8°. *New York, Kirk & Mercein*, 1817.

——— Rime of the ancient mariner. Illustrated. 51 pp. 8°. *London, Sampson Low & Co*, 1857.

Coles (Elisha.) An English dictionary. 184 l. unp. 16°. *London, R. and J. Bonwicke and others*, 1724.
[Imperfect; leaf 184 wanting.]

——— The same. Newly corrected and improved. 184 l. unp. 18°. *London, J. Walthoe and others*, 1732.

Coles (Elisha). Dictionary, English-Latin, Latin-English. 18th ed. 8°. 2 p. l. 650 l. unp. *London, J. Bonwicke and others,* 1772.
[Imperfect, leaves wanting at the end.]

Coley (Henry). Clavis astrologiæ elimata; or, a key to the whole art of astrology, new filed and polished. 62 p. l, 759 pp. 12°. [*London,* 1676?]
[Title wanting.]

Collaert (Adriaan). Vita B. virginis Teresiæ. [25 estampes.] oblong fol. *Antverpiæ, apud A. Collardum & C. Galleum,* 1613. S.
[*With* GALLAEUS (Philippe). Acta. etc.

Colleçao de opusculos reimpressos relativos á historia das navegações, viagens, e conquistas dos Portuguezes. Publicada pela academia real das sciencias. v. 1. xii. 139, 4 l. sm. 4°. *Lisboa,* 1844.

CONTENTS.

Relaçam verdadeira dos trabalhos q̃ ho governador dõ Fernãdo de Souto e certos fidalgos portugueses passarom no descobrimẽto da prouincia da Frolida. Agora nouamẽte feita per hũ fidalgo Deluas [d' Elvas].

Collection of nearly 500 fac-similes of the water-marks used by the early paper makers, during the latter part of the 14th, and early part of the 15th centuries. [*anon.*] 25 pl. fol. *London,* 1840.

Collection of seventy-nine black-letter ballads and broadsides, printed 1559 to 1597. With introduction and notes. xxxvi, 319 pp. 12°. *London, J. Lilly,* 1867.

Collection of several treatises concerning the reasons and occasions of the penal laws, viz: i. The execution of justice in England, not for religion, but for treason: 17th Dec. 1583. ii. Important considerations, by the secular priests: printed A. D. 1601. iii. The jesuits reasons unreasonable. 4 p. l. 131 pp. sm. 4°. *London, Richard Royston,* 1677. (*With* Jesuits' loyalty, *London,* 1677.)

Collection de mémoires et de relations sur l'histoire ancienne du Canada. [*anon.*] 8°. *Québec, William Cowan et fils,* 1840.

Collection orientale. Manuscrits inédits de la bibliothèque royale, traduits et publiés par l'ordre du roi. 8 v. fol. *Paris, Imprimerie royale,* 1836–55. S.

CONTENTS.

Le Bhâgavata Purâna, traduit par E. Burnouf. 3 v.
Firdousi (Abou'lkasim). Le livre des rois: traduit par J. Mohl. 4v.
Reshid-Eddin. Histoire des Mongols de la Perse. Traduite par É. M. Quatremère. v. i.

Collier (William Francis, *LL. D.*) Pictures of the periods: a sketch book of old English life. xii, 287 pp. 12°. *Edinburgh, W. P. Nimmo,* 1865.

Collin de Plancy (Jacques Auguste Simon). Le diable peint par lui-même, ou galerie de petits romans et de contes merveilleux, extrait et traduit des écrivains les plus respectables. 2e éd. xl, 318 pp. 1 pl. 8°. *Paris, P. Mongie aîné,* 1825.

——— Histoire du manneken-piss, racontée par lui-même. Avec des appendices. 192 pp. 1 pl. 24°. *Bruxelles, A. Lacrosse,* 1824.

Collings (*Rev.* John). Responsoria ad erratica pastoris; the shepherds wandrings discovered, in a revindication of the great ordinance of God: gospel preachers and preaching. 180 pp. sm. 4°. *London, R. Tomlins,* 1652.

Collins (William). Poetical works. 8°. *Edinburgh,* 1794.
[Anderson's Brit. poets, v. 9.]

Colman (Henry). European life and manners; in familiar letters to friends. 2 v. xxiv, 360 pp. xvi, 392 pp. 12°. *Boston, Little & Brown,* 1849.

Colombat de l'Isère (Marc, *M. D.*) A treatise upon the diseases and hygiene of the organs of the voice. Translated by J. F. W. Lane. 2d ed. xii, 220 pp. 1 pl. 18°. *Boston, Redding & Co.* 1857.

Colon, *or* Colombo, (Cristoforo). *See* **Novus** orbis, *Roterodami,* 1616.

Colon *or* Colombo (Fernando). Historie. Nelle quali s' hà particolare, e vera relatione della vita e de' fatti dell' ammiraglio, D. Christoforo Colombo, suo padre. Nuouamente di lengua spagnuola tradotta nell' italiana dal Alfonso Vlloa. 24 p. l. 489 pp. 5 l. 24°. *Venetia, Iseppo Prodocimo,* 1678.

Colonial policy, with hints upon the formation of military settlements, and observations on the boundary question pending between this country and the United States. [*anon.*] 2d ed. 40 pp. 8°. *London, James Cochrane & Co.* 1835.

Colonna (Egidio). Theoremata de corpore Christi. xxxx l. paged. fol. [n. p.] *Baldassare,* 1481. S.

Colonna (Fabio). De glossopetris. [*With* **Scilla** (Agustino), De corporibus, marinis.]

Colonna (Francesco). Songe de poliphile, traduction libre de l'Italien, par J. G. Legrand. 2 v. in 1. 2 p. l. 228 pp; 217 pp. 18°. *Paris, Didot,* 1804.

Colquhoun (John). Sporting days. vii, 255 pp. 16°. *Edinburgh, Blackwood & sons,* 1866.

Colton (Calvin). The Americans. xii, 389 pp. 12°. *London, Westley & Davis,* 1833.

Colton (Walter). Deck and port; or, incidents of a cruise in the U. S. frigate Congress to California, with sketches of Rio Janeiro, Valparaiso, Lima, Honolulu, and San Francisco, 12°. *New York, A. S. Barnes & Co.* 1850. s.

Columbia college, (*N. Y.*) Addresses of the newly appointed professors, (Charles A. Joy, Francis Lieber, Charles Davies, C. M. Nairne,) with an introductory address by W. Betts, February, 1858. 4 p. l. 201 pp. 8°. *New York, Trustees Col. college,* 1858.

——— Catalogue of the governors, trustees, and officers, and of the alumni and other graduates from 1754 to 1864. 112 pp. 8°. *New York, D. Van Nostrand,* 1865. s.

Columbian eloquence, being the speeches of the most celebrated American orators, as delivered in the trial of Hon. Samuel Chase. 3 v. 300, 220, 247 pp. 18°. *Baltimore, S. Butler & S. Cole,* 1806.

Columbian (The) magazine; or, monthly miscellany. [Sept. 1786 to Dec 1789.] v. 1–3. 8°. *Philadelphia, T. Seddon, W. Spotswood, and others,* 1786–89.

Columella (Lucius Junius Moderatus). De re rustica. (*With* **Libri** de re rustica.)

——— De arboribus. (*With* the same.)

Columna. *See* **Colonna.**

Coluthus. Helenæ raptus. Græce et Latine. [*With* NEANDER (Michael). Opus aureum, etc.]

——— The same. The rape of Helen. Translated by Mr. C. 8°. *Edinburgh,* [1792.] [Anderson's British poets, v. 5.]

Colvin (John B.) Historical letters; a brief but general view of the history of the world, civil, military, and religious, to 1820. 2d ed. vi, 290 pp. 16°. *Georgetown, (D. C.) J. Milligan,* 1821.

Combes (François). Histoire générale de la diplomatie européenne. Histoire de la formation de l'équilibre européen par les traités de Westphalie et des Pyrénées. xii, 404 pp. 8°. *Paris, E. Dentu,* 1854.

——— The same. Histoire de la diplomatie slave et scandinave; suivie des négociations de Ponce de La Gardie. D'après des documents contemporains. 420 pp. 8°. *Paris, E. Dentu,* 1856.

Comestor (Pierre). Historia scholastica, magnā sacre scripture partem, que et in serie et in glossis crebro diffusa erat, breuiter cōplectens. 255 l. 16°. *Lugduni,* 1543. [*colophon* 1542.]

Comfield (*Mrs.* Amelia Stratton). Alida; or, miscellaneous sketches of incidents during the late American war, with poems. 240 pp. 12°. *New York, Angell & Engel,* 1849.

Comingo (Henry G. *D.D.*) Memorial; containing his 25th anniversary discourse, proceedings of the anniversary meeting, two sermons Nov. 24th, and funeral discourse by C. C. Beatty. 62 pp. 8°. *Steubenville, (O.) Herald,* 1862. s.

Commercial (The) and financial chronicle; a weekly newspaper. July, 1866, to June, 1867. v. 3–4. sm. fol. *New York, W. B. Dana & Co.* 1866–67.

Commerelle (*abbé* de). An account of the culture and use of the mangel-wurzel, or root of scarcity. Translated from the French [by J. C. Lettsom]. 56 pp. 8°. *London, C. Dilly,* 1787.

Common sense cook book, containing plain directions for all dishes, from soup to dessert; [with] a chapter on beverages, food for infants, etc. 113 pp. 12°. *New York, J. C. Haney & Co.* [1867].

Companion (The) to the newspaper; and journal of facts in politics, statistics, and public economy, 1833. 2 p. l. 234 pp. sm. fol. *London, C. Knight,* 1834.

Company of royal adventurers of England trading into Africa. Answer of the company to the petition and paper of certain heads and particulars thereunto relating and annexed, exhibited to the honorable House of Commons by Sir Paul Painter, Ferdinando Gorges, Henry Batson, Benjamin Skutt, and Thomas Knights, on the behalf of themselves and others concerned in his majestie's plantations in America. 1 p. l. 18 pp. sm. 4°. [*London,*] 1667. [Imperfect.]

Compleat (The) cook. [*anon.*] 123 pp. 4 l. 24°. *London, N. Brooks,* 1655. [*With* **Queen's** closet opened. 1655.]

Compleat (A) system of magick; or, the history of the black-art, compiled from the best authorities, ancient and modern. 5, 403 pp. 8°. *London, J. Clarke and others,* 1729.

Comstock (John Lee). Readings on zoology. Part i. Mammalia and birds. 408 pp. 12°. *New York, Newman & Ivison,* 1853.

Comte (Auguste). Traité philosophique d'astronomie populaire. x, 48 pp. 1 pl. 8°. *Paris, Carilian-Goeury & V. Dalmont,* 1844. s.

Conant (*Mrs.* H. C.) The English bible. History of the translation of the holy scriptures into the English tongue. xv, 466 pp. 2 pl. 12°. *New York, Sheldon, Blakeman & Co.* 1856.

Conciones, sive orationes, ex græcis latinisque historicis excerptæ. 10 p. l. 288 pp. 2 l. fol. [n. p.] *H. Stephanus*, 1570. s.

Concise (A) historical account of all the British colonies in North-America, comprehending their rise, progress, and modern state. [*anon.*] 196 pp. 8°. *London, J. Bew*, 1775.

Conduct (The) of the Dutch relating to their breach of treaties with England. With a full account of the case of Jeronimy Clifford. [*anon.*] 220 pp. 8°. *London, W. Bristow*, 1760.

Conduct (The) of the two B——rs [Barriers] vindicated. [*anon.*] 37 pp. 12°. *London, M. Cooper*, 1749. [With **Examination** of principles and conduct of the two Barriers. 12°. *London*, 1749.

Cone (Solomon). The harmonia; a new collection of easy songs. obl. 18°. *Albany, J. Ernst*, 1850.

Confederate (The) first reader; containing selections in prose and poetry, as exercises for younger children. [*anon.*] 120 pp. 16°. *Richmond, G. L. Bidgood*, 1864.

Confederate States (so called). Army regulations, with the articles of war. 12°. *Richmond*, 1861.

——— General orders from the adjutant and inspector general's office for 1863. Compiled under authority by R. H. P. Robinson. 16°. *Richmond*, 1864.

——— Instructions for the guidance of the medical officers of the navy. 40 pp. 12°. *Richmond, Macfarlane & Fergusson*, 1864.

——— Official reports of battles. Published by order of congress. 671 pp. 8°. *Richmond, Enquirer press*, 1862.

——— Ordnance instructions for the navy. 3d ed. xix, 171, cix pp. 21 pl. 8°. *London, Saunders, Otley & Co.* 1864.

——— Regulations for the army, 1863. 2d ed. 12°. *Richmond*, 1863.

——— Regulations for the navy, 1862. iv, 239 pp. 16°. *Richmond, Macfarlane & Fergusson*, 1862.

——— Regulations for the subsistence department. 54 pp. 16°. *Richmond, Ritchie & Dunnavant*, 1862.

Conference of the governor of Massachusetts bay with the sachems of the eastern Indians, Arrowsick island, August 9–12th, 1717. 13 pp. sm. 4°. *Boston, B. Green*, 1717.

Conference with the eastern Indians, Falmouth, 1726. 20 pp. sm. 4°. [*Boston*, 1726?]

Conference with the eastern Indians, Falmouth, July, 1727. 27 pp. sm. 4°. *Boston, S. Kneeland*, 1754.

Conference of his excellency, Jonathan Belcher, and the eastern Indians, Falmouth, 1732. 23 pp. sm. 4°. *Boston, B. Green*, 1732.

Conference at the fort at St. George's, York county, August 4th, 1742, between his excellency, William Shirley, and the sachems of the eastern New England Indians. 19 pp. sm. 4°. *Boston, J Draper*, 1742.

——— The same. [imp: p. 19 in ms.]

Confession (A) of faith owned and consented to by the elders and messengers of the churches in the colony of Connecticut in New England, assembled at Say-brook, September 9th, 1708. [*anon.*] 99 pp. 18°. *New London, Thomas Short*, 1710.

Congar (*Capt.* Obadiah). *See* **Cheever** (*Rev.* Henry). Autobiography, etc.

Congress (library of). Alphabetical catalogue of the library of congress. Authors. 1236 pp. 8°. *Washington, government printing office*, 1864.

——— Catalogue of additions, for the years ending Dec. 1, 1864, 1865, and 1866. 3 v. 8°. *Washington, government printing office*, 1864–66.

——— Catalogue of the library of congress. Chap. i. Ancient history, 77 pp. 8°. *Washington, Smithsonian institution*, 1854.

Congressional (The) globe: containing the debates and proceedings of the 39th congress, 1st and 2d sessions. (Dec. 1865 to March 1867). By F. and J. Rives. 8 v. 4°. *Washington, Cong. globe office*, 1866–67.

Congreve (William). Essay concerning humor in comedy. pp. 66–73. [Appended to **Morris** (Corbyn). Essay, etc. *London*, 1744.]

——— Poetical works. 8°. *Edinburgh*, 1793. [Anderson's Brit. poets, v. 7].

Connecticut. An account of the number of inhabitants in the colony of Connecticut, Jan. 1, 1774. [with the same] for Jan. 1, 1756. 9 l. fol. *Hartford, E. Watson*, 1774.

——— The code of 1650, a compilation of the earliest laws and orders of the general court of Connecticut, also the constitution adopted by the towns of Windsor, Hartford, and Weathersfield in 1638–9, and extracts from the blue laws. 119 pp. 18°. *Hartford, Silas Andrus*, 1830.

——— The same. 199 pp. 18°. *Hartford, Silas Andrus and Son*, 1843.

Connecticut. Journal of the house of representatives. May session, 1867. 8°. *Hartford, Case, Lockwood & Co.* 1867.

——— Journal of the senate. May session, 1867. 8°. *Hartford, Case, Lockwood & Co.* 1867.

——— Public documents of the legislature. May session, 1867. 8°. *Hartford, Case, Lockwood & Co.* 1867.

——— Third to sixth annual reports of the superintendent of common schools, 1848–51. 4 v. in 1. 8°. *Hartford and New Haven,* 1848–51. s.

——— Reports of the commissioner of the school fund, 1818, 1819, 1825, and 1849. 8°. *Hartford,* 1819–49.

——— Fourth annual report of the board of commissioners of common schools. 60 pp. 8°. *Hartford, Case & Co.* 1842.
[*With* the preceding].

Connecticut historical society. Collections. v. 1. xii, 332 pp. 8°. *Hartford,* 1860.

Conner (James). Specimens of light face printing types and ornaments. 209 l. unp. 8°. *New York, S. Hoyt & Co.* 1832.

——— (*and* sons). Specimens of printing types, and ornaments. 191 l. unp. 4°. *New York,* 1855. s.

Conrad (Timothy Abbott). Check list of the invertebrate fossils of North America. Eocene and oligocene. iv, 41 pp. 8°. *Washington,* 1866.
[Smithsonian miscel. coll. v. 7.]

——— Description of cretaceous and tertiary fossils. [**Emory** (W. H.) Report on the U. S. and Mexican boundary survey, v. 1.]

——— Fossil shells [of Chile]. *With* **Gilliss** (J. M.), U. S. astron. exped., v. 2.]

——— Fossils of the miocene formation of the United States. xvi, 80 pp. 44 pl. 8°. *Philadelphia, J. Dobson,* 1845. s.
[Imperfect; wanting plate 33.]

——— Fossils of the tertiary formations of the United States. 80 pp. 49 pl. 8°. *Philadelphia, J. Dobson,* 1838. s.
[Imperfect; 6 plates wanting.]

——— The same. [Imperfect; 5 plates wanting.]

——— New fresh water shells of the United States, with colored illustrations, and a monograph of the genus anculotus; also a synopsis of the American naiades. 12°. *Philadelphia,* 1834. s.

——— Nouvelles coquilles d'eau douce des États-Unis, suivis de la monographie du genre anculotus de Say et du tableau synoptique des naiades d'Amérique. De l'Anglais par J. C. Chenu. [Extract.] 36 pp. 4 pl. 8°. *Paris, Bibliothèque conchyliologique,* 1845. s.

Considerations on the choice of public rulers; on the extent of their powers; and on the best means of securing the advantages and reforming the abuses of popular elections. [*anon.*] vi, 156 pp. 8°. *New York, T. S. Arden,* 1805.

Constable (H. Strickland). Observations suggested by the cattle plague, about witchcraft, credulity, superstition, parliamentary reform, and other matters. 99 pp. 8°. *London, Dalton & Lucy,* 1866.

Constant de Rebecque, (Henri Benjamin). Adolphe; anecdote trouvée dans les papiers d'un inconnu. Nouv. éd. suivie des ouvrages: Quelques réflexions sur le théâtre allemand et sur la tragédie de Wallstein, et de l'Esprit de conquête et de l'usurpation. 388 pp. 16°. *Paris, Charpentier,* 1839.

——— De la religion, considérée dans sa source, ses formes, et ses développements. 5 v. 8°. *Paris, Bossange,* 1824–31.

——— Du polythéisme romain, considéré dans ses rapports avec la philosophie grecque et la religion chrétienne; précédé d'une introduction de J. Matter. 2 v. lix, 283 pp; 384 pp. 8°. *Paris, Béchet ainé,* 1833.

Contarini (Alvise). Relazione del congresso di Munster. 103 pp. 4°. *Venezia, Antonelli,* 1864. s.

Controversy (The) touching the old stone mill, in the town of Newport, R. I. with remarks. [*anon.*] 91 pp. 16°. *Newport, E. Hammett, jr.* 1851.

Contzen (Adam). Disceptatio de secretis societatis Jesv. 190 pp. 16°. *Mogvntiæ, J. Volmar,* 1617.

Conversations on ritualism. 77 pp. 12°. *New York, Hurd and Houghton,* 1867.

Conversations-lexikon. Allgemeine deutsche real-encyclopädie für gebildeten stände. 11e auflage. v. 1–10. A–O. 8°. *Leipzig, Brockhaus,* 1864–66.

Conybeare (William John). Essays, ecclesiastical and social. Reprinted, with additions, from the Edinburgh review. xi, 440 pp. 8°. *London, Longman,* 1855. s.

CONTENTS.

Essay i. The church in the mountains.
ii. Church parties.
iii. Ecclesiastical economy.
iv. Vestries and church rates.
v. Mormonism.
vi. Agitation and legislation against intemperance.

Conyngham (*Capt.* D. P.) The Irish brigade and its campaigns, with [sketch] of the Corcoran legion and the principal officers. 599 pp. 12°. *New York, W. McSorley & Co.* 1867.

Conring (Hermann). De antiqvitatibvs academicis dissertationes septem, vna cvm eivs svpplementis. Recognovit Christoph Avg. Hevmannvs, adjecitqve bibliothecam historicam academicam. xxxii, 399 pp, 36 l. unp. 4°. *Gottingæ, Bib. acad.* 1739.

——— Dissertatio ad L. I. codicis Theodosiani de stvdiis liberalibvs vrb. Romæ et Constantinopolis. 68 pp. 8 l. unp. 4°. *Gottingæ,* [1739.] s.
[*With* the preceding.]

——— Introductio in universam artem medicam singulasqve ejus partes, etc. consimilis argumenti commentationes, cura ac studio Guntheri, Christophori Schelhammeri, cum præfatione Friderici Hoffmanni, etc. 2 v. in 1. 16 pp. 8 l. 424 pp. 121; 163 pp. 4°. *Halae, E. G. Crugius,* 1726. s.

Cook (Ann, *late Mrs. Beauchamp*). Letters to her friend in Maryland, containing a short history of her life. 91 pp. 12°. *Washington,* 1826. s.

Cooke (C.) Curiosities of occult literature. xii, 275 pp. 12°. *London, A. Hall,* [1863.]

Cooke (Charles Turner). Observations on the efficacy of white mustard seed in affections of the liver, internal organs, and nervous system, and on general management of health and life. 5th ed. 16°. *London,* 1828.

Cooke (John Esten). Wearing of the gray; being personal portraits, scenes, and adventures of the war. 601 pp. 10 pl. 8°. *New York, E. B. Treat & Co.* 1867.

Cooke (*Rev.* Samuel, *of Cambridge*). The violent destroyed and the oppressed delivered. Sermon preached at Lexington, Apr. 19, 1777, a memorial of the tragedy in that town, 1775. 31 pp. 8°. *Boston, T. Leverett & N. Bowes,* 1777.

Coolidge (Austin J.) *and* **Mansfield** (J. B.) History and description of New England, general and local. v. 1. Maine, New Hampshire, and Vermont. xxv, 1023 pp, 3 maps, 22 pl. 8°. *Boston, A. J. Coolidge,* 1864. s.

Cooper (*Rev.* Edward). The crisis; or, an attempt to show from prophecy the prospects and duties of the church of Christ. With inquiry into the probable destiny of England. 1st Am. ed. xxx, 196 pp. 12°. *Cincinnati, Morgan, Fisher & L'Hommedieu,* 1827.

Cooper (James G.) Catalogue of mollusca west of the Rocky Mountains, etc. s.
[*With* CALIFORNIA. Geological survey, 1867.]

Cooper (*Rev.* William, *of Boston*). The doctrine of predestination unto life. Preface by [B. Colman and others.] 4, 140 pp. 18°. *Boston, J. Edwards & H. Foster,* 1740.

——— The same. iii, 142 pp. 16°. *London, E. & C. Dilly,* 1765.

Coote (Henry Charles). A neglected fact in English history. [An essay on the Anglo-Saxon polity.] xi, 183 pp. 16°. *London, Bell & Daldy,* 1864.

Copenhagen. Forlagsforeningen. Almindeligt dansk-norsk forlagscatalog. 1–2 supplement. 233 pp; 112 pp. 8°. *Hauniae, Soc. bibliop.* 1841–45. s.

——— Bibliotheca regia. Codices orientales bibliothecæ regiæ hafniensis. Pars 1, Codices indicos continens. Pars 2, Codices hebraicos et arabicos continens. 2 v. x, 122 pp; xi, 188 pp. 4°. *Havniæ, Schultz,* 1846–51. s.

Copineau (*l'abbé*). Essai synthétique sur l'origine et la formation des langues. [*anon.*] xv, 464 pp. 2 l. 8°. *Paris, Rouault,* 1774.

Coppée (Henry). Select academic speaker. 572 pp. 8°. *Philadelphia, E. H. Butler & Co.* 1860.

Copway (George). Organization of a new Indian territory east of the Missouri river; arguments and reasons submitted to the members of the 31st congress of the United States. 32 pp. 8°. *New York, S. W. Benedict,* 1850.

Copy of the resolves of a council of churches, met at Northampton, 1742. 6 pp. 24°. *Boston, S. Kneeland & T. Green,* 1742.

Coquelin (Charles), *and* **Guillaumin** (Urbain Gilbert). Dictionnaire de l'économie politique, contenant l'exposition des principes de la science, l'opinion des écrivains qui ont le plus contribué à sa fondation et à ses progrès, la bibliographie générale de l'économie politique, etc. 2 v. xxvii, 791 pp; 2 p. l. 896 pp. 8 pl. 8°. *Paris, Guillaumin et Cie,* 1864.

Coquerel (Athanase Josué). Les forçats pour la foi. (1684, 1775.) 377 pp. 16°. *Paris, Lévy,* 1866.

——— First historical transformations of christianity. [Translated] by E. P. Evans. 264 pp. 16°. *Boston, Wm. V. Spencer,* 1867.

Corcoran (Peter). The fancy; a selection from [his] poetical remains, with a memoir of his life. xxx, 107 pp. 12°. *London, Taylor & Hessey,* 1820.

Corda (August Joseph). Beiträge zur flora der vorwelt. viii, 128 pp, 60 pl. 4°. *Prag, J. G. Calve,* 1845. s.

Cordier (Pierre Louis Antoine). An essay on the temperature of the interior of the earth. 94 pp. 12°. *Amherst, J. S. & C. Adams,* 1828. s.

Cordner (*Rev.* John). The vision of the pilgrim fathers; an oration before the New England society of Montreal, on 22d December, 1856; with the proceedings at the dinner. 54 pp. 8°. *Montreal, H. Rose,* 1857.

Cork and Orrery (John, *5th earl of*). *See* **Boyle** (John).

Cormatin Desoteux (Pierre Marie Felicité, *baron* de). *See* **Desoteux de Cormatin.**

Cormenin (Louis Marie de La Haye, *vicomte* de). De la centralisation. Par Timon. 2e éd. 159 pp. 24°. *Paris, Pagnerre,* 1842.

——— Livre des orateurs, [de la France] par Timon. [*pseudon.*] 13e éd. 547 pp. 27 pl. 8°. *Paris, Pagnerre,* 1844. s.

Cornalia (Emilio). Monografia del bombice del gelso. (*Bombyx mori Linn.*) (Extract). ix, 19, 288 pp. 15 pl. 4°. *Milano, I. R. Istituto lombardo de scienze, etc.* 1856. s.

Cornay (Joseph Émile, *de Rochefort*). Éléments de morphologie humaine. 246 pp. 2 pl. 16°. *Paris, Gide, Labé,* 1847. s.

——— Mémoire sur l'unité de spécialite des espèces humaines, et en particulier sur la concordance des vues des physiologistes relatives a l'état d'unité et de pluralité de ces espèces. 81 pp. 16°. *Paris, J. B. Baillière,* 1862. s.

——— Principes de physiologie et exposition de la loi divine d'harmonie; ou traité de la distribution légale des espèces dans la nature. 146 pp. 12°. *Paris, J. B. Baillière,* 1862. s.

Cornelius *Mechlenburgensis.* De puerorum morbis, et symptomatis tum dignoscendis, tum curandis liber, ex græcorum, latinorum et arabum placitis excerptus à Sebastiano Avstrio, Rubeaquensi, etc. 338 pp. 14 l. 24°. *Lvgduni, G. Rouillié,* 1549. s.

[*With* DUBOIS (J.) Ratio medendi, etc.]

Cornhill (The) magazine, July, 1866, to June, 1867. v. 14–15. 8°. *London, Smith, Elder & Co.* 1866–67.

Corniani (Giambattista). Riflessioni sulle monete; della legislazione relativamente all' agricoltura.

[Scrittori class. ital. di econ. pol. v. 39].

Cornut (Jacques Philippe). Canadensivm plantarvm aliarumque nondum editarum historia; cui adiectum est enchiridion botanicvm parisiense. 8 p. l. 238 pp. 1 l. 4°. *Paris, S. Le Moyne,* 1635.

Coronation anecdotes; or, select and interesting fragments of English coronation ceremonies. By Giles Gossip. [*pseudon.*] viii, 334 pp. 16°. *London, R. Jennings,* 1823.

Corradi (Sebastiano). Qvaestvra. Partes dvae, qvarvm altera de Ciceronis vita et libris, item de ceteris Ciceronibvs agit; altera Ciceronis libros permvltis locis emendat. 6 p. l. 398 pp. 8°. *Lipsiæ, J. Wendler,* 1754.

Correal (Francisco). Voyages aux Indes Occidentales, de 1666–97, traduits de l'Espagnol, avec une relation de la Guiane de Walter Raleigh, et le voyage de Narbrough à la mer du sud par le détroit de Magellan. Nouv. éd. 3 v. 16°. *Paris, André Callieau,* 1522.

——— The same. Traduits de l'Anglois. 3 v. 18°. *Amsterdam, J. F. Bernard,* 1722.

Corry (John). [Life of George Washington. 1st ed. vii, 349 pp. 1 pl. 12°. *New York,* 1807]?

[Title wanting].

Cortada (Juan). Historia de Portugal, hasta 1839. 433, 4 pp. 6 pl. 8°. *Barcelona, A. Brusi,* 1844.

[1 portrait wanting].

Cortambert (L.) *and* **Tranaltos** (F. de). Histoire de la guerre civile américaine, 1860–65. 2 v. 390 pp; 350 pp. 2 pl. 3 maps. 8°. *Paris, Amyot,* 1867.

Cortés (Fernando). La preclara narratione della Nuoua Hispagna del mare oceano, per Pietro Sauorgnano dal iddioma hispagniuolo in lingua latina conuersa. 77 l. sm. 4°. *Venetia, Bernardino de Viano de Lexona,* 1524.

——— Aliquot narrationes. *See* **Novus** orbis (Roterodami), 1616.

Cosin (John, *D. D.*) Scholastical history of the canon of the holy scriptvre. 18 p. l. 224 pp. 23 l. sm. 4°. *London, T. Garthwait,* 1657.

[*With* SPARROW (Anthony). Coll. of articles, etc. *Lond.* 1675].

Cosmographiae introdvctio cvm quibvsdam geometriæ ac astronomiæ principiis ad eam rem necessariis [auctore Hylacomyla, *i. e.* M. Waldseemüller]. Insuper quatuor Americi Vespucii nauigationes. 48 l. unp. sm. 4°. [*Deodate*], 1507.

[Imperfect; wanting probably 4 leaves.]

Cosmopolitanus (Evangelus). [*pseudon.*] *See* **Beyer** (August).

Cosmopolite (The). [Jan. to April 1866]. 8°. *Baltimore, De Leon & Co.* [1867.]

[No more issued.]

Costa (Ethbin Heinrich). Bibliographie der deutschen rechtsgeschichte. 4 p. l. 342 pp. 8°. *Braunschweig, C. A. Schwetschke,* 1858. s.

Costa (Oronzio Gabriele). Microdoride mediterranea; o descrizione de' poco ben conosciuti ed affatto ignoti viventi, minuti e micoscropici animali del Mediterraneo. v. 1. xviii, 80 pp. 13 pl. 8°. *Napoli, Stamperia dell' iride*, 1861. s.

Costa. *See* **Da Costa.**

Costé (François Auguste). Manuel de gréement, ou l'art d'équiper les vaisseaux et autres batimens de mer, de tout ce qui est nécessaire à leurs mouvemens. xvi, 281 pp. 8 tab. 8°. *Paris, Dezauche*, 1829. s.

Costigan (Arthur William). Sketches of society and manners in Portugal. 2 v. vi, 424 pp; iv, 424 pp. 8°. *London, T. Vernor*, 1787.

Cotolendi (Charles). Arlequiniana, ou les bons mots, les histoires plaisantes et agréables. Recueillies des conversations d'Arlequin. [*anon.*] 27 p. l. 354 pp. 6 l. 1 pl. 24°. *Paris*, [*Delaulne & Brunet*], 1694.

Cotta (Bernhard). Die Alpen. 2e ausgabe. viii, 328 pp. 6 pl. 8°. *Leipzig, T. O. Weigel*, 1851. s.

——— Deutschlands boden, sein geologischer bau und dessen einwirkungen auf das leben der menschen. 2 v. in 1, xi, 614 pp; 283 pp. 3 pl. 1 map. 8°. *Leipzig, F. A. Brockhaus*, 1854. s.

——— Die gesteinlehre. iv, 255 pp. 8°. *Freiberg, J. G. Engelhardt*, 1855. s.

——— The same. 2e auf. vi, 333 pp. 8°. *Freiberg, J. G. Engelhardt*, 1862. s.

——— Rocks classified and described; a treatise on lithology. English translation by P. H. Lawrence. xii, 425 pp. 12°. *London, Longmans*, 1866.

Cotton (Charles). *See* **Walton** (Isaac).

Cotton (Edward, *sergeant major.*) A voice from Waterloo; a history of the battle. 4th ed. enlarged. xix, 278 pp. 4 pl. 16°. *Mont St. Jean*, 1852.

Cotton (*Rev.* Henry). Typographical gazetteer. 2d ed. xviii, 393 pp. 8°. *Oxford, Univ. press*, 1831. s.

Cotton (John). Letter to Mr. [Roger] Williams. Wherein is showed that those ought to be received into the church who are godly, etc. [Edited by R. A. Guild.] 28 pp. 4°. *Providence, R. I.* 1866.
[Narragansett club publications, v. 1. pp. 285—312.]

——— Answer to master Roger Williams. Edited by J. L. Diman. 240 pp. 4°. *Providence, R. I.* 1867.
[Narragansett club publications, v. 2. pp. 1—240.]

Coughlan (*Rev.* L.) An account of the work of God in Newfoundland, North America. 192 pp. 16°. *London, W. Gilbert*, 1776.

Coulanges (Phillippe Emanuel, *marquis* de). Mémoires, suivis de lettres inédites de madame de Sévigné, de son fils, d'Arnauld de Pomponne, de Jean de La Fontaine, et d'autres personnages du même siècle. Publiée par M. de Monmerqué. xii, 512 pp. 4 pl. 8°. *Paris, J. J. Blaise*, 1820.

Counsel for emigrants, with original letters from Canada and the United States. 2d ed. [*anon.*] 156 pp. 1 map. 12°. *Aberdeen, John Mathison*, 1835.

Country (The) bard; or, the modern courtiers; a poem. [*anon.*] 2 p. l. 31 pp. 4°. *London*, 1741.

Course of psalms, selected from the new version for the services of the united church of England and Ireland, etc. by J. T. Barrett, *D. D.* 4th ed. corrected, with set of tunes selected by B. Jacobs. 252 pp. 16°. *Lambeth*, (*Eng.*) 1825.

Course (A) of sermons on the creed of pope Pius IV, preached at Bilston, 1840, by fourteen clergymen of the church of England. xxviii, 659 pp. 8°. *Wolverhampton, T. Simpson*, 1841.

Court anecdotes. [*anon.*] iv, 380 pp. 1 pl. 12°. *London, W. Sams*, 1825.

Court (The) of Atlantis. Containing a four years' history of that famous island, political and gallant. By several hands. [*anon.*] vi, 310 pp. 1 l. 12°. *London, J. Roberts*, 1714.

Court (The) of Neptune, and the curse of liberty; with other poems, on subjects connected with the late war. [*anon.*] 106 pp. 18°. *New York, Van Winkle, Wiley & Co.* 1817.

Courtenay (Francis Burdett, *M. D.*) A practical essay on the debilities of the generative system, their varieties, causes, treatment, and cure. 74 pp. *London, T. Hill*, 1838.

Courtisane (La) vertueuse. Histoire véritable. [*anon.*] 120 pp. 18°. *Lyon*, 1786.
[*With* Capucins (Les) sans barbe.]

Cousin (Victor). Histoire générale de la philosophie depuis les temps les plus anciens jusqu'au xixe siècle. 7e éd. vii, 598 pp. 8°. *Paris, Didier et Cie.* 1867.

——— Jacqueline Pascal. Premières études sur les femmes illustres et la société du xviie siècle. 3e éd. xxiii, 467 pp. 1 fac. sim. *Didier & Cie.* 1856.

——— La jeunesse de Mazarin. xxiv, 616 pp. 8°. *Paris, Didier et Cie.* 1865.

——— La société française au xviie siècle. 2 v. xxiii, 444 pp; 2 p. l. 480 pp. 8°. *Paris, Didier et Cie.* 1858.

Coustelier (Antoine Urbain). Lettres d'une demoiselle entretenue à son amant. [*anon.*] 2 p. l. 43 pp. 16°. *Cologne, [Paris] P. Marteau*, 1749.

[*With* VARENNES DE MONDASSE. Lettres de M. à son ami. 16°. *Amsterdam*, 1750.]

Couts (Joseph). Practical guide for the tailor's cutting room. vii, 166 pp. 44 pl. 4°. *Glasgow, Blackie & son*, [*about* 1850].

Couvret (Auguste). Calembours et jeux de mots des hommes illustres, anciens et modernes, précédés d'un éloge historique. 2 v. in 1. 211 pp. 202 pp. 16°. *Paris, Aubry*, 1806.

Covelli (Niccolò). *See* **Monticelli** (T.) *and* **Covelli.**

Covyn (Jakob). Bibliotheca nitidissima, sive catalogus præstantissimorum et insignium librorum. 242 pp. 8°. *Amstelœdami, A. Schouten*, [*about* 1747.]

Cowell (Benjamin). Spirit of '76 in Rhode Island. 352 pp. 8°. *Boston, A. J. Wright*, 1850. S.

Cowles (*Rev.* Henry, *D. D.*) Ezekiel and Daniel; with notes. *See* **Bible,** *English.*

Cowper (William). Private correspondence. 1st Amer. ed. 385 pp. 8°. *Philadelphia, E. Littell*, 1824. S.

——— *See* **Guyon** (Jeanne Marie Bouvier de La Mothe) *and* Cowper, (William). Poems. 24°. 1801.

Cox (*Mrs.* Ann C.) Family directory; or, forty years' experience of a practical housekeeper; with hints on health, farming [etc.] Selected from the best authors. xvi, 80 pp. 12°. *Columbus, (O.)* 1867.

Cox (Edward). Report on geology (in Owen's geology of Arkansas).

Cox (Francis Augustus, *D. D.*) *and* Hoby, (*Rev.* J.) The baptists in America; a narrative of the deputation from the baptist union of England to the United States and Canada. 476 pp. 12°. *New York, Leavitt, Lord & Co.* 1836.

Cox (George W.) Dictionary of science. *See* **Brande** (William Thomas).

Cox (Ross). Adventures on the Columbia river, including a residence of six years among various tribes of Indians. 335 pp. 8°. *New York, Harpers*, 1832. S.

Cox (William E.) Viage en las rejiones septentrionales de la Patagonia, 1862–3. viii, 273 pp. 1 map. 8°. *Santiago de Chile, Imprenta nacional*, 1863. S.

Coxe (Arthur Cleveland). The criterion; a means of distinguishing truth from error in questions of the times. With four letters on the Eirenicon of Dr. Pusey. 129 pp. 12°. *New York, H. B. Durand*, 1866.

Coxe (John Redman). *See* **Hippocrates** *and* Galenus.

Coxe (Richard S). A new critical pronouncing dictionary of the English language. Compiled from authors of the most improved reputation: with considerable additions. [*anon*]. xiv, 85 pp. 470 l. unp. 8°. *Burlington, (N. J.) D. Allinson & Co.* 1813.

Coxe (William). Travels into Poland, Russia, Sweden, and Denmark. 3d ed. 4 v. 8°. *London, Cadell*, 1787. S.

Coyer (Gabriel François). A supplement to lord Anson's voyage round the world, containing a discovery and description of the island of Frivola. xl, 63 pp. 8°. *London, A. Millar and others*, 1752.

Coyner (David H.) The lost trappers; a collection of interesting scenes and events in the Rocky Mountains; with a short description of California. 255 pp. 12°. *Cincinnati, J. A. & U. P. James*, 1847.

Cozens (Alexander). Principles of beauty relative to the human head. With a French translation. 3 p. l. 15, 15 pp. 19 pl. fol. *London, J. Dixwell*, 1778.

Cozzens (Frederic S.) Col. Peter A. Porter: a memorial delivered before the century, 1864. 54 pp. 8°. *New York, D. Van Nostrand*, 1865.

——— The sayings of Dr. Bushwhacker, and other learned men. 8, 213 pp. 12°. *New York, A. Simpson & Co.* 1867.

——— The wine press. [published monthly.] June 20, 1854 to May 20, 1855. v. 1, 96 pp. 8°. *New York, T. A. Gray*, 1855.

Crabb (George). English synonymes. 10th ed. lxiii, 535 pp. 8°. *New York, Harpers*, 1849.

——— Universal technological dictionary; or, familiar explanation of the terms used in all arts and sciences. 2 v. vii pp. 340 l; 296 l. 60 pl. 4°. *London, Baldwin, Cradock and Joy*, 1823.

Crabb (James). The gipsies' advocate; or, observations on the origin, character, manners, and habits of the English gipsies. 3d ed. 199 pp. 16°. *London, Nisbet*, 1832.

Cracraft (*Rev.* J. W.) Judaizing teachers, ancient and modern: or sacramental error refuted. vii, 156 pp. 12°. *Chicago, C. Scott & Co.* 1858.

Craig (B. F.) Weights and measures, according to the decimal system, with tables of conversion. 49 pp. 18°. *New York, Van Nostrand*, 1867.

Craig (Neville B.) Memoirs of major Robert Stobo. 18°. [*anon.*] *Pittsburgh, John S. Davidson*, 1854.

——— Sketch of the life and services of Isaac Craig. 70 pp. 18°. *Pittsburgh, J. S. Davidson*, 1854.

Craik (George Lillie.) The English of Shakespeare; illustrated in a philological commentary on his Julius Cæsar. Edited from 3d Lond. ed. by W. J. Rolfe. xvi, 386 pp. 12°. *Boston, Crosby & Ainsworth*, 1867.

Cramer (John Anthony). Geographical and historical description of ancient Greece. 3 v. 1 map. 8°. *Oxford, Clarendon press*, 1828.

Cranch (William). Memoir of the life, character, and writings of John Adams, read March 16, 1827, in Washington, at the request of the Columbian institute. 70 pp. 8°. *Washington, S. A. Elliot*, 1827.

[*With* SMITH (Samuel H.) Memoir of Thomas Jefferson. *Washington*, 1827.]

Cranmer (Thomas). Miscellaneous writings and letters. Edited by Rev. J. E. Cox. xv, 592 pp. 1 fac-sim. 8°. *Cambridge, (Eng.)* 1846.

[Parker society publications.]

——— Writings and disputations relative to the sacrament of the Lord's supper. Edited by Rev. J. E. Cox. xxxi, 444, 99 pp. 8°. *Cambridge. (Eng.) univ. press*, 1844.

[Parker society publications.]

Cranz (David). Historie von Groenland, enthaltend die beschreibung des landes und der einwohner. 2 v. 16°. *Barby, H. O. Ebers*, 1765.

Crashaw (Richard). Poetical works. 8°. *Edinburgh*, 1793.

[Anderson's Brit. poets, v. 4].

Crashawe (William). The Jesvite's gospel. 113 pp. 16°. *London*, 1610.

Crauford (David). Ovidius britannicus; or, love epistles in imitation of Ovid. 6 p. l. 152 pp. 16°. *London, J. Chantry*, 1703.

Crawford (J. Marshall). Mosby and his men. 375 pp. 12°. *New York, Carleton*, 1867.

Crawford (*Rev.* William). History of Ireland from the earliest period to the present time. 2 v. xxx, 350 pp; 387 pp. 8°. *Strabane, J. Bellew*, 1783.

Crawfurd (John). Journal of an embassy from the governor general of India to the courts of Siam and Cochin-China; exhibiting a view of the actual state of those kingdoms. 2d ed. 2 v. viii, 475 pp. 7 pl. 1 map; v. 459 pp. 6 pl. 1 map. 8°. *London, Colburn & Bentley*, 1830. s.

Crawley (Rawdon). Billiards; its theory and practice. 5th ed. vi, 180 pp. 18°. *London, Bickers & Bush*, 1860.

Crazy tales. [In verse. By A. S. *anon.*] 2d ed. xi, 151 pp. 18°. *London*, 1764.

Crébillon, (Claude Prosper Jolyot de). Mémoires de madame la marquise de Pompadour. Écrits par elle-même. [*anon.*] 2 v. in 1. 160, 136 pp. 16°. *Liége*, 1768.

NOTE.—This work is attributed to Crébillon by Oettinger, but its authorship is uncertain.

Creecy (James R.) Scenes in the south, and other miscellaneous pieces. 294 pp. 12°. *Washington, T. McGill*, 1860. s.

Cregeen (Archibald). Dictionary of the Manks language. 188 pp. 12°. *Douglas, J. Quiggin*, 1835. s.

Creigh (Alfred). History of the knights templar of the state of Pennsylvania; with constitution, etc. 394 pp. 12°. *Philadelphia, J. B. Lippincott & Co.* 1867.

Creighton (Henry). Ruins of Gour described, and represented in 18 views; with a topographical map. iii, 12 pp. 36 l. 1 map. 18 col. pl. 4°. *London, Black, Parbury & Allen*, 1817.

Creswell (Daniel, *editor*). [*See* **Euclides**. Geometry. *Cambridge*, 1819.]

Crétineau-Joly (Jacques). Histoire du sonderbund. 2 v. 536 pp; 540 pp. 8°. *Paris, Plon*, 1850.

Cretzschmar (Philipp Jakob). Säugethiere, und vögel, von Africa, 2 v. 1826. s.

[*With* RÜPPELL (W. P. E.) Atlas zu reise im nördlichen Afrika].

Crichton (Alexander). Ueber den climatischen zustand der erde vor der allgemeinen ueberschwemmung, etc. s.

[*With* CUVIER (G. L. C. F. D. *baron*). Ansichten von der urwelt, v. 2].

Cricket field (The); or, the history and the science of cricket. [By J. P. *anon.*] 238 pp. 1 pl. 16°. *Boston, Mayhew & Baker*, 1859.

Cristoforis (Luigi de). Relazione sopra alcune macchine all' esposizione di Londra del 1851. 140 pp. 1 pl. 8°. *Milano, G. Bernardoni*, 1852. s.

Critic (The) in parliament and in public since 1835. [*anon.*] 188 pp. 12°. *London, G. Bell*, 1841.

Critical (A) commentary on archbishop Secker's letter to the right hon. Horatio Walpole, concerning bishops in America. [*anon.*] 111 pp. 8°. *London, E. & C. Dilly*, 1770.

Critical and social essays; reprinted from the New York Nation. iv, 230 pp. 16°. *New York, Leypoldt & Holt*, 1867.

Crito Cantabrigiensis. [*pseudon*]. *See* **Turton** (Thomas, *M. D.*)

Croker (Thomas Crofton). Landscape illustrations of Moore's Irish melodies; with comments for the curious. 64 pp. 4 pl. 8°. *London, J. Power*, 1835.

Crombie (Alexander). Gymnasium, sive symbola critica. 3a ed. 2 v. cvii, 342 pp; 2 p. l. 486 pp. 8°. *Londini, R. Hunter*, 1828.

——— The same. Clavis gymnasii, editioni quartæ accomodata; sive exercitationes in symbolam criticam. 1 p. l. 122 pp. 8°. *Londini, R. Hunter*, 1832.

[*With* CROMBIE (A.) Gymnasium. 3a ed. 8°. *Londini*, 1828.]

Cromwell's bloody slaughter-house; or, his damnable designes laid and practiced by him and his negro's, in contriving the murther of his sacred majesty king Charles I, discovered. By a person of honor. [*anon.*] 24°. *London, James Davis*, 1660.

Crook (*Rev.* John). The design of christianity, with other books, epistles, and manuscripts; [and] a short account of his life, written by himself. lx, 416 pp. 8°. *London, J. Phillips*, 1791.

Crooke (Hilkiah). Mikrokosmographia. A description of the body of man, collected and translated out of all the best authors of anatomy. 7 p. l. 1011 pp. 1 l. fol. [*London,*] *W. Jaggard*, 1688.

Croquet; its principles and rules. By A. Rover, [*pseudon ?*] 66 pp. 2 pl. 18°. *Springfield, (Mass.) M. Bradley & Co.* 1867.

Crosby (Thomas). Builder's price book for 1823. [*anon.*] 24th ed. 170 pp. 12°. *London, Baldwin, Cradock & Joy*, 1823.

Croserio (C.) Homœopathic manual of obstetrics. From the French, by M. Coté. 153 pp. 12°. *Cincinnati, Moore, Anderson, Wilstach & Keys*, 1853.

Cross (James). Journals of several expeditions made in western Australia during the years 1829–32. xxii, 263 pp. 1 map. 18°. *London, J. Cross*, 1833.

Crosthwaite (John Clarke). Modern hagiology: an examination of the nature and tendency of some legendary and devotional works lately published. 2 v. xxiii, 308 pp; viii, 305 pp. 16°. *London, J. W. Parker*, 1846.

Crouch (Louisa J.) Early crowned: a memoir of Mary E. North. With introduction by R. S. Forster. 256 pp. 16°. *New York, Carlton & Porter*, 1866.

Crown (John). Ambitious statesman, or loyal favorite. 7 p. l. 88 pp. sm. 4°. *London, W. Abington*, 1679.

Crown (John). Andromache: a tragedy. 4 p. l. 48 pp. sm. 4°. *London, R. Bentley*, 1675.

——— Caligula: a tragedy. 4 p. l. 55 pp. sm. 4°. *London, R. Wellington*, 1698.

——— Calisto; or, the chaste nimph. 9 p. l. 82 pp. sm. 4°. *London, J. Magnes & R. Bentley*, 1675.

——— City politiques: a comedy. 4 p. l. 80 pp. sm. 4°. *London, R. Bentley*, 1683.

——— Countrey wit: a comedy. 4 p. l. 92 pp. sm. 4°. *London, J. Magnes & R. Bentley*, 1675.

——— Darius, king of Persia: a tragedy. 6 p. l. 71 pp. sm. 4°. *London, R. Bentley*, 1688.

——— English frier: a comedy. 6 p. l. 54 pp. sm. 4°. *London, J. Knapton*, 1690.

——— History of Charles the eighth of France; or, invasion of Naples by the French. 4 p. l. 79 pp. sm. 4°. *A. Isted*, 1672.

——— Juliana; or the princess of Poland: a tragicomedy. 6 p. l. 63 pp. sm. 4°. *London, W. Cademan*, 1671.

——— Married beau; or, curious impertinent: a comedy. 5 p. l. 68 pp. sm. 4°. *London, R. Bentley*, 1694.

——— Misery of civil war: a tragedy. 2 p. l. 72 pp. sm. 4°. *London, R. Bentley*, 1680.

——— The same. (Henry the sixth, the second part.) 2 p. l. 72 pp. sm. 4°. *London, R. Bentley*, 1681.

——— Regulus: a tragedy. 2 p. l. 63 pp. sm. 4°. *London, J. Knapton*, 1694.

——— Sir Courtly Nice; or, it cannot be: a comedy. 2d ed. 4 p. l. 52 pp. sm. 4°. *London, R. Bentley*, 1693.

——— Thyestes: a tragedy. 3 p. l. 56 pp. sm. 4°. *London, R. Bentley*, 1681.

Cruden (*Rev.* Alexander). A complete concordance to the holy scriptures. Condensed edition. iv, 568 pp. 8°. *New York, Lewis Colby*, 1845.

Cruikshank (George). Bachelor's own book, being the progress of Mr. Lambkin in the pursuit of pleasure and amusement, and also in search of health and happiness. 13 pl. obl 24°. *London, D. Bogue*, 1844.

Cruikshank (Robert). Cruikshank at home: a new family album of endless entertainment. With illustrations. 1st, 2d, and 3d series. 3 v. 16°. *London, W. Kidd*, [n. d. *about* 1840.]

Crummell (*Rev.* Alexander). The future of Africa: addresses, sermons, etc. delivered in the republic of Liberia. 354 pp. 12°. *New York, C. Scribner*, 1862.

Cruse (Englehart). Projector detected; or, some strictures on the plan of Mr. James Rumsey's steamboat. 14 pp. 18°. *Baltimore, J. Hayes,* 1788.

Cuba. Informe presentado a la real junta de fomento de agricultura y commercio de esta isla, 1833. iv, 153 pp. 4°. *Habana,* 1834. s.

——— Materiales relativos a la historia de la isla de Cuba. Recogidos y redactados por una comision especial. xvi, 274 pp. 2 l. 8°. [*Habana*], n. d. s.

Cuitt (George). Wanderings and pencillings amongst ruins of the olden time; a series of 73 etchings. With descriptive letter-press. 38 pp. 52 pl. fol. *London, Nattali & Bond,* 1855.

Culm rock; the story of a year. What it brought and what it taught. By Glance Gaylord. (*pseudon.*) 432 pp. 4 pl. 16°. *Boston, H. Hoyt,* [1867].

Cumberland (Richard, *LL. D.*) The observer, being a collection of moral, literary, and familiar essays. [*anon.*] 2d ed. 5 v. 8°. *London, C. Dilly,* 1788–90.

Cumming (John, *D. D.*) Last warning cry; with reasons for the hope that is in me. 327 pp. 8°. *New York, G. W. Carleton & Co.* 1867.

Cundall (Joseph). Photographic tour. *See* **Delamotte** (Philip H.) *and* **Cundall.**

Cunningham (J. W.) A world without souls. 170 pp. 18°. *Philadelphia, E. Earl,* 1815.

——— The velvet cushion. 151 pp. 18°. *Philadelphia, E. Earl,* 1815.
[*With* his "WORLD without souls."]

Cunningham (William M.) Cross' masonic chart, revised, containing the degrees of the ancient York rite, as worked in the U. S. [With] historical sketch of the origin and progress of free-masonry. 2d ed. 332 pp. 49 pl. 8°. *Philadelphia, Moss & Co.* 1867.

——— Manual of the ancient accepted Scottish rite, arranged to correspond with the ritual of the supreme council of the 33d degree for the northern masonic jurisdiction of the U. S. 3d ed. 286 pp. 12°. *Philadelphia, Moss & Co.* 1867.

Curiae canadenses, or the Canadian law courts; a poem, by Plinius Secundus. [*anon.*] 3 l. 126 pp. 8°. *Toronto, H. & W. Rowsell,* 1843.

Curione (Celio Secondo). Defence of the true and old authority of Christ's church. Translated by John Philpot. pp. 319–446.
[*In* PHILPOT (John). Examinations and writings. 8°. *Cambridge,* 1842.]

Curiosités anecdotiques. 404 pp. 18°. *Paris, Paulin,* 1855.
[Bibliothèque de poche].

Curiosités de l'archéologie et des beaux arts. vi, 493 pp. 18°. *Paris, Paulin,* 1855.
[Bibliothèque de poche].

Curiosités des inventions et découvertes. 471 pp. 18°. *Paris, Paulin,* 1855.
[Bibliothèque de poche].

Curiosités historiques. 380 pp. 18°. *Paris, Paulin,* 1855.
[Bibliothèque de poche].

Curiosités militaires. 416 pp. 18°. *Paris, Paulin,* 1855.
[Bibliothèque de poche].

Curiosités philologiques, géographiques, et ethnologiques. 370 pp. 18°. *Paris, Paulin,* 1855.
[Bibliothèque de poche].

Currey (Richard O.) Sketch of the geology of Tennessee. x, 128 pp. 1 map. 8°. *Knoxville, Kinsloe & Rice,* 1857. s.

Currie (William). A synopsis, or general view of the principal theories of diseases. 172 pp. 12°. *Philadelphia, E. Parker,* 1815. s.

Curry (John P.) Volunteers' camp and field book, containing information on the art of war. 144 pp. 18°. *Richmond, West & Johnston,* 1862.

Curtis's botanical magazine. Ed. by Sir W. J. Hooker. v. 92, (or 3d series, v. 22). 69 l. 66 pl. 8°. *London, L. Reeve & Co.* 1867.

Curtius (Ernst). Peloponnesos; eine historisch-geographische beschreibung der halbinsel. 2 v. vi, 495 pp. 9 maps; 639 pp. 21 maps. 8°. *Gotha, J. Perthes,* 1851–52. s.

Curwen (John Christian). Observations on the state of Ireland, principally directed to its agriculture and rural population. 2 v. xix, 435 pp; xii, 355 pp. 8°. *London, Baldwin, Cradock & Joy,* 1818.

Cushing (*Rev.* David). Divine judgments upon tyrants, and compassion for the oppressed; [commemorative] sermon at Lexington, Apr. 20, 1778. 28 pp. 8°. *Boston, Powars & Willis,* 1778.

Cushman (Robert). The sin and danger of self-love described; a sermon preached at Plimouth in New England in 1620. vi, 26 pp. 18°. *Boston,* 1724.
(Imperfect; title page, and pp. 23 to 26 wanting, supplied in Ms.)

Cusick (David). Sketches of the ancient history of the Six nations. 36 pp. 2 pl. 16°. *Lockport, Cooley & Lathrop,* 1828.

——— The same. 35 pp. 4 pl. 8°. *Lockport, Turner & McCollum,* 1848.

Cutler (Elbridge Jefferson). War poems. 59 pp. sq. 16°. *Boston, Little, Brown & Co.* 1867.

Cutler (Henry Stephen). The masonic harmonia; a collection of music for the use of the masonic fraternity. 120 pp. 12°. *New York, Masonic pub co.* 1867.

Cuvier (Georges Léopold Chrétien Frédéric Dagobert, *baron*). Discours sur les révolutions de la surface du globe. 5e éd. vi, 400 pp. 6 pl. 8°. *Paris, G. Dufour & E. D'Ocagne,* 1828. s.

——— The same. Ansichten von der urwelt, nach der zweiten originalausgabe verdeutscht .... von J. Nöggerath. 2 v. in 1. viii, 340 pp; xii, 220 pp. 8°. *Bonn, E. Weber,* 1822–26. s.

APPENDED.

[CRICHTON über das clima der urwelt].

——— Histoire des sciences naturelles pendant la deuxième moitié du xviiie siècle et une partie du xixe; complétée par Magdeleine de Saint-Agy. 2 v. 2 p. l. 351 pp; 440 pp. 8°. *Paris, Fortin, Masson & Cie.* 1843. s.

[*Note.*—The same as his Histoire des sciences naturelles, depuis leur origine, etc. v. 4–5].

——— Leçons d'anatomie comparée, recueillies et publiées par C. Duméril. 5 v. 8°. *Paris, Baudouin,* 1800–05.

CONTENTS.

v. 1. Organes du mouvement. xxxi, 521 pp. 9 tab.
v. 2. Organes des sensations. xvi, 697 pp.
v. 3—4. Organes de la digestion, circulation, respiration, voix. xxviii, 558 pp; xii, 539 pp.
v. 5. Organes de la génération, excrémentielles. vii, 368 pp. 52 pl.

——— The same. [Revues par F. G. Cuvier, Laurillard, et G. L. Duvernoy]. 2e éd. 8 v. in 9. 8°. *Paris, Crochard & Cie.* 1835–49. s.

CONTENTS.

v. 1. Généralités, et les organes du mouvement des animaux vertébrés.
v. 2. Organes du mouvement et ostéologie de la tête.
v. 3. Système nerveux, etc.
v. 4. Organes de mastication, etc.
v. 5. Organes d'alimentation des mollusques, animaux articulés et zoophytes.
v. 6—7. Description du fluide nourricier dans les quatre types, etc.
v. 8. Organes de génération et des sécrétions, etc.

——— Le règne animal distribué d'après son organisation. 4 v. 8°. *Paris, Déterville,* 1817. s.

——— The same. The animal kingdom arranged in conformity with its organization. The crustacea, arachnides, and insecta, by P. A. Latreille. Translated from the French, [2d ed]. with notes, etc, by H. McMurtrie. 4 v. 8°. *New York, Carvill,* 1831. s.

——— The same. New ed. with additions by W. B. Carpenter and J. O. Westwood. xxii, 706 pp. 44 pl. 8°. *London, A. Fullarton & Co.* 1849. s.

——— *See* **Guérin**. Iconographie du règne animal.

Cuvier (Frédéric). De l'histoire naturelle des cétacés, etc. lii, 416 pp. 22 pl. 8°. *Paris, Roret,* 1836. s.

——— Des dents des mammifères, considérées comme caractères zoologiques. lv, 258 pp. 103 pl. 8°. *Strasbourg, Levrault,* 1825. s.

——— Description des mammifères et des oiseaux les plus remarquables, etc. 2 v. 8°. s.

[*With* BUFFON. Oeuvres complètes. Supplément, 1831–32].

Cyprian (Johann). Historiæ animalivm continvatio.

[*With* FRANZ (Wolfgang). Historia animalivm. v. 2].

Cyrillus (*Saint, bishop of Jerusalem*). Speculum sapiencie, alias quadripartitus apologeticus vocatus. 59 l. unp. fol. [*Basileae,* 1473]. s.

Czerwiakowski (Ignacy Rafal). Opisanie roslin skrytopleiowych lekarskich i przemyslowych. Botaniki szczególnéj. 3 v. 8°. *Kraków, Drukarni uniwersytetu,* 1849–59. s.

Czjzek (Johann). Erläuterungen zur geognostischen karte der umgebungen Wiens. xxx, 104 pp. 8°. *Wien, W. Braumüller,* 1849. s.

Dablon (Claude). Relation de ce qui s'est passé de plus remarquable aux missions des pères de la compagnie de Jésus en la Nouvelle France, 1672 et 1673. v, 219 pp. 8°. *Nouvelle York, J. M. Shea,* 1861.

——— The same. 1673–79. v, 290 pp. 1 map. 8°. *Nouvelle York, J. M. Shea,* 1860.

Dabney (Richard). Poems, original and translated. 2d ed. 172 pp. 18°. *Philadelphia, Mathew Carey,* 1815.

Dabney (Robert L.) Life of Lieut. Gen. Thomas J. Jackson (Stonewall Jackson). 2 v. vi, 333 pp; xvi, 527 pp. 1 pl. 12°. *Edinburgh, Nisbet & Co.* 1864.

Da Costa (Emanuel Mendes). Historia naturalis testaceorum Britanniæ; or, the British conchology; in English and French. xii, 254, vii pp. 17 pl. 4°. *London, author,* 1778.

Da Costa (J. M.) Inhalations in the treatment of diseases of the respiratory passages, particularly as affected by the use of atomised fluids. 86 pp. 12°. *Philadelphia, J. B. Lippincott & Co.* 1867.

Dadd (George H.) Theory and practice of veterinary medicine and surgery, containing the curative treatment of diseases of horses and cattle, sheep and swine, and embracing all the latest information on the rinderpest and trichina. 782 pp. 1 pl. 8°. *Cincinnati, R. W. Carroll & Co.* 1867.

Daelli (G.) A relic of the Italian revolution of 1849; album of engravings [illustrative of European politics], with descriptions in English, Italian, and French. 29 pp. 50 pl. obl. 4°. *New Orleans, Gabici,* [1850?] s.

Daggett (John). Sketch of the history of Attleborough, [Ms.] from its settlement to the present time. 136 pp. 8°. *Dedham, H. Mann,* 1834.

Daggett (*Rev.* Naphtali). Faithful serving of God and our generation. A sermon occasioned by the death of Rev. Thos. Clap, president of Yale college. 39 pp. sm. 4°. *New Haven, B. Mecom,* [1767?]

Dagley (Richard). Gems, selected from the antique, with descriptive illustrations by Rev. George Croly. [*anon.*] 4°. *London,* 1704. s.

Daguin (P. A.) Traité élémentaire de physique théorique et expérimentale, avec les applications a la météorologie et aux arts industriels. 3 v. 8°. *Toulouse, E. Privat,* 1855–60. s.

Daily (William M. *D. D.*) Discourses from the pulpit. 306 pp. 1 pl. 12°. *Cincinnati, R. W. Carroll & Co.* 1865.

Daily national intelligencer. July 1866, to June 1867. 2 v. fol. *Washington,* 1866-67.

Daily prayers. Part i. Revised and compiled by the committee of the Cleveland conference. Translated by Isaac M. Wise. 120 pp. 16°. *Cincinnati, Block & Co.* [1857].

[Same in Hebrew. 144 pp. 16°. With the preceding.]

Dalberg (Eric von, *editor*). Suecia antiqua et hodierna. 3 v. in 1. oblong fol. *Holmiae,* [1693–1714]. s.

[Wanting title page.]

Dalbiac (William Wilks). Law list [for 1861]; comprising the judges and officers of the different courts of justice in England and Wales, [etc.] xxiv, 951 pp. 16°. *London, V. & R. Stevens & sons,* [1861].

Dale (*Rev.* James W.) Classic baptism. An inquiry into the meaning of the word βαπτιζω, as determined by the usage of classical Greek writers. 354 pp. 8°. *Philadelphia, Wm. Rutter & Co.* 1867.

Dall, (Caroline H.) The college, the market and the court; or, woman's relation to education, labor and law. xxxv, 499 pp. 12°. *Boston, Lee & Shepard,* 1867.

Dallas (E. S.) The gay science. 2 v. xviii, 334 pp; xvi, 334 pp. 8°. *London, Chapman & Hall,* 1866.

Dallas (*Sir* George). Biographical memoir of Sir Peter Parker. 111 pp. 4°. *London, Longmans,* 1815.

Dallas (William S.) A natural history of the animal kingdom, etc. 817 pp. 2 pl. 8°. *London, &c., R. Griffin & Co.* 1860. s.

Dallaway (James). *See* **Rundle** (Thomas).

Dallington (Robert). Aphorismes. *See* **Guicciardini** (F.)

Dalrymple (Campbell, *Lieut. Col.*) Extracts from a military essay on the raising, arming, clothing, and discipline of the British infantry and cavalry. 31 pp. 8 pl. 12°. *Philadelphia, Humphreys, Bell and Aitken,* 1776.

[With Simes (Thomas). New military dictionary. 1776. Wanting 3 pl.]

Dalrymple (*Sir* David, *lord* Hailes). Remarks on the history of Scotland. vi, 284 pp. 18°. *Edinburgh, Balfour & Smellie,* 1773.

Dalton (John, *D. C. L.*) Meteorological observations and essays. 2d ed. xx, 244 pp. 8°. *Manchester, Harrison & Crossfield,* 1834. s.

——— On the phosphates and arseniates; microcosmic salt; acids, bases and water; and a new and easy method of analysing sugar. 4 v. in 1. 46 pp. 12°. *Manchester, J. Harrison,* 1840–42. s.

Daly (César). L'architecture privée au 19e siècle sous Napoléon iii. Nouvelles maisons de Paris et de ses environs. 2 v. in 3. fol. *Paris, A. Morel & Cie.* 1864.

CONTENTS.

v. 1. Hotels privés.
v. 2. Maisons à loyer.
v. 3. Villas suburbaines.

Dalzel (Andrew). History of the university of Edinburgh from its foundation. With a memoir of the author [by C. Innes. Edited by D. Laing]. 2 v. vi, 280 pp; x, 481 pp. 1 pl. 8°. *Edinburgh, Edmonston & Douglass,* 1862.

Damberger (Christian Frederick [*pseudon.*]). Travels through the interior of Africa from the Cape of Good Hope to Morocco, in the years 1781 to 1797. xxiv, 523 pp. 8°. *Charlestown, (Mass.) S. Etheridge,* 1801.

Dana (E.) A description of the bounty lands of Illinois; also the principal roads and routes through the United States. 108 pp. 12°. *Cincinnati, Looker, Reynolds & Co.* 1819.

Dana (James, *D. D.*) Two discourses: 1, on the commencement of a new year; 2, on the completion of the eighteenth century, delivered in New Haven, January, 1801. 68 pp. 8°. *New Haven, W. W. Morse,* 1801.

Dana (James Dwight). System of mineralogy, comprising the most recent discoveries. 4th ed. 2 v. in 1. 320, 533 pp. 8°. *New York, Appletons,* 1858. s.

——— Supplements to Dana's mineralogy. 1st to 7th, by the author; 8th to 10th, by Geo. J. Brush. 10 v. in 1. 8°. *New Haven, Am. journal of science,* 1855–62. s.

Dana (T. Freeman, *M. D. and* Samuel L. *M. D.*) Outlines of the mineralogy and geology of Boston and its vicinity. With a geological map. 8°. *Boston,* 1818.

Dancourt (Florent Carton). Les œuvres de théatre. 4e éd. 8 v. 16°. *Paris, compagnie des libraires,* 1742.

CONTENTS.

v. 1. Les fonds perdus; Le chevalier à la mode; Les bourgeoises à la mode; L'été des coquettes; La folle enchère.
v. 2. La maison de campagne; L'impromptu de garnison; La parisienne; La femme d'intrigues; La désolation des joueuses; La gazette; L'opéra de village.
v. 3. Les vendanges; Le tuteur; La foire de Besons; Les vendanges de Suresne; La foire Saint Germain; Le moulin de Javelle; Les eaux de Bourbon; Prologue et divertissemens nouveaux pour Circe, tragédie en machines.
v. 4. Les vacances; Renaud et Armide; La loterie; La charivary; Le retour des officiers; Les curieux de Compiègne; Le mari retrouvé; Nouveau prologue, et nouveaux divertissemens pour la comédie de l'inconnu.
v. 5. Les fées; Les enfans de Paris; La feste de village; Les trois cousines; Colin-Maillard.
v. 6. L'opérateur Barry; Nouveau prologue, et nouveaux divertissemens pour la comédie des amans magnifiques; La galant jardinier; Le diable boiteux; Second chapitre du diable boiteux; La trahison punie; Madame Artus.
v. 7. Les agioteurs; La comédie des comédiens, ou l'amour charlatan; L'amour charlatan; Céphale et Procris; Sancho Pança.
v. 8. L'inpromptu de Suresne; L'inpromptu de Livry; Divertissement de Sceaux; Les festes nocturnes du cours; Le vert galant; Le prix de l'arquebuze; La métempsicose des amours; La déroute du Pharaon.

Danes (Peter Ludwig). Generalis temporum, notis ab orbe condito usque ad annum 1736. 474 pp. 16°. *Lovanii, M. van Overbeke,* [1741].

Danet (Pierre). Magnum dictionarium latinum et gallicum. 4°. 580 l. *Parisiis, J. Barbou,* 1744.

Dangy (—.) *See* **Daugis** (—.)

Daniel (George). Catalogue of [his] library, and other objects of art and vertu, sold July, 1864. v, 222 pp. 8°. *London, Sotheby,* 1864.

——— Democritus in London; with notes festivous, etc. [*anon.*] 312 pp. 18°. *London, W. Pickering,* 1852.

Daniel (J.) Rinderpest, human plagues, and the small pox; their cause and prevention. 16 pp. 16°. *Macclesfield (Eng.) author,* 1865.

Daniel (Samuel). The collection of the history of England. 4th ed. With continuation unto the raigne of Henry vii. By John Trussell. 4 p. l. 262 pp. sm. fol. *London, J. Williams,* 1850.

——— Poetical works. 8°. *Edinburgh,* 1793.
[Anderson's Brit. poets, v. 4.]

Daniell (Samuel). Sketches representing the native tribes, animals and scenery of southern Africa, engraved by William Daniell. 52 pp. 48 pl. 4°. *London, W. Daniell and W. Wood,* 1820.

Daniell (William). Sketches of a voyager. 27 pl. obl. 8°. [*London, about* 1814].

Danielssen (Daniel C.) *See* **Koren** (J.) *and* **Danielssen.** Pectinibranchiernes Udviklings-historie.

Dänische bibliothec; oder sammlung von alten und neuen gelehrten sachen aus Dännemarck. 5 pts. in 2 v. 16°. *Copenhagen,* 1738–44. s.

Dankers (Jasper), *and* **Sluyter** (Peter) Journal of a voyage to New York, and a tour in several of the American colonies in 1679-80. Translated from the Dutch, by Henry C. Murphy. xlv, 440 pp. 12 pl. 8°. *Brooklyn, N. Y.* 1867.
[Long Island hist. soc. publications, v. 1.]

Dante Alighieri. Divine comedy, translated by H. W. Longfellow. 3 v. 4°. *Boston, Ticknor & Fields,* 1867.

CONTENTS.

v. 1. The Inferno. xii, 413 pp.
v. 2. The Purgatorio. viii, 410 pp.
v. 3. The Paradiso. viii, 452 pp.

——— First canticle, (Inferno,) of the divine comedy. Translated by T. W. Parsons. 216 pp. 4°. *Boston, De Vries, Ibarra & Co.* 1867.

——— The new life. Translated by C. E. Norton. 149 pp. 4°. *Boston, Ticknor & Fields,* 1867.

Danvers (Mass.) Account of the centennial celebration, June 16, 1852; with the proceedings of the town in relation to the donation of George Peabody. 208 pp. 19 pl. 8°. *Boston, Dutton & Wentworth,* 1852. s.

——— Proceedings at the reception and dinner in honor of George Peabody, October 9, 1856. With an historical sketch of the Peabody institute. vii, 195 pp. 18 pl. 8°. *Boston,* 1856. s.

Danz (J. And.) Interpres Ebraeo-Chaldævs, omnes vtriusque linguæ idiotismos dextere explicans. Ed. 3a. 361 pp. 42 l. 16°. *Jenæ, J. F. Bielck,* 1715.

D'Arblay (Frances Burney, *madame.*) Evelina; or, the history of a young lady's introduction to the world. xlix, 456 pp. 12°. *New York, Derby & Jackson,* 1858.

Dareste (Rodolphe). La justice administrative en France; ou, traité du contentieux de l'administration. viii, 688 pp. 8°. *Paris, Durand,* 1862.

Darlington (William, *M. D.*) Agricultural botany; an enumeration and description of useful plants and weeds which merit notice, or require the attention of American agriculturists. 12°. *Philadelphia,* 1847. s.

——— Flora cestrica; an attempt to enumerate and describe the flowering and filicoid plants of Chester county, Pa. xxiii, 640 pp. 1 map. 12°. *West Chester, author,* 1837. s.

——— Florula cestrica; an essay towards a catalogue of the phænogamous plants, native and naturalized, growing in the vicinity of the borough of West Chester, in Chester county, Pa. xx, 152 pp. 3 pl. 8°. *West Chester, author,* 1826. s.

Darnley (*Sir* Charles). *See* **Vermont** (*marquis* de) and **Darnley.** London and Paris. *London,* 1823.

Darondeau (B.) *and* **Chevalier** (E.) Physique: observations météorologiques et magnétiques. *See* **Vaillant,** (A. N.) Voyage, etc.

Daru (Pierre Antoine Noël Bruno, *comte*). Notions statistiques sur la librairie. 44 pp. 4°. *Paris, F. Didot,* 1827. s.

Darwin (Charles). Journal and remarks.

With FITZROY (Robert) and others. Narrative of the ships Adventure and Beagle. v. 3.

——— Monograph on the fossil balanidæ and verrucidæ of Great Britain. 4°. *London,* 1854. s.

[Palæontographical society publications.]

——— Monograph on the fossil lepadidæ, or pedunculated cirripedes of Great Britain. 4°. *London,* 1851. s.

[Palæontographical society publications.]

——— On the origin of species by means of natural selection, or the preservation of favoured races in the struggle for life. 4th ed. with additions. 8°. *London, J. Murray,* 1866.

——— The same. 432 pp. 12°. *New York, D. Appleton & Co.* 1860. s.

Darwin (Erasmus). Phytologia; or, the philosophy of agriculture and gardening, with the theory of draining morasses, etc. viii, 556 pp. 12 pl. 8°. *Dublin, P. Byrne,* 1800. s.

——— Temple of nature; or, the origin of society; a poem, with philosophical notes. 200 pp. 2 l. 144 pp. 8°. *Baltimore, Bonsal & Niles,* 1804.

Daubenton (Louis Jean Marie). *See* **Buffon** (G. L. L. *comte* de), and **Daubenton.** Histoire naturelle.

Daubrée (Gabriel Auguste). Études et expériences synthétiques sur le métamorphisme et sur la formation des roches cristallines. vii, 127 pp. 4°. *Paris, Acad. de sciences,* 1860. s.

Daudin (François Marie). Histoire naturelle, générale et particulière des reptiles. 8 v. 8°. *Paris, Dufart,* 1802–03. s.

——— Traité élémentaire et complet d'ornithologie, ou histoire naturelle des oiseaux. v. 1–2. 474 pp, 8 pl; 473 pp, 21 pl. 4°. *Paris, Bertrandet,* 1800. s.

[No more published.]

CONTENTS.

v. 1. Généralités.
v. 2. Oiseaux sédilipèdes.

Daughter (The) of Zion awakened, and putting on strength. [By] M. F. [*anon.*] 19 pp. sm. 4°. [n. p.] 1677.

Daughters (The) of the prairie. [*anon.*] 301 pp. 3 pl. 16°. *Boston, Amer. tract soc.* 1865. s.

Daugis, *or* **Dangy** (——). Traité sur la magie, le sortilège, les possessions, obsessions, et maléfices. Par M. D. [*anon.*] 2 p. l. xxiv, 204, 18 pp. 16°. *Paris, P. Prault,* 1732.

Daunou (Pierre Claude François). Analyse des opinions diverses sur l'origine de l'imprimerie. [pp. 311–424 of v. 1 of Lambinet's Origine, etc.] s.

Daurignac (J. M. S.) History of the society of Jesus, from its foundation to the present time. Translated by Jas. Clements. 2 v. xvi, 421 pp; 372 pp. 12°. *Cincinnati, J. P. Walsh,* 1865.

Dauton. *See* **Auton** (Jehan d').

Dauzats (Adrien). *See* **Blanchard** (P.) *and* **Dauzats.** San Juan de Ullùa. *Paris,* 1839.

Davaine (C.) Recherches sur la génération des huitres. 50 pp. 2 pl. 8°. *Paris, E. Thunot & Cie.* 1853. s.

——— Traité des entozoaires et des maladies vermineuses de l'homme et des animaux domestiques. xcii, 838 pp. 8°. *Paris, Baillière,* 1860.

Davanzati (Bernardo). Lezione delle monete, con la notizia de'cambj.

[SCRITTORI class. ital. di econ. pol. v. 43.]

Daveis (Charles Stewart, *LL.D.*) An address delivered on the commemoration at Fryeburg, May 19, 1825, [of Lovel's fight.] 64 pp. 8°. *Portland, James Adams, jr.* 1825.

Davenant (*Sir* William). Gondibert: an heroick poem. 88 pp, 2 l. 314 pp, 3 l. 4°. *London, John Holden,* 1651.

——— Poetical works. 8°. *Edinburgh,* 1793.
[Anderson's British poets, v. 4.]

Davenport (A. Benedict). A history and genealogy of the Davenport family, in England and America, from A. D. 1086 to 1850. 398 pp. portrait. 12°. *New York,* 1851.

Davenport (Bishop). History of the United States; for the use of schools. New ed. 173 pp. 18°. *Philadelphia, U. Hunt & son,* 1850. s.

Davenport (*Rev.* John). The profession of the faith at his admission into one of the churches of God in New England. [*anon.*] 8 pp. sm. 4°. *London, John Handcock,* 1642.

Davesiès de Pontès (Lucien). Études sur l'Angleterre; réformes sociales. 2e éd. xii, 612 pp. portrait. 16°. *Paris, Lévy,* 1867.

——— The same. Social reform in England. Translated by the widow of the author. 12°. *London, Cassell, Petter & Galpin,* 1866.

David (*l'abbé* P.) History of the campaigns of general Pichegru, 1794–5, with memoirs of generals Pichegru, Jourdan, etc. Translated from the French. xxiv, 268 pp. 8°. *London, G. & J. Robinson,* 1796.

Davidson (John, *F. R. S.*) Notes taken during travels in Africa. 3 p. l. 218 pp. 3 pl. 4°. *London, T. L. Cox,* 1839.

Davidson (Thomas). Monograph of the British fossil brachiopoda. 8 v. in 3. 4°. *London,* 1852-65.
[Palæontographical society.]

CONTENTS.

Introduction: i. On the anatomy of terebratula. By Richard Owen. ii. On the intimate structure of the shells of brachiopoda. By W. Carpenter. iii. On the classification of the brachiopoda. By Thomas Davidson. v. 1.
Part i. Monograph of British tertiary brachiopoda. v. 1.
Part ii. Monograph of British cretaceous brachiopoda. v. 1.
Part iii. Monograph of British oolitic and liasic brachiopoda. v. 1.
Part iv. Monograph of British permian brachiopoda. v. 2.
Part v. Monograph of British carboniferous brachiopoda. v. 2.
Part vi. Monograph of British Devonian brachiopoda.

Davies (Benjamin). Some account of the city of Philadelphia. 93 pp. 16°. *Philadelphia, R. Folwell,* 1794.

Davies (Charles). Arithmetic. 360 pp. 12°. *New York, A. S. Barnes & Co.* 1848. s.

——— The same. 52d ed. 360 pp. 12°. *New York, A. S. Barnes & Co.* 1850. s.

——— Intellectual arithmetic. 179 pp. 16°. *New York, A. S. Barnes & Co.* 1854. s.

——— Outlines of mathematical science for the school room. 168 pp. 16°. *New York, A. S. Barnes & Co.* 1867.

Davies (*Sir* John). Historical relations: or, a discovery of the true causes why Ireland was never entirely subdued until the reign of king James I. 4 p. l. unp. 123 pp. 16°. *Dublin, S. Hyde,* 1733.
[*With* DAVIS (*Sir* John). Immortality of the soul. 16°. *Dublin,* 1733.]

——— Letter to the earl of Salisbury [concerning corbes, erenachs, and termon lands.] 44 pp. 8°. *Dublin, T. Ewing,* 1774.
VALLANCEY (C.) Collectanea de rebus Hibernicis. v. 1. No. 2.]

——— Poem on the immortality of the soul. With essay, by T. Sheridan. 96 pp. 16°. *Dublin, Hyde & Dobson,* 1733.

——— Poetical works. 8°. *Edinburgh,* 1793.
[Anderson's Brit. poets, v. 2.]

Davies (*Rev.* Samuel). Sermons on important subjects, with an essay on the life and times of the author, by Albert Barnes. 4th ed. 3 v. 12°. *New York, R. Carter,* 1845.

Davies (Thomas A.) How to make money and how to keep it. 322 pp. 12°. *New York, Carleton,* 1867.

Daviler. *See* **Aviler** (D'.)

Davis (Andrew Jackson). Arabula; or, the divine guest. Containing a new collection of gospels. 403 pp. 12°. *Boston, W. White & Co.* 1867.

Davis (Henry Winter). Speeches and addresses delivered in congress, etc. With sketch of his life, being an oration by J. A. J. Creswell. 596 pp. portrait. 8°. *New York, Harpers,* 1867.

Davis (Isaac, *of Dover, Del*). The defence of Davis, on the charge of using undue influence over Laws, in devising his estate. 21 pp. 12°. *Dover, (Del). J. B. Wootten,* (1806?)

Davis (John, *judge of U. S. dist. court, Mass.*) Discourse before the Massachusetts historical society, Boston, Dec. 22, 1813, in commemoration of the landing at Plymouth in 1620, with notes. 31 pp. 8°. *Boston, John Eliot,* 1814.

Davis, (John, *of Salisbury, Eng.*) The American mariners; or, the Atlantic voyage, [with] a vindication of the American character [and] naval annals: or a summary of the actions fought during the late war between the ships of Great Britain and those of the United States. [*anon.*] xii, 384 pp. 16°. *Salisbury, Brodie & Downing,* [1822].

Davis (Jonas Abraham). Autobiography of a convert from Judaism to christianity. 119 pp. 12°. *Knoxville, (Tenn.) Register office,* 1850. s.

Davis (Minnie S.) Rosalie and her two homes. (Round Hill stories). 191 pp. 16°. *Boston, R. A. Ballou,* 1866.

Davis (N. S.) A text-book of agriculture. 187 pp. 12°. *New York, S. S. & W. Wood,* 1848. s.

Davis (*Mrs.* R. H.) Waiting for the verdict. 361 pp. 4 pl. 8°. *New York, Sheldon & Co.* 1868.

Davis (W. W. H.) History of the 104th Pennsylvania regiment, from August 22, 1861, to September 30, 1864. 364 pp. 6 pl. 8°. *Philadelphia,* 1866.

Davity (Pierre). Descriptio orbis. *See* **Linda** (L. de).

Davy (Charles). Letters upon subjects of literature, with an explanation of the Greek musical modes. 2 v. xii, 423 pp; 541 pp. 15 pl. 8°. *Bury St. Edmunds, J. Rackham,* 1787.

Davy (John Tanner). The Devon herd book. 4 v. in 1. 486 pp. 2 pl. 8°. *Exeter, W. Roberts,* 1851–63.

Dawson (John William). On the conditions of the deposition of coal, more especially as illustrated by the coal formation of Nova Scotia and New Brunswick. [With] appendix. Descriptive list of carboniferous plants. (Extract). 77 pp. 9 pl. 8°. [*London*], *Geological soc.* 1866. s.

Day (Albert, *M. D.*) Methomania; a treatise on alcoholic poisoning. With an appendix by H. R. Storer, *M. D.* 70 pp. 16°. *Boston, J. Campbell,* 1867.

Day (Angel). The English secretorie; or, methode of writing of epistles and letters. [2d ed.?] 6 p. l. 441 pp. 5 l. 16°. *London, W. Stansby,* 1592.

Day (George Edward, *D. D.*) A genealogical register of the descendants, in the male line, of Robert Day, of Hartford, Conn, who died in the year 1648. 2d ed. 129 pp. 8°. *Northampton,* (*Mass.*) *J. & L. Metcalf,* 1848.

Day (Henry N.) The art of discourse; a system of rhetoric. xvi, 343 pp. 12°. *New York, C. Scribner & Co.* 1867.

——— Elements of Logic. x, 237 pp. 12°. *New York, C. Scribner & Co.* 1867.

——— Grammatical synthesis. The art of English composition. xii, 356 pp. 12°. *New York, C. Scribner & Co.* 1867.

Day (Thomas). Reflections upon the present state of England, and the independence of America. 3d ed. 129 pp. 12°. *London, J. Stockdale,* 1783.

Dean (Richard). Essay on the future life of brutes, introduced with observations upon evil. 2 v. xxx, 113 pp; xxi, 118 pp. 16°. *Manchester, J. Harrop,* 1767.

Dean (Silas). A brief history of the town of Stoneham, Mass. 36 pp. 12°. *Boston, S. R. Hart,* 1843.

Deane (*Rev.* Samuel, *D. D.*) *See* Smith (*Rev.* Thomas), *of Falmouth, Me.* Journals. *Portland,* 1849.

Dearing (*Rev.* Arthur). An essay on the fugitive slave law of 1850. *See* **Lewis** (John W.) Life of Charles Bowles.

Dearn (T. D. W. *architect*). Designs for lodges and entrances to parks, paddocks, and pleasure grounds. New ed. 4 p. l. 19 pp. 20 pl. fol. *London, J. Taylor,* 1823.

Debes (Lucas Jacobson). Faeroæ and Faeroa reserta: a description of the islands and inhabitants of Foeroe. Englished by J(ohn) S(terpin). 12 p. l. 408 pp. 2 maps. 18°. *London, W. Iles,* 1676.

DeBow (James D. B.) Mortality statistics of the 7th census of the United States, 1850. 304 pp. 8°. *Washington, A. O. P. Nicholson,* 1855. s.

——— De Bow's review, July 1866, to June 1867. New series, v. 2–3. [Complete series, v. 33–34]. 8°. *New York,* 1866–67.

DeBure (Guillaume). Catalogue des livres de la bibliothèque de feu M. le duc de La Vallière. 1e partie. 3 v. 8°. *Paris, DeBure,* 1783. s.

De Bure (J. Jacques, *and* Marc Jacques). Catalogue des livres rares et précieux de la bibliothéque de le comte de MacCarthy Reagh. 2 v. xxviii, 583 pp. 2 pl; 473 pp. 8°. *Paris, De Bure,* 1815. s.

De Candolle (Augustin Pyramus). *See* **Candolle.** s.

Decloux (A.) *and* **Doury** (—). Histoire archéologique, descriptive, et graphique de la saint-chapelle du palais. 48 pp. 25 col. pl. fol. *Paris, A. Morel,* 1865.

De Coetlogon (Dennis). An universal history of arts and sciences. 2 v. vi, 1203 pp. 12 l; 1244 pp. 13 l. 34 pl. fol. *London, J. Hart,* 1745.

De Coin (Robert L.) History and cultivation of cotton and tobacco. vi, 306 pp. 1 map. 12°. *London, Chapman & Hall,* 1864.

Decremps (Henri). Codicile de Jérôme Sharpe, professeur de physique amusante. 328 pp. 1 pl. 8°. *Paris, Lesclapart,* 1787.

——— Les petites aventures de Jérôme Sharp. [*anon.*] 336 pp. 1 pl. 8°. *Bruxelles, Dujardin,* 1789.

Decremps (Henri). Supplément à la magie blanche dévoilée. viii, 287 pp. 8°. *Paris, Lesclapart,* 1788.

Dedu (—, *M. D.*) De l'ame des plantes. 24°. *Leide, P. Vander Aa,* 1685. s.
[*With* GREW (N.) Anatomie des plantes. pp. 247–310].

Deems (James M.) Vocal music simplified. 4°. *Baltimore,* 1849. s.

Deeth (Sylvanus G.) Sale catalogue of valuable books, containing over 100,000 volumes. 156 pp. 8°. *Washington,* 1860. s.

Defence (A) of the protestant bible, as published by the bible societies, against the charge of Rev. Dr. Ryder, that it does not contain the whole of the written word of God. By Akroatees. [*anon.*] 68 pp. 8°. *New York, Leavitt, Trow & Co.* 1844.

Defence of the settlers of Honduras against the unjust and unfounded representations of Col. Geo. Arthur. [With] an account of the descent of the Spaniards on the settlement, 1798. [*anon.*] 101 pp. fol. *Jamaica,* [*W. I.*] *A. Aikman,* 1824.

Defence (The) of Stonington, (Connecticut), against a British squadron, August, 1814. 57 pp. 4°. *Hartford,* 1864.

Defoe (Daniel). An account of the societies for reformation of manners in England and Ireland. [*anon.*] 3d ed. 15 p. l. 132 pp. 7 l. 16°. *London, Aylmer,* 1700.

——— Memoirs of [a cavalier] Col. Andrew Newport. [*pseudon.*] New ed. 439 pp. 8°. *London, E. Jeffery & R. Faulder,* 1792.
[Wanting portrait].

——— Memoirs of Capt. George Carleton, an English officer; including anecdotes of the war in Spain under the earl of Peterborough. Written by himself. [*pseudon.*] 4th ed. xxiii, 463 pp. 8°. *Edinburgh, Constable & Co.* 1809.

——— The same. 149 pp. *London, J. Davis,* 1811.
[Royal military chronicle. v. 1].

——— Minutes of the negotiations of Mons'r Mesnager at the court of England, towards the close of the last reign. Written by himself. [*pseudon.*] 326 pp. 12°. *London, S. Baker,* 1717.

——— Religious courtship; being historical discourses on the necessity of marrying religious husbands and wives only. With appendix, of the necessity of taking none but religious servants. [*anon.*] 7th ed. 4 p. l. 351 pp. 1 pl. 16°. *London, J. Hodges,* 1750.

——— The same. vi, 274 pp. 18°. *Glascow, J. & M. Robertson,* 1789.

Defoe (Daniel), **Richardson** (Samuel) *and others.* A tour through the whole island of Great Britain. Interspersed with useful observations. 7th ed. 4 v. 16°. *London, Rivington,* 1769.

De Forest (J. W.) Miss Ravenel's conversion from secession to loyalty. 521 pp. 12°. *New York, Harpers,* 1867.

Degland (Come Maquet?) *and* **Gerbe** (Z.) Ornithologie européenne, ou catalogue descriptif, analytique et raisonné des oiseaux observés en Europe. 2e éd. 2 v. xxx, 610 pp; xv, 637 pp. 8°. *Paris, J. B. Baillière,* 1867.

Deguin (——, *prof. of physics*). Cours élémentaire de physique. 6e éd. 2v. viii, 484 pp. 6 pl; 466 pp. 6 pl. 8°. *Paris, E. Belin,* 1848. s.

Dehon (*Rev.* Theodore). Discourse, the Sunday following the death of Gen. George Washington. 17 pp. sm. 4°. *Newport, H. Barber,* 1800.

Déjean (Pierre François Marie Auguste, *comte*). Catalogue des coléoptères de la collection du comte Déjean. viii, 136 pp. 3 l. *ms.* 8°. *Paris,* 1821. s.
[Imperfect; title page wanting.]

——— The same. 3e éd. 8°. *Paris,* 1837. s.

De Kay (James E.) Anniversary address on the progress of the natural sciences in the United States, before the lyceum of natural history, New York, 1826. 78 pp. 8°. *New York, G. and C. Carvill,* 1826.

Dekker (G. J.) Beredeneerd woordenboek voor de hollandsche en fransche talen; [ou] dictionnaire raisonné hollandais et français, etc. 2 v. vi, 1127 pp; iii, 1371 pp. 16°. *Brussel, Meline, Cans & Cie.* 1841. s.

De la Beche (*Sir* Henry Thomas). A geological manual. viii, 535 pp. 8°. *Philadelphia, Carey & Lea,* 1832.

——— The geological observer. xxxii, 846 pp. 8°. *London, Longmans,* 1851. s.

——— Report on the geology of Cornwall, Devon, and West Somerset. xxviii, 648 pp. 13 pl. 8°. *London, Longmans,* 1839. s.

——— Vorschule der geologie. Nach dem "geological observer," bearbeitet von Dr. Ernst Dieffenbach. xviii, 624 pp. 8°. *Braunschweig, Vieweg,* 1853. s.

Delafond (O.) Traité sur la maladie de sang des bêtes à laine, suivi de l'étude comparée de cette affection avec la fièvre charbonneuse, etc. viii, 224 pp. 8°. *Paris, F. Locquin,* 1843. s.

Delamarche (A.) *and* **Dupré** (J.) Météorologie et magnétisme. 4 v. 8°. *Paris, A. Bertrand*, 1847–50. s.
[*With* Cécille (J. B. F. M.) Campagne dans les mers de l'Inde et de la Chine.]

Delamotte (Philip H.) *and* Cundall (Joseph). Photographic tour among the abbeys of Yorkshire. With descriptive notices by J. R. Walbran and W. Jones. 50 pp. 23 pl. fol. *London, Bell and Daldy*, 1856.

Delany (Martin Robison). The condition, elevation, emigration, and destiny of the colored people of the United States, politically considered. 215 pp. 12°. *Philadelphia, King & Baird*, 1852.

Delany (Patrick, *D. D.*) Revelation examined with candor. Or, a fair enquiry into the sense and use of the several revelations as they are found in the Bible. [*anon.*] 3d ed. 2 v. xxxi, 282 pp; lxxi, 296 pp. 8°. *London, C. Rivington*, 1735.

Delaunay (Charles Eugène). Traité de mécanique rationelle. 619 pp. 8°. *Paris, Langlois & Leclercy*, 1856.

Delaval (Edward Hussey). An experimental inquiry into the cause of the permanent colours of opake bodies. 128 pp. 8°. *Warrington, W. Eyres*, 1785.

Delaware (The) register and farmer's magazine, [edited] by William Huffington. v. 1-2. 3 p. l. 480 pp; 2 p. l. 490 pp. 8°. *Dover, [Del.] S. Kimmey*, 1838-39.

Delén (Carl.) Engelskt och svenskt lexikon. 4°. *Stockholm*, 1806. s.

——— Ordbok i fabelläran, eller allmän mythologi. 2 v. 2 p. l. 638 pp; 690 pp. 8°. *Stockholm, C. Delén*, 1831–36. s.

——— Swedish and English pocket dictionary. 2 p. l, 626 pp. 24°. *Orebro, N. M. Lindh*, 1829. s.

Delepierre (Joseph Octave). An essay on the mythological and symbolical history of the rose. From the German by C. W. 35 pp. 8°. *London, Trübner & Co.* [1865?]

——— Macaronéana andra, overum nouveaux mélanges de littérature macaronique. 179 pp. sm. 4°. *Londres, Trübner*, 1862.

Deleschamps (Pierre). Des mordans, des vernis, et des planches, dans l'art du graveur; ou traité complet de la gravure. xv, 284 pp. 4 pl. 8°. *Paris, Huzard*, 1836. s.

Delezenne (——. *physicist*). Notes sur la polarisation: suite. 2 v. 108 pp, 2 pl; 104 pp, 2 pl. 8°. *Lille, Soc. royale des sciences*, 1834-35.

Delfico (Melchiorre). Memoria sulla libertà del commercio.
[Scrittori class. ital. di econ. pol. v. 39.]

Délices (Les) et les galanteries de l'Isle de France. [*anon.*] 2 v. in 1. 6 p. l. 272 pp, 2 l; 276 pp. 2 l. 18°. *Cologne, P. Marteau*, 1709.

De Liefde. *See* **Liefde.**

Delille (Jacques, *l'abbé*). The gardens; a poem. Translated from the French by Mrs. Montolieu. 2d ed. 147 pp. 8°. *London, T. Bensley*, 1805.

Delmar (Alexander). International almanac for 1866; or, hand-book of geographical [etc.] statistics, relating to every country. 128 pp. 8°. *New York*, 1866.

——— Statistics of the United States, compiled under the authority of the secretary of the treasury, for the "Paris exposition" of 1867. 72 pp. 8°. *Washington*, 1867.

Del Mar (Emanuel). Guia para la conversacion en Español é Ingles. Habiéndose añadido, etc. par Francisco Javier Vingut. xlii, 17, 157 pp. 12°. *New York, Lockwood & son*, 1854. s.

Delmotte (Henri Florent). Voyage pittoresque et industriel dans le Paraguay-roux et la Palingénésie Australe. Par Tridace-Nafé-Théobrôme de Kaout't 'Chouk, gentilhomme breton. [*pseudon.*] 48 pp. 8°. *Mons, E. Hoyois-Derely*, [1835].

De Man (J. C.) *See* **Van den Broecke** (J. C.) *and* **De Man.** De cholera asiatica. 1850.

Demarest (John T.) *and* **Gordon** (William R.) Christocracy, or essays on the coming and kingdom of Christ; with answer to the objections of postmillenarians. 403 pp. 12°. *New York, A. Lloyd*, 1867.

Demorests' monthly magazine, Jan. 1865 to Dec. 1866. v. 1—2. 4°. *New York, W. J. Demorest*, 1865–66.

De Morgan (Augustus). Elements of trigonometry and trigonometrical analysis. vii, 143 pp. 12°. *London, Taylor & Walton*, 1837. s.

——— The connexion of number and magnitude; an attempt to explain the fifth book of Euclid. iv, 87 pp. 12°. *London, Taylor & Walton*, 1837. s.
[*With* his Elements of trigonometry.]

——— Preface to Ramchundra. Treatise on maxima and minima, etc. xxiii pp. 8°. *London, W. H. Allen & Co.* 1859. s.
[*With* Ramchundra. Treatise on maxima, etc. 1850.]

Demosthenes. The i. ii. iii. philippics. [Gr.] With historical introductions and critical and explanatory notes. By M. J. Smead. 3d ed. [?] xvi, 249 pp. 12°. *Boston, Wm. H. Dennet,* 1866.

——— Select popular orations. [Gr.] With notes and a chronological table by J. T. Champlin. 2d ed. vii, 237 pp. 12°. *Boston, J. Munroe & Co.* 1855.

Denecourt (C. F.) Les délices de la forêt de Fontainebleau. 3e éd. 126 pp. 1 map. 1 pl. 8°. *Fontainebleau, chez l'auteur,* [1845.]

——— Souvenirs historiques et pittoresques de Fontainebleau; avec l'itinéraire descriptif du palais et de la forêt. 89 pp. 3 l. 1 map. 1 pl. 8°. *Fontainebleau, chez l'auteur,* [1845.]
[*With* the preceding.]

Denham (*Sir* John). The true presbyterian without disguise; or, a character of a presbyterian's ways and actions. 10 pp. 12°. *London,* 1705.
[*With* SECRET history of the calves-head club. *London,* 1705.]

Denier (Tony). [*pseudon?*] Amateur's handbook, and guide to home or drawing room theatricals. 86 pp. 16°. *New York,* 1866.

Denina (Giacomo Maria Carlo). Istoria della Italia occidentale. 6 v. 8°. *Torino, G. Balbino, etc.* 1809.

Denis (Michael). Annalivm typographicorvm supplementvm. 2 pts. in 2 v. 4°. *Viennæ,* 1789. s.

Denis (Nicolas). *See* **Denyse** (Nicolas).

Denman (Thomas). The obstetrical remembrancer; or, aphorisms on natural and difficult parturition, etc. augmented by Michael Ryan; with additions by Thomas F. Cock. 258 pp. 24°. *New York, S. S. & W. Wood,* 1848.

Dennis (John). An essay on the navy. [*anon.*] 53 pp. sm. 4°. *London, J. Dennis,* 1702.

Denny (*major* Ebenezer). Military journal. May 1, 1781—May 31, 1795. With memoir by W. H. Denny. pp. 205—498. 8 pl. 8°. *Philadelphia,* 1860.
[Penna. hist. soc. memoirs, v. 7.]

Denny (Henry). Monographia anoplurorum Britanniæ; or, an essay on the British species of parasitic insects belonging to the order anoplura of Leach. xxiv, 262 pp. 26 pl. 8°. *London, H. G. Bohn,* 1842. s.

Dent (*Capt.* Digby). The defence to the complaint made against him by rear-admiral Knowles. 56 pp. 12°. *London,* 1749.

Denys (Nicolas). Description géographique et historique des costes de l'Amériqve septentrionale. Avec l'histoire naturelle du païs. 2 v. 16 p. l. 267 pp; 480 pp. 3 l. 18°. *Paris, Louis Billaine,* 1672.

Denyse (Nicolas). Gemma predicantium. 16 p. l. unp. clxvii l. 4°. *Basilee, Jacobus de Pfortzen,* 1516.

——— The same. 16 p. l. unp. ccxvi l. 16°. *Parisiis, F. Regnault,* 1522.

Depping (Georges Bernard), *and* **Michel** (Francisque Xavier). Wayland Smith. A dissertation on a tradition of the middle ages. From the French, with additions by S. W. Singer. 4 p. l. xcii pp. 16°. *London, W. Pickering,* 1847.

De Puydt (R.) Rapport officiel de la commission d'exploration dans l'Amérique Centrale; au conseil général de la compagnie belge de colonisation. 203 pp. 3 pl. 8°. [n. p. *about* 1840.]

De Ronde (*Rev.* Lambertus). The true spiritual religion, in two discourses. xvi, 262, 9 pp. 12°. *New York, John Holt,* 1767.

Derosne (—) *and* **Cail** (—), *engineers.*) De la elaboracion del azucar en las colonias, y de los nuevos aparatos a mejorarla; trad. por José Luis Casaseca. 216 pp. 4°. *Habana, Imp. del gobierno,* 1844. s.

Derrotero de las islas Antillas, de las costas de Tierra Firme, y de las del Seno Mejicano. 2a ed. 6 p. l. 591 pp. sm. 4°. *Madrid, Imp. real,* 1820. s.

Desaguliers (Jean Théophile). A course of experimental philosophy. 2 v. xii, 475 pp. 32 p. l; xv, 575 pp. 46 pl. 4°. *London, W. Innys,* 1744–45. s.

Descamps (Jean Baptiste). La vie des peintres flamands, allemands, et hollandois. Avec des portraits. 4 v. 8°. *Paris, C. A. Jombert,* 1753–64. s.

——— Voyage pittoresque de la Flandre et du Brabant. 406 pp. 5 l. 16°. *Amsterdam, et Bruxelles, J. Moris,* 1772. s.

——— *and* **Dezallier** d'Argenville (Antoine Joseph). La vie des peintres flamands et hollandais par Descamps, réunie à celle des peintres italiens et français par d'Argenville. 4 v. in 2. 8°. *Marseille, J. Barile,* 1840–43.

Deschamps (Pierre.) Notice biographique et bibliographique sur Gabriel Peignot. Par P. D. [*anon.*] 60 pp. 8°. *Paris, J. Techener,* 1857.

Description (A) of South Carolina. containing many curious and interesting particulars relating to the civil, natural, and commercial history of that colony. [*anon.*] viii, 110 pp. 8°. *London, R. & J. Dodsley,* 1761.

Description (A) of the windward passage and gulf of Florida, with the course of the British trading ships to and from the island of Jamaica. 2d ed. [*anon.*] 23 pp. 2 l. 1 map. 4°. *London, J. Applebee and others*, 1739.

Descroizelles (François Antoine Henri.) Notices sur l'alcali-mètre, et autres tubes chimico-métriques, et sur un petit alambic, pour l'essai des vins. 2e éd viii, 144 pp. 1 pl. 8°. *Paris, auteur*, 1818.

Desdouits (L. M.) La physique en action; ou applications utiles et intéressantes de cette science. 2 v. 443 pp; 453 pp. 8°. *Paris, J. Lecoffre, et Cie.* 1846. s.

Deshayes (Gérard Paul). Description des animaux sans vertèbres découverts dans le bassin de Paris. Text, 3 v. Atlas. 2 v. 4°. *Paris, J. B. Baillière*, 1860-66.

CONTENTS: *text.*

v. 1. Mollusques acéphalés dimyaires. 912 pp.
v. 2. Mollusques acéphalés monomyaires et brachiopodes. Mollusques céphalés. 1e. partie. 968 pp.
v. 3. Mollusques céphalés. 2e partie. Mollusques céphalopodes. 667 pp.

CONTENTS: *atlas.*

v. 1. Mollusques acéphalés. 89 pl.
v. 2. Mollusques céphalés et mollusques céphalopodes. 107 pl.

——— Description des coquilles caractéristiques des terrains. vii, 264 pp. 14 pl. 8°. *Paris, F. G. Levrault*, 1831. s.

——— Description des coquilles fossiles des environs de Paris. 2 v. 390 pp. Atlas 15 pp. 116 pl. 4°. *Paris, auteur*, 1824. (Atlas bound with v. 1.) s.

CONTENTS.

v. 1. Conchifères.
v. 2. Mollusques.

Desjardins (Marie C. H.) *See* **Villedieu**, (*Madame.*)

Deslauriers (———). Les fantaisies de Bruscambille. [*pseudon.*] *Lyon*, 1618. [Reprint.] 315 pp. 18°. *Bruxelles, A. Mertens et fils*, 1863.

Deslongchamps (Auguste L. A. Loiseleur.) *See* **Loiseleur-Deslongchamps.**

Desmarest (Anselme Gaëtan). Mammalogie; ou, description des espèces de mammifères. 2 pts. in 1 v. 555 pp. 4°. *Paris, Agasse*, 1820-22. s.

Desmoulins (Camille). The history of the Brissotins; or, part of the secret history of the revolution, in answer to Brissot's address to his constituents. Translated from the French. 2d ed. 2 p. l. 68 pp. 8°. *London, J. Owen*, 1794.

[*With* Brissot de Warville, (J. P.) Address to his constituents. 8°. *London*, 1794.]

Des Moulins (Charles.) Catalogue raisonné des phanérogames de la Dordogne. (Suite). 178 pp. 8°. *Bordeaux, Th. Lafargue*, 1849.

——— Étude sur les cailloux roulés de la Dordogne, 1865. 60 pp. 8°. *Bordeaux, Codere, Degréteau et Poujol*, 1866. s.

[Suite du bassin hydrographique du Conzeau.]

Des Murs (Parfait O.) Traité général d'oologie ornithologique au point de vue de la classification. xix, 640 pp. 8°. *Paris, F. Klincksieck*, 1860. s.

——— *See* **Chenu** (J. C.) **Des Murs** (P. O.) *and* **Verreaux** (J.)

Desoteux de Cormatin (Pierre Marie Felicité, *baron*). Travels of the duke de Chatelet in Portugal, revised by J. F. Bourgoing. Translated by J. J. Stockdale. 2 v. viii, 295 pp.; 244 pp. 10 l. 1 map. 1 pl. 8°. *London, J. & J. J. Stockdale*, 1809.

Desperiers (Bonaventure). Les contes, ou nouvelles récréations et joyeux devis. Avec un choix des anciennes notes de Bernard de La Monnoye et de Saint Hyacinthe, augmentées par P. L. Jacob [Paul Lacroix]: et d'une notice littéraire par C. Nodier. 322 pp. 16°. *Paris, Gosselin*, 1843.

Despretz (César Mansuète). Traité élémentaire de physique. 3e éd. iv, 884 pp. 16 pl. 8°. *Paris, Méquignon-Marvis*, 1832. s.

Destutt de Tracy (Antoine Louis Claude, *comte*). Observations sur le système actuel d'instruction publique. viii, 80 pp. 1 tab. 8°. *Paris, Panckoucke*, 1801. s.

(*With* PRINCETON, NASSAU HALL COLLEGE. Catalogue of the graduates, 1805.

Desvaux (A. N.) Essai d'ichtyologie des côtes océaniques et de l'intérieur de la France. 175 pp. 2 pl. 8°. *Angers, Cosnier et Lachèse*, 1851. s.

De Tornos (Alberto). *See* **Tornos.**

Deutscher zeitungs-catalog. Verzeichniss der in deutscher sprache erscheinenden periodischen schriften. 3e ausgabe. 8°. *Leipzig*, 1845. s.

Devens (*Rev.* Samuel Adams). Sketches of Martha's Vineyard, and other reminiscences of travel at home, etc. viii, 207 pp. 16°. *Boston, J. Munroe & Co.* 1838.

De Voe (Thomas F.) The market assistant, containing a brief description of every article of human food sold in the public markets of New York, Boston, Philadelphia, and Brooklyn. 455 pp. 1 pl. 12°. *New York, Hurd & Houghton*, 1867.

Devonshire (*Duchess* of). *See* **Cavendish** (Georgiana).

Dewalque (G.) Description des fossiles, etc. *See* **Chapuis** (F.) *and* **Dewalque**.

D'Ewes (*Sir* Simonds). A compleat journal of the votes, speeches and debates, both of the house of lords and house of commons throughout the whole reign of Queen Elizabeth. [Revised and published by P. Bowes.] 6 p. l. 689 pp. 8 l. fol. *London, J. Robinson*, 1708.

De Wint (P.) *See* **Light** (Henry).

De Witt (Jan). Fables, moral and political, with large explications. Translated from the Dutch. [*anon.*] 2 v. 15 p. l. 381 pp. 9 l; vii, 391 pp. 8 l. 1 pl. 12^c^. *London*, 1703.

Dezallier d'Argenville (Antoine Joseph). L'histoire naturelle éclaircie dans deux de ses parties principales, la lithologie et la conchyliologie. [*anon.*] 4 p. l. 491 pp. 33 pl. 4°. *Paris, De Bure*, 1742.

——— Vie des peintres italiens et français. *See* **Descamps** (Jean Baptiste), *and* **Dezallier**, Vie des peintres. *Marseille*, 1840–43.

Dialogue (A) between Timothy and Philatheus. In which the principles of a book entituled Rights of the christian church [by Tindal] are fairly stated and answered. By a layman. [*anon.*] 2d ed. 2 v. 485 pp; 512 pp. *London, B. Lintott*, 1709–10.

Dialogues in a library. [View of the creation, and of the moral and political world. *anon.*] vi, 278 pp. 12°. *London, G. G. & J. Robinson*, 1797.

Diaz de Fonseca. *See* **Suasso Diaz** de Fonseca. Theory of infantry movements, 1846.

Diaz del Castillo (Bernal). Historia verdadera de la conqvista de la Nueva España. 6 p. l. 254 l. 5 l. fol. *Madrid*, 1632.

Dibdin (Charles). Observations on a tour through almost the whole of England, and a considerable part of Scotland, in a series of letters. 2 v. 404 pp; 408 pp. 61 pl. 4°. *London, G. Goulding*, [1801-2].

Dibdin (Thomas Frognall, *D. D.*) A bibliographical, antiquarian, and picturesque tour in France and Germany. 2d ed. 3 v. 12 pl. 8°. *London, Jennings & Major*, 1829.

——— The history of Cheltenham, and an account of its environs, with a concise display of the county of Glocester. xii, 358 pp. 1 pl. 8°. *Cheltenham, H. Ruff*, 1803.

——— An introduction to the knowledge of rare and valuable editions of the Greek and Latin classics. Preceded by an account of polyglot bibles. 2d ed. lxiii, 572 pp. 8°. *London*, 1804.

Diccionario universal de historia y de geografía. 7 v. 8°. *Mexico, Andrade*, 1853–55. s.

——— Apéndice al diccionario universal de historia y de geografía. Coleccion de articulos relativos á la república mexicana. 3 v. 8°. *Mexico, Andrade*, 1855–56. s.

[Forming v. 8–10 of the preceding.]

Diceto (Ralph de). Historia compendiosa de regibus Britonum. fol. *Oxoniæ*, 1691.

[Gale (Thomas) *and* Fell (John). Rerum anglicarum scriptores veteres. *Oxoniæ*, 1684–91. v. 3.]

Dickens (Charles). American notes for general circulation. 126 pp. 2 pl. 8°. *Boston, Ticknor & Fields*, 1867.

——— The same. [Globe edition.] 335 pp. 1 pl. 16°. [*New York, Hurd & Houghton*, 1867.] (*With* Christmas stories, Globe ed.)

——— The same. [Diamond ed.]

[*With* Oliver Twist. Diamond ed. sq. 16°. *Boston, Ticknor & Fields*, 1867.]

——— Barnaby Rudge. [Globe ed.] Illustrated by Darley and Gilbert. 3 v. in 1. 16°. *New York, Hurd & Houghton*, 1867.

——— The same. [With sketches by Boz. part ii.] Riverside edition. Illustrated by Darley [and others.] 4 v. in 2. 630 pp. 21 pl; 641 pp. 23 pl. 12°. *New York, Hurd & Houghton*, 1867.

——— The same, and Hard times. [Diamond ed.] Illustrations by S. Eytinge, jr. 523 pp. 16 pl. sq. 18°. *Boston, Ticknor & Fields*, 1867.

——— Le baron de Grogzwig. Traduit de l'anglais par E. de La Bédollière. 20 pp. 12°. *Paris*, 1841,

[Included in Pléiade, La.]

——— Bleak House. [Globe ed.] Illustrated by Darley and Gilbert. 4 v. in 1. 4 pl. 16°. *New York, Hurd & Houghton*, 1867.

——— The same. [Diamond ed.] With illustrations by S. Eytinge, jr. ix, 498 pp. 16 pl. sq. 18°. *Boston, Ticknor & Fields*, 1867.

——— Christmas books. [Riverside ed.] Illustrated. 2 v. in 1. 300, 300 pp. 14 pl. 12°. *New York, Hurd & Houghton*, 1867.

——— Christmas stories. Pictures from Italy and American notes. [Globe edition.] Illustrated by Darley and Gilbert. 4 v. in 1. 1,295 pp. 4 pl. 16°. *New York, Hurd & Houghton*, 1867.

——— David Copperfield. [Globe ed.] Illustrated by Darley and Gilbert. 4 v. in 1. 4 pl. 16°. *New York, Hurd & Houghton*, 1867.

Dickens (Charles). David Copperfield. [Diamond ed.] With illustrations by S. Eytinge, jr. viii, 494 pp. 16 pl. 18°. *Boston, Ticknor & Fields,* 1867.

——— Dombey and son. [Globe ed.] Illustrated by Darley and Gilbert. 4 v. in 1. 4 pl. 16°. *New York, Hurd & Houghton,* 1867.

——— The same. [Diamond ed.] With illustrations by S. Eytinge, jr. vii, 501 pp. 16 pl. sq. 18°. *Boston, Ticknor & Fields,* 1867.

——— Great expectations. [Globe ed.] 2 v. in 1. 336, 334 pp. 2 pl. 16°. [*New York,*] *Hurd & Houghton,* 1867.

——— The same. [Diamond ed.] sq. 16°. (*With* "Tale of two cities." Diamond ed. pp. 203–460. 19 pl.)

——— Hard times for these times. [Globe ed.] 333, 338 pp. 2 pl. 16°. [*New York, Hurd & Houghton,* 1867.]

——— The same. [Diamond ed.] sq. 18°. (*With* Barnaby Rudge. Diamond ed. pp. 373–523.)

——— The haunted man and the ghost's bargain. 34 pp. 8°. *New York, Harpers,* 1849.

——— Little Dorrit. [Globe ed.] Illustrated by Darley and Gilbert. 4 v. in 1. 1,231 pp. 4 pl. 16°. *New York, Hurd & Houghton,* 1867.

——— The same. [Diamond ed.] With illustrations by S. Eytinge, jr. ix, 480 pp. 16 pl. sq. 18°. *Boston, Ticknor & Fields,* 1867.

——— Martin Chuzzlewit. [Globe ed.] Illustrated by Darley and Gilbert. 4 v. in 1. 14 pl. 16°. *New York, Hurd & Houghton,* 1867.

——— The same. [Riverside ed.] Illustrated by Darley [and others]. 4 v. in 2. 44 pl. 12°. *New York, Hurd & Houghton,* 1867.

——— The same. [Diamond ed.] Illustrations by S. Eytinge, jr. xiii, 480 pp. 16 pl. sq. 18°. *Boston, Ticknor & Fields,* 1867.

——— Nicholas Nickleby. [Globe ed.] 4 v. in 1. 16°. *New York, Hurd & Houghton,* 1867.

——— The same. [Diamond ed.] Illustrated by S. Eytinge, jr. sq. 18°. *Boston, Ticknor & Fields,* 1861.

——— The same. [Riverside ed.] Illustrated by Darley [and others]. 4 v. in 2. 43 pl. 12°. *New York, Hurd & Houghton,* 1867.

——— Old curiosity shop. [Globe ed.] Illustrated by Darley and Gilbert. 3 v. in 1. 3 pl. 16°. *New York, Hurd & Houghton,* 1867.

——— The same; and Reprinted pieces. [Diamond ed.] With illustrations by S. Eytinge, jr. x, 480 pp. 4 pl. sq. 18°. *Boston, Ticknor & Fields,* 1867.

——— The same. [With reprinted pieces and sketches by Boz. Part I. Riverside ed.] Illustrated by Darley [and others.] 4 v. in 2. 602 pp. 17 pl; 636 pp. 35 pl. 12°. *New York, Hurd & Houghton,* 1867.

——— Oliver Twist. [Globe ed.] Illustrated by Darley and Gilbert. 2 v. in 1. 318, 300 pp. 2 pl. 16°. *New York, Hurd & Houghton,* 1867.

——— The same. [Riverside ed.] 2 v. in 1. 318, 300 pp. 16°. *New York, Hurd & Houghton,* 1867.

——— The same. Also pictures from Italy, and American notes for general circulation. [Diamond ed.] Illustrations by S. Eytinge, jr. xi, 487 pp. 16 pl. sq. 18°. *Boston, Ticknor & Fields,* 1867.

——— Our mutual friend. [Globe edition.] Illustrated by Darley and Gilbert. 4 v. in 1. 1,206 pp. 4 pl. 16°. *New York, Hurd & Houghton,* 1867.

——— The same. [Diamond ed.] With illustrations by S. Eytinge, jr. pp. 479. sq. 18°. *Boston, Ticknor & Fields,* 1867.

——— Pictures from Italy. [Globe edition.] 250 pp. 1 pl. 16°. [*New York, Hurd & Houghton,* 1867.] (*With* Christmas stories. Globe ed.)

——— The same.

[*With* Oliver Twist. Diamond ed. sq. 18°. *Boston, Ticknor & Fields,* 1867.]

——— Reprinted pieces. [Globe ed.] 16°. (*With* "Hard times." pp. 63–338, and "Old curiosity shop." pp. 211–298. Globe ed.)

——— The same. [Diamond ed]. sq. 18°. (*With* "Old curiosity "shop, pp. 321–480. Diamond ed.)

——— The same. [Riverside ed.] (*With* "Old curiosity shop." Riverside ed. v. 2. pp. 211–298.)

——— Sketches by Boz. [Globe ed.] 2 v. in 1. 338 pp. 331 pp. 2 pl. 16°. *New York, Hurd & Houghton,* [1867].

——— The same. [Riverside ed.] 338 pp. 25 pl; 331 pp. 17 pl. 12°. *New York, Hurd & Houghton,* 1867.

(Part I with "Old curiosity shop." v. 2. Part II with "Barnaby Rudge." v. 2. Riverside ed.)

——— A tale of two cities. [Globe ed.] Illustrated by Darley and Gilbert. 2 v. in 1. 259, 256 pp. 2 pl. 16°. *New York, Hurd & Houghton,* 1867.

——— The same; and Great expectations. [Diamond ed.] Illustrations by S. Eytinge, jr. v, 460 pp, 25 pl. sq. 18°. *Boston, Ticknor & Fields,* 1867.

——— *and others.* Mugby junction. 32 pp. 8°. *London,* 1866. [*With* "All the year round," v. 16].

Dickenson (*Rev.* Jonathan). God's protecting providence evidenced in the deliverance of Robert Barrow, with other persons from the sea, and also from the cannibals of Florida. 89 pp. 16°. *London*, 1700.

Dickinson (*Rev.* Jonathan). Familiar letters to a gentleman upon important subjects in religion. v, 424 pp. 16°. *Boston, Rogers & Fowle*, 1745.

——— The reasonableness of christianity, in four sermons. xiv, 175 pp. 24°. *Boston, S. Kneeland*, 1732.

Dickson (A. F.) Hazael; or, know thyself. 18°. *Philadelphia*, 1857. s.

Dickson (Samuel, *M. D.*) Principles of the chronothermal system of medicine; with fallacies of the faculty. 1st Am. from 3d London ed. With introduction and notes by Mrs. Turner. 4 p. l. 228 pp. 8°. *New York, J. S. Redfield*, 1846. s.

Dickson (William S. *D.D.*) A narrative of [his] confinement and exile. 2d ed. xv, 371 pp. 8°. *Dublin, John Stockdale*, 1812.

——— Three sermons on scripture politics. 118 pp. 8°. *Dublin, John Stockdale*, 1812.

[*With* his Narrative of confinement and exile. *Dublin*, 1817.]

Dictionnaire françois-berbère. [Dialect écrit et parlé par les kabaïles de la division d'Alger.] [*anon.*] iv, 656 pp. 4°. *Paris, Imprimerie royale*, 1844. s.

Didier (Franklin J.) Franklin's letters to his kinsfolk, from Edinburgh, London, etc. during the years 1818–20. 2 v. xii, 192 pp; 200 pp. 8°. *Philadelphia, J. Maxwell*, 1822.

Didot (Ambroise Firmin). L'Imprimerie, etc. *See* **Exhibition** of 1851.

Diemerbroeck (Isbrand van). Disputationum practicarum pars prima et secunda, de morbis capitis et thoracis. ed. 2a. 4 p. l. 326 pp. 24°. *Trajecti-ad-Rhenum, T. ab Ackersdyck*, 1664. s.

[*With* Marchetti (P.) Observationum medico-chirurgicarum sylloge.]

Dierks (Th.) Prüfung der im herzogthum Oldenburg errichteten wittwen-und waisencassen. Vom pupillenschreiber. Nebst einem anhange, die untersuchungen des Dr. Tiarks. 159 pp. 8°. *Jever, D. Grosse*, [Leipzig, Orthaus], 1846. s.

Dieu (Lodewick de). Rvdimenta lingvæ Persicæ. Accedvnt duo priora capita Geneseos, ex persica translatione Jac. Tawusi. 95 pp. sm. 4°. *Lvgduni Batavorvm*, 1639.

[*With* Wasmuth (M.) Grammat. arab. 1654.]

Diez (Heinrich Friedrich von). Über inhalt und vortrag, enstehung und schicksale des königlichen buchs, aus dem türkisch-persisch-arabischen des Waassi Aly Dschelebi. 214 pp. 8°. *Berlin, J. F. Weiss*, 1811. s.

——— Denkwürdigkeiten von Asien in künsten und wissenschaften, alterthümern, religion und regierungsverfassung. Aus handschriften, etc. gesammelt. 2 v. xxviii, 314 pp; xii, 1079 pp. 8°. *Berlin, Nicolai*, 1811–15. s.

——— Unfug und betrug in der morgenländischen litteratur. 600 pp. 8°. *Halle, Waisenhaus*, 1815. s.

Digby (*Sir* Kenelm). Observations upon Religio medici.

[*With* Browne (*Sir* Thomas). Religio medici. *London*, 1672.]

Digby (Kenelm Henry). Evenings on the Thames; or, serene hours, and what they require. [*anon.*] 2 v. 345 pp; 373 pp. 16°. *London, Longmans*, 1860.

Digges (Thomas). Alæ sev scalæ mathematicæ. 48 l. unp. sm. 4°. *Londini*, 1573.

Dilday (E.) Plain and concise method of garment cutting. 24 pp. 8°. *St. Louis, author*, 1856. s.

Dillon (Frank). Sketches in the island of Madeira. 14 pp. 12 pl. fol. *London, Paul & Dominic Colnaghi & Co.* 1850.

Dillon (Wentworth, *Earl of Roscommon*). Poetical works. 8°. *Edinburgh*, 1793.

[Anderson's Brit. poets, v. 6.]

Dilworth (Thomas). A new guide to the English tongue. New Amer. ed., with additions. 132 pp. 16°. *Harrisburgh, John Wyeth*, 1811.

Dilworth (W. H.) Life of Alexander Pope, with a view of his writings. 151 pp. 18°. *London, Woodgate & Brooks*, 1760.

Dimmock (Charles H.) The modern; a fragment. 24 pp. 8°. *Richmond, J. W. Davies & sons*, 1866.

Dinaux (Arthur Martin). Trouvères, jongleurs, et ménestrels du nord de la France et du midi de la Belgique. 4 v. 8°. *Paris, Téchener*, 1837–63.

CONTENTS.

v. 1. Les trouvères cambrésiens. 3e éd. 3 p. l. 193 pp.
v. 2. Les trouvères de la Flandre et du Tournaisis. viii, 374 pp.
v. 3. Les trouvères artésiens. vii, 483 pp.
v. 4. Les trouvères brabançons, hainuyers, liégeois, et namurois. xl, 717 pp.

Dinsmoor (Robert). Incidental poems, accompanied with letters, and a sketch of the author's life. xxiv, 264 pp. 12°. *Haverhill*, [*Mass.*] *A. W. Thayer*, 1828.

Diogenes. [A weekly journal.] 1853–55. 5 v. [Illust.] 4°. *London*, 1853–55.

Dionigi (Marianna Candidi). Viaggi in alcune città del Lazio che diconsi fondate dal re Saturno. 36 l. 30 pl. obl. fol. *Roma, autore,* 1809–12. s.

Dionysius Areopagita. Opera omnia, et commentarii quibus illustrantur. G. Pachymeræ paraphrasis Græce et Latine, cum adnotationibus B. Corderii. Ed. aucta. 2 v. xxxii, 674 pp; xvi, 475 pp. fol. *Venitiis, A. Zatta,* 1755–6.

Dionysius Periegetes. Geographia [Gr. et Lat.] emendata et locupletata additione scil. geographiæ hodiernæ græco carmine pariter donatæ. [Ab Edwardo Wills.] Ed. 4ª. 4 p. l. 124 pp. 4 l. 14 maps. 12°. *Londini, J. & J. Knapton and others,* 1726.
(Imp.; 2 plates wanting.)

——— De situ orbis cum Antonii Bechariae procemio in traductionem. 31 l. unp. sm. 4°. *Christoferus de Pensis dictus Mandello,* 1498.

Dioscorides Pedacius *or* Pedanius. De medica materia libri vi, interprete Marcello Virgilio: cū eiusdē annotationibus; nuperque deligētissime excusi. 6 p. l. 352 l. 6 l. fol. *Florentiae, Haeredes P. Iuntæ,* 1518. s.

Directorium anglicanum, being a manual of directions for the right celebration of the holy communion, for the saying of matins and even song, and for the performance of other ceremonies, according to the ancient use of the church of England. 3d ed. Edited by F. G. Lee. li, 371 pp. 10 pl. 8°. *London, Bosworth,* 1866.

Discourse (A) concerning generosity. [*anon.*] 9 p. l. 143 pp. 24°. [n. p. or d.]
[Title wanting.]

Discourse (A) concerning the original of the powder-plot; together with a relation of the conspiracies against Queen Elizabeth, and the persecutions of the protestants in France to the death of Henry the fourth, collected [from various authors.] 4 p. l. 195 pp. sm. 4°. *London, John Leigh,* 1674.
With THOU (J. A. de). History of the bloody massacres. *London,* 1674.

Discourse (A) of the dukedom of Modena, containing the origine, antiquity, government, manners and qualities of the people, temperature of the climate, and nature of soil. [*anon.*] 30 pp. 8°. *London, W. Crook,* 1674.

Disraeli (Benjamin). Parliamentary reform: a series of speeches delivered in the house of commons, 1848–1866. Edited by M. Corry. 2d ed. xi, 478 pp. *London, Longmans,* 1867.

——— The revolutionary epick. x, 176 pp. 16°. *London, Longman,* 1864.

Disraeli (Isaac). The calamities and quarrels of authors. New ed. Edited by B. Disraeli. vii, 552 pp. 12°. *London, Routledge,* 1859. s.

Disturnell (John). A guide between Washington, Baltimore, Philadelphia, New York and Boston; also routes of travel from Boston to Buffalo, and from New York to Montreal. 62 pp. 16°. *New York, J. Disturnell,* 1846. s.

——— A guide through the middle, northern and eastern States. 18°. *New York,* 1847. s.

——— The influence of climate in North and South America. 8°. *New York,* 1867.

——— United States national register and calender for 1851–52. 12°. *New York,* 1850. s.

——— United States register, or, blue book for 1866. 100 pp. 8°. *New York, S. Tousey,* 1866.

——— The same for 1867, containing political and statistical information. 102 pp. 12°. *New York, S. Tousey,* 1866.

Dix (Dorothea L.) Memorial to the legislature of Massachusetts [protesting against the confinement of the insane in almshouses and prisons.] 32 pp. 8°. *Boston, Munroe & Francis,* 1843. s.

Dix (John A.) Sketch of the resources of the city of New York. [*anon.*] 104 pp. 8°. *New York, G. & C. Carvill,* 1827.

Dixon (Edward H. *M. D.*) Back-bone; photographed from "the Scalpel." 396, viii pp. Portrait. 12°. *New York, R. M. De Witt,* 1866.

——— A treatise on diseases of the sexual system, adapted to popular instruction. 10th ed. with an appendix. xii, 312 pp. 12°. *New York, R. M. De Witt,* [1867.]

Dixon (William Hepworth). New America. With illustrations. 2 v. 8°. *London, Hurst & Blackett,* 1867.

Dizionario dei termini di medicina, chirurgia, veterinaria, farmacia, storia naturale, botanica, fisica, chimica, etc. publicato in Francia da Bégin, Boisseau, Dupuy, Jourdan, Montgarny, Richard, e Sanson. [Trad.] da dottori A. Leone, G. B. Fantonetti ed A. Omodei. Ed. 2ª. 856 pp. 8°. *Milano, soc. d. ann. univ. d. scienze, etc.* 1834. s.

Djami. *See* **Jami.**

Dobell (Sydney). The Roman. A dramatic poem. By Sydney Yendys. [*anagram*]. 2d ed. 2 p. l. 166 pp. 12°. *London, R. Bentley,* 1852.

Dobson (Edward). Rudiments of the art of building. xvi, 174 pp. 16°. *London, J. Weale,* 1849. s.

——— The same. 3d ed. xiv, 154 pp. 16°. *London, J. Weale,* 1859.
[*With* GARBETT (E. L.) Rudimentary treatise on the principles of design. 16°. *London,* 1850].

Docte (Henri Le). *See* **Le Docte** (Henri.)

Doctrina christiana en lengua española y mexicana; hecha por los religiosos de la ordē de sctō Domingo. Agora nueuamēte corregida y emēdada. [*anon.*] 9 p. l. unp. 147 l. sm. 4°. *Mexico, Juā Pablos,* 1550.

Documents furnished by the British government under the third article of the convention of St. Petersburg, 1822; and Bayly's list of slaves, remaining on Tangier island, and H. B. M. ships of war, after the ratification of the treaty of Ghent. 112 pp. 8°. *Washington, Gales & Seaton,* 1827.

Documents relating to the settlement of the church of England by the act of uniformity of 1662. Edited by Rev. Geo. Gould. With historical introduction by Peter Bayne. vi, 142, 516 pp. 8°. *London, W. Kent & Co.* 1862.

Dod (Charles R.) Parliamentary companion. 35th year [1867]. 319 pp. 32°. *London, Whittaker,* 1867.

Dodd (George). The curiosities of industry and the applied sciences. 16 v. in 1. 8°. *London, G. Routledge & Co.* 1852. s.

CONTENTS.

Calculating and registering machines. 24 pp.
Chemistry of manufactures. 24 pp.
Corn and bread: what they are to machinery. 24 pp.
Electricity: industrial applications of. 24 pp.
Fire and light: contrivances for their production. 24 pp.
Glass and its manufacture. 24 pp.
Gold: in the mine, the mint, and the workshop. 24 pp.
India-rubber and gutta-percha. 24 pp.
Paper: its applications and its novelties. 24 pp.
Printing: its modern varieties. 24 pp.
Ship (A) in the nineteenth century. 24 pp.
Steam power and water power. 24 pp.
Wool and silk. Fur and feathers. 24 pp.

Dodd (*Rev.* William, *LL. D.*) Poems. viii, 271 pp. 12°. *London, D. Leach,* 1767.

——— Reflections on death. 240 pp. 16°. *Philadelphia, R. Johnson,* 1806.

Dodd (William, *A. M.*) Three weeks in Majorca. viii, 169 pp. 16°. *London, Chapman & Hall,* 1863.

Doddridge (Philip, *D. D.*) Some remarkable passages in the life of Col. James Gardiner, [with] the sermon occasioned by his heroick death. 3d ed. 157 pp. 16°. *Boston,* 1748.

——— The same. 263 pp. 16°. *Boston, Lincoln & Edmands,* 1811. s.

Dodge (Joshua). Sermon at Haverhill, [on second centennial anniversary of the landing at Plymouth]. 28 pp. 8°. *Haverhill, Burrill and Hersey,* 1821.

Dodge (Mary Abigail). Wool-gathering. By Gail Hamilton. [*pseudon.*] 335 pp. 12°. *Boston, Ticknor & Fields,* 1867.

Dodge (William Sumner). A waif of the war; or, the history of the 75th Illinois infantry, embracing the entire campaigns of the army of the Cumberland. 242 pp. 8°. *Chicago, Church & Goodman,* 1866.

——— History of the old second division, army of the Cumberland—commanders McCook, Sill, and Johnson. 582, 51 pp. 10 pl. 4 maps. 8°. *Chicago, Church & Goodman,* 1864.

Dogs' (The) plea; or, reasons submitted by the barking fraternity of Great Britain to the men, their masters, showing why dogs ought to be exempted from taxes. [*anon.*] 26 pp. 8°. *London, R. Griffiths,* 1753.

Dolce (Lodovico). Le ter'ze rime, 1542.
[*With* BERNI (F.) Tutte le opere, etc.]

Döll (J. Ch.) Flora des grossherzogthums Baden. 3 v. 1429 pp. 8°. *Carlsruhe, G. Braun,* 1862. s.

Domeyko (Ignacio). Tratado de ensayos, tanto por la via seca como por la via humeda, de toda clase de minerales y postes de cobre, ploms, plata, oro, mercurio, etc. con descripcion de los caracteres de los principales minerales y productos de las artes en America, y en particular en Chile. 3 p. l. 341, xviii pp. 2 pl. 8°. *Serena, imprenta del colejio,* 1844. s.

——— The same. 2ª ed. viii, 458, xviii pp. 5 pl. 8°. *Valparaiso, imprenta del Diario,* 1858. s.

Donald Fraser. (A novel). 224 pp. 16°. *New York, R. Carter & Bros.* 1867.

Donaldson, (Paschal). Odd-Fellows' pocket text-book. Revised by G. Bertram. 558 pp. 1 pl. 32°. *Philadelphia, Moss & Co.* 1867.

——— Odd-Fellows' text-book and manual. Revised by George Bertram. 366 pp. 12°. *Philadelphia, Moss & Co.* 1867.

Donaldson (Thomas Leverton). Architectural maxims and theorems, and a lecture on the education and character of the architect. xii, 105 pp. 8°. *London, J. Weale,* 1847.

Donaldson (Walter). Recollections of an actor. [1800–1846]. viii, 360 pp. 16°. *London, J. Maxwell & Co.* 1865.

Donaldson (William). North America, a descriptive poem, representing the voyage to America, etc. 19 pp. 4°. *London, J. Shepeard,* 1757.

Donandt (Ferdinand). Versuch einer geschichte bremischen stadtrechts. Mit einer einleitung über die entstehung und fortbildung der bremischen verfassung bis zum jahre 1433. 2 v. in 1. xxi, 352 pp.; iv, 387 pp. 8°. *Bremen, J. G. Heyse,* 1830. s.

Doni (Anton Francesco). La zvcca, divisa in cinqve libri di gran ualore. 8 p. l. 316 l. 18°. *Venetia, F. Rampazetto,* 1565.

Donn (Benjamin). The British mariner's assistant. 424 pp. 12°. *London, B. Law,* 1774.

Donne (John). Poetical works. 8°. *Edinburgh,* 1793.
[Anderson's Pritish poets, v. 4.]

Donne (William Bodham). Essays on the drama. vii, 256 pp. 12°. *London, Parker & son,* 1858.

Donoho (Thomas Seaton). Ivywall. 348 pp. 12°. *Washington, McGill,* 1860.

Dorat (Claude Joseph). Les sacrifices de l'amour; ou, lettres de la vicomtesse de Sénanges, et du chevalier de Versenai; suivies de Sylvie et Moléshoff. [*anon.*] Nouv. éd. 2 pts. in 1 v. xiii, 300 pp; 276 pp. 16°. *Amsterdam,* 1772.

Dorchester. The taxable valuation of the polls and estates, and amount of tax in the town, for the year 1850. 119 pp. 8°. *Boston, David Clapp,* 1850. s.

Doré. By a stroller in Europe. 386 pp. 12°. *New York, Harpers,* 1857. s.

Doris (Charles). Amours secrettes des quatre frères de Napoléon. Par M. le baron B * * *. [*anon.*] 2 v. in 1. 2e éd. 264 pp. 16°. *Paris, G. Mathiot,* 1816.

Dornfeld (J.) Der rationelle weinbau und die weinbereitungs-lehre. xv, 472 pp. 8°. *Heilbronn, A. Scheurlen,* 1864. s.

Dorr (David F.) A colored man round the world. By a quadroon. [*anon.*] 192 pp. 1 pl. 8°. (n. p.) 1858.

Dorset (*earl of*). *See* **Sackville** (Charles).

Dorsey (*Mrs.* Anna H.) The student of Blenheim forest; or, the trials of a convert. 2d revised ed. 346 pp. 16°. *Baltimore, J. Murphy & Co.* 1867.

Dorsey (Sarah A.) Recollections of Henry Watkins Allen. 420 pp. 12°. *New York, M. Doolady,* 1866.

Douce (Francis). Catalogue of books, etc. *See* **Bodleian** library.

Douglas (Gawain, *bishop of Dunkeld*). Select works. With memoirs of the author by Rev. —— Scott. lxi, 150 pp. 18°. *Perth, Morison & son,* 1787.
[*With* DUNBAR (William). Poems. 1788. Title wanting].

Douglass (Amanda M.) In trust; or, Dr. Bertraud's household. 383 pp. 12°. *Boston, Lee & Shepard,* 1866.

——— Stephen Dane. (A novel). 353 pp. 12°. *Boston, Lee & Shepard,* 1867.

Douglass (C. C.) Report of the assistant geologist of Michigan. (**Houghton** (Douglass). Reports on geology of Michigan. doc. No. 4).

Dove (Heinrich Wilhelm). Klimatologische beiträge. 1er theil. viii, 296 pp. 2 maps. 8°. *Berlin, D. Reimer,* 1857. s.
[No more published].

Dover (N. H.) and Great Falls directory; also Salmon Falls (Me.) directory [for 1867]. By Dean Dudley. 115, 32 pp. 8°. *Dover, (N. H.) D. Lothrop & Co.* 1867.

Dow (Alexander). History of Hindostan; [from the death of Akbar to Aurungzebe 1612–66]. With an enquiry into the state of Bengal, etc.
[v. 3 of FERISHTA'S history of Hindostan. 3 v. 4°. *London,* 1770–72.]

Dow (*Rev.* Lorenzo). History of cosmopolite; or, Lorenzo's journal; containing his experience and travels, to 1814. 360 pp. 1 pl. 16°. *New York, John C. Totten,* 1814.

——— The dealings of God, man, and the devil, as exemplified in [his] life, experience, and travels. 4th ed. 704 pp. 12°. *Norwich, (Ct.) William Faulkner,* 1833.

Dowling (Charles Hutton). Iron works. Practical formulæ and rules for finding the strain and breaking weight of wrought-iron bridges. 31 pp. 16°. *London, John Weale,* 1866.

Downey (Stephen W.) Play of destiny, as played by actors from the kingdom of the dead in the theatre of the universe. 76 pp. 8°. *New Creek, (W. Va.)* 1867.

Downing (Clement). A compendious history of the Indian wars; with an account of Angria, the pyrate. Also an account of John Plantain, a pyrate at Madagascar. iv, 238 pp. 18°. *London, T. Cooper,* 1737.

Downing (C. Toogood). The stranger in China; or, the Fanqui's visit to the celestial empire in 1836–7. 2 v. 248 pp; 232 pp. 12°. *Philadelphia, Lea & Blanchard,* 1838. s.

Dozy (*Dr.* F.) *and* **Molkenboer** (J. H.) Prodromus florae bryologicae surinamensis. 54 pp. 19 pl. 4°. *Harlemi, Erven Loosjes,* 1854. s.

Dragon (Le) rouge, ou l'art de commander les esprits célestes, aériens, terrestres, infernaux. 107 pp. 18°. *Nismes, Gaude,* 1823.

Drake (Benjamin). Life of Tecumseh, and of his brother, the prophet. With a historical sketch of the Shawanoe Indians. 235 pp. 12°. *Cincinnati, E. Morgan & Co.* 1841.

Drake (Daniel, *M. D.*) Discourses before the Cincinnati medical library association. 93 pp. 12°. *Cincinnati, Moore & Anderson,* 1852.

Drake (Edward Cavendish). A new universal collection of authentic voyages and travels, selected from the best writers. 796 pp. 10 maps. 56 pl. fol. *London, J. Cooke,* 1768.

——— The same. fol. *London, J. Cooke,* 1770.

Drake (*Sir* Francis). Sir Francis Drake revived. Being a summary and true relation of foure severall voyages by the said Drake to the West Indies. Collected out of the notes of Sir F. Drake, P. Nichols, F. Fletcher, and of divers other gentlemen. 1 pl. sm. 4°. *London, N. Bourne,* 1653.

CONTENTS.

Sir Francis Drake revived. 87 pp.
The world encompassed. 108 pp. 1652.
A summarie and true discourse of Sir F. D's. West Indian voyage. 41 pp. 1652.
A full relation of another voyage into the West Indies. pp. 43–60. 1652.

——— The same.
[Imperfect; title, 2 p. l. and 1 pl. wanting.]

——— Le voyage cvrievx, faict avtovr du monde. [Trad. par F. de Louvencourt, sieur de Vauchelles.] 4 p. l. 230 pp. 16°. *Paris, A. Robinot,* 1641.

Drake (Samuel Gardner). Biography and history of the Indians of North America. 3d ed. 518, xxx pp. 8 pl. 8°. *Boston, O. L. Perkins,* 1834.

——— The same. 10th ed. xii, 696, xvi pp. 10 pl. 8°. *Boston, B. B. Mussey,* 1848.

——— A brief memoir of Sir Walter Raleigh. 35 pp. 1 pl. 8°. *Boston,* 1862.

——— Memoir of the life and writings of Rev. Thomas Prince. 12 pp. 1 pl. 8°. *Boston, C. C. P. Moody,* 1852.

——— A memoir of Rev. Cotton Mather. 16 pp. 1 pl. 8°. *Boston, C. C. P. Moody,* 1851.

——— The witchcraft delusion in New England: its rise, progress, and termination, as exhibited by Cotton Mather and Robert Calef. With preface, introduction, and notes. 3 v. sm. 4°. *Roxbury, (Mass.) W. E. Woodward,* 1866.
(Woodward's historical series, Nos. 5–7.)

Draper (Henry). On the construction of a silvered glass telescope, 15½ in. aperture, and its use in celestial photography. iii, 55 pp. 4°. *Washington,* [*Sm. Inst.*] 1864.
[SMITHSONIAN contributions. v. 14.]

Draper (John William). History of the American civil war. 3 v. v. i. Causes of the war to the close of president Buchanan's administration. 567 pp. 8°. *New York, Harpers,* 1867.

——— A treatise on the forces which produce the organization of plants. With appendix containing memoirs on capillary attraction, electricity, and the chemical action of light. xi, 216 pp. 4 pl. 4°. *New York, Harpers,* 1844. s.

Drapiez (Auguste). Cours complet d'histoire naturelle médicale et pharmaceutique. 2 v. 342 pp; 498 pp. Atlas, 160 pl. 8°. *Bruxelles, H. Dumont,* 1835. s.

——— Indicateur minéralogique.
[*With* BRARD (C. P.) Nouveaux élémens de minéralogie, 1838.]

——— Notice sur l'établissement géographique de Bruxelles. 107 pp. 1 pl. 8°. *Bruxelles,* 1842. s.

Drasche (Anton, *M. D.*) Die epidemische cholera. xiv, 387 pp. 2 col. maps. 8°. *Wien, C. Gerold's sohn,* 1860. s.

Drayton (Michael). Poetical works. 8°. *Edinburgh,* 1793.
[Anderson's Brit. poets, v. 3.]

Drennan (William). A letter to his excellency, earl Fitzwilliam, lord lieutenant, etc. of Ireland. [*anon.*] 3d ed. 51 pp. 8°. *Dublin, J, Chambers,* 1795.

Dreuillette (Gabriel). Narré du voyage faict pour la mission des Abnaquiois et des connaissances tirez de la Nouvelle Angleterre. [Et] epistola ad dominum Joannem Wintrop, etc. 45 pp.
[*With* RECUEIL de la négociation entre la N. France et la N. Angleterre, 1648. *New York,* 1866.]

Dreux-Brézé (Scipion, *marquis* de). Documens historiques ou discours, précédés d'une introduction sur les constitutions, par M. A. Delaforest. 2 v. 431 pp; 422 pp. 8°. *Paris, C. Gosselin,* 1842. s.

Dreux du Radier (Jean François, *and others*). Essai historique, critique, philologique, politique, moral, littéraire et galant, sur les lanternes. Par une société de gens de lettres. [*anon.*] xii, 156 pp. 16°. *Dôle,* [*Paris,*] *Lucnophile & Cie,* 1755.

Drewry (George Overend, *M. D.*) Cholera and typhus. 17 pp. 8°. *London, Williams and Norgate,* 1866.

——— Dyspepsia and nervous derangement: their connection, causes, and treatment, with hints on diet. 40 pp. 8°. *London, Williams & Norgate,* 1865.

Dreyss (Christian). Chronologie universelle; suivie de la liste des grands états anciens et modernes, avec les tableaux généalogiques des familles de France et des principales maisons régnantes d'Europe. xi, 904 pp. 16°. *Paris, Hachette,* 1853.

Drown (S. DeWitt). Record, and historical view of Peoria, [Ill.] 164 pp. 12°. *Peoria, E. O. Woodcock*, 1850.

Droysen (Johann Gustav). Geschichte der preussischen politik. Zweiter theil: die territoriale zeit. 2e abtheilung. vi, 520 pp. vi, 643 pp. 8°. *Leipzig, Veit & Co.* 1859. s.

——— Das leben des feldmarshalls grafen York von Wartenburg. Neue ausg. 2 v. iv, 432 pp; 636 pp. 12°. *Berlin, Veit & Co.* 1854. s.

Druitt (Robert). The principles and practice of modern surgery. New Am. from last London ed. By F. W. Sargent. 576 pp. 8°. *Philadelphia, Lea & Blanchard*, 1848. s.

Drumann (Wilhelm). Ideen zur geschichte des verfalls der griechischen staaten. 776 pp. 8°. *Berlin, Nicolai*, 1815. s.

Drummond (William, *of Hawthornden*). Poetical works. *Edinburgh*, 1793.
[Anderson's Brit. poets, v. 4.]

Drummond (*Sir* William), *and* **Walpole** (*Rev.* Robert). Herculanensia, or archeological and philological dissertations, concerning a manuscript found among the ruins of Herculaneum. xv pp. 2 l. 198 pp. 3 pl. 4°. *London, W. Bulmer & Co.* 1810.

Drummond (*Rev.* William Hamilton). The giant's causeway; a poem. xxiv, 204 pp. 2 maps. 6 pl. 8°. *Belfast, Joseph Smyth*, 1811.

Dryden (John). Albion and Albanus. An opera. 6 p. l. 30 pp. sm. fol. *London, J. Tonson*, 1685.

——— Alexander's feast. 5 p. l. 20 pp. sm. 4°. *London, J. & R. Tonson*, 1736.

——— The same. 8 pp. sm. 4°. *Birmingham, T. Chapman*, 1774.

——— All for love; or, the world well lost. 10 p. l. 78 pp. 1 l. sm. 4°. *London, H. Herringman*, 1678.

——— Amboyna; a tragedy. 6 p. l. 59 pp. 1 l. sm. 4°. *London, H. Herringman*, 1673.

——— Amphitryon; or, the two Sosa's. A comedy. 2d ed. 3 p. l. 57 pp. 1 l. sm. 4°. *London, J. Tonson*, 1694.

——— The assignation; or, life in a nunnery. 6 p. l. 62 pp. sm. 4°. *London, H. Herringman*, 1678. [Imperfect.]

——— Aureng-zebe; a tragedy. 6 p. l. 67 pp. 1 l. sm. 4°. *London, H. Herringman*, 1692.

——— Cleomenes, the Spartan heroe. A tragedy. 8 p. l. 72 pp. sm. 4°. *London, J. Tonson*, 1692.

——— Conquest of Granada. 5th ed. 9 p. l. 124 pp. 1 l. sm. 4°. *London, H. Herringman*, 1695.

——— The same. 7 p. l. 158 pp. 1 l. sm. 4°. [*n. d.*] [Imp; title and 1 p. l. wanting].

——— Don Sebastian; a tragedy. 8 p. l. 132 pp. 1 l. sm. 4°. *London, J. Hindmarsh*, 1690.

——— An evening's love; a comedy. 10 p. l. 89 pp. 2 l. sm. 4°. *London, H. Herringman*, 1671.

——— Fables, with engravings by lady Diana Beauclerc. xviii, 241 pp. 9 pl. fol. *London, J. Edwards*, 1797.

——— The Indian emperour. 4 p. l. 68 pp. 1 l. sm. 4°. *London, H. Herringman*, 1681.

——— The kind keeper; a comedy. 6 p. l. 65 pp. 1 l. sm. 4°. *London, R. Bentley*, 1680.

——— King Arthur; a dramatic opera. 6 p. l. 51 pp. 1 l. sm. 4°. *London, J. Tonson*, 1691.

——— Love triumphant; a tragi-comedy. 5 p. l. 82 pp. 1 l. sm. 4°. *London, J. Tonson*, 1694.

——— Marriage-a-la-mode; a comedy. 4 p. l. 63 pp. 1 l. sm. 4°. *London, H. Herringman*, 1698.

——— The mistaken husband; a comedie. 4 p. l. 70 pp. 1 l. sm. 4°. *London, J. Magnes*, 1675.

——— Poetical works. 8°. *Edinburgh*, 1793.
[Anderson's Brit. poets, v. 6.]

——— The rival ladies; a tragi-comedy. 6 p. l. 68 pp. sm. 4°. *London, H. Herringman*, 1669.

——— Secret love, or the maiden-queen. 4 p. l. 57 pp. 2 l. sm. 4°. *London, H. Herringman*, 1679.

——— Sir Martin Mar-All; a comedy. [*anon.*] 2 p. l. 59 pp. 1 l. sm. 4°. *London, H. Herringman*, 1678.

——— The Spanish fryar. 5 p. l. 83 pp. 1 l. sm. 4°. *London, R. & J. Tonson*, 1681.

——— The state of innocence, and fall of man; an opera. 8 p. l. 38 pp. sm. 4°. *London, H. Herringman*, 1684.

——— The tempest; a comedy. 3 p. l. 62 pp. sm. 4°. *London, H. Herringman*, 1690.

——— Troilus and Cressida; a tragedy. With preface containing the grounds of criticism in tragedy. 12 p. l. 69 pp. 1 l. sm. 4°. *London, A. Swall*, 1679.

——— Tyrannick love; a tragedy. 5 p. l. 58 pp: 1 l. sm. 4°. *London, H. Herringman*, 1695.

——— The wild gallant; a comedy. 4 p. l. 78 pp. 1 l. sm. 4°. *London, H. Herringman*, 1669.

Drysdale (C. R. *M. D.*) Prostitution medically considered, with some of its social aspects. 41 pp. 8°. *London, R. Hardwicke*, 1866.

Dschami. *See* **Jami.**

Dub (Julius). Die anwendung des elektromagnetismus, mit besonderer berücksichtigung der telegraphie. xvi, 645 pp. 8°. *Berlin, J. Springer*, 1863. s.

——— Der elektromagnetismus. xxii, 516 pp. 8°. *Berlin, J. Springer*, 1861. s.

DuBartas (Guillaume de Saluste). [Poetical works]. Translated by Joshua Sylvester. 17 p. l. 617 pp. sm. 4°. *London*, 1605.

CONTENTS.

First weeke: or birth of the world.
Second weeke: or childhood of the world.
Fragments and other small workes.

Dublin university magazine. July 1866 to June 1867. v. 68–69. 8°. *Dublin, G. Herbert*, 1866–67.

Dubois (E.) *See* **Posthumous** parodies.

Dubois *or* Sylvius (Jacques). Ratio medendi morbis internis prope omnibus. 216 pp. 2 l. 24°. *Lvgdvni, G. Rouille*, 1549. s.

Ducatel (Julius T.) Report of the geologist [of Maryland, for 1834–36. 8°. *Annapolis, state printing office*, 1835–37.] s.
[Maryland geology, v. 1.]

——— Report of the geologist [of Maryland, for 1837.] 40 pp. 8°. [*Annapolis, state printing office*, 1838.] s.
[Maryland geology, v. 1.]

Du Chaillu (Paul B.) Explorations and adventures in equatorial Africa. 531 pp. 1 pl. 1 map. 8°. *New York, Harper & Bros.* 1861. s.

——— Journey to Ashango-Land; and further penetration into equatorial Africa. With map and illustrations. xxiv, 501 pp. 22 pl. 1 map. 8°. *New York, D. Appleton & Co.* 1867.

Duché (*Rev.* Jacob). Observations on a variety of subjects. By [Tamoc Caspipina, *pseudon.*] a gentleman of foreign extraction who resided some time in Philadelphia. x, 241 pp. 16°. *Philadelphia, John Dunlap*, 1774.

Duchesne (Édouard Adolphe). De la prostitution dans la ville d'Alger depuis la conquête. 231 pp. 8°. *Paris, J. B. Baillière*, 1853.

Duchesne (Jean). Essai sur les nielles, gravures des orfèvres florentins du xve siècle. xii, 381 pp. 8°. *Paris, Merlin*, 1826. s.

——— Notice des estampes exposées à la bibliothèque royale, formant un aperçu historique des produits de la gravure. 3e éd. xx, 215 pp. 8°. *Paris, Heideloff*, 1837. s.

Duchesne *or* Quercetanus (Joseph). Diæteticon polyhistoricon. Opvs vtiqve varivm, magnæ utilitatis ac delectationis, quod multa historica, philosophica, et medica, tàm conseruandæ sanitati, quàm varijs curandis morbis necessaria contineat. vi, 463 pp. 3 l. 1 pl. 12°. *Parisiis, C. Morell*, 1606. s.

Du Choul (Guillaume). Verhandeling van den godtsdienst der oude Romeinen, verrijkt met een groot getal medalien. Vit het Fransch vertaelt door M. Smallegange. 4 p. l. 339 pp. 17 l. 4°. *Amsteldam, J. en G. Janssonius van Waesberge*, 1684.

——— Verhandeling van de legerschikking en krygstucht der Romeinen, van de badstoven en oude oeffeningen der Grieken en Romeinen. Uit het Fransch vertaelt door M. Smallegange. 4 p. l. 147 pp. 2 l. 4°. *Amsteldam, J. en G. Janssonius van Waesberge*, 1684.

Dudevant (Amandine Lucile Aurore Dupin, *madame*). Le chateau des désertes. Par George Sand. [*pseudon.*] 251 pp. 18°. *Bruxelles, Meline, Cans et Cie.* 1851.

——— Consuelo. Nouv. éd. 3 v. 16°. *Paris, M. Lévy frères*, 1856.

Dudley (Dean). History of the council of Nice: a world's christian convention, A. D. 325. 87 pp. 8°. *Boston, T. O. H. P. Burnham*, 1860.

Dudley (*Miss* Elizabeth). The life of Mary Dudley, including an account of her religious engagements, and extracts from her letters. [With] some account of the illness and death of her daughter, Hannah Dudley. 380 pp. 8°. *London, editor*, 1825.

Duesberg. *See* **Mannert** (Conrad).

Dufail (Noel). Discours d'aucuns propos rustiques, facécieux et de singulière récréation: ou les ruses et finesses de Ragot. [Nouv. éd.] 4 p. l. 174 pp. 1 l. 16°. [*Paris*,] 1732.

Duff (P. *merchant*). North American accountant; embracing single and double entry book-keeping. 192 pp. 8°. *New York, author*, 1848. s.

Dufferin (Harriot Georgina Hamilton Blackwood, *lady*). Lispings from low latitudes; or, extracts from the journal of the hon. Impulsia Gushington. [*pseudon.*] 98 pp. obl. fol. 23 pl. *London, John Murray*, 1863.

Duflot de Mofras (——). Exploration de l'Orégon, des Californies, et de la Mer Vermeille, 1840–42. 2 v. 514 pp, 4 pl; 524 pp. 4 pl. 8°. Atlas, 14 maps. 3 pl. fol. *Paris, A. Bertrand*, 1844. s.

Dufour (Guillaume Henri). Strategy and tactics. Translated from the French by W. P. Craighill. 400 pp. 12°. *New York, D. Van Nostrand*, 1864.

Dufrénoy (Pierre Armand). Traité de minéralogie. 2e éd. 4 v. Atlas, 236 pl. 8°. *Paris, V. Dalmont*, 1856–59. s.

Du Fresnoy (Charles Alphonse). The art of painting, translated into English, by John Dryden. 2d ed. 8 p. l. lxviii, 397 pp. 3 l. 16°. *London, Bernard Lintott*, 1716.

Dufresnoy (Nicolas Lenglet). *See* **Lenglet-**Dufresnoy.

Du Fresny (Charles Rivière). Amusemens sérieux et comiques. Par M. de Fontenelle. [*pseudon.*] 2 p. l. 288 pp. 8 l. 18°. *Paris, C. Barbin*, 1701.

Dugdale (*Sir* William). Chronica juridicialia: or, an abridgment and continuation of Dugdale's Origines juridiciales. 2d ed. 7 p. l. 209, 19 pp. 44 l. 12°. *London, J. Worrall*, 1739.

——— Perfect copy of all summons of the nobility to the great councils and parliaments of this realm, from the xlix of king Henry iii, until these present times. 6 p. l. 580 pp. 13 l. fol. *London, R. Clavell*, 1685.

Duguay-Trouin, (René). Mémoires [depuis 1689 jusqu'à 1712] publ. par Pierre de Villepontoux. Continués jusqu' en 1736 par P. F. Godard de Beauchamps. xlviii, 288 pp. 8 pl. 12°. *Amsterdam, P. Mortier*, 1748.

Duhamel (Jean Marie Constant). Lehrbuch der reinenmechanik. Deutsch bearbeitet .... von Wilhelm Wagner. 2 v. in 1. viii, 312 pp; viii, 300, 96 pp. 8°. *Braunschweig, Vieweg*, 1853. s.

Duhamel du Monceau (Henri Louis), *and* Tillet (—). Histoire d'un insecte que devore les grains de l'Angoumois. 3 p. l. 314 pp. 3 pl. 16°. *Paris, Guerin & Delatour*, 1762. s.

Dujarday (*Madame* H.) Résumé des voyages, découvertes et conquêtes des Portugais en Afrique et en Asie, aux xve et xvie siècles. 2 v. iv, 400 pp; 331 pp. 8°. *Paris, H. Fournier, jeune*, 1839.

Duke (Basil W.) History of Morgan's cavalry. 578 pp. 1 pl. 8°. *Cincinnati, Miami Pub. Co.* 1867.

Duke (Richard). Poetical works. 8°. *Edinburgh*, 1793.
[Anderson's Brit. poets, v. 6].

Du Laurens (Henri Joseph). Le compère Mathieu, ou les bigarrures de l'esprit humain. [*anon.*] 4 v. 24°. *Paris, André*, 1801.

——— Imirce, ou la fille de la nature. [*anon.*] 3 p. l. 378 pp. 16°. *Berlin, [Hollande]*, 1765.

Dumarquez (Louis Joseph). Les délassemens d'un paresseux. Par un C. R. D'E. A. C. D. L. [*anon.*] vi, 224 pp. 24°. *Pigritiopolis, et se vend à Lille, Vanackère*, 1790.

Du Marsais (César Chesneau). Essai sur les préjugés. Ouvrage contenant l'apologie de la philosophie par Mr. D. M. 2 p. l. 394 pp. 1 l. 16°. *Londres, [Amsterdam, Mich. Rey]*, 1770.
Note.—Ascribed by Quérard to Holbach; by Delaulnaye in the Biog. univ. to an unknown writer.

Dumas (Alexandre Davy). Catherine Blum. iv, 184 pp. 16°. *London, Routledge*, 1861.

——— Un Gil-Blas en Californie. 323 pp. 16°. *Paris, Lévy*, 1861.

——— Les grands hommes en robe de chambre. Louis xiii et Richelieu. 3 v. 24°. *Bruxelles, Kiessling, Schnée et Cie.* 1855.

Dumas *fils*, (Alexandre). Antonine. 319 pp. 16°. *Paris, Lévy, frères*, 1856.

——— La boite d'argent—un paquet de lettres—le prix de pigeons—le pendu de la piroche—ce que l'on voit tous les jours—césarine. 304 pp. 16°. *Paris, Lévy frères*, 1862.

——— La vie à vingt ans. 320 pp. 12°. *Paris, M. Lévy*, 1856.

Dumas (Alphonse). The lady with the golden hair. [A tale]. 314 pp. 16°. *London*, 1866.

Dumas (J.) Études sur les inondations: causes et remède. 174 pp. 5 pl. 8°. *Valence, auteur*, 1857. s.

Dumas (Jean Baptiste). Leçons sur la philosophie chimique recueillis par M. Bineau. 430 pp. 8°. *Paris, Bechet*, 1837. s.

——— Die philosophie der chemie. Vorlesungen gesammelt von Bineau und ... übertragen von C. Rammelsberg. viii, 387 pp. 8°. *Berlin, C. G. Lüderitz*, 1839. s.

——— Manures, ameliorators and stimulants; modes of manufacture and application. The nutrition of plants. Tr. by C. Morfit, etc. 40 pp. 8°. *New York, Greeley & McElrath*, 1848. s.
[Farmer's library, v. 3].

Dumay (Louis.) The estate of the empire; or, an abridgement of the laws and government of Germany. Translated into French. Now rendered into English. 8 p. l. 345 pp. 9 l. 18°. *London, R. Royston*, 1664.

Duméril (André Marie Constant). Zoologie analytique; ou, méthode naturelle de classification des animaux. xxxii, 344 pp. 8°. *Paris, Allais*, 1806. s.

——— *and* (Auguste). Muséum d'histoire naturelle de Paris. Catalogue méthodique de la collection des reptiles. 1–2e livraison. iv, 224 pp. 8°. *Paris, Gide & Baudry*, 1851. s.
[No more published.]

Duméril (André Marie Constant) *and* **Bibron** (Gabriel.) Erpétologie générale; ou, histoire naturelle complète des reptiles. 9 v. in 10. Atlas, 120 col. pl. 8°. *Paris, Roret,* 1834–54. S.

CONTENTS.

v. 1. Généralités des reptiles, et celles des chéloniens. xiv. 446 pp.
v. 2. Chéloniens; généralités de sauriens. ii, 680 pp.
v. 3-5. Sauriens, iv, 518 pp. ii, 572 pp. viii. 855 pp.
v. 6-7. Ophidiens. xii. 610 pp. xvi, xii, 1536 pp.
v. 8. Batraciens. iii, 784 pp.
v. 9. Batraciens urodèles; Catalogue méthodique de tous les reptiles, xx, 340 pp.

Duméril (Auguste.) Des poissons voyageurs qui sont dits poissons anadromes et catadromes. 31 pp. 8°. *Paris, S. Raçon & Cie.* [1861.]? S.

Du Mersan (Marion). Histoire du cabinet des médailles antiques et pierres gravées, avec une notice sur la bibliothèque royale, etc. iv. 191 pp. 8°. *Paris, M. Du Mersan,* 1838. S.

——— Notice sur Marion DuMersan. [extract.] 5 pp. 8°. *Paris, Carpentier-Méricourt* [n. d.]
[*With* Du Mersan, (M.) Hist. du cabinet.]

Dumont (G. M. Butel.) *See* **Butel-Dumont.**

Dumortier (Barthélemy Charles), *and* **Beneden** (P. J. van.) Histoire naturelle des polypes composés d'eau douce, ou des bryozoaires fluviatiles. 130 pp. 7 col. pl. 4°. *Bruxelles, Acad. royale de Belgique,* 1850. S.

Dun (R. G. & Co.) The mercantile agency reference book. [v. 21.] July, 1866. 432 pp. 4°. *New York, R. G. Dun & Co.* 1866.

——— The same. [v. 22.] Jan. 1867. 690 l. unp. 4°. *New York, R. G. Dun & Co.* 1867.

——— The same. [v. 25.] July, 1867. 4°. *New York, R. G. Dun & Co.* [1867.]

Dunart (Émile). Histoire de manneken-piss, d'après des documents inédits, suivie d'une notice historique sur la fontaine de manneken piss. 120 pp. 1 pl. 24°. *Bruxelles, J. B. Tircher,* 1847.

Dunbar (E. Dunbar). Social life in former days. Illustrated by letters and family papers. [1st series.] viii, 422 pp. 8°. *Edinburgh, Edmonston & Douglas,* 1865.

——— The same. 2d series. viii, 199 pp. 8°. *Edinburgh, Edmonston & Douglas,* 1866.

Dunbar (Edward E.) Romance of the age; or, the discovery of gold in California. 134 pp. 3 pl. 12°. *New York, D. Appleton & Co.* 1867.

Dunbar (John R.) Club-foot. S.
[With Carmoly (E.) History of the Jewish physicians.]

Dunbar (Sophia). Family tour around the coasts of Spain and Portugal, 1860–61. viii, 184 pp. 16°. *Edinburgh, Blackwood & sons,* 1862.

Dunbar (William). Select poems. Part first. From the ms. of Geo. Bannatyne. 100 pp. 18°. *Perth, Morison & Son,* 1788.

Duncan (John, *of Scotland*). An essay on genius; or, the philosophy of literature. 264 pp. 8 l. 8°. *Edinburgh, W. Blackwood,* 1814.

Duncan (Jonathan). The religious wars of France, from the accession of Henry the second to the peace of Vervins. viii, 340 pp. 1 pl. 16°. *London, J. Rickerby,* 1840.

Duncan (J. Matthews). Fecundity, sterility, and allied topics. xvi, 378 pp. 8°. *Edinburgh, A. & C. Black,* 1866.

Duncan (William, *prof. of philosophy, Aberdeen.*) The elements of logick. 5th ed. vi, 364 pp. 16°. *London, R. & J. Dodsley,* 1764.

Dundonald (*9th earl of*). *See* **Cochrane** (Archibald).

D'Unger (Robert). The historical cabinet. The American continent; its discovery and conquest, description, etc. 72 pp. 1 pl. 12°. *Philadelphia, J. J. Fullmer & Co.* 1854. S.

Dungersheim, Dungerstein, *or,* **Tungersheim** (Hieronymus). Confutatio apologetici cuiusdā sacre scripture falso inscripti. cxxvii l. paged, 5 l. unp. 4°. *Lipsiae, Vuolfgangus Monacesius,* 1514.
[*With* Denyse (N.) Gemma predicantium. *Basilee,* 1516. Imperfect; wanting all after 5th leaf at end].

Dunglison (Robley). Medical lexicon. A dictionary of medical science. 927 pp. 8°. *Philadelphia, Blanchard & Lea,* 1851. S.

Dunker (Wilhelm Bernhard Rudolph Hadrian). Mollusca japonica descripta et tabulis tribus iconum illustrata. iv, 36 pp. 3 pl. 4°. *Stuttgartiae, E. Schweizerbart,* 1861. S.

Dunlap (William). André; a tragedy in five acts. With authentic documents respecting André; consisting of Letters to Miss Seward, The cow chace, Proceedings of the court martial, etc. *New York, T. and J. Swords,* 1798.

Dunn (*Rev.* John). A collection of curious observations on the nations of Asia, Africa, and America. Translated from the French. 2 v. vi, 411 pp; 404 pp. viii l. 12°. *London,* 1750.

Dunning (A. G.) An ancient, classical, and scriptural geography. 37 pp. 1 map. 4°. *New York,* 1850. S.

Dunton (John, *bookseller*). Dunton's ghost; or, a speech to the most remarkable persons in church and state. [*anon.*] viii, 10 pp. sm. 4°. *London, Baker and others,* [*about* 1733.]

Dunton (John, *mariner*). A true iovrnall of the Sally fleet. 2 p. l. 40 pp. 1 map. sm. 4°. *London, J. Dawson,* 1637.

Du Pan (Mallet). *See* **Mallet du Pan** (J.)

Dupin (André Marie Jean Jacques). Bibliothèque choisie des livres de droit. 8°. *Paris,* 1832.

[*With* CAMUS (A. G.) Profession d'avocat. v. 2].

Dupin (François Pierre Charles.) Constitution, histoire et avenir des caisses d'épargne de France. xxviii, 344 pp. 24°. *Paris, Didot,* 1844. s.

Du Plessis Mornay. *See* **Mornay.**

Duplex (George, *pseudon?*) *See* **Matter**; its forms and governing laws.

Du Ponceau (Peter Stephen). Mémoire sur le système grammatical des langues de quelques nàtions indiennes de d'Amérique du nord. xvi, 464 pp. 8°. *Paris, A. Pihan de La Forest,* 1838. s.

Du Pont de Nemours (Pierre Samuel). Sur l'éducation nationale dans les États-Unis d' Amérique. [*Ms.* presented to T. Jefferson and dated 15 Juin, 1800]. 96 pp. 4°. s.

[*With* PRINCETON college; catalogue of the graduates of Nassau hall, 1805].

Dupotet de Sennevoy (J.) Cours de magnétisme en sept leçons. 2e éd. vi, 503 pp. 8°. *Besançon, Bintot,* 1840. s.

Dupré (Alphonse). Relation d'un voyage en Italie. 2 v. xxiii, 445 pp; 525 pp. 1 pl. 8°. *Paris, A. Boucher,* 1826.

Dupré (J.) *See* **Delamarche** (A.) *and* **Dupré.** Météorologie, etc.

Dupuy (*Miss* Eliza A.) Ashleigh: a tale. 112 pp. 8°. *Cincinnati, H. B. Pearson,* 1854.

——— Celeste: the pirate's daughter. 152 pp. 8°. *Cincinnati, Stratton & Barnard,* 1849.

Dura (Giuseppe). Catalogo di libri antichi e rari vendibili in Napoli. 1007 pp. 8°. *Napoli, G. Cardamone,* 1861. s.

Durand (Ursin). *See* **Art**(l') de vérifier les dates, etc.

Durande (Amédée). Joseph, Carle, et Horace Vernet. Correspondance et biographies. 360 pp. 16°. *Paris, Hetzel,* 1865.

Durazzo (——, *of Genoa*). Catalogo della biblioteca di un amatore bibliofilo. [*anon.*] 251 pp. 8°. *Italia,* [*about* 1840]. s.

Durbin (John P. *D. D.*) Observations in the east, chiefly in Egypt, Palestine, Syria, and Asia Minor. 9th ed. 2 v. xi, 347; x. 299 pp. 2 maps. 12°. *New York, Harpers,* 1847.

Dureau de La Malle, (Adolphe J. C. Auguste). Province de Constantine. Recueil de renseignemens pour l'expédition ou l'établissement des Français dans cette partie de l'Afrique Septentrionale. xv, 315 pp. 1 map. 8°. *Paris, Gide,* 1837. s.

Durey de Noinville,(Jacques Bernard). Dissertation sur les bibliothèques. [*anon.*] 156 pp. 2 l. 16°. *Paris, H. Chaubert,* 1758. s.

——— Table alphabétique des dictionnaires, en toutes sortes de langues, et sur toutes sortes de sciences et d'arts. [*anon.*] iv. 88 pp. 16°. *Paris, H. Chaubert,* 1758. s.

[*With* his Dissertation sur les bibliothèques.]

D'urfey (Thomas). Stories, moral and comical, in verse and prose. 6 p. l. 257 pp. 16°. *London, F. Leach,* 1691.

Durieu (Jean Louis Marie Eugène), *and* **Roche** (Germain). Répertoire de l'administration et de la comptabilité des établissemens de bienfaisance. 2 v. vii, 603 pp; 851 pp. 8°. *Paris, P. Dupont & Cie.* 1842. s.

Durocher (J. *Prof. at Rennes*). Essay on comparative petrology. Tr. by Samuel Houghton, 26 pp. 2 tab. 8°. *Dublin, McGlashan & Gill,* 1859. s.

Dusseau (J. L.) Catalogue de la collection d'anatomie humaine, comparée et pathologique de MM. G. et W. Vrolik. xvi, 464 pp. 8°. *Amsterdam, W. J. DeRoever Kröber,* 1865. s.

Dutertre (H. B.) Annuaire de l' imprimerie et de la librairie françaises et étrangères; année 1845. 16°. *Paris, Leriche,* 1845. s.

Dutoit (Eugene). Die ovariatomie in England, Deutschland und Frankreich. lx, 237 pp. 8°. *Würzburg, Stahel,* 1864. s.

Dutrochet (Réné Joaquim Henri). Mémoires pour servir a l'histoire anatomique et physiologique des végétaux et des animaux. 3 v. xxxi, 576 pp; 573 pp. 30 pl. 8°. *Paris, J. B. Baillière,* 1837. s.

——— Recherches anatomiques et physiologiques sur la structure intime des animaux et des végétaux, et sur leur motilité. 232 pp. 1 tab. 2 pl. 8°. *Paris, J. B. Baillière,* 1824. s.

Duttenhofer (*Prof.*) Ueber die emancipation der neger. 94 pp. 8°. *Noerdlingen, C. H. Beck,* 1855.

Duval (Guillaume). Synopsis analytica doctrinæ peripateticæ.

[*With* ARISTOTELES. Opera, ed. 1619.]

Duvergier de Hauranne (Prosper). Histoire du gouvernement parlementaire en France, 1814–1848. v. 8. 8°. *Paris, Lévy,* 1867.

Dwight (Henry E.) Travels in the north of Germany in 1825 and 1826. iv. 454 pp. 1 pl. 8°. *New York, Carvill,* 1829. s.

Dwight (Theodore W.) Our municipal law and the best mode of acquiring a knowledge of it. pp. 1–55.

[COLUMBIA college inaugural addresses. 8°. *New York,* 1859.]

Dwight (Timothy, *D. D.*) A discourse on some events of the last century, delivered in New Haven, Jan. 7, 1801. 56 pp. 8°. *New Haven, Ezra Read,* 1801.

——— Travels in New England and New York. 4 v. 8°. *New Haven, T. Dwight,* 1821–2.

Dye (John Smith). History of the plots and crimes of the great conspiracy to overthrow liberty in America. vi, 388 pp. 8 pl. 8°. *New York,* 1866.

Dyer (George, *bookseller*). Restoration of the ancient modes of bestowing names on the rivers, hills, vallies, plains, and settlements of Britain. 295 pp. 4 l. 8°. *Exeter, G. Dyer,* 1805.

Dyer (John). Grongar hill and other poems. 8°. *Edinburgh,* 1794.
[Anderson's Brit. poets, v. 9.]

——— Poems. v, 188 pp. 3 pl. 16°. *London, R. & J. Dodsley,* 1761.

——— The same. Grongar hill; the ruins of Rome; the fleece. 190 pp. 3 pl. 12°. *London, J. Dodsley,* 1770.

Dyer (Thomas H.) Pompeii: its history, buildings, and antiquities. xvi, 579 pp. 1 map. 8 pl. 8°. *London, Bell & Daldy,* 1867.

Dzialynski (Adam Titus, *comes* de Kóscielec). Collectanea, vitam resque gestas Joannis Zamoyscii magni cancellarii et summi ducis reipublicæ polonæ illustrantia. 3 p. l. 307 pp, 9 pl. 4°. *Posnaniæ, L. Merzbach,* 1861. s.

——— Liber geneseos illustriss. familie Schidlovicie, 1531. 16 l, 17 pl. fol. *Paris, [auctor,* 1848].

——— Lites ac res gestæ inter Polonos ordinemque cruciferorum. 3 v. 4°. *Posnaniæ, L. Merzbach,* 1855–57. s.

Dzondi (Carl Heinrich). Nuovo e sicuro metodo di guarire la sifilide in tutte le sue forme. Aggiuntivi altri metodi curativi antisifilitici di rinomati medici, dal Pietro Lichtenthal. 2ª ed. 224 pp. 12°. *Milano, G. Pirola,* 1846. s.

Eagle (G. Barnard). Mesmerism, clairvoyance, and animal magnetism explained. Also, a hand-book of magic. 36 pp. 16°. *London, Chapman & Co.* 1858.

Ealtze (Frederick). The new table book. Pictures for young and old parties. With "a copy of verses" to each picture, and a page for "everybody's favorite." Edited by Mark Lemon. 52 l. 26 pl. 4°. *London, Bradbury, Evans & Co.* 1867.

Earle (Jabez). Sacramental exercises. 103 pp. 24°. *Boston, D. & Z. Fowle,* 1756.

Earle (John Milton). Land and fresh water shells of Massachusetts. s.
[*In* HITCHCOCK (E.) Catalogue of animals, etc. of Mass.]

Earle (Pliny, *M. D.*) History, description, and statistics of the Bloomingdale asylum for the insane. 136 pp. 1 pl. 8°. *New York, Egbert, Hovey & King,* 1848. s.

Early English Text Society. Ayenbite of inwyt; or, remorse of conscience. In the Kentish dialect, 1340 A. D. by Dan. Michel. Edited by R. Morris. 6 p. l. c, 359 pp. 8°. *London, Trübner,* 1866. [No. 23.]

——— Clene maydenhod. [From ms. ab. 1370 A. D.] A supplement to "Hali meidenhad." Edited by F. J. Furnivall. 7 pp. 8°. *London, Trübner,* 1867. [*In* No. 25.]

——— Hymns to the Virgin and Christ, the parliament ot devils, and other religious poems. Edited by F. J. Furnivall. xviii, 139 pp. 8°. *London, Trübner,* 1867. [No. 24.]

——— Pilgrim's sea-voyage. A supplement to "The stacions of Rome." 8°. *London, Trübner,* 1867. [*In* No. 25; pp. 35 to 40.]

——— Religious pieces in prose and verse. Edited from MS. (*cir.* 1440,) by G. G. Perry. xii, 106 pp. 8°. *London, Trübner,* 1867. [No. 26.]

——— Romans of Partenay, or of Lusignen: otherwise known as the tale of Melusine. Translated from the French of La Coudrette, (about 1500—1520, A. D.) Edited, with introduction, [etc.] by W. W. Skeat. xx, 299 pp. 8°. *London, Trübner,* 1866. [No. 22.]

——— Stacions of Rome. [In verse, from MS. 1370 A. D. and in prose, from MS. ab. 1460—1470 A. D.] and the Pilgrim's sea-voyage; with Clene maydenhod. [From MS. ab. 1370 A. D.] A supplement to "Political, religious and love poems," and "Hali meidenhad." xvi, 40, 8, 16 pp. 8°. *London, Trübner,* 1867. [No. 25.]

Earnest (An) and affectionate address to the people called methodists. 2d ed. [*anon.*] 47 pp. 18°. *London, B. Dod,* 1745.
[*With* WILSON (Thomas). Christianity made easy. 5th ed. *London,* 1743.]

Eastburn (*Rev.* James Wallis), *and* **Sands** (Robert C.) Yamoyden; a tale of the wars of king Philip. xi, 339 pp. 16°. *New York, James Eastburn,* 1820.

Eastern hospitals and English nurses. By a lady volunteer. [*anon.*] 2 v. xii, 328 pp; ix, 273 pp. 2 pl. 12°. *London, Hurst & Blackett,* 1856.

East India Company. General report on the administration of the Punjab, for 1849–51. xvi, 336 pp. 2 maps. fol. *London, East India Co.* 1854. s.

Eastman (F. S.) A history of the state of New York. viii, 279 pp. 16°. *New York, E. Bliss*, 1828.

Eastman (*Mrs.* Mary). Dacotah; or, the life and legends of the Sioux around fort Snelling. xi, xxxi, 268 pp. 3 pl. 12°. *New York, J. Wiley*, 1849.

Easton (Pa.) library company. Catalogue of the books. 99 pp. 8°. *Phillipsburg, Cooley & Wise*, 1855. s.

Easy lessons in reading; with an English and Maráthi vocabulary. [*anon.*] vi, 170 pp. 12°. *Bombay, Am. mission press*, 1851. s.

Eaton (Amos). Geological nomenclature for North America, founded upon geological surveys taken under the direction of Stephen Van Rensselaer. 31 pp. 3 maps. 8°. *Albany, Packard & Van Benthuysen*, 1828. s.

——— Geological text-book, etc. with applications to agriculture and the arts. 63 pp. 8°. map. *Albany*, 1830. s.

[*With* BAKEWELL (R.) Introduction to geology. 8°. *New Haven*, 1829.]

Eaton (*Rev.* Asa.) Historical account of Christ church, Boston. Discourse. 39 pp. 8°. *Boston, J. W. Ingraham*, 1824.

Eaton (Francis B.) History of Candia [N. H.] once known as Charmingfare, with notices of the early families. 152 pp. 1 map. 8°. *Manchester, J. O. Adams*, 1852.

Eaton (Paul). Stuart Sharpe: a romance. 78 pp. 8°. *London, G. Berger*, [1839.]

[Hazlitt's romancist and novelists' libr. v. 6.]

Eberhard (Johann August). Synonymisches handwörterbuch der deutschen sprache. xvi, 583 pp. 8°. *Wien, B. P. Bauer*, 1807. s.

Ebert (Friedrich Adolf). Die bildung des bibliothekars. Zur handschriftenkunde. 2e ausg. 2 v. in 1. 68, xv. 238 pp. 8°. *Leipzig, Steinaker & Wagner*, 1820–25.

——— Bibliothecæ guelferbytanæ codices graeci et latini classici. 179 pp. 8°. *Lipsiæ, Steinacker*, 1827. s.

[*With* the preceding.]

Eberth (C. Joseph). Untersuchungen über nematoden. 3 p.l. 77 pp. 9 pl. 4°. *Leipzig, W. Engelmann*, 1863. s.

Ecce Deus. Essays on the life and doctrine of Jesus Christ, with controversial notes on "Ecce Homo." [*anon.*] 363 pp. 16°. *Boston, Roberts Bros*, 1867.

Ecce Deus-Homo; or, the work and kingdom of the Christ of scripture. [*anon.*] 207 pp. 12°. *Philadelphia, J. B. Lippincott & Co.* 1868.

Ecclesiastical histories of Eusebius, Socrates, Sozomen and Theodoret. Translated and abridged by [Samuel] Parker. With their lives [and] an abridgment of Evagrius Scholasticus. 3d ed. 651 pp. 11 l. 5 pl. 4°. *London, C. Rivington*, 1729.

Echard (Laurence). Gazetteer's or newsman's interpreter; a geographical index of all the empires, kingdoms, islands, provinces, peninsulas, [etc.] in Asia, Africa, and America. 6th ed. 2 parts in 1 v. 137, 113 l. 16°. *London, J. & J. Knapton*, 1732.

[Title of part 1 wanting.]

Echoes from the south; comprising the most important speeches, proclamations, and public acts during the late war. 211 pp. 12°. *New York, E. B. Treat & Co.* 1866.

Eck (Heinrich). Ueber die formationen des buntens sandsteins und des muschelkalks in Oberschlesien, und ihre versteinerungen. viii, 149 pp. 2 pl. 1 tab. 8°. *Berlin, J. F. Starcke*, 1865. s.

Eclectic (The) and congregational review. New series. July, 1866, to Dec. 1867. v. 11-13. 8°. *London, Jackson, Walford & Hodder*, [1866–67].

Eclectic (The) magazine of foreign literature, science, and art. W. H. Bidwell, editor. Jan. to Dec. 1867. New series. v. 5–6. 8°. *New York*, 1867.

Eclectic (The) medical journal. Edited by J. M. Scudder, M. D. Jan. 1864 to Dec. 1867. v. 24–27. 8°. *Cincinnati, J. M. Scudder*, 1864–67.

Economist, (The) weekly commercial times, bankers' gazette, and railway monitor; a political, literary, and general newspaper. July, 1866, to June, 1867. v. 24, part 2. v. 25 part 1. folio. *London*, [1867].

Ecsamen de los delitos de infidelidad a la patria. Ed. españ. 2 v. in 1. xi, 164, 170 pp. 8°. *Madrid, Of. estab. central*, 1842.

Ecton (John). Thesaurus rerum ecclesiasticarum. An account of the valuations of all the ecclesiastical benefices in England and Wales. 2d ed. revised by Browne Willis. xl, 704 pp. *London, J. & P. Knapton and others*, 1754.

——— *See* **Lloyd** (John.)

Edda. Den ældre edda. En samling af de nordiske folks aeldste sagn og sange, ved Saemund Sigfússon kaldet hin Frode. Oversat og forklaret ved Finn Magnusen. 4 v. 18°. *Kjöbenhavn, Gyldendalsk*, 1821–23.

Edda. Den ældre edda. Samling af norrone oldkvad, indeholdende Nordens ældste gude- og heltesagn. Udgivet af P. A. Munch. xviii, 216 pp. 4°. *Christiania, P. T. Mallings,* 1847. s.

Eddius (Stephanus). Vita S. Wilfridi, episcopi eboracensis. fol. *Oxoniæ,* 1691.

[GALE (Thomas) *and* FELL (John). Rerum anglicarum scriptores veteres. *Oxoniæ,* 1684-91. v. 3.]

Eddy (Daniel C. *D. D.*) The angels' whispers; or, echoes of spirit voices. New ed. 258 pp. 16°. *Boston, H. Wentworth,* 1866.

——— The heroines of the church; or, lives and sufferings of female missionaries in heathen lands. New ed. 290 pp. 16°. *Boston, H. Wentworth,* 1866.

——— The young man's friend. New ed. 260 pp. 16°. *Boston, H. Wentworth,* 1866.

——— The young woman's friend; or, the duties, trials, loves, and hopes of woman. New ed. 250 pp. 16°. *Boston, H. Wentworth,* 1866.

Eddy (*Rev.* Richard). History of the 60th regiment New York state volunteers, from July 1861, to Jan. 1864. xii, 360 pp. 12°. *Philadelphia, R. Eddy,* 1864.

Ede (George). The management of steel. 4th ed. 221 pp. 12°. *New York, Appleton,* 1867.

Eden (*Hon.* Emily). "Up the country." Letters written to her sister, from the upper provinces of India. 2 v. vi, 302 pp; 263 pp. 12°. *London, R. Bentley,* 1866.

Eden (William, *afterwards lord* Auckland). Four letters to the earl of Carlisle, on perversions of political reasoning; on the war between Great Britain, and France and Spain; the public debts; the representations of Ireland respecting a free-trade; population, revenue laws respecting commerce, public œconomy. 3d ed. 232, xi pp. 16°. *London, B. White & T. Cadell,* 1780.

Edged tools. By the author of the "Win and wear series." [*anon.*] 316 pp. 16°. *New York, R. Carter and brothers,* 1867.

Edgeworth (Maria). The absentee. 234 pp. 16°. *London, Routledge,* 1856.

——— Ennui, and Emilie De Coulanges, being tales of fashionable life. 241 pp. 16°. *London, Routledge,* 1856.

——— Manœuvring, Madame de Fleury, and The dun. 237 pp. 16°. *London, Routledge,* 1856.

——— Vivian, and Almeria: being tales of fashionable life. 248 pp. 16°. *London, Routledge,* 1856.

Edgeworth (Richard Lovell). Essay on the construction of roads and carriages. [with appendices.] ix, 202, 81, 194 pp. 4 pl. 8°. *London, Johnson & Co.* 1813.

Edinburgh. Advocates' library. Catalogue of printed books. Parts 1-2. A.—Beyle. 4°. *Edinburgh, Blackwood,* 1863-64. s.

——— Royal college of physicians. Catalogue of the library. 8°. *Edinburgh,* 1863. s.

——— Select subscription library. Catalogue. xvi, 580 pp. 8°. *Edinburgh, Neill & Co.* 1842. s.

——— The same. 1st and 2d supplement to the catalogue. 9, 5,40 pp. 8°. *Edinburgh, J. Johnstone, etc.* 1848-52. s.

[*With* catalogue, 1842.]

——— Society of writers to his majesty's signet. Catalogue of the library. xxxi, 761 pp. 108 l. 4°. *Edinburgh, Society, etc.* 1805. s.

——— The same. 4 pts. with a general index. 5 v. 4°. *Edinburgh,* 1826-37. s.

——— University. Academic annual for 1840, consisting of contributions in literature and science. By alumni of the university. lxviii, 237 pp. 12°. *Edinburgh, A. & C. Black,* 1840. s.

——— ——— Catalogus librorum ad rem medicam spectantium in bibliotheca academiæ edinburgenæ, secundum auctorum nomina disponitur. Ed. altera. 8°. *Edinburgh,* 1798. s.

——— ——— Nomina eorum qui gradum medicinæ doctoris adepti sunt. 1705-1845. vi, 280 pp. 8°. *Edinburgh, Neill & Co.* 1846. s.

Edinburgh (The) encyclopædia; conducted by David Brewster, etc. A—Z. 18 v. 4°. *Edinburgh, W. Blackwood, etc.* 1830. s.

Edinburgh medical journal. v. 12. pts. 1-2. July, 1866, to July, 1867. 2 v. 8°. *Edinburgh,* 1867.

Edinburgh (The) review, or critical journal. Jan. to Oct. 1867. v. 125-126. 8°. *London, Longmans,* 1867.

Ed. Lee and sailor Dick: a boy's trials and triumphs. (Round hill stories.) 196 pp. 16° *Boston, R. A. Ballou,* 1866.

Edlin (A.) Treatise on the art of bread-making. xxiv, 221 pp. 16°. *London, Vernor & Hood,* 1805.

Edmond (Charles). Voyage dans les mers du nord à bord de la corvette la Reine Hortense. 8°. *Paris,* 1857. s.

APPENDED.—Notices scientifiques.

Relation nautique par A. G. Du Buisson.
Partie physiologique et médicale, par Drs. Bellebon et Guérault.
Partie géologique, par E. B. de Chancourtois et Ferri-Pisani.

Edmonds (John W.) Report upon the disturbance at the Potawatamie payment. 47 pp. 8°. *New York*, 1837.

——— Report on the claims of creditors of the Potawatamie Indians of the Wabash in 1836–37. 95 pp. 8°. *Scatcherd & Adams*, 1837.

Edwards (Bela Bates). Biography of self-taught men: with an introduotory essay. 642 pp. 16°. *Boston, Tilton & Co.* 1859.

Edwards (Carlton). In memory: [being a selection from his writings, with a memoir]. iv, 272 pp. 1 photog. portrait. *Albany, Printed for priv. distrib.* 1863. s.

Edwards (Edward). Administrative economy of the fine arts in England. 376 pp. 8°. *London, Saunders & Otley*, 1840. s.

Edwards (Frederic E.) A monograph of the eocene mollusca, or description of shells from the older territories of England. pp. 1–330. pl. 1–33. 4°. *London, Palæontographical soc.* 1849–50. s.

(No more published.)

Edwards (George, *M. D. of London*). Aggrandisement and national perfection of Great Britain; the means of paying off its public debt within the space of 30 years; of accomplishing the national improvements, etc. including the art of ameliorating land to the greatest advantage. 2 v. in 1. vi, 384 pp; 2 p. l. 313 pp. 4°. *London, J. Debrett*, [1787].

Edwards (George, *F. R. S.*) *and* **Catesby** (Mark). Sammlung verschiedener ausländischer und seltener vögel; worinnen ein jeder derselben nicht nur auf das genaueste beschrieben, sondern auch in einer richtigen und sauber illuminirten abbildung vorgestellet wird, von Johann M. Seligmann [und Georg Leonhard Huth.] 9 v. in 4. fol. *Nürnberg, J. J. Fleischmann*, 1749–76. s.

Edwards (H. Sutherland). The three Louisas: a novel. 3v. 12°. *London, Tinsley*, 1862.

Edwards (Henri Milne). Histoire naturelle de coralliares, ou polypes proprement dits. Text, 3 v. atlas, 8°. *Paris, Roret*, 1857–60.

——— Leçons sur la physiologie et l'anatomie comparée de l'homme et des animaux. v. I—VIII, pt. 1. 8°. *Paris, V. Masson*, 1857–63. s.

——— Mélanges carcinologiques. (extract). 2 v. 1 p. l. 192 pp, 23 pl. 4°. *Paris, Annales des sciences naturelles, etc.* 1851–54. s.

——— Recherches anatomiques, physiologiques, et zoologiques sur les polypes. (extracts). 7 v. in 1. 8°. *Paris, Annales des sciences naturelles*, 1835–38. s.

CONTENTS.

Mémoire sur un nouveau genre, etc. (Alcyonides). 11 pp, 2 pl.
Observations sur les alcyons proprement dits. 10 pp, 3 pl.
Recherches sur les eschares. 49 pp, 5 pl.
Observations sur les polypiers fossiles du genre eschare. 24 pp, 4 pl.
Note sur un nouveau genre de polypiers fossiles eschariens (Mélicérite). 12 pp, 3 pl.
Mémoire sur les crisies, les hornères, etc. (Tubuliporiens). 46 pp, 11 pl.
Observations sur la nature et le mode de croissance des polypiers. [14] pp.

——— **Blanchard** (Émile), *and* **Lucas** (Hippolyte). Muséum d'histoire naturelle de Paris. Catalogue de la collection entomologique—classe des insectes. Ordre des coléoptères. iv, 240 pp. 8°. *Paris, Gide & Baudry*, 1850.

[No more published.] s.

——— *and* **Haime** (Jules). Monograph of the British fossil corals. 4°. *London*, 1850–54.

[Palæontographical society.] s.

——— *See* **Audouin** (J. V.) *and* **Edwards** (H. M.) Hist. nat. de la France.

Edwards (John, *D. D.*) A compleat history, or survey of all the dispensations and methods of religion, as represented in the old and new testament. 2 v. xvi, 774 pp. 1 pl. 12°. *London, D. Brown*, 1699.

Edwards (John N.) Shelby and his men; or the war in the west. 551 pp. 1 pl. 1 map. 8°. *Cincinnati, Miami pub. Co.* 1867.

Edwards (*Rev.* Jonathan, *senior*). The distinguishing marks of a work of the spirit of God applied to that uncommon operation that has lately appeared on the minds of many of the people in New England. With a preface by the Rev. Mr. Cooper, of Boston. 76 pp. 12°. *London, S. Mason*, 1742.

——— A faithful narrative of the surprising work of God in the conversion of many hundred souls in Northampton, in a letter to Dr. Colman. With prefaces by Drs. Watts and Guyse. xvi, 132 pp. 8°. *London, J. Oswald*, 1737.

——— The same. 125 pp. 16°.

[Another edition; title wanting].

——— A history of the work of redemption. 402 pp. 8°. *New York, R. Hodge*, 1786.

——— Humble attempt to promote an explicit agreement and visible union of God's people thro' the world, in extraordinary prayer, for the revival of religion and the advancement of Christ's kingdom on earth. 188 pp. 18°. *Boston, D. Henchman*, 1747.

——— A treatise concerning religious affections. 499 pp. 8°. *Elizabethtown, (N. J.) Shepard Kollock*, 1787.

Edwards (*Rev.* Jonathan, *senior*). Humble inquiry into the rules of the word of God, concerning the qualifications requisite to a complete standing and full communion in the visible christian church. With an appendix by Mr. [Thomas] Foxcroft. sm. 4°. v, 136, 16 pp. *Boston, S. Kneeland*, 1749.

——— A farewell-sermon, preached in Northampton, June 22, 1750. 36 pp. 16°. *Boston, S. Kneeland,* 1751.

——— Misrepresentations corrected, and truth vindicated, in a reply to Rev. Solomon Williams's book, entitled The true state of the question concerning the qualifications necessary to lawful communion in the christian sacraments. iv, 173 pp. 2 l. 1 pl. 8°. *Boston, S. Kneeland,* 1752.

Edwards (*Rev.* Morgan). Materials towards a history of the American baptists in Pennsylvania. v. i. 132 pp. 1 pl. 16°. *Philadelphia, Joseph Crukshank & Isaac Collins,* 1770.

——— Materials towards a history of the baptists in Jersey. v. ii. 155 pp. 16°. *Philadelphia, Thomas Dobson,* 1792.
(Hazard coll. pam. v. 107).

Edwards (Pierrepont). Practical guide for British shipmasters, to United States ports. viii, 323 pp. 12°. *London, Longmans,* 1866.

Edwards (William Frederic). Recherches sur les langues celtiques. xix, 538 pp. 8°. *Paris, imp. royale,* 1844. s.

Egan (Pierce). Boxiana; or, sketches of ancient and modern pugilists. [Illustrated]. 8°. *London,* 1823–29.

——— The same. New series. 2 v. 8°. *London,* 1828–29.

Egede (Hans). Det gamle Grönlands nye perlustration, eller naturel-historie. 6 p. l. 131 pp. 1 map, 11 pp. sm. 4°. *Kiöbenhavn, Groth,* 1741.

——— The same. Description et histoire naturelle du Groenland. Traduite en François par Mr. D. R. D. P. 16°. *Copenhague et Genève,* 1763.

Egede (Hans Saabye). Brudstykker af en dagbog holden i Grönland i aarene, 1770–1778. 154 pp. 16°. *Odense,* 1816.

——— The same. Bruchstükke eines tagebuches gehalten in Grönland 1770–78. Aus dem dänischen übersetzt von G. Fries, mit einer vorrede. xcii, 191 pp. 1 map. 12°. *Hamburg, Perthes & Besser,* 1817. s.

Egede (Paul). Efterretninger om Grönland, uddragne af en journal holden fra 1721 til 1788. 6 pl. 284 pp. 3 pl. 1 map. 16°. *Kiöbenhavn,* 1789.

Egger (Émile). Mémoires de littérature ancienne. xxiii, 520 pp. 8°. *Paris, Durand,* 1862.

——— Mémoires d'histoire ancienne et de philologie. xi, 516 pp. 2 pl. 8°. *Paris, Durand,* 1863.

Eggerling (H. W. E.) Beschreibung der Vereinigten Staaten von Nord America, den deutschen auswanderern gewidmet. 2e aufl. 12°. *Mannheim, Löffler,* 1833.

Egleston (Thomas, *jr.*) Catalogue of minerals, with their formulæ, etc. xiii, 42 pp. 8°. *Washington, Sm. Inst.* 1863.
(Smithsonian miscel. coll. v. 7.)

——— The same. 34 pp. 8°. *New York, School of mines,* 1866. s.

——— A check list of the silicates, with their formulæ and crystalline systems, etc. 12 pp. 8°. *New York,* 1866. s.

——— Diagrams to illustrate the lectures on crystallography delivered at the school of mines of Columbia college. x pp. 38 pl. 8°. *New York,* 1866. s.

Eglin (Raphael). Captivitatis babylonicæ historia. *See* **Helwig** (Christoph). Elenchi judaici. *Lugduni in Batavis,* 1702.

Egyptian dream-book and fortune-teller, containing an alphabetical list of dreams, with their signification. 16°. *New York,* 1866.

Ehninger (J. W.) A series of etchings suggested by Hood's bridge of sighs. 2 p. l. 8 pl. obl. fol. *New York, G. P. Putnam,* 1851.

Ehrenström (Marianne d'). Notices sur la littérature et les beaux arts en Suède. 7 p. l. 347 pp. 8°. *Stockholm, Eckstein,* 1826. s.

Ehrentempel des neunzehnten jahrhunderts. In biographien berühmter zeitgenossen. 3 v. 8°. *Leipzig, Spamer,* 1852–55. s.

CONTENTS.

v. 1. Humboldt, von H. Klenckè. xvi, 224 pp. 2 pl.
2. Wellington. xvi, 307 pp. 7 pl.
3. Von Stein. ix, 217 pp. portrait.

Eichenfeld (Joseph von), *and* **Endlicher** (Stephen). Analecta grammatica, maximam partem anecdota. xxvi, 571 pp. 1 pl. 8°. *Vindobonæ, F. Beck,* 1837.

Eichstädt (Heinrich Carl Abraham). Opvscvla oratoria. Orationes, memoriæ, elogia. Ed. 2a. xxxii, 804 pp. 8°. *Jenæ, Mauke,* 1850. s.

Eichthal (Gustave d'). Histoire et origine des Foulahs, ou Fellans. xii, 296 pp. 1 pl. 8°. *Paris, Dondey-Dupré,* 1841.

Eichwald (Eduard). Naturhistorische skizze von Lithauen, Volhynien und Podolien, in geognostisch-mineralogischer, botanischer, und zoologischer hinsicht. 3 p. l. 256 pp. 3 pl. 4°. *Wilna, J. Zawadzki*, 1830. s.

Eisenlohr (W.) Lehrbuch der physik. 6e aufl. vi, 657 pp. 8°. *Stuttgart, Krais & Hoffmann*, 1852. s.

Ejercicio cotidiano, ú horas divinas. [*anon.*] v, 458 pp. 24°. *Bogotá, F. Tórres Amaya*, 1854.

Elcock (Ephraim). Animadversions on a book called a Plea for non-scribers. 3 p. l. 61 pp. sm. 4°. *London, Richard Wodnothe*, 1651.

Elder (Cyrus). My gift. [Poems.] 104 pp. 12°. *New York, N. Tibbals & Co.* 1867.

Elderfield (Christopher). The civil right of tythes. By C. E. [*anon.*] 4 p. l. 344 pp. sm. 4°. *London, J. Holden*, 1650.

Elderhorst (William). Chemical report. [*With* Owen's first report on geology of Arkansas.]

Eldredge (Mira). Drops of water from many fountains. 216 pp. 16°. *New York, Foster & Palmer*, 1867.

Élémens d'économie politique, suivis de quelques vues sur l'application des principes de cette science aux règles administratives. xxi, 384 pp. 8°. *Paris, Fantin*, 1817. s.

Élie de Beaumont (Jean Baptiste Armand Louis Léonce). Note sur les systèmes de montagnes les plus anciens de l'Europe. [Extract.] 128 pp. 8°. *Paris, Soc. géol. de France*, 1847. s.

Eliot (*Rev.* Andrew). A burning and shining light extinguished. Sermon [on the death] of Rev. John Webb, 1750. 42 pp. 12°. *Boston, Joshua Winter*, [1750?]
[*With* Walley (*Rev.* Thomas.) Balm in Gilead. *Cambridge*, 1670].

Eliot (*Rev.* John). The day-breaking, if not the sun-rising of the gospell with the Indians in New England. [*anon.*] 25 pp. sm. 4°. *London, Fulk Clifton*, 1647.

——— A late and further manifestation of the gospel amongst the Indians in New-England. 4 p. l. 23 pp. sm. 4°. *London*, 1655.

——— Learned conjectures of John Eliot, touching the Americans, of new and notable consideration, written to Mr. Thorowgood. 2 p. l. 67 pp. 4°. *London, Henry Brome*, 1660.
[Appended to Thorowgood (*Rev.* Thomas). Jews in America. *London*, 1660.]

——— *See* **Bible**, *Indian, Massachusetts.*

——— *and* **Mayhew** (*Rev.* Thomas). Tears of repentance; or, a further narrative of the progress of the gospel amongst the Indians in New-England. 18 p. l. 46 pp. sm. 4°. *London, Peter Cole*, 1653.

Eliot (William Greenleaf, *D. D.*) Discourses on the doctrines of christianity. 16th [ed.] 168 pp. 16°. *Boston, Amer. Unit. assoc.* 1867.

——— Early religious education considered as the divinely appointed way to the regenerate life. 128 pp. 16°. *Boston, Crosby, Nichols & Co.* 1855.

——— Lectures to young men. 8th ed. 190 pp. 16°. *Boston, Amer. Unit. assoc.* 1867.

——— Lectures to young women. 8th ed. 196 pp. 16°. *Boston, Am. Unit. assoc.* 1867.

Elis (Carl). Chronik der alten bischofstadt Halberstadt. 122 pp. 8°. *Halberstadt, C. B. Elis*, 1859. s.

Ellen: a poem for the times. [*anon.*] 48 pp. 12°. *New York, Carleton*, 1867.

Ellet (*Mrs.* Elizabeth F.) Family pictures from the bible. 2 p. l. 223 pp. 12°. *New York, G. P. Putnam*, 1849. s.

Elliot (Stephen). An address to the literary and philosophical society of South Carolina, 1814. 20 pp. 4°. *Charleston, W. P. Young*, 1814.

Elliott (Charles). The sabbath. 106 pp. 12°. *Philadelphia, Presbyt. bd. of pub.* [1867].

Elliott (Charles Boileau). Letters from the north of Europe; or, journal of travels. xxiii, 475 pp. 8°. *London, H. Colburn & R. Bentley*, 1832.

Elliott (Charles W.) Remarkable characters and places of the holy land. 640 pp. 12 pl. 1 map. 8°. *Hartford, (Conn.) J. B. Burr & Co.* 1867.

Elliott (Franklin Reuben). Fruit book; or, the American fruit-grower's guide in orchard and garden. 503 pp. 12°. *New York, C. M. Saxton*, 1854.

Elliott (Robert). Original sketches. *See* **Views** in India, China, etc.

Ellis (Alexander John). The alphabet of nature; or, contributions towards a more accurate analysis and symbolization of spoken sounds: with some account of the principal phonetic alphabets hitherto proposed. vii, 194 pp. 8°. *Bath, I. Pitman*, 1845.

Ellis (Benjamin). The medical formulary; being a collection of prescriptions. 8th ed. With numerous additions. By Samuel George Morton. 272 pp. 8°. *Philadelphia, Lea & Blanchard*, 1846. s.

Ellis (Charles Mayo). The history of Roxbury town. part i. 146 pp. 8°. *Boston, Samuel G. Drake*, 1847.

Ellis (Daniel). Thrilling adventures of D. Ellis, the Union guide of east Tennessee, during the southern rebellion. 430 pp. 12°. *New York, Harpers*, 1867.

Ellis (Henry). A voyage to Hudson's bay by the Dobbs galley, and California, in 1746–7, for discovering a north-west passage. xxviii, 336 pp. 1 map. 8 pl. 8°. *London, H. Whitridge*, 1748.

Ellis (*Sir* Henry). Journal of the proceedings of the late embassy to China. 382 pp. 8°. *Philadelphia, A. Small*, 1818. s.

Ellis (*Rev.* J. *D. D.*) A defence of the thirty-nine articles of the church of England, [with] the Lambeth articles. 3 p. l. 177 pp. 18°. *London, R. Bonwicke and others*, 1710.

Ellis (Samuel). The history of the order of the sons of temperance, from 1842 to 1848. Revised ed. 238 pp. 12°. *Boston, Stacy, Richardson & Co.* 1848.

Ellis (*Rev.* William). Polynesian researches during a residence of nearly eight years in the Society and Sandwich islands. New ed. 4 v. 16°. *London, H. G. Bohn*, 1859. s.

Elwes (Alfred). Legend of the mount; or, the days of chivalry. 95 pp. 1 pl. 16°. *London, E. Wilson*, 1866.

Ely (Ezra Stiles, *D. D.*) The journal of the stated preacher to the hospital and almshouse in the city of New York, for 1811. [*anon.*] 300 pp. 12°. *New York, Whiting & Watson*, 1812.

Emblemata anniversaria academiæ altorfinæ, stvdiorvm ivventvtis exercitandorvm cavsa proposita et variorvm orationibvs exposita. 6 pl. 153 l. 3 l. sm. 4°. *Norimbergæ, Levinus Hvlsius*, 1597.

Emerson (Charles N.) Internal revenue guide; containing the law of June 30, 1864, as amended March 3, 1865, July 13, 1866, and March 2, 1867. 402 pp. 8°. *Springfield, (Mass.) S. Bowles & Co.* 1867.

Emerson (*Mrs.* Eleanor Read). Memoirs, with some of her writings. To which is added Rev. [Samuel] Worcester's sermon occasioned by her death. 2d ed. 96 pp. 16°. *Boston, Lincoln & Edmands*, 1809.

Emerson (Ralph Waldo). May-day and other pieces. iv. 205 pp. 12°. *Boston, Ticknor & Fields*, 1867.

——— Nature. [Including commodity, beauty, language, and discipline. 1st ed.] 95 pp. 12°. *Boston, J. Munroe & Co.* 1836.

——— Representative men; seven lectures. vii, 143 pp. 16°. *London, H. G. Bohn*, 1850. s.

CONTENTS.

Uses of great men; Plato; Swedenborg; Montaigne; Shakspeare; Napoleon; Goethe.

Emerson (William). System of astronomy. xii, 368 pp. 12 pl. 8°. *London, J. Nourse*, 1769.

Emmich (Matthias). Geneviève de Brabant. Traduit du Latin, par É. de La Bédollière. 24 pp. 12°. *Paris*, 1841.

Emmons (Ebenezer). Birds of Massachusetts. s.

[*In* Hitchcock (E.) Catalogue of animals, etc. of Mass.]

——— Report on the geological survey of North Carolina. xvi, 314 pp. 8°. *Raleigh, H. D. Turner*, 1852. s.

——— Report of the North Carolina geological survey. Agriculture of the eastern counties; [also] description of the fossils of the marl beds: illustrated. xvi, 315 pp. 8°. *Raleigh, H. D. Turner*, 1858.

——— Reports on the geology [of New York].

[New York. Annual reports on the geological survey. v. 1–5.]

Emmons (Richard, *M. D.*) The battle of Bunker hill. 2d ed. 144 pp. 12°. *New York, Sackett & Sargent*, 1839.

——— The same; or, temple of liberty. 2d ed. 144 pp. 1 pl. 12°. *Boston*, 1841.

——— The same. 6th ed. 144 pp. 12°. *Boston*, 1856.

——— The same. An historic poem. 10th ed. 144 pp. 1 pl. 12°. *Boston*, 1865.

——— The defence of Baltimore [in 1814] and death of general Ross. 48 pp. 16 l. 16°. *Washington, William Emmons*, 1831.

Emory (William H.) Notes of a military reconnoissance from fort Leavenworth, in Missouri, to San Diego, in California, including parts of the Arkansas, Del Norte, and Gila rivers. 416 pp. 8°. *Washington, Wendell & Van Benthuysen*, 1848.

——— Report on the United States and Mexican boundary survey, made under the direction of the secretary of the interior. 8 v. in 3. 4°. *Washington, Government press*, 1857–59.

CONTENTS.

v. 1, pt. 1. [Itinerary, etc.] xi, 253 pp. 1 map 57 pl.
v. 1, pt. 2. Geological reports of C. C. Parry and Arthur Scott. Palæontology and geology, by James Hall. Description of cretaceous and tertiary fossils, by T. A. Conrad. viii, 174 pp. 1 col. map, 21 pl.
v. 2, pt. 1. Botany of the boundary. Introduction by C. C. Parry. Botany by John Torrey. 270 pp. 61 pl. Cactaceæ, by George Engelmann. 78 pp. 75 pl.

Emory (William H.) Notes, etc.—Continued.
v. 2, pt. 2. Zoology of the boundary.
Mammals, by S. F. Baird. 62 pp. 27 pl.
Birds, by S. F. Baird. 32 pp. 25 col. pl.
Reptiles, by S. F. Baird. 35 pp. 41 pl.
Ichthyology, by Charles Girard. 85, ii pp. 41 pl.

Enchyridion Leonis [iii] papæ. [*pseudon.*] 162 pp. 18°. *Romæ,* 1670.

Encyclopédie d'architecture: journal mensuel publié sous la direction de Victor Calliat et Adolphe Lance. 12 v. 4°. *Paris, Bance,* 1851-62.

Encyclopédie des gens du monde: répertoire universel des sciences, des lettres, et des arts. Par une société de savans, etc. [Sous la direction de J. H. Schnitzler.] 44 v. in 22. 8°. *Paris, Treuttel & Würtz,* 1833-44.

Enfield (William). A general pronouncing dictionary. 5th ed. xxiv, 392 pp. 24°. *London, Baldwin, Cradock & Joy,* 1816. s.

——— Institutes of natural philosophy. 5th ed. By Samuel Webber. xviii, 216 pp. 16 pl. 8°. *Boston, Hilliard, Gray & Co.* 1832. s.

Engel (Carl). An introduction to the study of national music; comprising researches into popular songs, traditions, and customs. xi, 435 pp. 1 pl. 8°. *London, Longmans,* 1866.

Engel (Ferdinand). Axonometrical projections on the most important geometrical surfaces. Drawings in descriptive geometry. Preface by Dr. Joachimsthal. 10 pp. 19 pl. obl. fol. *New York, H. Goebeler,* 1855. s.

Engel (Samuel). Extraits raisonnés des voyages faits dans les parties septentrionales de l'Asie et de l'Amérique. 4°. *Lausanne,* 1779.

Engelmann (George, *M. D.*) Cactaceæ of the (U. S. and Mexican) boundary. 78 pp. 76 pl. 4°. [*Washington,* 1859]. s.

——— The same.
[EMORY (W. H.) Report on the U. S. and Mexican boundary survey. v. 2. pt. 1].

Engelmann (Wilhelm). Bibliotheca mechanico-technologica, oder verzeichniss der bis zur mitte des jahres 1843 in Deutschland erschienenen bücher, über alle theile der mechanischen und technischen künste und gewerbe, u. s. w. 2e auflage. vii, 503 pp. 8°. *Leipzig, W. Engelmann,* 1844. s.

England and France; or, a cure for the ministerial gallomania. [*anon.*] viii, 268 pp. 12°. *London, J. Murray,* 1832.

England illustrated, or a compendium of the natural history, geography, topography, and antiquities, ecclesiastical and civil, of England and Wales. [*anon.*] 2 v. 4 p. l. xiii, 426 pp; 2 p. l. 490 pp. 51 maps. 27 pl. 4°. *London, R. & J. Dodsley,* 1764.

Englefield (*Sir* Henry C.) *See* **Moses** (Henry). Vases, etc.

English (The) compendium: or, rudiments of honour; containing the genealogies of all the nobility of England, their titles, posts, and seats. 11th ed. [*anon.*] 3 v. 24°. *London, C. Hitch,* 1760.

English (The) constitution fully stated; with animadversions on Mr. Higden's mistakes about it. [*anon.*] 108 pp. 8°. *London,* 1710.

English (The) pilot. Describing the seacoasts, etc. in the whole northern navigation. 78 pp. 31 maps. fol. *London, J. Mount,* 1775.

English (George Bethune). Five pebbles from the brook. A reply to "a defence of christianity," by Edward Everett. vi, 124 pp. 16°. *Philadelphia,* 1824.

Enquiry (An) into and detection of the barbarous murther of [Arthur Capel,] the late earl of Essex. [*anon.*] 2 p. l. 75 pp. sm. 4°. [*London*], 1689.

Enquiry (An) into the Caledonian project, with a defence of England's procedure in relation thereunto. [*anon.*] 54 pp. numb. as 92 pp. sm. 4°. *London, J. Nutt,* 1701.

Enquiry (An) respecting the capture of Washington by the British. By Spectator. [*anon.*] 32 pp. 16°. *Washington,* 1816.

Enslin (Theodor Johann Christian Friedrich). Bibliothek der handlungswissenschaft; oder verzeichniss der vom jahre 1750 bis 1845 in Deutschland erschienenen bücher über alle theile der buchhandlungskunde und deren hülfswissenschaften. 2e auflage, von Engelmann. vi, 225 pp. 8°. *Leipzig, W. Engelmann,* 1846. s.
[*With* GRÄSSE (J. G. T.) Bibliotheca magica].

Ensor (George). On national government. 2 v. vi, 456 pp; iv, 487 pp. 8°. *London, J. Johnson,* 1810.

Epictetus. Works; consisting of his discourses, in four books, the enchiridion, and fragments. A translation by T. W. Higginson. xvi, 437 pp. 12°. *Boston, Little, Brown & Co.* 1866.

——— Enchiridion.
[*With* VEEN (O. van). Theatro moral de la vida humana. 1701].

Epigrammatum anthologia palatina, cum planudeis, et appendice nova epigrammatum veterum ex libris et marmoribus ductorum. Instruxit F. Dübner. Græce et Latine. v. 1. xxiv, 572 pp. 8°. *Parisiis, Didot,* 1864.
[DIDOT, Biblioth. grecque. v. 53.]

Erasmus *or,* Gerhardt (Desiderius). Familiarvm colloqviorũ formulæ, multis adiectis, non tantũ ad linguam pverilem expoliẽdam utiles, uerum etiam ad uitã instituendã; nuper recognitæ ab autore, et locupletatæ. [unp.] 16°. *Apud Basileam, Joan. Frob.* 1523. s.

Eratosthenes. *See* **Aratus.** Phænomena et diosemeia. *Oxonii,* 1672.

Ercilla y Zuñiga (Alonso de). La araucana. 2 pts. lvi, 298 pp; 413 pp. 1 map. 2 pl. 16°. *Madrid, A. de Sancha,* 1776.

Erckmann (Émile) *and* **Chatrian** (Alexandre). L'ami Fritz. 2e éd. 3 p. l. 341 pp. 16°. *Paris, Hachette,* 1865.

——— Contes des bords du Rhin. 4 p. l. 336 pp. 16°. *Paris, Hetzel,* 1862.

——— Histoire d'un conscrit de 1813. 3e éd. 2 p. l. 310 pp. 16°. *Paris, Hetzel et Lacroix,* [1864].

——— Histoire d'un homme du peuple. 2 p. l. 374 pp. 16°. *Paris, Hetzel et Lacroix,* [1865].

——— L'illustre docteur Mathéus. 3e éd. 2 p. l. 337 pp. 16°. *Paris, Hetzel et Lacroix,* [1859].

——— L'invasion; ou, le fou Yégof. 9e éd. 2 p. l. 318 pp. 16°. *Paris, Hetzel,* [1862].

——— Madame Thérèse. 8e éd. 2 p. l. 377 pp. 16°. *Paris, Hetzel et Lacroix,* [1863].

——— Waterloo; suite du conscrit de 1813. 5e éd. 2 p. l. 374 pp. 16°. *Paris, Hetzel et Lacroix,* [1865].

Erdl (Michael Pius). Entwicklung des menschen und des hühnchens im eie. Entwicklung der leibesform. 140 pp. 30 pl. 4°. *Leipzig, L. Voss,* 1845. s.

Erichson (Wilhelm Ferdinand). Genera et species staphylinorum, insectorum coleopterorum familiæ. viii, 955 pp. 5 pl. 8°. *Berolini, F. H. Morin,* 1840.

——— The same. Pars prior. 400 pp. 3 pl. 8°. *Berolini, F. H. Morin,* 1839. s.

Erlam (J. S.) Advice to builders, buyers, and renters of houses. 70 pp. 16°. *London, W. Shoberl,* 1851. s.

Erman (Adolph). Travels in Siberia. Translated from the German by W. D. Cooley. 2 v. xi, 495 pp; ix, 536 pp. 1 map. 8°. *London, Longmans,* 1848. s.

Ernesti (Johann August). Elements of interpretation. Translated from the Latin, with notes, by Moses Stuart. 3d ed. vii, 124 pp. 16°. *Andover, M. Newman,* 1827.

Erotopægnion. *See* **Priapeia.**

Erpenius *or* Van Erpe (Thomas). Rudiments de la langue arabe; supplément indiquant les différences entre le langage littéral et le langage vulgaire, par A. E. Hébert. iv, 132 pp. 8°. *Paris, Imprimerie royale,* 1844. s.

Ersch (Johann Samuel), Gruber (J. G. *and others, editors.*) Allgemeine encyclopädie der wissenschaften und künste. 140 v. 4°. *Leipzig, Gleditsch* [*und*] *Brockhaus,* 1818–66. s.

CONTENTS.

1e section. A—G. v. 1–84. A—Griechenland, 1818-66.
2e section. H—N. v. 1–31. H—Junius, 1827–55. [wanting v. 7, 18, 20.]
3e section. O—Z. v. 1–25. O—Phyxios, 1830–50. [No more published.]

——— Bibliographisches handbuch. *See* **Geissler** (C. A.)

Erskine (Ralph). Gospel sonnets; or, spiritual songs, [with] account of the author's life and writings. 356 pp. 18°. *Edinburgh, G. Caw,* 1788.

——— A paraphrase; or, large explicatory poem upon the song of Solomon. 144 pp. 18°. *Glasgow, R. Duncan,* 1770.

Erslew (Thomas Hansen). Almindeligt forfatter-lexicon for kongeriget Danmark med tilhörende bilande, fra 1814 til 1840. 2 v. 8°. *Kjöbenhavn, Forlagsforeningens forlag,* 1843. s.

(A.—R. only. v. 3 wanting.)

Erste dalmatinisch-kroatisch-slavonisch ausstellung abgehalten in Agram in 1864. 4 p. l. 271 pp. 8°. *Agram, A. Jakić,* 1864. s.

Erzinger (Heinrich). Lesebuch für landwirthschaftliche fortbildungsschulen, mit besonderer berücksichtigung der verhältnisse und bedürfnisse des württemb. bauernstandes. viii, 175 pp. 12°. *Stuttgart, Ebner & Seubert,* 1860. s.

Esche (Louise). Grandmother and granddaughter. From the German, by C. R. Corson. pp. 79–112.

[*With* STORM (Th.) Immen-see. 16°. *Phila.* 1863.]

Eschricht (Daniel Friedrich). Zoologisch-anatomisch-physiologisch untersuchungen über die nordischen wallthiere. v. i. xvi, 205 pp. 15 pl. 4°. *Leipzig, L. Voss,* 1849. s.

Esenbeck (Nees von). *See* **Nees von Esenbeck.**

Espinasse (Francis). Life and times of François-Marie Arouet, calling himself Voltaire. v. i. iv, 620 pp. 8°. *London, Chapman & Hall,* 1866.

Esprit (Jacques). Discourses on the deceitfulness of human virtues. Done out of French, by William Beauvoir. 8 p. l. 432 pp. 8°. *London, A. Bell,* 1706.

Espy (James Pollard). The human will; essays on moral accountability, the legitimate object of punishment, and the powers of the will. 95 pp. 8°. *Cincinnati, Dial office,* 1860.

Esquiros (Henri Alphonse). Cornwall and its coasts. vii, 304 pp. 12°. *London, Chapman & Hall*, 1865.

Essais d'anatomie; ou l'on explique clairement la construction des organes et leurs opérations méchaniques selon les nouvelles hypothèses. [*anon.*] 5 p.l. 189 pp. 24°. *Leide, P. Van der Aa*, 1686. s.

[*With* GREW (N.) Anatomie des plantes.]

Essay (An) on laughter. Translated from the French by P. Hiffernan. [*anon.*] xii, 140 pp. 18°. *London, T. Davies*, 1769.

Essay (An) on trade and commerce. [*anon.*] xvi, 302 pp. 8°. *London, S. Hooper*, 1770.

Essays on the principles of charitable institutions. [*anon.*] xi, 371 pp. 8°. *London, Longman*, 1836.

Essex, (*Earl of*). *See* **Capel** (Arthur).

Essex county (Mass.) Directory for 1866. 224, 152 pp. 8°. *Boston, Briggs & Co.* 1866.

[Title wanting.]

Estaing (Charles Hector, *comte* d'). Déclaration adressée au nom du roi à tous les anciens François de l'Amérique Septentrionale. fol. broadside. *À bord du vaisseau Languedoc, en rade de Boston, F. P. Demauge*, 1778.

Estancelin (Louis). Recherches sur les voyages et découvertes des navigateurs normands en Afrique, dans les Indes Orientales et en Amérique. xii, 261 pp. 8°. *Paris, Delaunay et A. Pinard*, 1832.

Estell & Co. The Liverpool commercial list, 1867–68. fol. *London*, 1866–67.

——— The London commercial list, 1867–68. fol. *London*, 1866–67.

——— The Manchester commercial list, 1867–68. fol. *London*, 1867.

Estes (Matthew). Defence of negro slavery, as it exists in the United States. 260 pp. 18°. *Montgomery, (Ala.)* 1846.

Esteve (Joaquin, *and others*). Diccionario catalan-castellano-latino. 2 v. in 1. 3 p.l. 419 pp; 429 pp. fol. *Barcelona, Tecla Pla*, 1803–05.

Estienne (Henri). De abvsv lingvæ græcæ in qvibvsdam vocibvs qvas latina vsvrpat admonitio. Io. Henr. Kromayeri adnotationibus nondvm editis instructam pvblicavit F. G. Roloffivs. 16 p.l. clii pp. 4 l. 16°. *Berolini, C. G. Nicolai*, 1736.

——— Epistolia, dialogi breves, orativncvlæ, poematia, ex variis vtriusque linguæ scriptoribus. 2 p.l. 276, 120 pp. 16°. *H. Stephanus*, 1577.

——— Ὁμηρου και Ἡσιοδου αγων. Homeri et Hesiodi certamen. Ex Homeri versibus lepide detortés consutum. Matronis et aliorvm parodiæ. 4 p.l. 181 pp. 16°. *H. Stephanus*, 1573.

[*With* ESTIENNE (Henri). Epistolia, etc. [1577.]

——— Introdvction av traité de la conformité des merveilles anciennes auec les modernes; ov, traité préparatif à l'apologie pour Hérodote. 32 p.l. unp. 680 pp. 16°. 1566.

——— The same. A world of wonders: or, an introdvction to a treatise touching the conformitie of ancient and moderne wonders. Continued by the author himselfe. Translated [from] the French. 2 pts. in 1 v. 9 p.l. unp. 358 pp. fol. *London, John Norton*, 1607. [Imperfect.]

État présent de la noblesse française. [*anon.*] xxiv, 1230 pp. 8°. *Paris, Brachelin-Deflorenne*, 1866.

Ethiopic didascalia; or, the Ethiopic version of the apostolic constitutions. With an English translation by T. P. Platt. xvi pp. 1 l. 131 pp. 5 l. 4°. *London*, 1834.

[Oriental translation fund.]

Etourneau (——). Les mormons. Préface par Pierre Vinçard. xi, 282 pp. 2 p.l. 18°. *Paris, Bestel*, 1856.

Ettingshausen (Constantin von). Die blattskelete der dikotyledonen, mit besonderer rücksicht auf die untersuchung und bestimmung der fossilen pflanzreste. xlvi, 308 pp. 95 pl. 4°. *Wien, Hof-und-staatsdruckerei*, 1861. s.

——— *and* **Pokorny** (Alois). Physiotypia plantarum austriacarum. Der naturselbstdruck in seiner anwendung auf die gefässpflanzen des österreichischen kaiserstaates, mit besonderer berücksichtigung der nervation in den flächenorganen der pflanzen. 500 pl. in 5 v. fol. *Wien, Hof-und-staatsdruckerei*, 1855–56. s.

Etzel (Anton von). Grönland geographisch und statistisch beschrieben. Aus dänischen quellschriften. xiv, 655 pp. 8°. *Stuttgart, J. G. Cotta*, 1860. s.

Etzler (J. A.) The paradise within the reach of all men, without labor, by powers of nature and machinery. 2 v. in 1. viii, 119 pp; 98 pp. 16°. *Pittsburgh, (Pa.) author*, 1833. s.

Euclides. The elements, viz: the first six books, with the eleventh and twelfth; also, the book of Euclid's data. By Robert Simson. [Also] Elements of plane and spherical trigonometry, etc. By Rev. A. Robertson. 24th ed. xii, 482 pp. 8°. *London, Longmans*, 1834. s

Euclides. The elements, etc. 419 pp. 3 pl. 8°. *Philadelphia, Desilver & Thomas*, 1834. s.

——— The same. Geometry, plane, solid, and spherical, in six books. With the theory of projection, etc. [*anon.*] viii, 272 pp. 8°. *London, Soc. for diff. of useful knowledge*, 1830. s.

——— The same. The first six books. *See* **Lardner** (D.)

——— The same. The geometry of Euclid; with annotations by Horatio Hubbell. 90 pp. 8°. *Philadelphia, J. B. Lippincott & Co.* 1861. s.

——— The same. A treatise of geometry, containing the first six books of Euclid's elements, with the elements of solid geometry. By D. Creswell. xxiii, 503 pp. 8°. *Cambridge, (Eng.) Deighton*, 1819. s.

——— The same. Elementi di geometria. Emendati . . . . da V. Flauti. 21ª ed. 2 v. in 1. lxxxviii, 341, c pp. 24 pl. 8°. *Napoli, Flauti*, 1852. s.

[FLAUTI. corso di geometria. v. iii].

Eugène (François Eugène de Savoie-Carignan, *prince*). Life of prince Eugene of Savoy. From his own original manuscript. Translated from the French. 67 pp. 8°. *London, J. Davis*, 1812.

[Royal military chronicle. v. 1].

Euler (Leonhard). Opuscula varii argumenti. 300 pp. 6 pl. 4°. *Berolini, A. Haude & J. C. Spener*, 1746. s.

CONTENTS.

1. Solutio problematis mechanici de motu corporum tubis mobilibus inclusorum.
2. Novæ tabulæ astronomicæ motuum solis ac lunæ.
3. Nova theoria lucis et colorum.
4. De perturbatione motus planetarum a resistentia ætheris orta.
5. Enodatio questionis; an materiæ facultas cogitandi tribui possit.
6. Recherches sur la nature des moindres particules des corps.

——— Elements of algebra. Translated from the French; with the notes of Bernouilli, etc. and the additions of Lagrange. [With] memoir of Euler, by Francis Horner. 5th ed. xxx, 593 pp. 8°. *London, Longmans*, 1840. s.

——— Vollständige anleitung zur niedern und höhern algebra; von Johann Philipp Grüson. 2 v. 7 p. l. 312 pp; 5 p. l. 403 pp. 8°. *Berlin, G. C. Rauck*, 1796. s.

Eumenes; a collection of papers exhibiting some of the errors and omissions of the constitution of New Jersey, to prove the necessity of a convention for its revision. [*anon.*] 149 pp. 2 l. 8°. *Trenton, G. Craft*, 1799.

Euripides. Tragedie, tradotte da Felice Bellotti. 477 pp. 8°. *Milano, A. F. Stella & figli*, 1829. s.

Eusebius Pamphilus. Animadversiones in Philostrati de Apollonio commentarios, de Hierocle. *See* **Philostratus**. Quæ svpersvnt omnia. *Lipsiae*, 1709.

——— Chronicon, id est temporvm breviarivm. 180 l. 4°. *Uenetijs, E. Ratdolt*, 1483. s.

——— Chronicon quod Hieronymus latinū facere curauit. 20 p. l. 175 l. paged. 1 l. unp. 4°. *Parisiis, H. Stephanus*, 1512. s.

——— Historia ecclesiastica. J. Christophorsono interprete. fol. *Coloniæ Agrippinæ*, 1581. s.

[*With* HISTORIAE eccl. scriptores graeci, 1581].

——— The same. Ruffino interprete. [*With* **Auctores** hist. eccl. fol. *Basileae*, 1523].

——— Ecclesiastical history. Translated and abridged by S. Parker.

[*With* Ecclesiastical histories, etc. 3d ed. 4°. *London*, 1729.]

Evagrius *scholasticus*. Historia ecclesiastica. fol. *Col. Agrippinae*, 1581. s.

[*With* HISTORIAE eccl. scriptores graeci, 1581].

——— Ecclesiastical history, translated and abridged by [Samuel] Parker.

[*With* ECCLESIASTICAL histories, etc. 4°. *London*, 1729].

Evans (Augusta T.) St. Elmo. A novel. 12°. *New York, Carleton*, 1867.

Evans (*Rev.* Christmas). Sermons: a new translation from the Welch; with a memoir of the author, by Rev. J. Cross. 304 pp. 2 pl. 8°. *Chicago*, 1867.

Evans (D. Morier). Speculative notes, and notes on speculation, ideal and real. x, 240 pp. 12°. *London, Groombridge*, 1864.

Evans (John). Builders' price-book. 44 pp. 16°. *Washington*, 1804.

——— *See* **Rose** (Philip) *and* **Evans** (John).

Evans (Lewis). Analysis of a general map of the middle British colonies in America; and of the country of the confederate Indians. 2d ed. iv, 32 pp. sm. fol. *Philadelphia, B. Franklin & D. Hall*, 1755.

Evans (Oliver). The young mill-wright and miller's guide. 5 pts. pp. 154, 175, 90, x. 8°. *Philadelphia*, 1795.

Eveleen Wilson, or the trials of an orphan girl. [*anon.*] 108 pp. 8°. *New York, H. Long & Co.* 1853.

Evelyn (John). Account of architects and architecture. 3 p. l. 75 pp. fol. *London*, 1706.

[*With* FRÉART de Chambray (Roland). Parallel of antient architecture with the modern. fol. *London*, 1707.]

Evening (The) post (New York daily). July, 1866 to June, 1867. 2 v. fol. *New York*, 1866–67.

Evening (The) star. (Washington daily). Jan. 1856 to June, 1867. 23 v. fol. [*Washington*, 1856–67].

Everest (*Rev.* Thomas R.) A popular view of homœopathy, exhibiting the present state of the science. 2d ed. xxv, 151 pp. 8°. *London, J. Baillière*, 1836. s.

Everett (David). Common sense in dishabille: or, the farmer's monitor. [With] a perpetual calendar, or economical almanack. 120 pp. 18°. *Worcester, Isaiah Thomas*, 1799.

Ewbank (Thomas). Indian remains, [from Chile].

[*With* GILLISS (J. M.) U. S. astron. exped. v. 2.]

Ewell (James). The medical companion, or family physician. 10th ed. 692 pp. 1 pl. 8°. *Philadelphia, Thomas, Cowperthwait & Co.* 1847. s.

Ewell (Thomas, *M. D.*) Letters to ladies, detailing important information concerning themselves and infants. 308 pp. 9 pl. 8°. *Philadelphia, W. Brown*, 1817.

Ewington (H.) The arcana of short-hand. New ed. 8 pp. 24°. *London, Baldwin, Cradock & Joy*, 1815.

Examination (An) of and some answer to a pamphlet, entitled, a narrative and defence of the proceedings of the ministers of Hampshire, who disapproved of Mr. Breck's settlement at Springfield [by a Boston clergyman. *anon*]. 98 pp. 8°. *Boston, H. Foster*, 1736.

Examination (An) of the principles and conduct of the two B'rs. (Barriers.) [*anon.*] 3d ed. 79 pp. 12°. *London, A. Price*, 1749.

Exceptions against Will. Rogers's cavills at J. P's complaint, etc. taken out of his sixth part of his Christian quaker. [*anon.*] 14 pp. sm 4°. *London, Benjamin Clark*, 1682.

Exhibition of 1851, London. Art journal illustrated. Catalogue of the industry of all nations, 1851. 4°. *London, G. Virtue*, [1851.] s.

——— Lectures on the results of the exhibition, delivered before the society of arts, manufactures, and commerce; 1–6, by Messrs. Whewell, De la Beche, Owen, Bell, Playfair, Lindley. 242 pp. 12°. *London*, 1852. s.

[Title wanting.]

——— L'imprimerie, la librairie et la papeterie à l'exposition universelle de 1851. Rapport du xviie jury présenté par M. Ambroise Firmin Didot. 2e éd. 142 pp. 8°. *Paris, Imprimerie royale*, 1854. s.

Exhibition of 1862, London. Special-catalog der gewerblichen ausstellung des zollvereins, herausgegeben von den commissarien der zollvereins regierungen. Mit einem anhange enthaltend anzeigen, illustrationen, und empfehlungen. viii, 196, cxv pp. 1 col. pl. 8°. *Berlin, R. Decker*, 1862. s.

Exhibition of 1865, Dublin. The illustrated record and descriptive catalogue. Compiled and edited by Henry Parkinson, P. L. Simmonds, etc. under the sanction of the executive committee. xvi, 570 pp. 25 pl. 8°. *London, E. & F. N. Spon*, 1866.

Explanations of the church service; or, a series of thoughts on the lessons, collects, epistles, and gospels, for young readers. By A. J. [*anon.*] 340 pp. 18°. *New York, H. B. Durand*, 1867.

Exposé (An) of facts concerning recent transactions relating to the corps of cadets of the United States military academy. [*anon*]. vii, 68 pp. 8°. *Newburgh, (N. Y.) U. C. Lewis*, 1819. s.

Expounder (The) expounded: or, annotations upon a short account of God's dealing with the Rev. Mr. G——e W—f—d. By R—ph J—ph—n of the inner temple. 82 pp. 16°. *London, W. & T. Payne*, 1740.

Exquemelin (Alexandre Olivier). Histoire des aventuriers flibustiers. Nouv. éd. augmentée de l'histoire des pirates anglois jusqu' à présent. 4 v. 16°. *Trévoux, par la compagnie*, 1775.

Extracts from humbugiana: or, the world's convention. A satire. By Quirk Ogee, *LL. D.* (*pseudon.*) 24 pp. 16°. *Gotham, (New York,)* 1847.

Extracts from the reports of her majesty's inspectors of schools. xix, 315 pp. 12°. *Warrington, Longmans*, 1862.

Extraordinary (The) life and adventures of Robin Hood, with Edward's cross, or the wife and the friend. [*anon.*] 71 pp. 24°. *Philadelphia, Freeman Scott*, 1827.

Eye (The): by Obadiah Optic. [*pseudon.*] 2 v. vi, 316 pp; viii, 316 pp. 16°. *Philadelphia, J. W. Scott*, 1808.

Eytelwein (Johann Albert). Summary of the most useful parts of hydraulics; chiefly extracted and abridged from Eytelwein's hand-buch. By T. Young. s.

(*With* TREDGOLD (F.) Tracts on hydraulics.)

Eyton (Thomas Campbell). Osteologia avium; or, a sketch of the osteology of birds. vi pp, 2 l, x, 229, vii pp, 114 pl. 4°. *Wellington, Salop, R. Hobson*, [1858–67.] s.

Faber (Frederick William). Hymns. vii, 196 pp. 12°. *Northampton, (Mass.) Bridgman & Childs*, 1867.

Faber (Friedrich). Naturgeschichte der fische Islands, mit einem anhange von den isländischen medusen und strahlenthieren. 206 pp. 4°. *Frankfort am Main, H. L. Bronner*, 1829. s.

——— Prodromus der isländischen ornithologie; oder, geschichte der vögel Islands. 2 p. l. 112 pp. 1 tab. 8°. *Kopenhagen, Verfasser*, 1822. s.

Faber (Théodore). Sketches of the internal state of France. Translated. 256 pp. 16°. *Philadelphia, Humphreys*, 1812. s.

Fabre (François Joseph). Descripcion de las alegorias pintadas en las bóvedas del real palacio de Madrid. 8°. *Madrid*, 1829.

Fabre (J. Antoine). Essai sur la théorie des torrens et des rivières. xxxii, 284 pp. 8 pl. 4°. *Paris, Bidault*, 1797. s.

Fabre d'Olivet (N.) Les vers dorés de Pythagore expliqués, précédés d'un discours sur l'essence de la poésie. [*See* **Pythagoras.** Les vers dorés. 8°. *Paris*, 1813.]

Fabricius (Otto). Bibelingoak merdlāinnut imaloneet. [Bible teachings for children]. 68 pp. 16°. *Kiöbenhavnime, C. F. Skubart*, 1822.

——— Favna grœnlandica. xvi, 452 pp. 1 pl. 8°. *Hafniae et Lipsiae, Rothe*, 1780.

——— Forsög til en forbedret grönlandsk grammatica. Andet oplag. 388 pp. 16°. *Kiöbenhavn, C. F. Schubart*, 1801.

——— Den grönlandske ordbog, forbedret og foröget. viii, 795 pp. 16°. *Kjöbenhavn, C. F. Schubart*, 1804.

——— Okalluktuæt opernartut tersāuko Bibelimit. [True narratives from the Bible.] 256 pp. 16°. *Kiöbenhavnime, C. F. Skubart*, 1820.

——— *See* **Bible** (*Esquimaux*).

Fac simile di alcune imprese di stampatori italiani dei secoli xv e xvi. 2 p. l. 24 pl. 4°. *Milano, P. A. Tosi*, 1838. s.

Fac similes of the memorial stones of the last English ancestors of George Washington in the parish church of Brington, Northamptonshire, England, permanently placed in the state house of Massachusetts. 15 pp. fol. *Boston, W. White*, 1862.

Faeneste [*pseudon.*] *See* **Aubigné** (Théodore Agrippa d'). Aventures, etc.

Faerno (Gabriello). Centvm fabulæ ex antiquis avctoribus delectæ. 173 pp. 32°. *Antverpiæ, C. Plantin*, 1585.

[With Junius (A.) Emblemata. 1596.]

Fahnestock (George Wolff). A centennial memorial of Christian and Anna Maria Wolff, with brief records of their children and relatives. 113 pp. 2 pl. fol. *Philadelphia, Helfenstein*, 1863.

Fairbairn (William). Treatise on mills and mill-work. part i. 2d ed. xvi, 306 pp. 9 pl. 8°. *London, Longmans*, 1864.

——— Useful information for engineers. 3d series. xix, 330 pp. 12°. *London, Longmans*, 1866.

Fairbanks (George R.) The early history of Florida; lecture before the Florida historical society, April 15, 1857. 31 pp. 18°. *St. Augustine*, 1857.

Fairbanks (Lorenzo). Science and practice of book-keeping, by single and double entry. 448 pp. 8°. *Philadelphia, Sower, Barnes & Potts*, 1866.

Fairchild (*Rev.* Ashbel G.) Memoir of Mrs. Louisa A. Lowrie. With an introduction by Rev. E. P. Swift. 2d ed. 221 pp. portrait. 18°. *Philadelphia, W. S. Martien*, 1837. s.

Fairfax (Ferdinando). Memorial against the extension of the patents granted to Robert Fulton for improvements in propelling vessels by steam. 8 pp. 8°. *Washington, E. De Krafft*, 1816.

Fairfield (Sumner Lincoln). Abaddon, the spirit of destruction, and other poems. 157 pp. 8°. *New York, Sleight & Robinson*, 1830.

——— (*and* Jane). The life of Sumner Lincoln Fairfield. [With appendix: The sister of saint Clara and other poems]. 132 pp. 12°. *New York*, 1847.

Fairholme (George). General view of the geology of scripture. xv, 493 pp. 3 pl. 8°. *London, Ridgway*, 1833.

Fairholt (Frederick W.) Miscellanea graphica: representations of ancient, medieval, and renaissance remains in the possession of Lord Londesborough. The historical introduction by Thomas Wright. 84 pp. 50 l. 45 pl. fol. *London, Chapman & Hall*, 1856.

Falconer (*Capt.* Richard). The voyages, dangerous adventures and imminent escapes of R. Falconer. 2 p. l. 179 pp. 1 pl. 12°. *London, W. Chetwood and others*, 1720.

——— The same. 4th ed. 3 p. l. 216 pp. 3 l. 1 pl. 16°. *London, J. Marshall*, 1734.

Falconia Proba. Centones de vtriusque testamenti hystoriis ex carminibus Virgilii selecti. 19 l. unp. sm. 4°. *Oppenheym*, [n. d.]

Falkenstein (Carl). Geschichte der buchdruckerkunst in ihrer entstehung und ausbildung. Ein denkmal zur vierten säcularfeier der erfindung der typographie. xiv, 406 pp. 37 pl. 4°. *Leipzig, B. G. Teubner,* 1840. s.

Falkman (Ludvig B.) Upplysningar om kronans, kyrkornas och presterskapets inkomster af andeligt gods uti skäue, halland och bleokinge frän äldre tider till 1660, jemväl innehällande beskrifning ofuer och förklaring af 1569 ärs Lunds stifts landebok. 2 v. 10 p. l. 328 pp; 344 pp. 8°. *Lund, Berlingska boktryceriet,* 1848. s.

Fall of British tyranny; or, American liberty triumphant. Tragi-comedy. [*anon.*] viii, 64 pp. 12°. *Philadelphia,* 1776.
[Imperfect; title page in m. s.]

Fall river (Ms.) athenaeum library. Catalogue; with rules and by-laws. 36 pp. 16°. *Boston, Damrell & Moore,* 1855. s.

Falle (Philip). An account of the isle of Jersey. 10 p. l. 216 pp. 1 map. 16°. *London, J. Newton,* 1694.
[Imperfect; wanting map and pp. 1 and 2.]

Fallén (Carl Fredrik). Monographia cimicum Sveciae. 123 pp. 8°. *Hafniae, Proft,* 1807. s.

Falloux (Frédéric Alfred Pierre, *vicomte* de). Life and letters of madame Swetchine. Translated by H. W. Preston. xv, 369 pp. 12°. *Boston, Roberts Bros.* 1868.

Family (The) and ship medicine chest companion; being a compendium of domestic medicine, surgery, and materia medica. By a practising physician. [*anon.*] 416 pp. 12°. *Philadelphia, Lindsay & Blakiston,* 1851. s.

Family (The) treasure; a religious and literary monthly for 1865–66. v. 2–3. 8°. *Pittsburgh, (Pa.)* 1865–66.

Fanjat (*pseudon.*) *See* **Adresse[une]** illisible.

Fanning (*Captain*). A narrative of the adventures of an American navy officer, who served during part of the American revolution under Paul Jones. [*anon.*] 270 pp. 12°. *New York,* 1806.

Fanshawe (*Sir* Richard). Original letters during his embassies in Spain and Portugal. 4 p. l. 510 pp. 12°. *London, A. Roper,* 1702.

Farmer (Henry T. *M. D.*) Imagination; the maniac's dream, and other poems. 163 pp. 12°. *New York, Kirk & Mercein,* 1819.

Farmer's (The) magazine. July 1866, to June 1867. 3d series. v. 30–31. 8°. *London, Rogerson & Tuxford,* [1866–67].

Farnham (Thomas J.) Travels in the great western prairies, the Anahuac and Rocky mountains, and in the Oregon territory. 112 pp. 8°. *New York, Greeley & McElrath,* 1843.

Farquharson (Martha). Allan's fault. 412 pp. 5 pl. 16°. *Philadelphia, presby'n board of pub.* [1866.]

Farrar (Timothy). Manual of the constitution of the United States of America. xii, 532 pp. 8°. *Boston, Little, Brown & Co.* 1867.

Fasciculus temporū omnes antiquorū cronicas complectens. *See* **Rolevinck** (Werner).

Fashionable (The) cypriad. Part 1. [*anon.*] 248 pp. 18°. *London, Henderson,* 1798.
[No more published.]

Fau (Julien), *and* **Chevalier** (Charles). Nouveau manuel complet du physicien-preparateur; ou description d'un cabinet de physique. 2 v. 406; 530 pp. 24°. Atlas, 88 pl. 8°. *Paris, Roret,* 1853. s.

Fauche (Pierre François). Réflexions sur la cession de la Guadeloupe à la couronne de Suède. 20 pp. 12°. *Londres, J. C. de Boffe,* 1813.

Faucher (Léon). Études sur l'Angleterre. 2 v. xxxi, 472 pp; 434 pp. 8°. *Paris, Guillaumin,* 1845.

Fauques (Marianne Agnès de). The last war of the beasts; a fable. Translated from the French. [*anon.*] vii, 244 pp. 12°. *London, C. G. Seyffert,* 1758.

Fauriel (Claude Charles). Chants populaires de la Grèce moderne, avec une traduction française, des éclaircissements, et des notes. 2 v. cxliv, 303 pp; 491 pp. 8°. *Paris, Dondey-Dupré,* 1824–25.

Favre (Alphonse). Notice sur les cartes géologiques de l'Angleterre. [Extrait.] 23 pp. 8°. *Genève, Bibliothèque univ.* 1847. s.

Favre (Eugène). Deutsches lesebuch. Lectures allemandes; ou, choix de versions faciles et graduées à l'usage des collèges et des gymnases de la Suisse française. 3e éd. 216 pp. 12°. *Genève, J. Kessmann,* 1853. s.

Favyn (André). The theater of honor and knighthood; or, a compendious chronicle and historie of the whole christian world. [Translated from the French by W. I.] 2 v. in 1. 9 p. l. 572; 538 pp. 11 pl. fol. *London, W. Jaggard,* 1623.

Faxardo (Diego Saavedra). *See* **Saavedra.**

Fay (H. A. *Capt. U. S. A.*) Collection of the official accounts in detail of all the battles fought by sea and land, between the United States and Great Britain, 1812–15. 295 pp. 8°. *New York, E. Conrad,* 1817.

Fearnside (William Gray) *and* **Harral** (T.) *editors.* History of London. *See* **Woods** (John), history, etc.

Febres (Andres). Diccionario hispano chileno, [y chileno hispano]. iv, 108 pp; iv, 87 pp. 12°. *Santiago,* 1846. s.

Feijoo y Montenegro (Benito Jeronimo). Obras escogidas. Con una noticia de su vida, [etc.] por V. de La Fuente. xliv, 609 pp. 8°. *Madrid, Rivadeneyra,* 1863.
[Bib. de autores españoles, v. 56].

Félibien d'Avaux (André). The tent of Darius explained; or, the queens of Persia at the feet of Alexander. Translated by Col. Parsons. 7 p. l. 51 pp. 1 pl. 4°. *London, W. Redmayne,* 1703. s.

Fellenberg, (L. Rudolph von). Analysen von antiken bronzen. [extract]. 12°. *Bern,* 1860.
[*With* MORLAT (A.) Articles]. s.

Fellens (Jean Baptiste). Louis Napoléon, sa vie politique et privée. Dessins par J. A. Beauce et H. Émy. 152 pp. 8°. *Paris, Marescqet,* 1852.

Feller (F. E.) Das gange der kaufmännischen arithmetik. Herausgegeben von Carl Gustav Odermann. 8e aufl. xii, 527 pp. 8°. *Leipzig, O. A. Schuly,* 1861. s.

Feller (Joachim). Oratio de bibliotheca academiæ lipsiensis paulina, cui duplex subjunctus est catalogus manuscriptorum. 32 l. unp. 4°. *Lipsiæ, Bucht,* 1676. s.
[*With* SCHÖTTGEN, (C.) Histoire, etc. 1722.]

Felt (Joseph Barlow, *D. D.*) The annals of Salem [Mass]. 611 pp. 8°. *Salem, W. & S. B. Ives,* 1827.

——— Statistics of towns, population, and taxation in Massachusetts.
[AMERICAN statistical association, collections, v. 1.]

Felton (Cornelius Conway). Greece, ancient and modern: lectures before the Lowell institute. 2 v. vi, 511 pp. portrait; iv, 549 pp. 8°. *Boston, Ticknor & Fields,* 1867.

Fénelon (François de Salignac de La Mothe).
——— Les aventures de Télémaque. xxxv, 234 pp. 2 pl; 275 pp. 1 map. 18°. *Londres, C. Spilsbury,* 1805.

——— The same. The adventures of Telemachus. Translated with notes, by J. Kelly. 2 v. 2 p.l. 295 pp; 304 pp. 26 pl. 16°. *London, J. Walthoe & T. Waller,* 1742–43.

——— Court of beauty; or, judgment of Venus; also, ethic tales and fables, invented for the education of a prince. From the French by D. Bellamy. 89 pp. 26 pl. 4°. *London,* 1768.
[*With* Bellamy, (Daniel), ethic amusements. 4°. *London,* 1768.]

Fénelon (François de Salignac de La Mothe). Demonstration of the existence and attributes of God. 263 pp. 12°. *Harrisburgh, (Pa.) William Gillmor,* 1811.

——— The same. Extracts from letters on the existence of God, [*etc.*] *See* **Catechism** on christian faith. *New York,* 1811.

——— Dialogues concerning eloquence; particularly that kind which is proper for the pulpit. Translated by W. Stevenson. 174 pp. 16°. *Boston, Farrand, Mallory & Co.* 1816. s.

——— Tales and fables, in French and English. Translated by D. Bellamy. New ed. 2 p. l. 78, 86 pp. 28 pl. 4°. *London, J. Deighton,*1789.

Fenestella (Lucius). [*pseudon.*] *See* **Fiocchi** (Andrea Domenico).

Fenn (Joseph). The complete accountant; being a system of arithmetic both theoretical and practical. 1 p. l. 168 pp. 5 l. 8°. *Dublin, A. McCulloh,* [*about* 1790]. s.

Fenner von Fenneberg (F.) Transatlantische studien. 243 pp. 12°. *Stuttgart, C. A. Sonnewald,* 1861.

Fenton (Elijah). Poetical works. 8°. *Edinburgh,* 1794.
[Anderson's Brit. poets, v. 7].

Feraud (F. G.) A new Spanish grammar. iv, 392 pp. 8°. *London, Dulau & Co.* 1809.

Fergola (Nicola). Della invenzione geometrica; opera postuma ordinata dal V. Flauti. lviii, 282, lxiv pp. 11 pl. 8°. *Napoli, Flauti,* 1842. s.

——— Trattati analitici delle sezione coniche e de' loro luoghi geometrici. 3a ed. con nuove note del Prof. Flauti. 6 p. l. xxviii, 422, 62 pp. 9 pl. 4°. *Napoli, Flauti,* 1840. s.

——— Trattato geometrico delle sezione coniche reprodotto da V. Flauti. lxxii, 297, lxx pp. 15 pl. 8°. *Napoli, Flauti,* 1851. s.

Ferguson (Adam). Institutes of moral philosophy. New ed. xii, 242 pp. 12°. *Basil, J. Decker,* 1800.

Ferguson (George). Table of the pay of commissioned officers, U. S. A. *See* **Jameson** (W. H. *jr.*) *and* **Ferguson** (G.)

Ferguson (James). Lectures on select subjects in mechanics, hydrostatics, pneumatics, and astronomy. New ed. xlvii, 463 pp. 11 pl. 8°. *London, T. Tegg,* 1843. s.

——— Astronomical part. *See* **Guthrie** (William). A new system of geography. ed. 1811.

Fergusson (James). Historical inquiry into the true principles of beauty in art, more especially with reference to architecture. Part 1, [consisting of introduction, and essays on Egyptian, western Asiatic, Grecian, Etruscan, and Roman art]. 8°. *London,* 1849. s.
[No more published].

Fergusson (James). Rock-cut temples of India. One hundred illustrations of architecture and natural history in western India. Photographed by major Gill. New ed. xii pp. 100 stereoscopic views. 8°. *London, Cundall, Downes & Co.* 1864.

Ferishta (Mohammed Kasim, *surnamed*). The history of Hindostan, translated from the Persian. With continuation [up to 1666] by Alexander Dow. 2d ed. 3 v. 4°. *London,* 1770–72. s.

Fernandez (Diego). Primera [y segunda] parte de la historia del Peru. 2 v. in 1. 2 p. l. 142 l; 130 l. sm. fol. *Sevilla, H. Diaz,* 1571.
[Imperfect; l. 1–4 of v. 2 wanting].

Fernandez (Juan Patricio). Relacion historial de las missiones de los Indios, que llaman Chiquitos. Sacada a luz por Geronimo Heràn. 7 p. l. 452 pp. table, 2 l. sm. 4°. *Madrid, M. Fernandez,* 1726.

Ferrario (Giulio). Le classiche stampe dal cominciamento della calcografia, compresi gli artisti viventi. cxiii, 401 pp. 8°. *Milano, Bravetta,* 1836. s.

Ferrario (Giuseppe). Statistica medico-economica di Milano dal secolo xv fino ai nostri giorni. 2 v. xvii, 658 pp; vii, 546 pp. 1 map. 8°. *Milano, Bernardoni,* 1838–50. s.

——— Statistica delle morti improvvise, e particolarmente delle morti per apoplessia nella città e nel circondario esterno di Milano dall' anno 1750 al 1834. 8°. *Milano,* 1834. s.

Ferreri di Labriano (Francesco Maria). Avgvstæ regiæqve Sabavdæ domvs arbor gentilitia. [898–1675]. [French and Latin]. 209 pp. 34 pl. fol. *Avgvstæ Tavrinorum, J. B. Zappata,* 1702. s.

Ferrero (Edward). The art of dancing, [with] a few hints on etiquette; also, the figures, music, etc. 181, 103 pp. 12°. *New York, E. Ferrero,* 1859.

Ferris (John Alexander). The financial economy of the United States illustrated, and the causes which retard the progress of California demonstrated. 356 pp. 1 pl. 12°. *San Francisco, A. Roman & Co.* 1867.

Ferro (Pascal Joseph). *See* **Bleile** (J.)

Ferry (Gabriel, *pseudon.*) *See* **Bellemare** (Louis de).

Férussac (André Étienne Just Paschal Joseph François d'Audebard, *baron* de) *and* **Orbigny** (Alcide Dessalines d'). Histoire naturelle générale et particulière des céphalopodes acétabulifères vivants, et fossiles. 24, 361 pp. Atlas, 144 pl. fol. *Paris, A. Lacour,* 1835–48.
[Imperfect]. s.

Fessenden (G. M.) The history of Warren, (R. I.) from the earliest times, with particular notices of Massasoit and his family. 125 pp. 18°. *Providence, H. H. Brown,* 1845.
[*With* TUSTIN, (*Rev.* J. P.) Dedication of baptist church in Warren. *Providence,* 1845.)

Festus (Sextus Pompeius). De verborum significatione fragmentum. *See* **Flaccus** (Marcus Verrius).

Fétis (François Joseph.) Biographie universelle des musiciens, et bibliographie générale de la musique. 8 v. 8°. *Bruxelles, Leroux,* etc. 1835–44.

Feuillet (Octave). La petite comtesse. Le parc. Onesta. 5e éd, 352 pp. 12°. *Paris, M. Lévy,* 1860.

Few (A) facts regarding the geological survey of Pennsylvania, exposing the erroneous statements and claims of J. P. Lesley. [By an assistant]. 22 pp. 8°. *Philadelphia, author,* 1859. s.

Few (A) plain directions for persons intending to proceed as settlers in Upper Canada. [With] a journal of the author's voyage across the Atlantic in 1819. By an English farmer. [*anon.*] vii, 100 pp. 1 map. 12°. *London, Baldwin, Cradock & Joy,* 1820.

Feyerabend *or* **Feierabend** (Sigmund *or* Sigismund). Theatrum diabolorum, das ist; warhafte eigentliche vnd kurtze beschreibung allerley grewlicher, schrecklicher, und abschewlicher laster. 5 p. l. 568 l. fol. *Franckfurt-am-Mayn, Peter Schund & Co.* 1575.

Fichte (Johann Gottlieb). On the nature of the scholar, and its manifestations. Translated by William Smith. 2d ed. 131 pp. 12°. *London, J. Chapman,* 1848. s.

Field (David Dudley, *D. D.*) A history of the town of Pittsfield, Mass. 80 pp. 1 map. 8°. *Hartford, Case, Tiffany & Burnham,* 1844.

——— A statistical account of the county of Middlesex, Connecticut. 154 pp. 8°. *Middletown, Clark & Lyman,* 1819.

Field (George). Rudiments of the painters' art; or, a grammar of colouring. viii, 170 pp. 6 pl. 16°. *London, Weale,* 1850. s.

Field (Henry M. *D. D.*) Additional chapters with appendix, to the second edition of The Atlantic telegraph. pp. 343–438. 16°. *New York, C. Scribner & Co.* 1867.

Fielding (Henry). Works; containing a journey from this world to the next; a voyage to Lisbon; the true patriot, etc. 297 pp. 12°. *New York, W. Durrell,* 1819.

Fielding (Sarah). Adventures of David Simple; and familiar letters between the principal characters in David Simple, and some others. [*anon*]. 5 v. 16°. *London, A. Millar*, 1744–53.

Fiery (The) cross; a tale of the great American war. By the author of "The black angel," etc. [*anon.*] 411 pp. 18°. *London, C. Clarke*, [1866].

Figaniere (Jorge Cesar de). Bibliographia historica portugueza. ix, 359 pp. 8°. *Lisboa, typog. do panorama*, 1850. s.

Figuier (Guillaume Louis). The vegetable world; being a history of plants, with their botanical descriptions and peculiar properties. Illustrated by M. Faguet. [Translated with preface by W. S. O.] 8°. *London, Chapman & Hall*, 1867.

——— The world before the deluge. 4th ed. 8°. *London, Chapman & Hall*, 1865.

Filangieri (Gaetano). Delle leggi politiche ed economiche.

(Scrittori class ital. di ecón. pol. v. 32.)

Filelfo (Francesco). Epistole. 5 p. l. unp. lxi l. sm. 4°. *Argentine*, 1495.

——— Orationes et nonnulla alia opera. clxvi l. paged. 4°. *B. de Zanis de Portesio, Venetiis*, 1491.

Filelfo (Giovanni Maria). Epistolae. 108 l. unp. sm. 4°. *Venetie, Joannes de Cereto*, 1492.

Fillmore (A. D.) Harp of Zion: a book of church music, [with] course of instruction, [etc.] 336 pp. obl. 16°. *Cincinnati, R. W. Carroll & Co.* [1867].

——— *and* (C. L.) The polyphonic, or juvenile choralist; containing music and hymns. 128 pp. obl. 32°. *Cincinnati, R. W. Carroll & Co.* [1863].

Filson (John). The discovery, settlement, and present state of Kentucke, with appendix containing the adventures of Daniel Boon, minutes of the Piankashaw council, account of the Indian nations in the U. S. and the stages and distances between Philadelphia and the falls of the Ohio. 118 pp. 12°. *Wilmington, James Adams*, 1784.

Finch (Louisa Thynne, *countess of Guernsey*). Fairburn's genuine edition of the death-bed confessions of the late countess of Guernsey to lady Anne H*******; with the q——'s [queen Caroline's] last letter to the king. [*anon.*] iv, 50 pp. 8°. *London, J. Fairburn*, [1821?]

Finden (Edward *and* W.) Tableaux of national character, beauty, and costume. With original tales in prose and poetry, written expressly for the work by the most popular authors of the day. 2 v. 209 pp. 61 pl. fol. *London, T. G. March*, 1843.

Fine (The) arts quarterly review, October, 1864, to January, 1865. v. 3. 8°. *London, Chapman & Hall*, [1865].

——— The same. July, 1866, to June, 1867. New series. v. 1–2. 8°. *London, Day & son*, [1866–67].

Finishing (The) stroke. Being a vindication of the patriarchal scheme of government; wherein Mr. Hoadly's examination of this scheme is considered. [*anon.*] 12°. *London, printed by the booksellers*, 1711.

Finlay (Hugh). Journal, during his survey of the post-offices between Falmouth and Casco bay, in the province of Massachusetts, and Savannah, in Georgia; begun 13th September, 1773, and ended 26th June, 1774. [With introduction by F. H. Norton]. 4°. *Brooklyn, privately printed*, 1867.

Finney (*Rev.* Charles G.) Lectures on revivals of religion. 438 pp. 12°. *New York, Leavitt, Lord & Co.* 1835.

——— Sermons on important subjects. 3d ed. vi, 277 pp. 8°. *New York, J. S. Taylor*, 1836.

Finsch (Otto). Index ad C. L. Bonaparte conspectum generum avium. 23 pp. 8°. *Lugduni-Batavorum, E. J. Brill*, 1865. s.

——— *and* **Hartlaub** (Gustav). Beitrag zur fauna Centralpolynesiens. Ornithologie der Viti-Samoa und Tonga-inseln. xxxix, 290 pp. 14 col. pl. 8°. *Halle, H. W. Schmidt*, 1867. s.

Fiocchi (Andrea Domenico). Lucii Fenestele de Romanorum magistratibus liber. 22 l. unp. sm. 4°. [n. p. *about* 1480].

Note. Falsely attributed to L. Fenestella.

——— The same. De Ro[manorum] magistratibus: restitutus industria Joannis Camertis. 35 l. unp. sm. 4°. *Vienne, H. Victor*, 1510.

Fiorentino (Paolo). *See* **Paolo** fiorentino.

Fiorillo (Johann Dominic). Geschichte der zeichnenden künste in Deutschland und den Vereinigten Niederlanden. 4 v. 8°. *Hannover, Hahn*, 1815–20. s.

Firdúsi (Abú'l Kasim Hasan Ben Mohammed et Túsí, *known as*). Le livre des rois, par Abou'lkasim Firdousi. Publié, traduit, et commenté par Jules Mohl. 4 v. fol. *Paris, imp. royale*, 1838–55. s.

[Collection orientale].

Firenzuola (Agnolo). Novelle.

[*In* POGGIALI, (G.) Novelle fiorentini. 18°. *Milan*, 1815].

First (The) book of geometry, including plane and solid geometry, and an introduction to trigonometry. 3 p. l. 84 pp. 32°. *London, Soc. for prom. christ. knowledge,* 1835. s.

First lessons in botany. By Theodore Thinker. [*pseudon*]. 141 pp. 1 pl. 16°. *New York, A. S. Barnes & Co.* 1851. s.

First (The) settlers of New England; or, conquest of the Pequods, Narragansetts, and Pokanokets. By a lady of Massachusetts. [*anon.*] 282 pp. 1 pl. 18°. *Boston, Munroe & Francis,* [*about* 1822].

Firth (William). Remarks on the recent state trials, and the rise and progress of disaffection in the country. 8°. *London,* 1818.

Fischer (Friedrich Ernst Ludwig). Enumeratio plantarum novarum a cl. Schrenk lectarum. 113 pp. 2 pl. 8°. *Petropoli, G. Fischer,* 1841. s.

Fischer (Kuno). Commentary on Kant's critick of pure reason; translated from the history of modern philosophy. With introduction, notes, etc. by J. P. Mahaffy. 12°. *London, Longmans,* 1866.

Fischer (Leopold Heinrich). Orthoptera europæa. xx, 454 pp. 18 pl. 4°. *Lipsiæ, G. Engelmann,* 1854. s.

Fischer (—— *major*). Memoir über die karte von Kleinasien. *See* **Kiepert** (H.)

Fisher (A. *quakeress*). A few lines in love to such that frequent the meetings of the quakers. 8 pp. sm. 4°. *London, T. Sowle,* 1694.

Fisher (Alexander). A journal of a voyage of discovery to the arctic regions, in H. M. ships Hecla and Griper, in 1819–20. 3d ed. xi, 520 pp. 2 maps. 8°. *London, Longman,* 1821.

Fisher (George, *accomptant*). Arithmetic, in the plainest and most concise methods hitherto extant. 334 pp. 16°. *Paisley, A. Weir,* 1780.

Fisher (Joseph). Where shall we get meat? The food supplies of western Europe; being letters written in reply to the question, where is England to get meat? during a tour in [western Europe] in 1865. [Also] a paper on the production of food, read at the international social science congress at Berne, 1865. xvi, 272 pp. 16°. *London, Longmans,* 1866.

Fisher (Thomas). Dial of the seasons; or, a portraiture of nature. 217 pp. 8°. *Philadelphia, Carey & Hart,* 1845.

Fisk (Fidelia). Recollections of Mary Lyon, with selections from her instructions to the pupils of Mt. Holyoke female seminary. 333 pp. 1 pl. 12°. *Boston, Am. tract soc.* [1866].

Fisk (*Rev.* George). A memorial of Egypt, the Red sea, the wildernesses of Sin and Paran, Mount Sinai, Jerusalem, and other localities of the Holy Land, visited in 1842. 2d ed. 451 pp. 2 pl. 12°. *New York, Robert Carter,* 1847.

Fitch (George W.) Outlines of physical geography. Revised by A. J. Robinson. With questions, etc. by C. C. Morgan. vi, 112 pp. 15 maps. 4°. *New York, Ivison,* 1867.

Fitch (John). The original steamboat supported; or, a reply to Mr. James Rumsey's pamphlet, shewing the true priority of John Fitch, and the false datings, etc. of James Rumsey. 34 pp. 8°. *Philadelphia, Z. Poulson,* 1788.

Fitz-Geffrey (*Rev.* Charles). The life and death of Sir Francis Drake: poem. xxiii, 101 pp. 12°. *Lee Priory (Kent), John Warwick,* 1819.

Fitz Gerald (F.) An expanding currency, for preventing injurious fluctuations in the rate of discount, and consequent stagnation of trade. 2d ed. 20 pp. 8°. *London, Delizy, Davies & Co.* 1866.

Fitzgerald (Percy). Charles Townshend, wit and statesman. xv, 360 pp. 1 pl. 12°. *London, R. Bentley,* 1866.

Fitzinger (Leopold Joseph). Bilder-atlas zur wissenschaftlich-populären naturgeschichte der vögel. 1 p. l. 164 pl. col. 4°. *Wien,* 1864. s.

—— Neue classification der reptilien nach ihren natürlichen verwandtschaften. 4 p. l. 66 pp. 1 tab. 4°. *Wien, J. G. Heubner,* 1826. s.

—— Systema reptilium, fasciculus primus: amblyglossæ. 110, vi pp. 8°. *Vindobonæ, Braumüller & Seidel,* 1843. s.

—— Wissenschaftlich-populäre naturgeschichte der säugethiere in ihren sämmtlichen hauptformen. Nebst einer einleitung in die naturgeschichte überhaupt. 6 v. 8°. Atlas, 123 pl. (in 248 col. fig.) 4°. *Wien, k. hof-und staatsdruckerei,* 1860–61. s.

Fitzmaurice (George William Hamilton, *viscount Kirkwall*). Four years in the Ionian islands. Their political and social condition, with a history of the British protectorate. xiii, 305 pp; viii, 336 pp. 12°. *London, Chapman & Hall,* 1864.

Fitzwilliam (G. W.) The pleasures of love; being amatory poems, original and translated, from the Asiatic and European languages. xii, 188 pp. 4 pl. 16°. *London, J. Cundee,* 1806.

Flaccus (Marcus Verrius). Fragmenta post editionem augustinanam denuo collecta atque digesta. Sexti Pompei Festi fragmentum ad fidem ursiniani exemplaris recensitum, etc. Edidit A. E. Egger. xxiv, 358 pp. 18°. *Parisiis, Bourgeois-Maze,* 1838. s.

Flack (*Captain of the Texan rangers*). A hunter's experiences in the southern states of America; account of the quadrupeds and birds, the objects of chase in those countries. 2 p. l. 359 pp. 8°. *Londou, Longmans,* 1866.

——— The Texan rifle-hunter; or, field sports on the prairie. viii, 333 pp. 12° *London, J. Maxwell & Co.* 1866.

Flambo: a brief treatise on the persecuting and dangerous character of popery. By a presbyter of the diocese of New York. [*anon.*] 80 pp. 12°. *New York, Pudney & Russell,* 1855. s.

Flammen der liebe; ein katholisches gebetbuch zur verehrung des göttlichen herzens Jesu, beim besuche des heiligsten altarssakramentes; bearbeitet von Joseph Peter. 349, 64 pp. 4 pl. 32°. *New York, Benziger Bros,* 1866.

Flanagan (Thomas). A history of the church in England, from the earliest period to 1850. 2v. xx, 633 pp; x, 549 pp. 8°. *London, C. Dolman,* 1857.

Flanders (W. A.) Nature's bee book; a manual [of] bee culture. 3d ed. 64 pp. 18°. *Mansfield (O.) L. D. Myers & Bro.* 1867.

Flaubert (Gustave). Madame Bovary; mœurs de province. 2 v. in 1. 490 pp. 16°. *Paris, Lévy,* 1858.

Flauti (Vincenzio). Analisi algebrica delle quantità determinate. 5ª ed. xviii, 256, xvi pp. 8°. *Napoli, autor,* 1844. s.

——— Geometria di sito sul plano e nello spazio. Parte i, 3ª ed. xlix, 208, xxiv pp. 18 pl. 8°. *Napoli, autor,* 1842. s.

——— Della trigonometria rettilinea e sferica libri sei. 14ª ed. xxxix, 176, xlviii pp. 7 pl. 8°. *Napoli, autor,* 1846. s.

——— *See* **Archimedes**; *also* **Euclid**; *also* **Fergola** (N.)

Flavel (*Rev.* John). Husbandry spiritualized; or, the heavenly use of earthly things, etc. 295 pp. 12°. *Elizabethtown, (N. J.) S. Kollock,* 1794. s.

Flaxman (John). Compositions of the "acts of mercy;" engraved by F. C. Lewis. 8 pl. obl. fol. *London, Misses Flaxman & Denman,* 1831.

——— Lectures on sculpture. 2d ed. [With] address on the death of T. Banks, and of Canova; and an address on the death of Flaxman, by Sir R. Westmacott. x. 303 pp. 52 pl. 8°. *London, H. G. Bohn,* 1838. s.

Fleetwood (William, *bishop of Ely*). Chronicon preciosum; or, an account of English money, the price of corn and other commodities, for the last 600 years. [*anon.*] 8 p. l. 181 pp. 3 l. 12°. *London, C. Harper,* 1817.

Fleischmann (C. L.) Erwerbszweige, fabrikwesen und handel der Vereinigten Staaten von Nordamerika. 2ᵉ ausg. 2 p. l. 617 pp. 8°. *Stuttgart, F. Kohler,* 1852. s.

Fleming (Robert). The history of hereditary right, from Cain to Nero. 2d ed. 8 p. l. 156 pp. 12°. *London, A. & W. Bell,* 1717.

Fletcher (Ebenezer). Narrative of captivity and sufferings. 4th ed. 24 pp. 16°. *New Ipswich, (N. H.)* 1827.

——— The same. Narrative of a soldier of the revolution, written by himself. With introduction and notes, by C. I. Bushnell. 86 pp. 8°. *New York, (privately printed),* 1866.

Fletcher (Giles). Christ's victory and triumph. 8°. *Edinburgh,* 1793.
[Anderson's Brit. poets, v. 4.]

Fletcher (Henry Charles). History of the American war. Third and fourth years of the war. v. 3. 8°. *London, R. Bentley,* 1866.
[Completing the work.]

Fletcher (Phineas). Piscatory eclogues, with other poetical miscellanies. 8, 151 pp. 2 l. 12°. *Edinburgh, Kincaid & Creech,* 1771.

——— Poetical works. 8°. *Edinburgh,* 1793.
[Anderson's Brit. poets, v. 4.]

Fleury (Claude). A short history of the Israelites. Translated from the French by Ellis Farneworth. vi, 240 pp. 8°. *London, J. Whiston,* 1756.

Fleury (Lamé). *See* **Lamé**-Fleury (Jules Raymond).

Flindall (John Morris). Amateur's pocket companion; or, description of engraved British portraits, curious books, etc. 141 pp. 24°. *London, Gale, Curtis & Fenner,* 1812. s.

Flint (Austin, *M. D.*) The physiology of man; designed to represent the existing state of physiological science, as applied to the functions of the human body: alimentation, digestion, absorption, lymph, and chyle. 556 pp. 8°. *New York, Appletons,* 1867.

Flint (Henry M.) Mexico under Maximilian. 258 pp. 12°. *Philadelphia,* [*etc.*] *National pub. co.* [1867].

Flint (Timothy). Biographical memoir of Daniel Boone, interspersed with incidents in the early annals of [Kentucky]. 252 pp. 16°. *Cincinnati, George Conclin,* 1842.

Flint (Timothy). Biographical memoir of Daniel Boone, etc. 215 pp. 16°. *Cincinnati, George Conclin,* 1842.

Flloyd (Thomas). Bibliotheca biographica: a synopsis of universal biography, ancient and modern. 3 v. 8°. *London, J. Hinton and others,* 1760.

Flora parvula; or, gleanings from favourite flowers. [*anon.*] iv, 87 pp. 8°. *London, W. Macintosh,* [1860]?

Florez (Henrique). Clave historial, con que se abre la puerta à la historia eclesiastica y politica, etc. Ed. 12ª. xxxviii, 447 pp. 1 map. 1 pl. sm. 4°. *Madrid, Ibarra,* 1786.

Florian (Jean Pierre Claris de). Guillermo Tell, libertador de la Suiza: y Andres Hofer, el "Tell" del Tirol. Con la vida del autor. xx, 254 pp. 2 pl. 16°. *Nueva York, Appletons,* 1866.

[The life of Hofer is a compilation by the translator.]

Florida. Journal of proceedings of a convention of delegates to form a constitution for the people of Florida, at St. Joseph, Dec. 1838. 120, 20 pp. 8°. *St. Joseph,* 1839.

Florus (Lucius Annaeus). *See* **Justinus** *and* **Florus.** Epithome, etc.

Flourens (Marie Jean Pierre). Cuvier. Histoire de ses travaux. 2ᵉ éd. 12°. *Paris, Paulin,* 1845. s.

——— De l'instinct, et de l' intelligence des animaux. 2ᵉ éd. 207 pp. 16°. *Paris, Paulin,* 1845. s.

——— Recueil des éloges historiques lus dans les séances publiques de l'académie des sciences. 1ᵉ série. 412 pp. 12°. *Paris, Garnier,* 1856. s.

Flower (Benjamin). Flower's political review, and monthly register. Jan. 1807, to July 1811. 9 v. 8°. *Harlow, M. Jones,* 1807–11.

Flower (William Henry). Diagrams of the nerves of the human body. 8 pp. 6 pl. fol. *London, J. Churchill,* 1861. s.

Foa (*madame* Eugénie). *pseudon. for* Rodrigues (Eugénie Rebecca). Boy artists; or, sketches of the childhood of Michael Angelo, Mozart, Haydn, Watteau, and Sebastian Gomez. From the French. 176 pp. 2 pl. 16°. *Boston, E. P. Dutton & Co.* 1868.

Foderé (François Emmanuel, *M. D.*) Traité de médecine légale et d'hygiène publique, ou de police de santé. [2ᵉ éd.] 6 v. 8°. *Paris, Mame,* 1813.

Foigny (Gabriel). New discovery of terra incognita Australis, or the southern world. 4 p. l. 186 pp. 24°. *London, John Dunton,* 1693.

Foissac (Pierre). De la météorologie dans ses rapports avec la science de l'homme, et principalement avec la médecine et l'hygiène publique. 2 v. 508 pp; 520 pp. 8°. *Paris, J. B. Baillière,* 1854. s.

Foix-Pino (F. L.) Galerie choisie d'hommes célèbres de l'antiquité grecque et romaine. 357 pp. 100 pl. 16°. *Amsterdam,* 1823.

Folard (Jean Charles de). Commentaire [sur Polybe] ou un corps de science militaire.

[*With* Polybius, Histoire. *Paris.*]

——— The same. Nouvelles découvertes sur la guerre, dans une dissertation sur Polybe. 2ᵉ éd. xxxii, 272 pp. 4 pl. 18°. *Brusselle, F. Foppens,* 1724.

Folengo (Teofilo). Orlandino di Limerno [o, merlino.] pitocco. Nuovamente stampato, et arrichito di annotazioni. xi, 249 pp. 18°. *Parigi, Molini,* 1773.

Folger (Robert M.) Exchange tables of British sterling in United States and English currency. 211 pp. 8°. *New York, author,* 1849. s.

Follen (Theodor Christian Charles). Practical grammar of the German language. xvii, 282 pp. 12°. *Boston, Hilliard & Co.* 1828.

Folsom (Benjamin). A compilation of biographical sketches of distinguished officers in the American navy. 187 pp. 8°. *Newburyport, Horatio G. Allen,* 1814.

Fonseca (Fabian de), *and* **Urrutia** (Carlos de). Historia general de real hacienda. 6 v. sm. 4°. *Mexico, V. G. Torres,* 1845–53. s.

Fontaine, *or* **La Fontaine** (Jean). A tale of the Huguenots; or, memoirs of a French refugee family. With an introduction, by F. L. Hawks, D. D. 266 pp. 16°. *New York,* 1838.

Fontaine (P. Jules). Manuel de l'amateur d'autographes. 8°. *Paris, Morta,* 1836. s.

Fontaine. *See* **La Fontaine.**

Fontanini (Giusto). Biblioteca dell' eloquenza italiana; con le annotazioni del signor [Apostolo] Zeno. 2 v. 4°. *Venezia, Pasquali,* 1753. s.

Fonte (Bartolommeo). In Persivm poetam explanatio [et opusculum de mensuris et ponderibus.] 90 l. unp. sm. 4°. *Florentiæ, Sanctus Jacobvs de Ripoli,* 1477.

Fontenelle (Bernard Le Bovier de). A discovery of new worlds, from the French. [*anon.*] Made English by Mrs. A. Behn. 22 p. l. 158 pp. 16°. *London, Wm. Canning,* 1688.

——— History of oracles, and the cheats of the pagan priests. Made English [by A. B.] 2 pts. in 1 v. 10 p. l. 227 pp. 2 l. 16°. *London,* 1688.

Fontenelle (Bernard Le Bovier de). Lettres galantes [du chevalier D'Her]. Translated by Geo. Russel.

[*With* RUSSEL (George). Works. v. 2. 12°. *Cork*, 1769.]

Fontenelle (Julia de). *See* **Julia** de Fontenelle.

Foot (Joseph I.) Historical address at West Brookfield, Mass. Nov. 27, 1828; with Capt. Thomas Wheeler's narrative. 96 pp. 12°. *West Brookfield, Merriam & Cooke*, 1843.

Forbes (Charles Stuart). A standing navy; its necessity and organization. v, 120 pp. 16°. *London, J. Murray*, 1861.

Forbes (Edward). Monograph of the echinodermata of the British territories. [Echinoderms of the crag.] vii, 36 pp. 4 l. 4 pl. 4°. *London*, 1852. s.

[Palæontographical society. No more published.]

Forbes (*Rev.* John, *of Alford*). Certain records, etc. *See* **Scot** (*Rev.* William, *of Cupar*). State of the kirk of Scotland. *Edinburgh*, 1846.

Forbin (Louis Nicolas Philippe Auguste, *comte* de). Voyage dans le Levant en 1817–18. 2e éd. 5 p. l. 460 pp. 1 pl. 8°. *Paris, Delaunay*, 1819.

Force (William Q.) The builder's guide. vi, 80 pp. 16°. *Washington, Peter Force*, 1842.

——— Picture of Washington and its vicinity for 1850; also, the Washington guide. viii, 188 pp. 38 pl. 18°. *Washington, W. Q. Force*, 1850.

Ford (Edward). The most famous, delectable, and pleasant history of Parismus, prince of Bohemia. 12th impression. 2 pts. 2 p. l. 184 pp; 235 pp. 12 pl. sm. 4°. *London, J. Wright*, 1684.

Ford (E. L.) Madelaine Darth. [A novel]. 71 pp. 8°. *Chicago, Western news Co.* 1867.

Ford (Henry A.) History of Putnam and Marshall counties, embracing an account of the settlement of Bureau and Stark counties. vii, 160 pp. 18°. *Lacon, (Ill.) author*, 1860. s.

Ford (Richard). Hand-book for travelers in Spain. 2d ed. lxii, 645 pp. 2 maps. 12°. *London*, 1847. s.

Forde *or* **Ford** (Thomas). Foenestra in pectore; or, familiar letters. 3 p. l. 158 pp. 16°. *London, W. Grantham*, 1660.

[*With* his Virtus rediviva, etc. 16°. *London*, 1660].

——— Fragmenta poetica; or, poetical diversions. 24 pp. 16°. *London, W. Grantham*, 1660.

[*With* his Virtus rediviva, etc. 16°. *London*, 1660].

Forde *or* **Ford** (Thomas). A theatre of wits, ancient and modern, represented in a collection of apothegmes. 3 p. l. 90 pp. 16°. *London, W. Grantham*, 1660.

[*With* his Virtus rediviva, etc. 16°. *London*, 1660].

——— Virtus rediviva; or, a panegyrick on the late K. Charles I, second monarch of Great Britain. 5 p. l. 27 pp. 3 l. 16°. *London, W. Grantham*, 1660.

Fordun (John de). Scotichronicon, sive Scotorum historia. fol. *Oxoniæ*, 1691.

[GALE (Thomas) *and* FELL (John). Rerum anglicarum scriptores veteres. v. 3. *Oxoniæ*, 1684–91].

Forme (The) of prayers and administration of the sacraments, etc. used in the English congregation at Geneva. [*anon.*] 6 p. l. 28 pp. sm. 4°. *London*, 1643.

Forney (John W.) Letters from Europe. 406 pp. portrait. 12°. *Philadelphia, T. B. Peterson & Bros.* [1867].

Forrest (James). Some account of the origin and progress of trinitarian theology in the 2d and succeeding centuries, and of the manner in which its doctrines supplanted the unitarianism of the primitive church. 4th Am. ed. x, 104 pp. 4 charts. 12°. *Boston, Nichols & Noyes*, 1867.

Forster (Edward, *F. R. S.*) Collection of engravings from the Italian, Flemish, Dutch, and English schools. 52 pl. fol. *London, W. Miller*, 1830. s.

Forster (Johann Reinhold). Observations made during a survey round the world, on physical geography, natural history, and ethic philosophy. iv, 649 pp. 1 map, 1 tab. 4°. *London, G. Robinson*, 1778. s.

——— *See* **Kalm** (Peter).

Forster (Thomas Farleigh). Flora tonbrigiensis; or, a catalogue of plants growing wild in the neighborhood of Tonbridge Wells. vii, 216 pp. 12°. *London, R. & A. Taylor*, 1816. s.

Forster (Thomas Ignatius Maria). Recueil de ma vie, mes ouvrages et mes pensées. 3e éd. xxxvii, 122 pp. 18°. *Bruxelles, A. Stapleaux*, 1837. s.

——— Éloge de chiens favoris. [*anon.*] Traduit de l'Anglais. 34 pp. 1 pl. 18°. *Bruxelles, Deltombe*, 1840. s.

(*With* his "Recueil de ma vie," etc.)

Forsyth (Joseph). Remarks on antiquities, arts, and letters, during an excursion in Italy, 1802–3. 3d ed. xv, 672 pp. 16°. *Geneva, P. G. Ledouble*, 1824. s.

Forsyth (William, *surveyor*). Plats of subdivisions of the city of Washington, D. C. 4 p. l. 62 pl. fol. *Washington, R. A. Waters*, 1856.

Fortia d'Urban (Agricole Joseph François Xavier Pierre Esprit Simon Paul Antoine, *marquis* de). Essai sur l'origine de l'écriture, sur son introduction dans la Grèce et son usage jusq'au temps d'Homère. 306 pp. 4 pl. 8°. *Paris, H. Fournier*, 1832. s.

Fortini (Pietro). Novelle.
[*In* v. 1 of NOVELLE di autori senesi. 18°. *Milano*, 1815].

Fortmann (Heinrich). Abriss der oldenburgischen geschichte bis auf unsere zeit, für den bürger und landmann. 138 pp. 16°. *Oldenburg, J. H. Stalling*, 1836. s.

Fortnightly (The) review. Edited by George Henry Lewes. Aug. 15, to Dec. 1, 1866. v. 6. 8°. *London, Chapman & Hall*, 1866.

——— The same. Edited by John Morley. Jan. to Dec. 1867. New series. v. 1–2. (Whole series v. 7–8). 8°. *London, Chapman & Hall*, 1867.

Foss (H.) *See* **Sagen** (L.) *and* **Foss** (H.) Bergens beskrivelse.

Foss (John). A journal of captivity and sufferings at Algiers. 2d ed. 189 pp. 16°. *Newburyport, A. March*, (1798?)

Foss (*Dr.* R.) Die geschichte des deutschen volkes. [Ein erläuterung zum] grossen bildern dargestellt von Karl Heinrich Hermann. 8 p. l. 434 pp. 8°. *Gotha, J. Perthes*, 1854. s.

Foster (B. F.) The merchant's manual. 252 pp. 12°. *Boston, Perkins & Marvin*, 1838.

Foster (*Rev.* Benjamin F.) Debate on universalism. *See* **Lozier** (J. H.) *and* Foster.

Foster (G. G. *editor*). The gold regions of California. 80 pp. 8°. *New York, Dewitt & Davenport*, 1848.

Foster (John Welch). Memorial. [Letters, addresses, and religious writings]. Edited by A. P. Peabody. vi, 400 pp. portrait. 12°. *Portsmouth (N. H.) J. F. Shores, jr.* 1852. s.

Fothergill (Samuel). Discourses, delivered extempore at several meeting-houses of the people called quakers. xv, 270 pp. 16°. *Philadelphia, B. & J. Johnson*, 1800.

Foucaud (Édouard). Les artisans illustres. 2 p. l. 643 pp. 8°. *Paris, Béthune & Plon*, 1841. s.

Foudras (*Marquis* de). Soudards et Lovelaces. 317 pp. 16°. *Paris, Cadot*, [1860].

Fouqué. *See* **La Motte Fouqué.**

Four (The) colonies of Australia; [with] an account of the discovery of gold. [*anon.*] 64 pp. 16°. *London, Cradock & Co.* [1852?]

17

Fourcroy (Antoine François de). Élémens d'histoire naturelle et de chimie. 5e éd. 5 v. 8°. *Paris, Cuchet*, 1794. s.

Fournier (Édouard). Variétés historiques et littéraires; recueil de pièces volantes, rares et curieuses, en prose et en vers, revues et annotées. v. 1–4. 16°. *Paris, P. Jannet*, 1855–56.

Fowler (George). Wandering philanthropist; or, letters from a Chinese, written during his residence in the United States. Discovered and edited by George Fowler. 300 pp. 18°. *Philadelphia, Geo. Fowler, and B. Graves*, 1810.

Fowler (John). Journal of a tour in the state of New York, in 1830, and return to England by the Western islands. 333 pp. 12°. *London, Whittaker, Treacher and Arnot*, 1831.

Fowler (Orson S. *and* L. N.) Phrenology proved, illustrated, and applied. 4th ed. 420 pp. 12°. *Philadelphia, Fowler & Brevoort*, 1839.

Fowler (P. H. *D. D.*) Employers and the employed; their relation and duties to each other. 180 pp. 18°. *Utica, Wm. S. Taylor*, 1865.

Fowler (Thomas, *M. D.*) Medical report of the effects of blood-letting, sudorifics, and blistering, in the cure of the acute and chronic rheumatism. xxi, 287 pp. 6 l. 8°. *London, J. Johnson*, 1795.

Fox (Charles). A portrait of George Washington, from an original drawing, as he appeared while reviewing the army, Boston, 1776; with its history and evidence of correctness. 37 pp. 1 pl. 8°. *Boston, Crocker & Brewster*, 1851.

Fox (Charles James). Speech at Shakespeare tavern, Covent Garden, Oct. 10, 1797, with speech of T. Erskine. 24 pp. 8°. *London*, 1797.
[*With* TURNBULL (Robert J.) Visit to the Philadelphia prison. *London*, 1797.]

Fox (George). A collection of many select and christian epistles, letters, and testimonies. v. 2. 575 pp. fol. *London, T. Sowle*, 169[illegible].
[Imperfect; wanting last two leaves.]

——— A few words to all such (whether papists or protestants) as observe dayes contrary to Christ and his apostles. Also, the quaker's challenge to the papists; and the quaker's testimony concerning magistracy. By G. F. [*anon.*] 14 pp. sm. 4°. *London*, 1669.

——— Gospel truth demonstrated, in a collection of doctrinal books. 7 p. l. 1090 pp. 2 l. fol. *London, T. Sowle*, 1706.

Fox (George). A journal, or historical account of the life, etc. of George Fox. [With a preface by William Penn.] 3d ed. lix, 679 pp. 14 l. fol. *London, W. Richardson & S. Clark*, 1765. s.

Fox (Henry Richard Vassall, *3d lord Holland*). Some account of the lives and writings of Lope Felix de Vega Carpio, and Guillen de Castro. 2 v. xv, 261 pp; vii, 232 pp. 12 pl. 12°. *London, Longmans*, 1817.

Fraas (Carl). Die ackerbaukrisen und ihre heilmittel. Ein beitrag zur wirthschaftspolitik des ackerbauschutzes. ix, 255 pp. 8°. *Leipzig, F. A. Brockhaus*, 1866. s.

Fraas (Oscar). Die nutzbaren minerale Württembergs zusammengestellt. viii, 208 pp. 8°. *Stuttgart, Ebner & Seubert*, 1860. s.

Fracastoro (Girolamo). Opera omnia. Accesserunt Andreæ Navagerii orationes duæ, carminaque nonnulla. 6 p. l. 285, 32 l. 4°. *Venetiis, Ivnta*, 1555. s.

CONTENTS.

De stellis; de causis criticorum dierum; de sympathia et antipathia; de contagionibus et de contagiosis morbis; de poetica dialogus; de intellectione dialogus; de anima dialogus; de vini temperatura; syphilidis libri tres; Joseph, poema; carmina.

Fragments of the history of Bawlfredonia; containing an account of the discovery and settlement of that great southern continent, and of the formation and progress of the Bawlfredonian commonwealth. By Herman Thwackius. [*anon.*] 164 pp. 8°. [*Baltimore?*] *American booksellers*, 1819.

France. Affaires étrangères. Documents diplomatiques, 1866. (*Livre jaune*, Nos. 6–7.) 2 v. fol. *Paris*, 1866.

—— The same. 1867. Nos. 8–9. 2 v. fol. *Paris*, 1867.

—— Catalogue général des cartulaires des archives départementales; publié par la commission des archives départementales et communales. viii, 285 pp. 4°. *Paris, Imp. royale*, 1847. s.

—— Catalogue général des livres composant les bibliothèques du département de la marine et des colonies. 5 v. 8°. *Paris, Imprimerie royale*, 1838–43. s.

—— Code de l'instruction primaire, contenant l'historique de la législation primaire depuis 1789, etc. 2e éd. 392 pp. 8°. *Paris, P. Dupont*, 1834. s.

—— Le code noir, ou, édit du roy, servant de règlement pour le gouvernement et l'administration de justice et la police des isles françoises de l'Amérique, et pour la discipline et le commerce des nègres et esclaves dans ledit pays. Donné à Versailles au mois de Mars, 1685. 14 pp. sm. 4°. *Paris, Veuve Saugrain*, 1718.

—— Commission pour l'examen de certaines questions de législation commerciale. Enquête sur les sucres. 324 pp. 4°. *Paris, Ministère du commerce, etc.* 1829. s.

—— The same. Enquête sur les fers. 368 pp. 4°. *Paris, Renard*, [1828]. s.

—— Ordonnance provisoire sur l'exercise et les manœuvres de la cavalerie, rédigée par ordre du ministre de la guerre. 3e éd. xxiii, 498; 8 pp. 16°. *Paris, Magimel*, 1815. s.

—— Rapport au roi sur l'instruction secondaire. 358 pp. 4°. *Paris, Imp. royale*, 1843. s.

—— Tableau général numérique par fonds des archives départementales antérieures à 1790. Publié par la commission des archives départementales et communales. 2 p. l. 253 pp. 4°. *Paris, Imp. nationale*, 1848. s.

—— Tableau de la situation des établissements français dans l'Algérie en 1840, 1841, 1843–44. 3 v. 4°. *Paris, Imp. royale*, 1841–45. s.

Franceson (E. F.) Grammatik der spanischen sprache. 3e ausg. xii, 401 pp. 8°. *Leipzig, F. Fleischer*, 1850.

Francis (Samuel W. *M. D.*) Biographical sketches of distinguished living New York physicians. 228 pp. 16°. *New York, G. P. Putnam & son*, 1867.

Francisci *born* Finx (Erasmus). Neu-polirter geschichtkunst-und sitten-spiegel auslandischer völcker. 15 p. l. 1550 pp. 15 l. 52 pl. fol. *Nürnberg, J. A. Endters*, 1670.

—— Ost-und west-indischer wie auch sinesischer lust-und stats-garten. [Illustrated]. 3 v. in 1. 11 p. l. 1762 pp. 17 l. fol. *Nürnberg, J. A. Endters*, 1668.

Franck (Adolphe). Esquisse d'une histoire de la logique, précédée d'une analyse étendue de l'organum d' Aristote. 316 pp. 8°. *Paris, Hachette*, 1838. s.

—— Études orientales. xi, 477 pp. 8°. *Paris, Lévy*, 1861.

Francklin (William). Voyage du Bengal à Chyraz in 1787–88. Traduit de l'Anglais par L. Langlès. 2 v. 18°. *Paris, Crapelet*, 1798. s.

Francoeur (Louis Benjamin). Uranographie, ou traité élémentaire d'astronomie. 5e éd. xiv, 512 pp. 8 pl. 8°. *Paris, Bachelier*, 1837. s.

—— An introduction to linear drawing. Translated by Wm. B. Fowle. (2d ed.) viii, 88 pp. 2 pl. 12°. *Boston, Hilliard, Gray, Little & Wilkins*, 1828. s.

Francoeur (Louis Benjamin) **Robinet** (—) **Payen** (Anselme) *and* **Pelouze** (Edmond). Abrégé du grand dictionnaire de technologie; ou, nouveau dictionnaire des arts et métiers, etc. Augmenté par M. Drapiez. 2 v. 2 p. l. 617 pp; 2 p. l. 678 pp. 8°. *Bruxelles, soc. belge de librairie*, 1837. s.

Frank on the lower Mississippi. By Harry Castleman. (*pseudon.*) 236 pp. 3 pl. 16°. *Cincinnati, R. W. Carroll & Co.* 1868.

Fränkel (Ludwig, *M. D.*) Practische heilmittellehre für die krankheiten des kindlichen alters. 2e aufl. x, 310 pp. 12°. *Berlin, Veit & Co.* 1840. s.

Frankenheim (M. L.) Völkerkunde. Charakteristik und physiologie der völker. viii, 559 pp. 8°. *Breslau, Trewendt & Granier*, 1852. s.

Franklin (A. W.) American cottage library; or, useful facts, figures, and hints, for everybody. 190 pp. 4 pl. 12°. *New York, Burgess, Stringer & Co.* 1848.

Franklin (Benjamin). Autobiography. Ed. by Jared Sparks. vi, 154 pp. 12°. *London, H. G. Bohn*, 1850. s.

——— The same. 8°. [n. p. or d.]

[Imperfect; title wanting].

——— The same. Life of Franklin, written by himself. 2d Am. ed. 197 pp. 16°. *Philadelphia, Benjamin Johnson*, 1794.

——— Experiments and observations on electricity, [with] letters and papers on philosophical subjects. [4th ed.] iv, 496 pp. 8 l. 5 pl. 4°. *London, D. Henry*, 1769.

——— Two tracts: information to those who would remove to America; and remarks concerning the savages of North America. [*anon.*] 39 pp. 8°. *London, John Stockdale*, 1784.

——— Way to wealth, and advice to a young tradesman.

[pp. 97 to 130 of WEEMS' (Mason L.) Immortal mentor. 321 pp. *Philadelphia*, 1796].

Franks (David). The New York directory, 1786. *See* **New York**, city.

Franque (Johann Baptist). Dissertatio inauguralis anatomico-physiologica de serpentum quorumdam genitalibus ovisque incubatis. 44 pp. 2 pl. 4°. *Tubingæ, L. F. Fues*, 1817. s.

Franque (Otto von). Der vorfall der gebärmutter in anatomischer und klinischer beziehung. vi, 69 pp. 7 pl. 4°. *Würzburg, Stahel*, 1860. s.

Franz (Johann Michael). Abhandlung von den grenzen der bekannten und unbekannten welt alter und neuer zeit, als eine kurze einleitung zu einer parallelen erdbeschreibung. 4 p. l. 59 pp. 1 map. 4°. *Nürnberg, G. P. Monath*, 1762.

Franze (Wolfgang). Historia animalivm; in qua plerorumque animalium præcipue proprietates ad usum εικονολογικὸν breviter accommodantur; cum commentariis et supplementis Johannis Cypriani. 4 parts in 2 v. 17 p. l. 3624. 12 l. pp. portrait. 103 l. 4°. *Francofurti, G. Lesch*, 1712. s.

Fraser (Donald). The American magazine of wonders and marvellous chronicle. 2 v. 508 pp. 2 l; 510 pp. 2 l. 8 pl. 8°. *New York, Southwick & Pelsue*, 1809.

Fraser (William). The Stirlings of Keir, and their family papers. 4°. *Edinburgh, Stevenson*, 1858. s.

Fraser's magazine for town and country. July, 1866 to Dec. 1867. v. 74–76. 8°. *London, Longmans, Green & Co.* [1866–67].

Fraunhofer (Joseph von). Bestimmung des brechungs und farbenzerstreuungs-vermögens verschiedener glasarten. [Extract]. pp. 193–226. 3 pl. 4°. *München, K. akad. der wissenschaften*, 1814. s.

[With the following.]

——— Neue modification des lichtes durch gegenseitige entwirkung und beugung der strahlen, und gesetze derselben. [Extract]. 76 pp. 6 pl. 4°. *München, K. akad. der wissenschaften*, [*about* 1810.]

Fréart (Roland, *sieur de Chambray*). Parallel of the antient architecture with the modern. made English [from the French] by J. Evelyn. 2d ed. 10 p. l. 115 pp. 40 pl. fol. *London, D. Brown, etc.* 1707.

Frederic II, (*king of Prussia, surnamed the great*). Posthumous works. Translated from the French by T. Holcroft. 13 v. 8°. *London, G. G. J. & J. Robinson*, 1789.

CONTENTS.

v. 1. History of my own times.
v. 2–3. History of the seven-years' war.
v. 4. Memoirs from the peace of Hubertsburg, to the partition of Poland, and of the Bavarian war; the Bavarian succession; Bavarian state papers; present state of politics in Europe.
v. 5. Essay on forms of government and on the duties of sovereigns; dialogues of the dead; character of Charles XII; examination of the work Système de la nature; commentary on Blue Beard of Dom Calmet; innocence of errors of the understanding; school of the world, a comedy, by Satyricus; elegy of the city of Berlin; preface to Voltaire's Henriade; Tantalus at law, a comedy; portrait, epitaph, etc. of Voltaire.
v. 6–8. Correspondence with Voltaire.
v. 9. Correspondence with Jordan.
v. 10. Correspondence with the marquis d'Argens.
v. 11. Correspondence with d'Alembert,
v. 12. Correspondence with d'Alembert, Condorcet, Grimm, and d'Arget.
v. 13. Correspondence with the prince of Prussia and Gen. Fouquet; miscellanies; essay on German literature; moral dialogue; eulogium on Voltaire.

Fredet (Peter, *D. D.*) Modern history; from the coming of Christ to 1867. With questions. 22d ed. 566, 38 pp. 12°. *Baltimore, J. Murphy & Co.* 1867.

Free thoughts occasioned by the heads of agreement assented to by the United ministers in and about London; formerly called presbyterian and congregational. [*anon*]. 35 pp. sm. 4°. *London, Tim. Goodwin,* 1691.

[*With* HEADS of agreement, etc. *London,* 1691].

Freebooter (The). v. 1, 1823-24. 4, 427 pp. 8°. *London, J. Chappel & son,* 1824.

Freeman (James, *D. D. and* **Cary,** *Rev.* Samuel). Funeral sermons, preached at King's chapel, Boston. [Occasioned by the deaths of Mrs. Susan Bulfinch, Rev. Samuel Cary, and Joseph Coolidge]. 68 pp. 8°. *Boston, Phelps,* 1820.

Freeman (Strickland). The art of horsemanship, altered and abbreviated, according to the principles of Sir Sidney Medows. 3 p. l. xix, 244 pp. 15 pl. 4°. *London, W. Bulmer & Co.* 1806.

Freemason's pocket companion. With a complete collection of songs, etc. [*anon.*] 240 pp. 16°. *Glasgow, Tait, Brown & Tait,* 1771.

Freer (Martha Walker). The regency of Anne of Austria, queen of France, mother of Louis xiv. 2 v. xxxii, 368 pp; 451 pp. 1 pl. 8°. *London, Tinsley Bros.* 1866.

Fréjus (Roland de). The relation of a voyage made into Mauritania in Africk. Englished out of French. 4 p. l. 119 pp. 18°. *London, M. Pitt,* 1671.

Frémont (John Charles). Geographical memoir upon upper California. 8°. *Washington,* 1848.

[*With* EMORY (W. H.) Notes of a military reconnoisssance, etc.]

——— Report of the exploring expedition to the Rocky mountains in 1842, and to Oregon and north California in 1843-44. 693 pp. 2 maps. 23 pl. 8°. *Washington, government pr.* 1845.

[Senate doc. 174, 28th congress, 2d session.]

——— The same. 2d ed. 278 pp. 8°. *Washington, Taylor, Wilde & Co.* [1845 ?] s.

——— A report of an exploration of the country between Missouri river and the Rocky mountains, on the line of the Kansas and Great Platte rivers. 207 pp. 1 map. 1 pl. 8°. *Printed for the senate, Washington,* 1843.

French (Benjamin Brown). Fitz Clarence: a poem. 31 pp. 8°. *Washington, Blair & Rives,* 1844.

——— The changes of earth, a poem delivered before the Capitol hill institute in the city of Washington. 15 pp. 8°. [*Washington,* 1845 ?]

French (Benjamin Franklin). Biographia Americana; or historical and critical account of the lives, actions, and writings of the most distinguished persons in North America. By a gentleman of Philadelphia. [*anon.*] vii, 356 pp. 8°. *New York, D. Mallory,* 1825.

——— Memoirs of eminent female writers, of all ages and countries. [*anon.*] vii, 183 pp. 2 pl. 24°. *Philadelphia, T. Desilver,* 1827. s.

French (D'Arcy A.) English grammar simplified. In two lectures. 42 pp. 12°. *Galena, author,* 1846. s.

French (George). History of Col. Parke's administration, whilst he was captain general and chief governor of the Leeward islands; with account of the rebellion in Antegoa. 6 p. l. 427 pp. 16°. *London,* 1717.

French-Onondaga (A) dictionary, from a manuscript of the seventeenth century. [*anon.* Edited] by J. G. Shea. viii, 103 pp. 8°. *New York, Cramoisy press,* 1860.

[Library of American linguistics, I.]

French phraseology. [*anon.*] 2d ed. iv, 260 pp. 24°. *London, author,* 1814. s.

Freneau (Philip). Miscellaneous works, containing his essays and additional poems. xii, 429 pp. 16°. *Philadelphia, Francis Bailey,* 1788.

Frerichs (Friedrich Theodor). Die bright'sche nierenkrankheit und deren behandlung. xii, 286 pp. 1 pl. 8°. *Braunschweig, Vieweg,* 1851. s.

Fresenius (C. Remigius). Anleitung zur qualitativen chemischen analyse, u. s. w. Mit eine vorwort von Justus Liebig. 8e aufl. xxiv, 307 pp. 8°. *Braunschweig, Vieweg,* 1853. s.

——— Anleitung zur quantitativen chemischen analyse. 3e aufl. xx, 619 pp. 8°. *Braunschweig, Vieweg,* 1853. s.

——— Lehrbuch der chemie. xxiii, 657 pp. 8°. *Braunschweig, Vieweg,* 1847. s.

——— A system of instruction in qualitative chemical analysis. 4th ed. Edited by J. L. Bullock. xxii, 310 pp. 8°. *London, J. Churchill,* 1855. s.

Fresny (C. R. du). *See* **Du Fresny.**

Fréville (A. F. J.) Histoire des nouvelles découvertes faites dans la mer du sud en 1767-1770. 2 v. xlviii, 522 pp; 572 pp. 2 l. 1 pl. 8°. *Paris, De Hansy, le jeune,* 1774.

Frey (A.) Manuel nouveau de typographie. Imprimerie, contenant les principes théoriques et pratiques de l'imprimeur-typographe. 2 v. x, 518 pp. 7 pl. 18°. *Paris, Roret,* 1835. s.

Freytag (Gustav). The lost manuscript: a novel. Translated [from the German] by Mrs. Malcolm. 3 v. 12°. *London, Chapman & Hall*, 1835.

Frick (*Dr.* J.) Die physikalische technik; oder anleitung zur anstellung von physikalischen versuchen und zur herstellung von physikalischen apparaten. 2e aufl. xxiii, 588 pp. 8°. *Braunschweig, Vieweg*, 1856. s.

Fridriksson (H. Cr.) *See* **Ingerslev** (C. F.) *and* **Fridriksson.**

Friedreich (J. B.) Die realien in der Iliade und Odyssee. xl, 728 pp. 8°. *Erlangen, F. Enke*, 1851.

Friedrich (Johannes Christoph.) Kritische erörterungen zum übereinstimmenden ordnen und verzeichnen öffentlicher bibliotheken. 110 pp. 8°. *Leipzig, Dyk*, 1835. s.

Friedrike (Sophie Wilhelmine, *of Prussia, margravine of Baireuth*). Mémoires. 2 v. ii, 405 pp; 352 pp. 8°. *Brunswick, Colburn*, 1812.

Friendly (The) disputants; or, future punishment reconsidered. By Aura. [*anon.*] x, 490 pp. 12°. *London, Hall, Virtue & Co.* 1859.

Friendly (A) rebuke to one parson Benjamin [Hoadly]; particularly relating to his quarrelling with his own church, and vindicating the dissenters. By one of the people called quakers. [*anon.*] 32 pp. 12°. *London, E. Moore*, 1719.

Frisch (Johann Leonhard). Nouveau dictionnaire des passagers; françois-allemand et allemand-françois. Neuo aufl. 2 v. in 1. 6 p. l. 508 l. 186 l. 8°. *Leipzig, J. F. Gleditsch*, 1746. s.

Frisch (*Dr.* P.) Die staaten von Mexico, Mittel und Südamerica in ihren geschichtlich-politischen, administrativen, handels-und cultur-beziehungen, seit ihrer unabhängigkeitserklärung bis zum jahre 1850. xxiv, 297 pp. 8°. *Lübeck, A. Dittmer*, 1853.

Friswell (T. Hain). Familiar words; an index verborum, or quotation hand-book, with parallel passages of phrases which have become imbedded in our English tongue. 2d ed. xvi, 420 pp. 12°. *London, S. Low, son, & Marston*, 1866.

Fritz (Théodore). Esquisse d'un système complet d'instruction et d'éducation et de leur histoire. 3 v. 8°. *Strasbourg, Schmidt & Grucker*, 1841.

Fröbel (Friedrich). L'éducation de l'homme. Traduit de Allemand par la baronne de Crombrugghe. xv, 397 pp. 1 pl. 8°. *Bruxelles, F. Claasen*, 1861.

Fröbel (Julius). America, Europa und die politischen gesichtspunkte der gegenwart. x, 213 pp. 12°. *Berlin, J. Springer*, 1859.

Frobisher (*Prof.* J. E.) New and practical system of the culture of voice and action; with readings and recitations. 262 pp. 18°. *New York, Ivison & Co.* 1867.

Frobisher (Martin). De Angli navigatione in regiones occidentis et septentrionis narratio historica, ex gallico sermone in latinum translata per Joan. Tho. Freigivm. 44 l. unp. 18°. *Noribergæ, Catharina Gerlachin, et hæredes Johannis Montani*, 1580.

——— Three voyages in search of a passage to Cathaia and India by the northwest, 1576–78. Edited by R. Collinson. xxvi, 376 pp. 1 pl. 1 map. 8°. *London*, 1867.
[Hakluyt soc. publications, v. 38.]

Froebel. *See* **Fröbel.**

From dawn to dark in Italy; a tale of the reformation in the 16th century. [*anon.*] 441 pp. 12°. *Boston, Am. tract soc.* [1865.]

From Mayfair to Marathon. [*anon.*] viii, 428 pp. 12°. *London, R. Bentley*, 1853.

Fromberg (Emanuel Otto). Essay on the art of painting on glass. From the German. 116 pp. 16°. *London, J. Weale*, 1851. s.

Fromherz (Carl). Geognostiche beschreibung des Schönbergs bei Freiburg im Breisgau. viii, 36 pp. 1 col. pl. 4°. *Freiburg, Groos*, 1837. F.

Frommann (C. *M.D.*) Untersuchungen über die normale und pathologische anatomie des rückenmarks. 2 v. viii, 123 pp. 4 pl; 130 pp. 6 pl. 4°. *Jena, F. Frommann*, 1864–67. s.

Fronmüller (G. F. Christoph). The epistles general of Peter and Jude. [Commentaries.] *See* **Bible,** *English*, Commentary, by Lange (J. P.) *and others.*

Frost (John). American generals, embracing a complete military history of the United States. 8°. *Philadelphia*, 1848. s.

——— The beauties of French history. 252 pp. 16°. *New York, Harpers*, 1846. s.

——— Thrilling incidents of the wars of the United States. [*anon.*] 600 pp. 8°. *Philadelphia, Carey & Hart*, 1848. s.
[Title wanting.]

Frothingham (Richard, *jr.*) History of the siege of Boston, and of the battles of Lexington, Concord, and Bunker Hill. x, 420 pp. 3 pl. 3 maps. 8°. *Boston, Little & Brown*, 1849.

——— Life and times of Joseph Warren. xix, 558 pp. portrait. 8°. *Boston, Little, Brown & Co.* 1865.

Froude (James Anthony). History of England, from the fall of Wolsey to the death of Elizabeth. Reign of Elizabeth. v. 3-4. 8°. *London, Longmans,* 1866.

——— Short studies on great subjects. 2 v. 3 p. l. 320 pp; 3 p. l. 311 pp. 12°. *London, Longmans,* 1867.

——— The same. 534 pp. 12°. *New York, C. Scribner & Co.* 1868.

Fry (Caroline). The listener. 6th ed. 2 v. vi, 362 pp; 335 pp. 16°. *Edinburgh, Nisbet & Co.* 1836.

Fry (*Mrs.* Elizabeth). Elizabeth Fry; or, the christian philanthropist. [A compilation. *anon.*] 450 pp. portrait. 12°. *Philadelphia, Am. S. S. union,* 1851. s.

Fry (J. Reese). A life of Gen. Zachary Taylor. 332 pp. 12°. *Philadelphia, Grigg, Elliot & Co.* 1848.

Fuchs (Christian Joseph). Handbuch der allgemeinen pathologie der haussäugethiere. xvi, 500 pp. 8°. *Berlin, Veit & Co.* 1843. s.

——— Pathologische anatomie der haussäugethiere. xvi, 447 pp. 8°. *Leipzig, Veit & Co.* 1859. s.

Fulchiron (Jean Claude). Voyage dans l'Italie méridionale. 2e éd. 4 v. 8°. *Paris, Pillet,* 1844. s.

Full (A) and accurate report of the proceedings in the case of the borough of Trinity college, Dublin, as heard before a select committee of the house of commons, 1791. [*anon.*] 277 pp. 8°. *Dublin, Charles Mills,* 1791.

Full (A) reply to Lieut. Cadogan's Spanish hireling, etc. and Lieut. Mackay's letter concerning the action at Moosa. Wherein the impartial account of [Oglethorpe's] expedition to St. Augustine [Fla.] is clearly vindicated. [*anon.*] viii, 63 pp. 12°. *London, J. Huggonson,* 1743.

Fuller (Andrew S.) Forest tree culturist: a treatise on the cultivation of American forest trees, with notes on the most valuable foreign species. 188 pp. 12°. *New York, G. E. & F. W. Woodward,* 1866.

——— The grape culturist. New ed. 286 pp. 12°. *New York, O. Judd & Co.* 1867.

——— The small fruit culturist. 276 pp. 12°. *New York, O. Judd & Co.* [1867].

Fuller (Daniel). Political class-book of the state of Pennsylvania. 120 pp. 12°. *Philadelphia, Biddle,* 1853. s.

Fullom (S. W.) Rome, under Pius IX. viii, 312 pp. 12°. *London, C. J. Skeet,* 1864.

Fulton (Robert). [Letter to] Aaron Ogden. 7 pp. 8°. [n. p. 1815?]
[Title-page wanting].

Funeral (The) sermons, orations, epitaphs, and other pieces, on the death of Rev. Patrick Forbes. From the original edition of 1635. With biographical memoir and notes by C. F. Shand. cxvi, 474 pp. 8°. *Edinburgh, Spottiswoode society,* 1845.

Furetière (Antoine). Le roman bourgeois; ouvrage comique. Nouv. éd. avec des notes historiques et littéraires par Édouard Fournier. Précédée d'une notice par C. Asselineau. 350 pp. 16°. *Paris, P. Jannet,* 1854.

Furman (Wood). History of the Charleston association of Baptist churches in South Carolina. 238 pp. 16°. *Charleston, J. Hoff,* 1811.

Fürstenberg (M. H. F.) Die krätzmilben der menschen und thiere. v, 240 pp. 15 pl. 4°. *Leipzig, W. Engelmann,* 1861. s.

Fuss (G.) **Sawitsch** (A.) *and* **Sabler** (G.) Beschreibung der zur ermittelung des höhenunterschiedes zwischen dem schwarzen und dem caspischen meere. Im auftrag der kaiserlichen akademie der wissenschaften, 1836-37, herausgegeben von W. Struve. cxviii, 408 pp. 2 pl. 4°. *St. Petersburg, k. akad. der wissenchaften,* 1849. s.

Fuster (Justo Pastor). Biblioteca valenciana de los escritores que florecieron hasta nuestros dias. Con adiciones y enmiendas a la de Ximeno. 2 v. 7 p. l. xxi, 356 pp; 4 p. l. 548 pp. fol. *Valencia, J. Mompe,* 1827. s.

——— Breve vocabulario valenciano y castellano de las voces mas obscuras ó anticuadas.
[pp. 313-356 of v. 1 of the preceding].

Fyfe (Alexander). The royal martyr, Charles I. A tragedy. 3 p. l. 64 pp. sm. 4°. *London, J. Morphew,* 1709.
[Imperfect; wanting pp. 65, etc. at the end].

Gabb (William M.) Synopsis of the mollusca of the cretaceous formation. (Extract.) 201 pp. 8°. *Philadelphia, Am. phil. soc.* 1861. s.

——— *See* **California**. Geological survey.

Gachard (Louis Prosper). Correspondance de Guillaume le taciturne, prince d'Orange; suivie de pièces inédites sur l'assassinat de ce prince. 6 v. 8°. *Bruxelles, C. Muquardt,* 1847-66.

Gadsden (Christopher Edwards, *D. D.*) An essay on the life of Rev. Theodore Dehon. 341 pp. 8°. *Charleston, (S. C.) A. E. Miller,* 1833.

Gaffarel (Jacques). Cvriositez inovyes, svr la scvlptvre talismaniqve des Persans, horoscope des patriarches, et lectvre des estoilles. 7 p. l. 315 pp. 16°. *Roven, Jean Bovley,* 1631.

Gage (*Mrs.* Frances Dana). Poems. 252 pp. 16°. *Philadelphia, J. B. Lippincott & Co.* 1867.

——— Elsie Magoon, or the old still-house in the hollow. A tale of the past. 324 pp. 12°. *Philadelphia, J. B. Lippincott & Co.* 1867.

Gage (Thomas). The history of Rowley, anciently including Bradford, Boxford, and Georgetown. xvii, 484 pp. 1 pl. 12°. *Boston, F. Andrews,* 1840.

Gailhabaud (Julius). Denkmäler der baukunst. Unter mitwirkung von F. Kugler und J. Burckhardt herausgegeben von L. Londe. 4 v. 4°. *Hamburg,* 1852. s.

Galatian (Andrew B.) History of Scranton, Providence, Dunmore, Waverly, and Humphreysville, with accounts of the coal companies [etc.] Also, directory and business advertiser for 1867–68. 416 pp. 8°. *Scranton, (Pa.) author,* 1867.

Galaxy (The). An illustrated magazine of entertaining reading. May 1866, to Oct. 1867. v. 1–4. 8°. *New York, W. C. & F. P. Church,* 1866–67.

Gale (George, *LL. D.*) The Gale family records in England and the United States: [with] the Nottingham family of New England, and Bogardus, Waldron, and Young families of New York. 254 pp. 4 pl. 12°. *Galesville, (Wis.) Leith & Gale,* 1866.

Gale (L. D.) Report on the geology of New York county.

[NEW YORK, STATE, annual reports on geol. survey. v. 3.]

Gale (Thomas, *surgeon*). Certaine workes of chirurgerie, nevvlie compiled. 8 pl. unp. 112 p.l. 6 l. unp. 12°. *London, Thomas East,* 1586.

[*With* VIGO (G. de), Whole work. 12°. *London,* 1586.]

Gale (Thomas), *and* **Fell** (John). Rerum anglicarum scriptores veteres. 3 v. fol. *Oxoniæ,* 1684–91.

CONTENTS.

v. 1. Rerum anglicarum veterum, [opera J. Fell et W. Fulman] tom. 1. 1684.
Ingulfi croylandensis historia.
Petri blesensis continuatio ad historiam Ingulfi.
Chronica de Mailros.
Annales burtonenses.

v. 2. Historiæ anglicanæ scriptores quinque. [nunc primum in lucem editi a T. Gale.] 1687.
Annales de Margan.
Chronicon Thomæ Wikes salisburiensis monasterii.
Annales waverleienses.
Gaufridus Vinisauf. Itinerarium regis Anglorum.
Richardi et aliorum in terram Hierosolymorum.
Chronica Walteri Hemingford de gestis regum Angliæ.

v. 3. Historiae britanicae, saxonicae, anglo-danicae, scriptores xv. Opera T. Gale. 1691.
Gildæ de excidio Brittaniæ liber querulus.
Vita S. Wilfridi auctore Eddio Stephano.
Nennii historia Britonum.
Joannis Asserii chronicon fani Sancti Neoti.
Polychronicon Ranulphi Higdeni.
Willielmus malmesburiensis de antiquitate Glastoniensis ecclesiæ.
Wilhelmi malmesburiensis liber v. de pontificibus.
Historia ramesiensis.
Historiæ eliensis liber.
Chronica Joannis Wallingford.
Randulphi de Diceto historia compendiosa de regibus Britonum.
De partitione provinciæ in schiras, et episcopatus et regna.
Joannis Fordun Scoti chronicon.
Flacci Alcwini de pontificibus et sanctis ecclesiæ eboracensis, poema.
Appendix antiquitatum brittanicarum.

Galenus (Claudius). De simplicivm medicamentorvm facvltatibus libri vi. Theod. Gerardo goudano interprete. 12 p. l. 352 pp. 24°. *Lvgdvni, G. Gazellus,* 1589. s.

——— *See* **Hippocrates.**

Galerie des artistes; ou portraits des hommes célèbres dans la peinture, la sculpture, la gravure et la musique, pendant les trois siècles de la renaissance. 110 pp. 52 pl. 8°. *Paris, Société des amis des arts,* 1836. s.

Galerie impériale et royale du Belvédère à Vienne, gravée par les meilleurs artistes, avec un texte explicatif de chaque sujet, publiée par Charles Haas. 4 v. in 2. 4°. *Francfort sur Maine, A. Osterrieth,* [*about* 1850.]

Galfridus le Baker de Swinbroke. Chronicon Angliæ, temporibus Edwardi ii, et Edwardi iii. Edidit J. A. Giles. xi, 271 pp. 8°. *Londini, J. Bohn,* 1847.

Galiani (Ferdinando). Correspondence inédite avec Mme d'Epinay, d'Holbach, Grimm, et autres personnages du 18e siècle. Éd. revue et accompagnée de notes, par M***. Précédé d'une notice historique sur la vie de l'auteur, par Ginguené. et du Dialogue sur les femmes. 2 v. civ, 348 pp; 519 pp. 8°. *Paris, Treuttel & Würtz,* 1818.

——— Un napolitain du dernier siècle. Contes, lettres et pensées de l'abbé Galiani. Avec introduction et notes par P. Ristelhuber. xi, 144 pp. 18°. *Paris, librairie centrale,* 1866.

——— Della moneta; dialogues sur le commerce de blés; estratto del discorso sulla perfetta conservazione del grano.

[SCRITTORI class. ital. di econ. pol. v. 3–6.]

Galiberti (Casimiro). Quien mal vive mal muere. Trad. del idioma italiano. 4 p. l. 250 pp. 4°. *Madrid, G. Ramirez,* 1745. s.

Galicia (Faustino C.) Silabario de idioma mexicano. 17 pp. 18°. *Mexico, M. Castro,* 1849.

Galilei (Galileo). Nuncius sidereus. *See* **Gassendi** (Pierre). Institutio astronomica. *Londini,* 1683.

Gall (James). The first initiatory catechism, with the ten commandments and the Lord's prayer in the Ojibwa [Chippeway] language. Translated by P. Dougherty and D. Rodd. 69 pp. 16°. *Grand Traverse Bay, [Mich.] Presb. for. miss.* 1847.

Gallagher (William D.) Erato, number iii. (Cadwallen and other poems.) 60 pp. 16°. *Cincinnati, Alexander Flash*, 1837.

——— Facts and conditions of progress in the northwest; a discourse before the historical society of Ohio. 85 pp. 8°. *Cincinnati, H. W. Derby, & Co.* 1850.

Galland (Antoine). Les paroles remarquables, les bons mots, et les maximes des Orientaux. Traduction de leurs ouvrages en Arabe, en Persan et en Turc. Avec des remarques. [*anon.*] 8 p. l. 344 pp. 17 l. 24°. *La Haye, L. & H. Van Dole*, 1694.

Gallardo (Bartolomé José, *assisted by others*). Ensayo de una biblioteca española de libros raros y curiosos. v. 2. [Babia to Funes.] 8°. *Madrid, Rivadeneyra*, 1866.

Gallatin (Albert). Ethnology, etc.
[*With* EMORY (W. H.) Notes of a military reconnoissance, etc. Appendix I.]

Gallaudet (Thomas H.) Picture defining and reading book. Also, New Testament stories in the Ojibwa [Chippeway] language. 123 pp. 16°. *Boston, Am. board for. miss.* 1835.

——— Scripture biography; from Adam to Noah. [*Choctaw text.*] 88 pp. 18°. *New York, Am. tract soc.* [*about* 1850.] s.

——— Scripture biography; the history of Abraham. [*Choctaw text.*] 88 pp. 18°. *New York, Am. tract soc.* [*about* 1860.] s.
[*With* the preceding.]

——— Scripture biography; the history of Joseph. [*Choctaw text.*] 42 pp. 18°. *New York, Amer. tract soc.* (n. d.)
[*With* the preceding.]

——— Scripture biography; the history of Moses. [*Choctaw text.*] 207 pp. 18°. *New York, Am. tract soc.* [*about* 1850.) s.

Galle (Philippe, *engraver*). Acta apostolorvm delineata a Martino Hemskerchio et Iohanne Stradano. T. Gallæus edidit. 35 pl. obl. fol. *Antuerpie, P. Gallaeus,* [*about* 1600.] s.

Galletti (Johann Georg August). Allgemeine weltkunde; oder encyklopädie für geographie, statistik und staatengeschichte, umgearbeite von H. F. Brachelli und M. Falk. 12e. aufl. 1358 pp. 27 maps. 3 pl. 4°. *Wien, C. A. Hartleben*, 1859.

Gallichon (F. C. de La Roche). *See* **La Roche Gallichon.**

Gallois (Charles André Gustave Léonard). Histoire des journaux et des journalistes de la révolution française, (1789–96.) 2 v. 575 pp. 4 pl; 511 pp. 22 pl. 8°. *Paris, soc. de l'industrie fraternelle*, 1845–46. s.

Gallois (Jean Le). (*See* **Le Gallois** (Jean).

Galloway (Joseph). An account of the war in the middle colonies. Extracted from a late author. [*anon.*] 2d ed. 56 pp. 18°. *London*, 1780.

Gallup (Joseph A. *M.D.*) Outlines of the institutes of medicine. In three parts. 2 v. 416 pp. 1 pl; 460 pp. 8°. *Boston, Otis, Broaders & Co.* 1839. s.

CONTENTS.

Physiology, v. 1.
Pathology, v. 1–2.
Therapeutics, v. 2.

——— Sketches of epidemic diseases in the state of Vermont, from the first settlement to 1815, [with] remarks on pulmonary consumption. 419 pp. 8°. *Boston, Wait & sons*, 1815.

Gally (Henry, *D. D.*) Some considerations upon clandestine marriages. 2d ed. 4 p. l. 164 pp. 8°. *London, J. Hughs*, 1750.

Galt (John). The fatal whisper. Haddad-ben-Ahab. 13 pp. 8°. *London*, 1841.
[Hazlitt's romancist and novelist's lib. v. 2.]

——— The unguarded hour. The painter. The book of life. 20 pp. 8°. *London*, 1841.
[Hazlitt's romancist and novelist's lib. v. 4].

——— *See* **George** the third, his court, etc.

Galt (John M. *M. D.*) The treatment of insanity. viii, 579 pp. 8°. *New York, Harpers*, 1846. s.

Galtruchius (P.) *See* **Gaultruche.**

Galvani (Luigi). Abhandlung über die kräfte der thierischen elektrizität auf die bewegung der muskeln, nebst einigen schriften der Valli, Carminati, und Volta. Herausgegeben von Johann Mayer. xxviii, 183 pp. 4 pl. 16°. *Prag, J. G. Calve*, 1793. s.

Galvão, *or* **Galvano** (Antonio). The discoveries of the world unto the yeere 1555. Translated from the Portuguese by Richard Hakluyt. 97 pp. sm. 4°. *London*, 1601.

Gamba (Bartolommeo). Delle novelle italiane in prosa bibliografia. xv, 225 pp. 8°. *Venezia, Alvisopoli*, 1833. s.

——— Serie degli scritti impressi in dialetto veneziano. 276 pp. 18°. *Venezia, Alvisopoli*, 1832. s.

——— Serie dell' edizioni de testi di lingua italiana. 2 pts. in 1 v. 722 pp. 18°. *Milano, stamperia reale*, 1812. s.

——— The same. Serie dei testi di lingua e di altre opere importanti nella italiana letteratura scritte dal secolo xiv al xix. 4a ed. xxv, 795 pp. 1 pl. 8°. *Venezia, Gondoliere*, 1839.

Gambold (*Rev.* John). Works. With the life of the author. xxiii, iv, 276 pp. 1 pl. 12°. *Bath, S. Hazard,* 1789.

Gamgee (John). Dairy stock; its selection, diseases, and produce; with a description of the Brittany breed. v, 311 pp. 2 l. 3 pl. 12°. *Edinburgh, T. C. Jack,* 1861.

Gamond (Thomé de), *and* **Belly** (Félix). Carte d'étude pour le tracé et le profil du canal de Nicaragua, précédée de documents publiés sur cette question par F. Belly. 90 pp. 1 map. 4°. *Paris, Dalmont & Dunot,* 1858.

Gand. *See* **Ghent.**

Gandolfi (Giovanni). Sulla genesi e cura dello scirro e del cancro. xiv, 410 pp. 8°. *Milano, G. Chiusi,* 1845. s.

Ganganelli (Giovanni Vincenzo Antonio). *See* **Clement** XIV, *pope.*

Ganilh (Charles). Essai politique sur le revenu public des peuples de l'antiquité, du moyen age, des siècles modernes, et spécialement de la France et de l'Angleterre depuis le milieu du 15e siècle jusqu' au 19e. 2 v. 420 pp; 503 pp. 8°. *Paris, Giguet et Michaud,* 1806. s.

Gano (*Rev.* John). Biographical memoirs, written principally by himself. 151 pp. 16°. *New York, Southwick & Hardcastle,* 1806.

Ganot (A.) Traité élémentaire de physique expérimentale et appliquée, et de météorologie. 6e éd. 806 pp. 12°. *Paris, l'auteur,* 1856. s.

Garbet (Edward Lacy). Rudimentary treatise on the principles of design in architecture. viii, 264 pp. 16°. *London, J. Weale,* 1850.

Garcia (Francisco Gregorio). Origen de los Indios de el nvevo mvndo, e Indias Occidentales. 14 p. l. 535 pp. 12 l. 16°. *Valencia, Pedro Patricio Mey,* 1607.

Garcia (Pedro Andres), *and* **Los Reyes** (José Maria de). Diario de la expedicion de 1822, a los campos del sud de Buenos-Aires, desde Moron hasta la sierra de la Ventana. vii, 178 pp. iii pl. fol. *Buenos-Aires, imprenta del estado,* 1836.

Garcia de Palacio (Diego). *See* **Palacios** (D. G. de).

Garcia de Saavedra (Juan Gallego). *See* **Saavedra.**

Garcia y Cubas (Antonio). Memoria para servir á la carta general de la república mexicana. 166 pp. 1 map. 8°. *México, Andrade y Escalante,* 1861. s.

Garden (Alexander). Anecdotes of the American revolution. Second series. ix, 240 pp. 12°. *Charleston, A. E. Miller,* 1828.

Gardener's (The) chronicle and agricultural gazette, 1864 to 1866. 3 v. fol. *London, W. Bradbury and F. M. Evans,* 1864–66.

Gardenier (Barent, *editor*). *See* **Examiner** (The); containing political essays, etc.

Gardin-Dumesnil (Jean Baptiste). Synonymes latins, et leurs différentes significations. xlviii, 526 pp. 16°. *Paris, Simon,* 1777.

Gardiner (John, *M. D.*) Untersuchung der beschaffenheit, ursache, und kur des podagra's, und einiger damit verbundener krankheiten; nebst dem guten rath für podagrister von Dr. Kentish, aus dem Englischen übersetzt, und mit einiger anmerkungen begleitet von Christian Friderich Michaelis. xxxii, 264 pp. 8°. *Leipzig, J. F. Junius,* 1792. s.

Gardiner (John), *and* **Hepburn** (David). The American gardener. 3d ed. viii, 308 pp. 16°. *Washington, W. Cooper, jr.* 1826.

Gardiner (*Lieut.* Lion). A history of the Pequot war. 36 pp. 4°. *Cincinnati, J. Harpel,* 1860.

Gardiner (*Capt.* Richard). Account of the expedition to the West Indies against Martinique, 1759. 2 p. l. 75 pp. 2 maps. 4°. *London, Z. Stuart, John Baskerville,* 1759.

——— The same. 3d ed. 91 pp. 4°. *Birmingham, John Baskerville,* 1762.

——— The same. Relation de l'expédition aux Indes Occidentales contre Martinique, 1759. 3e éd. 91 pp. 4°. *Birmingham, John Baskerville,* 1762.

[*With* the preceding].

Gardiner (Me.) Directory for 1867–68. *See* **Augusta,** Hallowell, and Gardiner directory for 1867–68.

Garland *or* **Garlandia** (John de). Floretus sancti Bernardi in se continens sacre theologie et canonum flores. 51 l. unp. sm. 4°. *Colonie,* 1501.

NOTE.—This poem is placed under Garland on the authority of Rivet, Hist. litt. de France, v. 8.

Garneau (F. X.) Voyage en Angleterre et en France, 1831–33. 252 pp. 16°. *Québec, A. Coté & Cie.* 1855. s.

Garnier (*Rev.* Thomas). Domestic duties. A series of sermons. viii, 123 pp. 16°. *London, J. Laver,* 1851.

Garouville (——). L'amant oisif. Contenant cinquante nouvelles espagnoles. [*anon*]. 3 v. in 1. 3 p. l. 420 pp. 1 pl. 18°. *Brusselles, G. De Backer,* 1711.

Garovaglio (Santo). Alcuni discorsi sulla botanica, fasc. iii. Ed. 2^a. 81, 92 pp. 8°. *Pavia, Eredi Bizzoni,* 1865. s.

——— Enumeratio muscorum omnium in Austria inferiore hucusque lectorum, etc. viii, 48 pp. 8°. *Viennæ, U. Klopf,* 1840. s.

Garrard (Lewis H.) Wah-to-yah, and the Taos trail. vi, 349 pp. 12°. *Cincinnati, H. W. Derby*, 1850.

Garretson (Ferdinand V. D.) Carmina yalensia; a complete and accurate collection of Yale college songs, with piano accompaniment. 88 pp. 8°. *New York, Taintor Bros & Co.* [1867].

Garth (*Sir* Samuel). Poetical works. 8°. *Edinburgh*, 1793.

[Anderson's Brit. poets, v. 7].

Garwood (*Rev.* John). The million-peopled city; or, one-half of the people of London made known to the other half. x, 317 pp. 16°. *London, Wertheim & Macintosh*, 1853.

Gascoigne (*Sir* Bernard). Description of Germany, its government, [etc.]

[Pp. 1-63 of BROWN (T.) Miscellanea aulica. *London*, 1702.]

Gascons (Les) en Hollande; ou, aventures singulières de plusieurs gascons. [*anon.*] 2 v. 378 pp; 284 pp. 8°. [n. p.] 1767.

Gasparin (Adrien Étienne Pierre, *comte* de). Cours d'agriculture. v. 1-2. 8°. *Paris, Bureau de la maison rustique*, 1843-44. s.

[Wanting v. 3.]

Gasparin (Valérie Boissier, *comtesse* de). Au bord de la mer—reveries d'un voyageur. [*anon.*] 2e éd. 353 pp. 16°. *Paris, Lévy*, 1866.

——— The same. By the sea shore; reveries of a traveller. Authorized translation. 243 pp. 16°. *Edinburgh, Edmonston & Douglas*, 1867.

——— Camille. [*anon.*] 298 pp. 16°. *Paris, Levy*, 1866.

——— The same. Authorized translation. 235 pp. 16°. *Edinburgh, Edmonston & Douglas*, 1867.

Gassendi (Pierre). Institutio astronomica; cui accesserunt Galilei Galilei nuncius sidereus, et Johannis Kepleri dioptrice. Ed. 3a. 8 p. l. 199, 173 pp. 4 pl. 12°. *Londini, H. Dickinson*, 1683.

Gassies (J. B.) Tableau méthodique et descriptif des mollusques terrestres et d'eau douce de l'Agenais. 209 pp. 4 pl. 8°. *Paris, J. B. Baillière*, 1849. s.

Gaston (William, *LL. D.*) An address before the American whig, and Cliosophic societies of the college of New Jersey, 1835. 2d ed. 32 pp. 8°. *Princeton, R. E. Hornor*, 1835.

Gastrell (Francis, *D. D. bishop of Chester*). Considerations on the trinity. 44 pp. 8°. *Oxford*, 1825.

[*With* RANDOLPH (John, *Bishop of London*). Enchiridion theologicum, v. 1.]

Gattey (François). Éléments du nouveau systême métrique, suivis des tables de rapports des anciennes mesures agraires avec les nouvelles. 216 pp. 8°. *Paris, Bailly*, 1801. s.

Gaubil (J.) Catalogue synonymique des coléoptères d'Europe et d'Algérie. 296 pp. 8°. *Paris, Maison*, 1849. s.

Gauché (——, *architect*). Divers projets d'édifices proposés en 1841, pour transférer la bibliothèque royale dans les xie ou xiie arrondissemens de Paris. 6 p. l. 5 pl. fol. [*Paris*], *Mantoux*, 1845. s.

Gaucherel (Léon). Exemples de décoration appliqués à l'architecture et à la peinture depuis l'antiquité jusqu'á nos jours. 1e partie. 4°. *Paris, A. Morel*, 1857.

[No more published].

Gaudin (Charles Th.), *and* **Strozzi** (*marquis* Carlo). Contributions à la flore fossile italienne. 4e mémoire. Travertins toscans. [Extract]. 30 pp. 7 pl. 4°. *Zurich, soc. helvétique*, 1860. s.

Gaudin (Marc Antoine Augustin). Traité pratique de photographie; exposé complet des procédés relatifs au daguerréotype. iv, 248 pp. 8°. *J. J. Dubochet*, 1844. s.

Gaultruche *or* Gautruche (Pierre, *or* Denis). Poetical histories; a collection of stories necessary for a perfect understanding of the Greek and Latine poets. Now Englisht. With two treatises, one of the curiosities of old Rome; the other containing the hieroglyphics of Ægypt. By Marius d'Assigny. 10 p. l. 285, 200 pp. 10 l. unp. 16°. *London, Moses Pitt*, 1671.

Gauss (Carl Friedrich), *and* **Weber** (Wilhelm). Resultate aus den beobachtungen des magnetischen vereins im jahre 1836-38. 3 v. in 1. 8°. *Göttingen, Dieterich*, 1837-39. s.

——— The same. Im jahren 1839-1841. 3 v. in 1. 8°. *Leipzig, Weidmann*, 1840-43. s.

Gauthier (Aubin). Histoire du somnambulisme, chez tous les peuples, sous les noms divers d'extases, songes, oracles et visions. 2 v. 455 pp; 440 pp. 8°. *Paris, Malteste et Cie.* 1842.

——— Introduction au magnétisme. 494 pp. 8°. *Paris, Dentu*, 1840. s.

——— Introduction philosophique à l'étude de la géologie. 292 pp. 8°. *Paris, V. Masson*, 1853. s.

Gauthier (François Louis). Traité contre l'amour des parures, et le luxe des habits. 2e éd. [*anon*]. xii, 250 pp. 24°. *Paris, A. M. Lottin*, 1780.

Gautier (Théophile). Poésies nouvelles. Émaux et camées: théatre; poésies diverses. 283 pp. 12°. *Paris, Charpentier*, 1863.

Gautruche (Pierre, *or* Denis). *See* **Gaultruche.**

Gavarni *or* Chevalier (*called* Sulpice Paul). Madame Acker. Nouvelle. 25 pp. 12°. *Paris*, 1842.

[Included in PLÉIADE, La.]

Gavarret (J.) Télégraphie électrique. 428 pp. 12°. *Paris, V. Masson*, 1861. S.

Gay (*Rev.* Ebenezer, *D. D.*) The untimely death of a man of God lamented. Sermon preach'd at the funeral of Rev. John Hancock, Braintree; who died May 7th, 1744. 25 pp. 12°. *Boston, S. Kneeland & T. Green*, 1744.

[*With* WALLEY (*Rev.* Thomas). Balm in Gilead, *Cambridge*, 1670.]

Gay (John). ? The Mohocks; a tragi-comical farce. 4 p l. 21 pp. 12°. *London, Bernard Lintott*, 1712.

——— Poetical works. 8°. *Edinburgh*, 1794.

[Anderson's Brit. poets, v. 8].

Gay (Marie Françoise Sophie Nichault de Lavalette, *Mme.*) Physiologie du ridicule, par une société de gens ridicules. 356 pp. 18°. *Bruxelles, J. P. Meline*, 1833.

Gayarré (Charles). History of Louisiana. [v. iii.] The American domination. viii, 693 pp. 8°. *New York, W. J. Widdleton*, 1866.

——— Philip II. of Spain. With an introductory letter, by George Bancroft. iv, 366 pp. 1 pl. 8°. *New York, W. J. Widdleton*, 1866.

Gaye (Giovanni). Carteggio inedito d'artisti dei secoli xiv, xv, xvi. Pubblicato ed illustrato con documenti pure inediti; con facsimile. 3 v. 8°. *Firenze, Molini*, 1839–40.

Gaylord (Glance, *pseudon ?*) *See* **Culm** rock.

Gayot (Eugène). Hippologiques. iv, 349 pp. 8°. *Paris, Guiraudet & Jouaust*, 1845. S.

Gazette de France. 3 Aoust, 1778 —— 29 Juin, 1779. 2 v. pp. 277–486; 246 pp. 4°. *Paris*, 1779.

[Imperfect; v. i. Nos. 63 and 64 wanting. V. 2. No. 23 wanting.]

Gazzettiere (Il) americano. *See* **American Gazetteer.**

Geinitz (Hans Bruno). Das königliche mineralogische museum in Dresden, geschildert auf hohe veranlassung. 2 p. l. 110 pp. 2 pl. 8°. *Dresden, Blochmann*, 1858. S.

——— Gäa von Sachsen. Enleitung in die flora von Sachsen von Ludwig Reichenbach. viii, 225 pp. 8°. *Dresden, Arnold*, 1843. S.

CONTENTS.

COTTA (Bernhard). Geognostische skizze von Thuringen.
GEINITZ (Hans Bruno). Das nördlich und östlich von königreiche Saschen gelegene land, zwischen der Mulde und der Queiss und der vereinigten Bober.
——— *and* GUTBIER (Christian August von). Die versteinerungen von Obersachsen und der Lausitz.
NAUMANN (Carl). Geognostische skizze des königreichs Sachsen.
REICHENBACH (Heinrich Gottlieb Ludwig). Vegetationsverhältnisse innerhalb der grenzen der flora von Sachsen; Eigenthümlichkeit der vegetation einzelner districten.
SCHIFNER (Albert). Obersachsen und die Lausitz in physikalisch-geographischer beziehung.

——— *and* **Liebe** (Carl). Ueber ein aequivalent der takonischen schiefer Nordamerikas, in Deutschland und dessen geologische stellung. pp. 25–52. (extract.) iv, 52 pp. 8 l. 8 pl. 4°. *Dresden, K. Leopold. Carol. deutsche Akad.* 1866. S.

Geissler (Christian Anton). Bibliographisches handbuch der philologischen literatur der Deutschen von der mitte des 18ten jahrhunderts. Nach J. S. Ersch bearbeitet. 3a aufl. xi pp. 257 l. 8°. *Leipzig, F. A. Brockhaus*, 1845. S.

Geldard (James). Hand-book on cotton manufacture; or, a guide to machine-building, spinning and weaving, with examples, calculations, and tables. 298 pp. 12 pl. 12°. *New York, J. Wiley & son*, 1867.

Gellert (Christian Fürchtegott). Life; with a course of moral lessons. Taken from a French translation of the original German, by Mrs. M. Douglas, 2d ed. 3 v. 18°. *London, Hatchard & Son*, 1810.

Gelli (Giambattista). Discovrs fantastiques. Traduits en François, par C. D. K. [i. e. Cl. de Kerquifinon.] 336 pp. 18°. *Lyon, Clemens Bavdin*, 1575.

Gelston (John). Education of the deaf and dumb poor of Ireland. *See* **Ringland** (J.) *and* **Gelston.**

Gelzer (Heinrich). Die drei letzten jahrhunderte der schweizergeschichte; mit besondrer berücksichtigung der geistigen und religiösen zustände und der sittengeschichte. 2 v. xiv, 204 pp; xiv, 316 pp. 8°. *Aarau u. Thun, J. J. Christen*, 1838–39.

Gemelli-Careri (Giovanni Francesco). Voyage autour du monde, traduit de l'italien par [Eustache Lenoble]. 6 v. 16°. *Paris, Étienne Ganeau*, 1719.

CONTENTS.

v. i. Turquie.
v. ii. Perse.
v. iii. Indostan.
v. iv. Chine.
v. v. Isles Philippines.
v. vi. Nouvelle Espagne.

——— The same. Nouv. éd. 6 v. 60 pl. 16°. *Paris, Étienne Ganeau*, 1727.

[v. iv. imperfect: wanting pp. 540–553 ?]

Genealogy (The) of Corca Laidhe. Edited by J. O'Donovan. 144 pp. 8°. *Dublin*, 1849.
[Celtic soc. publ. No. 3.]

Genealogy of the family of Anthony Stoddard of Boston. 23 pp. 8°. *Boston, Coolidge & Wiley*, 1849.

General Taylor and his staff. 284 pp. 12°. *Philadelphia, Grigg, Elliott & Co.* 1848.

General (A) view of the fine arts, critical and historical. [By a lady. *anon.*] With an introduction by D. Huntington. 477 pp. 12°. *New York, G. P. Putnam*, 1851. s.

Gengembre (Philippe W.) *and* Brown (J. H.) Elements of English grammar, on a progressive system. xii, 213 pp. 12°. *Philadelphia, Hayes & Zell*, 1855.

Genius (The) of Erin, Columbia's freedom, Flights of fancy, Lucinda, etc. being part first of a series of poems, by a citizen of South Carolina. [*anon.*] 190 pp. 12°. *Charleston, D. J. Dowling*, 1835.

Genovesi (Antonio). Lezione di economia politica.
(SCRITTORI class. ital. di econ. pol. v. 7–10.)

Gentleman's (The) magazine and historical review. By Sylvanus Urban, gent. July, 1866 to Dec. 1867. New series. v. 2–4. Complete series. v. 221–223. 8°. *London, Bradbury, Evans & Co.* 1866–67.

Gentleman's pocket farrier, showing how to use a horse on a journey. With remedies. [*anon.*] New ed. 36 pp. 24°. *Louth, J. Jackson*, 1809.

Genty (L.) Influence de la découverte de l'Amérique sur le bonheur du genre-humain. 3 p. l. 352 pp. 1 pl. 12°. *Orléans*, 1787.
[Title wanting.]

Genuine account of the life and actions of James McLean, highwayman. [*anon.*] 33 pp. 12°. [*London*, 1750 ?]

Geoffrey de Vinsauf. Itinerarium regis Anglorum Richardi et aliorum in terram Hierosolymorum. fol. *Oxoniæ*, 1687.
[GALE (Thomas) *and* FELL (John). Rerum anglicarum scriptores veteres, *Oxoniæ*, 1684–91. v. 2.]

Geoffroy (Étienne François). Tractatus de materia medica, sive de medicamentorum simplicium historia, virtute, de lectu et usu. 3 v. 8°. *Parisiis, J. Desaint & C. Saillant*, 1741. s.

Geoffroy (Étienne Louis]. Histoire abrégée des insectes de Paris. 2 v. 4°. [*Paris*], *Durand*, 1764.

——— The same. Nouv éd. 2 v. xxviii, 556 pp; 744 pp. 22 pl. 4°. *Paris, Calixte-Volland*, 1799. s.

Geoffroy-Saint-Hilaire (Étienne). Cours de l'histoire naturelle des mammifères. 691 pp. 8°. *Paris, Pichon et Didier*, 1829. s.

Geoffroy-Saint-Hilaire (Isidore). Acclimatation et domestication des animaux utiles. 4e éd. xvi, 534 pp. 8°. *Paris, Librairie agricole*, 1861.

——— Domestication et naturalisation des animaux utiles; rapport général à la ministère de l'agriculture. 3e éd. xi, 204 pp. 12°. *Paris, Dusacq*, 1854.

——— Histoire générale et particulière des anomalies de l' organisation chez l'homme et les animaux; ou, traité de tératologie. 3 v. 8°. *Bruxelles, Soc. belge de librairie*, 1837.

——— Histoire naturelle générale des règnes organiques, principalement étudiée chez l'homme et les animaux. v. 2–3. 523 pp; 539 pp. 8°. *Paris, V. Masson*, 1859–62.

——— Muséum d'histoire naturelle de Paris. Catalogue méthodique de la collection des mammifères, de la collection des oiseaux, etc. 2 p. l. xv, vii, 96 pp. 8°. *Paris, Gide & Baudry*, 1851. s.
(No more published.)

Geographia classica: the geography of the ancients, so far described as it is contained in the Greek and Latin classicks. 8th ed. 6 pp. 29 maps. obl. 4°. *London, J. & P. Knapton*, 1747. s.

Geological society of London. The quarterly journal. v. 22. 1866. 8°. *London*, 1866.

George III, (*king of England*). Correspondence with lord North, from 1768 to 1783. Ed. from the originals, with an introduction and notes, by W. B. Donne. 2 v. xcii, 307 pp; 452 pp. 8°. *London, John Murray*, 1867.

Georgi (Carl August, *M. D.*) Karl Heinrich Ferdinand Schütze auf Schweta. Ein bild seines lebens, nach seinen eigenen mündlichen und schriftlichen mittheilungen gezeichnet. 158 pp. 8°. *Leipzig, F. A. Brockhaus*, 1861. s.

Georgi (Johann Gottlieb, *M. D.*) Description de la ville de St. Pétersbourg et de ses environs. Traduite de l'Allemand, [par S. H. Catel]. xvi, 404 pp. 1 map. 12°. *St. Pétersbourg, J. Z. Logan*, 1793.

Georgi (Theophilus *or* Gottlieb). Allgemeines europäisches bücher-lexicon. 5 v. in 2. fol. *Leipzig, auctor*, 1742–53. s.

——— (Erste) — drittes supplement zu dessen lexicon. 3 v. in 2. fol. *Leipzig, T. Georgi*, 1750–58. s.

Georgia (University of). Catalogue of books in the library. By Williams Rutherford, jr. 192 pp. 8°. *Athens, (Ga.) college*, 1858. s.

Georgia (University of). Supplement to the printed catalogue. 1849. [Mss. 8 l. 8°.] s.

Georgia Mississippi company. Grant to the Georgia Mississippi company, the constitution thereof, and extracts relative to the company's lands. Published by order of the directors. 28 pp. 8°. *Augusta, J. E. Smith*, 1795.

Gera (Francisco). De la fabrication du fromage. Trad. de l'Italien par V[ict]or Rendu. 2 p. l. 251 pp. 2 pl. 8°. *Paris, Roret*, 1843.

Geraldini (Alessandro). Itinerarivm ad regiones svb æqvinoctiali plaga constitvtas. 20 p. l. 284 pp. 18 l. 18°. *Romæ, Gulielmus Facciotti*, 1631.

Gerard (Alexander). Account of Koonawur in the Himalaya. Edited by G. Lloyd. xiii, 308, xxvi pp. 1 map. 8°. *London, Madden & Co.* 1841.

——— Attempt to penetrate the Garoo, etc. *See* **Lloyd** (*Sir* William.)

Gérard (Pierre Auguste Florent). Ferdinand Rapédius de Berg. Mémoires et documents pour servir à l'histoire de la révolution brabançonne [de 1787–89]. 2 v. 8°. *Bruxelles, Demanet*, 1842–43. s.

Gérardin (Sébastien). Tableau élémentaire d' ornithologie; ou, histoire naturelle des oiseaux que l'on rencontre communément en France. 2 v. cxi, 396 pp; 2 p. l. 523 pp. 8°. *Paris, Tourneisen fils*, 1806. s.

Gerardus *Cremonensis*. *See* **Gherardo.**

Gerbe (Z.) *See* **Degland** (C. D.) *and* **Gerbe.**

Gerhard (*Dr.* Eduard). Neuerworbene antike denkmäler des königlichen museums zu Berlin. 3 v. in 1. 8°. *Berlin, Druckerei der K. Akad. der Wissenschaften*, 1836–46. s.

CONTENTS.

v. 1–3. Nachtrag zum verzeichniss der vasensammlung.
v. 2. Vasensammlung No. 1630—1690.

Gerhard (James W.) Ostrea; or, the loves of the oysters. A lay by A. Fishe Shelly. [*pseudon.*] 72 pp. 12°. *New York, T. J. Crowen*, 1857.

Gerhard (W. W. *M. D.*) Clinical lectures. 8°. *Philadelphia*, 1848.
[*With* Graves (R. J.) Clinical medicine.]

Gerlac (Pieter *or* Peterssen). Ignitum cum Deo soliloquium. Edidit J. Strange. 132 pp. 24°. *Coloniæ, J. M. Heberle*, 1849.

Germar (Ernst Friedrich). Coleopterorum species novæ, aut minus cognitæ, descriptionibus illustratæ. [Insectorum species, v. 1.] xxiv, 622 pp. 2 p. 8°. *Halæ, J. C. Hendel*, 1824. s.
[No more published.]

——— Die im bernstein befindlichen hemipteren und orthopteren.
[*With* Berendt (G. C.) Die im bernstein reste, etc. v. 2. 1856.]

Gerstäcker (Friedrich). Wanderings and fortunes of some German emigrants. Translated by David Black. viii, 310 pp. 12°. *London, D. Bogue*, 1848.

Gervais (Paul). Histoire naturelle des mammifères. 2 v. xxiv, 418 pp. 32 pl; 344 pp. 68 pl. 8°. *Paris, L. Curmer*, 1854–55. s.

——— Listes des ouvrages et mémoires de zoologie et d'anatomie comparée. 8 pp. 8°. *Montpellier, Boehm*, 1852. s.
[*With* Gervais (P.) Mammifères.]

Gervaise (Nicolas). Histoire naturelle et politique du royaume de Siam. 8 p. l. 324 pp; 4 l. 1 map. 4°. *Paris, C. Barbin*, 1688. s.

Gesner (Abraham, *F. G. S.*) Third and fourth reports on the geological survey of the province of New Brunswick. 2 v. in 1. xiv, 88 pp. 101 pp. 8°. *Saint-John, H. Chubb*, 1841–42. s.

Geysbeek (P. G. Witsen). Biographisch, anthologisch, en critisch woordenboek der nederduitsche dichters. 6 v. 8°. *Amsterdam, C. J. Schleijer*, 1821–27.

Gfrörer (August F.) Kritische geschichte des urchristenthums. Philo und die jüdisch-alexandrinische theosophie. 2e auflage. 2 pts. in 1 v. lxxvi, 536 pp. 8°. *Stuttgart, G. Schweizerbart*, 1835. s.

Ghent. Bibliotheca gandavensis. Catalogue méthodique de la bibliothèque de l'université de Gand; précédé d'une histoire de cette bibliothèque, etc. par Aug. Voisin. Jurisprudence. lxxxii, 394 pp. 1 pl. 8°. *C. Annoot-Broeckman*, 1839. s.

Gherardo *da Cremona, or* Gherardo *di Sabbionetta.* Astronomical geomancy. Translated by R. Turner. pp. 231—318.
[*With* Agrippa von Nettesheim (H. C.) Occult philosophy. 1783.]

Ghost stories; collected with a view to counteract the vulgar belief in ghosts and apparitions. Illust. by Darley. 192 pp. 10 pl. 12°. *New York, J. Miller*, 1865.

Ghostly colloquies. By the author of "letters from Rome." [*anon.*] 267 pp. 12°. *New York, Appleton & Co.* 1856.

Giannetasio (Niccolò Partenio). Piscatoria et navtica. 4 p. l. 347 p. 11 pl. 18°. *Neapoli, typis regiis*, 1685.

Gianutio. *See* **Mantia,** Orazio Gianutio della.

Gibbon (Edward). History of the decline and fall of the Roman empire. 5th Amer. ed. 4 v. 8°. *New York, Harpers,* 1835. s.

Gibbon (Lardner). Exploration of the valley of the Amazon. *See* **Herndon** (W. L.) *and* **Gibbon.**

Gibbons (J. S.) Public debt of the United States, [comprising] its organization, its liquidation, administration of the treasury, the financial system. xii, 276 pp. 12°. *New York, Appletons,* 1867.

Gibbs (George). Dictionary of the Chinook jargon, or trade language of Oregon. xiv, 44 pp. 8°. *Washington,* 1863.

[Smithsonian miscel. coll. v. 7].

——— Instructions for research relative to the ethnology and philology of America. iii, 51 pp. 8°. *Washington,* 1863.

[Smithsonian miscel. coll. v. 7].

Gibbs (Josiah Willard). Teutonic etymology: the formation of Teutonic words in the English language. 139 pp. 16°. *New Haven, (Conn.) Peck, White & Peck,* 1860.

Gibson (*Rev.* Charles B.) Life among convicts. 2 v. x, 304 pp; viii, 305 pp. portrait. 12°. *London, Hurst & Blackett,* 1863.

Gibson (Edmund, *bishop of London*). Pastoral letters to the people of his diocese. 192 pp. 8°. *Oxford,* 1825.

[*With* RANDOLPH (John, *bishop of London*). Enchiridion theologicum, v. 2].

Gibson (William, *M. D.*) Institutes and practice of surgery. 7th ed. 503 pp; 478 pp. 34 pl. 8°. *Philadelphia, Kay & Bro.* 1845.

Gibson (William Sidney). Miscellanies, historical and biographical; being a second series of essays, lectures, and reviews. iv, 385 pp. 8°. *London, Longmans,* 1863.

Giebel (Christian Gottfried Andreas). Allgemeine palæontologie; entwurf einer systematischen darstellung der fauna und flora der vorwelt. viii, 413 pp. 8°. *Leipzig, A. Abel,* 1852. s.

——— Fauna der vorwelt, mit steter berücksichtigung der lebenden thiere. Monographisch dargestellt. v. i. 1–4: ii, 1: iii, 1. 8°. *Leipzig, F. A. Brockhaus,* 1847–56. s.

[No more published, down to 1867.]

CONTENTS.

v. i. Wirbelthiere.
Abth. i. Säugethiere. xi, 281 pp. 1847.
" 2. Vögel und amphibien. xi, 217 pp. 1847.
" 3. Fische. xii, 467 pp. 1848.
v. ii. Gliederthiere.
Abth. i. Insecten und spinnen. xviii, 511 pp. 1856.
v. iii. Mollusken.
Abth. i. Cephalopoden. xvi, 856 pp. 1852.

——— De geognostica septentrionalis Hercyniæ fastigii constitutione. 33 pp. 8°. *Halis, Ploetz,* 1848. s.

——— Paläozoologie; entwurf einer systematischen darstellung der fauna der vorwelt. viii, 359 pp. 8°. *Merseburg, Rulandt,* 1846. s.

——— Die silurische fauna des Unterharzes nach C. Bischof's sammlung bearbeitet. 72 pp. 7 pl. 4°. *Berlin, G. Bosselmann,* 1858.

Gilbert (*Dr.* J.) *and* Martin (C. A. F.) Précis d'histoire naturelle. 2 v. 549 pp; 500 pp. 8°. *Paris, bibliothèque ecclésiastique,* 1839–40. s.

CONTENTS.

v. i. Géologie, minéralogie, botanique.
v. ii. Anatomie, physiologie, zoologie.

Gilbert (James). Modern atlas of the earth, with an introduction to physical and historical geography, by Robert Mudie. xx, 228, 52 pp. 56 maps. 2 pl. 4°. *London, H. G. Collins,* [*about* 1840]. s.

Gilbert (John T.) History of the viceroys of Ireland; with notices of the castle of Dublin. xxxvi, 613 pp. 8°. *Dublin, J. Duffy,* 1865.

Gilbert (Joseph Henry). Growth of barley and clover by different manures. *See* **Lawes** (J. B.) *and* Gilbert.

Gilbert (Linney). India illustrated; an historical and descriptive account. viii, 232 pp. 21 pl. 8°. *London,* [n. d.]

Gilbert (Louis). La marbrerie; 120 planches gravées représentant des travaux de marbrerie; monuments funéraires, cheminées, autels, fonts baptismaux, dallages, etc. 4°. *Paris, A. Morel, & Cie.* 1860.

Gilbert (William, *M. D.*) De magnete, magneticisqve corporibus, et de magno magnete tellure. viii, 240 pp. fol. *Londini, P. Short,* 1600.

Gilbert (William). De profundis. A tale of the social deposits. 2d ed. viii, 444 pp. 16°. *London, A. Strahan,* 1866.

Gildas. De excidio Brittaniæ liber querulus. fol. *Oxoniæ,* 1691.

[GALE (Thomas) *and* Fell (John). Rerum anglicarum scriptores veteres. *Oxoniæ,* 1684–91. v. 3.]

Gildemeister (Johann). Scriptorum arabum [Masûdii, Ibn Hauqualis, Abulfadæ, Qazvînii] de rebus indicis loci et opuscula inedita. [Latine et Arabice, cum commentatione.] Fasciculus primus. xiv, 223, 80 pp. 8°. *Bonnæ, H. B. König,* 1838.

[No more published.]

Giles (*Rev.* Chauncey). Lectures on the nature of spirit, and of man as a spiritual being. 206 pp. 12°. *New York, New Jerusalem pub.* 1867.

Gill (John). The scriptures the only guide in matters of religion. 44 pp. 16°. *London, G. Keith,* 1751.

[Imperfect; pp. 3 and 4 wanting].

Gillet (Joseph A.) The Cambridge course of elementary physics. *See* **Rolfe** (W. J.) *and* **Gillet** (J. A.)

Gillett (*Rev.* E. H.) Ancient cities and empires; their prophetic doom, read in the light of history and modern research. 302 pp. 20 pl. 12°. *Philadelphia, Presbyt. pub. com.* [1867].

——— England two hundred years ago. 363 pp. 5 pl. 16°. *Philadelphia, Presbyt. board of pub.* [1866].

——— History of the presbyterian church in the United States of America. 2 v. xxiv, 576 pp; xii, 605 pp. 8°. *Philadelphia, Presb. pub. com.* 1864.

——— Life and times of John Huss. 2d ed. 2 v. xx, 632 pp; xiii, 651 pp. 8°. *Boston, Gould & Lincoln,* 1864.

Gilliland (William). Journal and other papers.

[*See* WATSON (Winslow C.) Pioneer history of the Champlain valley, etc.]

Gilliss (James Melville). The U. S. naval astronomical expedition to the southern hemisphere, during the years 1849–52. v. i, ii, iii, and vi. 4°. *Washington, Gov. print.* 1855–56.

[No more published.]

CONTENTS.

v. i. Chile; its geography, climate, earthquakes, government, social condition, mineral and agricultural resources, commerce, etc. xiii, 556 pp. 3 maps, 11 pl.

v. ii. The Andes and pampas, by A. MacRae; minerals, by J. L. Smith; Indian remains, by T. Ewbank; mammals, by S. F. Baird; birds, by J. Cassin; reptiles, fishes, and crustacea, by C. Girard; shells, by A. A. Gould; dried plants, by A. Gray; living plants and seeds, by W. D. Brackenridge; fossil mammals, by J. Wyman; fossil shells, by T. A. Conrad. ix, 300 pp. 2 maps, 35 pl.

v. iii. Observations to determine the solar parallax. By J. M. Gilliss. cclxxxviii, 492 pp.

v. vi. Magnetical and meteorological observations. xlviii, 420 pp.

Gilman (Daniel Coit). A historical discourse, delivered in Norwich, Connecticut, Sept. 7, 1859, at the bi-centennial celebration of the settlement of the town. 2d ed. with additional notes. 8°. *Boston,* 1859.

Gilman (*Rev.* Samuel). A week among autographs. pp. 371–460.

[App. to GILMAN, (Caroline). Poetry of travelling in the United States. 16°. *N. Y.* 1838].

Gilmore (James R.) Life of Jesus, according to his original biographers, with notes. By Edmund Kirke. [*pseudon.*] 297 pp. 16°. *Boston, Lee & Shepard,* 1867.

——— On the border. By Edmund Kirke. [*pseudon.*] 333 pp. 12°. *Boston, Lee & Shepard,* 1867.

Gilpin (Bernard). Sermon preached before king Edward vi, 1552.

[*With* GILPIN (William). Lives of Latimer and Gilpin. 3d ed. 8°. *London,* 1780].

Gilpin (William, *M. A.*) The life of Hugh Latimer, bishop of Worcester. 197 pp. 3 l. 12°. *London, J. & J. Rivington,* 1755.

——— The lives of Hugh Latimer and of Bernard Gilpin. 3d ed. viii, 368 pp. 8°. *London, R. Blamire,* 1780.

——— The lives of John Wickliff, and of lord Cobham, John Huss, Jerome of Prague, and Zisca. 2d ed. 10, 272 pp. 5 l. 5 pl. 8°. *London, J. Robson,* 1766.

Gilpin (William). The central gold region. The grain, pastoral, and gold regions of North America. With some new views of its physical geography, and observations on the Pacific railroad. 194 pp. 6 maps. 8°. *Philadelphia, Sower, Barnes & Co.* 1860.

Gioacchimo calabrese. Vaticinia Joachimi abbatis calabri. *See* **Merlin.**

Girac (Emilius). Appendix and notes to Marx's theory of musical composition. vi, 166 pp. 8°. *New York, Mason Bros.* [1854].

——— The same.

[Supp. to MARX's theory of musical composition].

Girard (Charles, *M. D.*) Ichthyology.

[*With* EMORY (W. H.) Report on the U. S. and Mexican boundary survey. v. 2, pt. 2].

——— Mammals. s.

[*With* BAIRD (Spencer F.) Outlines of zoology].

——— Reptiles, fishes, and crustacea [of Chile].

[*With* GILLISS (J. M.) U. S. astron. exped. v. 2].

Girard college. *See* **Bache** (A. D.) Meteorological observations, etc.

Girardin (Émile de). De l'instruction publique en France. 464 pp. 32°. *Paris, A. Desrez,* 1840. s.

——— The same. 3e éd. 481 pp. 16°. *Paris, Mairet et Fournier,* 1842.

Girardin (Saint Marc). De l'instruction intermédiare, et de son état dans le midi de l'Allemagne. 2 pts. in 1 v. viii, 415 pp. 8°. *Paris, F. G. Levrault,* 1835–39. s.

Giraud (Pierre François Félix Joseph). Campagne de Paris en 1814, précédée d'un coup d'œil sur celle de 1813. 6e éd. 124 pp. 8°. *Paris, A. Eymery,* 1814. s.

——— The same. Official narrative of the campaign in France, 1814, preceded by a view of that of 1813. With Buonaparte's bulletins from the armistice to [his] abdication. pp. 493–576. 1 pl. 8°. *London,* 1814.

[Royal military chronicle, v. 3].

Giraudeau (Bonaventure). Introductio ad linguam graecam. Ed. nova. xii, 431 pp. 8°. *Avenione, F. Seguin*, 1821. s.

Girault (A. L. A.) Astronomie simplifiée. 236 pp. 32°. *Paris, Librairie des écoles*, 1836. s.

Girault (A. N. *Prof. at Annapolis*). The French student's manual. 4th ed. 480 pp. 12°. *Philadelphia, H. Perkins*, 1848. s.

Girault de St. Fargeau (Eusèbe). Bibliographie historique et topographique de la France; ou catalogue de tous les ouvrages depuis le xve siècle jusq'au mois d'avril, 1845. 8°. *Paris, F. Didot*, 1845. s.

Girtanner (Christoph). Ausführliche darstellung des darwin'schen systems der praktischen heilkunde, nebst einer kritik desselben. 2 v. lvi, 599 pp; xxxviii, 468 pp. 8°. *Göttingen, J. G. Rosenbusch*, 1799. s.

Gisborne (Thomas). The principles of moral philosophy investigated, and applied to the constitution of civil society. With remarks on the decision of the house of commons, April 2, 1792, respecting the abolition of the slave trade. 4th ed. xi, 466 pp. 8°. *London, T. Cadell & W. Davies*, 1798.

Gíslason (Conrad). Dönsk ordabok med islenzkum thydingum. vi, 596 pp. fol. *Kaupmannahöfn, B. Luno*, 1851. s.

Gistel (Johannes). Die mysterien der europäischen insectenwelt. Ein geheimer schlüssel für sammler aller insecten-ordnungen und stände, etc. xii, 530 pp. 12°. *Kempten, T. Dannheimer*, 1856. s.

——— Naturforscher diess und jenseits der oceane. 372 pp. 16°. *Straubing, J. Schorner*, 1856. s.

Givry (——). Pilote français. Instructions nautiques (partie des côtes septentrionales de France comprise entre la pointe de Barfleur et Dunkerque). viii, 493 pp. 12 pl. 4°. *Paris, Dépôt de la marine*, 1842. s.

——— The same. (Entre les casquets et la point de Barfleur. Environs de Cherbourg.) vi, 139 pp. 2 pl. 4°. *Paris, Dépôt de la marine*, 1845. s.

——— The same. (Entre le phare des Héaux de Bréhat et le phare du cap de la Hogue.) viii, 543 pp. 16 pl. 4°. *Paris, Dépôt de la marine*, 1851. s.

Glaisher (James, *F. R. S.*) On the meteorology of England, the south of Scotland, and parts of Ireland, 1851—1859. 21 pts. in 1 v. 8°. *London, British met. soc.* 1851–59. s.

Glas (George). Canary islands. *See* **Abreu de Galineo** (Juan de).

Glascock (William N.) Naval sketch book; or, the service afloat and ashore. [*anon.*] 2 v. in 1. xxiv, 251 pp; 286 pp. 12°. *London, H. Colburn*, 1826.

Glasgow university. Catalogus impressorum librorum in bibliotheca academiae glasguensis. Labore A. Arthur. 596 pp. fol. *Glasguæ, in aedibus academicis*, 1791. s.

——— A supplement to the catalogue of books in the university library. 2 p. l. 520 pp. 8°. 8°. *Glasgow, A. & J. M. Duncan*, 1825. s.

——— A second supplement to [same.] 2 p. l. 800 pp. 8°. *Glasgow, University press*, 1836. s.

——— Catalogue of books bought from August 20th, 1844, till August 20th, 1846, for the university library, out of the compensation fund allowed by government on the abolition of privilege under the copyright act. xxxviii, 730 pp. 8°. *Glasgow, G. Richardson*, 1846. s.

Glasl (Carl). Excursionsbuch; oder, anleitung alle körper der drei naturreiche zu sammeln, zuzubereiten, in sammlungen aufzustellen und zu erhalten, etc. vii, 142 pp. 8°. *Wien, W. Braumüller*, 1863. s.

Glasse (Francis). Memoirs of Andrew Winpenny, count de deux sous. 224 pp. 8°. *London*, 1841.
[Hazlitt's romancist and novelist's lib. v. 3.]

Glauber (Johann Rudolph). Operis mineralis partes i, ii. 16°. *Amsterodami*, 1651–52. s.

Glendenning (Robert). The pinetum. *London*, 1858. *See* **Gordon** (George).

Glenn (James). The mysteries of nature revealed; or, the identity of light, heat, and electricity fully established. 55 pp. 8°. *New York, author*, 1846. s.

Gliddon (George R.) Ancient Egypt; her monuments, hieroglyphics, history, and archæology. 66 pp. 8°. *New York, J. Winchester*, 1843. s.

——— No. 2. An appeal to the antiquaries of Europe on the destruction of the monuments of Egypt. 2 p. l. 160 pp. 8°. *London, J. Madden & Co.* 1841.

Gloger (Constantin Lambert). Das abändern der vögel durch einfluss des klima's, etc. xxxii, 159 pp. 8°. *Breslau, A. Schulz & Co.* 1833. s.

Gloria Patri. Prayers, chants, and responses for public worship. [Universalist]. 214 pp. 12°. *Boston, R. A. Ballou*, 1866.

Glossographia anglica nova; or, a dictionary interpreting hard words of whatever language, used in English. [*anon.*] 2d ed. 337 l. unp. 8°. *London, D. Brown*, 1719.

Glover (Anna). Glover memorials and genealogies. An account of John Glover of Dorchester, and his descendants. ix, 602 pp. 8°. *Boston, D. Clapp & son*, 1867.

Gmelin (Carl Christian). Flora badensis alsatica et confinium regionum cis et transrhenana, plantas exhibens. 4 v. 8°. *Carlsruhae, Müller*, 1805-26. s.

Gmelin (Samuel Gottlieb). *See* **Histoire**, etc. dans la Russie.

Gneist (Rudolf). Das englische verwaltungsrecht; mit einschluss des heeres, der gerichte und der kirche, geschichtlich und systematisch. 2 v. xv, 1374 pp. 8°. *Berlin, J. Springer*, 1867.

Godard (Ernest). Études sur la monorchidie et la cryptorchidie chez l'homme. [Extract.] 164 pp. 4 pl. 8°. *Paris, soc. de biologie*, 1857. s.

Godart (Jean Baptiste). Histoire naturelle des lépidoptères, ou papillons, de France. v. 1-4. 8°. *Paris, Crevot*, 1821-22. s.
[Wanting v. 5-8.]

——— Tableau méthodique des lépidoptères, ou papillons, de France, etc. Diurnes. 64 pp. 8°. *Paris, Crevot*, 1823. s.
[*With* GODART, hist. nat. des lépidoptères de France, v. 2.]

Godby (James). Italian scenery; representing the manners, customs, and amusements of the states of Italy; containing thirty-two coloured engravings, by J. Godby, from original drawings by P. Van Lerberghi: the narrative by M. Buonaiuti. 41 l. unp. 32 pl. fol. *London, T. M'Lean*, 1823.

Godet (Charles H.) Énumération des végétaux vasculaires du Jura suisse et français, plus spécialement du canton de Neuchâtel. vi, 233 pp. 8°. *Neuchâtel, H. Wolfrath*, 1851. s.

——— Flore du Jura; ou, description des végétaux vasculaires, etc. xvi, 872 pp. 8°. *Neuchâtel, auteur*, 1853. s.

Godey's lady's book. Edited by Mrs. S. J. Hale and L. A. Godey. July 1866, to June 1867. v. 73-74. 8°. *Philadelphia, Louis A. Godey*, 1866-67.

Godfrey (Thomas, *jr.*) Juvenile poems on various subjects, with The prince of Parthia, a tragedy. xxv, 223 pp. 4°. *Philadelphia, Henry Miller*, 1765.

Godwin (S. P.) Heart-breathings, or the soul's desire expressed in earnestness; a series of prayers, [etc.] for "the home circle." 123 pp. 18°. *Philadelphia, J. B. Lippincott & Co.* 1867.

Godwin (Thomas, *D. D.*) Moses and Aaron: Civil and ecclesiasticall rites vsed by the Hebrewes. 3d ed. 4 p. l. 332 pp. 6 l. sm. 4°. *London, J. Haviland*, 1628.

——— Romanæ historiae anthologia, recognita et avcta. An English exposition of the Roman antiquities. [New ed.] 4 p. l. 277 pp. 11 l. sm. 4°. *Oxford, H. Cripps*, 1628.
[*With* GODWIN (Thomas). Moses and Aaron. *London*, 1628.]

Goedart (Jean). Metamorphoses naturelles; ou, histoire des insectes. 3 v. 18°. *Amsterdam, P. Mortier*, 1700. s.

Goepp (Charles). New Rome. *See* **Poesche** (Theo.) *and* **Goepp** (C.)

Goeppert. *See* **Göppert**.

Goës (Bento de). Journey from Agra to Cathay. 66 pp.
[*With* YULE (Henry). Cathay, etc. v. 2.]

Goes (Damião de). Chronica do serenissimo senhor rei D. Manoel, novamente dada a luz por Reinerio Bocache. 3ª ed. 4 p. l. 609 pp. sm. fol. *Lisboa, M. Manescal da Costa*, 1749.

——— Legatio magni Indorvm imperatoris presbyteri Joannis, ad Emanuelem Lusitaniæ regem, anno Domini, mdxiii. Item de Indorum fide, ceremoniis, religione, etc. Item aliquot Cornelij Graphei, ad eundem Damianum carmina. 36 l. unp. 18°. *Anvers, Joan. Grapheus*, 1532.

Goethe. *See* **Göthe**.

Golding (Arthur). *See* **Testaments** (The) of the twelve patriarches.

Goldstein (Isaac). Jesus of Nazareth. An authentic ancient tale. 170 pp. 5 pl. 16°. *New York, Goldstein & Co.* 1866.

Goltz (Hubert). Vivæ omnivm fere imperatorvm imagines, a C. Ivlio Cæsare vsque ad Carolvm v. et Ferdinandvm ejvs fratrem, ex antiqvis vetervm nvmismatis solertissime ac fideliter advmbratae. [*anon.*] 173 l. 139 pl. fol. *Antverpiæ, H. Goltz*, 1557.

Gomara (Francisco Lopez de). Hispania victrix. Historia general de las Indias; cō todo el descubrimiento y cosas notables que han acaescido dende que se ganaron hasta el año de 1551. Con la conquista de Mexico, y de la Nueua España. 2 pts. in 1 v. 2 p. l. cxxxvii l. fol. *Medina, Guillermo de Millis*, 1553.

——— Historia de Mexico, con el descvbrimiento de la Nueua España conquistado por Fernando Cortes. 349, 11 l. 18°. *Anvers, Juan Lacio*, 1554.

——— The same. La segunda parte de la historia general de las Indias, que contiene la conquista de Mexico, y de la Nueua España. 340 l. 18°. *Anuers, Martin Nucio*, 1554.

Gomara (Francisco Lopez de). Histoire generalle des Indes Occidentales et terres nevves qui jusques à présent ont esté descouuertes. Traduite en François par M. Fumée. [*anon.*] 6 p. l. 355 l. 15 l. 16°. *Paris, Michel Sonnius,* 1578.

——— The same. 5e éd. 4 p. l. 485 l. 18 l. 16°. *Paris, Michel Sonnius,* 1605.

——— The same. The pleasant historie of the conquest of the West India, now called New Spain. Atchieued by Hernando Cortes. Translated out of the Spanish tongue, by T[homas] N[icholss]. 4 p. l. 305 pp. 5 l. sm. 4°. *London, Thomas Creede,* 1596.

Gomberville. *See* **Le Roy** de Gomberville.

Gonzague (Louis de, *duc* de Nevers.) *See* **Nevers.**

Good stories. Parts i–ii. 200 pp. 6 pl. 223 pp. 4 pl. sq. 16°. *Boston, Ticknor & Fields,* 1867.

CONTENTS.

Part I. DeQuincey (T.) The avenger.
Hawthorne (N.) Peter Goldthwaite's treasure.
Hood (T.) The defaulter.
Spicer (H.) Madonna.
Vaughan (H.) Coldstream.
Winthrop (T.) Love and skates.
Part II. Bellows-mender (The) of Lyons.
Blacksmiths (The) of Holsby.
Lee (H.) The Scotsman's tale.
Macnish (R.) The metempsychosis.
Penitent (A) confession.
Small-change (The) family.
Uninvited (The).

Good thoughts for priest and people; or, short meditations for every day in the year, [etc.] Translated from the German by Rev. Theo. Noethen. 383 pp. 12°. *Albany, Weed, Parsons & Co.* 1866.

Goodale (S. L.) The principles of breeding: or, the reproduction and management of domestic animals. 164 pp. 12°. *Boston, Crosby, Nichols, Lee & Co.* 1861.

Goodrich (Charles A.) History of the United States of America to 1850, with the constitution of the U. S. 418 pp. 12°. *Boston, Jenks, Palmer & Co.* 1850. s.

——— The same. Revised to the present time, by W. H. Seavey. 320, 28 pp. 12°. *Boston, Brewer & Tileston,* 1867.

——— Stories on the history of Connecticut for young persons. 203 pp. 18°. *Hartford, D. F. Robinson & Co.* 1829.

Goodrich (Frank Boott.) The tribute book; a record of the munificence, self-sacrifice, and patriotism of the American people during the war for the union. 512 pp. 7 pl. 8°. *New York, Derby & Miller,* 1865.

Goodrich (Samuel Griswold). Natural history, illustrating and describing the animal kingdom, with its wonders and curiosities: showing the habits, [etc.] of animals and their relation to agriculture, [etc.] 2 v. xvi, 680 pp. 16 pl; viii, 680 pp. 16 pl. 8°. *New York, A. J. Johnson,* 1868.

——— Pictorial history of Greece; ancient and modern. Revised ed. 371 pp. 1 map. 12°. *Philadelphia, E. H. Butler & Co,* 1855. s.

——— Histoire des États Unis d'Amérique. 352 pp. 12°. *Philadelphie, E. H. Butler & Cie.* 1855. s.

——— Historietas morales para la infancia. 352 pp. 12°. *Nueva York,* 1867. *D. Appleton y Ca.*

——— Petite histoire universelle. 331 pp. 12°. *Philadelphie, E. H. Butler & Cie.* 1855.

——— Peter Parley's universal history. Elohi nulistanitolv kanohesgi. [Common school history. Translated into Cherokee. 53 chap. in **Cherokee** messenger. 8°. *Cherokee,* 1844–46.]

Goodwin (*Rev.* Harvey). Elementary course of mathematics. 5th ed. xiv, 631 pp. 8°. *Cambridge, Deighton, Bell & Co.* 1857. s.

Göppert (Heinrich Robert). Der bernstein und die in ihm befindlichen pflanzreste der vorwelt.

[*With* BERENDT (G. C.) Die im bernstein reste, etc.]

——— Ueber die wärme-entwickelung in den pflanzen, deren gefrieren, und die schutzmittel gegen dasselbe. xiv, 272 pp. 8°. *Breslau, J. Max & Co.* 1830.

Gorani (Giuseppe). Mémoires secrets et critiques des cours, des gouvernemens, et des moeurs des principaux états de l'Italie. 3 v. 16°. *Paris, Buisson,* 1794. s.

Gordon (*Sir* Cosmo). Life and genius of lord Byron. 80 pp. 1 pl. 8°. *London, Knight & Lacey,* 1824.

[Miscellaneous pam. v. 56.]

Gordon (George), *and* **Glendenning** (Robert). The pinetum: being a synopsis of all the coniferous plants at present known, with descriptions, history, and synonymes. xxii, 353 pp. 8°. *London, H. G. Bohn,* 1858. s.

Gordon (*Rev.* James). Terraquea; or, a new system of geography and modern history. 4 v. 8 maps. 8°. *Dublin, W. Porter,* 1793–98.

[NOTE.—v. 1, 2d ed. v. 2–4, 1st ed.]

Gordon (Patrick). Geography anatomiz'd: or, the geographical grammar. 11 p. l. 432 pp. 17 maps. 8°. *London, Knapton and others,* 1733.

Gordon (Thomas). Cato's letters. *See* **Trenchard** (John), *and* **Gordon** (T.)

Gordon. A tale. A poetical review of Don Juan. [*anon.*] 79 pp. 8°. *London, T. & J. Allman,* 1821.

[Miscellaneous pam. v. 56.]

Gorges (*Sir* Ferdinando). America painted to the life. Publisht by F. Gorges, Esq. 396 pp. 9 l. sm. 4°. *London, N. Brooks,* 1659.

CONTENTS.

A description of New England. 51 pp. [Imperfect: 2 p. l. wanting.]
A briefe narration of the originall undertakings of the advancement of plantations into America. 57 pp. 1658.
A true history of the originall undertakings of plantations. [Running title: Wonder-working providence of Sion's saviour. By Capt. Ed. Johnson.] 236 pp. 1658.
The history of the Spaniards' proceedings in America, from Columbus to the later times. 52 pp.

Gori (Antonio Francesco). Dactyliotheca smithiana. Volumen primum, gemmarum ectypa complectens. Volumen alterum, historiam glyptographicam exhibens. 2 v. xix, 97 pp; 3, ccxcvii pp. 100 pl. fol. *Venetiis, J. B. Pasquale,* 1767.

——— Monumentum, sive columbarium libertorum et servorum Liviæ Augustæ et Cæsarum, Romæ detectum in via appia, 1726. xxxvi, 254 pp. 21 pl. fol. *Florentiæ, typis regiæ celsitudinis,* 1727.

Görres (Johann Joseph). La mystique divine, naturelle, et diabolique, traduit de l'Allemand par M. Charles Sainte-Foi. 5 v. 8°. *Paris, Poussielgue-Rusaud,* 1854–5.

Gorton (Samuel). Simplicitie's defence; or, innocency defended, being unjustly accused by that seven-headed church-government united in New England. 8 p. l. 111 pp. sm. 4°. *London, John Macock,* 1646.

Gosky (Martin). Arbustum, seu arboretum poetice; variis arborum figuris et signaturis, varioque carminis genere et variorum authorum applausu germinans et determinans vitam cum fama Augusti ducis brunovicensis et lunaeburgensis. 72 p. l. unp. 585 l. fol. *Wolfenbüttel, J. & H. Stern,* 1650. s.

Goss (Warren Lee). The soldier's story of the captivity at Andersonville, Belle Isle, and other rebel prisons. 273 pp. 4 pl. 12°. *Boston, Lee & Shepard,* 1867.

Gosse (Philip Henry). A handbook to the marine aquarium. viii, 47 pp. 12°. *London, J. Van Voorst,* 1855. s.

——— A manual of marine zoology for the British Isles. 2 v. xi, 203 pp; iv, 239 pp. 16°. *London, J. Van Voorst,* 1855–56. s.

——— Natural history. Fishes. viii, 357 pp. 16°. *London, Soc. prom. christ. knowledge,* 1851. s.

——— Natural history. Mammalia. vi, 302 pp. 16°. *London, Soc. prom. christ. knowledge,* 1848. s.

Gosse (Philip Henry). Natural history. Mollusca. viii, 328 pp. 16°. *London, Soc. prom. christ. knowledge,* 1854. s.

——— Natural history. Reptiles. iv, 296 pp. 16°. *London, Soc. prom. christ. knowledge.* 1850. s.

——— The ocean. xii, 360 pp. 2 pl. 12°. *London, Soc. for prom. christ. knowledge,* [1845]. s.

——— The romance of natural history. xiv, 372 pp. 12 pl. 12°. *Boston, Gould & Lincoln,* 1861. s.

——— A text-book of zoology, for schools. 450 pp. 12°. *London, Soc. prom. christ. knowledge,* 1851. s.

Gosselmann (Carl August). Resa i Colombia, ären 1825 och 1826. Andra uppl. 2 v. in 1. 275 pp. 1 pl. 1 map; 302 pp. 1 pl. 8°. *Stockholm, J. Hörberg,* 1830.

Göthe (Johann Wolfgang von). Faust. Eine tragödie. Neue auflage. 288 pp. 18°. [Interleaved as 4°.] *Stuttgart, J. S. Cotta,* 1825. s.

——— The same. Faustus, from the German. viii, 86 pp. 26 pl. 4°. *London, Boosey & sons, and Rodwell & Martin,* 1821.

——— The same. A dramatic poem. Translated into English prose, with notes, by A. Hayward. 2d ed. cviii, 350 pp. 8°. *London, E. Moxon,* 1834.

——— The same. A tragedy. Translated into English verse, by John Hills. xxi, 369 pp. 16°. *London, Whittaker & Co.* 1840.

——— The same. Part the second. From the German, by A. Gurney. viii, 336 pp. 8°. *London, Senior, Heathcote & Senior,* 1842.

——— The same. A tragedy. Translated by Lewis Filmore. 8°. *London,* 1866.

[Masterpieces of foreign literature.]

——— Göethe's letters to Leipzig friends. Edited by Otto Jahn. Translated by R. Slater. x, 305 pp. 3 pl. 12°. *London, Longmans,* 1866.

Gottlieb (D. J.) Lehrbuch der reinen und technischen chemie. xii, 756 pp. 8°. *Braunschweig, Vieweg,* 1853. s.

Gottwald (Christoph). Museum gottwaldianum. 111 pl. fol. [*Gedani, auctor,* 1714]. s.

Goud (Clarkson). The plan of redemption. *See* **Welcome** (J. C.) *and* **Goud** (C.)

Goudar (*madame* Sara). Oeuvres mêlées. 2 v. in 1. xii, 203 pp; 2 pl. 198 pp. 16°. *Amsterdam,* 1777.

CONTENTS.

v. 1. Lettres sur les divertissements du carnaval de Naples et de Florence.
v. 2. Remarques sur la musique italienne et sur la danse.

Gouget des Landres (*juge*). Nouvelle législation de l'impôt et du crédit public. vi, 232 pp. 8°. *Paris, Delaunay*, 1816. s.

Gough (John). History of the people called quakers. 4 v. 8°. *Dublin, R. Jackson*, 1789-90.

Gould (Augustus Addison). Crustacea of Massachusetts.

[*With* HITCHCOCK (E.) Catalogue of animals, etc. of Mass.]

——— History of New Ipswich. *See* **Kidder** (Frederic) *and* **Gould** (A. A.)

——— Shells [of Chile].

[*With* GILLISS (J. M.) U. S. astron. exped. v. 2].

Gould (Edward S.) Good English; or, popular errors in language. 12°. *New York, C. Scribner*, 1867.

Gould (James L.) Guide to the royal arch chapter. *See* **Sheville** (John) *and* **Gould** (J. L.)

Gould (Marcus T. C.) The art of short-hand writing. Revised stereotype ed. 40 pp. 18°. *Philadelphia, U. Hunt*, 1841.

Gould (S. Baring). *See* **Baring-Gould.**

Gouldman (Francis). A copious dictionary in three parts: i. The English before the Latin. ii. The Latin before the English. iii. The proper names of persons and places. 4th ed. 767 pp. unp. 4°. *Cambridge, (Eng.) John Hayes*, 1778.

Gouvion Saint-Cyr (Laurent, *marquis*). Journal des opérations de l'armée de Catalogne en 1808 et 1809. vii, 503 pp. 8°. *Paris, Anselin et Pochard*, 1821.

Government of the commonwealth of England, Scotland, and Ireland, as publicly declared at Westminster, Dec. 16, 1653, with the oath of the lord protector for observing the same. 46 pp. sm. 4°. *London, William Du Gard and Henry Hills*, 1653.

Gozzi (Carlo). Mémoires écrits par lui-même. Traduction libre par Paul de Musset. 300 pp. 16°. *Paris, Charpentier*, 1848.

Graah (Wilhelm August). Undersögelses-reise til östkysten af Grönland. Efter kongelig befaling, udförd i aarene 1828-31. xviii, 216 pp. 8 col. pl. 1 map. 4°. *Kiöbenhavn, J. D. Quist*, 1832.

Gräberg *af Hemsö* (Jacob). Saggio istorico su gli scaldi, o antichi poeti scandinavi. xvi, 253 pp. 8°. *Pisa, Molini*, 1811. s.

——— Specchio geografico e statistico dell'impero di Marocco. 364 pp. 8 pl. 1 map. 8°. *Genova, Tipog. Pellas*, 1834. s.

Gracian (Balthazar). Art of prudence; or, companion for a man of sense. With notes by Amelot de La Houssaie. Translated from the Spanish by Mr. Savage. 2d ed. 14 p. l. 280 pp. 12°. *London, Jonah Bowyer*, 1705.

Graesse. *See* **Grässe.**

Grafström (A.) Ett är i Sverge. *See* **Sandberg** (J. G.)

Graham (*Sir* James Robert George). Corn and currency: in an address to the land owners. 2d ed. 116 pp. 8°. *London, J. Ridgway*, 1826.

Graham (Sylvester). Philosophy of sacred history, considered in relation to human aliment and the wines of scripture. Edited by H. S. Chubb. 580 pp. 12°. *New York, Fowler & Wells*, 1855. s.

Graham (Thomas). Elements of chemistry. v. 1. 696 pp. 8°. *London*, 1848. s.

[Imperfect; wanting title, table of contents, etc.]

——— The same. Part i. [Inorganic]. 2d Am. from [2d London] ed. Edited, with notes, by Robert Bridges. 430 pp. 8°. *Philadelphia, Blanchard & Lea*, 1852. s.

Grahame (Thomas). A treatise on internal intercourse and communication in civilized states, and particularly in Great Britain. [Part 1, Railways.] xiii, 160 pp. 8°. *London, Longmans*, 1834.

Grainger (James). The sugar cane: a poem. With notes. vii, 167 pp. 4°. *London, R. & J. Dodsley*, 1764.

Grammar of the Huron language, by a missionary of the village of Huron Indians. Translated from the Latin by J. Wilkie. [*anon.*] pp. 94-198.

[*With* QUEBEC. Lit. and hist. soc. transactions, v. 2.]

Grant (Allan, *pseudon.*) *See* **Wilson** (James Grant).

Grant (*Mrs.* Anne). Memoirs of an American lady: with sketches of manners and scenery in America, as they existed previous to the revolution. viii, 344 pp. 16°. *New York, Samuel Campbell*, 1809.

——— The same. 295 pp. 12°. *New York, D. Appleton & Co.* 1846.

Grant (Asahel). The Nestorians; or, the lost tribes: containing evidence of their identity; with sketches of travel in ancient Assyria, Armenia, Media, and Mesopotamia. x, 338 pp. 1 map. 8°. *London, J. Murray*, 1841.

Grant (E. B.) Beet-root sugar and cultivation of the beet. 158 pp. 16°. *Boston, Lee & Shepard*, 1867.

Grant (James.) The king's own borderers. A military romance. 3 v. 12°. *London, Routledge*, 1865.

Grant (*Capt.* John). London bills of mortality. *See* **Graunt.**

Grant (John W.) Lenore; translated, with some original poems. 52 pp. 16°. *London, Murray & Co.* 1865.

Granville (*or* Greenville, George, *viscount Lansdowne.*) Poetical works. 8°. *Edinburgh,* 1794.
[Anderson's Brit. poets, v. 7.]

Grapheus (Cornelius). *See* **Schryver** (Cornelius).

Graphic sketches illustrating the costume, habits, and character of the aborigines of America. [Part 1, The natives of Virginia, by John Wyth, 1585–88.] 15, 39 l. 8°. *New York, J. & H. G. Langley,* 1841.

Grässe (Johann Georg Theodor). Bibliotheca magica et pneumatica; oder, wissenschaftlich geordnete bibliographie der wichtigsten in das gebiet des zauber wunder und sonstigen aberglaubens werke. iv, 175 pp. 8°. *Leipzig, W. Engelmann,* 1843. s.

——— Bibliotheca psychologica; oder, verzeichniss der wichtigsten über der menschen und thierseelen, und die unsterblichkeitslehre schriftsteller. vi, 60 pp. 8°. *Leipzig, W. Engelmann,* 1845.
[*With* his Bibliotheca magica.]

——— Trésor de livres rares et precieux; ou nouveau dictionnaire bibliographique. v. 6. in 2 parts. R–Z. 543, 523 pp. 4°. *Dresde, R. Kuntze,* 1865–66.

Grasse (Will de, *pseudon.*) *See* **Swallows** on the wing, etc.

Grassmann (Hermann). Die ausdehnungslehre, vollständig und in strenger form bearbeitet. xii, 388 pp. 8°. *Berlin, T. C. F. Enslin,* 1862. s.

Gratton (John). A journal of [his] life. With a collection of his books and manuscripts. xxiv, 432 pp. 8°. *London, Assigns of J. Sowle,* 1720.

CONTENTS.

Journal of life; of baptism; prisoner's vindication; of the Lord's supper; treatise of tithes.

Gratz. Statistischer ausweis der grazer handels- und gewerbekammer, 1855, 1856. 2 v. 8°. *Gratz, J. A. Kienreich,* 1857. s.

Gratz (Clemens Lorenz). Commentatio de codice sacro interpretando. Sacra scriptura num eodem modo interpretanda sit, quo reliquos antiquitatis libros interpretari solemus. 95 pp. 8°. *Campoduni,* 1832. s.

Grauert (Wilhelm). Zweites deutsches lesebuch. [Turner-schulbücher, II.] 192 pp. 16°. *New York, C. Steiger,* 1867.

Graunt (*Capt.* John). Natural and political observations upon the bills of mortality. 5th ed. 19 p. l. 150 pp. 16°. *London, J. Martyn,* 1676.

Gravenhorst (Johann Ludwig Carl). Systematische uebersicht und nachweisung der merkwürdigsten gegenstände im zoologischen museum der universität Breslau. [*anon.*] 48 pp. 8°. [*Breslau,* 1823]. s.

——— Das zoologische museum der universität Breslau. xviii, 288 pp. 1 pl. 8°. *Breslau, Gross, Barth & Co.* 1832. s.

Graves (*Rev.* Richard). Euphrosyne; or, amusements on the road of life. [*anon.*] 2d ed. 2 v. viii, 308 pp; xvii, 211 pp. 2 pl. 12°. *London, S. Dodsley,* 1780.

——— The festoon: a collection of epigrams, ancient and modern; with an essay on that species of composition. [*anon.*] 2d ed. xxiv, 213 pp. 16°. *London, Robinson & Roberts,* 1767.

——— The spiritual Quixote; or, the summer's ramble of Mr. Geoffrey Wildgoose. 2 v. 331 pp; 351 pp. 18°. *Providence, (R. I.) Robinson & Howland,* 1816.

Graves (Robert James, *M. D.*) System of clinical medicine. With notes and a series of lectures, by W. W. Gerhard. 3d Am. ed. 751 pp. 8°. *Philadelphia, Barrington & Haswell,* 1848. s.

Graves (W.) Two letters respecting the conduct of rear-admiral Graves in North America, from July to November, 1781. 39 pp. 4°. [*London,* 1782]?

Gravesande (Willem Jakobus). Mathematical elements of natural philosophy confirmed by experiments; or, an introduction to Sir Isaac Newton's philosophy. [From the Latin]. By T. T. Desaguliers. 2 v. xxii, 259 pp. 33 pl; xvi, 285 pp. 25 pl. 8°. *London, J. Senex, etc.* 1731–37. s.
[v. 1, 5th ed. 1737; v. 2, 4th ed. 1731].

Gravier (Jacques). Lettre sur les affaires de la Louisiane. 18 pp. 8°. *Nouvelle York, J. M. Shea,* 1865.
[*With* RELATION des affaires du Canada 1696, 1865].

——— Relation de ce qvi s'est passé dans la mission de l'immaculée conception, au pays des Illinois, 1693–4. 65 pp. 16°. *Manate, J. M. Shea,* 1857.

——— Relation ou journal du voyage en 1700, depuis le pays des Illinois jusqu'à l'embouchure du Mississipi. 68 pp. 16°. *Nouvelle York, J. M. Shea,* 1859.

Gray (Asa, *M. D.*) Dried plants [from Chile].
[*With* GILLISS (J. M.) U. S. astron. exped. v. 2].

Gray (Asa, *M. D.*) A manual of the botany of the northern United States, etc. [The mosses and liverworts, by Wm. S. Sullivant]. xxviii, 739 pp. 14 pl. 8°. *New York, Ivison,* 1859. s.

Gray (John Edward). Manual of the land and fresh-water shells of the British islands. (*See* **Turton** (W.)

Gray (Maria Emma). Figures of molluscous animals, selected from various authors. 5 v. 8°. *London, Longmans,* 1859. s.

Gray (Robert). Letters during the course of a tour through Germany, Switzerland, and Italy, in 1791-92. ix, 468 pp. 8°. *London, F. & C. Rivington,* 1794.

Gray (Samuel Frederick). A natural arrangement of British plants, according to Jussieu, De Candolle, Brown, etc. With an introduction to botany. 2 v. xxviii, 824 pp. 1 pl; viii, 757 pp. 8°. *London, Baldwin, Cradock, and Joy,* 1821.

Gray (Thomas). Poems. 121 pp. 12°. *London, J. Dodsley,* 1768.

Gray (William C.) Life of Abraham Lincoln. 200 pp. 3 pl. 16°. *Cincinnati, Western tract and book soc.* 1867.

Grayson (Eldred, *pseudon.) See* **Standish**, the puritan.

Grazzini (Antonfrancesco, *detto il Lasca).* Le bene. [Novelle]. 3 v. in 2. 16°. *Milano, G. Silvestri,* 1815.

Great Britain. Calendar of the state papers relating to Ireland, of the reign of Elizabeth, 1574-1585. Edited by H. C. Hamilton. cxliv. 718 pp. 8°. *London, Longmans,* 1867.

——— A catalogue of the books in the admiralty library. 403 pp. 8°. *London, admiralty,* 1858. s.

——— The same. A supplement, etc. 138 pp. 8°. *London, admiralty,* 1865. s.

——— Catalogue of books belonging to the treasury library. 135 pp. 8°. *London, Eyre & Spottiswoode,* 1853.

——— A collection of all the proclamations, declarations, articles, and ordinances passed by his highness the lord protector and his council. 766, 106 pp. fol. *London, H. Hills,* 1654-55.

——— Convention between the crowns of Great Britain and Spain, concluded at the Prado on the 14th of January, 1739, N. S. 28 pp. sm. 4°. [n. p. *about* 1739.]
[Imperfect; title page wanting.]

——— The humble address of the lords spiritual and temporal, in parliament assembled, presented to her majesty, 13th March, 1705, relating to the province of Carolina, and the petition therein mentioned. With her majestie's answer thereto. 4 pp. fol. *London, Charles Bill,* 1705.

——— A list of the general and field officers; of the officers in the several regiments; and a succession of colonels, 1775, 1777. 2 v. 8°. *London, J. Millan,* 1775-77.

——— The same. List of the officers of the army. [With] the officers of the militia forces, etc. 1781-82. 2 v. 8°. [*London, war office,* 1781-82].

——— The same. List of the officers of the army. 32d ed. 8°. [*London, war office,* 1784.]

——— Minutes of the committee of council on education. Correspondence, financial statements, etc; and reports by her majesty's inspectors of schools. 1851-1866. 18 v. 8°. *London, W. Clowes, etc.* 1852-66.

——— The same. Schools of parochial unions, England and Wales. Reports by her majesty's inspectors of parochial union schools. 1848-50, 1852-56. 3 v. 8°. *London, W. Clowes, etc.* 1850-56.

——— Navy list, from Dec. 1866, to Sept. 1867. 4 v. 16°. *London, J. Murray,* 1866-67.

——— Reports from the commissioners appointed to execute the measures recommended by the house of commons, respecting the public records of Ireland: with supplements and appendixes. 1810-15. [nos. 1-5.] 571 pp. 21 pl. fol. [*London, Gov't. print.* 1819.]

——— Reports from the select committee of the house of commons appointed to inquire into the state of the public records of the kingdom, [with analysis of the principal matters referred to in the records, rolls, etc. in the several public repositories]. 667 pp. 17 pl. fol. [*London, L. Hansard,* 1800.]
[Imperfect; pl. v. a. v. b. and vi wanting; 10 pl. of the public records of Ireland inserted.]

——— The report of the select committee [of the house of commons] on emigration in 1826, with a brief analysis of the evidence and appendix. 177 pp. 8°. *London, John Murray,* 1827.

——— Report from the select committee [of the house of commons] on the silk trade. 1050 pp. fol. [*London,* 1832].

——— Reports on normal schools for 1855; by her majesty's inspectors of schools. 90 pp. 2 pl. 8°. *London, Eyre & Spottiswoode,* 1856.

——— Reports received from her majesty's secretaries of embassy and legation, respecting coal. With an appendix, and reports as to coal production in British colonies. 136 pp. 8°. *London, Harrison & sons,* 1867.

Great Britain. Eleventh and twelfth reports of her majesty's civil service commissioners. 2v. 8°. *London, Eyre & Spottswoode,* 1866–67.

——[Parliamentary reports and papers]: session of 1866. 77 v. fol. *London, Eyre & Spottiswoode,* 1866.
[V. 49, 62, wanting.]

Great (The) conspiracy: [with] full secret of the assassination plot; and account of J. H. Surratt, etc. 198 pp. 8°. *Philadelphia, Barclay & Co.* 1866.

Great Falls, [N. H.] Directory for 1867. *See* **Dover** and Great Falls directory.

Great (The) metropolis; or, guide to New York for 1849. 179 pp. 1 map. 24°. *New York, H. Wilson,* 1849.

Greding (Johann Ernst). Vermischte medicinische und chirurgische schriften. Herausgegeben von K. W. Greding. 8 p. l. 320 pp. 16°. *Altenburg, Richter,* 1781. s.

Greece to the close of 1825. A review of the revolutionary state of Greece, etc. By a resident amongst the Greeks. [*anon.*] pp. 233–349.
[*With* BULWER (*Sir* H. L. E.) Autumn in Greece. *London,* 1826.]

Greeley (Horace). Der grosse conflikt in Amerika. Die geschichte der grossen rebellion in den Vereinigten Staaten von Nord-Amerika nach ihren ursachen, fortschritten und resultaten. Aus dem Englischen übersetzt von W. Grauert. v. 2. 749 pp. 10 pl. 1 map. 8°. *Hartford, O. D. Case & Co.* 1867.

Green (Francis). "Vox oculis subjecta;" a dissertation on the art of imparting speech, and the knowledge of language, to the naturally deaf, and (consequently) dumb. By a parent. [*anon.*] xvi, 224 pp. 12°. *London, B. White,* 1783.

Green (Horace, *M. D.*) Observations on the pathology of croup, etc. xi, 115 pp. 1 pl. 12°. *New York, J. Wiley,* 1849. s.

Green (Jonathan H.) Exposure of the arts and miseries of gambling. 4th ed. 336 pp. 12°. *Philadelphia, G. B. Zieber & Co.* 1847.

Green (William Henry). Elementary Hebrew grammar. viii, 58, 26 pp. 12°. *New York, John Wiley & son,* 1866.

Greene (Barnaby Edward). The classic: a poem. *See* **Anacreon,** Sappho, and others. *London,* 1768.

Greene (B. F.) The magnetism of ships, and the deviations of the compass. [A series of papers from the transactions of foreign societies, by Poisson [and others,] with other papers and documents. Reprinted by order of the secretary of the navy. Edited, and the memoir of Poisson translated, by B. F. Greene.] 771 pp. 13 pl. 5 tables. 8°. *Washington, Govt. printing office,* 1867.

Greene (George Washington). Nathaniel Greene: an examination of some statements in the ninth volume of Bancroft's history of the United States. 86 pp. 8°. *Boston, Ticknor & Fields,* 1866.

Greene (Samuel S.) A grammar of the English language. 323 pp. 12°. *Philadelphia, Cowperthwait & Co.* 1867.

Greene (Thomas A.) Marine shells of Massachusetts.
[*With* HITCHCOCK (E.) Catalogue of animals, etc. of Mass.]

Greenleaf (*Rev.* Jonathan). A history of the churches of all denominations in the city of New York. 379 pp. 18°. *New York, E. French,* 1846.

—— Sketches of the ecclesiastical history of the state of Maine. 293, 77 pp. 12°. *Portsmouth, (N. H.) H. Gray,* 1821.

Greenwood (Isaac). A philosophical discourse concerning the mutability and changes of the material world, read upon the news of the death of Thomas Hollis. 2 p. l. 24 pp. 8°. *Boston, S. Gerrish,* 1731.
[*With* WIGGLESWORTH (Edward). Blessedness of the dead, etc. *Boston,* 1731.]

Greenwood (James). Curiosities of savage life. 3d ed. v. 1. xiv, 418 pp. 8 pl. 8°. *London, S. O. Beeton,* 1865.

Greg (Robert Philips), *and* **Lettsom** (William G.) Manual of the mineralogy of Great Britain and Ireland. xvi, 483 pp. 8°. *London, J. Van Voorst,* 1858.

Gregg (Alexander, *D. D.*) History of the old Cheraws; containing an account of the aborigines of the Pedee, the first white settlements, [etc.] A. D. 1730 to 1810. viii, 546 pp. 4 maps. 8°. *New York, Richardson & Co.* 1867.

Gregory (James J. H.) Squashes; how to grow them. 69 pp. 16°. *New York, O. Judd & Co.* [1867].

Gregory (Samuel). History of Mexico from the earliest times to the present. 100 pp. 8°. *Boston, F. Gleason,* 1847.

Greiss (C. B.) Lehrbuch der physik. viii, 559 pp. 8°. *Wiesbaden, C. W. Kreidel,* 1863. s.

Grellmann (Heinrich Moritz G.) Dissertation on the gipseys, with an historical enquiry concerning their origin. 4 p. l. xiii, 210 pp. 8°. *London, W. Ballintine,* 1807.

Grelot (Guillaume Joseph). A late voyage to Constantinople. Made English by J. Philips. 7 p. l. 243 pp. 4 l. 14 pl. 16°. *London, J. Playford,* 1683.

Greswell (William Parr). A view of the early Parisian Greek press; including the lives of the Stephani; notices of other contemporary Greek printers of Paris, etc. Edited by E. Greswell. 2 v. xix, 412 pp; vii, 413 pp. 8°. *Oxford, D. A. Talboys*, 1833. s.

Greville (—— *esq.*) British India analyzed. The provincial and revenue establishments of Mahomedan and British conquerors in Hindostan stated and considered. 3 v. 2 p. l. viii, lxiii, 960 pp. 8°. *London, R. Faulder*, 1795.

Greville (Robert Kaye). Botany of India.
[pp. 117-157 of v. 3 of MURRAY (Hugh). Account of British India. *N. Y.* 1833-36].

Grew (Nehemiah). Anatomie des plantes. 5 p. l. 246 pp. 11 l. 1 pl. 24°. *Leide, P. Vander Aa*, 1685. s.

——— Cosmologia sacra: or, a discourse of the universe as it is; the creation and kingdom of God. Portrait. fol. *London*, 1701.

——— *and* **Boyle** (Robert). Recueil d'expériences et observations curieuses sur le combat, qui procède du mélange des corps, sur les saveurs, et sur les odeurs. 108 pp. 24°. *Leide, P. Vander Aa*, 1685. s.
[*With* GREW (N.) Anatomie des plantes].

Grey, *of Howick*, (Henry George, 3*d earl*). Parliamentary government considered with reference to reform. New ed. xxiii, 360 pp. 8°. *London, John Murray*, 1864.

Gridley (*Rev.* John). History of Montpelier, [Vt.] a discourse delivered on thanksgiving day, Dec. 8, 1842. 48 pp. 8°. *Montpelier, E. P. Walton & Sons*, 1843.

Griffin (John J.) A practical treatise on the use of the blowpipe in chemical and mineral analysis. xvi, 308 pp. 24°. *Glasgow, Griffin*, 1827. s.

Griffin (M.) Impressions of Germany. By an American lady. [*anon.*] 451 pp. 12°. *Dresden, B. G. Teubner*, [1866].

Griffith (Mattie). Poems. Now first collected. 167 pp. 12°. *New York, D. Appleton & Co.* 1853.

Griffith (Robert Eglesfeld.) A universal formulary: containing the methods of preparing and administering officinal and other medicines. 567 pp. 8°. *Philadelphia, Lea & Blanchard*, 1850. s.

——— Dispensatory. *See* **Christison** (R.); *also*, **Mayne** (J.)

Griffith (William.) Posthumous papers bequeathed to the East India company. Journals of travels in Assam, Burma, Bootan, Affghanistan, and the neighboring countries. xxxii, 529 pp. 1 map. 18 pl. 8°. *Calcutta, bishop's coll. press*, 1847. s.

——— Posthumous papers, etc. Itinerary notes of plants collected in the Khasyah and Bootan mountains, 1837-38; in Affghanistan, etc. 1839-41. Arranged by John McClelland. lxix, 435 pp. 1 map. 3 pl. 8°. *Calcutta, J. F. Bellamy*, 1848. s.

——— Posthumous papers, etc. Notulae ad plantas asiaticas. Arranged by John McClelland. 4 v. 8°. *Calcutta, bishops' college press*, 1847-54. s.

——— Posthumous papers, etc. Icones plantarum asiaticarum. Arranged by John McClelland. 4 v. in 2. 28 pp. 661 pl. 4°. *Calcutta, bishops' college press*, 1847-54. s.
[Plates to the preceding].

CONTENTS OF NOTULAE, AND ICONES.

v. 1. Development of organs in phanerogamous plants. viii, 255 pp; pl. 1-62.
v. 2. On the higher cryptogamous plants. pp. 256-628, viii; pl. 63-138.
v. 3. Monocotyledonous plants. 436, xii pp. pl. 139-359.
v. 4. Dicotyledonous plants. xli, 764 pp. pl. 360-661.

Grillet (Jean), *and* **Béchamel** (François Jean). A journal of travels into Guiana in 1674. 2 p. l. 68 pp. 16°. *London, Buckley*, 1698.
[*With* ACUÑA (Cristoval d'). Relation of the great river of the Amazons. viii, 190 pp. 16°. *London*, 1698.]

Grimaldi (Giuseppe Ceva). Considerazioni sulle pubbliche opere della Sicilia di quà, dal faro dai Normanni sino ai nostri tempi. 247, civ pp. 8°. *Napoli, Tipografia flautina*, 1839. s.

——— Itinerario da Napoli a Lecce, e nella provincia di terra d'Otranto nell' anno 1818, di G. C. G. [*anon.*] 260 pp. 8°. *Napoli, Porcelli*, 1821. s.

Grimes (J. Stanley). Geonomy; a theory of the ocean currents and their agency in the formation of the continents; to which is added astrogenea; a new theory of the formation of planetary systems. 206 pp. 16°. *Albion, (Mich.)* 1866.

Grimm (Jacob Ludwig Carl). Geschichte der deutschen sprache. 2 v. xvi, 1035 pp. 8°. *Leipzig, Weidmann*, 1848. s.

——— *and* **Grimm** (Carl Wilhelm). Deutsches wörterbuch. v. 1-3. v. 4. pt. 1. A—Fromm. portrait. 4°. *Leipzig, S. Hirzel*, 1854-63.

——— The same. Fortgesetzt von Rudolph Hildebrand und Karl Weigand. v. 4. pt. 2. Fromm.—Fül. v. 5. pts. 1-5. K—Klippe. 4°. *Leipzig, S. Hirzel*, 1864-67.

Grimshaw (William). An etymological dictionary, or analysis of the English language. viii pp. 154 l. 16°. *Philadelphia, Lydia R. Bailey,* 1821.

——— An exposition of the situation, character and interests of the American republic. 31 pp. 16°. *Philadelphia,* 1822.

——— The history of France, from the foundation of the monarchy to the death of Louis xvi. 302 pp. 16°. *Philadelphia, Towar & Hogan,* 1829.

——— History of the United States, from their first settlement as colonies to the cession of Florida, in 1821. 3d ed. 308 pp. 12°. *Philadelphia, L. R. Bailey,* 1822.

——— The same. To 1840. 336 pp. 12°. *Philadelphia, Grigg, Elliot & Co.* 1847. s.

——— The same. To the peace with Mexico, in 1848. 371 pp. 12°. *Philadelphia, Grigg, Elliot & Co.* 1849. s.

Grindlay (Robert Melville). Scenery, costumes, and architecture, chiefly on the western side of India. 2 v. 25 l. 18 pl; 37 l. 18 pl. fol. *London, Ackermann, and Smith, Elder & Co.* 1826–30.

Grisebach (August Heinrich Rudolph). Spicelegium flora rumelicæ et bithynicae. 2 v. xii, 407 pp. 8°. *Brunsvigae, Vieweg,* 1843–44. s.

——— Ueber die vegetationslinien des nord-westlichen deutschland. 104 pp. 8°. *Gottingen, Vandenhoeck & Ruprecht,* 1847. s.

Griswold (Rufus Wilmot). Napoleon and the marshals of the empire. [*anon.*] 2 v. 348 pp. 372 pp. 16 pl. 12°. *Philadelphia, Carey & Hart,* 1848. s.

Gritti *or* (Rocco Gritti). Dell' ottalmoscope e delle malattie end-oculari per esso riconoscibili. 440 pp. 6 pl. 8°. *Milano, Tipografia del patronato,* 1862. s.

Groans (The) of the plantations; or, a true account of their grievous and extreme sufferings by the heavy impositions upon sugar, and other hardships. Relating more particularly to the island of Barbados. 35 pp. sm. 4°. *London, M. Clark,* 1689.

Groesbeck (John). Crittenden commercial arithmetic and business manual. (Abridged edition.) 216 pp. 12°. *Philadelphia, E. C. & J. Biddle,* 1867.

Gröningen university. Catalogus librorum bibliothecæ universilatis quœ Groningae est curante J. R. Van Eerde. 3 pts. in 3 v. fol. *Groningae, I. Oomkens,* 1833–51. s.

Gronovius *or* **Grönhof** (Johann Friedrich). Lectiones plautinae, quibus non tantum fabulæ plautinæ et terentianæ, verum etiam Cæsar, Cicero, Livius, Virgilius, Ovidius, etc. illustrantur. Ac. vita auctoris. xxxvi, 398 pp. 8°. *Amstelædami, J. Hoffman,* 1740. s.

——— Flora virginica, exhibens plantas, quas Johannes Claytonius in Virginia crescentes observauit, collegit et obtulit. 6 p. l. 176 pp. 4 l. 1 map. 4°. *Lugduni Batavorum,* 1762. s.

Grose (*Captain* Francis). Advice to the officers of the British army: with some hints to the drummer and private soldier. [*anon.*] iv, 134 pp. 1 pl. 16°. *London, J. Kearsley,* 1783.

Gross (*Dr.* H.) Comparative materia medica. Edited by C. Hering. xxxii, 520 pp. 8°. *Philadelphia, F. E. Boericke,* 1867.

Gross (Samuel D.) A practical treatise on the diseases and injuries of the urinary bladder, prostate gland, and urethra. 826 pp. 8°. *Philadelphia, Blanchard & Lea,* 1851. s.

Grove (*Rev.* Henry). A system of moral philosophy. Published by Thomas Amory. 2 v. 24 p. l. 420 pp; 10 p. l. 610 pp. 10 l. 8°. *London, J. Waugh,* 1749.

Gruithuisen (Franz von Paula). Anthropologie, oder von der natur des menschlichen lebens und denkens. xxxx, 478 pp. 8°. *München, J. Lentner,* 1810. s.

——— Beyträge zur physiognosie und eautognosie. xxiii, 446 pp. 4 pl. 8°. *München, I. J. Lentner,* 1810. s.

——— Die naturgeschichte im kreise der ursachen und wirkungen; oder die physik historisch bearbeitet. xx, 276 pp. 1 tab. 8°. *München, J. Lentner,* 1810. s.

——— Naturgeschichte des gestirnten himmels. xxxvi pp. 13 l. 428 pp. 8°. *München, C. A. Fleischmann,* 1836. s.

——— Organozoonomie; oder, ueber das niedrige lebensverhältniss, als propädevtik zur anthropologie. xxiv, 239 pp. 1 tab. 8°. *München, I. J. Lentner,* 1811. s.

——— Siegfried, oder kurze biographie des verstandes bis auf dem zwist mit seinen kindern. 18°. *München, Lentner,* 1812. s.

——— Über die natur der kometen. 368 pp. 4 pl. 12°. *München, I. J. Lentner,* 1811. s.

Gründliche anweisung vögel auszustopfen, und besonders gut zu conserviren. [*anon.*] xxiv, 88 pp. 16°. *Leipzig, A. F. Böhme,* 1788. s.

Gruner (Carl Ernst, *editor*). Homœopathic pharmacopœia, compiled by order of the German central union of homœopathic physicians. Authorized English, from 2d German ed. x, 224 pp. 8°. *Leipzig, C. H. Arnold,* 1855. s.

Gruner (Christian Gottfried). Censvra librorvm hippocrateorvm, qva veri a falsis, integri a svppositis segregantvr. 9 p. l. 206 pp. 4 l. 8°. *Vratislaviae, J. F. Kornius*, 1772. s.

Gruson (L.) Blicke in das universum, mit specieller beziehung auf unsere erd. viii, 351 pp. 3 pl. 8°. *Leipzig, Gräbner*, 1853. s.

Gruter (Janus). *See* **Seneca**, *and* **Publius Syrus.** Singulares sententiae.

Guarini (Giovanni Battista). Madvigavx amovrevx. Traduits d'Italien en vers françois. Par monsieur P[icot]. 6 p. l. 178 pp. 18°. *Paris, Gvillavme de Lvynes*, 1664.

Guarini (Giovanni). Dizionario farmaceutico magistrale ed officinale, etc. 6ª ed. 6 p. l. 400 pp. 8°. *Napoli, V. Puzziello*, 1843. s.

Guasco (Ottavio de.) De l'usage des statues chez les anciennes. Essai historique. [*anon.*] xxiii, 505 pp. 2 l. 14 pl. 4°. *Bruxelles, J. L. de Boubers*, 1768.

Gubler (Adolphe). Études sur l'origine et les conditions de développement de la mucédinée du muguet (*oidium albicans*): mémoire. 75 pp. 8°. *Paris, Acad. imp. de médicine*, 1858. s.

Guégan (Henri). A compendious and easy grammar for teaching and learning the French language. xx, 52 pp. 8°. *Washington, P. Force*, 1831. s.

——— Tachygraphie; ou, art d'écrire aussi vite qu'on parle. 2e éd. 32 pp. 3 pl. 8°. *Paris, l'auteur*, 1818.

Guénon (François). A treatise on milch cows. Translated from the French, by N. P. Trist. With introductory remarks on the cow and the dairy. By John S. Skinner. 32, 24 pp. 8°. *New York, Greeley & McElrath*, 1846. s.

Guenot (C.) Vengeance of a Jew. [A tale]. 224 pp. 12°. *Philadelphia, E. Cummiskey*, 1867.

Guer (Jean Antoine). Mœurs et usages des Turcs, leur religion, leur gouvernement civil, militaire, et politiqve, avec un abrégé de l'histoire ottomane. 2 v. 493 pp; 547 pp. 27 pl. 4°. *Paris, Coustelier*, 1746–47.

Guéranger (Édouard). Leçons de chemie appliquées à l'agriculture. 3 p. l. iv, 584 pp. 4°. *Paris, Julien, Lanier & Cie.* 1850. s.

Guéranger (Prosper). Life of Saint Cecilia, virgin and martyr. Translated from the French. 404 pp. 12°. *Philadelphia, P. F. Cunningham*, 1866.

Guérin (Félix Édouard). Iconographie du "règne animal" de M. le baron Cuvier, ou représentation d'après nature, etc. 2 v. 8°. *Paris*, 1829, *etc.* s.
[Imperfect; v. i, and title of v. ii. wanting].

Guérin (Georges Maurice de). Journal, with an essay by Sainte Beuve. Edited by G. S. Trébutien. Translated by E. T. Fisher. 153 pp. 16°. *New York, Leypoldt & Holt*, 1867.

Guérin-Méneville (——). Insectes.
[*With* Lefebvre (C. T.) Voyage en Abyssinie. v. 6.]

Guernsey (Egbert). History of the United States of America. 7th ed. 456 pp. 12°. *New York, Cady & Burgess*, 1850. s.

Guettée (Réné François). The papacy; its historic origin and primitive relations with the eastern churches. Translated from the French, with biographical notice. With introduction, by A. C. Coxe. 383 pp. 12°. *New York, Carleton*, 1867.

Guevara (Antonio de). Vita, gesti, costvmi, discorsi, lettere di Marco Aurelio con la gionta di molte cose, che nello spagnuolo non erano, e delle cose spagnuole, che mãcauano nella tradottione italiana. [*anon.*] 148 l. 3 l. 18°. *Vinegia, F. di Aldo*, 1546.

Guggenbühl (Louis). The Abendberg, an Alpine retreat for the treatment of infant cretins. By L. G. [*anon.*] With introduction by J. Coldstream. 79 pp. 16°. *Edinburgh, W. P. Kennedy*, 1848. s.

Guicciardini (Francesco). Aphorisms, civill and militarie; amplified with authorities and exemplified with historie out of the first quarterne of Fr. Guiccardine. By Robert Dallington. 2d ed. 3 p. l. 339 pp. sm. fol. *London, R. Allot*, 1629.

——— A brief inference upon Gvicciardine's digression, in the fourth part of the first quarterne of his historie. Effaced out of the originall by the inquisition. 61 pp. sm. fol. *London, R. Allot*, 1629.
[*With* the preceding.]

Guichenot (Adolphe). Reptiles et poissons.
[*With* Lefebvre, (C. T.) Voyage en Abyssinie. v. 6].

Guide (A) to the Central park, New York. With a map of the proposed improvements. [*anon.*] 30 pp. 12°. *New York, C. M. Saxton, Barker & Co.* 1859.

Guide to the White mountains and the lakes of New Hampshire. [*anon.*] 72 pp. 16°. *Concord, (N. H.) Tripp & Osgood*, 1851. s.

Guide to West Point and the U. S. military academy. 105 pp. 1 pl. 4 maps. 18°. *New York, D. Van Nostrand*, 1867.

Guild (Reuben Aldridge). Biographical introduction to the writings of Roger Williams. 60 pp. 4°. *Providence, (R. I.)* 1866.
[Narragansett club publications. v. 1. pp. 1-60].

——— History of Brown university, with illustrative documents. xv, 443 pp. 5 pl. 4°. *Providence, Press Co.* 1867.

Guillaume d'Auvergne, (*abp. of Paris*). Postilla sup. epistolas et evangelia. 215 l. fol. [*Argentorati, about* 1469].

——— Tractatus de sacramentis, cur deus homo, et de penetencia. cxxxii l. fol. [*Norimbergæ, Anton Koburger*, 1496?]

——— [Tractatus] de vniverso. cxlix l. 1 l. unp. fol. [*Norimbergæ, Anton Koburger*, 1496?]

Guillaumin (Urbain Gilbert). Dictionnaire de l'économie politique. *See* **Coquelin** (C.) *and* **Guillaumin** (U. G.)

Guillelmus (Petrus). *See* **Guillaume** d'Auvergne.

Guillemin (Amédée). Causeries astronomiques. Les mondes; voyage pittoresque dans l'univers visible. xii, 336 pp. 12°. *Paris, Lévy*, 1861. s.

Guiteras (Pedro J.) Historia de la isla de Cuba; con notas e ilustraciones. 2 v. xvi, 417 pp; vi, 421 pp. 12°. *Nueva York, Jorge R. Lockwood*, 1865-66.

Guizot (Élisabeth Charlotte Pauline de Meulan). Les enfants: contes. Nouvelle éd. Augmentée de moralités en vers par Mlle. Élise Moreau. xi, 268 pp. 8 pl. 8°. *Paris, Didier*, 1862.

Guizot (François Pierre Guillaume). Histoire de la civilisation en France depuis la chute de l'empire romain. 3e éd. 4 v. 8°. *Paris, Didier*, 1843. s.

——— Histoire général de la civilisation en Europe. 5e éd. xiv, 435 pp. 1 pl. 8°. *Paris, Didier*, 1842. s.

——— Histoire de la révolution d'Angleterre, depuis l'avénement de Charles Ier jusqu'à sa mort. 3e éd. 2 v. xxxi, 395 pp; vi, 464 pp. 2 pl. 8°. *Paris, Didier*, 1841. s.

——— Mémoires pour servir à l'histoire de mon temps. 8 v. 8°. *Paris, Lévy*, 1858-66.

——— History of the English revolution of 1640, from the accession of Charles I to his death. Translated by William Hazlitt. 515 pp. 12°. *New York, Appletons*, 1846.

——— The last days of the reign of Louis Philippe. viii, 573 pp. 8°. *London, R. Bentley*, 1867.
[Forming v. 8 of the author's memoirs].

——— Meditations on the actual state of christianity, and the attacks which are now being made upon it. Translated. ix, 367 pp. 12°. *London, J. Murray*, 1866.

Gulzara, princess of Persia; or, the virgin queen. Collected from the original Persian. [*anon.*] xiii, 248 pp. 8°. *London, J. Souter*, 1816.

Gumaer (Peter E.) Thoughts and contemplations in relation to the motions of the heavenly bodies. 174 pp. 12°. *New York, W. J. Baner*, 1851. s.

Gumilla (José). Histoire naturelle, civile, et géographique de l'Orénoque et des principales rivières qui s'y jettent. Traduite de l'Espagnol sur la 2e éd. par M. Eidous. 3 v. 16°. *Avignon*, 1758.

Gundlach (Juan). Revista y catalogo de las aves cubanas. (Extract.) 110 pp. 1 tab. 8°. *Habana, Rep. fis. nat. de Cuba*, 1865-66. s.

——— Revista y catalogo de los mamiferos cubanos. Extract. (17 pp.) 8°. *Habana, Rep. fis. nat. de Cuba*, 1866. s.

Gunning (J. W.) Leerboek der scheikunde. 2 v. viii, 231 pp. 5 pl; viii, 244 pp. 1 pl. 12°. *Schoonhoven, S. E. Vanhooten*, 1858. s.

CONTENTS.

v. 1. De scheikunde der nietmetalen.
v. 2. De scheikunde der metalen.

Gunning (W. M.) Onderzoekingen over bloedsbeweging en stasis. 61 pp. 8°. *Utrecht, Schryver*, 1857. s.

Günther (Albert). Handbuch der medicinischen zoologie. viii, 244 pp. 8°. *Stuttgart, E. Schweizerbart*, 1858. s.

Gurley (*Rev.* Ralph Randolph.) Mission to England, in behalf of the American colonization society. xii, 264 pp. 12°. *Washington, Wm. W. Morrison*, 1841.

Gurney (John Henry). A descriptive catalogue of the raptorial birds in the Norfolk and Norwich museum. Part I, containing serpentariidæ, polyboridæ, vulturidæ. 90 pp. 8°. *Norwich, author*, 1864. s.

Gurney (Thomas). Brachygraphy: or an easy and compendious system of short-hand, improved by Joseph Gurney. 14th ed. 76, 12 pp. 18°. *London, W. B. Gurney*, 1817. s.

Gurowski (Adam). Diary: 1863-64-65. 413 pp. 12°. *Washington, W. H. & O. H. Morrison*, 1866.

Gustavus Selenus. (*pseudon.*) *See* **Mantia** *and* **Brunswick-Luneburg.**

Gutbier (Aegidius). Lexicon syriacum, continens omnes n[ovi] t[estamenti] syriaci dictiones et particulas, etc. vii p. l. 146 pp. xxv l. 16°. *Hamburg, Autor,* 1667.

——— Notæ criticæ in novum testamentum syriacum, etc. 55 pp. 16°. *Hamburgi,* 1667.
[*With his* Lexicon syriacum. 16°. 1667.]

Gutbier (Christian August von). *See* **Geinitz** (H. B.) Gäa von Sachsen.

Gutch (John Mathew). Observations, or notes, upon the writings of the ancients, and upon the introduction of the art of printing. 170 pp. 8°. *Bristol, J. M. Gutch,* 1827.

Guthrie (William). A new system of modern geography; or, a geographical, historical and commercial grammar. 1st Am. ed. 2 v. 572 pp; 704 pp. 49 maps. 4°. *Philadelphia, M. Carey,* 1795-96.

——— The same. With astronomical part by James Ferguson. x, 1,115 pp. 29 maps. 4°. *London, Rivington,* 1811.

Gütle (Johann Conrad). Kunst in kupfer zu stechen, zu raidiren, und zu aezen, etc. von Abraham Bosse. 3 v. in 1. 16°. *Nürnburg und Altdorf, J. C. Monath, und Kuszler,* 1795-96. s.

Gutteridge (William). The universal gauger of Great Britain and Ireland. xlvi, 504 pp. 12°. *London, Baldwin, Cradock & Co.* 1821.

Gutterson (A. C.) Cantata of the months and seasons; adapted to the closing of singing classes, day schools, etc.
[*With* PALMER (H. R.) The song queen. pp. 71-96.

Guyétant (Sébastien). Le guide médical des maitres et maitresses de pension, curés, dames de charité, et autres personnes, etc. 2e éd. vii, 419 pp. 8°. *Paris, L. Hachette,* 1842. s.

——— Le médecin de l'age de retour et de la vieillesse; ou, conseils aux personnes qui ont passé l'age de 45 ans. xvi, 487 pp. 8°. *Paris, Dufey,* 1836.

Guyot (Arnold). A collection of meteorological tables, with other tables useful in practical meteorology. 4 v. in 1. 8°. *Washington, Smithsonian Inst.* 1852. s.

Guyot (Guillaume Germain)? Nouvelles récréations physiques et mathématiques. [4e] éd. 92 pl. 3 v. 8°. *Paris,* 1799. s.

CONTENTS.

v. I. Aimant; électricité. xvi, 553 pp; 32 pl.
v. II. Géométrie et perspective: catoptrique; dioptrique; feu; air; air inflammable; eau. iii, 380 pp. 48 pl.
v. III. Nombres; adresse et combinaisons; mécanique; écriture occulte. 399 pp. 22 pl.

Guys (Henri). Voyage en Syrie; peinture des mœurs mussulmanes, chrétiennes et israélites. 412 pp. 8°. *Paris, J. Rouvier,* 1855. s.

Guzman (Fernan Perez de). Cronica del señor rey don Juan, segundo de este nombre, en Castilla y en Leon. xx, 636 pp. fol. *Valencia, B. Monfort,* 1779.

Haan (Willem de). Specimen philosophicum inaugurale, exhibens monographiam ammoniteorum et goniatiteorum. ii, 168 pp. 8°. *Lugduni Batavorum, H. W. Hazenberg,* 1825. s.

Haast (Julius, *provincial geologist*). Report on the formation of the Canterbury plains, [New Zealand]. 63 pp. 3 maps, etc. fol. *Christ Church, J. E. Fitzgerald,* 1864. s.

——— Report on the geological survey of the province of Canterbury. 31 pp. fol. *Christ Church, J. E. Fitzgerald,* 1864. s.

Hacker (William). Monitorial ritual for the order of high priesthood.
[pp. 73 to 192 of "CHAPTER and council manual." 24°. *Cincinnati, J. Ernst & Co.* 1867].

Hacket (John, *bishop of Lichfield*). Scrinia reserata: a memorial of John Williams, keeper of the great seal of England, etc. 2 parts in 1 v. 228, 239 pp. Portrait. fol. *London,* 1693.

Hackley (Charles W.) Elementary course of geometry. 12°. *New York, Harpers,* 1847. s.

——— A treatise on algebra, containing the latest improvements. xv, 504 pp. 8°. *New York, Harpers,* 1846. s.

——— School algebra. xi, 226 pp. 8°. *New York, Harpers,* 1847. s.

——— A treatise on trigonometry, plane and spherical, etc. with tables. xix, 372, pp. 60 l. unp. 8°. *New York, G. P. Putnam,* 1851. s.

Hadley (George). Grammatical remarks on the practical and current dialect of the jargon of Hindostan, with a vocabulary. 169 pp. 18°. [*London*], 1797. s.

Haeser (*Dr.* Heinrich). Historisch-pathologische untersuchungen. Als beiträge zur geschichte der volkskrankheiten. 2 v. xiii, 331 pp; xviii, 543 pp. 8°. *Leipzig, G. Fleischer,* 1841. s.

Hagen (Friedrich Heinrich von der). Nibelungen. Einzige handschrift der ältesten darstellung. 60 pp. 2 facs. 8°. *Berlin, J. A. Stargardt,* 1853.

Hagen (*Dr.* Friedrich Wilhelm). Physiologische untersuchungen. Studien im gebiete der physiologischen psychologie. iv, 96 pp. 8°. *Braunschweig, Vieweg,* 1847. s.

Hagen (G.) Über wellen auf gewässern von gleichmässiger tiefe. 79 pp. 1 pl. 4°. *Berlin, k. akad. der wissenschaften,* 1862. s.

Hagen (Hermann August). Bibliotheca entomologica. Die litteratur über das ganze gebiet der entomologie bis zum jahre 1862. 2 v. xii, 566 pp; 512 pp. 8°. *Leipzig, W. Engelmann,* 1862–63. s.

——— Monographie des caloptérygines, etc. *See* **Selys-Longchamps** *and* **Hagen.**

Hagn (Theodorich, *editor*). Urkundenbuch für die geschichte des benedictiner stiftes kremsmüenster, seiner pfarreien und besitzungen, 777–1400. viii, 404 pp. 8°. *Wien, k. hof- und staatsdruckerei,* 1852. s.

Haidinger (Wilhelm). Handbuch der bestimmenden mineralogie. 2e ausg. xxxvi, 630 pp. 8°. *Wien, W. Braumüller,* 1850.

Haig (James). Philosophy; or, the science of truth. xxvi, 303 pp. 12°. *London, Saunders, Otley & Co.* 1861.

Hailes (D. Dalrymple, *lord*). *See* **Dalrymple.**

Hair (T. H.) *and* **Ross** (M.) A series of views of the collieries in the counties of Northumberland and Durham, with descriptive sketches, and a preliminary essay on coal, and the coal trade. iv, 51 pp. 42 pl. fol. *Newcastle-upon-Tyne, Madden & Co.* 1844.

Hakluyt Society. Works issued by the society. v. 31–38. 8°. *London,* 1863–67.

CONTENTS.

ANDAGOYA (Pascual de). Narrative containing the earliest notice of Peru. Translated [from the Spanish], and edited by C. R. Markham. v. 34.
BARBOSA (Duarte). The coasts of east Africa and Malabar in the 16th century. From the Spanish, by H. E. J. Stanley. v. 35.
BARTHEMA (Ludovico di). Travels in Syria, Arabia, Persia, India, etc. 16th century. Translated [from the Italian], by J. W. Jones, and edited by Rev. G. P. Badger. v. 31.
CIEZA DE LEON (Pedro). Travels in 1532–50, from Darien to La Plata. Translated [from the Spanish], and edited by C. R. Markham. v. 33.
FROBISHER (*Sir* Martin). Three voyages, with a selection from letters in the state paper office. Edited by R. Collinson. v. 38.
JORDANUS *or* JOURDAN DE SERVREE (——, *friar*). Mirabilia descripta; wonders of the east. Translated from the Latin, and edited by H. Yule. v. 32.
YULE (Henry). Cathay, and the road thither. Translated and edited by H. Yule. v. 36–37.

Haldat Du Lys (Charles Nicolas Alexandre). Exposition de la doctrine magnétique; ou, traité philosophique, historique, et critique du magnétisme. viii, 320 pp. 8°. *Nancy, Grimblot & Raybois,* 1852. s.

Haldeman (Samuel Stehmann). Invertebrates.
[*With* BAIRD (Spencer F.) Outlines of zoology.]

Haldorsen (Björn). Lexicon islandico-latino-danicum. Cura R. K. Raskii editum. Præfatus est P. E. Müller. 2 v. in 1. xxxiv, 488 pp; 520 pp. 4°. *Havniæ, J. H. Schuboth,* 1814.

——— The same. 2 v. 4°. *Havniæ,* 1814. s.
[Imperfect; title-page of v. 1 wanting.]

Hale (Edwin M. *M. D.*) Homœopathic materia medica; or, the new remedies: their description and application. 2d ed. 1142 pp. 8°. *Detroit, E. A. Lodge,* 1867.

——— A systematic treatise on abortion. 347 pp. 2 pl. 8°. *Chicago, C. S. Halsey,* 1866.

Hale (*Rev.* George, *D. D.*) Sketches. *See* **Kirkpatrick** (*Rev.* Jacob, *jr.*) Kirkpatrick memorial, etc.

Hale (Lucretia P.) The lord's supper and its observance. [With preface by Rev. E. E. Hale.] 181 pp. 16°. *Boston, Walker, Fuller & Co.* 1866.

——— The service of sorrow. v, 249 pp. 16°. *Boston, American Unit. assoc.* 1867.

Hale (*Sir* Matthew). Contemplations, moral and divine. 2 pts. in 1 v. viii, 558 pp. 12°. *London, D. Brown* [*and others,*] 1711.

——— The primitive origination of mankind, considered and examined according to the light of nature. 5 p. l. 380 pp. 1 pl. fol. *London, W. Godbid,* 1677.

Hale (Salma). History of the United States, from their first settlement to the close of Mr. Tyler's administration in 1845. 326, 28 pp. 12°. *Cooperstown,* (*N. Y.*) *H. & E. Phinney,* 1846. s.

Halem (Gerhard Anton von). Geschichte des herzogthums Oldenburg. 3 v. 16°. *Oldenburg, G. Stalling,* 1794-96. s.

——— Statistisches hand-buch für das departement der Wesermundungen, 1813. xxii, 330 pp. 12°. *Bremen, G. Jöntzen,* [1813.] s.

Half tints. Table d'hôte and drawing room. [*anon.*] 232 pp. 12°. *New York, D. Appleton & Co.* 1867.

Half-yearly (The) abstract of the medical sciences; being an analytical and critical digest of the principal British and continental medical works, published in the preceding six months. Jan. 1865, to June, 1867. v. 41–45. 12°. *London, J. Churchill & sons,* 1867.

Halhed (Nathaniel Brassey, *M.P.*) A calculation on the commencement of the milennium; and a short reply to Dr. Horne's pamphlet entituled "Sound argument, dictated by common sense," with observations on the "Age of credulity." 28 pp. 18°. *Philadelphia, R. Campbell,* 1795.

Haliburton (Thomas Chandler). The old judge; or, life in a colony. 239 pp. 8°. *New York, Stringer & Townsend,* 1849.

Halifax, (1*st marquis of,* George Savile). *See* **Savile** (George).

Halifax (4*th earl of*). *See* **Montague** (Charles).

Hall (A. Oakey). Old Whitey's Christmas trot; a story for the holidays. 237 pp. sq. 16°. *New York, Harpers*, 1857. s.

Hall (Charles H. *D. D.*) True protestant ritualism; being a review of a book entitled "The law of ritualism." 210 pp. 16°. *Philadelphia, J. B. Lippincott & Co.* 1867.

Hall (Charles W.) Twice taken: an historical romance of the maritime British provinces. 242 pp. 16°. *Boston, Lee & Shepard*, 1867.

Hall (David). An epistle of love and caution to the quarterly and monthly meeting of friends in Great Britain, or elsewhere. 3d ed. 46 pp. 12°. *London, L. Hinde*, 1750.

Hall (Edward Brooks, *D. D.*) Memoir of Mary L. Ware, wife of Henry Ware, jr. 11th [ed.] vii, 434 pp. 1 pl. 12°. *Boston, Am. Unit. Assoc.* 1867.

——— Sermons; with a brief memoir. xviii, 162 pp. 16°. *Boston*, 1867.

Hall (Edward H.) Northern tour. *See* **Appleton** (D.) Hand-book of American travel.

Hall (*Col.* Francis). Colombia; its present state in respect of climate, soil, productions, population, government, commerce, revenue, manufactures, arts, literature, manners, education, and inducements to emigration. 131 pp. 12°. *Philadelphia, A. Small*, 1825. s.

Hall (Frederick, *M. D.*) Letters from the east and from the west. xi, 168 pp. 8°. *Washington, F. Taylor & W. M. Morrison*, 1840. s.

Hall (*Rev.* James). The pearl of great price. 139 pp. 12°. *New York, J. Miller*, 1867.

Hall (*Prof.* James, *of Albany, N. Y.*) Key to a chart of the successive geological formations, with an actual section from the Atlantic to the Pacific ocean. 72 pp. 18°. *Boston, Gould & Lincoln*, 1852. s.

——— Geological formations and organic remains.

[*With* Frémont (J. C.) Report of the exploring expedition to Rocky mountains in 1842, etc. Ed. *Washington*, 1845.]

——— Palæontology and geology.

[*With* Emory (W. H.) report on the U. S. and Mexican boundary survey, v. i.]

——— Reports on geology.

[New York. Annual reports on geol. survey. v. 2–5.]

Hall (*judge* James). The romance of western history. 420 pp. 1 pl. 12°. *Cincinnati, Applegate & Co.* 1857.

——— Statistics of the west, at the close of the year 1836. xviii, 284 pp. 12°. *Cincinnati, J. A. James & Co.* 1837.

——— The west; its commerce and navigation. vii, 328 pp. 16°. *Cincinnati, H. W. Derby & Co.* 1848.

Hall (John, *D. D.*) History of the presbyterian church in Trenton, N. J. from the first settlement of the town. 453, vii pp. 1 pl. 12°. *New York, A. D. F. Randolph*, 1859.

Hall (Joseph, *bishop of Norwich*). Satires. 8°. *Edinburgh*, 1793.

[Anderson's Brit. poets, v. 2.]

Hall (Joseph). The iron question, considered in connection with theory, practice, and experience, with special reference to "the Bessemer process." 73 pp. 2 pl. 8°. *London, Hamilton, Adams & Co.* 1857. s.

Hall (Marshall, *M. D.*) Aperçu du système spinal. 246 pp. 16°. *Paris, Masson*, 1855.

Hall (Samuel Carter). The baronial halls, picturesque edifices, and ancient churches of England. From drawings executed under the superintendence of Mr. Harding. v. 1–2. 4°. *London*, 1845–46. s.

[v. 3 wanting].

Hall (William). The abominations of mormonism exposed, containing facts and doctrines during seven years' residence among them, 1840–47. 155 pp. 16°. *Cincinnati, I. Hart & Co.* 1852.

Hall. *See* **Halle.**

Hallam (Henry). Introduction to the literature of Europe. 2 v. 416 pp; 462 pp. 8°. *New York, Harpers*, 1841.

——— View of the state of Europe during the middle ages. 4 v. 8°. *Philadelphia, J. Dobson & son*, 1821.

——— The same. Supplemental notes. xvi, 418 pp. 8°. *London, J. Murray*, 1848. s.

Halle *or* **Hall** (Edward). [Union of the two noble and illustre famelies of Lancastre and Yorke, with all the actes done in the tymes of bothe the one linage and of the other, beginnyng at the tyme of king Henry the fowerth, and proceadyng to the reigne of kyng Henry the eight. fol. *London, Richard Grafton*, 1548–50].

COLLATION.

Henry iv. xxxii l. table, 2 l. unp; Henry v. 51 pp. 2 l. Henry vi. cii, 3 l. Edward iv. lxi, 4 l. Edward v. xxiiii l. Henry iv. xxxii, 1 l. Richard iii. 2 l. Henry vii. lxi, 3 l. Henry viii. cclxiii, 9 l.

[Imperfect; wanting leaves previous to fol. 1, and the last 4 leaves of final table].

——— The same.

[Very imperfect].

Halleck (Henry Wager). Papers on practical engineering. Bitumen: its varieties and uses, compiled from various sources. 206 pp. 4 pl. 8°. *Washington, Peter Force*, 1841.

Haller (Albrecht von). Elementa physiologiæ corporis humani. 8 v. 4°. *Lausannæ, M. M. Bosquet, & Soc.* 1757–66. s.

CONTENTS.

v. i. Fibra; vasa; circuitus sanguinis; cor.
v. ii. Sanguis; ejus motus; humorum separatio.
v. iii. Respiratio; vox.
v. iv. Cerebrum; nervi; musculi.
v. v. Sensus, externi et interni.
v. vi. Deglutitio; ventriculus; omenta; lien; pancreas; hepar.
v. vii. Intestina; chylus; urina; semen; muliebria.
v. viii. Fetus hominisque vita.

——— Opera minora. 3 v. 4°. *Lausannæ,* 1762–68. s.

CONTENTS.

v. i. Anatomica: Partes corporis humani.
v. ii. Generatio.
v. iii. Opuscula pathologica.

——— Letters to his daughter on the truths of the christian religion. 2d ed. xxxii, 278 pp. 16°. *London, J. Murray,* 1793.

Haller (Gottlieb Emanuel von). Conseils pour former une bibliothèque historique de la Suisse. 18°. *Berne,* 1771.

Hallervord (Johann). Bibliotheca curiosa. 4 p. l. 415 pp. 4°. *Regiomonti et Francofurti, sumtibus M. Hallervordi,* 1676. s.

Halliday (Samuel B.) The little street sweeper; or, life among the poor. 356 pp. 1 pl. 12°. *New York, Phinney, Blakeman & Mason,* 1861. s.

Halliwell (James Orchard). Brief description of the ancient and modern manuscripts preserved in the public library, Plymouth, [England], with some fragments of early literature hitherto unpublished. 239 pp. 4°. *London, C. & J. Adlard,* 1853. s.

——— Catalogue of chap-books, garlands, and popular histories. iv, 190 pp. 12°. *London,* 1849.

——— Dictionary of archaic and provincial words. 2d ed. 2 v. viii, 960 pp. 8°. *London, J. R. Smith,* 1850.

——— Some account of a collection of several thousand bills, accounts, and inventories, illustrating the history of prices between the years 1650 and 1750, with copious extracts from old account books. 4°. *London, privately printed,* 1852. s.

[*Note.*—The originals of this collection form fifty-four volumes, and are deposited in the library of congress.]

Hallowell (Me.) Directory for 1867–68. *See* **Augusta**, Hallowell, and Gardiner directory for 1867–68.

Halls of the Montezumas: or, Mexico in ancient and modern times. [*anon.*] 136 pp. 4 pl. 8°. *New York, J. C. Burdick,* 1848.

Halsted (*rear admiral* Edward Pellew). A turret navy for the future; an appeal to the parliament of 1866. 18 pp. 1 pl. 4°. [*London, author*], 1866.

Halsted (Oliver Spencer). Theology of the Bible; itself the teacher, and its own interpreter. [A critical essay on the meaning of the words, soul, spirit, ghost, death, paradise, hell, satan, devil, heaven, and resurrection]. iv, 632 pp. 8°. *Newark, (N. J.) the author,* 1866.

——— The same. 2d ed. With appendix. xvi, 632, xii pp. 8°. *Newark, author,* 1866.

Hamberger (Georg Christoph). Das gelehrte Teutschland; oder, lexicon der jetzt lebenden schriftsteller. Fortgesetzt von J. G. Meusel, J. S. Ersch, und J. N. S. Lindner. 5te ausg. 23 v. in 24. 12°. *Lemgo, Meyer,* 1796–1834.

Hamburg. Hamburgische rath-und bürgerschlüsse, 1856, 1859, 1861. 3 v. 4°. *Hamburg,* [*Rathe,*] 1857–62. s.

——— Hamburgischer botanischer garten. Verzeichniss von hauspflanzen, staudengewächsen, bäumen und gesträuchen welche abgegeben werden können. 79 pp. 8°. *Hamburg, J. A. Meissner,* 1853. s.

——— Katalog der commerz-bibliothek. vi, viii, 618, xix pp. 4°. *Hamburg, H. G. Voigt,* 1841. s.

Hamilton (Alexander). Letter concerning the public conduct and character of John Adams. 2d ed. 54 pp. 8°. *New York, John Lang,* 1800.

[*With* ADAMS (John). Correspondence, *Boston,* 1809.]

——— *and* **Madison** (James). Letters of Pacificus and Helvidius on the proclamation of neutrality of 1793, [with] the proclamation. 102 pp. 8°. *Washington, J. and G. S. Gideon,* 1845.

Hamilton (*Mrs.* Cospatrick Baillie). Views in the Mediterranean, Grecian archipelago, Bosphorus, Black sea, etc. 12 pl. col. fol. *London, Day & son,* 1857.

Hamilton (G. *M. D.*) Elements of vegetable and animal physiology. Edited by D. M. Reese. 2 v. in 1. 162, 144 pp. 12°. *New York, A. S. Barnes and Co.* 1849. s.

Hamilton (*Mrs.* Jane). Leaves gathered in the daily walks of life. By the compiler of "Drifted snow flakes," etc. [*anon.*] 224 pp. sq. 18°. *Philadelphia, author,* [1867].

Hamilton (William, *of Bangour*). Poems on several occasions. 262 pp. 16°. *Edinburgh, W. Gordon,* 1760.

——— Poetical works. 8°. *Edinburgh,* 1794.

[Anderson's Brit. poets, v. 9.]

Hamilton (*Sir* William). Collection of Etruscan, Greek, and Roman antiquities from [his] cabinet [Fr. and Eng. text, by D'Hancarville]. 4 v. fol. *Naples*, 1766–67.
[Imperfect: v. 3–4 wanting.]

——— Collection of engravings from ancient vases, mostly of fine Greek workmanship, discovered in the kingdom of the two Sicilies. [Fr. and Eng.] Published by W. Tischbein. 4 v. fol. *Naples*, 1791–95.
[Continuation of the preceding. v. 4 wanting.]

——— Observations on mount Vesuvius, mount Etna, and other volcanos. 2d ed. iv, 179 pp. 1 map. 4 pl. 12°. *London, T. Cadell*, 1773.

Hamilton (*Rev.* William). Letters concerning the northern coast of the county of Antrim. Containing a natural history of its basaltes. viii, 195 pp. 1 map. 8°. *London, G. Robinson & Co.* 1786. s.

Hamilton (*Rev.* William), *and* **Irvin** (*Rev.* S. M.) An Ioway grammar, illustrating the principles of the language used by the Ioway, Otoe, and Missouri Indians. 152 pp. 18°. *Ioway & Sac mission, (Iowa?)* 1848. s.

Hamley (Edward Bruce). Lady Lee's widowhood. New ed. 416 pp. 12 pl. 12°. *Edinburgh, Blackwood & sons*, 1856.

——— The same. [*anon.*] 148 pp. 8°. *New York, Harpers*, 1853.

Hamm (*Dr.* Wilhelm). Lust, lob und trost der edlen landwirthschaft. Lieder und lebensbuch fur die landwirth. xv, 307 pp. 16°. *Frankfurt-a-M. J. D. Sauerländer*, 1862. s.

Hammarsköld (Laurentius). Svenska viiterheten. Historiskt-kritiska anteckningar. 2ª upplagan, af P. A. Sonden. xvi, 647 pp. 8°. *Stockholm, Q. Hæggström*, 1833. s.

——— Utkast till de bildande konsternas historia, i foerelaesningar. x, 460 pp. 12°. *Stockholm, O. Grahn*, 1817. s.

Hammer-Purgstall (Joseph von). Über die länderverwaltung unter dem Chalifate. [Extract.] xiv, 264 pp. 8°. *Berlin, K. akad. d. wissenschaften*, 1835. s.

Hammond (James). Love elegies. 30 pp. 16°. *Edinburgh, W. Ruddiman*, 1759.
[Select collection modern poems. *Edinburgh*, 1758.]

——— Poetical works. 8°. *Edinburgh*, 1794.
[Anderson's Brit. poets, v. 8.]

Hammond (Samuel H.) Wild northern scenes; or, sporting adventures with the rifle and the rod. 341 pp. 4 pl. 12°. *New York, Derby & Jackson*, 1857.

Hammond (William A. *M. D.*) Experimental researches relative to the nutritive value and physiological effects of albumen, starch, and gum, when singly and exclusively used as food. 79 pp. 8°. *Philadelphia, author*, 1857. s.

——— On sleep and insomnia. [Extract.] 36 pp. 8°. *New York, Medical journ.* 1865. s.

——— Treatise on hygiene, with special reference to the military service. 604 pp. 1 pl. 8°. *Philadelphia, Lippincott*, 1863. s.

Hamon (Henry). New York stock exchange manual. 405 pp. 12°. *New York, J. F. Trow*, 1865.

Hamond (Walter). Paradox. Proving that the inhabitants of Madagascar, or St. Laurance, (in temporall things,) are the happiest people in the world; with a briefe description of that island. 2 p. l. 16 l. sm. 4°. *London, N. Butter*, 1640.

Hampole, *or*, **Pampolitanus** (Richard). *See* **Rolle**, (*of Hampole*).

Hampson (R. T.) Origines patriciæ; or a deduction of European titles, of nobility and dignified offices, from their primitive sources. xv, 428 pp. 8°. *London, H. C. Causton*, 1846.

Hamst (Olphar; *anagram for* Thomas Ralph, *or* Ralph Thomas?) A martyr to bibliography: a notice of the life and works of Joseph-Marie Quérard, bibliographer. 48 pp. 8°. *London, J. R. Smith*, 1867.

Hanaford (*Mrs.* Phebe Ann). The captive boy in Terra del Fuego; being an authentic narrative of the loss of the ship Manchester, and the adventures of the sole white survivor. 231 pp. 4 pl. 16°. *New York, Carlton & Porter*, [1867].

——— Frank Nelson; or, the runaway boy. 296 pp. 16°. *Boston, W. H. Hill*, 1866.

Hancock (John). The constitution and government of the United States; with questions and answers. With the late amendments. xiv, 130 pp. 1 pl. 18°. *Philadelphia, King & Baird*, 1867.

Hancock (Sallie J.) The Montanas: or, under the stars. A romance. 320 pp. 12°. *New York, Carleton*, 1866.

Haney (Jesse C.) Guide to authorship; [with] instructions in composition, hints as to preparation of mss. etc. 110 pp. 12°. *New York, Haney & Co.* [1867].

——— Phonographic hand-book: being an introduction to Munson's complete phonographer. 71 pp. 12°. *New York, J. C. Haney & Co.* [1867].

Hanin (L.) Nouveaux élémens de botanique. 2ᵉ éd. xx, 204, 9 pp. 16°. *Paris, Crochard*, 1812. s.

Hankel (W. G.) Elektrische untersuchungen. I. Über die messung der atmosphärischen elektricität nach absolutem maase. [Extract.] 222 pp. 2 pl. 8°. *Leipzig, K. S. Ges. d. wissenschaften,* [1857]. s.

Hankey (Thomson). The principles of banking, its utility and economy; with remarks on the working and management of the bank of England. 123 pp. 8°. *London, E. Wilson,* 1867.

Hanley (Sylvanus). An illustrated and descriptive catalogue of recent bivalve shells. Forming an appendix to the index testaceologicus. xviii, 392 pp. 16 pl. 8°. *London, Williams & Norgate,* 1842–56. s.

——— Ipsa Linnæi conchylia. The shells of Linnæus, determined from his manuscripts and collections. 556 pp. 5 pl. col. 8°. *London, Williams & Norgate,* 1855. s.

Hanna (John Smith). A history of the life and services of captain Samuel Dewees. Also, reminiscences of the revolutionary struggle and late war with Great Britain. 360 pp. 1 pl. 16°. *Baltimore, Robert Neilson,* 1844.

Hannett (John). Bibliopegia; or, the art of bookbinding, in all its branches. 4th ed. 166 pp. 11 pl. 12°. *London, Simpkin, Marshall & Co.* 1848. s.

Hansard's parliamentary debates. 3d series. April 27, 1866, to June 17, 1867. v. 183–187. 5 v. 8°. *London, C. Buck,* 1863–67.

Hansen (Peter Andreas). Tables de la lune, construites d'après la principe newtonien de la gravitation universelle. 10 p. l. 511 pp. 4°. *Londres, Eyre & Spottiswoode,* 1857. s.

——— Ueber die chronometer, etc. 55 pp. 8°. *Altona, Perthes & Besser,* 1836. s.
[*With* NAUMANN (C. F.) Table of mineralogical species, 1833].

Hanson (J. W.) History of the old towns Norridgewock and Canaan, comprising Norridgewock, Canaan, Starks, Skowhegan, and Bloomfield, [Maine], to the year 1849. 371 pp. 12°. *Boston, Coolidge & Wiley,* 1849.

Hanssen (Lorens). Grönlandsfarerne i aaret 1777, en fœdrenelandsk tildragelse. xix pp. 4 l. 143 pp. 16°. *Fridericia, G. Elmenhoff,* 1806.

Hanway (Jonas). Historical account of the British trade over the Caspian Sea; with journal of travels from England through Russia and Persia and back; with the revolutions of Persia and history of Nadir [Shah] Kouli. 2d ed. 2 v. xxvii, 468 pp. 9 maps. 20 pl. 4 l; xx, 460 pp. 9 l. 1 map. 7 pl. 4°. *London, T. Osborne,* 1754. s.

Hanway (Jonas). The revolutions of Persia. [1707—1750]. 2 v. xv, 255 pp; vii, 301 pp. 10 l. 1 map. 1 pl. 4°. *London, Dodsley,* 1753.
[v. 3 and 4 of his historical account of British trade over the Caspian, etc.]

Happel (Eberhard Guerner). Mundus mirabilis tripartitus; oder, wunderbare welt in einer kurtzen cosmographia fürgestellet. 3 v. 3 maps. sm. 4°. *Ulm, M. Wagner,* 1687–89.

Harbaugh (Henry). Heaven; or, an earnest and scriptural inquiry into the abode of the sainted dead. 8th ed. 290 pp. 12°. *Philadelphia, Lindsay & Blakiston,* 1853.

——— Youth in earnest; as illustrated in the life of Theodore David Fisher. 238 pp. 16°. *Philadelphia, S. R. Fisher & Co.* 1867.

Harbin (George). The hereditary right of the crown of England asserted, and the true English constitution vindicated from the misrepresentations of Dr. Higden. By a gentleman. [*anon.* Attributed to Hilkiah Bradford]. 4 p. l. 274, lxiii pp. fol. *London, R. Smith,* 1713.

Harbison (Massy). Narrative of [her] sufferings from Indian barbarity. Communicated by herself. With some account of the history, etc. of the Indians. Edited by John Winter. 4th ed. 12°. *Beaver, (Penn.)* 1836.

Harcourt (Robert). A relation of a voyage to Guiana. 8 p. l. 71 pp. sm. 4°. *London, W. Welby,* 1613.

Hardcastle (Lewis B.) The young American's elocutionist. vii, 150 pp. 12°. *New York, C. Shepard & Co.* 1854. s.

Hardegg (Leopold Ferdinand). Dissertatio inauguralis, sistens observationes quasdam de vario arsenici in animalia effectu. 28 pp. 8°. *Tubingæ, auctor,* 1817. s.

Hardenberg (Carl August, *prinz* von). *See* **Mémoires** d'un homme d'état.

Harding (James D.) Picturesque views of Ireland. *See* **Newenham** (R. O'C.)

Hardinge (George). Miscellaneous works in prose and verse. Edited by J. Nichols. 3 v. 8°. *London, J. Nichols,* 1818.

CONTENTS.

v. 1. Memoirs of the author.
Charges in the courts of general sessions.
Eighteen sermons by a layman.
Speeches.
Substance of letters to Edmund Burke.
v. 2. Poetical works.
v. 3. Miscellanies in prose.

Hardt (Ignaz). Catalogus codicum manuscriptorum bibliothecæ regiæ bavaricæ. [Codices græci]. Edidit, notisque illustravit I. C. L. baro de Aretin. 5 v. 4°. *Monachii, J. E. Seidel,* 1806–12. s.

Hardwich (T. Frederick). A manual of photographic chemistry. 6th ed. 12°. *London, J. Churchill,* 1861. s.

Hardy (Philip Dixon). Wellington: a poem. 103 pp. 4°. *London, K. Causton,* 1814.

Hardy (Thomas Duffus). Report to the master of the rolls, upon the documents in the archives and public libraries of Venice. 107 pp. 8°. *London, Longmans,* 1866.

Hare (Thomas). The election of representatives, parliamentary and municipal. 3d ed. xlvii, 350 pp. 12°. *London, Longmans,* 1865.

Harford (John Scandrett.) Life of Thomas Burgess, bishop of Salisbury. xv, 557 pp. 1 pl. 8°. *London, Longmans,* 1840.

Harkness (Albert). An introductory Latin book. ix, 162 pp. 12°. *New York, D. Appleton & Co.* 1866.

Harleian miscellany (The): or, a collection of scarce, curious, and entertaining pamphlets and tracts, as well in manuscript as in print, found in the late earl of Oxford's library. Interspersed with historical, political, and critical notes [by W. Oldys. 1st ed.] 8 v. 4°. *London, T. Osborne,* 1744–46.

——— A selection from the Harleian miscellany of tracts, which principally regard the English history; of which many are referred to by Hume. vii, 571 pp. fol. *London, C. & G. Kearsley,* 1793.

Harless (Emil, *M.D.*) Populäre vorlesungen aus dem gebiet der physiologie und psychologie. x, 293 pp. 8°. *Braunschweig, Vieweg,* 1851. s.

Harless (Gottlieb Christoph). Introdvctio in historiam lingvæ græcæ. Ed. alt. 2 v. in 3. 8°. *Altenburgi, Richter,* 1792–95. s.

——— Supplementa ad introductionem in historiam lingvæ Græcæ. 2 v. [in 1.] iv, 382 pp; viii, 390 pp. 8°. *Jenæ, Bibliop. acad.* 1804–06. s.

Harlow (S. R.), *and* **Boone** (H. H.) Life sketches of the state officers, senators, and members of the assembly of the state of New York, in 1867. 418 pp. 1 pl. 8°. *Albany, Weed, Parsons & Co.* 1867.

Harnisch (C.) Bildliche darstellungen in arabeskenform zu Göethe's Faust. Text, 4 pp. 6 pl. fol. *Berlin, G. Reimer,* 1832.

Harper (L.) Preliminary report on the geology and agriculture of the state of Mississippi. vii, 351 pp. 1 col. map. 7 pl. etc. 8°. *Jackson, state printer,* 1857. s.

Harper's hand-book for travellers in Europe and the East. By W. Pembroke Fetridge. 6th year. 12°. *New York, Harpers,* 1867.

——— New monthly magazine, Dec. 1866 to Nov. 1867. v. 34–35. 8°. *New York, Harper & Bros.* 1865–67.

——— Weekly. A journal of civilization. Jan. 1866, to Dec. 1867. v. 10–11. fol. *New York, Harper & Bros.* 1866–67.

Harrington (J.) Josephine; or, the Romish poison. 102 pp. 8°. *New York, Burgess & Day,* [*about* 1850].

Harris (*Mrs.* Caroline). History of [her] captivity and providential release [from the Camanche Indians]. 24 pp. 1 pl. 8°. *New York, Perry & Cook,* 1838.

Harris (Chapin A. *M. D.*) Dictionary of dental science, biography, bibliography and medical terminology. 780 pp. 8°. *Philadelphia, Lindsay & Blakiston,* 1849. s.

——— The same. A dictionary of medical terminology, dental surgery, and the collateral sciences. 3d ed. revised by F. J. S. Gorgas, M. D. 743 pp. 8°. *Philadelphia, Lindsay & Blakiston,* 1867.

Harris (Elijah P.) The chemical constitution and chronological arrangement of meteorites. 132 pp. 8° *Göttingen, W. F. Kaestner,* 1859. s.

Harris (George W.) Sut Lovingood. Yarns spun by a nat'ral born durn'd fool. 299 pp. 12°. *New York, Dick & Fitzgerald,* 1867.

Harris (John, *D. D. F. R. S.*) Remarks on some late papers relating to the universal deluge, and to the natural history of the earth. 10 p. l. 270 pp. 12°. *London, R. Wilkin,* 1697.

Harris (John, *D. D. pres. of new college, London.*) Mammon; or, covetousness the sin of the Christian church. 10th ed. xvi, 311 pp. 8°. *London, T. Ward & Co.* 1836.

Harris (Thaddeus Mason, *D.D.*) A masonic eulogy, 1794. 16 pp. 4°. *Worcester, Isaiah Thomas,* 1794.

——— A textuary; or, guide to preachers in the selecting of texts. 40 pp. 8°. *Boston, Cummings & Hilliard,* 1818.

Harris (Thaddeus William). Insects of Massachusetts. s.

[*In* HITCHCOCK (E.) Catalogue of animals, etc. of Mass.]

——— A treatise on some of the insects of New England, injurious to vegetation. 2d ed. viii, 513 pp. 8°. *Boston, White & Potter,* 1852. s.

Harris (William, *D. D.*) Historical and critical account of the life and writings of Charles I. 4 p. l. 428 pp. 8°. *London, R. Griffith,* 1758.

Harris (William *D. D.*) Historical and critical account of the life and writings of James I. xv, 255 pp. 2 l. 8°. *London, J. Waugh,* 1753.

——— Historical and critical account of the life of Oliver Cromwell. With appendix. 2d ed. 4 p. l. 543 pp. 8°. *London, W. Strahan,* 1772. s.

Harris (William Cornwallis). Wild sports of Southern Africa. 5th ed. xxvi, 359 pp. 1 map. 26 pl. 8°. *London, H. G. Bohn,* 1852.

Harris (*Sir* William Snow). Rudimentary treatise on magnetism. 2 v. in 1. viii, 159 pp. 1 pl; vi, 186 pp. 12°. *London, J. Weale,* 1850–52. s.

Harrison (*Capt.* David). The melancholy narrative of [his] distressful voyage and miraculous deliverance, on his voyage from Fayal to New York. Written by himself. 1 p. l. 67 pp. 8°. *London, James Harrison,* 1766.

Harrison (Joseph, *jr.*) Essay on the steam boiler; [also] report of committee, constituted by the Franklin institute, on the Harrison boiler, and list of patents for improvements in steam boilers. 219 pp. 7 pl. 16°. *Philadelphia, J. B. Lippincott & Co.* 1867.

Harrison (W. H.) Montfort: a poem. 94 pp. 16°. *London, Smith and Elder,* 1818.
[*With* TAYLOR (George). Mental claims of the sexes. *London,* 1821].

Harrisson (David, *jr.*) Voice from the Washingtonian home; an institution for the reformation of the inebriate. xii, 322 pp. 1 pl. 12°. *Boston, Redding & Co.* 1860.

Harsha (David Addison). Life of Philip Doddridge, D. D. with notices of some of his cotemporaries and specimens of his style. 249 pp. 1 pl. 8°. *Albany, J. Munsell,* 1865.

Hart (Adolphus M.) Life in the far west; or, the comical, quizzical, and tragical adventures of a hoosier. 131 pp. 8°. *Cincinnati, H. B. Pearson,* [*about* 1854].

Hart (Joseph C.) The romance of yachting: voyage the first. 2 pts in 1 v. 332 pp. 12°. *New York, Harpers,* 1849.

Hartcliffe (John). Treatise of the moral and intellectual virtues. 24 p. l. 414 pp. 16°. *London, C. Harper,* 1691.

Harte (F. Bret, *pseudon?*) Condensed novels, and other papers. Comic illustrations by F. Bellew. 307 pp. 6 pl. 12°. *New York, Carleton,* 1867.

Harte (Henry H.) Notes. *See* **Laplace** (P. S.) Treatise on celestial mechanics.

Harte (Walter). Poetical works. 8°. *Edinburgh,* 1794.
[Anderson's Brit. poets, v. 9].

Hartford (Conn.) Geer's Hartford city directory for 1867–68. Compiled by E. Geer. 533 pp. 1 map. 16°. *Hartford, (Conn.) steam printing co.* 1867.

——— Hartford young men's institute. Catalogue of the library and reading room. 359 pp. 8°. *Hartford, Case, Tiffany & Burnham,* 1844. s.

——— ——— Catalogue of books added to the library since 1844. 32 pp. 8°. *Hartford, Case, Tiffany & Burnham,* 1848.
[*With* catalogue of 1844].

Hartig (Ernst). Untersuchungen über die heizkraft der steinkohlen Sachsens. Unter aufsicht von J. B. Schneider, ausgeführt und bearbeitet. [Nebst] die heizversuche des Dr. [P. W.] Brix. x, 589 pp. 4 pl. 4°. *Leipzig, W. Engelmann,* 1860. s.
[*With* STEINKOHLEN (Die) des königreichs Sachsen, etc. v. 3].

Harting (Pieter). Das mikroskop. Theorie, gebrauch, geschichte und gegenwärtiger zustand desselben. Aus d. hollandischen von F. W. Theile. xix, 950 pp. 1 pl. 8°. *Braunschweig, Vieweg,* 1859. s.

——— The same. Deutsche originalausgabe, vom verfasser revidirt und vervollständigt. Herasugegeben von F. W. Theile. 2ᵉ aufl. 3 v. 8°. *Braunschweig, F. Vieweg & sohn,* 1866. s.

Hartlaub (Gustav.) Systematischer index zu Felix de Azara's Apuntamientos para la historia natural de los páxaros del Paraguay y Rio de la Plata. vi, 29 pp. 4°. *Bremen, C. Schünemann,* 1847. s.

——— *See* **Finsch** (O.) *and* **Hartlaub.**

Hartley (John). Researches in Greece and the Levant. 2d ed. 5 p. l. unp. 383 pp. 2 maps. 12°. *London, Seeley & Burnside,* 1833.
[Imperfect; 1 map wanting].

Hartmann (Carl Friedrich Alexander). Der autodidaktische mineralog; oder leichtfassliche anleitung zum selbststudium der mineralogie. vi, 286 pp. 7 pl. 8°. *Leipzig, E. Schäfer,* 1854. s.

——— Der heutige standpunkt des deutschen eisenhüttengewerbes in statistischer und ökonomisch-technischer beziehung; sowie vergleichung der eisenhütten-industrien in Britannien, Belgien, Frankreich, Schweden, u. s. w. xii, 263 pp. 6 tab. 8°. *Leipzig, Veit & Co.* 1861. s.

——— Mineralogie, in sechs und zwanzig vorlesungen. xxvi, xlviii, 452 pp. 8°. *Ilmenau, B. F. Voigt,* 1829. s.

Hartmann (Moritz). The last days of a king; an historical romance. Translated from the German, by M. E. Niles. 198 pp. 12°. *Philadelphia, J. B. Lippincott & Co.* 1857.

Hartshorne (Henry, *M. D.*) Essentials of the principles and practice of medicine. A handy book for students and practitioners. 417 pp. 12°. *Philadelphia, H. C. Lea,* 1867.

Hartt (C. Frederick). Fossils, etc.
[*With* BAILEY (L. W.) Geology of southern New Brunswick].

Harvard College. Catalogue of the library. [By B. Peirce]. With 1st supplement. 4 v. 8°. *Cambridge, (Mass.) E. W. Metcalf & Co.* 1830–34. s.

——— A catalogue of the law library. 4th ed. 354 pp. 8°. *Cambridge, Metcalf & Co.* 1846. s.

——— Catalogus collegii harvardiani, seu universitatis cantabrigiensis. xv, 110, 51 pp. 8°. *Cantabrigiæ, Acad. typogr.* 1848. s.

——— The same. Catalogus senatus academici et eorum qui honoribus academicis donati sunt xxi, 150, 48 pp. 8°. *Cantabrigiæ,* 1860. s.

——— Pietas et gratulatio collegii cantabrigiensis apud Novanglos, cum Georgius tertius regnare incipit. [*anon.*] xiv, 106 pp. 4°. *Bostoniæ, J. Green et J. Russell,* 1761.

Harvey (Gideon, *M. D.*) Morbus anglicus; or, the anatomy of consumptions. 2d ed. 128 pp. 1 pl. 16°. *London, T. Johnson,* 1672.

——— Discourse of the plague; its nature, causes, etc. 2d ed. 16°. *London,* 1673.
[Pp. 129–144 of his Morbus anglicus; imperfect.]

Harvey (Henry). History of the Shawnee Indians, from 1681 to 1854. 316 pp. 16°. *Cincinnati, E. Morgan & sons,* 1855.

Harvey (William Henry). A manual of the British marine algæ. lii, 252 pp. 27 col. pl. 8°. *London, J. Van Voorst,* 1849. s.

Hasler & Co. Beschreibung der münsterkirche und ihrer merkwürdigkeiten in Basel, mit abbildungen. 22 pp. 18 pl. fol. *Basel, Hasler & Cie.* 1842. s.

Hassaurek (Friedrich). Four years among Spanish-Americans. x, 401 pp. 12°. *New York, Hurd & Houghton,* 1867.

Hassell (J.) Drawing magazine. [plates.] 4 v. 16°. [*London, about* 1850].

Hastings (Sally). Poems; to which is added an account of a tour to the west in 1800. 220 pp. 16°. *Lancaster,* [*Pa.*] *W. Dickson,* 1808.

Hastings (Thomas, *engraver*). Etchings from the works of Ric. Wilson, with some memoirs of his life. 19 pp. 39 pl. 4°. *London, Hurst, Robinson & Co.* 1825.

Hastings (Thomas), *and* **Warriner** (Solomon). Musica sacra; or, Springfield and Utica collections united; consisting of psalm and hymn tunes, anthems and chants. 2d ed. iv pp. 136 l. unp. 8°. *Utica, William Williams,* 1819.

Hastings (Warren). The answer to the articles exhibited by the knights, citizens, and burgesses in parliament assembled, in maintenance of their impeachment against him for high crimes and misdemeanours. 261 pp. 8°. *London, J. Murray,* 1788.

Haswell (Charles H.) Engineers' and mechanics' pocket-book. 21st ed. 663 pp. 16°. *New York, Harper & Bros.* 1867.

Hatborough (Pa.) Union library company. The charter and laws, with a catalogue of books. 6th ed. 116 pp. 18°. *Norristown, (Pa.) National defender office,* 1858. s.

Hatin (Louis Eugène). Bibliographie historique et critique de la presse périodique française, [1631–1865]. 2 p. l. cxvii, 660 pp. 1 pl. 8°. *Paris, Didot,* 1866.

Hau Kiou choaan [*or*, choaon, the accomplished woman], or the pleasing history. A translation from the Chinese language. [Also] the argument of a Chinese play, a collection of Chinese proverbs, and fragments of Chinese poetry. [Re-translated from a Portuguese Ms. by Tho. Percy, bishop of Dromore]. With notes. 4 v. 12°. *London, R. & J. Dodsley,* 1761.

Haug (Martin). *See* **Rig-Veda-Sanhita.**

Haughton (*Rev.* Samuel, *prof. of geol. Dublin univ.*) Outlines of a new theory of muscular action. 27 pp. 12°. *London, Williams & Norgate,* 1863. s.

——— The solar and lunar diurnal tides of the coasts of Ireland. (Extract). 109 pp. 4°. *Dublin, royal Irish academy,* 1855. s.

Haupt (Leopold), *and* **Schmaler** (Johann Ernst). Volkslieder der Wenden in den Ober- und Nieder-Lausitz. 2 v. xvi, 392 pp; xii, 332 pp. 5 pl. 4°. *Grimma, J. M. Gebhardt,* 1841–43. s.

Hauranne (Prosper Duvergier de). *See* **Duvergier** de Hauranne.

Hauréau (Jean Barthélemy). Singularités historiques et littéraires. iii, 325 pp. 16°. *Paris, Lévy,* 1861.

Haussez (Charles Lemercher de Longpré, *baron* d'). Great Britain in 1833. 2 v. 212 pp; 200 pp. 12°. *Philadelphia, Carey, Lea & Blanchard,* 1833.

Havana. Memoria acerca del estado de la enseñanza en la universidad de la Habana desde su fundacion hasta Octubre de 1864. 162 pp. 8°. *Habana,* [*universidad*], 1865. s.

Haven (Alice Bradley). Good report: morning and evening lessons for lent. 318 pp. 16°. *New York, Appletons,* 1867.

Haven (C. C.) Annals of the city of Trenton, [N. J.] with random remarks and historic reminiscences. 31 pp. 8°. *Trenton, N. J.* 1866. [*With* his Thirty days in N. J. ninety years ago].

——— Thirty days in New Jersey ninety years ago: an essay revealing new facts in connection with Washington and his army, in 1776 and 1777. 72 pp. 1 pl. 1 map. 8°. *Trenton, [N. J.]* 1867.

Haven (Samuel F.) Historical address before the citizens of Dedham, Sept. 21, 1836. 8°. 79 pp. *Dedham, Herman Mann,* 1837.

Haverhill (The) and Bradford [Mass.] directory for 1867. By Langford & Chase, Boston. 138, 20 pp. 12°. *Haverhill, [Mass.] J. V. Smiley,* 1867.

Havet (Alfred). French manual: a new method of acquiring a conversational knowledge of the French language; with a dictionary. Revised ed. xxxii, 112 pp. 12°. *New York, Appletons,* 1867.

Hawes (Joel, *D. D.*) An address delivered at Hartford, Nov. 9, 1835, the close of the second century from the settlement of the city. 80 pp. 12°. *Hartford, Belknap and Hamersley,* 1835.

——— Sermons, experimental and practical. An offering to home missionaries. 407 pp. 12°. *New York, R. Carter & Bros.* 1867.

——— A tribute to the memory of the pilgrims, and a vindication of the congregational churches of New England. 2d ed. 176 pp. 12°. *Hartford, D. Burgess & Co.* 1836.

Hawker (Peter). Instructions to young sportsmen in all that relates to guns and shooting. 1st Am. from 9th London ed. [With] the hunting and shooting of North America, etc. By Wm. T. Porter. 459 pp. 12 pl. 8°. *Philadelphia, Lea & Blanchard,* 1846. s.

Hawkins (Benjamin W.) Comparative osteology. *See* **Huxley** (T. H.) *and* **Hawkins.**

Hawkins (*Sir* Christopher). Observations on the tin trade of the ancients in Cornwall, and on the "Ictis" of Diodorus Siculus. 80 pp. 8°. *London, J. J. Stockdale,* 1811. s. [Wanting 1 plate].

Hawkins (John Sidney). An inquiry into the nature and history of Greek and Latin poetry; more particularly of the dramatic species. xv, 479 pp. 10 l. 8°. *London, E. Williams,* 1817.

Hawkins (Joseph). History of a voyage to the coast of Africa, and travels into the interior of that country. 179 pp. 1 pl. 18°. *Philadelphia, S. C. Ustick & Co.* 1797. [Imperfect; pp. 65–68 wanting].

Hawkins (*Sir* Richard). A discourse of the nationall excellencies of England. [*anon.*] 7 p. l. 248 pp. 8°. *London, Henry Fletcher,* 1658.

Hawks (Francis Lister, *D. D.*) Romance of biography. [Richard the lion-hearted]. 2d ed. 273 pp. 6 pl. 16°. *New York, J. S. Dickerson,* 1855. s.

Hawn (F.) Report of the geological survey of Miami county, Kansas. *See* **Swallow** (G. C.) *and* **Hawn.**

Hawtrey (*Rev.* Montague John Gregg). An earnest address to New Zealand colonists, with reference to their intercourse with the native inhabitants. vi, 140 pp. 16°. *London, J. W. Parker,* 1840.

Hay (John). De rebvs iaponicis, indicis et pervanis, epistolae recentiores. 4 p. l. 968 pp. 25 l. 12°. *Antverpiæ, Martinus Nutius,* 1605.

Hay (Richard). Vindication of Elizabeth More from the imputation of being a concubine, and her children from the tache of bastardy. 1723. Reprinted. viii, 224 pp. 8°. *Edinburgh, W. Adams,* 1826.

Hayden (F. V. *M. D.*) Palæontology of the upper Missouri. *See* **Meek** (F. B.) *and* **Hayden** (F. V.)

Hayden (Horace H.) Geological essays; or, an inquiry into some of the geological phenomena in America and elsewhere. viii, 412 pp. 8°. *Baltimore, J. Robinson,* 1820. s.

Haydn (Joseph). Dictionary of dates, for universal reference. American supplement, and biographical index, by G. P. Putnam. 61, 100 pp. 8°. *New York, G. P. Putnan & son,* 1867.

Hayes (Isaac I. *M. D.*) An arctic boat journey in the autumn of 1854. [2d ed.] xxv, 387 pp. 12 pl. 2 charts. 12°. *Boston, Ticknor & Fields,* 1867.

——— The open polar sea: a narrative of a voyage of discovery towards the north pole, in the schooner "United States." xxiv, 454 pp. 10 pl. 8°. *New York, Hurd & Houghton,* 1867.

Hayes (John L.) Memorial of the iron manufacturers of New England, asking for a modification of the tariff of 1846. 39 pp. 8°. *Philadelphia, C. Sherman,* 1850.

——— The probable influence of icebergs upon drift. 28 pp. 8°. [n. p. *about* 1844?] [With the preceding].

Haym (Niccola Francesco). Biblioteca italiana; ossia notizia de libri rari italiani. 4 v. in 2. 8°. *Milano, S. Silvestri,* 1803. s.

Haynes (D. F.) The romance of the castle. 106 pp. 8°. *London,* 1841.
[Hazlitt's romancist and novelist's lib. v. 3].

Haynes (Thomas). Treatise on improved culture of the strawberry, raspberry, gooseberry, and currant. 5 p. l. 112 pp. 4 col. pl. 8°. *London, Sherwood, Jones & Co.* 1823.

Hayward (John). The Massachusetts directory; being the first part of the New England directory. 192 pp. 18°. *Boston, John Hayward,* 1835.

——— New England gazetteer. 9th ed. 257 l. unp. 12°. *Concord, (N. H.) J. S. Boyd & W. White,* 1839. s.

Hayward (J. Henry). Poetical pen-pictures of the war: selected from our union poets. 3d ed. 408 pp. 12°. *New York, J. H. Hayward,* 1864.

Hazlitt (William, *editor*). The romancist and novelist's library. New series. 6 v. 8°. *London, J. Clements,* 1841.
[*Note.*—The contents will be found in the catalogue under the names of the authors].

Hazlitt (William Carew). British Columbia, and Vancouver island. viii, 247 pp. 1 map. 16°. *London, Routledge & Co.* 1858.

——— Hand-book to the popular poetical and dramatic literature of Great Britain, from the invention of printing to [1660]. Parts 1–9. A—M. xii, 564 pp. 8°. *London, J. Russell Smith,* 1867.

Head (*Sir* Edmund Walker). A hand-book of the history of the Spanish and French schools of painting. Intended as a sequel to Kugler. xiv, 373 pp. 16°. *London, J. Murray,* 1848. s.

Head (*Sir* Francis Bond). The emigrant. 5th ed. 3 p. l. 441 pp. 12°. *London, J. Murray,* 1847.

Headley (Joel Tyler). The Alps and the Rhine; a series of sketches. New ed. vii, 138 pp. 12°. *New York, Baker & Scribner,* 1848. s.

——— Farragut, and our naval commanders. With portraits, etc. 609 pp. 8°. *New York, E. B. Treat & Co.* 1867.

——— The great rebellion; a history of the civil war in the United States. 2 v. 506 pp. 15 pl; 702 pp. 12 pl. 8°. *Hartford, Am. publishing co.* 1866.

——— Miscellanies. viii, 298 pp. 1 pl. 12°. *New York, Baker & Scribner,* 1850. s.

——— The power of beauty. [Three essays, Esther, Ruth, Alfieri]. iv, 107 pp. 3 pl. 16°. *New York, J. S. Taylor,* 1850.

——— The sacred mountains. 175 pp. 11 pl. 12°. *New York, Baker & Scribner,* 1847. s.

——— Sketches and rambles. xi, 241 pp. 12°. *New York, Baker & Scribner,* 1850. s.

Headley (*Rev.* Phineas Camp). Life and military career of major-general William Tecumseh Sherman. 368 pp. 12°. *New York, W. H. Appleton,* 1865.

——— Massachusetts in the rebellion. A record of the historical position of the commonwealth, and the services of the leading statesmen, the military, the colleges, and the people, in the civil war of 1861–65. xii, 688 pp. 8 pl. 8°. *Boston, Walker, Fuller & Co.* 1866.

Heads of agreement assented to by the united ministers in and about London, formerly called presbyterian and congregational. [*anon.*] 2 p. l. 16 l. sm. 4°. *London,* [1691?]
[Title wanting.]

——— The same. Also articles for the administration of church discipline agreed upon at Say-Brook, September 9th, 1708. [*anon.*] 26 pp. 18°. *New London, T. Short,* 1710.
[*With* CONFESSION of faith, owned at Say-Brook, *New London,* 1710.]

Heard (James). A practical grammar of the Russian language, with a key. xiv, 323, 197 pp. 12°. *St. Petersburg, Sleunine,* 1827. s.

Hearn (William Edward). Plutology; or the theory of the efforts to satisfy human wants. xii, 475 pp. 8°. *London, Macmillan,* 1864.

Hearne (Samuel). A journey from Prince of Wales's fort in Hudson's bay, to the northern ocean, in the years 1769–72. xliv, 458 pp. 1 map. 8 pl. 4°. *London, A. Strahan & T. Cadell,* 1795.

——— The same. l, 459 pp. 1 map. 8 pl. 8°. *Dublin, P. Byrne,* 1796.

Heath (Laban). Greatly improved and enlarged infallible government counterfeit detector, with designs from original plates. 2d ed. 39 pp. 16 pl. 16°. *Boston, L. Heath,* 1866.

——— The same. Banking house and counting room edition. 39 pp. 15 pl. 4°. *Boston, L. Heath,* [1867].

Heath (Noble). The people's spelling book. 168 pp. 12°. *Philadelphia, author,* 1857.

——— A treatise on arithmetic. 455 pp. 12°. *Philadelphia, T. E. Chapman,* 1855. s.

Heath (Robert). Natural and historical account of the islands of Scilly; [with] a general account of Cornwall. viii, xvi, xiii, 456 pp. 1 map. 8°. *London, Manby & Cox,* 1750.

Heather (John Fry). A treatise on mathematical instruments. vi, 183 pp. 2 pl. 12°. *London, J. Weale,* 1849. s.

Heathside farm. A tale of country life. [*anon.*] 2 v. 291 pp; 299 pp. 12°. *London, T. C. Newby,* 1863.

Hebenstreit (Johann Ernst). Mvsevm richterianvm; continens fossilia, animalia, vegetabilia marina, illustrata iconibvs et commentariis. 384 pp. 14 pl. fol. *Lipsiae, C. Fritsch,* 1743.

Hebenstreit (Wilhelm). Wissenschaftlich-literärische encyklopädie der aesthetik. 2e ausg. lxxxvii, 994 pp. 8°. *Wien, C. Gerold,* 1848. s.

Hébert (A. E. *capitaine des ingénieurs.*) Différences entre le langage littéral et le langage vulgaire. s.

[*With* Erpenius (T.) Rudiments de la langage arabe].

Heckel (Jakob), *and* **Kner** (Rudolph). Die süsswasserfische der östreichischen monarchie; mit rücksicht auf die angränzenden länder. xii, 388 pp. 8°. *Leipzig, W. Engelmann,* 1858. s.

Hecker (John). The scientific basis of education demonstrated. xx, 167, xxiv pp. 12 pl. 8°. *New York, author,* 1867.

Hédelin (François). *See* **Aubignac** (F. Hédelin, *abbé* d').

Hedley (J. H.) Anviisning til hurtig og grundig at lære det engelske sprog. Efter Dr. Ahn's methode. 3e oplag. 222 pp. 12°. *Bergen, E. B. Giertsen,* 1864. s.

Hedwig (Johann). Theoria generationis et fructificationis plantarvm cryptogamicarvm Linnaei. 164 pp. 37 pl. 4°. *Petropoli, Acad. imp. scientiarum,* 1784. s.

Heeren (Arnold Hermann Ludwig). Ancient Greece. Translated from the German, by George Bancroft. Also, three historical treatises: 1. Political consequences of the reformation. 2. Rise, etc. of political theories. 3. Rise and growth of the continental interests of Great Britain. New ed. xii, 518 pp. 8°. *London, H. G. Bohn,* 1847. s.

——— Historical researches into the politics, intercourse, and trade of the Carthaginians, Ethiopians, and Egyptians. Translated from the German. 2d ed. 8, xxxii, 520 pp. 2 pl. 1 map. 8°. *London, H. G. Bohn,* 1857. s.

——— Historical researches into the politics, intercourse, and trade of the principal nations of antiquity: Asiatic nations. 2 v. xvi, 368 pp. 1 pl. 1 map; 472 pp. 3 pl. 8°. *London, H. G. Bohn,* 1854. s.

CONTENTS.

v. 1. Persians, Phœnicians, Babylonians.
v. 2. Scythians, Indians. Appendixes.

——— A manual of ancient history with regard to constitutions, etc. Translated from the German. 6th ed. With a biographical sketch of the author. xvi, xxx, 413 pp. 8°. *London, H. G. Bohn,* 1854. s.

——— A manual of the history of the political system of Europe and its colonies. [1492-1776]. From 5th German ed. xxxii, 540 pp. 8°. *London, H. G. Bohn,* 1857. s.

Heider (Eduard J.) Systematische anleitung zum traçiren der eisenbahnen. 2e aufl. 8 p. l. 167 pp. 8°. *Leipzig, J. L. Schrag,* 1860. s.

Heinecken (Carl Heinrich von). Idée générale d'une collection complete d'estampes. Avec une dissertation sur l'origine de la gravure. 8 p. l. 520 pp. 16 l. 28 pl. 8°. *Leipsic, J. P. Kraus,* 1771. s.

Heinemann (H. von). Die schmetterlinge Deutschlands und der Schweiz systematisch bearbeitet. I. Grossschmetterlinge. xxiii, 850 pp. 8°. *Braunschweig, Vieweg,* 1859. s.

——— Tabellen zur bestimmung der schmetterlinge Deutschlands und der Schweiz. 118 pp. 8°. *Braunschweig, Vieweg,* 1859. s.

[*With* the preceding.]

Heinrich (Carl). Tyskt och svenskt handlexikon. 3e upplagan. 2 v. in 1. 480 pp; 528 pp. sq. 18°. *Stralsund, Löffler,* 1836. s.

Heinrich (J.) Landwirthschaftliche beschreibung der guts-wirthschaft Castell; nebst einem vorworte über bewirthschaftung grösserer güter in den nordöstlichen Schweiz und den nachbarstaaten. xxiv, 357 pp. 9 pl. 8°. *Zürich, C. Beyel,* 1845. s.

Heinsius (Johannes Wilhelm). Allgemeines bücher-lexicon, oder vollständiges alphabetisches verzeichniss aller von 1700 bis zu ende [1861] erschienenen bücher, welche in Deutschland und in den durch sprache und literatur damit verwandten ländern gedruckt worden sind. 20 v. in 15. 4°. *Leipzig, J. F. Gleditsch,* 1812-28; *F. A. Brockhaus,* 1836-63.

CONTENTS.

v. 1-4. A—Z. 1700-1810. Neue auflage.
v. 5. A—Z. 1811-15.
v. 6. A—Z. 1816-21. Herausgegeben von C. G. Kayser.
v. 7. A—Z. 1822-27. Herausgegeben von C. G. Kayser.
v. 8 in 2 v. A—Z. 1828-34. Herausgegeben von O. A. Schulz.
v. 9 in 2 v. A—Z. 1835-41. Bearbeitet von O. A. Schulz.
v. 10. A—Z. 1842-46. Bearbeitet von L. F. A. Schiller.
v. 11. A—Z. 1847-51. Von L. F. A. Schiller.
v. 12. A—Z. 1852-56. Von L. F. A. Schiller.
v. 13. A—Z. 1857-61. Von C. R. Heumann.

Heiss (Johann von). Histoire de l'empire. 2 v. 9 p. l. lxix, 523 pp. 3 p. l. 740 pp. 10 pl. 4°. *Amsterdam, Wetsteins & Smith,* 1733.

Held (Joseph). Staat und gesellschaft vom standpunkte der geschichte der menschheit und des staats. 3 v. 8°. *Leipzig, F. A. Brockhaus,* 1861-65.

CONTENTS.

v. 1. Grundanschauungen über staat und gesellschaft. xxiv, 598 pp.
v. 2. Volk und regierung, mit besonderer rücksicht auf die entwickelung der gesellschaft und des staats in Deutschland. xxix, 796 pp.
v. 3. Der verfassungsmässige oder constitutionelle staat. xxiv, 1,020 pp.

Helena's household; a tale of Rome in the first century. [*anon.*] 3 p. l. 422 pp. 12°. *New York, R. Carter & brothers,* 1867.

Hellenbroek (*Rev.* Abram). A sermon from Canticles, on taking the little foxes. Translated from the Dutch. 31 pp. 16°. *Boston, S. Kneeland & T. Green,* 1742.

[*With* TENNENT (*Rev.* Gilbert). Necessity of holding fast the truth. *Boston,* 1743].

Heller (Joseph). Das leben und die werke Albrecht Dürer's. 297, 983 pp. 3 pl. 8°. *Bamberg, E. F. Kunz,* 1827. s.

Hellwig (Johann Christian Ludwig). Tabellarische uebersicht der ordnungen, familien und gattungen der säugethiere, nach Illiger's Prodromus systematis mammalium. viii, 118 pp. 8°. *Helmstadt, C. G. Fleckeisen,* 1819. s.

Helme (Elizabeth). The farmer of Inglewood forest. 162 pp. 8°. *London,* 1841.

[HAZLITT's romancist and novelists libr. v. 4.]

Helmont (Jean Baptiste van). Opera omnia. 19 p. l. 765 pp. 36 l. 4°. *Francofurti, J. J. Erythropilus,* [*Rothuet*] 1682. s.

——— Opuscula medica inedita. 8 p. l. 275 pp. 21 l. 4°. *Francofurti, J. J. Erythropilus,* 1682. s.

[*With* the preceding.]

Helper (Hinton Rowan). The impending crisis of the south: how to meet it. 15th thousand. 12°. *New York, J. B. Burdick,* 1860.

——— Nojoque: a question for a continent. 479 pp. 12°. *New York, G. W. Carleton & Co.* 1867.

Helvicus (Christophorus). *See* **Helwig** (Christoph).

Helwig, *or* **Helwich** (Christoph). Elenchi judaici. Antonii Probi oratio de monarchia regni Israelis. Raphaelis Eglini captivitatis babylonicæ historia. Cum T. Crenii præfatione, notis et indice. 88, 466 pp. 3 l. 18°. *Lugduni in Batavis, A. de Swart,* 1702.

——— The historical and chronological theatre. Faithfully done into English according to the two best editions, with additions. 11 p.l. 214 pp. 22 l. fol. *London, West & Crosley,* 1687.

Hemingford, *or* **Hemingburgh** (Walter *of*). Chronica de gestis regum Angliæ, mlxvi—mccc. fol. *Oxoniæ,* 1687.

[GALE (Thomas), *and* FELL (John). Rerum anglicarum scriptores veteres. *Oxoniæ,* 1684-91. v. 2.]

Hempel (Gustav). Geographische beschreibung der grossherzogthümer Mecklenburg-Schwerin und Mecklenburg-Strelitz. xiv, 147 pp. 16°. *Neu Strelitz, L. Dümmler,* 1829. s.

Henderson (John, *comedian*). Letters and poems. With anecdotes of his life, by John Ireland. xii, 206 pp. 8°. *London, J. Johnson,* 1786.

Henderson (Peter). Gardening for profit: guide to successful cultivation of the market and family garden. 243 pp. 12°. *New York, O. Judd & Co.* 1867.

Henderson (William). Notes on the folk-lore of the northern counties of England and the borders. With an appendix on household stories, by S. Baring Gould. xxvii, 344 pp. 1 pl. 12°. *London, Longmans,* 1866.

Henkel (Johann Friedrich). Anleitung zum chirurgischen verbande: umgearbeitet und mit vielen zusätzen versehen von J. C. Stark. Von neuem bearbeitet und mit zusätzen vermehrt von J. F. Dieffenbach. 558 pp. 40 pl. 8°. *Berlin, G. Reimer,* 1829. s.

[Wanting pl. xl.]

Henkle (W. D.) Algebra. *See* **Stoddard** (J. F.) *and* **Henkle.**

Henle (Julius). Handbuch der rationellen pathologie. 2 v. in 3. 8°. *Braunschweig, Vieweg,* 1854-55. s.

CONTENTS.

v. 1. Einleitung und allgemeiner theil. 3e aufl. 4 p. l. 357 pp.
v. 2. Specieller theil.
Abth. 1. Pathogenie. 2e aufl. viii, 835 pp. 3 pl.
Abth. 2. Symptomatogie und aetiologie. vi, 493 pp.

Hennekeler (Gysbert van). *See* **Van Hennekeler.**

Hennell (Sara S.) Christianity and infidelity; an exposition of the arguments on both sides. xii, 173 pp. 8°. *London, Hall, Virtue & Co.* 1857.

Hennepin (Louis). A new discovery of a vast country in America, extending above four thousand miles, between New France and New Mexico. With the continuation; giving an account of the attempts of the sieur La Salle upon the mines of St. Barbe. 2 v. in 1. 11 p. l. 299 pp; 16 p. l. 355 pp. 2 maps. 7 pl. 12°. *London, M. Bentley & others,* 1698.

Hennequin (Amand). Essai sur l'analogie des langues. 220 pp. 8°. *Besançon, Bintot,* 1838. s.

Henrici (Moritz). Die kupferstechkunst und der stahlstich; für männer vom fach und kunstfreunde. iv, 168 pp. 16°. *Leipzig, J. C. Hinrichs,* 1834. s.

Henriques (A. D. Y.) Modern mercantile calculator; a companion for the accountant and book-keeper. xv, 369 pp. 8°. *New York, J. M. Bradstreet & Son,* 1867.

Henry (David). The curiosities of London and Westminster described. [*anon.*] 2 v. 198 pp. 6 pl; 213 pp. 6 pl. 18°. *London, J. Harris,* [*about* 1790].

Henry (James, *M. D. pseudon?*) Notes of a twelve years' voyage of discovery in the first six books of the Eneis. xvi, 586 pp. 8°. *Dresden, Meinhold,* 1853. s.

Henry (Matthew). Miscellaneous writings. New ed. 4 p.l. 876 pp. 4°. *London, S. Bagster,* 1811.

CONTENTS.

Life of Mr. Philip Henry.
Sermons, tracts, and biography of eminent christians; sermon on the author's death by Rev. W. Tong.

Henry (William, *M. D.*) The elements of experimental chemistry. 2d Am. ed. With supplement, and theory of galvanism, by R. Hare, M. D. 3 v. [*illust.*] 8°. *Philadelphia, R. Desilver,* 1823.

Henschel (C. A.) Le système de mesures et de poids le plus commode, basé sur le pas naturel de l'homme, et projeté d'après l'analogie du système métrique. Trad. de l'Allemand. 35 pp. 2 pl. 8°. *Cassel, O. Bertram,* 1855. s.

Hentz (N. M.) Araneides, of Massachusetts. [*In* HITCHCOCK (E.) Catalogue of animals, etc. of Mass.]

Hentzner (Paul). Travels in England during the reign of Queen Elizabeth. Translated by Horace [Walpole,] late earl of Orford; with sir Robert Naunton's Fragmenta regalia; or, observations on Queen Elizabeth's times and favourites. viii, 152 pp. 11 pl. 8°. *London, Edward Jeffery,* 1797.

Herald (The) of health, and journal of physical culture, devoted to hygienic medication, bodily development, and laws of life. M. L. Holbrook, M. D. editor. Jan. to Dec. 1867. new series, v. 9–10. (complete series, v. 43–44.) viii, 302, 304 pp. 8°. *New York, Miller, Wood & Co.* [1867.]

Herbarius. Das kreüter buch, oder herbarius. Das buch von allen kreütern, wurtzlen vnd andern dingen, wie mans bruchen soll zü gesundtheit der menschen, von neüwem corrigiert vnd gebessert. [*anon.*] 186 l. fol. *Strassburg, Balthassar Beck,* 1528.

Herbert, Herbers, *or* **Hébert.** Extraits du Dolopathos. Par Le Roux de Lincy. *See* **Loiseleur Deslongchamps,** (A. L. A.) Essai sur les fables, etc.

Herbert (Henry William). Ruth Whalley; or, the fair puritan. A romance of the Bay province. 72 pp. 8°. *Boston, H. L. Williams,* 1845.

Herbich (Franz). Stirpes rariores bucovinæ; oder, die seltenen pflanzen der Bucovina. 65 pp. 8°. *Stanislawon, author,* 1853. s.

Herborn (Nikolaus). De Indis convertendis. *See* **Novus orbis.** *Roterodami,* 1616.

Herchenbach (Wilhelm). Aus der mansarde; eine wahre geschichte. 188 pp. 1 pl. 12°. *Regensburg, G. J. Manz,* 1866.

——— Bagdad, die königin der wüste; erzählung. 192 pp. 1 pl. 12°. *Regensburg, G. J. Manz,* 1866.

——— Ein verlorenes leben; erzählung. 188 pp. 1 pl. 12°. *Regensburg, G. J. Manz,* 1866.

——— In der mühle; erzählung. 188 pp. 1 pl. 12°. *Regensburg, G. J. Manz,* 1866.

Hering (C. J.) De kultuur en de bewerking van het suikerriet, benevens eene beschryving van al de toestellen tot de suikerbereiding en tot het destilleren van rum. 3 v. in 1. 21 pl. 8°. *Rotterdam, H. Nijgh,* 1858. s.

Hering (J. H.) Bespiegeling over neêrlandsch waternood, 14–15 Nov. 1775. 2 v. xvi, 38, 245 pp. 7 pl; viii, 335 pp. 3 pl. 8°. *Amsterdam, Lovering & Allart,* 1776. s.

———The same. 21–22 Nov. 1776. xxviii, 32, 238 pp. 5 pl. 8°. *Amsterdam, J. Allart,* 1776. s.

Herkern *or* Herkeren. Insha i Herkérn. The forms of Herkern corrected from a variety of manuscripts, translated into English: with an index of Arabic words explained, by F. Balfour. [Arabic and English]. 266 pp. 4°. *Calcutta,* 1781.

Hermann (Carl Heinrich). Geschichte des deutschen volkes. Erläuterung zu einige bildern. *See* **Foss** (R.)

Hermann (Paul). Lapis materiæ medicæ lydivs. 1737. s.
[*With* TEICHMEYER (H. F.) Institutiones materiæ medicæ.]

Hermannsen. *See* **Herrmannsen.**

Hermetical (The) triumph: or, the victorious philosophical stone, translated from the French. [With] the ancient war of the knights, translated from the German. [*anon.*] xxvi, 147, 39 pp. 1 pl. 18°. *London, P. Hanet,* 1723.

Hermogenes *Tarsensis.* De dicendi generibvs, sive formis orationum libri ii. Latinitate donati, etc. scholiis explicati atque illustrati, a Joan. Stvrmio. 16 p. l. 399 pp. 8 l. 16°. [*Argentorati*], *J. Rihelius,* 1571.

——De ratione tractandæ grauitatis occultæ liber, latinitate donatus, etc. scholiis explicatus atque illustratus a Joan. Stvrmio. 12 p. l. 79 pp. 16°. [*Argentorati*], *J. Rihelius,* 1571.
[*With* the preceding.]

Hernandez (Francisco). Nova plantarvm, animalivm et mineralivm mexicanorvm historia. A Nardo Antonio Recchio digesta, a Io. Terentio, Io. Fabro, et Fabio Colvmna notis illustrata. 14 p. l. 960 pp. 95 pl. fol. *Romae,* 1651. s.

Herndon (William Lewis), *and* Gibbon (Lardner). Exploration of the valley of the Amazon. 2 v. 8°. *Washington, public printer,* 1854.

CONTENTS.

Part 1. Herndon's report. iv, 417 pp. 16 pl.
Part 2. Gibbon's report. x, 339 pp. 36 pl.

Herodotus. History, translated from the Greek, by Isaac Littlebury. 2 v. xiv. 447 pp. 8 l; 430 pp. 8 l. 8°. *London, E. Castle,* 1709.

——The same. Translated from the Greek, with notes. By J. Lempriere. vol. i. xl, 459 pp. 8°. *London, T. Cadell,* 1792.
[No more published.]

Herrera y Tordesillas (Antonio de). Descripcion de las Indias Occidentales. 2 p. l. 96 pp. 14 maps. fol. *Madrid, Juan Flamenco,* 1601.
[*With* v. 1 and 4 of HERRERA, historia general de los hechos de los Castellanos, etc. 4 v. fol. 1601-15.]

——The same. Description des Indes Occidentales. Translatée d'Espagnol en François. 4 p. l. 103 pp. 14 maps. fol. *Amsterdam, M. Colin,* 1622.

——The same. Novvs orbis, sive descriptio Indiæ Occidentalis. Metaphraste C. Barlæo. 6 p. l. 44 l. fol. *Amstelodami, M. Colin,* 1622.

——Historia general de los hechos de los Castellanos en las islas y tierra firme del mar oceano. En quatro decadas, 1492–1531. v. 1–2. fol. *Madrid, Juan Flamenco,* 1601.

——The same. [Continuation, 4 decades. 1532–54]. v. 3–4. fol. *Madrid, Juan de La Cuesta,* 1615.

——The same. Histoire générale des voyages et conqvestes des Castillans dans les isles et terre-ferme des Indes Occidentales. Traduite de l'Espagnol par N. de La Costa. 9 p. l. 789 pp. 6 l. 4°. *Paris, De La Coste and others,* 1671.

——Verscheide zee en land-togten gedaan in de West-Indien: d'eerste, door Jean Ponce de Leon, naar Florida in 1512. De andere gedaan door Pamphilio de Narvaes op't eiland Cuba, in 1513. In't Spaans beschreven door Antonius Herrera en nu aller-eerst in't Nederduyts vertaald. 77 pp. 3 l. 4 pl. 16°. *Leyden, P. Van der Aa,* 1706.

Herrick-Schäffer (Gottlieb August Wilhelm). Nomenclator entomologicus. Verzeichniss der europäischen insecten. 2 v. in 1. iv, 116 pp; viii, 244 pp. 8 pl. 12°. *Regensburg, F. Pustel,* 1835–40. s.

Herrmannsen (A. N.) Indicis generum malacozoorum primordia. Nomina subgenerum, generum, familiarum, tribuum, ordinum, classium, etc. 2 v. xxviii, 660 pp; xiii, 717 pp. 8°. *Cassellis, T. Fischer,* 1846–49. s.
[Imperfect.]

——Indicis generum malacozoorum supplementa et corrigenda. vi, 140 pp. 8°. *Cassellis, T. Fischer,* 1852. s.

Herrod (G.) Grammar of the Maskoke or Creek language. *See* **Buckner** (H. F.) *and* **Herrod.**

Herschel (*Sir* John Frederick William). Outlines of astronomy. 6th ed. xxiv, 714 pp. 7 pl. 8°. *London, Longman,* 1859. s.

——The telescope. [From the Encyclopædia Britannica.] vii, 190 pp. 16°. *Edinburgh, Black,* 1861. s.

——Treatise on astronomy. New ed. with a preface, by S. C. Walker. 417 pp. 12°. *Philadelphia, Carey, Lea & Blanchard,* 1836. s.

Hertz (B.) Catalogue of his collection of Assyrian, Babylonian, Egyptian, Greek, Etruscan, Roman, Indian, Peruvian, and Mexican antiquities. 156 pp. 6 pl. 4°. *London, Thimm,* 1851. s.

Hertz (Henrik). King Réné's daughter, a Danish lyrical drama. Translated by Theodore Martin. xii, 100 pp. 12°. *New York, Leypoldt & Holt,* 1867.

Herz (Henri). Mes voyages en Amérique. 328 pp. Portrait. 16°. *Paris, A. Faure,* 1866.

Herzog (*Dr.* Eduard). Kurze andeutungen über die kaltwassercur. iv, 102 pp. 1 pl. 8°. *Dresden, E. Pietzsch,* 1842. s.

Hesiodus. De opere et die, enarrationes Phil. Melancth. vna cvm elegantissima authoris praefatione. 44 l. 16°. *Parisiis, Jac. Bogards,* 1543.

——Works and days, Theogony. Translated by T. Cooke. 8°. *Edinburgh,* [1792–94].
[Anderson's Brit. poets, v. 5.]

Hesiodus. Les œuvres, traduction nouvelle, enrichie de notes et du combat d'Homère et d'Hésiode, par [P. L. C.] Gin. viii, 303 pp. 16°. *Paris, Gueffier,* 1785.

——— *and* Orpheus. Hesiods werke, und Orfeus der Argonaut, von Johann Heinrich Voss. 354 pp. 16°. *Heidelberg, Mohr & Zimmer,* 1806. s.

Hess (J.) Catalog des antiquarischen bücherlagers. No. v. 292 pp. 8°. *Ellwangen, J. Hess,* 1861. s.

Hessische medicinalordnung und gesetze, welche das sanitätswesen im lande überhaupt betreffen. 498 pp. 16°. *Cassell, H. Schmiedt,* 1778. s.

Hessler (J. Ferdinand). Lehrbuch der technischen physik, fortgesetzt von Fr. Jo. Pisko. 3e aufl. 2 v. xii, vii, 1373, lxx, 11 pp. *Wien, W. Braumüller,* 1866. s.

Hetherington (William M. *D. D.*) Memoir of Alexander Wilson.

[*With* WILSON (A.) *and* BONAPARTE (C. L.) American ornithology. 4 v. 1831.]

Hethum, *or* Haiton, *or* Aiton. Haithoni armeni historia orientalis, quae et de Tartaris inscribitur.

[*With* Marco Polo, libri tres de regionibus orientalibus. *Coloniæ,* 1671.]

Heuglin (Theodor von). Reisen in nord-ost Afrika, von Chartum nach Abyssinien. x, 136 pp. 3 pl. 3 maps. 8°. *Gotha, J. Perthes,* 1857. s.

Heuschling (Philippe François Xavier Théodore). Essai sur la statistique générale de la Belgique. 2e éd. viii, 444 pp. 1 map. 8°. *Bruxelles, L'établiss. géog.* 1841. s.

——— The same. Supplément à la 2e éd. 3 p. l. 116 pp. 8°. *Bruxelles, P. Vandermaelen,* 1844. s.

——— Des naissances dans la ville de Bruxelles, considérées dans leur rapport avec la population. (Extract.) 41 pp. 4°. *Bruxelles, Comm. cent. de statistique,* 1843. s.

——— Sur l'accroissement de la population de la Belgique, 1831 à 1840. (Extract.) 20 pp. 4°. *Bruxelles, Com. cent. de statistique,* [1843]. s.

[*With* the preceding.]

——— Recensement général. [Extract.) 21 pp. 4°. *Com. cent. de statistique,* [1844?] s.

[*With* the preceding.]

——— Sur le mouvement de l'état civil en Belgique, 1841 à 1844. (Extract.) 38 pp. 4°. *Bruxelles, Com. cent. de statistique,* (1844?] s.

[*With* the preceding,]

——— Statistique du royaume de Bavière. (Extract.) 37 pp. 4°. *Bruxelles, Com. cent. etc.* [1844.] s.

[*With* the preceding.]

Heuter (Pontus). Rerum bvrgvndicarvm libri sex. 4 p. l. 192 pp. 6 l; 6 p. l. 99 pp. fol. *Antverpiæ, C. Plante,* 1583–84. s.

Hewett (D.) The American traveller; or, national directory, containing an account of the roads in the United States, with a description of the country, and a geographical and statistical view of the U. S. 440 pp. 16°. *Washington, Davis & Force,* 1825.

——— Self-taught stenographer; or, a new and complete system of short-hand. 2d ed. 16 pp. 12°. *Washington, James Wilson,* 1824.

Hewett (James D.) The votary; a narrative poem. 123 pp. 12°. *New York, G. W. Carleton & Co.* 1867.

Hewitt (Girart). Minnesota; its advantages to settlers. Being a synopsis of its history and progress, climate, [etc.] 6th ed. 30 pp. 8°. *St. Paul, (Minn.)* 1867.

Heyden (Carl Heinrich Georg von). Reptilien. Atlas zur der reise im nördlichen Africa von Rüppell. 24 pp. 6 col. pl. fol. *Frankfort am Main, H. L. Brönner,* 1827. s.

Heyfelder (J. F.) Über resectionen und amputationen. 7 p. l. 269 pp. 4 pl. 4°. *Breslau und Bonn, k. leop. carol. acad. d. nat.* 1854. s.

Heylyn *or* **Heylin** (Peter, *D. D.*) Cosmographie; containing the chorographie and historie of the whole world, and all the principall kingdoms, provinces, seas, and isles thereof. [1st fol. ed.] 6 p. l. 1052 pp. 9 l. 4 maps. fol. *London, H. Seile,* 1652.

——— Cyprianus anglicus: or, the history of the life and death of William [Laud] lord archbishop of Canterbury. 2 p. l. 511 pp. fol. *London, A. Seile,* 1681.

——— Ecclesia restaurata; or, the history of the reformation of the church of England. With life of the author by John Barnard. Edited by James C. Robertson. 2 v. ccxii, xvi, 302 pp; x, 496 pp. 8°. *Cambridge, Eccles. hist. soc.* 1849.

——— Keimelia ecclesiastica. Historical and miscellaneous tracts, and an account of [his] life [by George Vernon]. xxviii pp. 10 l. 747 pp. 12 l. portrait. fol. *London, Charles Harper,* 1681.

CONTENTS.

Ecclesia vindicata, or the reformation of the church of England justified.
History of the Sabbath.
Historia quinquarticularis, or the judgment of the western churches on the five points of Arminianism.
Discovery and removal of the stumbling block of disobedience and rebellion, cunningly laid down in the subject's way by Calvin.
De jure paritatis episcoporum.

Heyse (Johann Christian August). Handwörterbuch der deutschen sprache. Ausgeführt von Dr. K. W. L. Heyse. 3 v. 8°. *Magdeburg, W. Heinrichshofen,* 1833–49. s.

Heywood (James, *F. R. S.*) Academic reform and university representation. xv, 335 pp. 8°. *London, E. T. Whitfield,* 1860.

Heywood (Joseph C.) Antonius: a dramatic poem. 272 pp. 16°. *New York, Hurd & Houghton,* 1867.

——— Herodias: a dramatic poem. 251 pp. 16°. *New York, Hurd & Houghton,* 1867.

Heywood (Peter, *captain English navy*). The Brazil pilot. iv, 107, 3 pp. 8°. *London, W. Faden,* 1818.

Hibernia fire engine company, No. 1 [of Philadelphia]. Visit to the cities of New York, Boston, Brooklyn, Charlestown, and Newark, in 1858. Memorial. 108 pp. 18 pl. 4°. *Philadelphia, J. B. Chandler,* 1859. s.

Hichborn (Benjamin). An oration, delivered March 5, 1777, at the request of the inhabitants of Boston, to commemorate the bloody tragedy of March 5, 1770. 18 pp. 4°. *Boston, Edes & Gill,* 1777.

Hickcox (John H.) History of the bills of credit, or paper money issued by New York, from 1709 to 1789. 3 p. l. 150 pp. 8°. *Albany, J. H. Hickcox & Co.* 1866.

Hicks (T.) A complete treatise of urines. By T. H. [*anon.*] 6 p. l. 88 pp. 18°. *London, H. Bonwicke,* 1703.

Hieover (Harry, *pseudon.*) *See* **Bindley** (Charles).

Hierocles *Grammaticus.* Synecdemus.
[*With* ANTONINUS Augustus. Vetera Romanorum itineraria. Ed. Amstelaedami, 1735].

Higden (Ralph). Polychronicon. fol. *Oxoniæ,* 1691.
[*With* GALE (Thomas) *and* FELL (John). Rerum anglicarum scriptores veteres. *Oxoniæ,* 1684–91. v. 3].

Higden (William). View of the English constitution; with respect to the sovereign authority of the prince, and the allegiance of the subject. 4 p. l. 112 pp. 12°. *London, S. Keble,* 1709.

Higgins (S. W.) Report on the topography of Michigan. pp. 45–65. s.
[HOUGHTON (Douglass). Reports, etc. Doc. No. 3].

Higginson (*Rev.* Francis). New England's plantation; or, a short and trve description of the commodities and discommodities of that country. [*anon.*] 11 l. unp. sm. 4°. *London, Michael Sparke,* 1630.
[Map wanting.]

Higginson (*Rev.* John). Our dying saviour's legacy of peace. 5 p. l. 205 pp. 18°. *Boston, John Usher,* 1686.

Higginson (Stephen). Ten chapters in the life of John Hancock. The writings of Laco, as published in the Mass. centinel, 1789. [*pseudon.* 2d ed.] 68 pp. 8°. *New York,* 1857.

Higgons (Bevill). A short view of English history: to the revolution, 1688. 2 p. l. 374 pp. 12°. *Hague, T. Johnson,* 1727.

Hildebertus *Cenomanensis.* Hymn to the trinity. *See* **Benedict** (E. C.)

Hildebrand (Bror Emil). Anglosachsiska mynt, i svenska konigl. myntkabinet, finna i Sveriges jord; [or] monnaies anglo-saxonnes du cabinet royal du Stockholm, toutes trouvées en Suède. 5 p. l. cxxv, 332 pp. 1 map. 10 pl. 4°. *Stockholm, P. A. Norstedt & söner,* 1846. s.

Hildebrand (Rudolf). Deutsches wörterbuch. *See* **Grimm** (Jacob L. C.)

Hildreth (Samuel Prescott). Biographical and historical memoirs of the early pioneer settlers of Ohio, with incidents and occurrences in 1775. 539 pp. 6 pl. 8°. *Cincinnati, H. W. Derby & Co.* 1852.

Hill (Aaron). Works: consisting of letters and poems, with an essay on acting. 2d ed. 4 v. 8°. *London,* 1754.

CONTENTS.

v. 1–2. Letters.
v. 3–4. Poems, and essay on acting.

——— Poetical works. 8°. *Edinburgh,* 1794.
[Anderson's Brit. poets, v. 8.]

Hill (*Mrs.* A. P.) House-keeping made easy. New family receipt book for the kitchen. Particularly adapted to the south; with directions for carving, etc. 427 pp. 12°. *New York, J. O'Kane,* 1867.

Hill (Carl Johann Daniel). Matheseos fundamenta nova analytica. Pars 1ª mathesin universalem comprehendens. 48, 226 pp. 4°. *Londini Gothorum, Bülow,* 1860. s.

Hill (H. A.) *See* **Bible,** *Mohawk.*

Hill (Ira). An abstract of a new theory of the formation of the earth. 211 pp. 12°. *Baltimore, N. G. Maxwell,* 1823.

Hill (John, *LL. D.*) The synonymes of the Latin language, with critical dissertations upon the force of its prepositions. xiv, 782, vii pp. 4°. *Edinburgh, Manners & Miller,* 1804.

Hill (*Sir* Richard). An apology for brotherly love and for the doctrines of the church of England, in a series of letters to Rev. Charles Daubeny. [With] a sermon by bishop Babington. xv, 212, 42, 10 pp. 8°. *London, Cadell & Davies,* 1798.

Hill (Richard, *M. D.*) Letters. *See* **Smith** (John Jay).

Hill (*Rev.* Rowland). A collection of psalms and hymns. 4th ed. xv, 272 pp. 4°. *London, A. Paris,* 1798.

Hill (S. S.) Travels in the Sandwich and Society islands. xii, 428 pp. 1 pl. 12°. *London, Chapman & Hall,* 1856.

Hill (William, *D. D.*) A history of the rise, progress, genius, and character of American presbyterianism. xv, 224 pp. 8°. *Washington, J. Gideon, jr.* 1839.

Hillard (George Stillman). Discourse before the New England society of New York, Dec'r 22, 1851, [on the pilgrim fathers of New England]. 31 pp. 8°. *New York, George F. Nesbitt & Co.* 1852.

——— A first-class reader. 504 pp. 12°. *Boston, Hickling, Swan & Co.* 1856.

——— Six months in Italy. 5th ed. xii, 563 pp. 12°. *Boston, Ticknor & Fields,* 1856. s.

Hillhouse (Augustus L.) An essay on the history and cultivation of the olive tree. [2d ed.] 54 pp. 1 col. pl. 8°. *Paris, L. T. Cellot,* 1820. s.

Hillhouse (William). A dissertation, in answer to a late lecture on the political state of America, [with] a poem spoken at the same time. 23 pp. 12°. *New Haven, T. & S. Green,* [1789?]

Hilliard d'Auberteuil (Michel René). Essais historiques et politiques sur les Anglo-Américains, [et sur la guerre de l'Amérique]. 2 v. xii, 303 pp; vi, 307 pp. atlas, 8 maps. 10 pl. 4°. *Bruxelles,* [*auteur*], 1782.

——— Mis[s] Mac Réa, roman historique. xii, 146 pp. 18°. *Philadelphie,* 1784.

Hillier (George). Narrative of the attempted escapes of Charles I from Carisbrook castle, and of his detention in the isle of Wight, 1647–48. Including the letters of the king to Col. Titus. xiv, 335 pp. 2 pl. 12°. *London, R. Bentley,* 1852.

Hillside (A. M.) A familiar compend of geology. For the school and family. 150 pp. 1 pl. 1 chart. 12°. *Philadelphia, Sower, Barnes & Potts,* 1866.

Hilpert (Joseph Leonhard). Englisch-deutsches und deutsch-englisches wörterbuch; [or,] a dictionary of the English and German, and the German and English language. 4 parts in 2 v. 4°. *Leipzig, B. Hermann,* 1846.

CONTENTS.

v. 1. English and German. xvi, 464 pp; 624 pp.
v. 2. Deutsch-englisch. xx, 658 pp; 1010 pp.

Hilton (David, *pseudon.*) *See* **Wheeler** (D. Hilton.)

Hilton (William). A relation of discovery made on the coast of Florida. 34 pp. sm. 4°. *London, Simon Miller,* 1664.

Hind (Henry Youle). A preliminary report on the geology of New Brunswick; together with a special report on the distribution of the "Quebec group" in the province. 293 pp. 8°. *Fredericton, G. E. Fenety,* 1865. s.

Hinds (John, *pseudon.*) *See* **Bell** (J.)

Hines (David Theodore). The life, adventures, and opinions of D. T. Hines, written by himself. 195 pp. 12°. *New York, Bradley & Clark,* 1840.

Hinterhäuser (Johann Baptist). Christus, die fundamentalidee des alten und neuen testamentes. xv, 110 pp. 8°. *Eichstätt, P. Brönner,* 1836. s.

Hinton (Richard J.) The rebel invasion of Missouri and Kansas, and the campaign of the army of the border, against General Sterling Price, 1864. 2d ed. 351 pp. 8 pl. 8°. *Chicago, Church & Goodman,* 1865.

Hints on common politeness. [*anon.*] 96 pp. 18°. *Boston, D. C. Colesworthy,* 1867.

Hippisley (*Sir* John Cox). Prison labour, etc. Correspondence concerning the introduction of tread-mills into prisons, with other matters of prison discipline. iv, 228 pp. 1 pl. 8°. *London, W. Nicol* 1823.

Hippocrates. Opera omnia, græce et latine, edita industria Ioan-Antonidæ Van der Linden. 2 v. in 1. 18 p. l. 788 pp. 2 pl; 1034 pp. 67 l. 8°. *Lugduni-Batavorum, Gaasbeeck,* 1665. s.

——— Ächte medizinische schriften, mit einem alphabetischen repertorium der sätze und materien, herausgegeben von Fr. v. P. Gruithuisen. xxx, 407 pp. 16°. *München, I. J. Lentner,* 1814. s.

——— Aphorismi novi operibus nunc primum collecti, studio Jacobi Sponii. 12 p. l. 436 pp. 9 l. 24°. *Lugduni, Anissonii & Rigaud,* 1689. s.

——— The prognostics and crises. Translated from the Greek; with critical and explanatory notes. By Henry William Ducachet. 126 pp. 12°. *New York, J. Eastburn & Co.* 1819. s.

——— *and* **Galenus.** The writings of Hippocrates and Galen, epitomised from the original Latin translations. By John Redman Coxe. 681 pp. 8°. *Philadelphia, Lindsay & Blakiston,* 1846. s.

Hippolytus redivivus; id est, remedium contemnendi sexum muliebrem. Autore S. I. E. D. V. M. W. A. S. [*anon.*] 96 pp. 24°. [n. p.] 1644.

Hirsch (A.) Longitude, etc. *See.* **Plantamour** (E.) *and* **Hirsch.**

Hirtius (Aulus). De bello alexandrino, africo, hispano. s.

[*With* ANNIUS. Commentaria, ed. 1498.]

Histoire de l'ancien Tobie, et de son fils le jeune Tobie. L'histoire de la vaillantise de la veûve Judith. Le vertueux fait de la noble et honneste dame Susanne, avec la sentence du jeune prophète Daniel. Ensemble l'histoire de la belle reine Esther. [En caractères de civilité]. 40 l. 18°. *Lille, Gilles-Eustache Vroye,* [n. d.]

Histoire de Foulques Fitz-Warin. [*anon.*] Publiée d'après un manuscrit du musée britannique, par F. Michel. xx, 112 pp. 8°. *Paris, Sylvestre,* 1840.

Histoire de la vie, des amours, et du procès du fameux Louis Dominique Cartouche. [*anon.*] 89 pp. 1 pl. 18°. *Paris,* [*about* 1721].

Histoire des découvertes faites par divers savans voyageurs, [Pallas, Gmelin, Lepechin, etc.] dans plusieurs contrées de la Russie et de la Perse, [abrégée de l'Allemand par Frey des Landres.] 6 v. 8°. *Berne,* 1779–87. s.

Histoire des vestales et de leur culte; d'après Plutarque, Tacite, Suetone, etc. Traduit de l'Italien. Par B. Cartoux. [*anon.*] xv, 124 pp. 3 pl. 18°. *Paris, Le Fuel,* [*about* 1830].

Histoire d'un peuple nouveau; ou, découverte d'une isle à 43 dégrés 14 minutes de latitude méridionale; par David Tompson, à son retour de la Chine en 1756. [*anon.*] 2 parts in 1 v. vi, 158 pp; 1 p. l. 138 pp. 16°. *London, Société de libraires,* 1757.

Histoire générale des larrons. Par F. D. C. lyonnois. [*anon.*] 3 pts. in 1 v. 16°. *Paris, A. Covlon,* 1639.

Histoire littéraire de la France; ouvrage commencé par des religieux benedictins de la congrégation de saint Maur, et continué par les membres de l'académie des inscriptions et belles-lettres. v. 23–24. 4°. *Paris, Didot,* 1856–63.

[*Note.*—v. 23 has an index to vols. 16–23.]

Historia et cartularium monasterii sancti Petri, Glouceslriæ. v. 2–3. Ed. by W. H. Hart. 8°. *London, Longmans,* 1865–67.

[Chronicles of Great Britain and Ireland during the middle ages].

Historiæ ecclesiasticæ scriptores graeci, nempe; Eusebius, Socrates scholasticus, Theodoretus, Sozomenus, Euagrius scholasticus, J. Christophorsono interprete. Recogniti a Suffrido Petro leovardiensi, adiecto indice. 14 p. l. 944 pp. 13 l. fol. *Coloniæ Agrippinæ, hæredes Arnoldi Birckmanni,* 1581. s.

Historiæ romanæ scriptores, latini et græci, minores. Opera F. Sylburgii. 3 v. fol. *Francofvrdi, A. Wecheli hæredes,* 1588–90. s.

CONTENTS.

v. 1. Fasti capitolini, a C. Sigonio suppleti. Messalla Coruinus; L. Florus; Velleius Paterculus; Sex. Aurelius Victor; Sex. Rufus; Eutropius; Casiodori chronicon; Jornandis, lib. 1. Iulius Exsuperantius 4 p. l. xxviii. 859 pp.

v. 2. Suetonius Tranquillus; Aelius Spartianus; Julius Capitolinus; Vulcatius Gallicanus; Aelius Lampridius; Trebellius Pollio; Flavius Vopiscus; Ammianus Marcellinus; Pomponius Lætus; Ioann. Baptista Egnatius; Ausonii epigrammata; Imperatorum catalogus; Romanæ urbis descriptio. 8 p. l. 887 pp.

v. 3. Scriptores graeci minores, qvi partim ab vrbe condita, partim ab Avgvsto imperio, res romanas memoriæ prodiderunt; Fasti græci ac latini; Eutropius; Dionis epitome; Herodianus; Zosimus; Juliani Cæsares; Olympiodorus; E Suida excerptæ Cæsarum vitæ; Imperatorum series chronologica duplex. 4 p. l. 1052, 70 pp.

Historical collections; or, a brief account of the most remarkable transactions of the two last parliaments, held and dissolved at Westminster and Oxford. [*anon.*] 3 p. l. 302 pp. 1 pl. 16°. *London, S. Neale,* 1681.

Historical (An) essay on the ambition and conquests of France, with some remarks on the French revolution. [*anon.*] 355 pp. 8 l. 8°. *London, J. Debrett,* 1797.

Historical outlines of political catholicism: its papacy, prelacy, priesthood, people. [*anon.*] xii, 220 pp. 8°. *London, Chapman & Hall,* 1853.

Historical (The) magazine, and notes and queries concerning the antiquities, history, and biography of America. Jan. to Dec. 1867. 2d series, v, 1–2. 8°. *Morrisania,* [*N. Y.*] *H. B. Dawson,* [1867].

Historical (An) review and directory of North America, containing a geographical, political, and natural history of the British and other European settlements, the united and apocryphal states, etc; and an account of the Indian nations. By a gentleman immediately returned from a tour of the continent. [*anon.*] 2 v. xxviii, 268 pp; ix, 377 pp. 16°. *Cork, W. Matthews,* 1801.

History (A) and description of the Baltimore and Ohio railroad. By a citizen of Baltimore. [*anon.*] 200 pp. 1 map. 6 pl. size? *Baltimore, J. Murphy & Co.* 1853. s.

History (The) of the American revolution, and monthly register of the United States. [Jan. 1805–June 1806]. v. i. vii, viii, 384 pp. 8°. *Charleston,* (*S. C.*) *G. M. Bounetheau,* 1806.

[No more published].

History of the British empire from 1765 to 1783, containing an impartial history of the origin, progress, and termination of the American revolution. By a society of gentlemen. [*anon.*] 2 v. 475 pp; 452, 59 pp. 2 pl. 8°. *Philadelphia, R. Campbell & Co.* 1798.

History of the establishment and progress of the christian religion in the islands of the South sea. [*anon.*] x, 387 pp. 1 map. 16°. *Boston, Tappan & Dennet,* 1841.

History (The) of faction, alias hypocricy, alias moderation. [*anon.*] 4 p. l. 176 pp. 16°. *London, B. Bragg,* 1705.

History (The) of Francis-Eugene, prince of Savoy. By an English officer. [*anon.*] 2d ed. 2 p. l. 343 pp. 6 l. 1 map. portrait. 16°. *London, J. Hodges,* 1742.

History (The) of Jane Grey, queen of England: with a defence of her claim to the crown. [*anon.*] xii, 168 pp. 1 pl. 18°. *London, T. Wilkins,* 1792.

History (The) of the late conspiracy against the king and the nation. [*anon.*] 195 pp. 16°. *London, D. Brown,* 1696.

History (The) of the new world, called America. [*anon.*] 180 pp. 24°. *Dublin, R. Jackson,* [1776]?

History of North and South America, [with] impartial enquiry into the present American disputes. [*anon.*] 2 v. 4 p. l. 276 pp; 3 p. l. 280 pp. 24°. *London, J. Whitaker,* 1776.

History (The) of Robespierre, political and personal. [*anon.*] iv, 136 pp. 1 pl. 8°. *London, C. Whittingham,* 1794.

History (The) of Theodore I, [Theodor Stephan von Neuhoff], king of Corsica. [*anon.*] 139 pp. 8°. *London, J. Roberts,* 1743.

History (The) of two acts, entitled an act for the safety and preservation of his majesty's person and government against treasonable and seditious practices and attempts, and an act for the more effectually preventing seditious meetings and assemblies. [*anon.*] xlviii, 828 pp. 8°. *London, G. G. and J. Robinson,* 1796.

History (The) of the war in America between Great Britain and her colonies, from its commencement to 1783. [*anon.*] 3 v. 8°. *Dublin, booksellers,* 1779–85.

History of the war between the United States and Mexico. [*anon.*] 168 pp. 8 pl. 8°. *Philadelphia, Zieber & Co.* 1847.

History of the Westminster election, 1784. [With 15 caricature plates by Gillray. *anon.*] xi, 538 pp. 15 pl. 4°. *London,* 1784.

Hitchcock (David). Poetical works; containing the shade of Plato, knight and quack, and the subtlety of foxes. xvi, 164 pp. 16°. *Boston, Etheridge & Bliss,* 1806.

Hitchcock (Edward). First anniversary address before the association of American geologists, April 5th, 1841. 48 pp. 8°. *New Haven, B. L. Hamlen,* 1841. s.

——— (*editor*). Catalogues of the animals and plants of Massachusetts. 142 pp. 8°. *Amherst, J. S. & C. Adams,* 1835. s.

CONTENTS.

EARLE (John Milton). Land and fresh water shells. pp. 22–30.
EMMONS (Ebenezer). Birds. pp. 8–14.
GOULD (Augustus Addison). Crustacea. pp. 28–30.
GREENE (Thomas A.) Marine shells. pp. 18–28.
HARRIS (Thaddeus William). Insects. pp. 33–81.
HENTZ (N. M.) Araneides. pp. 30–32.
HITCHCOCK (Edward). Mammalia, pp. 6–7. Radiata. Catalogue of plants growing without cultivation, pp. 82–132.
SMITH (D. S. C. H.) Reptilia. p. 14.
SMITH (J. V. C.) Fishes. pp. 15–18.

Hitchcock (Enos). Memoirs of the Bloomsgrove family. In a series of letters containing sentiments on a mode of domestic education suited to society, government, and manners in the U. S. of A. 2 v. 298 pp; 300 pp. 16°. *Boston, Thomas & Andrews,* 1793.
[Imperfect; pp. 277, 278, 299, 300, of v. 1, wanting].

Hitopadésa. The book of good counsels: from the Sanskrit. By E. Arnold. xii, 167 pp. 4 pl. 12°. *London, Smith, Elder & Co.* 1861.

Hittell (John S.) The resources of California. 3d ed. xv, xvi, 462 pp. 12°. *San Francisco, A. Roman & Co.* 1867.

Hittorff (Jaques Ignace). Architecture moderne de la Sicile; ou, recueil des plus beaux monumens religieux, et des édifices publics et particulièrs les plus remarquables de la Sicile. 5 p. l. 66 pp. fol. *Paris, J. T. Hittorff,* 1835. s.

——— Description des cérémonies et des fêtes qui ont eu lieu pour le baptême de son altesse royale monseigneur Henri Charles Ferdinand Marie Dieudonné d'Artois, duc de Bordeaux. Recueil des décorations exécutées dans l'église de Notre Dame de Paris. 2 p. l. ii, 19 pp. 12 pl. fol. *Paris, P. Renouard,* 1827. s.

——— Description de la rotonde des panoramas élévée dans les Champs-Élysées: précédée d'un aperçu historique. 29 pp. 5 pl. 4°. *Paris, revue de l'architecture,* 1842. s.

Hive (The), or weekly entertaining register. 2 v. 432 pp; 428 pp. 8°. *London, J. Onwhyn,* [*about* 1830].

Hoadly (Benjamin, *D. D. bishop of Bangor*). Refutation of bishop Sherlock's arguments against a repeal of the test and corporation acts. vii, 78 pp. 8°. *London, C. Dilly,* 1787.

Hoadly (E. S.) Method for the piano-forte. *See* **Mason** (Wm.) *and* **Hoadly** (E. S.)

Hoare (*Sir* Richard Colt). The ancient history of South Wiltshire. 254 pp. 3 l. 76 pl. fol. *London, W. Bulmer, for W. Miller,* 1812. s.

——— The ancient history of North Wiltshire. 123, 127 pp. 6 l. 50 pl. fol. *London, W. Bulmer, for Lackington, etc.* 1819. s.

Hoare (William Henry). The veracity of the book of Genesis, with the life and character of the inspired historian. xxii, 303 pp. 8°. *London, Longmans,* 1860.

Hobart (Benjamin). History of the town of Abington, Plymouth county, Massachusetts, from its first settlement. xix, 453 pp. 12°. *Boston, T. H. Carter & son,* 1866.

Hobart (Nathaniel). Life of Emanuel Swedenborg, with some account of his writings. [With] a lecture on the mission of Swedenborg, by Sampson Reed, and an article on the New Jerusalem church. 4th ed. iv, 246 pp. 1 pl. 12°. *Boston, W. Carter & Bro.* 1862.

Hobart (*Rev.* Noah). A second address to the members of the episcopal separation in New England, occasioned by the exceptions made to the former by Dr. Johnson, Mr. Wetmore, Mr. Beach, and Mr. Caner. 172 pp. 1 l. 12°. *Boston, D. Fowle,* 1751.

Hobart & Robbins. Specimens of printing types and ornaments, from the New England type and stereotype foundry. 151 l. 4°. *Boston, Dutton & Wentworth,* 1851. s.

Hobbes (Thomas). Opera philosophica quæ latine scripsit omnia. 2 v. 6 p. l. 479 pp; 661 pp. 7 l. 1 pl. 4°. *Amstelodami, J. Blaev,* 1668.

——— The same. Collecta studio Gulielmi Molesworth. 5 v. 8°. *Londini, J. Bohn,* 1839–45.

CONTENTS.

v. 1. T. Hobbes vita, authore seipso.
Vitæ Hobbianæ auctarium authore R. Blackbourne.
Tho. Hobbes vita, carmine expressa, authore seipso.
Elementorum philosophia de corpore.
v. 2. Elementorum philosophia de homine, de cive, de imperio, de religione.
v. 3. Elementorum philosophia de homine, de civitate, de civitate christiana, de regno tenebrarum.
v. 4. Examinatio et emendatio mathematicæ hodiernæ.
Dialogus physicus de natura aëris.
Problemata physica, propositiones xvi de magnitudine circuli, et duplicatio cubi.
De principiis et ratiocinatione geometrarum et de mediis proportionalibus in genere.
Quadratura circuli, cubatio spherae, duplicatio cubi.
v. 5. Rosetum geometricum.
Lux mathematica.
Principia et problemata aliquot geometrica antehac desperata, nunc breviter explicata.
Tractatus opticus.
Objectiones ad Cartesii meditationes.
Epistolæ.
Praefatio in Mersenni ballisticam.
De mirabilibus Pecci, (seu, de caverna Peak dicta).
Historia ecclesiastica.

Hobhouse (John Cam, *lord Brougton*). Journey through Albania, and other provinces of Turkey in Europe and Asia to Constantinople, during 1809–10. 2d ed. 2 v. 1153 pp. 22 pl. 2 maps. 4°. *London,* [*B. McMillan*], 1813. s.

Hodenberg (Wilhelm von). Calenberger urkundenbuch. 1e–9e abth. 4°. *Hannover,* 1855–58.

[Abtheilungen 2-4, not yet published.]

——— Hoyer urkundenbuch. 8 pts in 3 v. 4°. *Hannover,* 1855–56.

Hodge (Michael). An oration before St. Peter's lodge, Newburyport, June 24, 1802. 15 pp. 4°. *Newburyport, A. March,* 1802.

Hodges (Richard M. *M. D.*) Practical dissections. 2d ed. 286 pp. 12°. *Philadelphia, H. C. Lea,* 1867.

Hodges (William). Voyage pittoresque de l'Inde, 1780–1783. Traduit de l'Anglais, par L. Langlès. 2 v. xxvii, 222 pp; 252 pp. 18°. *Paris, Delance,* 1805. s.

[Collection portative de voyages, v. 4–5. Atlas in 8°. wanting.]

Hodgkin (Thomas, *M. D.*) Lectures on the morbid anatomy of the serous and mucous membranes. 2 v. 10 p. l. 402 pp; 12 p. l. 541 pp. 8°. *London,* 1836–40. s.

Hodgson (William). The lives, sentiments, and sufferings of some of the reformers and martyrs before, since, and independent of the Lutheran reformation. 465 pp. 12°. *Philadelphia, J. B. Lippincott & Co.* 1867.

Hodson (*Mrs.* Margaret Holford). Wallace; or, the fight of Falkirk. 256 pp. 8°. *Philadelphia, J. & A. Y. Humphreys,* 1810.

Hoe (Robert, & Co.) Catalogue of printing presses, etc. 138 pp. 8°. *New York,* [1867].

Hoefer (Jean Chrétien Ferdinand). Histoire de la chimie depuis les temps les plus reculés jusqu'à notre époque, etc. 2 v. xi, 510 pp; viii, 518 pp. 8°. *Paris, bureau de la revue scientifique, etc.* 1842–43. s.

Hoefle (Mark Aurel). Chemie und mikroskop am krankenbette. x, 483, 200 pp. 3 pl. 8°. *Erlangen, F. Enke,* 1848. s.

Hoek (Martinus). De kometen van de jaren 1556, 1264, en 975, en hare vermeende identitert. vii, 94 pp. 1 pl. 4°. *'s Gravenhage, Van Cleef,* 1857. s.

Hoff (Carl Ernst Adolf von). Geschichte der durch überlieferung nachgewiesenen natürlichen veränderungen der erdoberfläche. 5 v. 8°. *Gotha, J. Perthes*, 1822–41. s.

CONTENTS.

v. i. Veränderungen in dem verhältnisse zwischen land und meer.
v. ii. Geschichte der vulcane und der erdbeben.
v. iii. Zusätzen zu den beiden ersten theilen.
v. iv–v. Chronik der erdbeben und vulcan-ausbrüche von 3460 [B. C.] bis 1832 [A. D.]

Hoffmann (Ernst Theodor Amadeus). Le conseiller Krespel. Traduit de l'Allemand par É. de Labédollière. 40 pp. 12°. *Paris, L. Curmer*, 1841.
[In PLÉIADE, La.]

Hoffmann (Friedrich). De studio medico recte pertractando.
[*With* CONRING (H.) Introductio in universam artem medicam. Ed. 1726.]

Hoffmann (*Dr.* Hermann). Pflanzenverbreitung und pflanzenwanderung. 144 pp. 8°. *Darmstadt, G. Jonghaus*, 1852. s.

Hoffmann (Samuel Friedrich Wilhelm). Bibliographisches lexicon der gesammten litteratur der Griechen. 2e ausg. 3 v. 8°. *Leipzig, A. F. Böhme*, 1838–45. s.

——— Handbuch zur bücherkunde für lehre und studium der beiden alten klassischen und deutschen sprache. x, 467 pp. 8°. *Leipzig, C. Cnobloch*, 1838. s.

Hoffmann (*Dr.* Wilhelm). Die geschichte des handels, der erdkunde und schifffahrt aller völker und staaten, von der frühesten zeit bis auf die gegenwart. 2e aufl. vi, 609 pp. 4 tab. 8°. *Leipzig, O. Wigand*, 1847. s.

Hoffmeister (Werner Friedrich Ludwig Albert). Die bis jetzt bekannte arten aus der familie der regenwürmer. 43 pp. 1 col. pl. 4°. *Braunschweig, Vieweg*, 1845. s.

Hofland (Barbara). The unloved one, a domestic story. 160 pp. 8°. *New York, Harpers*, 1844.

Hofmann (Joseph, *M. D.*) Das regelwidrige weibliche becken. iv, 107 pp. 8°. *München, Verfasser*, 1839. s.

Hogan (Edmund). The prospect of Philadelphia, and check on the next directory. 2 pts. in 1 v. 180 pp. 12°. *Philadelphia, Francis and Robert Bailey*, 1795.

Hogarth (William). Les satyres de Guillaume Hogarth. (English text.) 2 p. l. 79 pl. fol. *Londres, R. Sayer*, 1768. s.

——— Zeichnungen nach den originalen in stahl gestochen, etc. 2 abtheile in 1 v. 7 p. l. xxiv, 994 pp. 8°. *Stuttgart, Literatur-comptoir*, 1840.

CONTENTS.

Abth. 1. Zeichnungen mit der vollständigen erklärung von G. C. Lichtenberg und einer lebensgeschichte von F. Kottenkamp. 3 p. l. xxiv, pp. 1–539.
Abth. 2. Zeichnungen mit der vollständige erklärung von F. Kottenkamp. 4 p. l. pp. 561–994.

Hogrewe (Johann Ludwig). Beschreibung der in England seit 1759 angelegten und jetzt gröstentheils vollendeten schiffbaren kanäle. Nebst einem versuch einer geschichte der inländischen schiffahrt. 6 p. l. vi, 164 pp. 12 pl. 4°. *Hannover, H. M. Pockwitzt*, 1780. s.

Hohmann (Christian Heinrich). Practical course of instruction in singing. Part 1, exercises and songs for younger classes. 38 pp. sq. 18°. *Boston, O. Ditson*, 1856. s.

Hoikehonua. He mau palapala aina a me-na niele no ka hoikehonua. 16 pp. 8 col. maps. 18°. *Lahainaluna*, 1840.

Hoisington (Henry Richard, *editor*). The oriental astronomer: a complete system of Hindu astronomy, (Tamil and English). 2 v. in 1. 2 p. l. 177 pp; 145 pp. 8°. *Jaffna, Am. mission press*, 1848. s.

Holbach (Paul Henri Thiry, *baron* d'). Le bon sens du curé J[ean] Meslier. Suivi de son testament. [Publiés par Voltaire.] 380 pp. 16°. *Paris & Bruxelles*, [*about* 1792].

Holbein (Hans). The dance of death, engraved by W. Hollar. [Preface and description of plates by F. Douce, with the daunce of Macaber, by John Lydgate.] 1 p. l. 81 pp. 32 pl. 23 l. 1 pl. 16°. *London, J. Simco*, 1792. s.

——— The same. [New ed.] 12°. *London*, 1804. s.

Holberg (Ludvig). An introduction to universal history. Translated by G. Sharpe. A new edition, revised by W. Radcliffe. xxv, 354 pp. 8°. *London, L. Davis* [*and others*], 1787.

——— Nicolai Klimii iter svbterranevm, novam tellvris theoriam ac historiam qvintæ monarchiæ adhvc nobis incognitæ exhibens. [*pseudon.*] 380 pp. 4 pl. 16°. *Hafniae, J. Preuss*, 1741.

Holbrook (*Rev.* Anthony). Christian essays upon the immorality of uncleanness and duelling; two sermons. 46 pp. 12°. *London, J. Wyat*, 1727.

Holbrook (John Edwards). North American herpetology; or, a description of the reptiles inhabiting the United States. 5 v. 147 col. pl. 4°. *Philadelphia, J. Dobson*, 1842.

Holcombe (Henry *D. D.*) The first fruits, in a series of letters. 228 pp. 16°. *Philadelphia, Ann Cochran*, 1812.

Holcroft (Thomas). Tales in verse. 2 v. x, 170 pp; 142 pp. 18°. *London, H. D. Symonds*, 1806.

Holden (Frederic A.) Genealogy of the descendants of Banfield Capron, 1660–1859. 263 pp. 12°. *Boston, G. C. Rand & Avery*, 1859. s.

Holden (Horace). A narrative of the shipwreck, captivity, and sufferings, of Horace Holden and Benj. H. Nute on the Pelew and Lord North's islands. 133 pp. 18°. *Boston, Russell, Shattuck & Co.* 1836.

Holeman (*Rev.* F. R.) Christian poems. 227 pp. 18°. *Claremont (N. H.) Manuf. Co.* 1865.

Holford (George). The destruction of Jerusalem, an absolute and irresistible proof of the divine origin of christianity. [*anon.*] 3d Am. ed. 132 pp. 16°. *Pottstown, John Royer*, 1820.

Holford (*Miss* Margaret). *See* **Hodson** (*Mrs.* Margaret H.)

Holgate (Jerome B.) American genealogy; being a history of some of the early settlers of North America and their descendants. 244 pp. 4°. *Albany, J. Munsell*, 1848. s.

Holl (Friedrich). Handbuch der petrefactenkunde. 2 p. l. 489 pp. 4 pts. in 1 v. 16°. *Dresden, R. G. Hilscher*, 1829–30. s.

Holland (H. R. Fox, 3*d lord*). *See* **Fox** (Henry Richard Vassall).

Holland (Josiah Gilbert). Christ and the twelve; as painted by the poets. 504 pp. 6 pl. 8°. *Springfield, (Mass.) G. Bill & Co.* 1867.

——— Kathrina; her life and mine, in a poem. 14th ed. 287 pp. 12°. *New York, C. Scribner & Co.* 1867.

Holland (Saba Smith, *lady*). Memoir of Sydney Smith, with a selection from his letters. Edited by Mrs. Austin. 2 v. 378; 511 pp. 12°. *New York, Harpers*, 1855. s.

Holland. *See* **Netherlands.**

Hollard (Henri). Précis d'anatomie comparée, etc. 466 pp. 3 pl. 12°. *Bruxelles, H. Dumont*, 1836. s.

Holley (O. L.) A gazetteer of the state of New York; with the census of 1840, and the tables of distances. [*anon.*] 479 pp. 1 map. 1 pl. 12°. *Albany, J. Disturnell*, 1842.

Hollick (Frederick). Neuropathy; or, the true principles of the art of healing the sick. 14, 193 pp. 1 col. pl. 16°. *Philadelphia, national publishing co.* 1847. s.

Hollingsworth (S.) An account of the present state of Nova Scotia. [*anon.*] viii, 157 pp. 8°. *Edinburgh, W. Creech*, 1786.

Hollister (Hiel). Pawlet [Vt.] for one hundred years. 272 pp. 12°. *Albany, J. Munsell*, 1867.

Hollister (Ovando J.) The mines of Colorado. vii, 450 pp. 1 map. 12°. *Springfield, (Mass.) S. Bowles & Co.* 1867.

Holloway (Benjamin). Originals physical and theological, sacred and profane; or, essay towards a discovery of the first descriptive ideas in things, by discovery of the simple or primary roots in words. [With discourses on the hidden manna, and on the tree of life.] 2 v. 13 p. l. 439 pp; 433 pp. 6 l. 8°. *Oxford, printed at the theatre*, 1751.

Holmberg (Axel Emanuel). Nordbon under hednatiden. Populär framställing af våra förfäders älsta kultur. 4 p. l. 302 pp. 2 pl. 8°. *Stockholm, J. Beckman*, 1852. s.

Holmboe (Christopher Andreas). Det norske sprogs væsentligste ordforraad, sammenlignet med sanskrit og andre sprog af samme aet. xx, 496 pp. 4°. *Wien, k. hof og stats-trykkerie*, 1852. s.

——— Descriptio ornamentorum maximam partem aureorum et numorum saeculi viii et ix in praedio Hoen, in parochia Eger, in diocesi Norwegiæ agershusiensi, anno 1834 repertorum. 16 pp. 2 pl. 4°. *Christianiæ, Lehmann*, 1835. s.

——— Det oldnorske verbum, oplyst ved sammenligning med sanskrit og andre sprog af samme aet. 4°. *Christiania*, 1848. s.

Holmes (*Rev.* Abiel). Sermon preach'd at Cambridge, first Lord's day in the nineteenth century. 27 pp. 8°. *Cambridge, (Mass.) William Hilliard*, 1801.

Holmes (J. H. H.) Treatise on the coal mines of Durham and Northumberland. xxii, 259 pp. 7 pl. 8°. *London, Baldwin, Cradock, & Joy*, 1816.

Holmes (*Mrs.* Mary J.) The Cameron pride; or, purified by suffering. A novel. 415 pp. 12°. *New York, G. W. Carleton & Co.* 1867.

Holmes (Oliver Wendell). The guardian angel. xii, 420 pp. 12°. *Boston, Ticknor & Fields*, 1867.

Holyoke (Edward). The doctrine of life; or, of man's redemption by the seed of Eve, the seed of Abraham, etc. 9 p. l. 426 pp. ix l. sm. 4°. *London, Nath. Ekins*, 1658.

Homans (J. Smith). Merchants' and bankers' almanac for 1865–1867. 3 v. 8°. *New York, J. S. Homans*, 1865–67.

Home (*Sir* Everard). Lectures on comparative anatomy; in which are explained the preparations in the Hunterian collection. 4 v. 4°. *London, G. & W. Nicol,* 1814. s.

——— The same. v. 5–6. Supplement. 2 v. viii, 437 pp; vi, 68 pp. 68 pl. 4°. *London, Longmans,* 1828. s.

Home evangelization; a view of the wants and prospects of our country. By one of the secretaries of the American tract society. 18°. *New York,* [*about* 1850]. s.

Homer (James Lloyd). Nahant, and other places on the north shore. vii, 48 pp. 8°. *Boston, William Chadwick,* 1848.

Homerus. Opera græco-latina quæ extant omnia. Operam contulit S. Castalio. 10 p. l. 292, 318 pp. fol. *Basiliae, Brylinger,* 1567. s.

——— The works of Homer, including the Iliad and the Odyssey, [translated by Pope; and] the battle of the frogs and mice, translated by Parnell. Revised by W. H. Melmoth. vi, 7, 654 pp. 5 l. 1 map, 39 pl. 4°. *London, A. Hogg,* [*about* 1780].

——— The Iliad. Faithfully translated into unrhymed English metre. By F. W. Newman. xxii, 435 pp. 12°. *London, Walton & Maberly,* 1856.

——— ——— The same. Translated into English accentuated hexameters, by Sir J. F. W. Herschel. xvi, 549 pp. 8°. *Cambridge, Macmillan & Co.* 1866.

——— Burlesque translation [of the first twelve books of the Iliad, by Thomas Brydges]. [*anon.*] From 4th London ed. 2 v. 189; 221 pp. 24 pl. 16°. *New York,* 1809.

——— Versione letterale dell' Iliade, [di Melchior Cesarotti.] 7 v. in 8. 8°. *Firenze, Molini, Landi, e Ca.* 1804–07. s.
[General index wanting.]

——— Le combat des rats et des grenouilles. Traduit du Grec par M. Trianon. 34 pp. 12°. *Paris,* 1841.
[Included in PLÉIADE, La.]

Homiliarius doctorum. *See* **Thierry** (Jean, *of Langres*).

Hone (William). Facetiæ and miscellanies, with one hundred and twenty engravings, drawn by George Cruikshank. 2d ed. 8°. *London, William Hone,* 1827.

——— Table book. 2 v. 859; 888 pp. 8°. *London, W. Hone,* 1827–28.

Honeywood (St. John). Poems, with some pieces in prose. viii, 159 pp. 16°. *New York, T. & J. Swords,* 1801.

Hood (Charles). Practical treatise on warming buildings by hot water; on ventilation, the laws of radiant and conducted heat, the chemical constitution of coal, and the combustion of smoke. 2d ed. xii, 348 pp. 8°. *London, Whittaker,* 1844. s.

Hood (John W. *M. D.*) Principles and practice of medicine, in a series of essays. xvi, 263 pp. 8°. *Philadelphia, Thomas, Cowperthwait & Co.* 1848. s.

Hood (Samuel). A brief account of the society of the friendly sons of St. Patrick; with biographical notices of members, and extracts from minutes. [*anon.*] 112 pp. 1 pl. 12°. *Philadelphia, W. S. Young,* 1844.

Hood (Thomas, *jr. and others*). Rates and taxes, and how they were collected. xi, 277 pp. 1 pl. 16°. *London, Groombridge & sons,* 1866.

Hook (Walter Farquhar, *D. D.*) Lives of the archbishops of Canterbury. v. 5. xvi, 524 pp. 8°. *London, R. Bentley,* 1867.

Hooker (Joseph Dalton). Himalayan journals. Notes of a naturalist in Bengal, the Sikkim and Nepal Himalayas, the Khasia mountains, etc. New ed. 2 v. 8°. *London, John Murray,* 1855. s.

——— Genera plantarum. *See* **Bentham** (Geo.) *and* **Hooker** (J. D.)

Hooker (Worthington). The child's book of nature. 3 v. in 1. 12°. *New York, Harpers,* 1857. s.

CONTENTS.

Part 1. Plants.
Part 2. Animals.
Part 3. Air, water, heat, light, etc.

Hookham's original circulating library. New catalogue. 284 pp. 8°. *London,* [1805?] s.

Hooper (George, *D. D. bishop of Bath and Wells*). Works. [With preface by T. Hunt]. xiii, 693 pp. 1 pl. fol. *Oxford, J. Fletcher,* 1757.

CONTENTS.

Calculation of the credibility of human testimony.
Church of England free from the imputation of popery.
De Valentinianorum haeresi conjecturae.
Discourse concerning lent.
Discussion of the controversy between the church of England and the church of Rome concerning the infallible guide.
Emendationes ad Tertulliani adversus Valentinianos tractatum.
Enquiry into the ancient measures.
Eight sermons.
In benedictionem patriarchae Jacobi conjecturae.

——— An inquiry into the state of the ancient measures, the Attick, the Roman, and the Jewish, with appendix concerning our old English money and measures of content. [*anon.*] 12 p. l. 475 pp. 8°. *London, R. Knaplock,* 1721.

Hooper (Robert, *M. D.*) Lexicon medicum; or, medical dictionary. With additions by S. Akerly, M. D. 4th Amer. ed. 2 v. in 1. 472 pp; 367 pp. 23 l. 8°. *New York, Harpers,* 1829.

Hooper (William, *M. D.*) Rational recreations, in which the principles of numbers and natural philosophy are elucidated; among which are all those commonly performed with cards. 4 v. 8°. *London, L. Davis,* 1774. s.

Hope (A. J. Beresford). *See* **Beresford**-Hope.

Hope (Thomas). Costume of the ancients. New ed. 2 v. xvi, 50 pp. 6 l. 300 pl. 8°. *London, H. G. Bohn,* 1841. s.

——— Historical essay on architecture. 3d ed. 3 v. 8°. *London, J. Murray,* 1836–40.

CONTENTS.

v. 1. Text. xx, 526 pp.
v. 2. Plates. xii pp. 97 pl.
v. 3. Index. 90 pp.

Hopf (Carl). Historisch-genealogischer atlas seit Christi geburt bis auf unsere zeit. Abth. 1. Deutschland. v. 1. xvi, 449 pp. fol. *Gotha, F. A. Perthes,* 1858. s.

Hopkins (David). *See* **Richardson** (J.) Vocabulary, Persian, Arabic, and English, 1810.

Hopkins (Jesse). The patriots' manual; interesting to every American citizen. 220 pp. 16°. *Utica, W. Williams,* 1828.

Hopkins (John Henry, *D. D. bishop of Vermont*). History of the church, in verse. Composed for the use of bible-classes, [etc.] in the protestant episcopal church in the United States. 256 pp. 12°. *New York, W. I. Pooley,* 1867.

Hopkins (Samuel, *A. M.*) Historical memoirs relating to the Housatunnuk Indians; or, account of the propagation of the gospel among that tribe, under the ministry of John Sergeant. 1 p. l. 182 pp. 8°. *Boston, S. Kneeland,* 1753.

Hopkins (Samuel, *D. D.*) An inquiry concerning the future state of those who die in their sins. 2 p. l. vi, 194 pp. 12°. *Newport, S. Southwick,* 1783.

Hopkinsian (The) magazine, 1826–27. Rev. Otis Thompson, editor. v. 2. iii, 583 pp. 8°. *Providence, Field & Co.* 1826.

Hopper (Edward). One wife too many; or, Rip Van Bigham. A tale of Tappan Zee. 262 pp. 16°. *New York, Hurd & Houghton,* 1867.

Hoppin (James M.) Old England; its scenery, art, and people. v, 468 pp. 16°. *New York, Hurd & Houghton,* 1867.

Hoppus (E.) Hoppus's tables of measuring; or, practical measuring made easy; with curious observations on measuring timber. 18th ed. lx, 226 pp. 8°. *London, Rivington,* 1823.

Horatius Flaccus (Quintus). Opera expurgata, notis anglicis illustrata. Cura Thomæ Dugdale, jun. xvii, 359 pp. 8°. *Philadelphiæ, S. W. Conrad,* 1815. s.

——— Opera, cum notis gallicis. viii, 275 pp. 24° *Parisiis, A. Delalain,* 1832. s.

——— The works of Horace, [Lat.] with English notes, etc. By Charles Anthon. A new ed. xxv, 731 pp. 12°. *New York, Harpers,* 1849. s.

——— Works, in English verse, by [W.] Duncombe, J. Duncombe, and other hands. With notes, historical and critical, [and] many imitations. 2d ed. 4 v. 16°. *London, B. White, [and others],* 1767.

——— Odes, satires, epistles, and art of poetry. Translated by P. Francis. 8°. *Edinburgh,* [1792–94].
[Anderson's Brit. poets, v. 1].

——— Odes and epodes, satires, epistles, and art of poetry, construed literally, and word for word, by Rev. Dr. Giles. 352 pp. 18°. *London, J. Cornish,* [1859].

——— Satiren aus dem lateinischen übersetzt und mit einleitungen und erläuternden anmerkungen versehen von C. M. Wieland. 2 v. in 1. 312 pp; 254 pp. 8°. *Leipzig, Weidmann,* 1804. s.

Horner (G. R. B. *M. D.*) Diseases and injuries of seamen; with remarks on their enlistment, naval hygiene, and the duties of medical officers. 252 pp. 12°. *Philadelphia, Lippincott, Grambo & Co.* 1854.

Hörnes (*Dr.* Moriz). Verzeichniss der fossil-reste aus 135 fundarten des tertiär-beckens von Wien. 74 pp. 3 tab. 8°. *Wien, W. Braumüller,* 1848. s.
[*With* Czjzek's erläuterungen, etc.]

Horsburgh (James). India directory; or, directions for sailing to and from the East Indies, China, New Holland, Cape of Good Hope, Brazil, etc. 2d ed. with supplement. 2 v. in 1. 5 p. l. xxvi, 446 pp; 3 p. l. 551, 50 pp. 4°. *London, author,* 1817–18. s.

Horse owner's friend; a treatise on all diseases and accidents of the horse, with their treatment. [*anon.*] 256 pp. 24°. *Ann Arbor, (Mich.) Chase,* 1867.

Horsford (Eben Norton). Report on the geology of Cattaraugus county.
[*With* NEW YORK, *State*, annual reports on the geological survey. v. 4.]

——— Report on the phrenological classification of J. Stanley Grimes. Adopted by the Albany phrenological society. 28 pp. 12°. *Albany, J. Munsell*, 1840. s.

——— Untersuchungen über glycocoll und einiger seiner zersetzungsproducte. [Extract.] 57 pp. 8°. *Giessen, Ann. d. chemie*, 1846. s.

Horsmanden (Daniel). A journal of proceedings in the detection of the conspiracy formed by some white people, in conjunction with negro and other slaves [at New York]. vi, 205, xvi pp. 4°. *New York, James Parker*, 1744.

Hortense de Beauharnais, (Eugénie, *queen of Holland*). Romances composées et mises en musique. *See* **Mémoires** sur madame la duchesse de St. Leu. *Londres*, 1832.

Horticulturist (The) and journal of rural art and rural taste. Jan. to Dec. 1867. New series. v. 22. 8°. *New York, F. W. Woodward*, 1867.

Horton (R. G.) Youth's history of the great civil war in the United States, 1861–65. 2d ed. 384 pp. 16°. *New York, Van Evrie, Horton and Co.* 1866.

Horton (William, *M. D.*) Report on the geology of Orange county.
[NEW YORK, *State*, annual reports on the geol. survey. v. 2.]

Hoskins (Nathan). A history of Vermont, from its discovery and settlement to 1830. 316 pp. 16°. *Vergennes, (Ind.) J. Shedd*, 1831.

Hoskyns (Chandos Wren). Occasional essays. 256 pp. 16°. *London, Longmans*, 1866.

Höst (Georg). Efterretninger om öen Sanct Thomas og dens gouverneurer, fra 1769 indtil 1776. xx, 203 pp. 12°. *Kiöbenhavn, N. Moller og son*, 1791.

Hostmann (F. W. *M. D.*) Over de beschaving van negers in Amerika, door kolonisatie met Europeanen. 2 v. lxvi, 346 pp; 463 pp. 8°. *Amsterdam, J. C. A. Sulpke*, 1850.

Hotchkiss (*Capt.* Jed.) *and* Allan (William). The battlefields of Virginia. Chancellorsville. 152 pp. 5 maps. 1 pl. 8°. *New York, D. Van Nostrand*, 1867.

Hotho (H. G.) Die malerschule Huberts Van Eyck nebst deutschen vorgängern und zeitgenossen. v. i, ii, lief. 1. 12°. *Berlin, Veit & Co.* 1855–58. s.

CONTENTS.

v. i. Geschichte der deutschen malerei bis 1450. xvii, 490 pp.
v. ii. Flandrische malerei des xv. jahrhhunderts. 1e lief. ix, 244 pp.

Hough (Franklin B.) History of Duryée's brigade, during the campaign in Virginia under Gen. Pope, and in Maryland under Gen. McClellan, in 1862. 200 pp. 1 pl. 8°. *Albany, J. Munsell*, 1864.

——— The northern invasion of October, 1780; a series of papers relating to the expeditions from Canada under Sir John Johnson and others, against the frontiers of New York. With an introduction and notes. 224 pp. 1 pl. 1 map. 8°. *New York*, 1866.
[Bradford club publications, No. 6.]

——— *See* **New York**, *State*, Convention manual.

——— (*editor*). *See* **Washington** (George). Washingtoniana, etc. 1865.

Houghton (Douglass). First and second annual reports of the state geologist [of Michigan], and documents. 3 v. 8°. *Lansing*, 1838–39. s.

CONTENTS OF DOCUMENTS.

Douglass (C. C.) Report of assistant geologist. pp. 66–77.
Higgins, (J. W.) Report of topographer. pp. 45–65
Hubbard (Bela). Report of assistant geologist. pp. 79–123
Sayer (Abram). Report of zoologist. pp. 1–15.
Wright (John). Report of botanist. pp. 17–44.

Houghton (J.) *and* **Bristol** (T. W.) Reports on the geography, topography, and geology of the mineral region of Lake Superior. 109 pp. map. 16°. *Detroit, Charles Wilcox*, 1846.

Houghton (John, *F. R. S.*) Husbandry and trade improv'd; revised by Richard Bradley. 3 v. 8°. *London, Woodman & Lyon*, 1727.

Houghton gallery. A set of prints, engraved after the most capital paintings, in the collection of H. I. M. the empress of Russia, lately in the collection of the earl of Orford, at Houghton, in Norfolk. [With plans of Houghton hall and estate]. 2 v. 5 p. l. 81 pl; 4 p. l. 71 pl. fol. *London, J. & J. Boydell*, 1788.

Hours at home; a popular monthly, devoted to religious and useful literature. Edited by J. M. Sherwood. Nov. 1866—Apr. 1867. v. 4. 4°. *New York, C. Scribner & Co.* [1865].

House carpenters' book of prices, and rules for measuring and valuing work. 35 pp. 12°. *Philadelphia, R. Folwell*, 1801.

Household tales and traditions of England, Germany, France, Scotland, etc. [*anon.*] 188 pp. 16°. *London, E. Lumley*, [*about* 1850].

Houston (*Mrs.* M. C.) Hesperos; or, travels in the west. 2 v. viii, 293 pp. 12°. *London, J. W. Parker*, 1850.

Houston (Samuel). Letter to Gen. Santa Anna. 8 pp. 8°. *Washington*, 1852.

Houtteville (Alexandre Claude François). Religion chrétienne prouvée par les faits. Avec un discours sur la méthode des principaux auteurs qui ont écrit pour et contre le christianisme depuis son origine. cciv, 476 pp. 4°. *Paris, Greg. Dupuis,* 1722.

Hovey (Alvah, *D. D.*) The state of the impenitent dead. 168 pp. 16°. *Boston, Gould & Lincoln,* 1859. s.

How (*Rev.* Thomas Y.) A vindication of the protestant episcopal church, in a series of letters addressed to Rev. Samuel Miller. xxxvi, 492 pp. 8°. *New York, Eastburn, Kirk & Co.* 1816.

Howard (Luke). Seven lectures on meteorology. 2d ed. vi, 218 pp. 16°, *London, Harvey & Darton,* 1843. s.

Howard (Robert). Revelations of Egyptian mysteries, and allegories of the Greek lyric poets clearly interpreted. History of the works of nature, with a discourse on health, according with the wisdom of the ancients. viii, 284 pp. 8°. *London, H. Colburn,* 1850.

Howe (Henry). Historical collections of Virginia, with sketch of the District of Columbia. 544 pp. 19 pl. 1 map. 8°. *Charleston, (S. C.) W. R. Babcock,* 1847. s.

——— Times of the rebellion in the west; a collection of miscellanies. 252 pp. 8°. *Cincinnati, F. A. Howe,* 1867.

Howe (Nathaniel). Century sermon in Hopkinton, Dec. 24, 1815. 2d ed. 8°. 31 pp. *Andover, Flagg & Gould,* 1817.

Howell (George Rogers). Early history of Southampton, L. I. With genealogies. 318 pp. 12°. *New York, J. N. Hallock,* 1866.

Howell (James). A German diet, or the ballance of Europe. 4 p. l, 187 pp. 4 l. 1 pl. fol. *London, H. Moseley,* 1653.

Howells (William D.) Italian journeys. 320 pp. 12°. *New York, Hurd & Houghton,* 1867.

——— Venetian life. 2d ed. 401 pp. 12°. *New York, Hurd & Houghton,* 1867.

Howitt (William). A country book; for the field, the forest, and the fireside. 3d ed. viii, 392 pp. 8 pl. 16°. *London, Routledge & Co.* 1858.

Howse (Joseph). A grammar of the Cree language; [with] analysis of the Chippeway dialect. xx, 324 pp. 8°. *Cirencester, J. G. F. & J. Rivington,* 1844.

Howson (Henry). Information and estimates relating to foreign patents. 48 pp. 12°. *Philadelphia, U. S. and European Pat. Off.* [1866].

Hoxse (John). The Yankee tar. A narrative of his voyages and hardships. 200 pp. 16°. *Northampton, John Metcalf,* 1848.

Hoyt (David W.) A genealogical history of John Hoyt of Salisbury, and David Hoyt of Deerfield, (Mass.) and their descendants: with some account of the earlier Connecticut Hoyts. 144 pp. 3 pl. 8°. *Boston, C. Richardson,* 1857.

Hoyt (Epaphras). Practical instructions for military officers, [with] a new military dictionary. viii, 480 pp. 14 pl. 12°. *Greenfield, [Mass.] J. Denio,* 1811.

Hoyt (Jesse). Letters from Jesse Hoyt, to the secretary of the treasury, explanatory of the action of George Poindexter and his colleagues, commissioners for the investigation of the affairs of the custom-house at New York. 139 pp. 8°. *New York, Evening post,* [1842?] s.

Huarte de San Juan (Juan). Essame de gl'ingeni de gl'hvomini per apprender le scienze. Tradotto dalla lingua spagnuola da C. Camilli. 12 p. l. 367 pp. 16°. *Venetia, Aldo,* 1586.

Hubbard (Bela). Report of the assistant geologist of Michigan. s.

[*With* HOUGHTON (Douglass). Report on the geology of Michigan, Doc. No. 5.]

Hubbard (John N.) Sketches of border adventures in the life and times of Maj. Moses Van Campen, a surviving soldier of the revolution. 310 pp. 8°. *Bath, [N. Y.] R. L. Underhill & Co.* 1842.

Hubbard (S.) The temperance melodist. 12°. *Boston, Kidder & Cheever,* 1852. s.

Hubbard (*Rev.* William). The present state of New England; a narrative of the troubles with the Indians, from 1607 to 1677, with a discourse about the war with the Pequods in 1637, [and a narrative of the troubles with the Indians from Pascataqua to Pemmaquid]. 6 p. l. 131, xiii, 88 pp. sm. 4°. *London, Tho. Parkhurst,* 1677.

Hübener (J. W. P.) Flora der umgegend von Hamburg, städtischen gebietes, holstein-lauenburgischen und luneburgischen antheils. xliv, 523 pp. 8°. *Hamburg, J. A. Meissner,* 1846. s.

Huber (Therese). Die geschichte des Cevennen-kriegs. 16°. *Stuttgart, Cotta,* 1834. s.

Hubley (Benrard *or* Bernard). The history of the American revolution. v 1. 1774–75. [No more published.] 606 pp. 8°. *Northumberland, [Pa.] A. Kennedy,* 1805.

Hübner (Jacob). Verzeichniss bekannter schmetterlinge. 431, 72 pp. 8°. *Augsburg, Hübner,* 1816. s.

Hudson (Thomas). Comic songs. 7th, 8th, 9th, 11th, and 12th collections. 36 pp. each. 18°. *London, T. Hudson,* 1826-31.

Huerne de La Mothe (François Charles). Libertés de la France, contre le pouvoir arbitraire de l'excommunication. xxxvi, 255 pp. 16°. *Amsterdam,* 1761.

Hufeland (Christoph Wilhelm). L'art de prolonger la vie humaine, traduit sur la 2e éd. de l'Allemand. 2 parts in 1 v. xvi, 358 pp. 8°. *Lausanne, Hignon & Cie.* 1809.

Huffington (William). *See* **Delaware** Register. *Dover,* 1838-39.

Hug (Johannes Leonhard). Bemerkungen über die aeginetischen bildwerke. 4°. *Freiburg, Wagner,* 1835. s.

Hugel (Julius von), *and* **Schmidt** (C. F.) Die gestüte und meiereien des königs Wilhelm von Wurttemberg. xvi, 220 pp. 7 col. pl. 4°. *Stuttgart, Ebner & Seubert,* [1861.] s.

Huggins (John Richard Desborus). Hugginiana; or, Huggins' fantasy, being a collection of the most esteemed literary productions. 2d ed. 288 pp. 9 pl. 16°. *New York, H. C. Southwick,* 1808.

Hughes (Jabez). Miscellanies in verse and prose. viii p. l. 292 pp. 8°. *London, John Watts,* 1737.

Hughes (John). Poetical works. 8°. *Edinburgh,* 1793.

[Anderson's Brit. poets, v. 7].

Hughes (Thomas Smart). History of England, from the death of George II. to the present time. [1760—1835.] 5 v. 8°. *Paris, Baudry,* 1835-36. s.

Hughes (W.) The American physitian; or, a treatise of the roots, plants, trees, herbs, etc. in the English plantations in America. viii p. l. 159 pp. 24°. *London, William Crook,* 1672.

Hugo (Marie Victor). The king's fool; or, le roi s'amuse. iv, 44 pp. 8°. *London,* [1841?]

[Hazlitt's romancist and novelist's lib. v. 5.]

——— Lucretia Borgia; a dramatic tale. Translated from the French by W. T. Haley. viii, 39 pp. 8°. *London,* [1841?]

[Hazlitt's romancist and novelist's lib. v. 5.]

Hull (Joseph Hervey). English grammar, by lectures. 107 pp. 16°. *Hagerstown, J. H. Hull,* 1823.

Hullah (John), *and* **Sharland** (Joseph B.) The grammar school chorus; containing Wilhem's method of teaching vocal music; also, selections for devotional exercises, [etc.] in one, two, and three parts. 183 pp. 8°. *Boston, O. Ditson & Co.* [1866].

Hulot (——). Instruction sur le service de l'artillerie. Revue et augmentée, par Bigot. 3e éd. xii, 283 pp. 2 tab. 2 pl. 12°. *Paris, Magimel,* 1813. s.

Hulshoff (Maria Aletta). Peace republican's manual; or, the French constitution of 1793; the declaration of the rights of man and of citizens; debates on this constitution in the national convention, [etc.] vii, 161 pp. 8°. *New York, J. Tiebout,* 1817.

Hülsse (*Dr.* J. A. *editor.*) Grösseren logarithmisch-trigonometrisch tafeln. s.

[*With* VEGA (G. von.) Sammlung, etc.]

Humbert (Jean). Mythologie grecque et romaine; ou, introduction à la lecture des poètes. 3e éd. viii, 295 pp. 12°. *Paris, B. Duprat,* 1847.

Humboldt (Carl Wilhelm von). Über die Kawi-sprache auf der insel Java. 3 v. 4°. *Berlin, k. Akad. der wissenschaften,* 1836-39. s.

CONTENTS.

v. I. Einleitung über die verschiedenheit des menschlichen sprachbaues, und ihren einfluss auf die geistige entwicklung des menschen-geslechts. *Buch* i. Verbindungen zwischen Indien und Java.
v. II. Buch ii. Kawi-sprache. Buch iii. Malayischen sprachstamm. Abschnitt 1. Stammverwandtschaft der malayischen sprachen. Abs. 2. Betrachtung der einzelnen sprachen des stammes, etc.
v. III. Abs. 3. Sprachen der südsee inseln. Abs. 4. Vergleichende grammatik der südsee sprachen, und beiläufig des malayischen sprachstammes überhaupt, von [J. C. E.] Buschmann.

Humboldt (Friedrich Heinrich Alexander von). Ansichten der natur, mit wissenschaftlichen erläuterungen. v. 1. viii, 334 pp. 16°. *Tübingen, J. G. Cotta,* 1808. s.

[No more published.]

——— The same. Aspects of nature in different lands and different climates. Translated by Mrs. Sabine. 475 pp. 8°. *Philadelphia, Lea & Blanchard,* 1849. s.

——— The same. Views of nature; or, contemplations on the sublime phenomena of creation. Trans. from the German by E. C. Otté and H. G. Bohn. xxx, 452 pp. 2 pl. 12°. *London, H. G. Bohn,* 1850. s.

——— The same. Tableaux de la nature, ou considérations sur les déserts, sur la physionomie des végétaux, et sur les cataractes de l'Orénoque. Trad. de l'Allemand par J. B. B. Eyriès. 2 v. x, 240 pp; 240 pp. 16°. *Paris, F. Schoell,* 1808. s.

Humboldt (Friedrich Heinrich Alexander von). Cosmos: sketch of a physical description of the universe. Translated from the German by E. C. Otté; [assisted, v. 4 by B. H. Paul, v. 5, by W. S. Dallas]. 5 v. 1 pl. 12°. *London, H. G. Bohn*, 1849–58.

——— Correspondance scientifique et littéraire; recueillie, publieé, et précédeé d'une notice, etc. par de La Roquette; suivie de la biographie des correspondants de Humboldt, etc. xliv, 466 pp. 2 l. 2 pl. 8°. *Paris, E. Ducrocq*, 1865. s.

——— Kritische untersuchungen über die historische entwickelung der geographischen kenntnisse von der neuen welt, und die fortschritte der nautischen astronomie in d. 15ten und 16ten Jahrhundert. Aus dem Französischen übersetzt von J. L. Ideler. 3 v. 8°. *Berlin, Nicolai*, 1836–52.

——— Letters to Varnhagen von Ense, 1827–58, with extracts from Varnhagen's diaries, and letters to Humboldt. Translated from the 2d German ed. by F. Kapp. 407 pp. portrait. 12°. *New York, Rudd & Carleton*, 1860. s.

——— *and* **Bonpland** (Aimé). Personal narrative of travels to the equinoctial regions of the new continent during the years 1799–1804. Translated into English by Helen Maria Williams. 2 v. xii, li, 289 pp; 299 pp. 8°. *London, Longmans*, 1814.

——— The same. 432 pp. 8°. *Philadelphia, M. Carey*, 1815.

Hume (David). The history of England, from the invasion of Julius Cæsar to the revolution in 1688, with his life, written by himself. 8 v. portrait. 8°. *Edinburgh, Hill & Doig*, 1810.

——— The same. Continued to the death of George II. by T. Smollett. 8°. *London*, 1832. s.

Humphrey (*Mrs.* E. J.) Six years in India, as seen by a lady missionary. 286 pp. 18°. *New York, Carlton & Porter*, 1866.

Humphrey (George). Museum calonnianum: specification of the various articles which compose the magnificent museum of natural history collected by M. de Calonne in France. [*anon.*] 84 pp. 8°. *London*, 1797. s.
[With ms. corrections, etc. by the author].

Humphreys (*Col.* David). An essay on the life of Israel Putnam. 187 pp. 16°. *Hartford, Hudson & Goodwin*, 1788.

——— The same. 144 pp. 18°. *Brattleboro', W. Fessenden*, 1812.

——— The same. With a (poetical) address to the armies of the United States, and a poem on the happiness of America. 285 pp. 1 pl. 16°. *Philadelphia, W. McCarty*, 1811.

Humphreys (*Col.* David). The life and heroic exploits of Israel Putnam. 190 pp. 18°. *New York, Ezra Strong*, 1834.

——— Miscellaneous works. [Poems, and life of Israel Putnam]. 348 pp. 8°. *New York, Hodge, Allen & Campbell*, 1790.

Hungerford (James). The old plantation, and what I gathered there in an autumn month. 369 pp. 12°. *New York, Harpers*, 1859.

Hunt (Cornelius E.) The Shenandoah; or, the last confederate cruiser. 273 pp. 12°. *New York, G. W. Carleton & Co.* 1867.

Hunt (*Rev.* Daniel). History of Pomfret, [Ct.] A discourse delivered on the day of annual thanksgiving, in the first church, in Pomfret, Nov. 19th, 1840. 35 pp. 8°. *Hartford, J. Holbrook*, 1841.

Hunt (John, *M. D.*) Hours of reflection on honor and pleasure. 324 pp. 18°. (*n. p.*) 1845.

Hunt (Leigh) *and* **Lee** (S. Adams). The book of the sonnet. [With preliminary essays]. 2 v. xiv, 340 pp; vi, 344 pp. 16°. *Boston, Roberts Bros.* 1867.

Hunt (Robert). The poetry of science; or, studies of the physical phenomena of nature. xxiv, 463 pp. 8°. *London, Reeve, Benham & Reeve*, 1848. s.

Hunt (Thomas Sterry). *See* **Logan** (*Sir* W. E.) *and* Hunt (T. S.) Sketch of the geology of Canada.

Hunt's merchant's magazine. *See* **Merchant's** magazine and commercial review.

Hunter (Charles, *M. D.*) On the speedy relief of pain and other nervous affections, by means of the hypodermic method. 64 pp. 8°. *London, Churchill*, 1865.

Hunter (John, *surgeon*). A treatise on the venereal disease, with copious additions, by P. Ricord, edited, with notes, by F. J. Bumstead. 520 pp. 8 pl. 8°. *Philadelphia, Blanchard and Lea*, 1853. s.

Hunter (John H.) Analytic history, for schools, founded upon the Esquisses historiques of D. Levi Alvares. 312 pp. 12°. *New York, D. Fanshaw*, 1848. s.

Hunter (Robert, *royal gov. of N. Y.*) State of the case in dispute between the queen and the late assemblies, of the province of New York arising from the refusal of the latter to admit of any amendments from the council, to money bills. [*anon.*] 8 pp. fol. *New York, W Bradford*, 1713.

Huntington (*Prof.* Ezra A.) Notes on the epistle to the Hebrews. 134 pp. 8°. *Auburn, [N. Y.] Wm. J. Moses*, 1866.

Hurdis (James). The village curate, a poem. [*anon.*] 148 pp. 16°. *Newburyport, (Mass.) Blunt & Robinson,* 1793.

Hurlbert (William Henry). General McClellan and the conduct of the war. 312 pp. 2 maps. 12°. *New York, Sheldon & Co.* 1864.

Hurt (G. *M. D.*) Epidemic cholera: its causes, pathology, etc. and the best means for its prevention and cure; with a glossary, explaining all technical terms. 127 pp. 8°. *Saint Louis, P. M. Pinckard,* 1867.

Huss (*Dr.* Magnus). Chronische alkoholskrankheit, oder alcoholismus chronicus. Ein beitrag zur kenntniss der vergiftungs-krankheiten, nach eigener und anderer erfahrung. Aus dem Schwedisch übersetzt mit aenderungen und zusätzen des verfassers, von Gerhard van dem Busch. xix, 574 pp. 8°. *Stockholm, C. E. Fritze,* 1852. S.

Husson (Henri Marie). Report on the magnetical experiments made by the commission of the royal acad. of medicine, of Paris, read June 21, and 28, 1831. Translated from the French, with an introduction, by Charles Poyen St. Sauveur. 172 pp. 16°. *Boston, H. D. Hitchcock,* 1836.

Hutchings (Thomas Gibbons). The medical pilot; or, new system. 7 p. l. 300 pp. 12°. *New York,* [*author,*] 1855. S.

Hutchinson (Francis, *bishop of Down and Connor*). An historical essay concerning witchcraft. xv, pp. 2 l. 270 pp. 8°. *London, R. Knaplock,* 1718.

Hutchinson (John). Philosophical and theological works. Edited by R. Spearman and J. Bate. [3d ed.] 12 v. 2 pl. 8°. *London, J. Hodges,* 1748-49.

CONTENTS.

v. i-ii. Moses's principia.
v. iii. Moses's sine principio.
v. iv. Confusion of tongues, and trinity of the Gentiles.
v. v. Power, essential and mechanical.
v. vi. Glory or gravity essential, or cherubim explained.
v. vii. The Hebrew writings perfect.
v. viii. The religion of Satan.
v. viii-ix. The data in christianity.
v. x. The human frame.
v. xi. Glory mechanical.
v. xii. Tracts.

——— The use of reason recovered by the data in christianity. Part ii. 371 pp. 12°. *London, G. Strahan,* 1739.

Hutchinson (*Capt.* John Hely). *See* **Wilson** *sir* R. F. *etc.*) Trial of, 1816.

Hutchinson (*Rev.* Roger). Works. Edited by J. Bruce. xv. 350 pp. 8°. *Cambridge, university press,* 1842.
[Parker society publications, No. 4.]

CONTENTS.
Biographical notice; image of God, or laymans' book; sermons on the Lord's supper, etc.

Hutton (Charles). The principles of bridges. 2d ed. 104 pp. 8°. *London, author,* 1801. S.
[*With* SMEATON (J.) Experimental enquiry, etc.]

Hutton (*Rev.* W.) Hutton's book of nature laid open; revised and improved, by Rev. J. L. Blake. 252 pp. 1 pl. 18°. *New York, Harpers,* 1846. S.

Huxham (John, *M. D.*) Essay on fevers, with a dissertation on the malignant, ulcerous sore throat. 4th ed. xvi, 336 pp. 8°. *London, J. Hinton,* 1764.

Huxley (Thomas Henry). Lectures on the elements of comparative anatomy. On the classification of animals, and on the vertebrate skull. xi, 303 pp. 8°. *London, Churchill,* 1864. S.

——— On our knowledge of the causes of the phenomena of organic nature. 157 pp. 12°. *London, B. Hardwicke,* 1862. S.

——— *and* **Hawkins** (Benjamin Waterhouse). An elementary atlas of comparative osteology; the objects selected and arranged by Prof. Huxley, and drawn on stone, by B. W. Hawkins. 3 p. l. 12 l. 12 pl. fol. *London, Williams & Norgate,* 1864.

Huygens *or* **Hugenius** (Christian). The celestial worlds discovered: conjectures concerning the inhabitants, productions, etc. vi, 160 pp. 5 pl. 16°. *London, T. Childe,* 1698.

Hyatt (T. Hart). Hand-book of grape culture, [wine manufacture] etc. 279 pp. 12°. *San Francisco, H. H. Bancroft & Co.* 1867.

Hyde (*Mrs.* Anne M.) The American boy's life of Washington. 255 pp. 12 pl. 16°. *New York, J. Miller,* 1868.

Hyde (Edward, 1*st earl of Clarendon*). The history of the rebellion and civil wars in England, [with] an historical view of the affairs of Ireland. New ed. 6 v. 8°. *Boston, Wells & Lilly,* 1827.

——— State papers, 1621—[1674]; containing the materials from which his history of the great rebellion was composed. [Collected and edited by Richard Scrope, Thomas Monkhouse, John Douglas, bishop of Salisbury, and others]. 3 v. fol. *Oxford, Clarendon press,* 1767-86.

Hyde (J. Burrows). Treatment and uses of peat and peaty material, designed expressly for the instruction of farmers, and owners of peat lands. 81 pp. 18°. *New York, Baillière bros.* 1866.

Hymnal of the presbyterian church. Ordered by the general assembly. 598 pp. 12°. *Philadelphia, Presbyterian board,* 1867.

Hymns from various authors, for the use of the unitarian church at Washington. 212 pp. 24°. *Washington, W. Cooper,* 1821.

Hymns of the higher life. [Selected by B. K. P.] 224 pp. sq. 18°. *New York, Broughton & Wyman,* 1868.

Hymns to the Virgin and Christ, The parliament of devils, and other religious poems. Edited by F. J. Furnivall. xviii, 139 pp. 8°. *London, N. Trübner & Co.* 1867.
[Early English text society, No. 24.]

Hyneman (Leon). The origin of freemasonry. 177 pp. 8°. *Philadelphia, Masonic Mirror,* 1858. s.

Ibn Batuta. *See* **Batuta.**

Ibn Zafer, *or* **Djafer.** *See* **Mohammed ibn abi Mohammed ibn Zafer.**

Icazbalzeta (Joaquin Garcia). Documentos para la historia de Mexico. v. 1-2. 8°. *Mexico, V. G. Torres,* 1852-53. s.

CONTENTS.

v. 1-2. Sumario de la residencia tomada à D. Fernando Cortes.

——— The same. Documentos para la historia de Mexico. 4ª série. v. 1-7. 8°. *Mexico, V. G. Torres,* 1856—57. s.

CONTENTS.

v. 1. Continuacion de los materiales para la historia de Sonora.
v. 2. Sinaloa y Sonora. Materiales, etc.
v. 3-4. Nueva-Vizgaya. Documentos, etc.
v. 5. Establecimiento i progresos de las misiones de la Antigua California.
v. 6-7. Noticias de la Nueva California por el R. P. Fr. F. Palou. Agresiones y hazañas de tres Apaches.

——— The same. cliii, 544 pp. 8°. *Mexico, J. M. Andrade,* 1858. s.

CONTENTS.

Historia de los Indios de Nueva España, por Fr. Toribio Motolinia. pp. 1-277.
Noticias de la vida y escritos de fray Toribio de Motolinia, por J. F. Ramirez. cliii. pp.
Varios documentos del siglo xvi. pp. 279-537.

Iceland. Catalog over Islands stifts-bibliothek. xxxvi, 180 pp. 12°. *Kjöbenhavn, L. J. Jacobsen,* 1828. s.

Icilius (G.) Experimental physik. Ein leitfaden bei vorträgen. 2 p. l. 704 pp. 8°. *Hannover, Schmorl & von Seefeld,* 1855. s.

Ida Wilmot, "the queen of the household." [*anon.*] 192 pp. 16°. *Boston, R. A. Ballou,* 1866.
[Round Hill stories.]

Idalia; a novel. By "Ouida." [*pseudon.*] 594 pp. 12°. *Philadelphia, J. B. Lippincott & Co.* 1867.

Ides (Evert Ysbrandt). Three years travels from Moscow over-land to China. Printed in Dutch; now faithfully done into English. 6 p. l. 110 pp. 1 map. 29 pl. 4°. *London, W. Freeman,* 1706.

Idiomatic sentences, in English and Panjabi. [*anon.*] 130, 130, iv pp. 12°. *Lodiana, Amer. presbyt. miss. press,* 1846. s.

Ierne; or, anecdotes and incidents during a life chiefly in Ireland. With notices of people and places. By a retired civil engineer. [*anon.*] 1st series. xvi, 344 pp. 5 pl. 12°. *London, Partridge & Co.* 1861.

Ilicino (Bernardo). *See* **Lapini** (Bernardo).

Illiger (Johann Carl Wilhelm). Versuch einer systematischen vollständigen terminologie für das thierreich und pflanzenreich. xlvi, 469 pp. 8°. *Helmstädt, C. G. Fleckeisen,* 1800. s.

Illinois. Annual report of the adjutant general for 1862. 8°. *Springfield,* 1863. s.

——— H. C. Chandler & Co.'s railway business directory and shippers' guide, for the state of Illinois. xxiv, 936, 190 pp. 1 map. 8°. *Indianapolis, H. C. Chandler & Co.* 1868.

——— Reports of the Illinois state hospital for the insane. 1847-62. 422 pp. 8°. *Chicago, Fulton & Co.* 1863. s.

Illustrated arctic news. Facsimile of the Illustrated arctic news, published on board H. M. S. Resolute, in search for Sir John Franklin, Lieut. S. Osborne, and G. F. McDougall, editors. 2 p. l. 57 pp. fol. *London, Ackerman & Co.* 1852.

Illustrated London news. July 1866, to June 1867. v. 49-50. fol. *London,* 1866-67.

Illustration (An) of the wisdom and equity of an indulgent providence, in a similar treatment of all creatures on this globe. [*anon.*] xxii, 247 pp. 8°. *London, John Noon,* 1761.

Impartial (An) historical narrative of those momentous events which have taken place in this country from 1816 to 1823. [*anon.*] 56 pp. 5 pl. 2 facs. fol. *London, R. Bowyer,* 1823.

Impartial observations to be considered by the king, ministers, and people of Great Britain. [*anon.*] 27 pp. 4°. [*London,* 1763?]

Imperiali (Francesco). La faoniade. Inni ed odi di Saffo tradotti dal testo greco in metro italiano, da S[osare] I[tomeio] P[astore] A[rcade]. [*pseudon.*] xiii, 99 pp. 18°. *Crisopoli, C. Bodoniani,* 1792.

Impressions of the west and south during a six weeks' holiday. [*anon.*] 83 pp. 8°. *Toronto, Armour & Co.* 1858.

Imray (Keith, *M.D.*) A popular cyclopædia of modern domestic medicine, etc. 1st Am. ed. To which are prefixed by the editor, popular treatises upon anatomy, physiology, surgery, dietetics, etc. 855 pp. 1 col. pl. 8°. *New York, Gates, Stedman & Co.* 1849. s.

Inajut-Ullah *or* **Inatulla** (*of Delhi*). Tales, translated from the Persian, [by Alexander Dow]. 2 v. ix, xvii, 275 pp; 245 pp. 18°. *London, T. Becket,* 1768.

Inatulla (*of Delhi*). *See* **Inajut-Ullah.**

Incidents and sketches connected with the early history and settlement of the west. [*anon.*] 72 pp. 9 pl. 8°. *Cincinnati, J. A. & U. P. James,* 1853.

Independent (The). (A religious weekly). Dec. 1848, to Dec. 1867. 17 v. fol. *New York,* 1848-67.

Index [expurgatorius] librorvm prohibitorvm, cvm regvlis confectis per patres à tridentina synodo delectos. Avctoritate Pii iiii. primùm editus; postea verè à Syxto v. auctus, et nvnc demvm S. D. N. Clementis papæ viii. iussu recognitus, et publicatus. Instrvctione adiecta de exequendæ prohibitionis, etc. 21 p. l. 55 l. 18°. *Coloniæ, G. Cholinus,* 1598. s.

——— The same. Index librorum prohibitorum a Sixto v. papa confectus et publicatus; at vero a successoribus ejus in sede romana suppressus. Edente Josepho Mendham. vi, 47 pp. 4°. *Londini, J. Duncan,* 1835.

Indian battles, murders, sieges, and forays in the southwest. Narratives of Gen. Hall [and others]. 100 pp. 8°. *Nashville,* 1853.

Indian songs of peace, with a proposal for erecting Indian schools, and a postscript introducing Yariza, an Indian maid's letter. [*anon.*] 27 pp. 12°. *New York, J. Parker & W. Wayman,* 1752.

Indiana. Brevier legislative reports; embracing short-hand sketches of the journals and debates of the general assembly. By Ariel and W. H. Drapier, reporters. v. 6 and 8. 8°. *South Bend, (Ind.) Forum job office,* 1863-66.

——— Documents and annual reports of the officers of public institutions for 1864. 858 pp. 8°. *Indianapolis, J. J. Bingham,* 1865.

——— Documents of the general assembly. 41st session, 1861, 42d, 43d, 1863, 43d regular, 1865, 45th session, 1867. 7 v. 8°. *Indianapolis,* 1861-67.

——— Journal of the house of representatives, special session 1861, 43d, 1863, 44th, 1865, and called session, 1865. 4 v. 8°. *Indianapolis,* 1861-65.

——— Journal of the senate. Called session 1858, 40th sess. 1859, special sess. 1861, 44th sess. 1865, called sess. 1865, 45th sess. 1867. 6 v. 8°. *Indianapolis,* 1858-67.

——— Report of the adjutant general; containing rosters of officers and men, and historical memoranda of Indiana regiments. v. 6-7. 699 pp; 781 pp. 8°. *Indianapolis, S. M. Douglass,* 1867.

——— Report (thirteenth) of the superintendent of public instruction, being the second biennial report, for 1863 and 1864. By Samuel L. Rugg. 240 pp. 8°. *Indianapolis, J. J. Bingham,* 1865.

——— Report (annual) of the treasurer of state for the fiscal year ending Oct. 31, 1865. 11 pp. 8°. *Indianapolis, S. M. Douglass,* 1866.

——— Reports of the officers of state to the governor for 1860-61, 1863. 2 v. 8°. *Indianapolis,* 1862-64.

——— Registry law, and an act regulating general elections, and prescribing the duties of officers in relation thereto. 20 pp. 8°. *Indianapolis, A. H. Conner,* 1867.

——— School laws, as amended in 1865 and 1867; with opinions, instructions, and judicial decisions relating to common schools, and to the officers thereof. Prepared by the superintendent of public instruction. 72 pp. 8°. *Indianapolis, A. H. Conner,* 1867.

Indiana gazetteer; or, topographical dictionary of the state of Indiana. 3d ed. 440 pp. 8°. *Indianapolis, E. Chamberlain,* 1849.

Indiana institute for the education of the blind. Twentieth annual report of the trustees and superintendent. 93 pp. 8°. *Indianapolis, S. M. Douglass,* 1866.

Indiana state board of agriculture. Annual reports: 1st and 2d. 2 v. 8°. *Indianapolis, J. P. Chapman,* 1852-53.

Indiana state library. Catalogue. Compiled by J. R. Bryant. 96 pp. 8°. *Indianapolis, J. C. Walker,* 1859. s.

Indiana university. Annual report, including the catalogue for 1866-7. 48 pp. 1 pl. 8°. *Indianapolis, A. H. Conner,* 1867.

Indianapolis. Edwards's annual directory. 1867. 412, cxv pp. 8°. *Indianapolis, Edwards & Boyd,* 1867.

——— Logan's directory for 1867[-68]. xxiv, 357 pp. 8°. [*Indianapolis,*] *Logan & Co.* 1867.

Industrial and social position of women, in the middle and lower ranks. [*anon.*] xv, 419 pp. 12°. *London, Chapman & Hall,* 1857.

Ingelow (Jean). Story of doom, and other poems. vi, 290 pp. 1 pl. 16°. *Boston, Roberts bros.* 1867.

Ingemisco. [A novel.] By Fadette. [*pseudon.*] 12°. *New York,* 1867.

Ingenhousz (Jean). Nouvelles expériences et observations sur divers objets de physique. 2 v. xxvii, 498 pp. 4 pl; xx, 574 pp. 8°. *Paris, P. T. Barrois*, 1785-89. s.

Ingeröe (Julie). Et aar i Utah; eller, mormonismens hemmeligheder. 62 pp. 12°. *Chicago, "Skandinavens" office*, 1867.

Ingerslev (C. F.) *and* Fridriksson (H. Cr.) Stutt kennslubók i landafrœdinni. vi, 304 pp. 12°. *Reykjavik, Prentzmidjn Islands*, 1854. s.

Ingersoll (Jared). Letters relating to the stamp act. iv, 68 pp. sm. 4°. *New Haven*, 1766.

]Title page wanting.]

Ingersoll (Lurton Dunham). Iowa and the rebellion, a history. 3d ed. 743 pp. 8°. *Philadelphia, J. B. Lippincott and Co.* 1867.

Ingoldsby (Thomas, *pseudon.*) *See* **Barham** (R. H.)

Ingraham (Joseph Holt). Beatrice, the goldsmith's daughter. 93 pp. 8°. *New York, Williams brothers*, 1847.

——— Edward Austin. 66 pp. 8°. *Boston, F. Gleason*, 1842.

——— Edward Manning. 120 pp. 8°. *New York, Williams brothers*, 1847.

——— Ringold Griffitt. 100 pp. 8°. *Boston, F. Gleason*, 1847.

——— Spectre steamer, and other tales. 100 pp. 8°. *Boston*, 1846.

Ingraham (Joseph W.) Geographical index to the historical map of Palestine. 96 pp. 8°. *Boston, Thomas B. Wait and J. W. Ingraham*, 1828.

Ingulph. Historia. fol. *Oxoniæ*, 1684.

[*In* GALE (Thomas), *and* FELL (John). Rerum anglicarum scriptores veteres. *Oxoniæ*, 1684-91. v. 1.]
Note.—Sir Francis Palgrave has demonstrated that this work is an historical novel, composed by a monk of the thirteenth or fourteenth century, and therefore falsely attributed to Ingulph, who lived in the eleventh century.

Innes (Cosmo). Memoir of Thomas Thomson, advocate. xi, 251 pp. 8°. *Edinburgh, Bannatyne club*, 1854. s.

Institut impérial de France. Annuaire pour 1866-67. 2 v. 18°. *Paris*, 1866-67.

Institution (The) of civil engineers. Catalogue of the library, etc. viii, 228 pp. 8°. *London, institution*, 1851. s.

——— The same. 2d ed. viii, 412 pp. 8°. *London, institution*, 1866. s.

Intellectual (The) house-keeper; or, hints to females. [*anon.*] 47 pp. 16°. *Boston, Russell, Odiorne and Co.* 1835.

Internal (The) revenue record and customs journal. A weekly register of official information on internal revenue and customs, Jan. to June, 1867. v. 5. 4°. *New York, P. Vr. Vanwyck*, [1867.]

Investor's (The) monthly manual, in connection with the economist. A newspaper for investors in stocks. Jan. 1866 to Dec. 1867. v. 2-3. sm. fol. *London*, [*D. Aird*, 1866-67].

Invisible (The) spy. By Exploralibus. [*pseudon.*] 4 v. 16°. *London, T. Gardner*, 1755.

Invisibles: an explanation of phenomena commonly called spiritual. [*anon.*] 331 pp. 12°. *Philadelphia, J. B. Lippincott & Co.* 1867.

Iowa. The census returns of the different counties. 1856, 59, 62, 65. 4 v. in 1. 12°. *Iowa city, and Des Moines, State printer*, 1857-65.

——— The debates of the constitutional convention, 1857. W. B. Lord, reporter. 2 v. ii, 1096, 103 pp. 8°. *Davenport, Luse, Lane & Co.* 1857.

——— Journal of the constitutional convention, 1857. 406 pp. 12°. *Muscatine, J. Mahin*, 1857.

——— Journals of the senate and house, 1855-1866. 18 v. 8° and 12°. *Iowa city, and Des Moines, State printer*, 1865-66.

——— Legislative documents compiled by order of the general assembly, 1857. [Sen. doc.], 1860-66. 7 v. 8° and 12°. *Iowa city, and Des Moines, State printer*, 1857-66.

——— Report of the adjutant general, 1863-66. 5 v. 8°. *Des Moines, F. W. Palmer*, 1863-67.

——— Reports [annual] of the state agricultural society, for 1857, 1859-65. 7 v. 8° and 12°. *Des Moines, Teesdale & Palmer*, 1858-66.

Irby (Charles Leonard), *and* **Mangles** (James). Travels in Egypt and Nubia, Syria, and the Holy Land. viii, 150 pp. 12°. *London, John Murray*, 1847.

Ireland (Joseph N.) Records of the New York stage, from 1750 to 1860. 2 v. iv, 663 pp; vi, 746 pp. 8°. *New York, T. H. Morrell*, 1866-67.

Ireland (William Henry). Napoleon anecdotes: illustrating his mental energies; and the characters and actions of his contemporary statesmen and warriors. 3 v. 16°. *Boston, Wells & Lilly*, 1830.

Ireland. Report from the committee of secrecy, of the house of commons in Ireland, as reported by lord Castlereagh, Aug. 21, 1798, [on the united Irishmen's conspiracy]. 184, 83 pp. 8°. *London, J. Debrett*, 1798.

——— Report from the committee of secrecy, of the house of lords in Ireland, as reported by John, earl of Clare, chancellor, Aug. 30, 1798, [on the united Irishmen's conspiracy]. 53 pp. 8°. *London, J. Debrett*, 1798.

[*With* the preceding.]

Irvin (Christopher). Historiæ Scoticæ nomenclatura latino-vernacula. 7 p. l. 253 pp. 18°. *Edinbruchii, Gideon Schaw*, 1682.

Irvine (Alexander). The London flora. xvi, 340 pp. 12°. *London, Smith, Elder & Co.* 1838. s.

Irving (C.) Catechism of practical chemistry; a familiar introduction to that interesting science. 5th Am. ed. by M. J. Kerney. 85 pp. 1 pl. 24°. *Baltimore, J. Murphy & Co.* 1854. s.

Irving (David, *LL. D.*) Elements of English composition. New ed. x, 318 pp. 8°. *London, R. Phillips*, 1809.

——— Lives of Scotish writers. 2 v. in 1. vii, 384; 385 pp. 12°. *Edinburgh, A. & C. Black*, 1850. s.

Irving (Theodore). The conquest of Florida, under Hernando de Soto. 2 v. xii, 296; 315 pp. 8°. *London, Edward Churton*, 1835.

Irving (Washington). A book of the Hudson. Collected from the various works of Diedrich Knickerbocker. Edited by Geoffrey Crayon. [*pseudon.*] 215 pp. 16°. *New York, G. P. Putnam*, 1849. s.

——— A history of New York, by Diedrich Knickerbocker. [*pseudon.*] 2 v. xxiii, 268 pp; 258 pp. 1 pl. 12°. *New York, Inskeep & Bradford*, 1809.

Isenkrahe (Caspar). Helicinae titanicae anatome. 27 pp. 1 pl. 8°. *Bonnae, Auctor*, 1866. s.

[Wanting 1 plate.]

Isidorus *Hispalensis.* Ethimologiarum libri viginti. fol. *Augustae Vindelicorum, G. Zainer*, 1472. s.

Isla (José Francisco de). Historia del famoso predicador fray Gerundio de Campazas, alias Zotes. Por Francisco Lobon de Salazar. [*pseudon.*] 5 v. 18°. *Madrid, Ramos*, 1822. s.

Islands landnamabok. Hoc est: liber originum Islandiae. Versione latina, nec non indicibus illustratus [a Johanne Finnaeo]. 4°. *Havniae, A. F. Stein*, 1774.

Isocrates. Paræenesis; hoc est præcepta de officiis ad Demonicum; oratio ad Nicoclem de regno, etc. (Gr. et Lat.) 4 p. l. 147 pp. 24°. *Londini, J. Heptinstall*, 1699. s.

CONTENTS.

Paræenesis, etc. Agapeti expositio admonitoria ad Justinianum imperatorem.
De regno, ex Diogene et ex Ecphante.
Senecae, Proverbia: De moribus.
Theoctisti sententiæ, adversus molles et negligentes.

Isselt (Michael von). *See* **Surius** (Lorenz) *and* **Isselt** (M. von). Commentarivs brevis rervm in orbe gestarvm. *Coloniæ*, 1586.

Italy. Statistica del regno d'Italia. Istruzione pubblica e privata. Istruzione primaria, 1863–64. cxv, 229 pp. 4°. *Firenze, Tofani*, 1866. s.

——— The same. Sanità pubblica. Il cholera-morbus nel 1865. xxiii, 112 pp. 4°. *Firenze, G. Barbèra*, 1867. s.

Itinerarium Hierosolymitanum.

[*With* ANTONINUS (Augustus). Vetera Romanorum itineraria. Ed. *Amstelaedami*, 1735].

Ivernois (François d', *LL. D.*) An historical and political view of the constitution and revolutions of Geneva in the eighteenth century. Translated by J. Farrell. xxx, 374 pp. 8°. *Dublin, W. Wilson*, 1784.

Ives (Edward, *M. D.*) A voyage from England to India, 1754, and an historical narrative of the operations of the squadron and army in India, 1755–57. Also, a journey from Persia to England, by an unusual route. xii, 506 pp. 1 map. 11 pl. 4°. *London, Dilly*, 1773.

Ives (Joseph C.) Report upon the Colorado river of the west, explored in 1857–58. 367 pp. 1 map. 34 pl. 4°. *Washington, gov. printing office*, 1861.

CONTENTS.

Part 1. General report. 131 pp.
2. Hydrographic report. 14 pp.
3. Geological report. By J. S. Newberry. 154 pp.
4. Botany. By A. Gray, J. Torrey, G. Thurber, and G. Engelmann. 30 pp.
5. Zoology [birds]. By S. F. Baird. 6 pp.
Appendix. Astronomical observations. 32 pp.

Izard (*Maj. Gen.* George). Official correspondence with the department of war, relative to the military operations of the American army under [his] command on the northern frontier of the United States in 1814 and 1815, vii, 152 pp. 8°. *Philadelphia, T. Dobson*, 1816.

Jackson (Andrew). Proclamation [on nullification, December 10, 1832]. 25 pp. 8°. *London, Richard Phillips*, [1833?]

[*With* PRIOR (James). Narrative of a voyage in the Indian seas. *London.*]

Jackson (Charles Thomas). First annual report on the geology of the state of New Hampshire. 164 pp. 8°. *Concord, C. Barton*, 1841. s.

——— First, second, and third annual reports on the geology of the state of Maine. 3 v. in 1. 8°. *Augusta*, 1837–39. s.

Jackson (Frederick). The victim of chancery: or, a debtor's experience. 208 pp. 12°. *New York, J. F. Trow*, 1841.

Jackson (J. W.) Ethnology and phrenology, as an aid to the historian. 324 pp. 12°. *London, Trübner & Co.* 1863.

Jackson (R. M. S.) The [Alleghany] mountain. [Also, medical essays, entitled: Æsculapius, Hygeia, Antæus the giant, Pan a symbol of the universe]. xii, 632 pp. 12°. *Philadelphia, J. B. Lippincott & Co.* 1860. s.

Jackson (William, *of Exeter*). The four ages; [with] essays on various subjects. 454 pp. 8°. *London, Cadell & Davies*, 1798.

Jackson (*Maj.* William). Eulogium on the character of general Washington, pronounced 22 Feb. 1800. New ed. 44 pp. 8°. *Philadelphia, John Ormrod*, 1800.
[*With* WASHINGTON (George). Monuments of patriotism. *Philadelphia*, 1800].

Jacob (P. L. *bibliophile; pseudon.*) *See* **Lacroix** (Paul).

Jacob (Stephen). Poetical essay, delivered at Bennington, on the anniversary of the 16th of August, 1777. 8 pp. 8°. *Hartford, Watson & Goodwin*, 1779.

Jacobaeus *or* **Jacobsen** (Holger). Museum regium; seu catalogus rerum tam naturalium, quam artificialium, quæ in basilica bibliothecæ Christiani v. Hafniae asservantur. 8 p. l. 206 pp. 37 pl. fol. *Hafniae, J. Schwetgen*, 1696. s.

Jacobi (Louis). Idées générales sur la maladie; méthodes qui en découlent; application du traitement des fièvres graves. 113 pp. 4°. *Strasbourg, Berger-Levrault*, 1850. s.

Jacobs (Christian Friedrich Wilhelm). The first part of [his] Latin reader adapted to Bullion's Latin grammar. By Peter Bullions. 6th ed. 336 pp. 12°. *New York, Pratt, Woodford & Co.* 1846. s.

——— *and* **Ukert** (Friedrich August). Beiträge zur altern litteratur; oder, merkwürdigkeiten der herzog. öffentlichen bibliothek zu Gotha. 6 pts. in 3 v. 8°. *Leipzig, Dyk*, 1835–43. s.

Jacobs (*Rev.* Peter). Journey from Rice lake to the Hudson's Bay territory, and returning, 1852; with account of his life, and history of the Wesleyan mission. 96 pp. 16°. *New York*, 1857.

Jacquemin (Émile). L'Allemagne agricole, industrielle et politique; voyages faits en 1840-42. iv, 459 pp. 8°. *Paris, bureau d'agriculture*, 1842. s.

Jacquemont (Victor.) Correspondance avec sa famille et plusieurs de ses amis, pendant son voyage dans l'Inde. [1828–1831.] 2 v. 360 pp; 356 pp. 1 map. 16°. *Bruxelles, A. Peeters*, 1834.

Jacques (D. H.) Philosophy of human beauty; hints towards physical perfection: showing how to acquire and retain bodily symmetry, health, [etc.] 244 pp. 21 pl. 12°. *New York, Miller, Wood & Co.* 1867.

Jaeger (Georg Friedrich von). De ichthyosauri sive proteosauri fossilis speciminibus in agro bollensi in Würtembergia repertis. 14 pp. 2 pl. fol. *Stutgardiæ, Cotta*, 1824. s.

——— Ueber die fossilen säugethiere, welche in Würtemberg aufgefunden worden sind. 2 v. in 1. 3 p. l. 230 pp. 20 pl. 4°. *Stuttgart, C. Erhard*, 1835–39. s.

——— Ueber die wirkungen des arseniks auf pflanzen. viii, 115 pp. 8°. *Stuttgart, E. Schweizerbart*, 1864. s.

Jaenisch (C. F. de). Chess preceptor; a new analysis of the openings of games. Translated by George Walker. xx, 291 pp. 8°. *London, Longmans*, 1847.

Jal (A.) Virgilius nauticus. Examen des passages de l'Enéide qui ont trait à la marine. [extract.] 107 pp. 8°. *Paris, imprimerie royale*, 1843. s.

Jamaica (The) movement, for promoting the enforcement of the slave-trade treaties, and the suppression of the slave-trade. [*anon.*] 430 pp. 8°. *London, C. Gilpin*, 1850.

James I (*king of England*). Βασιλικον Δωρον; or, king James's instructions to his dearest sonne, Henry the prince. [With portrait by R. White.] 16°. *London*, 1682.

James (George Payne Rainsford). Bertrand de la Croix; or, the siege of Rhodes. 25 pp. 8°. *London*, 1841.
[Hazlitt's romancist and novelist's lib. v. 3].

——— Thirty years since; or, the ruined family. xi, 383 pp. 1 pl. 8°. *London, Simpkin, Marshall & Co.* 1848.

James (Henry). Old and new theology, and the church of Christ not an ecclesiasticism. xv, 198 pp. 16°. *London, Longmans*, 1861.

James (John, *M. D.*) The American household book of medicine: containing directions on diseases, bathing, diet, etc.; adapted to popular use and ready reference. 810 pp. 3 pl. 8°. *Cincinnati, R. W. Carroll & Co.* 1866.
[Imperfect; wanting pp. 33–48].

James (Joseph), *and* **Moore** (Daniel). A system of exchange with almost all parts of the world; [with] the India directory for purchasing drugs and spices in the East Indies. 180 pp. 16°. *New York, J. Furman*, 1800.
[Imperfect; wanting pp. 5–12].

James (Thomas). Strange and dangerovs voyage in his intended discouery of the northwest passage into the South sea. 3 p. l. 120 pp. 11 l. 16°. *London, J. Partridge*, 1633.

James (William Dobein). A sketch of the life of Francis Marion, and history of his brigade. 181, 39 pp. 8°. *Charleston, (S. C.) Gould & Riley,* 1821.

Jameson (*Mrs.* Anna Murphy). Studies, stories, and memoirs. 408 pp. 1 pl. 24°. *Boston, Ticknor & Fields,* 1859.

Jameson (Horatio Gates, *M. D.*) American domestic medicine; or, medical admonisher. 2d ed. with additions. 574 pp. 8°. *Baltimore, John D. Toy,* 1818.

Jameson (Robert). Climate, geology, and mineralogy of India.

[pp. 158-257 of v. 3 of MURRAY (Hugh). Account of British India. 3 v. 8°. *N. Y.* 1833-36].

Jameson (William H. *jr.*) *and* **Ferguson** (George). Table of pay of the commissioned officers of the [U. S.] army, under the law of the 39th Congress. 4°. [*Washington,* 1867].

Jamieson (Milton). Journal and notes of a campaign in Mexico: containing a history of co. C, of the second regiment of Ohio volunteers. 105 pp. 8°. *Cincinnati, Ben. Franklin printing house,* 1849.

Janet's home. [A novel. *anon.*] 2 v. 411 pp; 428 pp. 16°. *London, Macmillan,* 1863.

Janeway (James). Invisibles, realities, demonstrated in the holy life and triumphant death of John Janeway. 3d ed. 177 pp. 24°. *Boston, B. Eliot,* 1703.

[pp. 25-26, and table of contents, imperfect.]

Janeway (*Rev.* James). A token for children: an account of the conversion and exemplary lives of several young children; with a token for the children of New England. 156 pp. 18°. *Boston, Z. Fowle,* 1771.

Janin (Jules Gabriel). Béranger et son temps. 2 v. 176 pp; 120 pp. 2 pl. 18°. *Paris, Pincebourde,* 1866.

——— Un hiver à Paris. Nouv. éd. 282 pp. 18 pl. 8°. *Paris, Ve. Janet,* [1847].

——— Prosper Chavigni and Letitia Laferti; or, Le chemin de traverse. 172 pp. 8°. *London,* [1841?]

[Hazlitt's romancist and novelist's lib. v. 5].

——— Sketches of Genoa, Pisa, and Florence; with a description of the cathedral of Milan. Translated by Mrs. M. H. Robinson. 144 pp. 12°. *Philadelphia, Lippincott,* 1854. s.

Janita's cross. By the author of "St. Olave's." [*anon.*] 3 v. 12°. *London, Hurst & Blackett,* 1864.

Janse (L.) Bijdrage tot het onderzoek naar de oorzaken der geslachtsverhouding bij de geboorten. viii, 171 pp. 2 pl. 8°. *Middleburg, Abrahams,* 1853. s.

Janson (Christopher). Norske dikt. 5 p. l. 195 pp. 16°. *Bjorgvin, E. B. Giertsen,* 1867. s.

Jarves (James Jackson). History of the Hawaiian islands, embracing their antiquities, mythology, etc. 3d ed. 240 pp. 8°. *Honolulu, C. E. Hitchcock,* 1847.

Jay (*Rev.* William). Memoirs of the life and character of the Rev. Cornelius Winter. xxi, 478 pp. 8°. *Bath, M. Gye,* 1808.

Jay (William, *judge, Westchester co. N. Y.*) Slavery in America; or, an inquiry into the character and tendency of the American colonization, and the American anti-slavery societies. With an introduction by S. H. Cox. xxiv, 198 pp. 12°. *London, F. Westley & A. H. Davis,* 1835.

Jeaffreson (John Cordy). A book about lawyers. 2 v. viii, 359 pp; vii, 431 pp. 8°. *London, Hurst & Blackett,* 1867.

Jebb (John, *D. D. bp. of Limerick*). Works theological, medical, political and miscellaneous. With memoirs of the author, by J. Disney. 3 v. 8°. *London, T. Cadell,* 1787.

CONTENTS.

v. 1. Life; theological lectures at Cambridge; new harmony of the gospels; letters on subscription to the liturgy and thirty-nine articles.
v. 2. Miscellaneous, and medical.
v. 3. Miscellaneous; every man his own priest; academical papers, political papers, index.

Jefferson (Thomas). An essay towards facilitating instruction in the Anglo-Saxon and modern dialects of the English language. 43 pp. 4°. *New York, J. F. Trow,* 1851.

——— Manual of parliamentary practice, [with] the rules and orders of the senate and house of representatives, and joint rules of the two houses. 220 pp. 16°. *Washington, Davis & Force,* 1820.

——— Notes on the state of Virginia. With an appendix relative to the murder of Logan's family. 356 pp. 16°. *Trenton, Wilson & Blackwell,* 1803.

Jefferson college, (*Washington, Miss.*) The charter and statutes, with a historical sketch of the institution, etc. [With] a catalogue of its library, apparatus, etc. 90 pp. 8°. *Natchez, The book and job office,* 1840. s.

Jefferys (Thomas). Natural and civil history of the French dominions in North and South America. 2 pts. in 1 v. fol. *London,* 1760. s.

Jeffrey (Francis). Extract of the review of lord Byron's Hours of idleness, from the Edinburgh review, No. 22. [*anon.*] 8 pp. 8°. *London, Wilton & son,* 1820.

[*With* BYRON. The Giaour. Ed. 1813.]

Jeffreys (John Gwyn). British conchology; or, an account of the mollusca which now inhabit the British isles and the surrounding seas. v. 1–4. 12°. *London, J. Van Voorst,* 1862–67.

CONTENTS.

v. 1. Land and fresh water shells. 9 pl.
v. 2–4. Marine shells. 27 pl.

Jeffreys (Julius, *F. R. S.*) Views upon the statics of the human chest, animal heat, and determinations of blood to the head. xix, 233 pp. 8°. *London, Longmans,* 1843. s.

Jenkins (Geoffrey, *pseudon.*) *See* **Legislative** sketches.

Jenkins (John). Art of writing reduced to a plain and easy system. xlviii, 68 pp. 2 l. 8°. *Cambridge,* [*printed at Andover, Flagg & Gould*], 1813.

Jenkins (John S.) History of political parties in the state of New York, 1783 to 1849. 2d ed. 580 pp. 12°. *Auburn, Alden & Parsons,* 1849.

Jenkins (Thornton A.), *and* **Bache** (Richard). Reports on improvements in the lighthouse system, and collateral aids to navigation. 8°. [*Washington, Gov't printer,* 1846.] s.

Jennings (Isaac *M. D.*) The tree of life; or, human degeneracy: its nature and remedy, as based on orthopathy. 279 pp. 12°. *New York, Miller, Wood & Co.* 1867.

Jennings (James). A lecture on the history and utility of literary institutions. xii, 122 pp. 8°. *London, Sherwood, Jones & Co.* 1823.

Jennings (Louis J.) Eighty years of republican government in the United States. xv, 288 pp. 12°. *London, J. Murray,* 1868.

Jennings (Robert). The horse and other live stock. With [their] diseases, and remedies for each, their history and varieties, their crossing and breeding, etc. Horse, 384 pp. Cattle, 340 pp. Sheep, 243 pp. Swine, 87 pp. Poultry, 170 pp. 1 pl. 8°. *Philadelphia, J. E. Potter & Co.* [1866].

——— Sheep, swine, and poultry; embracing the history and varieties of each; the best modes of breeding, etc. 490 pp. 16°. *Philadelphia, Potter & Co.* [1864].

Jennings (Samuel K. *M. D.*) A compendium of medical science, or fifty years' experience in the art of healing, etc. 592 pp. 1 pl. 8°. *Tuskaloosa, (Ala.) M. J. Slade,* 1847. s.

Jenny and the insects. [*anon.*] 298 pp. 7 pl. 12°. *Philadelphia, Am. S. S. union,* 1857.

Jenyns (Soame). Free enquiry into the nature and origin of evil, and reflections on several subjects.

[*With* MISCELLANEOUS pieces. v. 2. 12°. *London, Dodsley,* 1761.]

Jephson (Robert). Roman portraits, a poem: with historical remarks and illustrations. xxiv, 277 pp. 20 pl. 4°. *London, F. & J. Robinson,* 1794.

Jerdon (T. C.) The birds of India, being a natural history of all the birds known to inhabit continental India, etc. 2 v. in 3. 8°. *Calcutta, author,* 1862–64. s.

Jérôme (Jérôme Bonaparte, *king of Westphalia*). Mémoires et correspondance du roi Jérôme et de la reine Cathérine. v. 7. 8°. *Paris, Dentu,* 1866.

Jesse (John Heneage). Memoirs of the life and reign of king George the third. 3 v. 8°. *London, Tinsley bros.* 1867.

Jessen (Carl F. W.) Botanik der gegenwart und vorzeit in culturhistorischer entwickelung. xxii, 495 pp. 8°. *Leipzig, F. A. Brockhaus,* 1864. s.

——— Über die lebensdauer der gewächse. [Extract.] 188 pp. 4°. *Breslau, etc. k. Leop. Carol. akad. der nat.* 1854. s.

Jessen (*Dr.* P.) Versuch einer wissenschaftlichen begründung der psychologie. viii, 715 pp. 8°. *Berlin, Veit & Co.* 1855. s.

Jesuits' (The) loyalty, manifested in three treatises written by them against the oath of allegiance; with a preface, showing the pernicious consequence of their principles as to civil government. Also, three other treatises concerning the reasons of the penal laws. [*anon.*] 48, 132 pp. sm. 4°. *London, R. Royston,* 1677.

Jewel (*Rev.* John, *bishop of Salisbury*). Works. Edited by Rev. John Ayre. 4 v. 8°. *Cambridge, Univ. press,* 1845–50.

[Parker society publications.]

CONTENTS.

v. 1. Sermon preached at Paul's cross; correspondence with Dr. Cole; reply to Harding's answer: of private mass; of communion; of prayers in a strange tongue; of the supremacy; of real presence; of being in many places; of elevation of the sacrament; of adoration of the sacrament.
v. 2. Reply to Harding, continued: exposition of St. Paul's epistles to the Thessalonians; sermons; of the sacraments.
v. 3. Apology of the church of England, with defence of apology.
v. 4. Defence of apology, continued; epistle to Scipio; view of a seditious bull; treatise on the holy scriptures; letters, and miscellaneous pieces.

——— Apologia ecclesiæ anglicanæ. 90 pp. 8°. *Oxford,* 1825.

[*With* RANDOLPH (John, *bishop of London*). Enchiridion theologicum, v. 1.]

Jewett (Charles Coffin). Notices of public libraries in the United States. 207 pp. 8°. *Washington, Smithsonian inst.* 1851.

Jewett (Charles Coffin). On the construction of catalogues of libraries, and stereotyped titles. vi, 78 pp. 8°. *Washington, Smithsonian inst.* 1852.

Jewish nation; containing an account of their manners and customs, rites and worship, laws and polity. [*anon.*] iv, 452 pp. 1 pl. 12°. *London, Rel. tract soc.* 1848.

Jobert (Antoine Claude Gabriel). Ideas; or, outlines of a new system of philosophy. 141 pp. 16°. *London, Simpkin, Marshall & Co.* 1848. s.

——— The philosophy of geology. [3d ed.] 184 pp. 16°. *London, Whittaker & Co.* [1852]. s.

Jobert de Lamballe (Antoine Joseph). Des appareils électriques des poissons électriques. 2 v. in 1. xiii, 104 pp. 8°. atlas, 11 pl. obl. fol. *Paris, J. B. Baillière,* 1858. s.

Jobson (D. Wemys). History of the French revolution [to the death of Robespierre]. 3d ed. 338 pp. 8°. *London, author,* 1853. s.

Jöcher (Christian Gottlieb). Allgemeines gelehrten lexicon. Fortzsetzung und ergänzungen; von H. W. Rotermund, K—L. v. 3. 4°. *Delmenhorst, G. Jöntzen,* 1810.

Joel (M.) Schlüssel zu den aufgaben in der russischen grammatik nach Ollendorff's methode. 3e aufl. durchgesehen von Paul Fuchs. 2 p. l. 205 pp. 12°. *Frankfurt a. M. C. Jügel,* 1865. s.

——— H. G. Ollendorff's neue methode in sechs monaten eine sprache lesen, etc. Anleitung zur erlernung der russischen sprache, etc. 3e aufl. Durchgesehen von Paul Fuchs. viii pp. 2 l. 669 pp. 12°. *Frankfurt a. M. C. Jügel,* 1865.

Jogues (Isaac). Novum Belgium; description de Nieuw Netherland, et notice sur René Goupil. 44 pp. 1 map. 8°. *New York, J. M. Shea,* 1862.

John, of Salisbury. Opera omnia nunc primum in unum collegit et cum codicibus manuscriptis contulit J. A. Giles. 5 v. 8°. *Oxonii, J. H. Parker,* 1848.

CONTENTS.

v. i–ii. Epistolæ.
v. iii–iv. Polycraticus, sive de nugis curialium et vestigiis philosophorum.
v. v. Opuscula; vita Anselmi cantuariensis; vita S. Thomae [à Becket].

John Bull. [A weekly newspaper]. Dec. 17, 1820—Dec. 31, 1859. v. 1–39. fol. *London,* 1821-59.

Johns (*Rev.* Charles Alexander). British birds in their haunts. xxxii, 626 pp. 8°. *London, Soc. for promoting christ. knowl.* 1862. s.

Johnson (Charles). History of the lives and actions of the most famous highwaymen, murderers, street robbers, etc. with the voyages and plunders of the most noted pirates. 484 pp. 17 pl. fol. *London,* 1734.

[Imperfect; title wanting. Also pp. 21–22; 105–6; 477–84, and plates on pp. 91, 132, 136, 188, 203, 228, 278, 372, and 483].

Johnson (Cuthbert W.) Our house and garden; what we see, and what we do not see, in them. vii, 287 pp. 12°. *London, W. Ridgway,* 1864.

Johnson (*Capt.* Edward). A history of New England, from the English planting in the yeere 1628, untill the yeere 1652. [Running title: Wonderworking providence of Zion's saviour in New England.] 2 p. l. 239 pp. sm. 4°. *London, Nath. Brooke,* 1654.

——— The same. sm. 4°. *London,* 1658.

[*With* Gorges (Ferdinando). America painted to the life. sm. 4°. *London,* 1659. Purports to be written by Gorges.]

——— The same. Wonder-working providence of Sion's saviour in New England. [Second title:] A history of New England. From the English planting in the yeere 1628, untill the yeere 1652. London, 1654. [Reprinted] with an historical introduction and an index by W. F. Poole. cliv, 265 pp. 1 fac-sim. sm. 4°. *Andover, W. F. Draper,* 1867.

Johnson (Frank G. *M. D.*) Aid to teachers and students in natural philosophy; being the key to Dr. Johnson's philosophical charts. 60 pp. 10 pl. 12°. *New York, A. Ranney,* 1856. s.

——— The Nicolson pavement, and pavements generally. 128 pp. 8°. *New York, W. C. Rogers & Co.* 1867.

Johnson (George William). A dictionary of modern gardening. Edited, with additions, by David Landreth. 635 pp. 12°. *Philadelphia, Lea & Blanchard,* 1847. s.

Johnson (Henry). Introduction to logography; or, the art of arranging and composing for printing with words intire, instead of single letters. 65 pp. 8°. *London, J. Walter,* 1773.

Johnson (L.) Specimens of printing types and ornaments. 388 l. 8°. *Philadelphia,* 1844. s.

——— The same. Second supplement to the specimen book of plain and fancy types cast at the type and stereotype foundry of L. Johnson. 4°. *Philadelphia, L. Johnson,* [1849]. s.

——— Specimens of printing types, plain and ornamental. 382 l. 4°. *Philadelphia, Johnson & Co.* 1859.

Johnson (Lorenzo D.) The spirit of Roger Williams. 94 pp. 16°. *Boston, Cassady & March,* 1839.

Johnson (*Mrs.* M. O.) The century plant, and other poems. By the author of "Linwood." [*anon.*] 144 pp. 12°. *Boston, W. V. Spencer,* 1867.

Johnson (Overton), *and* **Winter** (William H.) Route across the Rocky Mountains, with a description of Oregon and California. 152 pp. 8°. *Lafayette, (Ind.) J. B. Semans,* 1846.

Johnson (*Rev.* Samuel, *chaplain to lord W. Russell*). Works. xxviii, 488 pp. fol. *London, A. Bell,* 1710.

CONTENTS.

Abrogation of king James according to the English constitution.
Essay concerning parliaments at a certainty.
Julian, the apostate, with a comparison of popery and paganism.
Sermons and tracts.
Several reasons for the establishment of a standing army.
Tracts on passive obedience.
Vindication of magna charta, with a true copy.

——— An argument proving that the abrogation of king James, and the promotion of the prince of Orange, was according to the English constitution. 62 pp. sm. 4°. *London,* 1692.

Johnson (Samuel, *the lexicographer*). A dictionary of the English language, etc. To which are prefixed a history of the language, and an English grammar. 2d ed. 2 v. 27 p. l. 279 l; 375 l. fol. *London, J. & P. Knapton, etc.* 1755. S.

——— Schatzung keine tiranney. Ein antwort auf die entschlüsse und addressen des amerikanischen congresses. 58 pp. 8°. *Braunschweig, F. Waisenhaus,* 1777.

[*With* Remer (Julius August). Amerikanisches archiv. v. 2.]

Johnson (S. W.) Rural economy: containing a treatise on pisé building, on buildings in general, on the culture of the vine, and on turnpike roads. viii, 246 pp. 8 pl. 8°. *New Brunswick, Riley & Co.* 1806.

Johnson (Samuel W.) Peat and its uses, as fertilizer and fuel. 168 pp. 12°. *New York, O. Judd & Co.* 1866.

Johnson (*Mrs.* Susanna). A narrative of [her] captivity, containing an account of her sufferings, during four years, with the Indians and French. 2d ed. 144 pp. 18°. *Windsor, (Vt.) Alden Spooner,* 1807.

——— The same. 3d ed. 178 pp. 16°. *Windsor, Thomas M. Pomroy,* 1814.

Johnson (Theodore T.) Sights in the gold region, and scenes by the way. xii, 278 pp. 12°. *New York, Baker & Scribner,* 1849.

Johnson (Walter Rogers). The coal trade of British America, with researches on the characters and practical values of American and foreign coals. 179 pp. 8°. *Washington, Taylor & Maury,* 1850.

——— Notes on the use of anthracite in the manufacture of iron, with some remarks on its evaporating power. vi, 159 pp. 12°. *Boston, Little & Brown,* 1841.

——— Report on American coals. v, 607 pp. 3 pl. 8°. *Washington, Gales & Seaton,* 1844.

[*With* United States patent office report, 1844.]

Johnson (William, *D. D.*) Deus nobiscum: a narrative of a great deliverance at sea. 4th ed. 5 p. l. 35 pp. 16°. *London, J. Marshall,* 1734.

[*With* Falconer (*Capt.* Richard). Voyages. *London,* 1734].

Johnson (*Sir* William). [Letter giving an account of the battle of lake George]. 3 pp. 4°. [*n. p.* 1755]?

Johnston (Adam S.) The soldier boy's diary-book; or, memorandums of the alphabetical first lessons of military tactics, 1861–64. 139 pp. 16°. *Pittsburgh,* 1866.

Johnston (Alexander Keith). The physical atlas of natural phenomena. 122 pp. 24 pl. 4°. *Philadelphia, Lea & Blanchard,* 1850. S.

Johnston (A. R.) Journal, [1846].

[*With* Emory (W. H.) Notes of a military reconnoissance.]

Johnston (George, *M. D.*) The botany of the eastern borders. xii, 336 pp. 14 pl. 8°. *London, J. Van Voorst,* 1853. S.

——— The flora of Berwick-upon-Tweed. 2 v. in 1. xxiv, 242 pp; 335 pp. 8 pl. 12°. *Edinburgh, Carfrae,* 1829–31. S.

——— A history of the British zoophytes. xii, 341 pp. 44 pl. 8°. *Edinburgh, W. H. Lizars,* 1838. S.

Johnston (James Finlay Weir). Elements of agricultural chemistry and geology. 6th ed. xiv, 410 pp. 12°. *Edinburgh, Blackwood,* 1852. S.

——— The same. With an American preface, by Simon Brown. vi, 381 pp. 12°. *New York, C. M. Saxton,* 1853. S.

Johnston (John, *M. D.*) *See* **Jonston** (Johann).

Johnston (Samuel B). Letters written during three years residence in Chili, with an account of the revolutionary struggle of that province. 204 pp. 12°. *Erie, (Pa.) R. J. Curtis,* 1816.

Joliet (——.) *See* **Marquette** (Jacques), *and* **Joliet**. Voyage et découverte de quelques pays de l'Amérique Séptentrionale. *Paris,* 1681.

Jollivet (Adolphe). Documents américains. Annexion du Texas; émancipation des noirs; politique de l'Angleterre. [La dépêche de M. Calhoun à M. King, à Paris; la lettre de Hammond, etc.] 40 pp. 8°. *Paris; Bruneau,* 1845.

——— The same. 3e série. Les États-Unis d'Amérique et l'Angleterre. Annexion du Texas, l'Orégon. 74 pp. 8°. *Paris, Bruneau,* 1845.

Jomard (Edme François). De la collection géographique créée à la bibliothèque royale. 104 pp. 8°. *Paris, E. Duverger,* 1848. s.

——— Fragments sur l'uniformité à introduire dans les notations géographiques sur les antiquités américaines, et sur divers points de géographie. 45 pp. 8°. *Paris, L. Martinet,* [*about* 1847].

——— Observations sur le voyage au Darfour, [parle cheikh Mohammed Ebn Omar el Tounsy,] suivies d'un vocabulaire du langue des habitants et de remarques sur le nil blanc supérieur. 76 pp. 1 map. 8°. *Paris, B. Duprat,* 1845. s.

Jomini (Henri, *baron* de). Atlas militaire et portatif pour l'intelligence des relations des dernières guerres publiées sans plans; notamment pour la vie politique et militaire de Napoléon. Planches; légendes. 1 v. 36 pl. fol. 4°. *Paris,* 1827–40. s.

——— Histoire critique et militaire des guerres de la révolution, [1e période, 1792–94]. 6 v. 8°. *Paris, Anselin et Pochard,* 1820. s.

Jonas (S. F.) Die kräfte der erd und der sie umgebenden weltkörper. xii, 227 pp. 4 pl. 8°. *Lüneburg, Herold & Wahlstab,* 1838. s.

——— Populäre anleitung zur praktischen und theoretischen astronomie. xiii, 239 pp. 12 pl. 8°. *Leipzig, A. Reimann,* 1835. s.

Jonckbloet (W. J. A.) Geschiedenis der middener-landsche dichtkunst. 3 v. 8°. *Amsterdam, P. N. Van Kampen,* 1851–55.

Jones (Amanda F.) Poems. 203 pp. 16°. *New York, Hurd & Houghton,* 1867.

Jones (Charles A.) The outlaw, and other poems. 72 pp. 16°. *Cincinnati, J. Drake,* 1835.

Jones (Charles C. *of the middle temple*). Recollections of royalty, from the death of William Rufus, in 1100, to that of the cardinal of York, the last of the Stuarts, in 1807. 2 v. xxxvi, 399 pp; xix, 490 pp. 3 l. 8°. *London, Saunders & Otley,* 1828.

Jones (Charles Colcock, *D. D.*) The religious instruction of the negroes in the United States. xiii, 277 pp. 12°. *Savannah, T. Purse,* 1842.

——— A catechism of scripture doctrine and practice. 154 pp. 18°. *Philadelphia, Presbt. board of pub.* [1852].

Jones (Charles C. *jr.*) Monumental remains of Georgia. Part 1. 119 pp. 1 pl. 8°. *Savannah, J. M. Cooper & Co.* 1861.

Jones (Evan). Brief specimens of Cherokee grammatical forms, [with alphabet].

[CHEROKEE messenger, Nos. 1, 2, 6, 7, and 9. 8°. *Cherokee,* 1844–46.]

——— *See,* also, **Cherokee** messenger.

Jones (George, *M. R. S. I.*) The first jubilee oration upon the life, character, and genius of Shakspeare, originally pronounced at Stratford-upon-Avon, April 23, 1836. 4th ed. 2 p. l. 38 pp. 8°. *London, Longmans,* 1844.

[App. to JONES (George). Tecumseh. *London,* 1844].

——— The life and history of General Harrison. 2 p. l. 176 pp. 8°. *London, Longmans,* 1844.

[App. to JONES (George). Tecumseh. *London,* 1844.]

——— Tecumseh and the prophet of the west; an original historical Israel-Indian tragedy. 9 p. l. 113 pp. 8°. *London, Longmans,* 1844.

Jones (Henry Bence). Ueber gries, gicht, und stein; zunächst eine anwendung von Liebig's thierchemie auf die verhüting und behandlung dieser krankheiten. Uebersetzt von Hermann Hoffmann. xi, 136 pp. 8°. *Braunschweig, Vieweg,* 1843. s.

Jones (Horatio Gates). The Levering family; a genealogical account of Wigard Levering and Gerhard Levering, and their descendants. 10, 193 pp. 7 pl. 8°. *Philadelphia, King & Baird,* 1858.

——— Report of the committee of the Hist. Soc. of Pennsylvania, of their visit to N. Y. at the celebration of the two hundredth birth day of W. Bradford. 14 pp. 8°. *Philadelphia, King & Baird,* 1863.

Jones (Ichabod Gibson, *M. D.*) The American eclectic practice of medicine. To which are appended the posthumous writings of T. V. Morrow, M. D. 2 v. 788 pp; xi, 862 pp. 8°. *Cincinnati, Moore, Anderson, Wilstach & Keys,* 1853–54. s.

——— The American eclectic practice of medicine. Extended, by Wm. Sherwood. 2 v. 806 pp; 806 pp. 8°. *Cincinnati, Moore, Wilstach, Keys & Co.* 1857–58. s.

Jones (James, and Henry, & Co.) Illustrated catalogue of plumbers' materials. ix, 167 pp. 8°. [*New York,* 1867].

Jones (*Rev.* John G.) Appeal to all christians against the practice of social dancing. 66 pp. 18°. *St. Louis, P. M. Pinckard,* 1867.

——— Concise history of the introduction of protestantism into Mississippi and the southwest. 257 pp. 12°. *St. Louis, P. M. Pinckard,* 1866.

Jones (John Matthew). The naturalist in Bermuda; a sketch of the geology, zoology, and botany; with meteorological observations. Assisted by major J. W. Wedderburn and J. L. Hurdis. xii, 200 pp. 1 map. 12°. *London, Reeves & Turner,* 1859. s.

Jones (J. Seawell). Memorials of North Carolina. 87 pp. 8°. *New York, Scatcherd & Adams,* 1838.

Jones (*Sir* John Thomas). Journaux des siéges entrepris par les alliés en Espagne, pendant les années 1811–12; suivis de deux discours sur l'organization des armées anglaises, etc. Trad. de l'Anglais, par G[osselin]. viii, xvi, 464 pp. 9 pl. 8°. *Paris, Anselin & Pochard,* 1821. s.

[Wants plate ix.]

Jones (Joseph, *M. D. of Athens, Ga.*) Observations on malarial fever. 84 pp. 8°. *Augusta, (Ga.) South. med. and surg. journal,* 1858. s.

——— Observations on some of the physical, chemical, physiological and pathological phenomena of malarial fever. (Extract). 419 pp. 8°. *Philadelphia, Collins,* 1859. s.

Jones (Lloyd). Progress of the working class. *See* **Ludlow** (J. M.)

Jones (Samuel, *D. D.*) A treatise of church discipline, and a directory. By appointment of the Philadelphia baptist association. 38 pp. 16°. *Philadelphia, S. C. Ustick,* 1798.

Jones (Shubael T.) Ready calculations upon business transactions; comprised in tables on buying, selling, and manufacturing. 171 pp. 16°. *Boston, the author,* 1855. s.

Jones (Thomas Rupert). A monograph of the entomostraca of the cretaceous formation of England. 2 p. l. 40 pp; 7 l. 7 pl. 4°. *London, Palæontographical society,* 1849. s.

——— A monograph of the fossil estheriæ. x, 132 pp. 1 tab. 5 pl. 5 l. 4°. *London, Palæontographical society,* 1863.

——— A monograph of the tertiary entomostraca of England. xii, 68 pp. 6 l. 6 pl. 4°. *London, Palæontographical society,* 1856. s.

[*With* JONES. Monograph of the entomostraca of the cretaceous formation].

Jones (Thomas Wharton). Principles and practice of ophthalmic medicine and surgery. 2d Am. ed. 500 pp. 4 pl. 12°. *Philadelphia, Blanchard & Lea,* 1856. s.

Jones (*Rev.* William). Memoirs of the life, ministry and writings of Rev. Rowland Hill. xiv, 368 pp. 2 pl. 8°. *London, J. Bennett,* 1834.

Jones (*Sir* William). A grammar of the Persian language. 7th ed. xxiii, 198 pp. 4°. *London, W. Bulmer & Co.* 1809. s.

Jones (W. Alfred). Characters and criticisms. 2 v. viii, 289; iv, 268 pp. 12°. *New York, I. Y. Westervelt,* 1857.

——— Memorial of David S. Jones. With notices of the Jones family of Queen's county. 99 pp. 12°. *New York, Stanford & Swords,* 1849.

Jonghe *or* **Junius** (Adriaan de). Emblemata. 167 pp. 32°. *Lugdvni Batavorvm, ex officina Plantiniana, F. Rapheleng,* 1596.

Jonnès (Alexandre Moreau de). *See* **Moreau de Jonnès.**

Jonson (Ben). Poetical works. 8°. *Edinburgh,* 1793.

[Anderson's Brit. poets, v. 4.]

Jonston (Johann). Historiæ natvralis de arboribvs et plantis libri x, tabvlis 137 ab illo celeberrimo Mathia Meriano aeri incisis ornati, ex scriptoribvs tam antiqvis, qvam recentioribvs, etc. 2 v. 214 pp. 63 pl; 274 pp. 74 pl. fol. *Heilbrvnn, F. J. Eckebrecht,* 1768–69. s.

——— Historiæ natvralis de piscibvs et cetis libri v, etc. 228 pp. 47 pl. fol. *Heilbrunn, F. J. Eckebrecht,* 1767. s.

——— Historiæ natvralis de serpentibvs libri duo. 57 pp. 11 pl. fol. *Heilbronnæ, F. J. Eckebrecht,* 1757. s.

——— Historiæ natvralis de exangvibvs aqvaticis libri iv, etc. 84 pp. 20 pl. fol. *Heilbrunn, F. J. Eckebrecht,* 1767. s.

[*With* JONSTON (J.) Hist. nat. de serpentibus.]

——— Theatrum universale de avibus, etc. 4 p. l. 247 pp. 62 pl. fol. *Heilbrvnn, F. J. Eckebrecht,* 1756. s.

——— Theatrvm vniversale omnivm animalivm insectorvm. 3 p. l. unp. 212 pp; 2 l. unp. 28 pl. fol. *Heilbronn, F. Eckebrecht,* 1768. s.

——— Theatrum vniversale omnivm animalivm qvadrvpedvm, etc. 8 p. l. 242 pp. 80 pl. fol. *Heilbrunn, F. J. Eckebrecht,* 1755. s.

——— Histoire naturelle et raisonnée des différens oiseaux qui habitent le globe, etc. Trad. du latin, etc. Et précédée de l'histoire particulière des oiseaux de la ménagerie du roi, peints par [N.] Robert. Pour servir de suite à l'histoire des insectes, etc. de Mérian. 2 v. in 1. 24 pp. 23 pl.; 2 p. l. 64 pp. 62 pl. fol. *Paris, L. C. Desnos,* 1773–74. s.

Jörg (Eduard). Darstellung des nachtheiligen einflusses des tropenklima's auf bewohner gemässigter zonen, und des verlaufes und der behandlung der tropenkrankheiten, des gelben fiebers und der asiatischen cholera. xvi, 576 pp. 8°. *Leipzig, Arnold*, 1851. s.

Jörg (Johann Christian Gottfried). Zeugung des menschen und der thiere. xvi, 350 pp. 8°. *Leipzig, P. G. Kummer*, 1815. s.

Jorio da Paterno (Filippo). Della coltivazione delle cereali, con osservazioni relative al regno di Napoli. viii, 308 pp. 8°. *Napoli, Tipografia del Vesuvio*, 1838. s.

Jornandes. De rebus Gothorum. fol. *Augustae Vindelicorum, Miller*, 1515. .s

Josephus (Flavius). Genuine works, containing xx books of the Jewish antiquities, vii books of the Jewish war, and the life of Josephus, written by himself. Translated by William Whiston, revised by Samuel Burder. 2 v. 572 pp. 15 pl; 541 pp. 13 l. 5 pl. 4°. *New York, T. Kinnersley*, 1821. s.

——— Wars of the Jews, with history of the siege and destruction of Jerusalem. Epitomized and translated by Sir Roger L'Estrange. 107 pp. 18°. *Glasgow*, 1785.

Joubert (F. E.) Manuel de l'amateur d'estampes, faisant suite au Manuel du libraire, Précédé d'un essai sur le génie, considéré comme principe des beaux-arts, etc. 3 v. 8°. *Paris, auteur*, 1821. s.

Joubert (Joseph). Some of the "thoughts" of Joseph Joubert. Translated by George H. Calvert. 163 pp. 16°. *Boston, W. V. Spencer*, 1867.

Jouher, Djauher, *or* Djewahir. The tezkereh al vakiat; or, private memoirs of the Moghul emperor Humāyūn. Translated from the Persian language by C. Stewart. pp. viii, 127. 4°. *London*, 1832.

[Oriental translation fund publ.]

Journal (The) of agriculture. July, 1863, to April, 1866. New [second] series. 2 v. 8°. *London and Edinburgh*, 1865–[66].

——— The same. July, 1866, to June, 1867. Third series. v. 1—2. 8°. *Edinburgh and London*, [1866–67].

Journal (The) of applied chemistry. Devoted to chemistry as applied to the arts, manufactures, metallurgy, and agriculture. Jan. 1866, to Dec. 1867. v. 1—2. sm. fol. *New York, Dexter & Co.* 1866–67.

Journal (A) of the expedition up the river St. Lawrence, from the embarkation at Louisbourg 'til after the surrender of Quebeck. By the sergeant major of Gen. Hopson's grenadiers. [*anon.*] 24 pp. 16°. *Boston, Fowle & Draper*, 1759.

Journal (A) of a tour in Italy in 1821. With a description of Gibraltar. By an American. [*anon.*] 468 pp. 10 pl. 8°. *New York, A. Paul*, 1824. s.

Journal of a tour and residence in Great Britain, during 1810 and 1811, by a French traveller. [*anon.*] 2 v. xiii, 382 pp; 360 pp. 8°. *Edinburgh, Geo. Ramsay & Co.* 1815.

Journal (A) of a young man of Massachusetts, who was captured by the British, and confined at Melville Island, Halifax, Chatham, Eng. and at Dartmoor prison. [*anon.*] 228 pp. 1 pl. 12°. *Boston, Rowe & Hooper*, 1816.

Journal de la guerre du Micissippi contre les Chicachas, 1739–40. Par un officier de l'armée de M. de Nouaille. [*anon.*] 92 pp. sm. 4°. *Nouvelle York, J. M. Shea*, 1859.

Journal général de l'imprimerie et de la librairie. 2e sér. v. 7–10. 1863–66. 1e partie. Bibliographie. 2e partie. Chronique. 8 v. 8°. *Paris, Pillet*, 1863–66.

Journals of several expeditions made in western Australia during 1829 to 1832, under sanction of the governor, Sir James Stirling. xxii, 263 pp. 1 map. 16°. *London, J. Cross*, 1833.

Joursanvault (——). Catalogue analytique des archives de M. le baron de Joursanvault, contenant manuscrits, chartes, et documens originaux concernant l'histoire générale de France, etc. 2 v. xi, 373 pp; 298 pp. 8°. *Paris, J. Techener*, 1838. s.

Joutel (—). Journal historique du dernier voyage que feu M. de Sale fit dans le golfe de Mexique, pour trouver l'embouchure, et le cours de la rivière de Missicipi. xxxiv, 386 pp. 16°. *Paris, Estienne Robinot*, 1713.

——— The same. A journal of the last voyage performed by De La Sale to the Gulph of Mexico, to find the mouth of the Mississippi. Translated from the French. xxix, 205, v pp. 1 map. 12°. *London, A. Bell and others*, 1714.

——— The same. [New ed. with altered title:] Journal of his voyage to Mexico: his account of the great river Missasipi, etc. 16 p. l. 210 pp. 1 map. 8°. *London, B. Lintot*, 1719.

Jouy (Victor Joseph Étienne). État actuel de l'industrie française, 1819. lxvi, 221 pp. 8°. *Paris, L'Huillier*, 1821. s.

Juan y Santacilia (Jorge), *and* **Ulloa** (Antonio de). Voyage historique de l'Amérique Meridionale, [voyage au Pérou]; qui contient une histoire des Yncas du Pérou, et les observations astronomiques et physiques, faites pour déterminer la figure et la grandeur de la terre, [traduit de l'Espagnol par É. Mauvilon]. 2 v. 12 p. l. 554 pp; 309 pp. 56 pl. 4°. *Amsterdam et Leipzig, Arkstee & Merkus,* 1752.

Jubinal (Michel Louis Achille). Lettres à M. le comte de Salvandy sur quelques-uns des manuscrits de la bibliothèque royale de La Haye. 262 pp. 8°. *Paris, Didron,* 1846. s.

——— Mystères inédits du 15e siècle. 2 v. lii, 397 pp; xix, 411 pp. 8°. *Paris, Techener,* 1837.

——— Nouveau recueil de contes, dits, fabliaux, et autres pièces inédites des 13e, 14e, et 15e siècles, pour faire suite aux collections Le Grand d'Aussy, Barbazan, et Méon. Mis au jour pour la 1e fois. 2 v. vii, 387 pp; 444 pp. 8°. *Paris, E. Pannier,* 1839-42.

——— Recherches sur l'usage et l'origine des tapisseries à personnages dites historiées, dépuis l'antiquité jusqu'au 16e siècle inclusivement. 96 pp. 4 pl. 8°. *Paris, Challamel,* 1840. s.

——— Un nouvel épisode de l'affaire Libri. 80 pp. 8°. *Paris, Didron,* 1851. s.

Judson (Adoniram, *D. D.*) Christian baptism; a sermon preached in the Lal bazar chapel, Calcutta, Sept. 27, 1812. 71 pp. 1 pl. 8°. *Boston, Lincoln & Edmands,* 1817.

Judson (*Mrs.* Ann Haseltine). A particular relation of the American baptist mission to the Burman empire. 315 pp. 12°. *Washington, John S. Meehan,* 1823.

Judson (*Mrs.* Emily Chubbuck). Memoir of Sarah B. Judson. By "Fanny Forrester." [*pseudon.*] 8th ed. 250 pp. 18°. *New York, L. Colby & Co.* 1848. s.

Julia de Fontenelle (Jean Sébastian Eugène). Manuel complet du blanchiment et du blanchissage, nettoyage et dégraissage, des fils et étoffes de chanvre, lin, coton, laine, soie, etc. 2 v. iv, 295 pp; 231 pp. 3 pl. 18°. *Paris, Roret,* 1834. s.

Julien (Félix). Courants et révolutions de l'atmosphère et de la mer; comprenant une théorie nouvelle sur les déluges périodiques. vi, 240 pp. 8°. *Paris, Lacroix & Baudry,* 1860. s.

Jullien (Marc Antoine). Essai général d'éducation physique, morale, et intellectuelle. 2e éd. xvi, 496 pp. 8°. *Paris, Dondey-Dupré,* 1835. s.

——— Exposé de la méthode d'éducation de Pestalozzi. 2e éd. xl, 568 pp. portrait. 8°. *Paris, L. Hachette,* 1842. s.

Juncker (Christian). Historische nachricht von der öffentlichen bibliotheqve des fürstl. gymnasii zu Eisenach; nebst einem discours von einigen in den thur und furstl. sächsischen landen öffentlichen bibliotheqven, etc. 102 pp. 4°. *Eisenach, M. Urban,* 1709. s.

[*With* SCHÖTTGEN (C.) Historie derer buchhändler, etc.]

Junghuhn (Franz Wilhelm). Java; seine gestalt, pflanzendecke, und innere bauert. Ins Deutsche übertragen von J. K. Hasskarl. 3 v. 8°. *Leipzig, Arnold,* 1852-54. s.

Jungmann (Josef). Historie literatury české. Druhé wydání. vi, 772 pp. Portrait. 8°. *Praze, F. Rziwnatz,* 1849. s.

Jung-Stilling (Johann Heinrich). Scenes in the world of spirits. Translated from the 3d original ed. xiv, 282 pp. 16°. *New Market, (N. C.) Henkel & Co.* [*about* 1815].

Junius (Adrian). *See* **Jonghe** (Adriaan van).

Junius. A complete collection of Junius's letters, with those of Sir William Draper. 2 p. l. 177 pp. 8°. *London, A. Thomson,* 1770.

——— The same. 2 v. vii, 208 pp. 19 l; 356 pp. 18°. *London, Henry Sampson Woodfall,* [1772?]

——— The same. 1st Am. ed. 2 p. l. 283 pp. 6 l. 16°. *Philadelphia, Richard and Hall,* 1791.

——— The same. 2 v. xxxv, 274 pp; v, 318 pp. 21 pl. 8°. *London, Vernor and Hood,* 1801.

——— The same, with notes and illustrations, by Robert Heron. v, vi, 613 pp; 2 p. l. 466 pp. 2 l. 8°. *Philadelphia, Robert Carr,* 1804.

——— The same. New ed. 2 v. xxxi, 252 pp; 284 pp. 21 pl. 12°. *London, Vernor and Hood, and others,* 1805.

——— The same. With notes and an enquiry concerning the real author, by John Almon. 2 v. lxxxiv, 355 pp; iv, 385 pp. 2 pl. 12°. *London, Phillips,* 1806.

——— The same. Including letters under other signatures (now first collected), confidential correspondence with Mr. Wilkes, and private letters to Mr. H. S. Woodfall. 3 v. xiii, 336, 248 pp; xi, 516 pp; xiii, 511 pp. 6 pl. 8°. *London, F. C. & J. Rivington,* 1812.

——— The same. 300 pp. 24°. *New York, D. Huntington,* 1813.

——— The same. 2 v. xii, 210, 279 pp; xiii, 513 pp. 6 pl. 8°. *Philadelphia, Bradford and Inskeep,* 1813.

——— The same. 2d ed. 3 v. viii, 588 pp; xi, 517 pp; xiii, 510 pp. 6 pl. 8°. *London, F. C. and J. Rivington, and others,* 1814.

Junius. A complete collection of Junius's letters, with those of Sir William Draper. 2 v. 216 pp; 215 pp. 2 pl. 18°. *Boston, N. H. Whitaker*, 1827.

——The same. With new evidence as to the authorship, and analysis, by Sir Harris Nicolas. [Ed. by John Wade.] 2 v. x, 480 pp; xc, 458 pp. 12°. *London, Henry G. Bohn*, 1850.

Jürgens (Friedrich?) Jedermann sein eigener liqueur-fabrikant! Ausführliche mittheilungen über die fabrikation von liqueuren auf kaltern wege; nebst genauer anweisung zur bereitung verschiedener arten weine, extracte, etc. 44 pp. 12°. *Milwaukee, (Wis.) author*, 1867.

Jurine (Louis). Histoire des monocles qui se trouvent aux environs de Genève. xvi, 258 pp. 22 pl. 4°. *Genève, J. J. Paschoud*, 1820. s.

—— Nouvelle méthode de classer les hyménoptères et les diptères. v. 1, Hyménoptères. 320, 4 pp. 14 col. pl. 4°. *Genève, J. J. Paschoud*, 1807. s.
[No more published.]

Jussieu (——). Catalogue de la bibliothèque scientifique de MM. de Jussieu. (Sale catalogue). xv, 464 pp. 8°. *Paris, H. Labitte*, 1857. s.

Just (A) defence of the royal martyr, Charles I, from the false aspersions in Ludlow's memoirs, and other virulent libels. [*anon.*] 2 v. in 1. 8 p. l. 199 pp; 223 pp. 12°. *London, A. Roper* [*and others*], 1699.

Justinus. Historiæ philippicæ. Secundum vetustissimos codices prius neglectos recognovit, brevi adnotatione critica et historica instruxit F. Duebner. xxv, 439 pp. 8°. *Lipsiae, B. G. Teubner*, 1831. s.

—— *and* **Florus** (Lucius Annaeus). Iustini et L. Flori epithome. [Ed. Marcus Antonivs Sabellicvs]. 68 l. fol. [*n. p. about* 1475.] s.

Juvenalis (Decimus Junius). Satyræ cum commentar. D. Calderi et G. Valle. clxliii l. 8°. *Lugduni, J. de Vingle*, 1495.

—— The satires, translated [by Thomas Sheridan?] With notes [on] the laws and customs of the Greeks and Romans. 2d ed. xvi, 416 pp. 8°. *London, D. Browne*, 1745.

—— Tenth satire, in English verse, by Henry Higden. 8 p. l. 58 pp. 5 l. sm. 4°. [*London*, 1683].

—— Les trois satiriques latins traduits en vers français, par L. V. Raoul. I. Juvénal. 6e éd. 424 pp. 8°. *Bruxelles, Wouters, Raspoet & Cie.* 1842. s.

—— *and* **Persius** Flaccus (Aulus). [Satires] translated and illustrated, as well with sculpture as notes, by Barten Holyday. 6 p. l. 341 pp. 1 map. 3 pl. fol. *Oxford, F. Oxlad and others*, 1673.

—— The satyrs, translated into English verse, by [J.] Dryden. To which is prefix'd a discourse concerning satyr. 5th ed. cxi, 296 pp. 23 pl. 18°. *London, J. Tonson*, 1726.

Juvigny (Jean Antoine Rigoley de). *See* **Rigoley** de Juvigny.

Juville (—— *surgeon*). Traité des bandages herniaires. xxxiv, 238 pp. 8°. *Paris, Belin*, 1786. s.

Kabus, *or* **Kawus**, *or* **Jawus** (Kje, *or* Kaï). Buch des Kabus, oder lehren des persischen königs Kjek-Jawus für seinen sohn Ghilan schach, aus dem Türkisch-persisch-arabischen. Uebersetzt und erläutert von H. F. von Diez. 3 p. l. 867 pp. 8°. *Berlin, Nicolai*, 1811. s.

Kahl (Emil). Mathematische aufgaben aus der physik, nebst auflösungen. 2 v. in 1. x, 165; 137 pp. 8°. *Leipzig, B. G. Teubner*, 1857. s.

Kai-Kaöus, *or* **Kje** Kawus. *See* **Kabus.**

Kalm (Peter). Beschreibung der reise nach dem Nördlichen Amerika; eine uebersetzung von J. A. Murray. 3 v. 8°. *Göttingen, Vandenhoeck*, 1754–64. s.

—— Histoire naturelle et politique de la Pensylvanie, et de l'établissement des quakers dans cette contrée. Traduite de l'Allemand [par J. P. Rousselot de Surgy]. xx, 372 pp. 1 map. 16°. *Paris, Ganeau*, 1768.

Kamenski (Bantisch). Age of Peter the great. With notes and preface, by Ivan Golovin. viii, 272 pp. 12°. *London, T. C. Newby*, 1851.

Kämpz (Ludwig Friedrich). Prelezioni alla meteorologia. Versione dal Tedesco di V. Kohler e L. Del Re, con note di Martins e Bravais. viii, 884 pp. 6 pl. 8°. *Napoli, Stamperia dell' Iride*, 1846. s.

Kant (Immanuel). Allgemeine naturgeschichte und theorie des himmels. Neue aufl. 12 p. l. 143 pp. 12°. *Zeitz, W. Webel*, 1798. s.

Kao (Dionysius). Short description of the vast empire of China. pp. 113—210. 1 pl.
[*With* IDES (E. Y.) Three years' travels from Moscow, etc. *London*, 1706.]

Kapp (Friedrich). Geschichte der deutschen einwanderung in Amerika. v. i. Geschichte der Deutschen im staate New York bis 1800. vii, 411 pp. 1 map. 8°. *New York, E. Steiger*, 1867.

Karlamagnus saga ok kappa Hans. I norsk bearbeidelse fra det trettende aarhundrede. Udgivet af C. R. Unger. cv, 567 pp. 1 pl. 8°. *Christiania, H. J. Jensen*, 1859–60.

Karmarsch (Carl). Handbuch der mechanischen technologie. 4e aufl. xiv, xii, 1715 pp. 8°. *Hannover, Helwing*, 1866-67.

Karr (Jean Baptiste Alphonse). Contes et nouvelles. 270 pp. 16°. *Paris, L. Hachette et Cie.* 1856.

——— Sous les tilleuls. 2 v. in 1. 252; 228 pp. 18°. *Paris, Garnier*, 1850.

——— Voyage autour de mon jardin. Nouv. éd. 326 pp. 16°. *Paris, Lévy*, 1861.

Karsten (Gustav C.) Lehrgang der mechanischen naturlehre. 3 v. in 1. 8°. *Kiel, Akad. buchhandlung*, 1851-53. s.

Kästner (Abraham Gotthelf). Geschichte der mathematik. 4 v. 8°. *Göttingen, J. G. Rosenbusch*, 1796—1800. s.

[Geschichte der künste und wissenschaften, abtheil vii.]

Katekismuse Luterim aglega. [Lutheran catechism, in the Esquimaux.] 24 pp. 18°. *Kiobenhavnime, C. F. Schubart*, 1816.

Kauffman (C. H.) The dictionary of merchandize and nomenclature in all European languages. With history [etc.] of such natural productions as form articles of commerce. 4th ed. xlviii, 396 pp. 8°. *London, T. Boosey*, 1815.

Kauffmann (François Joseph). Considérations sur le diagnostic de quelques maladies du foie. 55 pp. 4°. *Strasbourg, Berger-Levrault*, 1848. s.

Kaup (Johann Jacob). Classification der säugethiere und vögel. x, 144 pp. 2 tab. 2 pl. 8°. *Darmstadt, C. W. Leske*, 1844. s.

Kaura (Johann B.) Bauentwürfe im byzantinischen style, nebst projecten im dorischen style. 2 p. l. 70 pl. fol. *Leipzig, Spamer*, 1855. s.

Kavanagh (Julia). Daisy Burns; a tale. 3 v. 12°. *London, R. Bentley*, 1853.

Kavanaugh (*Mrs.* Russell). Original dramas, dialogues, declamations and tableaux vivants, for school exhibitions, [etc.] 252 pp. 16°. *Louisville, J. P. Morton & Co.* 1867.

Kay (Joseph). The social condition and education of the people in England. 323 pp. 12°. *New York, Harpers*, 1863.

Kayser (Christian Gottlob). Index locupletissimus librorum qui inde ab anno mdccl usque ad annum mdccclxiv in Germania et in terris confinibus prodierunt. Vollständiges bücher-lexicon, [etc.] Bearbeitet von G. W. Wuttig. A-Z. 1859-1864. v. 15-16. 567 pp; 592 pp. 4°. *Leipzig, T. O. Weigel*, 1866.

——— Sachregister zum kayser'schen bücherlexicon. 1750-1832. Von L. Schumann. viii. 511 pp. 4°. *Leipzig, L. Schumann*, 1838. s.

Kayser (Wilhelm Carl). Historia critica tragicorum graecorum. xxxviii, 332 pp. 8°. *Gottingae, Dieterich*, 1845. s.

Keath (*Sir* William). *See* **Keith.**

Keating (Geoffry). General history of Ireland. Translated from the original Irish by Dermod O'Connor. 556 pp. 12°. *Dublin, J. Duffy*, 1857.

Keating (William H.) Narrative of an expedition to the source of St. Peter's river, lake Winnepeek, etc. 2 v. xiii, 458 pp; 248, clvi pp, 9 pl. 8°. *London, Geo. B. Whitaker*, 1825.

Keber (Gotthard August Ferdinand). Mikroskopische untersuchungen über die porosität der körper. Nebst einer abhandlung über den eintritt der samenzellen in das ei. Mit zusätzen, von M. Barry. xvi, 183 pp. 2 pl. 4°. *Königsberg, Bornträger*, 1854. s.

Kehoe (Simon D.) Indian club exercise, with figures and positions; also, general remarks on physical culture. 123 pp. 4°. *New York, F. A. Brady*, 1867.

Keightley (Thomas). Outlines of universal history; written for Lardner's cyclopædia. 540 pp. 12°. *Philadelphia, Hogan & Thompson*, 1851. s.

Keilhau (Balthazar Mathias, *editor*). Gaea norvegica, von mehreren verfassern. 4 p. l. 516 pp. 7 pl. etc. 4°. *Christiania*, 1838-50. s.

CONTENTS.

Böbert (C. F.) Über serpentingebilde im urgebirges auf Modun.
Boeck (C.) Übersicht der bisher in Norwegen gefundenen formen der trilobiten.
Keilhau (B. M.) Christianias uebergangs territorium.
— Über den bau der felsenmasse Norwegens.
Munch (P. A.) Übersicht der orographie Norwegens.
Scheerer (Th.) Ueber den Norit und die auf der insel Hitteroe und in dieser gebirgsart vorkommenden mineralien reichen granitgange.
Vibe (A.) Hohenmessungen in Norwegen.
— Zweite sammlung von höhenmessungens in Norwegen.

Keily (A. M.) Prisoner of war; or, five months among the Yankees. By A. Rifleman, esq. gent. [*pseudon.*] 120 pp. 8°. *Richmond, West & Johnston*, 1865.

Keith (*Rev.* George). The presbyterian and independent visible churches in New England and elsewhere brought to the test, etc. vi, 230 pp. 18°. *London*, 1691.

[Title page imperfect].

Keith (*Rev.* Patrick). A botanical lexicon; or, expositor of the terms, facts, and doctrines of the vegetable physiology, brought down to the present time. 416 pp. 8°. *London, Orr & Co.* 1837.

Keith (*Sir* William). A collection of papers and other tracts, [concerning politics and commerce]. 2d ed. xxiv, 228 pp. 18°. *London, Jacob Loyseau*, 1749.

Keller (Ferdinand). Bauriss des klosters St. Gallen, vom jahr 820. Im facsimile herausgegeben und erläutert. 41 pp. 1 pl. 4°. *Zürich, Meier & Zeller,* 1844. s.

Kellerhoven (F.) *and* **Michiels** (Alfred). Chefs d'œuvre des grand maitres reproduits en couleur, par F. Kellerhoven. Texte par A. Michiels. Première série. 13 l. 6 pl. fol. *Paris, Didot,* [1864].

Kelley (Hall J.) A geographical sketch of Oregon, [with] a new map of the country. 80 pp. 8°. *Boston, J. Howe,* 1830.

Kellogg (Edward). New monetary system. Revised from his work on "labor and other capital," with numerous additions. Ed. by Mary K. Putnam. 366 pp. 12°. *New York, Rudd & Carleton,* 1861.

Kellogg (T. D.) United States mercantile register for 1867-68. *See* **United States.**

Kells (David). "The ways of the world." Being a history of the life of D. Kells, the hero of seven battles. 24 pp. 8°. *Adrian, (Mich.) author,* 1867.

Kelly (Ebenezer Beriah). An autobiography. 100 pp. 12°. *Norwich, (Conn.) J. W. Stedman,* 1856.

Kelly (Hugh). The babler. [Periodical essays]. 2 v. x, 286 pp; xiv, 285 pp. 16°. *London, J. Newberry and others,* 1767.

Kelly (Walter Keating). Syria and the Holy Land, their scenery and their people. viii, 451 pp. 8°. *London, Chapman & Hall,* 1844.

Kelly (William). An excursion to California, over the prairie, Rocky Mountains, and great Sierra Nevada. 2 v. x, 342 pp; viii, 334 pp. 12°. *London, Chapman & Hall,* 1851.

Kelsall (Charles). Remarks on the state of modern Sicily, with notes on ancient Sicily. pp. 295-365. 1 pl.

[*With* CICERO (M. T.) Two last pleadings against Verres, translated. 8°. *London,* 1812.]

Kemble (John Mitchell). Horæ ferales; or, studies in the archaeology of the northern nations. Edited by R. G. Latham and A. W. Franks. 251 pp. 34 pl. 4°. *London, Lovell, Reeve & Co.* 1863.

Kemp (Heinrich). De loco et ambitu vermium classis in systemate. 39 pp. 8°. *Bonnae, formis carthusianis,* 1864. s.

Kempis (Thomas à). Of the imitation of Christ. Translated from the Latin by John Payne. xliv, 211 pp. 16°. *Philadelphia, J. Crukshank,* 1783.

——— Kristusimik mallinguāursut. [Esquim. Of the imitation of Christ]. Pelesiunermit Paviamit Egedemit, narkingniarkikfarallóarå A. F. Hönnib. 6 p. l. 168 pp. 24°. *Kjobenhavnime, C. F. Skubart,* 1824.

Kemys (Lawrence). *See* **Keymis.**

Kendall (E. Otis). Elementary treatise on descriptive geometry. s.

[*With* WALKER (T.) Elements of geometry. *Phila* 1843.]

Kendall (Henry Edward, *jr.*) Designs for schools and school houses, parochial and national. 16 l. 19 pl. fol. *London, J. Williams & Co.* 1847. s.

Kendall (James, *D. D.*) Sermon before the society for propagating the gospel among the Indians and others in North America, at their anniversary, November 7, 1811. 44 pp. 8°. *Boston, John Eliot, jr.* 1812.

Kennaway (John H.) On Sherman's track; or, the South after the war. x, 320 pp. 12°. *London, Seeley, Jackson & Halliday,* 1867.

Kennedy (*Rev.* John). A new method of stating and explaining the scripture chronology, upon Mosaic astronomical principles. viii, 431 pp. 8°. *London, J. Kennedy,* 1751.

Kennedy (Joseph G. C.) History and statistics of the state of Maryland, according to the returns of the seventh census of the United States, 1850. v, 104 pp. fol. *Washington, Gideon & Co.* 1852.

Kennedy (Patrick). Legendary fictions of the Irish Celts. xiv, 352 pp. 12°. *London, Macmillan,* 1866.

Kennedy (Samuel M.) First loves; with sketches of the poets. 502 pp. 12°. *Chicago, author,* 1867.

Kennedy (Thomas). Poems. 334 pp. 16°. *Washington, Daniel Rapine,* 1816.

Kennedy (William). A short narrative of the second voyage of the Prince Albert, in search of Sir John Franklin. xiv, 202 pp. 4 pl. 1 map. 12°. *London, W. H. Dalton,* 1853. s.

Kennet (White, *bishop of Peterborough*). A sermon before the lords spiritual and temporal, at Westminster, 1719. 28 pp. sm. 4°. *London, W. Taylor,* 1720.

Kenny (W. S.) Practical chess exercises. 239 pp. 16°. *London, T. & J. Allman,* 1818.

Kenrick (William, *LL. D.*) Rhetorical grammar of the English language: rudiments of articulation, pronunciation, and prosody displayed. 90 pp. 8°. *London, T. Cadell & W. Longman,* 1784.

Kent (James). Outline of a course of English reading. Edited with additions, by H. A. Oakley. viii, 120 pp. 12°. *New York, G. P. Putnam & Co.* 1853. s.

Kentuckian (The) in New York; or, the adventures of three southerns. By a Virginian. [*anon.*] 2 v. 223 pp; 219 pp. 12°. *New York, Harpers*, 1834.

Kentucky. Message of the acting governor, to the house of representatives, communicating the correspondence between the Kentucky and Tennessee commissioners on the boundary line, with the reports of the Kentucky commissioners. 40 pp. 8°. *Frankfort, Kendall & Russells*, 1820.

——— Report of the adjutant general, 1861–66. 2 v. vii, 985 pp; 981, 178 pp. 4°. *Frankfort, T. H. Harney*, 1866–67.

Kepler (Johann). Opera omnia. Edidit Ch. Frisch. v. 1—6. 8°. *Francofurti a. M. etc. Heyder & Zimmer*, 1858–66. s.

——— Tabulæ rudolphinæ, supputated to the meridian of Uraniburge. Afterwards digested into a most accurate and easie compendium by Johannes Baptista Morinvs. 103 pp. 12°. *London*, 1675.

——— Dioptrice. *See* **Gassendi** (Pierre). Institutio astronomica. *Londini*, 1683.

Ker (*Mrs.* Anne). Edric, the forester; or, the mysteries of the haunted chamber. 64 pp. 8°. *London*, 1841.

[Hazlitt's romancist and novelist's lib. v. 3.]

Kéralio Robert (Louise Félicité Guinement de). *See* **Robert** (Louise Félicité Guinement).

Kératry (Auguste Hilarion). Inductions morales et physiologiques. 4 p. l. ii, 451 pp. 8°. *Paris, Maradan*, 1817.

Kerhallet (Charles Philippe de). Manuel de la navigation à la côte occidentale d'Afrique. 2ᵉ éd. 2 v. xxviii, 430 pp. 2 maps; xv, 475 pp. 8°. *Paris, P. Dupont*, 1857–58. s.

——— The same. Vues de côtes. 3 p. l. 22 pl. 4°. *Paris, Dépôt de la marine*, 1852. s.

Kerl (Simon). Treatise on the English language. xx, 536 pp. 12°. *Philadelphia, J. B. Lippincott & Co.* 1859. s.

Kerney (M. J. *A. M.*) A compendium of ancient and modern history, to 1867. 30th ed. 431 pp. 12°. *Baltimore, J. Murphy & Co.* 1867.

Kerr (Orpheus C. *pseudon.*) *See* **Newell** (Robert H.)

Kerr (James). Domestic life, character, and customs of the natives of India. xii, 381 pp. 12°. *London, Allen & Co.* 1865.

Kerr (W.) Report of the progress of the geological survey of North Carolina, 1866. 66 pp. 8°. *Raleigh, W. E. Pell*, 1867. s.

Kerst (S. Gottfried). Die Plata-staaten, und die wichtigkeit der provinz Otuquis, und des Rio Bermego. 2 p. l. 138 pp. 1 map. 8°. *Berlin, Veit u. Co.* 1854. s.

Kessler (Hermann Friedrich). Die lebensgeschichte von *ceuthorhynchus sulcicollis* Gyllenhal, und *nematus ventricosus* Klug. 65 pp. 8°. *Marburg*, 1866. s.

Kett (Henry). Flowers of wit; or, a choice collection of bon mots, antient and modern. 2 v. in 1. xxiv, 216; 222 pp. 16°. *London, Lackington, Allen & Co.* 1814.

Kettle (Rupert). Strikes and arbitrations. 48 pp. 12°. *London, Simpkin, Marshall & Co.* 1866.

Kew gardens, a sketch; St. Mark's eve in Yorkshire, and other tales. Selected from Chambers' miscellany. vii, 144 pp. 12°. *Philadelphia, Lippincott, Grambo & Co.* 1854. s.

Key of heaven; or, manual of prayer. New ed. 512 pp. 32°. *New York, P. J. Kenedy*, 1867.

Keye *or* Keyen (Otto). Kurtzer entwurff von Neu-Niederland vnd Guajana einander entgegen gesetzt, vmb den vnterscheid zwischen warmen und kalten landen herauss zu bringen. 10 p. l. sm. 4°. *Leipzig*, 1572.

Keymis (Lawrence). A relation of the second voyage to Guiana, performed in the yeare 1596, [by direction of Sir Walter Raleigh]. 32 l. unp. 16°. *London, Thomas Dawson*, 1596.

Keynotes of American liberty; comprising important speeches, proclamations, and acts of congress, from the foundation of the government; with a history of the flag. [*anon.*] 273 pp. 2 pl. 12°. *New York, E. B. Treat & Co.* 1866.

Keyserling (Alexander, *Graf*), *and* **Krusenstern** (Paul von). Wissenschaftliche beobachtungen auf einer reise in das Petschora-land, 1843. iii, 469 pp. 4°. *St. Petersburg, C. Kray*, 1846. s.

CONTENTS.

Geographische ortsbestimmungen, von P. von Krusenstern.
Geognostische beobachtungen, von A. von Keyserling.
Beitrage zur geographie und hydrographie des Petschora landes, P. v. Krusenstern.

Keysler (Johann Georg). Dissertatio de cvltv solis, Freji et Othini. pp. 761–771. 16°. s.

[*With* Schede (Elias). De diis germanis. *Halae*, 1728.]

Kidder (Frederic). Expeditions of Capt. John Lovewell, and his encounters with the Indians; including a particular account of the Pequaket battle, with a history of that tribe; and a reprint of Rev. Thos. Symmes' sermon. 138 pp. 1 map. 4°. *Boston, Bartlett and Halliday*, 1865.

Kidder (Frederic). Military operations in eastern Maine and Nova Scotia during the revolution, with notes and memoir of Col. John Allan. x, 336 pp. 1 map. 8°. *Albany, J. Munsell*, 1867.

——— *and* **Gould** (Augustus A.) The history of New Ipswich (N. H.) 488, iv pp. 2 maps. 10 pl. 8°. *Boston, Gould & Lincoln*, 1852.

Kidder (K. P.) Guide to apiarian science, being a practical treatise in every department of bee culture and bee management. 175 pp. 12°. *Burlington, (Vt.) S. B. Nichols*, 1858. s.

Kidgell (*Rev.* John). Fables originales. Original fables. 2 v. 5 p. l. 127, xviii pp; 2 p. l. pp. 128–221, xx pp. 16°. *London, J. Robson*, 1763.

Kielsen (Frederik Christian). Icones amphibiorum. iv pp. 42 pl. 8°. *Hafniae, C. Steen*, 1835. s.

Kiepert (Heinrich). Historisch-geographischer atlas der alten welt. 13e aufl. 30 pp. 13 maps. obl. 4°. *Weimar, Geog. institut*, 1860. s.

——— (*Editor*). Memoir über die construction der karte von Kleinasien und türkisch Armenien, in 6 blatt, von v. Vincke, Fischer, v. Moltke und Kiepert. Nebst mittheilungen über die physikalisch, geographischen verhältnisse der neu erfarschten landstriche. Redigirt von Dr. H. Kiepert. 2 p. l. 194 pp. 4 maps. 8°. *Berlin, S. Schropp & Co.* 1854. s.

Kieser (Dietrich Georg). Elemente der psychiatrik. Grundlage klinischer vorträge. xvi, 490 pp. 11 pl. 8°. *Bonn, E. Weber*, 1855. s.

Kimball (Harriet McEwen). Hymns. 83 pp. 12°. *Boston, E. P. Dutton & Co.* 1867.

Kimball (James William). Friendly words with fellow-pilgrims. 262 pp. 18°. *Boston, Am. tract soc.* 1867.

Kimber (Thomas). Life of Vauban.
[*With* VAUBAN (S. L. de). Fortification, etc. Ed. 1861.]

Kincaid (Alexander). History of Edinburgh, [with] gazetteer of the county. viii, 336, 59 pp. 2 pl. 16°. *Edinburgh, N. R. Cheyne*, 1787.

Kinderling (Johann Friedrich August). Geschichte der nieder-sächsischen oder sogenanten plattdeutschen sprache, vornehmlich bis auf Luther's zeiten. xxxii, 414 pp. 8°. *Magdeburg, G. C. Keil*, 1800. s.

Kindersley (*Mrs.* N. E.) Letters from the island of Teneriffe, Brazil, the Cape of Good Hope, and the East Indies. 301 pp. 1 pl. 12°. *London, J. Nourse*, 1777.

King (Albert Freeman Africanus, *M. D.*) Essay on the ligation and management of the umbilical cord at childbirth. 37 pp. 8°. *Washington, (D. C.) Wm. H. Moore*, 1867.

King (Charles William). Hand-book of engraved gems; with illustrations. xiii, 396 pp. 29 pl. 8°. *London, Bell & Daldy*, 1866.

King (John, *M. D.*) American eclectic obstetrics. 2d ed. 768 pp. 1 pl. 8°. *Cincinnati, Moore, Wilstach & Baldwin*, 1866.

——— Causes, symptoms, diagnosis, pathology, and treatment of chronic diseases. 1,607 pp. 8°. *Cincinnati, Moore, Wilstach & Baldwin*, 1867.

King (Thomas). Shop fronts and exterior doors, for the use of the architect, builder, and joiner. 18 pl. fol. *London, J. Weale*, [1836].

King (William, *LL. D. principal of St. Mary's Hall*). Apology or vindication of himself. 46 pp. 4°. *Oxford, S. Parker*, 1755.

——— Opera. viii, 327 pp. 1 pl. 4°. [*London*, 1736–60].

——— The toast. An heroick poem, written originally in Latin by Frederick Scheffer; now done into English with notes by Peregrine O'Donald. [*pseudon.*] lxvi, 232 pp. 1 pl. 4°. *London*, 1736.
[*With* the preceding].

King (William, *LL. D. of London*). Poetical works. 8°. *Edinburgh*, 1793.
[Anderson's Brit. poets, v. 6].

King (William, *prof. at Galway*). A monograph of the permian fossils of England. xxxviii, 258 pp. 29 pl. 4°. *London, palæontographical society*, 1859. s.

Kinglake (Alexander William). Eōthen; or, traces of travel brought home from the east. 93 pp. 8°. *New York, W. H. Colyer*, 1845.

Kingman (Bradford). History of North Bridgewater, Mass. from [1645 to 1866], with family registers. xii, 696 pp. 36 pl. 1 map. 8°. *Boston, author*, 1866.

Kingsbury (C. P.) An elementary treatise on artillery and infantry, adapted to the service of the United States. x, 203 pp. 12°. *New York, G. P. Putnam*, 1849. s.

Kingsbury (Harmon). Law and government: the origin, nature, extent, and necessity of divine and human government, and of religious liberty. 235 pp. 16°. *New York, C. M. Saxton*, 1849.

Kingsley (Charles). Good news of God: sermons. vi, 370 pp. 16°. *New York, Burt, Hutchinson & Abbey*, 1859.

Kingsmill (Joseph). Chapters on prisons and prisoners, and the prevention of crime. 3d ed. viii, 508 pp. 8°. *London, Longman & Co.* 1854.

Kingston (William H. G.) The cruise of the "Frolic." xi, 395 pp. 4 pl. 12°. *London, Low, son & Marston*, 1865.

——— Western wanderings; or, a pleasure tour in the Canadas [and the United States]. 2 v. xvi, 343 pp. 1 pl; viii, 324 pp. 1 pl. 12°. *London, Chapman & Hall*, 1856. s.

Kingston-upon-Hull. (Subscription library at). A catalogue of the library. xxix, 672 pp. 8°. *Liverpool, library*, 1822. s.

——— A supplementary catalogue, containing the books admitted since 1822. xiv, pp. 673–915. 8°. *Hull, library*, 1836. s.

——— The same. Containing the works admitted since 1836. xxviii, pp. 917–1470. 8°. *Hull, library*, 1855. s.

——— A list of books admitted from November 15, 1859, to November 15, [1862]. 3 v. 8°. *Hull, library*, 1860–62. s.

Kinney (Elizabeth C.) Poems. viii, 226 pp. 12°. *New York, Hurd & Houghton*, 1867.

Kirby (Joshua). Dr. Brook Taylor's method of perspective made easy, both in theory and practice. 2d ed. 2 v. in 1. xvi, 78 pp. 22 pl; 84 pp. 8 l. 29 pl. 4°. *Ipswich, author*, 1755. s.

——— The perspective of architecture. [Also: a description and use ot a new architectonic sector]. 3 p. l. ii, 82, 60 pp. 25, 74 pl. fol. [*London*, 1761].

Kirby (W. F.) A manual of European butterflies. xii, 153 pp. 2 pl. 12°. *London, Williams & Norgate*, 1862. s.

Kirby (William), *and* **Spence** (William). Introduction to entomology. 7th ed. xxviii, 607 pp. 12° *London, Longmans*, 1859. s.

Kircher (Athanasius). Lingua aegyptiaca restitvta; opvs tripartitvm. Una cum supplemento. viii p. l. 32 l. pp. 33–622. 32 l. 4°. *Romæ, Hermann Scheus*, 1643. s.

——— Magneticvm natvrae regnvm, sive disceptatio physiologica de triplici in natura rerum magnete. 138 pp. 4°. *Romæ, I. de Lazaris*, 1667.

——— Prodromvs coptvs sive aegyptiacvs. xiii p. l. 338 pp. 1 l. 4°. *Romæ, Typis S. Cong. de propag. fide*, 1636. s.

Kirchhoff (G.) Researches on the solar spectrum, and the spectra of the chemical elements. Translated by Henry E. Roscoe. iv, 36 pp. 3 pl. 4°. *Cambridge, Macmillan & Co.* 1862. s.

Kirchmaier (Georg Caspar). Disputatio geographico-historica de origine, aditu atqve fama gentium americanarum. 12 l. sm. 4°. *Wittebergæ, J. Haken*, 1659.

Kirkes (William Senhouse), *and* **Paget** (James). Manual of physiology. 2d Am. ed. 568 pp. 12°. *Philadelphia, Blanchard & Lea*, 1853. s.

Kirkland (*Mrs.* Caroline M. Stansbury). A new home: who'll follow? or, glimpses of western life. 24°. *London*, 1844.

[*With* Lee (Mrs. Hannah F.) The log-cabin. *London*, 1844].

Kirkland (Frazar). Pictoral book of anecdotes and incidents of the war of the rebellion, embracing the most remarkable anecdotical events of the great conflict in the United States, from 1830 to [1865]. Illustrated. 705 pp. 9 pl. 8°. *Hartford, Hartford pub. co.* 1867.

Kirkpatrick (*Rev.* Jacob, *jr.*) The Kirkpatrick memorial; or, biographical sketches of father and son, and a selection from the sermons of the Rev. Jacob Kirkpatrick, jr. The sketches by Rev. George Hale. Edited by W. M. Blackburn. 312 pp. 12°. *Philadelphia, Westcott & Thomson*, 1867.

Kirkpatrick (James, *of Belfast*). An historical essay upon the loyalty of presbyterians in Great Britain and Ireland, from the reformation to 1713. [*anon.*] xv, 564 pp. Index. 2 l. sm. 4°. [n. p.] 1713.

[Index imperfect].

Kirkpatrick (*Col.* William). An account of the kingdom of Nepaul, in 1793. xix, 386 pp. 1 map. 15 pl. 4°. *London, W. Miller*, 1811.

Kirkwall (*viscount*). *See* **Fitzmaurice** (Geo. William Hamilton).

Kirkwood (Daniel, *LL. D.*) Meteoric astronomy: a treatise on shooting-stars, fire-balls, and aërolites. 129 pp. 2 pl. 12°. *Philadelphia, J. B. Lippincott & Co.* 1867.

Kirkwood (James P. *C. E.*) *See* **Brooklyn** water works and sewers.

Kittlitz (F. H. von). Kupfertafeln zur naturgeschichte der vögel. 1-3 hefte, 28 pp. 36 col. pl. 8°. *Frankfurt am Main, J. D. Sauerländer*, 1832–33.

[No more published.]

Kitto (John). An illustrated history of the holy Bible. Edited by Alvan Bond. xii, 701 pp. 4 pl. 3 maps. 8°. *Norwich, (Conn.) H. Bill*, 1868.

Klaproth (Jules Henri). Grammaire générale. Théorie des signes; aperçu de l'origine des diverses écritures de l'ancien monde (extract). 96 pp. 8°. *Paris, Encyc. mod. de Courtin*, [1823.] s.

[Title page wanting.]

Klaproth (Jules Henri). Verzeichniss der chinesischen und mandschuischen bücher und handschriften der königlichen bibliothek zu Berlin. viii, 188, 68 pp. fol. *Paris, König. druckerei*, 1822. s.

Klee (Frederik Alexander Gottlieb). Le déluge; considérations géologiques et historiques sur les derniers cataclysmes du globe. Éd. française. 3 p. l. 333 pp. 16°. *Paris, Masson*, 1847.

Klein (Jacob Theodor). Historiæ piscium naturalis promovendæ missus i–v. 5 v. in 1. 4°. *Gedani, Schreiber*, 1740–49. s.

——— Tentamen herpetologiæ. iv, 72 pp. 2 pl. 4°. *Leidae, etc. E. Luzac, jun.* 1755. s.

Kleinschmidt (Samuel). Grammatik der grönländischen sprache, mit theilweisem einschluss des Labrador dialects. x, 182 pp. 8°. *Berlin, G. Reimer*, 1851. s.

Klemm (Friedrich Gustav). Zur geschichte der sammlungen für wissenschaft und kunst in Deutschland. 2e aufl. 8°. *Zerbst, Kummer*, 1838. s.

Klencke (P. F. Hermann). Alexander von Humboldt; ein biographisches denkmal. 2e aufl. xii, 252 pp. 8°. *Leipzig, Spamer*, 1852. s.

Klim (Nikolaus, *pseudon.*) *See* **Holberg** (Ludvig von).

Kloss (*Dr.* Georg). Catalogue of his library, including many original and unpublished manuscripts, and printed books with ms. annotations of Philip Melancthon. xxiii, 343 pp. 8°. *London, S. Sotheby & son, and others*, 1835.

Klüpfel (Carl). Wegweiser durch die litteratur der Deutschen. *See* **Schwab** (G.) *and* Klüpfel.

Knapp (Georg Ludwig). Beschreibung des hallischen waisenhauses. *See* **Schulze** (J.L.)

Knapp (Samuel Lorenzo). The picturesque beauties of the Hudson river and its vicinity, in a series of views, from original drawings, by distinguished artists. With descriptive illustrations. Part 1. 16 pp. 3 pl. 4°. *New York, J. Disturnell*, 1835.

Knappe (Julius). Versuch einer entwickelung des begriffes der exzeptionen, mit rücksicht auf die beweislast. x, 127 pp. 8°. *München, G. Jaquet*, 1835.

Kner (Rudolph). Süsswasserfische. *See* **Heckel** (J.) *and* **Kner** (J.)

Knight (H. *lady Luxborough*). Letters to William Shenstone. iv, 416 pp. 8°. *London, J. Dodsley*, 1775.

Knight (Richard Payne). A discourse on the worship of Priapus, and its connection with the mystic theology of the ancients. New ed. [With] an essay on the worship of the generative powers during the middle ages of western Europe. [*anon.* by J. O. Halliwell]. xvi, 254 pp. 40 pl. 4°. *London, privately printed*, 1865.

Knight (Samuel, *D. D.*) The life of Dr. John Colet; with some account of the masters and more ancient scholars of St. Paul's school. New ed. xx, 439 pp. 8°. *Oxford, Clarendon press*, 1823. s.

Knight (Thomas F.) Shore and deep sea fisheries of Nova Scotia. viii, 113 pp. 8°. *Halifax, prov. gov't*, 1867. s.

Knighton (*Rev.* F.) Primary grammar. iv, 67 pp. 16°. *Philadelphia, R. E. Peterson & Co.* 1852.

Knighton (William). Elihu Jan's story; or, the private life of an eastern queen. vii, 210 pp. 12°. *London, Longmans*, 1865.

Knights (Sarah Kemble). The journal of madame Knight [on a journey from Boston to New York] in 1704. 70 pp. 12°. *New York, Wilder & Campbell*, 1825.

Knutt (Frigida, *pseudon.*) *See* **Snow** angel.

Kobell (Franz von). Tafeln zur bestimmung der mineralien mittelst einfacher chemischer versuche, etc. 3e aufl. 70 pp. 8°. *München, J. Lindauer*, 1838.

[*With* NAUMANN (C. F.) Table, etc. 1833].

Koch (Albrecht C.) Reise durch einen theil der Vereinigten Staaten von Nordamerika, 1844–46. 162 pp. 2 pl. 8°. *Dresden, Arnold*, 1847. s.

Koch (Christophe Guillaume de). Tableau des révolutions de l'Europe, depuis le bouleversement de l'empire romain en occident jusqu'à nos jours. 4 v. 8°. *Paris, F. Schoell*, 1807. s.

Koch (C. L.) Die im bernstein befindlichen crustaceen, myriapoden, arachniden und apteren der vorwelt. s.

[*With* BERENDT (G. C.) Die im bernstein reste, etc. v. 1. 1854].

Koch (Fr. C. L.) Die mineral-regionen der obern halbinsel Michigan's (N. A.) am Lake Superior und die Isle Royale. 248 pp. 1 map. 8°. *Gottingen, Dieterich*, 1852. s.

Koch (Gabriel). Die indo-australische lepidopteren-fauna in ihrem zusammenhang mit der europaeischen, nebst den drei hauptfaunen der erde. xii, 119 pp. 1 col. pl. 8°. *Leipzig, L. Denicke*, 1865. s.

Koenig. *See* **König.**

Koestlin (Carl Heinrich). Dissertatio inauguralis medica, sistens animadversiones de materiis narcoticis regni vegetabilis, earumque ratione botanica. 76 pp. 8°. *Tubingae, litteris hopfferianis*, 1808. s.

Köhler (Carl). Briefe aus America. Ein lehrreicher wegweiser für deutsche auswanderer. 2e aufl. viii, 288 pp. 6 pl. 12°. *Darmstadt, G. G. Lange*, 1854.

Kohli (Ludwig). Handbuch einer historisch-statistisch-geographischen beschreibung des herzogthums Oldenburg, sammt der erbherrschaft Jever, und Lübeck und Birkenfeld. 2e ausg. 2 v. in 3. 8°. *Oldenburg, Schulze*, 1844. s.

Kohlman (*Rev.* Anthony). Unitarianism philosophically and theologically examined; a refutation of [its] leading principles. 2 v. viii, 296 pp; 265 pp. 8°. *Washington, Henry Guegan*, 1821–22.

Kohlrausch (Friedrich). History of Germany, from the earliest period to the present time. xv, 700 pp. 8°. *London, Chapman & Hall*, 1844. s.

Kokscharow (Nikolai von). Materialien zur mineralogie Russlands. 4 v. 8°. atlas, pl. 1–64. 4°. *St. Petersburg, A. Jacobson*, 1853–58. s.

[Wanting all after v. 4, p. 96, and pl. 64.]

Kolenati (Friedrich A.) Meletemata entomologica. 5 v. in 1. 8°. *Petropoli, Imp. acad. sc.* 1845–46. s.

CONTENTS.

v. 1. Insecta Caucasi, coleop. pentamera carnivora 88 pp. 2 pl.
v. 2. Hemiptera Caucasi, tesseratomidæ. 132 pp. pl. 3—11.
v. 3. Brachelytra Caucasi. 44 pp. pl. 12—14.
v. 4. Hemiptera Caucasi, pentatomidæ. 64 pp. pl. 15—16.
v. 5. Insecta Caucasi. 169 pp. pl. 17—19.

Kölliker (Albrecht). Handbuch der gewebelehre des menschen. x, 637 pp. 8°. *Leipzig, W. Engelmann*, 1852. s.

——— The same. 2e aufl. xx, 675 pp. 8°. *Leipzig, W. Engelmann*, 1855. s.

——— Mikroskopische anatomie, oder gewebelehre des menschen, v. 2. Specielle gewebelehre. 1 v. in 2 v. xi, 555 pp. 4 col. pl; xii, 784 pp. 8°. *Leipzig, W. Engelmann*, 1850–54. s.

[No more published].

——— Die schwimmpolypen oder siphonophoren von Messina. vii, 96 pp. 12 col. pl. 4°. *Leipzig, W. Engelmann*, 1853. s.

König (Gustav). The life of Martin Luther, and the reformation in Germany. [*anon.* Adapted from König]. With an introduction by Theophilus Stork. viii, 360 pp. 16 pl. 8°. *Philadelphia, Lindsay & Blakiston*, 1854.

——— *and* **Thäter** (Julius). Güldenes A. B. C. Gezeichnet von G. König; gestochen von J. Thäter. 25 l. unp. obl. 18°. *Gotha, J. Perthes*, 1863. s.

Koninck *or* **De Koninck** (Laurent Guillaume de). Description des animaux fossiles qui se trouvent dans le terrain carbonifère de Belgique. iv, 650 pp. atlas, 63 pl. 4°. *Liége, H. Dessain*, 1842–44. s.

——— The same. Supplément. pp. 651—746. pl. 56—60. 4°. *Liége, H. Dessain*, 1851. s.

——— Mémoire sur les fossiles paléozoïques recueillis dans l'Inde par Fleming. Suivi de la description des brachiopodes fossiles de l'Inde, par T. Davidson. [Extract]. 44 pp. 12 pl. 8°. *Liége, H. Dessain*, 1863. s.

——— Recherches sur les animaux fossiles. 1e partie. Monographie des genres Productus et Chonetes. xvii, 246 pp. 20 pl. 4°. *Liége, H. Dessain*, 1847. s.

[No more published.]

Kopp (Hermann). Geschichte der chemie. 4 v. 8°. *Braunschweig, Vieweg*, 1843–47. s.

——— The same. 4 v. in 2. 8°. *Braunschweig, Vieweg*, 1843–47. s.

Koppe (Johann Christian). Mecklenburgs schriftsteller von den ältesten zeiten bis jetzt. 95 pp. 16°. *Rostock, Adler*, 1816.

Körner (Friedrich). *See* **Thomas** (Louis). Buch der welt, 1854–55.

Kort begrijp der hollandsche schipvaerden nae Nova Zembla.

[pp. 103–114 of La Peyrère (I. de). Nauwkeurige beschrijvingh van Groenland. 1678.]

Kort begryp seven persoonen op Spitsbergen gestorven.

[pp. 120–28 of La Peyrère (I. de). Nauwkeurige beschrijvingh van Groenland, 1678].

Körte (*Dr.* Wilhelm). Die sprichwörter und sprichwörtlichen redensarten der Deutschen. Neue ausg. xl, 568 pp. 8°. *Leipzig, F. A. Brockhaus*, 1847.

Kosciusko (Tadeusz). Manœuvres of horse-artillery adapted to the service of the U. S.

[Part ii of Exercise for garrison and field ordnance. By an officer of the U. S. artillery. 8°. *New York*, 1812].

Kossuth (Lajos). Authentic life of Louis Kossuth, with a full report of his speeches delivered in England. [*anon.*] 136 pp. 15 pl. 8°. *London, Bradbury & Evans*, 1851. s.

Kotschy (Theodor). Reise in den cilicischen Taurus über Tarsus. Mit vorwort von Carl Ritter. x, 443 pp. 1 pl. 2 maps. 8°. *Gotha, J. Perthes*, 1858. s.

Kotzebue (August Friedrich Ferdinand von). Historical, literary, and political anecdotes and miscellanies. 3 v. 16°. *London, H. Colburn*, 1807.

——— The noble lie; a comedy, being the conclusion of the Stranger. Translated from the German. vii, 39 pp. 8°. *London, R. Pitkeathley*, 1799.

——— The negro slaves; a dramatic historical piece. Translated from the German. x, 142 pp. 8°. *London, Cadell & Davies*, 1796.

Kotzebue (Moritz von). Narrative of a journey into Persia, in the suite of the imperial Russian embassy. Translated from the German. 4 p. l. 328 pp. 5 pl. 8°. *London, Longman, Hurst & Co.* 1819.

Kowalewski (Joseph Sgepan). Dictionnaire mongol, russe, français. 3 v. xiii, 2690 pp. 4°. *Kasan*, 1844–49. s.

Kowalski (——). Recherches sur les mouvements de Neptune, suivies des tables de cette planète. 179 pp. 8°. *Kasan, imprimerie de l'université*, 1855. s.

Kracheninnikow *or* Krascheninnikoff (Stepan Petrovich). Beschreibung des landes Kamtschatka. Mit landkarten und kupferbildern, herausgegeben von T. Jefferys. Yn das deutsche übersetzet und mit anmerkungen erläutert, von J. Köhler. xvi, 344 pp. 3 pl. 4 maps. 4°. *Lemgo, Meyer*, 1766.

——— The same. Description du Kamtchatka. [v. 3 of CHAPPE d'AUTEROCHE. Voyage en Sibérie. *Paris*, 1768].

Krafft (Albrecht). Die arabischen, persischen und türkischen handschriften der k. k. orientalischen akademie zu Wien. xx, 208 pp. 8°. *Wien, Mechitaristen*, 1842. s.

Kraft (Jens Edvard). Norsk forfatter-lexicon. 1814–1856. Ordnet og udgivet af C. C. A. Lange. 728 pp. portrait. 8°. *Christiania, Johan Dahl*, 1863. s.

Kragh (Peter). Okalluktuàutit sajmâubingmik annékbingmiglo Jesuse-kristusikut. [Relation of salvation through the mediatorship of Christ Jesus]. 4 p.l. 292 pp. 18°. *Kjöbenhavnime, F. de Tengnagel*, 1830.

Krascheninnikof. *See* **Kracheninnikow.**

Krasinski (Valerian *count*). Panslavism and Germanism. 3 p. l. 328, xxii pp. 1 map. 16°. *London, T. C. Newby*, 1848.

Kratz (Arthur). La guerre d' Amérique. Résumé des opérations militaires et maritimes. [Extrait de la revue maritime et coloniale]. 116 pp. 3 maps. 8°. *Paris, Bertrand*, 1866.

Kraus (Johann Baptist Carl). Handbuch über den montanistischen staatsbeamten- gewerken-und gewerkschaftl. beamten-stand des österreichischen kaiserstaates für 1849. v. 1. 206 pp. 8°. *Wien, F. Ullrich*, 1849. s.

Krause (Wilhelm). Allgemeine und specielle hydrotherapie; oder, die grundsätze der priesznitz'schen heilverfahrens. 2e aufl. xii, 251 pp. 8°. *Stuttgart, Scheitlin & Krais*, 1851. s.

Krauss (Christian Ferdinand Friedrich). Die südafrikanischen crustaceen. 68 pp. 4 pl. 4°. *Stuttgart, E. Schweizerbart*, 1843. s.

Krebs (Henry J.) The West Indian marine shells, with some remarks. [*anon.*] 3 p. l. 137 pp. 12°. *Copenhagen, W. Laub*, 1864. s.

Kreissle von Hellborn (Heinrich). Franz Schubert: a musical biography. From the German, by Edward Wilberforce. 287 pp. 16°. *London, W. H. Allen*, 1866.

Krepp (Frederick Charles). The sewage question, [with] a description of Captain Liernur's system for daily removal of fæcal solids, fluids, and gases by pneumatic force. xvi, 208 pp. 8°. *London, Longmans*, 1867.

——— Statistical book-keeping: being a simplification and abbreviation of the common system by double entry. vii, 180 pp. 4°. *London, Longmans*, 1858.

Kresz (C.) Le pêcheur français: traité de la pêche, à la ligne et aux filets, en eau douce. viii, 361 pp. 24 pl. 16°. *Paris, Audot*, 1818.

Kreüter buch. *See* **Herbarius.**

Kröyer (Henrik Nikolaj). Danmark's fiske. 3 v. in 4. 8°. *Kjöbenhavn, S. Trier*, 1838–53. s.

——— Forsög til en monografisk fremstilling af krebsdyrslægten sergestes. 85 pp. 5 pl. 4°. *Kjöbenhavn, Bianco Luno*, 1856. s.

[*With* KRÖYER (H.) Monografisk fremstilling, etc. 4°. *Kjöbenhavn*, 1842.]

——— Monografisk fremstilling af slaegten hippolyt's nordiske arter, med bidrag til dekapodernes udviklings historie. 152 pp. 6 pl. 4°. *Kjöbenhavn, Bianco Luno*, 1842. s.

——— Naturhistorisk lærebog for de förste begyndere. 5en udgabe. 3 p. l. 133 pp. 12°. *Kjöbenhavn, C. A. Reitzel*, 1851. s.

——— The same. 6en oplage. 12°. *Kjöbenhavn*, 1855. s.

Krüdner (Juliane von, *born* Wietinghoff). Valérie. [Nouvelle]. xxxvi, 264 pp. 12°. *Paris, Charpentier*, 1855.

Kruger (*Dr.* F.) The first discovery of America, and its early civilization. Translated and enlarged from the German, by W. L. Wagener. 134 pp. 12°. *New York, Sheldon & Co.* 1863.

Kruger (Fr. J.) Wohin soll der Deutsche auswandern? Entwurf einer deutschen kolonialpolitik. 75 pp. 16°. *Hamburg, F. Schuberth,* 1857.

Kruse (Friedrich Carl Hermann). Chronicon Nortmannorum Wariago-Russorum, nec non Danorum, Sveonum, Norwegorum, inde ab 777, usque ad 1379. xvi, 478 pp. 4°. *Dorpati, auctor,* 1851. s.

——— Necrolivonica; oder, alterthümer Liv-Esth-und Curlands bis zur einführung der christlichen religion in den k. russischen Ostsee-gouvernments; nebst plänen und charten. 44 pl. 1 map. fol. *Dorpat,* 1842. s.

Krusenstern (Adam Ivan von). Beyträge zur hydrographie der grössern oceane, als erläuterung einer karte der ganzen erdkreises. 4 p. l. 248 pp. 4°. *Leipzig, P. F. Kummer,* 1819. s.

——— The same. Recueil de mémoires hydrographiques, pour servir d'analyse et d'explication à l'atlas de l'océan pacifique. Avec supplémens. 3 v. 4°. *Saint Pétersbourg, Imp. du depart. de l'instruc. publ.* 1824–25. s.

Krusenstern (Paul von). Petschora-land. *See* **Keyserling** (S.)

Küchenmeister (Friderich). On animal and vegetable parasites of the human body. Translated from 2d German ed. by E. Lankester. 2 v. xix, 452 pp. 8 pl; xvi, 287 pp. 6 pl. 8°. *London, Sydenham society,* 1857.
[Sydenham society publications].

Kugler (Franz Theodor). Handbuch der kunstgeschichte. xxiv, 920 pp. 8°. *Stuttgart, Ebner & Seubert,* 1842. s.

Kuhl (Heinrich). Beiträge zur zoologie und vergleichenden anatomie. 2 v. in 1. 5 p. l. 151 pp; 2 p. l. 212 pp. 11 pl. 4°. *Frankfurt-am-Main, Hermann,* 1820. s.

——— Buffoni et Daubentoni figurarum avium coloratarum nomina systematica. Edidit Theodorus Van Swinderen. 2 p. l. 28 pp. 4°. *Groningae, J. Oomkens,* 1820. s.

——— Conspectus psittacorum. (Extract). 104 pp. 3 col. pl. 4°. *k. Leop. Carol. akad. der natur wissenschaften,* 1820. s.

Kühn (Otto Bernhard). System der anorganischen chemie. xxii, 729 pp. 8°. *Göttingen, Vandenhoeck & Ruprecht,* 1848. s.

Kühne (Willie). Myologische untersuchungen. 4 p. l. 226 pp. 1 pl. 8°. *Leipzig, Veit & Co.* 1860. s.

Kuinoel *or* **Kühnöl** (Christian Gottlieb). Commentarivs in libros novi testamenti historicos. Ed 3a. 4 v. 8°. *Lipsiae, J. A. Barth,* 1823–27.

CONTENTS.

v. 1. Evangelium Matthæi.
2. Evangelium Marci et Lvcae.
3. Evangelium Johannis.
4. Acta apostolorum.
[v. 1–3. 3a ed. v. 4. 2a ed.]

Kummer (S. Agnes). An epitome of English history; with questions for examination. 129 pp. 12°. *Baltimore, J. S. Waters,* 1866.

Kunth (Carl Sigismund). Enumeratio plantarum omnium hucusque cognitarum, secundum familias naturales disposita, adjectis characteribus, differentiis et synonymis. v. 1–iv. in 5. 8°. *Stutgardiae, J. G. Cotta,* 1833–43.
[No more published.] s.

CONTENTS.

v. 1. and supp. Agrostographia synoptica, sive enumeratio graminearum omnium, etc. 606 pp; 436 pp. 20 l. unp. 40 pl.
v. 2, Cyperographia synoptica, sive enumeratio cyperacearum omnium, etc. 592 pp.
v. 3. Enumeratio aroidearum, typhinearum, pandanearum pluvialium, juncaginearum, alismacearum, butomearum, palmarum, gunicearum, philydrearum, restiacearum, centrolepidearum et eriocaulearum omnium, etc. 644 pp.
v. 4. Enumeratio xyridearum, mayacearum, commelynearum, pontederiaceearum, melanthacearum; uvulariearum, liliacearum et asphodelearum omnium. 752 pp.

Kunze (Carl Ferdinand). Der kindermord. viii, 288 pp. 8°. *Leipzig, Veit & Co.* 1860. s.

Kunzek (August). Die lehre vom lichte. 455 pp. 5 pl. 8°. *Lemberg, J. Millikowski,* 1836. s.

——— Studien aus der höheren physik. vi, 386 pp. 8°. *Wien, W. Braumüller,* 1856. s.

Kupffer (A. T. *editor*). Observations météorologiques faites à Arkhangel. [extract]. 243 pp. 4°. *Saint Pétersbourg, acad. imp. des sciences,* [1842]. s.

——— Observations météorologiques, faites à l'académie impériale des sciences, etc. de 1822–33, et calculées. [extract]. 214 pp. 4°. *Saint Pétersbourg, acad. imp. des sciences,* 1836. s.

Kurtz (Henry). The [united] brethren's encyclopedia. The united counsels and conclusions of the brethren at their annual meetings, [etc.] 202 pp. 8°. *Columbiana, (Ohio), author,* 1867.

Kurz (Franz Seraphine). Oesterreichs militärverfassung in älteren zeiten. viii, 457 pp. 8°. *Linz, C. Haslinger,* 1825. s.

Küstel (Guido). Nevada and California processes of silver and gold extraction. 327 pp. 11 pl. 8°. *San Francisco, Frank D. Carlton,* 1863.

Kuster (Charles de). Notice sur la serre de palmiers.
[*With* FISCHER (F. E. L.) *and* MEYER (C. A.) Sertum petropolitanum, etc. Decas 2a. 1852].

Kutscher (Franz Jacob). Amerika. Et bidrag til Vestindiens geographie-natur- og folkehistorie, oversat af C. B. Hallager. v. 1. x, 446 pp. 16°. *Kiöbenhavn, M. J. Sébbelow*, 1804.

Kysell (Melchior). Icones biblicæ veteris et novi testamenti. 241 pl. 4°. *Augustae Vindelicorum, M. Kysell*, 1679. s.

La Barre de Beaumarchais (Antoine de). Amusemens littéraires; ou, correspondance politique, historique, philosophique, critique, et galante. 3 v. 18°. *La Haye, Jean van Duren*, 1740.

Labarte (Jules). Histoire des arts industriels au moyen âge et à l'époque de la renaissance. Texte. v. 1-3. 8°. Album. 2 v. 4°. *Paris, A. Morel & Cie*, 1864-65.

Labarthe (Pierre). Voyage au Sénégal, pendant les années 1784-5, d'après les mémoires de Lajaille. Avec des notes sur la situation de cette partie de l'Afrique jusqu' en l'an x. xii, 262 pp. 1 map. 8°. *Paris, Dentu*, 1802. s.

Labat (Jean Baptiste). Nouveau voyage aux isles [françoises] de l'Amérique. Nouv. éd. 8 v. 4 maps. 92 pl. 16°. *Paris, Théodore Le Gras*, 1742.

Labbe (Philippe). Bibliotheca nummaria. *See* **Teissier** (A.) Catalogus, etc. s.

La Beche. *See* **De la Beche.**

Labédollière (Émile Gigault de). Histoire de la guerre du Mexique, 1861 à 1866. 76 pp. 2 maps. sm. fol. *Paris, G. Barba*, [1866].

Labillardière (Jacques Julien Houton de). Voyage in search of La Pérouse, during the years 1791-94, [with a vocabulary of the Malay and other Polynesian tongues]. Translated from the French, by John Stockdale. 2 v. xxxii, 487 pp; 344, ciii pp. 46 pl. 8°. *London, John Stockdale*, 1800.
[Imperfect; pl. 27, 42, 44, and 45 wanting.]

Laborde (Alexandre Louis Joseph, *comte* de). Description des nouveaux jardins de la France et de ses anciens chateaux. [En Franç, en Anglais, et en Allem. Les dessins par C. Bourgeois]. 130 pl. fol. *Paris, Bourgeois*, 1808-15. s.

Laborde (Jean Benjamin de). Histoire abrégée de la Mer du Sud, ornée de plusieurs cartes. 3 v. 8°. *Paris, P. Didot*, 1791.

Laborde (Léon Emmanuel Simon Joseph, *comte* de). Commentaire géographique sur l'Exode et les Nombres. [Avec le text en Latin et en Français]. fol. *Paris, Renouard et Cie.* 1841.

——— Débuts de l'imprimerie à Strasbourg; ou, recherches sur les travaux mystérieux de Gutenberg dans cette ville. 83 pp. 5 pl. 8°. *Paris, Techener*, 1840. s.

——— Débuts de l'imprimerie à Mayence et à Bamberg; ou, description des lettres d'indulgence du pape Nicolas v, Pro regno Cypri, imprimées en 1454. 31 pp. 10 pl. 4°. *Paris, Techener*, 1840.

——— Histoire de la gravure en manière noire. 8°. *Paris, Techener*, 1839. s.

——— De l'organisation des bibliothèques dans Paris.
[Lettres 1, 2, 4 and 8. No more published.]

CONTENTS.

1e Lettre. La bibliothèque royale occupe le centre topographique et intellectuel de la ville de Paris. 24 pp. 2 pl. 8°. *Paris, A. Franck*, 1845.
2e Lettre. Revue critique des projets présentés pour la déplacement de la bibliothèque royale. 56 pp. 4 pl. 8°. *Paris, A. Franck*, 1845. s.
4e Lettre. Le palais mazarin et les habitations de ville et de campagne au 17e siècle. 124 pp. 7 pl. 8°. *Paris, A. Franck*, 1845. s.
——— The same. [2e ptie. notes]. pp. 121-408. 2 facs. 8°. *Paris, A. Franck*, 1846.
8e Lettre. Étude sur la construction des bibliothèques. 52 pp. 13 pl. 8°. *Paris, A. Franck*, 1845.

——— Recherches sur ce qu'il s'est conservé dans l'Egypte moderne de la science des anciens magiciens. 23 pp. 4°. *Paris, J. Renouard & Cie*, 1841. s.

——— Journey through Arabia Petræa to Mount Sinai, and the excavated city of Petra. 2d ed. xxviii, 340 pp. 1 map. 8°. *London, John Murray*, 1838.

Laboulaye (Édouard René Lefebvre). Histoire des États-Unis, 1620—1789. 2e éd. 3 v. 16°. *Paris, Charpentier*, 1867.

——— Fairy book: fairy tales of all nations. Translated by Mary L. Booth. 12°. *New York, Harpers*, 1867.

——— Finette: a legend of Brittany. Translated from the French. 90 pp. 3 pl. 8°. *Boston, J. E. Tilton & Co.* 1867.

La Bourdonnais (L. C. de). Nouveau traité du jeu des échecs. xvi, 376 pp. 8°. *Bruxelles, Hauman et Cie.* 1842.

Labree (Lawrence). Rebels and tories; or, the blood of the Mohawk! A tale of the American revolution. 202 pp. 8°. *New York, Dewitt & Davenport*, [1851].

La Cava; or, recollections of the Neapolitans. [*anon.*] 338 pp. 8°. *London, Saunders, Otley & Co.* 1860.

Lacépède (Bernard Germain Étienne de La Ville, *comte* de). Histoire naturelle, comprenant les cétacés, les quadrupèdes ovipares, les serpents et les poissons. Nouv. éd. précédée de l'éloge de Lacépède par Cuvier. Avec des notes de A. G. Demorest. 2 v. xii, 668 pp. 24 col. pl; 647 pp. 12 col. pl. 8°. *Paris, Furne et Cie*, 1855. s.

Lachmann (W. *M. D.*) Physiographie des herzogthumes Braunschweig und des Harzgebirges, [etc.] 2 v. in 1. xix, 291 pp; xii, 316 pp. 2 maps. 8°. *Braunschweig, Vieweg,* 1851–52.

Lackington (James). Confessions, in a series of letters to a friend. vii, 169 pp. 24°. *New York, John Wilson & D. Hitt,* 1808.

——— Memoirs of the forty-five first years of his life. New ed. 540 pp. portrait. 8°. *London, author,* 1793.

Lackland (Thomas, *pseudon?*) Homespun; or, five and twenty years ago. 346 pp. 16°. *New York, Hurd & Houghton,* 1867.

Laco [*pseudon.*] *See* **Higginson** (Stephen).

Lacordaire (Jean Baptiste Henri). Vie de saint Dominique, précédée du mémoire pour le rétablissement en France de l'ordre des frères prêcheurs; et suivie de la lettre sur le saint siége. 3e éd. 695 pp. 8°. *Paris, Sagnier & Bray,* 1844. s.

Lacordaire (Jean Théodore). Monographie des érotyliens, famille de l'ordre des coléoptères. xiv, 543 pp. 8°. *Paris, Roret,* 1842. s.

Lacoste *père et fils aîné.* Polytypie. 22 l. [figures]. 4°. [*Paris, about* 1850].

Lacroix (Paul). Bibliothèque dramatique de monsieur de Soleinne. Catalogue rédigé par P. L. Jacob, bibliophile. [*pseudon.*] 9 parts in 4 v. 8°. *Paris, Alliance des arts,* 1843–45. s.

CONTENTS.

v. 1. Théâtre oriental; grec et romaine; latine moderne; ancien théâtre françois; théâtre françois moderne jusqu' à Racine. xvi, 322 pp. Supplément au tome 1. 44 pp. [Wanting pp. 5-20].
v. 2. Théâtre françois depuis Racine jusqu' à V. Hugo, théâtre des provinces; théâtre françois à l'étranger. 391 pp.
v. 3. Suite du théâtre françois; recueils manuscrits, etc. ballets; théâtre burlesque et de société; proverbes dramatiques; pièces satiriques; pièces en patois; dialogues. viii, 368 pp.
v. 4. Théâtre italien, espagnol, portugais, allemand, anglais, suédois, flamand, hollandois, russe, polonais, turc, grec et valaque. xi, 226 pp.
v. 5. Appendice au tome 3. Autographes, 56 pp. Tome 5. le partie. Écrits relatifs au théâtre; estampes et dessins; autographes, vii, 260 pp. Dernière partie. Livres doubles et livres omis; corrections et additions. vi, 88 pp. Table générale [des auteurs] et table des ouvrages relatifs au théâtre; rédigée par M. Goizet. iv, 144 pp. Prix des livres du premier volume. 12 pp.

——— Curiosités de l'histoire du vieux Paris. Par P. L. Jacob, bibliophile. [*pseudon.*] 364 pp. 18°. *Paris, A. Delahays,* 1858.

——— Énigmes et découvertes bibliographiques. Par P. L. Jacob, bibliophile. [*pseudon.*] viii, 371 pp. 16°. *Paris, Lainé,* 1866.

——— Lettres à M. Hatton, juge d'instruction au sujet de l' incroyable accusation intentée contre M. Libri, etc. 64 pp. 8°. *Paris, Paulin,* 1849. s.

Lacroix (Silvestre François). Anleitung zur ebenen und sphärischen trigonometrie. Neu übersetzt von Ludwig Ideler. xviii, 335 pp. 6 pl. 8°. *Berlin, Duncker & Humblot,* 1822. s.

La Croix de Chevrières (Jean Baptiste de). Estat présent [1688] de l'église et de la colonie françaíse, dans la Nouvelle-France. [2e éd.] ix, 102 pp. 8°. *Québec, A. Coté & Cie.* 1856. s.

La Croix du Maine (François Grusdé, *sieur* de). Premier volvme de [sa] bibliothèqve, qui est vn catalogue général de toutes sortes d'autheurs, qui ont escrit en François depuis cinq cents ans et plus, etc. 22 p. l. 558 pp. fol. *Paris, Abel L'Angelier,* 1584. s.
[No more published.]

La Croze (Cornand de); *or,* **La Croze** (Jean.) A historical grammar; or a chronological abridgment of universal history. Translated from the French by Lucy Peacock. Revised and enlarged by Caleb Bingham. 228 pp. 16°. *Boston, C. Bingham,* 1802.

Ladame (Paul, *M. D.*) Symptomatologie und diagnostik der hirngeschwülste. viii, 264 pp. 1 pl. 8°. *Würzburg, Stahel,* 1865. s.

Lady's almanac for 1867. 128 pp. 32°. *Boston, Lee & Shepard,* 1867.

Laet (Jan de). Notæ ad dissertationem Hugonis Grotii de origine gentium americanarum. 3 p. l. 223 pp. 18°. *Amstelodami, Elzevir,* 1643.

——— Novvs orbis; seu, descriptionis Indiæ Occidentalis libri xviii. 16 p. l. 690 pp. 9 l. 14 maps. fol. *Lvgd. Batav. apud Elzevirios,* 1633.

——— The same. L'histoire dv nouveau monde; ou, description des Indes Occidentales. 14 p. l. 632 pp. 6 l. 14 maps. fol. *Leyde, B. & A. Elseuiers,* 1640.

——— Responsio ad dissertationem secundam Hvgonis Grotii de origine gentium americanarum. 2 p. l. 116 pp. 4 l. 18°. *Amstelodami, Elsevir,* 1644.

Laetus (Pomponius). *See* **Leto** (Giulio Pomponio).

Lafayette (M. J. P. R. Y. Gilbert Motier, *marquis* de). Memoirs, correspondence, and manuscripts. 1777–81. Published by his family. v. 1. xiv, 552 pp. 1 pl. 8°. *New York, Saunders & Otley,* 1837.

Lafforgue (Pierre C. Théodore, *known as T. Robertson*). The whole French language. Ed. by Louis Ernst. xi, 605 pp. 12°. *New York, R. Lockwood,* 1855.

La Fontaine (Alphonse de). Faune du pays Luxembourg; ou, manuel de zoologie, contenant la description des animaux vertèbrés observés dans le pays de Luxembourg.—[Oiseaux.] 326 pp. 8°. *Luxembourg, V. Buck,* 1865–66. s.

Lafontaine (August Heinrich Julius). Gemähldesammlungzur veredlung des familienlebens. [Die brüder; oder, der wildfang.] 2 v. in 1. 435, 471 pp. 16°. *Berlin, J. D. Sander,* 1807.

——— Man of nature; or, nature and love; from the German of Miltenberg. [*pseudon.*] By W. Wennington. New ed. xx, xxvii, 447 pp. 8°. *London, W. Wennington,* 1807.

La Fontaine (Jean de). Contes et nouvelles en vers. Nouv. éd. [avec dessins] par R. de Hooge. 2 v. 7 p. l, 240 pp. 1 l; 4 p. l. 273 pp. 1 l. 62 pl. 18°. *Amsterdam, Brunel & Lucas,* 1709–32.

——— Fables choisies, mises en vers par La Fontaine, et par luy reveuës, corrigées et augmentées de nouveau. 4 pts. in 1 v. 18°. *La Haye, H. van Bulderen,* 1688.

[pp. 175–6 imperfect.]

——— Fables. Translated by E. Wright. jr. 8°. *London,* 1866.

[Masterpieces of foreign literature.]

——— Opuscules inédits.

[pp. 451–557 of COULANGES, (P. E. *marquis* de). Mémoires, etc.]

——— *and others.* Fables inédites des 12e, 13e, et 14e siècles, et fables de la Fontaine rapprochées de celles de tous les auteurs qui avoient, avant lui, traité les mêmes sujets. Précédées d'une notice sur les fabulistes, par A. C. M. Robert. 2 v. cclxii, 368 pp; 601 pp. 80 pl. 8°. *Paris, Étienne Cabin,* 1825.

La Fontaine. *See* also, **Fontaine.**

La Force (Caumont de); *or,* **La Force** (Charlotte Rose de). Histoire secrète des amours de Henri iv. roy de Castile, surnommé l'impuissant. [*anon.*] 180 pp. 18°. *La Haye, M. Roguet,* [1736?]

——— Histoire secrète de Bourgogne. [Éd. publiée par J. B. de La Borde]. 3 v. 18°. *Paris, Didot,* 1782.

La Gasca (Mariano). Genera et species plantarum quae aut nova sunt, aut nondum recte cognoscuntur. 8 p. l. 35 pp. 8°. *Matriti, Typographia regia,* 1816. s.

Lagemans (E.) Recueil des traités et conventions conclus par le royaume des Pays-bas avec les puissances étrangères, depuis 1813 jusqu'à nos jours. 4 v. 8°. *La Haye, A. Belinfante,* 1858–59.

Lagus (Wilhelm Gabriel). Biographiska anteckningar om Äbo hofrätts presidenter och ledamöter jemte förteckning öfrer secreterare och advocat-fiscaler der städes intill der 12 Nov, 1823, då nofrätten firade sin andra secular-fest. (Äbo hofrätts historia, delen i.) xxxiii, 596 pp. 8°. *Helsingfors, J. C. Frenckell & son,* 1834. s.

Laing (John, *surgeon*). A voyage to Spitzbergen; an account of that country, of the zoology of the north; of the Shetland isles, and of the whale fishery. 3d ed. 165 pp. 12°. *Edinburgh, Tait,* 1820.

Laing (John). The theory of business. viii, 240 pp. 12°. *London, Longmans,* 1867.

Laire (François Xavier). Specimen historicum typographiæ romanæ xv saeculi. xiv p. l. 1 l. 308 pp. 4°. *Romae, Monaldini,* 1778.

Lairesse (Gérard de). Het groot schilderbook. 2 v. in 1. sm. 4°. *Amsterdam, Willem de Coup,* 1707. s.

Lajaille (—— de). *See* **Labarthe** (Pierre). Voyage au Sénégal. s.

Lakenman (Seger). Ontwerp van een onkostbaar en zeker middel, om de westvriesche zeedyken, door het afknagen van't paalwerk zeer gevaarlyk geworden, in de aanstaande zomer 1733 te stellen, buiten eenig gevaar van doorbrake, schoon de zeewormen voortragen, etc. 2 p. l. 23 pp. 2 maps. fol. *Amsterdam, erven van J. Ratelband & Co.* 1733. s.

Lallemant (Jêrome). Lettres envoiées de la Novvelle France au Jacques Renault. 49 pp. 2 l. 12°. *Paris, Cramoisy,* 1670. [*Privately reprinted by James Lennox, New York,* 1855.]

[*With* LE MERCIER (F.) Copie de devx lettres. 1656.]

Lally (Thomas Arthur, *comte* de, *baron* de Tollendal). Memoirs of count Lally; consisting of pieces addressed to his judges, [with] accounts of the prior part of his life, his condemnation and execution. 8 p. l. 375 pp. 8°. *London, F. Newberry,* 1766.

Lama (Giuseppe de). Vita del cavaliere Giambattista Bodoni, e catalogo cronologico delle sue edizioni. 2 v. 4°. *Parma,* 1816. s.

Lamartine (Marie Alphonse de). Biographies and portraits of some celebrated people. 2 v. 384 pp; 424 pp. 12°. *London, Tinsley bros.* 1866.

CONTENTS.

v. 1. Lord Chatham, William Pitt, Shakspeare.
v. 2. Shakspeare, Charlotte Corday, madame Roland, Mirabeau, Danton, Vergniaud.

——— The past, present, and future of the republic. Trans. from the French. 163 pp. 12°. *New York, Harpers,* 1850. s.

——— Raphael. Blätter aus dem zwanzigsten jahre. Deutsch von Friedrich Müller. 280 pp. 24°. *Stuttgart, k. hofbuchdruckerei,* 1849. s.

La Martinière. *See* **Bruzen** de La Martinière.

Lamb (*lady* Caroline). Poetical effusions, letters, anecdotes, and recollections. 12°.
[pp. 147 to 196 of NATHAN (I.) Fugitive pieces and reminiscences of Lord Byron].

Lamb (Edward Buckton). Studies of ancient domestic architecture, with observations on the application of ancient architecture to the pictorial composition of modern edifices. 30 pp. 20 pl. fol. *London, J. Weale,* 1846.

Lambert (Anne Thérèse de Marguenat de Courcelles, *marquise* de). Essays on friendship and old age. Translated from the French by a lady. 142 pp. 8°. *London, J. Dodsley,* 1780.

Lambert (Charles). Traité sur l'hygiène et la médecine des bains russes et orientaux. 2e éd. xiv, 406 pp. 8°. *Paris, C. Lambert,* 1842.

Lambert (Charles R.) Poems, and translations from the German of Goethe, Schiller, Chamisso, Uhland, etc. xii, 224 pp. 16°. *London, Whittaker & Co.* 1850.

Lambert (T. S. *M. D.*) Human anatomy, physiology, and hygiene. 456 pp. 8 pl. 12°. *Hartford, Brockett, Hutchinson & Co.* 1854. s.

——— Primary systematic human physiology, anatomy, and hygiene. 178 pp. 12°. *New York, Wm. Wood & Co.* 1867.

Lambin (Denis). In Q. Horatium Flaccum commentarii, etc. Ed. nova. 2 v. vi, 564 pp; xxx, 641 pp. 8°. *Confluentibus, J. Hoelscher,* 1829. s.

Lambinet (Pierre). Origine de l'imprimerie, d'après les titres authentiques, l'opinion de Daunou et celle de Van Praet; suivie de l'histoire de la stéreotypie. 2 v. 8°. *Paris, H. Nicolle,* 1810. s.

Lambinus (Dionysius). *See* **Lambin** (Denis).

Lamé (Gabriel). Cours de physique de l'école polytechnique. 2e éd. 731 pp. 17 pl. 8°. *Bruxelles, H. Dumont,* 1836. s.

——— Leçons sur la théorie mathématique de l'élasticité des corps solides. 335 pp. 1 pl. 8°. *Paris, Bachelier,* 1852. s.

Lamé-Fleury (Jules Raymond). L'histoire de la découverte de l'Amérique, racontée à la jeunesse. 2e éd. viii, 280 pp. 18°. *Paris, Dufart,* 1844.

——— The same. 3e éd. iv, 276 pp. 24°. *Paris, Borrani et Droz,* 1850.

La Mettrie (Julien Offray de). L'homme machine. [*anon.*] 10 p. l. 109 pp. 18°. *Leyde, É. Luzac fils,* 1748.

Lamont (Johann). Astronomie und erdmagnetismus. [Extract.] viii, 289 pp. 5 pl. 8°. *Stuttgart, Neue encycl. für wissensch. u. künste,* 1851. s.

——— Magnetische ortsbestimmungen ausgeführt an verschiedenen puncten des königreichs Bayern und an einigen auswärtigen stationen. 2 v. 199, cccc pp. 18 pl; 191, ccxcii pp. 26 pl. 8°. *München, F. S. Hübschmann,* 1854–56. s.

CONTENTS.

v. I. Allgemeinen grundlagen zur bestimmung des laufes der magnetischen curven in Bayern.
v. II. Nähere bestimmungen über den verlauf der magnetischen curven.

——— Untersuchungen über die richtung und stärke des erdmagnetismus an verschiedenen puncten des südwestlichen Europa. 198, cxv pp. 13 pl. 4°. *München, F. S. Hübschmann,* 1858. s.

La Mothe (F. C. Huerne de). *See* **Huerne de La Mothe.**

Lamothe (Léonce de). Compte rendu de la Gironde, etc. *See* **Rabanis** (J.) *and* **Lamothe** (L. de).

Lamothe-Langon (Étienne Léon, *baron* de). La duchesse de Grammont. Par la comtesse O. D. [*pseudon.*] 2 v. 518 pp; 508 pp. 8°. *Paris, Schwartz et Gagnot,* 1843.

La Motte Fouqué (Friedrich Carl Heinrich, *baron* von).

——— The four seasons. 96, 52, 42, 120 pp. 18°. *London, E. Lumley,* [1846.]

NOTE.—Under this general title are included Undine, [spring], Two captains, [summer], Aslauga's knight, [autumn], and Sintram, [winter].

CONTENTS.

Undine. A new translation, with illustrations, xxiv, 96 pp.
The two captains, a romance. From the German. 52 pp.
Aslauga's knight, a romance. From the German. 42 pp.
Sintram and his companions. 120 pp.

——— Sintram and his companions. From the German. 120 pp. 18°. *London, E. Lumley,* 1848.

——— Undine; or, the spirit of the waters. Translated from the German by the Rev. Thomas Tracy. 49 pp. 8°. *London,* 1841.
[HAZLITT's romancist and novelist's lib. v. 2.]

——— The same. Illustrations by H. W. Herrick. iv, 116 pp. 6 pl. 18°. *New York, Hurd & Houghton,* 1867.

——— The same. Esquisses pour servir á illustrer Ondine. Dessinées et gravees á l'eau forte, par J. E. G. [German and French.] 34 l. unp. 57 pl. 4°. *Londres, W. Nicol,* 1843.

Lamouroux (Jean Victor Félix). Histoire des polypiers coralligènes flexibiles, vulgairement nommés zoophytes. lxxxiv, 559 pp. 19 pl. 8°. *Caen, F. Poisson,* 1816. s.

Lamporecchi *or* Ranieri-Lamporecchi (——). Mémoire sur la persécution qu'on fait souffrir en France à M. Libri, accompagné des adhésions, etc. 2e éd. 82 pp. 8°. *Londres, Barthes & Lowell*, 1850. s.

Lampredi (Giovanni Maria). Comercio de los pueblos neutrales en tiempo de guerra. Traducida al Castellano por don Cesareo de Nava Palacio. 18°. *Madrid*, 1793.

[*With* MOLLOY (Charles). Derecho maritimos, etc. v. 4.]

Lamson (Alvan). History of the first church and parish in Dedham. 104 pp. 8°. *Dedham, (Mass.) Herman Mann*, 1839.

Lamson (David R.) Two years' experience among the shakers. 212 pp. 1 pl. 18°. *West Boylston, (Mass.) The author*, 1848. s.

Lancaster (Joseph). Improvements in education, as it respects the industrious classes of the community. 1st Am. from 2d London ed. iv, 39 pp. 8°. *New York, Collins*, 1804. s.

[*With* PRINCETON college. Catalogue of the graduates of Nassau Hall, 1805.]

Lancelot (Claude). Tour to Alet and La Grande Chartreuse.

[*With* SCHIMMELPENNINCK (M. A). Tour, etc. 1816.]

Lancereau (Édouard, *editor*). Chrestomathie hindie et hindouie. iv, 134 pp. 8°. *Paris, Imp. nationale*, 1849. s.

——— Vocabulaire hindi-hindoui-français. 144 pp. 8°. *Paris, Imp. nationale*, 1849. s.

[*With* the preceding.]

Lancet (The). A journal of British and foreign medicine, physiology, surgery, chemistry, criticism, literature, and news. July 1866, to June 1867. 2 v. 8°. *London*, 1866–67.

Lancetti (Vincenzo). Pseudonimia; ovvero tavole alfabetiche de' nomi finti o supposti degli scrittori, con la contrapposizione de' veri. 4 p. l. 1, 449 pp. 8°. *Milano, L. di G. Pirola*, 1836. s.

Lancia de Brolo (Federico). Statistica della istruzione publica in Palermo, 1859. 186 pp. 8°. *Palermo, A. Russitano*, 1860. s.

Landgrebe (*Dr.* Georg). Naturgeschichte der vulcane. 2 v. viii, 499 pp; iv, 450 pp. 8°. *Gotha, J. Perthes*, 1855. s.

Landis (Simon M.) Sense and nonsense in relation to all topics concerning human affairs. 306 pp. 12°. *Philadelphia, author*, 1867.

Landrin (H. *engineer*). De l' or: de son état dans la nature, de son exploitation, de sa métallurgie, de son usage, et de son influence en économie politique. xxiv, 300 pp. 12°. *Paris, A. Franck*, 1851.

Landstad (Magnus Brostrup). Norske folkeviser. xx, 868 pp. 22 l. 8°. *Christiania, Chr. Tönsbergs*, 1853. s.

Lane (Charles). A dictionary, English and Burmese. 3 p. l. 468 pp. 4°. *Calcutta, Ostelle & Lepage*, 1841. s.

Lane (Horace). Wandering boy, careless sailor, and result of inconsideration. 224 pp. 24°. *Skaneateles, (N. Y.) L. A. Pratt*, 1839.

Lang (John Dunmore, *D. D.*) Religion and education in America. viii, 474 pp. 16°. *London, Ward & Co.* 1840.

Lange (Christian C. A. *editor*). *See* **Kraft** (Jens E.)

Lange (Johann Peter, *D. D. and others*). A Commentary on the holy scriptures. *See* **Bible**, *English*.

Langethal (Christian Édouard). Die gewächse des nordlichen Deutschlands. Mitr einem blüthen kalenden. vi, 498 pp. 8°. *Jena, F. Luden*, 1843. s.

Langhorne (John). Fables of Flora. 73 pp. 12°. *London, T. Rickaby*, 1794.

Langland (William). The vision of William concerning Piers Plowman. [Also] Vita de Dowel, Dobet, et Dobest. Edited by W. W. Skeat. Vernon text. Part 1. xliii, 158 pp. 8°. *London, Trübner & Co.* 1867.

[Early English text soc. publ. No. 28].

Langlé (Joseph Adolphe Ferdinand). Les contes du gay sçavoir; ballades, fabliaux, et traditions du moyen age; ornés de vignettes imitées des manuscrits, par Bonington et Monnier. [Avec des notes et un glossaire.] 3 p. l. cxlvi, 48 pp. 8°. *Paris, F. Didot*, [1828].

Langlès (Louis Mathieu). Contes, fables, et sentences, tirés de différens auteurs arabes et persans, avec une analyse du poëme de Ferdoussy, sur les rois de Perse. [*anon.*] xliv, 179 pp. 24° *Paris, Royez*, 1788.

Langlois (Eustache Hyacinthe). Essai historique et descriptif sur la peinture sur verre, ancienne et moderne, [etc.] suivi de la biographie des plus célèbres peintres verriers. xvi, 302 pp. 7 pl. 8°. *Rouen, C. Frère*, 1832. s.

Langman (Christopher, *and others*). A true account of the voyage of the Nottingham galley, of London, John Dean, commander, from the river Thames to New England, near which place she was cast away on Boon island, Dec. 11, 1710, by the captain's obstinacy. 4 p. l. 36 pp. 16°. *London, S. Popping*, 1711.

Langsdorff (Georg Heinrich von). Voyages and travels [of Cook, Forster, etc.] in various parts of the world. 2 v. xxii, 362 pp. 3 l. unp; 4 p. l. unp. 386 pp. 3 l. unp. 1 map. 21 pl. 4°. *London, H. Colburn,* 1813–14.

——— The same. 2 v. in 1. 617 pp. 9 l. 1 pl. 8°. *Carlisle, (Pa.) G. Philips,* 1817.

Langtoft (Peter). Chronicle of Pierre de Langtoft, in French verse, from the earliest period to the death of king Edward I. Edited by T. Wright. v. 1. xxx, 497 pp. 8°. *London, Longmans,* 1866.

[Chronicles of Great Britain and Ireland during the middle ages.]

Langworthy (Edward). Memoirs of the life of lieut. col. Charles Lee; with his political and military essays and letters. [*anon.*] 2d Amer. ed. viii, 284 pp. 12°. *New York, T. Allen,* 1793.

Langworthy (Lucius H.) Dubuque; its history, mines, Indian legends, etc. 82 pp. 8°. *Dubuque, literary institute,* 1855.

Lanjuinais (Jean Denis, *comte* de). Réfutation du [8e] chapitre du Contrat social de Rousseau, entitulé: De la religion civile.

[*With* TOROMBERT (C. L. H.) Principes du droit pol.]

Lankester (Edwin *M. D.*) Cholera: what is it? and how to prevent it. 93 pp. 18°. *London, G. Routledge & sons,* 1866.

Lanman (Charles). Adventures of an angler in Canada, Nova Scotia, and the United States. xii, 322 pp. 1 pl. 12°. *London, R. Bentley.* 1848.

——— Dictionary of the United States congress. 3d ed. Revised to July 28, 1866. 4 p. l. 602 pp. 8°. *Washington, government printing office,* 1866.

——— Life of William Woodbridge. 236 pp. portrait. 8°. *Washington, Blanchard & Mohun,* 1867.

La Noue (Odet de). The profit of imprisonment. Translated by Josvah Sylvester. pp. 619–662.

[*With* Du Bartas (G. de S.) Poetical works. ed. *London,* 1605].

Lansdowne (*Lord*). *See* **Granville** (George).

Lansens (P.) Alouden staet van Vlaenderen, voor en gedurende het leenvaevig bestier, geuolgd van bene beknopte etymologische en geschied-kundige beschryuing der steden, en der parochien. xii, 498 pp. 4 l. 8°. *Brugge, Van C. De Moor,* 1841. s.

Lantier (Étienne François de). The travels of Antenor in Greece and Asia: including some account of Egypt. Translated from the French. 3 v. 8°. *London, Longman & Rees,* 1799.

Lanzi (Luigi). Notizie della scultura degli antichi i dei vare suoi stili. xxxi, 83 pp. 19 pl. 2a ed. 8°. [*Fiesole*], *Poligrafia fiesolana,* 1824.

——— Histoire de la peinture en Italie, depuis la renaissance des beaux-arts, jusques vers la fin du 18e siécle. Traduite de l'Italien sur la 3e éd; par Mme. A. Dieudé. 5 v. 8°. *Paris, H. Sequin, etc.* 1824. s.

La Peyrère (Isaac de). Bericht von Gröhnland gezogen aus zwo chroniken: einer alten ihslandischen, und einer neuen danischen. Jetso aber deutsch gegäben, und um desto färtiger ihn zu gebrauchen unterschihdlich eingeteihlet von Henrich Sivers. 3 p. l. 70 pp. 1 map. 2 pl. sm. 4°. *Hamburg, Johan Nauman & J. Wolf,* 1674.

——— The same. Nauwkeurige beschrijvingh van Groenland; verdeelt in twee boecken, 't erste van't oud (nu verloorne) Groenlandt; 't tweede van't nieuw Groenland, door S. de V. [*anon.*] 3 p. l. 128 pp. 2 maps. sm. 4°. *Amsterdam, Jan Claesz ten Hoorn,* 1678.

——— The same. Relation dv Groenland. 8 p. l. 278 pp. 1 map. 1 pl. 16°. *Paris, A. Covrbe,* 1647.

——— The same.

[Imperfect: wanting title, map and plate].

——— Relation de l'Islande. 20 p. l. 108 pp. 1 map. 16°. *Paris, T. Jolly,* 1663.

——— The same.

[*With* LA PEYRÈRE (Isaac de). Relation dv Groenland. *Paris,* 1647.]

Lapini (Bernardo), *called* Glicino, *or* Ilicino, *or,* da Montalcino (Bernardo). Novelle.

[NOVELLE di autori senesi. v. 2. 18°. *Milano,* 1815.]

La Place (Guislain François Marie Joseph de). Leçons françaises de littérature et de morale. *See* **Noel** (F. J.) *and* **La Place** (G. F. M. J. de.)

La Place (Pierre Simon, *marquis* de). A treatise of celestial mechanics. Translated from the French, and elucidated with explanatory notes, by Henry H. Harte. 2 v. xii, 276 pp; ix, 419 pp. 4°. *Dublin, University press,* 1822–27.

Laporte (François L. de; *comte* de Castelneau). *See* **Castelneau.**

La Primaudaie (F. Hélie de). Le commerce et la navigation de l'Algérie avant la conquête française. 319 pp. 1 map. 8°. *Paris, Lahure,* 1860. s.

La Primaudaye (Pierre de). The French academie. [Part first]. Wherein is discoursed the institution of manners, and whatsoever else concerneth the good and happie life of all estates and callings. Translated by T. B. 5th ed. 13 p. l. 752 pp. 5 l. sm. 4°. *London, T. Adams,* 1614.

La Primaudaye (Pierre de). The French academie. Second part. Wherein as it were by a natural historie of the body and soule of man, all the parts of the frame of man are handled, and chiefly the nature, power, works and immortalitie of the soul. 12 p. l. 600 pp. sm. 4°. *London, George Bishop*, 1605.
[With the preceding.]

——— The same. Third volume. Contayning a notable description of the whole world. Englished by R. Dolman. 8 p. l. unp. 439 pp. sm. 4°. *London, G. Bishop*, 1601.
[With the preceding.)

Lara (Alvear y). *See* **Alvear y Lara.**

Larcom (Lucy). Breathings of the better life. [Extracts, chiefly in prose, from various writers]. vii, 285 pp. 16°. *Boston, Ticknor & Fields*, 1867.

Lardner (Dionysius). Hand-book of natural philosophy. Hydrostatics, pneumatics, and heat. xv, 408 pp. 1 pl. 12°. *London, Walton & Maberly*, 1855. s.

——— The same. Optics. xvi, 432 pp. 1 pl. 12°. *London, Walton & Maberly*, 1856. s.

——— The same. Electricity, magnetism and acoustics. xix, 425 pp. 1 pl. 12°. *London, Walton & Maberly*, 1856. s.

——— The same. Mechanics. xvi, 403 pp. 1 pl. 12°. *London, Walton & Maberly*, 1856. s.

——— The first six books of Euclid, with a commentary and geometrical exercises. A treatise on solid geometry, etc. 4th ed xx, 332 pp. 8°. *London, J. Taylor*, 1834. s.

——— The same. 7th ed. xx, 332 pp. 8°. *London, J. Taylor*, 1840. s.

——— Railway economy; a treatise on the new art of transport, etc. 442 pp. 12°. *New York, Harper & brothers*, 1850. s.

Larmont (M.) Paris, London, and New York medical adviser and marriage guide. 30th ed. 410 pp. 28 pl. 12°. *New York, E. Banister*, 1859.

La Roche-Aymon (Antoine Charles Étienne Paul, *marquis* de). Des troupes légères; ou réflexions sur l'organisation, l'instruction et la tactique de l'infanterie et de la cavalerie légères. xx, 610 pp. 2 pl. 8°. *Paris, Magimel, Anselin & Pochard*, 1817.

La Roche Flavin (Bernard de). Treize lieures des parlemens de France, esqvels est amplement traicté de levr origine et institvtion, et des présidents, conseillors, gens du roy, [etc]. 14 p. l. 1216 pp. 8°. *Genève, Mathiev Berjon*, 1621.

La Rochefoucauld (François, *duc* de). Moral reflections and maxims. Newly made English from the Paris ed. xvi, 95, 8 pp. 8°. *London, A. Bell*, 1706.
[*With* ESPRIT (J.) Discourses, etc.]

La Rochefoucault Liancourt (François Alexandre Frédéric, *duc* de). Travels through the United States of North America, the country of the Iroquois, and upper Canada, in the years 1795–97. Translated by H. Neuman. 2 v. xxiii, 642 pp. 6 l; 1 p. l. 680 pp. 8 l. 3 maps. 4°. *London, R. Phillips*, 1799.

La Roche Gallichon (F. C. de). Sendschreiben, betreffend die wiederfindung des alten Grönlands. 102 pp. 12°. *Kopenhagen, C. F. Holm*, 1787.

Laromiguière (Pierre). Leçons de philosophie, ou essai sur les facultés de l' âme. 2e éd. 2 v. 447 pp; 484 pp. 8°. *Paris, Brunot-Labbe*, 1820.

Larousse (Pierre). Grand dictionnaire universel du xixe siècle, français, historique, géographique, mythologique, bibliographique, littéraire, artistique, scientifique, etc. v. 1–2. A-Bzo. fol. *Paris, Larousse et Boyer*, 1866–67.

La Rue (Gervais de). Essais historiques sur les bardes, les jongleurs, et les trouvères normands et anglo-normands. 3 v. 8°. *Caen, Marcel*, 1834.

La Sale *or* La Salle (Antoine). L'hystorye et plaisante cronicque du petit Jehan de Saintré et de la jeune dame des belles cousines, sans autre nom nommer. [*anon.*] Publiée par J. M. Guichard. xxxi, 297 pp. 16°. *Paris, Gosselin*, 1843.

——— Les quinze joyes de mariage. Nouv. ed. avec une notice bibliographique et des notes. xvi, 180 pp. 18°. *Paris, P. Jannet*, 1853.

La Salle (J. B. de). Conduite des écoles chrétiennes. 236 pp. 3 tab. 16°. *Paris, J. Moronval*, 1838. s.

Las Casas *or* Casaus (Bartolomé de). Aqui se contiene vna disputa, o controuersia: entre Bartholome de Las Casas y el doctor Hines de Sepulueda. 61 l. sm. 4°. *Seuilla, Sebastiã Trugillo*, 1552.

——— Aqui se cõtienẽ treynta proposiciones muy juridicas. 10 l. sm. 4°. *Seuilla, Sebastiã Trugillo*, 1552.

——— Aqui se cõtienẽ vnos auisos y reglas para los confessores. 16 l. unp. sm. 4°. *Seuilla, Sebastian Trugillo*, 1552.

——— Brevissima relacion de la destrvycion de las Indias [etc.] 214 l. sm. 4°. *Seuilla, Sebastian Trugillo*, 1552.

Note.—The above ed. of the "Brevissima relacion" contains also the following tracts, the leaves being paged continuously with the foregoing.

Las Casas *or* Casaus (Bartolomé de).—*Continued.*

CONTENTS.

Aqvi se contienen treynta proposciones muy juridicas. 51-60 l.
Aqvi se contiene vna dispvta, o controversia entre el obispo don fray Bartolome de Las Casas y el dotor Gines de Sepulueda. 60-121 l.
Este es vn tratado sobre la materia de los Indios que se han hecho en ellas esclauos. 122-157 l.
Entre los remedios para reformacion de las Indias. 158-209 l.
Pedaço de vna carta, y relacion que escriuio cierto hombre de los mismos que andauã en estas estaciones. 210-214 l.

——— Breuissima relacion de la destruycion de las Indias. 54 l. sm. 4°. *Seuilla, Sebastiano Trugillo,* 1552.

——— The same. The Spanish colonie, or briefe chronicle of the acts and gestes of the Spaniardes in the West Indies. Translated into English by M. M. S. 60 l. unp. sm. 4°. *London, W. Brome,* 1583.

——— The same. [Account of the first voyages and discoveries made by the Spaniards in America. 3 p. l. 248 pp. 2 p. l. 8°. *London,* 1699?]

[Title wanting. This vol. contains the dispute between Las Casas and Dr. Sepulveda.]

——— The same. Le miroir de la tyrannie espagnole perpetrée aux Indes Occidentales. 68 l. sm. 4°. *Amsterdam, Jan E. Cloppenburg,* 1620.

——— The same. [Imperfect, wanting l. 68. *With* CLOPPENBURG (Jan Everhardts), Miroir de la cruelle et horrible tyrannie espagnole. *Amsterdam,* 1620].

——— The same. Tyrannies et crvavtez des Espagnols commises es Indes Occidentales. 11 p. l. 214 pp. sm. 4°. *Roven, Jacqves Cailloüe,* 1630.

——— The same. Relation des voyages et des découvertes que les Espagnoles ont fait dans les Indes Occidentales. 4 p. l. 354 pp. 2 l. 1 pl. 18°. *Amsterdam, J. Louis de Lorme,* 1698.

[This vol. contains the dispute between Las Casas and Dr. Sepulueda.]

——— The same. Istoria, ò breuissima relatione della distrvttione dell' Indie Occidentali. Tradotta in Italiano dall' Giacomo Castellani. 4 p. l. 150 pp. sm. 4°. *Venetia, Marco Ginammi,* 1643.

——— The same. Narratio regionum indicarum per Hispanos qvosdam devastatarum verissima. 138 pp. sm. 4°. *Oppenheimii, Johan. Theod. de Bry,* 1614.

——— The same. Regionvm indicarum per Hispanos olim devastatarum accuratissima descriptio. 112 pp. sm. 4°. *Heidelbergae, Gvilielmi Walteri,* 1664.

Las Casas *or* Casaus (Bartolomé de). Entre los remedios para reformaciõ de las Indias. 53 l. sm. 4°. *Seuilla, Jacome Crõberger,* 1552.

——— Este es vn tratado sobre la materia de los Yndios qui se han hecho esclauos. 36 l. sm. 4°. *Seuilla, Sebastiã Trugillo,* 1552.

——— La liberta pretesa dal supplice schiauo indiano. Tradotto in Italiano per opera di Marco Ginammi. 155 pp. sm. 4°. *Venetia, Marco, Ginammi,* 1640.

——— Il svpplice schiauo indiano. Tradotto in Italiano per opera di Marco Ginammi. 118 pp. sm. 4°. *Venetia, Marco Ginammi,* 1636.

——— Tratado cõprobatorio del imperio soberano y principado uniuersal que los reyes de Castilla y Leon tienen sobre las Indias. 80 l. unp. sm. 4°. *Seuilla, Sebastian Trugillo,* 1553.

Las Cases (Emmanuel Dieudonné Marin Joseph, *comte* de). Mémorial de sainte Hélène; journal ou se trouve consigné, jour par jour, ce qu'a dit et fait Napoléon durant dix-huit mois. Nouv. éd. 9 v. 16°. *Paris, H. L. Delloye,* 1840.

Laschamps (F. Bigorie de). *See* **Bigorie** de Laschamps (F.)

Lasor a Varea (Alfonso, *anagram*). *See* **Savonarola,** (Rafaello).

Laterrade (Jean François). Flore bordelaise et de la Gironde. 4e éd. 612 pp. 12°. *Bordeaux, T. Lafargue,* 1846. s.

Latham (John). A general synopsis of birds. 3 v. in 6. 4°. *London, B. White, etc.* 1781-85. s.

——— The same. Supplement. 313 pp. 13 pl. 4°. *London, Leigh & Sotheby,* 1787. s.

——— The same. Supplement ii. 396 pp. 23 pl. 4°. *London, Leigh, Sotheby & son,* 1801. s.

——— Index ornithologicus, sive systema ornithologiæ; complectens avium divisionem in classes, ordines, genera, species, ipsarumque varietates. 2 v. xviii, 920 pp. 4°. *Londini, auctor,* 1790. s.

——— The same. Supplementum. lxxiv pp. 4°. *Londini, G. Leigh, J. & S. Sotheby,* 1801.

[*With* LATHAM. Supplement ii, etc. 1801.]

Latham (Wilfred). States of the river Plate; their industries and commerce. vi, 200 pp. 8°. *London, Longmans,* 1866.

Latin and English poems. By a gentleman of Trinity college, Oxford. [*anon.*] 179 pp. 16°. *London, C. Bathurst,* 1741.

Latreille (Pierre André). Crustacea, arachnides, et insecta. s.

[*With* CUVIER (G. L. C. D.) Règne animal. v. 3.]

Latreille (Pierre André). *See* **Sonnini** (C. N. S.) *and* Latreille. Hist. nat. de reptiles. 1799.

Latrobe (*Rev.* Christian Ignatius.) Journal of a visit to south Africa, with some account of the missionary settlements of the United Brethren. 2d ed. xi, 580 pp. 1 map. 4 pl. 8°. *London, L. B. Seeley,* 1821. s.

Latter (Thomas). A grammar of the language of Burmah. lvi, 203 pp. 4°. *Calcutta, Thacker & Co.* 1845. s.

Laudonnière (René Goulaine de). L'histoire notable de la Floride sitvé es Indes Occidentales, contenant les trois voyages faits en icelle per certains capitaines et pilotes françois [sous J. Ribaut, en 1562, 1564, et 1565]: à laquelle a esté adiousté vn quatriesme voyage fait par le capitaine Gourgues [en 1567], mise en lumière par M[artin] Basanier. 8 p. l. 124 l. 16°. *Paris, Guillaume Auuray,* 1586.

Laughton (George, *D.D.*) The history of ancient Egypt. xiv, 362 pp. 1 pl. 8°. *London, T. Cadell,* 1774.

Laugier (André). Cours de chimie générale. 3 v. 8°. *Paris, Pichon & Didier,* 1829. s.

Launoi (Jean de). De scholiss a caro lo magno instauratis. *See* **Mabillon** (Jean). Iter germonicum.

Laurens (*Col.* John). Army correspondence in the years 1777–8. Now first printed from original letters to his father, Henry Laurens. With memoir by W. G. Simms. 250 pp. portrait. 8°. *New York,* 1867.
[Bradford club series, No. 7.]

Laurens. *See* **Du Laurens.**

Laurent (Paul Marie). La guerre du Mexique de 1862 à 1866. Journal de marche du 3e chasseurs d'Afrique. 352 pp. 16°. *Paris, Amyot,* 1867.

Laurentie (Pierre Sébastien). Lettres à un père sur l'éducation de son fils. 239 pp. 18°. *Paris, Lagny,* 1836. s.

——— Lettres à un curé sur l'éducation du peuple. 248 pp. 18°. *Paris, Lagny,* 1837. s.

Laurop (C. P.) Handbuch der forst-und jagdliteratur, vom jahre 1829 bis 1845. 2 v. in 1. xiv, 180 pp; 134 pp. 8°. *Frankfurt am Main, Sauerländer,* 1844–46. s.

Lausitz. Bibliothek, der oberlausitzischen gesellschaft der wissenschaften. 2 v. 4 p. l. 635 pp; 580 pp. 2 l. 8°. *Görlitz, Gesellschaft,* 1819. s.

La Vacquerie (Jean de). De mvltiplici haereticorvm tentatione. Cvi accessit sermo per eundem habitus, in baptismo duorum adolescentium terræ Almericæ. 68 l. 18°. *Parisiis, Chesneau,* 1561.

Laval (Victor Lottin de). *See* **Lottin de Laval** (Victor).

La Vallière (Louise Françoise de La Baume Le Blanc, *duchesse* de). Vie. [*anon.*] 142 pp. 18°. [*Cologne,* 1695.]
[Title page wanting.]

Lavater (Johann Heinrich). Introduction to the study of the anatomy of the human body; for the use of painters, sculptors, and artists. Translated from the German. vi, 120 pp. 27 pl. 8°. *London, R. Ackerman,* 1824.

La Vega (Garsias Laso de, *the Inca*). La Florida del Ynca. Historia del adelantado Hernando de Soto, y de otros heroicos caualleros españoles è indios. 7 p. l. 351 pp. 6 l. sm. 4°. *Lisbona, Pedro Crasbeeck,* 1605.

——— Histoire des Yncas rois du Pérou, traduite de l'Espagñol [par J. Baudouin]. On a joint à cette éd. l'histoire de la conquête de la Floride [traduite par P. Richelet. Suivie de la découverte d'un pays plus grand que l'Europe, situé dans l'Amérique entre Nouveau Mexique, et la mer glaciale: par La Hontan.] 2 v. 19 p. l. 540 pp. 8 l; xxiii, 373 pp. 1 l. 2 maps. 16 pl. 4°. *Amsterdam, Jean Frederick Bernard,* 1737.

La Vega (Gonzales de). Review of the report of the committee on foreign affairs, of the senate of the United States, relative to the Tehuantepec matters. [*anon.*] 106 pp. 8°. [n. p.] 1852.

Lavoisier (Antoine Laurent). Elements of chemistry. Translated from the French by Robert Kerr. 4th ed. 592 pp. 13 pl. 8°. *Philadelphia, M. Carey,* 1799. s.

Lavy (Filippo). Museo numismatico Lavy, appartenente alla accademia delle scienze di Torino. 2 v. 3 p. l. 447 pp. 7 pl; 483 pp. 2 pl. 4°. *Torino, Stamperia reale,* 1839–40. s.

Law (Andrew). The art of singing, in three parts; to wit: 1. The musical primer. 2. The christian harmony. 3. The musical magazine. 4th ed. Printed upon a new plan. 3 parts in 1 v. 160, 96 pp. obl. 18°. *Cambridge,* [*Mass.*] *W. Hilliard,* 1803.

Law (Henry, *C. E.*) The rudiments of civil engineering. 2 v. in 1. viii, 89 pp. 2 p. l; 152 pp. 1 p. l. 16°. *London, J. Weale,* 1848–49. s.

——— The same. New ed. 2 pts. in 1 v. viii, 101 pp; viii, 152 pp. 16°. *London, J. Weale,* 1859.

——— *and* **Burnell** (G. R.) Rudiments of civil engineering; and the rudiments of hydraulic engineering. iv, 126 pp. 6 pl. 16°. *London, J. Weale,* 1852.
[*With* LAW (Henry). Civil engineering. *London,* 1859.]

Law (John, *judge and M. C.*) Address before the Vincennes historical society, 1839. 48 pp. 1 map. 8°. *Louisville, Prentice & Weissinger,* 1839.

Law (Thomas). Considerations tending to render the policy questionable of plans for liquidating, within the next four years, the six per cent. stocks of the United States. 22 pp. 8°. *Washington, S. A. Elliott,* 1826.

——— Proposition for creating means for commencing the Chesapeake and Ohio canal, (Cumberland), with report of committee thereon. 1 fol. sheet. [*Washington,* 1827?]

——— A reply to certain insinuations published as an article in the sixty-eighth number of the Quarterly review. 27 pp. 8°. *Washington,* 1824.

——— (*and others*). Report of the proceedings of the committee appointed at a meeting in Washington, in 1824, to present a memorial to congress praying for the establishment of a national currency. 40 pp. 8°. *Washington, Way & Gideon,* 1824.

Law (*Rev.* William). An humble, earnest, and affectionate address to the clergy. 2d ed. 3 p.l. 208 pp. 8°. *London, M. Richardson,* 1764.

Lawes (John Bennett), *and* **Gilbert** (Joseph Henry). Experimental inquiry into the composition of some of the animals fed and slaughtered as human food. [Phil. Trans. 1859.] pp. 493-680. 4°. *London, Taylor & Francis,* 1860. s.

——— On the growth of barley by different manures, continuously on the same land. 80 pp. 8°. *London, Roy. agricult. soc.* 1858. s.

——— Report of experiments on the growth of red clover by different manures. Part i. 24 pp. 8°. *London, Roy. agricult. soc.* 1860. s.

Lawrence (George Alfred). A bundle of ballads. [*anon.*] 141 pp. 12°. *London, Tinsley bros.* 1864.

Lawrence (William, *surgeon*). A treatise on the diseases of the eye. New ed. Edited, with additions, by Isaac Hays. 859 pp. 12 pl. 8°. *Philadelphia, Lea & Blanchard,* 1847. s.

Lawrence academy (*Groton, Mass.*) Catalogue of the library. 207 pp. 1 pl. 8°. *Lowell, S. J. Varney,* 1850. s.

——— Catalogue of the officers and students of Lawrence academy, from the time of its incorporation. 108 pp. 8°. *Groton, academy,* 1855. s.

[*With* the preceding].

——— The jubilee of Lawrence academy, at Groton, Mass. July 12, 1854. 76 pp. 5 pl. 8°. *New York, academy,* 1855. s.

Lawson (George). On the occurrence of "cinchonaceous glands" in galiaceæ, and the relations of that order to cinchonaceæ. (Extract). 8 pp. 1 pl. 8°. (*London,*) *Annals and mag. of nat. hist.* 1854. s.

Lawson (George C.) Sherman's campaign through the Carolinas. [22 verses]. 1 sheet fol. n. p. (1865?)

[*With* SHARLAND (George). Knapsack notes, etc. 8°. 1865].

Lawson (John). The history of Carolina: description and natural history, with the present state thereof. And a journal of a thousand miles, travel'd thro' several nations of Indians. 3 p. l. 258 pp. sm. 4°. *London, W. Taylor & J. Baker,* 1714.

——— New voyage to Carolina, [with rare plate]. 2 p. l. 258 pp. sm. 4°. *London,* 1708.

[*With* STEVENS (John). Voyages and travels. 1708. Title wanting].

Layard (Austen Henry). Nineveh and its remains. 2 v. in 1. 326 pp; ii, 373 pp. 40 pl. 1 map. 8°. *New York, G. P. Putnam,* 1851. s.

Layres (Augustus). Belles-lettres. (Book ii of "Elements of composition.") 240 pp. 12°. *San Francisco, A. Roman & Co.* 1867.

——— Elements of composition, belles-lettres, and oratory. 166 pp. 12°. *San Francisco, A. Roman & Co.* 1867.

Lazarus (Emma). Poems and translations, written between the ages of fourteen and seventeen. viii, 297 pp. 12°. *New York, Hurd & Houghton,* 1867.

Lea (Albert M.) Notes on Wisconsin territory. 53 pp. 1 map. 18°. *Philadelphia, H. S. Tanner,* 1836.

Lea (Henry Carey). Historical sketch of sacerdotal celibacy in the christian church. 601 pp. 8°. *Philadelphia, Lippincott & Co.* 1867.

Lea (Isaac). Contributions to geology. 227 pp. 6 pl. 8°. *Philadelphia, Carey, Lea & Blanchard,* 1833. s.

CONTENTS.

Tertiary formation of Alabama. New tertiary fossil shells from Maryland and New Jersey. New genus of fossil [foraminiferous] shells from New Jersey. Tufaceous lacustrine formation of Syracuse, N. Y.

Leach (William Elford). Mélanges zoologiques, trad. de l'Anglais par J. C. Chenu. (Extract). 24 pp. 9 pl. 8°. *Paris, Bibliothèque conchyliologique,* 1845. s.

Leaming (*Rev.* Jeremiah). A defence of the episcopal government of the church: containing remarks on two late noted sermons on presbyterian ordination. 73 pp. 12°. *New York, J. Holt,* 1766.

Leavitt (Jonathan). Memoir, by a sister. [With compositions in prose, and select poems. *anon.*] 283 pp. 1 pl. 18°. *New Haven, S. Converse,* 1822.

Leavitt (T. H.) Facts about peat as an article of fuel. Its origin, localities, [etc.] 3d ed. 316 pp. 1 pl. 12°. *Boston, Lee & Shepard,* 1867.

Lebert (Hermann). Abhandlungen aus dem gebiete der praktischen chirurgie und der pathologischen physiologie. Mit besondere rücksicht auf die dieffenbach'sche klinik. xxvi, 597 pp. 8°. *Berlin, Veit & Co.* 1848. s.

——— Klinik des acuten gelenkrheumatismus. viii, 149 pp. 8°. *Erlangen, F. Enke,* 1860. s.

Le Blanc (Vincent). Les voyages famevx, qu'il a faits depuis l'aage de douze ans iusques à soixante, aux quatre parties du monde. Le tout recueilly de ses mémoires par le sieur Covlon. 3 pts. in 1 v. 4°. *Paris, G. Clovsier,* 1648.

CONTENTS.

1. L'Asie et les Indes Orientales. 4 p. l. 276 pp. 2 l.
2. L'Afrique. 179 pp. 2 l.
3. Constantinople, pp. 1–14; Italie, pp. 15–25; Guinée, pp. 26–35; l'Amérique, pp. 36–136. 136 pp. 2 l.

Lecerf (Pierre Louis). La science et la raison humaine, en présence des maux et des dangers qui menacent l'ordre social. 100 pp. 8°. *Caen, [auteur,]* 1851. s.

Le Cerf de La Viéville (Philippe). Bibliothèque historique et critique des auteurs de la congrégation de St. Maur. 6 p. l. 492 pp. 5 l. 16°. *La Haye, P. Gosse,* 1726. s.

Lechford (Thomas). Plain dealing; or, news from New England [1642]; with introduction and notes by J. Hammond Trumbull. xl, 211 pp. sm. 4°. *Boston, Wiggin & Lunt,* 1867.
[Library of N. England history, v. 4.]

Le Clerc (Jean). Account of the earl of Clarendon's History of the civil wars. Done from the French, by J. O. 2 parts in 1 v. 12°. *London,* 1710.

——— Funeral oration upon the death of Philip a Limborch; also, an oration concerning the excellence and usefulness of ecclesiastical history, pronounced Sept. 6, 1702.
[*In* HUGHES (Jabez). Miscellanies, pp. 204—263. *London,* 1737.]

Le Clerc (Joseph Victor). Discours sur l'état des lettres en France, au quatorzième siècle. 602 pp. 4°. *Paris, F. Didot frères,* 1863.
[V. xxiv of HISTOIRE littéraire de la France.]

Leclerc-Thouin (Oscar). L'agriculture de l'ouest de la France, étudiée plus spécialement dans le département de Maine-et-Loire. xvi, 484 pp. 1 map. 8°. *Paris, Bouchard-Huzard,* 1843. s.

Leclerq (Chrétien). Nouvelle relation de la Gaspésie; qui contient les mœurs et la religion des sauvages gaspésiens, Porte-Croix, et d'autres peuples de l'Amérique Septentrionale, dite le Canada. 14 p. l. 572 pp. 18°. *Paris, Amable Auroy,* 1691.

Le Cœur (J. *M.D.*) Des bains de mer. Guide médical et hygiénique du baigneur. 2 v. in 1. x, 468 pp; 401 pp. 8°. *Caen, l'auteur,* 1846. s.

Lecomte (Ferdinand). Guerre de la sécession. Esquisse des événements militaires et politiques des États-Unis de 1861–65. 2 v. 2 p. l. 288 pp; 2 p. l. 390 pp. 6 maps. 8°. *Lausanne, Tanera,* 1866–67.

Le Comte (Louis, *Jesuit.*) Memoirs and observations in a journey through China. Translated from the Paris edition. 12 p. l. 527 pp. 2 pl. 12°. *London, Benj. Tooke,* 1697.

Leconte (John L. *M.D.*) List of the coleoptera of North America. Part I. 78 pp. 8°. *Washington, Sm. inst.* 1863–66.
[Smithsonian miscel. coll. v. 6.]

——— New species of North American coleoptera. Part I. 177 pp. 8°. *Washington, Sm. inst.* 1863–66.
[Smithsonian miscel. coll. v. 6.]

Lecouteux (Édouard). Traité élémentaire de l'agriculture du département de la Seine. [Extract.] xii, 215 pp. 16°. *Paris, Soc. royale centrale d'agriculture,* 1840. s.

Lectures delivered before the Young men's christian association, in Exeter Hall, London, from Nov. 1853, to Feb. 1854. viii, 485 pp. 12°. *New York, R. Carter & bros.* 1855. s.

Ledebur (Leopold von). Das königliche museum vaterländischer alterthümer im schlosse Monbijou zu Berlin. xi, 226 pp. 6 pl. 8°. *Berlin, Druckerei der k. akad. der wissenschaften,* 1838. s.

Lederer (John). The discoveries of John Lederer, from Virginia to the west of Carolina. Translated out of Latin, by Sir William Talbot. 3 p. l. 27 pp. 1 map. sm. 4°. *London, S. Heyrick,* 1672.

Le Docte (Henri). Mémoire sur la chemie et la physiologie végétales, et sur l'agriculture. 900 pp. 8°. *Bruxelles, Hayez,* 1849. s.

Ledran (Henri François). Tratado ó reflexiones sacadas de la practica acerca de las heridas de armas de fuego. Traducido al Español, par Felix Galisteo y Xiorro. 6 p. l. 239 pp. 16°. *Madrid, P. Marin,* 1774. s.

Le Duc (W. G.) Minnesota year book for 1852. 98 pp. 12°. *St. Paul, (Minn.) W. G. Le Duc*, 1852. S.

Ledwich (*Rev.* Edward). [*In* **Vallancey** (C.) Collectanea de rebus hibernicis. v. 1–5. 8°. *Dublin*, 1774–90].

CONTENTS.

i. Essay on the study of Irish antiquities. 32 pp. [v. 2, no. 6.]
ii. Dissertation on the round towers in Ireland. 23 pp. [v. 2, no. 6.]
iii. Memoirs of Dunamase and Shean castle. 12 pp. [v. 2, no. 6.]
iv. History and antiquities of Irish town and Kilkenny. 212 pp. 4 pl. [v. 2, no 9.]
v. Observations on Irish antiquities with application to the ship temple near Dundalk. 12 pp. [v. 3, no. 11.]

Ledyard (John). A journal of Capt. Cook's last voyage to the Pacific ocean, and in quest of a northwest passage between Asia and America. 1776–79. 208 pp. 12°. *Hartford, Nathaniel Patten*, 1783.

Lee (*Gen.* Charles), *and* Burgoyne (*Gen.* John). Briefe bey gelegenheit der ankunft des letztern in Boston. 8 pp. 8°. *Braunschweig, F. Waisenhaus*, 1777.

[*In* REMER (Julius August). Amerikanisches archiv. v. 1.)

Lee (*Mrs.* Hannah F.) The log-cabin; or, the world before you. [*anon.* Also,] A new home: who'll follow? or, glimpses of western life, by Mrs. Mary Clavers. [*pseudon.* for Mrs. Caroline M. Kirkland.] 448 pp. 1 pl. 24°. *London, J. S. Pratt*, 1844.

Lee (Henry, *D. D.*) Anti-scepticism: or, notes upon each chapter of Mr. Lock's Essay concerning humane understanding. 16 p. l. 432 pp. fol. *London, Clavel and Harper*, 1702.

Lee (Jesse). A short account of the life and death of Rev. John Lee. 179 pp. 24°. *Baltimore, J. W. Butler*, 1805.

Lee (J. K. *capt.* 1*st reg. Virginia vol.*) Volunteer's hand book: containing an abridgement of Hardee's infantry tactics. 25th ed. 96 pp. 16°. *Richmond, (Va.)* 1861.

Lee (Margaret). Dr. Wilmer's love; or, a question of conscience. A novel. 416 pp. 12°. *New York, D. Appleton & Co.* 1868.

Lee (Mary Elizabeth). Poetical remains. With a biographical memoir by S. Gilman. xl, 224 pp. 1 pl. 16°. *Charleston, Walker & Richards*, 1851.

Lee (*Rev.* Samuel). Contemplations on mortality. vii, 149 pp. 18°. *Boston, (N. E.) Samuel Phillips*, 1698.

——— Ελεοθριαμβος; or, the triumph of mercy in the chariot of praise. A treatise of preventing secret and unexpected mercies, with some mixt reflexions. [*anon.*] 4 p. l. 194 pp. 18°. *Boston, B. Green for Benjamin Eliot*, 1718.

Lee (Weyman). An essay to ascertain the value of leases and annuities for years and lives, and to estimate the chances of the duration of lives. xix, 470 pp. 8°. *London, S. Birt*, 1738. S.

Leech (Samuel). Thirty years from home; or, a voice from the main deck: experience in British and American navies. 305 pp. 18°. *Boston, John M. Whittemore*, 1847.

Leechdoms, wortcunning, and starcraft, of early England; being documents illustrating the history of science in this country before the Norman conquest. Collected and edited by Oswald Cockayne. v. 3. 8°. *London, Longmans*, 1866.

[Chronicles of Great Britain and Ireland in the middle ages.]

Leedom (B. J.) Voyage to Harlem thirty years ago, and other poems. 111 pp. 12°. *Philadelphia, T. E. Zell*, 1867.

Leeds (W. H.) Rudimentary architecture: for the use of beginners. The orders, and their aesthetic principles. 3d ed. viii, 139 pp. 16°. *London, J. Weale*, 1854.

Lees (Frederic Richard, *M. D.*) Argument for the legislative prohibition of the liquor traffic. 320 pp. 12°. *Manchester, United kingdom alliance*, 1857. S.

——— Inquiry into the reasons and results of the prescription of intoxicating liquors in the practice of medicine. 144 pp. 16°. *London, Trübner*, 1866.

——— One hundred objections to a Maine law. 128 pp. 12°. *Manchester, U. K. alliance*, 1857.

[*With his* ARGUMENT for prohibition of the liquor traffic].

Leeven en daden der doorluchtighste zee-helden en ontdeckers van landen deser eeuwen. Door V. D. B. [*anon.*] 2 v. in 1. 344 pp; 310 pp. 27 pl. 4°. *Amsterdam, J. Claesz ten Hoorn & J. Bouman*, 1676.

Leewis *or* **Leuwis** (Dionysius de). Quattuor nouissima, [de morte videlicet, extremo judicio, inferno, et regno celorum], cum multis exemplis pulcherrimis. [*anon.*] 56 l. sm. 4°. *Dauentrie, Richardus Pafraet*, 1502.

NOTE.—Also printed with the title CORDIALE quattuor, etc.

Lefebure (Louis F. H.) Concordance des trois systêmes de Tournefort, Linnæus, et Jussieu, par le systême foliare. 75 pp. 2 l. 8°. *Paris, Th. Desoer*, 1816. S.

Lefebure. *See, also,* **Lefebvre.**

Lefebvre (Charlemagne Théophile, *editor*). Voyage en Abyssinie, exécuté pendant les années 1839-43, par une commission scientifique, composée de T. Lefebvre, A. Petit, Quartin Dillon, [et] Vignaud. Publié par ordre du roi. 6 v. 8°. atlas. 3 v. fol. *Paris, A. Bertrand*, 1845-50. S.

CONTENTS.

1e. partie. Relation historique, Par T. Lefebvre. 2 v. xci, 395 pp. 4 pl; 337 pp. 4 pl. 1 map 8°. Notice sur le commerce de la Mer Rouge et de l'Abyssinie. 148 pp. [*With* v. 2].
2e. partie. Itinéraire. Description et dictionnaire géographiques. Physique et météorologie, statistique, ethnologie, linguistique, archéologie. v. 3. xxiii; 439 pp. atlas. 3 p. l. 59 pl. fol.
3e. partie. Histoire naturelle, botanique. Par A. Richard [alias] Tentamen floræ Abyssinicæ, [etc.] auctore Achille Richard. v. 4-5. xi, 472 pp; 515 pp. atlas, 3 pp. 102 pl. fol.
4e. partie. Histoire naturelle, zoologie. Par O. Des-Murs [oiseaux], Florent Prévost [mammifères], Guichenot [reptiles et poissons], et Guérin-Méneville [insectes]. v. 6. 398 pp. atlas. 40 col. pl. fol.

Lefebvre (Tannegui). *See* **Lefevre** (Tannegui).

Lefebvre Laboulaye (Édouard René). *See* **Laboulaye.**

Le Fevre (Tannegui). Compendious way of teaching antient and modern languages, practised by Tanaquil Faber; observations by Ascham, Carew, Milton, Locke, etc: essay on rational grammar, new method of domestick education, etc. 4th ed. By T. Philips. 8 pl. 321 pp. 8°. *London, W. Meadows*, 1750.

Le Franc (——, *ancien supérieur des Eudistes de Caen*). Le voile levé pour les curieux; ou, le secret de la révolution de France révélé, à l'aide de la franç-maçonnerie; suivi de la conjuration contre la réligion catholique et les souverains. [Par le même.] Nouv. éd. 2 v. in 1. 115, 261 pp. 8°. *Paris*, 1816. S.

Le Gallois (Pierre). Traité des plus belles bibliothèques de l'Europe. 6 p. l. 240 pp. 24°. *Paris, E. Michalles*, 1685. S.

Legende (Ye) of St. Gwendoline. [*anon.*] By an American lady. With photographs by Addis, from drawings by J. W. Ehninger. 55 pp. 8 photogr. 4°. *New York, G. P. Putnam*, 1867.

Legendre (Adrien Marie). Elements of geometry. Translated from the French, by John Farrar. 2d ed. xv, 224 pp. 12 pl. 8°. *Cambridge, (N. E.) Hilliard & Metcalf*, 1825.

——— The same. With additions and modifications, by M. A. Blanchet. Translated from the French. 11th ed. by F. H. Smith. 312 pp. 8°. *Baltimore, Kelly & Piet*, 1867.

Legends and traditionary stories. [*anon.*] 270 pp. 24°. *London, E. Lumley*, [1843].

Legge (James, *D. D.*) The Chinese classics. Translated into English, with preliminary essays and explanatory notes. v. 1. The life and teachings of Confucius. vi, 338 pp. 12°. *London, Trübner & Co.* 1867.

Legh (Thomas). Account of a journey into Syria.

[Chap. iv of MACMICHAEL (W.) Journey from Moscow to Constantinople. 4°. *London*, 1819.]

Legislative sketches from a reporter's note book. By Geoffrey Jenkins. [*pseudon.*] 93 pp. 16°. *Albany, Weed, Parsons & Co.* 1866.

Legouvé (Ernest Wilfrid). Médée: tragédie en trois actes et en vers. [Avec la] traduction italienne de Joseph Montanelli. 155 pp. 12°. *Paris, Lévy*, 1856.

Le Grand (Antoine). Man without passion: or, the wise stoick, according to the sentiments of Seneca. Englished by G. R. 8 p. l. 285 pp. 16°. *London, C. Harper*, 1675.

Lehmann (J. G. C.) *and* **Petersen** (C.) Ansichten und baurisse der neuen gebäude für Hamburgs öffentliche bildungsanstalten, kurz beschrieben und in verbindung mit dem plan für die künftige aufstellung der stadtbibliothek. iv, 122 pp. 9 pl. 4°. *Hamburg, J. A. Meissner*, 1840. S.

Lehmanowski (Lewis Ferdinand). The fall of Warsaw. A tragedy. 59 pp. 18°. *Annapolis, Geo. S. M'Kiernan*, 1840.

Leibnitz (Gottfried Wilhelm von). Causa Dei asserta per justitiam ejus, cum caeteris ejus perfectionibus, cunctisque actionibus conciliatam. [*anon.*] 48 pp. 12°. *Amsterdam, I. Troyel*, 1710.

[*With his* "Essais de théodicée," éd. 1710].

——— Essais de théodicée, sur le bonté de Dieu, la liberté de l'homme, et l'origine du mal. [*anon*]. 3 v. in 1. 26 p. l. 660 pp. 12°. *Amsterdam, I. Troyel*, 1710.

——— Protogaea. Edita a C. L. Scheidio. xxvi, 88 pp. 12 pl. 4°. *Goettingae, J. G. Schmid*, 1749. S.

——— Réflexions sur l'ouvrage que M. Hobbes a publié en Anglais, de la liberté, de la necessité et du hazard. [*anon.*] 99 pp. 12°.

[App. to his "Essais de théodicée," 1710 éd.]

——— (*Editor.*) Novissima sinica historiam nostri temporis illustratura. 2ª ed. 14 p. l. 175 pp. 6 l. 16, 128 pp. 2 pl. 18°. [*Ultrajecti, W. Broedeleth*,] 1699.

——— ——— Scriptores rervm brvnsvicensivm illvstrationi inservientes, antiqvi omnes et religionis reformatione priores. 3 v. 4°. *Hanoveræ, M. Foerster*, 1707-11. S.

Leich (Johann Heinrich). De origine et incrementis typographiae lipsiensis liber singularis, ubi varia de litterariis urbis studiis et viris doctis inseruntur. Accedit librorum sec. xv. excusorum ad Maitairii annales supplementum. 5 p. l. 147 pp. sm. 4°. *Lipsiae, Bern. Christoph Breitkopf,* 1740.

Leidy (Joseph, *M. D.*) Cretaceous reptiles of the United States. v, 135 pp. 20 pl. 4°. *Washington, Sm. Inst.* 1864.

[*In* Smithsonian contrib. v. 14].

——— Description of the remains of extinct mammalia and chelonia.

(*With* Owen (D. D.) Report of a geological survey of Wisconsin. 1852.]

Leigh (Edward). A systeme or body of divinity: consisting of ten books. 15 p. l. 873 pp. 9 l. sm. fol. *London, W. Lee,* 1654.

Leipsic. Catalogus librorum manuscriptorum qui in bibliotheca senatoria asservantur. Ed. A. G. R. Naumann. Codices orientalium linguarum descripserunt H. O. Fleischer et F. Delitzsch. xxiv, 562, lvi pp. 15 pl. 4°. *Grimae, J. M. Gebhardt,* 1838. s.

——— Katalog des vom 15 Aug. bis 15 Sept. 1853 öffentlich versteigerten münz kabinetes der stadtbibliothek zu Leipzig. Von J. J. Leitzmann. vi, 508, 62 pp. 8°. *Leipzig,* 1853. s.

Leland (Charles Godfrey). Union Pacific railway, eastern division; or, three thousand miles in a railway car. 95 pp. 8°. *Philadelphia, author,* 1867.

Lelewel (Joachim). Album d'un graveur polonais. 22 pp. 43 pl. obl. 4°. *Posen, J. C. Zupanski,* 1854.

——— Dzieje polski J. Lelewel potocznym sposobem opowiedzial,do nich dwanas 'cie krajobraz'ow skres'lil. Wyd. 3e. 175 pp. 4 maps. 2 tab. 24°. *Bruxella, Kalussowski i Spólki,* 1837. s.

——— Études numismatiques et archéologiques. v. i. Type gaulois, ou celtiqne. 468 pp. 8°. *Bruxelles, Voglet,* 1841. s.

[No more published].

——— Géographie du moyen age. 4 v. in 3. 6 maps. 8°. Atlas, 49 maps. fol. *Bruxelles, Pilliet,* 1852. s.

——— Histoire de Pologne. 2 v. xx, 388 pp. 1 pl; 359 pp. 8°. Atlas, 12 pl. obl. 4°. *Lille, Vanackère,* 1844. s.

[Atlas *with* his Album d'un graveur polonais, 1854].

——— Numismatique du moyen-age, considérée sous le rapport du type. 2 v. in 3. 8°. Atlas, 4°. *Paris, J. Straszéwicz,* 1835. s.

Le Long (Jacques). Bibliotheca sacra seu syllabus omnium ferme sacrae scripturae editionum et versionum, cum notis criticis. [Curante Nic. Desmolets]. 2 v. in 1. xxvi, 1222 pp. fol. *Parisiis, F. Montalant,* 1723. s.

Lemaire (Charles). Manuel de l'amateur de cactus. 125 pp. 16°. *Paris, Duverger,* [1845]. s.

Lemaire (C. L.) Hist. nat. des oiseaux. *See* **Prévost** (F.) *and* **Lemaire.**

Le Maire (Jacques). Journal et miroir de la navigation avstrale. pp. 104-178. 3 maps. 6 pl. fol.

[*With* Herrera (A. de). Description des Indes Occidentales. fol. *Amsterdam,* 1622].

——— The same. Ephemerides, sive descriptio navigationis australis. l. 45-75. fol.

[*With* Herrera (A. de). Novvs orbis, sive descriptio Indiæ Occidentalis. fol. *Amstelodami,* 1622].

——— The same. Spieghel der avstralische navigatie. 8 p. l. 70 pp. 13 l. 3 maps. 4 pl. fol. *Amsterdam,* 1622.

[*With* Herrera, (A. de). Nievwe werelt, etc. Ed. *Amsterdam,* 1622].

——— The same. Specvlvm Orientalis Occidentalisque Indiæ navigationvm, 1619. *See* **Spilberg** (Georg von).

Le Maistre d'Anstaing (J.) Recherches sur l'histoire et l'architecture de l'église cathédrale de Notre-Dame de Tournai. v. 1. xxvi, 403 pp. 1 pl. 8°. *Tournai, Massart & Janssens,* 1842. s.

Lemay (Léon Pamphile). Essais poétiques. [Avec l'Évangeline de Longfellow, traduite en vers français]. 320 pp. 8°. *Québec, G. E. Desbarats,* 1865.

Lembeye (Juan). Aves de la isla de Cuba. 137 pp. 20 col. pl. 8°. *Habana, Imp. del Tiempo,* 1850. s.

Le Mercier (François). Copie de devx lettres envoiées de la Novvelle France, au père procureur des missions de la compagnie de Jésvs. *Paris, Cramoisy,* 1656. [Reprint, 28 pp. 12°. *New York, privately printed by James Lennox,* 1855?]

Lémery (Louis, *M. D.*) A treatise of all sorts of foods, both animal and vegetable; also, of drinkables. From the French, by D. Hay, M. D. 3d ed. xii, 372 pp. 12 l. 16°. *London, W. Innys,* 1745.

Le Moine (J. M.) Ornithologie du Canada. Quelques groupes d'après la nomenclature du Smithsonian institution, etc. 1e. et 2e. partie. [Les oiseaux de proie et les palmipèdes]. 398 pp. 12°. *Québec, auteur,* 1860-61.

Le Moine (Louis, *le chevalier*). Abrégé de l'histoire de Suède. 2 v. vi, 429 pp; 450 pp. 8°. *Paris, A. Bertrand,* 1844. s.

Lemoyne (Pierre). La gallerie des femmes fortes. 36 p. l. 452 pp. 12 l. 20 pl. 24°. *Leiden, J. Elsevier*, 1660.

Lengerke (Alexander von). Beiträge zur kenntniss der landwirthschaft in den königl. preuss. staaten. v. 1-2. 12°. *Berlin, Veit & Co.* 1846-47. s.
[v. 3-6 wanting].

——— Entwurf einer agricultur-statistik des preussischer staates, 1842-43. xii, 202 pp. 8 tab. 8°. *Berlin, Veit & Co.* 1847. s.

Lenglet Dufresnoy (Nicolas). Recueil de dissertations anciennes et nouvelles sur les apparitions, les visions, et les songes. Avec une préface historique. 4 v. 16°. *Avignon et Paris, Leloup*, 1751.

——— Tablettes chronologiques de l'histoire universelle, sacrée et profane, ecclésiastique et civile, depuis la création du monde jusqu'à l'an 1775. 2 v. 10 p. l. ccxxx, 623 pp; 2 p. l. xvi, 872 pp. 16°. *Paris, frères De Bure*, 1778.

——— New method of studying history. [With] a catalogue of the chief historians of all nations, their best editions, and characters of their writings. Translated from the French by R. Rawlinson. 2 v. 360 pp. 4 l; 550 pp. 25 l. 12°. *London, W. Burton*, 1728.

Lenhossék (Michael von). Physiologia medicinalis. 5 v. 8°. *Pestini, J. S. Trattner*, 1816-18. s.

Lenning (C.) [*pseudon.*] *See* **Mossdorf** (Friedrich).

Lenormand (Louis Sébastien). Nouveau manuel complet du relieur. Nouv. éd. 254 pp. 18°. *Paris, Roret*, 1840. s.

Lenormant (Charles). Cours d'histoire ancienne. Introduction á l'histoire de l'Asie occidentale. x, 384 pp. 1 map. 8°. *Paris, C. Heideloff*, 1838. s.

Lènström (Carl Julius, *M. D.*) Konsttheoriernas historia. 339 pp. 8°. *Upsala, Lef fler & Sebell*, 1839. s.

Lenthe (F. C. G.) Verzeichniss der grossherzoglichen gemälde-sammlung welche sich auf dem alten schlosse in Schwerin befindet. vi, 173, 6 pp. 8°. *Schwerin, Hofbuchdruckerei*, 1836. s.

Leo (Heinrich). Geschichte der italienischen staaten. 5 v. 8°. *Hamburg, F. Perthes*, 1829. s.
[Imperfect; title of v. 2, wanting.]

Leonard (Levi W. *D. D.*) History of Dublin, N. H. with address by Charles Mason, and the proceedings at the centennial celebration, June 17, 1852; with a register of families. [*anon.*] vi, 433 pp. 1 map. 25 pl. 8°. *Boston, T. Wilson & son*, 1855.

Léonard (Nicholas Germain). Œuvres. 5e éd. 3 v. in 1. 24°. *Avignon, J. A. Joly*, 1795.

CONTENTS.

v. 1. Idylles.
v. 2. Les saisons, poëme.
v. 3. Alexis, roman pastoral.
Poésies diverses.
Le temple de Gnide.
Lettre sur un voyage aux Antilles.
Supplément aux poésies.

Leonhard (Carl Cäsar von). Lehrbuch der geognosie und geologie. 2e aufl. xxii, 1056 pp. 9 pl. 8°. *Stuttgart, E. Schweizerbart*, 1846. s.
[Naturgeschichte, v. 3.]

——— Popular lectures on geology. Translated by J. G. Morris, and edited by F. Hall. 400 pp. 9 pl. 12°. *Baltimore, N. Hickman*, 1839-41. s.

——— *See* **Buch** (Das) der geologie.

Léotaud (Antoine, *M. D.*) Oiseaux de l'ile de la Trinidad, (Antilles). xx, 560, viii, iv pp. 8°. *Port d'Espagne, (Trinidad,) Chronicle publishing office*, 1866.

Le Paulmier de Grentemesnil (Julien). De morbis contagiosis libri septem. 8 p. l. 552 16 l. 16°. *Francofvrti, C. Marnius*, 1601.

Lepechin (Ivan Ivanovitch, *joint author*). *See* **Histoire** des découvertes, etc. dans la Russie et dans la Perse. s.

Le Pelletier de Saint-Fargeau (Louis Michel). Monographia tenthredinetarum, synonimia extricata. xvii, 176 pp. 8°. *Parisiis, F. G. Levrault*, 1823. s.

Le Pois (Antoine). Discovrs svr les médalles et gravevres antiques, principalement romaines. 10 pl. 159 l. sm. 4°. *Paris, Mamert Patisson*, 1579.

Le Prince (Nicolas Thomas). Essai historique sur la bibliothèque du roi, et sur chacun des dépôts que la composent, etc. [*anon.*] xxii, 343 pp. 18°. *Paris, Belin*, 1782. s.

Le Prince de Beaumont (Joanne). Les Américaines; ou la preuve de la religion chrétienne par les lumières naturelles. Nouv. éd. 6 v. 16°. *Paris, Saint-Michel et Brunot-Labbe*, 1811.

Lepsius (Carl Richard). Die chronologie der Aegypter. v. i. Einleitung und kritik der quellen. xxvi, 554 pp. 4°. *Berlin, Nicolai*, 1849. s.

——— Denkmäler aus Ägypten und Äthiopien, nach den zeichnungen der von seiner majestät dem könige von Preussen Friedrich Wilhelm iv. nach diesen ländern gesendeten, 1842-45, wissenschaftliche expedition. 36 pp. 4°. *Berlin, Nicolai*, 1849. s.

Lepsius (Carl Richard). Über einige berührungspunkte der ägyptischen, griechischen, und römischen chronologie. [Extract]. 82 pp. 4°. *Berlin, K. Akad. der wissenschaften,* 1859. S.

——— Koenigliche musen; abtheilung der aegyptischen alterthümer; die wandgemaelde der verschiedenen raeume. 37 tafeln nebst erklaerung. obl. fol. *Berlin,* 1855. S.

——— Königsbuch der alten Ägypter. 2 v. 4 p. l. 178, 23 pp; 3 p. l. 73 pl. 4°. *Berlin, W. Hertz,* 1858. S.

CONTENTS.

v. 1. Text und dynastieentafeln.
v. 2. Die hieroglyphischen tafeln.

——— Zwei sprachvergleichende abhandlungen. 2 p. l. 150 pp. 2 tab. 8°. *Berlin, F. Dümmler,* 1836. S.

CONTENTS.

1. Über die anordnung und verwandtschaft des semitischen, indischen, äthiopischen, alt-persischen, und alt-ägyptischen alphabets.
2. Über die ursprung und die verwandtschaft der zahlwörter in der indogermanischen, semitischen, und der koptischen sprache.

——— Das todtenbuch der Ägypter nach dem hieroglyphischen papyrus in Turin, mit-einem vorworte zum ersten male herausgegeben. 4°. *Leipzig,* 1842. S.

——— Standard alphabet for reducing unwritten languages and foreign graphic systems to a uniform orthography in European letters. 2d ed. xvii, 315 pp. 8°. *Berlin, W. Hertz,* 1863. S.

Lerch (——, *surgeon*). Unnersòutiksak ernisuksiortunnut kaládlit nunácn nêtunnut. Underretning for Jordemödre i Grönland. [Danish and Esquimaux]. Pellesimit Peter Kraghmit. 4 l. 63 pp. 16°. *Kjobenhavnime, F. F. de Tengnagel,* 1829.

Lerebours (Nicholas Marie Paymal) *and* **Secrétan**, *opticians*). Catalogue et prix des instruments d'optique, de physique, de chimie, de mathématiques, d'astronomie et de marine, etc. viii, 244 pp. 8°. *Paris,* 1853. S.

Leroy (Charles François Antoine). Traité de géométrie descriptive, suivi de la méthode des plans cotés, et de la théorie des engrenages cylindriques et coniques. 3e éd. 2 v. texte, xx, 432 pp; atlas, 71 pl. 4°. *Paris, Bachelier,* 1850.

——— Traité de stéréotomie, comprenant la théorie des ombres, la perspective linéaire, la gnomonique, la coupe des pierres et la charpente. Texte. xvi, 483 pp. 4°. atlas, 74 pl. fol. *Liége, Avanzo et Cie.* 1845.

[Imperfect; atlas wanting.]

Leroy (P. L.) Narrative of the singular adventures of four Russian sailors who were cast away on the desert island of East Spitzbergen. Translated from the German original. pp. 45 to 118. 8°. *London,* 1774.

[*With* STAEHLIN-STORCKSBURG, (J. von).

Le Roy de Gomberville (Marin). *See* **Nevers** (*duc* de). Les mémoires.

Lery (Jean). Historia navigationis in Brasiliam, quæ et America dicitvr. 31 p. l. 341 pp. 8 l. 1 pl. 16°. [*Genevae*], *E. Vignon,* 1586.

——— The same.

[*With* BENZONI (Girolamo). Historia Indiae Occidentalis. [*Genevae*], 1586.]

Le Saint (L.) L'isthme de Suez. iv, 175 pp. 1 map. 16°. *Paris, Hachette,* 1866.

Le Saulnier de Vauhello (——). Mémoire sur les attérrages des côtes occidentales de France, et précis des opérations hydrographiques et astronomiques faites en 1828–29. 88 pp. 1 pl. 4°. *Paris, Imp. royale,* 1833. S.

Lescarbot (Marc). Histoire de la Novvelle France. Contenant les navigations, découvertes et habitations faites par les François és Indes Occidentales et Nouvelle France souz l'avœu et authorité de noz roys très chrétiens, et les diverses fortunes d'iceux en l'execution de ces choses, depuis cent ans jusques à hui. 2e éd. 24 p. l. 877 pp. 2 maps. 16°. *Paris, Jean Millot,* 1611.

——— Les mvses de la Novvelle France. 66 pp. 16°. *Paris, Jean Millott,* 1612.

[*With* LESCARBOT (M.) Histoire de la Novvelle France, *Paris,* 1611].

——— Noua Francia: or, the description of that part of New France which is one continent with Virginia. Translated out of French by P[ierre] E[rondelle. *anon.*] 307 pp. sm. 4°. *London,* 1609.

[Imperfect; wanting title and p. 1.]

Lescurel (Jehannot de). Chansons, ballades, et rondeaux. Publiés pour la première fois, par Anatole de Montaiglon. 68 pp. 16°. *Paris, P. Jannet,* 1855.

Lesley (Joseph, *jr.*) Topographical and geological reports. S.

[*With* OWEN, (D. D.) Reports of the geological survey of Kentucky, v. 4.]

Leslie (*Rev.* Charles). A short and easie method with the deists, [and discourse concerning episcopacy]. 8th ed. [*anon.*] 132 pp. 12°. *London, J. Applebee,* 1723.

——— The same. 38 pp. 8°. *Oxford,* 1825.

[*With* RANDOLPH (John, *bishop of London*). Enchiridion theologicum, v. 2.]

——— The snake in the grass; or Satan transform'd into an angel of light; discovering the subtilty of many of the quakers. 3d ed. xliv pp. 3 l. 370 pp. 12°. *London, C. Brome,* 1698.

Lesné (Mathurin Marie). Lettre d'un relieur français à un bibliographe anglais. [T. F. Dibdin]. 28 pp. 8°. *Paris, l'auteur,* 1822. s.

Lesquereux (Leo). Botanical and palaeontological report. s.

[*With* OWEN (D. D.) Second report on the geology of Arkansas].

——— On the origin and formation of prairies. [Extract.] 19 pp. 8°. *New Haven, Amer. journ. sci.* 1865. s.

——— Palaeontological reports of the fossil flora of Kentucky.

[*With* OWEN (D. D.) Reports of the geological survey of Kentucky, v. 4].

——— Quelques recherches sur les marais tourbeux en général. 8°. *Neuchatel,* 1844. s.

Lesseps (Ferdinand, *vicomte* de). Percement de l'isthme de Suez. Exposé et documents officiels. 280 pp. 2 maps. 8°. *Paris, H. Plon,* 1855. s.

Lesser (Friedrich Christian). Insecto-theologia. Oder, versuch, wie ein mensch durch betrachtung der insecten zur erkentniss Gottes gelangen kann. 2e aufl. 5 p. l. 528 pp. 17 l. 1 pl. 16°. *Frankfurt, Michael Blockberger,* 1740. s.

Lessing (Gotthold Ephraim). Laokoon; oder, über die grenzen der mahlerey und poesie, [etc.] Neue aufl. von C. G. Lessing. 8 p. l. 380 pp. 8°. *Berlin, C. F. Voss & sohn,* 1788.

——— Nathan the wise. A dramatic poem. Translated by Ellen Frothingham. Preceded by a brief account of the poet and his works, and followed by an essay on the poem, by Kuno Fischer. xxiii, 259 pp. 16°. *New York, Leypoldt & Holt,* 1868.

Lesson (René Primevère). Manuel de mammalogïe, ou histoire naturelle des mammifères. 18°. *Paris, Roret,* 1827. s.

——— Traité d'ornithologie; ou, tableau méthodique des ordres, sous-ordres, familles, tribus, genres, sous-genres et races d'oiseaux, etc. xxxii, 659 pp; atlas, xii pp. 119 pl. 8°. *Paris, F. G. Levrault,* 1831. s.

——— Voyage autour du monde enterpris par ordre du gouvernement sur la corvette la Coquille. 2 v. 510 pp; 547 pp. 2 l. 41 pl. 8°. *Paris, Pourrat,* 1838–39.

L'Estrange (Hammond). Observator observed; or, animadversions upon [Heylin's] observations on the history of king Charles [the first], with the observator's rejoinder. [*anon.*] 47 pp. sm. fol. *London, E. Dod,* 1656.

[*With* L'ESTRANGE (Hamon). Reign of king Charles. *London,* 1656.]

——— The reign of king Charles [the first.] An history disposed into annals. [*anon.*] 2d ed. enlarged. 5 p. l. 274 pp. 3 l. sm. fol. *London, H. Seile,* 1656.

L'Estrange (*Sir* Roger). Toleration discuss'd; in two dialogues. [*anon.*] 4 p. l. 350 pp. 18°. *London, H. Brome,* 1670.

[*With* MORE (Henry). Exposition of the seven epistles, etc. 18°. *London,* 1669.]

Lesuire (Robert Martin), *and* **Louvel** (——). The savages of Europe. [*anon.*] From the French. iii, 144 pp. 4 pl. 16°. *London, Dryden Leach,* 1764.

Letchworth (Thomas). Twelve discourses delivered chiefly at the meeting house of the people called quakers, in the park, Southwark. 248 pp. 12°. *Salem, (Mass.) Thomas C. Cushing,* 1794.

Letera de la nobil cipta [Zhaval] nouamente ritrouata alle Indie, con li costumi e modi del suo re et soi populi: li modi del suo adorare, con la bella vsanza de le donne loro: et de le dua persone ermafrodite donate da quel re al capitano de larmata. Data in Peru adi xxv di Nouembre del mdxxxiiii. [*anon.*] 4 l. unp. 12°. [*n. p. about* 1534].

Leti (Gregorio). History of the cardinals of the Roman church, from the time of their first creation to the election of the present pope, Clement the ninth. From the Italian, by G. H. 3 pts. in 1 v. 2 p. l. 330 pp. fol. *London, John Starkey,* 1670.

Leto (Giulio Pomponio) De Romanorũ magistratibus: sacerdotiis: jurisperitis: et legibus ad M. Pantagathum libellus. 10 l. sm. 4°. [*n. p. about* 1500.] s.

[*With* FIOCCHI (A. D.) De Romanorvm, etc.]

Letourneur (Thomas Marie). Mode de commandement; ou, essai sur la théorie générale de la manœuvre des vaisseaux et autres bâtiments de guerre. 384 pp. 8°. *Lefournier & Deperiers,* 1832. s.

——— The same. Dictionnaire des commandements, faits avec le sifflet, à bord des bâtiments de guerre. 2e éd. faisant suite au mode de commandement. 42 pp. 8°. *Lefournier & Deperiers,* 1834. s.

[*With* the preceding.]

Letronne (Jean Antoine). Recherches pour servir à l'histoire de l'Égypte pendant la domination des Grecs et des Romains, tirées des inscriptions grecques et latines. lx, 524 pp. 8°. *Paris, Boulland-Pardieu,* 1823.

Lette (Adolph), *and* **Rönne** (Ludwig von). Die landes-kultur-gesetzgebung des preussischen staates. 2er band mit 1e abth. 2 v. xi, 1032 pp; x, 868 pp. 8°. *Berlin, Veit & Co.* 1853–54. s.

Letter (A) addressed to two great men on the prospect of peace. [*anon.*] 1 p. l. 56 pp. 12°. *London, A. Millar*, 1760.

Letter (A) from a cobler to the people of England on affairs of importance. [*anon.*] 17 pp. 12°. *London*, 1756.

Letter (A) on the present state of the Spanish West Indies, to P. H. [by J. N. *anon.*] 7 pp. sm. 4°. *London, J. Applebee and others*, 1739.

[*With* DESCRIPTION of the windward passage and gulf of Florida. *London*, 1739.]

Letter (A) to the author of the pamphlet called an Answer to the Hampshire narrative [respecting Rev. Robert Breck]. 84 pp. 12°. *Boston*, 1737.

Letter (A) to Rev. Andrew Croswell on the satyrical drollery last commencement day. By Simon, the tanner. [*anon.*] 12°. *Boston, Ezekiel Russell*, 1771.

Letter (A) to general Hamilton, occasioned by his letter to president Adams. By a federalist. Aristides. [*anon.*] 10 pp. 8°. [*Boston*, 1809.]

[*With* ADAMS (John). Correspondence. *Boston*, 1809.]

Letter (A) to a member of parliament, containing a proposal for bringing in a bill to revise, amend, or repeal certain obsolete statutes called the ten commandments. [*anon.*] 38 pp. 12°. *London, R. Minors*, 1738.

Letter (A) to Rev. Jedediah Morse, author of the American universal geography, [a defence of Williamsburg, Va.] By a citizen of Williamsburg. [*anon.*] 16 pp. 8°. *Richmond, Thomas Nicolson*, 1795.

Letter (A) to the people of England on the present situation and conduct of national affairs. [*anon.*] 58 pp. 12°. *London, J. Scott*, 1755.

Letter (A) to king William iii. on the English monarchy. 2d ed. [*anon.*] 15 pp. sm. 4°. *London, J. Darby*, 1699.

Letter (A) written to Dr. Burnet, giving an account of cardinal Pool's secret powers. By W. C. [Sir William Coventry. *anon.*] 40 pp. sm. 4°. *London, Richard Baldwin*, 1685.

Letters and conversations on the Indian missions in the states of New York and Ohio. [*anon.*] 112 pp. 18°. *Boston, Mass. s. s. union*, 1831.

Letters by a South Carolinian. Sketches of some Virginians. [*anon.*] 89 pp. 18°. *Norfolk, C. Bonsal*, 1827.

Letters from an American loyalist in Upper Canada, to his friend in England, on a pamphlet published by John Mills Jackson, entitled a View of the province of Upper Canada. [*anon.*] 104 pp. 8°. [*Halifax*, 1807]?

Letters from the prisons and prison-ships of the revolution. With notes by H. R. Stiles, M. D. 49 pp. 8° *New York, privately printed*, 1865.

[Wallabout prison-ship series, No. 1.]

Letters (The) of Fabius, in 1788, on the federal constitution; and in 1797 on the present situation of public affairs. [*pseudon.* By John Dickinson.] iv, 202 pp. 8°. *Wilmington, (Del.) W. C. Smyth*, 1797.

Letters (The) of Papinian; in which the conduct, present state, and prospects of the American congress are examined. [*pseudon.*] v, 130 pp. 16°. *New York, Hugh Gaine*, 1779.

Letters of a Nova Scotian, and of Scævola on Canadian politics. [*anon.*] 106 pp. 8°. *Quebec, T. Cary & Co.* 1828.

Letters on the internal political state of Spain, 1821–23. By G. G. D. V. Translated from the original French manuscript. [*anon.* By Guillaume de Vaudoncourt.] 8 p. l. 412 pp. 8°. *London, L. Relfe*, 1824.

Letters on the subject of the concert of princes, and the dismemberment of Poland and France. By a calm observer. [*anon.*] 2d ed. 4 p. l. 991 pp. 8°. *London, G. & J. Robinson*, 1793.

Lettieri (Francesco). Catalogus codicum saeculo xv impressorum qui in regia bibliotheca borbonica adservantur, ordine alphabetico digestus notisque bibliographicis illustratus. 3 v. fol. *Neapoli, regia typog.* 1828–33. s.

——— The same. Supplementum. 276 pp. fol. *Neapoli, regia typographia*, 1841. s.

Lettres d'un sauvage depaysé; contenant une critique des mœurs du siécle, et des réflexions sur des matières de religion et de politique. [*anon.*] 2 parts in 1 v. 205; 219 pp. 24°. *Amsterdam, Jean François Jolly.* [n. d.]

Lettres édifiantes et curieuses concernant l'Asie, l'Afrique, et l'Amérique. Publiées sous la direction de Louis Aimé Martin. 4 v. 8°. *Paris, Auguste Desrez*, 1839–43.

[v. 1 imperfect, wanting all after p. 520.]

CONTENTS.

v. 1. Grèce, Turquie, Syrie, Arménie, Perse, Égypte, Amérique Septentrionale.
v. 2. Guyanes, Pérou, Californie, Chili, Paraguay, Brazil, Buénos Ayres, Indoustan, Bengale, Gingi, (Madras) Golconde, Maduré, Tanjaour, Marhate.
v. 3. Chine.
v. 4. Chine, Indo-Chine, Océanie.

Lettsom (William G.) *See* **Greg** (R. P.) *and* **Lettsom**, Mineralogy of Great Britain.

Leuckart (Friedrich Sigismund). Allgemeine einleitung in die naturgeschichte. 130 pp. 8°. *Stuttgart, E. Schweizerbart*, 1832. s.

[Naturgeschichte, v. 1.]

——— Neue wirbellose thiere des Rothen meers. *See* **Rüppells** (W. P. E.) *and* **Leuckart** (F. S.)

Leunis (Johannes). Analytischer leitfaden für den ersten wissenschaftlichen unterricht in der naturgeschichte. 3 v. in 1. 8°. *Hannover, Hahn,* 1852–57. s.

CONTENTS.

v. 1. Zoologie. iv, 145 pp. 1852.
v. 2. Botanik. 2e aufl. xii, 183 pp. 1857.
v. 3. Oryktognosie und geognosie.

——— Schul-naturgeschichte. Eine analytische darstellung der drei naturreiche, etc. 3 v. in 1. 8°. *Hannover, Hahn,* 1853–56. s.

CONTENTS.

v. 1. Zoologie. 3e aufl. vi, 330 pp. 1856.
v. 2. Botanik. 3e aufl. xii, 332 pp. 1855.
v. 3. Oryktognosie und geognosie.

——— Synopsis der drei naturreiche. 3 v. 8°. *Hannover, Hahn,* 1853–56. s.

CONTENTS.

v. 1. Mineralogie und geognosie. Bearbeitet von F A. Roemer. xiv, 464 pp. 4 pl.
v. 3. Zoologie. 3e aufl. 670 pp.
[Wanting botanik and zoologie. Heft ii, abth. 2.]

Levasseur (A). Lafayette en Amérique en 1824 et 1825; ou, journal d'un voyage aux États-Unis. 2 v. 509 pp; 632 pp. 9 pl. 1 map. 8°. *Paris, Baudouin,* 1829.

Lever (Christopher). The historie of the defendors of the catholique faith, Henry 8, Edward 6, queen Marie, queen Eliz. James 1; [with] observations, divine, politique, morall. 31, 371 pp. sm. 4°. *London, N. Fussell & H. Moseley,* 1627.
[Imperfect; wanting 1 pl.]

Levezow (Conrad von). Verzeichness der antiken denkmäler im antiquarium des königlichen museums zu Berlin. Erste abth. Gallerie der vasen. 24 pl. 8°. *Berlin, Duncker & Humblot,* 1834. s.

Levi (David). A defense of the old testament, in a series of letters, addressed to Thomas Paine. 240 pp. 16°. *New York, N. Judah* 1797.

Lévi (Éliphas). Histoire de la magie avec une exposition claire et précise de ses procédés, de ses rites et de ses mystères. xvi, 560 pp. 16 pl. 8°. *Paris, G. Baillière,* 1860.

Levi (Leone, *editor*). Wages and earnings of the working classes, with their economic condition, drawn from authentic and official sources, in a report to M. T. Bass, M. P. lix, 140 pp. 8°. *London, John Murray,* 1867.

Lévi-Alvarés (David Eugéne). Analytic history, for schools. 12°. *New York,* 1848. *See* **Hunter** (John H.) s.

Levison (J. L.) Mental culture. viii, 300 pp. 16°. *London, author,* 1833.

Lévizac (Jean Pons Victor Lecoutz de). *See* **Moysant** (F.) *and* **Lévizac**. Bib. port. des ecrivains français.

Lévy (Michel). Traité d'hygiéne publique et privée. 4e éd. 2 v. viii, 924 pp; 2 p. l. 992 pp. 8°. *Paris, J. B. Baillière,* 1862.

Lewes (*Rev.* Daniel). The joy of children walking in truth. A sermon at the Boston-lecture, August 15, 1723. 28 pp. 16°. *Boston, D. Henchman,* 1723.
[*With* WALLEY, (*Rev.* Thomas). Balm in Gilead. *Cambridge,* 1670].

Lewes (George Henry). Life and works of Goethe, with sketches of his contemporaries. 2 v. xx, 435 pp; xii, 478 pp. 12°. *Boston, Ticknor & Fields,* 1856. s.

Lewis (Evan). An address to christians of all denominations, on the inconsistency of admitting slave-holders to communion and church membership. 19 pp. 16°. *Philadelphia, S. C. Atkinson,* 1831.

Lewis (Henry). The English language; its grammar and history. 82 pp. 16°. *London, Williams & Norgate,* 1866.

Lewis (John W.) Life, labors, and travels of elder Charles Bowles, with an essay on the character and condition of the African race. Also, an essay on the fugitive law of the U. S. congress of 1850, by Rev. Arthur Dearing. 285 pp. 12°. *Watertown, (N. Y.) Ingalls & Stowell,* 1852.

Lewis (Matthew Gregory). My uncle's garret window. 21 pp. 8°. *London,* 1841.
[HAZLITT'S romancist and novelist's lib. v. 1.]

——— Raymond and Agnes; or, the bleeding nun. 78 pp. 8°. *London,* 1841.
[HAZLITT'S romancist and novelist's lib. v. 4.]

Lewis (Meriwether). Documents accompanying a bill making compensation to messieurs Lewis and Clarke, and their companions, presented the 23d January 1807. 8 pp. 8°. *Washington, A. & G. Way,* 1807.

——— *and* **Clarke** (William). Travels to the source of the Missouri river and across the American continent to the Pacific ocean. Performed by order of the government of the U. S. in the years 1804–5–6. xxiv, 663 pp. 1 map. 4°. *London, Longmans,* 1814. s.

——— The same. New ed. 3 v. 8°. *London, Longman,* 1817.

Lewisham free grammar school. Bibliothecae colfanæ catalogus. Catalogue of the library [etc.] founded by Abraham Colfe. By W. H. Black. lvi, 176 pp. 1 pl. 8°. *London, governors of the grammar school,* 1831. s.

Lexington (*Ky.*) Directory of the city of Lexington and of the county of Fayette, for 1838 and '39. By Julius P. B. MacCabe. 136 pp. 16°. *Lexington, J. C. Noble,* 1838.

Lexington (*Ky.*) library company. A catalogue of books, [etc.] With its charter, laws, and regulations. xvi, 172 pp. 12°. *Lexington, (Ky.) T. Smith,* 1821. s.

——— The same. Additions to the catalogue of books, [etc.] from 1821 to the present, [etc.] 113 pp. 8°. *Lexington, (Ky.) A. W. Elder,* 1852. s.

[*With* LEXINGTON Catalogue, 1821].

Leybourn (William). Dialing: plain, concave, convex, etc. Shewing [also] how to make dials. 5 pl. 330 pp. 23 pl. fol. *London, A. Churchill,* 1682.

Leycester (John, *pseudon?*) Civil warres of England. *See* **Ricraft** (Josiah). *London,*1649.

Leyden university. Catalogus librorum manuscriptorum, qui inde ab anno 1741 bibliothecae Lugduno Batavae accesserunt. Descripsit Jacobus Geel. 4 p. l. 307 pp. 4°. *Lugduni Batavorum, E. J. Brill,* 1852. s.

Leydig (*Dr.* Franz). Naturgeschichte der daphniden, (crustacea cladocera). iv, 251 pp. x pl. 4°. *Tübingen, Laupp & Siebeck,* 1860. s.

Lezay-Marnezia (Claude François Adrien, *marquis* de). Lettres écrites des rives de l'Ohio. viii, 144 pp. 8°. *Paris, au Fort-Pitt, et se trouve à Prault,* 1801.

Levins (Peter). Manipulus vocabulorum: a rhyming dictionary of the English language. Edited, with an alphabetical index, by H. B. Wheatley. xv, 368 pp. 8°. *London, Trübner,* 1867.

[Early English text soc. pub. No. 28].

——— The same. A dictionary of English and Latin words, arranged in the alphabetical order of the last syllables. Re-edited, with an alphabetical index, by H. B. Wheatley. 3 p. l. xv, 370 pp. sm. 4°. *London,* 1867.

[Camden soc. pub. No. 95].

L'Hermite (François). Poésies galantes et héroiqves. 3 p. l. 80, 27, 368 pp. 7 pl. 4°. *Paris, J. B. Loyson,* 1662.

L'Huillier (Simon). Principiorum calculi differentialis et integralis expositio elementaris. xxviii, 339 pp. 9 pl. 4°. *Tubingæ, J. G. Cotta,* 1795. s.

Liancourt (*le duc de*). *See* **La Rochefoucault-Liancourt.**

Libanius *Sophista.* Praelvdia oratoria lxii. Declamationes xlv, et dissertationes morales. His accedunt monodiæ, inuectivæ, etc. F. Morellus nunc primum edidit, idemque latine vertit. 2 v. 44 p. l. 948 pp. 17 l; 8 p. l. 735 pp. 12 l. fol. *Parisiis, C. Morel,* 1606–27. s.

Liber facetiarum: a collection of curious and interesting anecdotes. [*anon.*] 1st Amer. ed. 336 pp. 24°. *Boston, G. Williams,* 1811.

Liber librorum: its structure, limitations, and purpose. [*anon.*] 232 pp. 16°. *New York, Scribner & Co.* 1867.

Liber monasterii de Hyda: comprising a chronicle of the affairs of England, from the settlement of the Saxons to the reign of king Cnut; and a chartulary of the abbey of Hyde, in Hampshire, A. D. 455–1023. Edited by E. Edwards. cxiv, 468 pp. 1 fac-sim. 8°. *London, Longmans,* 1866.

[Great Britain: chronicles and memorials during the middle ages].

Liberty and property vindicated, and the St——pm——n burnt. By a friend to the liberty of his country. [Elizaphan of Parnach. *pseudon.*] 15 pp. 8°. *Boston,* 1766.

Liberty of conscience; or, the sole means to obtaine peace and truth. [*anon.*] 5 p. l. 62 pp. sm. 4°. (*n. p.*) 1643.

Libri-Carrucci della Sommaja (Guglielmo Bruto Icilio Timoleonte). Lettre à M. Barthélemy Saint Hilaire. 31 pp. 8°. *Londres, Barthès & Lowell,* 1850. s.

——— Lettre à M. de Falloux, contenant le récit d'une odieuse persécution, et le jugement porté sur cette persécution par les hommes les plus compétents, etc. 2e éd. xvi, 327 pp. 8°. *Paris, Paulin,* 1849. s.

——— Lettre à M. le président de l'institut de France. 72 pp. 8°. *Londres, Barthès & Lowell,* 1850. s.

——— Réponse au rapport de M. Boucly. 98 pp. 8°. *Londres, Schulze & Cie.* 1848. s.

Libri de re rustica. 54 p. l. 295 l. 8°. *Venetiis, Aldvs,* 1533. s.

CONTENTS.

Cato (Marcus Porcius). De re rustica.
Columella (Lucius Junius Moderatus). De re hortensi et villatica.
Palladius (Rutilius Taurus Æmilianus). De insitionibus.
Varro (Marcus Terentius). De re rustica.

Lichtenthal (Peter). Manuale bibliografico del viaggiatore in Italia concernente località, storia, arte, scienze, antiquaria e commercio, etc. 2a ed. xiv, 412 pp. 12°. *Milano, L. di Giacomo Pirola,* 1834. s.

Licteriis (F. de). *See* **Lettieri** (F. de).

Liddon (Henry Parry). The divinity of our lord and saviour Jesus Christ. Eight lectures before the university of Oxford. xix, 776 pp. 8°. *Oxford, Rivingtons,* 1867.

[Bampton lectures, for 1866.]

Liebe (Carl Theodor). Das alter der in reussischen oberlande brechenden dachschiefer. s.

[*With* GEINITZ (H. B.) Aequivalent der takonischen schiefer Nordamerika's in Deutschland, 1866.]

Liebe (Christian Sigismund). Gotha nvmaria; sistens thesavri fridericiani nvmismata antiqva. Accedunt ex Andreæ Morellii specimine vniuersæ rei numariæ antiquæ excerpta, et epistolæ tres Ez. Spanhemii. 7 p. l. xxvi, 544 pp. 14 l. 2 pl. fol. *Amstelædami, Wetstenii et Smith,* 1730. s.

Lieber (Francis). The ancient and the modern teacher of politics. An introductory discourse to a course of lectures on the state. Delivered, Oct. 10, 1859, in the law school of Columbia college. 35 pp. 8°. *New York,* 1860.

——— The character of the gentleman. 3d ed. 121 pp. 16°. *Philadelphia, J. B. Lippincott & Co.* 1864.

——— Inaugural address, Columbia college, 1858. [History, political philosophy, political economy, and university education.]

[*With* COLUMBIA COLLEGE. Addresses, etc. pp. 55-116. *New York,* 1858.]

——— Reflections on the changes which may seem necessary in the present constitution of the state of New York; elicited and published by the New York union league club. 50 pp. 8°. *New York,* 1867.

Liebig (Justus von). Anleitung zur analyse organischer körper. 72 pp. 1 tab. 3 pl. 8°. *Braunschweig, Vieweg,* 1837.

[*With* NAUMANN (C. F.) Table of mineralogical species, 1833.]

——— The same. 2e aufl. viii, 130 pp. 8°. *Braunschweig, Vieweg,* 1853.

——— Grundsätze der agricultur-chemie, mit rücksicht auf die in England angestellten untersuchungen. 2e aufl. 3 p. l. 152 pp. 8°. *Braunschweig, Vieweg,* 1855. s.

——— Animal chemistry; or, organic chemistry in its applications to physiology and pathology. Edited by W. Gregory. 48 pp. 4°. *New York, J. Winchester,* 1842. s.

——— Familiar lectures on chemistry, in its relations to physiology, dietetics, agriculture, commerce, and political economy. 3d ed. xx, 536 pp. 12°. *London, Taylor, Walton & Maberly,* 1851. s.

Liefde, *or* De Liefde (John). Six months among the charities of Europe. 2 v. xi, 421 pp; vi, 490 pp. 15 pl. 12°. *London, A. Strahan,* 1865.

Life (The) and adventures of Paul Jones. [*anon.*] 64 pp. 8°. *New York, W. H. Graham,* 1846.

Life (The) and adventures of Joe Thompson. A narrative founded on fact. Written by himself. [*pseudon.*] 3d ed. 2 v. xxiv, 310 pp; xii, 348 pp. 2 p. l. 16°. *London, J. Hinton,* 1763.

Life (The) and confession of John Johnson, the murderer of James Murray, with some particulars of his family. [*anon.*] 26 pp. 8°. *New York, Brown & Tyrell,* 1824.

Life (The) and public services of major gen. Zachary Taylor, with graphic accounts of the battles [in Mexico, and] all his letters and despatches. [*anon.*] 60 pp. 7 pl. 16°. *Philadelphia, Turner & Fisher,* 1848.

Life and remains of Wilmot Warwick. Edited by his friend Henry Vernon. [*pseudon.*] 326 pp. 12°. *London, J. Ridgway,* 1828.

Life in India; or, Madras, the Neilgherries, and Calcutta. [*anon.*] 528 pp. 35 pl. 18°. *Philadelphia, Am. S. S. Union,* 1855. s.

Life in New York, in doors and out of doors. [*anon.*] 48 l. 8°. *New York, Bunce & bro.* 1851.

Life insurance; its nature, origin, and progress. [*anon.*] 87 pp. 6 l. (tables.) 12°. *New York, C. B. Norton,* 1852. s.

Life (The) of Oliver Cromwell. By a gentleman of Oxford. [*anon.*] 247 pp. 16°. *London, T. Thompson,* 1748.

Life (The) of Daniel Dana, *D.D.* By members of his family. With a sketch of his character, by W. B. Sprague. vii, 279 pp. 1 pl. 12°. *Boston, J. E. Tilton & Co.* 1866.

Life (The) of the danseuse Mlle. Fanny Elssler. 32 pp. 8°. *Philadelphia,* [*about* 1850.]

Life (The) of Thomas J. Jackson ["Stonewall Jackson"]. By an ex-cadet. [*anon.*] 2d ed. 196 pp. 12°. *Richmond, J. E. Goode,* 1864.

Life (The) of Sir William Phips. [*anon.*] 5 p. l. 110 pp. 18°. *London, Nathaniel Hiller,* 1697.

Life (The) of William Merchant Richardson, LL.D. [*anon.*] 90 pp. 16°. *Concord,* [*N. H.*] *I. S. Boyd & W. White,* 1839.

Life (The) of gen. Zachary Taylor; with numerous illustrative anecdotes and embellishments. [*anon.*] 214 pp. sq. 16°. *Philadelphia, Lindsay & Blakiston,* 1847.

Life (The) of the Rev. William Tennent; [with] an account of his being three days in a trance. [*anon.*] 128 pp. 24°. *Hartford, S. Andrus & son,* 1845.

Life (The) of George Washington. [*anon*]. 144 pp. 24°. *Boston, Isaiah Thomas, jr.* 1815.

Life, speeches, and public services of John Bell, [with a sketch of the life of Edward Everett. *anon.*] 118 pp. 16°. *New York, Rudd & Carleton*, 1866.

Liggins (*Rev.* John). One thousand familiar phrases in English and Romanized Japanese. 2d ed. 59 pp. 8°. *New York, Hurd & Houghton*, 1867.

Light (*Maj.* Henry), *and* **De Wint** (P.) Sicilian scenery. 66 l. 62 pl. sm. fol. *London, Rodwell & Martin*, 1823.

Lightbody (James). The gauger and measurer's companion. With a true method for brewing strong ale. 5 p. l. 120 pp. 16 l. 18°. *London, John Everingham*, 1694.

Liljeborg (Wilhelm). Bidrag till kännedom om den inom Sverige och Norrige förekommande crustaceer af tanaidernas familj. [Extract.] 31 pp. 4°. *Upsala, K. acad.* 1864. s.

——— Om den inom Skåne förekommande crustaceer af ordningarne cladocera, ostracoda och copepoda. xv, 222 pp. 27 pl. 8°. *Lund, Berling*, 1853. s.

——— Systematisk öfversigt af de gnagande däggdjuren, *Glires*. [Extract.] 59 pp. 3 tab. 4°. *Uppsala, K. akad.* 1866. s.

Liljegren (Johan C.) Run-arkunder. xii, 307 pp. 12°. *Stockholm, Norstedt*, 1833. s.

Lilly (William). Merlini anglici ephemeris; or, astrological judgments for the year 1671. 48 l. 18°. *London, J. Macock*, 1671. s.

Linage Veitia. *See* **Veitia Linage** (J. de).

Lind (John). Anmerkungen über die vornehmsten acten des dreyzehnten parlements von Groszbritannien. 334 pp. 8° *Braunschweig, F. Waisenhaus*, 1778.

[*With* REMER (Julius August). Amerikanisches archiv. v. 3).

Linda (Lukasz de). Descriptio orbis et omnium ejus rerumpublicarum. 3 p. l. 1448 pp. 7 l. 18°. *Jenae, Matthias Birckner*, 1670.

[NOTE.—Lenglet-Dufresnoy asserts that this book is merely a translated extract from Les états et empires du monde, of Pierre Davity.]

Linde (Samuel Bogumil). Slownik jezyka polskiego. Wydanie drugie, poprawne i pomnozone staraniem i nakladem Zakladu Narodowego Imienia Ossolinskich. 6 v. 4°. *Lwów, w drukarni Zakladu Ossolinskich*, 1854–60.

——— The same. v 1–4. [A–P. only]. 4°. *Lwów*, 1854–58. s.

Lindeberg (Peter). Chronicon rostochiense posthumum. 174 pp. 9 l. 4°. *Rostochii, S. Myliander*, 1596. s.

——— Commentarii rerum memorabilium in Europa, 1786–91. Quibus Regiomontani, Stoëfleri, Ranzovii, et aliorum praedictiones de anno mirabili confirmantur. 8 p. l. 176 pp. 6 l. 4°. *Hamburgi, J. Wolff*, 1591. s.

[*With* his Chronicon rostochiense, etc. 1596.]

Linden (Jan Antoonije van der). Manductio ad medicinam.

[*With* CONRING (H.) Introductio in universam artem medicam. Ed. 1726.]

Lindley (John). Introduction to the natural system of botany. First Am. ed. with an appendix, by John Torrey. xxix, 393 pp. 2 pl. 8°. *New York, G. & C. Carvill*, 1831. s.

——— The vegetable kingdom; or, the structure, classification and uses of plants, illustrated upon the natural system. xviii, 911 pp. 1 pl. 8°. *London, Bradbury & Evans*, 1846. s.

Lindsay (Alexander William Crawford, *lord*). Progression by antagonism; a theory involving considerations touching the present position, duties, and destiny of Great Britain. xii, 110 pp. 3 tab. 8°. *London, J. Murray*, 1846.

Lindsay (*Rev.* John). A voyage to the coast of Africa in 1758, containing an account of the expedition to, and the taking of the island of Goree, by a squadron commanded by hon. Augustus Keppel. 4 p. l. 110 pp. 1 map. 7 pl. 4°. *London, S. Paterson & others*, 1759.

Lindsay (Robert, *of Pitscottie*). Chronicles of Scotland. Published from several old manuscripts. [Ed. by J. G. Dalyell]. 2 v. xxxi, 639 pp. 8°. *Edinburgh, Constable*, 1814.

Lines on the departure of a great poet [lord Byron], from his country. [*anon.*] 2d ed. 15 pp. 8°. *London, J. Booth*, 1816.

[Misc. pamphlets. v. 56].

Lingard (John, *D. D.*) Catechetical instructions on the doctrines and worship of the catholic church. 2d ed. 2 p. l. 139 pp. 16°. *New York, Casserly & sons*, 1842.

Linguet (Simon Nicolas Henri). Memoirs of the Bastile. Translated from the French. 2 pts. in 1 v. iv, 114, 162 pp. 16°. *London, G. Kearsly*, 1783.

Linköpings bibliotheks handlingar. 2 v. 10 p. l. 378 pp; 3 p. l. 426 pp. 16°. *Linköping, G. W. Londicer & Björckegrens*, 1793. s.

Linn (William, *D. D.*) Discourses on the signs of the times. iv, 200 pp. 8°. *New York, Thomas Greenleaf*, 1794.

Linné (Carl von). Egenhändiga anteckningar af Carl Linnaeus om sig sielf, med anmärkningar och tillagg. xxviii, 248 pp. 13 l. 1 tab. 6 pl. 4°. *Stockholm, A. Afzelius*, 1823. s.

Linné (Carl von). Museum Ludovicæ Ulricæ reginæ Suecorum, in quo animalia rariora, exotica imprimis insecta et conchilia describuntur, etc. 4 p. l. 111 pp. 8°. *Holmiæ, L. Salvius,* 1764. s.

——— Opera. v. 2. Systema, genera, species plantarum uno volumine. Editio critica, adstricta, conferta, sive codex botanicus linnaeanus. Ed. Herrmannus Eberhardus Richter. xxxii, 1102, 202 pp. 4°. *Lipsiae, O. Wigand,* 1835–40.
[No more published].

——— Philosophia botanica; in qva explicantvr fundamenta botanica, cum definitionibus partium, exemplis terminorum, observationibus rariorum. 3 p. l. 362 pp. 10 pl. 8°. *Stockholmiæ, G. Kiesewetter,* 1751. s.
[*With* LINNÉ. Systema naturæ. *Lipsiæ,* 1748].

——— Reisen durch Oeland und Gothland, 1741. Aus dem Schwedischen. 16 p. l. 364 pp. 1 map. 2 pl. 8°. *Halle, J. J. Curt,* 1764. s.

——— Systema naturæ; in quo naturæ regna tria secundum classes, ordines, genera, species, systematice proponuntur. Ed. 2a. 2 p. l. 80 pp. 8°. *Stockholmiæ, G. Kiesewetter,* 1740. s.

——— The same. Cvrante Mich. Gottl. Agnethlero. Ed. altera auctior. 88 pp. 8°. *Halæ Magdebvrgicæ,* 1747. s.

——— The same. Sistens regna tria naturæ, in classes et ordines, genera et species redacta, secundum sextam stockholmiensem ed. 3 p. l. 224 pp. 15 l. 9 pl. 8°. *Lipsiae, G. Kiesewetter,* 1748. s.

——— The same. Secvndvm classes, ordines, genera, species, etc. Praefatvs est J. J. Langivs. Ad ed. 10m reformatam holmiensem. 4 p. l. 1380 pp. 8°. *Halae Magdebvrgicae, J. J. Cvrt,* 1760. s.

——— The same. Ex editione duodecima in epitomen redactum, et praelectionibus academicis accommodatum a J. Beckmanno. Animalia vegetabilia. 2 v. in 3. 240 pp; 356 pp. 8°. *Gottingæ, Vandenhöck,* 1772. s.

Linoli (Odoardo). Se l'infiammazione abbia facoltà di rigenerare o distruggere la fibra vivente; memorie tre. 152 pp. 8°. *Lucca, L. Guidotti,* 1844. s.

Linton (*Mrs.* E. Lynn). Lizzie Lorton of Greyrigg. 3 v. 12°. *London, Tinsley,* 1866.

——— Sowing the wind. A novel. 3 v. 12°. *London, Tinsley,* 1867.

——— Witch stories. 428 pp. 12°. *London, Chapman & Hall,* 1861.

Lipenius *or* Lipen (Martin). Bibliotheca realis ivridica. Post F. G. Strvvii et G. A. Jenichenii cvras emendata. 2 v. in 1. x, 860 pp; 476, 351 pp. fol. *Lipsiae, J. Wendler,* 1757.

——— Bibliothecæ realis ivridicae svpplementa ac emendationes, cura A. F. Schott, R. C. de Senkenberg, L. G. Madihn. 3 v. fol. *Lipsiae et Vratislaviae, C. Fritsch,* 1785–1820.

——— Tractatus de navigatione Salomonis ophirica. 1 p. l. 28 l. 826 pp. 1 l. 18°. *Wittebergæ, Hartmann,* 1682.

Lippard (George). Blanche of Brandywine, a romance. 351 pp. 8°. *Philadelphia, G. B. Zieber & Co.* 1846.

——— The midnight queen; or, leaves from New York life. 110 pp. 8°. *New York, Garrett & Co.* [*about* 1850].

——— The Nazarene; or, the last of the Washingtons. 240 pp. 8°. *Philadelphia, G. B. Zieber & Co.* 1846.
[Imperfect.]

——— Paul Ardenheim, the monk of Wissahickon. 2 v. 536 pp. 8°. *Philadelphia, T. B. Peterson,* 1867.

——— Washington and his generals; or, legends of the revolution; with a biographical sketch of the author, by Rev. C. Chauncey Burr. iv, 538, xxvii pp. 8°. *Philadelphia, G. B. Zieber & Co.* 1847.

Lippe (Adolphe). Text book of materia medica. 714 pp. 8°. *Philadelphia, A. J. Tafel,* 1866.

Lippincott (Sarah J. Clarke). Records of five years. By Grace Greenwood. [*pseudon.*] vi, 222 pp. 16°. *Boston, Ticknor & Fields,* 1867.

——— Stories and sights of France and Italy. By Grace Greenwood. [*pseudon.*] With illustrations. vi, 291 pp. 6 pl. 16°. *Boston, Ticknor & Fields,* 1867.

Lipscomb (A. A.) Life of Rev. Charles W. Jacobs. 96 pp. 18°. *Baltimore, Matchett & Neilson,* 1839.

Lipsius (Richard Adelbert). De Clementis Romani epistola ad Corinthios priore disquisitio. Pars prior. 107 pp. 8°. *Lipsiae, F. Brockhaus,* 1855. s.

Lira (La) argentina; ó coleccion de las piezas poèticas, dadas a luz en Buenos-Ayres durante la guerra de su independencia. vii, 515 pp. 1 chart. 8°. *Buenos-Ayres,* 1824.

Lisch (Georg Christian Friedrich). Albrecht ii, herzog von Mecklenburg, und die norddeutschen landfrieden; ein versuch bei der jubelfeier der vollendeten funfzig-jährigen regierung des grossherzogs Friederich Franz von Mecklenburg-Schwerin, am 24 April, 1835. 84 pp. 8°. *Schwerin, Kürschner,* 1835. s.

Lisle (James George Semple). Life; containing a faithful narrative of his alternate vicissitudes of splendor and misfortune. Written by himself. 2d ed. xxii, 382 pp. 1 pl. 8°. *London, W. Stewart,* 1800.

List (A) of all places, pensions, sinecures, etc. with salaries and emoluments arising therefrom; also, a view of the national debt, with account of the receipt and expenditure of the public money. By a commoner. [*anon.*] xx, 213 pp. 12°. *London, J. Blacklock,* 1816.

List (A) of general and staff officers, and of officers serving in regiments in North America under Sir William Howe, K. B. [*anon.*] 56 pp. 12°. *Philadelphia, McDonald & Cameron,* 1778.

List of patents granted by the United States, for the encouragement of arts and sciences from 1790 to 1828. 118, xxiv, 8 pp. 8°. *Washington, S. Alfred Elliot,* 1828.

Literary leisure; or, recreations of Solomon Saunter, esq. [A weekly publication. Sept. 26, 1799–Dec. 18, 1800.] 2 v. vi, 379 pp; iv, 357 pp. 12°. *London, W. Miller,* 1802.

Littérature (La) française contemporaire; recueil de morceaux [des] écrivains du xixe siècle. iv, 310 pp. 12°. *New York, Leypoldt & Holt,* 1868.

Little (The) corporal. For boys and girls. July, 1865 to June, 1867. v. 1–4 in 1 sm. fol. [*Chicago, A. L. Sewell,* 1865–67.]
[Title-page wanting].

Little Rock and Fort Smith railroad company. Annual report of the president, made to the governor; including the report of the special agent. 96 pp. 8°. *Little Rock, state of Arkansas,* 1866. s.

Littleton (Adam). Latine dictionary, in four parts: i. English-Latine. ii. Latine-classical. iii. Latine proper. iv. Latine-barbarous. 4th ed. 4 v. in 1. 4°. *London, W. Rawlins, etc.* 1703. s.

Littré (Maximilien Paul Émile). Dictionnaire de la langue française. v. 1. A–H. 2 p. l. lix, 2080 pp. 4°. *Paris, Hachette,* 1863.

Littrow (Joseph Johann von). Die doppelsterne. 174 pp. 1 pl. 8°. *Wien, F. Beck,* 1835. s.
[*With* LITTROW. Geschichte der gravitation, etc. 1835].

——— Geschichte der entdeckung der allgemeine gravitation durch Newton. 100 pp. 8°. *Wien, F. Beck,* 1835. s.

———Sterngruppen und nebelmassen des himmels. 87 pp. 3 pl. 8°. *Wien, F. Beck,* 1835. s.
[*With* LITTROW. Geschichte der gravitation, etc. 1835].

——— Ueber kometen. Mit einem anhange über den im jahre 1835 erscheinenden halleyschen kometen. Von Carl L. Littrow. Neue aufl. xvi, 223 pp. 2 pl. 8°. *Wien, C. Gerold,* 1835. s.

——— Vermischte schriften. Herausgegeben von C. L. v. Littrow. 3 v. 8°. *Stuttgart, Hoffmann,* 1846. s.

——— Die wunder des himmels, oder gemeinfassliche darstellung des weltsystems. 2^e^ aufl. x, 814 pp. 24 pl. 8°. *Stuttgart, Hoffmann,* 1837. s.

Livermore (George). Remarks on the publication and circulation of the scriptures. 31 pp. 8°. *Cambridge,* [*Ms.*] 1849.

Liverpool free public library. Catalogue. vi, 277, viii pp. 4°. *Liverpool, G. M'Corquodale & Co.* 1855. s.

——— Catalogue of the free lending library for the south district. 132 pp. 8°. *Liverpool, T. Brakell,* 1857. s.

Lives (The) of the most eminent modern painters, who have lived since, or were omitted by Mons. De Piles. By J. B. [James Burgess. *anon.*] 14 p. l. 140 pp. 8°. *London, T. Payne,* 1754.
[*With* PILES (Roger de). Art of painting, etc. 3d ed. 8°. *London,* 1754].

Livingston (John). Livingston's law register, for 1852. With a list of newspapers in the U. S. by J. C. G. Kennedy. 291, 1–48 pp. 8°. *New York, J. Livingston,* 1852.
[The "list of newspapers" is defective after p. 48.]

——— Portraits of eminent Americans now living, with biographical memoirs. 4 v. 8°. *New York, author,* 1853–54. s.

CONTENTS.

Alcorn, James L. v. 4.
Allen, Stephen M. v. 3.
Amonett, James J. v. 4.
Anderson, Samuel. v. 2.
Anspach, John. v. 3.
Ayer, Richard H. v. 1.
Badger, Luther. v. 2.
Barbee, William. v. 4.
Barnard, William T. v. 4.
Barringer, Daniel M. v. 1.
Bash, Henry M. v. 3.
Battle, William H. v. 2.
Baxter, Eli H. v. 3.
Bell, Montgomery. v. 4.
Biddle, Horace P. v. 1.
Bierce, Lucius V. 3.
Bottum, Nathan H. v. 4.
Bowles, Joshua B. v. 2.
Bowman, James L. v. 1.
Boutelle, Timothy. v. 3.
Brierly, Benjamin. v. 4.
Brigham, Josiah. v. 1.
Brisbane, A. H. v. 3.
Brooks, Charles. v. 3.
Brooks, Nathan C. v. 3.
Brown, Aaron V. v. 1.
Brown, Edwin R. v. 4.
Brown, Samuel A. v. 1.
Brown, William G. v. 3.
Bullock, William F. v. 1.
Burnet, Jacob. v. 1.
Calhoun, James M. v. 4.
Campbell, David. v. 4.
Campbell, James. v. 3.
Campbell, John C. v. 1.
Catchings, Thomas J. v. 4.
Catron, John. v. 2.
Chamberlain, Ebenezer M. v. 4.
Chapman, John B. v. 4.
Chapman, John G. v. 4.
Christy, William. v. 3.
Church, Leonard. v. 1.
Clark, Lincoln. v. 4.
Clarke, William B. v. 1.
Clay, John R. v. 1.
Cleveland, Elijah. v. 4.
Coale, James M. v. 3.
Colt, James B. v. 1.
Converse, E. A. v. 3.

Livingston (John). Portraits, etc.—*Continued.*

Cooper, David. v. 4.
Coopwood, Thomas. v. 2.
Cothren, William. v. 4.
Coxe, Richard S. v. 1.
Crawford, Joel. v. 3.
Crey, Frederick. v. 3.
Croskey, Joseph R. K. v. 4.
Cullom, E. North. v. 4.
Culver, Reuben. v. 1.
Cushing, Caleb. v. 3.
Cushman, Henry W. v. 3.
Cutler, Pliny. v. 1.
Darby, John F. v. 1.
Davis, Charles D. v. 4.
Davis, D. A. v. 4.
Davis, Jefferson. v. 3.
Day, Joseph. v. 4.
Dean, Gilbert. v. 1.
Dean, Hosea J. v. 4.
Deford, Benjamin. v. 4.
Deforest, Richard. v. 4.
Devens, David. v. 1.
De Witt, Alexander. v. 1.
Dexter, S. Newton. v. 2.
Dickerson, Cornelius S. v. 4.
Diffenderffer, Henry. v. 4.
Dixon, Archibald. v. 2.
Dobbin, James C. v. 3.
Dobbins, Miles G. v. 4.
Dobyns, John Porter. v. 1.
Dowdell, James F. v. 4.
Downes, George. v. 1.
Duffee, Francis H. v. 4.
Dutton, Henry. v. 2.
Eaves, Nathaniel R. v. 2.
Eddy, Zechariah. v. 3.
Edmonds, John W. v. 2.
Emmons, H. H. v. 2.
Everhart, William. v. 4.
Everitt, Abraham. v. 4.
Farrar, Edwin. v. 4.
Finlayson, John. v. 3.
Fisher, George. v. 3.
Fogg, Francis B. v. 2.
Fontaine, Edmund. v. 4.
Foster, Lafayette S. v. 1.
Fletcher, Elijah. v. 4.
Freelon, Thomas W. v. 4.
Fuller, Henry H. v. 1.
Garland, Hugh A. v. 2.
George, Robert. v. 4.
Gilmer, John A. v. 1.
Goodwyn, Robert H. v. 1.
Gordon, George H. v. 1.
Gott, James R. v. 3.
Gould, Jacob. v. 1.
Gove, Charles F. v. 4.
Grace, William P. v. 1.
Graves, Calvin. v. 1.
Gridley, Albert G. v. 1.
Grier, Robert C. v. 2.
Griswold, Hiram. v. 1.
Guthrie, James. v. 3.
Haldeman, S. S. v. 4.
Hall, Samuel. v. 1.
Hall, Willard. v. 2.
Hamilton, Allen. v. 1.
Hanly, Thomas B. v. 4.
Harper, Joseph M. v. 1.
Harrington, Samuel M. v.1.
Harris, James C. v. 4.
Harris, Thomas. v. 4.
Hayne, Isaac W. v. 1.
Hayt, Samuel A. v. 3.
Hitchcock, Peter. v. 3.
Hogg, Joseph L. v. 4.
Hood, Charles C. v. 4.
Howard, W. G. v. 4.
Hoyt, Hiram. v. 4.
Hubbs, Paul K. v. 4.
Humphreys, West H. v. 2.
Hunt, Benjamin F. v. 2.
January, Andrew M. v. 2.
Jones, Lazarus J. v. 4.
Keith, Charles F. v. 2.
Knapp, Isaac. v. 4.
Knowles, John A. v. 2.
Kock, Charles. v. 3.
Labauve, Zenon. v. 1.
Landes, John. v. 2.
L'Amoreaux, James. v. 4.
Lawrence, William. v. 1.
Layton, William E. v. 4.
Lee, Oliver H. v. 3.
Long, Stephen H. v. 4.
Lumpkin, Joseph H. v. 2.
McClelland, Robert. v. 3.
McClure, William B. v. 1.
McDugald, John G. v. 4.
McHenry, John H. v. 3.
McKay, Donald L. v. 3.
McLean, John. v. 2.
Mann, Horace. v. 4.
Marchbanks, Andrew J. v.2.
Marcy, William L. v. 3.
Marsh, Mulford. v. 1.
Marshal, Benjamin. v. 3.
Mason, William. v. 1.
Meeker, Bradley B. v. 1.
Merrick, Pliny. v. 1.
Mills, William H. v. 2.
Miner, Hiram J. v. 2.
Monkur, J. C. S. v. 3.
Moody, Dexter. v. 4.
Moreland, John F. v. 3.
Munn, Ira Y. v. 4.
Nash, John W. v. 2.
Nelson, Thomas, v. 2.
Norton, George W. v. 2.
Orr, James L. v. 2.
Overton, Archibald W. v. 2.
Owen, C. M. v. 4.
Paddock, Loveland. v. 1,
Parker, William. v. 1.
Parkhurst, Nathan C. v. 4.
Patterson, Angus. v. 1.
Peabody, George. v. 3.
Perry, Benjamin F. v. 2.
Perry, Horatio J. v. 4.
Peters, Frederick G. v. 3.
Phillips, Willard. v. 1.
Pickens, Ezekiel. v. 1.
Pierce, Franklin. v. 3.
Pillow, Gideon J. v. 2.
Pirtle, Henry. v. 2.
Pomeroy, Noah. v. 1.
Pope, John. v. 2.
Pratt, O. C. v. 4.
Prentiss, Samuel. v. 2.
Prescott, William B. v. 4.
Printup, Daniel S. v. 2.
Reeder, Robert S. v. 4.
Rice, Harvey. v. 4.
Ross, William. v. 3.
Rost, Pierre A. v. 1.
Rothwell, Andrew. v. 4.
Rowland, John S. v. 4.
Russell, William J. v. 3.
Saunders, Isaac. v. 1.
Schaeffer, Emanuel. v. 4.
Scott, Christopher C. v. 4.
Seal, Roderick. v. 4.
Seibels, John J. v. 4.
Shelton, George. v. 3.
Silliman, R. D. v. 4.
Simmons, James P. v. 3.
Simon, Edward. v. 3.
Sisson, David. v. 4.
Smith, John P. v. 4.
Smith, Joseph. v. 4.
Smith, Joseph H. v. 3.
Smith, William R. v. 1.
Snyder, Jacob R. v. 4.
Starr, Parley. v. 4.
Tallmadge, Darius. v. 1.
Taylor, John. v. 4.
Taylor, William. v. 4.
Teall, Oliver. v. 1.
Toland, Hugh H. v. 4.
Towson, Nathan. v. 3.
Train, Asa W. v. 3.
Turner, Jesse. v. 1.
Van Antwerp, Verplanck. v. 3.
Walbridge, Hiram. v. 4.
Walker, Henry C. v. 4.
Walker, Thomas A. v. 4,
Wallis, John C. v. 4.
Walworth, Reuben H. v. 2.
Ward, Marcus L. v. 4.
Warner, Hiram. v. 1.
Warren, Lott. v. 2.
Washington, W. H. v. 3.
Wheeler, Alfred. v. 2.
White, John B. v. 4.
White, John J. v. 4.
White, Philo. v. 4.
Whittemore, Thomas. v. 1.
Williams, Archibald. v. 2.
Wilson, Daniel A. v. 2.
Wilson, Joel W. v. 3.
Woodruff, Edward. v. 4.
Woodson, David M. v. 2.
Woodward, John L. v. 4.

Livingston (John Henry, *D. D.*) A dissertation on the marriage of a man with his sister-in-law. 179 pp. 8°. *New Brunswick, Deare & Smith,* 1816.

Livingston (John R. *and* Robert J.) Memorial to the legislature of New York respecting steamboats. 43 pp. 8°. [*n. p.* 1814?]

——— Petition to the legislature of New Jersey respecting steamboats, with the laws of New York and New Jersey [concerning them]. 52 pp. 8°. *New York, Pelsue & Gould,* 1814.

Livingston (Robert R.) Essay on sheep: their varieties; account of the merinoes of Spain, France, etc. 186 pp. 8°. *New York, State,* 1809.

Livingston (*Gov.* William). A letter to John [Ewer], bishop of Landaff, occasioned by his sermon on the 20th of February, 1767, in which the American colonies are loaded with great and undeserved reproach. 2 p. l. 25 pp. 12°. *New York,* 1768.

Livingstone (David). Travels and researches in South Africa, [abridged]. from the personal narrative. 440 pp. 9 pl. 12°. *Philadelphia, J. W. Bradley,* [1858]. s.

——— Missionary travels and researches in South Africa. xxiv, 732 pp. 44 pl. 3 maps. 8°. *New York, Harpers,* 1857.

Livius (Titus). Ab urbe condita liber tricesimus tertius. Ad codicis bambergensis et editionum antiquarum fidem edidit J. T. Kreyssig. cxxiv, 400 pp. 8°. *Misenae, Klinkicht,* 1839. s.

——— The history of Titus Livius, with the entire supplement of Freinsheim. Translated into English, with notes. 3 v. 8°. *London, J. Davis,* 1814-15.

——— Romerske historie. Oversat af J. Geelmuyden. 1e hefte, indeholdende 1ste og 2den bog. 3 p. l. 204 pp. 12°. *Bergen, E. B. Giertsen,* 1863. s.

Llorente (Juan Antonio). Portrait politique des papes, jusqu' en 1822. 2 v. xi, 359 pp; 320 pp. 8°. *Paris, Béchet,* 1822.

Lloyd (David). Fair warnings to a careless world. [*anon.*] 24°. *York,* 1666.

[*With* PROGNOSTICATION forever. 24°. *London,* 1653?]

Lloyd (John). Thesaurus ecclesiasticus: an improved edition of the Liber valorum, containing an account of the valuation of all the livings in England and Wales. xi, 504 pp. 8°. *London, T. N. Longman*, 1796.

[*Note.*—This work may be considered as an improved form of Ecton's Thesaurus].

Lloyd (L.) The game birds and wild fowl of Sweden and Norway; together with an account of the seals and salt-water fishes of those countries. xx, 599 pp. 48 col. pl. 8°. *London, Day & son*, 1867. s.

Lloyd (Samuel). The New Jersey annual register for 1846. 143 pp. 24°. *Trenton, Robert Gosman*, 1845.

Lloyd (*Sir* William). Narrative of a journey from Caunpoor to the Himalaya mountains; and captain Alexander Gerard's account of an attempt to penetrate by Bekhur to Garoo and lake Manas-arowara. xv, 347 pp; 323 pp. 2 maps. 8°. *London, J. Madden & Co.* 1846. s.

Lloyd (William, *son of the bishop of Worcester*). Series chronologica Olympiadum, Pythiadum, Isthmiadum, Nemeadum, quibus veteres Græci tempora sua metiebantur. 4 p. l. xlii pp. 3 l. fol. *Oxoniæ, E theatro sheldoniano*, 1700. s.

Lobon de Salazar (Francisco). [*pseudon.*] *See* **Isla** (José Francisco de).

Local loiterings, and visits in the vicinity of Boston. By a looker-on. [*anon.*] 147 pp. 12°. *Boston, Redding & Co.* 1845.

Locke (D. R.) Nasby papers. [*pseudon.*] With an introduction by G. A. Sala. viii, 88 pp. 12°. *London, Ward, Lock & Tyler*, 1866.

——— "Swingin round the cirkle." By Petroleum V. Nasby. [*pseudon.*] His ideas of men, politics, and things, during 1866. Illustrated by Nast. 299 pp. 8 pl. 12°. *Boston, Lee & Shepard*, 1867.

Locke (E.) *and* **Nourse** (S.) The school melodist. 160 pp. obl. 18°. *Cincinnati, Moore, Wilstach, Keys & Co.* 1854. s.

Locke (John). Geological report.

[*With* Owen (D. D.) Report of a geological exploration of Iowa, Wisconsin, and Illinois, p. 116.]

Locke (*Rev.* William Henry). The story of the regiment, [11th Pa. vols.] 401 pp. 2 pl. 12°. *Philadelphia, J. B. Lippincott & Co.* 1868.

Lockhart (George). Memoirs concerning the affairs of Scotland, from queen Anne's accession to the throne, to the union in 1707. With an account of the design'd invasion from France, in 1708. [*anon.*] xxx, 420, 23 pp. 8°. *London, J. Baker*, 1714.

Lockhart (John Gibson). Ancient Spanish ballads; historical and romantic. Translated, with notes. New ed. With illustrations by Allan, etc. borders and vignettes by Owen Jones. 117 l. 6 pl. 3 illum. 4°. *London, J. Murray*, 1841. s.

——— Peter's letters to his kinsfolk. By Peter Morris. [*pseudon.*] 2d Am. ed. 520 pp. 8°. *New York, Harpers*, 1820. s.

——— Reginald Dalton. [*anon.*] 2 v. 258 pp; 296 pp. 12°. *New York, Harpers*, 1823.

Lockman (John). History of the cruel sufferings of the protestants, and others, by popish persecutions in various countries: with a view of the reformation. xii, 345 pp. 13 l. 16°. *London, J. Clarke*, 1760.

Lockwood (Luke A.) Masonic law and practice, with forms. 144 pp. 12°. *New York, Masonic pub. & manuf. co.* 1867.

Loder (Justus Christian von). Anfangsgründe der chirurgie. 304 pp. 8°. *Jena, Akad. buchhandlung*, 1799. s.

——— Anfangsgründe der physiologischen anthropologie und der staats-arzneykunde. 3e aufl. xvi, 674 pp. 8°. *Weimar, Industrie-comptoirs*, 1800. s.

Lodge (Edmund). The genealogy of the existing British peerage, with brief sketches of the family histories of the nobility. With engravings of the arms. viii, 410 pp. 88 pl. 8°. *London, Saunders & Otley*, 1832.

Loève-Veimars (François Adolphe). Résumé de l'histoire de la littérature allemande. viii, 476 pp. 24°. *Paris, L. Janet*, 1826.

Loew (Hermann). *See* **Löw**.

Löfling (Peter). Reisebeschreibung nach den spanischen ländern in Europa und America, 1751—1756, nebst beobachtungen über die merkwürdigen gewächse; herausgegeben von Carl von Linné. Aus dem Schwedischen übersetzt durch A. B. Kölpin. 2e aufl. 16 pp. 8 l. 406 pp, 1 l. 2 pl. 8°. *Berlin, G. A. Lange*, 1776.

Logan (Thomas M.) Report on the medical topography and epidemics of California. [Extract.] 75 pp. 8°. *Philadelphia, Am. med. assoc.* 1865. s.

Logan (*Sir* William E.) *and* **Hunt** (Thomas Sterry). Sketch of the geology of Canada, etc. Translated from the French. 8°. *Paris*, 1855. s.

[*With* Taché. Canada at the universal exhibition of 1855, pp. 413—454.]

Loiseleur Deslongchamps (Auguste Louis Armand). Essai sur les fables indiennes et sur leur introduction en Europe. Suivi du Roman des sept sages de Rome en prose, publié, avec une analyse et des extraits du Dolopathos, par Le Roux de Lincy. Pour servir d'introduction aux Fables des 12e, 13e, et 14e siècles publiées par M. Robert. 185, xlv, 298 pp. 8°. *Paris, Techener,* 1838.

Lombard (B.) Tableaux synoptiques de l'histoire de France, depuis les Gaulois jusqu'en 1840; avec les synchronismes de l'histoire générale. 4e éd. 85 pp. 2 maps. obl. 4°. *Paris, Daubrée,* 1843.
[Imperfect; title wanting.]

Lombardini (Elia). Saggio idrologico sul Nilo. 74 pp. 3 maps. 4°. *Milano, R. istituto lombardo di scienze e lettere,* 1864. S.

Loménie (Louis Léonard de). Galerie des contemporains illustres; par un homme de rien. [*pseudon.*] 4e éd. 10 v. 18°. *Paris, A. René & Cie.* [1844–47]. S.

CONTENTS.

Abd el-Kader, v. 8.
Ampère, v. 10.
Arago, v. 4.
Auber, v. 4.
Ballanche, v. 3.
Balzac, v. 3.
Béranger, v. 1.
Barante, v. 9.
Berryer, v. 1.
Bertrand, v. 7.
Berzélius, v. 7.
Bosio, v. 6.
Broglie, de, v. 2.
Brougham, v. 5.
Bugeaud, v. 9.
Carrel, v. 8.
Charles, l'archiduc, v. 4.
Chateaubriand, v. 1.
Cherubini, v. 9.
Cobden, v. 10.
Colettis, v. 7.
Constant, v. 8.
Cooper, v. 8.
Cormenin, v. 2.
Cousin, v. 5.
Cuvier, v. 9.
Czartorisky, v. 12.
David (d' Angers), v. 8.
Decazes, v. 8.
Delacroix, v. 6.
Delaroche, v. 7.
Delavigne, v. 4.
Dumas, (A.) v. 5.
Duperré, v. 4.
Dupin aîné, v. 1.
Dupuytren, v. 8.
Espartero, v. 3.
Fourier, v. 10.
Garnier-Pagès, v. 2.
Gay-Lussac, v. 6.
Gérard, v. 6.
Goethe, v. 10.
Guizot, v. 5.
Hugo, (Victor), v. 1.
Humboldt, v. 5.
Ibrahim-Pacha, v. 1.
Ingres, v. 2.
Jackson (Andrew), v. 9.
Lacordaire, v. 5
Lafayette, v. 5.
Laffitte, v. 1.
Lamartine, v. 1.
Lamennais, v. 1.
Larrey, v. 5.
Manzoni, v. 6.
Marmont, v. 5.
Martignac, v. 9.
Mauguin, v. 3.
Maurocordatos, v. 5.
Metternich, v. 2.
Meyerbeer, v. 3.
Mickiewicz, v. 3.
Mohammed-Aly, v. 2.
Molé, v. 2.
Moncey, v. 4.
Montalembert, v. 10.
Moore, Thos. v. 7.
Nesselrode, v. 8.
Nodier, C. v. 7.
O'Connell, v. 3.
Oudinot, v. 7.
Palmerston, v. 3.
Pasquier, v. 6.
Peel, v. 4.
Pellico, v. 4.
Périer, v. 6.
Reschid-Pacha, v. 7.
Rosa, M. de La, v. 4.
Rossini, v. 3.
Royer-Collard, v. 4.
Russell, Ld. John, v. 4.
Saint Simon, v. 10.
Sainte-Beuve, v. 9.
Salvandy, v. 10.
Sand, George, v. 2.
Schelling, v. 10.
Schlegel, A. W. v. 9.
Scott, Walter, v. 9.
Scribe, v. 3.
Sebastiani, v. 8.
Sismondi, v. 7.
Soult, v. 1.
Spontini, v. 10.
Talleyrand, v. 7.
Thiers, v. 1.
Thierry, v. 3.
Thorwaldsen, v. 9.
Tieck, v. 8.
Toreno, v. 6.
Uhland, v. 9.
Vernet, v. 4.
Vigny, A. de, v. 2.
Villèle, v. 6.
Villemain, v. 4.
Wellington, v. 2.

London. Catalogue of sculpture, paintings, engravings, and other works of art belonging to the corporation, together with books not included in the catalogue of the Guildhall library. Part i. 98 pp. 8°. *London, corporation,* 1867. S.

——— A catalogue of the library of the corporation of the city. iv, 376 pp. 8°. *London, corporation,* 1840.

——— The same. An alphabetical index to the catalogue [etc.] up to the present time. 176 pp. 8°. *London, corporation,* 1846. S.

——— General catalogue of books published in London since 1700; with sizes and prices. 152, 10, 14 pp. 8°. *London,* 1779–83. S.
[*With* appendix and supplement to 1783].

London (The) catalogue of books, with their sizes, prices, and publishers, 1810 to 1831. [*anon.*] 335 pp. 8°. *London, R. Bent,* 1831.

London (The) catalogue of books published in Great Britain, with their sizes, prices, and publishers' names, 1814–1846. viii, 542 pp. 8°. *London, T. Hodgson,* 1849. S.

——— The same. Supplement, 1846–1849. 122, 56 pp. 8°. *London, T. Hodgson,* 1846–49. S.

——— The same. Classified index, 1814–46. vii, 283 pp. 8°. *London, T. Hodgson,* 1848. S.

——— The same. Classified index, 1816–51. xiv, 285 pp. 8°. *London, T. Hodgson,* 1853. S.

London as it is to-day; where to go and what to see during the great exhibition. [*anon.*] ii, 437, vi pp. 12°. *London, H. G. Clarke & Co.* 1851. S.
[Imperfect.]

London athenæum; rules and regulations; list of members, 1850, and donations to the library, 1849; with addenda for 1851. 18°. *London,* 1851. S.

London board of trade. Catalogue of the library. 2 p. l. 648 pp. 8°. *London, board of trade,* 1866. S.

London, Edinburgh, and Dublin philosophical magazine and journal of science. 4th series. vols. 32–33. July, 1866, to June, 1867. 8°. *London,* 1866–67.

London (The little) directory of 1677. The oldest printed list of the merchants and bankers of London. Reprinted from the exceedingly rare original. [*anon.*] xxii pp. 64 l. 24°. *London, J. C. Hotten,* 1863.

London (The) encyclopædia; or, universal dictionary of science, art, literature, and practical mechanics, [etc.] By the original editor of the Encyclopædia metropolitana, [Thomas Curtis]. 22 v. (A–Z.) 8°. *London, T. Tegg, etc.* 1829. S.

London (The) gazette, Jan. 1859 to Sept. 1867. 27 v. sm. fol. *London, Harrison & sons*, [1859–67].

London library. Catalogue. By Robert Harrison. 3d ed. xxxii, 930 pp. 8°. *London, library*, 1865. s.

London (Royal college of surgeons). Synopsis of arrangement followed in the classed catalogue of books, [etc.] 4 p. l. 36 pp. 8°. *London*, 1838. s.

[*With* CATALOGUE. v. 2. 1840.]

London (Royal society of). Philosophical transactions for 1866. v. 156. 925 pp. 43 pl. 4°. *London, Taylor & Francis*, 1856.

London and provincial medical directory, inclusive of the medical directory for Scotland, and the medical directory for Ireland, and general medical register, 1867. 968 pp. 8°. *London, J. Churchill*, 1867.

Long (George). Classical geography. *See* **Hughes** (William), *and* **Long** (George).

——— The conduct of life; a series of essays. xi, 239 pp. 12°. *London, J. Murray*, 1845.

——— *and* **Porter** (George R.) Geography of Great Britain. Part i, England and Wales. iv, 540 pp. 8°. *London, R. Baldwin*, 1850.

Longfellow (Henry Wadsworth). Poetical works. Complete edition. viii, 363 pp. 18°. *Boston, Ticknor & Fields*, 1867.

——— Outre-mer; a pilgrimage beyond the sea. 2 nos. in 1 v. [*anon.*] 208 pp. 8°. *Boston, Hilliard, Gray & Co.* 1833–34.

——— Évangéline. [Traduite en vers français, par L. P. Lemay]..

[*With* LEMAY (L. P.) Essais poétiques].

Longhena (Francesco). Notizie biografiche di Giuseppe Longhi.

[*With* LONGHI (G.) La calcografia, 1830].

Longhi (Giuseppe). La calcografia propriamente detta; ossia l'arte d'incidere in ramo coll' acqua forte, col bulina, e colla punta; ragionamenti. v. 1. concernante la teorica dell' arte. xxxii, 437 pp. 1 pl. 8°. *Milano, Stamperia reale*, 1830. s.

——— The same. Die kupferstecherei; oder, die kunst in kupfer zu stechen und zu äzen. 2 v. 4 p. l. 368 pp; vi, 194 pp. 2 pl. 16°. *Hildburghausen u. Meiningen, Kesslring*, 1837. s.

CONTENTS.

v. 1. Theoretischer theil, aus dem italiänischen übersetzt, von C. Barth.
v. 2. Practischer theil, von C. Barth.

Longinus *or* Dionysius Longinus. Treatise of loftiness or elegancy of speech. Translated out of French, by J. Pulteney. 10 p. l. 167 pp. 18°. *London, J. Holford*, 1680.

——— The same. Traité du sublime; ou, du merveilleux dans le discours. Traduit du Grec. [Avec des remarques sur Longin]. 8 p. l. 190 pp. 6 l. 1 pl. 18°. [*Paris, D. Thierry*, 1683].

[*With* BLAINVILLE (de). Oeuvres diverses du sieur D * * *. 18°. *Paris*, 1683.]

Long Island historical society. Memoirs. v. 1. Journal of a voyage to New York, in 1679–80. viii, xlvii, 440 pp. 12 pl. 8°. *Brooklyn, (N. Y.) L. I. hist. soc.* 1867.

Longking (Joseph). Notes on the epistle to to the Hebrews. *See* **Bible**, *English*.

Longpérier (Henri Adrien Prévost de). Description des médailles du cabinet de M. de Magnoncour. 2 l. 139 pp. 2 pl. 8°. *Paris, Didot*, 1860. s.

Longstreet (Augustus B.) Georgia scenes, characters, incidents, etc. in the first half century of the republic. [*anon.*] 235 pp. 12°. *Augusta, S. R. Sentinel office*, 1835.

Lonicer (Philipp). Chronicorvm tvrcorvm tomi duo. 8 p. l. 208 pp. 7 l. 16°. *Francofvrti, Feyerabendt*, 1584.

Lonsdale (Edward Francis, *M. D.*) Observations on the treatment of lateral curvature of the spine. xvi, 116 pp. 8°. *London, J. Churchill*, 1847.

Loomis (Elias). Elements of plane and spherical trigonometry, etc. vi, 148 pp. 8°. *New York, Harpers*, 1848. s.

——— The same. 14th ed. 193 pp. 8°. *New York, Harpers*, 1858. s.

——— The recent progress of astronomy; especially in the United States. 257 pp. 12°. *New York, Harpers*, 1850. s.

——— Tables of logarithms of numbers, and of lines and tangents for every ten seconds of the quadrant, etc. xvi, 150 pp. 8°. *New York, Harpers*, 1848. s.

——— Treatise on arithmetic. viii, 359 pp. 12°. *New York, Harpers*, 1856. s.

Loomis (Justin R.) Elements of the anatomy and physiology of the human system. 211 pp. 4 col. pl. 12°. *New York, Lamport, Blakeman & Law*, 1853. s.

Loomis (*Rev.* William Isaacs). Discovery of the origin of gravitation, and the majestic motive force which generated the diurnal and yearly revolutions of the heavenly bodies. 82 pp. 8°. *Martindale Depot, (N. Y.) T. Holman*, 1866.

Lord (David N.) Louis Napoleon. Is he to be the imperial chief of the ten kingdoms and the anti-christ? 551 pp. 12°. *New York, F. Knight*, 1866.

——— Visions of paradise: an epic. v. 1. 415 pp. 12°. *New York, author*, 1867.

Lord (John). Modern history, from Luther to the fall of Napoleon. xv, 544 pp. 12°. *Philadelphia, Thomas, Cowperthwait & Co.* 1849. s.

Lord (W. B.) Sea fish, and how to catch them. 2d ed. viii, 118 pp. 18°. *London, Bradbury & Evans,* [1863].

Lorek (*Dr.* C. G.) Flora prussica. Abbildungen sämmtlicher bis jetzt aufgefundener pflanzen Preussens. 4 p. l. 210 pl. col. 8°. *Königsberg, Unzer,* 1826.

——— Zur flora prussica. [Explanation of plates of Flora prussica.] 51 pp. 8°. *Königsberg, Schultz,* 1830. s.
[*With* the preceding.]

Lorenz (Eduard Georg Heinrich). De chorea St. Viti. 30 pp. 8°. *Rostochii, auctor,* 1842. s.

Loring (Thomas, *of Raleigh, N. C.*) *See* **Wilmington** (N. C.) Proceedings, etc.

Losa. *See* **Loza.**

Lösche (Gustav Eduard). Ueber periodische veränderungen des windes an der erdoberfläche, nach beobachtungen zu Dresden, 1853–58. xix, 136, 205 pp. 1 pl. 8°. *Dresden, Meinhold,* 1865. s.

Los Rios (José Amador de). Historia critica de la literatura española. v. 1–7. [Siglo i–xvi.] 8°. *Madrid, J. Rodriguez,* 1861–65.

Los Santos (Domingo de). Vocabulario de la lengua Tagala. 2 pts. in 1 v. 4 pl. 738 pp; 118 pp. fol. [*Manila?*] *Tomas Oliva,* 1835. s.

Lossing (Benson J.) The Hudson, from the wilderness to the sea. Illustrated. sm. 4°. *New York, Virtue & Yorston,* 1866.

——— Life and times of Philip Schuyler. v. 1. 504 pp. 2 pl. 8°. *New York, Mason bros.* 1860.
[No more published.]

——— Life of Washington; a biography, personal, military, and political. 3 v. 8°. *New York, Virtue & Co.* 1860. s.

——— Martha Washington. 24 pp. portrait. 8°. *New York, J. C. Buttre,* 1861.

——— Vassar college and its founder. 175 pp. portrait. 8°. *New York, C. A. Alvord,* 1867.

Lotharius dyaconus, *or* Lottario dei Conti, *afterward pope Innocent iii.*) Liber de miseria conditionis hũane. 28 l. 4°. *Nurmberg, F. Creusner,* 1477. s.

Lottin de Laval (Victor). Gallanteries du maréchal de Bassompierre. 4 v. in 2. portrait. 8°. *Paris, Hortel & Ozanne,* 1839.

Lotus of the good law. Lotus de la bonne loi, traduit du Sanscrit, par E. Burnouf, accompagné de mémoires relatif au buddhisme. *See* **Saddharma** pundarika.

Loudon (Archibald). A selection of some of the most interesting narratives of outrages committed by the Indians in their wars with the white people. [With] an account of their manners, customs, traditions, etc. 2 v. xii, 355 pp; 569 pp. 16°. *Carlisle, (Pa.)* [*printed at Whitehall, N. Y.*] *A. Loudon,* 1808–11.

——— Wonderful magazine, and extraordinary museum. 504 pp. 8°. *Carlisle, (Pa.) A. Loudon,* 1808.

Loudon (*Mrs.* Margracia). Philanthropic economy; or, the philosophy of happiness, practically applied to the social, political and commercial relations of Great Britain. viii, 312 pp. 8°. *London, E. Churton,* 1835.

Loughridge (*Rev.* R. M. *and* Winslett (David). Nakcokv esyvhiketv. Muskokee [or Creek] hymns [in the original.] 3d ed. 216 pp. 24°. *New York, Presb. mission house,* 1859.

Louis (Bonaparte,) *king of Holland.* Documents historiques et réflexions sur le gouvernement de la Hollande. [1806–10.] 3 v. 8°. *Londres, Lackington,* 1820.

Louisiana. Debates in the convention for the revision of the constitution, 1864. 643 pp. 8°. *New Orleans, W. R. Fish,* 1864.

——— Documents of the second legislature. 1st and 2d sessions. 2 v. 8°. *New Orleans, J. O. Nixon,* 1866–67.

Louisville. Directory for 1838–9. By G. Collins. 6 p. l. 180 pp. 16°. *Louisville, J. B. Marshall,* 1838.

Louvel (——). The savages of Europe. *See* **Lesuire** (R. M.) *and* **Louvel.**

Louvet (L.) Curiosités de l'économie politique. 4 p. l. 440 pp. 16°. *Paris, A. Delahays,* 1861.

Love (William De Loss). Wisconsin in the war of the rebellion; a history of all regiments and batteries sent to the field, and deeds of her citizens. 1140 pp. 27 pl. 8°. *Chicago, Church & Goodman,* 1866.

Loveday (Robert). Letters, domestick and foreign. 7th ed. 7 p. l. 272 pp. 16°. *London, O. Blagrave,* 1684.

Lovemore (*Sir* Charles, *pseudon.*) *See* **Manley** de La Riviere (*Mrs.*)

Lovzinski *or* Lowzinsky (*baron* de). History of, with remarkable occurrences in the life of count [Casimir] Pulaski. 108 pp. 24°. *New York, Robert Moore,* 1807.

Löw (Hermann). Die europäischen bohrfliegen (*trypetidae*). 2 p. l. 128 pp. 26 phot. pl. 8°. *Wien, K. hof und staatsdruckerei,* 1862. s.

——— Monographs of the diptera of North America. Edited by R. Osten-Sacken. 2 pts. xxiv, 221 pp. 2 pl; xii, 360 pp. pl. 3 to 7. 8°. *Washington,* 1864–67.
[Smithsonian Miscel. Coll. v. 6.]

Löw (Johann Franz). Tractatvs novissimvs de variolis, et morbillis, etc. Cui accessit apodix medica de morbis infantum. 6 p. l. 472 pp. 7 l. 4°. *Norimbergæ, J. Zieger & G. Lehmann*, 1699. s.

Low, (Sampson), son & Co. American catalogue of books; or, English guide to American literature, since 1800. 8°. *London*, 1856. s.

Lowe (Edward Joseph). Natural history of new and rare ferns. viii, 192 pp. 72 col. pl. 8°. *London, Groombridge*, 1862. s.

——— A treatise on atmospheric phœnomena. 375 pp. 12°. *London, Longmans*, 1846.

Lowe (Martha Perry). Love in Spain, and other poems. iv, 232 pp. 12°. *Boston, Wm. V. Spencer*, 1867.

Lowell (James Russell). A fable for critics. [*anon.*] 78 pp. 12°. *New York, G. P. Putnam*, 1848.

Lowell (*Mass.*) City documents. 12 v. in 1. 8°. *Lowell, Knapp & Morey*, 1866. s.

——— City school library catalogue. 3 p. l. 214 pp. 8°. *Lowell, S. N. Merrill*, 1868. s.

Löwenorn (Paul de). Beretning om en reise, foretaget i aarene 1782 og 1783, med fregatten Pröven, for at undersöge de i Dannemark forfœrdigce söe-længde uhrer. Udgivet af det kongelige danske videnskabers selskab. 4°. *Kiöbenhavn*, 1785.

Löwenstern (Isidor). Le Mexique. Souvenirs d'un voyageur. viii, 467 pp. 8°. *Paris, A. Bertrand*, 1843.

Lower Canada (The) watchman. 491 pp. 18°. *Kingston, (U. C.) James Macfarlane*, 1829.

Löwig (Carl). Chemie der organischen verbindungen. 2e aufl. 2 v. xxxvii, 1023 pp; xxxiv, 1754 pp. 8°. *Braunschweig, Vieweg*, 1846. s.

——— Grundriss der organischen chemie. xxxiv, 474 pp. 8°. *Braunschweig, Vieweg*, 1852. s.

Low-life: or, one half of the world knows not how the other half live. In a true description of a Sunday as it is usually spent within the bills of mortality. [*anon.*] 2d ed. viii, 103 pp. 8°. *London, the author*, [*about* 1740].

[*With* HISTORY (The) of Theodore I, king of Corsica, *London*, 1743].

Lowrie (John C.) Two years in upper India. 276 pp. 1 map. 12°. *New York, Carters*, 1850. s.

Lowrie (*Rev.* Walter M.) The land of Sinim; or, an exposition of Isaiah xix, 12, together with a brief account of the Jews and christians in China. 2d ed. 147 pp. 18°. *Philadelphia, W. S. Martien*, 1850. s.

Lowth (George T.) The wanderer in western France. viii, 360 pp. 1 map. 1 pl. 8°. *London, Hurst & Blackett*, 1863.

Lowville academy. Semi-centennial anniversary, 1858. 133 pp. 4 pl. 8°. *Lowville, [N. Y.] home committee*, 1859.

Loyalist (The) poetry of the revolution. [Edited by Winthrop Sargent]. xi, 213 pp. 2 l. sm. 4°. *Philadelphia, Collins*, 1857.

Loza *or* Losa (Francisco). Vida del siervo de Dios, Gregorio Lopez. A qve se añaden los escritos del apocalypsi, y tesoro de medecina. 4a ed. 12 p. l. 441 pp. 1 pl. sm. 4°. *Madrid, Juan de Ariztia*, 1727.

Lozier (*Rev.* John Hogarth). Debate on universalism between Rev. J. H. Lozier and Rev. B. F. Foster, July, 1867. 87 pp. 8°. *Indianapolis, Downey & Brouse*, 1867.

Lübsen (Heinrich Burchard). Ausführliches lehrbuch der arithmetik und algebra. Mit einem vorwort von H. C. Schumacher. xii, 319 pp. 12°. *Oldenburg, W. Berndt*, 1835. s.

Luca (Paolo Anania de). Esame e proposta di ciò che manca per la compilazione di un trattato di acustica, compiuto ed applicabile alle arti. 144 pp. 8°. *Napoli, Fibreno*; 1841. s.

Lucas (Charles Jean Marie). De la réforme des prisons; ou, de la théorie de l'emprisonnement. 3 v. ciii. 390 pp; 463 pp; 631 pp. 8°. *Paris, Legrand & Descauriet*, 1838. s.

Lucas (Eduard). Kurze anleitung zur obstkultur. vii, 94 pp. 4 pl. 8°. *Ravensburg, Dorn*, 1866. s.

Lucas (Eliza). Journal and letters of Eliza Lucas. [Ed. by Mrs. H. P. Holbrook]. 30 pp. 4°. *Privately printed, Wormsloe, (N. C.)* 1850.

Lucas (Fielding, *jr.*) Specimens of printing types and ornaments cast at the Baltimore type and stereotype foundry. 241 pp. 8°. *Baltimore, F. Lucas, jr.* 1851. s.

Lucas (Hippolyte). Catalogues des coléoptères. *See* **Edwards** (H. Milne), **Blanchard** (E.) *and* **Lucas** (H.)

Lucas (Jean André Henri). De la minéralogie. [Extract]. 86 pp. 8°. *Paris, nouv. dict. d'hist. nat.* 1818. s.

Lucas (Margaret). Account of the convincement and call to the ministry of M. L. 111 pp. 16°. *Stanford, (N.Y.) H. & J. F. Bull*, 1803.

Lucia Darc. A novel. By Filia. [*pseudon.*] 138 pp. 8°. *New York, M. Doolady*, 1867.

Lucianus. Dialogus quomodo solus nudus per Acheronta transuehi potest; una cū contentione trium summorum ducum de artis imperatoriæ presidencia apud inferos sub Minone judice. [Per J. Aurispam in Latinum versus]. 5 l. [unp.] sm. 4°. *Liptzik, Jacobus Thanner,* 1500.

Lucretius Carus (Titus). De rerum natura libri sex. Accesserunt variæ lectiones. 2 p. l. 370 pp. 7 pl. 4°. *Londini, J. Tonson,* 1712.

——— The same. Interpretatione et notis illustravit Thomas Creech. Ed. alt. 16, 367 pp. 51 l. 8°. *Londini, M. Matthews,* 1717. s.

——— The same. Of the nature of things; in six books. Translated by T. Creech. 8°. *Edinburgh,* [1792–94].

[Anderson's Brit. poets, v. 5.]

——— The same. Translated with commentaries, by T. Busby. 2 v. clxxxiii, 242 pp; cxxvii, 312 pp. 1 pl. 4°. *London, J. Rodwell, etc.* 1813.

Lucubrations of Humphrey Ravelin, esq. [*pseudon.*] 414 pp. 8°. *London, Whittaker,* 1823.

Lüdecking (Heinrich). Englisches lesebuch; erster theil. Mit einem wörterbuche. viii. 238 pp. 8°. *Wiesbaden, Kreidel & Neidner,* 1858.

Ludlow (Edmund). Memoirs. With a collection of original papers. 3 v. 12°. *Vevay,* 1698–99.

Ludlow (Fitz-Hugh). Little brother; and other genre-pictures. 293 pp. 12°. *Boston, Lee & Shepard,* 1867.

Ludlow (John Malcolm), *and* **Jones** (Lloyd). Progress of the working class, 1832–67. xv, 304 pp. 16°. *London, Strahan,* 1867.

Ludvigh (Samuel). Der roman meines lebens in Europa. 239 pp. 8°. *Baltimore, verfasser,* 1858. s.

Luigi Gonzaga, (*St.*) *See* **Aloysius** Gonzaga, (*St.*)

Lujan (Francisco de). Memoria de la comision encargada de formar el mapa geológico de la provincia de Madrid y el general del reino. 88 pp. 2 tab. 3 maps. 4°. *Madrid, Ministro de fomento,* 1853. s.

Luke Darrell, the Chicago newsboy. [*anon.*] 377 pp. 16°. *Chicago, Tomlinson brothers,* 1866.

Lully *or* **Lulli** (Raymond). Philosophical and chymical experiments. [Translated] by R. Turner. 16°. *London, J. Cottrel,* 1657.

[*With* PARACELSUS, of chymical transmutation. pp. 97–166. 1657.]

Lumsden (Matthew, *LL. D.*) A grammar of the Persian language; comprising a portion of the elements of Arabic inflexion, etc. 2 v. xxxiii, 458 pp; 582 pp. fol. *Calcutta, T. Watley,* 1810. s.

Lund (Theodore). The children of the frontier. (Edited by Mrs. L. B. Gow). 16°. *New York,* 1867.

Lundie (*Mrs.* J. C.) America as I found it. [*anon.*] xii, 380 pp. 16°. *London, James Nisbet & Co.* 1852.

Lunn (John Robert). Of motion. xii, 132 pp. 8°. *Cambridge, (Eng.) Deighton, Bell & Co.* 1859. s.

Lunt (George). Three eras of New England, and other addresses, with papers critical and biographical. 264 pp. 12°. *Boston, Ticknor & Fields,* 1857.

Lussana (Filippo). Monografia delle vertigini, e ricerche di fisiologia nevrologica. [Extract]. 471 pp. 4 pl. 8°. *Milano, soc. delle scienze, etc.* 1858. s.

——— Monografia delle nevralgie bracchiali. Con appendice intorno alla angina pectoris. viii, 316 pp. 8°. *Milano, G. Chiusi,* 1859. s.

——— Sulla pellagra studj pratici. [Extract]. 356 pp. 1 pl. 8°. *Milano, Ann. univ. di med.* 1859. s.

Luthardt (Christian Ernst). De compositione evangelii Joannei. xiii, 92 pp. 8°. *Erlangae, Kunstmann,* 1852. s.

Lütké (Friedrich). Voyage autour du monde, par ordre de l'empéreur Nicolas I, 1826–29. 3 v. 7 maps. 8°. atlas, fol. *Paris, Didot,* 1835.

Luxborough (*lady*). *See* **Knight** (H.)

Luynes (Honoré Théodoric Paul Joseph d'Albert, *duc* de). Mémoire sur le sarcophage et l'inscription funéraire d'Esmunazar, roi de Sidon. 4°. *Paris, H. Plon,* 1856. s.

Luzan (Ignacio de). La poetica, ó reglas de la poesia en general. 2 v. 16°. *Madrid,* 1789.

Lyall (Robert). Travels in Russia, the Krimea, the Caucasus, and Georgia. 2 v. xxii, 527 pp; xv, 534 pp. 8°. *London, T. Cadell,* 1825.

Lycett (John). Supplementary monograph on the mollusca from the Stonesfield slate, great oolite, forest marble, and cornbrash. 4°. *London, palaeontographical society,* 1863. s.

——— *See* also **Morris** (J.) *and* **Lycett.**

Lydgate (John). The dance of Macaber, with preface by F. Douce. s.

[*With* HOLBEIN (H.) Dance of death. 16°. *London,* 1790].

Lyell (*Sir* Charles). The geological evidences of the antiquity of man, with remarks on theories of the origin of species by variation. x, 518 pp. 2 pl. 8°. *Philadelphia, G. W. Childs,* 1863. s.

——— A manual of elementary geology. Reprinted from 4th ed. xxxii, 512 pp. 1 pl. 8°. *New York, D. Appleton & Co.* 1853. s.

——— Principles of geology. 8th ed. xvi, 811 pp. 12 pl. 1 map. 8°. *London, J. Murray,* 1850. s.

——— Travels in North America in 1841–42; with geological observations on the United States, Canada, and Nova Scotia. 2 v. in 1. vii, 251 pp; vi, 197 pp. 12°. *New York, Wiley & Halsted,* 1856. s.

Lyman (Payson Williston). History of Easthampton, [Mass.] its settlement and growth; its material, educational, and religious interests; [also], a genealogical record of its original families. 192, 2 pp. 12°. *Northampton, (Mass.) Trumbull & Gere,* 1866.

Lynch (John, *titular bishop of Tuam*). Cambrensis eversus; seu potius historica fides in rebus hibernicis Giraldo Cambrensi abrogata; ostendit Gratianus Lucius, hibernus. Edited, with translation and notes, by Rev. M. Kelly. 3 v. 12°. *Dublin,* 1848–51.
[Celtic soc. publ. No. 2].

Lynch (William F.) Narrative of the United States expedition to the river Jordan and the Dead sea. 6th ed. xx, 509 pp. 2 maps. 8°. *Philadelphia, Lea & Blanchard,* 1849.

——— The same. 332 pp. 12°. *Philadelphia, Lea & Blanchard,* 1850. s.

Lynn (The) directory, for 1867. Also, a directory of Swampscott. By Sampson, Davenport & Co. 306 pp. 1 map. 8°. *Lynn, (Mass.) J. M. Munroe,* [1867].

Lynn library association. Catalogue of the library. xii, 84 pp. 16°. *Lynn, (Mass.) W. W. Kellogg,* 1856. s.

Lyon (George Francis). The sketch-book, during eight months' residence in Mexico. No. 1. [No more published]. 3 p. l. 10 pl. fol. *London, J. Dickinson,* 1827.

Lyon (Sydney S.) Topographical geological reports, and palæontological report.
[*With* OWENS (D. D.) Reports of the geological survey of Kentucky. v. 1, 2, 3, 4].

Lyra *or* **Lire** (Nicolas de). Dicta de sacramēto [eukaristie]. 12 l. unp. sm. 4°. *Colonie, Arnold Therhoern,* [*about* 1480].
[*With* AQUINO (*Saint* Tommaso d'). De corpore Christi. *Coloniæ,* n. d.]

——— Preceptoriū; siue expositio tripharia breuis et utilis in decalogū legis diuine, cum aliis tractatulis. 88 l. unp. 24°. *Colonie, Hermanus Bomgart de Ketwych,* 1495.

Lyrics on love. With translations and imitations from the French and Italian languages. By J. J. M. [*anon.*] 14 p. l. 109 pp. 18°. *London, J. F. Hughes,* 1807.

Mabel Ross, the sewing girl. By the author of "Luke Darrell, the Chicago newsboy." [*anon.*] 432 pp. 5 pl. 16°. *Chicago, Tomlinson Bros.* 1866.

Maberly (Joseph). The print collector: an introduction to the knowledge necesssary for forming a collection of ancient prints, [etc.] [*anon.*] viii, 211 pp. 4°. *London, Saunders & Otley,* 1844. s.

Mabillon (Jean). Iter germanicum. Præmissa est præfatio J. A. Fabricii. 11 p. l. 103 pp. 16°. *Hamburgi, C. Liebezeit,* 1717. s.

McAlpine (John). Genuine narratives and concise memoirs, from his emigration to America in 1773, to 1779, under command of generals Carleton and Burgoyne. vi, 72 pp. 18°. [*n. p.*] 1788.

Macaulay (Thomas Babington, *baron*). History of England from the accession of James II. v. 1–4. 8°. *New York and Philadelphia, Harpers, and E. H. Butler & Co.* 1849–56. s.

——— The same. 5th ed. v. 1–2. 8°. *London, Longmans,* 1849.

McCabe (James D. *jr.*) Life and campaigns of general Robert E. Lee. With maps. 717 pp. portrait. 6 maps. 8°. *New York, Blelock & Co.* 1867.

Maccalla (*Rev.* W. L.) Debate on christian baptism. *See* **Campbell** (Alexander).

McClellan (George, *M. D.*) Principles and practice of surgery. Edited by his son, John H. B. McClellan. 432 pp. 8°. *Philadelphia, Grigg, Elliot & Co.* 1848. s.

McClelland (Alexander, *D. D.*) Sermons. Edited by R. W. Dickinson, D. D. xvi, 424 pp. 12°. *New York, R. Carter & Bros.* 1867.

McClenachan (Charles T.) The book of the ancient and accepted Scottish rite of freemasonry; containing instructions in all the degrees. 624 pp. 2 pl. 12°. *New York, Masonic pub. and manuf. Co.* 1867.

M'Cleod [Malcolm, *D. D. pseudon?*] History of witches. 98 pp. 24°. *New Haven, Sidney's press,* 1811.
[Imperfect; wanting pp. 98–107.]

M'Clintock (John *D. D.*) A second book in Greek, etc. forming a sufficient Greek reader. 12°. *New York, Harpers,* 1850. s.

M'Clintock (John *D. D.*) Second book in Latin; containing syntax, and reading lessons in prose. xl, 296 pp. 12°. *New York, Harpers,* 1853.

——— *and* Strong (James, *S. T. D.*) Cyclopædia of biblical, theological, and ecclesiastical literature. v. 1. A–B. vi, 947 pp. 8°. *New York, Harpers,* 1867.

M'Clung (John A.) Sketches of western adventure; containing an account of the most interesting incidents connected with the settlement of the west, from 1755 to 1794; with appendix. 360 pp. 16°. *Philadelphia, Grigg & Elliot,* [*printed at Maysville, Ky.*] 1832.

——— The same. 315 pp. 16°. *Cincinnati, U. P. James,* 1839.

M'Clure (*Sir* Robert John Le Mesurier). Despatches from the discovery ship "Investigator," off Point Warren and Cape Bathurst. 45 pp. 1 map. 8°. *London, J. Betts,* 1853.

MacConmidhe *or* MacNamee (Gilla Brighde). Poem on the battle of Dun. Edited by J. O'Donovan. [Irish and Eng.] pp 145–183. 8°. *Dublin,* 1849.
[Celtic soc. publ. no. 3.]

McCorkle (John M. S.) A manual of masonic jurisprudence; with decisions on masonic law, and forms. 178 pp. 16°. *Louisville, author,* 1867.

McCoy (Frederick, *prof. in the university of Melbourne, Australia.*) Contributions to British palæontology, [etc.] Republished from the "Annals and magazine of natural history." viii, 272 pp. 1 pl. 8°. *Cambridge, Macmillan & Co.* 1854. s.

McCrie (Thomas). Istoria del progresso e dell' estinzione della riforma in Italia nel secolo sedicesimo; tradotta dall' Inglese. vii, 432 pp. 8°. *Parigi, Baudry,* 1835. s.

Macculloch (John, *M.D.*) System of geology, with a theory of the earth, and an explanation of its connexion with the sacred records. 2 v. 512 pp; 483 pp. 8°. *London, Longmans,* 1831.

McCulloch (John Ramsay). A dictionary, practical, theoretical, and historical, of commerce and commercial navigation, with supplement. New ed. xvi, 1269, 118 pp. 1 map. 8°. *London, Longmans,* 1838.

——— The same. New ed. xxiv, 1510 pp. 7 maps. 8°. *London, Longmans,* 1852.

——— A dictionary, geographical, statistical, and historical. New ed. revised by Frederick Martin. v. 4. 8°. *London, Longmans,* 1866.
[Completing the work].

McCulloh (Richard S.) A manual containing tables to be used by the revenue officers of the U. S. with glass hydrometers indicating the per cents by volume of alcohol in spirituous liquors. 212 pp. 16°. [n. p.] *Treasury dept. U. S.* 1849. s.

——— The proceedings of the late director of the mint, in relation to the official misconduct of Franklin Peale, esq. chief coiner, and other abuses in the mint. 79 pp. 8°. *Princeton, (N. J.) author,* 1853. s.

——— Report of scientific investigations relative to the chemical nature of saccharine substances, and the art of manufacturing sugar. [Senate doc.] 212 pp. 7 pl. 8°. *Washington, Government print.* 1847.

——— Report of the computation of tables, to be used with the hydrometer recently adopted for use in the U. S. custom-houses. 168 pp. 6 pl. 8°. *Washington, Gov. print.* 1851.

McCurdy (D.) The new American order of arithmetic. 260 pp. 16°. *Baltimore, Armstrong & Berry,* 1850.

M'Dermot (M.) A new and impartial history of Ireland, from the earliest accounts to the present time. 4 v. 8°. *London, J. M'Gowan,* 1820–23.

Macdiarmid (John). An inquiry into the system of national defence in Great Britain. 2 v. x, 448 pp; vi, 483 pp. 8°. *London, C. & R. Baldwin,* 1805.

Macé (——). L'abbé en belle humeur. Nouvelle galante. [*anon.*] 234 pp. 32°. *Cologne, Pierre Marteau,* 1705.

Macé (Jean). History of a mouthful of bread; and its effect on the organization of men and animals. Translated from the 8th French ed. by Mrs. Alfred Gatty. 1st Amer. ed. 398 pp. 12°. *New York, Am. news co.* 1866.

——— Home fairy tales. Translated by Mary L. Booth. 304 pp. 14 pl. 12°. *New York, Harper & bros.* 1867.

Maceuen (Malcolm). A mosaic from Italy, and other poems. 69 pp. 12°. *Philadelphia, Mason & co.* 1867.

M'Ewen (*Rev.* William). The most remarkable types, figures, and allegories of the old testament. 336 pp. 16°. *Danbury, S. Nichols,* 1803.

Mac-Geoghegan (J.) The history of Ireland, ancient and modern. Translated from the French by P. O'Kelly. 622 pp. 1 pl. 8°. *Dublin, J. Duffy,* 1849.

McGill (John, *D. D.*) Our faith, the victory: or, a comprehensive view of the principal doctrines of the christian religion, [i. e. of the catholic church]. 493 pp. 12°. *Baltimore, Kelly & Piet,* 1865.

McGill (P. M. *C. E.*) The wrongs and rights of labor shown, and a remedy proposed. 112 pp. 8°. *Washington, Gibson bros.* 1857.

McGill university, Montreal. Calendar, 1862–66. Examination papers, 1861–65. 4 v. 8°. *Montreal, J. C. Becket,* 1862–66. s.
[1863 wanting.]

Macgowan (John). Infernal conference; or, dialogues of devils on the many vices which abound in the civil and religious world. 2 v. in 1. vii, 239 pp; 243 pp. 1 pl. 24°. *London, W. Baynes,* 1813.

Machiavelli (Niccolò). Tutte [sue] opere, divise in v. parti, et di nvovo con somma accvratezza ristampate. [Ed. dalla Testina]. 4°. [*n. p.*] 1550.

CONTENTS.

p. i. Historie fiorentine, 8 libri. 8, 351 pp.
p. ii. Il principe. La vita di Castrvccio Castracani. Il modo che tenne il duca Valentino per ammazzare Vitellozzo Vitelli, Oliverotto da Fermo, il signor Pagolo, et il dvca di Gravina. I ritratti della cose della Francia, et dell' Alamagna. 2, 116 pp.
p. iii. Discorsi sopra la prima deca di T. Livio. 3 libri. 14, 304 pp.
p. iv. I sette libri dell'arte della guerra. 168 pp.
p. v. L'asino d'oro, con tvtte l'altre sve operette. 170 pp.

——— The same. Opere. [Pubblicate da Antonio Conti]. 10 v. 8°. portrait. *Firenze, N. Conti,* 1818–21.

CONTENTS.

v. i–iii. Historie fiorentine.
v. iii. Frammenti historici; vita di Castruccio; discorsi sopra la prima deca di Tito Livio.
v. iv. Discorsi [continued]; il principe.
v. v. Sentenze diverse; discorso sulla riforma; sommario delle cose di Lucca; rittratti di Francia; ritratti dell' Alamagna; dell'arte della guerra; provvisioni per istituire milizie nazionali; visita fatta per fortificare Firenze, etc.
v. vi. Discorso sulla liugua; novella di Belfagor; descrizione della peste di Firenze, 1527; capitoli per una bizzarra compagnia; allocuzione fatta ad un magistrato, etc; discorso morale; commedie.
v. vii. Poesie; canti carnascialeschi.
v. viii–x. Legazioni, spedizioni, commissioni, etc.
v. x. Lettere familiari; la mente di un uomo di stato.

——— The same. Opere, scelte da Giuseppe Zirardini. 662 pp. 1 l. portrait. 8°. *Parigi, Baudry,* 1851.

CONTENTS.

Istorie fiorentine.
Il principe.
I discorsi sopra la prima deca di Tito Livio.
Vita di Castruccio.
Ritratti delle cose di Francia e di Alamagna.
Peste di Firenze.
Belfagor, novella.
Dialogo sulla lingua.
Mandragola, commedia.
Poesie.
Lettere familiari.
La mente di un uomo di stato.

——— De' discorsi politici, e militari libri tre, scritti da Amadio Nicollvcci. [*anagram*]. 6 p. l. 399 pp. 8°. *Venetia, Marco Ginammi,* 1630.

Machin (John). The laws of the moon's motion according to gravity. 71 pp. 8°. s.
[*With* NEWTON (*Sir* I.) Mathematical principles of natural philosophy. 2 v. ed. 1729].

Macilwain (George). Memoirs of John Abernethy. viii, 434 pp. 12°. *New York, Harpers,* 1853. s.

Macintosh (George). Biographical memoir of the late Charles Macintosh, F. R. S. [With fifty seven autographs]. xix, 188 pp. 10 pl. 8°. *Glasgow, Blackie & Co.* 1847.

McIntosh (John). The discovery of America by Christopher Columbus; and the origin of the North American Indians. 152 pp. 8°. *Toronto, W. J. Coates,* 1836. s.

——— The origin of the North American Indians; with a description of their manners and customs. 311 pp. 12°. *New York, Nafis & Cornish,* 1843.

McIntosh (R. M.) Tabor; or, the Richmond collection of sacred music. 296 pp. oblong 8°. *New York, F. J. Huntington & Co.* 1866.

McIntosh. *See* **Mackintosh.**

Macirone (Francesco). Interesting facts relating to the fall and death of Joachim Murat, king of Naples, the capitulation of Paris in 1815, and the second restoration of the Bourbons. 167 pp. 8°. *London, Ridgways,* 1817.

M'Iver (Colin). An essay concerning the unlawfulness of a man's marriage with his sister by affinity; with a review of the various acts of the Presbyterian church in America, touching this and similar connexions. 163 pp. 18°. *Philadelphia, H. Hooker,* 1842.

M'Jilton (*Rev.* J. N.) Poems. 360 pp. 12°. *Boston, Otis, Broaders & Co.* 1840.

Mack (Alexander). A short and plain view of the rights and ordinances of the house of God. Also [E. L. Gruber's] ground-searching questions answered. English translation, accompanied with the original German. 148 pp. 8°. *Columbiana, (Ohio),* 1860.
[*With* KURTZ (H.) The united brethren's encyclopædia].

Mackay (Charles). Memoirs of extraordinary popular delusions. 2 v. 384 pp; 384 pp. 12°. *Philadelphia, Lindsay & Blakiston,* 1851.

——— The same. Memoirs of commercial delusions: embracing historical sketches of the Mississippi scheme, and the South sea bubble. pp. 233–342. 12°. *New York,* 1845.
[*In* HUNT (Freeman). Library of commerce. v. 1.]

McKeever (Harriet B.) Eleanor's three birthdays. Illustrated by Schell. 295 pp. 4 pl. 16°. *Philadelphia, Porter & Coates,* [1867].

——— Lucy Forrester's triumph. Illustrated by Schell. 298 pp. 4 pl. 16°. *Philadelphia, Porter & Coates,* [1867].

——— Mary Leslie's trials. Illustrated by Schell. 301 pp. 4 pl. 16°. *Philadelphia, Porter & Coates,* [1867].

——— Sunshine; or, Kate Vinton. 2d ed. 372 pp. 16°. *Philadelphia, Lindsay & Blakiston,* 1859.

McKeevor (Thomas, *M. D.*) A voyage to Hudson's Bay during 1812. 2 p. l. 96 pp. 6 pl. 8°. *London, R. Phillips & Co.* 1819.

Mackenna (B. Vicuña). *See* **Vicuña Mackenna** (Benjamin).

Mackenzie (Alexander). Tableau historique et politique du commerce des pelleteries dans le Canada, depuis 1608 jusqu'à nos jours. Traduit de l'Anglais par J. Castéra. 310 pp. 8°. *Paris, Dentu,* 1807.

Mackenzie (Colin). Ten thousand receipts, in all the useful and domestic arts. New ed. revised to April, 1867. 496 pp. 8°. *Philadelphia, T. E. Zell & Co.* 1867.

Mackenzie (*Sir* George). A defence of the antiquity of the royal line of Scotland. With a true account when the Scots were govern'd by kings in the isle of Britain. 4 p. l. 204 pp. 16°. *London, R. Chiswell,* 1685.

Mackenzie (George, *M. D.*) The lives and characters of the most eminent writers of the Scots nation; with an abstract and catalogue of their works. 3 v. in 1. fol. *Edinburgh, James Watson,* 1708–22.

Mackenzie (Robert Shelton). Tressilian and his friends. 372 pp. 12°. *Philadelphia, J. B. Lippincott & Co.* 1859.

Mackenzie (William L.) Sketches of Canada and the United States. xxiv, 504 pp. 8°. *London, E. Wilson,* 1833.

McKerrell (John). A grammar of the Carnátaca language. vi, 196, 15 pp. 4°. *Madras, college press,* 1820. s.

Mackey (James L.) A grammar of the Benga language. 60 pp. 1 tab. 12°. *New York, mission house,* 1855. s.

Mackintosh (*Sir* James). Defence of the French revolution, [with the French constitution of 1791]. 175, 22 pp. 8°. *Philadelphia, William Young,* 1792.

Mackintosh. *See* **McIntosh.**

MacLauchlan (Henry). Memoir written during a survey of the eastern branch of the Watling street, in the county of Northumberland, from Bewclay to Berwick-upon-Tweed. 62 pp. 8°. *London, privately printed,* 1864. s.

McLeod (Alexander Charles). Acholic diseases; comprising jaundice, diarrhœa, dysentery, and cholera, with a dissertation on bile, the bilious function, and the action of cholalogues. xxviii, 230 pp. 12°. *London, Churchill & sons,* 1866.

McLeod (Donald). History of Wiskonsan; including a geological and topographical description of the territory, with a correct catalogue of all its plants. 310 pp. 1 map. 12°. *Buffalo, Steele's press,* 1846.

Macleod (*Rev.* Xavier Donald). Devotion to the blessed virgin Mary in North America, with a memoir of the author, by John B. Purcell. xxiii, 461 pp. portrait. 8°. *New York, Virtue & Yorston,* 1866.

Maclure (William). Essay on the formation of rocks. 32 pp. 8°. *Philadelphia, J. Wilbank,* 1838. s.

[*With* Maclure (W.) Observations on geology of the U. S. Ed. 1817].

——— Observations on the geology of the United States of America. 129 pp. 1 map. 1 pl. 8°. *Philadelphia, A. Small,* 1817. s.

——— Observations on the geology of the West India islands, from Barbadoes to Santa Cruz, inclusive. 17 pp. 8°. *New Harmony, Ind.* 1832. s.

[*With* Maclure (W.) Observations on the geology of the U. S. 1817].

MacMahon (Thomas O'Brien). The candor and good nature of Englishmen exemplified. xii, 292 pp. 8°. *London, Bew,* 1777.

MacMahon (T. W.) Cause and contrast: an essay on the American crisis. xv, 190 pp. 8°. *Richmond, (Va.) West & Johnston,* 1862.

[Imperfect: wanting all after p. 190].

Macmichael (William). Journey from Moscow to Constantinople, 1817–18. vi, 269 pp. 5 pl. 4°. *London, J. Murray,* 1819.

Macmillan's magazine. Edited by D. Masson. Nov. 1865 to Oct. 1867. v. 13–16. 8°. *London and Cambridge, Macmillan & Co.* 1866–67.

Macnamara (*Capt.* M. H.) The Irish ninth in bivouac and battle; or, Virginia and Maryland campaigns. 306 pp. 12°. *Boston, Lee & Shepard,* 1867.

Mac Namee (Gilla Brighde). *See* **Mac Conmidhe.**

M'Nemar (Richard). The Kentucky revival; with a brief account of the entrance and progress of shakerism in Ohio and Kentucky. New ed. 118 pp. 16°. *Albany, E. & E. Hosford,* 1808.

Macoy (Robert). A cyclopedia of freemasonry; embracing Oliver's dictionary of symbolical masonry. Edited by Robert Macoy. Illustrated. 556 pp. portrait. 12°. *New York, Masonic pub. co.* 1867.

——— The same. 2d ed. 628 pp. portrait. 12°. *New York, Masonic pub. co.* 1867.

McPherson (Edward). Political manual for 1866 and 1867, of executive, legislative, judicial, politico-military, and general facts, from Apr. 15, 1865, to Apr. 1, 1867, and including the development of the presidential and congressional plan of reconstruction. iv, 262 pp. 8°. *Washington,* [*author*], 1867.

——— The same, for 1867, including a classified summary of facts from July 4, 1866, to Apr. 1, 1867, including the action of congress on reconstruction. 135 pp. 8°. *Washington, Philp & Solomons,* 1867.

Macpherson (James). *See* **Ossian.**

Macquart (J.) Facultés intérieures des animaux invertébrés. lxxxii, 272 pp. 8°. *Lille, L. Danel,* 1850. s.

Macquer (Joseph). Elements of the theory and practice of chymistry. Translated from the French [by Andrew Reid]. 3d ed. 2 v. xix, 416 pp, 6 pl; viii, 432 pp. 8°. *London, J. Nourse,* 1775. s.

Macquereau *or* Macqueriau (Robert). Histoire générale de l'Europe depuis la naissance de Charles-Quint jusqu 'au cinq juin mdxxvii. [Publiée avec des notes par l'abbe Jean Noel Paquot]. xvi, 346 pp. 4°. *Louvain, Imprimerie acad.* 1765. s.

——— The same. [Partie 2d.] Durant les années 1527-1529. [Par J. Barrois]. xlii, 366 pp. 4°. *Paris, Techener,* 1831. s.

MacRae (*Lieut.* Archibald, *U. S. N.*) The Andes and Pampas.

[*With* GILLISS (J. M.) U. S. astron. exped. v. 2.]

M'Sherry (Richard, *M. D.*) El Puchero; or, a mixed dish from Mexico, embracing General Scott's campaign, with sketches of military life. 247 pp. 12°. *Philadelphia, Lippincott,* 1850.

M'Ure *alias* **Campbel** (John). A view of the city of Glasgow; or, an account of its origin, rise and progress. 8 p. l. 381 pp. 16°. *Glasgow, James Duncan,* 1736.

[Imperfect: 5 pl. wanting].

Mac Walter (J. G.) The modern mystery; or, table rapping; its history, philosophy, and general attributes. viii, 175 pp. 12°. *London, J. F. Shaw,* 1854.

Madame Fontenoy. By the author of Mademoiselle Mori. [*anon.*] 224 pp. 16°. *London, J. & C. Mozley,* 1864.

Madden (*Sir* Frederick). Privy purse expenses of the princess Mary, with a memoir. ccv, 285 pp. 8°. *London, W. Pickering,* 1831.

Madden (Frederick W.) History of Jewish coinage, and of money in the Old and New Testament. xii, xi, 350 pp. 1 pl. 8°. *London, B. Quaritch,* 1864.

Madden (Samuel, *D. D.*) The reign of George vi. xxi, 192 pp. 16°. *London, W. Nicoll,* 1763.

Madison (James). Letters of Helvidius. *See* **Hamilton** (A.) *and* **Madison** (J.)

Madison (*Indiana*) library association. Catalogue of the books. 106 pp. 8°. *Madison, (Ind.) Courier office,* 1856. s.

Madison (*Wisconsin*) directory, and business advertiser. By Wm. N. Seymour. 1st annual ed. 192 pp. 18°. *Madison, W. N. Seymour,* 1855. s.

——— The same for 1866, compiled by B. W. Suckow, with a history of Madison by J. Y. Smith. 175 pp. 2 maps. 12°. *Madison, B. W. Suckow,* 1866.

Mädler (Johann Heinrich). Der mond, etc. *See* **Beer** (W.) *and* **Mädler.**

Madrid. Repertorio general; ó indice alfabético de los principales habitantes de Madrid. vi, 264 pp. 8°. *Madrid, J. M. Alegria,* 1851.

Maercker. *See* **Märcker.**

Maffei (Giovanni Pietro). Historiarvm indicarvm libri xvi. Selectarvm, item, ex India epistolarum, eodem interprete, libri iv. Accessit Ignatii Loyolae vita. 2 p. l. 541 pp. 18 l. 1 map. fol. *Coloniae Agrippinae, Arnold Mylius,* 1593.

Maffei (Scipione dè). A comparison of the use of inscriptions and medals.

[*With* LENGLET Du Fresnoy (N.) New method of studying history. v. 1. pp. 323-360. 12°. *London,* 1728.]

Maffitt (*Rev.* John Newland). A voice from the ocean, sermon, delivered July 31, 1842, to the memory of Rev. George G. Cookman. 31 pp. 8°. *Washington, Peter Force,* 1842.

Maga excursion papers. 304 pp. 16°. *New York, G. P. Putnam & son,* 1867.

[Reprinted from Putnam's monthly].

Maga social papers. 296 pp. 16°. *New York, G. P. Putnam & son,* 1867.

[Reprinted from Putnam's monthly].

Maga stories. 325 pp. 16°. *New York, G. P. Putnam & son.*

[Reprinted from Putnam's monthly.]

Magdeleine de Saint-Agy. *See* CUVIER (G. L. C. D.) Histoire des sciences naturelles.

Magician (The), and "the holy alliance," or "the spirit of the book." Melodrama. 28 pp. [*anon.*] 16°. *Philadelphia*, 1820.

Magini (Giovanni Antonio). Commentarii in Ptolemæum. *See* **Ptolemæus** (Claudius). Geographia universa. *Arnhemii*, 1597.

——— Novæ coelestivm orbivm theoricæ congruentes cum obseruationibus N. Copernici. 17 p. l. 314 pp. 12°. *Mogvntiaci, J. Albinvs*, 1608.

Maglathlin (Henry B.) New practical arithmetic. Prepared to accompany the mathematical series of Greenleaf. 12°. *Boston, R. S. Davis & Co.* 1866.

——— The same. 324 pp. 12°. *Boston, R. S. Davis & Co.* 1867.

Magnan (Dominique). La ville de Rome; ou, description abrégée de cette superbe ville, ornée de 425 planches en taille douce. 4 v. fol. *Rome, Casaletti, Venan, etc.* 1778.

Magnusen (Finn). *See* **Edda**. Den ældre edda, etc. 1821–23.

Mahabaráta. Sâvitri; épisode du Mahabaráta. Traduit de Sanskrit par G. Pauthier. 53 pp. 12°. *Paris*, 1841.

[Included in PLÉIADE (La).]

Mahan (Dennis H.) Elementary course of military engineering. Part ii, permanent fortifications. 8°. *New York, Wiley*, 1867.

Mahon (*lord*). *See* **Stanhope** (Philip Henry, 5*th earl*).

Mahoney (James W.) The Cherokee physician; or, Indian guide to health, as given by Richard Foreman, a Cherokee doctor. 3d ed. 304 pp. 12°. *New York, J. M. Edney*, 1857. s.

Mai (Emanuel). Catalog des bücher-lagers. v. 1. xiii, 430 pp. 8°. *Berlin, C. Schultze*, 1854. s.

Maillard (Olivier). Histoire de la passion de Jésus-Christ, composée en 1490, publiée en 1828, comme monument de la langue française au xve siècle. Avec une notice sur l'auteur, des notes, etc. par G. Peignot. 2e éd. xxiv, 119 pp. sm. fol. *Paris, Crapelet*, 1835.

Maimbourg (Louis). Libri tres de historia Lutheranismi, 1517–46. *See* **Seckendorf** (Veit Ludewig von.) Commentarius de Lutheranismo, *Francofurti*, 1692.

Mainardi (Gaspare). Lezione di introduzione al calcolo sublime. 2 v. vi, 208 pp; 173 pp. 1 pl. 8°. *Paris, Bizzoni*, 1836–39. s.

Maine. Act to provide for the education of youth. 52 pp. 12°. *Augusta, W. T. Johnson*, 1851.

Maine. Catalogue of state library, 1850. With appendix, 1854. 248, 47 pp. 8°. *Augusta, W. T. Johnson*, 1850–54. s.

——— Documents published by order of the legislature, 1867. 2 v. 8°. *Augusta, Stevens & Sayward*, 1867.

——— Eleventh annual report of the secretary of the board of agriculture, 1866. 8°. *Augusta, Stevens & Sayward*, 1866.

——— Fifth report of the board of education, 1851. 170 pp. 12 pl. 12°. *Augusta, W. T. Johnson*, 1851.

[*With* the preceding].

——— Fourth annual report of the superintendant of common schools, 1857. 143 pp. 8 pl. 8°. *Augusta, Stevens & Sayward*, 1858.

——— Laws relating to public schools. Compiled by E. Flint, sec. of state. vii, 64 pp. 16°. *Augusta, Stevens & Sayward*, 1867.

——— Report of the adjutant general, for 1864–65. 8°. *Augusta, Stevens & Sayward*, 1866. s.

Mair (John). Book-keeping methodized. With appendix. 3d ed. xiv, 288 pp. 12°. *Edinburgh, W. Sands and others*, 1749.

——— The same. 5th ed. xiv, 416 pp. 8°. *Edinburgh, W. Sands and others*, 1757.

——— An introduction to Latin syntax, with an epitome of ancient history. 311 pp. 16°. *Baltimore, S. & W. Meeter*, 1824.

——— The same. Revised by A. R. Carson. With exercises by David Patterson. viii, 248 pp. 16°. *New York, Collins & Hannay*, 1828.

Mairobert (Pidansat de). *See* **Pidansat de Mairobert** (M. F.)

Maissin (Eugène). Mexique et Texas. *See* **Blanchard** (P.) San Juan de Ullùa. *Paris*, 1839.

Maistre d'Anstaing. *See* **Le Maistre d'Anstaing**.

Maitland (Robert T.) Systematische beschrijving der dieren, welke in Noord Nederland of aan deszelfs kusten voorkomen, etc. xxxviii, 234 pp. 8°. *Leyden, Vander Hoek*, 1851. s.

Maitland (William). The history of London, from its foundation to the present time. [1737. 1st ed.] 8 p. l. 800 pp. 5 l. 17 pl. fol. *London, S. Richardson*, 1739.

Maittaire (Michael). Annales typographici. 6 v. in 9. 4°. *Hagæ-Comitum, etc. Vaillant, etc.* 1719–41. s.

CONTENTS.

v. 1. Annales typographici ab artis inventæ origine ad annum 1500. 6 p. l. 388 pp. 1 pl. *Hagæ-Comitum, J. Vaillant*, 1719.

v. 2. Annales typographici ab anno 1500 ad annum 1536 continuati. 1 v. in 2. 4 p. l. viii, iv, 860

Maittaire (Michael). Annales typographici.—*Continued.*

pp. 2 pl. *Hagæ-Comitum, Vaillant & N. Prevost,* 1722.

v. 3. Annales typographici ab anno 1536 ad annum 1557 continuati; cum appendice. 5 p. l. 925 pp. *Hagæ-Comitum, Vaillant & N. Prevost,* 1725.

v. 4. Annales typographici ab artis inventæ origine ad annum 1664. Ed. nova. xiv, 791 pp. 1 l. *Amstelodami, P. Humbert,* 1733.

v. 5. Annalium typographicorum tomus v et ultimus; indicem in tomos præeuntes complectens. (A–K.) viii, 536 pp. *Londini, W. Darres & C. Du Bosc,* 1741.

v. 6–7. Supplementum. 1 v. in 2. *See* DENIS (M.)

Major (Thomas). Ruins of Paestum, otherwise Posidonia, in Magna Græcia. 45 pp. 24 pl. fol. *London, T. Major,* 1768.

Makkari (Al). *See* **Ahmed Ibn Mohammed.**

Mako de Kerek-Gede (Palko). Compendiaria matheseos institvtio in vsvm avditorvm philosophiae. Editio altera, emendata. 377 pp. 9 pl. 12°. *Vindobonae, J. T. de Trattner,* 1766.

——— Compendiaria physicae institvtio in vsvm avditorvm philosophiae. Editio altera emendata. 2 parts. 10 p. l. 348 pp; 2 p. l. 419 pp. 1 l. 17 pl. 12°. *Vindobonae, J. T. de Trattner,* 1766.

Malaguti (François). Leçons de chemie agricole, 1847. iv, 456 pp. 1 tab. 12°. *Rennes, Verdier,* 1848. s.

Malan (*Rev.* Cæsar Henri Abraham). The Swiss peasant. [In Cherokee]. Asuwisi ageyo. [With] The one thing needful. Sudalegi udulvdiyu. [*anon.*] 24 pp. 24°. *Park Hill, mission press,* 1848.

Malcolme (*Rev.* David). An essay on the antiquities of Great Britain and Ireland. [With] an attempt to show an affinity betwixt the languages, etc. of the ancient Britons and the Americans of the isthmus of Darien. 256 pp. 12°. *Edinburgh, T. & W. Ruddimans,* 1738.

Malespine (A.) Les États-Unis en 1865, d'après les documents officiels communiqués au congrès. 48 pp. 8°. *Paris, E. Dentu,* 1865.

Malham (*Rev.* John). Naval gazetteer; or, seaman's complete guide. 1st Am. ed. 2 v. xlvi, 436 pp; 573 pp. 17 maps. 8°. *Boston, W. Spotswood & J. Nancrede,* 1797.

Malherbe (François de). Le bouquet de fleurs de Sénèque.

[*With* LA RUE (G. de). Essais hist. sur. les bardes, etc. v. 3. pp. 357–382].

Maling (E. A.) Song birds, and how to keep them. New ed. xii, 159 pp. 16°. *London, Smith, Elder & Co.* 1863.

Mallard (Harriet). Thoughts of heaven. [In verse]. 48 pp. 16°. [*New York, Baker & Godwin,* 1867.]

Mallet (David). Poetical works. 8°. *Edinburgh,* 1794.

[Anderson's Brit. poets, v. 9.]

Mallet (Paul Henri). Histoire de la maison et des états de Mecklenbourg. [Jusqu' à l'an 1503]. 2 v. in 1. 4 p. l. 292 pp. 4°. *Suerin, G. Baerensprvng,* 1796. s.

——— Northern antiquities; or, a description of the manners, customs, religion, and laws of the ancient Danes and other northern nations, with a translation of the Edda [of Snorro Sturleson]. Translated, with Goranson's Latin version of the Edda. 2 v. 5 p. l. lvi, 415 pp; 3 p. l. xxxix, 356 pp. 8°. *London, T. Carman & Co.* 1770.

Mallet du Pan (Jacques). Considerations on the nature of the French revolution, and on the causes which prolong its duration. Translated from the French. 4 p. l. 114 pp. 8°. *London, J. Owen,* 1793.

[*With* BRISSOT DE WARVILLE (J. P.) Address to his constituents. 8°. *London,* 1794].

Malmesbury (William *of*). De antiquitate glastoniensis ecclesiæ. fol. *Oxoniæ,* 1691.

[GALE (Thomas), and FELL, (John). Rerum anglicarum scriptores veteres. *Oxoniæ,* 1684–91. v. 3].

——— Liber V. de pontificiis. fol. *Oxoniæ,* 1691.

[GALE (Thomas), and FELL, (John.) Rerum anglicarum scriptores veteres. *Oxoniæ,* 1864–91. v. 3].

Malo (Amand). Éléments de comptabilité rurale, théorique et pratique. vii, 164 pp. 16°. *Paris, L. Hachette,* 1841. s.

Malo (Charles, *editor*). Livre d'amour, ou folastreries du vieux temps. [Choix de lays, balades, etc. des xi—xve siècles. *anon.*] 188 pp. 3 pl. 8°. *Paris, L. Janet,* [1821.]

Malone (Edmond). Catalogue of early English poetry. *See* **Bodleian** library.

Maltby (Isaac). The elements of war. xxiv, 208 pp. 18 pl. 16°. *Boston, Wait & Co.* 1811.

Malte-Brun (Malthe Conrad Bruun, *called*). A system of universal geography: or, a description of the world, on a new plan, according to the great natural divisions of the globe, with analytical, synoptical, and elementary tables. With additions and corrections by James G. Percival, [and memoir of the author by J. J. N. Huot]. 3 v. 8°. *Boston, S. Walker,* 1834.

——— The same. v. 1–3. 8°. *Philadelphia, A. Finley,* 1827.

[Wanting, v. 4–5.]

Malte Brun (Victor Adolphe), **Eyriès** (Jean B. B.) **Klaproth** (Henri J. de), *and others*).

Nouvelles annales des voyages, de la géographie, et de l'histoire. Année 1865. 4 v. 5 maps. 8°. *Paris, A. Bertrand,* [1865–66].

——— Annales des voyages, de la géographie, de l'histoire, et de l'archéologie. Année 1866. 4 v. 7 maps. 8°. *Paris, Challamel,* 1867.

Malton (William D.) Company and battalion drill illustrated. 4th ed. xv, 242 pp. 60 pl. 8°. *London, Clowes & sons,* 1860.

Maly (Joseph Carl). Nachträge, zu Maly's enumeratio plantarum phaneragamicarum imperii austriaci, etc. *See* **Neilreich** (August).

Mammatt (Edward). A collection of geological facts and practical observations, intended to elucidate the formation of the Ashby coalfield, etc. xii, 101 pp. 1 map. 133 pl. 4°. *Ashby-de-la-Zouch, W. Hextall,* 1836. s.

Man and the conditions that surround him; his progress and decline, past and present. [*anon.*] 365 pp. 12°. *New York, G. W. Carleton & Co.* 1867.

Manassi (Niccolò). Oracoli politici; cioè sentenze, et docvmenti nobili, et illustri raccolti da tutti gli antichi, e principali auttori hebrei, greci, et latini. Co i fiori de gli apoftemmi di Plutarco. 4 p. l. 92 pp. 16°. *Venetia, Aldo,* 1590.

Manby (George William). Essay on the preservation of shipwrecked persons. 94 pp. 8°. *London, Longmans,* 1812. s.

Manchester (*England*) free library. Catalogue of the books. Reference department. Prepared by A. Crestadoro. vii, 975 pp. 8°. *London, S. Low, son, & Marston,* 1864. s.

Manchester (*New Hampshire*) directory, etc. With an almanac for 1860. No. vi. By Adams, Sampson & Co. 192 pp. 16°. *Manchester, (N. H.) Fisk & Stearns,* 1860. s.

Mandeville (H. *D. D.*) An introduction to the author's "Course of reading," etc. 212 pp. 12°. *New York, D. Appleton & Co.* 1848. s.

Mañèr (Salvador Joseph). Defensa de la dissertacion critico-historica sobre el juicio universal, contra la impugnacion de un docto anonimo. 30 p. l. 168 pp. 4°. *Madrid, Imprenta del reyno,* [1742?] s.

Manesca (L.) The French reader, etc. to which is added a table of the French verbs, etc. 286, 26 pp. 12°. *Philadelphia, Thomas, Cowperthwait & Co.* 1851. s.

Mangin (Edward). The parlor window; or, anecdotes, original remarks on books, etc. vi, 179 pp. 18°. *London, E. Lumley,* 1841.

Mangles (James). Papers and despatches relating to the Arctic searching expeditions of 1850–52. With maps. 2d ed. 8°. *London,* 1852. s.

——— Travels in Egypt, etc. *See* **Irby** (C. L.), *and* **Mangles**.

Manilius (Marcus). Astronomicon libri v. 165 pp. 2 l. 24°. *Lvgduni, J. Tormaesius & G. Gazeius,* 1551.

——— The same, [book first]. The sphere, made an English poem; with annotations and an astronomical appendix. By Edward Sherburne. 8 p. l. 221 pp. 3 l. 4 pl. fol. *London, N. Brooke,* 1675.

——— The same. The five books, containing a system of the ancient astronomy and astrology; together with the philosophy of the stoicks. Done into English verse, [by Thomas Creech]. With notes. 68, 134, 88 pp. 4 l. 6 pl. 12°. *London, J. Tonson,* 1697.

Manley de La Riviere (*Mrs.* N.?) The adventures of Rivella; or the history of the author of the Atalantis. By Sir Charles Lovemore. [*pseudon.*] Done into English from the French. iv, 120 pp. 12°. *London,* 1714.

——— Memoirs of Europe, towards the close of the eighth century, written by Eginardus, secretary and favourite to Charlemagne. [*pseudon.*] 8 p. l. 380 pp. 8°. *London, J. Morphew,* 1710.

——— Secret memoirs and manners of several persons of quality of both sexes. From the new Atalantis. [*anon.*] 2d ed. 2 v. vi, 264 pp. 1 pl; 6 p. l. 272 pp. 1 pl. 8°. *London, J. Morphew,* 1709.

Mann (A. Dudley). Letter to the citizens of the slave-holding states, in relation to a weekly Atlantic ferry line between Chesapeake Bay and Milford Haven. 30 pp. 16°. *London, J. Miller,* 1856.

Mann (Horace). Life and works. Edited by Mrs. Mary Mann. v. 1–3. 8°. *Boston and Cambridge, H. B. Fuller, and editor,* 1865-68.

CONTENTS.

v. 1. Life, by Mrs. Mary Mann. 602 pp.
v. 2. Lectures, and annual reports, on education. xii, 571 pp.
v. 3. Annual reports on education. xii, 758 pp.

Mann (Nicholas). Of the true years of the birth and of the death of Christ. 10 p. l. 212 pp. 8°. *London, J. Wilcox,* 1733.

Mann's black book of the British aristocracy. 72 pp. 18°. *Philadelphia, H. Hooker,* 1848.

Manne (Louis Charles Joseph de). Catalogue des livres de feu M. de Manne suivi de manuscrits, lettres autographes, et autres documents provenant du cabinet de M. d'Anville. viii, 264 pp. 8°. *Paris, François,* 1863. s.

Mannering (May. *pseudon?*). Climbing the rope; or, "God helps those who try to help themselves." 224 pp. 4 pl. 16°. *Boston, Lee & Shepard*, 1868.

Mannert (Conrad). Géographie ancienne des états barbaresques, d'après l'Allemand par L. Marcus et Duesberg. xxxvi, 803 pp. 8°. *Paris, Roret*, 1842. S.

——— Geschichte der unmittelbaren nachfolger Alexanders des grossen. xvi, 384 pp. 8°. *Leipzig, Dyk*, 1787. S.

Manneville (William). English grammar simplified. xvi pp. 18°. *London, Simpkin, Marshall & Co.* 1850. S.

Manni (Domenico Maria). Istoria del decamerone di Giovanni Boccaccio. xxx, 672 pp. 2 pl. 4°. *Firenze*, 1742.

Manning (Robert). England's conversion and reformation compared. [*anon.*] 1st Am. from 5th Dublin ed. 314 pp. 10 l. 16°. *Lancaster, (Pa.) George Daly*, 1813.

——— The same; or, the young gentleman directed in the choice of his religion. [With] a brief enquiry into the general grounds of the catholick faith. Divided into four dialogues. [*anon.*] lv, 330 pp. 16°. *Antwerp, R. C. and C. F.* 1725.

Mansfield (Joseph). Hope: a poem delivered in the chapel of Harvard university at a public exhibition. 15 pp. sm. 4°. *Cambridge, (Mass.) W. Hilliard*, 1800.

Mansfield (Robert Blachford). The log of the Water Lily, 1851–52, on the Rhine, Neckar, Main, Moselle, Danube, etc. iv, 124 pp. 8 pl. 16°. *London, N. Cooke*, 1854.

Manstein (Christoph Hermann von). Contemporary memoirs of Russia, from 1727 to 1744. First edited in English by David Hume, and now re-edited by a Hertfordshire incumbent. xv, 416 pp. 8°. *London, Longmans*, 1856.

Mant (Richard, *bishop of Down and Connor*). Feriae anniversariae. Observance of the church's holy-days no symptom of popery; shown from the testimony of her most approved children, 1547—1800. vol. 1, the feasts; vol. 2, the fasts. 2 v. xi, 256 pp; xvi, 315 pp. 18°. *London, J. W. Parker*, 1847.

Mantia (Orazio Gianutio della), *and* **Brunswick**-Lüneburg (August, *herzog* von). Works of Gianutio and Gustavus Selenus on the game of chess. [*pseudon.*] Translated and arranged by J. H. Sarratt. 2 v. xxi, 233 pp; 240 pp. 12°. *London, J. Ebers*, 1817.

Manual exercise, as ordered by his majesty in 1764. 35 pp. 12°. *Philadelphia, Humphreys, Bell, and Aitken*, 1776.

[*With* Simes (Thomas). New military dictionary. Ed. 1776.]

Manual (A) of flax culture and manufacture. 48 pp. 8°. *Rochester, D. D. T. Moore*, 1863. S.

CONTENTS.

Bragdon (Charles D.) Hemp and flax in the west.
Brooks (Hugh T.) Flax as a domestic institution.
Dewey (Chester). Botanical descriptions of flax and hemp.
Goodsell (N.) Flax culture and manufacture in the United States and Great Britain.
Newcomb (William). Practical essay on flax culture.
New York State agricultural society (Committee of). Report on flax and machinery for making flax-cotton.
Phin (John). The structure of textile fibres.
Williams (Samuel). Flax growing in Seneca county, N. Y.

Manual (The) of rank and nobility; or, key to the [British] peerage. [*anon.*] xx, 598 pp. 1 pl. 8°. *London, Saunders & Otley*, 1828.

Manual (A) prepared for the use of a private school. [*anon.*] Printed—not published. 2 pl. 152 pp. 12°. *Boston, J. Munroe & Co.* 1855. S.

Manuzio (Paolo), *and* **Ragazzoni** (Girolamo). Commentarivs Pauli Manucii in M. Tvllii Ciceronis epistolas, etc. Accedvnt scholia ejvsdem et Hieronymi Ragazonii in easdem Ciceronis epistolas commentarivs. Cvravit Christ. Gottl. Richtervs. 2 v. vi, 606 pp; xxx, 609—1,048 pp. 68 l. 8°. *Lipsiae, S. L. Crvsivs*, 1780.

Manwaring (Christopher). Essays, historical, moral, political, and agricultural. 204 pp. 12°. *New London, Samuel Green*, 1828.

Marat (Jean Paul). A philosophical essay on man. Being an attempt to investigate the principles and laws of the reciprocal influence of the soul on the body. [*anon.*] 2d ed. 2 v. in 1. 271 pp; 263 pp. 8°. *London, H. Setchel*, 1775.

Marbach (Gotthard Oswald). Enkyklopädie der experimental-physik, der astronomie, geographie, chemie, physiologie, chronologie, nach dem grade ihrer verwandtschaft mit der physik. 5 v. in 4. 8°. *Leipzig, O. Wigand*, 1834–38. S.

Marban (Pedro). Arte de la lengva moxa, con su vocabulario, y cathecismo. 7 p. l. 664, 142 pp. 12°. *Lima, Joseph de Contreras*, 1701. S.

Marcellus (Marie Louis Jean André Charles Demartin du Tirac, *comte* de). Vingt jours en Sicile. xiv, 441 pp. 8°. *Paris, Debécourt*, 1841. S.

——— Souvenirs de l'Orient. 2 v. viii, 464 pp; 556 pp. 2 l. 1 map. 2 pl. 8°. *Paris, Debécourt*, 1839. S.

Marcet (Jane Haldimand). Conversations on chemistry. Revised by Thomas Cooper from the 5th London ed. 2 v. 264 pp; viii, 264 pp. *Philadelphia, M. Carey,* 1818. s.

Marcgraf de Liebstad (Georg). Historiæ rervm naturalivm Brasiliæ libri viii. s.

[*With* PISO (W.) and MARCGRAF. Historia natvralis Brasiliae, 1648].

March (Charles W.) Reminiscences of congress. 2d ed. viii, 295 pp. 1 portrait. 12°. *New York, Baker & Scribner,* 1850. s.

March (Walter, *pseudon.*) *See* **Shoepac** recollections.

Marchesini (Giovanni). Mammetractus. [Sive, mammothreptus. Expositio in singulos libros bibliorum]. Omnium scriptorum veterum vsque in nos celebris est et nota traductio, etc. 151 l. unp. fol. *Argentorati,* [*about* 1500]. s.

Marchetti (Pietro de'.) Observationum medico-chirurgicarum rariorum sylloge. 112 pp. 24°. *Amstelodami, P. Le Grand,* 1665. s.

Märcker (Traugott). Monumenta zollerana. *See* **Stillfried** (R. von) *and* **Märcker**.

Marcou (Jules). Le Niagara quinze ans après. Addition, etc. [Extracts.] 15 pp. 1 pl. 8°. *Paris, Soc. géol. etc.* 1865. s.

——— Une reconnaissance géologique au Nebraska. [Extract.] 16 pp. 8°. *Paris, Soc. géol. etc.* 1864. s.

——— Notice sur les gisements des lentilles trilobitifères taconiques de la Pointe Lévis, au Canada. [Extract.] 12 pp. 8°. *Paris, Soc. géol. etc.* 1864. s.

Marcusen (Johann, *M. D.*) Die familie der mormyren; eine anatomisch-zoologische abhandlung. 162 pp. 20 pl. 4°. *St. Pétersburg, Acad. imp. des sciences,* 1864. s.

Marcy (E. E.) Christianity and its conflicts, ancient and modern. xi, 480 pp. 12°. *New York, D. Appleton & Co.* 1867.

Mardochai (Isaac Nathan), *or* **Natan** (Isaak). Concordantiarvm hebraicarvm capita, quae sunt de vocum expositionibus. Translata per Antonium Reuchlinum. 10 p. l. 981 pp. fol. *Basiliæ, Henric-Petri,* 1556.

[*With* REUCHLIN (A.) Exegesis, etc.]

Maréchal (Pierre Sylvain). Pour et contre la Bible. xxxv, 404 pp. 8°. *Paris, Louis,* 1801.

Margan *or* Margam abbey. Annales de Margan, sive chronica abbreviata a tempore sancti Edwardi, regis ultimi de progenie Anglorum. [*anon.*] fol. *Oxoniæ,* 1687.

[GALE (Thomas), and FELL (John). Rerum anglicarum scriptores veteres. *Oxoniæ,* 1684–91. v. 2.]

Margaret Chester. [*anon.*] 316 pp. 2 pl. 16°. *Boston, Mass. S. S. soc.* 1867.

32

Margaret, the pearl of Navarre. [*anon.*] 239 pp. 16°. *New York, Am. tract soc.* 1867.

Mariana (Juan). Summarivm ad historiam Hispaniae, eorvm qvae accidervnt annis seqventibvs. 41 pp. 5 l. unp. 4°. *Mogvntiæ, D. ac D. Aubri & C. Schleich,* 1619.

[*With* AGUSTIN (A.) *and* URSINI (F.) De Romanorvm gentibvs. *Mogvntiæ,* 1619].

Marianini (Stefano). Memorie di fisica sperimentale. Anno I—IV, 1837–40. 4 v. 8°. *Modena, tipografia camerale,* 1838–41. s.

——— Saggio di esperienze elettrometriche. 206 pp. 8°. *Venezia, Alvisopoli,* 1825. s.

Marie de France. Lai des deux amants. Lai du Bisclaveret. [Mise en prose.] 21 pp. 12°. *Paris,* 1842.

[Included in PLÉIADE (La).]

Marie Antoinette de Lorraine (Josèphe Jeanne, *queen of France*). Correspondance secrète, avant et après le voyage de Varennes.

[*With* SOUVENIRS historiques, I, 1835].

Marieni (Luigi). Tavole di ragguaglio de' principali pesi medici dell'Europa. 8°. *Milano,* 1814. s.

[*With* SZERLECKI (L. A.) Dizionario di terapeutica].

Marignolli (Giovanni de'). Recollections of travels in the east. [India, 1838—53.] 83 pp.

[*With* YULE (Henry). Cathay, etc. v. 2.]

Marigny. *See* **Taitbout** de Marigny (E.)

Maritime capture. Shall England uphold the capture of private property at sea? By a lawyer. [*anon.*] 40 pp. 8°. *London, Trübner & Co.* 1866.

Maritime scraps; or, scenes in the frigate United States, during a cruise in the Mediterranean. By a man-of-war's-man. [*anon.*] 108 pp. 12°. *Boston,* 1838.

Markham (Clements Robert). Franklin's footsteps; a sketch of Greenland and of the Parry isles. vii, 143 pp. 1 map. 16°. *London, Chapman & Hall,* 1853.

Markham (*Mrs. pseudon.*) *See* **Penrose** (*Mrs.* E. C.)

Markham (William, *archbishop of York*). A sermon before the incorporated society for the propagation of the gospel in foreign parts, at their anniversary, 1777, with abstract of the proceedings of the society, 1776–7. 104 pp. sm. 4°. *London, T. Harrison,* 1777.

Markoe (Peter). The reconciliation; or, the triumph of nature; a comic opera. 48 pp. 12°. *Philadelphia, Richard & Hall,* 1790.

Marlow (Christopher), *and* **Chapman** (Geo.) Hero and Leander; a poem. A new ed. revised; with a critical preface, [by S. W. Singer]. lxvi pp. 2 pl. 124 pp. 16°. *Chiswick, C. Whittingham,* 1821.

Marly; or, the life of a planter in Jamaica. [*anon.*] 2d ed. 2 p. l. 364 pp. 8°. *Glasgow, Griffin & Co.* 1828.

Marmion (Shakerley). Cupid and Psyche. A [poetical] legend. [Edited by S. W. Singer.] xxxix, 105 pp. 16°. *Chiswick, C. Whittingham,* 1820.

Marmocchi (F. C.) Raccolta di viaggi dalla scoperta del nuovo continente fino a dì nostri. 19 v. 8°. *Prato, Giachetti,* 1840–47.
[Imperfect; wanting v. 19.]

CONTENTS.

v. 1–2. Navarrete, (M. F. de, *editor*). Narrazione dei quattro viaggi intrapresi da C. Colombo per la scoperta del nuovo continente. 1492–1504.
v. 3–4. Marcellus, (M. L. J. A. C. *visconte* di.) Rimembranze intorno all' Oriente.
v. 5. Xeres (F.) Relazione del conquisto del Perù e della provincia di Cuzco chiamata Nuova Castiglia; Viaggi di A. Vespucci; Viaggi di A. di Ojeda, trad. d' Inglese di W. Irving, da B. Poli; Viaggio di P. A. Niño e di C. Guerra; Viaggio di V. Yañes Pinzon; Viaggio di D. di Lepe e di R. di Bastides; Viaggio de D. Nicuesa, trad. d'Inglese di W. Irving, da B. Poli; Viaggi di Ponçe de Leon; Gomara (F. L. di). Viaggio di V. Nuñez di Balboa; Avventvre di Valdivio e dei suoi compagni, e destino dell'astrologo Micer Codro, trad. d'Inglese di W. Irving, da B. Poli; Viaggio del F. Magellano.
v. 6. Lafond di Lurcy (G.) Viaggio in Cina pell' Atlantico, il mare delle Indie, le isole della Sonda e le Filippine.
v. 7–9. Viaggi da Delhi a Lahora, Cabul, Buckara, ec. di Alessandro Burnes.
v. 10. Montesinos (F.) Memorie e tradizioni storiche dell antico Perù; Velasco (G. di.) Viaggi, relazioni e memorie relative al regno di Quito; Torozomoc (A. di.) Storia antiqua del Messico.
v. 11. Viaggi, lettere, relazioni e memorie relative alla scoperta ed alla conquista del Messico di F. Hernandez e G. di Grigialva, F. Cortes, Alva Ixtlilxochitl, B. Las Casas, F. da Bologna.
v. 12. Lafond di Lurcy (G.) Viaggio nell' America spagnuola in tempore delle guerre dell' independenza.
v. 13. Robinson (Giovanni). Viaggio in Siria e in Palestina.
v. 14. Lafond di Lurcy (G.) Viaggio nella Polinesia e nelle isole circonvicine dell' Australia.
v. 15. Burckhardt (J. L.) Viaggi in Arabia.
v. 16. Mitchell (*Sir* T. L.) Viaggi nell' interno dell' Australia o Nuova Olanda.
v. 17. Saint-Pierre (J. B. de) e Leguével (B. F.) Viaggi al Madagascar, alle isole Comore ed all' isola di Francia.
v. 18. Volney (C. F. C. de). Viaggio agli Stati Uniti dell' America Settentrionale; Chesney (F. R.) Viaggio nelle contrade di Mesopotamia, di Chaldea, e di Assiria; Hoskins [G. A]. Viaggio a Meroe e in Etiopia.

Marquart (John). United States key for mathematical self-instruction on the mechanical sliding rule, commonly called the carpenter's rule. 66 pp. 1 tab. 18°. *Philadelphia, C. Sherman,* 1850. s.

Marquette (Jacques), *and* Joliet (——). Voyage et découverte de quelques pays et nations de l'Amérique Septentrionale. 43 pp. 1 map. 16°. *Paris, Estienne Michallet,* 1681.

Marriott (William). A collection of English miracle plays, or mysteries, with a historical view of this description of plays. lxiii, 271 pp. 8°. *Basel, Schweighauser & Co.* 1838.

Marryat (Florence). *See* **Church** (*Mrs.* Ross).

Marsais (Du). *See* **Du Marsais.**

Marsden (William). A grammar of the Malayan language. lii, 225 pp. 4°. *London, Cox & Baylis,* 1812. s.

Marsden (William, *M. D.*) Symptoms and treatment of malignant diarrhœa, better known by the name of Asiatic or malignant cholera. 3d ed. 64 pp. 16°. *London, H. Renshaw,* 1865.

Marsh (George Perkins). Apology for the study of English. pp. 57–93. *N. Y.* 1859.
[*With* COLUMBIA COLLEGE inaugural addresses.]

Marshall (*Rev.* Charles). Sion's travellers comforted, and the disobedient warned. [With life of the author]. Compiled by W. Penn. 63 p. l. 332 pp. 16°. *London, T. Sowle,* 1704.

Marshall (John, *chief justice of the U. S.*) Het leven van George Washington, uit deszelfs oorspronglijke papieren onder toezigt van Bushrod Washington. Uit het Engelsch door J. Werninck. Met platen en kaarten. 10 v. in 6. 8°. *Haarlem, A. Loosjes,* 1805-09.

Marshall (Joseph). Travels through Holland, Flanders, Germany, Denmark, Sweden, Lapland, Russia, and Poland, in 1768–70. 2d ed. 3 v. 8°. *London, J. Almon,* 1773.

Marshall (Nathaniel). The penitential discipline of the primitive church for the first 400 years after Christ: [with] its declension from the fifth century downwards to its present state. [*anon.*] xiv, 255, 59 pp. 2 l. 8°. *London, W. Taylor,* 1714.

Marshall (Stephen). Copy of a letter in vindication of himself, and his ministry; with Lawfulnesse of the parliament's taking up arms demonstrated. 30 pp. sm. 4°. *London, Samuel Gellibrand,* 1643.

Marshall (*Rev.* Walter). The scriptural doctrines of justification, faith, and holiness: being the substance of [his] treatise on gospel sanctification. xi, 180 pp. 16°. *London, J. Buckland & S. Gardner,* 1766.
[*With* LIVING christianity. ed. *London,* 1766].

Marsigli (Luigi Ferdinando). Description du Danube, depuis la montagne de Kalenberg en Autriche, jusqu'au confluent de la rivière Jantra dans la Bulgarie. Traduite du Latin. 6 v. 283 pl. fol. *La Haye, J. Swart,* 1744. s.

—— Histoire physique de la mer. [Trad. par D. Le Clerc]. 4 pl. xi, 173 pp. 2 maps. 44 pl. fol. *Amsterdam,* 1725. s.

Marsters (Thomas). The poetical manual; or, British and classical anthology of past times. 2 v. xxiv, 460 pp; 622 pp. 16°. *Lynn, (Eng.) Newman & Co.* 1833.

Martainville (——). Moniteur secret; ou, chronique scandaleuse de la cour de Napoléon, de sa famille, et de ses agents. Nouv. éd. 2 v. in 1. iii, 216 pp; 220 pp. 8°. *Paris*, 1836.

Martenet (Simon J.) Map of Maryland. Atlas ed. 15 l. 22 maps. 4°. *Baltimore, author*, 1866.

Martens (Carl von). Geschichte der innerhalb der gegenwärtigen gränzen des königreichs Württemberg vogefallenen kriegerischen ereignisse A. C. 15–A. D. 1815. xvi, 845 pp. 8°. *Stuttgart, K. Hofbuchdruckerei*, 1847. s.

—— Le guide diplomatique. 5e éd. Entièrement refondue par M. F. H. Geffcken. 3 v. in 2. 8°. *Leipzig, F. A Brockhaus*, 1866.

Martialis (Marcus Valerius). [Epigrammata; cum] Nicolai Perotti cornucopia, sive commentariis linguæ latinæ. 48 p. l. 634 pp. 1 l. fol. *Mediolani, Nicolaus Gorgonzola*, 1507.

Martigny (——, *l'abbé*). Dictionnaire des antiquités chrétiennes, contenant le résumé de tout ce qu'il est essentiel de connaître sur les origines chrétiennes jusqu'au moyen âge exclusivement. 4 pl. viii, 676 pp. 8°. *Paris, Hachette*, 1865.

Martin (Benjamin). Philosophia britannica: or, a new and comprehensive system of the Newtonian philosophy, astronomy, and geography. 4th ed. 3 v. 8°. *London, Rivington* 1788. s.

—— New and compendious system of optics. xxiv, 295 pp. 34 pl. 8°. *London, J. Hodges*, 1740. s.

Martin (Bon Louis Henri). History of France to 1789. Translated by Mary L. Booth. v. 13, 14: Age of Louis xiv; xxii, 563 pp; viii, 543 pp. v. 15, 16: Decline of the monarchy; xvi, 546 pp; viii, 623 pp. 8°. *Boston, Walker, Fuller & Co.* 1865–66.

Martin (C. A. F.) Précis d'histoire naturelle. *See* **Gilbert** (J.) *and* **Martin** (C. A. F.)

Martin (David). Histoire de la bible, contenant le vieux et le nouveau testament. Enrichie de plus de 350 figures en taille-douce. 2 parts in 1 v. 4 p. l. 310 pp. 1 pl; 4 p. l. 198 pp. 1 pl. 4°. *Amsterdam, M. Schagen*, 1724. s.

Martin (Frederick). Commercial handbook of France. x, 394 pp. 3 maps. 12°. *London, Longmans*, 1867.

Martin (*Rev.* James). The angler's guide. xii, 191 pp. 1 pl. 16°. *London, G. Cox*, 1854.

Martin (James H.) The orthoëpist; containing a selection of all those words of the English language usually pronounced improperly, etc. 151 pp. 12°. *New York, A. S. Barnes & Co.* 1851. s.

Martin (Louis Aimé). *See* **Lettres** édifiantes. 4 v. éd. 8°. *Paris*, 1839–43.

Martin (Luther). The genuine information delivered to the legislature of the state of Maryland, relative to the proceedings of the general convention lately held at Philadelphia. viii, 93 pp. 16°. *Philadelphia, E. Oswald*, 1788.

Martin (Robert Montgomery). History of the British colonies. 5 v. 8°. *London, J. Cochrane & Co.* 1834.

Martin (W. C. Linnæus). A general introduction to the natural history of mammiferous animals, with a particular view of the physical history of man, and the more closely allied genera of the order quadrumana, or monkeys. Illustrated. 545 pp. 12 pl. 8°. *London, Wright & Co.* 1841. s.

—— *See* **Youatt** (William), *and* **Martin**. On cattle.

Martin de Nantes, (*le père.*) Relation succinte et sincère de la mission dans le Brézil, parmis les Indiens appelés Carivis. 8 p. l. 233 pp. 1 l. 24°. *Qvimper, Jean Perier*, [*about* 1706].

Martin. *See also* **Martyn.**

Martineau (Harriet). History of the peace; being a history of England from 1816 to 1864. With an introduction, 1800 to 1815. 4 v. 8°. *Boston, Walker, Fuller & Co.* 1865–66.

—— Household education. viii, 326 pp. 16°. *London, E. Moxon*, 1849.

Martineau (James). Endeavors after the christian life. Discourses. [1st and 2d series.] New ed. 551 pp. 12°. *Boston, J. Munroe & Co.* 1858.

—— Studies of christianity; timely thoughts for religious thinkers. Edited by W. R. Alger. xlix, 494 pp. 12°. *Boston, Am. unit. assoc.* 1866.

Martingale (Hawser. *pseudon.*) *See* **Sleeper** (Jacob S.)

Martini (Francesco). Trattato di architettura civile e militare. Con dissertazioni e [vita da C. Promis]. 2 v. xvi, 341 pp. 1 portrait; 356 pp. 4°. Atlas. fol. *Torino, Chirio e Mina*, 1841. s.

Martini (Lorenzo). Aemilivs; seu de vita instituenda. 2 v. 309 pp; 301 pp. 24°. *Taurini, P. Marietti*, 1824. s.

—— Elementi di polizia medica. 5 v. in 3. 8°. *Torino*, 1824–25. s.

Martins (Charles). Des climats de la France, et de leur influence sur son agriculture et le génie de ses habitants. [Extract.] 26 pp. 8°. *Paris, météorologique de la France,* 1850. s.

——— Mémoire sur les températures de la Mer Glaciale, à la surface, à de grandes profondeurs, et dans le voisinage des glaciers du Spitzberg. [Extrait.] 75 pp. 1 pl. 8°. *Paris, Arthus Bertrand,* 1848. s.

[GAIMARD'S voyage en Scandinavie, etc.]

Martire d'Anghiera (Pietro). De rebvs oceanicis et novo orbe, decades tres. Item eivsdem de babylonica legatione, libri iii. Et item de rebus æthiopicis, etc. liber Damiani a Goes. 24 p. l. 655 pp. 15 l. 16°. *Coloniæ, G. Calenius,* 1574.

——— The same. The decades [fyrst—thyrde] of the newe worlde of West India, conteynyng the nauigations and conquestes of the Spanyards, with the description of the landes and ilandes lately founde in the west ocean pertaynyng to Spayne. Translated by R. Eden. 2 p. l. 166 l. 12°. *Guil. Powell,* 1555.

——— The same. Decades of the ocean. 7–184 l.

[*In* EDEN (Rich.) History of trauayle. 12°. 1577.]

——— The same. The historie of the West Indies. Published in Latin by Hakluyt, and translated by Lok. [Eight decades.] 3 p. l. 318 l. 12°. *London, A. Hebb,* 1597.

——— Der newen weldt, etc. *Basel,* 1582. *See* **Benzoni** (Girolamo), *and* **Martire.**

——— De insulis nuper repertis. *See* **Novus** orbis. *Roterodami,* 1616.

Martire Vermigli (Pietro). *See* **Vermigli** (Pietro Martire).

Martius (Carl Friedrich Philipp von). Beiträge zur ethnographie und sprachenkunde Brasiliens. Wörtersammlung brasilianischer sprachen. xxi, 548 pp. 8°. *Erlangen, Junge,* 1863. s.

——— The same. 2 v. ix, 202 pp; xxi, 548 pp. 8°. *Leipzig, F. Fleischer,* 1867.

——— Catalogue de la bibliothèque américaine. 34 l. 4°. *Munich,* 1848.

——— Reise in Brasilien. *See* **Spix** (J. B.)

——— Syllabus praelectionum de botanica pharmaceutico-medica. 34 pp. 8°. *München, Verfasser,* 1852. s.

——— Systema materiae medicae vegetabilis brasiliensis. xxvi, 155 pp. 8°. *Lipsiae, F. Fleischer,* 1843. s.

——— Wegweiser für die besucher des k. botanischen gartens in München. vi, 169 pp. 1 pl. 16°. *München, C. Kaiser,* 1852. s.

Martius (Ernst Wilhelm). Erinnerungen aus meinem neunzig-jahrigen leben. xvi, 328 pp. 8°. *Leipzig, L. Voss,* 1847. s.

Martyn (Benjamin). Reasons for establishing the colony of Georgia. [*anon.*] 48 pp. 1 map. 1 pl. 4°. *London, W. Meadows,* 1733.

——— The same. 2d ed. 48 pp. 1 map. 1 pl. 4°. *London, W. Meadows,* 1733.

[Map wanting].

Martyn (*Mrs.* S. T.) The English exile; or, William Tyndale at home and abroad. 237 pp. 16°. *New York, Am. tract soc.* 1867.

——— The Hopes of Hope castle; or, the times of Knox and queen Mary Stuart. 16°. *New York, Am. tract soc.* 1867.

——— Lady Alice Lisle, the last of the English martyrs. [*anon.*] 276 pp. 16°. *New York, Am. tract soc.* [1867].

Martyn (W. Carlos). A history of the English puritans. 496 pp. 12°. *New York, Am. tract soc.* [1867].

——— History of the Huguenots. 528 pp. 12°. *New York, Am. tract soc.* [1866].

——— Life and times of Martin Luther. 550 pp. 12°. *Am. tract soc.* [1866].

——— The pilgrim fathers of New England. A history. 432 pp. 12°. *New York, Am. tract soc.* [1867].

Martyr (Peter). *See* **Martire** d'Anghiera (Pietro).

Martyr (Peter, *the reformer*). *See* **Vermigli** (Pietro Martire).

Marvin (Enoch M. *D. D.*) The work of Christ; or, the atonement considered in its influence upon the intelligent universe. 137 pp. 16°. *St. Louis, P. M. Pinckard,* 1867.

Marvin (Henry). Complete history of Lake George; intended as a guide. 102 pp. 1 map. 18°. *New York, Sibells & Maigne,* 1853. s.

Marx (Adolph Bernhard). Theory and practice of musical composition. Translated from the 3d German ed. and edited by H. S. Saroni. 5th Amer. ed. With appendix and notes, by E. Girac. 406, 166 pp. 8°. *New York, Mason bros.* [1851]. s.

Marx (Francis). The Serf and the Cossack. A sketch of the condition of the Russian people. 48 pp. 16°. *London, Trübner & Co.* 1854.

Maryland. (*Province*). Proceedings of the convention of the province of Maryland, held at Annapolis, May 8, 1776. 29 pp. sm. 4°. *Annapolis, Frederick Green,* [1776?]

——— The same. June 21, 1776. 33 pp. sm. 4°. *Annapolis, Frederick Green,* [1776?]

[*With* proceedings of May 8, 1776.]

——— The same. August 14, 1776. 91 pp. 4°. *Annapolis, Frederick Green,* [1776?]

Maryland (*Province.*) Proceedings *continued.* June 22, 1774; November 21, 1774; December 8, 1774; April 24, 1775; and July 26, 1775. 26 pp. 4°. *Annapolis, Frederick Green,* [1775?]

——— The same. December 7, 1775. 62 pp. sm. 4°. *Annapolis, Frederick Green,* [1776?]

——— *(State).* Catalogue of the library of the state of Maryland. By David Ridgely. [With additions to December, 1840, in ms.] 8°. *Annapolis, J. Hughes,* 1837.

——— Geological survey. Reports. 13 v. in 2. 8°. *Annapolis, state printer,* 1834-40. s.

CONTENTS.

ALEXANDER (John Henry). Engineers' reports on the topographical survey for 1834-36.
DUCATEL (Julius T.) Reports of the geologist. 1834-40. Report on iron manufacture.

——— Journal of the proceedings, [including "documents,"] of the senate and house of delegates, January session, 1865. 2 v. 8°. *Annapolis, R. P. Bayley,* 1865.

——— The same. Extra session, 1866. 2 v. 8°. *Annapolis, Haverstick & Longneckers,* 1866.

——— The same. January session, 1867. 2 v. 8°. *Annapolis, H. A. Lucas,* 1867.

——— Report of the committee of grievances and courts of justice of the Maryland house of delegates, on the recent mobs and riots in the city of Baltimore. v, 347 pp. 8°. *Annapolis, J. Green,* 1813.

——— Report of the select committee appointed to inquire into the expediency of repealing the act to provide for completing a new map and geological survey of the state. 4 pp. 8°. *Annapolis,* 1839.. s.

[*With* MARYLAND. Geological survey].

——— Votes and proceedings of the house of delegates, November session, 1793. 124 pp. fol. [*Annapolis,* 1794?]

[Imperfect; some pp. wanting at close].

Maryland institute for the promotion of the mechanic arts. Catalogue of books in the library. Classified and alphabetically arranged by titles. 176 pp. 8°. *Baltimore, J. Young,* 1865. s.

Marzenado (Santa Cruz de). *See* **Santa Cruz** de Marzenado (A.)

Mascardi (Agostino). Dissertationes de affectibvs sive pertvrbationibvs animi, et ethicæ prolvsiones. 4 p. l. 490 pp. 9 l. 18°. *Mediolani, F. Vigoni,* 1667.

Masch (G. M. C.) Geschichte des bisthums Ratzeburg. xvi, 780 pp. 8°. *Lübeck, F. Aschenfeldt,* 1835. s.

Masini (Eliseo). Sacro arsenale; ouero, prattica dell'officio della santa inqvisitione. Di nuouo corretto, et ampliato. [*anon.*] 8 p. l. 528 pp. 16°. *Bologna, G. Longhi,* 1679.

Masius *or* **Maase** (Hector Gottfried von der). Antiqvitatum mecklenburgensium schediasma historico-philologicum, cum notis Andreæ Borrichii. 8 p. l. 166 pp. 16°. *Lubecœ, J. Weidemeyer,* 1700. s.

——— De existentia dæmonis, qvatenus è naturæ lumine innotescit, dissertatio. 40 pp. 16°. s.

[*App.* to his Antiqvitatum mecklenb. schediasma, etc.]

Mason (Charlotte). The lady's assistant for regulating and supplying the table; being a complete system of cookery: with appendix on the breeding and management of poultry. 10 p. l. 422, 25 pp. 10 l. 8°. *London, J. Walter,* 1801.

Mason (*Miss* Emily V.) The southern poems of the war, collected and arranged. 456 pp. 12°. *Baltimore, J. Murphy & Co.* 1867.

——— The same. 2d rev. ed. 524 pp. 1 pl. 12°. *Baltimore, J. Murphy & Co.* 1868.

Mason (George). A supplement to Johnson's English dictionary. vii, 134 pp. 8°. *New York, H. Caritat,* 1803.

Mason (George C.) Reunion of the sons and daughters of Newport, R. I. August 23, 1859. 298 pp. 12°. *Newport, F. A. Pratt & Co.* 1859. s.

Mason (*major* John). A brief history of the Pequot war. Introduction by Rev. Thomas Prince. 4 p. l. x, 22 pp. 16°. *Boston, S. Kneeland,* 1736.

[Imperfect; 2 p. l. in ms.]

Mason (*Rev.* William). Heroic epistle to sir William Chambers, [*anon.*] 16 pp. 4°. *London, J. Almon,* 1763.

Mason (William), *and* **Hoadly** (E. S.) A method for the piano-forte. American fingering. 239 pp. 1 pl. 4°. *New York, Mason bros.* [1867].

Massachusetts. *(Colony).* A journal of the proceedings of [the] commissioners appointed by Spencer Phips, lieut. gov. of Massachusetts bay, to treat with the eastern Indians. [*anon.*] 16 pp. sm. 4°. *Boston, J. Draper,* 1752.

——— Journal of the house of representatives of his majesty's province of the Massachusetts bay, begun and held at Boston, May 28th, 1755. [72? pp.] fol. *Boston, S. Kneeland,* 1755.

[Imperfect; some pages wanting at the end].

——— *Commonwealth.* Debates, resolutions, and other proceedings of the convention of the commonwealth of Massachusetts, at Boston, Jan. 1788, for the purpose of ratifying the constitution recommended by the grand federal convention. 216 pp. 12°. *Boston, Adams & Nourse, and others,* 1788.

Massachusetts. (*Commonwealth.*) Fourth to ninth annual reports to the legislature, relating to the registry and returns of births, marriages, and deaths in Massachusetts, for 1845–50. By the secretary of state. 6 v. in 1. 8°. *Boston, Dutton & Wentworth,* 1845–51. s.

——— Reports and other documents relating to the state lunatic hospital at Worcester, Mass. Printed by order of the senate. 200 pp. 8°. *Boston, Dutton & Wentworth,* 1837.

Massachusetts college of pharmacy. Catalogue of the materia medica, and of the pharmaceutical preparations, with the uniform prices. 59 pp. 12°. *Boston, college,* 1854. s.

Massachusetts historical society. Proceedings, 1866–67. xvi, 524 pp. 2 portraits. 8°. *Boston, Wiggin & Lunt,* 1867.

Massachusetts horticultural society. A catalogue of the library. 65 pp. 8°. *Boston, H. W. Dutton & son,* 1867. s.

Massachusetts register, 1867, containing a record of state and county officers, and a directory of merchants, manufacturers, etc. v. 95. 8°. *Boston,* 1867.

Massie (James William, *D. D.*) The slave: hunted, transported, and doomed to toil; a tale of Africa. iv, 176 pp. 16°. *Manchester, J. Lowndes,* 1846.

Massmann (Hans Ferdinand). Atlas zu dem werke [von J. Scheible]: Die baseler todtentänze in getreuen abbildungen, [etc.] Sammt einem anhange: Todtentänze in holzschnitten des fünfzehnten jahrhunderts. 1 p. l. 49 pl. 4°. *Leipzig, Expedition des klosters,* 1847. s.

Masson (Alexander Frédéric Jacques, *marquis* de Pezay). Épitre à mon ami.

[*With* DORAT (Claude Joseph). Le pot-pourri, etc. 8°. 1764].

Masson (Jean). P. Ovidii Nasonis vita ordine chronologico sic delineata, ut poëtæ fata et opera veris assignentur annis, notisque philologicis et historicis illustrentur, etc. 3 p. l. 242 pp. 6 l. 18°. *Amstelodami, Jansson,* 1708. s.

Mastalier (Adolphus Edward). Ischel, [Switzerland. A hygienic essay, with special reference to the sanative advantages of Ischl]. 106 pp. 8°. *Leipzig, B. Tauchnitz, jun.* 1850.

Masters (Robert). History of the college of Corpus Christi and the b. virgin Mary in the university of Cambridge, of its principal members, etc. Part 1. 4 p. l. 212, 84, 54 pp. 6 pl. 4°. *Cambridge, (Eng.) J. Bentham,* 1753. s.

——— The same. Part 2. History of its principal members. 3 p. l. pp. 213–428. App. pp. 85–115. 9 l. 1 pl. 4°. [*Cambridge,* 1755]. s.

Mather (Cotton, *D. D.*) Ecclesiastes; or, the life of Mr. Jonathan Mitchel. xxxii, 100 pp. 24°. *Boston, B. Green and J. Allen,* 1697.

[Imperfect; title p. and 2 p. l. wanting.]

——— Essays to do good. 108 pp. 24°. *New York, Am. tract soc.* [*about* 1820].

——— India christiana. A discourse delivered unto the commissioners for the propagation of the gospel among the American Indians; [with] several instruments relating to the design of propagating our religion in the eastern as well as the western Indians. 120 pp. 18°. *Boston, B. Green,* 1721.

——— The life of the renowned John Eliot. 4 p. l. 152 pp. 18°. *Boston, B. Harris and J. Allen,* 1691. s.

——— [Manuductio ad ministerium.] Student and preacher; or, directions for a candidate of the ministry, [new ed. with] a literal translation of [the] Latin preface [by H. Welford]. xvi, 260 pp. 16°. *London, T. Scollick & J. Matthews,* 1789.

——— The present state of New England; a discourse on the necessities and advantages of a public spirit. 46 pp. 24°. *Boston, S. Green,* 1690.

——— Psalterium americanum; the book of psalms in blank verse. xxxv, 426 pp. 18°. *Boston, Benj. Eliot,* 1718.

——— The wonders of the invisible world; being an account of the tryals of several witches, lately executed in New England, etc. and of several remarkable curiosities therein occurring. With observations upon the nature, number, and operations of devils. Narrative of a late outrage in Swedeland. Some councels directing a due improvement of the terrible things lately done in New England. A discourse upon the more ordinary devices of Satan, *Boston,* 1693. [Reprint, 247 pp. ms. 4°. *Boston,* 1866.]

[*With* DRAKE (S. G.) Witchcraft delusion in New England, v. 1.]

——— *and others.* The principles of the protestant religion maintained, and the churches of New England in the profession and exercise thereof defended, against all the calumnies of one George Keith. viii, 156 pp. 24°. *Boston, Richard Pierce,* 1690.

——— The same.

[Imperfect: wanting 4 pp. at end].

Mather (*Rev.* Eleazar). A serious exhortation to the present and succeeding generation in New England. 4 p. l. 31 pp. sm. 4°. *Cambridge, (Mass.) S. Green and M. Johnson,* 1671.

——— The same. 2d ed. 2 p. l. 31 pp. sm. 4°. *Boston, John Foster,* 1678.

[*With* WALLEY (*Rev.* Thomas). Balm in Gilead. *Cambridge,* 1670].

Mather (Increase, *D. D.*) A brief history of the war with the Indians in New England, from June 24, 1675, to August 12, 1676. 4 p. l. 51, vii pp. sm. 4°. *London, Richard Chiswell,* 1676.
[pp. 2, 43, 45, imperfect.]

——— A discourse concerning comets. 6 p. l. 143 pp. 24°. *Boston,* 1683.
[Imperfect; title page wanting.]

——— Doctrine of divine providence opened and applyed; also, sundry sermons. 4 p. l. 148 pp. 18°. *Boston, Joseph Brunning,* 1684.

——— The greatest sinners exhorted and encouraged to come to Christ now, [with other sermons]. 3 p. l. 146 pp. 24°. *Boston, Joseph Brunning,* 1686.

——— The great blessing of primitive counsellours. 23 pp. sm. 4°. *Boston, B. Harris,* 1693.

——— Heaven's alarm to the world. 2d impression. 4 p. l. 38 pp. 24°. *Boston, Samuel Sewale,* 1682.
[*With* MATHER (Increase). Discourse concerning comets. 24°. *Boston,* 1653.]

——— The latter sign discoursed of, in a sermon. 30 pp? 24°.
[*With* MATHER, (Increase). Discourse concerning comets, *Boston,* 1653.]

——— The mystery of Christ opened and applied in several sermons. vi, 212 pp. 24°. *Boston,* 1686.

——— A sermon wherein is shewed that the church of God is sometimes a subject of great persecution. 3 p. l. 24 pp. sm. 4°. *Boston, Samuel Sewall,* 1682.

——— A sermon, wherein is shewed that excess in wickedness doth bring untimely death. 2d ed. 37 pp. 18°. *Boston, J. Brunning,* 1685.

——— Some important truths about conversion. xxii, 260 pp. 24°. *Boston, John Edwards,* 1721.

——— The same. 2d ed. xxii, 258 pp. 18°. *Boston, Boone,* 1721.
[Imperfect. Some pp. wanting at the close.]

——— De successu evangelii apud Indos Occidentales in Nova-Anglia: epistola ad Johannem Leusdenum. 8 pp. 18°. *Ultrajecti, W. Broedeleth,* 1699.
[*With* LEIBNITZ (G. W.) Novissima sinica, 1699].

Mather (Richard). A reply to Mr. Rutherford; or, defence of the answer to Mr. Herle's booke against the independency of churches. 6 p. l. 109 pp. sm. 4°. *London, J. Rothwell & H. Allen,* 1647.

Mather (Samuel, *D. D.*) An apology for the liberties of the churches in New England; [with] discourse concerning congregational churches. 4 p. l. ix, 216 pp. 12°. *Boston, D. Henchman,* 1738.

——— An attempt to show that America must be known to the ancients, [with] appendix concerning the American colonies. 35 pp. 8°. *Boston, T. Leverett & H. Knox,* 1773.

Mather (*Rev.* Samuel, *of Windsor, Conn.*) The self-justiciary convicted and condemned. A discourse concerning the necessity of renouncing our own righteousness. 82 pp. 24°. *Boston, D. Henchman,* 1740.
[Imperfect: wanting pp. 3-4.]

Mather (William W.) Reports on geology.
[NEW YORK, *State.* Annual reports on geol. survey. v. 1-5.]

Mathéron (Philippe). Catalogue méthodique et descriptif des corps organisés fossiles du département des Bouches du Rhone, et lieux circonvoisins; précédés d'un mémoire sur les terrains supérieurs au grès bigarré du S. E. de la France. [extract]. 269 pp. 41 pl. 8°. *Marseilles, Soc. de statistique,* 1842. S.

Mathews (Cornelius). Pen and ink panorama of New York city. 209 pp. 18°. *New York, J. S. Taylor,* 1853. S.

Mathias (Thomas James, *editor*). Componimenti lirici dè più illustri poeti d'Italia. 3 v. 1 pl. 16°. *Londra, Bulmer e Ca.* 1802.

——— The same. Aggiunta ai componimenti lirici. 3 v. 3 pl. 16°. *Londra, Bulmer e Ca.* 1808.

——— Poesie liriche e varie. Nuova ed. 3 v. in 1. 12°. *Napoli, A. Nobile,* 1825.

Mathieu (P. F.) Histoire des miraculés et des convulsionnaires de Saint Médard. viii, 491 pp. 16°. *Paris, Didier et Cie.* 1864.

Matienzo (Juan de). Dialogvs relatoris et advocati pintiani senatvs, in quo varia proponuntur ad renunciatorum, advocatorum et judicum munera. 6 p. l. 151 pp. 20 l. fol. *Pintiæ, L. Sanchez,* 1604. S.
[*With* VALDES (Juan). De dignitate, etc.]

Matigny (Hubert de). De la disparition de la monnaie d'argent et de son remplacement par la monnaie d'or; ou, situation monétaire de la France, en 1859. 2ᵉ éd. 168 pp. 8°. *Paris, auteur,* 1859. S.

Matlack (Timothy). An oration, 1780, before the American philosophical society. 27 pp. 4°. *Philadelphia, Styner & Cist,* 1780.

Matson (N.) Map of Bureau county, Illinois, with sketches of its early settlement. 88 pp. 8 pl. 26 maps. sm. 4°. *Chicago, G. H. Fergus,* 1867.

Mattei (Paschal de'). Devotion to the holy guardian angels in the form of considerations, prayers, [etc. From the Italian]. 230 pp. 32°. *Baltimore, Kelly & Piet,* 1866.

Matter; its forms and governing laws. By George Duplex. *(pseudon?)* viii, 166 pp. 12°. *London, Bradbury & Evans,* 1857.

Matthäi (Johann Friedrich). Verzeichniss der königlich sächsischen gemälde-galerie zu Dresden. 2 v. in 1. x, 240, xii pp; 130, vi pp. 1 pl. 8°. *Dresden, [Galerie,]* 1835. s.

Matthew (George F.) Geology.

[*With* BAILEY (L. W.) Geology of southern New Brunswick].

Matthews (James N.) My holiday; how I spent it: being some rough notes of a trip to Europe and back, in 1866. 275 pp. 12°. *Buffalo, M. Taylor,* 1867.

Matthiae (August Heinrich). Animadversiones in hymnos homericos, cum prolegomenis de cujusque consilio, partibus, ætate. xvi, 464 pp. 8°. *Lipsiæ, Weidmann,* 1800. s.

Matthieu (Pierre). Concernant la mort déplorable de Henry iv, roy de France. Ensemble vn panégyriqve et vn discovrs fvnèbre. 216 pp. 16°. [*Genève, A. Pernet,*] 1620.

[v. 2 of MATTHIEU (Pierre). Histoire de France, *Genève,* 1620].

——— Histoire de France et des choses memorables aduenues aux prouvinces estrangères durant sept années de paix [1598–1604] dv regne dv roy Henri iv, roy de France et de Nauarre. 2 v. 20 p. l. 728 pp. 39 l; 8 p. l. 844 pp. 16°. *Genève, Balthazar & Pernet,* 1620.

Mattison (Hiram). The resurrection of the dead; considered in the light of history, philosophy, and divine revelation. With an introduction by Rev. M. Simpson, *D. D.* 3d ed. 405 pp. 12°. *Philadelphia, Perkinpine and Higgins,* 1866.

Maturin (Charles Robert). Fatal revenge; or, the family of Montorio. 4th ed. 255 pp. 8°. *London,* 1840.

[HAZLITT'S romancist and novelist's lib. v. 1.]

Maudsley (Henry, *M. D.*) Physiology and pathology of the mind. xv, 442 pp. 8°. *New York, D. Appleton & Co.* 1867.

Maunder (Samuel). The treasury of knowledge. Part i. Being a new and enlarged dictionary of the English language. Part ii. Comprising a new universal gazetteer. 2 v. in 1. 198 p. l. 346 pp. 2 pl. 18°. *London, S. Maunder,* 1830.

Maundrell (Henry). A journey from Aleppo to Jerusalem, at easter, 1697. 5th ed. [with] a journey to the banks of the Euphrates. 6 p. l. 145, 10 pp. 15 pl. 12°. *Oxford, Theatre,* 1732.

Maurepas (Jean Frédéric Phelippeaux, *comte* de). Mémoires [depuis 1749 jusqu'en 1772, redigés par N. N. de Sallé et publ. par J. L. G. Soulavie]. 3 v. 8°. *Paris, Buisson,* 1792.

Maurice (Matthias). Faith encouraged, in a plain exposition of Heb. vi, 4–6. x, 26, 1 John v, 16. xvi, 262 pp. 16°. *London, J. Clark,* 1726.

Maury (Mathew Fontaine). Explanations and sailing directions to accompany the wind and current charts, etc. 318 pp. 12 pl. 4°. *Washington, C. Alexander,* 1851. s.

——— The same. 4th ed. 413 pp. 19 pl. 4°. *Washington, C. Alexander,* 1852.

——— The same. 7th ed. enlarged. xxvi, 869 pp. 34 l. 23 pl. 4°. *Philadelphia, E. C. & J. Biddle,* 1855.

——— The same. 8th ed. 2 v. xxxvi, 383 pp. 39 pl. 12 charts; vii, 874 pp. 6 pl. 4°. *Washington, C. Wendell,* 1858–59.

——— Investigations of the winds and currents of the sea. [From the appendix to the Washington astronomical observations for 1846]. 126 pp. 4°. *Washington, C. Alexander,* 1851. s.

——— A new theoretical and practical treatise on navigation. viii, 216, 174 pp. 9 pl. 8°. *Philadelphia, Key & Biddle,* 1836. s.

——— Wind and current charts. Gales in the Atlantic. 2 pl. 24 maps. 4°. *Washington,* 1857.

——— Die physische geographie des meeres. Deutsch bearbeitet von Dr. C. Boettger. xii, 268 pp. 6 pl. 8°. *Leipzig, G. Mayer,* 1856. s.

Maury (Sarah Mytton). An Englishwoman in America. An appendix contains the history of the emigrant surgeons' bill. cxviii, 251, 204, 16 pp. 8°. *London, Thomas Richardson & son,* 1848.

Mauvillon (Jacques). The history of Prussia, particularly during the reign of the late king Frederick William. [*anon.*] 7 p. l. 525 pp. 12°. *London, R. Manby,* 1756.

NOTE.—A compilation from Mirabeau's writings upon Prussia.

Maximilian (Alexander Philipp, *prinz von Wied-Nieuwied*). Beiträge zur naturgeschichte von Brasilien. 4 v. in 6. 8°. *Weimar, Landes industrie comptoirs,* 1825–33. s.

CONTENTS.

v. 1. Amphibien. xxii, 614 pp. 3 pl.
v. 2. Säugthiere. 622 pp. 5 pl.
v. 3–4. Vögel. 1280, xii pp. 1 pl; 946, viii pp. 2 pl.

Maximilian (Alexander Philipp, *prinz von Wied-Nieuwied*). Reise in das innere Nord-America in den jahren 1832–34. 2 v. xvi, 654 pp; xxii, 687 pp. atlas, 81 pl. 1 map. 4°. *Coblenz, J. Hoelscher*, 1839–41. s.

——— Reise nach Brasilien in den jahren 1815–17. 2 v. xxxvi, 385 pp. 11 pl; xviii, 346 pp. 8 pl. atlas, 22 pl. 3 maps. 4°. *Frankfurt am M. H. L. Brönner*, 1820–21. s.

——— Verzeichniss der auf seiner reise in Nord-Amerika beobachteten säugethiere. (Extract). 240 pp. 4 pl. 8°. *Berlin, Archiv für naturgeschichte*, 1862. s.

Maxims and observations, moral and physical, with characters from the most approved authors. [*anon.*] viii, 184 pp. 12° *London, J. Bladon*, 1788.

Maxwell (Alexander). Plurality of worlds. 2d ed. viii, 265 pp. 8°. *London, A. Maxwell*, 1820.

Maxwell (John S.) The czar, his court and people, including a tour in Norway and Sweden. 368 pp. 12°. *New York, Baker & Scribner*, 1848. s.

Maxwell (William). An oration commemorative of the Rev. John Holt Rice, D. D. 33 pp. 8°. *Richmond, (Va.) R. J. Smith*, 1832.

May (Walter W.) A series of fourteen sketches made during the voyage up Wellington channel in search of Sir J. Franklin, with a short account of each drawing. 7 pp. 14 pl. fol. *London, Day & son*, 1865.

Mayer (Carl von). Heraldisches A. B. C. buch, das ist: wesen und begriff der wissenschaftlichen heraldik, ihre geschichte, literatur, theorie und praxis. xv, 523 pp. 65 pl. 8°. *München, C. Wolf*, 1857. s.

Mayhew (*Rev.* Experience). Indian converts; or, some account of the lives and dying speeches of a number of the christianized Indians of Martha's Vineyard, in New England. xxiv, 275 pp. 12°. *London, S. Gerrish*, 1727.

——— *See* **Bible** (*Indian, Massachusetts*).

Mayhew (Jonathan, *D. D.*) A defence of the observations on the charter and conduct of the society for the propagation of the gospel in foreign parts, against an anonymous pamphlet, [by Rev. Henry Caner,] falsely intitled A candid examination of Dr. Mayhew's observations. 144 pp. 8°. *Boston, R. & S. Draper, and others*, 1763.

——— The same.

[*With* MAYHEW (Jonathan). Observations on the charter of the soc. for the prop. of the gospel in foreign ports. *Boston*, 1763].

Mayhew (Jonathan, *D. D.*) A discourse concerning unlimited submission and non-resistance to the higher powers, with reflections on the resistance made to king Charles i. 18°. First printed at *Boston*, 1750.

[*With* BARON (R.) Pillars of priestcraft shaken. v 2. pp. 259–335. *Lond.* 1752].

——— The expected dissolution of all things, a motive to universal holiness. Two sermons. 76, 5 pp. 16°. *Boston, Edes & Gill*, 1755.

[*With* MAYHEW (Jonathan). Striving to enter in, etc. *Boston*, 1761.]

——— Observations on the charter and conduct of the society for the propagation of the gospel in foreign parts. 176 pp. 8°. *Boston, R. & S. Draper*, 1763.

——— Remarks on an anonymous tract [by archbishop Secker], entitled, An answer to Dr. Mayhew's observations on the charter and conduct of the society for the propagation of the gospel in foreign parts. 86 pp. 8°. *Boston, R. & S. Draper*, 1764.

[*With* MAYHEW (Jonathan). Observations, etc. *Boston*, 1763].

——— Striving to enter in at the strait gate, and the connexion of salvation therewith. Two sermons. 83 pp. 16°. *Boston, R. Draper & others*, 1761.

Mayhew (*Rev.* Thomas). Tears of repentance. *See* **Eliot** (*Rev.* John), *and* **Mayhew** (Thomas).

Mayne (F.) Voyages and discoveries in the arctic regions. 140 pp. 16°. *London, Longmans*, 1855. s.

Mayne (John). A dispensatory and therapeutical remembrancer. Revised by R. Griffith. 329 pp. 12°. *Philadelphia, Lea & Blanchard*, 1848.

Mayne (Zachary). Two dissertations concerning sense and the imagination, with an essay on consciousness. [*anon.*] 4 p. l. 431 pp. 8°. *London, J. Tonson*, 1728.

Mazaudier (——, *engineer*). Guide pratique d'architecture navale, avec un appendice sur les bateaux à vapeur. 492 pp. 8°. 13 pl. 4°. *Paris, Desauche*, 1835. s.

[Text and plates bound together.]

Mazzini (Giuseppe). Life and writings. v. 1–4. v. 1 and 3, autobiographical and political; v. 2 and 4, critical and literary. 12°. *London* [*printed at Edinburgh*], *Smith, Elder & Co.* 1864–67.

Mazzocchi (Jacopo). Epigrammata antiqvæ vrbis [Romæ]. 10 p. l. clxxxi pp. 9 l. fol. *Romæ, J. Mazochius*, 1521.

Mead (H. E.) Kentucky and Tennessee. A complete guide to their railroads, stations and distances, connections north and south; their rivers, landings, [etc.] 147 pp. 4 maps. 24°. *Louisville, H. E. Mead,* 1867.

Mead (Mathew). The almost christian discovered; or, the false professor tried and cast. Published by elder James Reid. 226 pp. 16°. *Winchester, (Va.) J. Foster,* 1819.

Mead (Peter B.) An elementary treatise on American grape culture and wine making. 483 pp. 8°. *New York, Harpers,* 1867.

Meade (George Gordon). Report of the survey of the north and northwest lakes. 48 pp. 3 maps. 8°. *Detroit, Daily free press,* 1859. s.

Meade (Thomas). A reply to a paper, circulated under the name of the lord bishop of Lincoln [G. Pretyman Tomline]: the object of which is to counteract a verdict in an action brought by Thomas Meade against Rev. Charles Daubeny, in 1792. viii, 347 pp. 8°. *Bath, R. Cruttwell,* 1806.

Meade (William, *D. D.*) Companion to the font and the pulpit. 147 pp. 12°. *Washington, J. & G. S. Gideon,* 1846.

Meadows (F. C.) A new French and English pronouncing dictionary, on the basis of Nugent's. In two parts, with an abridged grammar. Corrected and improved by George Folsom. 3 p. l. 50, 352, 376 pp. 18°. *New York, Alexander V. Blake,* 1840.

Meares (John). Voyages in the years 1788–89, from China to the northwest coast of America; [with] a narrative of a voyage in 1786, from Bengal, in the ship Nootka. 10 p. l. xcvi, 372 pp. 54 l. 3 maps. 23 pl. 4°. *London, J. Walter,* 1790.

Mears (John W. *D. D.*) The beggars of Holland, and the grandees of Spain. A history of the reformation in the Netherlands, A. D. 1200—1578. 477 pp. 8 pl. 1 map. 16°. *Philadelphia, Presb. pub. com.* [1867].

Mease (James, *M. D.*) A geological account of the United States; comprehending a description of their animal, vegetable, and mineral productions, antiquities, and curiosities. 4 p. l. 496, xiv pp. 5 pl. 18°. *Philadelphia, Birch & Small,* 1807.

Mechanics' (The) magazine and journal of engineering, agricultural machinery, manufactures, and ship-building. July, 1866, to Dec. 1867. New series. v. 16–17; complete series, v. 85–87. 4°. *London, Robertson, Brooman & Co.* [1866–67].

Mechthildis (*Saint*). Revelationes selectæ. Textum cognovit A. Heuser. 183 pp. 24°. *Coloniæ, J. M. Heberle,* 1854.

Meckel (Johann Friedrich). System der vergleichenden anatomie. 5 v. 8°. *Halle, Renger,* 1821–31. s.

——— Traité général d'anatomie comparée. Traduit par MM. Riester et Sauson. (v. i–vii). Alph. Sauson et Th. Schuster. (v. viii). Th. Schuster. (v. ix–x). 10 v. 8°. *Paris et Rouen,* 1828–38. s.

Medary (Samuel). The new constitution, [of Ohio]. 26 nos. in 1 v. 408 pp. sm. fol. *Columbus (O.)* 1849.

Medleys (The) for the year 1711, with the five Whig examiners. 59, 479 pp. 24°. *London, John Darby,* 1712.

Medows (*Sir* Sidney). Art of horsemanship, etc. *See* **Freeman** (Strickland).

Meek (Fielding Bradford). Check list of the invertebrate fossils of North America. Miocene. ii, 32 pp. 8°. *Washington,* 1864.

[SMITHSONIAN miscel. coll. v. 7.]

——— The same. Cretaceous and jurassic. ii, 40 pp. 8°. *Washington,* 1864.

[SMITHSONIAN miscel. coll. v. 7.]

——— *See* **California** geological survey.

——— *and* **Hayden** (F. V.) Palæontology of the upper Missouri: a report upon collections made principally in 1855–56. Invertebrates. Part 1. ix, 136 pp. 5 pl. 4°. [*Washington, Sm. inst.*] 1865.

[SMITHSONIAN contrib. v. 14.]

Meelführer (Rodolph Martin). Accessiones ad T. J. ab Almeloveen bibliothecam promissam et latentem. 8 p. l. 176 pp. 16°. *Noribergæ et Lipsiæ, A. Otto,* 1699. s.

[*With* ALMELOVEEN (T. J. ab.) Bib. promissa, etc.]

Méhégan (Guillaume Alexandre, *chevalier* de). Zoroastre, histoire: [ou, de l' origine des Guèbres]. Traduit du Chaldéen. [*anon.*] 60, x pp. 18°. [*Paris, about* 1751].

[*With* CAPUCINS (Les) sans barbe, etc].

Meier (Georg Friedrich). The merry philosopher; or, thoughts on jesting. From the German. 2 p. l. 213 pp. 18°. *London, J. Newberry,* 1764.

Meiffren Laugier, *baron* de Chartrouse. *See* **Temminck** (C. J.)

Meigs (J. Forsyth, *M. D.*) Practical treatise on the diseases of children. 675 pp. 12°. *Philadelphia, Lindsay & Blakiston,* 1848. s.

Meikle (James, *surgeon*). Metaphysical maxims: or, thoughts on the nature of the soul, free will, and the divine prescience. 2d ed. 142 pp. 16°. *Edinburgh, J. Ogle,* 1811.

Mela (Pomponius). Libri de situ orbis tres, adiectis J. Vadiani helvetii in eosdem scholiis; addita quoque in geographia catechesi, et epistola Vadiani ad Agricolam digna lectu. 23 p. l. 133 l. fol. *Viennae Pannoniae, Lucas Alantse, per J. Lingrenium*, 1518. s.

Melanchthon *or* **Schwarzerd** (Philipp). Ethicæ doctrinæ elementa, et enarratio libri quinti ethicorvm [Aristotelis]. 8 p. l. 302 pp. 16°. *Vitebergæ*, 1566. s.

——— Initia doctrinæ physicæ, dictata in academia witebergensi. 6 p. l. 206 l. 16°. *Vitebergæ*, 1567. s.

[*With his* Ethicæ doctrinæ elementa].

Melbourn (Julius). Life and opinions. 239 pp. 12°. *Syracuse, Hall & Dickson*, 1847.

Melchior (Hans Böchman). Den danske stats og Norges pattedyr. Udgivet af Sophus Zahle. xvi, 298 pp. 13 pl. 8°. *Kjöbenhavn, Gyldendalk*, 1834. s.

Melcombe (*lord*). *See* **Dodington** (G. B.)

Melho, Melo, *or* **Mello** (Francisco Manoel de). Historia de los movimientos, separacion y guerra de Cataluña en tiempo de Felipe iv. [Con la vida del autor.] Nueva ed. xxvi, 475 pp. 16°. *Madrid, Sancha*, 1808.

Meline (James F.) Two thousand miles on horseback. Santa Fé and back. A summer tour through Kansas, Nebraska, Colorado, and New Mexico, in 1866. x, 317 pp 1 map. 16°. *New York, Hurd & Houghton*, 1867.

Melish (John). A geographical description of the United States, with the contiguous British and Spanish possessions. 2d ed. 180 pp. 8°. *Philadelphia, J. Melish*, 1816.

——— The same. 3d ed. 8°. *Philadelphia, author*, 1818. s.

——— A statistical view of the United States; containing a geographical description of the United States, and of each state and territory. 45 pp. 18°. *Philadelphia, author*, 1822.

[*With* the preceding].

——— The traveller's directory through the United States. [2d ed.] xix, 183 pp. 2 maps. 18°. *Philadelphia, author*, 1822.

Mellen (George S.) One thousand choice recipes, mysteries and disclosures, touching every branch of business, [etc.] New ed. 103 pp. 18°. *Lewiston, (Me.) G. S. Mellen*, 1866.

Mellin (Georg Samuel Albrecht). Encyclopädisches wörterbuch der kritischen philosophie. 6 v. in 11. 8°. *Leipzig, etc. F. Frommann*, 1797—1804. s.

Mello (Francisco Manoel de). *See* **Melho.**

Melpomene divina; or, poems on christian themes. By Christopher Laomedon Pindar. [*pseudon.*] 310 pp. 18°. *Philadelphia, J. B. Lippincott & Co.* 1867.

Melton (Edward). Zeldzaame en gedenkwaardige zee- en landreizen door Egypten, West-Indien, Perzien, Turkien, Oost-Indien, en d'aangrenzende gewesten, 1660–1667. 3 p. l. 495 pp. 4 l. 20 pl. 4°. *Amsterdam, Jan ten Hoorn*, 1681.

Melvil *or* **Melville** (*Sir* James). Memoirs: containing an impartial account of the most remarkable affairs of state during the sixteenth century; more particularly relating to England and Scotland. Published by George Scott. 3d ed. xx, 408 pp. 15 l. 8°. *London, D. Wilson*, 1752.

Melville (G. J. Whyte). Digby Grand: an autobiography. 2d ed. 12°. *London, J. W. Parker & son*, 1857.

——— Kate Coventry: an autobiography. 2d ed. 322 pp. 12°. *London, J. W. Parker & son*, 1856.

Melville (Herman). Omoo: a narrative of adventures in the south seas. 389 pp. 12°. *New York, Harpers*, 1847. s.

——— Typee; a peep at Polynesian life, during a four months' residence in a valley of the Marquesas. Revised ed. 307 pp. 12°. *New York, Wiley and Putnam*, 1847.

——— The same. xiv, 307 pp. 12°. *New York, Harpers*, 1849.

Memminger (J. D. G. von). Beschreibung von Württemburg. 3e auflage. xvi, 848 pp. 1 table. 8°. *Stuttgart, J. G. Cotta*, 1841. s.

Memoir of Charles Gordon Lennox, fifth duke of Richmond. [*anon.*] xi, 348 pp. 1 pl. 8°. *London, Chapman & Hall*, 1862.

Memoir of the Rev. W. A. B. Johnson, missionary in Sierra Leone, 1816–23. With prefatory remarks by Rev. W. Jewett. [*anon.*] xiii, 430 pp. 1 map. 16°. *London, Seeley*, 1852.

Mémoire historique et instructif sur l'Hospice de la maternité. [Rédigé par MM. Hucherard, Sausseret, et Girault]. xiv, 140 pp. 4°. *Paris, Imprimerie des hospices civiles*, 1808. s.

Mémoires de monsieur le marquis de * * *. Écrits par lui-même. [*anon.*] 3 p. l. 202 pp. 18°. *Paris, Coustelier*, 1728.

[*With* Capucins (Les) sans barbe, etc.]

Mémoires militaires sur la campagne de l'armée belgique dans les Pays-Bas autrichiens, pendant 1790. Par un officier de l'armée. [*anon.*] xi, 169 pp. 8°. *Londres, Spilbury*, 1791. s.

Mémoires sur le Canada, 1749–60. 207 pp. 2 l. 8°. *Québec, T. Cary & Cie.* 1838.

Mémoires sur madame [Hortense Beauharnais Bonaparte] la duchesse de St. Leu, ex-reine de Hollande; suivis des romances composées et mises en musique par elle-même. [*anon.*] xi, 84 pp. 13 pl. obl. 4°. *Londres, Colburn & Bentley*, 1832.

Mémoires tirés des papiers d'un homme d'état, [le prince de Hardenberg] sur les causes secrètes qui ont déterminé la politique secrète des cabinets dans les guerres de la révolution; par M. le comte d'Allonville, [Alphonse de Beauchamps, etc]. 3 v. 8°. *Bruxelles, Wahlen*, 1838–41.

Memoirs of an unfortunate young nobleman [James Annesley], returned from thirteen years' slavery in America, where he had been sent by his cruel uncle. [*anon.*] 3 v. 277 pp; 235 pp; 215 pp. 16°. *London, J. Freeman*, 1743–47.

Memoirs of Ferdinand VII, king of the Spains. By Don ***** advocate of the Spanish tribunals. Translated from the Spanish by M. J. Quin. [*anon.*] vii, 307 pp. 8°. *London, Hurst, Robinson & Co.* 1824.

[NOTE.—Œttinger represents this book as written by Quin himself.]

Memoirs of Frederick and Margaret Klopstock. Translated from the German [by Miss Elizabeth Smith. *anon.*] xii, 236 pp. 12°. *Bath, R. Cruttwell*, 1808.

Memoirs of the dead, and tomb's remembrancer. [*anon.*] 300 pp. 16°. *Baltimore, editors*, 1806.

Memoirs of the life and adventures of Tsonnonthonan, a king of the Indian nation called Roundheads. [*anon.*] 2 v. xx, 189 pp; viii, 210 pp. 16°. *London, J. Knox*, 1763.

Memoirs of the life and times of Sir Thomas Deveil. [*anon.*] 83 pp. 8°. *London, M. Cooper*, 1748.

Memoirs of the Nutrebian court. [*anon.*] 2 v. in 1. 3 p. l. 236 pp; 3 p. l. 256 pp. 1 pl. 16°. *London, M. Laugham*, 1747.

Memoranda concerning Baltimore city and its surroundings. 93 pp. 1 map. 12°. *Baltimore, W. M. Innes*, 1860.

Memphis (*Tenn.*) City directory, 1867–8. Also a classified business register [and] city and county record. T. M. Halpin, compiler. 339 pp. 8°. *Memphis, Bulletin pub. co.* 1867.

Men (The) of the time; or, sketches of living notables. [*anon.*] 564 pp. 12°. *New York, Redfield*, 1852. s.

Men (The) of the war. Francis Joseph, the prince ot Prussia, prince Paskiewitsch, Baraguay d'Hilliers, the king of Greece, St. Arnaud, Reschid Pacha, Gortschakoff, Orloff, vice-adm. Parseval-Deschenes, vice-adm. Hamelin, the Sultan, Omar Pacha, Menschikoff. [*anon.*] 2 p. l. 156 pp. 16°. *London, D. Bryce*, [1864].

Ménant (Joachim). Observations sur la peine de mort. 2e éd. 20 pp. 8°. *Paris*, 1846. s.

Mendell (*Miss* ——), *and* Hosmer (*Miss* Harriet). Notes of travel and life [in the United States]. 288 pp. 12°. *New York, for the authors*, 1854.

Mendham (Joseph). *See* **Index** librorum prohibitorum a Sixto v. confectus.

Mendoza (Iñigo Lopez de). *See* **Lopez** de Mendoza.

Mengarini (*Rev.* Gregory). A Selish or Flathead grammar, [*or*] grammatica linguæ selicæ. viii, 122 pp. 8°. *New York, Cramoisy press*, 1861. s.

[Shea's library of American linguistics, ii.]

Mengin-Fondragon (Pierre Charles Joseph, *baron* de). Lettres à ma fille; ou, conseils sur l'éducation. xii, 240 pp. 18°. *Paris, Debécourt*, 1843. s.

Mengotti (Francesco). Del commercio de' Romani dalla prima guerra punica a Constantino; il colbertismo; ossia, della libertà di commercio de' prodotti della terra.

[SCRITTORI class. ital. di econ. pol. v. 36].

Mengs (Anton Raphael). Opere. Aumentate dall' avvocato Carlo Fea. xlvi, 445 pp. portrait. 4°. *Roma, Pagliarini*, 1787. s.

Menke (Theodor). Orbis antiqui descriptio in usum scholarum. Ed 2a. 5 p. l. 17 maps. 4°. *Gotha, Perthes*, 1854. s.

Mennechet (Édouard). Leçons de littérature française classique, [etc.] Tirées des Matinées littéraires. 393 pp. 12°. *New York, Leypoldt & Holt*, 1868.

Menon (——). La cuisinière bourgeoise; précédée d'un manuel. 12e éd. 16°. *Paris, Moronval*, 1841.

Méon (Dominique Martin). Nouveau recueil de fabliaux et contes inédits des poètes français des xiie—xve siècles. 2 v. viii, 500 pp; 482 pp. 2 pl. 8°. *Paris, Chassériau*, 1823.

Mercantile agency United States business directory for 1867, containing the names of merchants, manufacturers, and traders. By R. G. Dun & Co. 821 pp. 4°. *New York, John F. Trow*, 1867.

Mercator, *or* **Kaufmann** (Gerhardt). Historia mvndi; or, Mercator's atlas. Containing his cosmographicall description of the fabricke and figure of the world. By the studious industry of Ivdocvs Hondy [Hondt]. Englished by W. S[altonstall]. 12 p. l. 58, 930 pp. 16 l. 191 maps. fol. *London, M. Sparke & S. Cartwright,* 1635.

Mercey (Frédéric Bourgeois de). Assyrie. 19 l. *ms.*

[*With* GOBINEAU, (A. de). Essai sur l'inégalité des races humaines, v. 2.]

Merchant's (The) magazine and commercial review. Edited by W. B. Dana. Jan. to Dec. 1867. v. 56–57. 8°. *New York, W. B. Dana & Co.* 1867.

Mercier (Alfred). Biographie de Pierre Soulé, 101 pp. 12°. *Paris, Dentu,* 1848. s.

Mercier (Louis Sébastien). Tableau de Paris. [*anon.*] xi, 556 pp. 16°. *Hambourg, Virchaux,* 1781. s.

Mercure (Le) françois. [Composé par Jean Richer jusqu'en 1635, et continué par Théop. Renaudot jusqu'en 1644.] 1605–1644. 25 v. 12°. *Paris,* 1617–48.

Mercure historique et politique, contenant l'état présent de l'Europe, Nov. 1686 à Dec. 1777. [Rédigé par Sandras de Courtilz, Bayle, La Brune, Saint Élier, Guyot, Rousset, Le Fèvre et autres]. 183 v. 18°. *Parme et La Haye,* 1686–1777.

[Imperfect: v. 44, Jan.–June 1708, wanting].

Meredith (Henry). Account of the gold coast of Africa, with a brief history of the African company. viii, 264 pp. 1 map. 8°. *London, Longmans,* 1812. s.

Merewether (John, *D. D.*) A statement of the condition and circumstances of the cathedral church of Hereford. 89 pp. 10 pl. 8°. *Hereford, W. H. Vale,* 1842.

Mérian (Marie Sibylle). Histoire générale des insects de Surinam, et de toute l'Europe; contenant les descriptions des plantes, fleurs et fruits, dont ils se nourrissent, etc. 3e éd. revue, etc. par Buchoz. 3 v. fol. *Paris, L. C. Desnos,* 1771. s.

Mérimée (Prosper). Chronique du règne de Charles ix. Suivie de La double méprise, et de la Guzla; [ou, choix de poésies illyriques]. Nouv. éd. 443 pp. 16°. *Paris, Charpentier,* 1856.

——— Colomba; suivi de La mosaïque et autres contes et nouvelles. Nouv. éd. 450 pp. 16°. *Paris, Charpentier,* 1854.

——— Les deux héritages; suivis de L'inspecteur général, et des Débuts d'un aventurier. 369 pp. 16°. *Paris, Lévy,* 1853.

——— Épisode de l'histoire de Russie: les faux Démétrius. 452 pp. 16°. *Paris, Lévy,* 1855.

——— Études sur l'histoire romaine; guerre sociale; conjuration de Catilina. 430 pp. 16°. *Paris, Lévy,* 1853.

——— Mélanges historiques et littéraires. 382 pp. 16°. *Paris, Lévy,* 1855.

Merivale (Herman). Memoirs of Sir Philip Francis. *See* **Parkes** (Joseph).

Merleker (Carl Friedrich). Geschichte der geographie und der geographischen entdeckungen, in verbindung mit der 'geschichte der schiffahrt, der kolonien, etc. xii, 214 pp. 8°. *Darmstadt, C. W. Leske,* 1839. s.

Merle d'Aubigné (Jean Henri). The protector: a vindication. 3d ed. 426 pp. 8°. *London, Oliver & Boyd,* 1848.

Merlin *or* Merdhyn (Ambrose). Prophetia anglicana et romana, una cum libris explanationvm Alani de Insvlis. Addita svnt vaticinia Joachimi abbatis calabri. 8 p. l. 325 pp. 1 l. 18°. *Francofvrti, J. J. Porssius,* 1608.

Merrem (Blasius). Beitraege zur naturgeschichte; [nebst beitraege zur geschichte des amphibien]. 3 v. in 1. 4°. *Essen, etc.* 1792–1829. s.

CONTENTS.

v. 1. Beitraege zur naturgeschichte, etc. 4 p. l. 47 pp. 12 col. pl. *Duisburg, author,* 1790.
v. 2. Beitraege zur geschichte der amphibien. 2e aufl. 47 pp. 2 col. pl. *Essen, G. D. Baedeker,* 1829.
v. 3. Beitraege zu geschichte der schlangen. ii, 141 pp. 13 col. pl. *Essen, G. D. Baedeker,* 1821.

——— Vermischte abhandlungen aus der thiergeschichte. 3 p. l. 172 pp. 7 pl. 4°. *Göttingen, V. Vossiegel,* 1781. s.

——— Versuch eines systems der amphibien. xv, 191 pp. 1 pl. 8°. *Marbvrgi, J. C. Krieger,* 1820.

Merrill (Orsamus C.) An oration delivered at the meeting-house in Bennington, on the 4th of July, 1806. 56 pp. 16°. *Bennington, [Vt.] Benjamin Smead,* [1806?]

Merry (The) droll; or, pleasing companion. Including some poetical recreations. [*anon.*] vii, 184 pp. 18°. *London, C. Parker,* 1769.

Merryweather (George, *pseudon?*) Kings the devil's viceroys and representatives on earth. 456 pp. 8°. [*n. p.*] *author,* 1838.

Merzdorf (J. F. L. Th.) Bibliothekarische unterhaltungen. 2 v. lxxxvi, 173 pp; vi, 239 pp. 8°. *Oldenburg, W. Berndt,* 1844–50. s.

Metcalf (Samuel L.) A collection of some of the most interesting narratives of Indian warfare in the west, containing an account of the adventures of Daniel Boone; with the expeditions of generals Harmer, Scott, etc. [and Col. James Smith's narrative]. 270 pp. 12°. *Lexington, (Ky.) William G. Hunt,* 1821.

Metcalfe (Samuel L. *M. D.*) Caloric; its mechanical, chemical and vital agencies, in the phenomena of nature. [2d ed.] 2 v. 630 pp; 481 pp. 8°. *Philadelphia, J. B. Lippincott & Co.* 1859.

Meteorological register for the years 1822–25, from observations made by the surgeons of the army, at the military posts of the United States. 63 pp. 8°. *Washington, E. DeKrafft*, 1826. s.

Meteyard (Eliza). The hallowed spots of ancient London; made memorable by the struggles of our forefathers for civil and religious freedom. xii, 291 pp. sm. 4°. *London, Marlborough & Co.* 1862.

——— Life of Josiah Wedgwood. With an introductory sketch of the art of pottery in England. With illustrations. 2 v. xxxv, 504 pp, 1 pl; xxiv, 643 pp. 4 pl. 8°. *London, Hurst & Blackett*, 1865.

Metz (Friedrich). Geschichte des buchhandels und der buchdruckerkunst. 2 v. in 1. vi, 340 pp; 136 pp. 8°. *Darmstadt, Jonghaus*, 1835. s.

Meugy (Jules). De l'extinction de la prostitution. Pétition au sénat—session de 1865. Suivie du discours de M. Dupin sur le luxe effréné des femmes. 3e éd. 71 pp. 16°. *Paris, Garnier*, [1866].

Meusel (Johann Georg). Das gelehrte Teutschland, fortgesetzt. *See* **Hamberger** (J. G.)

——— Lexikon der vom jahr 1750 bis 1800 verstorbenen teutschen schriftstellern. 15 v. 8°. *Leipzig, G. Fleischer*, 1802–16.

——— Teutsches künstlerlexikon oder verzeichniss der jetztlebenden teutschen künstler. Nebst einem verzeichniss sehenswürdiger bibliotheken, kunst-münz-und naturalienkabinete in Teutschland und in der Schweitz. 2e ausg. 3 v. 8°. *Lemgo, Meyer*, 1808–14. s.

Mexia (Pedro). The historie of all the Romane emperors, beginning with Caivs Jvlivs Cæsar, and successively ending with Rodolph the second now raigning. Englished by W. Traheron. 5 p. l. 890 pp. fol. *London, M. Lovvnes*, 1604.

Mexican letters. Containing humorous and satirical observations on the manners, customs, religion and policy of the English, French, Spaniards, and Americans. [*anon.*] 2 v. xii, ix, 264 pp; 280 pp. 12°. *London, W. Goldsmith*, 1773.

Mexico. Código fundamental de los estados-unidos mexicanos. 92 pp. 2 l. 18°. *Mexico, V. G. Torres*, 1847.

Mexico. Dimision del ministerio [1852]. 12 pp. 8°. *Mexico, V. G. Torres*, 1852.

——— Memoria en cumplimiento del articulo 120, de la constitucion federal. 28 pp. 8 tab. 8°. *Mexico, Impr. del supr. gobierno*, 1825.

——— Memoria leida en las camaras en 1851. 43 pp. fol. *Mexico, V. G. Torres*, 1851.

——— Memoria sobre el estado de la agricultura ó indústria de la republica, 1845. 75 pp. 8°. *Mexico, J. M. Lara*, 1846. s.

Meyendorf (Georg von). Voyage d'Orenbourg à Boukhara, fait en 1820, à travers les steppes qui s'étendent à l'est de la mer d' Aral et au-dela d' l'ancien Jaxartes. Revu par A. Jaubert. vii, 508 pp. 1 map. 7 pl. 8°. *Paris, Dondey-Dupré*, 1826.

Meyer (Christian Friedrich Hermann von). Über die reptilien und säugethiere der verschiedenen zeiten der erde. 150 pp. 8°. *Frankfurt a. M. S. Schmerber*, 1852. s.

——— Zur fauna der vorwelt. Fossile saeugethiere, voegel und reptilien aus dem molassemergel von Oeningen. viii, 52 pp. 12 pl. fol. *Frankfurt am Main, H. Keller*, 1845. s.

——— The same. Die saurier des muschelkalkes, mit rücksicht auf die saurier aus buntem sandstein und keuper. viii, 167 pp. 70 pl. fol. *Frankfurt am Main, H. Keller*, 1847–55. s.

Meyer (Christian Paul). Museum meyerianum, sive catalogus rerum naturalium, et nonnullarum artefactarum, quas Meyer collegit. iv, 276 pp. 8°. *Trajecti ad Rhenum, B. Wild & J. Altheer, etc.* 1802.

Meyer (H. A.) *and* **Möbius** (Carl August). Fauna der kieler bucht. v. 1. Die hinterkiemer, oder opisthobranchia. xxx, 86 pp. 26 pl. 4°. *Leipzig, W. Engelmann*, 1865. s.

Meyer (Hermann J.) Neues konversationslexikon, ein wörterbuch des allgemeinen wissens. 2e aufl. 15 v. A—Z. 8°. *Hildburghausen, Bibliographischen institut*, 1861–67.

Meyer (*Dr.* J.) Land, volk und staat der schweizerischen eidgenossenschaft. 2 v. 384 pp; 209 pp. 18°. *Zurich, F. Schulthess*, 1861.

Mezzofanti (Giuseppe, *cardinale*). Catalogo della libreria; compilato da Filippo Bonifazj. 139 pp. 8°. *Roma, Fratelli Pallotta*, 1851. s.

Micali (Giuseppe). Antiche monumenti per servire all' opera intitolata l'Italia avanti il dominio dei Romani. xi pp. 60 pl. fol. *Firenze*, [*autore*,] 1817. s.

Michaelis (H. C.) Quæstiones de bello punico primo. 188, xii pp. 8°. *Trajecti ad Rhenum, C. Van der Post, jun.* 1846. s.

Michaux (François André). Voyage à l'ouest des monts Alléghanys, dans les états de l'Ohio, du Kentucky, et du Tennessée, et retour à Charleston par les Hautes-Carolines, 1802. vi, 312 pp. 1 map. 8°. *Paris, Levrault, Schoell et Cie.* 1804.

Michel (*Dan*). Ayenbite of Inwyt; or, remorse of conscience. In the Kentish dialect, 1340 A.D. Translated from the French of Lorens, or Laurentius. Edited by R. Morris. 6 p. l. c, 359 pp. 8°. *London, Trübner,* 1866.
[Early English text society publ. No. 23.]

Michel (Francisque Xavier). Wayland Smith. *See* **Depping** (G. B.) *and* **Michel**.

Michelet (Jules). Histoire de France au dix-huitième siècle. Louis xv et Louis xvi. v. 17. 486 pp. 8°. *Chamerot & Lauwereyns,* 1867.

Michelet (*madame* Jules). The story of my childhood. From the French by Mary F. Curtis. xii, 218 pp. 16°. *Boston, Little, Brown & Co.* 1867.

Michhailofski-Danilefski (Alexsander). History of the campaign in France, in 1814, translated from the Russian. 414 pp. 1 map. 8 plans. 8°. *London, Smith, Elder & Co.* 1839.

Michiels (Alfred). Chefs d'œuvres des grands maitres. *See* **Kellerhoven** (F.) *and* **Michiels**.

Michigan. Census and statistics, 1854. 413 pp. 8°. *Lansing, G. W. Peck,* 1854. s.

——— Documents accompanying the journal of the house of representatives: 1843, '48, '50, '57, '59, '61, '65. 7 v. 8°. *Detroit and Lansing,* 1843–65.
[*With* Senate documents.]

——— Documents accompanying the journal of the senate: 1843, '49, '50, '55, '57, '61, '65. 7 v. 8°. *Detroit and Lansing,* 1843–65.

——— Joint documents of the legislature: 1850, '51, '53, '55, '57, '59—'65. 12 v. 8°. *Lansing,* 1850–65.

——— First biennial report of the progress of the geological survey of Michigan, embracing observations on the geology, zoölogy, and botany of the lower peninsula. 339 pp. 8°. *Lansing, Hosmer & Kerr,* 1861. s.

CONTENTS.

Part 1. Geology. By A. Winchell.
Part 2. Zoology. Report of the state zoologist, M. Miles.
Part 3. Botany. By N. H. Winchell.

——— Journal of the house of representatives, 1861; extra session, 1862, 1863, 1865. 7 v. 8°. *Lansing,* 1861–63.
[*With* Senate journal, extra session.]

——— Journal of the senate, 1835–37. Extra session, 1862, 1863, 1865. 4 v. 8°. *Detroit and Lansing,* 1835–65.

——— Reports of the superintendent of public instruction [school reports], 1855–57, 1859–66. 9 v. 8°. *Lansing,* 1858–66.

——— Transactions of the state agricultural society, 1857. v. 9. 592 pp. 8°. *Lansing,* 1859.

——— Third annual report of the secretary of the state board of agriculture, 1864. 254 pp. 8°. *Lansing,* 1865.

Michigan (The) teacher; organ of the state teachers' association, and of the department of public instruction. W. H. Payne [and others], editors. Jan. 1866, to Dec. 1867. [v. 1–2.] 8°. *Ypsilanti, Payne, Whitney & Goodison,* 1866–67.

Middendorp (Jakob). Academiarvm orbis christiani libri dvo. 12 p. l. 301 pp. 16°. *Coloniæ, Cholinus,* 1572. s.

Middleton (Christopher). A vindication of [his] conduct in a voyage for discovering a northwest passage, in answer to Arthur Dobbs. 206, 48 pp. 8°. *London,* 1743.

Middleton (Conyers). A dissertation concerning the origin of printing in England. 29 pp. sm. 4°. *Cambridge,* [*Eng.*] *W. Thurlbourn,* 1735.

Miège (Guy). The new state of England under their majesties k. William and q. Mary. By G. M. [*anon.*] 17 p. l. 828 pp. 18°. *London, J. Robinson,* 1691.

Miertsching (Johann A.) Journal de voyage au pole nord. 2e éd. 143 pp. 1 map. 12°. *Genève, J. Cherbuliez,* 1857.

Miéville (Antoine). Manuel du citoyen vaudois, à l'usage des campagnes et des écoles. 272 pp. 12°. *Lausanne, E. Vincent,* 1846. s.

Mifflin (Samuel W.) Methods of location; or, modes of describing and adjusting railway curves and tangents, as practiced by the engineers of Pennsylvania. 47 pp. 16°. *Philadelphia, Daniels & Smith,* 1850.

Mignet (François Auguste Alexis). Mémoires historiques. 3e éd. 534 pp. 12°. *Paris, Charpentier,* 1854.

——— Notices et portraits historiques et littéraires. 3e éd. 2 v. iv, 422 pp; 488 pp. 12°. *Paris, Charpentier,* 1854.

Mignonette; found among the flowers and weeds of Hillsdale. [*anon.*] 379 pp. 16°. *Boston, B. Smith,* 1868.

Mikailofski-Daniefski. *See* **Michailofski.**

Miles (James W.) Philosophic theology; or, ultimate grounds of all religious belief based in reason. xii, 234 pp. 8°. *Charleston,* [*S. C.*] *J. Russell,* 1849.

Miles (M. *M. D.*) Zoology of Michigan. *See* **Michigan.** Geological survey.

Miles (Pliny). American mnemotechny; or, the art of memory, theoretical and practical. 2 pts. in 1 v. 5th ed. 480 pp. 12°. *New York, M. H. Newman & Co.* 1848. s.

——— Statistical register and book of general reference and quotations. A compilation. 2d ed. 200 pp. 12°. *New York, M. H. Newman & Co,* 1849. s.

Milet (Pierre). Relation de sa captivité parmi les Onneiouts en 1690–91. 56 pp. 8°. *Nouvelle York, J. M. Shea,* 1864. s.

Militärische briefe eines verstorbenen an seine noch lebenden freunde, historischen, wissenschaftlichen, kritischen, und humoristischen inhalts. [*anon.*] 3 v. 8°. *Adorf, Verlags-büreau,* 1841–44.

NOTE.—Purports to be written by the spirit of C. von Clausewitz.

Milizia (Francesco). De l'art de voir dans les beaux arts. Traduit de l'Italien; suivi des institutions propres à les faire fleurir en France, et d'un état des objets d'arts dont ses musées ont été enrichis par la guerre de la liberté, par le général Pommereul. 4 p. l. 316 pp. 8°. *Paris, Bernard,* 1798. s.

——— Memorie degli architetti antichi e moderni. 4ª ed. 2 v. lxxix, 263 pp; 331 pp. 8°. *Bassano, Remondini,* 1785. s.

Mill (David). Dissertationes selectae varia s. litterarum et antiquitatis orientalis capita exponentes et illustrantes. 4 p. l. 447 pp. 23 l. 18°. *Trajecti ad Rhenum, J. Broedelet,* 1724.

Mill (James). History of British India [to 1805]. 3 v. 4°. *London, Baldwin, Cradock, & Joy,* 1817. s.

Mill (John Stuart). Considerations on representative government. viii, 365 pp. 12°. *New York, Harpers,* 1862.

——— Dissertations and discussions, political, philosophical, and historical. v. 3. 8°. *London, Longmans,* 1867.

——— Inaugural address; delivered to the university of St. Andrews, Feb. 1, 1867. 99 pp. 8°. *London, Longmans,* 1867.

——— On liberty. 223 pp. 12°. *Boston, Ticknor, & Fields,* 1863.

——— Thoughts on parliamentary reform. 2d ed. 58 pp. 8°. *London, J. W. Parker & son,* 1859.

——— Die inductive logik. Eine darlegung der philosophischen principien wissenschaftlicher forschung, insbesondere der naturforschung. Nach dem Englischen in's Deutsche übertragen von J. Schiel. lx, 654 pp. 8°. *Braunschweig, Vieweg,* 1849. s.

Millar (John). An historical view of the English government, from the settlement of the Saxons in Britain to the accession of the house of Stewart. 5 p. l. 506 pp. 10 l. 8°. *Dublin, Grueber & McAllister,* 1789.

Miller (Eli P. *M. D.*) A treatise on the cause of exhausted vitality; or, abuses of the sexual function. 131 pp. 12°. *New York, J. A. Gray & Green,* 1867.

Miller (George). Latter struggles in the journey of life; or, the afternoon of my days. [By a] country bookseller. 406 pp. 8°. *Edinburgh, J. Colston,* 1833.

Miller (Joe, *pseudon. for* John Mottley?) Jests; or, the wits' vade-mecum. 153 pp. 1 pl. 32°. *London, Allman & son,* [n. d.]

——— Joe Miller's jests, with copious additions. Edited by Frank Bellew. iv, 287 pp. 12°. *New York,* 1865.

Miller (*Rev.* John, *chaplain to the forces in N. Y.*) A description of the province and city of New York; with plans of the city and several forts as they existed in 1695. 43 pp. 8°. *London, T. Rodd,* 1843.

Miller (J. R.) The history of Great Britain from the death of George ii, to the coronation of George iv; designed as a continuation of Hume and Smollett. x, 464 pp. portrait. 8°. *London, Jones & Co.* 1829.

Miller (John Sebastian). An illustration of the sexual system of Linnaeus. v. 1. 106 pp. 106 pl. col. 8°. *London, author,* 1779. s.

——— The same. v. ii. An illustration of the termini botanici of Linnaeus. 86 pp. 86 pl. col. 8°. *London, author,* 1789. s.

Miller (Josiah). Our hymns; their authors and origin. xvi, 416 pp. 12°. *London, Jackson, Walford & Hodder,* 1866.

Miller (*Mrs.* O. D.) Twilight stories, for the little ones. 191 pp. 16°. *Boston, R. A. Ballou,* 1866.

[Round Hill stories.]

Miller (Samuel, *D. D.*) A sermon on the burning of the theatre at Richmond. 45 pp. 16°. *New York, Whiting and Watson,* 1812.

[*With* WITHERSPOON (John). Serious inquiry into the nature and effects of the stage. *New York,* 1812.]

Miller (*Rev.* Samuel). Treatise on Mercersburg theology; or, Mercersburg and modern theology compared. 131 pp. 16°. *Philadelphia, S. R. Fisher & Co.* 1866.

Miller (William Allen). Elements of chemistry, theoretical and practical. 3 v. 8°. *London, J. W. Parker & son,* 1851–62. s.

CONTENTS.

v. 1. Chemical physics.
v. 2. Inorganic chemistry.
v. 3. Organic chemistry.

Millet (Joshua). A history of the baptists in Maine. 472 pp. 12°. *Portland, Day & Co.* 1845.

Milligan (Robert). Reason and revelation; or, the province of reason in matters pertaining to divine revelation defined and illustrated, and the paramount authority of the holy scriptures vindicated. 445 pp. 8°. *Cincinnati, R. W. Carroll & Co.* 1868.

Millin de Grand Maison (Aubin Louis). Peintures de vases antiques, vulgairement appelés étrusques, tirées de différentes collections et gravées par A. Clener, accompagnées d'explications par A. L. Millin. 2 v. xx, 124 pp. 72 pl; 146 pp. 78 pl. fol. *Paris, P. Didot,* 1808–10. s.

——— Voyage dans les départemens du midi de la France. 4 v. in 5. 8°. Atlas, 4°. *Paris, L'imprim. impér.* 1807–11.

Millon (Eugène.) Éléments de chimie organique, comprenant les applications à la physiologie animale. 2 v. 636 pp; 771 pp. 8°. *Paris, J. B. Baillière,* 1845–48. s.

Millot (Claude François Xavier). Elements of ancient history. Translated from the French. 2 v. viii, 504 pp; viii, 519 pp. 8°. *New York, Mott & Lyon,* 1797.

Mills (Frederick C.) The wine guide; with remarks upon the treatment of spirits, bottled beer, and cider. 64 pp. 24°. *London, Groombridge & sons,* 1861.

Mills (Lewis E.) Glimpses of southern France and Spain. 2 p. l. 153 pp. 16°. *Cincinnati, R. Clarke & Co.* 1867.

Mills (Robert). American pharos; or, lighthouse guide: with a general view of the coast. 134 pp. 8°. *Washington, Thompson & Homans,* 1832. s.

Milman (*Rev.* Henry Hart). Belshazzar: a dramatic poem. 126 pp. 16°. *Boston, Wells & Lilly,* 1822.

Milner (John, *D. D.*) The key of heaven; a manual of prayer. New ed. 480 pp. 1 pl. 24°. *Baltimore, J. Murphy & Co.* [1867].

Milner (Mary). The life of Isaac Milner, D. D. 2d ed. xvi, 456 pp. 1 pl. 16°. *London, Seeley, Burnside & Seeley,* 1844.

Milnes (Richard Monckton, *lord Houghton*). Poems of many years. New ed. xi, 275 pp. 16°. *Boston, Ticknor & Co.* 1846.

Milton (John). A defense of the people of England. In answer to Salmasius's defense of the king. [Translated by Robert (?) Washington.] 16°. [*Amsterdam,*] 1692.

——— Εικονοκλαστης, in answer to a book intitul'd Εικων βασιλικη, the portraicture of king Charles the first. 16°. *Amsterdam,* 1690.

——— An old looking-glass for the laity and clergy of all denominations; being considerations touching the likeliest means to remove hirelings out of the church of Christ. x, 74 pp. 16°. *Philadelphia, R. Bell,* 1770.

——— Paradise lost. [With] an account of [Milton's] life. 12th ed. [Elijah Fenton's 1st ed.] xxviii, 350 pp. 23 l. 13 pl. 16°. *London, J. Tonson,* 1725.

——— The same. Illustrated by Gustave Doré. Edited with notes and a life of Milton, by Robert Vaughan. fol. *London, Cassell,* [1866].

——— The same. New ed. with explanatory notes. 16°. *New York,* 1867.

——— Poetical works, with life of the author. 348 pp. 16°. *Brookfield,* [*Mass.*] *I. Thomas, jr.* 1810.

——— Pro popvlo anglicano defensio, contra Salmasii defensionem regiam. 10 p. l. 244 pp. 24°. *Londini, Dv. Gard.* 1653.

——— Story of our first parents, selected from Milton's Paradise lost. By Mrs. Siddons. iv, 190 pp. 1 pl. 8°. *London, J. Murray,* 1822.

Milwaukee (Young men's association of the city of). Catalogue of the library. 181 pp. 8°. *Milwaukee,* [*Wis.*] *Daily news printing establishment,* 1861. s.

Minding (Julius). Ueber die geographische vertheilung der säugethiere. 103 pp. 4°. *Berlin, Enslin,* 1829. s.

Minifie (William). A text book of geometrical drawing. 127 pp. 56 pl. 8°. *Baltimore, W. Minifie & Co.* 1849. s.

——— The same. With illustrations for drawing plans, sections and elevations of buildings and machinery; and an essay on the theory of color, in its application to drawing, [etc.] 162 pp. 56 pl. 8°. *New York, D. Van Nostrand,* 1868.

Minneapolis, (*Minnesota*). Merwin's directory, 1867. 264 pp. 8°. *Minneapolis, H. Merwin,* 1867.

Minnesota. Executive documents for 1866. 8°. *St. Paul, Pioneer print co.* 1867.

——— Journal of the senate and house of representatives. 9th session. 2 v. 364 pp; 406 pp. 8°. *St. Paul, M. J. Clum,* 1867.

Minnesota historical society. Collections for the year 1864, and for 1867. 2 v. 84 pp; 62 pp. 8°. *St. Paul,* [*Society,*] 1865–67.

Minutes of the convention of delegates from the synod of the presbyterian church of New York and Philadelphia, and from the associations of Connecticut, held annually from 1766 to 1775, inclusive. 68 pp. 8°. *Hartford, E. Gleason,* 1843.

Minutoli *or* Menuminutoli (Julius, von). Die canarischen inseln, ihre vergangenheit und zukunft. 5 l. 259 pp. 8°. *Berlin, S. Wolff,* 1854. S.

Mirabeau (Honoré Gabriel Riquetti, *comte* de). Histoire secréte de la cour de Berlin; ou, correspondance d'un voyageur françois, depuis le mois de Juillet 1786 jusqu'au 19 Janvier 1787. Ouvrage posthume. [*anon.*] 2 v. in 1. xvii, 318 pp; 376 pp. 12°. [*Alençon, Malassis,*] 1789.

Mirabella e Alacogne (Vincenzo). Dichiarazioni della pianta dell' antiche Siracuse, e d'alcune scelte medaglie d'esse, e de' principi che quelle possedettero. 128, 126 pp. 16 pl. fol. *Napoli, L. Scoriggio,* 1614.

Mirick (B. L.) The history of Haverhill, Massachusetts. 277 pp. 1 pl. 12°. *Haverhill, A. W. Thayer,* 1832.

Mirone (*monsieur* de, *pseudon.*) *See* **Saumery** (— de). L'heureux imposteur. *Utrecht,* 1740.

Mirrour (The) of government, both ecclesiasticall and civill. [*anon.*] 5 p. l. 151 pp. sm. 4°. *London, Thomas Gibbs,* 1658.

Miscellaneous (A) collection, consisting of an original letter of Columbus, original poetry, etc. With selections, by M. H. [*anon.*] 132 pp. 4°. *London, T. Davison,* 1803.

Miscellaneous pieces. v. i, containing poems, translations and essays. v. ii, containing a free enquiry into the nature and the origin of evil, and reflections on several subjects. [*anon.*] 2 v. 287 pp; xxx, 257 pp. 12°. *London, R. & J. Dodsley,* 1761.

Miscellany of knowledge; a new work, by several gentlemen, on different subjects; viz: lectures on natural philosophy: poetry on different subjects; a twelve-month's tour through America; political hints for the perusal of the legislature. [*anon.*] 6 p. l. 302 pp. 1 l. 12°. *London,* 1792.

Missa de sancto angelo cvstode. 2 l. fol. *Venetiis, Ciera,* 1617.
[*With* MISSALE romanvm. *Venetiis,* 1598.]

Missa sacratissimi rosarii beatissimæ virginis Mariæ. 2 l. fol. *Venetiis, B. Ciera,* 1617.
[*With* MISSALE romanvm. *Venetiis,* 1598.]

Missa sancti Caroli [Borromæi] episcopi et confessoris. 2 l. fol. *Venetiis, Ciera,* 1618.
[*With* MISSALE romanvm. *Venetiis,* 1598.]

Missæ propriæ festorvm ordinis fratrvm minorvm. 10 l. fol. *Venetiis, B. Ciera,* 1598.
[*With* MISSALE romanvm. *Venetiis,* 1598.]

Missæ sancti Gregorii papæ, pro vivis et defvnctis. 2 l. fol. *Venetiis, Ciera,* 1617.
[*With* MISSALE romanvm. *Venetiis,* 1598.]

Missale romanvm. 20 p. l. 273 l. 1 pl. fol. *Venetiis, B. Ciera,* 1598.

Missale romanvm, ex decreto concilij tridentini restitutum. 31 p. l. 640, cxvi, 7, 28, 3, 12 pp. 8 pl. fol. *Antverpiæ, Soc. lib. off. eccl.* 1633. S.

Mission (La) moderne, par un prisonnier de la Bastille. [*anon.*] 2e éd. 68 pp. 12°. *Paris,* 1790.

Missionary records. North America. [*anon.*] viii, 423 pp. 18°. *London, Relig. tract soc.* [*n. d.*]

Missionary remains; or, sketches of the lives of [Jeremiah] Evarts, [Elias] Cornelius, and [Benjamin B.] Wisner. [*anon.*] With an introduction by Samuel H. Cox. 143 pp. 18°. *New York, Taylor & Gould,* 1835.

Missirini (Melchior). Della vita di Antonio Canova. Libri quattro. 523 pp. 3 pl. 8°. *Prato, frat. Giachetti,* 1824. S.

Misson (François Maximilien). A new voyage to Italy, with observations on Germany, Switzerland, Savoy, Geneva, Flanders, and Holland. 4th ed. 2 v. in 4. 12°. *London, R. Bonwicke* [*and others*], 1714.

Missouri. Journal of the state convention, held in Jefferson city, July, 1861, Oct. 1861, June, 1862, June, 1863. 4 v. 8°. *St. Louis, G. Knapp & Co.* 1861–63.

——— Journal of the state convention, held at St. Louis, Jan.–April. 1865. 287 pp. 8°. *St. Louis (Mo.) Democrat office,* 1865.

Mistanguet (——). Les plaisantes idées du sievr Mistanguet. Ensemble la genealogie de Mistanguet et de Bruscambille. [*anon.*] 79 pp. 16°. *Paris, Iean Millot,* 1615.

Mitchel *or* Mitchil (Jonathan). Letter to his brother [on conviction of sin]. 17 pp. 18°. [*n. p.* 1649?]

Mitchel (Martin), *and* Osborn (Joseph H). Geographical and statistical history of the county of Winnebago; with a general view of the state of Wisconsin. 120 pp. 16°. *Oshkosh, Mitchel & Smith,* 1856.

Mitchell (Donald G.) Rural studies, with hints for country places. viii, 295 pp. 12°. *New York, C. Scribner & Co.* 1867.

Mitchell (Elisha). Elements of geology, with an outline of the geology of North Carolina. 141 pp. 1 map. 8°. [*n. p.*] 1842. s.

Mitchell (John M.) The herring; its natural history and national importance. xii, 372 pp. 6 pl. col. 8°. *Edinburgh, Edmonston & Douglas*, 1864.

Mitchell (Joseph). Missionary pioneer; or, a memoir of John Stewart [a man of colour], founder of the mission among the Wyandotts, at Upper Sandusky, Ohio. 96 pp. 24°. *New York, J. C. Totten*, 1827.

Mitchell (S. Augustus). An accompaniment to Mitchell's reference and distance map of the United States, with a general view of the United States. 324 pp. 16°. *Philadelphia, Mitchell & Hinman*, 1834.

——— Mitchell's geographical reader: a system of modern geography. 600 pp. 12°. *Philadelphia, Thomas, Cowperthwait & Co.* 1840.

——— New traveller's guide through the United States. 118 pp. 1 col. map. 24°. *Philadelphia, Thomas, Cowperthwait & Co.* 1850. s.

Mitchell (S. Augustus, *jr.*) New general atlas; containing maps of the various countries of the world, plans of cities, etc. together with valuable statistical tables. [New ed.] 27 pp. 91 maps. 4°. *Philadelphia, S. A. Mitchell*, 1867.

——— Easy introduction to the study of geography. sq. 12°. *Philadelphia, S. A. Mitchell*, 1866.

Mitchell (Thomas). The gospel crown of life; a system of philosophical theology. xxv, 417 pp. 1 pl. 12°. *Albany, J. Munsell*, 1851.

Mitre (Bartolomé). Historia de [Manuel] Belgrano. 2 v. 644 pp; 553 pp. 8°. *Buenos Aires, Mayo*, 1859. s.

Mittermaier (Carl, *M.D.*) Madeira und seine bedeutung als heilungsort. viii, 158 pp. 8°. *Heidelberg, J. C. B. Mohr*, 1855. s.

Mnemonika: or, chronological tablets, exhibiting in a methodical manner the most remarkable occurrences, from the creation of the world to the present period. [*anon.*] 346 pp. 18°. *Baltimore, E. J. Coale*, 1812.

Möbius (August Ferdinand). Die elemente der mechanik des himmels. xx, 315 pp. 2 pl. 8°. *Leipzig, Weidmann*, 1843. s.

Möbius (Carl August). Das aquarium des zoologischen gartens zu Hamburg. 4e aufl. 55 pp. 8°. *Hamburg, Zool. gesellschaft*, 1866. s.

——— Fauna der kieler bucht. *See* **Meyer** (H. A.) *and* **Möbius** (C. A.)

Mocquet de Meaux (Jean). Voyages en Afriqve, Asie, Indes Orientales et Occidentales. 4 p. l. 442 pp. 6 l. 5 pl. 16°. *Roven, Jacqves Caillové*, 1645.

Moebius. *See* **Möbius.**

Moehring. *See* **Möhring.**

Moeller. *See* **Möller.**

Moerch. *See* **Mörch.**

Moffat (*Mrs.* A. S.) One-armed Hugh, the little corn merchant; or, Ralph and Tib. 506 pp. 5 pl. 16°. *Boston, Graves & Young*, 1866.

Moffat (*Rev.* James C.) Life of Thomas Chalmers. 2d ed. 435 pp. 12°. *Cincinnati, Moore, Anderson, Wilstach & Keys*, 1853.

Moffitt (*Mrs.* Mary Anna). The nobleman and the teacher; or, the youth's defense. An Irish story. 253 pp. 16°. *New York, J. Craft*, 1867.

Mohammed ibn abi Mohammed ibn Zafer, *or* **Djafer.** Solwan el mota; ossiano, conforti politici. Versione italiana di M. Amari. lxxvii, 352 pp. 12°. *Firenze, F. Le Monnier*, 1851.

Mohammed Kasim, *surnamed* **Ferishta.** *See* **Ferishta.**

Mohammed Wali Ullah. *See* **Wali.**

Mohan Lal. Travels in the Panjab, Afghanistan and Turkistan to Balk, Bokhara, and Herat; and a visit to Great Britain and Germany. xxvii, 528 pp. 8°. *London, Allen & Co.* 1846.

Mohl (Hugo von). Grundzüge der anatomie und physiologie der vegetabilischen zelle. 152 pp. 1 pl. 8°. *Braunschweig, Vieweg*, 1851. s.

Mohl (Jules de). Commentaires sur le livre des rois. *See* **Firdúsi.**

Mohr (D. M. Nicolas). Forsog til islandsk naturhistorie. xvi, 413 pp. 7 pl. 8°. *Kjöbenhavn, C. F. Holm*, 1786. s.

Mohr (Francis), *and* **Redwood** (Theophilus). Practical pharmacy; the arrangements, apparatus, and manipulations of the pharmaceutical shop and laboratory. Edited by William Proctor, jr. 576 pp. 8°. *Philadelphia, Lea & Blanchard*, 1849. s.

Mohr (Friedrich). Commentär zur preussischen pharmacopoe, nebst übersetzung des textes. 2e aufl. 2 v. xx, 485 pp; 459 pp. 8°. *Braunschweig, Vieweg*, 1853–[54]. s.

——— Lehrbuch der pharmaceutischen technik. 2e aufl. xii, 545 pp. 8°. *Braunschweig, Vieweg*, 1853. s.

Möhring (Paul Heinrich Gerhard). Avivm genera. 88 pp. 8°. *Bremae, G. G. Rump*, 1752. s.

Moir (David Macbeth). The bridal of Borthwick. 11 pp. 8°. *London*, 1841.
[Hazlitt's romancist and novelist's lib. v. 4].

Molbech (Christian). Om offentlige bibliotheker. 4 p. l. 220 pp. 8°. *Kiöbenhavn, Gyldendalske boghandlivgs forlag,* 1829. s.

Molesworth (James T.), *and* **Candy** (Thomas *and* George). A dictionary, Murathee and English. xviii, 1162 pp. 4°. *Bombay, authors,* 1831. s.

Molina (Alonso de). Vocabolario en lengva castellana y mexicana. 2 v. in 1. 4 p. l. 121 l; 3 p. l. 162 l. fol. *Mexico, Antonio de Spinosa,* 1571.

Molina, (Felipe). Bosquejo de la republica de Costa Rica. 128 pp. 5 pl. 9 maps. 8°. *Nueva York, S. W. Benedict,* 1851. s.

——— Costa Rica and New Grenada. An inquiry into the question of boundaries. 54 pp. 1 map. 8°. *Washington, R. A. Waters,* 1853.

——— Memoir of the boundary question pending between Costa Rica and Nicaragua. 40 pp. 1 map. 8°. *Washington, Gideon & Co.* 1851.

Molina (Giovanni Ignazio). Versuch einer naturgeschichte von Chili. Aus dem Italiänischen übersetzt von J. D. Brandis. 9 p. l. 328 pp. 1 map. 8°. *Leipzig, F. G. Jacobäer,* 1786. s.

Moll (C. L.), *and* **Reuleaux** (F.) Die festigkeit der materialien, namentlich des guss-und schmiedeisens. viii, 72 pp. 8°. *Braunschweig, Vieweg,* 1853. s.

Moll (Louis). Rapport sur l'état de la production des bestiaux en Allemagne, en Belgique, et en Suisse. [Extract.] 86 pp. 8°. *Paris, Bureau de la maison rustique,* 1842. s.

Mollard (John). Art of cookery. New ed. xv, 323 pp. 12°. *London, Whittaker & Co.* 1836.

Moller (Johann). Bibliotheca septentrionis eruditi. i. Alb. Bartholini liber de scriptis Danorum, Norwagorum, et Islandorum, a J. Mollero illustratus. ii. Joh. Schefferi Svecia literata, a Mollero illustrata. iii. Joh. Molleri introductio ad historiam ducatuum slesvicensis et holsatici, rerum scriptores recensens, [etc.] iv. Ejusdem præfatio de gentium borealium scriptoribus. 4 v. in 1. 16°. *Lipsiæ, G. Liebezeit,* 1698–99.

Möller (Johann Heinrich). Catalogus librorum tam manuscriptorum quam impressorum a beato Seetzenio in oriente emti in bibliotheca gothana asservantur. v. 1. particulas i. et ii. complectens. [Theologia; historia; philologia; carmina; opera rhetorica; MSS.] vi, 278, 28 pp. 4°. *Gothæ, C. Glaeser,* 1821–26. s.
[No more published.]

——— De numis orientalibus in nummophylacio gothano asservatis commentatio prima. Nummos chalificarum et dynastiarum cuficos exhibens. Ed. altera. iv, 188 pp. 1 pl. 4°. *Gothæ, C. Glaeser,* 1826. s.

——— The same. Commentatio altera. Numos dynastiarum recentiores exhibens. 2 p. l. 62 pp. 4°. *Gothæ, C. Glaeser,* 1830. s.
[*With* the preceding.]

——— Orbis terrarum antiquus. Schul-atlas der alten welt, nach D'Anville, Mannert, Uckert, Reichard, etc. Mit kurzer abriss der alten geographie. 23^e aufl. 14 pp. 15 maps. 4°. *Gotha, Perthes,* [1851]. s.

Mollhausen (Baldwin). Tagebuch eine reise vom Mississippi nach den küsten der Südsee. Eingeführt von A. von Humboldt. 5 p. l. xv, 496 pp. 13 pl. 1 map. 4°. *Leipzig, Mendelssohn,* 1858. s.

Molloy (Charles). De jure maritimo et navali; or, a treatise of affairs maritime and of commerce. 12 p. l. 433 pp. 7 l. 8°. *London,* [1676?]
[Imperfect: wanting title-page.]

——— The same. Derecho maritima y naval; ó tratado de los negocios maritimos y del comercio. Traducida al Castellano por D. Cesareo de Nava Palacio. 4 v. 16°. *Madrid,* 1793.

Moltke (*freiherr* von). Memoir über die karte von Kleinasien. *See* **Kiepert** (H.) *and* **Moltke.**

Molza (Francesco Maria). Le ter'ze rime, 1542.
[*With* BERNI (F.) Tutte le opere, etc.]

Mommsen (Theodor). The history of Rome. Translated by Rev. W. P. Dickson. v. iv. parts 1 and 2. viii, 619 pp. 12°. *London, R. Bentley,* 1866.

Momoro (Antoine François). Traité élémentaire de l'imprimerie; ou, le manuel de l'imprimeur. [2e éd.?] iv, 347 pp. 36 pl. 8°. *Paris, Ve. Taillard & fils,* 1796.

Monardes (Nicolas). Joyfvll nevves ovt of the newe founde worlde; wherein is declared the rare and singular vertues of diuerse and sundrie hearbes, trees, oyles, plantes, and stones, with their aplications as well for physicke as chirurgerie. Englished [out of Spanish] by John Frampton. 3 parts in 1 v. 3 p. l. 109 l. 1 l. sm. 4°. *London, Willyam Norton,* 1577.

Monceau (Duhamel du). *See* **Duhamel** du Monceau.

Moncrieff (John). An inquiry into the medicinal qualities and effects of aerated alkaline water. 102 pp. 16°. *Baltimore, Edward J. Coale,* 1810.

Moncrif (François Augustin Paradis de). *See* **Paradis** de Moncrif.

Mondasse (Varennes de). *See* **Varennes** de Mondasse.

Mone (Franz Joseph). Quellensammlung der badischen landesgeschichte. Im auftrage der regierung herausgegeben. v. i. viii, 564 pp. 4°. *Karlsruhe, C. Macklot,* 1848. S.
[No more published.]

Monfalcon (Jean Baptiste). Précis de bibliographie médicale, [etc.] viii, 554, viii pp. 18°. *Paris, Baillière,* 1827. S.

Mongitore (Antonino). Bibliotheca sicula; sive de scriptoribus siculis, qui tum vetera, tum recentiora saecula illustrarunt, notitiæ locupletissimæ. 2 v. xxviii, 420 pp; 301, 108 pp. fol. *Panormi, C. Bua,* 1707–14.

Monk (The) of the mountains; or, a description of the joys of paradise; with the destiny of the nations of the earth for one hundred years to come. By the hermit himself. [*anon.*] 256 pp. 1 portrait. 8°. *Indianapolis, Downey & Brouse,* 1866.

Monneken (Karel). *See* **Virulus** (C.)

Monro (Alexander). New Brunswick; with a brief outline of Nova Scotia and Prince Edward island; their history, geography, and statistics. vii, 385 pp. 2 maps. 8°. *Halifax, R. Nugent,* 1855. S.

Monro (Alexander, *jr. M. D.*) The structure and physiology of fishes, explained and compared with those of man and other animals. 128 pp. 44 pl. fol. *Edinburgh, C. Elliot,* 1785. S.

Monroe (James, *pres't U. S.*) The people the sovereigns; being a comparison of the government of the United States with those of the republics which have existed before, with the causes of their decadence and fall. Edited by S. L. Gouverneur. 274 pp. 12°. *Philadelphia, J. B. Lippincott & Co.* 1867.

Monselet (Charles). Rétif de la Bretonne: sa vie, ses ouvrages, etc. 210 pp. 16°. *Paris, Alvarès fils,* 1854.

Monson (W. I.) Extracts from a journal [during a tour in Istria and Dalmatia, and in Sicily, Malta, and Calabria]. xiii, 254 pp. 2 pl. 8°. *London, Rodwell & Martin,* 1820.

Montagne (Jean François Camille). Sylloge generum specierumque cryptogamarum, etc. xxiv, 498 pp. 8°. *Parisiis, J. B. Baillière,* 1856. S.

Montagu (George). Testacea britannica; or, natural history of British shells. xxxvii, 606 pp. 16 pl. 4°. *London, J. White,* 1803.

Montagu (George). The same. Supplement. v, 183 pp. 14 pl. 4°. *London, J. White,* 1808.
[*With* MONTAGU (G.) Testacea britannica].

Montague (Charles, *earl of Halifax*). Poetical works. 8°. *Edinburgh,* 1793.
[Anderson's Brit. poets, v. 6.]

Montalboddo *or* **Fracanzano,** da Montalboddo (——). Itinerariũ portugallẽsiũ e Lusitania in Indiã et inde in occidentem et demum ad aquilonem. 8 p. l. 88 l. 4°. *Milan,* 1508.
[Imperfect: wanting index.]

——— The same. Newe unbekanthe landte und ein newe weldte in kurtz zeythe verganger erfunden. 68 l. sm. 4°. *Nureinbergk, Georg Stüchsz,* 1508.

Montalembert (Marc René, *marquis* de). La fortification perpendiculaire; ou, essai sur plusieurs manières de fortifier la ligne droite, le triangle, le carré, et tous les polygônes, de quelqu' étendue qu'en soient les côtés, en donnant à leur défense une direction perpendiculaire, etc. [L'art défensif, etc.] v. 1–5. 4°. *Paris, Barrois,* 1776–84. S.

——— The same. [v. 8. Divers mémoires.] S.

CONTENTS.

Observations sur les nouveaux forts qui ont eté exécutés, et qui doivent l'être pour la défense de la rade de Cherbourg, etc. viii, 26 pp. 4°. *Paris,* [*auteur*], 1790.
Mémoire sur les casemates exécuteés à Cherbourg, etc. vi, 76 pp. 11 pl. 4°. *Paris,* [*auteur*], 1790.
Mémoire sur l'effet du canon dans les casemates. 10 pp. 4°.
Réponse au col. d'Arçon, sur son Apologie des principes observés dans le corps du génie. 24 pp. 4°. *Paris,* [*auteur*], 1790.
[Wanting v. 6, 7, and 9–11].

Montanari (Geminiano). Della moneta.
[SCRITTORI class. ital. di econ. pol. v. 44.]

Montauban (Jean). Relation du voyage en Guinée, en l'année 1695. 3 p. l. 38 pp. 18°. *Amsterdam, J. L. de Lorme,* 1698.
[*With* LAS CASAS (B. de). Relation des voyages des Espagnols. *Amsterdam,* 1698.]

Montefiore (Joshua). American trader's compendium; containing laws, customs, and regulations of the United States relative to commerce. xii, 304 pp. 8°. *Philadelphia, Samuel R. Fisher, jr.* 1811.

Montémont (Albert). Voyages en Amérique; par Christophe Colomb, Fernand Cortez, Pizarre, Cabral, Humboldt, Basil Hall, Mistress Trollope, Ross, Parry, Franklin, Bulloch, Watterton, Head, Walsh. Traduit par Albert Montémont. 320 pp. 1 map. 8 pl. fol. *Paris, J. Bry ainé,* 1854.

Montesquieu (Charles de Secondat, *baron* de). Le temple de Gnide. Nouv. éd. vii, 104 pp. 9 pl. 8°. *Paris, Le Mire,* 1772. S.

Monthly register and review of the United States. *See* **History** (The) of the Am. revolution and monthly register of the U. S. v. 1. *Charleston*, 1806.

Monti (Luigi). A reader of the Italian language. Extracts in prose and poetry: with notes. ix, 348 pp. 12°. *Boston, Little, Brown & Co.* 1855.

Monticelli (Teodoro). Opere. [7 v. in] 3. 4°. *Napoli, Stabl. tipog. dell' aquila.* 1841–43. S.

CONTENTS.

v. 1. Su l'economia delle acque da ristabilirsi nel regno di Napoli. 4a ed. 59 pp. 1841.
Memoria sull' origine delle acque del Sebeto, di Napoli antica, di Pozzuoli, etc. 44 pp. 1 pl. 1840.
In agrum puteolanum camposque phlegraeos commentarium. 31 pp. 1840.
Su la pastorizia del regno di Napoli. 90 pp. 1840.
Del trattamento delle api in Farignana. 109 pp. 1 pl. 1840.
v. 2. Descrizione dell' eruzione del Vesuvio. 2a ed. 335 pp. 2, 4 pl. 1813.
v. 3. Descrizione, cont'd. Vita P. Carolini; Elogio di V. Petagna. Prodromo della mineralogia vesuviana. 431 pp. 19 pl.

——— *and* Covelli (Niccola). Prodromo della mineralogia vesuviana. v. i. Orittognosia. xxxiv, 483 pp. atlas. 19 pl. 8°. *Napoli, Tramater*, 1825. S.

Montigny (—— de, *and others*). Relation de la mission du Missisipi du séminaire de Québec en 1700. Par MM. de Montigny, Buisson de St. Cosme, et Thaumur de La Source. 66 pp. 8°. *Nouvelle York, J. M. Shea*, 1861. S.

Montoya (Antonio Ruiz de). *See* **Ruiz de Montoya.**

Montreux (Nicolas de). Athlette, pastovrelle; ov fable bocagère. Par Ollenix du Montsacré. [*pseudon.*] 35 l. 24°. *Tovrs, I. Mettayer*, 1592.
[*With* the following].

——— Le premier livre des bergeries de Ivlliete. Auquel par les amours des bergers et bergères l'on voit les effects différents de l'amour, etc. avec plusieurs echoz, énigmes, chansons, sonnets, etc. De l'inuention d'Ollenix du Montsacré. [*pseudon.*] 5e éd. 6 p. l. 291 l. 24°. *Tovrs, G. Drobet*, 1592.

——— The same. Le second livre des bergeries de Ivlliette, etc. Ensemble, les œuures poëtiques de la docte bergère Ivlliette. 3e éd. 4 p. l. 482 l. 24°. *Tovrs, de Montr'oeil & Iean Richer*, 1592.

——— The same. Le troisième livre. Auec pareils enrichissemens de diuerses poësies et discours. Ensemble la Diane, pastourelle ou fable. 4 p. l. 402 l. 24°. *Tovrs, Iamet Mettayer*, 1594.

——— The same. Le quatriesme livre. Ensemble la tragédie d'Isabelle. 5 p. l. 400, 634 pp. 24°. *Paris, Gvil. des Rues*, 1595.

——— The same. Le cinqviesme livre. Suyte et conclusion des diuerses amours des bergers et bergères. 6 p. l. 808 pp. 24°. *Paris, A. Savgrain & G. des Rves*, 1598.

Montulé (Édouard de). Voyage en Amérique, en Italie, en Sicile, et en Égypte. 1816–19. 2 v. 8°. 466 pp; 448 pp. Atlas, 59 pl. obl. fol. *Paris, Delaunay*, 1821.

——— A voyage to North America, and the West Indies in 1817. 102 pp. 2 pl. 8°. *London, Sir R. Phillips & Co.* 1821.

Monypenny (David). Remarks on the poor laws, and on the method of providing for the poor, in Scotland. 2d ed. xxiii, 389 pp. 8°. *Edinburgh, T. Clark*, 1836.

Moodey (Samuel). Life and death of Joseph Quasson, Indian. 2 p. l. 41 pp. 18°. *Boston, S. Gerrish*, 1726.

Moody (James). Narrative of [his] exertions and sufferings in the cause of government since the year 1776. Written by himself. With an introduction and notes, by C. I. Bushnell. 98 pp. 4 pl. 8°. *New York, privately printed*, 1865.

Moody (Joshua). A practical discourse concerning communion with God in his house. 3 p. l. 109 pp. 18°. *Boston, J. Brunning*, 1685.

Moody (Sophy). What is your name? a popular account of the meanings and derivations of christian names. x, 313 pp. 12°. *London, R. Bentley*, 1863.

Moonshine. [Poems. *anon.*] 2 v. viii, 260 pp; 271 pp. 6 l. 12°. *London, Longmans*, 1814.

Moore (Clement C. *LL. D.*) Poems. 216 pp. 12°. *New York, Bartlett & Welford*, 1844.

Moore (Cornelius). Leaflets of masonic biography; or, sketches of eminent freemasons. 3d ed. 420 pp. 12°. *Cincinnati, Macoy & Sickels*, 1864.

Moore (David). A system of exchange. *See* **James** (Joseph), *and* **Moore.**

Moore (Frank, *editor*). Anecdotes, poetry, and incidents of the war, north and south, 1860–65. Collected by Frank Moore. 560 pp. 11 portraits. 8°. *New York, J. Porteus*, 1867.

Moore (George). Tales of the passions. [The married man: in which is attempted an illustration of the passion of jealousy.] xi, 455 pp. 8°. *London, G. Wilkie & J. Robinson*, 1811.

Moore (H. N.) Life and services of general Anthony Wayne. 210 pp. 8 pl. 18°. *Philadelphia, J. B. Perry*, 1845.

Moore (James, *M. D. surgeon, U. S. A.*) Complete history of the great rebellion; or, the civil war in the United States, 1861-1865. With introduction by R. Shelton Mackenzie. 12°. *Philadelphia*, 1867.

——— The Kimeliad. A poem. 65 pp. 18°. *Philadelphia, J. B. Rodgers*, 1867.

Moore (J. Hamilton). The young gentleman and lady's monitor, and English teacher's assistant. 6th ed. vi, 378 pp. 17 l. 4 pl. 16°. *New York, H. Gaine*, 1790.
[Imperfect; wanting pp. 343-52].

Moore (*Rev.* James Lovell). The columbiad: an epic poem on the discovery of America and the West Indies by Columbus. 455 pp. 8°. *London, F. & C. Rivington*, 1798.

Moore (John, *M. D.*) A view of society and manners in France, Switzerland, Germany, and Italy. 2 v. in 1. 281 pp. 8°. *Philadelphia, R. Bell*, 1783.

Moore (John M.) Adventures of Tom Stapleton. 120 pp. 8°. *New York, Garrett & Co.* [*about* 1850].

Moore (John S.) Abrah, the conspirator. A tragedy. 51 pp. 16°. *Washington, W. Adam*, 1847.

Moore (*Rev.* Martin). Memoirs of the life and character of Rev. John Eliot. 174 pp. 24°. *Boston, T. Bedlington*, 1822.

Moore (M. B.) Dixie elementary spelling book. 120 pp. 16°. *Raleigh, (N. C.) Branson & Farrar*, 1864.

——— First Dixie reader. 63 pp. sq. 24°. *Raleigh, (N. C.) Branson & Farrar*, 1863.

Moore (Rachel Wilson). Journal kept during a tour to the West Indies and South America in 1863-64. With notes from the diary of her husband; [and] his memoir, by G. Truman. 274 pp. 12°. *Philadelphia, T. E. Zell*, 1867.

Moore (Thomas). Intercepted letters; or, the two-penny post bag; [with] trifles reprinted. By Thomas Brown, the younger. [*pseudon.*] xiii, 109 pp. 2 l. 18°. *Philadelphia, Moses Thomas*, 1813.

Moore (William V.) Indian wars of the United States, from the discovery to the present time. 321 pp. 12°. *Philadelphia, R. W. Pomeroy*, 1840.

Moorman (J. J. *M. D.*) Mineral waters of the United States and Canada, and general directions for reaching mineral springs. 507 pp. 5 pl. 1 map. 12°. *Baltimore, Kelly & Piet*, 1867.

Moquin-Tandon (Chrétien Horace Bénédict Alfred). Histoire naturelle des mollusques terrestres et fluviatiles de France. 2 v. viii, 416 pp; 646 pp. atlas, 54 pl. 8°. *Paris, J. B. Baillière*, 1855. s.

——— Monographie de la famille des hirudinées. 151 pp. 6 pl. 4°. *Paris, Gabon et Cie.* 1827. s.

Mora y Villamil (Ygnacio de). Elementos de fortification. 2ª ed. 2 v. viii, 281 pp. 15 pl; 264 pp. 10 pl. 18°. *Mexico, I. Cumplido*, 1855. s.

Morabin (Jacques). The history of Cicero's banishment. Translated from the French. xxxii, 343 pp. 8°. *London, J. Bowyer*, 1725.

Morcelli (Stefano Antonio). Inscriptiones commentariis svbjectis. xvi, 418 pp. 1 l. 4°. *Romæ, Givnchi*, 1783. s.

Mörch (Johan Christian). Kadallit pelleserkångoæta Hans Egedib okallōutėi unnukorsiutit ajokærsukkaminut. Kakortormiut niuvertorigalloænnit mânalo titârnekartisimarsut Peter Kraghmit. 188 pp. 16°. *Kjöbenhavnime, Fabritius*, 1837. s.

Mörch (O. A. L.) Catalogus conchyliorum quae reliquit C. P. Kierulf, etc. 3 p. l. 34 pp. 2 pl. 8°. *Hafniæ, Trier*, 1850.

Mordecai (Alfred). Artillery for the United States land service as devised and arranged by the ordnance board. 13 pts. in 1 v. 141 col. pl. 8°. *Washington, U. S. government print.* 1848-49. s.

——— Report of the military commission to Europe in 1855-56. With rifled infantry arms, by Julius Schön. 232 pp. 21 pl. 4°. *Washington, U. S. government print.* 1860.

More miseries!! addressed to the morbid, the melancholy, and the irritable. By Sir Fretful Murmur. [*pseudon.*] xv, 176 pp. 16°. *London, H. D. Symonds*, 1806.

More (Hannah). Christian morals. 332 pp. 18°. *New York, Eastburn, Kirk & Co.* 1813.

More (Henry). An antidote against idolatry: with application to the doctrine of the council of Trent. 7 p. l. 140 pp. 8°. *London, J. Flesher*, 1669.
[*With* MORE (Henry). Exposition of the seven epistles, etc. 18°. *London*, 1669].

——— An explanation of the grand mystery of godliness; or, a representation of the gospel. xxx, 546 pp. 14 l. fol. *London, W. Morden*, 1660.

——— An exposition of the seven epistles to the seven churches. 33 pl. 184 pp. 18°. *London, J. Flesher*, 1669.

——— A modest enquiry into the mystery of iniquity; [with the apology for his writings]. 6 p. l. 567 pp. 13 l. fol. *London, W. Morden*, 1664.

Moreau-Christophe (Louis Malthurin). De l'état actuel et de la réforme des prisons de la Grand-Bretagne. 340 pp. 1 pl. 8°. *Paris, Imprimerie royale,* 1838. s.

Moreau de Jonnès (Alexandre). Statistique de l'Espagne. 318 pp. 1 map. 8°. *Paris, Cosson,* 1834. s.

Morel (Andreas). *See* **Liebe** (Christian Sigismund). Gotha nvmaria. *Amstelædami,* 1730.

Morel (Jules, *abbé*). Éléments de critique; ou, recherches des différentes causes de l'altération des textes latins. 276 pp. 8°. s.
[*With* QUANTINS (M.) Dictionnaire raisonné de diplomatique chrétienne. *Paris,* 1846].

Morel (J. M.) Tableau de l'école de botanique du jardin des plantes de Paris. Par un botaniste. [*anon.*] 107 pp. 8°. *Paris, Didot,* 1800. s.

Morel Vindé (Charles Gilbert, *vicomte* de), *and* **Bénard** (—). Cabinet de Paignon. État détaillé et raissonné des dessins et estampes dont il est composé, (etc.) 192, 420 pp. 4°. *Paris, Madame Huzard,* 1810. s.

Morell (John Reynell). Russia and England. Their strength and weakness. 2 p. l. 95 pp. 16°. *London, Trübner,* 1854.

Morelli (Jacopo). Bibliotheca Maphæi Pinellii descripta et annotationibus illustrata. 6 v. in 3. 8°. *Venetiis, C. Palesio,* 1787. s.

Moreni (Domenico). Bibliografia storico-ragionata della Toscana; o sia, catalogo degli scrittori che hanno illustrata la storia delle città, luoghi, e persone della medesima. 2 v. xii, 531 pp; xii, 551 pp. 4°. *Firenze, D. Ciardetti,* 1805.

Moret (M. *avocat*). Le moyen âge pittoresque; vues et fragments d'architecture, meubles, armes, décors, en Europe du 10e au 17e siècle, avec une explication. 5 pts. in 2 v. 180 pl. fol. *Paris, Veith & Hauser* [1838–44]. s.

Moreton (J. B.) Manners and customs in the West India islands; with the method of conducting a sugar plantation. Also, the treatment of slaves and the slave-trade. 192 pp. 8°. *London, W. Richardson and others,* 1790.

Morfit (Campbell), *and* **Mucklé** (Alexander). Chemical and pharmaceutic manipulations. 482 pp. 2 pl. 8°. *Philadelphia, Lindsay & Blakiston,* 1849. s.

——— *See* **Booth** (J. C.) *and* **Morfit**. Recent improvements in the chemical arts.

Morford (Henry). Over sea; or, England, France and Scotland, as seen by a live Amercan. 371 pp. 1 pl. 12°. *New York, Hilton & Co.* 1867.

Morgan (George Cadogan). Lectures on electricity. 2 v. lxxxv, 247 pp; 477 pp. 2 pl. 16°. *Norwich,* [*Eng.*] *J. March,* 1794. s.
[v. ii imperfect; title wanting].

Morgan (*Rev.* Henry). Ned Nevins, the newsboy; or, street life in Boston. 15th thousand. 428 pp. 6 pl. 16°. *Boston, Lee & Shepard,* 1867.

Morgan (John, *M. D.*) A discourse upon the institution of medical schools in America. xxvi, 63 pp. 12°. *Philadelphia, W. Bradford,* 1765.

Morgan (John, *of Hobart, Van Diemen's Land*). Life and adventures of William Buckley, 32 years a wanderer amongst the aborigines of the then unexplored country around Port Phillip, now the province of Victoria. xiv, 208 pp. 1 pl. 12°. *Tasmania, A. Macdougall,* 1852. s.

Morgan (John Minter). The christian commonwealth. ii, 44 pp. 3 pl. fol. *London, Longmans, Green & Co.* 1849.

——— The same. Colonie chrétienne. Traduit de l'Anglais. pp. 46–90. fol. *Londres, Longmans, Green & Co.* 1849.
[*With* the preceding].

——— Revolt of the bees. [*anon.*] 272 pp. 1 pl. 8°. *London, Longmans,* 1826.

Morgan (Sydney Owenson, *lady*). Lay of an Irish harp; or, metrical fragments. 152 pp. 18°. *New York, D. & G. Bruce,* 1808.

——— The O'Briens and the O'Flahertys; a national tale. 4 v. in 2. 12°. *Philadelphia, Carey, Lea & Carey,* 1828.

Morgan (*Sir* Thomas Charles, *and lady*). Book without a name. 2 v. vi, 279 pp; 282 pp. 12°. *New York, Wiley & Putnam,* 1841.

Morgenstern (Carl von). Reise in Italien im jahr 1809. 3 pts in 1. 4 p. l. xxii, 806 pp. 1 pl. 8°. *Dorpat, M. G. Grenzius,* 1811–13. s.

Morgenstern (Philipp, *editor*). Tvrba philosophorum; das ist, das buch von der güldenen kunst, neben andern authoribus, welche mit einander 36 bücher in sich haben. [Verdeutscht aus] der lateinischen sprach. 7 p. l. 560 pp. 16°. *Basel, Königs,* 1613.

Morghen (Raffaele). Principes du dessein. *See* **Volpato** (G.) *and* **Morghen**.

Morhof (Daniel Georg). Polyhistor literarius, philosophicus, et practicus; cum accessionibus Joannis Frickii et Joannis Molleri. Ed. 3^a^. Cui præfationem notitiamque diariorum litterariorum Europæ præmisit Io. Albertus Fabricius. 3 v. in 2. 21 p. l. 1072 pp. 3 pl; 604 pp. 4°. *Lubecæ, P. Broeckmann,* 1732. s.

CONTENTS.

v. 1. Polyhistor literarius.
v. 2–3. Polyhistor philosophicus et practicus.

Morigia (Paolo). Histoire de l'origine de tovtes les religions qvi ivsqves à présent ont esté au monde. Traduit d'Italien. 8 p. l. 451 pp. 6 l. 18°. *Paris, R. Coulombel*, 1578.

Morin (Arthur Jules). Aide-mémoire de mécanique pratique. viii, 330 pp. 8°. *Metz, Thiel*, 1857. s.

——— Leçons de mécanique pratique. Résistance des matériaux. 456 pp. 6 pl. 8°. *Paris, L. Hachette*, 1853. s.

——— Rapport sur les comparaisons des kilogrammes, etc. *See* **Regnault** (H. V.) **Morin**, *and* **Brix**.

Morin (Jean Baptiste, *editor*). *See* **Kepler** (Johann). Tabulæ rudolphinæ. *London*, 1675.

Morison (John, *D. D.*) Family prayers for every morning and evening throughout the year. 3d ed. 780 pp. 1 pl. fol. *London, Fisher, son & Co.* [1838].

Moritz (Julius). *See* **Thomas** (Louis).

Morley (John). Edmund Burke: a historical study. xv, 312 pp. 8°. *London, Macmillan*, 1867.

Morlot (A.) Allgemeine bemerkungen über die alterthumskunde. 15 pp. 8°. *Bern, Haller*, 1859. s.

[*With* MORLOT, "Some general views on archæology]."

——— Erläuterungen zur geologischen übersichtskarte der nordöstlichen Alpen. viii, 212 pp. 1 col. map. 8°. *Wien, Braumüller & Seidel*, 1847. s.

——— Études géologico-archéologiques, en Danemark et en Suisse. pp. 262–328. 8°. *Lausane, Soc. vaudoise des sciences nat.* 1860. s.

[*With* "Some general views on archæology]."

——— A happy man. [Biography of Edward Meystre.] 11 pp. 8°. *Lausanne, Pache*, 1855. s.

[*With* "Some general views on archæology]."

——— Une première leçon de géologie. 15 pp. 8°. *Lausanne, Pache*, 1852. s.

[*With* "Some general views on archæology."]

——— Some general views on archæology. [Reprinted from the "Geologist."] 12 pp. 12°. *London, Geologist*, 1860. s.

Mormons (The); or, knavery exposed. Giving an account of the discovery of the golden plates, building a temple, establishment of a bank, [etc.] Documents printed by order of the senate of the U. S. 24 pp. 8°. *Frankford, (Pa.) E. G. Lee*, 1841.

Mornay *or* **Duplessis Mornay** (Philippe de, *seigneur du Plessis Marly*). The mysterie of iniqvitie; that is to say, the historie of the papacie. Englished by Samson Lennard. 9 p. l. 661 pp. fol. *London, A. Islip*, 1612.

35

Morogues (P. M. S. Bigot de). *See* **Bigot de Morogues.**

Morren (Édouard). Dissertation sur les feuilles vertes et coloriées. 222 pp. 2 pl. 8°. *Gand, C. Arnout Braeckman*, 1858. s.

Morres (Hervey Redmond, *2d lord Mountmorres*). The danger of the political balance of Europe. Translated from the French of the king of Sweden. xxiv, 201 pp. 18°. *Dublin, Chamberlain & Rice, etc.* 1790.

Morris (Corbyn). An essay towards fixing the true standards of wit, humor, raillery, satire, and ridicule, [with] an analysis of the characters of an humorist, Sir John Falstaff, Sir Roger De Coverley, and Don Quixote. xxxiv, xxxii, 75 pp. 8°. *London, J. Roberts*, 1744.

Morris (Francis Orpen). A natural history of the nests and eggs of British birds. 3 v. 8°. *London, Groombridge*, 1853–56. s.

Morris (I. J.) A philosophical and practical grammar of the English language. xx, 192 pp. 12°. *New York, Miller & Holman*, 1857. s.

Morris (John, *F. G. S.*) A catalogue of British fossils; with references to their geological distribution and to the localities in which they have been found. 2d ed. viii, 372 pp. 8°. *London, author*, 1854. s.

——— *and* Lycett (John). A monograph of the mollusca from the great oolite, chiefly from Minchinhampton and the coast of Yorkshire. 2 v. in 1. 4°. *London, Palæontographical society*, 1850–53. s.

CONTENTS.

v. 1. Univalves. viii, 130 pp. 15 l. 15 pl.
v. 2. Bivalves. 148 pp. 15 l. 15 pl.

Morris (J. C.) A dictionary, English and Teloogoo. 2 v. 3 pl. 586 pp; 532 pp. 4°. *Madras*, 1835–39. s.

Morris (John G.) Life of John Arndt [Arnd]. 237 pp. portrait. 18°. *Baltimore, T. N. Kurtz*, 1853. s.

Morris (Lewis, *chief justice of N. Y. and prov. governor of N. J.*) Observations on the reasons given by Mr. [John] Hamilton's advisers, for his detaining the seals of the province of New Jersie, after the demand made of them by Lewis Morris, president of the council and commander-in-chief of the province of New Jersie. 11 pp. fol. [*New York*, 1736?]

——— Opinion and argument of the chief justice of the province of New York, concerning the jurisdiction of the supream court of the said province, to determine causes in a court of equity. 15 pp. fol. *New York, J. Peter Zenger*, 1733.

Morris (Lewis, *hydrographer*). Plans of the principal harbours, bays, and roads, in St. George's and the Bristol channels; with hints on improvements necessary for the security of navigation on the coast of Wales. New ed. by William Morris. xii, 21 pp. 32 maps. fol. *Shrewsbury, Sandford and Maddocks,* 1801.

Morris (Peter, *pseudon.*) *See* **Lockhart** (J.G.)

Morris (Robert, *LL. D.*) The dictionary of freemasonry. 518 pp. 12°. *Chicago, J. C. W. Bailey,* 1867.

Morris (William). The life and death of Jason, a poem. 363 pp. 12°. *London, Bell and Daldy,* 1867.

Morrison (John H. *D. D*). Disquisitions and notes on the gospels: Matthew. *See* **Bible** (*English*). New Testament.

Morrison (Robert, *D. D.*) Vocabulary of the Canton dialect. 2 v. in 1. 8°. *Macao, East India Co.'s press,* 1828. s.

Morrison (R. J.) The solar system as it is, and not as it is represented. 214 pp. 10 pl. 8°. *London, Piper, Stephenson & Spence,* 1857. s.

Morrison (William M.) Morrison's stranger's guide to the city of Washington and its vicinity. vi, 144 pp. 18 pl. 24°. *Washington, W. M. Morrison,* 1852. s.

——— The same. Stranger's guide for Washington city. Illustrated. [New ed.] 58 pp. 28 pl. 3 diag. 18°. *Washington, W. H. & O. H. Morrison,* 1868.

Morrow (T. V. *M. D.*) Posthumous writings. v. 1. 1853. s.

[*With* JONES (I. G.) American eclectic practice].

Morse (Edward S.) A classification of mollusca, based on the principle of cephalization. [Extract.] 20 pp. 1 pl. 8°. *Salem, Essex institute,* 1865. s.

Morse (Jedidiah, *D. D.*) The American gazetteer; a full account of the American continent; also of the West India and other appendant islands. 3d ed. 312 l. 8°. *Boston, Thomas and Andrews,* 1810.

——— American geography; or, a view of the present situation of the United States of America. 3d ed. xvi, 536 pp. 2 maps. 8°. *Dublin, John Jones,* 1792.

——— The American universal geography; or, a view of the present state of the known world, and of the United States in particular. 7th ed. 2 v. 898 pp; 859 pp. 6 maps. 8°. *Charlestown, Lincoln & Edmands, etc.* 1819.

——— Geography made easy. An abridgment of the American universal geography. 214 pp. 18°. *New Haven,* 1784?

[Imperfect; title wanting].

——— The same. 4th ed. 432 pp. 9 maps. 16°. *Boston, J. Thomas & E. J. Andrews,* 1794.

——— The same. 18th ed. 364 pp. 2 maps. 12°. *Boston, Thomas & Andrews,* 1816. s.

——— The same. 2d Troy, from the 16th Boston ed. 364 pp. 16°. *Troy, Parker & Bliss,* 1816.

——— The same. 22d ed. By Sidney E. Morse. 368 pp. 16°. *Boston, Richardson & Lord,* 1820.

——— The same. A new system of geography, ancient and modern, for the use of schools. 25th ed. 342 pp. 16°. *Boston, Richardson & Lord,* 1826.

——— History of America, in two books: containing, i, a general history of America; ii, a concise history of the late revolution. [*anon.*] 3d ed. iv, 356 pp. 2 maps. 12°. *Philadelphia, T. Dobson,* 1798.

Morse (O. A.) Vindication of the claim of Alex. M. W. Ball to the authorship of the poem, Rock me to sleep, mother. 72 pp. 8°. *New York, M. W. Dodd,* 1867.

Morse (Sidney E.) A new system of modern geography; or, a view of the present state of the world. vi, 376 pp. 8°. *Boston, G. Clark,* 1822.

Morton (A.) The charmed scarf. 8 pp. 8°. *London,* 1841.

[HAZLITT's romancist and novelist's lib. v. 3.]

Morton (Nathaniel). New England's memorial; or, the most memorable passages of the providence of God manifested to the planters of New England, with special reference to New Plimouth. 5 p. l. 248 pp. 18°. *Boston, Daniel Henchman,* 1721.

——— The same. viii, 208 pp. 16°. *Newport, (R. I.) S. Southwick,* 1772.

Morton (Samuel George). Medical formulary. *See* **Ellis** (B.)

Morton (Thomas, *of Clifford's inn*). New English Canaan; or, new Canaan: containing an abstract of New England, composed in three bookes. 188 pp. 2 l. sm. 4°. *Amsterdam, J. F. Stam,* [1637?]

[Title-page wanting].

Moschus. Idyllia. *See* **Theocritus.** Idyllia. [*n. p.*] 1579.

——— Idyls. Translated by F. Fawkes. 8°. *Edinburgh,* [1792].

[Anderson's Brit. poets. v. 5].

Mosdorf (Friedrich). *See* **Mossdorf.**

Mosel (Ignaz Franz Edler von). Geschichte der kaiserl. königl. hof-bibliothek zu Wien. viii, 398 pp. 2 pl. 8°. *Wien, Beck*, 1835. s.

Moses (Henry). Vases from the collection of Sir Henry Englefield, drawn and engraved. [English and French texts]. 62 pp. 40 pl. 8°. *London, Rodwell & Martin*, 1819. s.

Mossdorf (Friedrich). Allgemeines handbuch der freimaurerei. Zweite aufl. von Lenning's encyklopädie der freimaurerei. [*pseudon.*] 3 v. 8°. *Leipzig, F. A. Brockhaus*, 1863–67.

Mot (Maurice Adolphe, *pseudon?*). A French grammar and dictionary, with an infallible method for learning the pronunciation. 248, 17 pp. 12°. *Philadelphia, Moss & brother*, 1853.

Motherby (George, *M. D.*) A new medical dictionary, or general depository of physic. Revised and corrected by George Wallis, M. D. 5th ed. xii, 811 pp. 5 l. 33 pl. fol. *London, J. Johnson, etc.* 1801.
[Imperfect; wanting plate 15].

Mother's (The) thorough resource book: comprising self-discipline of the expectant mother; general management during infancy and childhood; also, children's complaints, etc. [*anon.*] iv, 252 pp. 12°. *London, Ward & Lock*, [1862].

Motolinea (*fray* Toribio de, *or* de **Benavente**). Historia de los Indios de Nueva España. *See* **Icazbalzeta** (J.) Coleccion, etc.

Mott (*Rev.* George S.) The resurrection of the dead. 230 pp. 16°. *New York, N. Tibbals*, 1866.

Mott (John Thomas). The last days of Francis the first, and other poems. 147 pp. 16°. *London, W. Pickering*, 1843.

Mott (Valentine). New elements of operative surgery. *See* **Velpeau** (A. L. M.)

Mouette (Germain). Travels in the kingdoms of Fez and Morocco. 115 pp. 1 map. sm. 4°. [*London*, 1700]?
[*With* STEVENS (John). Voyages and travels].

Moufet (Thomas, *M. D.*) Health's improvement; or, rules comprising and discovering the nature, method, and manner of preparing all sorts of food used in this nation. Corrected and enlarged by Christopher Bennet. viii, 296 pp. sm. 4°. *London, S. Thomson*, 1655.

Moulton (Joseph W.) History of the state of New York, part ii. Novum Belgium. viii, pp. 333—428. 8°. *New York, E. Bliss & E. White*, 1826.

Mount Auburn cemetery. Catalogue of lots, with the names of the proprietors, etc. 12°. *Boston*, 1857. s.

Mountain (George J.) Songs of the wilderness. xxviii, 153 pp. 4 pl. 16°. *London, F. & J. Rivington*, 1846.

Mountmorres (*lord*). *See* **Morres** (Hervey Redmond, 2d *lord* **Mountmorres**).

Mouradja d'Ohsson (Charles, *or* Constantin). Histoire des Mongols; depuis Tchinguiz-khan jusqu'à Timour Beg, ou Tamerlan. 4 v. 8°. *La Haye, Les frères Van Cleef*, 1834–35.

Moureau (Jules). Le salaire et des associations co-opératives; étude économique. 254 pp. 16°. *Paris, Guillaumin*, 1866.

Mourey (C. V.) La vraie théorie des quantités prétendues imaginaires. 2e éd. xii, 106 pp. 16°. *Paris, Mallet-Bachelier*, 1861.

Mourt (George). Relation; or, journal of the plantation at Plymouth; with introduction and notes, by Henry M. Dexter. xlvii, 176 pp. 2 maps. sm. 4°. *Boston, J. K. Wiggin*, 1865.
[Library of New England history, No. 1].

Mousson (Albert). Die physik auf grundlage der erfahrung. 2 v. vi, 291 pp. 11 pl; 2 p. l. 424 pp. 13 pl. 8°. *Zürich, Schulthess*, 1858. s.

Mowaffak-ed-din Abû Mohammed Abd-el-latif ben Yusuf. Relation de l'Égypte; suivie de divers extraits d'écrivains orientaux, et d'un état des provinces et des villages de l'Égypte dans le 14e siècle; le tout traduit et enrichi de notes, par Silvestre de Sacy. xxiv, 752 pp. 4°. *Paris, Treuttel et Würtz*, 1810.

——— The same. Denkwürdigkeiten Egyptens. Aus dem Arabischen übersezt von S. F. G. Wahl. 16°. *Halle, Verlag des Waisenhauses*, 1790. s.

Mowris (James A. *M. D.*) History of the 117th N. Y. volunteers, (fourth Oneida), from its organization, August, 1862, till June, 1865, 315 pp. 12°. *Hartford, Case, Lockwood & Co.* 1866.

Moxon (Joseph). Regulæ trium ordinum literarum typographicarum; or, the rules of the three orders of print letters. 2d ed. 2 p. l. 52 pp. 7 pl. sm. 4°. *London, James Moxon*, 1693.

Moysant (François), *and* **Lévizac** (Jean Pons Victor Lecoutz de). Bibliothèque portative des écrivains françois; ou choix des meilleurs morceaux extraits de leurs ouvrages. 3 v. 8°. *Londres, Dulau et Co.* 1803.

Mozley (*Rev.* James Bowling). Eight lectures on miracles. 2d ed. xxviii, 382 pp. 8°. *London, Rivingtons*, 1867.
[Bampton lectures, 1865].

Mudge (Z. A.) The christian statesman; a portraiture of Sir Thomas Fowell Buxton; with sketches of British antislavery reform. 268 pp. 4 pl. 16°. *New York, Carlton & Porter,* 1865.

——— The forest boy: a sketch of the life of Abraham Lincoln. For young people. 321 pp. 4 pl. 16°. *New York, Carlton & Porter,* [1867].

Mudie (Robert). Attic fragments, of characters, customs, opinions, and scenes. [*anon.*] 379 pp. 8°. *London, Knight & Lacey,* 1825.

——— Pictures of India; geographical, historical, and descriptive. 2d ed. 2 v. xvi, 415 pp; vi, 445 pp. 1 map. 1 pl. 16°. *London, Whittaker, Treacher & Co.* 1832.

Mueller *or* Müller (Ferdinand). Analytical drawings of Australian mosses. Fasc. 1. 7 pp. 20 pl. 8°. *Melbourne, J. Ferres,* 1864. s.

——— Australian vegetation in its bearings on the occupation of the territory, etc. 38 pp. 8°. *Melbourne, Blundell & Co.* 1867. s.

——— Fragmenta phytographiæ Australiæ. 4 v. 8°. *Melbourne, J. Ferres,* 1858–64. s.

——— The plants indigenous to the colony of Victoria, [Australia]. v. 1. Thalamifloræ. viii, 242 pp. 23 pl. 4°. *Melbourne, J. Ferres,* 1860–62. s.

——— The same. Lithograms. [v. 2, atlas]. 3 p. l. 66 l. unp. 66 pl. 4°. *Melbourne, J. Ferres,* 1864–65. s.

——— The vegetation of the Chatham islands. 2 p. l. 86 pp. 7 pl. 8°. *Melbourne, J. Ferres,* 1864. s.

Mueller. *See also* **Müller.**

Muffett (Thomas, *M. D.*) *See* **Moufet** (T.)

Mühlbach (Luise, *pseudon.*) *See* **Mundt** (*Mrs.* Clara).

Mühry (A. *M. D.*) Allgemeine geographische meteorologie; oder, versuch einer uebersichtlichen darlegung des systems der erd-meteoration in ihrer klimatischen bedeutung. xii, 203 pp. 2 maps. 8°. *Leipzig, etc. C. F. Winter,* 1860. s.

——— Beitraege zur geo-physik und klimatographie. Heft i–iii in 2 v. viii, 92 pp; xiii, 213 pp. 8°. *Leipzig, C. F. Winter,* 1863. s.

CONTENTS.

v. 1. Zur geographischen meteorologie; zur klimatologie.
v. 2–3. Über das klima der hoch Alpen.

Muirhead (Lockhart). Journals of travels in parts of the late Austrian Low Countries, France, the Pays de Vaud, and Tuscany, in 1787 and 1789. 428 pp. 8°. *London, T. N. Longman & O. Rees,* 1803.

Mulder (E.) Historisch-kritisch overzigt van de bepalingen der aequivalent-gewigten van 13 enkelvoudige ligchamen: (zwavel, selenium, tellurium, phosphorus, arsenicum, chloor, kalium, zilver, bromium, iodium, fluorium, silicium, en borium). 157 pp. 8°. *Utrecht, D. Post Uiterweer,* 1853. s.

Mulder (Gerhard Jan). Versuch einer allgemeinen physiologischen chemie. xii, vi, 1,291, 15 pp. 20 pl. 8°. *Braunschweig, Vieweg,* 1849–51. s.

Mulder (L.) Historisch-kritisch overzigt van bepalingen der aequivalent-gewigten van 24 metalen. 2 p. l. 336 pp. 1 pl. 8°. *Utrecht, D. P. Uiterweer,* 1853. s.

Mulgrave (C. J. Phipps, *2d baron*). *See* **Phipps** (C. J.)

Mullala (James, *LL. D.*) A delineation of the British constitution, from the origin to the present period. 3 v. in 2. 8°. *Dublin, J. Mullala,* 1798–1801.

Müller (Adolf *and* Carl). Charakterzeichnungen der vorzüglichsten deutschen singvögel. vii, 112 pp. 11 pl. 8°. *Leipzig, C. F. Winter,* 1865. s.

Müller (*Dr.* Carl). Synopsis muscorum frondosorum omnium hucusque cognitorum. 2 v. viii, 812 pp; 772 pp. 8°. *Berolini, A. Foerstner,* 1849–51. s.

Müller (C. H. *of Breslau*). Elemente der elektricität. *See* **Singer** (G. J.)

Müller (Carl Ottfried). Die Etrusker. 2 pts. or 4 books in 1 v. xiv, 456, 374 pp. 1 pl. 8°. *Breslau, J. Max & Komp.* 1828. s.

——— Handbuch der archäologie der kunst. 2e ausg. 8°. *Breslau, J. Max & Co.* 1835. s.

——— Dissertations on the Eumenides of Æschylus. From the German. 2d ed. xii, 224 pp. 1 pl. 12°. *London, Parker & son,* 1853.

Müller (*Dr.* Friedrich, *prof. at Vienna*). Reise der Novara: linguistischer theil.

[*With* WÜLLERSTORF-URBAIR (B. von). Reise der Novara].

Müller (Friedrich Max, *prof. at Oxford*). Lectures on the science of language. From 2d London ed. 416 pp. 12°. *New York, C. Scribner,* 1862. s.

——— The same. 2d series. 622 pp. 12°. *New York, C. Scribner,* 1865. s.

Müller (Gerhard Friedrich). Voyages et découvertes faites par les Russes le long des côtes de la mer glaciale et sur l'océan oriental, tant vers le Japon que vers l'Amérique. On y a joint l'histoire du fleuve Amur et des pays adjacens, depuis la conquête des Russes. Traduits de l'Allemand par Dumas. 2 v. xii p. l. 388 pp; iv, 207 pp. 11 l. 1 map. 18°. *Amsterdam, M. M. Rey,* 1766.

Müller (Johannes von). Vier und zwanzig bücher allgemeiner geschichtens, besonders der europäischen menschheit. Herausgegeben [von] J. G. Müller. 2e aufl. 3 v. 12°. *Tübingen, J. G. Cotta,* 1811.

Muller (John, *prof. at Woolwich*). A treatise containing the elementary part of fortification, regular and irregular. 2d ed. xvi, 240 pp. 34 pl. 8°. *London, J. Nourse,* 1756.

Müller (Johannes, *M. D. prof. at Berlin*). Über die bisher unbekannten typischen verschiedenheiten der stimmorgane der passerinen. [Extract]. 71 pp. 6 pl. 4°. *Berlin, k. akad. der wissenschaften,* 1847. s.

——— *and* **Troschel** (Franz Hermann). System der asteriden. xx, 134 pp. 12 pl. 4°. *Braunschweig, Vieweg,* 1842. s.

Müller (Johann, *prof. of physics at Freiburg*). Grundriss der physik und meteorologie. vi, 520 pp. 8°. *Braunschweig, Vieweg,* 1846. s.

——— The same. 4e aufl. 534 pp. 8°. *Braunschweig, Vieweg,* 1853. s.

——— The same. Principles of physics and meteorology. 635 pp. 1 col. pl. 8°. *Philadelphia, Lea & Blanchard,* 1848. s.

——— Lehrbuch der physik und meteorologie. *See* **Pouillet** (C. S. M.) Lehrbuch.

Müller (Johann Georg). Aus dem künstlerischen nachlasse von J. G. M. Enthaltend entwürfe zu architektonischen abhandlungen, gedichte, und tafeln. Mit einer lebensskizze Müller's und notizen herausgegeben von J. M. Ziegler. 3 p. l. 19 pp. 43 pl. fol. *Winterthur, J. Wurster & Co.* 1860. s.

Müller (Johann Sebastian). *See* **Miller** (J. S.)

Müller (Johann Wilhelm, *baron* von). Beiträge zur ornithologie Afrika's. lief 1–5. 24 l. unp. 20 col. pl. 4°. *Stuttgart, königl. hofbuchdruckerei,* 1853–54. s.

[No more published.]

——— The same. Description de nouveaux oiseaux d'Afrique, nouvellement découverts et dessinés d'après nature; pour servir de suite aux planches enluminées de Buffon, etc. livr. 1–5. 24 l. unp. 20 col. pl. 4°. *Stuttgart, imp. royale,* 1853–54. s.

[No more published].

Müller (L.) Numismatique d'Alexandre le grand. Suivie d'un appendice contenant les monnaies de Philippe ii. et iii. et accompagnée de planches et tables. xiv, 402 pp. 8°. Atlas, 29 pl. 6 l. 4°. *Copenhague, B. Luno,* 1855.

Müller (Otho Friedrich). Zoologia danica; sev, animalivm Daniæ et Norvegiæ rariorvm ac minvs notorvm descriptiones et historia. 2 v. in 1. vii, 103 pp; 124 pp. 8°. *Havniæ et Lipsiæ, Weygand, J. G. Müller,* 1779–84. s.

Müller (Ferdinand). *See* **Mueller** (Ferdinand).

Muloch (Dinah Maria, *Mrs.* Craik). Two marriages. [*anon.*] 301 pp. 12°. *New York, Harpers,* 1867.

Münch (Friedrich). Amerikanische weinbauschule. Anleitung zur anlegung des weinberges, [etc.] 2e aufl. 142 pp. 16°. *St. Louis, C. Witter,* 1867.

Munch (Peter Andreas). Det norske folks historie. v. 1. 3 p. l. 804, xii pp. 1 map. 8°. *Christiania, C. Tonsberg,* 1851.

——— Übersicht der orographie Norwegens. 1850. s.

[*With* KEILHAU (B. M.) Gaea norvegica, iii].

Munchausen at the pole; or, the surprising and wonderful adventures of a voyage of discovery. By Capt. Munchausen. [*pseudon.*] 5 p. l. 164 pp. 1 pl. 12°. *London, J. Johnston,* 1819.

Munck (Hans). Kort begrijp des reyssoeckende tusschen Groenland en America een wegh nae Ooost-Indien.

[*With* LA PEYRÈRE (I. de). Nauwkeurige beschrijvingh van Groenland. pp. 87–100. 1678].

Munde (Carl, *M. D.*) Die gräfenberger wasserheilanstalt und die priessnitzische curmethode. viii, 256 pp. 12°. *Leipzig, Hartleben,* 1845. s.

Mundt (Clara Müller). Berlin and Sans-Souci; or, Frederick the great and his friends. By L. Mühlbach. [*pseudon.*] 12°. *New York, D. Appleton & Co.* 1867.

——— Bernthal; or, the son's revenge. From the German. 8°. *New York, D. Appleton & Co.* 1867.

——— The daughter of an empress. An historical novel. Translated from the German, by Nathaniel Greene. 255 pp. 4 pl. 8°. *New York, D. Appleton & Co.* 1867.

——— The empress Josephine. An historical sketch of the days of Napoleon. From the German, by Rev. W. Binet. Illustrated by G. Fay. 280 pp. 8 pl. 8°. *New York, D. Appleton & Co.* 1867.

——— Frederick the great and his court. An historical romance. Translated from the German of Louise Mühlbach [*pseudon.*] by Mrs. C. Coleman and her daughters. iv, 434 pp. 12°. *New York, D. Appleton & Co.* 1866.

——— The same. 12°. *New York,* 1867.

——— Frederick the great and his family. An historical novel. By L. Mühlbach. [*pseudon.*] Translated from the German by Mrs. C. Coleman and her daughters. iv, 300 pp. 4 pl. 8°. *New York, D. Appleton & Co.* 1867.

Mundt (Clara Müller). Henry viii. and his court; or, Catharine Parr, a historical novel. From the German of Louise Mühlbach. [*pseudon.*] By H. N. Pierce. 2 v. in 1. 142, 143 pp. 12°. *Mobile, (Ala.) S. H. Goetzel,* 1865.

——— The same. 418 pp. 12°. *New York, D. Appleton & Co.* 1867.

——— Joseph ii. and his court. An historical novel. From the German of Louise Mühlbach. [*pseudon.*] by Adelaide De V. Chaudron. 4 v. in 1. 12°. *Mobile, (Ala.) S. H. Goetzel,* 1864.

——— The same. iv, 343 pp. 4 pl. 8°. *New York, D. Appleton & Co.* 1867.

——— Louisa of Prussia and her times. An historical novel. 2 p. l. 277 pp. 4 pl. 8°. *New York, D. Appleton & Co.* 1867.

——— Marie Antoinette and her son. An historical novel. 301 pp. 8 pl. 8°. *New York, D. Appleton & Co.* 1867.

——— The merchant of Berlin. An historical novel. Translated from the German by A. Coffin. 12°. *New York, D. Appleton & Co.* 1867.

——— Napoleon in Germany. Napoleon and Blücher. An historical novel. By L. Mühlbach. [*pseudon.*] From the German by F. Jordan. 301 pp. 8 pl. 8°. *New York, D. Appleton & Co.* 1867.

——— The same. Napoleon and the queen of Prussia. An historical novel. By L. Mühlbach. [*pseudon.*] From the German by F. Jordan. 245 pp. 8 pl. 8°. *New York, D. Appleton & Co.* 1867.

Munguia (Clémente de Jesus). Obras diversas. Primera serie. 3 v. in 1. 8°. *Morelia, [Mexico,] I. Arango,* 1842. s.

CONTENTS.

v. 1. Los principios de la iglesia católica comparados con los de las escuelas racionalistas en sus relaciones con la enseñanza [etc.] Memoria instructiva sobre el origen, progresos y estado actual de la enseñanza [etc.] en el seminario tridentino de Morelia. Del pensamiento y su enunciacion considerado en sí mismo, en sus relaciones, y en sus leyes. Parte 1a. 3 p. l. 526 pp.
v. 2–3. The same. 2a–3a parte. 509 pp; 385 pp.

——— The same. Segunda serie. 3 v. in 1. 8°. *Mexico, Imprenta de la voz de la religion,* 1852. s.

CONTENTS.

v. 1. Estudios fundamentales sobre el hombre, [etc.] Examen filosofico sobre las relaciones del orden natural y el sobrenatural, [etc.] Parte 1a. 3 p. l. 615, ix pp.
v. 2. The same. Parte 2a. 93, ii pp.
v. 3. Disertacion sobre el estudio de la lengua castellana. [etc.] Discurso sobre el establecimiento de la catedra de bella literatura en el seminario de Morelia, [etc.] Disertacion sobre la elocuencia religiosa, [etc.] Arengas [etc.] Discurso civico pronunciado en la plaza principal de Morelia, [etc.] 1838. Ensayos de critica, [etc.] 423, iii pp.

Munguia (Clemente de Jesus). Platicas doctrinales y sermones, precedidos de una disertacion sobre la oratoria sagrada. lviii, 193 pp. 3 l. 8°. *Morelia, O. Ortiz,* 1851. s.

Muños de Castro (Pedro). Exaltacion magnifica de la betlemitica rosa de la mejor americana Jerico. Con octavario plenissimo de sermones predicados. 12 p. l. unp. 84 l. sm. 4°. *Mexico, M. de Benavides, viuda de J. de Ribera,* 1697.

Munson (James E.) Complete phonographer. 236 pp. 8°. *New York, R. K. Johnston,* 1867.

Münster (Sebastian). Dictionarivm Hebraicum jam recognitum, et ex rabinis auctum et locupletatum. 496 l. 16°. *Basileæ, Froben & Episcopius,* 1539.

Murchison (H.) Conservatives and 'liberals,' their principles and policy. 2d ed. xxix, 49 pp. 8°. *London, Saunders, Otley & Co.* 1866.

Murdoch (David, *D. D.*) The Dutch dominie of the Catskills; or, the times of the "bloody Brandt." 471 pp. 12°. *New York, Derby & Jackson,* 1861.

Murger (Henry). Le pays latin. Nouv. éd. 353 pp. 12°. *Paris, M. Lévy,* 1857.

Murhard (Friedrich Wilhelm August). Litterteratur der mathematischen wissenschaften; bibliotheca mathematica. 2 v. xvi pp. 3 p. l. 256 pp; xii pp. 3 p. l. 436 pp. 8°. *Leipzig, Breitkopf & Härtel,* 1797–98. s.

——— [The same. v. 3–5.] Litteratur der mechanischen und optischen wissenschaften. 3 v. in 1. 8°. *Leipzig, Breitkopf & Härtel,* 1803–05. s.

Murphy (Henry). The conquest of Quebec; an epic poem. 2 p. l. xix pp. 2 l. 308 pp. 12°. *Dublin, W. Porter,* 1790.

Murphy (Henry C.) Jacob Steendam. A memoir of the first poet in New Netherland, with his poems descriptive of the colony. 59 pp. 1 pl. 8°. *The Hague, Giunta d'Albani,* 1861.

Murphy (Jacob). Über die grundregeln der gothischen bauart. Aus dem Englischen übersetzt von J. D. E. W. Engelhard. vi, 54 pp. 11 pl. 4°. *Darmstadt, C. W. Leske,* [1828]. s.

Murray (Charles Augustus). The prairie-bird. 207 pp. 8°. *New York, Harpers,* 1847.

Murray (Hannah *and* Mary). The toilet. [Emblematic illustrations, with moral precepts]. Edited by Mrs. S. W. Smith. 20 pp. 8°. *Washington, W. Ballantyne,* 1867.

Murray (Hugh, *and others*). Historical and descriptive account of British India. 3 v. 1 map. 18°. *New York, Harpers*, 1833-36.

CONTENTS.

V. 1—2. Murray (Hugh). History. 296 pp; 333 pp.
V. 3. Ainslie (Whitelaw). Medical observations. pp. 258-272.
Dalrymple (Clarence). Navigation between England and India. pp. 326-370.
Greville (Robert Kaye). Botany. pp. 117-157.
Jameson (Robert). Climate, geology, mineralogy. pp. 158-257.
Rhind (William). Spasmodic cholera. pp. 273-278.
Wallace (William). Astronomy and mathematics. 279-325 pp.
Wilson (James). Zoology. pp. 11-116.

Murray (*Rev.* James, *of Newcastle*). Sermons to asses. [*anon.*] 5th ed. 63 pp. 18°. *Philadelphia, J. Dunlap*, 1770.

——— Sermons to doctors in divinity; being the second volume of sermons to asses. viii, 144 pp. 18°. *Philadelphia, J. Dunlap*, 1783.
[*With* the preceding.]

Murray (John, *London publisher*). Hand-book for travellers in southern Germany, Bavaria, Austria, Tyrol, Salzburg, Styria, the Austrian and Bavarian Alps, etc. 3d ed. xiv, 486 pp. 1 map. 12°. *London, J. Murray*, 1844. s.

——— Hand-book for travellers in the Ionian islands, Greece, Turkey, Asia Minor, and Constantinople; including a description of Malta. New ed. lxix, 408 pp. 4 maps. 12°. *London, J. Murray*, 1845. s.

——— Hand-book for travellers in Switzerland and the Alps of Savoy and Piedmont. lxii, 420 pp. 3 maps. 3d ed. 12°. *London, J. Murray*, 1846. s.

——— Hand-book for travellers in northern Italy: Sardinia, Lombardy and Venice, Parma and Piacenza, Modena, Lucca, Massa-Carrara, and Tuscany, as far as the Val d'Arno. 3d ed. xxxii, 608 pp. 3 maps. 12°, *London, J. Murray*, 1847. s.

——— Hand-book for travellers on the continent: Holland, Belgium, Prussia and northern Germany. 8th ed. 12°. *London, J. Murray*, 1851. s.

——— Hand-book for travellers in Spain. *See* **Ford** (Richard).

——— Official hand-book of church and state. By S. Redgrave. 12°. *London, J. Murray*, 1854.

Murray (John, *M. D. of Edinburgh*). Elements of materia medica and pharmacy. 2 v. xv, 394 pp; viii, 351 pp. 8°. *Edinburgh, Neill & Co.* 1804.

Murray (John, *of London, F. S. A.*) Manuel de l'électricité atmosphérique, etc. Traduit de l'Anglais, par Anatole Riffault. vi, 264 pp. 3 pl. 24°. *Paris, Roret*, 1831. s.

Murray (Lindley). An abridgement of [his] English grammar. With appendix. 95 pp. 18°. *Washington, D. Rapine*, 1818.

——— English grammar. xii, 282 pp. 16°. [*n. p. n. d.*]
[Title page wanting.]

——— The same. Adapted to the different classes of learners. 228 pp. 16°. *Windsor, (Vt.) N. C. Goddard*, 1836. s.

——— Introduction to the English reader, [with] rules for assisting children to read with propriety. Improved ed. 153 pp. 12°. *Georgetown, (D. C.) S. S. Rind*, 1830.
[Imperfect].

Mursinna (Friedrich Samuel). Geschichte der entdekkung von Amerika. 4 p. l. 400 pp. 1 pl. 12°. *Halle, Renger*, 1795.

Musæus. The loves of Hero and Leander. Translated by F. Fawkes. 8°. *Edinburgh*, [1792].
[Anderson's Brit. poets, v. 5].

Musaeus (Johann Carl August). Select popular tales. From the German. 168 pp. 16°. *London, E. Lumley*, [*about* 1850].

Musée des Thermes et de l'hotel de Cluny. Catalogue et description des objets d'art de l'antiquité, du moyen-age et de la renaissance. 240 pp. 8°. *Paris, Vinchon*, 1851. s.

Musée royal. Explication des ouvrages de peinture, sculpture, architecture, gravure et lithographie des artistes vivans exposés, 1er Mars, 1836. 228 pp. 18°. *Paris, Vinchon*, 1836. s.

——— The same. Ouvrages exposés le 15 Mars, 1844. 345 pp. 16°. *Paris, Vinchon*, 1844. s.

Musée royal bourbon. (Guide pour le); contenant les peintures anciennes, les monumens égyptiens, les sculptures, etc. Par F. Verde, J. Pagano et C. Bonucci. Trad. par C. J. J. xv, 235 pp. 8°. *Naples, Fibreno*, 1831. s.
[*With* PALMERINI. Opere di Morghen].

Museo capitolino. [Illustrato da Bottari e N. Foggini]. 4 v. fol. *Roma*, 1741-83. s.
[v. 4 wanting].

CONTENTS.

v. 1. Immagines d'vomini illustri. 2 p. l. 48 pp. 90 pl.
2. I busti imperiali. 2 p. l. 83 pp. 83 pl.
3. Statue. viii, 174 pp. 91 pl.

Muses (The) choice; or, the merry follow. [*anon.*] 3d ed. 144 pp. 18°. *London, J. Warcus*, 1759.

Musschenbroek (Pieter van). Elementa physicae. Ed. alt. 8 p. l. 600 pp. 26 pl. 1 map. 8°. *Lugduni-Batavorum, S. Luchtmans*, 1741. s.

Muzio (Girolamo). La varchina. *See* **Varchi** (Benedetto). L'ercolano. *Padova,* 1744.

Mvskoke mopunvkv, nakchokv setempohetv. Translation of Introduction to the shorter [presbyterian] catechism into the Creek language, by R. M. Loughridge, [with alphabet]. 31 pp. 8°. *Park Hill,* 1846.

Myers (*Capt.* John). Life, voyages, and travels, with description of the northwest trade. 410 pp. 8°. *London, Longman, Hurst & Co.* 1817.

Myers (P. Hamilton). The emigrant squire. 109 pp. 8°. *Philadelphia, T. B. Peterson,* 1853.

Myles (William). A chronological history of the people called methodists, of the connexion of John Wesley, from 1729 to 1802. 3d ed. xii, 357 pp. 16°. *London, Jaques & Co.* 1803.

Myricio (Giovanni, *knight commander of St. John of Malta*). Opuscvlvm geographicvm rervm totius ejus negotii rationem complectens. 3 p. l. 136 pp. 1 map. sm. fol. *Ingolstadii, W. Eder,* 1590.

Myritius (Johannes). *See* **Myricio** (Giovanni).

Nack (James). The immortal; a dramatic romance, and other poems. With a memoir, by P. Morris. iv, 172 pp. 16°. *New York, Stringer & Townsend,* 1850.

Nadar. [*pseudon.*] *See* **Tournachon** (Felix).

Nagler (G. K.) Neues allgemeines künstlerlexicon, [etc.] 22 v. 8°. *München, E. A. Fleischmann,* 1835–52. s.
[V. 20–22 wanting].

Na Haawina Kamalii. Na mea Eaoaina Kamalii, ma ke kula sabati. 152 pp. 12°. *Honolulu, Paipalapala a na missionari,* 1838. s.

Nalson (*Rev.* John, *LL. D.*) The countermine; or, a short but true discovery of the dangerous principles, and secret practices of the dissenting party, especially the presbyterians. [*anon.*] 7 p. l. 317 pp. 12°. *London, Jonathan Edwin,* 1677.

Namur (Jean Pie). Bibliographie paléographico-diplomatico-bibliologique générale, [etc.] 2 v. xxvii, 227 pp; vi, 306 pp. 8°. *Liége, P. J. Collardin,* 1838. s.

——— Histoire des bibliothèques publiques de la Belgique. 3 v. 8°. *Bruxelles, F. Parent,* 1840. s.

CONTENTS.

v. 1. Bibliothèques de Bruxelles. xi, 320 pp.
v. 2. Bibliothèque de Louvain. xi, 282 pp. 1 pl.
v. 3. Bibliothèque de Liége. viii, 206 pp. 1 pl.

——— Manuel du bibliothécaire, accompagné de notes, [etc.] iv, 368 pp. 8°. *Bruxelles, J. B. Tircher,* 1834. s.

Nannini (Remigio). Civill considerations vpon many and sundrie histories, and principallie vpon those of Guicciardin. Done into French by Gabriel Chappuys, and out of French into English, by W. T. 9 p. l. 252 pp. 5 l. 4°. *London, M. Lownes,* 1601.

Napier (*Sir* Charles James). Records of the Indian command, comprising all his general orders, remarks on courts martial, etc. Compiled by John Mawson. xiv, 244, lix pp. 1 pl. 8°. *Calcutta, R. C. Lepage & Co.* 1851.

Napier (E. Elers). Excursions along the shores of the Mediterranean. 2 v. xviii, 352 pp; x, 387 pp. 2 pl. 12°. *London, H. Colburn,* 1842.

Napier (James Robert, *joint author*). *With* **Watts** (Isaac, *and others*). Shipbuilding, etc.

Napiersky (Carl Ed.) Index corporis historico-diplomatici Livoniae, Esthoniae, Curoniae; oder, kurzer auszug aus derjenigen urkunden-sammlung welche mit unterstützung Alexander I zusammengebracht worden ist, etc. 1198–1631. 2 v. in 1. xvii, 375 pp; 414 pp. fol. *Riga & Dorpat, E. Frantz,* 1833–35. s.

Naples. Catalogus bibliothecae latinae veteris et classicae manuscriptae, quae in regio neapolitano museo borbonico adservatur. Descriptus a Cataldo Jannellio. xii, 302 pp. 4°. *Neapoli, ex regia typographia,* 1827. s.

——— Codices graeci mss. regiae bibliothecae borbonicae neapolitanæ [descripti atque illustrati a Salv. Cyrillo.] 2 v. 4°. *Neapoli, Regia typog.* 1826. s.

——— Regii neapolitani archivi monumenta edita ac illustrata [A. D. 703–1000.] 2 v. xlviii, 284, xxi pp; 3 p. l. 198 pp. 4°. *Neapoli, Regia typog.* 1845–49. s.

Napoleon I. Correspondance inédite, officielle et confidentielle, avec les cours étrangères, les princes, les ministres et les généraux français et étrangers, en Italie, en Allemagne, et en Égypte. 7 v. 12°. *Paris, C. L. F. Panckoucke,* 1819–20.

——— Military maxims. Translated by colonel D'Aguilar. 250 pp. 18°. *Dublin, Milliken & son,* 1831.

Napoleon III. Extinction du paupérisme. 27 pp. fol. *Londres,* 1849.
[*With* Morgan (John M.) Christian commonwealth. *London,* 1849].

——— The same. Extinction of pauperism. Translated from the French. 23 pp. fol. *London,* 1849.
[*With* the preceding].

Napoli-Signorelli (Pietro). Storia critica de' teatri antichi e moderni. 10 v. in 5. 8°. *Napoli, V. Orsino,* 1813.

Narbrough (*Sir* John). *See* Correal (Francisco). Voyages aux Indes Occidentales. *Paris,* 1522.

Narragansett club. Publications. (First series.) v. 1-3. 4°. *Providence,* [*R. I.*] *press Co.* 1866-67.

CONTENTS.

v. 1. Biographical introduction to the writings of Roger Williams. By R. A. Guild.
Key into the language of America. By Roger Williams. Edited by J. H. Trumbull.
Letter of Mr. John Cotton to Roger Williams, and Mr. Cotton's letter examined and answered, by Roger Williams. Edited by R. A. Guild.
v. 2. Answer to master Roger Williams, by John Cotton. Edited by J. L. Diman.
Queries of highest consideration. By Roger Williams. Edited by R. A. Guild.
v. 3. The blovdy tenent of persecution. By Roger Williams.

Narrative (A) of the case of Mrs. Mary Catherine Cadière, against father John Baptist Girard, with father Girard's remarks thereon. [*anon.*] 36 pp. 16°. *London, J. Wilford,* 1731.

Narrative (A) of the circumstances which attended the separation of lord and lady Byron: remarks on his domestic conduct, and refutation of calumnies by public writers. [*anon.*] 22 pp. 8°. *London, R. Edwards,* 1816.
[Misc. pamphlets. v. 56].

Narrative of the extraordinary life of John Conrad Shafford, the Dutch hermit. [*anon.*] 24 pp. 1 pl. 12°. *New York, C. L. Carpenter,* 1840.

Narrative (A) of the life and sufferings of Mrs. Jane Johns, who was wounded and scalped by Indians in east Florida. [*anon.*] 24 pp. 8°. *Baltimore, Lucas & Deaver,* 1837.

Narrative (A) of the loss of the Kent, by fire, in the bay of Biscay, March, 1825. By a passenger. [*anon.*] 68 pp. 18°. *New York, Saxton & Miles,* 1842.

Narrative [of travels in Europe], in two parts: written in 1812. [*anon*]. 238 pp. 1 map. 8°. *London, J. Compton,* 1813.

Nasby (Petroleum Vesuvius, *pseudon.*) *See* **Locke** (D. R.)

Nash (E.) The farmer's practical horse-farriery. 198 pp. 12°. *Auburn, E. Nash,* 1858. S.

Nash (Francis H.), *and* **Bristow** (George F.) Cantara; or, teacher of singing. A complete text-book for schools. 144 pp. 8°. *New York, A. S. Barnes & Co.* 1867.

Nation (The). A weekly journal, devoted to politics, literature, science, and art. July, 1866, to June, 1867. v. 3-4. 4°. *New York,* 1866-67.

National association for the promotion of social science. Transactions: 1866. Edited by G. W. Hastings. xliv, 810 pp. 8°. *London, Longmans,* 1867.

National quarterly review. Edited by E. J. Sears. Dec. 1866, to Sept. 1867. v. 14-15. 8°. *New York, E. J. Sears,* 1867.

National (The) republican. [Washington daily.] Nov. 1860, to Dec. 1867. v. 1-7, in 14 v. fol. *Washington,* 1860-67.

Natt (*Rev.* George W.) Plain sermons on personal religion. 408 pp. 1 pl. 12°. *Philadelphia, J. B. Lippincott & Co.* 1867.

Natter (Johann Lorenz). Traité de la méthode antique de graver en pierres fines, comparée avec la méthode moderne. xxxix, 54 pp. 1 l. 37 pl. fol. *Londres, J. Haberkorn & Co.* 1754.

Naturgeschichte der drei reiche. Allgemeine einleitung in die naturgeschichte. 16 v. in 13. 8°. atlas, 3 v. in 1. 4°. *Stuttgart, E. Schweizerbart,* 1832-46. S.

CONTENTS.

BISCHOFF (Gottlieb W.) Lehrbuch der botanik. v. iv-vi, 1836-40.
BLUM (J. Reinhard). Lehrbuch der oryctognosie. v. ii, 1845.
——— Lithurgik, oder mineralien und felsarten nach ihrer ökonomischer-hinsicht. v. xvi, 1840.
BRONN (H. G.) Handbuch einer geschichte der natur. v. xiii-xv, 1841-49.
LEUCKART (F. S.) Allgemeine einleitung in die naturgeschichte. v. i, 1832.
LEONHARD (Carl Cäsar von). Lehrbuch der geognosie und geologie. v. iii, 1846.
VOIGT (F. S.) Lehrbuch der zoologie. v. vii-xii, v. vii-xii. 1835-40.

Natürliche geschichte der schöpfung. *See* **Vestiges** of the natural history of creation.

Naudé (Gabriel). Bibliographia politica. 271 pp. 23 l. 32°. *Lugd. Batav. J. Maire,* 1642.

Naumann (Carl). Geognostische skizze des königreiches Sachsen.
[*With* GEINITZ (H. B.) Gäa von Sachsen.]

Naumann (Carl Friedrich). Elemente der mineralogie. 5e aufl. xvi, 460 pp. 8°. *Leipzig, W. Engelmann,* 1859.

——— Lehrbuch der reinen und angewandten krystallographie. 2 v. x, 516 pp. 22 pl; vii, 556 pp. 17 pl. 8°. *Leipzig, F. A. Brockhaus,* 1830.

——— A table of mineralogical species. 34 pp. 8°. *Cambridge, J. & J. J. Deighton,* 1833. S.

Naumann (Johann Andreas). Naturgeschichte der vögel Deutschlands, nach eigenen erfahrungen entworfen, aufs neue herausgegeben von J. F. Naumann. [Mit 337 taf. col.] 12 v. 8°. *Leipzig, G. & E. Fleischer,* 1820-44.

——— The same. 13er theil: nachträge, zusätze und verbesserungen, von J. H. Blasius, E. Baldamus, und F. Sturm. 484, 316 pp. taf. col. 338-391. 8°. *Stuttgart, Hoffmann,* 1860.

Naunton, *Sir* Robert. Fragmenta regalia. 8°. *London, E. Jeffery,* 1797.

[*With* HENTZNER (Paul). Travels, etc. *London,* 1797].

Nautical (The) magazine and naval chronicle for 1866. A journal of papers on subjects connected with maritime affairs. viii, 696 pp. 2 pl. 2 maps. 8°. *London, Simpkin, Marshall & Co.* 1866.

Navagero (Andrea). Orationes duae, habitae una in funere B. Liviani; altera in funere L. Lavretani; carminaq. nonnulla. 4°. *Venetiis, Ivnta,* 1555. s.

[*With* FRACASTORO (G.) Opera omnia, 1555].

Navarrete (Martin Fernandez.) Disertacion sobre la historia de la náutica, y de las ciencias matemáticas que han contribuido á sus progresos entre los Españoles. 421 pp. 8°. *Madrid, Real academia de la historia,* 1846. s.

Neal (Daniel). The history of the puritans, [1517—1688. 1st ed.] xvi, 648 pp. 8°. *London, Richard Hett,* 1732.

——— The same. [2d ed.] 2 v. xxiii, 900 pp. 16 l; xx, 883 pp. 14 l. 1 pl. 4°. *London, J. Buckland,* 1754.

Neander (Michael, *editor*). Opus aureum et scholasticvm, in qvo continentvr Pythagoræ carmina aurea, Phocylidis, Theognidis, et aliorum poemata. [Graece et Latine]. 3 v. in 1. 789 pp; 268 pp; 8 l. 191 pp. 4°. *Lipsiae, J. Steinman,* 1577. s.

CONTENTS.

Apophthegmata. Libri duo.
Arion. Historia poetica.
Coluthus. Helenæ raptus.
Gnomologici. Libri duo.
Lucianus. Somnium, seu gallus.
Mithridates, poema historicum.
Nereus marinus de Troiæ excidio.
Nilus episcopus. Praecepta de pietate et moribus.
Phocylides. Poema admonitorium.
Pythagoras. Carmina aurea.
Quintus smyrnæus. De Troiae excidio; reditus Graecorum.
Theognis. Gnomologia.
Tryphiodorus. De Troiæ excidio.

Nebraska *territory.* Journals of the council and house of representatives. 1st to 12th session, 1865–67. 23 v. 8°. *Omaha,* 1855–67.

[Wanting, house journal, 1st session].

Necker (Jacques). Of the importance of religious opinions. From the French. 230 pp. 16°. *Boston, Thomas Hall,* 1796.

Necker de Saussure (Albertine Adrienne). L'éducation progressive; ou, étude du cours de la vie. 3e éd. 2 v. xxxii, 342 pp; 568 pp. 12°. *Paris, Garnier,* 1856.

Necrology: being memoirs of the lives of eminent and extraordinary characters. [*anon.*] 2d ed. v, 653 pp. 6 l. 8°. *London, Lackington, Allen & Co.* 1805.

Neebe (*Rev.* Fr.) A complete practical grammar of the German language. 8 p. l. 223 pp. 8°. *London, Williams & Norgate,* 1847. s.

Needham (John Turberville). Nouvelles observations microscopiques, avec des découvertes intéressantes sur la composition et la décomposition des corps organisés. [Traduites de l'Anglais par L. A. Lavirotte]. xviii, 524, xxix pp. 8 pl. 16°. *Paris, Ganeau,* 1750. s.

Néel (Louis Balthasar). History of Maurice, count Saxe; and of the wars of Europe in which he was concerned. Translated from the French. [*anon.*] 2 v. vii, 302 pp; 284 pp. 16°. *London, T. Osborne,* 1753.

Nees von Esenbeck (Christian Gottfried). Die allgemeine formenlehre der natur als vorschule der naturgeschichte. xiv, 182 pp. 6 pl. 8°. *Breslau, E. Leuckart,* 1852. s.

——— Beobachtungen und betrachtungen auf dem gebiete des lebens-magnetismus, oder vitalismus. 136 pp. 24°. *Bremen, C. Schüremann,* 1853. s.

——— Genera et species asterearum. xiv, 309 pp. 1 tab. 8°. *Norimbergae, L. Schrag,* 1833. s.

——— Hymenopterorum ichneumonibus affinium monographiae, genera europaea et species illustrantes. 2 v. in 1. xii, 320 pp; 448 pp. 8°. *Stuttgartiae, J. G. Cotta,* 1834. s.

Nehiro-iriniui aiamihe massinahigan. [Catholic church services in the Santeux dialect of the Chippeway language?] 96 pp. 18°. *Uabistiguiatsh, (Quebec), Brown & Gilmore,* 1767.

Neidhard (Charles, *M. D.*) Diphtheria, as it prevailed in the United States, 1860–62, [with] historical account of its phenomena, its nature and homoeopathic treatment. 176 pp. 8°. *New York, Wm. Radde,* 1867.

——— On the efficacy of crotalus horridus in yellow fever; also in malignant, bilious, and remittent fevers. 82 pp. 8°. *New York, W. Radde,* 1860. s.

Neill (Edward Duffield). Terra Mariae; or, threads of Maryland colonial history. 260 pp. 12°. *Philadelphia, J. B. Lippincott & Co.* 1867.

Neill (Patrick). The fruit, flower, and kitchen garden. Adapted to the United States. From the 4th ed. xii, 427 pp. 1 pl. 12°. *Philadelphia, H. C. Baird,* 1851. s.

Neilreich (August). Nachträge zu Maly's enumeratio plantarum phanerogamicarum imperii austriaci universi. 348 pp. 8°. *Wien, W. Braumüller,* 1861. s.

Nelli (Giustiniano). Novelle.

(NOVELLE di autori senesi. v. 2. 18°. *Milano,* 1815].

Nemnich (Philipp Andreas). Allgemeines polyglotten-lexicon der naturgeschichte. 1 v. in 4. 9 p. l. 1591 pp. 4°. *Hamburg, Nemnich,* [1793–95]. s.

Nennius. Historia Britonum. fol. *Oxoniæ,* 1691.

[GALE (Thomas) *and* FELL (John). Rerum anglicarum scriptores veteres. *Oxoniæ,* 1684–91. v. 3].

Neri (Pompeo). Osservazioni sopra il prezzo legale delle monete; Discorso sopra la materia frumentaria.

[SCRITTORI class. ital. di econ. pol. v. 47–49].

Nervo (*baron* de). Les finances françaises sous la restauration, 1814–30. 3 v. 8°. *Paris, Lévy,* 1867.

Netherlands. Bijdragen en mededeelingen voor de statistick. I. Verslag over den staat der gestichten voor krankzinnigen 1857-59. 229 pp. 8°. *Gravenhage, Van Weelden en Mingeleh,* 1861. s.

——— Recueil van alle de placaten, ordonnantien, resolutien, instructien, etc. betreffende de admiraliteyten, convoyen, licenten, en verdere zee-taaken. 12 v. 4°. *Gravenhage, J. Scheltus,* 1730–73. s.

——— Recueil des traités depuis 1813. *See* **Lagemans** (E. G.)

——— Staats almanak, 1860. 496 pp. 8°. *Gravenhage, Van Cleef & Belinfante,* 1860. s.

——— Statistisch jaarboek. 8e en 9e jaargang. 2 v. 445 pp; 489 pp. 8°. *Gravenhage, Van Weelden & Mingelen,* 1859–60. s.

——— Verslag aan den koning over de openbare werken, 1850 tot 1853, 1853, 1855–59. 6 v. 5 maps. 1 pl. 4°. *Gravenhage, Van Weelden & Mingelen,* 1854–60. s.

——— Verslag over de verrigtingen aangaande het armbestuur, 1858. 183 pp. 8°. *Gravenhage,* 1860. s.

——— Verslag over de vermoedelijke gevolgen der doorgraving von de landenzte von Suez voor den handel en de reederijen von Nederland. 2 p. l. 260 pp. 2 maps. 8°. *Gravenhage, Van Weelden & Mingelen,* 1859. s.

Netscher (Pieter Marinus). Les Hollandais au Brésil; notice historique sur les Pays-Bas et le Brésil au 17e siècle. xxxii, 210 pp. 2 pl. 1 map. 8°. *La Haye, Belinfante,* 1853.

Neuling (F.) Praktische elementar-naturlehre. Oder das wissenswertheste aus der physik und chemie, mit besonderer beziehung auf das praktische leben. xii, 232 pp. 2 pl. 8°. *Wiesbaden, Kreidel & Niedner,* 1855. s.

Neumann (Carl). Theorie der elektricitäts- und wärme-vertheilung in einem ringe. x, 51 pp. 8°. *Halle, Waisenhaus,* 1864. s.

Neumann (Carl Friedrich). Geschichte der Vereinigten Staaten von America; bis zur inauguration des Abraham Lincoln. v. 3. xxxvi, 559 pp. 8°. *Berlin, C. Heymann,* 1866.

Neumüller (Anton, *M. D.*) De justa tartari emetici paratione dissertatio. 28 pp. 8°. *Landishuti, J. F. Rietsch,* 1856. s.

Nève (Félix Jean Baptiste Joseph). Essai sur le mythe des Ribhavas; premier vestige de l'apothéose dans le Véda, avec le texte sanscrit et la traduction française des hymnes, adressés à ces divinités. xvi, 479 pp. 8°. *Paris, B. Duprat,* 1847. s.

——— Études sur les hymnes du Rigvêda, avec un choix d'hymnes traduites en français. viii, 120 pp. 8°. *Louvain, etc. J. B. Ansiau, etc.* 1842. s.

Nevers (Louis de Gonzague, *duc* de). Les mémoires. [Rédigé par Le Roy de Gomberville]. 2 v. 13 p. l. 937 pp; 20 p. l. 596 pp. portrait. fol. *Paris, L. Billaine,* 1665.

Nevin (Alfred, *D. D.*) Words of comfort for doubting hearts. 71 pp. 24°. *New York, A. D. F. Randolph,* 1867.

New book of nonsense; a contribution to the Philadelphia great central fair. [*anon.*] 53 pl. obl. 18°. *Philadelphia, Ashmead & Evans,* 1864.

New (The) British theatre; selection of original dramas, not yet acted; with critical remarks by the editor. 4 v. 8°. *London, H. Colburn, etc.* 1814–15.

CONTENTS.

v. 1. The witness; the watch-house; intrigues of a day; the prophetess; the masquerade; Theodora; the word of honor; the bandit; the forgery; the genii.

v. 2. Sulieman; manœuvring; Villario; family politics; Thermopylæ; the sailor's return; the last act; the way to win her.

v. 3. The sorceress; a search after perfection; Villario; Gonzanga; the gondolier; the Spaniards; love, honor, and interest; Orpheus; the apostate, or Atlantis destroyed; father and son, or family frailties.

v. 4. Selim and Zuleika; woman's will; Hortensia; Apollo's choice; he must be married; fair crusader; Hector; the Savoyard; sixteen and sixty.

New (The) Buxton guide; a concise account of its mineral springs, hot baths, and curiosities of nature and art. [*anon.*] 81 pp. 1 map. 9 pl. 16°. *Macclesfield, J. Swinnerton,* [1823].

New (A) canto [to Don Juan. *anon.*] 16 pp. 8°. *London, W. Wright,* 1819.

[Misc. pamphlets, v. 56].

New (The) discussion of the trinity; containing notices of Prof. Huntington's defence of that doctrine, reprinted from "the Christian examiner," etc. With sermons by Rev. T. S. King and Dr. O. Dewey. viii, 244 pp. 12°. *Boston, Am. unit. assoc.* 1867.

New (The) foundling hospital for wit. Being a collection of fugitive pieces, in prose and verse. [Edited by John Almon]. New ed. 6 v. 16°. *London, J. Debrett,* 1784.

New (A) history of the Grecian states, from their earliest period to their extinction by the Ottomans. [*anon.*] 140 pp. 2 l. 6 pl. 18°. *Lansingburgh, (N. Y.) S. Tiffany,* 1794.

New (A) pocket companion for Oxford; or, guide through the university; with a tour to Blenheim, Ditchley, Hythorp, Nuneham, and Stow. [*anon.*] New ed. 2 p. l. 160 pp. 1 map. 6 pl. 16°. *Oxford, Prince & Cooke,* 1784.

New (A) pocket dictionary of the English and Danish languages. English-Danish, Danish-English. [*anon.*] 2 v. in 1. vii, 765 pp. sq. 24°. *Leipzig, C. Tauchnitz,* [*about* 1860].

New school of arts, science and manufactures. [*anon.*] 2 v. iv, 683 pp; iv, 708 pp. 25 pl. 8°. *Nottingham, R. Dowson,* 1817.

New (A) system of practical domestic economy, [with] estimates of household expenses. [*anon.*] 3d ed. xii, 402, 76 pp. 11 l. 16°. *London, Colburn & Co.* 1823.

New and old principles of trade compared; or, a treatise on the principles of commerce between nations, with appendix. [*anon.*] 8°. *London,* 1788. s.

Newark library association. Catalogue of the library. 148 pp. 8°. *Newark, Douglass & Starbuck,* 1857. s.

New Bedford (*Mass.*) Free public library. Catalogue. vii, 355 pp. 8°. *New Bedford, B. Lindsey,* 1858. s.

Newberry (John S.) Geological report.

[*With* Ives (J. C.) Report upon the Colorado river, etc.]

Newburyport (*Mass.*) Public library. Catalogue. 207 pp. 8°. *Newburyport, W. H. Huse & Co.* 1857. s.

Newcastle (Margaret Cavendish, *duchess of*). *See* **Cavendish** (Margaret).

New Castle (*Delaware.*) library company. A catalogue of books, [with] the act of incorporation, and the by-laws of the company. 114 pp. 12°. *New Castle, J. C. Clark,* 1840. s.

[Interleaved, and with manuscript additions].

Newell (Robert H.) Avery Glibun; or, between two fires. A romance. By Orpheus C. Kerr. [*pseudon.*] 2 v. in 1. 301 pp. 8°. *New York, G. W. Carleton & Co.* 1867.

New England agricultural society. Second annual report, 1865. 268 pp. 45 pl. 12°. *Boston, J. E. Tilton & Co.* 1866.

New England company. Report by a committee, of their proceedings for the civilization and conversion of Indians, blacks, and pagans, in the British colonies in America and the West Indies, 1829, 1832, 1840, 1846. 4 v. in 1. 3 maps. 12°. *London,* 1829–46. s.

New England (The) historical and genealogical register, Jan. 1865 to Oct. 1867. v. 19–21. 8°. *Boston, N. E. hist. gen. society,* 1865–67.

New England mercantile union directory, 1849. 324 pp. 7 maps. 8°. *New York, Pratt & Co.* 1849. s.

New England patriot; being a candid comparison of the principles and conduct of the Washington and Jefferson administrations. [*anon.*] 148 pp. 8°. *Boston, Russell & Carter,* 1810.

New England's first fruits; in respect, first, of the conversion of some, conviction of divers, preparation of sundry of the Indians. 2. Of the progresse of learning in the colledge at Cambridge, in Massachusetts bay. [*anon.*] 26 pp. sm. 4° *London, Henry Overton,* 1643.

Newenham (Robert O'Callahan). Picturesque views of the antiquities of Ireland, drawn on stone, by James D. Harding. 2 v. in 1. 6 p. l. 25 pp. 111 pl. 4°. [*London*], *T. & W. Boone,* 1830.

Newes from divers countries: as from Spaine, Antwerpe, Collin, Venice, Rome, the Turke, and the prince Doria. 20 pp. sm. 4°. *London, Valentine Sims,* 1597.

Newgate (The) monthly magazine; or, calendar of men, things, and opinions. Sept. 1824, to Aug. 1826. Edited by William Campion. 2 v. viii, 568 pp; 2 p. l. 571 pp. 8°. *London, R. Carlile,* 1825–26.

New Hampshire. Articles in addition to and amendment of the constitution of the state of New Hampshire, agreed to by the convention, and submitted to the people [in 1792]. 33 pp. 8°. *Exeter, H. Ranlet,* 1792.

——— Journal of the house of representatives, July 1, 1767, to March 24, 1768. 60 pp. fol. [*n. p.* 1768]?

——— A journal of the house of representatives at the Concord session, June, 1787. Portsmouth session, Jan. 1788. Concord session, Nov. 1788. Concord session, June, 1793. Exeter session, Dec. 1793. Amherst session, June, 1794. 6 v. 12°. *Portsmouth,* 1787–94.

——— A journal of the senate at the Exeter session, Sept. 1786. Charlestown session, Sept. 1787. Portsmouth session, Jan. 1788. Exeter session, Nov. 1792. Concord session, June, 1793. 5 v. 12°. *Portsmouth,* 1787–93.

New Hampshire. Report of the adjutant general, for the year ending June 4, 1866. v. 1. xxxii, 716 pp. 8°. *Concord, G. E. Jenks,* 1866.

New Hampshire (The) annual register and United States calendar for 1867. By Edson C. Eastman, No. 46. No. 23, new series. 142 pp. 18°. *Concord, E.C. Eastman,* [1866].

New Hampshire (The) political manual for 1867. Compiled by George E. Jenks. 231 pp. 18° *Concord, McFarland & Jenks,* [1867].

New Hampshire (The) book, being specimens of the literature of the granite state. 391 pp. 12°. *Nashville, Charles T. Gill,* 1844.

New Haven colony. Nevv Haven's settling in New England, and some lawes for government. *London, Chapman,* 1656. Reprinted. 30 l. 4°. *Hartford, Case, Lockwood & Co,* 1858.

Newhouse (S. *and others*). The trapper's guide; a manual of instructions for capturing all kinds of fur-bearing animals, and curing their skins; with observations on the fur trade, etc. Edited by J. H. Noyes. 118 pp. 1 pl. 8°. *Wallingford, (Conn.) Oneida community,* 1865. s.

New hymn and tune book; an offering of praise for the Methodist episcopal church. Edited by Philip Philips. 432, 63 pp. 8°. *New York, Carlton & Porter,* 1867.

New Jersey. Analytical index to the colonial documents in the state paper offices of England. Compiled by H. Stevens. Edited, with notes, etc. by W. A. Whitehead. xxx, 504 pp. 8°. *New York, Appletons,* 1858.
[N. J. hist. coll. v. 5].

——— Documents of the ninety-first legislature of the state, and twenty-third under the new constitution. 1395 pp. 8°. *New Brunswick, J. F. Babcock,* 1867.

——— Journal of the twenty-third senate; being the ninety-first session of the legislature. 1109 pp. 8°. *Newark, F. F. Patterson,* 1867.

——— Minutes of votes and proceedings of the ninety-first general assembly, 1867. 1456 pp. 8°. *Camden, S. Chew,* 1867.

New Jersey state library. Catalogue of books. 8°. *Trenton,* 1853. s.

Newman (Edward). Sphinx vespiformis: an essay [on zoological classification]. 54 pp. 8°. *London, Westley & Davis,* 1832. s.

Newman (Francis W.) Handbook of modern Arabic; a practical grammar, with examples, etc. in a European type. xx, 190 pp. 12°. *London, Trübner & Co.* 1866.

Newman (Jeremiah Whitaker). The lounger's common-place book; or, miscellaneous anecdotes. [*anon.*] 4 v. 8°. *London, Kerby & Co.* 1796–99.

——— The same. A new volume of the lounger's common-place book. [*anon.*] 2 p. l. 252 pp. 8°. *London, Longman,* 1807.

Newman (Samuel). A concordance to the holy scriptures; [with] the books of the apocrypha. By S. N. [*anon.*] 4th ed. 404 l. fol. *Cambridge, (Eng.) J. Hayes,* 1698.

New (The) monthly magazine. Edited by W. H. Ainsworth. Sept. 1866 to Dec. 1867. v. 138–141. 8°. *London, Chapman & Hall,* 1866–67.

New Orleans as it is. By a resident. [*anon.*] 79 pp. 8°. [n. p.] 1850.

——— Catalogue of the library of the lyceum and library society, 1st district. 124 pp. 8°. *New Orleans, R. C. Kerr,* 1858. s.

New Plymouth. *See* **Plymouth.**

Newport (R. I.) Boyd's city directory, 1867. Compiled by Andrew Boyd. 280 pp. 12°. *Newport, A. J. Ward,* [1867].

New South Wales. Journal of the legislative council. v. 13. Session 1865–66. xvi, 893 pp. fol. *Sydney, Thomas Richards,* 1866.

New Testament. *See* **Bible.**

Newton (Charles T.) Travels and discoveries in the Levant. 2 v. xvi, 360 pp; xv, 275 pp. 3 maps. 38 pl. 8°. *London, Day & son,* 1865.

Newton (*Sir* Isaac). Arithmetica universalis; sive de compositione et resolutione arithmetica. Cum commentario Johannis Castillionei. 2 v. xviii, 310 pp. 24 pl; 288, 134 pp. 3 pl. 8°. *Amsterdam, M. M. Rey,* 1761. s.

——— The mathematical principles of natural philosophy. [Principia]. Translated by Andrew Motte. [With] the laws of the moon's motion, according to gravity. By John Machin. 2 v. 19 l. 320 pp. 25 pl; 406, viii pp. 19 pl. 71 pp. 8°. *London, B. Motte,* 1729. s.

——— The same. [With] Newton's system of the world. 1st Am. ed. with a life of the author, by N. W. Chittenden. 581 pp. 1 pl. 8°. *New York, D. Adee,* 1848. s.

——— Opticks; or, a treatise of the reflections, refractions, inflections, and colors of light. 2d ed. 4 p. l. 382 pp. 13 pl. 8°. *London, W. & J. Innys,* 1718. s.

Newton (John, *D. D.*) Authentic narrative of some remarkable and interesting particulars in his life, in letters to Rev. Mr. Haweis. [*anon.*] 4th ed. 3 p. l. 160 pp. 1 map. 1 pl. 16°. *London, J. Johnson,* 1775.

——— The same. 18°. *Hudson, (N. Y.)* 1808.

Newton (*Rev.* Richard). Bible blessings. 318 pp. 16°. *New York, Carter & bros.* 1866.

Newton's London journal of arts and sciences. New series, July 1866 to June 1867. v. 24–25. 8°. *London, Newton & son,* 1867.

New York (*City of*). Alms house commissioner. Annual report for 1848. 166 pp. 6 pl. 8°. *New York, McSpedon & Baker,* 1849. s.

——— The same. First—fifth annual report of the governors of the alms house, 1845–53. 5 v. 8°. *New York,* 1850–54. s.

——— Apprentices' and De Milt libraries. Catalogue. xi, 248 pp. 12°. *New York, J. W. Amerman,* 1855. s.

——— Central park. Third annual report of the board of commissioners, January 1860. 72 pp. 2 maps. 12 pl. 8°. *New York, W. C. Bryant & Co.* 1860.

——— The same. Tenth annual report, 1867. 4 pl. 4 maps. 8°. *New York,* 1867.

——— Chamber of commerce. Ninth annual report for the year 1866–67. 8°. *New York, J. F. Trow & Co.* 1867.

——— The same. Colonial records, 1768–1784. With historical and biographical sketches by J. A. Stevens, jr. 404, 172 pp. 7 pl. 2 maps. 8°. *New York, J. F. Trow & Co.* 1867.

——— Free school society. Account of [its] origin and progress. 70 pp. 8°. *New York, Collins & Co.* 1814.

——— General republican committee. A circular letter to their republican fellow-citizens throughout the state, in vindication of the measures of the general government. xxiii, 105 pp. 8°. *New York, Frank, White & Co.* 1809.

——— Hospital. Catalogue of the pathological cabinet, classified and arranged by Robert Ray, jr. With a memoir of the author. 364 pp. 1 pl. 8°. *New York, S. S. & W. Wood,* 1860. s.

——— Manual of the corporation for the years 1846, 1857, 1864, 1865, and 1866. By D. T. Valentine. 5 v. 16°. *New York,* 1847–67.

——— Mercantile library association. Systematic catalogue of books in the collection. xi, 271 pp. 8°. *New York, Harpers,* 1837. s.

——— The same. A supplementary catalogue of books added, 1837–40. 1 p. l. 271–386 pp. 8°. *Association,* 1840.

[*With* the preceding].

——— Metropolitan fire department. Annual reports of the board of commissioners for 1865–66. 110 pp. 4 pl. 8°. *New York, Baker & Godwin,* 1867.

——— New York directory for 1786. By David Franks. Republished. 80 pp. 1 map. 18°. *New York, John Doggett, jr.* 1851.

New York (*City of*). The same, and register, for the year 1789. 144 pp. 16°. *New York, Hodge, Allen & Campbell,* 1789.

——— The same. Longworth's American almanack, New York register, and city directory for [1797]. 340 pp. 16°. *New York, T. & J. Swords,* 1797.

——— The same. Directory for 1815, 1839, 1842, 1847–48, 1851–52. 5 v. 8°. *New York, Doggett,* 1815–51.

——— The same. Citizen and strangers' pictorial and business directory for the city of New York and vicinity, 1853. Solyman Brown, editor. 293 pp. sm. 4°. *New York, C. Spalding & Co.* 1853.

——— The same. Trow's New York city directory. Compiled by H. Wilson. v. 81. For the year ending May 1, 1868. 1141, 156, 41 pp. 8°. *New York, John F. Trow,* 1867.

——— The same. Wilson's copartnership directory for 1867–68. 8°. *New York, J. F. Trow,* 1867.

——— Society library. A catalogue of the books belonging to the New York society library, with the charter and by-laws. 2 p. l. 240 pp. Supplement. 135 pp. 8°. *New York, Library assoc.* 1813.

——— New York as it is, in 1837; including the city of Brooklyn. [*anon.*] 250 pp. 18°. *New York, J. Disturnell,* 1837.

New York daily tribune. July, 1866, to Dec. 1867. 3 v. fol. *New York,* 1866–67.

New York gazette, from Monday, Oct. 18, to Monday, Oct. 25, 1736, [containing the opinion of the council of New Jersey given to John Hamilton that the administration of the government is lawfully vested in him]. 4 pp. fol. *New York, W. Bradford,* 1736.

[*With* Morris, (Lewis). Observations on the reasons given by Mr. [John] Hamilton's advisers, etc. 11 pp. fol. [*New York*], 1736].

New York herald (daily). July, 1866, to Dec. 1867. 3 v. fol. *New York,* 1866–67.

New York (The daily) times. Jan. 1862 to Dec. 1865. 8 v. fol. *New York,* 1862–65.

New York (*City and county*). Board of education. Twelfth [and] fourteenth annual reports. 8°. *New York, W. C. Bryant & Co.* 1854–56.

New York (*Colony of*). A narrative of the proceedings subsequent to the royal adjudication, concerning the lands lately usurped by New Hampshire, [with] appendix, containing grants, acts of government, and other proofs, concerning the encroachments of New Hampshire. 28 pp. 33 l. sm. fol. *New York, John Holt,* 1773.

New York. (*Colony*). [Proceedings] in convention of the representatives of the state. 8°. *Fishkill, (N. Y.)* 1776.

——— Royal patent defining the boundaries between New York and Connecticut, and granting lands to certain persons mentioned therein. 8 pp. fol. [*New York*], 1731.

——— A state of the right of the colony of New York, with respect to its eastern boundary on Connecticut river, so far as concerns the late encroachments of New Hampshire, and also of [its] rights so far as concerns the grants formerly made by the French government of Canada, of lands on lake Champlain, and at, and to the southward of Cr n Point. 28 pp. sm. fol. *New York, H. Gaine*, 1773.

——— Votes and proceedings of the general assembly of the colony of New York, Feb. 15–26, 1757. 14 pp. fol. [*New York*], *James Parker*, 1757.

New York (*State of*). Annual reports of the regents of the university. 77th–79th. [1864–66.] 3 v. 8°. *Albany*, 1864–66.

——— Calendar of historical manuscripts in the office of the secretary of state. Edited by E. B. O'Callaghan. 2 parts. Part i. Dutch manuscripts, 1630–1664. xi, 423 pp. Part ii. English manuscripts, 1664–1776. xiv, 893 pp. 4°. *Albany, Weed, Parsons & Co.* 1865–66.

——— Calendar of N. Y. colonial manuscripts, indorsed land papers, in the office of the secretary of state. 1643–1803. 1087 pp. 8°. *Albany, Weed, Parsons & Co.* 1864.

——— Census for 1835. 56 sheets. fol. *Albany, Croswell, Van Benthuysen & Burt*, 1836.

——— Constitution, adopted in 1846. With a comparative arrangement of the constitutional provisions of other states, classified by their subjects. Prepared [for the] constitutional convention of 1867, by F. B. Hough. 4, 239 pp. 4°. *Albany, Weed, Parsons & Co.* 1867.

——— Documents of the senate and assembly. 89th session. 1866. 12 v. 8°. *Albany, C. Wendell*, 1866.

——— General index to the documents of the state, from 1777 to 1865. Prepared by O. Archer. 544 pp. 8°. *Albany, Weed, Parsons & Co.* 1866.

——— Journals of the senate and assembly. 89th session. 1866. 3 v. 8°. *Albany, C. Wendell*, 1866.

——— List of lands to be sold in April 1830, for arrears of taxes. 240 pp. 12°. *Albany, Croswell & Van Benthuysen*, 1829.

——— New York convention manual; prepared under the direction of [the] secretary of state, comptroller, and attorney-general. By F. B. Hough. 2 v. x, 586 pp; xxii, 462 pp. 1 chart. 8°. *Albany, Weed, Parsons & Co.* 1867.

CONTENTS.

v. 1. Constitutions.
v. 2. Statistics.

——— [Geological survey of the state. Annual reports to the legislature on the.] 5 v. in 3. 8°. *Albany, State printer*, 1837–41. s.

CONTENTS.

BECK (Lewis C.) Reports on the mineralogical and chemical departments (for 1836), v. i, p. 15; (1837), v. ii, p. 7; (1838), iii, 9; (1839), iv, 45; (1840), v, 5.
CARR (Ezra S.) Appendix to L. Vanuxem's report. Economical geology, iv, 385.
CONRAD (T. A.) Report on the palaeontological department (1837). ii, 107. Second do. (1838), iii, 57. Third do. (1839), iv, 199. Fourth do. (1840), v. 25.
—— First annual report on the geological survey of the third district (1836), vi, 155.
DEKAY (James E.) Letters on the botanical and zoological department. ii, 5.
—— Reports on the zoological departments, (1836) i, ii, (1838, 1839), iii, 7, 15.
EMMONS (Ebenezer). First annual report on the 2d geological district (1836), i, 197; second do. (1837), ii, 185; third do. (1838), iii, 201; fourth do. (1839), iv, 259; fifth do. (1840), v, 113.
—— *and* HALL (James). Communication relative to a place of deposit for the different specimens collected by the geologists. iii, 5.
GALE (L. D.) Report to W. W. Mather on the geology of New York county. iii, 177.
HALL (James). Second annual report of the fourth geological district (1837), ii, 287; third do. (1838), iii, 287; fourth do. (1839), iv, 389; fifth do. (1840), v, 149.
HORSFORD (Eben N.) Report to James Hall on the geology of Cattaraugus county. iv, 457.
HORTON (William). Report to W. W. Mather on the geology of Orange county. iii, 133.
MATHER (William W.) First report of the first geological district (1836), i, 61; second do. (1837), ii, 121; third do. (1838), iii, 69; fourth do. (1839), iv, 211; fifth do. (1840), v, 63.
TORREY (John). Reports on the botanical department, i, 9; iii, 113.
VANUXEM (L.) Second annual report of the third district, etc. (1837), ii, 253; third do. (1838), iii, 241; fourth do. (1839), iv, 355; fifth do. (1840), v. 137.
—— First annual report of the fourth district, etc. (1836), i, 185.

——— Insurance department. 1st–7th annual report of the superintendent. 8 v. 8°. *Albany*, 1860–66.

——— Manual for the use of the legislature of the state of New York, for 1838, 1840, 1844, 1845, 1854, 1856, 1858, 1859, 1861, 1863, 1865, and 1866; prepared by the secretary of state. 12 v. 18°. *Albany, State printers*, 1838–66.

——— Natural history of New York, Part 5. Palæontology. By James Hall. v. III. Containing descriptions and figures of the organic remains of the lower Helderberg group and the Oriskany sandstone. 1 v. in 2. 4°. *Albany, C. Van Benthuysen*, 1859–61.

New York (*State*). The official reports of the canal commissioners, and the acts of the legislature respecting navigable communications between the great western and northern lakes, and the Atlantic ocean. 174, 12 pp. 1 map. 8°. *New York, T. & W. Mercein*, 1817.

——— A record of the officers and privates of the regiments organized in the state of New York, to assist in suppressing the rebellion, as taken from the muster-in rolls. v. 5–6. 4°. *Albany, Weed, Parsons & Co.* 1866.

New York (The) almanac and weather book for the year 1857. 226 pp. 24°. *New York, Mason brothers*, 1857.

New York historical society. Catalogues of the books, tracts, newspapers, maps, charts, views, portraits, and manuscripts, in the library. 139 pp. 8°. *New York, J. Seymour*, 1813. s.

——— Catalogue of books, manuscripts, maps, etc. added to the library since January, 1839. 32 pp. 8°. *New York, J. W. Harrison*, 1840. s.

New York state agricultural society. Transactions for 1841. v. i. iv, 411 pp. 8 p. 8°. *Albany, T. Weed*, 1842.

——— The same. For 1861–1866. 6 v. 8°. *Albany, State printers*, 1862–67.

New York state business directory. 1867. By Sampson, Davenport & Co. 1036, 200 pp. 8°. *Albany, Sampson, Davenport & Co.* 1867.

New York state library. Catalogue: 1865. Law library: first supplement. 180 pp. 8°. *Albany, C. Van Benthuysen*, 1865.

New York state register, for 1843, 1844, 1845, 1846. Ed. by O. L. Holley. 4 v. in 3. 12°. *New York*, 1843–46.

Nibelungenlied (Das). Uebersetzt von G. O. Marbach. Mit holzschnitten nach originalzeichnungen von E. Bendemann und J. Hübner. 207 l. unp. 4°. *Leipzig, Wigand*, 1840. s.

Nicely (Wilson). The great southwest; or, plain guide for emigrants and capitalists, embracing a description of Missouri and Kansas. Also a township map of Missouri and Kansas. 115 pp. 1 map. 12°. *St. Louis, R. P. Studley & Co.* 1867.

Nicholas (Samuel Smith). Conservative essays, legal and political. v. 3. 155 pp. 8°. *Louisville, Bradley & Gilbert*, 1867.

——— *See, also,* **Nicolas.**

Nicholls (John). Recollections and reflections, personal and political, as connected with public affairs, during the reign of George iii. 302 pp. 12°. *Philadelphia, H. C. Carey & I. Lea*, 1822.

Nichols (Francis). The British compendium: or, rudiments of honour. The genealogy, etc. of the present nobility of England, coats of arms, etc. 4th ed. 2 p. l. 363 pp. 2 l. 65 pl. 32°. *London, H. Meere*, 1721.

——— The same. 9th ed. 2 v. iv, 596 pp. 24°. *London, J. & P. Knapton*, 1751. [Wanting v. 2].

Nichols (John Gough). Autographs of royal, noble, learned, and remarkable personages conspicuous in English history, from the reign of Richard ii to that of Charles ii, with some illustrious foreigners, engraved under the direction of Charles John Smith, [with] concise biographical memoirs. xiv pp. 63 l. iv pp. 55 fac-sim. pl. fol. *London, J. B. Nichols & son*, 1829.

Nichols (*Mrs.* Mary Gove). Mary Lyndon; or, revelations of a life. An autobiography. [*anon.*] 388 pp. 12°. *New York, Stringer & Townsend*, 1855.

Nichols (Rebecca S.) Bernice, and other poems. 216 pp. 1 pl. 12°. *Cincinnati, Shepard & Co.* 1844.

Nichols (William, *D. D.*) A conference with a theist; containing an answer to all the most usual objections of the infidels against the christian religion. 3d ed. 2 v. xvi, 516 pp. 6 l; 486 pp. 5 l. 2 pl. 12°. *London, Holland & Bowyer*, 1723.

Nicholson (N. A.) Science of exchanges. 3d ed. 108 pp. 8°. *London, E. Wilson*, 1865.

Nicholson (Peter). The carpenter's new guide: inclnding some observations and calculations on the strength of timber. 13th ed. By William Johnston. 117 pp. 83 pl. 4°. *Philadelphia, Grigg, Elliott & Co.* 1848. s.

Nicholson (William). An introduction to natural philosophy. 2 v. xx, 383 pp. 6 l. 19 pl; xi, 441 pp. 7 l. 7 pl. 8°. *London, J. Johnson*, 1782. s.

Nicholson. *See, also,* **Nicolson.**

Nicolai (Christoph Friedrich). Allgemeine deutsche bibliothek. 118 v. 8°. *Berlin, Kiel, und Stettin, F. Nicolai & C. E. Bohn*, 1766–96.

——— Anhang; [und] register, zum v. 1–12. 1 v. in 2. 1348 pp. 8°. *Berlin und Stettin, F. Nicolai*, 1771.

——— Anhang; [und] register, v. 13–24. 3 v. 8°. *Berlin und Stettin, F. Nicolai*, 1777.

——— Anhang; [und] register, v. 25–36. 6 v. 8°. *Berlin und Stettin, F. Nicolai*, 1780.

——— Anhang; [und] register, v. 37–52. 4 v. 8°. *Berlin und Stettin, F. Nicolai*, 1785.

Nicolai (Christoph Friedrich). Anhang; [und] register, v. 53–86. 5 v. in 6. 8°. *Berlin und Stettin, F. Nicolai,* 1791.

——— Neue allgemeine deutsche bibliothek. 107 v. in 106. 8°. *Kiel, Berlin, und Stettin, C. E. Bohn & F. Nicolai,* 1793–1806.

——— Anhang zum v. 1–28, nebst den registern. 6 v. 8°. *Kiel, C. E. Bohn,* 1797–1801.

——— Anhang zum v. 29–68, nebst registern. 4 v. 8°. *Berlin & Stettin, F. Nicolai,* 1802–3.

——— Die mitarbeiter an Friedrich Nicolai's Allgemeiner deutscher bibliothek nach ihren namen und zeichen in zwei registern, [von G. Parthey]. iv, 72 pp. 4°. *Berlin, Nicolai,* 1842.

NOTE.—The register of Allgemeine deutsche bibliothek, v. 87–117, constitutes v. 118. The register of Neue allgemeine deutsche bibliothek constitutes v. 105–107 of the series.

Nicolaides (Georgos). Topographie et plan stratégique de l'Iliade, avec une carte. xiv, 271 pp. 1 map. 8°. *Paris, L. Hachette & Cie.* 1867.

Nicolas (*Sir* Nicholas Harris). The court of queen Victoria; or, portraits of British ladies, distinguished by birth and rank: with biographical and genealogical memoirs. 81 pp. 10 pl. fol. *London, Hogarth,* 1845.

——— A full display of the whole peerage of England, which has existed at any period since the conquest. 2 v. 36, lxxxviii, 942 pp. 16°. *London, J. Nichols & son,* 1825.

——— The privy purse expenses of king Henry the eighth, from 1529 to 1531. xliv, 372 pp. 8°. *London, William Pickering,* 1827.

——— Privy purse expenses of Elizabeth of York; wardrobe accounts of Edward the fourth. With a memoir of Elizabeth of York. 2 p. l. civ, 205 pp. 8°. *London, William Pickering,* 1830.

——— The siege of Carlaverock. *See* **Walter,** *of Exeter.*

Nicolas. *See,* also, **Nicholas.**

Nicolay (*Rev.* Charles Grenfell). Atlas of physical and historical geography. *See* **Ansted** (D. T.) *and* **Nicolay.**

——— *and others.* A manual of geographical science; mathematical, physical, historical and descriptive. Maritime discovery. Theory of description and geographical terminology. 2 v. 8°. *London, J. W. Parker & son,* 1852–59.

Nicolet (H.) Atlas de physique et de météorologie agricoles. 10 pp. 6 l. 13 col. maps, fol. *Paris, Bachelier,* 1855. S.

Nicollet (Jean N.) Report intended to illustrate a map of the hydrographical basin of the upper Mississippi river. 170 pp. 8°. *Washington, Blair & Rives,* 1843. S.

[*With* FRÉMONT (J. C.) Report. *Washington,* 1845].

Nicolovius (Alfred). Johann Georg Schlosser's leben und literarischen wirken. iv, 284 pp. 8°. *Bonn, E. Weber,* 1844. S.

Nicolson (William, *archbishop of Cashel*). The English, Scotch, and Irish historical libraries. A short view and character of most of our historians, either in print or manuscript. With a letter to White Kennet. 3d ed. xvi, 590 pp. fol. *London, G. Strahan,* 1736.

Nicolson. *See,* also, **Nicholson.**

Nieberding (C. H.) Geschichte des ehemaligen niederstifts Münster, etc. Ein beitrag zur geschichte und verfassung Westphalens. 3 v. 12°. *Vechta, C. H. Fauvel,* 1840–52. S.

Niebuhr (Barthold Georg). Epitome of Niebuhr's history of Rome, with chronological tables and appendix, by Travers Twiss. xliii, 359 pp. 8°. *Oxford, D. A. Talboys,* 1836.

Niecollucci (Amadio, *anagram*). *See* **Machiavelli** (Niccolò).

Niemeyer (August Hermann). Beschreibung des hallischen waisenhauses. 8°. *Halle,* 1799. *See* **Schulze** (J. L.) etc.

Niemeyer (Johann Christian). Plan d'une académie des beaux arts en Italie, presénté aux états respectifs de l'Amérique. 20 pp. 4°. [*n. p. or d.*]

Nieremberg (Juan Eusebio). Firmamento religioso de lvzidos astros en algvnos claros varones de la compañia de Jesvs. 6 p. l. 808 pp. sm. fol. *Madrid, Maria de Quiñones,* 1644.

Nierses IV. (Klaiëtsi, *patriarch of Armenia*). Preces viginti quatuor linguis editæ. [Ed. P. Aucher.] iii p. l. 422 pp. 1 pl. 18°. *Venetiis, in insula S. Lazari,* 1823.

Niess (Johannes). Adolescens evropævs ab Indo, [Michaele Ayatvmo,] moribvs christianis informatus. 12 p. l. 450 pp. 8 l. 18°. *Dilingæ, Caspar Sutor,* 1629.

Nieuwentyt (Bernhart). The religious philosopher; or, the right use of contemplating the works of the Creator. Translated by J. Chamberlayne. 2d ed. 3 v. [illustrated.] 8°. *London, J. Senex,* 1721.

Night (The) side of New York. A picture of the great metropolis after night-fall. By members of the New York press. [*anon.*] Illustrations by F. Beard. 121 pp. 12°. *New York, J. C. Harvey & Co.* 1866.

Nightingale (Florence). Notes on nursing. New ed. xv, 221 pp. 8°. *London, Harrison,* 1860.

Nilsson *or* Nielsson (Sven). Illuminerade figurer till Skandinaviens fauna, med text utgifne. (Däggdjur och foglar). 2 v, 140 l. 100 col. pl; 155 l. 100 col. pl. 8°. *Lund, C. F. Berling*, 1832–40. s.

——— Petrificata suecana formationis cretaceæ. i. Vertebrata et mollusca. viii, 39 pp. 10 pl. 4°. *Londini Gothorum, Berling*, 1827. s.

——— Prodromus ichthyologiæ scandinavicæ. 2 p. l. 124 pp. 16°. *Lundæ, typis Berlingianis*, 1832. s.

——— Skandinavisk fauna. 4 parts in 5 v. 8°. *Lund, C. W. K. Gleerups, etc.* 1842–55. s.

CONTENTS.

1. Däggdjuren. 2e uppl. xviii, 656 pp. 1847.
2. Foglarna. 3e uppl. 2 v. xxxiv, 580 pp; 580 pp. 1858.
3. Amfibierna. 2 pl. iv, 119 pp. 1842.
4. Fiskarna. 3 pl. xxxiv, 768 pp. 1855.

——— Skandinaviska nordens ur-invänare, ett försök e komparativa ethnografien och ett bidrag till mennisko-slägtets utvechlings-historia. Första delen. 3 pl. xvi, 223 pp. 21 pl. 4°. *Lund, Berlingska boktryckeriet*, 1838–43. s.

Nilus (*asceta, St.*) Praeceptiones de vita pie, christiane ac honeste exigenda, græco-latine, a M. Neandro conversæ et expositæ, [etc.]

[*With* NEANDER (M.) Opus aureum, 1577. v. 2].

Nineteenth century; or, the new dispensation. An examination of the claims and assertions of E. S. By a layman. [*anon.*] xi, 425 pp. 1 pl. 12°. *New York, J. Allen*, 1852.

Nissen (Martinus). Norsk bog-fortegnelse. 1813–47. Med anhang. viii, 215 pp. 8°. *Kristiania, Feilberg & Landmark*, 1848. s.

Nitzsch (Carl Wilhelm). Die Gracchen und ihre nächsten vorgänger. 4 p. l. 456 pp. 8°. *Berlin, Veit & Co.* 1847. s.

Nitzsch (Christian Ludwig). Pterylographiæ avium pars prior. 52 pp. 4°. *Halae, Gebauer*, 1833. s.

[No more published].

——— The same. Pterylography. Translated from the German. Edited by P. L. Sclater. xi, 178 pp. 10 pl. fol. *London, R. Hardwicke*, 1867.

[Ray soc. publications].

Noad (Henry M.) Manual of electricity. 4th ed. 2 v. viii, 522 pp. 1 pl; 523–910 pp. 1 pl. 8°. *London, G. Knight & Co.* 1855–57. s.

Noah (Mordecai Manuel). Correspondence and documents relative to the attempt to negotiate for the release of the American captives at Algiers. 128 pp. 8°. *Washington*, 1816.

Noble (*Rev.* Samuel). An appeal in behalf of the views of the eternal world and state, and the doctrines of faith and life, held by the New church. 2d ed. 538 pp. 12°. *Boston, W. Carter & bro.* [*about* 1860].

——— The divine law of the ten commandments explained, according to both its literal and its spiritual sense. iv, 446 pp. 8°. *London, Simpkin, Marshall & Co.* 1848.

——— The plenary inspiration of the scriptures asserted. In six lectures. 3d ed. xvi, 354, lxi pp. 8°. *London, Hodson & son*, 1859.

Nodal (Bartolomè Garcia de *and* Gonçalo de). Relacion del viage al descubrimiento del estrecho nuevo de San Vicente, que hoy es nombrado de Maire, y reconocimiento del de Magalenes. 9 p. l. 162 pp. 1 l. 1 map. sm. 4°. *Cadiz, Manuël Espinosa de los Monteros*, [1766]?

Nodier (Charles Emmanuel). Bibliographie entomologique; ou, catalogue raisonné des ouvrages relatifs à l'entomologie et aux insectes, [etc.] viii, 64 pp. 18°. *Paris, Moutardier*, 1861. s.

——— Contes de la veillée. 358 pp. 12°. *Paris, Charpentier*, 1853.

——— Promenade de Dieppe aux montagnes d'Écosse. 334 pp. 1 map. 2 pl. 16°. *Paris, J. N. Barba*, 1821.

Noel (François Joseph Michel). Dictionarium latino-gallicum. Dictionnaire latin-françois. Nouv. éd. vii p. l. 1,037 pp. 8°. *Paris, Le Normant*, 1820.

——— Nouveau dictionnaire français-latin. 8e éd. viii, 1,044 pp. 8°. *Paris, Le Normant*, 1813.

——— *and* **La Place** (Guislain Fr. Mar. Jos. de). Leçons françaises de littérature et de morale. 19e éd. 2 v. xxiv, 730 pp. 8°. *Paris, Le Normant*, 1832–33.

Noinville (Jacques Bernard Durey de). *See* **Durey de Noinville.**

Nolan (Frederick). The Egyptian chronology analysed. xxxi, 480 pp. 8°. *London, Seeleys*, 1848.

Noll (Henry R.) The botanical class-book, and flora of Pennsylvania. 158, 452 pp. 16°. *Lewisburg, (Pa.) O. N. Worden*, 1852. s.

Nollet (Jean Antoine). Lectures in experimental philosophy. Translated by John Colson. xlviii, 278 pp. 18 pl. 8°. *London, J. Wren*, 1752. s.

Noorthouck (John). A new history of London, including Westminster and Southwark. 2 p. l. viii pp. 2 l. 902 pp. 21 l. 1 map. 41 pl. 4°. *London, R. Baldwin*, 1773.

Norcott (*Rev.* John). Baptism discovered, plainly and faithfully according to the word of God. 5th ed. 47 pp. 16°. *Philadelphia, Andrew Stuart*, 1764.

Nordhoff (Charles). Stories of the island world. 315 pp. 3 pl. 16°. *New York, Harpers,* 1857. s.

——— Whaling and fishing. 383 pp. 4 pl. 16°. *Cincinnati, Moore, Wilstach, Keys & Co.* 1856. s.

Noriac (Claude Antoine Jules Cayron, *dit*). Human follies. Translated from the 16th Paris ed. by G. Marlow. 224 pp. 16°. *Philadelphia, Leypoldt,* 1863.

Norman (W. H.) Exploration expedition. Letter reporting the return of the "Victoria" from the gulf of Carpentaria; together with reports and correspondence. 51 pp. fol. *Melbourne, J. Ferres,* 1862. s.

——— Exploration expedition. Report, together with copy of his journal on the late expedition to the gulf of Carpentaria. 31 pp. fol. *Melbourne, J. Ferres,* 1862. s.

Normand (L. *aîné*). Monuments funéraires choisis dans les cimetières de Paris et des principales villes de France. 2 v. in 1. 5 p. l. 72 pl; 1 p. l. 72 pl. 4°. *Paris, A. Morel & Cie.* 1863.

Normandy (A.) The commercial handbook of chemical analysis. xii, 640 pp. 12°. *London, Geo. Knight,* 1850. s,

——— Practical introduction to H. Rose's treatise on chemical analysis. Illustrated by synoptic tables and formulas. xii, 114 l. 7 tab. 8°. *London, W. Tegg & Co.* 1849. s.

Norris (Isaac). Journal during a trip to Albany, in 1745, and account of a treaty held there. iii, 31 pp. 4°. *Philadelphia, Hawthorne press,* 1867.

Norris (John). Practical discourses upon several divine subjects. 8 p. l. 350 pp. 12°. *London, S. Manship,* 1691.

Norris (Thaddeus). The American anglers' book; embracing the natural history of sporting fish, and the art of taking them. 604 pp. 8 pl. 8°. *Philadelphia, E. H. Butler & Co.* 1864. s.

——— The same. With instructions in fly-fishing, [etc.] New ed. 701 pp. 8 pl. 8°. *Philadelphia, E. H. Butler & Co.* 1865.

North (Milo Linus, *M. D.*) Saratoga waters; or, the invalid at Saratoga. 70 pp. 16°. *New York, M. W. Dodd,* 1840.

——— Saratoga waters; or, the invalid at Saratoga. 2d ed. 72 pp. 16°. *New York, Saxton & Miles,* 1843.

North American land co. Plan of association. Established February, 1795. 25 pp. 8°. *Philadelphia, R. Aitken & son,* 1795.

North (The) American review, for 1867. v. 104—105. 8°. *Boston, Ticknor & Fields,* 1867.

North (The) British review, Sept. 1866, to Dec. 1867. New series, v. 6–8. [Complete series, v. 45–47.] 8°. *Edinburgh, Edmonston & Douglas,* 1866–67.

North Carolina. Journal of the house of commons, 1785. 52 pp. fol. [*n. p.* 1786 ?]

——— Journal of the senate, 1785. 44 pp. fol. [*n. p.* 1786 ?]
[Imperfect; wanting pp. 1–8].

——— The same, 1786–7. 76 pp. fol. [*n. p.* 1787 ?]

North Carolina (Geological and natural history survey of). Part iii. Botany; containing a catalogue of the indigenous and naturalized plants of the state. By Rev. M[oses] A. Curtis, D.D. 158 pp. 8°. *Raleigh, N. C. institution for the deaf and dumb and the blind,* 1867. s.

Northcote (James). The life of Sir Joshua Reynolds, [etc.] 2d ed. 2 v. 339 pp; xii, 364 pp. 5 pl. 8°. *London, H. Colburn,* 1818. s.

North Missouri and eastern Kansas business directory for 1867–8. 455 pp. 8°. *Quincy, (Ill.) S. B. Wyckoff,* 1867.

Norton (*Rev.* Andrews). A statement of reasons for not believing the doctrines of trinitarians, concerning the nature of God and the person of Christ. 3d ed. With a [biography] of the author. l, 499 pp. 12°. *Boston, Am. unit. assoc.* 1867.

Norton (Charles B.) Literary register; or, annual book list, for 1856. 138 pp. 8°. *New York, C. B. Norton,* 1856. s.

Norton (George). Commentaries on the history, constitution, and chartered franchises of the city of London. xxiv, 541 pp. 8°. *London, H. Butterworth,* 1829.

Norton (*Rev.* John, *of Boston*). An answer to a dialogue entituled The meritorious price of man's redemption, [by William Pynchon]. 7 p. l. 270 pp. 2 l. 16°. *London,* [*about* 1648].
[Imperfect; title-page and 1 p. l. wanting; 2 l. at the end imperfect].

——— A discussion of that great point in divinity, the sufferings of Christ. 8 p. l. 270 pp. 16°. *London, Geo. Calvert,* 1653.

——— The orthodox evangelist; or, a treatise wherein many evangelical truths are briefly discussed, cleared, and confirmed. 7 p. l. 355 pp. sm. 4°. *London, Henry Cripps,* 1654.

Norton (William A.) A treatise on astronomy, spherical and physical; with problems and tables. 4th ed. xiv, 443, 115 pp. 15 pl. 8°. *New York, J. Wiley & son*, 1867.

Norway. Statistiske tabeller, udgivne efter foranstaltning af departementet for det Indre. 9e række. 236 pp. obl. fol. *Christiania, C. C. Werner & Co.* 1849. s.

Norwich. City directory; containing the names of the inhabitants of Norwich, Norwich town, Bean Hill, Yantic, Greenville, and part of Preston, [etc.] 1857. Compiled by William H. Boyd. viii, 157 pp. 1 pl. 8°. *Norwich, (Conn.) J. W. Stedman*, 1857.

Norwood (Joseph G.) Geological report of a survey of portions of Wisconsin and Minnesota.

[*With* OWEN (D. D.) Report of a geological survey of Wisconsin, 1852].

Notable women of olden time. [*anon.*] 301 pp. 9 pl. 16°. *Philadelphia, Amer. Sunday school union*, 1852. s.

Notes of a ramble through France, Italy, Switzerland, Germany, Holland, and Belgium; and of a visit to the scenes of "The lady of the lake," etc. By a lover of the picturesque. [*anon.*] 9 p. l. 464 pp. 8°. *London, Hamilton, Adams & Co.* 1836.

Notes on California and the placers; how to get there, and what to do afterwards. By one who has been there. [*anon.*] 128 pp. 2 pl. 8°. *New York, H. Long & bro.* 1850.

Notes and queries; a medium of intercommunication for literary men, general readers, etc. 3d series. July, 1866, to Dec. 1867. v. 10–12. sm. 4°. *London*, 1866–67.

Notice statistique sur la Guyane française. Extrait des notices statistiques sur les colonies françaises, imprimées en 1838, par ordre de M. le ministre des colonies. [Éd. par Ternaux-Compans, J. Lechevalier, Joly de Lotbinière.] 3 p. l. 176 pp. 1 col. map. 12°. *Paris, F. Didot*, 1843. s.

Notices of Sullivan's campaign; or, the revolutionary warfare in western New York, embodied in the addresses and documents connected with the funeral honors rendered to those who fell with Boyd in the Genessee valley. 191 pp. 1 pl. 18°. *Rochester, William Alling*, 1842.

Noticias biográficas, [biografia necrológica,] del exmo. señor don Lucas Alaman. [*anon.*] 59 pp. 1 pl. fol. *Mexico, R. Rafael*, 1853.

Notitia vtraqve cvm orientis tvm occidentis, vltra Arcadii Honoriiqve Cæsarvm tempora, [etc.] Præcedit Andreæ Alciati libellus, de magistratib, ciuilibusq; ac militaribus officijs, [etc.] Succedit descriptio urbis Romae que sub titulo Pub. Victoris circumfertur; et altera urbis constantinopolitanae incerto autore, [etc.] Svbiungitur, [etc.] Liber de rebvs bellicis, (etc.] Incerto autore. Item, [etc.] Disputatio Adriani Aug. et Epicteti philosophi. [Curavit S. Gelenius vel Ghelen]. 107 l. fol. *Basileæ, apud Hieronymvm Frobenivm et N. Episcopivm*, 1552. s.

Nott (Eliphalet, *D. D.*) Miscellaneous works. 240 pp. 8°. *Schenectady, William J. M'Carter*, 1810.

Nougaret (Pierre Jean Baptiste). Anecdotes des beaux-arts. Par M***. [*anon.*] v. 1. 18°. *Paris, Bastien*, 1776.

——— Londres, la cour et les provinces d'Angleterre, d'Écosse et d'Irlande; ou, esprit, mœurs, coutumes, habitudes privées des habitans de la Grande Bretagne. [*anon.*] 2 v. iv. 458 pp; 460 pp. 12°. *Paris, Briand*, 1816.

Nouveau dictionaire d'anecdotes historiques de l'amour. [*anon.*] 2 v. in 1. 18°. *Paris*, 1838.

Nouveau guide de conversations modernes en Russe, Allemand, Anglais et Français; ou, dialogues usuels et familiers, etc. Par Boltz, Fischer, Witcomb, et Bellinger. Nouv. éd. v, 236 l. 24°. *Berlin, B. Behr*, 1862. s.

Nouveaux mémoires secrets, pour servir à l'histoire de notre temps. 1823. [*anon.*] 457 pp. 8°. *Paris, Brissot Thivars*, 1829.

Nouvel abrégé de géographie moderne, suivi d'un appendice, et d'un abrégé de géographie sacrée. [*anon.*] 2e éd. xii, 277, xxxii, 16 pp. 12°. *Québec, Neilson et Cowan*, 1833.

Nouvelle biographie générale, depuis les temps les plus reculés jusq'à nos jours. Publiée sous la direction de J. C. F. Hoefer. v. 45–46. 8°. *Paris, Didot*, 1866.

[Completing the work.]

Nouvelles de la terre de Prestre Jehan.

[*With* Alcripe (P. d'). La nouvelle fabrique, etc.]

Nova Britannia; offering most excellent fruites by planting in Virginia. Exciting all such as be well affected to further the same. [*anon.*] 18 l. 12°. *London, Samvel Macham*, 1609.

Nova Scotia. Journal of the proceedings of the legislative council, 1866. fol. *Halifax, A. Grant*, 1866.

——— Journal of the proceedings of the house of assembly, 1866. fol. *Halifax, Compton & Co.* 1866.

Nova Scotia (The) magazine and comprehensive review of literature, politics, and news. [July—Dec. 1789. Edited by John Howe.] v. 1. viii, 480 pp. 3 l. 8°. *Halifax, editor*, 1789.

Novelle di autori senesi. [Pubblicate per cure di Gaetano Poggiali. ed. 2ª]. 2 v. xxxi, 398 pp; xxii, 386 pp. 2 pl. 18°. *Milano, Giovanni Silvestri*, 1815.

CONTENTS.

v. 1. Novelle di Gentile Sermini et di Pietro Fortini.
v. 2. Novelle del Ilicino, del Nelli, del Bargagli, del Sozzini, del Bandiera.

Novelties, inventions, and curiosities in arts and manufactures. [*anon.*] 3d ed. 267 pp. 16°. *London, G. Routledge & Co.* 1853. s.

Novi (Giuseppe). Il teatro della guerra dal Settembre al Novembre, 1860. iv, 116 pp. 8 tab. 8°. *Napoli, tipog. poliglotta*, 1861. s.

Novus orbis, id est, navigationes primæ in Americam. [Cura Balthasari Lydii]. 8 p. l. 570 pp. 18°. *Roterodami, J. L. Berewout*, 1616.

[Abridged from the collection of Grynœus].

CONTENTS.

Columbus, C. Navigatio.
Pinzon, V. Navigatio.
Vesputius, A. Navigatio.
Martyr, P. De insulis nuper repertis.
Cortes, F. De suis peregrinationibus.
Herborn, N. De Indis convertendis.
Varrerius, J. de. De Ophyra regione.

Nowell (Alexander). Catechismus, latine explicata. 133 pp. 8°. *Oxford*, 1825.

[*With* RANDOLPH (John, *bishop of London*). Enchiridion theologicum, v. 1.)

Noyes (George Rapall, *D. D.*) A collection of theological essays from various authors. With an introduction. 5th ed. xlvi, 512 pp. 12°. *Boston, Am. unit. assoc.* 1867.

——— Translations of Job, Psalms, etc. *See* **Bible** (*English*).

Noyes (*Rev.* Nicholas). New England's duty and interest to be an habitation of justice, and mountain of holiness. xi, 88 pp. 18° *Boston, B. Green & J. Allen*, 1698.

——— The same. [With an account of Indian plantations in Massachusetts, by Rev. G. Rawson, and S. Danforth.] xi, 99 pp. 18°. *Boston, B. Green & J. Allen*, 1698.

Nubila jubila britannico-stuartica, oder sonder vnd wunderbare glücks-verwandlung so sich zwischen den beyden Stuarten, Carln dem i. vnd Carln dem ii, königen über Gross-Britannien, vnd dem parlament. Vom 1625–62. [*anon.*] 13 p. l. 978 pp. 33 pl. 16°. *Frankfurt am Mayn, J. W. Ammons vnd W. Serlins*, 1662.

Nugæ criticæ. Occasional papers written at the seaside by Shirley. [*pseudon.*] 492 pp. 12°. *Edinburgh, Edmonston & Douglas*, 1862.

Nugent (Thomas). The grand tour; or, a journey through the Netherlands, Germany, Italy and France. [*With*] the European itinerary. 2d ed. 4 v. 16°. *London, D. Browne*, 1756.

Numan (A. *M. D.*) Verhandeling over de onvruchtbare runderen, bekend onder den naam van kweenen, in verband tot sommige andere dieren met misvormde geslachtsdeelen. xii, 85 pp. 4°. atlas, 23 pl. fol. *Utrecht, N. van der Monde*, 1843. s.

Nuñez (Alvar, *surnamed* Cabeça de Vaca). La relacion y comentariõs de lo acaescido en las dos jornadas que hizo a las Indias. 2 parts in 1 v. lvi. l. 2 l. 88 l. 12°. *Valladolid, Francisco Fernandez de Cordoua*, 1555.

——— The same. Narrative of Alvar Nuñez Cabeça de Vaca. Translated from the Spanish by Buckingham Smith. 138 pp. 9 maps. 4°. *Washington, privately printed by G. W. Riggs, jr.* 1851.

Nuovo dizionario italiano-tedesco e tedesco-italiano. Schul- und reise-taschen-worterbuch der italienschen und deutschen sprache. Ed. nuova. [Ital-Deutsch, und Deutsch-Ital.] 159 pp. 24°. *Lipsia, C. Tauchnitz*, [*about* 1850].

Nutt (David). A catalogue of theological books in foreign languages. 600 pp. 8°. *London*, 1857.

——— The same. Appendix. 106 pp. 8°. *London*, 1857.

Nyerup (Rasmus), *and* Kraft (Jens Edvard). Almindeligt litteraturlexicon for Danmark, Norge, og Island, etc. viii, 692 pp. 4°. *Kjöbenhavn, Gyldendal*, 1820. s.

Nyst (P. H.) Description des coquilles et des polypiers fossiles des terrains tertiaires de la Belgique. [Extract]. 697 pp. 15 pl. 4°. *Bruxelles, Acad. royale des sciences*, 1843. s.

Oates (George). Ne plus ultra interest tables, (seven per cent.) in which are shown the interest of any sum, from one dollar to five hundred dollars consecutively, for any length of time, from 1 to 360 days, by days. vi, 100 pp. obl. 16°. *Philadelphia, Lippincott, Grambo & Co.* 1850. s.

——— The same. From one dollar to one thousand dollars, [etc.] vi, 202 pp. obl. 16°. *Philadelphia, Lippincott, Grambo & Co.* 1850. s.

——— The same. From one dollar to ten thousand dollars, for any length of time, from one day to one year, by days, [etc.] vi, 183 pp. 4°. *New York, D. Appleton & Co.* 1851. s.

——— The same. (Six per cent.) in which are shown the interest on any sum from one dollar to five hundred dollars, for any length of time, from 1 day to 360 days, by days. vi, 112 pp. obl. 16°. *Philadelphia, Lippincott, Grambo & Co.* 1850. s.

Oates (George). Ne plus ultra interest tables, (six per cent.) in which are shown the interest of any sum, from one dollar to one thousand dollars, [etc.] 224 pp. obl. 16°. *Philadelphia, Lippincott, Grambo & Co.* 1850. s.

——— Tables of sterling exchange; in which are shown the value of a sterling bill, in federal money, from £1 to £10,000, [etc.] 207 pp. 8°. *New York, D. Appleton & Co.* 1851. s.

Oates (Titus). Eikon basilikē; or, the picture of the late king James, drawn to the life. 2d ed. 4 pts. in 1 v. 2 p. l. 558 pp. sm. 4°. *London, R. Baldwin,* 1696–97.

O'Beirne (James). New views of the process of defecation, and their application to pathology; with an analytical correction of Sir Charles Bell's views respecting the nerves of the face. 142 pp. 8°. *Washington, D. Green,* 1834. s.

Oberbauer (Julius C.) America und die sklaverei. 32 pp. 8°. *New York, Helmich & Stark,* 1854.

Obsequens (Julius). Qvae svpersvnt ex libro de prodigiis. Cvm animadversionibvs Joannis Schefferi et Francisci Ovdendorpii. Accedvnt svpplementa Conradi Lycosthenis, cvrante Joanne Kappio. 24 p. l. 250 pp. 27 l. 8°. *Cvriae Regnitianae, J. G. Vierlingivs,* 1772.

Observations on the authenticity of the gospels. By a layman. [*anon.*] viii, 101 pp. 16°. *Chicago, H. P. Chandler,* 1867.

Observations on church government by the presbytery of Springfield, (Ohio.) With the last will and testament of that body. [*anon.*] 23 pp. 16°. *Albany, E. & E. Hosford,* 1808.
[*With* M'NEMAR (Richard), Kentucky revival. 16°. *Albany,* 1808].

Observations on lord Bathurst's speech, [with official documents relative to Napoleon's imprisonment on St. Helena]. 173 pp. 16°. *New York, Kirk & Mercein,* 1818.

Observations on the new constitution, and on the fœderal and state conventions. By a Columbian patriot. [*anon.*] 22 pp. 8°. *New York,* 1788.

Observations on public principles and characters; with reference to recent events. [*anon.*] 62 pp. 12°. [*n. p.*] 1820.

Observations on doctor Stevens's history of Georgia. [*anon.*] 28 pp. 8°. *Savannah,* 1849.

Observations générales et impartiales sur l'affaire du Scioto. [*anon.*] 27 pp. 12°. *Paris, Fr. Didot le jeune,* 1790.

Observations sur l'instruction relative à la mort du duc de Bourbon, prince de Condé. [*anon.*] 272 pp. 8°. *Paris, G. Warée,* 1831. s.

O'Callaghan (Charles Williamson). Description of the Genesee country. [*anon.*] 37 pp. 1 pl. 2 maps. sm. 4°. *Albany, (N. Y.) L. Andrews & Co.* 1798.

O'Callaghan (Jeremiah). Usury, or interest proved to be repugnant to the divine and ecclesiastical laws, and destructive to civil society. 206 pp. 12°. *New York, J. O'Callaghan,* 1824.

Oceola Nikkanochee. Narrative of Oceola Nikkanochee, a young Seminole Indian, with a brief history of his nation and uncle. 4 p. l. 228 pp. 3 pl. 8°. *London, Hatchard,* 1841.

Ochsenheimer (Ferdinand). Die schmetterlinge von Europa. (v. i–iv). Fortsetzung von Friedrich Treitschke. (v. v–x). 10 v. in 7. 8°. *Leipzig, Fleischer,* 1807–35. s.

Ockel (E.) Anleitung zur aufzucht, erhaltung und benutzung der schafe. 2e aufl. viii, 192 pp. 4 pl. 8°. *Berlin, Veit u. Co.* 1846. s.

Ockley (Simon). Introductio ad linguas orientales. viii, 168 pp. 16°. *Cantabrigiae, Typis academicis,* 1706.

O'Connor (Henry). Connected essays and tracts, being a series of inferences deduced chiefly from the principles of the most celebrated sceptics. xxiv, 344 pp. 8°. *Dublin, Hodges & Smith,* 1837.

O'Connor (William D.) The ghost. Illustrated by T. Nast. 93 pp. 2 pl. sq. 16°. *New York, G. P. Putnam & son,* 1867.

O'Conor (Charles). [Writings;] *In* Vallancey (C.) Collectanea de rebus hibernicis. 8°. *Dublin,* 1774–90.

CONTENTS.

1. Reflections on the history of Ireland during the times of heathenism. 22 pp. [v. 3, No. 10].
2. Second letter on the heathen state and antient topography of Ireland. 28 pp. [v. 3, No. 10].
3. Third letter on the same. 27 pp. [v. 4, No. 13].

"**Odd-fellowship** examined, by the light of scripture and reason, by Rev. Joseph T. Cooper, D. D." re-examined according to the word of God, and official documents of the order. By a member of Harmony lodge, No. 16, I. O. O. F. [*anon.*] 172 pp. 12°. *Philadelphia, Higgins & Perkinpine,* 1856. s.

Ode to a friend, on our leaving, together, South Carolina. [*anon.*] 15 pp. 4°. *London, J. Dodsley,* 1783.

Odeleben (Ernst Otto Innocenz von). Relation circonstanciée de la campagne de 1813, en Saxe. Traduite de l'Allemand par M. Aubert de Vitry. 2 v. 308 pp; 334 pp. 8°. *Paris, Plancher,* 1817.

Odermann (Carl Gustav). Arithmetik. 1861. *See* **Feller** (F. E.) *and* **Odermann.**

Oderico *da Udine. See* **Odorico** *da Pordenone.*

Odiorne (Thomas). The progress of refinement; a poem, to which are added a poem on fame, and miscellanies. 176 pp. 1 pl. 18°. *Boston, Young & Etheridge,* 1792.

Odling (William). A manual of chemistry, descriptive and theoretical. Part i. 8°. *London, Longmans,* 1861. s.

Odorico *da Pordenone.* The eastern parts of the world described. 162 pp.

[*With* YULE (Henry). Cathay, etc. v. 1].

——— The same. [Text in Latin and Italian].

[*With* YULE (H.) Cathay, etc. v. 2].

Oehlenschläger (Adam Gottlob). Vaulundurs saga. A legend of Wayland Smith. From the German, by Eliz. Kinnear. 64 pp. 16°.

[*With* DEPPING (G. B.) *and* MICHEL (F. X.) Wayland Smith. *London,* 1847].

Oersted (Anders Sandöe). L'Amérique Centrale. Recherches sur sa flora et sa géographie physique. Liv. i. 3 p. l. 18 pp. 22 pl. 4°. *Copenhague, F. S. Muhle,* 1863. s.

——— De regionibus marinis. Elementa topographiæ historiconaturalis freti Öresund. 5 p. l. 90 pp. 2 col. pl. 8°. *Hauniæ, J. C. Scharling,* 1844. s.

Oersted (Hans Christian). Der mechanische theil der naturlehre. xxi, 349 pp. 8°. *Braunschweig, Vieweg,* 1851. s.

Oesterlen (Friedrich). Historisch-kritische darstellung der streits über die einheit oder mehrheit der venerischen contagien. xii, 343 pp. 8°. *Stuttgart, J. G. Cotta,* 1836. s.

Official list of officers who marched with the army under the command of major general Winfield Scott from Puebla upon the city of Mexico, and who were engaged in the battles of Mexico. 13 l. obl. 12°. *Mexico, Am. star print,* 1848.

O'Flaherty (Roderic). Ogygia; or, a chronological account of Irish events: collected from very ancient documents, and supported by the sacred and prophane writings of the first nations of the globe. Translated [from the Latin] by Rev. Jas. Hely. 2 v. lxxxiii, 4 l. 292 pp; 2 p. l. 419 pp. 12°. *Dublin, W. M'Kenzie,* 1793.

Ogden (E. D.) Tariff; or, rates of duties payable on goods imported into the United States of America; containing all recent circulars and decisions of the treasury department, to March 29, 1868. 158, 126 pp. 8°. *New York, Bogert, Kidder, & Nexsen,* 1867.

Ogilvie (John, *D. D.*) Philosophical and critical observations on the nature, characters and various species of composition. 2 v. vi, 447 pp; 359 pp. 8°. *London, G. Robinson,* 1784.

O'Halloran (Sylvester). An introduction to the study of the history and antiquities of Ireland, [with] appendixes. 4 p. l. xx, 384 pp. 5 pl. 4°. *London, J. Murray,* 1772.

Ohio. Annual message of the governor, to the fifty-seventh general assembly, 1867. 69 pp. 8°. *Columbus, L. D. Myers & Bro.* 1867.

——— Executive documents. Message, and reports to the general assembly, and governor of the state of Ohio, for the year 1865 and 1866. 4 v. 8°. *Columbus, R. Nevins,* 1866-67.

——— Fifth annual report of the state commissioner of common schools for year ending August 31, 1858. [By Anson Smyth.] 213, 2 pp. 8°. *Columbus, state printer,* 1859. s.

——— Journal of the senate and house of representatives of the state of Ohio for 1865-66. 4 v. 8°. *Columbus, R. Nevins,* 1867.

——— Report (20th annual) of the Ohio state board of agriculture, for 1865. 8°. *Columbus, R. Nevins,* 1866.

——— Report (8th, 9th, and 10th annual) of the commissioner of statistics for the years 1864-1866. 3 v. 8°. *Columbus, R. Nevins,* 1865-67.

——— Report of special committee on railroads and telegraphs, made to the senate, 1867. 197 pp. 8°. *Columbus, L. D. Myers & Bro.* 1867.

——— W. W. Reilly & Co.'s Ohio state business directory, [etc.] for 1853-4. Also, an advertising department. 425 pp; 328 pp. 2 maps. 8°. *Cincinnati, Morgan & Overend,* 1853. s.

Öhlenschläger. *See* **Oehlenschläger.**

Ohm (Georg Simon). Die galvanische kette, mathematisch bearbeitet. iv, 245 pp. 1 pl. 8°. *Berlin, T. H. Riemann,* 1827. s.

——— Grundzüge der physik, als compendium zu seinen vorlesungen. x, 563 pp. 8°. *Nurmberg, J. L. Schrag,* 1854. s.

Ohm (*Dr.* Martin). Die analytische und hohere geometrie in ihren elementen. Mit vorzüglicher berücksichtigung der theorie der kegelschnitte. x, 477 pp. 1 l. 8°. *Berlin, T. H. Riemann,* 1826.

——— Kurzes gründliches und leichtfassliches rechenbuch, zum unterricht auf gymnasien und bürgerschulen, zunächst für die schulanstalten in Thorn. xxxvi, 111 pp. 16°. *Berlin, Maurer,* 1818. s.

——— Lehrbuch der mechanik, zugleich mit den dazu nöthigen lehren der höhern analysis und der höhern geometrie. 3 v. 8°. *Berlin, T. C. F. Enslin,* 1836-38.

CONTENTS.

v. 1. Mechanik des atoms.
v. 2. Statik fester körper.
v. 3. Dynamik fester körper.

Ohm (*Dr.* Martin). Versuch einer kurzen, gründlichen und deutlichen, auch nicht-mathematikern verständlichen anweisung, etc. xxiv, 160 pp. 2 tab. 8°. *Berlin, T. H. Riemann,* 1827. s.

——— Versuch eines volkommen consequenten systems der mathematik. 2e ausgabe. 2 v. xxxiv, 418 pp; xxx, 455 pp. 2 pl. 12°. *Berlin, T. H. Riemann,* 1828–29.

CONTENTS.

v. 1. Arithmetik und algebra enthaltend.
v. 2. Algebra und analysis des Endlichen enthaltend.

Ohsson, Mouradja d'. *See* **Mouradja** d'Ohsson.

O-jib-ue spelling book, designed for the use of native learners. [*anon.*] 2d ed. 107 pp. 12°. *Boston, Am. board for. miss.* 1835.

Oken (Lorenz). Lehrbuch der natur-philosophie. 3 v. 8°. *Jena, F. Frommann,* 1809–11. s.

Okes (Thomas Verney). An account of the providential preservation of Eliz. Woodcock, who survived a confinement under the snow of nearly eight days and nights, in Feb. 1799. 43 pp. 12°. *Cambridge, F. Hodson,* [1799].

Okounéff (Nicolaj Alexandrowitsch). Considérations sur les grandes opérations de la campagne de 1812, en Russie; des mémoires sur les principes de la stratégie; de l'examen des trois armes, etc. Nouv. éd. augmentee de l'histoire de la campagne de 1800 en Allemagne et en Italie par Bulow. Traduit de l'Allemand par C. L. Sévelinges. 449 pp. 8°. *Bruxelles, J. B. Petit,* 1841.

Olaf. Olafs saga hins helga. Efter et gammelt pergaments-haandskrift i universitets-bibliotheket i Upsala. Udgivet af R. Keyser og C. R. Unger. xi, 150 pp. 8°. *Christiania, Feilberg & Landmarks,* 1849. s.

Olbers (Carl). Montanismen, kyrkhistorisk afhandling. 2 p. l. 140 pp. 8°. *Lund, Författare,* 1853. s.

Old (An) bushman, (*pseudon.*) *See* **Wheelwright** (H. W.)

Old England forever, or Spanish cruelty display'd; wherein the Spaniards right to America is impartially examined and found defective. [*anon.*] 320 pp. 1 pl. 16°. *London, the booksellers,* 1740.

Old (The) guard: a monthly journal devoted to the principles of 1776 and 1787. C. C. Burr, editor. Jan. 1865, to Dec. 1867. v. 3–5. 8°. *New York, Van Evrie, Horton & Co.* [1865–67].

Old (The) red house. [*anon.*] 388 pp. 3 pl. 16°. *Boston, H. Hoyt,* [1860].

Oldbug (John, *esq. pseudon.*) *See* **Withington** (*Rev.* Leonard).

Oldendorp (Christian Georg Andreas). Fuldstaendigt udtog af C. G. A. Oldendorp's missions-historie om de evangeliske broedres mission paa de Caraibiske der St. Thomas, St. Crux, og St. Jan. 16°. *Kjöbenhavn, J. R. Thiele,* 1784.

Olderico da Udine. *See* **Odorico** *da Pordenone.*

Oldericus de Portu Naono. *See* **Odorico** *da Pordenone.*

Oldmixon (John). Clarendon and Whitlock compar'd, [with a] comparison between the History of the rebellion and other histories of the civil war. [*anon.*] xxxvii, 344 pp. 9 l. 12°. *London, J. Pemberton,* 1727.

Oldoini (Bernardo). Ristretto dell' istorie del mondo, 1635–50. *See* **Torsellini** (Orazio).

Olin (Stephen, *D. D.*) College life; its theory and practice. 239 pp. 12°. *New York, Harpers,* 1867.

——— Travels in Egypt, Arabia Petræa, and the Holy Land. 8th ed. 2 v. xiv, 458; 478 pp. 12°. *New York, Harpers,* 1846.

Olina (Giovanni Pietro). Vccelliera; overo, discorso della natvra e proprietà di diversi vccelli, e in particolare di qve' che cantano; con il modo di prendergli, conoscergli, alleuargli, e mantenergli. 6 p. l. 81 pp. 66 pl. 4°. *Roma, A. Fei,* 1622.

Oliphant (Lawrence). Narrative of the earl of Elgin's mission to China and Japan, 1857–59. 645 pp. 1 pl. 8°. *New York, Harpers,* 1860. s.

——— On the present state of political parties in America. 30 pp. 8°. *Edinburgh, Blackwood & sons,* 1866.

Oliphant (Margaret O. W.) Agnes. 3 v. 16°. *London, Hurst & Blackett,* 1866.

——— Harry Muir; a story of Scottish life. [*anon.*] 3 v. in 1. 313 pp. 12°. *New York, D. Appleton & Co.* 1853.

——— Lilliesleaf; being a concluding series of Margaret Maitland. [*anon.*] New ed. 12°. *London,* 1856.

——— Madonna Mary. 3 v. 300 pp; 304 pp; 280 pp. 12°. *London, Hurst & Blackett,* 1866.

——— The same. 225 pp. 8°. *Boston, Littell,* [1867].

Oliveira (Francisco Xavier d'). Mémoires de Portugal, avec la bibliothèque lusitane. 2 v. 12 p. l. 384 pp; 8 p. l. 384 pp. 16°. *Amsterdam,* 1741. s.

Oliver (George, *D.D.*) A dictionary of symbolical masonry. 12°. *New York,* 1867.

[*With* Macoy (Robert). Cyclopedia of freemasonry. 1st ed. pp. 3–290. 2d ed. pp. 341–628. 12°. 1867].

Oliver (Isabella). Poems, on various subjects. 220 pp. 16°. *Carlisle, [Pa.] (A. Loudon's press, Whitehall,)* 1805.

Oliver Optic's magazine. Our boys and girls. Oliver Optic, [*pseudon.* for W. T. Adams,] editor. Jan. to Dec. 1867. v. 1–2 in 1. v, 728 pp. 10 l. 8°. *Boston, Lee & Shepard,* [1867].

Olivier (Antoine Guillaume). Entomologie. *See* **Sturm** (J.) Abbildungen, etc. 1802.

Olivier (J.) Fencing familiarized; or, a new treatise on the art of small sword. [French and English.] xlvii, 205 pp. 15 pl. 8°. *London, J. Bell,* 1780.

Ollenix du Montsacré. [*pseudon.*] *See* **Montreux** (Nicolas de).

Ollyffe (*Rev.* George). The madness of disaffection and treason against the present government. 7 p. l. 320 pp. 12°. *London, J. Downing,* 1724.

Olmsted (Denison, *LL. D.*) A compendium of astronomy. Revised by E. S. Snell. 194 pp. 12°. *New York, Collins & bro.* 1868.

Olmsted (Frederick Law). A journey in the back country. 492 pp. 12°. *New York, Mason Bros.* 1860. S.

Oltmanns (Jabbo). Nachtrag zu J. E. Bode's anleitung zur kenntniss des gestirnten himmels. *See* **Bode** (J. E.)

Omalius d'Halloy (Jean Baptiste Julien d'). Précis élémentaire de géologie. vii, 790 pp. 1 tab. 3 pl. 8°. *Paris, A. Bertrand,* 1843. S.

O'Meara (Barry Edward). Exposition of some of the transactions that have taken place at St. Helena, since the appointment of Sir Hudson Lowe as governor. xiv, 215 pp. 8°. *London, James Ridgway,* 1819.

——— Opinions of Napoleon Bonaparte of nations and persons, as delivered by him, from the years 1815 to 1818. Alphabetically arranged by W. Hough. 86 pp. 8°. *Calcutta, J. Pereira,* 1848.

Once a month: a magazine of miscellaneous selections. Oct. 1866 to Sept. 1867. v. 1–2. 8°. *Springfield, (Mass.) W. J. Holland & Co.* [1866–67].

One step; or, to what will it lead? [*anon.*] 125 pp. 1 pl. 8°. *Philadelphia, Am. Sunday school union,* 1853. S.

Opposite neighbors; or, the two lives, and their end. [*anon.*] 400 pp. 4 pl. 16°. *Philadelphia, Am. S. S. union,* [1867].

Orbigny (Alcide Dessalines d'). Cours élémentaire de paléontologie, et géologie stratigraphiques. 2 v. 299 pp; 847 pp. 12°. *Paris, V. Masson,* 1849–52. S.

——— Histoire naturelle des céphalopodes. *See* **Férussac** (A. É. J. P. F. de) *and* **Orbigny.**

——— Paléontologie française. Description zoologique et géologique de tous les animaux mollusques et rayonnés fossiles de France. Terrains crétacés. 6 v. in 12. 8°. *Paris, auteur,* 1840–53. S.

CONTENTS.

v. 1. Céphalopodes.
v. 2. Gastéropodes.
v. 3. Lamellibranches.
v. 4. Brachiopodes.
v. 5. Bryozoaires.
v. 6. Échinodermes.

——— The same. Terrains oolitiques, ou jurassiques. 2 v. in 4. 8°. *Paris, auteur,* 1842–1860. S.

CONTENTS.

v. 1. Céphalopodes.
v. 2. Gastéropodes.

——— Prodrome de paléontologie stratigraphique universelle des animaux mollusques et rayonnés. 3 v. 12°. *Paris, V. Masson,* 1849–52. S.

Orbigny (Charles). Keepsake d'histoire naturelle. Description des mammifères. Introduction. 48 pp. 8°. *Paris, Bazouge-Pigoreau,* [1840]. S.

Orbis lumen, et Atlantis ivga tecta retecta. 5 p. l. 1,450 pp. 5 l. 12°. *Franckfurt-am-Mayn, W. Serlin und G. Fickwirth,* 1656.

Orchestral journal. 25 l. in 1 v. 300 pl. 8°. *New York, [Firth, Pond & Co.]* 1856. S.

Order (The) for morning and evening prayer, and some other offices of the church of England. Ne Yakawea. Niyadewighniferage, Yondereanayendakhkwa. Translated into the Mohawk language [by Rev. —— Andrews and Rev. H. Barclay]. 3d ed. 208 pp. 12°. *Quebec,* 1780.

Order of worship for the reformed church. 388 pp. 12°. *Philadelphia, S. R. Fisher & Co.* 1867.

Orderly (The) book of that portion of the American army stationed at or near Williamsburg, Va. under gen'l Andrew Lewis, March 18th to August 28th, 1776. With notes and introduction by Charles Campbell. xi, 100 pp. sm. 4°. *Richmond, (Va.)* 1860.

[Hist. documents from the Old Dominion, No. 1].

Ordoñes de Cevallos *or* **Zeballos** (Pedro). Descriptio Indiae Occidentalis. 9 l. fol.

[*With* HERRERA (A. de). Novvs orbis, sive descriptio Indiae Occidentalis. fol. *Amstelodami,* 1622].

——— The same. Particvlière description de l'Inde Occidentale. pp. 201–227. fol.

[*With* HERRERA (A. de). Description des Indes Occidentales. fol. *Amsterdam,* 1622].

Ordoñes de Cevallos *or* **Zeballos** (Pedro). Eyghentlyche beschryvinghe van West Indien. 29 pp. fol. *Amsterdam*, 1621.

[*With* HERRERA (A. de). Nievwe Werelt, etc. Ed. *Amsterdam*, 1621].

Oregon. Journal of the house of representatives of the territory, 1855-6. 219, 179 pp. 8°. *Salem, A. Bush*, 1856. S.

—— Journal of the council of the legislative assembly of the territory, 1855-6. 195, 72 pp. 8°. *Salem, A. Bush*, 1856. S.

Orfila (Matthieu Joseph Bonaventure). Lehrbuch der toxicologie. Nach den 5en aufl. aus dem Französischen mit selbständigen zusätzen bearbeitet von Dr. G. Krupp. 2 v. vii, 601 pp; 720 pp. 8°. *Braunschweig, Vieweg*, 1854. S.

Orford (Horace Walpole, 4*th earl of*). *See* **Walpole.**

Oriental portfolio. Illustrations of the scenery, etc. of the East, from original drawings by Thomas Bacon. Ed. by H. H. Wilson. Nos. 1-2. engr. title, 10 l. unp. 10 pl. fol. *London, Smith, Elder & Co.* 1838-40.

Oriental translation fund. Publications. 40 v. 4°. 46 v. 8°. *London, etc.* 1829-58.

CONTENTS.

Ali Mohammed Khân. Political and statistical history of Gujarât. Translated from the Persian by James Bird. 8°. *London*, 1835.

Apostolical constitutions; or, canons of the apostles, in Coptic. With an English translation, by H. Tattam. 8°. *London*, 1848.

Batuta (Abu Abdallah Mohammed Ebn). Travels. From the Arabic by S. Lee. 4°. *London*, 1829.

Chodzko (Aleksander). Specimens of the popular poetry of Persia. Translated, with notes. 8°. *London*, 1842.

Critical essay on various Ms. works, Arabic and Persian, illustrating the history of Arabia, Persia, India, Egypt and Spain. Translated by J. C. 8°. *London*, 1832.

Cureton (William). Spicilegium syriacum; remains of Bardesan, Meliton, Ambrose, and Mara Bar Serapion. With English translation. 8°. *London*, 1855.

Customs and manners of the women of Persia, and their domestic superstitions. Translated from the Persian manuscript, by J. Atkinson. 8°. *London*, [*With* Ibrahim, *Basmajee*. War in Bosnia, etc.]

Dabistân; or, school of manners. [Ascribed to Mohsan Fâni]. From the Persian, with notes, by D. Shea and A. Troyer. 3 v. 8°. *Paris*, 1843.

Elisæus. History of Vartan; an account of the religious wars between the Persians and Armenians. Translated from the Armenian, by C. F. Neumann. 4°. *London*, 1830.

Ethiopic didascalia; or, the Ethiopic version of the apostolical constitutions, with an English translation, by T. P. Platt. 4°. *London*, 1834.

Evliyá Efendî Jelebi. Narrative of travels in Europe, Asia, and Africa, in the 17th century. From the Turkish, by J. von Hammer. V. 1 in 2 parts, and v. 2. 4°. *London*, 1834-50.

Firdûsî, Firdausî, *or* Firdousî (Abûl Kâsim Hasan Ben Mohammed Et-Tûsî, *surnamed*). The Shâh Nâmeh. Translated and abridged, with notes. By J. Atkinson. 8°. *London*, 1832.

Fortunate (The) union; a romance, translated from the Chinese original, with notes. To which is added, [Han Koong Tsew], a Chinese tragedy. By J. F. Davis. 2 v. 8°. *London*, 1829.

Garcin de Tassy (Joseph Héliodore). Histoire de littérature hindoui et hindoustani. 2 v. 8°. *Paris*, 1839-47.

Gholam Hussein, *Khan. Mir.* Siyar-ul-mutakherin: a history of the Mahomedan power in India during the last century. Revised from the translation of Haji Mustefa, and collated with the Persian original, by John Briggs. v. 1. 8°. *London*, 1832.

Hâji Khalfa (Mustafa Ben Abdallah, *surnamed*). History of the maritime wars of the Turks. From the Turkish, by J. Mitchell. Part I. 4°. *London*, 1831.

—— Lexicon bibliographicum et encyclopædicum. Edidit, latinè vertit, et commentario indicibusque instruxit G. Flügel. 7 v. in 6. 4°. *Leipzig*, 1835-58.

Hän Koong-Tsew; or, the sorrows of Hän. A Chinese tragedy. Translated by J. F. Davis. 4°. *London*, 1829.

Hariri (Abû Mohammed Kâsim Ben Ali, *surnamed* Al). Makamat; or, rhetorical anecdotes of Al Harirî of Basra. Translated from the Arabic, by T. Preston. 8°. *London*, 1850.

Harivansa, ou histoire de la famille de Hari; ouvrage formant un appendice du Mahabharata. Traduit sur l' original Sanscrit, par S. A. Langlois. 2 v. 4°. *Paris*, 1834-35.

Hatim Taï. Adventures of Hatim Taï. A romance. Translated from the Persian, by Duncan Forbes. 4°. *London*, 1830.

Hoeï-Lan-Ki; ou, l'histoire du cercle de craie: drame en prose et en vers. Traduit du Chinois, par S. Julien. 8°. *London*, 1832.

Hudsailian poems. Edited in Arabic, and translated by J. G. L. Kosegarten. v. 1. 4°. *London*, 1854.

Hussein Ali Khan Kirmanî. History of Hydur Naik, otherwise styled Hydur Ali. Translated from the Persian, by W. Miles. 8°. *London*, 1843.

—— History of the reign of Tipû Sultân [Tippoo Saib.] Translated from the Persian by W. Miles. 8°. *London*, 1844.

Ibrahim, *Basmajee.* History of the war in Bosnia during 1737-39. Translated from the Turkish by C. Fraser. 8°. *London*, 1830.

Iswara Krishna. Sânkhya Kârikâ, or memorial verses on the Sânkhya philosophy. Translated from the Sanscrit by H. T. Colebrooke. Also, the Bhâshya, or commentary, of Gaurapâda. Translated by H. H. Wilson. 4°. *Oxford*, 1837.

Jahangueir (*emperor of Hindoustan*). Memoirs written by himself. Translated from a Persian Ms. by David Price. 4°. *London*, 1829.

Jelâl Ed dîn Abd-er-rahman Ben Abi Bekr Es-Soyûtî. History of the temple of Jerusalem. Translated from the Arabic Ms. by James Reynolds. 8°. *London*, 1836.

Jelâl Ed-dîn Mohammed Ben Asad Es-Sadîkî Ed Dewânî. Practical philosophy of the muhammadan people; being a translation of the Akhlāk-i-Jalāly from the Persian. By W. F. Thompson. 8°. *London*, 1839.

Joseph ben Joshua ben Meir. Chronicles of the Sphardi, [to 1553]. Translated from the Hebrew by C. H. F. Bialloblotzky. 2 v. 8°. *London*, 1836.

Jouher. The Tezkereh al vakiāt; or, private memoirs of the Moghul emperor Humāyūn. Translated from the Persian by C. Stewart. 4°. *London*, 1832.

Kâlidâsa. Birth of the war-god. A poem. Translated from the Sanscrit into English verse by R. T. H. Griffith. 8°. *London*, 1853.

—— Kumâra Sambhava. Carmen, sanskrite et latine. Edidit A. F. Stenzler. 4°. *Berlin*, 1838.

—— Raghuvansa. Carmen, sanskrite et latine. Edidit A. F. Stenzler. 4°. *London*, 1832.

Kalpa Sûtra, and Nava Tatva: illustrative of the Jain religion and philosophy. Translated from the Mâgadhî, with remarks, by Rev. J. Stevenson. 8°. *London*, 1848.

Khallikan (Shems ed-din Abu'l Abbas Ahmed Ben Mohammed, *surnamed* Ibn). Biographical dictionary. Translated from the Arabic by baron Mac Guckin de Slane. v. 1-2. 4°. *Paris*, 1842-43.

Livre des recompenses et des peines, en chinois et en français. Accompagné de 400 légendes, anecdotes et histoires de la secte des Tao-ssé. Traduit par S. Julien. 8°. *Paris*, 1835.

Makkari (Shihab-ed-din Ahmed Ben Mohammed, *surnamed* Al). History of the Mohammedan dynasties in Spain. Translated with notes by Pascual de Gayangos. 2 v. 4°. *London*, 1840-43.

Makrizî (Takî Ed-din Abû'l Abbas Ahmed Ben Ali, *surnamed* El). Histoire des sultans mamlouks de l'Égypte. Traduit de l'Arabe, par Quatremère. v. 1-2. 4°. *Paris*, 1837-45.

Oriental translation fund—*Continued.*

Mâlik, (Jemâl ed-din Abû Abdallah Mohammed Ben Abdallah, *surnamed* Ibn). Alfiyya, ou la quintessence de la grammaire arabe. Publié en original, avec un commentaire, par Silvestre de Sacy. 8°. *Paris*, 1833.

Marsden, (William, *translator*). Memoirs of a Malayan family. Written by themselves, and translated from the original. 8°. *London*, 1830. (With Ibrahim, *Basmajee*. War in Bosnia.)

Mas'ûdi (Abû'l Hasan), Ali Ben Hosein, *called* El. Historical encyclopædia, entitled "Meadows of gold and mines of gems." Translated from the Arabic by Aloys Sprenger. v. 1. 8°. *London*, 1841.

Matthew (*of Edessa*). Chronique (962–1136) avec la continuation de Grégoire le prêtre jusqu'en 1162. (Bibl. hist. arménienne.) 8°. *Paris*, 1858.

Mémoires sur les contrées occidentales, traduits du Sanscrit en Chinois, en 648, par Hiouen-Thsang, et du Chinois en Français par S. Julien. [Index des mots sanscrits-chinois, v. 2.] 2 v. 8°. *Paris*, 1857–58.

Mirkhond, (Mohammed Ben Khondshah Ben Mahmûd, *surnamed*). History of the early kings of Persia. Translated from the Persian by David Shea. 8°. *London*, 1832.

Miscellaneous translations from the oriental languages. 2 v. 8°. *London*, 1831–34.

Mohammed Alî Hazîn. Life, 1692–1742, written by himself. Edited from two Persian manuscripts by F. C. Balfour. 8°. *London*, 1831.

——— The same. Translated, with notes, by F. C. Balfour. 8°. *London*, 1830.

[*With* the preceding.]

Mohammed Ben Mûsâ. Algebra. [Arabic and English]. Translated by F. Rosen. 8°. *London*, 1831.

Mohammed Moost'ujab khan buhadoor. Life of Hafiz ool Moolk, Hafiz Rehmut khan, by his son. Abridged and translated from the Persian by C. Elliot. 8°. *London*, 1831.

Naima. Annals of the Turkish empire, from A. D. 1591 to 1659. From the Turkish by C. Fraser. v. 1. [to 1617]. 4°. *London*, 1832.

Nazâmi, *or* Nizami (Abu Mohammed ben Yusuf). Lailî and Magnûn, a poem; from the Persian, by James Atkinson, 8°. *London*, 1836.

Neamet Ullah. History of the Afghans. Translated from the Persian by B. Dorn. 2 v. 4°. *London*, 1829–36.

Neumann (Carl Friedrich). Translations from the Chinese and Armenian, [History of the pirates of the China sea, from 1807 to 1810; catechism of the Shamans, or laws of Buddha; Vahram's chronicle of the Armenian kingdom of Cilicia;] with notes. 8°. *London*, 1831.

Nipon o Daï Itsi Ran; ou, annales des empereurs du Japon. Traduites par I. Titsingh. Précédé d'un aperçu de l'histoire mythologique du Japon, par J. Klaproth. 4°. *Paris*, 1834.

Otbî *or* Utbî (Abû'n Nasr Mohammed Ben Abdel jebbâr, El'). Kitab i-yamini; historical memoirs of the amîr Sabuktagîn and the sultân Mahmûd of Ghazna. Translated from the Persian version, by Rev. J. Reynolds. 8°. *London*, 1858.

Ouseley (*Sir* Gore). Biographical notices of Persian poets. With a memoir of Sir G. Ouseley, by J. Reynolds. 8°. *London*, 1846.

Paul (*of Aleppo*). Travels of Macarius, patriarch of Antioch. 2 v. 4°. *London*, 1829–36.

Râm Râz. Essay on the architecture of the Hindûs. With 48 plates. 4°. *London*, 1834.

Rigveda-Sanhitâ. Liber 1. Sanskrite et latine. Edidit F. Rosen. 4°. *London*, 1838.

Rinsifée de Sendai. San Kokf Tsou Ran To Sets; ou, aperçu général des trois royaumes. [Corée, Lieou Khieou, et Yeso.] Traduit de l'original japonais-chinois, par J. Klaproth. 8°. Maps and plates. 4°. *Paris*, 1832.

Sadik Isfahâni. Geographical works. Translated from the Persian by J. C. [Edited by Sir G. Ouseley.] 8°. *London*, 1832.

Sangermano (——). Description of the Burmese empire, translated from his MS. by W. Tandy, D.D. 4°. *Rome*, 1833.

Sanhitâ of the Sâma Veda. Translation by J. Stevenson. 8°. *London*, 1842.

Tabari (Abû Jafar Mohammed Ben Mohammed, *surnamed* El). Chronique; traduite sur la version persane, par L. Dubeux. 4°. *Paris*, 1836.

Tahcin-Uddin. Aventures de Kamrup; traduites de l' Hindoustani par Garcin de Tassy. 8°. *Paris*, 1834.

Timûr. Mulfûzat Timûry; or, autobiographical memoirs of the Moghul emperor Timûr. Translated by C. Stewart. 4°. *London*, 1830.

Vishnu purâna; a system of Hindu mythology and tradition. Translated from the Sanscrit, and illustrated with notes, by H. H. Wilson. 4°. *London*, 1840.

Yakkun Nattannawâ; a Cingalese poem, descriptive of the Ceylon system of demonology, [with] the practices of a capua or devil priest; and Kolan Nattannawâ: a Cingalese [masquerade] poem. Translated by John Callaway. 8°. *London*, 1829.

Zeen-ud-deen. Tohfut-ul-Mujahideen; an historical work [on Malabar] in the Arabic language, [1498–1579]. Translated into English by M. J. Rowlandson. 8°. *London*, 1833.

[*With* Tahcin Uddin. Les aventures, etc.]

Origin (on the) and progress of the north-west company of Canada, with a history of the fur trade. [*anon.*] 38 pp. 8°. *London, Cox, son & Baylis*, 1811.

[*With* GRAY (H.) Letters from Canada, 1809].

Orion (The): a monthly magazine of literature, science, and art. Ed. by William C. Richards. v. 1–3. 8°. *Penfield and Athens, (Ga.) W. Richards*, 1842–43.

Orlandini (Niccolò). Annvae litterae societatis Iesv, anni M. D. lxxxv, 362 pp. 18°. *Romae, In coll. societatis*, 1587.

Orléans (Pierre Joseph d'). The history of the revolutions in England under the family of the Stuarts, 1603–1690. 11 p. l. 328 pp. 7 l. 12°. *London, E. Curll*, 1711.

Orme (Robert). Historical fragments of the Mogul empire, of the Morattoes, and of the English concerns in Hindostan. [*anon.*] 1 p. l. 234 pp. 22 l. clxxiv pp. 3 maps. 12°. *London, C. Nourse*, 1782.

Orme (William). Memoirs of the life, writings, and religious connexions of John Owen. viii, 524 pp. 1 pl. 8°. *London, T. Hamilton*, 1820.

Ormerod (Oliver). The pictvre of a puritane, proving that the puritanes doe resemble the anabaptists. [With] a discovery of puritan papisme. 5 p. l. 81, 32 pp. sm. 4°. *London, Nathaniel Fosbrooke*, 1605.

Orosius (Paulus). Chronica, das ist: warhafftleeigentliche vnd kurtze beschreibung dess vmbkreiss vnd gelegenheit der ganzen welt. Von H. Boner verteutscht. 131 l. 3 l. fol. *Franckfurt a. M. P. Kesseler*, 1576.

Orpheus. Der argonaut. *See* **Hesiodus** *and* Orpheus, von J. H. Voss.

Orrery (Roger Boyle, 1st *earl* of). *See* **Boyle** (Roger).

Orsato (Sertorio). Monvmenta patavina. 9 p. l. 352 pp. 14 l. 1 pl. fol. *Patavii, P. Frambottus*, 1652.

Örsted. *See* **Oersted**.

Ortel (Abraham). Epitome theatri terrarvm. De nouo recognita a Michaele Coigneto. 267 pp. 138 maps. obl. 24°. *Antverpiae, in officina plantiniana,* 1612.

Ortes (Giammaria). Opere. [*In* Scrittori class. ital. di econ. pol. v. 21–27. v. 50].

CONTENTS.

1. Della economia nazionale. v. 21–23 and 50.
2. Riflessioni sulla popolazione delle nazioni per rapporto all' economia nazionale; delle scienze utili e delle dilettevoli per rapporto alla felicità umana ragionamento; calcolo sopra il valore delle opinioni, e sopra i piaceri e i dolori della vita umana; lettere. v. 24 and 50.
3. Errori popolari intorno all' economia nazionale considerati sulle presenti controversie tra i laici e i chierici in ordine al possedimento de' beni; lettere sulla religione e il governo de' popoli. v. 25–26.
4. Dei fidecommessi in proposito dei termine di mani-morte. v. 27.

Osann (G. W.) Grundzüge der lehre von dem magnetismus und der elektricität. viii, 183 pp. 8°. *Würzburg, Stahel,* 1847. S.

Osborn (Francis). Works, in four tracts. 8th ed. 6 p. l. 628 pp. 16°. *London, R. D.* 1682.

CONTENTS.

Advice to a son.
Memoires on queen Elizabeth and king James.
Miscellanies.
Political reflections on the government of the Turks.

Osborn (Laughton). Alice, or the painter's story. 262 pp. 12°. *New York, Doolady,* 1867.

——— Arthur Carryl, a novel, and other poems. [*anon.*] lvii, 357 pp. 8°. *New York, D. Appleton & Co.* 1841.

——— Calvary. Virginia. Tragedies. 4 p. l. 200 pp. 12°. *New York, Doolady,* 1867.

——— Handbook of young artists and amateurs in oil painting. By an American artist. [*anon.*] xxxvii, 398 pp. 12°. *New York, Wiley & Putnam,* 1845. S.

——— The silver head; The double deceit: comedies. 262 pp. 12°. *New York, Doolady,* 1867.

Osgood (Lucius). Progressive first reader. 108 pp. 16°. *Pittsburgh, A. H. English & Co.* 1855. S.

Osorio (Jeronymo). De rebvs Emmanvelis regis Lvsitaniæ, annis sex ac viginti, domi forisq. gestis libri duodecim. 16 p. l. 412 l. 18°. *Coloniæ Agrippinæ, apud hæredes Arnoldi Birckmanni,* 1574.

——— The same. The history of the Portuguese during the reign of Emmanuel. Translated from the Latin by James Gibbs. 2 v. 2 p. l. 376 pp; 388 pp. 8°. *London, A. Millar,* 1752.

Ossian. Poems of Ossian, the son of Fingal. [*pseudon.*] Translated by James Macpherson. New ed. 2 v. 306 pp; 315 pp. 6 pl. 16°. *New Haven, Duyckinck & Ronalds,* 1806.

——— The same. With dissertations on the æra and poems of Ossian, and a discourse on their authenticity. 2 v. 346 pp; 348 pp. 4 pl. 16°. *New York, Ezra Sargeant,* 1810.

Ostervald (J. F.) Recueil de hauteurs des pays compris dans le cadre de la carte générale de la Suisse. 123 pp. 13 l. 8°. *Neuchâtel, H. Wolfrath,* 1844–47.

——— *See,* also, **Select** views in Sicily.

Ostervald (Jean Rodolphe). Nourriture de l'âme; ou, recueil de prières pour tous les jours de la semaine, [etc.] Précédé d'un traité de la prière. 540 pp. 8°. *Jersey, Ph. Falle,* 1842.

Östgöthe (Thorgeir, *pseudon.*) Rest-ransakning med den S. k. fria pressen. 124 pp. 8°. *Stockholm, P. A. Norsted & söner,* 1839.

O'Sullivan (*Rev.* Mortimer). A guide to an Irish gentleman in his search for a religion. 304 pp. 16°. *Philadelphia, Carey, Lea & Blanchard,* 1833.

Other (The) side of the question; or, an attempt to rescue the characters of the two royal sisters, Q. Mary and Q. Anne, out of the hands of the d[uches]s d[owager] of ——— [Marlborough]? By a woman of quality. [*anon.*] 2 p. l. 467 pp. 12°. *London, T. Cooper,* 1742.

Otho *or* **Otto** (*bp. of Freisingen*). Rerum ab origine mundi ad ipsius vsq. tempora [A. D. 1146] gestarum libri viii. Eivsdem de gestis Friderici primi Aenobarbi Caes. Aug. libri ii. Radevici libri ii, prioribus additi, de eiusdē Friderici imp. gestis. 14 p. l. unp. cv l. 8 l. unp. lxxxiv l. fol. *Argentorati, M. Schvrer,* 1515. S.

Otis (Belle, *pseudon?*) The diary of a milliner. viii, 200 pp. 16°. *New York, Hurd & Houghton,* 1867.

Otis (F. N. *M. D.*) History of the Panama railroad, and the Pacific mail steamship company. [Also], a traveller's guide and business man's hand-book for the Panama R. R. [etc.] 317 pp. 30 pl. 1 map. 12°. *New York, Harpers,* 1867.

Otis (Harrison Gray). Eulogy on Alexander Hamilton. 23 pp. 8°. *New York, Isaac Collins & son,* 1804.

Ott (Adolph). The art of manufacturing soap and candles, embracing the modes of detecting frauds, [etc.] 193 pp. 1 pl. 12°. *Philadelphia, Lindsay & Blakiston,* 1867.

Otter (*Rev.* William). Life and remains of Edward Daniel Clarke, professor of mineralogy in the university of Cambridge. xii, 670 pp. 1 pl. 8°. *London, J. F. Dove,* 1824.

Otter (William, *senior*). History of my own times. 357 pp. 18°. *Emmitsburg, (Md.)* 1835.

Ottley (William Young). A collection of 129 fac-similes of scarce and curious prints, by the early masters of the Italian, German, and Flemish schools, illustrative of the history of engraving. xxxvi, xxv pp. 117 pl. 4°. *London, author*, 1828. s.

Otto (Friedrich Icilius). Ausführliches lehrbuch der anorganischen chemie. 3e aufl. 1 v. in 3. 8°. *Braunschweig, Vieweg*, 1855. s.
[GRAHAM-OTTO'S ausführliches lehrbuch der chemie. v. 2].

Otto (*Phrisingensis episcopus*). *See* **Otho**.

Otway (Thomas). Poetical works. 8°. *Edinburgh*, 1793.
[Anderson's British poets, v. 6].

Oudin (Casimir). Supplementum de scriptoribus vel scriptis ecclesiasticis a Bellarmino omissis ad annum 1460. 10 p. l. 720 pp. 66 l. 8°. *Parisiis, A. Dezallier*, 1686. s.

Our farm of four acres, and the money we made by it. [*anon.*] 6th ed. 124 pp. 1 pl. 12°. *London, Chapman & Hall*, 1859.

Our maid servants: a few friendly hints and counsels. By A. F. G. [*anon.*] 68 pp. 16°. *London, S. W. Partridge*, 1866.

Our summer retreats: a hand-book to all the chief waterfalls, springs, and other places of interest in the United States. [*anon.*] 64 pp. 12 pl. 18°. *New York, Nelson & sons*, 1858.

Our young folks. An illustrated [monthly] magazine for boys and girls. Edited by J. T. Trowbridge, Gail Hamilton, and Lucy Larcom. Jan. to Dec. 1867. v. 3. 8°. *Boston, Ticknor & Fields*, 1857.

Ouseley (*Sir* William Gore). Remarks on the statistics and political institutions of the United States, with some observations on the ecclesiastical system of America, her sources of revenue, etc. 226 pp. 8°. *Philadelphia, Carey & Lea*, 1832.

Outline (An) history of an expedition to California, containing the fate of The get all you can mining association. [*anon.*] obl. 18°. *New York*, 1849.

Ovid in London; a ludicrous poem, in six cantos. By a member of the university of Oxford. [*anon.*] 120 pp. 12°. *London, W. Anderson*, 1814.

Ovidius Naso (Publius). Excerpta ex scriptis. [By B. A. Gould]. vii, 287 pp. 12°. *Boston, Hilliard, Gray & Co.* 1835.

——— Fastorvm libri vi. Recensuit notisqve instrvxit Gottlieb Erdmann Gierig. xviii, 371 pp. 8°. *Lipsiæ, E. B. Schwickert*, 1812. s.

Ovidius Naso (Publius). Fastorum libri sex. Editore et interprete R. Merkelio. ccxciv, 320 pp. 8°. *Berolini, G. Reimer*, 1841. s.

——— Ibis. Translated into English verse: and the histories therein conteined, explained, by John Jones. 2d ed. 140 pp. 18°. *Oxford, R. Davis*, 1667.

——— Metamorphoses. Recensvit, varietate lectionis notisqve instrvxit Gottlieb Erdmann Gierig. 2 v. xxxii, 550 pp; 959 pp. 8°. *Lipsiæ, E. B. Schwickert*, 1804–7. s.

——— The same. Metamorphoses, [Latin text] with an English translation by J. Clarke. 4th ed. viii, 479 pp. 8°. *London, W. Clarke*, 1760.

——— The same. Metamorphosis, Englished by G[eorge) S[andys]. 326 pp. 2 l. portrait. fol. *London, William Stansby*, 1626.

——— The same. Englished, mythologiz'd, and represented in figures. [With] an essay to the translation of Virgil's Æneis. By G. S. [George Sandys]. 9 p. l. 303 pp. 9 l. 16 pl. fol. *London, Andrew Hebb*, 1640.

——— The same. With notes of Minellius, and prose version, by Nathan Bailey. xiii, 576 pp. 2 l. 12°. *Dublin, J. Exshaw*, 1774.

——— Metamorphoses, epistles, amours, art of love, remedy of love, and art of beauty. Translated into English verse by several eminent hands. [Published by Sir S. Garth.] 8°. *Edinburgh*, 1792.
[Anderson's Brit. poets. v. 1].

——— The same. Metamorphoses. [Translated into English verse] by John Benson Rose. 16°. *London*, 1866.

——— The same. Traduction en vers, avec des commentaires, par F. de Saint Ange. 2 v. xlv, 406 pp; 495 pp. 16 pl. 8°. *Paris, Déterville*, 1800.

——— Les œuvres galantes et amoureuses, contenant l'art d'aimer, le remède d'amour, les épitres et les élégies amoureuses. Nouv. éd. 2 v. in 1. 8, 215 pp; 204 pp. 8°. *Cythère*, 1774.

——— Amori. [Traduzione anacreontica di F. Cavriani]. 3 v. 18°. *Sulmona*, 1794.

Oviedo y Valdes (Gonzalo Fernandez de). Natural hystoria de las Indias. li, 2 l. fol. *Toledo, Remō de Petras*, 1526.

——— Historia general de las Indias. 4 p. l. cxciii l. fol. *Seuilla, Juam Cromberger*, 1535.

——— The same. Coronica de las Indias. La hystoria general de las Indias, agora nueuamente impressa corregida y emendada. 4 p. l. ccii pp. 1 l. fol. *Salamanca, Juan de Junta*, 1547.

Oviedo y Valdes (Gonzalo Fernandez de). The same. Historia general y natural de las Indias, islas y tierra-firme del mar oceano. Enriquecida con las enmiendas y adiciones del autor, é illustrada con la vida del mismo por J. A. de Los Rios. Primera parte. cvii, 632 pp. 5 pl. fol. *Madrid, Real academia de la historia,* 1851.

Owen (David Dale). First report of a geological reconnoissance of the northern counties of Arkansas, 1857–58. 256 pp. 9 pl. 8°. *Little Rock, Johnson & Yerkes,* 1858.

CONTENTS.

COX (Edward T.) Report (on geology). pp. 192–224.
ELDERHORST (William). Chemical report. pp. 143–191.
OWEN (D. D.) General report. pp. 1–142.

——— Second report of a geological reconnoissance of the middle and southern counties of Arkansas. 433 pp. 1 map. 16 pl. 8°. *Philadelphia, C. Sherman & son,* 1860. s.

CONTENTS.

COX (Edward T.) Second report (on geology). pp. 401–420.
LESQUEREUX (Leo). Botanical and palaeontological report. pp. 295–400.
OWEN (D. D.) Geological reconnoissance. pp. 1–153.
PETER (Robert). Chemical analysis, etc. pp. 163–287.

——— [First], second, third, and fourth reports of the geological survey of Kentucky, made during the years 1854–1859. 4 v. and atlas, 2 maps. 10 pl. 8°. *Frankfort, (Ky.) A. G. Hodges, etc.* 1856–61.

CONTENTS.

COX (Edward T.) Palæontological report of coal measure mollusca, v. 3.
LESLEY (Joseph, jr.) Topographical and geological report of the country along the outcrop base line, following the western margin of the eastern coal field. v. 4.
LESQUEREUX (Leo). Palæontological report of the fossil flora of the coal measures of the western Kentucky coal field. v. 3.
——— Report of the fossil flora, and of the stratigraphical distribution of the coal in the Kentucky coal fields. v. 4.
LYON (Sydney S.) Topographical geological reports, etc. v. 1, 2, 3, 4.
——— Palæontological report. v. 3.
OWEN (David Dale). General reports. v. 1, 2, 3, 4.
PETER (Robert). Chemical reports. v. 1, 2, 3, 4.

——— Report of a geological exploration of part of Iowa, Wisconsin, and Illinois, made in the autumn of 1839. 191 pp. 24 pl. 8°. *Washington, gov. print.* 1844.

[Senate doc. 28th cong. 1 sess. No. 407].
[*With his* REPORT of a geological reconnoissance of Indiana in 1837. *Indianapolis,* 1839].

——— Report of a geological reconnoissance of the state of Indiana, made in 1837. 34 pp. 8°. *Indianapolis, Osborn & Willets,* 1839.

——— The same. Second report of a geological survey of the state of Indiana, made in 1838. 54 pp. 8°. *Indianapolis, Osborn & Willets,* 1839.

[*With his* REPORT of a geological reconnoissance of Indiana in 1837. 8°. *Indianapolis,* 1839].

——— Report of a geological reconnoissance of the Chippewa land district of Wisconsin, and of a portion of the Kickapoo county, and of a part of Iowa and Minnesota. 134 pp. 1 map. 37 pl. 8°. *Washington, gov. print.* 1848.

[Senate U. S. 30th Cong. 1 sess. ex. doc. 57].
[*With his* REPORT of a geological reconnoissance of Indiana in 1837. 8°. *Indianapolis,* 1839].

——— Report of a geological survey of Wisconsin, Iowa, and Minnesota; and incidentally of a portion of Nebraska Territory. 638 pp. 21 maps, etc. 15 pl. 4°. *Philadelphia, J. B. Lippincott & Co.* 1852.

CONTENTS.

LEIDY (Joseph). Description of the remains of extinct mammalia and chelonia, from Nebraska Territory.
NORWOOD (Joseph G.) Geological report of a survey of portions of Wisconsin and Minnesota, 1847–50.
OWEN (David Dale). Geological survey of Wisconsin, Iowa, and Minnesota; description of new and imperfectly known genera and species of organic remains; additional chemical examinations.
——— *and* SHUMARD (Benjamin F.) Descriptions of one new genus, and twenty-two new species of crinoidea, from the carboniferous limestone of Iowa.
PARRY (C. C.) Systematic catalogue of plants of Wisconsin, Iowa, and Minnesota.
PRATTEN (Henry). Systematic catalogue of birds of Wisconsin and Minnesota.
SHUMARD (Benjamin F.) Local details of geological sections on the St. Peters, Mississippi, Wisconsin, Barraboo, Snake, and Kettle rivers.
WHITTLESEY (Charles). Geological report of that portion of Wisconsin bordering on the south shore of Lake Superior, 1849.

Owen (John, *D. D. the puritan divine*). The advantage of the kingdom of Christ. Sermon preached to the parliament, Oct. 24, 1651, a day of thanksgiving for the destruction of the Scots army at Worcester. 2 p. l. 34 pp. sm. 4°. *Oxford, L. Lichfield,* 1651.

Owen (*Rev.* N.) British remains; or, a collection of antiquities relating to the Britons. viii, 184 pp. 16°. *London, J. Bew,* 1777.

Owen (Richard). On the anatomy of terebratula. 4°. *London,* 1852.

[*With* DAVIDSON (T.) Monograph of the British fossil brachiopoda. Introduction. v. 1].

——— On the classification and geographical distribution of the mammalia, [with] appendix "on the gorilla," and "on the extinction and transmutation of species." 103 pp. 8°. *London, J. W. Parker & son,* 1859.

——— Lectures on the comparative anatomy and physiology of the invertebrate animals. 2d ed. viii, 689 pp. 8°. *London, Longman & Co.* 1855. s.

——— Monographs on the British fossil reptilia, from the oolitic formations. Parts 1–2. 44 pp. 11 l. 11 pl; 28 pp. 12 l. 12 pl. 4°. *London,* 1861–62.

[Palæontographical society publications].

Owen (Richard). A monograph on the fossil reptilia of the cretaceous formation. 7 p. l. 175 pp. 59 pl. 4°. *London,* 1857–64. s.
[Palæontographical society publications].

——— Monograph on the fossil reptilia of the Wealden and Purbeck formations. 128 pp. 37 l. 37 pl. 4°. *London,* 1853–64. s.
[Palæontographical society publications].

——— *and* **Bell** (Thomas). Monograph on the fossil reptilia of the London clay, and of the Bracklesham and other tertiary beds. 2 v. in 1. 5 p. l. 79, 4 pp. 40 l. 40 pl; 68 pp. 17 l. 17 pl. 4°. *London, Palæontographical society,* 1849–58. s.

CONTENTS.

Part 1. Chelonia. By Owen and Bell. v. 1.
Part 2. Crocodilia. By Owen. v. 2. pp. 5–50. pl. 1–11 and 2 a.
Part 3. Ophidia. By Owen. v. 2. pp. 51–68. pl. 12–16.

Owen (Robert Dale). Footfalls on the boundary of another world. 528 pp. 12°. *Philadelphia, J. B. Lippincott & Co.* 1865.

——— The wrong of slavery, the right of emancipation, and the future of the African race in the United States. 12°. *Philadelphia, J. B. Lippincott & Co.* 1864.

Owens (G.) A general directory and business guide of the principal towns in the upper country, embracing a portion of California; together with mining and statistical information concerning Idaho territory. 171 pp. 1 map. 8°. *San Francisco, A. Gensoul,* 1866. s.

Owenson (Sydney). *See* **Morgan** (S. Owenson, *lady*).

Oxenden (*Rev.* Ashton). Our church and her services. Adapted to the services of the protestant episcopal church in the United States, by Rev. F. D. Huntington, D. D. viii, 179 pp. 18°. *Boston, E. P. Dutton & Co.* 1866.

Oxford (*University of*). Catalogue of all graduates in divinity, law, medicine, arts, and music, who have regularly proceeded, or been created in the university of Oxford, between October 10, 1659, and December 31, 1850. vi, 808 pp. 8°. *Oxford, Univ. press,* 1851. s.

——— Catalogus codicum mss. qui in collegiis aulisque oxoniensibus hodie adservantur. Confecit H. O. Coxe. 18 v. in 2. 4°. *Oxonii, Typographeo academico,* 1852. s.

Oxholm (Peter Lotharius). De danske Vestindiske öers tilstand i henseende til population, cultur og finance-forvaltning, in anledning af nogle breve fra St. Croix. 84 pp. 5 pl. 16°. *Kiöbenhavn, J. F. Schultz,* 1797.

Oyárvide (Andres de). Memoria geografica de los viajes practicados desde Buenos Aires hasta el salto grande del Paraná, por las primeras y segundas partidas de la demarcacion de limites en la América Meridional, en conformidad del tratado preliminar de 1777, entre las coronas de España y Portugal. 1ª y 2ª parte. [1784–91.] 4 v. 8°. *Paris,* 1865–66.
[*With* Calvo (C.) Amérique latine. 1e période. v. 7–10. 1865–66].

Pacific coast business directory for 1867; also a gazetteer of the counties, cities, and towns, etc. Compiled by Henry G. Langley. 8°. *San Francisco, H. G. Langley,* 1867.

Packard (Frederick A.) A life of Robert Owen. 2d ed. 264 pp. 16°. *Philadelphia, J. B. Lippincott & Co.* 1868.

Packard (John H. *M. D.*) Lectures on inflammation. Delivered before the college of physicians of Philadelphia, under the bequest of Dr. Mütter. 276 pp. 12°. *Philadelphia, J. B. Lippincott & Co.* 1865.

Páez (*gen.* José Antonio). Autobiografia. v. 1. xiii, 576 pp. 2 pl. 8°. *Nueva York, Hallet & Breen,* 1867.

Paffenrode (Jan van). Der grieken en romeynen krijs-handel. 15 p. l. 392 pp. 7 l. 5 pl. fol. *Leyden, P. Van der Meersche,* 1686. s.

Page (David). Elements of geology. Edited by D. M. Reese. 332 pp. 12°. *New York, A. S. Barnes & Co.* 1849. s.

Page (Richard). A critical examination of the twelve resolutions of Mr. Joseph Hume, respecting the loan of fifteen millions for slave compensation; also, a review of the financial operations of the British government since 1794. viii, 278 pp. 8°. *London, Pelham Richardson,* 1839.

Pagès (François Xavier). Nouveaux dialogues des morts entre les plus fameux personnages de la révolution française et plusieurs hommes célèbres, anciens et modernes, morts avant la révolution. viii, 232 pp. 8°. *Paris, Laurens,* 1800.

Pagès (Léon). Bibliographie japonaise, ou catalogue des ouvrages relatifs au Japon, qui ont été publiés depuis le xve siècle jusqu'à nos jours. 67 pp. 4°. *Paris, B. Duprat,* 1859.

Paget (James). Manual of physiology, 1853. *See* **Kirkes** (W. S.) *and* **Paget.**

Paget (John). Hungary and Transylvania: with remarks on their condition—social, political, and economical. 2 v. 324 pp; 324 pp. 12°. *Philadelphia, Lea & Blanchard,* 1850. s.

Pagliardini (Tito). Une visite au familistère, ou maison de travailleurs de M. Godin-Lemaire, à Guise (Aisne). Traduit de l'Anglais. Extraite de la Revue des sciences sociales, Oct. 1865. 16°. *Paris,* 1866.

[*With* MOUREAU (Jules). Le salaire et des associations coopératives, pp. 203-236].

Pagnini (Giovanni Francesco). Saggio sopra il giusto pregio delle cose; della monetà e sopra il commercio dei Romani.

[SCRITTORI class. ital. di econ. pol. v. 2].

Paic (——) *and* **Scherb** (——). Cèrmagora. Eine umfassende schilderung des landes und der bewohner von Cèrmagora (Montenegro). 2e aufl. 253 pp. 12°. *Agram, F. Suppan,* 1851. s.

Paige (*Rev.* Lucius Robinson). An address at the centennial celebration in Hardwick, Mass. Nov. 15, 1838. 76 pp. 8°. *Cambridge, Metcalf, Torry & Ballou,* 1838.

——— Commentary on the new testament. *See* **Bible** (*English*).

Paine (John A. *jr.*) Catalogue of plants found in Oneida county and vicinity. (Extract.) 140 pp. 8°. *Albany,* [*Regents of the university,*] 1865. s.

Paine (Thomas). Works. 2 v. vi, 391 pp; 4 p. l. 368 pp. 8°. *Philadelphia, J. Carey,* 1797.

CONTENTS.

v. 1. Common sense.
Epistle to quakers.
The crisis.
Public good.
Letter to the abbé Raynal.
Dissertations on government, the bank, and paper money.
Miscellanies, in prose and verse.
v. 2. Prospects on the Rubicon.
Rights of man.
Letter to the author of the Republican.
Letter to the abbé Siéyes.
Address to the addressers.
Two letters to Lord Onslow.
Dissertation on first principles of government.
Letter to Dundas.
Decline and fall of the English system of finance.
Letter to the people of France.
Reasons for preserving the life of Louis Capet.
The age of reason. (wanting in this copy.)

——— The American crisis, and a letter to Sir Guy Carleton on the murder of Capt. Huddy. 1 p. l. 293 pp. 8°. *London, D. E. Eaton,* [1796].

Painter, gilder, and varnisher's companion: containing rules and regulations in everything relating to the arts of painting, gilding, varnishing, and glass-staining. 10th ed. vi, 246 pp. 12°. *Philadelphia, H. C. Baird,* 1867.

Pajeken (Clemens A.) Reise-erinnerungen und abenteuer aus der neuen welt, in ethnographischen bildern, mit einem vorwort von Friedrich Ruperti. iv, 168 pp. 12°. *Bremen, J. G. Heyse,* 1861.

Palacio (Diego Garcia de). Carta dirijida al rey de España; año 1576. Being a description of the ancient provinces of Guazacapan, Izalco, Cuscatlan, and Chiquimula, in the audiencia of Guatemala, 1576.

[*With* SQUIER (E. G.) Documents and relations concerning the discovery and conquest of America. 4°. *New York, C. B. Norton,* 1860].

Palacky (Frantisek). Dejiny národu ceskeho w Cechách a w Morawé dle půwodnich pramenů wyprawuje. Dílu i. 2 v. xvi, 406 pp; viii, 500 pp. 8°. *w. Praze, J. G. Kalve,* 1848-54. s.

——— Dějiny husitské dle puwodních pramenů wyprawuje. 2 v. xiv, 542 pp; viii, 447 pp. 8°. *w. Praze, J. G. Kalve,* 1850-51. s.

CONTENTS.

v. 1. Od roku 1403 do 1424.
v. 2. Od roku 1425 do 1439.

——— Altesten denkmaler der böhmischen sprache. *See* **Schafarik** (P. J.), *and* **Palacky**.

Paley (William, *D. D.*) Moral philosophy; with annotations by Richard Whately. vii, 246 pp. 8°. *London, J. W. Parker & son,* 1859. s.

——— A view of the evidences of christianity. With annotations by Richard Whately. viii, 407 pp. 8°. *New York, J. Miller,* 1860. s.

——— The same. 3d ed. viii, 424 pp. 12°. *Brunswick, (Me.) J. Griffin,* 1860.

Palfrey (John Gorham). Discourse at Barnstable, Sept. 3, 1839, at the second centennial anniversary of the settlement of Cape Cod. 50 pp. 8°. *Boston, Ferdinand Andrews,* 1840.

Palladius (Rutilius Taurus Aemilianus). De re rustica.

[*With* LIBRI de re rustica].

Pallas (Peter Simon). Lyst der plant-dieren, bevattende de algemeene schetzen der geslachten en korte beschryvingen der bekende zoorten. Vertaald door P. Boddaert. 654 pp. 14 pl. 8°. *Utrecht, A. van Paddenburg et J. van Schoonhover,* 1768. s.

——— Miscellanea zoologica, quibus novæ imprimis atque obscuræ animalium species describuntur et observationibus iconibusque illustrantur. xii, 224 pp. 14 pl. 4°. *Hagæ Comitum,* 1766. s.

——— The same. Naturgeschichte merkwürdiger thiere in welcher vornemlich neue und unbekannte thierarten durch kupferstiche, beschreibungen und erklärungen erläutert werden. Aus dem Lateinischen von E. G. Baldinger. 10 parts in 1 v. 4°. *Berlin, Reimer,* 1769-78. s.

Pallas (Peter Simon). Novae species qvadrvpedvm e glirivm ordine. viii, 388 pp. 27 pl. 4°. *Erlangae, W. Walther,* 1778. s.
——— Reise durch verschiedene provinzen des russischen reichs, in einem ausführlichen auszuge. 2 v. 4 p. l. 384 pp. 15 pl; 3 p. l. 464 pp. 2 pl. 8°. *Frankfurt, J. G. Fleischer,* 1776–77. s.
——— The same. Voyages en différentes provinces de l'empire de Russie, et dans l'Asie septentrionale. Traduits de l'Allemand, par Gauthier de La Peyronie. 5 v. texte. 4°. 1 v. planches. fol. *Paris, Lagrange,* 1789–93. [The plates are wanting]. s.
——— The same. Voyages dans plusieurs provinces de Russie et dans l'Asie septentrionale. Nouv. éd. revue par Lamarck et Langlès. 8 v. 8°. *Paris, Maradan,* 1794. s.
——— Zoographia russo-asiatica, sistens omnium animalium in extenso imperio russico, et adjacentibus maribus observatarum recensionem, etc. 3 v. 4°. *Petropoli, Caes. acad. scientiarum,* 1831. s.

CONTENTS.

v. 1. Lactantia. Aves. xxii, 568 pp. 16 col. pl.
v. 2. Aves. vii, 374 pp. 16 col. pl.
v. 3. Monocardia. vii, 428, cxxv pp. 6 col. pl.

——— *See,* also, **Histoire** des découvertes, etc. dans la Russe, etc.
Pallastrelli (B.) La città d'Umbria nell' Appennino piacentino: relazione. 75 pp. 9 pl. 4°. *Piacenza, A. del Majno,* 1864. s.
Pall Mall (The) gazette. An evening newspaper and review, July 1866, to Dec. 1867. v. 4–6. sm. fol. *London,* [*J. K. Sharpe,*] 1866–67.
Palma (Ricardo). Lira americana: coleccion de poesias de los mejores poetas del Peru, Chile, y Bolivia. 4 p. l. 656 pp. 8°. *Paris, Rosa y Bouret,* 1865.
Palmarius (Julius). De morbis contagiosis. *See* **Le Paulmier de Grentemesnil** (J.)
Palmer (Herbert). Memorials of godliness and christianity. 3 pts. 8th ed. ii, 36, ii, 28, ii, 18 pp. 24°. *Boston, Timothy Green,* 1713.
Palmer (H. R.) The song queen; a collection of music for singing classes, choirs, etc. Also, a cantata of the months and seasons, by A. C. Gutterson. 96 pp. obl. 16°. *Chicago, H. R. Palmer,* 1867.
Palmer (J.) Manual of astrology; or, the book of the stars. By Raphael. [*pseudon.*] 256 pp. 3 pl. 8°. *London, C. S. Arnold,* 1828.
——— Raphael's sanctuary of the astral art; or, elysium of astrology. By Raphael. [*pseudon.*] vii, 220 pp. 1 pl. 16°. *London, W. C. Wright,* [1834]?
——— Raphael's witch; or, the oracle of the future. By the author of the prophetic messenger. [*anon*]. 5th ed. 210 pp. 2 pl. 16°. *London, W. C. Wright,* 1856.
Palmer (John Williamson, *editor*). Folk songs. Selected. Illustrated from original designs. New ed. xl, 596 pp. 18 fac-sim. sm. 4°. *New York, C. Scribner & Co.* 1867.
——— The poetry of compliment and courtship: selected and arranged by J. W. Palmer. xx, 219 pp. 16°. *Ticknor & Fields,* 1868.
Palmer (Peter Sailly). History of Lake Champlain, from its first exploration by the French in 1609, to the close of 1814. 276 pp. 8°. *Albany, J. Munsell,* 1866.
Palmer (Ray, *D. D.*) Hymns of my holy hours, and other pieces. 103 pp, 12°. *New York, A. D. F. Randolph,* 1867.
Palmer (Samuel, *printer*). A general history of printing, etc. xii, 400 pp. 4°. *London, A. Bettesworth, C. Hitch & C. Davis,* 1733.
Palmer (Samuel, *bookseller*). A catalogue of books for 1860, in all languages. 188 pp. 8°. *London, S. Palmer,* [1860]. s.
Palmer (*Mrs.* Sarah A.) The story of aunt Becky's army-life. xix, 215 pp. 9 pl. 12°. *New York, J. F. Trow,* 1867.
Palmerini (Niccolò). Opere d'intaglio del cav. Raffaello Morghen, raccolte ed illustrate. 3ª ed. 2 p. 158 pp. 4 pl. 8°. *Firenze, N. Pagni,* 1824. s.
Palmieri (Giuseppe). Riflessioni sulla publica felicità relativamente al regno di Napoli; v. 37. Osservazioni sulle tariffe; Della ricchezza nazionale; v. 38.
[SCRITTORI class. Ital. di econ. pol. v. 37–38].
Palou (Francisco). Noticias de la Nueva California. s.
[*With* ICAZBALZETA. Documentos para hist. de Mexico. 4a serie. v. 6–7].
——— Relacion historica de la vida y apostolicas tareas del Junipero Serra, y de las misiones que fundó en la California septentrional. 14 p. l. 344 pp. 1 map. 1 pl. sm. 4°. *Mexico, Felipe de Zuñiga y Ontiveros,* 1787.
Panage, (*pseudon.*) *See* **Toussaint** (F. V.)
Panam (Pauline Adelaide Alexandre). Memoirs of a young Greek lady. xv, 305 pp. 1 pl. 12°. *London, Sherwood, Jones & Co.* 1823.
Pancirolli (Guido). Rerum memorabilium sive deperditarum partes duo. Ex Italico latine reddita ab Henrico Salmuth. 2 parts in 1 v. 6 p. l. 349 pp. 10 l; 4 p. l. 313 pp. 8 l. 4°. *Francoforti, Tampach,* 1631.

Pander (Christian Heinrich). Monographie der fossilen fische des silurischen systems der russisch-baltischen gouvernements. x, 91 pp. 9 pl. 4°. *St. Petersburg, k. akad. der wissenschaften*, 1856. s.

——— Über die saurodipterinen, dendrodonten, glyptolepiden und cheirolepiden des devonischen systems. ix, 90 pp. 4°. Atlas, 17 pl. fol. *St. Petersburg, Buchdruckerei der k. akad. der wissenschaften*, 1860. s.

Panizza (Bartolomeo). Osservazioni antropo-zootomico-fisiologiche. 110 pp. 10 pl. fol. *Pavia, Bizzoni*, 1830. s.

Panzer (Georg Wolfgang). Annales typographici ab artis inventæ origine ad annum 1536, post Maittairii, Denisii, aliorumque curas, [etc.] 11 v. 4°. *Norimbergæ, J. E. Zeh*, 1793—1803.

Panzer (Georg Wolfgang Franz). Index entomologicus, sistens omnes insectorum species in G. W. F. Panzeri favna insectorvm germanica descriptas atque delineatas. Pars i. Eleutherata. viii, 216 pp. 12°. *Norimbergæ, Felssecker*, 1813. s.

——— Kritische revision der insektenfaune Deutschlands. 2 v. xii, 144 pp; 6 l. 271 pp. 2 col. pl. 12°. *Nürnberg, Felssecker*, 1805–6.

Paoletti (Ferdinando). Estratto de' pensieri sopra l'agricoltura; I veri mezzi di render felici le società.
[SCRITTORI class. Ital. di econ. pol. v. 20].

Paoli (Paolo Antonio). Pæsti, quod Posidoniam etiam dixere rvdera. Dissertationes. [Ital. and Latin texts.] 170 pp. 44 pl. fol. *Romæ, Pagliarini*, 1784.

Paolo fiorentino. Breuiarium super totum corpus iuris canonici. 4 p. l. cxxix l. fol. *Mēmingen, A. Küne de Duderstat*, 1499.

Papers concerning the attack on Hatfield and Deerfield by a party of Indians from Canada, September 19th, 1677. 82 pp. 1 map. 8°. *New York, Bradford club*, 1859.
[Bradford club series, No. 1].

Papers for the schoolmaster. New series. v. 2. iv, 318 pp. 8°. *London, Simpkin, Marshall & Co.* 1866.

Papers presented to the committee appointed to inquire into the state and condition of the countries adjoining to Hudson's bay, and of the trade carried on there. 79 pp. fol. *London*, 1749.

Papers and despatches relating to the Arctic searching expeditions of 1850–51. With a few brief remarks as to the probable course pursued by Sir John Franklin. [*anon.*] 49 pp. 1 col. map. 8°. *London, F. & J. Rivington*, 1851.

Papworth (John W.), *and* W. Museums, libraries, and picture galleries, public and private, with illustrations. 8°. *London, Chapman Hall*, 1853. s.

Paracelsus *or* **Hoehenheim** (Philipp Aureolus Theophrastus Bombast von). Of the chymical transmutation, genealogy, and generation of metals and minerals. Translated by R. Turner. 78 pp. 16°. *London, R. Moon*, 1657.

——— Three books of philosophy written to the Athenians. Done into English by a young seeker of truth and holiness [H. Pinnell]. 70 pp. 16°. *London, L. Lloyd*, 1657.
[*With* PARACELSUS. Of chymical transmutation, 1657].

Paradis (Venture de). *See* **Venture** de Paradis (Jean Michel).

Paradis de Moncrif (François Augustin). Les chats. [*anon.*] viii, 204 pp. 6 l. 10 pl. 12°. *Rotterdam, J. D. Beman*, 1728.

Paraldus *or* Peraldus *or* de Petralta, *or* Peyrault, *or* Perrault. *See* **Perrault** (Guillaume). s.

Parburt (George R.) Anselmo; a poem. 148 pp. 12°. *San Francisco, H. H. Bancroft & Co.* 1865.

Paredes (Ignacio de). Promptuario manual mexicano, platicas y sermones. 614 pp. 1 pl. sm. 4°. *Mexico*, 1749.

Paris (Alexis Paulin). Le romancero françois. Histoire de quelques anciens trouvères, et choix de leurs chansons. x, 203 pp. 12°. *Paris, Techener*, 1833.

Paris (François Edmond), *and* Bonnefoux (*le baron* de). Dictionnaire de marine à voiles et à vapeur—Marine à vapeur. [*With* English and French vocabulary.] 2e éd. x, 740, 16 pp. 18 pl. 8°. *Paris, Bertrand*, [1859].

Paris guide. Par les principaux écrivains et artistes de la France. 2e éd. 2 v. xliv, 2162 pp. 8 maps. 129 pl. 12°. *Paris, Lacroix et Co.* 1867.

Parker (Henry, *of Lincoln's inn*). A discourse concerning puritans. A vindication of those who unjustly suffer by the mistake, abuse, and misapplication of that name. 3 p. l. 63 pp. sm. 4°. *London, Robert Bostock*, 1641.

Parker (*Rev.* John). The upward path; or, brief thoughts on christian salvation, [etc.] 123 pp. 16°. *Rochester, E. Darrow & bro.* 1857. s.

Parker (John Henry). Glossary of terms used in Grecian, Roman, Italian, and Gothic architecture, 2d ed. viii, 144 pp. 66 pl. 8°. *London, Charles Tilt*, 1838. s.

Parker (N. Howe). Iowa as it is in 1855; a gazetteer for citizens, and a hand-book for immigrants. 264 pp. 1 map. 12°. *Chicago, Keen & Lee, (printed Phila. Smith & Peters,)* 1855.

Parker (Richard Green). Exercises in rhetorical reading. 430 pp. 12°. *New York, A. S. Barnes & Co.* 1849. s.

——— *and* **Watson** (J. Madison). The national fifth reader; containing a treatise on elocution. 600 pp. 12°. *New York, A. S. Barnes & Co.* 1858. s.

Parker (*Mrs.* Rosa Abbott). Alexis the runaway; or, afloat in the world. 216 pp. 4 pl. 16°. *Boston, Lee & Shepard,* 1868.

——— Jack of all trades. 229 pp. 4 pl. 16°. *Boston, Lee & Shepard,* 1867.

Parker (Samuel, *bishop of Oxford*). A free and impartial censure of the Platonick philosphie; with an account of the Origenian hypothesis, concerning the preëxistence of souls. 2d ed. 6 p. l. 242 pp. 12°. *Oxford, H. Hall,* 1667.

——— Religion and loyalty. 8 p. l. 608 pp. 12°. *London, John Baker,* 1684.

Parker, (W. B.) Notes taken during the expedition [of] Capt. R. B. Marcy through unexplored Texas in 1854. 242 pp. 12°. *Philadelphia, Hayes & Zell,* 1856.

Parkes (Joseph). Memoirs of Sir Philip Francis, with correspondence and journals. Completed and edited by Herman Merivale. 2 v. xxxiii, 458 pp; viii, 566 pp. 2 portraits. 7 fac sim. 8°. *London, Longmans,* 1867.

Parkes (Samuel). Chemical catechism. xvii, 597 pp. 1 pl. 8°. *New York, Collins and Co.* 1818.

Parkinson (Sydney). Journal of a voyage to the South Seas, in his majesty's ship, the Endeavour, [1768–71. Edited by Stanfield Parkinson]. xxiii, 212, 22 pp. 1 map. 29 pl. 4°. *London, Richardson & Urquhart,* 1773.

Parkinson (*Rev.* William). A jubilee sermon, containing a history of the first baptist church in the city of New York. 106 pp. 12°. *New York, J. Gray,* 1846.

Parkman (Francis). The jesuits in North America in the seventeenth century. [Or,] France and England in North America. Part 2. lxxxix, 463 pp. 1 map. 8°. *Boston, Little, Brown & Co.* 1867.

Parliamentary (The) guide. (For 1837). xvi, 368 pp. 18°. *London, A. H. Baily & Co.* 1837. s.

Parlor tableaux and amateur theatricals. [*anon.*] 352 pp. 12°. *Boston, J. E. Tilton & Co.* 1867.

Parnell (Edward Andrew). A practical treatise on dyeing and calico printing. By an experienced dyer, assisted by several scientific gentlemen. [*anon.*] xxi, 704 pp. 10 pl. 8°. *New York, Harpers,* 1846.

Parnell (Thomas). Poetical works. 8°. *Edinburgh,* 1794.

[Anderson's British poets. v. 7].

Parny (Évariste Désiré Des Forges *vicomte* de). Œuvres. 5 v. 18°. *Paris, Didot,* 1808.

Parry (C. C.) Geology and botany.

[*With* Emory (W. H.) Report on the U. S. and Mexican boundary survey. 1857–59].

——— Systematic catalogue of plants of Wisconsin, Iowa, and Minnesota.

[*With* Owen (D. D.) Report of a geological survey of Wisconsin, etc. 1852].

Parry (*Rev.* Edward). Memoirs of rear-admiral Sir W. Edward Parry. xi, 403 pp. 1 map. 1 pl. 8°. *London, Longman,* 1857.

Parry (*Sir* William Edward). Journal of a third voyage for the discovery of a northwest passage in 1824–25, with appendix. 232 pp. 8°. *Philadelphia, H. C. Carey & I. Lea,* 1826.

Parsons (*lieut.* George Samuel P. *R. N.*) Nelsonian reminiscences. 251 pp. 12°. *Boston, Little & Brown,* 1843.

Parsons (John A.) A lecture on the human body. 51 pp. 8°. *New York, C. Shepard & Co.* 1854. s.

Parsons (*Rev.* Jonathan). The doctrine of justification by faith asserted and explained. 1 p. l. pp. 1–82. 18°. *Boston, Joseph Bay——t,* 1748.

[Imperfect: title-page and pp. 1–4 wanting; also pp. 83 and following].

——— Funeral sermon on the death of Rev. George Whitefield. 35 pp. 12°. *London, James Buckland,* 1771.

Parsons *or* **Persons** (Robert). The jesuit's memorial, for the intended reformation of England, under their first popish prince. With an introduction, by Edward Gee. 2 p. l. lvi pp. 8 l. 262 pp. 12°. *London, R. Chiswel,* 1690.

Note.—The author's title was simply "Memorial for the reformation of England."

Parsons (Sandford E.) The sawyer's companion; or, instructions for using and choosing both long and circular saws. 46 pp. 12°. *Wilkesbarre, (Va.) author,* 1857. s.

Parsons (Theophilus). Deus homo: Godman. viii, 455 pp. 8°. *Chicago, E. B. Myers & Chandler,* 1867.

Parsons (Usher, *M. D.*) Boylston prize dissertations on: i. inflammation of the periosteum; 2. eneuresis irritata; 3. cutaneous diseases; 4. cancer of the breast; also, remarks on animal and vegetable decomposition. 248 pp. 8°. *Boston, C. C. Little and J. Brown,* 1839. s.

Partington (Charles Frederick, *editor*). The British cyclopædia of natural history; comprising a scientific classification of animals, plants and minerals. 3 v. 8°. *London, Orr & Smith,* 1835–37. s.

——— Printers' complete guide: [with a] sketch of the history and progress of printing. 96 pp. 2 plates. 8°. *London, Sherwood, Gilbert, and Piper,* 1825.

Parton (James). Famous Americans of recent times. 473 pp. portrait. 8°. *Boston, Ticknor & Fields,* 1867.

CONTENTS.

Astor; Beecher, and his church; Bennett, and the New York herald; Theodosia Burr; Calhoun; Clay; Stephen Girard, and his college; Charles Goodyear; John Randolph; commodore Vanderbilt; Daniel Webster.

——— How New York city is governed. 48 pp. 16°. *Boston, Ticknor & Fields,* 1866.

——— Life and times of Aaron Burr. Enlarged ed. 2 v. xxii, 443 pp; xii, 431 pp. 2 pl. 12°. *New York, Mason bros.* 1864.

Paruta (Filippo), *and* **Agostini** (Leonardo). Sicilia nvmismatica, additis Hvberti Goltzii aliorumque Siciliæ descriptione, una cum in nvmismata singula explicationibus; edita studio Sigeberti Havercampi. Accedunt integræ Georgii Gvaltheri Siciliæ, adjacentium insvlarvm, atque Brvttiorvm tabvlæ antiqvæ, una cum G. Gvaltheri animadversionibus. Ed. nova. 3 v. fol. *Lvgdvni Batavorvm, P. van der Aa,* 1723.

[NOTE.—This work forms v. 6–8 of Grævius's Thesaurus antiq. et hist. Siciliæ].

Paseo pintoresco por la isla de Cuba. [*anon.*] 2 v. in 1. 290 pp; 47, 10 pp. 18 pl. obl. 24°. *Habana, Soler y Ca.* 1841–42.

Pasquali (Giambatista). Dell' arte di vedere nelle belle arti del disegno, secondo i principii di Sulzer e di Mengs. 167 pp. 12°. *Venezia, G. Pasquali,* 1781. s.

Pasquier (Étienne). Les recherches de la France. Augmentées en ceste dernière édition de trois liures entiers: Pour parler du prince; Pour parler de la loy; Pour parler d'Alexandre. 12 p. l. 1017 pp. 38 l. 1 pl. fol. *Paris, L. Sonnius,* 1621.

Pasquin (Anthony, *pseudon.*) *See* **Williams** (John).

Passerini (Carlo). Memoria sopra due specie d'insetti, nocivi uno alla vite (*Procris ampelophaga*), el altro alcavolo arboro. [*lixus octolineatus.* Extract]. 15 pp. 1 pl. 8°. [*Firenze,* 1829.] s.

——— Notizie sulla moltiplicazione in Firenze negli anni 1837–39, dell' uccello americano *paroaria cucullata.* 8 pp. 1 col. pl. fol. *Firenze, Pezzati,* 1841. s.

——— Osservaziomi sul baco danneggiatore delle ulive, e sulla mosca in cui si transforma. [Extract]. 9 pp. 1 pl. 8°. *Firenze, Giorn. agr. toscan.* 1829. s.

Passetems (Le) agréable; ou, nouveau choix de bon mots, avec des réflections. Par M. J. D. R[ochefort? 3e éd.] 2 v. in 1. 5 p. l. 320 pp; 340 pp. 16 l. 2 pl. 18°. *Rotterdam, J. Hofhout,* 1724.

Pastor (Tony, *pseudon?*). 201 Bowery songster. 72 pp. 24°. *New York, Dick & Fitzgerald,* [1867].

Pastor's (The) wife; or, memoirs of [*Mrs.*] E[liza M. S[aunders. *anon.*] 198 pp. portrait. 18°. *New York, Little, Rennie & Co.* 1867.

Pater (Erra, *pseudon.*) *See* **Prognostication** (A) forever.

Paterculus (Caius Velleius). Quae supersunt ex historiae romanae voluminibus duobus. Ex recensione D. Rvhnkenii. Edidit C. H. Frotscher. clxxxiv, 290 pp. 8°. *Lipsiae, C. H. F. Hartmann,* 1830. s.

Paterno (Filippo de Jorio da). *See* **Torio** da Paterno.

Paterson (Daniel). New and accurate description of direct and principal cross-roads of Scotland. 6th ed. ii, 31 pp. 12°. *London, E. Power & Co.* 1791.

[*With* his New and accurate description of cross-roads in England and Wales].

——— New and accurate description of direct and principal cross-roads in England and Wales. 9th ed. xxxvi, 386 pp. 12°. *London, T. N. Longman,* 1792.

——— Travelling dictionary; or, alphabetical table of distances of cities and towns in Great Britain from each other. 6th ed. 2 p. l. 216 pp. 12°. *London, T. N. Longman,* 1792.

[*With* his New and accurate description of cross-roads in England and Wales].

Paterson (*Lieut.* William). A narrative of four journeys into the country of the Hottentots and Caffraria, 1777–79. xii, 170 pp. 1 map. 17 pl. 4°. *London, J. Johnson,* 1780.

Patriot (The) preachers of the American revolution, with biographical sketches. [Ed. by Frank Moore.] 1766—1783. 368 pp. 12°. [New York], 1860.

Patriotism at home; or, the young invincibles. By the author of "Fred. Freeland." [*anon.*] 320 pp. 18°. *Boston, W. V. Spencer*, 1866.

Patten (George W. *U. S. A.*) Voices of the border. 361 pp. 12°. *New York, Hurd & Houghton*, 1867.

Patterson (Robert, *of Belfast*). Introduction to zoology. With illustrations. 2 pts. in 1 v. viii, 476 pp. 12°. *London, Simms & M'Intyre*, 1849.

Patterson (Robert, *reporter*). The reporter's assistant; an exposition of the reporting style of phonography. 52 pp. 18°. *Philadelphia, E. Webster*, 1849. S.

Pattilo (Henry). Sermons, etc. 296 pp. 18°. *Wilmington, J. Adams*, 1788.

Pattison (William). Poetical works. 8°. *Edinburgh*, 1794.
[Anderson's Brit. poets, v. 8].

Paul Venner; or, the forge and the pulpit. [*anon.*] 371 pp. 16°. *New York, Am. tract. soc.* 1867.

Paulding (James Kirke). The Bulls and the Jonathans; comprising John Bull and brother Jonathan, and John Bull in America. Edited by W. I. Paulding. 378 pp. 12°. *New York, C. Scribner & Co.* 1867.

——— The old continental; or, the price of liberty. [*anon.*] 2d ed. 2 v. in 1. 191 pp; 192 pp. 12°. *New York, Cady & Burgess*, 1851.

——— Tales of the good woman. By a doubtful gentleman. Edited by W. I. Paulding. 402 pp. 12°. *New York, C. Scribner & Co.* 1867.

Paulding (William Irving). Literary life of James K. Paulding. 397 pp. 12°. *New York, C. Scribner & Co.* 1867.

Paulian (Aimé Henri). La physique à la portée de tout le monde. 2 v. 416 pp; 415 pp. 1 pl. 8°. *Nismes, J. Gande & Co.* 1790–91.

Paulin (*chev.* G.) Théorie sur l'extinction des incendies; ou, nouveau manuel du sapeur-pompier, etc. Précédé de l'historique du corps des sapeurs-pompiers de Paris. xiv, 350 pp. 1 table. 18°. *Paris, Bachelier*, 1837. S.

Paulmy (Marc Antoine René de Voyer d'Argenson, *marquis* de). Choix de petits romans de différens genres. [*anon.*] 2 v. 2 p. l. 299 pp; 256 pp. 24°. *Paris, Gattey*, 1789.

CONTENTS.

v. 1. Histoire admirable du Juif errant, ou le roman de l'histoire universelle moderne; Histoire d'Odin.
v. 2. Les amours d'Aspasie de Milet; Les exilés de la cour d'Auguste.

Paulus (Christoph). Grundlinien der neuern ebenen geometrie, mit einer sammlung von mehr als 1,000 erläuterten aufgaben, einem anhang über die anwendung der neueren geometrie auf optik, [etc.] xii, 364 pp. 8°. *Stuttgart, W. Paulus*, 1853. S.
[Wanting atlas, 10 pl. 4°.]

Paulus *diaconus, or* Paul Warnefrid, *of Aquileia.* Historia de gestis Longobardorum. 4°. *Augustæ Vindelicorum*, 1615. S.
[*With* JORNANDES. De rebus Gothorum. 1615].

Paulus (Heinrich Eberhard Gottlob). Collectanea de vita B. de Spinoza.
[*With* SPINOZA (B. de). Opera omnia, 1802–03. v. 2. pp. 591—680.]

Paulus, *silentiarius.* Beschreibung der heiligen Sophia, etc.
[*With* SALZENBERG (W.) Altchristliche baudenkmale, etc. 1854].

Pauquet *frères* (—). Modes et costumes historiques. 2 p. l. 4 pp. 96 pl. col. 4°. *Paris, Pauquet frères*, [1864].

Pausanias. An extract out of Pausanias, of the statues, pictures, and temples in Greece. 251 pp. 8°. *London, W. Shropshire & B. Dod*, 1758.

Pause. *See* **Plantavit de la Pause** (Jean).

Pauw (Corneille de). Œuvres philosophiques. 7 v. 8°. *Paris, Bastien*, 1795.

CONTENTS.

v. 1–3. Recherches philosophiques sur les Américains.
v. 4–5. Sur les Égyptiens et les Chinois.
v. 6–7. Recherches philosophiques sur les Grecs.

Pavie (Théodore), *and* **Bertrand** (François Marie). Chrestomathie hindoustani. (Urdû et dakhui). 2 p. l. 108 pp. 64 l. 8°. *Paris, Dondey-Dupré*, 1847. S.

Paykull (Gustaf von). Fauna suecica. Insecta. [Coleoptera]. 3 v. in 1. 8°. *Upsaliae, Edman*, [1798]–1800. S.

Payne (C. Manuel). México y sus cuestiones financieras con la Inglaterra, la España y la Francia. vi, 346, 151 pp. 8°. *México, I. Cumplido*, 1862. S.

Payne (William, *teacher*). Introduction to the game of draughts. 4 p. l. 67 pp. 8°. *London, T. Payne*, 1756.

Payne *and* **Foss.** A catalogue of books in various languages, on sale. 328 pp. 8°. *London*, 1848. S.

Payva (Jacob). De societatis Jesv origine libellvs. 40 l. 18°. *Lovanii, Rutgerus Velpius*, 1566.
[*With* RUTILIUS (J.) Epistolæ indicæ. *Lovanii*, 1566].

Peabody (*Rev.* Andrew P.) Christian consolations. Sermons designed to furnish comfort and strength to the afflicted. 5th ed. viii, 438 pp. 12°. *Boston, Am. unit. assoc.* 1867.

——— Conversation; its faults and its graces. New ed. 152 pp. 12°. *Boston, W. H. Dennet*, 1867.

Peabody (*Rev.* Andrew P.) Lectures on christian doctrine. New ed. 263 pp. 12°. *Boston, Munroe & Co.* 1857.

Peabody (Ephraim, *D. D.*) An address, delivered at the centennial celebration in Wilton, N. H. Sept. 25, 1839, with an appendix. 103 pp. 8°. *Boston, B. H. Greene,* 1839.

Peacock (Lucy). Visit for a week; or, hints on the improvement of time. [*anon.*] 2 p. l. 275 pp. 1 pl. 16°. *Philadelphia, Ormrod & Conrad,* 1796.

Peard (W. *M. D.*) A year of liberty; or, salmon angling in Ireland, from February 1 to November 1. xii, 300 pp. 12°. *London, H. Cox,* 1867.

Pearsall (*Rev.* Richard). Contemplations on the ocean, harvest, sickness, and the last judgment. iv, 211 pp. 1 pl. 16°. *London, J. Oswald,* 1753.

Pearson (*Mrs.* Emily C.) Prince Paul: the freedman soldier. 359 pp. 2 pl. 16°. *Boston, Mass. S. S. soc.* [1867].

Pearson (John, *D. D. bishop of Chester*). Annales paulini. 22 pp. 8°. *Oxford,* 1825.

[*With* RANDOLPH (John, *bishop of London*). Enchiridion theologicum. v. 1].

Pearson (John, *F. R. S.*) Life of William Hey, F. R. S. New ed. 2 v. xciv, 200 pp; viii, 296 pp. 1 pl. 12°. *London, Seeley & Burnside,* 1827.

Peck (*Rev.* Francis). A complete catalogue of all the discourses written, both for and against popery, in the time of king James ii. 3 p. l. 61 pp. 4°. *London, A. Dodd,* 1835.

Peck (John M.) A new guide to the west: containing sketches of Ohio, Michigan, Indiana, Illinois, Missouri, Arkansas, Wisconsin and Iowa. 381 pp. 18°. *Cincinnati, D. Anderson,* 1848.

Peck (William Henry). The M'Donalds; or, the ashes of southern homes: a tale of Sherman's march. 192 pp. 12°. *New York, Metropolitan record office,* 1867.

Peckston (Thomas S.) Theory and practice of gas lighting. 2d ed. xii, 444 pp. 8°. *London, T. & G. Underwood,* 1823.

Péclet (Jean Claude Eugène). Traité de la chaleur considérée dans ses applications. 2e éd. texte. 2 v. 8°. ii, 456 pp; 483 pp. Atlas, 122 pl. 4°. *Paris, L. Hachette,* 1843. s.

——— Nouveaux documents relatifs au chauffage et à la ventilation des établissements publics. 2 p. l. 175 pp. 4°. *Paris, L. Hachette & Cie.* 1853. s.

——— Traité élémentaire de physique. 4e éd. entièrement refondu. 2 v. 424 pp. 20 pl; 404 pp. pl. 21–39. 8° *Bruxelles, société typographique belge,* 1838. s.

——— The same. 4e éd. revue et augmentée. 2 v. texte. vii, 719 pp; 683 pp. Atlas, 49 pl. obl. 8°. *Paris, L. Hachette & Cie.* 1847. s.

Pédroni *fils* (*prof. de chimie*). L'art du souffleur à la lampe et au chalumeau. 294 pp. 3 pl. 18°. *Paris, Roret,* 1849. s.

Peet (Harvey P.) Address delivered in commons hall at Raleigh on the occasion of laying the corner stone of the North Carolina institution for the instruction of the deaf and dumb. 47 pp. 8°. *New York, institution,* 1848. s.

Pegolotti *or* **Balducci-Pegolotti** (Francesco). Notices of the land route to Cathay, and of Asiatic trade in the first half of the 14th century. 28 pp.

[*With* YULE (Henry). Cathay, etc. v. 2. pp. 279–308].

Pegorier (César). Théologie chrétienne, qu'on explique en forme d'entretiens, pour la rendre plus claire et plus sensible. 2e éd. 2 p. l. 572 pp. 4°. *Amsterdam, L'Honoré & Chatelain,* 1726.

Peignot (Étienne Gabriel). Abrégé de l'histoire de France, etc. 2 v. lxiv, 432; xxx, 120 pp. 8°. *Paris, A. A. Renouard, etc.* 1819.

——— Les bourguignons salés: diverses conjectures des savans sur l'origine de ce dicton populaire, avec des notes. 43 pp. 8°. *Dijon, V. Lagier,* 1835.

——— Choix de testamens anciens et modernes, remarquables par leur importance, leur singularité, ou leur bizarrerie; avec des détails historiques et des notes. 2 v. in 1. xxiv, 431; 496 pp. 8°. *Paris, Renouard,* 1829.

——— Essai analytique sur l'origine de la langue française, et sur un recueil de monumens authentiques de cette langue, classés chronologiquement depuis le 9e siècle jusqu' au 17e, avec des notes historiques, [etc]. 8°. *Dijon, etc. V. Lagier,* 1835.

——— Essai historique sur la liberté d'écrire chez les anciens et au moyen âge, sur la liberté de la presse depuis le 15e siècle, et sur les moyens de répression dont ces libertès ont été l'objet dans tous les temps; et une chronologie des lois sur la presse de 1789 à 1831. xiii, 218 pp. 8°. *Paris, Crapelet,* 1832. s.

——— Mélanges littéraires, philologiques et bibliographiques, etc. xvi, 167 pp. 1 pl. 8°. *Paris, A. A. Renouard,* 1818. s.

Peirce (Benjamin). An elementary treatise on plane and solid geometry. xix, 150 pp. 6 pl. 12°. *Boston, W. H. Dennet,* 1867.

Peirce (Benjamin). Tables of the moon. 356 pp. 4°. *Cambridge, (Mass.) Metcalf & Co.* 1853. s.

Peirce (William Leigh). The year: a poem. 191, 75 pp. 18°. *New York, D. Longworth,* 1813.

Peirce. *See, also,* **Pierce.**

Pell (Ferris). A review of the administration and civil police of the state of New York, 1807–19. 184 pp. 8°. *New York, E. Conrad,* 1819.

Pelletan (Pierre). Dictionnaire de chimie générale et médicale. 2 v. xvi, 464 pp; 684 pp. 2 pl. 8°. *Paris, Bachelier,* 1822–24.

Pellico (Silvio). My prisons: memoirs of Silvio Pellico. [With a preface by Epes Sargent]. xxv, 307 pp. 12°. *Boston, Roberts bros.* 1868.

Pelloutier (Simon). Histoire des Celtes, et particulièrement des Gaulois et des Germains, depuis les tems fabuleux, jusqu'à la prise de Rome par les Gaulois. 2 v. 22 p. l. 574 pp; 6 p. l. 418 pp. 16°. *LaHaye, J. Beauregard,* 1750.

Pemberton (*Rev.* Ebenezer). The divine original and dignity of government asserted. [Election] sermon, May 31, 1710. 106 pp. 18°. *Boston, B. Green,* 1710.

Pemberton (Henry). Observations on poetry, especially the epic; occasioned by the late poem [of R. Glover] upon Leonidas. xii, 167 pp. 16°. *London, H. Woodfall,* 1738.

Pemberton (Robert). The natural method of teaching the elements of grammar. viii, 120 pp. 16°. *London, R. Pemberton,* 1851. s.

——— The natural method of teaching the technical language of anatomy, [etc.] xi, 163 pp. 16°. *London, author,* 1852. s.

Pemberton (Thomas). An historical journal of the American war. [*anon.*] 206 pp. 8°. *Boston, Joseph Belknap,* 1795.

[Mass. hist. society collections, v. 2].

Peñalver (Juan). Panlexico, v. 1; diccionario universal de la lengua castellana. 802, 42 pp. fol. *Madrid, J. Boix,* 1842.

Pencil (Mark). [*pseudon.*] *See* **White** Sulphur papers.

Penington (Mary). Brief accounts of my exercises from my childhood; left with my dear daughter, Gulielma Maria Penn. 39 pp. 8°. *Philadelphia,* 1848.

Penn (Granville). A christian's survey of all the primary events and periods of the world, from the commencement of history to the conclusion of prophecy. 8 p. l. 144 pp. 24°. *Alexandria, (D. C.) J. A. Stewart,* 1814.

Penn (William). A collection of [his] works. [With] a journal of his life. 2 v. 4 p. l. 911 pp; 2 p. l. 916 pp. fol. *London, assigns of J. Sowle,* 1726.

CONTENTS.

v. 1. Life. With tryal, travails into Holland and Germany, letters, petitions and speeches.
Truth exalted. 1668.
The sandy foundation shaken. 1668.
Innocency with her open face. 1668.
No cross, no crown. 1668.
Letter of love to the young convinced. 1669.
Liberty of conscience debated and defended. 1670.
Seasonable caveat against popery. 1670.
Truth rescued from imposture. 1670.
Christian quaker and his divine testimony. 1673.
Discourse of the general rule of faith and practice. 1673.
Letter to the council and senate of Embden. 1674.
Treatise of oaths. 1675.
England's present interest considered. 1675.
Saul smitten to the ground. 1675.
Address to protestants of all perswasions. 1679.
Some fruits of solitude. 1693.
Account of the rise and progress of the quakers. 1694.
Advice to his children. 1699.

v. 2. *Controversial:* Guide mistaken, and temporizing rebuked. 1668.
Serious apology for the principles and practices of the quakers. 1671.
Spirit of truth vindicated. 1672.
New witnesses prov'd old hereticks. 1672.
Plain dealing with a traducing anabaptist. 1672.
The proposed comprehension. 1672.
The spirit of Alexander the coppersmith justly rebuked. 1673.
Judas and the Jews combin'd against Christ and his followers. 1673.
Quakerism a new nickname for old christianity. 1673.
Invalidity of J. Faldo's vindication of his book call'd Quakerism no christianity. 1673.
Wisdom justified of her children. 1673.
Reason against railing, and truth against fiction. 1673.
Counterfeit christian detected and the real quaker justified. 1674.
Just rebuke to one and twenty divines. 1674.
Urim and Thummim. 1674.
Naked truth needs no shift. 1674.
A return to J. Faldo's reply. 1674.
Skirmisher defeated and truth defended. 1676.
Brief answer to a libel, call'd The quaker's opinions. 1678.
Brief examination, and state of liberty spiritual. 1678.
Defence of the duke of Buckingham's book of religion and worship. 1684.
Animadversions on the apology of the clamorous squire. 1684.
The new Athenians, no noble Bereans. 1692.
Reply to W. Penn's key. 1695.
Defence of a paper, entitled Gospel truths. 1698.
Doctrinal: Just measures. 1692.
A key, how to distinguish the religion professed by the quakers from the perversions of their adversaries. 1692.
Visitation to the Jews. 1695.
Primitive christianity reviv'd. 1695.
Testimony to the truth of God. 1698.
Political: England's great interest in the choice of a new parliament. 1679.
One project for the good of England, that is, our civil union is our civil safety. 1679.
A perswasive to moderation to church-dissenters, in prudence and good conscience. 1686.
Good advice to the church of England; etc. their duty, principle, and interest to abolish the penal laws and tests. 1687.
General description of Pennsylvania. 1683.

Penn (William). An account of [his] travels in Holland and Germany, in 1677, for the service of the gospel of Christ. 3d ed. 5 p. l. 240 pp. 16°. *London, J. Sowle,* 1714.

——— A brief account of the rise and progress of the people called quakers. 3 p. l. 88 pp. 12°. *Wilmington, (Del.) James Adams,* 1783.

[*Note.*—With general title-page: Three treatises, etc. the first by W. Penn].

——— A brief answer to a false and foolish libel called The quakers' opinions. By W. P. [*anon.*] 26 pp. sm. 4°. [*n. p.*] 1678.

——— England's present interest discovered, with honour to the prince and safety to the people. 2 p. l. 62 pp. sm. 4°. *London,* 1675.

——— A further account of the province of Pennsylvania and its improvements. 20 pp. sm. 4°. [*n. p.* 1685?]

[Imperfect; title page wanting; p. 20 imp.]

——— A key, opening the way to every capacity: how to distinguish the religion professed by the people called quakers, from the perversions and misrepresentations of their adversaries. 15th ed. 6 p. l. 48 pp. 16°. *London, T. S. Raylton & L. Hinde,* 1748.

——— Plain-dealing with a traducing anabaptist; or, three letters writ upon occasion of some slanderous reflections, given and promoted against William Penn by one John Morse. By W. P. [*anon.*] 19 pp. sm. 4°. [*n. p.*] 1672.

——— Proposals for a second settlement in the province of Pennsylvania. 1 l. broadside. 4°. *London, Andrew Sowle,* 1690.

——— A serious apology for the principles, etc. of the quakers. *See* **Whitehead** (George), *and* **Penn.**

——— The spirit of truth vindicated against that of error and envy, in a late malicious libel, intituled, The spirit of the quakers tryed, etc. By W. P. [*anon.*] 138 pp. sm. 4°. [*n. p.*] 1672.

Pennant (Thomas). Arctic zoology. 2 v. 4°. *London, H. Hughs,* 1784–85. S.

CONTENTS.

v. 1. Quadrupeds. 5 p. l. cc pp. 3 l. 185 pp. 9 pl.
v. 2. Birds. pp. 185–586. 7 l. pl. 9–23.

——— The same. Thiergeschichte der nördlichen polarländer. Aus dem Englischen, mit anmerkungen und zusätzen durch E. A. W. von Zimmermann. 2 v. 4°. *Leipzig, S. L. Crusius,* 1787. S.

CONTENTS.

v. 1. Einleitung und die naturgeschichte der vierfüssigen thiere. 7 p. l. 256, 180 pp. 9 pl.
v. 2. Naturgeschichte der vögel. pp. 181–568. pl. 9–23.

Pennant (Thomas). British zoology. 4 v. 8°. *London, B. White,* 1776–77.

CONTENTS.

v. 1. Quadrupeds, Birds. xxxii; 418 pp. 59 pl.
v. 2. Water-fowl. pp. 419–786. pl. 60, 103, 9.
v. 3. Reptiles, Fish. 425 pp. 73 pl.
v. 3. Crustacea, Mollusca, testacea. 154 pp. 93 pl.

——— Genera of birds. 3 p. l. xxv, 70 pp. 16 pl. 4°. *London, B. White,* 1781. S.

Pennsylvania. Annual report of the adjutant general for 1866. 8°. *Harrisburg,* 1867.

——— Brief view of the accounts of the treasury of Pennsylvania, from the commencement of the revolution to the 1st October, 1781. 237 pp. 8°. *Philadelphia, Hall & Sellers,* 1784.

——— Journal of the house of representatives, 1867. 8°. *Harrisburg, Singerly & Myers,* 1867.

——— Journal of the senate, 1867. 8°. *Harrisburg, Singerly & Myers,* 1867.

——— Miscellaneous documents, 1867. 2 v. 8°. *Harrisburg, Singerly & Myers,* 1867.

——— Minutes of the convention of the commonwealth of Pennsylvania, which commenced 24th Nov. 1789, for the purpose of reviewing, altering, and amending the constitution of this state. 222 pp. fol. *Philadelphia, Zechariah Poulson, jr.* 1789.

——— The same. Minutes of the grand committee of the convention, 24th Nov. 1789. 101 pp. fol. *Philadelphia, Z. Poulson, jr.* 1789.

——— Revised report made to the legislature, relative to the soldiers' national cemetery at Gettysburg, embracing an account of the origin of the undertaking; address of hon. E. Everett, with the dedicatory speech of pres. Lincoln, and maj. gen. O. O. Howard, delivered July 4, 1866, upon the dedication of the monument. 282 pp. 1 pl. 2 maps. 8°. *Harrisburg, Singerly and Myers,* 1867.

——— Reports of the heads of departments [executive documents] for 1866. 2 v. 8°. *Harrisburg, Singerly & Myers,* 1867.

——— Reports of the several railroad and canal companies for 1866. 8°. *Harrisburg, Singerly & Myers,* 1867.

——— Reports of the superintendent of common schools for 1855–59, 1862, 1865–67. 9 v. 8°. *Harrisburg,* 1856–68.

Pennsylvania free society of traders. The articles, settlement, and offices of the free society of traders in Pennsilvania. 8 l. unp. fol. *London, Benjamin Clark,* 1682.

Pennsylvania hospital. Catalogue of the medical library [By W. G. Malin.] xvi, 324 pp. 8°. *Philadelphia, T. A. Conrad,* 1829. S.

Pennsylvania hospital. Catalogue raisonné of the medical library. By Emil Fischer. xxvii, 750 pp. 8°. *Philadelphia, T. K. & P. G. Collins*, 1857. s.

——— Continuation of account from the 1st of May, 1754, to 5th of May, 1761. pp. 41 to 77. 4°. *Philadelphia, B. Franklin & D. Hall*, 1761.

——— Reports of the Pennsylvania hospital. v. I. 420 pp. 3 pl. 8°. *Philadelphia, Lindsay & Blakiston*, [1868].

Pennsylvania railroad guide. 40 pp. 1 map. 8°. *Philadelphia, T. & P. Collins*, 1855. s.

Pennsylvania state library. Catalogue. xii, 168 pp. 8°. *Harrisburg, E. Guyer*, 1839. s.

——— The same. Catalogue of miscellaneous books. xvi, 124 pp. 18°. *Harrisburg, Royal & Schroyer*, 1853. s.

Pennsylvania, University of. Catalogue of books belonging to the library of the university of Pennsylvania. 8°. *Philadelphia*, 1829.

Penrose (*Mrs.* Elizabeth Cartwright). History of France, to the reign of Louis Philippe. By Mrs. Markham. [*pseudon.*] Ed. by J. Abbott. 629 pp. 1 pl. 1 map. 12°. *New York, Harpers*, 1848. s.

Penrose (Thomas). Poems. viii, 120 pp. 16°. *Dublin, W. & H. Whitestone*, etc. 1782.

Pepe (Guglielmo). Mémoires, sur les principaux évènements politiques et militaires de l'Italie moderne. 3 v. 8°. *Paris, D'Amyot*, 1847.

Pepper (John Henry). Playbook of metals. viii, 504 pp. 1 pl. 12°. *London, Routledge*, 1861. s.

——— Scientific amusements for young people. 149 pp. 12°. *Philadelphia*, 1863.

[*With* PETERSON (R. E.) Familiar science. 2d ed 1863].

Pepys (*lady* Charlotte Maria). A journey on a plank from Kiev to Eaux-Bonnes, 1859. 2 v. x, 299 pp; v, 271 pp. 2 pl. 12°. *London, Hurst & Blackett*, 1860.

Pérault (Guillaume). *See* **Perrault.**

Perce (Elbert). The battle roll: an encyclopedia containing descriptions of the most famous and memorable land battles and sieges in all ages. 752 pp. 24 pl. 8°. *New York, Mason bros.* 1858.

Percheron (Achille Remi), *and* **Guérin-Méneville** (F. E.) Genera des insectes.

[*With* LEFEBVRE (C. T.) Voyage en Abyssinie, v. 6].

Percival (James Gates). Report on the geology of the state of Connecticut. 495 pp. 1 map. 8°. *New Haven, Osborn & Baldwin*, 1842. s.

——— Additions to System of universal geography. *See* **Malte-Brun** (M. C.) Universal geography. *Boston*, 1834.

Percy (Henry Algernon, *5th earl of Northumberland*). The regulations and establishment of the household [at Weasill and Lekinfleld, begun 1512. Edited by Thomas Percy. 2d ed.] xxvi, x, 464 pp. 2 l. 8°. *London, Pickering*, 1827.

Percy (Thomas, *bishop of Dromore*). Folio manuscript [of the Reliques of ancient English poetry]. Ballads and romances. Edited by J. W. Hales and F. J. Furnivall. v. 1 and v. 2, part 1. viii, 519 pp; xxxi, 264 pp. 8°. *London, Trübner*, 1867.

——— The same. Loose and humorous songs. Edited by J. W. Hales and F. J. Furnivall. viii, 120 pp. 8°. *London, Trübner*, 1867.

——— A key to the New Testament, giving an account of the several books, their contents, authors, and times, places, and occasions on which they were written. 148 pp. 16°. *Baltimore, E. J. Coale & Co.* 1822.

——— Miscellaneous pieces relating to the Chinese. [*anon.*] 2 v. 10 p. l. 232 pp; 248 pp. 18°. *London, R. & J. Dodsley*, 1762.

Péréfixe (Hardouin de Beaumont de, *abp. of Paris*). The history of Henry iv; surnamed the great, king of France and Navarre. Made English by J. D. 8 p. l. 400 pp. 16°. *London, J. Cottrel*, 1663.

Pereira (Gomez). Antoniana margarita; opvs nempe physicis, medicis ac theologis non minvs vtile qvam necessarivm. 16 l. 4°. *Methymnæ Campi, G. de Millis*, 1554.

——— Obiectiones Michaëlis à Palacios aduerssus nõnulla ex multiplicibus paradoxis Antonianæ margaritæ, et apologia eorundem. 18 l. 4°. *Methymnæ Campi, G. de Millis*, 1555.

[*With* the preceding].

Perez de Ribas (Andres). Historia de los trivmphos de nvestra santa fee entre gentes las mas barbaras y fieras del nuevo orbe: consequidos por los soldados de la milicia de la compañia de Jesvs en las missiones de la prouincia de Nueua-España. 20 p. l. 763 pp. fol. *Madrid, Alõso de Paredes*, 1645.

Perfect (William, *M. D.*) Poetic effusions; pastoral, moral, amatory, and descriptive. 2 p. l. 160 pp. 16°. *London, A. Milne*, 1796.

Périer (François). *See* **Perrier.**

Periers (Bonaventure des). *See* **Desperiers** (Bonaventure).

Peritsol, Parisol, *or* Farissol (Abraham). Itinera mundi, sic dicta, nempe cosmographia. Latina versione donavit et notas passim adjecit Thomas Hyde. 8 p. l. 196 pp. sm. 4°. *Oxonii, H. Bonwick*, 1691.

Perkins (Charles Callahan). Tuscan sculptors: their lives, works, and times. With illustrations. 2 v. lvi, 267 pp. 39 pl; vii, 267 pp. 6 pl. 4°. *London, Longmans*, 1864.

Perkins (C. H.), *and* **Stowe** (J. G.) A new guide to the sheet iron and boiler plate roller: a series of tables showing the weight of slabs and piles to produce boiler plates, sheet iron, etc. 2, 27 l. obl. 24°. *Philadelphia, H. C. Baird*, 1867.

Perkins (Frederic B.) The picture and the men; being biographical sketches of president Lincoln and his cabinet; with account of the artist, F. B. Carpenter, author of the painting, The first reading of the emancipation proclamation; with a key to the picture. 190 pp. 16°. *New York, A. J. Johnson*, 1867.

Perkins (George R.) Elements of geometry, with practical applications. iv, 308 pp. 12°. *Utica, H. H. Hawley & Co.* 1847. s.

Perkins (James Handasyd). Annals of the west; account of the principal events from the discovery of the Mississippi to 1845. xx, 591 pp. 8°. *Cincinnati, James R. Albach*, 1846.

Perkins (*Rev.* William). Workes. Newly corrected. v. 1. vi, 779 pp. fol. *London, Iohn Legatt*, 1612.

Pernety (Antoine Joseph). Histoire d'un voyage aux isles Malouines, fait en 1763 et 1764; avec des observations sur le détroit de Magellan, et sur les Patagons. Nouv. éd. 2 v. 8°. *Paris, Saillant & Nyon*, 1770.

——— The same. The history of a voyage to the Malouine [or, Falkland] islands, made in 1763–4, under M. de Bougainville, to form a settlement there; and of two voyages to the streights of Magellan. Translated from the French. 2d ed. 2 p. l. xvii, 294 pp. 5 maps. 11 pl. 4°. *London, W. Goldsmith*, 1773.

Perotti (Niccolò). Cornucopia: sive commentarii [super Martialis epigrammata, et super] linguam latinam. 48 p. l. 634 pp. 1 l. fol. *Mediolani, Nicolaus Gorgonzola*, 1507.

Perrault (Charles). Les hommes illustres qui ont paru en France pendant ce siècle; avec leurs portraits au naturel. 2 v. in 1. 5 p. l. 102 pp. 53 pl; 102 pp. 51 pl. fol. *Paris, A. Dezallier*, 1696–1700. s.

——— The same. Characters, historical and panegyrical, of the greatest men that have appeared in France during the last century. Rendered into English, by J. Ozell. 2 v. 14 p. l. 221 pp. 12°. *London, B. Lintott*, 1704–5.

Perrault (Guillaume). Summe, seu tractatus de viciis. 4°. [*Basileae*, 1475?]

Perrey (Alexis). Bibliographie séismique. Catalogue de livres, mémoires et notes sur les tremblements de terre et les phénomènes volcaniques. 183, 161, 70 pp. 8°. *Dijon, Rabutôt*, 1855–65.

——— Note sur les tremblements de terre en 1858, [et] en 1863–[64]; avec suppléments pour les années antérieures, 1843–63. [Extracts.] 3 v. 8°. *Bruxelles, Acad. royale de Belgique*, 1861–66. s.

Perrier *or* **Périer** (François). Icones et segmenta nobilium signorum et statuarum quae Romae extant, delineata atque in aere incisa, anno 1638–53. 2 p. l. 100 pl. fol. [*Romæ, n. d. about* 1653].

[Imperfect; title page wanting].

Perrin (James). An English-Kafir dictionary of the Zulu-Kafir language. 225 pp. 24°. *Pietermaritzburg, Church of England missions*, 1855. s.

Perrot (Antoine Marie.) Manuel du graveur; ou, traité complet de l'art de la gravure en tous genres. 255 pp. 1 tab. 4 pl. 18°. *Paris, Roret*, 1830. s.

——— Nouveau manuel complet du graveur. Nouv. éd. augmentée par F. Malepeyre. x, 289 pp. 1 tab. 4 pl. 18°. *Paris, Roret*, 1844. s.

Perrot (Claudius). Der priesteramts-kandidat. Vertrauliche mittheilungen an die kleriker des weltpriester und ordenstandes. 415 pp. 1 pl. 12°. *Einsiedeln & New York, Benziger bros.* 1867.

Perry (*Capt.* David, *of Chelsea, Vt.*) Recollections of an old soldier. 55 pp. 16°. *Windsor, (Vt.)* 1822.

Perry (George). Conchology; or, the natural history of shells. 4 pp. 62 l. 61 col. pl. fol. *London, W. Miller*, 1811. s.

Perry (John). The new London gleaner. 2 v. 456 pp; 443 pp. 14 pl. 8°. *London, J. Cundee*, 1809.

——— The new magazine of choice pieces: or, literary museum. 2 v. 448 pp; 438 pp. 16 pl. 8°. *London, J. Cundee*, [1810].

[Imperfect: 2 pl. wanting].

Persepolis illustrata: or, the ancient and royal palace destroyed by Alexander the great, illustrated and described, in 21 copper-plates. 1 p. l. 8 pp. 19 pl. fol. *London, S. Harding*, 1739.

Pershing (D. R.) A digest of the laws and decisions of the grand lodge of Indiana I. O. of G. T. Also decisions of the R. W. G. L. with funeral ceremonies, [etc.] 55 pp. 24°. *Philadelphia, "Good templar" office,* 1867.

Persius (Friedrich Ludwig). Architektonische entwürfe für den unterbau vorhandener gebäude. 8 pp. 24 pl. fol. *Potsdam, F. Riegel,* 1849. S.

Persius Flaccus (Aulus). Satirae. *See* **Juvenalis** (Decimus Junius), *and* **Persius** Flaccus.

Persoz (Jean François). Introduction à l'étude de la chimie moléculaire. 894 pp. 7 tab. 8°. *Paris, J. B. Baillière,* 1839. S.

Peschel (Carl Friedrich). Die kriegsbaukunst im felde. 2e aufl. Von Otto Andrée. xxxvi, 795 pp. 12 pl. 8°. *Leipzig, Arnold,* 1855. S.

Pesson-Maisonneuve (——.) Nouveau manuel complet du pêcheur français. Nouv. éd. Par [l'abbé R.] Moriceau. xvii, 354 pp. 32 pl. 18°. *Paris, Roret,* [1847]. S.

Petau (Denis). De doctrina temporum. Accesserunt notæ et emendationes quamplurimæ, quas codici propria manu auctor adscripsit, et J. Harduini præfatio ac dissertatio de lxx hebdomadibus. 3 v. fol. *Venetiis, B. Baronchelli,* 1757. S.

Petavius (Dionysius). *See* **Petau** (Denis).

Peter (Joseph). Flammen der liebe: ein katholisches gebetbuch zur verehrung des göttlichen herzens Jesu beim besuche des heiligsten altarssakramentes. 349 pp. 48°. *New York, C. & N. Benziger,* 1866.

Peter (Robert). Chemical analysis, etc.
[*With* OWEN (D. D.) Second report on the geology of Arkansas].

——— Chemical reports.
[*With* OWEN (D. D.) Reports of the geological survey of Kentucky. v. 1, 2, 3, 4].

Peterborough (Benedict, *abbot of*). Gesta regis Henrici secundi. The chronicle of the reigns of Henry ii, and Richard i. A. D. 1169–1192. Edited from the Cotton MSS. by W. Stubbs. 2 v. lxvii, 361 pp; clxiv, 386 pp. 8°. *London, Longmans,* 1867.
[Chronicles of Great Britain in the middle ages].

Petermann (Augustus). Historical summary of the search for Sir John Franklin. 30 pp. 8°. *London,* [*J. E. Taylor,* 1853?]

——— The search for Franklin, a suggestion to the British public. 24 pp. 1 map. 8°. *London, Longman & Co.* 1852.

——— The same.
[*With his* Historical summary, etc.]

Petermann (Julius Heinrich). Reisen im orient. 2 v. viii, 409 pp. 1 pl; xiv, 471 pp. 1 map. 8°. *Leipzig, Veit & Co.* 1860–61. S.
[v. 2 wanting].

Peters (Absalom, *D. D.*) Life and time; a birth-day memorial of seventy years. [A poem, with personal reminiscences]. 80 pp. sq. 16°. *New York, Sheldon & Co.* 1866.

Peters (Christian August Friedrich). Über die einige bewegung des Sirius. 31 pp. 4°. *Königsberg, E. J. Dalkowski,* 1851. S.

Peters (*Rev.* Hugh). Tales and jests. [With] a short account of his life. 51 pp. 1 pl. 8°. *London, J. Caulfield,* 1807.

Peters (John C. *M. D.*) Notes on the origin, nature, prevention, and treatment of Asiatic cholera. 2d ed. 200 pp. 12°. *New York, D. Van Nostrand,* 1867.

Peters (John R. *jr.*) Miscellaneous remarks upon the governments, history, religions, literature, arts, etc. of the Chinese, as suggested by an examination of the articles comprising the Chinese museum in the Marlboro' chapel, Boston. 8, 182 pp. 8°. *Boston, Eastburn,* 1845. S.

Peters (Richard). Agricultural enquiries on plaister of Paris. 109 pp. 8°. *Philadelphia, C. Cist & J. Markland,* 1797.

——— The same. [With a fac simile of Washington's handwriting and a sketch of his character. 2d ed.] xvi, 129, ix pp. 8°. *Philadelphia, Jane Aitken,* 1810.
[*With* PHILADELPHIA society for promoting agriculture. Memoirs. v. 2].

——— A statistical account of the Schuylkill permanent bridge, communicated to the Philadelphia society of agriculture, 1806. [*anon.*] 84 pp. 1 pl. 8°. *Philadelphia, J. Aitken,* 1807. S.
[*With* SMEATON (J.) Experimental enquiry, etc].

Peters (*Rev.* Samuel, *or* Samuel Andrew, *LL.D.*) History of Rev. Hugh Peters. vi, 155 pp. 12°. *New York,* 1807.

Peters (Wilhelm C. H.) Über die säugethiergattung *Solenodon.* (Extract). 22 pp. 3 pl. 4°. *Berlin, Akad. der wissenschaften,* 1863. S.

Petersburg, (*Va.*) Catalogue of the library of Petersburg. 82 pp. 8°. *New York, Appletons,* 1854. S.

Peterson (Robert E.) Familiar science; or the scientific explanation of common things. 558 pp. 16°. *Philadelphia, R. E. Peterson,* 1851.

——— The same. Revised ed. [With] scientific amusements for young people by J. H. Pepper. 591 pp. 12°. *Philadelphia, Sower, Barnes & Potts,* [1863].

——— The same. Common school ed. 146th thousand. 305 pp. 18°. *Philadelphia, Sower, Barnes & Potts,* [1866].

Petis (François). The history of Genghizcan. [based on Mirkhond, etc.] Translated [from the French] into English. ix, 448 pp. 1 map. 8°. *London, J. Darby,* 1722.

Petitpierre (Ferdinand Olivier, *or* Frédéric Louis). Thoughts on the divine goodness, displayed in future rewards and punishments. Translated from the French. xxii, 294 pp. 8°. *Bath, S. Hazard,* 1788.

Peto (*Sir* Samuel Morton). Resources and prospects of America, ascertained during a visit to the States in 1865. xv, 428 pp. 2 pl. 8°. *London, A. Strahan,* 1866.

——— The same. xii, 404 pp. 16°. *New York, A. Strahan & Co.* [*printed in London*], 1866.

——— Taxation: its levy and expenditures, past and future; being an inquiry into our financial policy. vii, 255 pp. 8°. *New York, D. Appleton & Co.* 1866.

Petöfi (Alexander). *See* **Petrovich** (Sándor).

Petot (———, *engineer.*) Recherches sur la chaufournerie, faites au port de Brest. [Extract.] iv, 176 pp. 4 pl. 8°. *Paris, Annales marit. et coloniales,* 1833. s.

Petra, *or* **Petri,** *or* **Peeters** (Hermann de). Compendiosa sermonū quinquaginta sup. dñicam orōnem compilatio. 123 l. unp. 4°. *Louanii, J. de Westfalia,* 1484.

Petrarca (Francesco). Trivmphi, [col commento di Glicino (o, Ilicino, ossia da Montalcino, o piutosto Bernardo Lapino,) e di F. Filelfo]. 128 l. unp. 3 pl. fol. [*Milano, A. Zaroto Parmense,* 1484].

——— Sonetti e canzone, [col commento di Glicino e di F. Filelfo]. cii l. fol. *Milano, A. Zaroto Parmense,* 1484.

[Imperfect; wanting l. lxviii—lxix].
[*With* PETRARCA (Francesco). Trivmphi. *Milano,* 1484].

Petri (Friedrich Erdmann). Gedrängtes handbuch der fremdwörter in deutscher schrift- und umgangsprache. 8ᵉ ausg. 2 v. 544 pp; 546 pp. 12°. *Dresden, Arnold,* 1838. s.

Petri (Hermann de). *See* **Petra** (Hermann de).

Petrovich (Sándor), *or* **Petöfi** (Alexander). Translations from Alexander Petöfi, the Magyar poet. By Sir John Bowring. viii, 239 pp. 16°. *London, Trübner & Co.* 1866. s.

Petrus *Blesensis. See* **Pierre** *de Blois.*

Pettibone (Daniel). Economy of fuel; or, description of his improvements of the rarefying air-stoves, for warming and ventilating, with or without the application of steam. 2d ed. 62 pp. 8°. *Philadelphia, author,* 1812. s.

Pettigrew (Thomas Joseph). Bibliotheca sussexiana. Descriptive catalogue, accompanied by historical and biographical notices of the manuscripts and printed books in the library of the duke of Sussex. 2 v. in 3 pts. ccxciv, 11 p. l. 516 pp; liii, 579 pp. 4 l. 1 pl. 4°. *London, Longman & Co.* 1827–39.

——— Memoirs of the life of vice-admiral lord viscount Nelson. 2 v. xxxiv, 501 pp; 668 pp. 5 pl. 8°. *London, T. & W. Boone,* 1849.

Petty (*Sir* William). An essay concerning the multiplication of mankind; with another essay in political arithmetic, concerning the growth of the city of London. 2d ed. 50 pp. 16°. *London, M. Pardoe,* 1686.

[*With* GRAUNT (John). Observations upon the bills of mortality. *London,* 1676].

——— Five essays in political arithmetic. [French and English]. 3 p. l. 51, 51 pp. 16°. *London, H. Mortlock,* 1687.

[*With* GRAUNT (John). Observations upon the bills of mortality. *London,* 1676].

——— Further observations upon the Dublin bills; or, accompts of the houses, hearths, baptisms, and burials in that city. 2d ed. 6, 8 pp. 5 l. 16°. *London, M. Pardoe,* 1686.

[*With* GRAUNT (John). Observations upon the bills of mortality. *London,* 1676].

——— Observations upon the cities of London and Rome. 4 pp. 16°. *London, H. Mortlock,* 1687.

[*With* GRAUNT (John). Observations upon the bills of mortality. *London,* 1676].

——— Two essays in political arithmetic concerning London and Paris. 2 p. l. 21 pp. 16°. *London, J. Lloyd,* 1687.

[*With* GRAUNT (John). Observations upon the bills of mortality. *London,* 1676].

Petzholdt (Alexander). Lectures to farmers on agricultural chemistry. 107 pp. 8°. *New York, Greeley & McElrath,* 1846. s.

[Farmers' library, v. 1.]

Petzholdt (Julius). Adressbuch deutscher bibliotheken. 3ᵉ ausg. vi, 179 pp. 16°. *Dresden, Adler & Dietze,* 1848. s.

——— The same. Nachträge zur zweiten auflage. iv, 96 pp. 16°. *Dresden, Adler & Dietze,* 1848. s.

[*With* his Adressbuch. Ed. 1848].

——— Bibliotheca bibliographica. Kritisches verzeichniss der das gesammtgebiet der bibliographie betreffenden litteratur des in- und auslandes in systematisches ordnung bearbeitet. xii, 939 pp 8°. *Leipzig, W. Engelmann,* 1866. s.

Peutinger (Conrad). De mirandis Germaniae antiqvitatibvs, sermones conuiuales. 18 l. unp. sm. 4°. *Argentorati, C. Egenolphus,* 1530.

Peverelly (Charles A.) Book of American pastimes, containing a history of the principal base-ball etc. clubs of the United States. 556 pp. 4 pl. 12°. *New York, the author*, 1866.

Peyrère (Isaac de La). *See* **La Peyrère.**

Peyton (John Lewis). The American crisis; or, pages from the note-book of a state agent during the civil war. 2 v. xii, 340 pp. 1 pl; vi, 329 pp. 12°. *London, Saunders, Otley & Co.* 1867.

Pfeiffer (Louis). Monographia heliceorum viventium. 3 v. 8°. *Lipsiae, F. A. Brockhaus*, 1848–53. s.

——— Monographia pneumonopomorum viventium, accedente fossilium enumeratione. xviii, 439 pp. 8°. *Cassellis, T. Fischer*, 1852. s.

Pfinzing (Melchior). Die geüerlicheiten vnd eins teils der geschichten des löblichē streitbaren vnd hochberümbten helds vnd ritters Tewrdanncks. [2e ausg.] 289 l. unp. fol. *Augspurg, Schönsperger*, 1519. s.

Pfnor (Rodolphe). Architecture, décoration, ameublement; époque Louis xvi. Avec un texte descriptif. 32 pp. 50 pl. fol. *Paris, A. Morel & Cie.* 1865.

——— Monographie du chateau de Heidelberg. Accompagnée d'un texte historique et descriptif. Par Daniel Ramée. 2 pts. in 1 v. 19 pp. 24 pl. fol. *Paris, A. Morel & Cie.* 1859.

——— Monographie du palais de Fontainebleau. Accompagnée d'un texte historique et descriptif, par Champollion-Figeac. 2 v. 23, 15 pp. 150 pl. fol. *Paris, A. Morel & Cie.* 1863.

Phædrus. Fables. Traduction nouvelle. Par Ernest Panckouke. 384 pp. 8°. *Paris, C. L. F. Panckouke*, 1839. s.

Phantom flowers; a treatise on the art of producing skeleton leaves. [*anon.*] 96 pp. 6 pl. 12°. *Boston, Tilton & Co.* 1866.

Pharmacopoea norvegica. Regia auctoritate edita. xxiii, 202 pp. 8°. *Christianiæ, Brögger & Christie*, 1854. s.

Phelan (Michael). Game of billiards. 8th ed. 255 pp. 4 l. 28 diagrams. 1 portrait. 12°. *New York, Dick & Fitzgerald*, 1867.

Phelan (William, *D. D.*) Remains; with a memoir, by John [Jebb], bishop of Limerick. 2 v. xxvi, 320 pp; 364 pp. 8°. *London, J. Duncan*, 1832.

CONTENTS.

V. 1. Memoir.
Donnellan lectures, 1819.
Discourses.
V. 2. History of the policy of the church of Rome in Ireland to the great rebellion.

Phelps (Austin, *D. D.*) The new birth; or, the work of the holy spirit. 253 pp. 16°. *Boston, Gould & Lincoln*, 1867.

Phelps (E. W.) Bee-keeper's chart; treatise on the instinct, habits, and management of the honey-bee. vii, 96 pp. 12°. *New York, C. M. Saxton*, 1854.

Philadelphia (Apprentices' library company). A catalogue of books belonging to the boys' department. 176 pp. 8°. *Philadelphia*, 1854. s.

——— A catalogue of books belonging to the girls' department. [etc.] 74 pp. 18°. *Philadelphia*, 1853. s.
[*With* the preceding.]

——— Catalogue of the books belonging to the library of the four monthly meetings of Friends of Philadelphia. 350 pp. 12°. *Philadelphia, Kite & Walton*, 1853. s.

——— Desilver's directory and stranger's guide, for 1835–36. 8°. *Philadelphia*, 1835.

——— Gopsill's city and business directory for 1867–8. Compiled by J. Costa. 1,690 pp. 1 map. 8°. *Philadelphia, J. Gopsill*, 1867.

——— McElroy's city directory for 1837, 1848, 1850, 1851, 1852, 1856, 1858, 1860, 1862, and 1867. 10 v. 8°. *Philadelphia*, 1837–67.

——— Library company of Philadelphia. A catalogue of books; [with] a short account of the institution. xl, 406 pp. 8°. *Philadelphia, Z. Poulson*, 1789.

——— The same. With the charter, laws, and regulations. xl, 616 pp. 8°. *Philadelphia, Bartram & Reynolds*, 1807.

Philadelphia (The) botanic sentinel and Thomsonian medical revolutionist. M. Mattson, editor. Aug. 1837, to Aug. 1838. v. 3. viii, 408 pp. sm. fol. *Philadelphia, J. Coates*, 1838.

Philadelphia society for promoting agriculture. Memoirs. v. 1–2. 8°. *Philadelphia, Jane Aitken*, 1808–11.

Philatelist (The): an illustrated magazine for stamp collectors. Dec. 1866, to Dec. 1867. v. 1. 8°. *London, E. Marlborough & Co.* 1867.

Philelphus (F.) *See* **Filelfo** (Francesco).

Philidor (François Antoine Daniçan, *called*). Chess rendered familiar by tabular demonstrations, as described by Philidor. With other critical situations and modes, and a concise introduction, by J. G. Pohlman. 3 p. l. 449 pp. 1 pl. 8°. *London, Baldwin, Cradock, & Joy*, 1819.

Philip (Maxwell). Emmanuel Appadocca; or, blighted life. 2 v. vi, 250 pp; 248 pp. 8°. *London, C. J. Skeet*, 1854.

Philippart (John). Memoirs and campaigns of Charles John [Bernadotte], prince royal of Sweden. xv, 390 pp. 1 pl. 8°. *Baltimore, Neal, Wills & Cole, etc.* 1815.

Philips (Ambrose). Poetical works. 8°. *Edinburgh,* 1794.

]Anderson's Brit. poets, v. 9.]

Philips (Erasmus). Miscellaneous works, consisting of essays, political and moral. 4 p. l. 508 pp. 8°. *London, Waller,* 1751.

CONTENTS.

Country gentleman. March 11 to Dec. 26, 1726.
Letter respecting the situation of affairs, 1749.
Political reflexions, 1722.
State of the nation, 1725.

——— The state of the nation, in respect to her commerce, debts, and money. 8 p. l. 152 pp. 12°. *London, Woodman & Lyon,* 1725.

Philips (John). Cyder: a poem. [*anon.*] 2 p. l. 88 pp. 1 pl. 12°. *London, J. Tonson,* 1708.

——— Poetical works. 8°. *Edinburgh,* 1793.

[Anderson's Brit. poets, v. 6.]

Philips (Miles). Voyages and adventures. 18°. *London,* 1824.

[Imperfect.]

Philipson (Rudolph George). Academisch proefschrift over den volkenregtelijken regel: "Schip is territoir." xii, 302 pp. 8°. *Zwolle, Erven J. J. Tijl,* 1864. s.

Phillippe (A.) Geschichte der apotheker bei den wichtigsten völkern der erde seit den ältesten zeiten. Aus den französischen übersetzt, und mit einer zusammen-stellung der förderer der pharmacie vermehrt von Hermann Ludwig. viii, 1,122 pp. 8°. *Jena, F. Mauke,* 1854–55. s.

Phillips (Charles). Speeches at the bar, and on various public occasions. 4th Amer. ed. xvi, 176 pp. 8°. *Alexandria, (D. C.) Hawe & Thomson,* 1820.

Phillips (Edward). The mysteries of love and eloquence; or, the arts of wooing and complimenting, etc. [*anon.*] 3d ed. 11 p. l. 318, 70 pp. 6 l. 1 pl. 12°. *London, J. Rawlins,* 1685.

——— The new world of words; or, universal English dictionary. 6th ed. [by John Kersey]. 347 l. 1 pl. fol. *London, J. Phillips, etc.* 1706.

——— The same. 7th ed. By John Kersey. 360 l. fol. *London, J. Philips,* 1720. s.

[Imperfect: leaves wanting at the end].

Phillips (E.) Report. 8°. *Washington,* 1844.

[*With* OWEN (D. D.) Report of a geological exploration of Iowa, Wisconsin, and Illinois. 1844. p. 159].

Phillips (John, *prof. of geology*). Figures and descriptions of the palæozoic fossils of Cornwall, Devon and West Somerset. xii, 231 pp. 60 pl. 8°. *London, Longmans,* 1841. s.

——— Illustrations of the geology of Yorkshire Part i. The Yorkshire coast. 2d ed. xii, 184 pp. 1 col. map. 14 pl. 4°. *London, J. Murray,* 1835. s.

——— Memoirs of William Smith, LL. D. author of the "Map of the strata of England and Wales." viii, 150 pp. 1 pl. 8°. *London, J. Murray,* 1844. s.

Phillips (John Arthur). The mining and metallurgy of gold and silver. xix, 532 pp. 1 map. 8 pl. 8°. *London, C. & F. Spon,* 1867.

——— Report on the property of the California borax company. [With] review by the company. 12, 14 pp. 8°. *San Francisco, Towne & Bacon,* 1866. s.

Phillips (Philip, *editor*). Singing pilgrim. [Hymns set to music]. With notes by J. W. Wiley. 8°. *New York,* 1866.

Phillips (*Rev.* Samuel). A word in season; or, the duty of the people to take and keep the oath of allegiance to God. viii, 213 pp. 24°. *Boston, Kneeland & Green,* 1727.

Phillips (Teresa Constantia). An apology for the conduct of Mrs. Teresia Constantia Phillips. 3 v. Portrait. 12°. *London, author,* 1748–49.

Phillips (William Barnet). The diamond cross; a tale of American society. 353 pp. 12°. *New York, Hilton & Co.* 1866.

Philostratus. Philostratorvm quae svpersvnt omnia. [Gr. et Lat.] Accessere Apolonii tyanensis epistolae, Evsebii liber adversvs Hieroclem, Callistrati descriptio statvarvm. Rec. G. Olearivs. 4 p. l. 43, 987 pp. fol. *Lipsiæ, T. Fritsch,* 1709.

Philp (Robert Kemp). The history of progress in Great Britain. First and second series. 3d ed. xii, 386 pp; vi, 384 pp. 3 maps. 20 pl. 8°. *London, Houlston & Wright,* 1866.

Philpot (*Rev.* John). Examinations and writings [with biography]. xxxi, 446 pp. 8°. *Cambridge, Univ. press,* 1842.

[Parker society publications].

Phin (John). Open air grape culture: [with] the manufacture of domestic wine. 375 pp. 12°. *New York, Sheldon & Co.* 1867.

Phipps (Constantine John, *2d baron Mulgrave*). Voyage au pole boréal, fait en 1773. Traduit de l'Anglois [par Jean Nicolas Demeunier]. xii, 259 pp. 2 l. 12 pl. 4°. *Paris, Saillant & Nyon,* 1775. s.

Phipps (Joseph). Dissertations on the nature and effect of christian baptism. 16°. *Philadelphia,* 1811.

[*With* WELL (William, *and others*). Doctrines of baptism, etc. pp. 43–71. 16°. 1811].

Phocylides. Poëma admonitorium. Græce et latine. s.

[*With* NEANDER (Michael). Opus aureum, etc.]

Phoebus (Philipp). Deutschlands kryptogamische giftgewächse. xii, 113 pp. 9 col. pl. 4°. *Berlin, A. Hirschwald,* 1838. s.

——— Ueber den leichenbefund bei der orientalischen cholera. viii, 340 pp. 8°. *Berlin, A. Hirschwald,* 1833. s.

——— Der typische frühsommer katarrh; oder, das sogenannte heu-fieber, heu-asthma. xvi, 284 pp. 1 tab. 8°. *Giessen, J. Ricker,* 1862. s.

Piazzi (Giuseppe). Lezione elementari di astronomia. 2 v. xix, 240 pp. 5 pl; viii, 446 5 pl. 8°. *Palermo, stamperia reale,* 1817. s.

——— Lehrbuch der astronomie. Aus dem Italienischen üb. von Johann Heinrich Westphal, mit einer vorrede des Gauss. 2 v. vi, 258 pp. 2 pl; 356 pp. 2 pl. 8°. *Berlin, G. Reimer,* 1822. s.

Pibrac (Guy du Faur, *or* Fevre, de La Boderie, *seigneur* de). Tetrastika, or the quadrains of Pibrac. Translated by Joshua Silvester. sm. 4°. *London, H. Lownes,* 1605.

[*With* DU BARTAS. [Poetical works]. pp. 669–715. *London,* 1605].

Picard (H.) A new pocket dictionary of the English and Dutch languages. i. English-Dutch. ii. Nederduitsch-englisch. 3d ed. by H. J. Vogin. 2 pts. in 1 v. 2 p. l. ix, 584 pp. sq. 18. *Gouda, G. B. Van Goor,* 1862.

Pichon (Thomas). Lettres et mémoires pour servir à l'histoire naturelle, civile, et politique du Cap Breton, depuis son établissement jusqu' à 1758. xvi, 327 pp. 16°. *La Haye, Pierre Gosse,* 1760.

Pickard (*Mrs.* Kate E. R.) The kidnapped and the ransomed; being the personal recollections of Peter Still and his wife "Vina," after forty years of slavery. With an introduction by S. J. May, and an appendix by W. H. Furness. 409 pp. 2 pl. 12°. *Syracuse, W. T. Hamilton,* 1856. s.

Picken (Andrew). The Canadas, as they at present commend themselves to the enterprize of emigrants, colonists, and capitalists. Compiled from documents furnished by John Galt. vii, 349, lxxxvii pp. 1 map. 16°. *London, E. Wilson,* 1832.

——— The deer-stalkers of Glenskiach. 54 pp. 8°. *London,* 1840.

[HAZLITT'S romancist and novelists' lib. v. 1].

——— Eisenbach; or, the adventures of a stranger. 30 pp. 8°. *London,* 1840.

[HAZLITT'S romancist and novelists' lib. v. 4].

——— The three Kearneys. 11 pp. 8°. *London,* 1841.

[HAZLITT'S romancist and novelists' lib. v. 4].

Pickering (Octavius). The life of Timothy Pickering. v. 1. xix, 549 pp. 1 pl. 8°. *Boston, Little, Brown & Co.* 1867.

Pickering (Timothy, *jr.*) An easy plan of discipline for a militia. 28, 169, 2 pp. 14 pl. 8°. *Salem, S. & E. Hall,* 1775.

Pickett (Albert J.) Eight days in New Orleans in February, 1847. 40 pp. 8°. *Montgomery, (Ala.) author,* 1847.

Pickett (James Chamberlain). Poems on various subjects. 106 pp. 8°. *Washington, author,* 1867.

Pictet (Bénédict). La théologie chrétienne, et la science du salut; ou, l' exposition des véritez révélés dans la Ste Écriture. Avec la réfutation des erreurs contraires, l'histoire de ces erreurs et les sentimens des anciens pères. 2 v. in 1. 3 p. l. 516 pp; 4 p. l. 456 pp. 4°. *Amsterdam, G. Gallet,* 1702.

Pictet *or* **Pictet-Barabon** (François Jules). Histoire naturelle générale et particulière des insectes névroptères. Famille des éphémérines. x, 300, 19 pp. 48 col. pl. 8°. *Genève, J. Kessmann,* 1843. s.

——— The same. Famille des perlides. xiii, 423, 23 pp. 53 col. pl. 8°. *Genève, J. Kessmann,* 1841. s.

——— Notices sur quelques anomalies de l'organisation. (Extract). 22 pp. 4 pl. 4°. *Genève, T. G. Fick,* 1855. s.

——— Recherches pour servir à l'histoire et à l'anatomie des phryganides. iii, 235 pp. 2 l. 20 col. pl. 4°. *Genève, Abraham Cherbuliez,* 1834. s.

——— Traité de paléontologie; ou, histoire naturelle des animaux fossiles considérés dans leurs rapports zoologiques et géologiques. 2e éd. v. i–iii. 8°. Atlas. pl. 1–84. 4°. *Paris, J. B. Baillière,* 1853–55. s.

[Wanting, v. 4; pl. 85–110].

——— *and* **Hagen** (Hermann). Die im bernstein befindlichen neuropteren der vorwelt.

[*With* BERENDT (G. C.) Die im bernstein, etc. v. 2. 1856].

Pictet (Marc Auguste). An essay on fire. Translated from the French by W. B. *M. D.* xi, 304 pp. 18°. *London, E. Jeffery,* 1791.

Pictorial (The) hand-book of London. Illustrated by Branston, Jewitt, and others. 910 pp. 1 map. 12°. *London, H. G. Bohn,* 1854. s.

Picture (The) of New York; or, the traveller's guide. [*anon.*] viii, 223 pp. 1 map. 18°. *New York, J. Riley & Co.* 1807.

——— The same, and stranger's guide. [*anon.*] v, 492 pp. 8 pl. 16°. *New York, A. T. Goodrich,* [*about* 1828].

Picture (A) of New York in 1846, with a short account of places in its vicinity. [*anon.*] iv, 172 pp. 2 l. 1 map. 18°. *New York, Homans & Ellis*, 1846.

Picturesque pocket companion and visitors' guide through Mount Auburn. [*anon.* With miscellanies.] Illustrated. 252 pp. 18°. *Boston, Otis, Broaders & Co.* 1839.

Pidansat de Mairobert (Mathieu François). Anecdotes sur M^e la comtesse du Barri. Nouv. éd. revue et corrigée. 2 p. l. 346 pp. 16°. *Londres, J. Adamsohn*, 1776.

Pièces du procès instruit contradictoirement au conseil supérieur de la Martinique, entre le procureur général, et la société des jésuites. [*anon.*] 191 pp. 12°. [*n. p. about* 1763].

Pierce (*Rev.* Bradford K.) Trials of an inventor: life and discoveries of Charles Goodyear. 224 pp. 16°. 1 portrait. *New York, Carlton & Porter*, 1866.

Pierce (Josiah). Address, May 26, 1836, the centennial anniversary of Gorham. 36 pp. 8°. *Portland, Charles Day & Co.* 1836.

Pierce. *See, also,* **Peirce.**

Pierpont (John). Introduction to the national reader, [etc.] 168 pp. 12°. *Boston, Richardson & Lord*, 1828. s.

Pierre Cœur, suivi de Georges et Louis; ou, l'orgueil vaincu par la générosité. [*anon.*] 4e éd. 139 pp. 18°. *Tours, Mame et Cie.* 1847.

Pierre de Blois. Opera omnia Petri Blesensis. Edidit J. A. Giles. 4 v. 8°. *Oxonii, J. H. Parker*, 1847.

CONTENTS.

v. 1–2. Epistolæ.
v. 3. Opuscula.
v. 4. Sermones, etc.

——— Continuatio ad historiam Ingulphi. fol. *Oxoniæ*, 1684.

[GALE (Thomas), *and* FELL (John). Rerum anglicarum scriptores veteres. *Oxoniæ*, 1684–91. v. 1].

Pierre (J. Isidore). Recherches sur la dilatation des liquides, etc. 6 v. in 1. 8°. *Paris, Bachelier, etc.* 1845–51. s.

——— Recherches sur la thermométrie. (Extract). 43 pp. 8°. *Caen, Acad. des sciences, etc.* 1851. s.

[*With* the preceding].

Piers (*Sir* Henry). A chorographical description of the county of West Meath. Written 1682. 126 pp. 1 map. 8°. *Dublin, T. Ewing*, 1774.

[VALLANCEY (C.) Collectanea de rebus hibernicis, v. 1, No. 1].

Piers Plowman, (*pseudon*). *See* **Langland** (William).

Pigoreau (Alexandre Nicolas). Catalogue des romans nouveaux, des mémoires, [etc.] des livres au rabais, qui se trouvent dans mon magazin. Appendice au 20e supplément à la bibliographie romancière. 16 pp. 8°. *Paris, Pigoreau*, 1830. s.

[*With* his Petite bibliographie, etc. Supp. 1–20].

——— Catalogue des romans nouveaux, [etc.] qui se trouvent chez Pigoreau, [etc.] 36 pp. 8°. *Paris*, 1831.

[*With* his Petite bibliographie. Supp. 1r–20e.]

——— Petite bibliographie biographico-romancière; ou, dictionnaire des romanciers. 1^r–20e supplément, 20 pts. in 1 v. 8°. *Paris, Pigoreau*, 1821–30. s.

Pigott (Charles). Political dictionary, explaining the true meaning of words, exemplified in the lives, morals, etc. of [many] illustrious persons. 198 pp. 18°. *New York, Thomas Greenleaf*, 1796.

Pike (James Shepherd). The financial crisis: its evils and their remedy. 38 pp. 8°. *New York, author*, 1867.

Pike (Joseph). An epistle to the national meeting of friends, in Dublin, concerning good order and discipline. 24 pp. 12°. *Wilmington, (Del.) James Adams*, 1783.

[*With* PENN (William). Account of the rise and progress of the people called quakers. 12°. *Wilmington*, 1783].

Pike (*Rev.* Samuel), *and* **Hayward** (*Rev.* Samuel). Religious cases of conscience answered in an evangelical manner. New ed. with introd. by H. A. Boardman. xxviii, 432 pp. 12°. *Philadelphia, Smith, English & Co.* [1859]. s.

Pike (Zebulon Montgomery). Exploratory travels through the western territories of North America, comprising a voyage from St. Louis, on the Mississippi, to the source of that river, and a journey through Louisiana and the northeastern provinces of New Spain, 1805 to 1807. xx, 436 pp. 1 map. 4°. *London, Longman, etc.* 1811.

Pikkert (H.) Le nouveau secrétaire de la cour; contenant une instruction pour se former dans le style épistolaire, etc. [*anon.*] Nouv. éd. viii, 590 pp. 16°. *Lyon, Bernuset*, 1780. s.

Piles (Roger de). The principles of painting, [with] the balance of painters. [Translated from the French]. xii, 300 pp. 4 l. 2 pl. 8°. *London, J. Osborn*, 1743.

——— The same. The art of painting, with the lives and characters of above 300 of the most eminent painters. [With] an essay towards an English school of painters, [by B. Buckeridge]. 3d ed. viii, 439 pp. 8°. *London, T. Payne*, [1754].

Pillet (René-Martin). Views of England, during a residence of ten years—six of them as a prisoner of war. Translated from the French. 296 pp. 16°. *Boston, Parmenter & Norton,* 1818.

Pim (Bedford Capperton Trevylian). The negro and Jamaica. Read before the anthropological society of London, Feb. 1, 1866. vii, 72 pp. 8°. *London, Trübner & Co.* 1866.

Pim (Jonathan). Condition and prospects of Ireland, and the evils arising from the present distribution of landed property. xxiii, 346 pp. 8°. *Dublin, Hodges & Smith,* 1848. s.

Pimentel (Francisco). Cuadro descriptivo y comparativo de las lenguas indigenas de México. 2 v. 8°. *México, Andrade y Escalante,* 1865.

——— La economia politica aplicada a la propiedad territorial en México. 267 pp. 8°. *México, J. Cumplido,* 1866. s.

——— Memoria sobre las causas que han originado la situacion actual de la raza indigena de México, y medios de remediarlo. 244 pp. 8°. *México, Andrade y Escalante,* 1864.

Pinaud (Auguste). Programme d'un cours élémentaire de physique. 5e éd. viii, 463 pp. 8 pl. 8°. *Toulouse, Bon & Privat,* 1848. s.

Pinchion *or* Pynchon (William). The Jewes synagogue; or, a treatise concerning the ancient orders and manner of worship used by the Jews in their synagogue assemblies. 4 p. l. 90 pp. sm. 4°. *London, John Bellamie,* 1652.

Pindar (Christopher Laomedon, *pseudon.*) *See* **Melpomene** divina; or, poems on christian themes.

Pinelli (Maffeo). Bibliotheca Pinelliana. A catalogue of [his] magnificent and celebrated library, of the Greek, Roman, and Italian authors, [by Giacomo Morelli], to be sold by auction, March, 1789, in London. xxviii, 538 pp. 8°. *London,* 1789.

Pinkerton (James N. *M. D.*) Sleep and its phenomena; an essay. 3 p. l. 141 pp. 16°. *London, E. Fry & son,* 1839.

Pinkerton (John). Modern geography. With an astronomical introduction by S. Vince. 2 v. clxv, 520 pp; 698 pp. 8°. *Philadelphia, John Conrad & Co.* 1804.

Pinneo (T. S.) Analytical grammar of the English language. 12°. *Cincinnati, W. B. Smith & Co.* 1850. s.

——— Exercises in false syntax: for the correction of errors in grammatical construction. 104 pp. 12°. *Cincinnati, Sargent, Wilson & Hinkle,* 1867.

Pinzon (Vicente Yañez). Navigatio. *See* **Novus** orbis. *Roterodami,* 1616.

Piola (Gabrio). Sull' applicazione de' principj della mecanica analitica del Lagrange ai principali problemi. xxvii, 252 pp. 4°. *Milano, I. r. istituto di scienze,* 1825. s.

——— Elogio di Bonaventura Cavalieri. Con note, postille matematiche, etc. xxxi, 154 pp. 1 l. 4°. *Milano, G. Bernardoni di Giovanni,* 1844. s.

Piomingo [*pseudon.*] *See* **Savage** (The). By Piomingo. *Philadelphia,* 1810.

Pirate (The) doctor; or, the extraordinary career of a New York physician. By a naval officer. [*anon.*] 126 pp. 8°. *New York, Garrett & Co,* [*about* 1850].

Piroli (Tommaso). Les monumens antiques du musée Napoléon, dessinés et gravés; avec une explication par J. G. Schweighaeuser. Publiés par F. et P. Piranesi. 4 v. 8°. *Paris, F. & P. Piranesi,* 1804–06. s.

Pisis (Raynerius de). *See* **Ranieri** *da Pisa.*

Pisko (Franz Joseph). Lehrbuch der technischen physik. *See* **Hessler** (J. F.)

Piso *or* **Le Pois**? (Willem). De aëribus, aquis et locis in Brasilia. *See* **Baerle** (Caspar). Rervm per octennivm in Brasilia gestarum historia. *Clivis,* 1660.

——— *and* **Marcgraf** de Liebstad (Georg). Historia natvralis Brasiliæ. 2 v. in 1. fol. *Lvgdvni Batavorvm, F. Hack,* 1648. s.

CONTENTS.

v. 1. Gulielmi Pisonis de medicina brasiliensi libri iv. 6 p. l. 122 pp. 1 l.
v. 2. Georgii Marcgraf de Liebstad historiæ rervm natvralivm Brasiliæ libri viii. 4 p. l. 293 pp. 3 l.

Pitcairn (Archibald, *and others*). Selecta poemata. xii, 145 pp. 4 l. 16°. *Edinburgi,* 1727.

Pitman (John). A discourse delivered at Providence, August 5, 1836, in commemoration of the first settlement of Rhode Island and Providence plantations, being the second centennial anniversary of the settlement of Providence. 72 pp. 8°. *Providence, B. Cranston & Co.* 1836.

Pitocco (Limerno, *pseudon.*) *See* **Folengo.**

Pitscottie (Robert Lindsay, *of*). *See* **Lindsay** (Robert).

Pitt (Christopher). Poetical works. 8°. *Edinburgh,* 1794.

[Anderson's Brit. poets, v. 8].

Pittilloch (Robert). Tracts, legal and historical. i. The hammer of iniquity. ii. The settling of the Scottish judicatories. iii. Oppression under colour of law. [From the editions of] 1659–89. iv, 14 pp; 10 pp; iv, 32 pp. 4°. *Edinburgh*, 1827.

Pittman (*capt.* Philip). The present state of the European settlements on the Mississippi; with a geographical description of that river. viii, 96 pp. 4 maps. 3 pl. 4°. *London, J. Nourse*, 1770.

Pittsburgh directory for 1815. 156 pp. 16°. *Pittsburgh, J. M. Riddle*, 1815.

——— and Allegheny business directory. By Isaac Harris. 105 pp. 25 l. 16°. *Pittsburgh, A. A. Anderson*, 1844.

Pius iv, *pope*. Societatis Iesv defensio adversus obtrectatores, ex testimonio et literis. 15, 9 l. 18°. *Lovanii, Rutgerus Velpius*, 1566.

Place (Conyers). Reason an inefficient guide to conduct mankind in religion. 204 pp. 12°. *London, J. Roberts*, 1735.

Plagemann (Johann Otto). Kleines handbuch der mecklenburgischen geschichte. xxxii, 428 pp. 12°. *Rostock, Adler*, 1809. s.

Plancy (J. A. S. Collin de). *See* **Collin de Plancy**.

Plantamour (Édouard). Résumé météorologique des dernières années, pour Genève et le Grand Saint Bernard, et tableaux des observations météorologiques et magnétiques faites à Genève et au Saint Bernard. 1846. [Extracts]. 135 pp. 19 l. 8°. [*Genéve*], *Archiv. sc. physiques et nat.* [*n. d.*] s.

——— Résumé météorologique de l'années 1848 [–57], pour Genève et le Grand Saint Bernard. 10 v. [in 2.] 8°. *Genève, F. Ramboz & Cie.* 1849–58.

[*With* the preceding.]

——— *and* **Hirsch** (A.) Détermination télégraphique de la différence de longitude entre les observatoires de Genève et de Neuchatel. [Extract]. 148 pp. 4 pl. 4°. *Genève, H. Georg*, 1864. s.

Plantation work the work of this generation. Written in true love to all such as are inclined to transplant themselves and families to the English plantations in America. [*anon.*] 1 p. l. 18 pp. sm. 4°. *London, Benjamin Clark*, 1682.

Plantavit de la Pause (Jean). Florilegium rabbinicum; complectens præcipuas ueterum rabbinorum sententias, versione latina et scoliis, illustratas. Cui accesserunt sexcenta Graecorum et Latinorum apofthegmata hebraice reddita. fol. *Lodove*, 1645. s.

Platea (Francesco de). Opvs restitvtionvm vsvrarvm et excomvnicationvm. 172 l. 4°. *Padve*, 1473. s.

Platform (A) of church discipline: gathered out of the word of God, and agreed upon by the elders and messengers of the churches assembled at Cambridge, in New England. [*anon.*] 70 pp. 16°. *Boston, Belcher & Armstrong*, 1808.

Platina, *or* **Piadena** (Bartolommeo de' Sacchi *called*). Liber de vita Christi ac pontificorvm omnivm. fol. [*Tarvisii*], 1485. s.

Platner (Ernst Zacharias), Bunsen (Christian Carl Josias), Gerhard (Eduard), *and others*. Beschreibung der stadt Rom. Mit beiträgen von B. G. Niebuhr, etc. 3 v. in 6. 8°. *Stuttgart, Cotta*, 1830–42. s.

Plato. Opera, [latine], a Marsilio Ficino traducta. 4 p. l. 444 l. fol. *Venetiis, B. de Choris et S. de Luero*, 1491. s.

——— Phaedon. Explanatvs et emendatvs prolegomenis et annotatione Danielis Wyttenbachii. lxii, 366 pp. 8°. *Lvgdvni Batavorvm, Haak & Honkoop*, 1810. s.

——— The republic, translated into English, with an analysis, and notes, by D. J. Vaughan, and J. Llewelyn Davies. 3d ed. xxxii, 370 pp. 18°. *London, Macmillan*, 1866.

Platt (J. C.) History of the British corn-laws. 12°. *New York*, 1845.

[*In* HUNT (Freeman). Library of commerce. v. 1. pp. 121–231].

Plautus (Marcus Accius). Seven comedies; Aulularia, Epidicus, Menæchmi, Mercator, Pseudolus, Trinummus, and Rudens. [Translated] by Rev. George Sackville Cotter. xi, 273 pp. 8°. *London, J. F. Dove*, 1827.

Plaw (John). Ferme ornée; or, rural improvements. New ed. 2 p. l. 14 pp. 38 pl. fol. *London, J. Taylor*, 1823.

Play (The) ground; or, out-door games for boys. [*anon.*] Illustrated. 120 pp. 16°. *New York, Dick & Fitzgerald*, 1866.

Playfair (William). British family antiquity; illustrative of the origin and progress of the rank, honours, and personal merit, of the nobility of the United Kingdom. 9 v. 4°. atlas. fol. *London, T. Reynolds & W. Playfair*, 1807–11. s.

CONTENTS.

v. 1–2. Peerage of England. xv, 680 pp. 24 col. pl; vii, 640, xxxvi pp.
v, 3. Peerage of Scotland. lxxiv, 811 pp.
v. 4–5. Peerage of Ireland. xxxii, 523, clii pp; 4 l. 420, cli. lxxxviii pp.
v. 6–7. Baronetage of England. xxvii, 831, cxcvi pp. 24 col. pl. 844 pp.
v. 8. Baronetage of Scotland. xl, 444, cccli, 36 pp.
v. 9. Baronetage of Ireland. lx, 437, ccx.iii, xlvii pp.

Playfair (William). The history of jacobinism. With an appendix by Peter Porcupine [W. Cobbett], containing a history of the American jacobins, commonly denominated democrats. 2 v. in 1. 385 pp; 301, xlviii pp. 8°. *Philadelphia, William Cobbett,* 1796.

Plea (A) for Urania; being a popular sketch of celestial philosophy. [*anon.*] xxxii, 387 pp. 12°. *London, Piper, Stephenson & Spence,* 1854.

Pleasant hours in foreign lands. A series of short romances. [*anon.*] 249 pp. 16°. *London, E. Lumley, about* [1850].

Pleasures (The) of human life: in a dozen dissertations on male, female, and neuter pleasures; with anecdotes. By Hilaris Benevolus & Co. [*pseudon. for* John Britton.] xvi, 223 pp. 6 pl. 16°. *London, Longmans,* 1807.

Pléiade (La). Ballades, fabliaux, nouvelles et légendes. Homère, Veda-Vyasa, Marie de France, Burger, Hoffmann, Ludwig Tieg [Tieck], Dickens, Gavarni. 332 pp. 12°. *Paris, L. Curmer,* 1842.

Plettner (*Dr.* F.) Die braunkohle in der Mark Brandenburg. 240 pp. 5 pl. 8°. *Berlin, W. Kertz,* 1852. s.

Plinius Secundus (Caius). Naturalis historiæ libri xxxvii. 322 l. fol. *Venetiis, Nicolas Jenson,* 1472.
[Imperfect: 33 l. wanting in the body of the work].

——— The same. 2 v. 48 p. l. 314 pp; 303 pp. 16°. *Venetiis, Aldus,* 1535–36. s.

——— The historie of the world; commonly called, the natvrall historie. Translated by Philemon Holland. 2 v. in 1. 28 p. l. 614 pp. 21 l; 6 l. 632 pp. 42 l. fol. *London, A. Islip,* 1634. s.

Plinius Caecilius Secundus (Caius). Epistolarvm libri decem, et panegyricvs. Ex recensione etc. Io. Matthiae Gesneri, qvibus Io. Michaelis Hevsingeri, Io. Christ. Theoph. Ernestii, suasque notas addidit Godofr, Henr. Schaefer. xc, 794 pp. 8°. *Lipsiæ, C. Fritsch,* 1805. s.

——— The same. The epistles of Pliny the younger. Translated from the original Latin, with notes. 2 v. vii, 300 pp; 268 pp. 16°. *Edinburgh, A. Donaldson,* 1767.

——— Panegyricvs liber Trajano dictvs cvm annotationibus D. Bavdii [et variorum]. 20 p. l. 427 pp. 21 l. 8°. *Lvgdvni Batavorvm, ex officina Hackiana,* 1675.

Ploennies (Luise von). Princess Ilse; a story of the Harz mountain. From the 24th German ed. by an American lady. With an introduction by J. L. Lincoln. Illustrated ed. 81 pp. 4 pl. 4°. *Boston, Gould & Lincoln,* 1867.

Pluche (Noël Antoine). The history of the heavens, considered according to the notions of the poets and philosophers, compared with the doctrines of Moses: an inquiry into the origine of idolatry. Translated from the French by J. B. De Fréval. 2d ed. 2 v. 4, 278 pp; xiii, 251 pp. 25 pl. 16°. *London. J. Osborn,* 1743.

Plumbe (John, *jr.*) Sketches of Iowa and Wisconsin, taken during a residence of three years in those territories. 101 pp. 12°. *St. Louis, Chambers, Harris & Knapp,* 1839.

Plumer (William S. *D. D.*) The rock of our salvation: a treatise respecting the natures, person, [etc.] of Jesus Christ. 519 pp. 12°. *New York, Am. tract soc.* [1867].

——— Studies of the book of psalms: a commentary, with doctrinal and practical remarks on the entire psalter. 1211 pp. 8°. *Philadelphia, J. B. Lippincott & Co.* 1867.

——— Vital godliness: a treatise on experimental and practical piety. 610 pp. 12°. *New York, Am. tract soc.* [1867].

Plumtre (*Rev.* James). Collection of songs, moral, sentimental, instructive and amusing. 3 v. 12°. *London, F. C. & J. Rivington,* 1824.

Plutarchus. Lives, from the original Greek, with notes and a new life of Plutarch. By J. and W. Langhorne. 6 v. 8°. *London, E. & C. Dilly,* 1770.

——— The same. Lives of celebrated Romans, condensed, [with an historical introduction by A. J. H.] 176 pp. 16°. *London, E. Lumley,* [1845].

——— On the delay of the deity in punishing the wicked. [Gr.] Revised ed. with notes by H. B. Hackett and W. S. Tyler. 171 pp. 12°. *New York, Appleton,* 1867.

——— De musica. Edidit Ricardus Volkmann. xxiv, 171 pp. 8°. *Lipsiae, B. G. Teubner,* 1856. s.

——— Fiori de gli apoftemmi di Plutarco.
[MANASSI, (N.) Oracoli politici. 16°. *Venetia,* 1590].

Pluvinel (Anthoine de). L' instruction dv roy en l'exercice de monter à cheval. [Avec une traduction allemande]. 3 p. l. 253 pp. 50 pl. fol. *Paris, M. Rvette,* 1629. s.

Plymouth (*Mass.*) A declaration of the warrantable grounds and proceedings of the first associates of the government of New Plymouth, [with] the general fundamentals of their laws. 24 pp. 12°. *Boston, Greenleaf,* 1773.

Plymouth (*Mass.*) First Plymouth patent: granted June 1, 1621. Edited by Charles Deane. 16 pp. 4°. *Cambridge, privately printed,* 1854.

Plymouth (*N. H.*) congregational church. Historical sketch, articles of faith and covenant, principles and rules, and catalogue of members, past and present. 44 pp. 12°. *Boston, J. E. Farwell & Co.* 1867.

Pock (Edmund). Historisch-chronologisch-geographische tabellen, von anfang der welt bis auf [1734]. 4 p. l. xii, 360 pp. 14 l. fol. *Augspurg, M. Wolff,* 1736. s.

Poems. By a collegian. [*anon.*] 95 pp. 12°. *Charlottesville, (Va.) C. P. M'Kennie,* 1833.

Poems on slavery, by Longfellow, Whittier, Southey, etc. iv, 232 pp. 16°. *London, Clarke, Beeton & Co.* 1853.

Poems and reflections by a young lady. [*anon.*] lxiii, 143 pp. 16°. *London, J. Booth,* 1815.

[*With* TAYLOR (George). Mental claims of the sexes, *London,* 1821].

Poesche (Theodore), *and* **Goepp** (Charles). The new Rome; or the United States of the world. 181 pp. 2 maps. 12°. *New York, G. P. Putnam & Co.* 1853.

Poetas castellanos anteriores al siglo xv. Coleccion hecha por T. A. Sanchez, continuada por P. J. Pidal y F. Janer. xlviii, 600 pp. 8°. *Madrid, M. Rivadeneyra,* 1864.

[Biblioteca de autores españoles. v. 57].

Poetical (A) epistle to his excellency, George Washington, from an inhabitant of the state of Maryland, [with] a short sketch of Washington's life and character. [*anon.*] 24 pp. 1 pl. 8°. *London, C. Dilly,* 1780.

Poetry (The) of Anna Matilda. [*anon.*] 4 p. l. 95 pp. 18°. *London, J. Bell,* 1788.

Poetry of the anti-jacobin. [By Gifford, Canning, Frere, and Ellis.] 4th ed. 3 p. l. 256 pp. 4°. *London, J. Wright,* 1801.

Poey (Felipe). Geografia fisica y politica de la isla de Cuba. Ed 17ª. 44 pp. 8°. *Habana, Barcina,* 1857. s.

——— Memorias sobre la historia natural de la isla de Cuba. 2 v. 463 pp; 442 pp. 53 pl. 8°. *Habana, Barcina,* 1851–58. s.

Poggendorff (Johann Christian). Lebenslinien zur geschichte der exacten wissenschaften seit wiederherstellung derselben. 20 pp. 3 pl. 4°. *Berlin,* 1853. s.

Poggiali (Gaetano Domenico). Novelle di alcuni autori fiorentini. [Ed. 2ª.] xxiii, 448 pp. 1 pl. 18°. *Milano, G. Silvestri,* 1815.

CONTENTS.

Alamanni (L.)
Bottari (G.)
Doni (A. F.)
Firenzuola (A.)
Legnajuolo (G.)
Machiavelli (N.)
Magalotti (L.)
Pulci (L.)
Salvucci (S.)

——— *See also,* **Novelle** di autori senesi.

Pohlman (J. G.) Chess, as described by Philidor. *See* **Philidor.**

Poinsett (Joel Roberts). Esposicion de la conducta politica de los Estados-Unidos, para con las nuevas republicas de America. 16 pp. 8°. *México, M. Ximeno,* 1827. s.

Pokorny (Alois). Österreichs holzpflanzen. Eine auf genaue berücksichtigung der merkmale der laubblätter gegründete floristische bearbeitung aller im österreichischen kaiserstaate bäume, sträucher, und halbsträucher. xxviii, 524 pp. 80 pl. 4°. *Wien, k. hof- und staatsdruckerei,* 1864. s.

——— Physiotypia plantarum austriacarum. *See* **Ettingshausen** (C.) *and* **Pokorny.**

Polari (Constant). Herinneringen eener reize naar Nieuw York, 1831–2. 220 pp. 8°. *Leiden, C. C. Van der Hoek,* 1833. s.

Polehampton (*Rev.* Arthur). Kangaroo land. xii, 269 pp. 1 pl. 12°. *London, R. Bentley,* 1862.

Polesi (Giacomo). Dictionnaire des idiotismes italiens-français et français-italiens. 2 v. in 1. 5 p. l. 235 pp; 300 pp. 12°. *Paris, Baudry,* 1829. s.

Polignac (Camille Armand Jules Marie de). L'union américaine après la guerre. iv, 48 pp. 8°. *Paris, Dentu,* 1866.

Political disquisitions proper for public consideration in the present state of affairs, in a letter to a noble duke. [*anon.*] 66 pp. 8°. *London, G. Kearsley,* 1763.

Political (A) and historical account of Lower Canada; with remarks on the present situation of the people, as regards manners, character, and religion. By a Canadian. [*anon.*] xvi, 275 pp. 8°. *London, W. Marsh & A. Miller,* 1830.

Pölitz (Carl Heinrich Ludwig). Die europäischen verfassungen seit dem jahre 1789 bis auf die neueste zeit. 2ᵉ auflage. 3 v. in 4. 8°. *Leipzig, F. A. Brockhaus,* 1832–33. s.

Pollard (Edward A.) Lee, and his lieutenants; comprising the early life, services, and campaigns of Gen. R. E. Lee, and his companions in arms, with a record of their campaigns and heroic deeds. 851 pp. 7 pl. 8°. *New York, E. B. Treat & Co.* 1867.

——— The lost cause: a new southern history of the war. With portraits. 752 pp. 24 pl. 8°. *New York, E. B. Treat & Co.* 1867.

——— Observations in the north; eight months in prison and on parole. 142 pp. 8°. *Richmond, E. W. Ayres,* 1865.

Polli (Giovanni). Degli effetti della sottrazione di sangue nell umano organismo. (Extract.) 200 pp. 8°. *Milano, Ann. univ. di med.* 1847. s.
[*With his* Ricerche ... sul sangue umano].

——— Dello stato della fibrina del sangue nelle infiammazione. (Extract). 50 pp. 8°. *Milano, Ann. univ. di med.* 1845. s.
[*With his* Ricerche ... sul sangue umano].

——— Di un nuovo metodo di analisi del sangue. (Extract). 32 pp. 8°. *Milano, Ann. univ. di med.* 1845. s.
[*With his* Ricerche ... sul sangue umano].

——— Ricerche ed esperimenti intorno alla formazione della cotenna nel sangue ed al suo valore sintomatico nelle malattie. (Extract). 167 pp. 8°. *Milano, Ann. univ. di med.* 1843. s.

——— Sulla quistione di esistenza della sifilide ereditaria. (Extract). 70 pp. 8°. *Milano, Ann. univ. di medicina,* 1847. s.

——— Cura delle sifilitiche; appendice. 12°. *Milano,* 1846. *See* **Dzondi** (C. H.)

Pollich (Johann Adam). Historia plantarum in palatinatu electorali sponte nascentium incepta, secundum systema sexuale digesta. 3 v. 8°. *Manheimii, C. F. Schwan,* 1776–77. s.

Pollini (Ciro). Catechismo agrario. 2ª ed. 488 pp. 8°. *Verona, Soc. tipografica,* 1821. s.

Polo (Marco). De regionibus orientalibus libri iii. Accedit Haithoni Armeni historia orientalis, quæ et de Tartaris inscribitur; itemque Andreæ Mulleri de Chataja disquisitio, inque ipsum Marcum Paulum præfatio et indices. 4 p. l. 25 pp, 8 l. 167 pp. 25 l. sm. 4°. *Coloniæ Brandenburgicæ, G. Schulz,* 1671.

Polybius. Historiarum libri quinque. Nicolaus Perottus e Græco traduxit. 74 l. fol. *Venetiis, Bernardinus,* 1498. s.
[*With* ANNIUS. Cōmentaria. fol. 1498].

——— The same. The general history, translated from the Greek by JamesHampton. ix, 11, 464 pp. 8°. *London, J. Davis,* 1811.

——— The same. Histoire nouvellement traduite du Grec, par Vincent Thuillier. Avec un commentaire, ou un corps de science militaire, etc. par M. de Folard. 6 v. 4°. *Paris, P. Gandouin, etc.* 1727–30. s.

Pomeroy (*Rev.* Benjamin). Shocks from the battery; or, sermons and sayings. With an introduction by J. T. Peck. 300 pp. 1 pl. 12°. *Albany, S. R. Gray,* 1867.

Pomfret (John). Poetical works. 8°. *Edinburgh,* 1793.
[Anderson's Brit. poets, v. 6].

Pompée (Pierre Philibert). Études sur l'éducation professionelle en France. xx, 412 pp. 16°. *Paris, Pagnerre,* 1863.

Pomponius Mela. *See* **Mela** (Pomponius).

Ponce (Nicolas), *and* **Godefroy** (M.) Recueil d'estampes représentant les différents évènemens de la guerre qui a procuré l'indépendance aux États Unis de l'Amérique. 2 maps. 14 pl. 4°. *Paris, N. Ponce et M. Godefroy,* [1784?]

Ponsin (J. N.) Nouvelle magie blanche dévoilée, physique occulte et cours complet de prestidigitation. 2 v. 312 pp; 314 pp. 8°. *Reims, A. Huet,* 1853–54.

Poole (Joshua). The English Parnassus; or, a help to English poesie. 15 p. l. 639 pp. 1 pl. 16°. *London, H. Brome,* 1677.

Poole (William Frederick). An alphabetical index to subjects treated in the reviews and other periodicals, etc. [1st ed.] 155 pp. 8°. *New York, G. P. Putnam,* 1848. s.

Poor (A) fellow. By the author of "Which: the right, or the left?" [*anon.*] 480 pp. 12°. *New York, Dick & Fitzgerald,* 1858. s.

Poor Sarah. [In Cherokee]. Uyoiyudvhnadegi seliulenitonvkanoshes-gi. [*anon.*] 18 pp. 24°. *Awu niyvsdigi walosudlawa tsuleyvtanvhi,* 1843.

Pope (Alexander). Essay on man. 49 pp. 16°. *London,* 1772.

——— Poetical works. 8°. *Edinburgh,* 1794.
[Anderson's Brit. poets, v. 8].

Pope (William). The triumphal chariot of friction; or, a familiar elucidation of the origin of magnetic attraction, etc. vii, 108 pp. 12 pl. 4°. *London, author,* 1829. s.

Popham (The) colony. A discussion of its historical claims, with a bibliography of the subject. [By W. F. Poole, and others]. 72 pp. 8°. *Boston, J. K. Wiggin & Lunt,* 1866.

Popular pastimes for field and fireside; or, amusements for young and old. By "Aunt Carrie." [*anon.*] 248 pp. 12°. *Springfield, (Mass.) M. Bradley & Co.* 1867.

Population en France et la question hydrologique. [*anon.*] 68 pp. 8°. *Paris,* 1858. s.

Porcacchi (Tomaso). Isole piv famose del mondo. 12 p. l. 201 pp. fol. *Venetia, S. Galignani & G. Porro,* 1576.
[The colophon is dated 1575].

Porcher (Francis Peyre, *M. D.*) The medical, poisonous, and dietetic properties of the cryptogamic plants of the U. S. (Extract). 126 pp. 8°. *New York, Am. medical association,* 1854. s.

Porny (Marc Antoine). Syllabaire françois; or, a French spelling book. 151 pp. 16°. *New York, D. Longworth,* 1815.

Porson (Richard). Adversaria. Notae et emendationes in poetas graecos. Ed. J. H. Monk [et] C. J. Blomfield. xvii, 334 pp. 8°. *Cantabrigiae, J. Smith,* 1812.

Porta (Giovanni Battista). La physionomie humaine.

[*With* v. 3. of ROBERT (L. J. A.) Nouvel essai sur la mégalantropogénésie. *Paris,* 1803].

Porta (Luigi). Delle malattie e delle operazioni della ghiandola tiroidea. 3 p. l. 164 pp. 4 pl. 4°. *Milano, G. Bernardoni,* 1849. s.

Portal (Placido). Intorno un ascesso al fegato guarito colla incisione. 32 pp. 8°. *Napoli, Filiatre-sebezio,* 1840. s.

——— Memorie medico-chirurgiche. v. ii. [Su gl'inconvenienti della cannula di Dupuytren per la cura della fistola lagrimale]. viii, 89 pp. 1 pl. 8°. *Napoli, presso l'osserv. med.* 1836. s.

[v. 1. wanting].

——— Storia di due casi d'allacciatura d'arterie, una alla femorale, l'altra all'iliaca esterna. 31 pp. 1 pl. 8°. *Napoli, Filiatre-sebezio,* 1839.

[*With* his Memorie medico-chirurgiche. v. 2]. S.

——— Sull' ernie osservazioni. 128 pp. 8°. *Napoli, Filiatre-sebezio,* 1842.

[*With* his Memorie medico-chirurgiche. v. 2].

——— Trattato di clinica chirurgica. 326 pp. 8°. *Trapani, P. Colajanni,* 1836. s.

[Wanting v. 2, etc.]

Porter (George Richardson). Geography of Great Britain. 8°. *London,* 1850. *See* **Long** (George), *and* **Porter**.

Porter (Jacob). Topographical description and historical sketch of Plainfield, Mass. 44 pp. 8°. *Greenfield, Prince & Rogers,* 1834.

Porter (Jane). The Scottish chiefs, a romance. 2 v. 408 pp; 410 pp. 16°. *New York, D. Longworth,* 1810.

[Imperfect; pp. 409–10 of v. 1 wanting].

——— Remarks on Sidney's aphorisms. *See* **Sidney** (*Sir* Philip).

Porter (J. G. V.) State of Ireland in 1866: its chief evils, and their best possible remedies. 2d ed. 35 pp. 8°. *Dublin, J. Chambers & son,* 1866.

Porter (*Rev.* John Leech). The giant cities of Bashan; and Syria's holy places. 377 pp. 4 pl. 12°. *New York, Nelson & sons,* 1866.

Porter (William T. *editor*). Hunting and shooting of North America, etc.

[*With* HAWKER (P.) Instructions to young sportsmen. *Phila.* 1846].

Porter (—, *M. D. of New York city*). Book of men, women, and babies. Laws of God applied to obtaining, rearing, etc. the natural, healthful, and beautiful in humanity. viii, 189 pp. 8°. *New York, Dewitt & Davenport,* 1855. s.

Porteus (Beilby, *bishop of London*). Death: a poetical essay. 4th ed. 20 pp. 16°. *Philadelphia, R. Bell,* 1773.

——— Tracts on various subjects. 6th ed. 528 pp. 8°. *London, T. Cadell,* 1836.

Portland (*Me.*) Directory for 1866–67. v. 8. By S. B. Beckett. 349 pp. 8°. [*Portland*] *B. Thurston & Co.* 1866.

Portland (The) sketch book, edited by Mrs. Ann S. Stephens. 289 pp. 12°. *Portland, Colman & Chisholm,* 1836.

Portlock (Joseph Ellison). Report on the geology of the county of Londonderry, and of parts of Tyrone and Fermanagh. xxxi, 784 pp. 54 pl. 8°. *Dublin, Stationery office,* 1843. s.

——— A rudimentary treatise on geology. vi, 182 pp. 1 pl. 12°. *London, J. Weale,* 1848. s.

Portraits of United States senators, with a biographical sketch of each. [*anon.*] 119 pp. 57 pl. 16°. *Claremont, (N. H.) Tracey, Kenney & Co.* 1856.

Portsmouth (*N. H.*) athenæum. Catalogue of books, [with] by-laws, and list of proprietors. 252 pp. 8°. *Portsmouth, (N. H.) C. W. Brewster & son,* 1862. s.

Pössnecker (W.) Die einheitliche ursache aller kräfte-erscheinungen im universum. vii, 88 pp. 8°. *München, E. H. Gummi,* 1863. s.

Postage stamp album, for the stamps of all nations. 210 pp. 4°. *Boston, Wm. H. Hill, jr. & Co.* 1865.

Postans (*Mrs.* Marianne). Cutch; or, random sketches of western India. xix, 283 pp. 1 map. 15 pl. 8°. *London, Smith, Elder & Co.* 1839. s.

Postans (Thomas). Personal observations on Sindh; the manners and customs of its inhabitants, and its productive capabilities. xv, 402 pp. 1 map. 1 pl. 8°. *London, Longman, Brown & Co.* 1843.

Post-boy (The) robb'd of his mail: or, letters of love, and miscellaneous subjects. [*anon.*] 2d ed. 2 v. in 1. xxii, 487 pp. 8°. *London, J. Sprint,* 1706.

Postel (Guillaume). Les tres-merveileuses victoires des femmes du nouveau monde. Avec la doctrine du siècle doré, ou de l'évangelike règne de Jésus. Sur l'imprimé à Paris, Jehan Ruelle, 1553. xx, 92, 27 pp. 16°. [*n. p. about* 1670].

Posthumous parodies and other pieces, composed by several of our most celebrated poets, but not published in any former edition of their works. [*anon.* By E. Dubois ?] xi, 103 pp. 8°. *London, J. Miller*, 1814.

Postlethwayt (Malachy). Great Britain's true system, to support the public credit. 4 p. l. cl, 363 pp. 8°. *London, A. Millar*, 1757.

Postscript (A) to John Bull, containing the history of the Crown-Inn, with the death of the widow. [*anon.*] 2d ed. 4 pts. in 1 v. 17, 19, 19 pp. 12°. *London, J. Moor*, [*about* 1750].
[Imperfect: 3d pt. wanting].

Pot (Le) au noir, et le pot au blanc, ou la verité dévoilée, la fourberie démasquée et la réligion papiste renversée. [*anon.*] 206 pp. 12°. *Rome*, 1787.

Pott (Johann Heinrich). Lithogéognosie; ou, examen chymique des pierres, et des terres en général, et du talc, de la topaze, et de la stéatite en particulier, avec une dissertation sur le feu, et sur la lumière. Ouvrages traduits de l'Allemand. viii, 431 pp. 1 pl. 16°. *Paris, J. T. Hérissant*, 1753. S.

——— The same. v. 2. Continuation de la lithogéognosie pyrotechnique; ou, l'on traite plus particulièrement de la connoissance des terres et des pierres, et de la manière d'en faire l'examen. [With appendix]. Table des effets des mélanges différents des terres. 72, ciii pp. 16°. *Paris, J. T. Hérissant*, 1753. S.

Potter (John). Archæologia græca; or, antiquities of Greece. New ed. 2 v. 3 p. l. 464 pp. 4 l; 5 p. l. 420 pp. 17 l. 8°. *London, G. G. & J. Robinson*, 1795. S.

Potter (Richard). An elementary treatise on mechanics. 4th ed. viii, 162 pp. 8°. *London, Walton & Maberly*, 1859. S.

——— Physical optics; or, the nature and properties of light. viii, 119 pp. 8°. *London, Walton & Maberly*, 1856. S.

Pouchet (Félix Archimède). Hétérogénie; ou, traité de la génération spontanée, basé sur de nouvelles expériences. xxxii, 672 pp. 3 pl. 8°. *Paris, J. B. Baillière*, 1859. S.

——— Histoire des sciences naturelles au moyen âge; ou, Albert le grand et son époque. v, 265 pp. 8°. *Paris, J. B. Baillière*, 1853. S.

Pouchot (*M.* ——) Memoir upon the late war in North America, between the French and English, 1755–60. Translated and edited by F. B. Hough. With notes and illustrations. 2 v. iv, 268 pp. 2 pl. 7 maps; 283 pp. 5 pl. 7 maps. 8°. *Roxbury, (Mass.) W. E. Woodward*, 1866.

Pouillet (Claude Servais Mathias). Élémens de physique expérimentale et de météorologie. 2e éd. 2 v. in 4. xi, 434 pp. 11 pl; 346 pp. 6 pl. 869 pp. 16 pl. 8°. *Paris, Béchet jeune*, 1832. S.

——— The same. 6e éd. vi, 836 pp; 852 pp. Atlas. 49 pl. 8°. *Paris, L. Hachette & Cie.* 1853. S.

——— Lehrbuch der physik und meteorologie, für deutsche verhältnisse frei bearbeitet, von Joh. Müller. 2e aufl. 2 v. x, 623 pp. 2 col. pl; 664 pp. 8°. *Braunschweig, Vieweg*, 1847. S.

——— The same. 4e aufl. 2 v. viii, 644 pp. 1 tab. 6 col. pl; 777 pp. 1 col. pl. 8°. *Braunschweig, Vieweg*, 1852. S.

Poullain de St. Foix (Germain François). Essais historiques sur Paris. 5e éd. 7 v. 16°. *Paris, Duchesne*, 1776–77.

Pousse (François). Examen des principes des alchymistes sur la pierre philosophale. [*anon.*] 10 p. l. 254 pp. 1 l. 16°. *Paris, Jollet*, 1711.

Poussin (Guillaume Tell). De la puissance américaine: origine, institutions, esprit politique, resources militaires, agricoles, commerciales et industrielles des États-Unis. 3e éd. 2 v. 492 pp; 448 pp. 8°. *Paris, Guillaumin & Cie.* 1848. S.

Powell (Thomas, *D. D.*) Human industry; or, a history of most manual arts. [*anon.*] viii, 188 pp. 16°. *London, H. Herringman*, 1661.

Power (Tyrone). The gipsy of the Abruzzo. 16 pp. 8°. [*London*, 1841].
[HAZLITT's romancist and novelist's library. v. 1].

Powers (The) of the air; or spiritualism: what it is, and what it is not. [*anon.*] 376 pp. 16°. *Dayton, (O.) United brethren pub. house*, 1867.

Pownall (Thomas). An account of the ship-temple near Dundalk, in Ireland. 10 pp. 1 pl. 8°.
[VALLANCEY (C.) Collectanea de rebus hibernicis. v. 3. No. 10].

——— The administration of the British colonies; wherein their constitutional rights and establishments are discussed and stated. 6th ed. 2 v. xv, 288 pp; xi, 308 pp. 8°. *London, J. Walter*, 1777.

Poyen de St. Sauveur (Charles). Report on magnetical experiments, etc. *See* **Husson** (H. M.)

Poynder (John). Human sacrifices in India. vii, 261 pp. 8°. *London, Hatchard & son*, 1827.

Pozzo (Andrea). Perspectivæ pictorum atque architectorum i–ii pars. 2 v. 222 pp. fol. *Augustæ Vindelicorum, J. Wolff*, 1719.

Pradt (Dominique Dufour de). Mémoires historiques sur la révolution d'Espagne. xxiv, 406 pp. 8°. *Paris, Rosa & Perronneau,* 1816.

Prætorius *or* Schultheiss? (Johann Augustin). Diascepsis juridica de philallilia connubiali. Von ehelicher gegen-liebe. 94 pp. sm. 4°. *Jenæ, Cassiter Müller,* 1579.

Prato (Catharina). Die süddeutsche küche auf ihrem gegenwärtigen standpuncte, mit berücksichtigung des thee's für anfängerinnin sowie für practische köchinnen zusammengestellt. 2e ausg. 8°. *Gratz,* 1861. s.

——— The same. 4e ausg. 4 p. l. 664 pp. 8°. *Gratz, A. Zimmermann,* 1864. s.

Pratt (*Rev.* Josiah, *and Rev.* John Henry). Memoir of Rev. Josiah Pratt. xv, 501 pp. 1 pl. 8°. *London, Seeleys,* 1849.

Pratt (Parley P.) A voice of warning; or, introduction to the faith and doctrine of the latter-day saints. 3d ed. 180 pp. 18°. *New York, J. W. Harrison,* 1842.

Pratt (Samuel Jackson). Harvest-home: consisting of supplementary gleanings, original dramas and poems, contributions of literary friends, etc. 3 v. 1 pl. 8°. *London, R. Phillips,* 1805.

Pratt (Zadock). Biography of Z. Pratt, of Prattsville, N. Y. [with] a portion of his addresses, letters, congressional reports, and speeches. xx, 506, xi pp. 8°. [*n. p. about* 1853].

Pratten (Henry). Systematic catalogue of birds of Wisconsin and Minnesota.

[*With* OWEN (D. D.) Report of a geological survey of Wisconsin, etc. 1852].

Prayer (A) book in the language of the six nations of Indians, containing the book of common-prayer of the protestant episcopal church; with forms of family and private devotion. By the Rev. Solomon Davis. 168 pp. 12°. *New York, Swords, Stanford & Co.* 1837.

Prayers and hymns for the church and the home, with selections of psalms. 122, 600 pp. 16°. *Boston, N. E. univ. pub. house,* 1865.

Prechtl (Johann Joseph). Praktische dioptrik als vollständige und gemeinfassliche anleitung zur verfertigung achromatischer fernröhre. xii, 296 pp. 4 pl. 8°. *Wien, J. G. Heubner,* 1828. s.

Précieuses (Les) qualités et propriétés de la petite poule noire, pour la découverte des trésors cachés. [*anon.*] 108 pp. 1 pl. 18°. *Paris,* 1843.

Predari (Francesco) Bibliografia enciclopedica milanese. xvi, 693 pp. 8°. *Milano, M. Carrara,* 1857.

Premunire: a ballad, relating the doughty deeds of the knight Decanus, or dean; his horse Capitulum, or chapter: and his squire, Canonicus. By D. Bird, esq. [*anon.*] 12 l. 9 pl. fol. *London, T. McLean,* 1848.

Prenties (S. W.) Narrative of a shipwreck on the island of Cape Breton, in a voyage from Quebec, 1780. iv, 115 pp. 18°. *London,* 1782.

Presbyterian church of the U. S. Constitution, adopted May 16, 1788; containing the confession of faith, the catechisms, the government and discipline, and the directory for worship. 4 p. l. 215 pp. 16°. *Philadelphia, T. Bradford,* 1789.

——— The same. 4 p. l. 215 pp. 16°. *Philadelphia, T. Bradford,* 1792.

——— Larger catechism; as received by the associate reformed church in North America. 105 pp. 18°. *Salem, Dodd & Rumsey,* 1812.

Present (The) state of the British court; or, an account of the civil and military establishment of England. To be published annually. [*anon.*] 4 p. l. 200 pp. 12°. *London, A. Bell,* 1720.

Present (The) state of the British empire in Europe, America, Africa, and Asia. [*anon.*] 3 p. l. 486 pp. 5 maps. 1 pl. 8°. *London, W. Griffin,* 1768.

Present (The) state of the controversy between the states of New York and New Hampshire on the one part, and the state of Vermont on the other. [*anon.*] 16 pp. 16°. *Hartford, (Ct.) Hudson & Goodwin,* 1782.

Present (The) state of the parties in Great Britain; particularly an inquiry into the state of the dissenters in England and the presbyterians in Scotland. [*anon.*] 4 p. l. 352 pp. 12°. *London, J. Baker,* 1712.

Present (The) state of the protestants in France. [*anon.*] 3 p. l. 31 pp. sm. 4°. *London, John Holford,* 1681.

Present (The) state of the republick of letters. [Edited by Andrew Reid]. 1728—1736. 18 v. 12°. *London, W. Innys,* 1728-36.

Pressencé (Edmond de). The Redeemer: a sketch of the history of redemption. Translated from the 2d ed. by Rev. J. H. Myers, D.D. 412 pp. 12°. *Boston, American tract soc.* [1867].

Pressler (Max Robert). Der messknecht und sein praktikum. 3e aufl. xiv, 459 pp. 1 tab. 12°. *Braunschweig, Vieweg,* 1862. s.

Prestel (M. A. F.) Das astronomische diagramm; ein instrument mittelst dessen der stand und gang einer uhr, das azimuth terrestrischer gegenstände, die mittagslinie, die abweichung der magnetnadel, der auf und untergang der gestirne bestimmt, und andere aufgaben der astronomischen geographie und nautischen astronomie, ohne rechnung gelöst werden können. xxi, 404 pp. 8°. *Braunschweig, Vieweg*, 1859. s.

——— Die periodischen und nicht periodischen veränderungen des barometerstandes, so wie die stürme und das wetter über der hannoverschen nordseeküste, als grundlage der sturm und wetter-prognose. 3 p. l. 150 pp. 2 pl. 4°. *Emden, Verfasser*, 1866. s.

Preston (Margaret J.) Beechenbrook; a rhyme of the war. 5th thousand. 106 pp. 12°. *Baltimore, Kelly & Piet*, 1867.

Preston (*Rev.* Thomas S.) The purgatorian manual; or, selection of prayers and devotions, with appropriate reflections, for the use of the members of the Purgatorian society in the diocese of New York. viii, 453 pp. 1 pl. 18°. *New York, P. O. Shea*, 1866.

Prétendu (Le) enfant supposé; ou, mémoires de la jeunesse du comte de Letaneuf. Par Mr. D. de Vaubreton. [*pseudon.*] 5 p. l. 263 pp. 24°. *La Haye, au dépens de la compagnie*, 1740.

Prevention (The) of panics; or, suggestions for an economical system of national finance in connection with the construction of public works, without subscriptions, loans, etc. By a civil engineer. [*anon.*] 3d ed. revised. 58 pp. 8°. *London, A. H. Baily & Co.* 1866.

Prévost (Florent). Mammifères.

[*With* LEFEBVRE (C. T.) Voyage en Abyssinie, v. 6].

——— *and* **Lemaire** (C. L.) Histoire naturelle des oiseaux exotiques. Avec 80 planches représentant 200 sujets peintes d'après nature par Paquet. [Avec appendice: de la chasse et de la préparation des oiseaux.] 156 pp. 80 col. pl. xii pp. 2 pl. 8°. *Paris, F. Savy*, [1864]. s.

Prévost d'Exiles (Antoine François). The life and entertaining adventures of Mr. Cleveland, natural son of Oliver Cromwell. [*anon.*] 2d ed. 3 v. 16°. *London, T. Astley*, 1741.

——— Manon Lescaut. [English translation.] 8°. *Boston*, 1845.

Preyer (William), *and* **Zirkel** (Ferdinand). Reise nach Island im sommer 1860. Mit wissenschaftlichen anhängen. viii, 499 pp. 1 pl. 1 map. 8°. *Leipzig, F. A. Brockhaus*, 1862. s.

Priapeia. Erotopægnion, sive priapeia veterum et recentiorum. [Ed. Franciscus J. Noël]. 6 p. l. vi, 188 pp. 16°. *Lutetiæ Parisiorum, C. F. Patris*, 1798.

Price (Edmund E.) The science of self-defence. A treatise on sparring and wrestling, [etc.] 130 pp. 16°. *New York, Dick & Fitzgerald*, [1867].

Price (*Capt.* Joseph). [Tracts on India politics, chiefly in connection with Warren Hastings' government.] v. 1–3. 8°. *London*, 1783.

Price (Owen). England displayed. fol. *London*, 1769. *See* **Russell** (P.), *and* **Price.**

Price (Richard, *D. D.*) Observations on the nature of civil liberty, the principles of government, and the justice and policy of the war with America; [with] State of the national debt. 5th ed. 4 p. l. 104 pp. 16°. *Charlestown, (S. C.) D. Bruce*, 1776.

——— The same. Anmerkungen über die natur der bürgerlichen freyheit, über die grundsätze regierung, und über die rechtmäszigkeit und politik des krieges mit Amerika. 108 pp. 8°. *Braunschweig, F. Waisenhaus*, 1777.

[*With* REMER (Julius August). Amerikanisches archiv. v. 1.]

Prichard (James Cowles). Researches into the physical history of mankind. 3d ed. 5 v. 8°. *London, Sherwood, Gilbert & Piper*, 1836–47. s.

CONTENTS.

v. 1. Introduction.
v. 2. African races.
v. 3. Europe.
v. 4. Asiatic nations.
v. 5. Oceanic and American races.

Prideaux (Humphrey). The old and new testament connected, in the history of the Jews and neighboring nations, from the declension of the kingdoms of Israel and Judah to the time of Christ. 2 parts in 1 v. xvi, 259 pp. 6 l; xii, 288 pp. 20 l. fol. *Dublin, A. Rhames*, 1719.

Prideaux (Matthias). An easy and compendious introdvction for reading all sorts of histories. 2d ed. 4 p. l. 351 pp. 19 l. sm. 4°. *Oxford, L. Lichfield*, 1650.

——— The same. 3d ed. with synopsis of councels, by J. Prideaux. 4°. *Oxford*, 1655. s.

Priest's (The) turf-cutting day. A historical romance. By T. C. M. [*anon.*] 82 pp. 12°. *New York, author*, 1841. s.

Priestley (Joseph, *LL. D.*) Discourses on various subjects. 385 pp. 8°. *Northumberland, (Pa.) John Binns*, 1805.

——— Experiments and observations on different kinds of air, and other branches of natural philosophy connected with the subject. 3 v. 8°. *Birmingham, T. Pearson*, 1790. s.

Primaudaye. *See* **La Primaudaye.**

Prime (Temple). Monograph of American corbiculadae. (Recent and fossil.) xi, 80 pp. 8°. *Washington, Sm. inst.* 1865.

[Smithsonian miscel. coll. v. 7].

Prince (L. Bradford). Articles of confederation *vs.* the constitution. The progress of nationality among the people and in the government. 125 pp. 12°. *New York, G. P. Putnam & son,* 1867.

Prince (*Rev.* Thomas). A chronological history of New England in the form of annals. 1602–1730. v. 1. and v. 2, no. 1–2 in 1 v. 5 p. l. xi, 20, 104, 254 pp; 64 pp. 1 l. 16°. *Boston, S. Gerrish & S. Kneeland,* 1736–[55].

[Imperfect; No. 3 of v. 2, and 9 pp. of table of subscribers wanting].

——— Some account of those English ministers, who have presided over the work of gospelizing the Indians on Martha's Vineyard and the adjacent islands. [*anon.*] 34 pp. 8°. *London, Samuel Gerrish,* 1727.

[*With* MAYHEW (*Rev.* Experience). Indian converts. *London,* 1727].

Prince (Thomas, *jr. editor*). *See* **Christian** (The) history. *Boston,* 1744.

Prince Edward island. The parliamentary reporter; or, debates and proceedings of the house of assembly, for the year 1861. D. Laird and J. D. Gordon, reporters. 137 pp. 4°. *Charlottetown, G. T. Haszard,* 1861. s.

Principles of English grammar and idiomatic sentences, in English and Maráthí. [*anon.*] 2d ed. 12°. xi, 284 pp. 12°. *Bombay, American mission press,* 1853. s.

Pringle (*Sir* John, *M. D.*) Discourse upon some late improvements of the means for preserving the health of mariners. 4°. *London,* 1784.

[*With* COOK (James). Voyage towards the south pole, etc. v. 2. pp. 365–396].

Prior (James, *R. N.*) Narrative of a voyage in the Indian seas, in the Nisus frigate, to the cape of Good Hope; isles of Bourbon, France, and Seychelles; to Madras; and the isles of Java, St. Paul, and Amsterdam, 1810–11. 112 pp. 2 maps. 1 pl. 8°. *London, Phillips,* [*about* 1815].

——— Voyage along the eastern coast of Africa, to Mosambique, Johanna, and Quiloa; to St. Helena; to Rio de Janeiro, Bahia, and Pernambuco in Brazil, in the Nisus frigate. 114, v pp. 2 maps. 1 pl. 8°. *London, Phillips and Co.* 1819.

Prior (Matthew). Poems on several occasions. 20 p. l. 506 pp. 3 l. portrait. fol. *London, J. Tonson,* 1718.

——— The same. Poetical works. 8°. *Edinburgh,* 1793.

[Anderson's Brit. poets, v. 7].

Prior (Matthew). Miscellaneous works; poems on several occasions; [with verses sent to Mr. Prior]. Copied for the press by Adrian Drift. 2d ed. x, 380, xcv pp. 1 pl. 12°. *London, A. Drift,* 1740.

Priscianus *grammaticus.* Libri omnes, etc. Rufini item de metris ionicis, et oratoriis numeris, etc. 14 p. l. 231 l. 8°. *Venitiis, Aldus,* 1527. s.

Pritchard (Andrew). Natural history of animalcules. 196 pp. 7 pl. 8°. *London, Whittaker & Co.* 1834. s.

Pritzel (Georg August). Iconum botanicorum index locupletissimus. An alphabetical register of upwards of 86,000 representations of phanerogamic plants and ferns, etc. xxxi, 1183 pp. 8°. *Berlin, F. Nicolai,* 1855. s.

Private letters from an American in England to his friends in America. [*anon.*] 163 pp. 18°. *London, J. Almon,* 1769.

Privileges (The) and practice of parliaments in England. [*anon.*] 2 p. l. 44 pp. 1 pl. sm. 4°. *London, Robert Harford,* 1680.

Probus *grammaticus.* De octo orationis membris ars minor.

[*With* EICHENFELD (J. von). Analecta grammatica. pp. 227–452. *Vindobonae,* 1837].

Probus *or* **Frommann**? (Antonius). Oratio de monarchia regni Israëlis.

[*With* HELWIG (Christoph.) Elenchi judaici, 1702].

Proceedings of the convention of congregational ministers of the commonwealth of Massachusetts, 1792. 18 pp. 4°. *Boston, S. Hall,* [1795].

Proceedings of the fifth convention of American instructors of the deaf and dumb, at Jacksonville, Ill. 1858. 376 pp. 8°. *Alton, (Ill.) Courier printing house,* 1859.

Proceedings of the fifty-sixth anniversary of the settlement of Hudson, (O.); with tables showing the longevity of the pioneer settlers. 36 pp. 8°. *Hudson, E. F. Chittenden & bro.* 1856. s.

Proceedings of the R. W. grand lodge of Pennsylvania, at Philadelphia, March 6th, 1865, A. L. 5865, in reference to the death of George Mifflin Dallas. 37 pp. 1 pl. 8°. *Philadelphia, King & Baird,* 1865. s.

Proclus *Diadochus.* Commentarius in Platonis Timaeum; græce recensebat C. E. Chr. Schneider. vi, 876 pp. 8°. *Vratislaviæ, E. Trewendt,* 1847. s.

Proeve over de middelen die tot bescherming van de zeevaart en koophandel en tot verdédiging van de binnen en buitenlandsche bezittingen der republicq in de Oost Indien en op't vaste land van América. [*anon.*] 256 pp. 8°. *Amsterdam, E. van Harrevelt,* 1783.

Profits of panics: showing how financial storms arise; who make money by them; who are the losers, and other revelations of a city man. By the author of "The bubbles of finance." [*anon*]. 108 pp. 16°. *London, S. Low, son, & Marston,* 1866.

Prognostication (A) forever, made by Erra Pater, a Jew, born in Jury, with a list of the principal fairs of England and Wales, the month, day, and place where they be kept, and the distances from one notable town to another, over all England. [*pseudon.*] 24°. *London,* [1653]?

Progress of her majesty queen Victoria and prince Albert, to Burghley house, Northamptonshire, Nov. 1844. [*anon.*] 3 p. l. 54 pp. 3 pl. 4°. *Northampton, Abel & sons,* 1844.

Pröhle (Heinrich). Feldgarben. Beiträge zur kirchengeschichte, literaturgeschichte und culturgeschichte. xix, 476 pp. 8°. *Leipzig, G. Gräbner,* 1859. S.

Pröll (Gustav). Gastein. Erfahrungen und studien aus wissenschaftlichem standpunkte. viii, 330 pp. 1 tab. 3 pl. 12°. *Wien, W. Braumüller,* 1862. S.

Prometheus in Atlantis; a prophecy of the extinction of the christian civilization. [*anon.*] 318 pp. 12°. *New York, G. W. Carleton & Co.* 1867.

Promis (Carlo). Cinque dissertazioni dell' arte dell' ingegnere e dell' artigliere in Italia, e degli scrittori di essa dal 1285 al 1560. 4°. *Torino,* 1841. S.

[*With* MARTINI (Francesco). Trattato di architettura. v. 2].

Prony (*baron* Gaspard Clair François Marie Riche de). Instruction élémentaire sur les moyens de calculer les intervalles musicaux, etc. 107, ii pp. 2 tab. 4°. *Paris, F. Didot frères,* 1832. S.

Propertius (Sextus Aurelius). Propertii monobiblos; or, that book of the elegies of Propertius, entitled Cynthia. Translated into English verse, with classical notes, by G. F. Nott? [Latin and English]. xix, 140 pp. 12°. *London, H. Payne,* 1782.

——— Élégies, traduites [en prose] par [P. de] Longchamps. [Avec le texte latin en regard.] xxiv, 610 pp. 8°. *Amsterdam, et se trouve à Paris chez Le Jay,* 1772.

Proposals to amend and perfect the policy of the government of the United States of America. [*anon.*] 36 pp. 16°. [*n. p.*] 1782.

Proteaux (A.) Practical guide for the manufacture of paper and boards. With additions, by L. S. Le Normand. Translated from the French, with notes, by H. Paine. [Also] a chapter on the manufacture of paper from wood, in the United States. By H. T. Brown. 285 pp. 6 pl. 8°. *Philadelphia, H. C. Baird,* 1866.

Protestant episcopal church in the U. S. Episcopal common praise. [A book] of psalms, hymns, [etc.] licensed for use in the protestant episcopal church, by the general convention of 1865. Set to music. 600 pp. 8°. *New York, A. S. Barnes & Co.* 1867.

Proud (Robert). The history of Pennsylvania in North America, from the original institution and settlement of that province, [etc.] in 1681, till after the year 1742; with an introduction respecting the life of William Penn, [etc.] With an appendix. 2 v. 508 pp. 1 portrait; 373, 146 pp. 1 map. 8°. *Philadelphia, Z. Poulson, jr.* 1797–98.

Prout (John Skinner). The castles and abbeys of Monmouthshire. 20 pp. 29 pl. fol. *London,* 1838.

Proverbs; or, the manual of wisdom. [With] the wise sayings, maxims, etc. of the ancients. [*anon.*] 2d ed. 2 p. l. vi, 146 pp. 18°. *London, Tabart & Co.* 1804.

Providence (*R. I.*) City documents; June, 1865, to June, 1867. 2 v. 8°. *Providence press co.* 1855–67.

——— Directory for 1866–67. 2 v. 270, 82 pp; 424 pp. 8°. *Providence, (R. I.) Sampson, Davenport & Co.* 1866–67.

Provoost (William, *and others*). Report of the committee of the council of New Jersey to Hon. Jno. Hamilton, in regard to the claims of Lewis Morris to the governorship of the province. [2 pp. of New York Gazette, Oct. 18–25, 1736. fol. *New York, W. Bradford,* 1736].

Prussia. Statistische nachrichten von den preussischen eisenbahnen. Bearbeitet von dem technischen eisenbahn-büreau, genannten ministeriums. 4 v. 4°. *Berlin, Ernst & Korn,* 1855–58. S.

Prynne (William). An exact chronological vindication and historical demonstration of the supreme ecclesiastical jurisdiction of our kings, in all matters, spiritual, as well as temporal. v. 3. 48 p. l. 1307 pp. fol. *London, Ratcliff and Daniel,* 1668.

——— The same. [2d ed.] The history of king John, king Henry iii, and king Edward i. 46 pl. 1307 pp. fol. *London, P. Chetwind,* 1670.

Prynne (William). The treachery and disloyalty of papists to their sovereignes; with the sovereigne power of parliaments and kingdomes. 2d ed. 2 p. l. 603 pp. sm. 4°. *London, M. Sparke,* 1643.

Ptolemæus (Claudius). Cosmographia. [Latine reddita a Jac. Angelo]. 144 l. unp. fol. *Vicenciæ, ab Hermano Leuilapide,* 1475.

——— The same. Geographia. Cum schematibus correctio a Marco Beneuentano et tractato de tribus orbis partibus a Ioanne Cotta. 141 l. unp. 34 maps. fol. *Rome, Evangelista Tosinus,* 1508.

——— The same. Geographie opus [cura Philesii, i. e. Matthiae Ringmann] castigatissime pressum. [Accedit J. Cottae de tribus orbis partibus tractatus]. 2 p. l. unp. 60 l. 1416 l. unp. 46 maps. fol. *Argentinæ, Io. Schott,* 1513.

——— The same. Geographiae libri viii. Quorum primus noua translatione Pirckheimheri et accessione commentarioli illustrior redditus est. Succedunt tabulæ ptolemaicæ, et compendium geographicae descriptionis opera S. Munsteri. 27 p. l. 195 pp. 54 maps. fol. *Basileæ, H. Petrus,* 1545.

——— The same. Geographiæ, libri viii, partim a B. Pirckheymero translati ac commentario illustrati. 106 p. l. 155 pp. 54 maps. fol. *Basileæ, H. Petrus,* 1552.

——— The same. Cum amplissimis ejusdem commentariis. Redacta a Ios. Moletio. 4 p. l. 112, 286 pp. 32 l. 64 maps. sm. 4°. *Venetiis, V. Valgrisius,* 1562.

——— The same. Vna cum tabularum expositionibus, quibus singulæ orbis partes, etc. describuntur. Auctore Jo. Ant. Magino. 2 v. in 1. 4 p. l. 47, 184 pp. 19 l; 292, 28 l. 63 maps. sm. fol. *Arnhemii, Jo. Janson,* 1597.

——— The same. Geografia, nuouamente tradotta di Greco in Italiano, da G. Rvscelli. 4 p. l. 358 pp. 24 l. 63 maps. sm. 4°. *Venetia, V. Valgrisi,* 1561.

——— The same. Ricorretta da G. Malombra. 39 p. l. 350 pp. 64 maps. sm. 4°. *Venetia, G. Zilletti,* 1574.

——— The same. Ricontrati et corretti da G. A. Magini. Tradotta L. Cernotti. 2 v. in 1. 2 p. l. 83 pp. 15 l. 212 l. 30 l. 64 maps. fol. *Venetia, G. Battista & G. G. Fratelli,* 1597–98.

——— The quadripartite; or, four books concerning the influences of the stars. Rendered into English, with notes, by John Whalley. [With MS. notes by J. Turton?] 2d ed. v. 219 pp. 107 blank l. 18°. *London, M. Sibly,* 1786.

Ptolemæus (Claudius). The same. The tetrabiblos; or, quadripartite. From the copy of Leo Allatius, with notes by J. Wilson. [xxviii], 224 pp. 1 pl. 16°. *London, W. Hughes,* [1828].

Public (The) spirit: a monthly magazine of choice literature. April to Sept. 1867. 8°. *Troy, (N. Y.) Le Grand Benedict,* 1867.

Publications relative to the difference of opinion between the governor and the council [of Maryland] on their respective powers. iv, 138 pp. 12°. *Annapolis, Frederick Green,* 1803.

Publisher's (The) circular and general record of British and foreign literature. Jan. to Dec. 1867. v. 30. 8°. *London, S. Low,* 1867.

Pückler-Muskau (Hermann Ludwig Heinrich von). Tour in Germany, Holland, and England, 1826–27. By a German prince. [Abridged translation. *anon.*] 2 v. xvi, 384 pp; x, 389 pp. 1 pl. 12°. *London, E. Wilson,* 1832.

——— The same. Mémoires et voyages. Lettres posthumes sur l'Angleterre, l'Irlande, la France, la Hollande, l'Allemagne, et l'Italie, traduites de l'édition allemande par J. Cohen. 6 v. in 3. 18°. *Bruxelles, J. P. Meline,* 1833–34.

Pugh (*Mrs.* Eliza Lofton). Not a hero. A novel. 131 pp. 8°. *New York, Blelock & Co.* 1867.

Pugin (Augustus). Paris and its environs, displayed in a series of two hundred picturesque views, with topographical and historical descriptions. 2 v. in 1. 100 pp. 100 pl; 102 pp. 102 pl. 4°. *London, Jennings & Chapin,* 1833.

Pugliatti (Carmelo). Cenno critico sulle opere medico-chirurgiche di Placido Portal. s.
[*With* PORTAL (P.) Memorie medico-chirurgiche, v. 2].

Pulsifer (David). Guide to Boston and vicinity. viii, 293 pp. 1 pl. 2 maps, 1 fac-sim. 16°. *Boston, A. Williams & Co.* 1867.

Pulszky (Terezia Walder), *and* **Pulszky** (Ferencz Aurelius). Memoirs of a Hungarian lady. With a historical introduction. 375 pp. 12°. *Philadelphia, Lea & Blanchard,* 1850.

Pulte (J. H. *M. D.*) Homœopathic domestic physician; containing the treatment of diseases; with popular explanations of anatomy, physiology, hygiene, and hydropathy; also, an abridged materia medica. 12°. *Cincinnati, H. W. Derby & Co.* 1850.

——— The same. 2d ed. 12°. *Cincinnati, H. W. Derby & Co.* 1851.

——— The same. 12°. *Cincinnati, H. W. Derby & Co.* 1852.

Pulte (J. H. *M. D.*) Organon der weltgeschichte. iii, 124 pp. 8°. *Cincinnati, C. F. Schmidt,* 1846. S.

Punch; or, the London charivari. July 1866, to June 1867. v. 51-52. 4°. *London, Bradbury & Evans,* 1866-67.

Punchard (George). History of congregationalism, from about A. D. 250 to the present time. 2d ed. v. 3. 12°. *New York, Hurd & Houghton,* 1867.
[Completing the work].

Purmann (Johann Georg). Sitten und meinungen der wilden in Amerika. Letzte aufl. [*anon.*] 4 v. 18°. *Wien, F. A. Schrambl,* 1790.

Puteanus (Erycius). *See* **Van der Putten** (Hendrick).

Putlitz (Gustav Heinrich G. E. zu). Forest voices. Translated from the German. C. A. Smith, editor. 102 pp. 12°. *Albany, J. Munsell,* 1866.

Putnam (Anna). Gold robin. (Kaleidoscope pictures). 237 pp. 16°. *Boston, N. E. publishing house,* 1866.

——— Kalid and Kittie. (Kaleidoscope pictures). 216 pp. 16° *Boston, N. E. publishing house,* 1866.

——— Pet circle. (Kaleidoscope pictures). 229 pp. 16°. *Boston, N. E. publishing house,* 1866.

Putnam (C. H.) Gospel by Moses, in the book of Genesis; or, the old testament unveiled. xi, 486 pp. 8°. *New York, E. H. Fletcher,* 1854.

Putten (Hendrik van der). *See* **Van der Putten.**

Putzer (*Dr.* Julius). Neuere wasserheilkunde. 256 pp. 8°. *Magdeburg, Heinrichshofen,* 1850. S.

Puydt (R. de). *See* **De Puydt.**

Pye (Henry James). Commentary on Aristotle. *See* **Aristoteles.**

——— Sketches on various subjects; moral, literary, and political. xii, 285 pp. 16°. *London, J. Bell,* 1796.

Pynchon. *See* **Pinchion.**

Pythagoras. Carmina aurea. [Græce et latine.]
[*With* NEANDER (Michael). Opus aureum. 4°. *Lipsiae,* 1777].

———The same. Les vers dorés, expliqués et traduits en vers eumolpiques français, précédes d'un discours sur l'essence et la forme de la poésie, par M. Fabre d'Olivet. 409 pp. 8°. *Paris, Treuttel & Würtz,* 1813.

Quackenbos (George P.) Illustrated school history of the United States. 460 pp. 12°. *New York, Appleton & Co.* 1857.

——— Practical arithmetic. 324 pp. 12°. *New York, D. Appleton & Co.* 1867.

Quadrado y De-Roó (Francisco de Paula). Elogio histórico del excelentisimo señor Don Antonio de Escaño. 8°. *Madrid, Real academia de la historia,* 1852. S.

Quantin (Maximilien). Dictionnaire raisonné de diplomatique chrétienne, contenant les notions nécessaires pour l'intelligence des anciens monuments manuscrits. Suivi d'un rapport au roi sur les archives départmentales, et des eléments de critique; ou, recherches des différentes causes de l'altération des textes latins, par l'abbé Morel. 1136 pp. 8°. *Paris, l'éditeur,* 1846. S.

Quarin (Joseph von). Animadversiones practicæ in diversos morbos. v, 270 pp. 8°. *Viennæ, R. Graeffer,* 1787. S.

Quarterly journal of microscopical science. Edited by E. Lankester and G. Busk. v. 7. New series. [Whole series v. 15.] 8°. *London, Churchill & sons,* 1867.

Quarterly (The) journal of science. Edited by J. Samuelson and W. Crookes. v. 4. 8°. *London, Churchill & sons,* 1867.

Quarterly (The) review. Jan'y to Oct. 1867. v. 122—123. 8°. *London, J. Murray,* 1867.

Quartier (Jacques). *See* **Cartier** (Jacques).

Quatremère (Étienne Marc). Mémoires géographiques et historiques sur l'Égypte, et sur quelques contrées voisines. Recueillis et extraits des manuscrits coptes, arabes, etc. de la bibliothèque impériale. 2 v. x, 525 pp; 532 pp. 8°. *Paris, F. Schœll,* 1811. S.

——— Observations sur quelques points de la géographie de l'Égypte, pour servir de supplément aux Mémoires, [etc.] 73 pp. 8°. *Paris, F. Schœll,* 1812. S.
[*With* his Mémoires géographiques, etc. v. 2].

——— Les Philistins. 36 l. MS.
[*With* GOBINEAU (A. de). Essai sur l'inégalité des races humaines, v. 2].

——— Introduction et notes à l'histoire des Mongols de la Perse. *See* **Reshíd-ed-dín.**

Quatremère de Quincy (Antoine Chrysostome). Histoire de la vie et des ouvrages des plus célèbres architectes du 11e siècle jusqu' à la fin du 18e, [etc.] 2 v. xii, 354 pp. 22 pl; vi, 376 pp. 25 pl. 8°. *Paris, J. Renouard,* 1830. S.

——— Monuments et ouvrages d'art antiques, restitués d'après les descriptions des écrivains grecs et latins, et accompagnés de dissertations archéologiques. 2 v. 3 p. l. viii, 160 pp. 7 pl; 4 p. l. 158 pp. 6 pl. 4°. *Paris, J. Renouard,* 1829. S.

Quatuor novissima. *See* **Leewis** (Dionysius de).

Quebec literary and historical society. Transactions. 2 v. xxxvi, 262, 73 pp; iii, 445, v pp. 2 maps. 12 pl. 8°. *Quebec*, 1829–31.

Queen's (The) closet opened. Incomparable secrets in physick, chirurgery, preserving, candying, and cookery. By W. M. [*anon.*] 5 p. l. 296 pp. 11 l. 24°. *London, N. Brooks*, 1655.

Quekett (John). A practical treatise on the use of the microscope. xxi, 464 pp. 9 pl. 8°. *London, H. Baillière*, 1848. s.

——— The same. 2d ed. xxii, 515 pp. 12 pl. 8°. *London, H. Baillière*, 1852. s.

Quenstedt (Friedrich August). Handbuch der mineralogie. viii, 728 pp. 8°. *Tübingen, H. Laupp*, 1855. s.

——— Methode der krystallographie. xvi, 412 pp. 7 pl. 8°. *Tübingen, C. F. Osiander*, 1840. s.

Quentin (Ch.) Account of Paraguay: its history, its people, and its government. From the French. 90 pp. 8°. *London, Trübner*, 1865.

Quercetanus (Joseph). *See* **Duchesne**.

Quételet (Lambert Adolphe Jacques). Histoire des sciences mathématiques et physiques chez les Belges. 479 pp. 8°. *Bruxelles, Hayez*, 1864. s.

——— Positions de physique. 2e éd. 3 v. 24°. *Bruxelles, J. B. Tircher*, 1834. s.

[Imperfect; v. 1 wanting title].

——— Sciences mathématiques et physiques chez les Belges au commencement du xixe siècle. iii, 754 pp. 8°. *Bruxelles, H. Thiry van Buggenhoudt*, 1866. s.

——— Sur le recensement de la population de Bruxelles en 1842. [Extract.] 139 pp. 1 map. 4°. *Bruxelles, Comm. cent. de statistique*, [1843]? s.

——— Sur la statistique criminelle du royaume uni de la Grand Bretagne. [Extract]. 13 pp. 4°. *Bruxelles, Comm. cent. etc.* [1844]? s.

[*With* the preceding].

——— Sur les tables de mortalité et de population. [Extract.] 24 pp. 4°. *Bruxelles, Comm. cent. etc.* [1846]? s.

[*With* the preceding].

Quevedo y Villegas (Francisco de). The pleasant history of the life and actions of Paul, the Spanish sharper. Translated by J. Stevens. 59 pp. 8°. *London*, 1841.

[HAZLITT'S romancist and novelist's lib. v. 2].

Quevedo Redivivus, *jr. pseudon. See* **Wright** (R. W.)

Quincy (Edmund). Life of Josiah Quincy, of Massachusetts. xii, 560 pp. 2 pl. 8°. *Boston, Ticknor & Fields*, 1867.

Quincy (Josiah). An address to the citizens of Boston, 17th Sept. 1830—the close of the second century from the first settlement. 68 pp. 8°. *Boston, J. H. Eastburn*, 1830.

Quincy (*Rev.* Samuel). Twenty sermons, preach'd in the parish of St. Philip, Charlestown, S. C. 12°. *Boston, John Draper*, 1750.

Quinet (Edgar). Philosophie de l'histoire de France. [Extract]. pp. 925–965. 8°.

[*With* GOBINEAU (A. de). Essai sur l'inégalité des races humaines. v. 4].

Quintana (Francisco de). The most entertaining history of Hippolyto and Aminta. Translated from the Spanish. 2 p. l. 391 pp. 18°. *London, A. Betteswort*h, 1718.

Quintette (The) orchestra; a collection of quadrilles, [etc.] arranged for two violins, clarinet, cornet, and bass. 48 pp. 4°. *Boston, O. Ditson & Co.* [1867].

Quintilianus (Marcus Fabius). Oratoriarum institutionū lib. xii, vna cū annotationibus R. Regii, G. Merulæ, et J. Badii Ascensii. 8°. cclvi l. fol. [*Parisiis*], *J. Badius Ascēsius & J. Paruus*, 1516.

——— The same. The 10th and 12th books of [his] institutions. [Latin.] With notes, by H. S. Frieze. 175 pp 12°. *New York, D. Appleton & Co.* 1865.

Quinto (Javier de). Discursos politicos sobre la legislacion y la historia del antiguo reino de Aragon. 513 pp. 8°. *Madrid, C. G. Alvarez*, 1848. s.

Quintus *Smyrnaeus*. Cointi smyrnaei Ilij excidij libri dvo, reditus Græcorum, capta Troia, liber vnvs. Expositi olim in schola ilfeldensi et editi nunc studio, [etc.] L. Rhodomanni Cherusci.

[*With* NEANDER (M.) Opus aureum, 1577].

Rabanis (J.), *and* **Lamothe** (Léonce de). Compte rendu des travaux de la commission des monuments et documents historiques et batiments civils, du département de la Gironde. 1848–49. 8°. *Paris*, 1849. s.

Racchia (P. *lieut. col. of engineers*). Précis analytique de l'art de la guerre. 6 p. l. 355 pp. 8°. *Turin, Chirio & Mina*, 1832. s.

Radakowitsch (Nikolas). Zur wärmelehre von standpunkte der emanationstheorie. xii, 371 pp. 8°. *Göttingen, Dieterichsche buchhandlung*, 1861. s.

Radde (Gustav). Reisen im süden von Ost-Siberien in den jahren 1855–1859, im auftrage der k. geographischen gesellschaft ausgeführt. 2 v. 4°. *St. Petersburg, Buchdruckerei der k. akademie der wissenschaften,* 1862–63. s.

CONTENTS.

V. 1. Die säugethierfauna. lv. 328 pp. 4 col. maps. 14 col. pl.
V. 2. Die festlands-ornis des südöstlichen Siberiens. 3 p. l. 392 pp. 15 col. pl.

——— The same. Berichte über reisen im süden von ŏ'st—Sibirien, etc. xxii, 719 pp. 2 maps. 11 pl. 8°. *St. Petersburg, Buchdruckerei der k. acad.* 1861.

Rader (Matthäus). Bavaria sancta. [v. 1.] 161 l. (60 pl.) 12 l. unp. fol. *Monaci, R. Sadler,* 1615. s.

Radevicus *or* **Radwig.** De Friderici imperatoris gestis. *See* **Otho**, *bishop of Freisingen.*

Radical (The). A monthly magazine, devoted to religion. Edited by Sidney H. Morse. Sept. 1865 to Aug. 1867. v. 1–2. 8°. *Boston, A. Williams & Co. and Adams & Co.* 1866–67.

Rafinesque-Schmalz (Constantine Samuel). American manual of the mulberry trees. 96 pp. 12°. *Philadelphia,* 1839.
[*With* his American nations, 1836].

——— The American nations: or, outlines of a national history of the ancient and modern nations of North and South America. 2 v. 260 pp; 292 pp. 12°. *Philadelphia, C. S. Rafinesque,* 1836.

——— Annals of nature; or, annual synopsis of new genera and species of animals, plants, etc. discovered in North America. 16 pp. 8°. *Lexington, (Ky.) Thomas Smith,* 1820. s
[No more published].

——— Atlantic journal, and friend of knowledge. [v. 1, nos. 1–8]. 912 pp. 8°. *Philadelphia,* [*author*], 1832–33.
[No more published].

——— Genius and spirit of the Hebrew bible. Including the biblic philosophy of celestial wisdom, religion, and theology, etc. The real ancient Obri knowledge restored. 264 pp. 12°. *Philadelphia, Eleutherium of knowledge,* 1838.
[*With* his American nations, 1836].

——— Ichthyologia ohiensis; or, natural history of the fishes inhabiting the river Ohio and its tributary streams. 8°. *Lexington, (Ky.)* 1820. s.

——— A life of travels and researches in North America and south Europe, 1802–1835. 148 pp. 12°. *Philadelphia, for the author,* 1836.
[*With* his American nations, 1836].

——— Medical flora; or, manual of the medical botany of the United States of North America. 2 v. xii, 268 pp. 99 pl. 12°. *Philadelphia, Atkinson,* 1828–30.
[Imperfect; v. 1. pp. 253–60, pl. 52 wanting].

——— Monographie des coquilles bivalves fluviatiles de la rivière Ohio. 31 pp. 4 pl. 8°. *Paris, Bibliothèque conchyliologique,* 1845. s.

——— Safe banking, including the principles of wealth. 136 pp. 12°. *Philadelphia, Divitial institution of N. A.* 1837.
[*With* his American nations, 1836].

Rafn (Carl Christian). Americas arctiske landes gamle geographie efter de nordiske oldskrifter. 48 pp. 3 maps. 8 pl. 8°. *Kjöbenhavn, S. L. Möllers,* 1845. s.

Ragazzoni. Commentarius in Ciceronis epistolas. *See* **Manuzio** (P.) *and* **Ragazzoni.**

Ragland (Thomas, *cadet*). Defence before a general court-martial, held at West-Point, in the state of New York, May, 1819. 24 pp. 8°. *Newburgh, (N. Y.) author,* 1819. s.
[*With* Exposé of facts, etc. 1819].

Ragon (F.) Histoire générale des temps modernes, depuis la prise de Constantinople par les Turcs (1453), jusqu'à la fin de la guerre d'Amérique (1783). 5e éd. 3 v. 8°. *Paris, Louis Colas,* 1845.

Railroads (The), history, and commerce of Chicago. Three articles published in the Daily democratic press. [*anon.*] 67 pp. 2 maps. 8°. *Chicago,* 1854.

Rainbow (The). 1st series originally published in the Richmond enquirer. [*anon.*] 72 pp. 8°. *Richmond, Ritchie and Worsley,* 1804.

Raleigh (*Sir* Walter). The arts of empire and mysteries of state discabinated. Published by John Milton. [2d ed.] 4 p. l. 238 pp. 18°. *London, J. Watts,* 1692.

——— The discovery of the large, rich, and bevvtiful empyre of Gviana, with a relation of the great and golden citie of Manoa [El dorado]. Performed in the year 1595. 8 p. l. 104 pp. sm. 4°. *London, Robert Robinson,* 1596.
[Title page imperfect.]

——— Judicious and select essayes and observations upon the first invention of shipping; the misery of invasive warre; the navy royal and sea-service; with his apologie for his voyage to Guiana. 5 p. l. 42 pp; 33 l. 46, 69 pp. 1 pl. 24°. *London, Humphrey Moseley,* 1650.

Ramchundra (——). A treatise on problems of maxima and minima solved by algebra. viii, 185 pp. 8 pl. 8°. *Calcutta, P. S. Drozario & Co.* 1850. s.
[With preface by Augustus De Morgan, and title-page. xxiii pp. *London, W. H. Allen & Co.* 1859].

Rám Ráz. Essay on the architecture of the Hindús. [With preface by Capt. Harkness]. xiv, 64 pp. 1 l. 48 pl. 4°. *London*, 1834.
[Oriental translation fund publications].

Rambles in Italy, 1816–17. By an American. [Theodore Lyman. *anon.*] 371 pp. 2 l. 8°. *Baltimore, N. G. Maxwell*, 1818.

Ramée (Daniel). Texte descriptif. *See* **Pfnor** (Rodolphe). Monographie du chateau de Heidelberg.

——— Introduction. Le moyen âge monumental. *See* **Chapuy** (N. M. J.) *and* **Ramée.**

Ramel, (*général* Jean Pierre). Relation de la déportation à Cayenne des citoyens Barthélemy, Pichegru, Willot, La Rue, etc. Contenant plusieurs faits relatifs au voyage, séjour et évasion de quelques-uns des déportés. 271 pp. 8°. *Hambourg*, 1799.

Ramière (*Rev.* H. *S. J.*) Apostleship (The) of prayer. Translated from the French. 393 pp. 12°. *Baltimore, J. Murphy & Co.* 1866.

Ramirez (José F.) Memorias, negociaciones y documentos para servir a la historia de las diferencias que han suscitado entre Mexico y los Estados Unidos. xiii, 944, xv pp. 8°. *Mexico, I. Cumplido*, 1853. s.

——— The same. Noticias históricas y estadisticas de Durango, (1849–1850.) 87 pp. 3 pl. 8°. *Mexico, I. Cumplido*, 1851. s.

Ramler (Carl Wilhelm). Lyrische blühmenlese. 2 v. xvi, 444 pp; xxxii, 404 pp. 6 l. 12°. *Leipzig, Weidmanns erben & Reich*, 1774. s.

Rammelsberg (Carl Friedrich). Handbuch der mineralchemie. lxx, 1,038 pp. 8°. *Leipzig, W. Engelmann*, 1860. s.

Ramon del Moral (Thomas). Curso elemental de geodesia. 240 pp. 6 pl. 8°. *México, V. G. Torres*, 1852. s.

Ramond de Carbonnières (*baron* Louis François Elisabeth). Mémoires sur le formule barométrique de la Mécanique céleste, et les dispositions de l'atmosphère qui en modifient les propriétés. xii, 275 pp. 4°. *Clermont-Ferrand, Landriot*, 1811. s.

Ramos de Arispe (Miguel). Memorial on the natural, political, and civil state of the province of Cohauila, Mexico, and those of the new kingdom of Leon, New Santander, and Texas, [etc.] Tran. from the Spanish. 47 pp. 8°. *Philadelphia, J. Melish*, 1814. s.

Ramsay *abbey.* Historia ramesiensis, sive liber de fundatione et benefactoribus coenobii ramesiensis. [*anon.*] fol. *Oxoniæ*, 1691.
[GALE (Thomas), and FELL (John). Rerum anglicarum scriptores veteres. *Oxoniæ*, 1684–91. v. 3].

Ramsay (André Michel). History of Henri de la Tour d'Auvergne, viscount de Turenne, marshal general of France. 2 v. 4 p. l. 496 pp. 5 l; 516 pp. 2 l. 8°. *London, J. Bettenham*, 1735.

Ramsbotham (Francis H.) Principles and practice of obstetric medicine and surgery, in reference to the process of parturition. New Am. ed. revised by the author, with notes and additions by William V. Keating. 648 pp. 64 pl. 8°. *Philadelphia, Blanchard & Lea*, 1855. s.
[Imperfect: pl. 12 wanting].

Rand (Edward Sprague, *jr.*) Garden flowers: how to cultivate them. 384 pp. 12°. *Boston, J. E. Tilton & Co.* 1866.

Rand (*Rev.* William). The late religious commotions in New England considered: an answer to Rev. Jonathan Edwards' sermon entitled, The distinguishing marks of a work of the spirit of God. With an examination of Rev. William Cooper's preface to Mr. Edwards's sermon. [*anon.*] 8°. *Boston, T. Fleet*, 1743.

Randall (Samuel S.) The common school system of the state of New York, etc. 408 pp. 8°. *Troy, (N. Y.) Johnson & Davis*, 1851. s.

——— Sheep husbandry in the south. 320 pp. 8°. *Philadelphia, J. S. Skinner & son*, 1848.

Randolph (Edmund). Letter on the federal constitution, October 16, 1787. 16 pp. 16°. [*n. p. about* 1787].

Randolph (John, *bishop of London*). Enchiridion theologicum; or, a manual for the use of students in divinity. 3d ed. 2 v. viii, 488 pp; 512 pp. 8°. *Oxford*, 1825.

CONTENTS.

v. 1. Catechism of Edward vi.
RIDLEY (Nicholas). Protestatio.
——— Treatise against transubstantiation.
JEWEL (John). Apollogia ecclesiæ anglicanæ.
NOWELL (Alexander). Catechismus.
TAYLOR (Jeremy). Advice to his clergy.
PEARSON (John). Annales paulini.
STILLINGFLEET (Edward). Mysteries of the christian faith.
——— Doctrine of the trinity and transubstantiation compared.
GASTREL (Francis). Considerations on the trinity.
v. 2. CONYBEARE (John). Discourse on miracles.
——— Scripture mysteries.
——— Subscription to articles of religion.
——— Expediency of a divine revelation.
——— Scripture difficulties.
GIBSON (Edmund). Pastoral letters.
LESLIE (Charles). Short and easy method with the deists.
BENTLEY (Richard). Remarks on free-thinking.

Randolph (P. B. *M. D.*) The rosicrucian's story: the wonderful things that happened to Mr. Thomas W. and his wife. 106 pp. 18°. *New York, S. Tousey*, 1863.

Rang (Sander). Manuel de l'histoire naturelle des mollusques et de leurs coquilles. iv, 390 pp. 8 pl. 1 chart. 18°. *Paris, Roret,* 1829. s

Rangabé (Alexander Riso). Greece: her progress and present position. From the French, [by C. K. Tuckerman], with an introduction. 102 pp. 4°. *New York, G. P. Putnam & son,* 1867.

Ranieri da Pisa. Pantheologia. Jacobi Florentini prefatio. 2 v. 431 l; 415 l. fol. [*Basileæ, Bertholdus, about* 1485.] s.

Ranke (Leopold von). Deutsche geschichte im zeitalter der reformation. [1486—1535.] 3 v. 8°. *Berlin, Duncker & Humblot,* 1839–40. s.

——— Französische geschichte, vornehmlich im sechzehnten und siebzehnten jahrhundert. 2^e^ aufl. 5 v. 8°. *Stuttgart, J. G. Cotta,* 1856–62. s.

Rankine (William John Macquorn). A manual of the steam engine and other prime movers. 3d ed. xxxii, 575 pp. 12°. *London, C. Griffin & Co.* 1866.

Ranking (John). Historical researches on the wars and sports of the Mongols and Romans; in which elephants and wild beasts were employed or slain. xv, 516 pp. 1 map. 10 pl. 4°. *London, Longman, Rees & Co.* 1826.

Ranking (W. H.), *and* **Radcliffe** (C. B.) *See* **Half-yearly** abstract of the medical sciences.

Raphael. [*pseudon.*] *See* **Palmer** (J.)

Rapin (René). Of gardens; a Latin poem Englished by Mr. Gardner. 19 p. l. 195 pp. 5 pl. 12°. *London, B. Lintott,* 1706.

Rapin de Thoyras (Paul). Acta regia; being the account of the history of England, grounded upon Rymer's Foedera. Containing a relation of the treaties, negotiations, battles. etc. [Transl. by S. Whatley]. 828 pp. 15. l. fol. *London, J. & P. Knapton,* 1732.

Rapport des commissaires pour explorer le Saguenay. [By Andrew and D. Stuart]. 197 pp. 4 pl. 12°. *Quebec, Neilson & Cowan,* 1829.

Raschid Eldin. *See* **Reshíd-ed-dín.**

Rates (The) of his majesties customes. 3 p. l. 104 pp. 24°. *Edinburgh, Anderson,* 1670.

Rathgeber (Georg). Annalen der niederländischen malerei, formschneide- und kupferstecherkunst. 2 v. in 1. 2 p. l. x, 444; 228 pp. fol. *Gotha, J. G. Müller,* 1844. s.

Rathke (Heinrich, *of Königsberg*). Entwicklungsgeschichte der wirbelthiere. Mit eine vorwort von A. Kölliker. viii, 201 pp. 8°. *Leipzig, W. Engelmann,* 1861. s.

——— Ueber die entwickelung der schildkröten. xvi, 268 pp. 10 pl. 4°. *Braunschweig, F. Vieweg & sohn,* 1848. s.

Raucourt (*Col.*) A manual of lithography; or, memoir on the lithographical experiments made in Paris, at the royal school of the roads and bridges. Translated from the French, by C. Hullmandel. 2d ed. xix, 138 pp. 2 pl. 8°. *London, Rodwell & Martin,* 1821. s.

Raulin (Victor), *and* **Leymerie** (Al.) Statistique géologique du département de l'Yonne. Statistique générale. Avec la carte géologique du département. xvi, 863 pp. 1 map. pl. 3–4. 8°. *Auxerre, Perriquet & Rouillé,* 1858. s.

——— Précis pour M. V. Raulin contre M. A. Leymerie, au sujet de la statistique géologique. 23 pp. 8°. *Bordeaux, G. Gounouilhon,* [1858]. s.
[*With* the preceding].

——— M. Raulin contre M. Leymerie, etc. 8 pp. 8°. *Bordeaux, G. Gounouilhon,* [1858]. s.
[*With* the preceding].

Raumer (Carl Georg von). Geschichte der pädagogik vom wiederaufbluhen klassischer studien bis auf unsere zeit. 2^e^ aufl. 4 v. in 5. 8°. *Stuttgart, S. G. Liesching,* 1846–54. s.

Raumer (Friedrich Ludwig Georg von). England im jahre 1835. 2 v. xiv, 599 pp; x, 547 pp. 12°. *Leipzig, F. A. Brockhaus,* 1836. s.

——— Über die geschichtliche entwickelung der begriffe von recht, staat und politik. 2^e^ auflage. 8°. *Leipzig, Brockhaus,* 1832. s.

Ravanel (Pierre). Bibliotheca sacra; sev, thesavrvs scripturæ. 2 v. 11 p. l. 1404 pp; 1544 pp. fol. *Genevæ, P. Chouët,* 1660.

——— The same. Additamenta nova. 2 pts. in 1 v. 3 p. l. 459 pp; 372 pp. 16 l. fol. *Genevæ, P. Chouët,* 1663.

Ravelin (Humphrey, *pseudon.*) *See* **Lucubrations,** etc.

Ravignan (Gustave François Xavier Delacroix de). Clément xiii et Clément xiv. v, 574 pp. 8°. *Paris, Julien, Lanier & Cie.* 1854. s.

Ravisius Textor (Joannes). *See* **Tixier de Ravisi** (Jean).

Ravoth (Friedrich W.) Grundriss der akiurgie, nebst einem anhang von 15 tafeln instrumenten-abbildungen. Als 4e aufl. von Schlemm's operations-uebungen am cadaver. xii, 401 pp. 16 pl. 8°. *Leipzig, Veit & Co.* 1860. s.

Rawleigh redivivus; or, the life and death of Anthony [Ashley Cooper], late [1st] earl of Shaftesbury. By Philanax Misopappas. [S. N. *pseudon.*] 8 p. l. 136 pp. 1 pl. 12°. *London, T. Malthus,* 1683.

Rawlings (Thomas). What shall we do with the Hudson's Bay territory? Colonize the "Fertile Belt," which contains forty millions of acres. 83 pp. 8°. *London, A. H. Baily & Co.* 1866.

Rawson (*Rev.* Grindal, *of Mendon*), *and* **Danforth**, (*Rev.* Samuel). Visit to the several plantations of Indians in the province of Massachusetts bay.

With NOYES (*Rev.* Nicholas). New England's duty. pp. 89–99. 1697].

——— *See* **Wunnamptamoe** sampooaonk, etc.

Rawson (Rawson W.) Report on the Bahamas, for 1864. 120 pp. pp. 8°. *London, stationery office*, 1866. s.

Rawson (*Sir* William). Present operations and future prospects of the Mexican mine association. 83 pp. 8°. *London, J. Hatchard & son, etc.* 1825.

Ray (Alexander). List of officers of the continental army who served to the end of the war; also, officers killed in battle or who died in the service. 44 pp. 8°. *Washington, J. & G. S. Gideon*, 1849.

Ray (John). Methodus plantarum nova, brevitatis et perspicuitatis causa synoptice in tabulis exhibita, etc. 11 p. l. 166 pp. 17 l. 16°. *Londini, H. Faithorne & J. Kersey*, 1682. s.

——— Synopsis methodica animalium quadrupedum et serpentini generis. 8 p. l. 366 pp. 4 l. 1 pl. 8°. *Londini, S. Smith & B. Walford*, 1693. s.

——— L'histoire naturelle; l'ornithologie. Traduite du Latin de Ray, augmentée d'un grand nombre de descriptions, etc. par M. [François] Salerne. 7 p. l. 464 pp. 31 pl. fol. *Paris, Debure*, 1767. s.

Ray (John Mead, *D. D.*) Synopsis; or, a comprehensive view of philosophical, political, and theological systems, from the creation to the present time. New ed. 320 pp. 8°. [*n. p. about* 1792].

Ray (William). Poems, on various subjects, religious, moral, sentimental, and humorous. [With] a sketch of the author's life, by himself. 254 pp. 12°. *Auburn, U. F. Doubleday*, 1821.

Raymond (Henry Augustus). *pseudon.* for *Mrs.* Sarah Scott. The history of Gustavus Ericson [Gustavus Vasa], king of Sweden. With an introductory history of Sweden, from the middle of the twelfth century. xiv p. l. 401 pp. 8°. *London, A. Millar*, 1761.

Raynal (Guillaume Thomas François). Philosophical and political history of the British settlements and trade in North America. From the French. 2 v. 16°. *Edinburgh*, 1776.

Read (Harriette Fanning). The haunted student. A romance of the fourteenth century. 396 pp. 12°. *Washington, author*, 1860.

Read (Jesse). A concise history of the Kehukee Baptist association. *See* **Burkitt** (L.) *and* **Read**.

Read (J. A. *and* D. F.) Journey to the gold diggins, by Jeremiah Saddlebags. obl. 18°. *New York, Stringer & Townsend*, 1849.

Read (John Meredith, *jr.*) Historical inquiry concerning Henry Hudson, his friends, relatives, and early life; his connection with the Muscovy company and discovery of Delaware bay. 209 pp. 8°. *Albany, J. Munsell*, 1866.

Reade (Charles). The eighth commandment. 379 pp. 8°. *London, Trübner*, 1860.

Ready (The) reckoner; or, trader's useful assistant. [*anon.*] 191 pp. 18°. *York, (Pa.) M. Carey*, 1798.

Real (The) advantages which ministers and people may enjoy, especially in the colonies, by conforming to the church of England. [*anon.*] 47 pp. 12°. [*n. p.*] 1762.

Reasons for adhering to our platform, as a rule of church-government, and objections against ruling elders answered. [*anon.*] 10 pp. 8°. *Boston, T. Fleet*, 1734.

[*With* WILLIAMS (*Rev.* John). Redeemed captive. *Boston*, 1734].

Réaumur (Réne Antoine Ferchault de). Mémoires pour servir à l'histoire des insectes. 6 v. in 12. 18°. *Amsterdam, P. Mortier*, 1737–48. s.

——— The art of hatching and bringing up domestic fowls of all kinds, at any time of the year, either by means of the heat of hot-beds, or that of common fire. Translated from the French. viii, 470 pp. 15 pl. 8°. *London, C. Davis*, 1750.

——— The natural history of bees. Translated from the French [of v. 5 of his "Mémoires pour servir à l'histoire des insectes"]. 7 p. l. 452 pp. 8 l. 12 pl. 8°. *London, J. & P. Knapton*, 1744.

Rebel brag and British bluster. By Owlsglass. [*pseudon.*] 111 pp. 12°. *New York, Amer. news co.* 1865.

Rebellion and opposition; or, the American war. [*anon.*] 2 p. l. 48 pp. sm. 4°. *London, S. Bladon*, 1780.

Rebellion (The) record; a diary of American events. Edited by Frank Moore. v. 10. 8°. *New York, D. Van Nostrand*, 1867.

Récamier (Jeanne Françoise Julie Adélaïde Bernard). Memoirs and correspondence. Translated from the French [of mad. Lenormant], and edited by Isaphene M. Luyster. 16°. *Boston, Roberts bros.* 1867.

Recchi (Nardo Antonio). Nova plantarvm historia. *See* **Hernandez** (F.)

Recollections of Rugby, by an old Rugbæan. [R. N. Hutton. *anon.*] 180 pp. 1 pl. 16°. *Cirencester, Hamilton & Adams,* 1848.

Recueil et abbrégé de tous les voyages, qui ont esté faicts devers le destroit de Magallanes. [*anon.*] pp. 179–195.

[*With* HERRERA (A. de). Description des Indes Occidentales. fol. *Amsterdam,* 1622].

——— The same. [Brevis narratio omnium, quae per fretvm magellanicvm institutae sunt, navigationum.] l. 76–83. fol.

[*With* HERRERA (A. de). Novvs orbis, sive descriptio Indiae Occidentalis. fol. *Amstelodami,* 1622].

Recueil de pièces sur la négociation entre la Nouvelle France et la Nouvelle Angleterre, ès années 1648 et suivantes. [*anon.*] 62 pp. 12°. *Nouvelle York, J. M. Shea,* 1866. S.

Reden (Friedrich Wilhelm von). Allgemeine vergleichende finanz-statistik. 2 v. in 3. 8°. *Darmstadt, C. Jonghaus,* 1851–56. S.

——— Allgemeine vergleichende handels-und gewerbs-geographie und statistik. xx, 608 pp. 8°. *Berlin, T. C. F. Enslin,* 1844. S.

[Imperfect: pp. wanting at close].

——— Erwerbs-und verkehrs-statistik des königstaats Preussen. 1 v. in 3. 8°. *Darmstadt, Jonghaus,* 1853–54. S.

——— Ost Europa. Kampf-gebiet und siegespreis in geschichtlich-statistischer darstellung. 8°. *Frankfurt am M., K. T. Völcker,* 1854–56. S.

CONTENTS.

Erste abth. Russlands kraft-elemente und einfluss mittel. viii, 383 pp.
Zweite abth. Die Türkei und Griechenland in ihrer entwicklungs-fähigkeit. viii, 369 pp.

Redfield (David A.), *and* **Campbell** (John D.) [Monthly] American railway register, [for] July 1867; containing alphabetical list of railway stations on the American continent. 168 pp. 16°. *Indianapolis, Redfield & Campbell,* 1867.

Redfield (William C.) Observations in relation to cyclones of the western Pacific. [Extract.] pp. 335–359. 1 map. 4°. [*n. p.* 1856].

[From Perry's Japan expedition, v. 2].

——— Observations on the hurricanes, etc. of the West Indies and the coast of the U. S.

[*With* BLUNT, (George W.) Way to avoid violent gales. *New York,* 1866].

Redwood (Theophilus). Practical pharmacy. *See* **Mohr** (F.) *and* **Redwood.**

Reech (F.) Théorie générale des effets dynamiques de la chaleur. [Extract.] 4°. *Paris,* 1854. S.

Reed (Isaac). Bibliotheca reediana. A catalogue of the library of the late I. Reed, [etc.] which will be sold by auction, Nov. 2, 1807. xii, 405 pp. 8°. *London,* 1807. S.

Reed (John). An explanation of the map of the city and liberties of Philadelphia. 24 pp. 4 l. 23 pp. 4 l. 4°. *Philadelphia, N. Brooks,* 1774.

Reed (Sampson). Lecture on Swedenborg. *See* **Hobart** (Nathaniel). Life of Swedenborg.

Reed (William B.) President Reed of Pennsylvania: a reply to George Bancroft and others. 132 pp. 8°. *Philadelphia, H. Challen,* 1867.

——— *and* **Hamilton** (John Church). President Joseph Reed of Pennsylvania: a correspondence. 29 pp. 8°. *Morrisania, (N. Y.)* 1867.

Rees (Abraham, *D. D. editor*). The cyclopædia; or, universal dictionary of arts, sciences, and literature. 1st Am. ed. revised, [etc.] by several literary and scientific characters. Text, 41 v. plates, 6 v. 4°. *Philadelphia, S. F. Bradford, etc.* [1806, etc.] S.

Reese (David Meredith, *M. D.*) Humbugs of New York; being a remonstrance against popular delusion. 267 pp. 12°. *New York, John S. Taylor,* 1838.

Reeve (Clara). The progress of romance, through times, countries, and manners. 2 v. in 1. 144, 136 pp. 12°. *Colchester, W. Keymer,* 1785.

Reeve (Lovell Augustus). Conchologia iconica; or, illustrations of the shells of molluscous animals. [105 v. in 9.] v. 7–15. 4°. *London, L. Reeve,* 1854–66.

Reeve (Thomas, *D. D.*) God's plea for Nineveh; or, London's precedent for mercy. 10 p. l. 341 pp. sm. fol. *London, printed by W. Wilson, for the author,* 1657.

Reeve (William). A dictionary, English and Carnatàca. 1204 pp. 4°. *Madras, college press,* 1824. S.

Reeves (John, *F. R. S.*) History of the government of the island of Newfoundland, with an appendix, containing the acts of parliament made respecting the trade and fishery. 3 p. l. 167, cxvi pp. 8°. *London, J. Sewell and others,* 1793.

Reflections upon the present state of affairs at home and abroad, particularly with regard to subsidies, and the differences between Great Britain and France. In a letter from a member of parliament to a constituent. [*anon.*] 60 pp. 12°. *London, J. Payne,* 1755.

Regimen sanitatis salernitanū necnō a mgrē Arnoldi di Nouavilla expositu. [*anon.*] 134 l. 4°. *Louanii, Johannes de Westphalia,* [*n. d.*] [*probably* 1482].

——— The same. Regimen sanitatis cum expositiōe magistri Arnaldi de Villanoua. 61 l. 4°. *Argeñ.* m. cccc. xci.

——— The same. Regimen sanitatis salernitanū. a Arnaldo de Villanoua expositū. Nouiter correctū ac emēdatū. 80 l. sm. 4°. *Argentorati,* 1491.

NOTE.—Though this celebrated treatise upon the "Regimen" is ascribed to Arnoldi di Villanuova by many authorities, in numerous editions and versions, and is included in his collected works, Tiraboschi claims it for "a certain Magnino, of Milan."

——— The same. Regimen sanitatis salernitanum. A poem. With an ancient translation, and an introduction and notes, by Sir Alexander Croke. xix, 199 pp. 12°. *Oxford, D. A. Talboys,* 1830.

Register (Seeley, *pseudon.*) *See* **Victor** (Metta Victoria Fuller).

Registres des baptesmes et sepultures qui se sont faits au Fort Duquesne, 1753–56. 12°. *Nouvelle York, J. M. Shea,* 1859. S.

Registro yucateco. Periodico literario, redactado por una sociedad de amigos. 3 v. 8°. *Merida,* (*Yucatan*), 1845–46.

Règles et constitutions de l institut des frères des écoles chrétiennes, approuvées par le pape Benoit. xiii, xvi, 132 pp. 1 portrait. 4°. *Paris, Poussielgue,* 1835. S.

Regnault (Henri Victor). Cours élémentaire de chimie. 2e éd. 4 v. 16°. *Paris, V. Masson,* [1850]? S.

[v. iv wanting].

——— Kurzes lehrbuch der anorganischen chemie, theilweise nach V. Regnault, selbständig bearbeitet von Adolph Strecker. 3e aufl. xxvii, 783 pp. 12°. *Braunschweig, Vieweg,* 1853. S.

——— **Morin** (Arthur Jules), *and* **Brix** (A.) Rapport sur les comparaisons qui ont été faites à Paris en 1859–60, de plusieurs kilogrammes en platine et en laiton, avec le kilogramme prototype en platine des archives impériales. Études sur les diverses circonstances qui peuvent influer sur l'exactitude des pesées. 85 pp. 1 pl. 4°. *Berlin, G. Hickethier,* 1861 S.

Regnault (Jules). Calcul des chances, et philosophie de la bourse. 2 p. l. 215 pp. 8°. *Paris, Mallet-Bachelier,* 1863.

Regnault-Warin (Jean Baptiste Joseph Innocent Philadelphe). Mémoires pour servir à la vie du général La Fayette, et à l'histoire de l'assemblée constituante. 2 v. 391 pp; 164 pp. 8°. *Paris, Hesse et Cie.* 1824.

Reichenbach (Anton Benedict). Der käferfreund. Anleitung die käfer zu sammeln und zu bestimmen, nebst aufzählung und beschreibung der bekanntesten europäischen, vorzüglich deutschen arten. xv, 244 pp. 12 col. pl. 8°. *Leipzig, T. Thomas,* [1857]. S.

Reichenbach (Carl von). Physikalisch-physiologische untersuchungen über die dynamide des magnetismus, der elektricität, der wärme, des lichtes, der krystallisation, des chemismus in ihren beziehungen zur lebens kraft. 2e aufl. xiv, 218 pp. 2 pl; vi, 240 pp. 1 pl. 8°. *Braunschweig, Vieweg,* 1850. S.

Reichenbach (Heinrich Gottlieb Ludwig). Anatomia mammalium. Pars i. Cetacea et pachydermata. Anatomie der säugethiere. 1e theil. Wallthiere und dickhäuter. 2 p l. 23 pp. 65 pl. 8°. *Lipsiae, F. Hofmeister,* 1845. S.

——— Avium systema naturale. Das naturliche system der vögel, [etc.] Vorläufer einer iconographie der arten der vögel aller welttheile, [etc.] Ornithologie méthodique; ou, exposé des genres des oiseaux de toutes les parties du monde, etc. Prodrome d'une iconographie des espèces des oiseaux, ou synopsis avium, etc. 2 v. viii, 36, xxx; xxxi, pp. 1 pp. atlas. 100 pl. 8°. *Dresden, etc. Expédition, etc.* 1850. S.

——— The same. 2 v; atlas. 4°.

——— Trochilinarum enumeratio ex affinitate naturali reciproca primum ducta provisoria. Ed. post illam Cabanisii 2a emendata. 12 pp. 8°. *Lipsiae, F. Hofmeister,* 1855. S.

[*With* REICHENBACH. Die vollständigste naturgeschichte. Die Vögel. v. 4. Trochilinae].

——— Vegetationsverhältnisse innerhalb der grenzen der flora von Sachsen; eigenthümlichkeiten der vegetation einzelner districte. S.

[*With* GEINITZ (H. B.) Gäa von Sachsen].

——— Die vollständigste naturgeschichte des in- und- auslandes. Die säugethiere. 8°. *Dresden und Leipzig, Expedition der vollständigsten naturgeschichte,* 1846, *etc.* S.

CONTENTS.

v. 1. Wallthiere; cetacea. v, 172 pp. 1846.
v. 2. Hufthiere. Abth. 1. Pachydermen und schweinsartige. 64 pp. 21 pl. [24–44].
v. 3. Wiederkäuer. 1. Hirsche, giraffen, antilopen u. s. w. vi, 166 pp. 51 pl.

[Wanting of v. 1, Wallthiere, plates (25); all of ovina et caprina, plates (22); all of v. 4 (Ferae).

Reichenbach (Heinrich Gottlieb Ludwig). Die vollständigste naturgeschichte. Die vögel. 4 v. in 10. 8° and 4°. *Dresden, etc. Expedition, etc.* 1847–54. S.

CONTENTS.

v. 1. Schwimmvögel; aves natatores. 113 col. pl. [1–111 c.]
v. 2. Sumpfvögel; aves grallatores. 75 col. pl. [112–186.]
v. 3. Rallen, taubenvögel und hühnervögel, wasserhühner u. rallen;—fulicariae et rallariae. 34 col. pl. [187–219].
Tauben und taubenartigen vögel; columbariae. 65 col. pl. [220–277.].
Hühnervögel; aves gallinaceae. 112 col. pl. [281–390.] v. 4 in 6. Baumvögel. 6 v. viz.
v. 4. Baumvögel. 1. Alcedinae, 44 or 41 col. pl. [391–430.] 2. Meropinae. 67 col. pl. [431–506.]
3. Scansoriae sittinae. 43 col. pl. 4. Certhinae. 62 col. pl. [507–615.]
5. Picinae. 66 col. pl. [616–681.] 6. Trochilinae. 176 col. pl. [679–855.]

——— [The same. Text]. Handbuch der speciellen ornithologie. Beschreibender text zu der vollständigsten kupfersammlung der vögel aller welttheile. 434 pp. 8°. *Dresden, etc. Expedition, etc.* 1851[–54]. S.

CONTENTS.

Alcedineae; meropinae; scansoriae (a. sittinae; b. tenuirostres [except trochilinae]; c. picinae).

——— [The same]. Die vollständigste naturgeschichte der tauben und taubenartigen vögel: wallnister, erdtauben, baumtauben, hocco's. Columbariæ; megapodinæ, peristerinæ, columbinæ, alectorinæ. 2 p. l. 162 pp. 8°. Atlas, 65 col. pl. 4°. *Dresden, etc. Expedition, etc.* [1851]? S.

[Atlas *with* REICHENBACH, Die vollständigste naturgeschichte, etc. Vögel. v. 3. *Wanting* nachträge. 9 pl].

——— The same. Die singvögel, als fortsetzung der vollständigsten naturgeschichte, und zugleich als central-atlas für zoologische gärten und für thierfreunde. x, 90 pp. 8°. 50 pl. 4°. *Dresden, etc. Expedition, etc.* 1862–64. S.

——— Die vollständigste naturgeschichte der vögel Neuhollands, etc. Ein beitrag zur naturgeschichte Australiens. xii, 248 pp; iv, 367 pp. 4°. 8°. *Dresden, etc. Expedition, etc.* 1850. S.

[Die völlstandigsten naturgeschichte der vögel. 2er band.]

Reichhardt (Paul Gottfried). Die druckorte des xv. jahrhunderts; nebst angabe der erzeugnisse ihrer erst-jährigen typographischen wirksamkeit. Mit einem anhange: verzeichniss der je ersten typographen, etc. x, 37 pp. 4°. *Augsburg, F. Butsch,* 1853. S.

Reid (James Seaton, *D. D.*) History of the presbyterian church in Ireland. 2 v. xv, 456 pp; xiv, 520 pp. 8°. *Edinburgh and London,* 1834–37.

Reid (Mayne). Bruin; the grand bear hunt. v, 371 pp. 8 pl. 12°. *Boston, Ticknor,* 1864.

——— The giraffe hunters. v, 298 pp. 16°. *Boston, Ticknor & Fields,* 1867.

——— The headless horseman; a strange tale of Texas. 408 pp. 8 pl. 12°. *New York, R. M. De Witt,* [1867].

Reiff (Carl Philipp). Dictionnaire russe-français, dans lequel les mots russes sont classés par familles. 2 v. lxiv, 1110, 279, 8 pp. 8°. *Saint Pétersbourg, H. Gretsch,* 1835–36. S.

——— New parallel dictionaries of the Russian, French, German, and English languages, in four parts. 4th part. English dictionary. With the explanation of the English words in Russian, French and German. New ed. xl, 848 pp. 8°. *Carlsruhe, author, etc.* 1862. S.

Reiffenberg (Frédéric Auguste Ferdinand Thomas, *baron* de). Annuaire de la bibliothèque royale de Belgique. 1e–9e année. 9 v. 16°. *Bruxelles, etc. C. Muquardt,* 1840–48. S.

[Vol. for 1849–50 wanting].

——— Principes de logique, suivis de l'histoire et de la bibliographie de cette science. 3 p. l. ii, 420 pp. 1 pl. 8°. *Bruxelles, L. Hauman & Cie.* 1833. S.

Reigart (J. Franklin). The inventor's and patentee's guide and pocket record, containing the U. S. patent laws, with notes of numerous decisions of the U. S. courts, etc. 180 pp. 18°. *Lancaster, (Pa.) Baer,* 1856. S.

Reinaert de vos; episch fabeldicht van de twaelfde en dertiende eeuw, met aenmerkingen en ophelderingen van J. F. Willems. 2e dr. [*anon.*] lxvii, 404 pp. 8°. *Gent, F. en E. Gyselynck,* 1850.

Reinaud (Joseph Toussaint). Fragments arabes et persans inédits relatifs à l'Inde, antérieurement au 11e siècle de l'ère chrétienne. [Par Modjmel-Altevarykh, d'Albyrouny, de Beladori.] 227 pp. 8°. *Paris,* 1845.

[*With* GILDEMEISTER (Johann). Scriptorum Arabum, etc.]

Reinhardt (Carl Wilhelm Theodor). Sarcoptis scabiei brevis historia. 25 pp. 8°. *Halis, auctor,* 1856. S.

Reinick (Robert). Lieder eines malers; mit randzeichnungen seiner freunde. 2 p. l. iv, 64 pp. 4°. *Düsseldorf, J. Buddaeus,* 1838. S.

Reinwald (C.) Catalogue annuel de la librairie française, 1866. 8°. *Paris, Reinwald,* 1867.

Reisseisen (Fr.) Ueber die structur, die verrichtung und den gebrauch der lungen. S.

[*With* SÖMMERRING (S. T. von), *and* REISSEISEN. Über die structur, etc. pp. 1–56].

Relaçam verdadeira dos trabalhos, etc. Virginia richly valued, by the description of the maine land of Florida, her next neighbour: out of the foure yeeres continuall trauell and discouerie for aboue one thousand miles east and west, of Don Fernando de Soto, and sixe hundred able men in his companie. Written by a Portugall gentleman of Eluas, and translated by Richard Haklvyt. [*anon.*] 4 p. l. 180 pp. sm. 4°. *London, Matthew Lownes,* 1609.

Relation de ce qui s'est passé de plvs remarqvable avx missions des pères de la compagnie de Jésvs, en la Novvelle France, 1676-77. [*anon.*] 165 pp. 12°. [*New York, privately printed by James Lenox,* 1855].

[*With* LE MERCIER (F.) Copie de devx lettres. 1656].

Relation des affaires du Canada, en 1696. Avec des lettres des pères de la compagnie de Jésus depuis 1696 jusqu'en 1702. [*anon.*] 73 pp. 8°. *Nouvelle York, J. M. Shea,* 1865. s.

Relation des missions et des voyages des evesques vicaires apostoliques [d'Héliopolis, de Berithe, et de Metellopolis], et de leurs ecclesiastiques [aux royaumes de Siam, de la Cochinchine, et du Tonquin], es années 1672-75. [*anon.*] 8 p. l. 389 pp. 12°. *Paris, C. Angot,* 1770.

Relation (A) of Maryland; together, a map of the countrey, the conditions of plantation, his majesties charter to the lord Baltimore, translated into English. [*anon.*] 1 p. l. 56, 25 pp. 1 map. sm. 4°. *London, W. Peasley,* 1635.

Religious mystery considered. [*anon.*] vii, 52 pp. 16°. *London, J. Chapman,* 1850.

Religious pieces in prose and verse. Edited from R. Thornton's MS. (cir. 1440), by G. G. Perry. xii, 106 pp. 8°. *London, N. Trübner & Co.* 1867.

[Early English text society publications. No. 26].

CONTENTS.

Dan Jon Gaytringe's sermon; The mirror of St. Edmund; The abbey of the holy ghost; Poem of William Nassyngton on the trinity and unity of God, etc; Hymns to Jesus Christ and the virgin; Of Sayne John the euaungelist; Hymns.

Remarkable convictions. By a writer to the signet. [*anon.*] ix, 260 pp. 12°. *Edinburgh, Wm. P. Nimmo,* 1865.

Remarks on the early corruptions of christianity; chiefly, so far as regards the trinity; and on prayer. By J. W. [*anon.*] 147 pp. 12°. *Philadelphia, J. Campbell,* 1867.

Remarks on a pamphlet entituled "A dissertation on the political union and constitution of the thirteen United States of North America." By a citizen of Philadelphia. With some observations, Whether all the western lands not purchased or conquered by the crown of Great Britain, antecedent to the late cession, ought not to be considered as ceded to the thirteen states jointly. By a Connecticut farmer. [*anon.*] 43 pp. 16°. [*n.p.*] 1784.

Remarks on the proposed plan of a federal government, addressed to the citizens of the United States of America, and particularly to the people of Maryland. By Aristides. [*pseudon.*] 42 pp. 12°. *Annapolis, Frederick Green,* [*about* 1788].

Remarks on the resolutions passed at a meeting of the noblemen, gentlemen, and clergy of the county of Warwick [to remonstrate against the proposed repeal of the corporation and test acts]; in three letters to the earl of Aylesford. [*anon.*] 47 pp. 8°. *Birmingham, J. Thompson,* 1790.

Remer (Julius August, *editor*). Amerikanisches archiv. 3 v. 8°. *Braunschweig, F. Waisenhaus,* 1777-78.

CONTENTS.

v. 1. PRICE (Richard). Anmerkungen über die natur der bürgerlichen freyheit, über die grundsätze regierung, und über die rechtmäszigkeit und politik des kriegs mit Amerika.
BURKE (Edmund). Rede womit er seinen vorschlag einer aussöhnung mit den colonien empfielet, 22 März 1775.
LEE (Charles), *and* BURGOYNE (John). Briefe bey gelegenheit der ankunft des letztern in Boston.
ANHANG zu Doctor Price's schrift, von der natur der bürgerlichen freyheit.

v. 2. JOHNSON (Samuel). Schatzung keine tiranney.
TUCKER (Josiah). Ein demüthige vorstellung an diejenigen verehrungswürdigen personen in Groszbrittanien und Irrland, welche geschicktesten sind zu urtheilen, und die tüchtigsten zu entscheiden, ob est für das beste der nation, mit den amerikanischen colonien vereinight zu bleiben, oder sich von ihnen zu trennen.
——— Berufung auf die gerechtigkeit und den vortheil der groszbrittanischen nation in den gegenwärtigen streitigkeiten mit Amerika.
——— Zweyte berufung auf die gerechtigkeit und den vortheil des volks, in absicht der maaszregeln gegen Amerika.

v. 3. LIND (John). Anmerkungen über die vornehmsten acten des dreyzehnten parlement von Groszbritannien.

Rémond des Cours (Nicolas). Histoire d'Eloïse et d'Abélard. Avec la lettre passionnée qu'elle lui écrivit. Traduite du Latin et accompagnée de deux autres avantures galantes fort singulières; [le marquis de Basin, et le chevalier de La Tour Landry]. 2 p. l. 140 pp. 24°. *La Haye, L. & H. Van Dole,* 1693.

[*With* COTOLENDI (C.) Arlequiniana. *Paris,* 1694].

Rémusat (Claire Elisabeth Jeanne Gravier de Vergennes, comtesse de). Essai sur l'éducation des femmes. Nouv. éd. 246 pp. 16°. *Paris, Charpentier,* 1842.

Remy (Jules). Voyage au pays des Mormons. Relation, géographie, histoire naturelle, histoire, théologie, moeurs et coutumes. 2 v. lxxxviii, 432 pp. 5 pl. 1 map; vii, 544 pp. 5 pl. 8°. *Paris, E. Dentu,* 1860.

Renaldini (Carlo). De resolutione, et compositione mathematica, libri dvo. 4 p. l. 535 pp. 15 l. fol. *Patavii, heredes P. Frambotti,* 1668.

——— Geometra promotvs. 88 pp. fol. *Patavii, P. M. Frambotti,* 1670.
[*With* the preceding].

Renan (Joseph Ernest). Les apôtres. lxiv, 388 pp. 8°. *Paris, Lévy frères,* 1866.

——— The same. The apostles. Translated from the French. 353 pp. 12°. *New York, G. W. Carleton & Co.* 1866.

——— Discours sur l'état des beaux-arts au [xive] siècle. 4°. *Paris,* 1863.
[*In* Histoire littéraire de la France. v. 24. pp. 603–757. 4°. *Paris,* 1863].

——— La poésie des races celtiques. 82 pp. 8°. *Paris, Lévy,* 1860.
[*In* RENAN. Essais de morale et de critique, 1860].

Renaudot (Théophraste). *See* **Mercure** françois.

Rendu (Ambroise Marie Modeste). Code universitaire; ou, lois, statuts et règlemens de l'université royale de France. 2e éd. xvi, 924 pp. 8°. *Paris, Hachette,* 1835. S.

——— De l'instruction secondaire, et spécialement des écoles secondaires ecclésiastiques. 2e partie. pp. 193–512. 8°. *Tours, Mame,* 1842. S.
[1e partie wanting.]

Rendu (Victor). Manuel d'agriculture. vi, 215 pp. 12°. *Paris, L. Hachette,* 1838. S.

Rennell (James). Memoir on the ruins of Babylon.
[*With* RICH (C. J.) Narrative, etc. pp. 107–134. 8°. *London,* 1839].

Rennie (James). Alphabet of angling, for the use of beginners. 136 pp. 16°. *London, H. G. Bohn,* 1849.

Rennie (John). Report and estimate of the grand southern canal, proposed to be made between Tunbridge and Portsmouth. 10 pl. 1 map. 4°. *London, E. Blackader,* 1810. S.

Renou (Jean Baptiste). Nouvelle méthode pour apprendre les langues hébraique et chaldaique. Avec le dictionnaire des racines hébraiques et chaldaiques, et de leurs dérivés. [*anon.*] Publiée par Jacques Le Long. 7 p. l. 386 pp. 12°. *Paris, Jacques Collombat,* 1708.

Renouard (Antoine Auguste). Annales de l'imprimerie des Alde; ou, histoire des trois Manuce et de leurs éditions. 2 v. xxviii, 250 pp. 20 l. 44 pp; ix, 149 pp. 3 l. 8°. *Paris, auteur,* 1803.

——— Annales de l'imprimerie des Estienne; ou, histoire de la famille des Estienne et de ses éditions. 2e éd. xix, 584 pp. 8°. *Paris, Renouard,* 1843. S.

Renshawe. A novel. By the author of "Mary Brandegee." Edited by Cuyler Pine. [*anon.*] 384 pp. 12°. *New York, G. W. Carleton & Co.* 1867.

Renwick (James). Treatise on the steam engine. 328 pp. 9 pl. 8°. *New York, Carvill,* 1830. S.

Renzi (Angelo Maria). La confession souterraine de la basilique de Saint Marc de Rome. (Extract). 7 pp. 8°. *Paris, Inst. historique,* 1845. S.
[*With his* Mémoire sur les Incas, etc].

——— Le guerre de Spartacus, en trois campagnes. 135 pp. 1 pl. 1 map. 8°. *Paris, l'auteur, etc.* 1832. S.

——— Histoire des Basques. (Extract). 12 pp. 8°. *Paris, Inst. historique,* 1850. S.
[*With his* Mémoire sur les Incas, etc].

——— Mémoire sur les Incas et sur les langues Aymara-Quichua. (Extract). 19 pp. 8°. *Paris, Inst. historique,* 1844. S.

——— Notice sur la grotte de Collepardo (Italie). (Extract). 4 pp. 8°. *Paris, Inst. historique,* 1840. S.
[*With his* Mémoire sur les Incas, etc].

——— Ouolofs; introduction à la grammaire de M. Lambert. (Extract). 27 pp. 8°. *Paris, Inst. historique,* 1842. S.
[*With his* Mémoire sur les Incas, etc].

——— Des peuples et des arts primitifs de l'Italie. (Extract). 8 pp. 8°. *Paris, Inst. historique,* 1842. S.
[*With his* Mémoire sur les Incas, etc].

——— [Revue des] mémoires de la société des antiquaires de l'Amérique du nord. Partie linguistique. (Extract). 15 pp. 8°. *Paris, Inst. historique,* 1842. S.
[*With his* Mémoire sur les Incas, etc.]

Reply (A) to fare thee well!!! Lines addressed to lord Byron. [*anon.*] 12 pp. 8°. *London, R. S. Kirby,* 1816.
[Miscellaneous pamphlets. v. 56].

Reply (A) to the Rev. Dr. George Junkin's treatise, entitled "Sabbatismos." By Justin Martyr. [*pseudon.*] 143 pp. 12°. *Philadelphia, T. E. Zell,* 1867.

Republican (The) from Aug. 27, 1819, to Dec. 29, 1826. 14 v. 8°. *London, R. Carlile,* 1819–26.

Reshíd-ed-dín Fadhlallah, *known as* **Er-Reshídí.** Histoire des Mongols de la Perse. Publiée, traduite en français, accompagnée de notes et d'un mémoire sur la vie et les ouvrages de l'auteur par E. M. Quatremère. v. 1. clxxv, 450 pp. fol. *Paris collection orientale, imp. royale,* 1836. s.
[No more published].

——— Cathay under the Mongols. 20 pp. 8°.
[*With* YULE (Henry). Cathay, etc. v. 2. *London,* 1866].

Residence (A) on the shores of the Baltic. Described in a series of letters. [*anon.*] 2 v. viii, 293 pp; vi, 286 pp. 12°. *London, J. Murray,* 1841.

Restif de La Bretonne (N. E.) *See* **Rétif de La Bretonne.**

Rétif de La Bretonne (Nicolas Edme). L'andrographe, ou idées d'un honnête-homme, sur un projet de réglement, pour opérer une réforme générale des moeurs. Avec notes. 2 v. 475 pp. 8°. *La Haie, Gosse & Pinet,* 1782.

——— La mimographe, ou idées d'une honnête femme pour la réformation du théâtre nationale. [*anon.*] 466 pp. 8°. *Amsterdam, Changuion,* 1770.

——— Le paysan perverti, ou les dangers de la ville. 4 v. in 2. 16°. *La Haye, et se trouve à Paris, chez Duchesne,* 1776.

Retslag *palindrome* for Galster? (Carl). Political sketches; twelve chapters of the struggles of the age. iv, 154 pp. 12°. *London, R. Theobald,* 1854.

Retz, *or* **Retzius** (Anders Johan). Faunae suecicae a Carolo a Linné; inchoatae pars prima, sistens mammalia, aves, amphibia et pisces Sueciae. x, 362 pp. 1 pl. 8°. *Lipsiae, S. L. Crusius,* 1800. s.
[No more published].

Retza *or* **Rota** (Franz von). Comestorium viciorum. 286 l. fol. *Nuremberge,* [*J. Sensenschmid & H. Kefer,*] 1470.

Retzsch (Friedrich August Moritz). Fantasien. Fancies; a series of subjects in outline. With prefatory remarks and descriptions, by Mrs. Jameson. xiii pp. 12 l. 6 pl. *London, etc. Saunders & Otley, etc.* 1834. s.

——— Gallery to Shakespeare's dramatic works, in outlines. 16 pts, with explanations. obl. 4°. *New York, G. & B. Westermann bros.* 1849.
[Imperfect: pts 5–16 wanting; pl. 1 of the Macbeth series, and all of text but pp. 1–16].

Reuchlin (Johann). Exegesis dictionvm in psalmos sex. 56 pp. fol. *Basiliae, H. Petrus,* 1554. s.

——— Tabvlae viginti, institvtiones in lingvam sanctam absolvtas complectentes. 72 l. fol. *Basiliae, H. Petrus,* 1554. s.
[*With his* Exegesis, etc.]

Reuleaux (*prof.* F.) Die festigkeit der materialien. *See* **Moll** (C. L.) *and* **Reuleaux.**

Reume (Auguste de). Variétés bibliographiques et littéraires. 204 pp. - pl. 8°. *Bruxelles, Dewasme,* 1848.

Reumont (Alfred von). La jeunesse de Catherine de Médicis. xvii, 388 pp. 1 pl. 12°. *Paris, Plon,* 1866.

Reuss (Jeremias David). Alphabetical register of all the authors actually living in Great Britain, Ireland, and in the united provinces of North America, with a catalogue of their publications, 1770–1790. xiv, xi, 459 pp. 8°. *Berlin & Stettin, F. Nicolai,* 1791.

Reveillé-Parise (Joseph Henri). Études de l'homme dans l'état de santé et dans l'état de maladie. 2 v. iv, 512 pp; 512 pp. 8°. *Paris, Dentu,* 1845.

——— Physiologie et hygiène des hommes livrés aux travaux de l'esprit. 4e éd. 2 v. 424 pp; 483 pp. 8°. *Paris, Dentu,* 1843.

——— Traité de la vieillesse, hygiénique, médical et philosophique. viii, 488 pp. 8°. *Paris, Baillière,* 1853.

Revere (John, *M. D.*) A summary of physiology. 430 pp. 8°. *Baltimore, Edward J. Coale & Co.* 1822.

Review of the "Biographical sketch" of John Vanderlyn, published by Wm. Dunlap, in his "History of the arts of design;" with some additional notices respecting Mr. Vanderlyn as an artist. By a friend of the artist. [*anon.*] 65 pp. 8°. *New York,* 1838.

Review (A) of Capt. Basil Hall's travels in North America, in 1827–28. By an American. [*anon.*] 149 pp. 8°. *London, R. J. Kennett,* 1830. s.

Review (A) of the letter addressed by W. A. Duer to C. D. Colden, in answer to strictures contained in his "Life of Robert Fulton." With appendix. [*anon.*] 27 pp. 8°. *New York,* 1818.

Review of the life and character of Lord Byron. From the British critic, April 1831. [*anon.*] viii, 95 pp. 18°. *London, Rivingtons,* 1833.
[Miscellaneous pamphlets, v. 56].

Review (A) of the proceedings of the Arctic searching expeditions, under command of Captain H. T. Austin, and W. Penny. [Nautical magazine, 1851–2. Arctic papers]. 30, 23, 22, pp. 1 map. 8°. *London, J. D. Potter,* 1851.

Reviews of a part of Prescott's history of Ferdinand and Isabella, [drawing a parallel between Elizabeth, queen of England, and Isabella], and of Campbell's lectures on poetry, [relating to Homer's Odyssey *anon.*] 199 pp. 12°. *Boston, J. H. Francis*, 1841.

Revue des deux mondes. 36e et 37e années. 2e période. Nov. 1866 to Dec. 1867. v. 66–72. 8°. *Paris,* [*J. Claye*], 1866–67.

Reybaud (Marie Roch Louis). L'industrie en Europe. 296 pp. 12°. *Paris, M. Lévy*, 1856.

——— Jérome Paturot à la recherche d'une position sociale. Nouv. éd. ix, 426 pp. 16°. *Paris, Lévy*, 1867.

Reyes *or* **Los Reyes** (José Maria de). Diario de la expedicion de 1822. *Buenos-Aires*, 1836. *See* **Garcia** (Pedro Andres), *and* **Los Reyes** (José Maria de).

Reynold-Chauvancy (Charles de). Code Reynold. Télégraphie nautique polyglotte à l'usage des armées navales et de la marine du commerce. 4 p. l. lxxxii, 229 pp. 64 l. 11 pl. 8°. *Paris, V. Dalmont*, 1855.

Reynolds (Edward, *D. D. bp. of Norwich*). A treatise of the passions and faculties of the soul of man. 9 p. l. 553 pp. 1 pl. sm. 4°. *London, R. Bostock*, 1656.

Reynolds (George W. M.) The soldier's wife. 202 pp. 8°. *New York, H. Long & brother*, 1853.

Reynolds (John, *of Exeter, Eng.*) The triumphs of God's revenge against the crying and execrable sinne of murther. In thirty severall tragical histories. 4th ed. fol. *London*, 1663.

Reynolds (John, *of Vermont*). Recollections of Windsor [Vt.] prison; containing sketches of its history and discipline. 252 pp. 1 pl. 12°. *Boston, A. Wright*, 1834.

Reynolds (John, *governor of Illinois, and M. C.*) My own times, embracing also the history of my life. 600, xxiii pp. 1 pl. 16°. *Belleville, (Ill.)* 1855.

Rhind (William). Spasmodic cholera.

[*With* MURRAY (Hugh). Account of British India. v. 3. pp. 273-278. *New York*, 1833-36].

Rhode Island. [Proceedings of the general assembly holden at Providence, Jan. 2, 1776. pp. 202 to 265.] 8°. *Providence, J. Carter*, 1776.

——— Report upon public schools and education, October, 1854. By E. R. Potter. 247 pp. 8°. *Providence, State*, 1855. s.

——— Report upon the census, 1865; with statistics of the population, agriculture, fisheries, and manufactures of the state. Prepared by E. M. Snow. cxi, 111 pp. 8°. *Providence, Press co.* 1867.

——— Thirteenth report upon the registration of births, marriages, and deaths for the year 1865. Prepared by E. M. Snow. vii, 87 pp. 8°. *Providence, Press co.* 1867.

Rhode Island (The) repository, a monthly magazine. [From April, 1814, to April, 1815.] v. 1. 672 pp. 3 portraits. 8°. *Providence, (R. I.) Robinson & Howland*, 1815.

Rhode (Johan). Introductio ad medicinam paulo accuratiorem, et bibliotheca medica.

[*With* CONRING (H.) Introductio in universam artem medicam. Ed. 1726].

Rhodes *or* **Rueda** (Alexandre de). Voyages et missions en la Chine et autres royaumes de l'Orient. Nouv. éd. ix, 448 pp. 8°. *Paris, Julien, Lanier & Cie.* 1854. s.

Rhodes (James A.) Adventures by sea and land; a cruise in a whale boat, during a year in the Pacific ocean and the interior of South America. 107 pp. 8°. *New York*, 1848.

Rhodes (William Barnes). Epigrams. In two books. 84 pp. 16°. *London, Wm. Miller*, 1803.

Ricci (Lodovico). Riforma degl' instituti pii della città di Modena.

[SCRITTORI class. Ital. di econ. pol. v. 41].

Riccoboni (Marie Jeanne Laboras de Mézières). Letters from Elizabeth Sophia de Valiere to her friend, Louisa Hortensia de Canteleu. Translated from the French by Mr. Maceuen. 2 v. 252 pp; 242 pp. 16°. *London, T. Becket*, 1772.

Rice (*Rev.* David). Epistles to the citizens of Kentucky; especially presbyterians. Also, Slavery inconsistent with justice and good policy, first printed in 1792. pp. 321—418.

[*With* BISHOP (Robert H.) History of the church in Kentucky. *Lexington*, 1824].

Rice (*Rev.* Nathan L.) An account of the lawsuit instituted against [him] for a pretended libel on the character of Rev. David Duparque, a Roman priest. With some remarks on celibacy and nunneries. 192 pp. 16°. *Louisville, (Ky.) D. Holcomb & Co.* 1837.

Rich (Claudius James). Narrative of a journey to the site of Babylon in 1811; memoir on the ruins; remarks on the topography of ancient Babylon, by Major Rennell, in reference to the memoir; with narrative of a journey to Persepolis. Edited by his widow. xlvii, 324 pp. 26 pl. 8°. *London, Duncan & Malcolm*, 1839.

Rich (Jeremiah). Pen's dexterity compleated. [With] the terms of the law compleat. By Samuel Botley. 30 pl. 16°. *London, E. Parker,* [1669].

Rich (Obadiah). Supplement to the Bibliotheca Americana nova. Part i. Additions and corrections, 1701 to 1800. 8°. *London,* 1841.

Richard (Achille). Élémens d'histoire naturelle médicale. 3 v. 8°. *Paris, Béchet,* 1831-35. S.

——— Tentamen floræ Abyssinicæ, etc. *See* **Lefebvre** (C. T.) Voyage en Abyssinie, v. 4-5.

——— Iconographie végétale. Texte. *See* **Turpin** (P. J. F.)

Richards (George, *of Portsmouth, N. H.*) Washington; an historical discourse. 80 pp. 4°. *Portsmouth, (N. H.) C. Peirce,* 1800.

[Imperfect].

Richards (T. Addison). Miller's guide to Saratoga springs and vicinity. Illustrated. 91 pp. 8 pl. 18°. *New York, J. Miller,* 1867.

——— Tallulah and Jocassee; or, romances of southern landscape, and other tales. 255 pp. 12°. *Charleston, Walker, Richards & Co.* 1852.

Richardson (Albert D.) Our new states and territories; being notes of a recent tour of observation through [the far west]. 80 pp. 8°. *New York, Beadle & Co.* 1866.

——— Beyond the Mississippi. Life and adventure on the prairies, mountains, and Pacific coast. 1857-1867. [Illustrated.] 572 pp. 16 pl. 1 map. 8°. *Hartford, (Conn.) American pub. Co.* 1867.

Richardson (Benjamin Ward, *M. D.*) For and against tobacco; or, tobacco in its relation to the health of individuals and communities. 75 pp. 8°. *London, J. Churchill & sons,* 1865.

Richardson (Charles James). Popular treatise on the warming and ventilation of buildings: showing the advantage of the improved system of heated water circulation. 3d ed. viii, 115 pp. 17 pl. 8°. *London, J. Weale,* 1856. S.

——— Studies of ornamental design. 4 p. l. 11 pl. fol. *London, J. Weale,* 1848.

Richardson (John, *B. D. of Emanuel coll. Camb.*) The canon of the new testament vindicated; in answer to the objections of J. T[oland] in his Amyntor. 2d ed. xii, 131 pp. 12°. *London, R. Sare,* 1701.

Richardson (John, *quaker*). An account of [his] life. vi, 236 pp. 8°. *Philadelphia, J. Crukshank,* 1783.

Richardson (John, *F. S. A.*) A vocabulary, Persian, Arabic, and English; abridged from the quarto edition of Richardson's dictionary, as edited by Charles Wilkins. By David Hopkins. viii, 643 pp. 8°. *London, F. & C. Rivington,* 1810. S.

Richardson (*Sir* John). Fishes. [Extract.] 74 pp. 17 col. pl. 8°. *London, Museum of nat. hist.* [*about* 1860]. S.

——— Ichthyology. [Extract.] 128 pp. 4°. *London, Encyclopædia britannica,* [1856]. S.

Richardson (*Rev.* J. *LL. B.*) Recollections, political, literary, dramatic, and miscellaneous, of the last half century. 2 v. in 1. xi, 304 pp; viii, 303 pp. 8°. *London, C. Mitchell,* 1856.

Richardson (Nathaniel K.) One hundred choice selections in poetry and prose. 180 pp. 12°. *Philadelphia, P. Garrett & Co.* 1866.

Richardson (Samuel). A tour through Great Britain. *See* **Defoe** (Daniel), **Richardson** (S.) *and others.*

Richardson (T. G. *M. D.*) Elements of human anatomy: general, descriptive, and practical. 2d ed. 671 pp. 8°. *Philadelphia, J. B. Lippincott & Co.* 1867.

Richardson (William, *professor at Glasgow*). The Indians; a tragedy. [*anon.*] iv, 81 pp. 12°. *London, C. Dilly,* 1790.

Riche de Prony. *See* **Prony.**

Richelet (Pierre). Dictionnaire portatif de la langue françoise, extrait du grand dictionnaire de Pierre Richelet. [Par l'abbé C. P. Gouget]. Nouv. éd. 2 p. l. 676 pp. 12°. *Lyon, Benoist Duplain,* 1770.

Richer (Jean). *See* **Mercure** françois.

Richmond (Va.) library. Catalogue of books. 107 pp. 8°. *Richmond, Macfarlane & Fergusson,* 1855. S.

Richmond during the war; four years' of personal observation. By a Richmond lady. [*anon.*] 389 pp. 12°. *New York, Carleton & Co.* 1867.

Richmond (*Rev.* James Cook). The Rhode Island cottage; or, a gift for the children of sorrow: a narrative of facts [in the life of Cynthia Taggart]. 1st English from 2d Am. ed. 160 pp. 24°. *Newport, (Isle of Wight), R. J. Denyer,* 1849.

Richmond (*Rev.* Legh). The dairyman's daughter. [In Cherokee]. Unvdi ganodisgi uwetsi ulenitolvi kanohesgi. 56 pp. 24°. *Park Hill, Mission press,* 1847.

——— A statement of facts, relative to the supposed abstinence of Ann Moore. 56, lxxvi pp. 8°. *Burton-on-Trent, J. Croft,* 1813.

Richter (Ernst Friedrich). Manual of harmony: a practical guide to its study. Translated from the German by J. P. Morgan. 219 pp. 8°. *New York, G. Schirmer,* [1867].

Richter (Eugen). Co-operative stores, their history, organization, and management. Based on the German work of E. Richter, with annotations and amendments, rendering the work specially adapted for use in the United States. 131 pp. 12°. *New York, Leypoldt & Holt,* 1867.

Richter (Otto Friedrich von). Wallfahrten im Morgenlande. Aus seinem tagebüchern und briefen dargestellt von J. P. G. Ewers. xviii, 715 pp. portrait. 8°. *Berlin, Reimer,* 1822. s.

Rickard (F. Ignacio). A mining journey across the great Andes. xvi, 314 pp. 2 maps. 12°. *London, Smith, Elder & Co.* 1863.

Rickey, Mallory and company. Catalogue raisonné, [etc.] of the most important works [etc.] published in the United States and England, [etc.] 259 pp. 8°. *Cincinnati,* 1860. s.

Rickman (Thomas). An attempt to discriminate the styles of architecture, in England, from the conquest to the reformation, [etc.] 3d ed. vii, 414 pp. 1 l. 14 pl. 8°. *London, Longmans,* [1825]. s.

——— The same. [With appendix on Saxon architecture, etc.] 5th ed. lvi, 238 pp. 1 l. lxii pp. 6 l. 8°. *London, J. H. Parker,* 1848. s.

Ricord (F. W.) Series of Roman history. The kings of Rome. 304 pp. 7 pl. 16°. *New York, A. S. Barnes & Co.* 1856. s.

——— The same. The republic of Rome. 308 pp. 5 pl. 16°. *New York, A. S. Barnes & Co.* 1856. s.

Ricord (Philippe). Additions, etc. *See* **Hunter** (John). Treatise on the venereal disease.

Ricraft (Josiah). A survey of England's champions, and truth's faithfull patriots. [With another title-page: Civil warres of England briefly related, 1641–48. Collected by J. Leycester]. 5 p. l. 174 pp. 22 pl. 8°. *London, J. Hancock,* 1649.

Riddell (John). Architectural designs for model country residences. 14 l. 40 pl. obl. fol. *Philadelphia, T. B. Peterson & bros.* [1867].

Riddell (*Mrs.* J. H.) George Geith of Fencourt. A novel. By F. G. Trafford. [*pseudon.*] x, 555 pp. 12°. *Boston, T. O. H. P. Burnham,* 1865.

Riddell (Robert). The modern carpenter and builder. New and original methods for every cut in carpentry, joinery, and hand-railing. 40 pp. 14 pl. 4°. *Philadelphia, H. Challen,* 1867.

Riddle (Edward). Treatise on navigation and nautical astronomy. vi, 299, 251 pp. 8°. *London, Baldwin, Cradock & Joy,* 1824.

Riddle (*Rev.* Joseph Esmond). Household prayers for four weeks; with additional prayers for special occasions, [etc.] 179 pp. 12°. *New York, J. Pott,* 1866. s.

Ridley (James). The schemer; or, universal satirist. By that great philosopher, Helter Van Scelter. [*pseudon.*] 278 pp. 3 l. 16°. *London, J. Wilkie,* 1763.

Ridley (Nicholas, *D. D. bishop of London*). Præfatio et protestatio habita Aprilis 20, in scholis publicis Oxonii, anno 1555; treatise against the error of transubstantiation. 59 pp. 8°. *Oxford,* 1825.

[*With* RANDOLPH (John) *bishop of London.* Enchiridion theologicum. v. 1].

Ridner (John P.) The artist's chromatic handbook. Being a practical treatise on pigments, [etc.] 144 pp. 12°. *New York, G. P. Putnam,* 1850. s.

Riedesel (Friederike Charlotte Luise von). Die berufs-reise nach Amerika. Briefe der generalin von Riedesel auf dieser reise, und während ihres sechsjährigen aufenthalts in America, zur zeit des dortigen krieges in den jahren 1776 bis 1783. x, 352 pp. 8°. *Berlin, Haude & Spener,* 1800.

——— The same. Letters and journals relating to the American revolution, and the capture of the German troops at Saratoga. From the German, by W. L. Stone. 235 pp. 3 pl. 8°. *Albany, J. Munsell,* 1867.

Riehl (W. H.) Land und leute. [Die naturgeschichte des volkes, als grundlage einer deutschen social-politik. v. 1.] 5^e^ aufl. xvi, 365 pp. 8°. *Stuttgart, J. G. Cotta,* 1861. s.

Riera (Joaquin Valentin). La mujer. Breves rasgos descriptivos de su naturaleza, fisica y moral con relacion á la sociedad. 150 pp. 12°. *New York, Familtor,* 1856. s.

Riess (Peter Theophilus). Die lehre von der reibungs elektricitat. 2 v. viii, 516 pp. 7 pl; viii, 592 pp. 5 pl. 8°. *Berlin, A. Hirschwald,* 1853. s.

Rietstap (J. B.) Armorial général, contenant la description des armoiries des familles nobles et patriciennes de l'Europe; précédé d'un dictionnaire des termes du blason. vi, 1171 pp. 5 pl. 8°. *Gouda, G. B. van Goor,* 1861.

Rietz (Johan Ernst). Skånska skolväsendets historia. 8 p. l. 655 pp. 8°. *Lund, Berling,* 1848. s.

Rigaud (Stephen Peter, *editor*). Correspondence of scientific men of the 17th century, including letters of Barrow, Flamsteed, Wallis, and Newton; from the collection of the earl of Macclesfield. 2 v. xv, 375 pp; 610 pp. 8°. *Oxford, University press*, 1841. s.

Rigby (Edward, *M.D.*) An essay on the uterine hæmorrhage which precedes the delivery of the full-grown fœtus. With a memoir of his life, by John Cross. 6th ed. lxi, 267 pp. 8°. *Norwich, Hunter*, 1822.

Right (The) of a state to grant exclusive privileges in roads, bridges, navigable waters, etc. vindicated by examination of the grant from the state of New York to Robert Livingston and Robert Fulton for exclusive navigation of vessels by steam or fire, on the waters of said state. [*anon.*] 44 pp. 8°. *New York, E. Conrad*, 1811.

Right (The) of tithes re-asserted. [*anon.*] 24 p. l. 486 pp. 16°. *London, H. Brome & R. Clavel*, 1680.

Right (The) way. [A weekly political newspaper]. Nos. 1–62. Dec. 18, 1865, to March 2, 1867. 2 v. in 1. fol. *Boston, Impartial suffrage league*, 1865–67.
[No more published].

Rights and wrongs of the north and the south: oil on the waters. [*anon.*] 436 pp. 12°. *Boston, J. E. Tilton & Co.* 1867.

Rigoley de Juvigny (Jean Antoine). De la décadence des lettres et des mœurs, depuis les Grecs et les Romains jusqu'à nos jours. 2e éd. vii, 552 pp. 16°. *Paris, Merigot*, 1787.

Rig-Veda-Sanhitá: the sacred hymns of the Brahmans, together with the commentary of Sayanacharya. [Sanskrit text]. Edited by Max Müller. v. 1–4. 4°. *London, W. H. Allen & Co.* 1849–62. s.

——— The same. A collection of ancient Hindu hymns, constituting the third and fourth Ashtakas, or books of the Rig-Veda. Translated from the Sanskrit. By H. H. Wilson. [v. 3.] xxiii, 524 pp. 8°. *London, W. H. Allen & Co.* 1857. s.

——— The same. The Aitareya Brahmanam of the Rigveda, containing the earliest speculations of the Brahmans on the meaning of the sacrificial prayers, and on the origin, performance, and sense of the rites of the Vedic religion. Edited by Martin Haug. With Sanscrit text. 2 v. ix, 89, 216, vi pp; vii, 535 pp. 12°. *Bombay, gov. central book depôt*, 1863. s.

Riley (Harvey). The mule. A treatise on the breeding, training, and uses, to which he may be put. 107 pp. 14 pl. 12°. *New York, Dick & Fitzgerald*, 1867.

Riley (H. H.) Puddleford papers; or, humors of the west. 359 pp. 12°. *New York, Redfield*, 1857.

Riley (James). An authentic narrative of the loss of the American brig Commerce, wrecked on the western coast of Africa, in 1815, with the sufferings of her surviving officers and crew, enslaved by the Arabs. xiv, 554, xxi pp. 1 map, 9 pl. 8°. *New York, T. & W. Mercein*, 1817.

Rimestad (C. W.) Zwei weltbegebenheiten. [China; die eroberung Pekings. Nordamerika; der zerfall der union]. Deutsch von H. Helms. 280 pp. 16°. *Leipzig, L. Wiedemann*, [1862].

Ringland (John), *and* **Gelston** (John). Report of a deputation from the national association for the education of the deaf and dumb poor of Ireland, who visited several institutions for the deaf and dumb in Great Britain. 80 pp. 1 tab. 16°. *Dublin, association*, 1856. s.

Rio (C. Andres del). Elementos de orictognosia, ó del conocimiento de los fosiles, segun el sistema de Bercelio, y segun los principios de A. G. Werner. 2a ed. vii, 680 pp. 8°. *Filadelfia, J. F. Hurtel*, 1832. s.

Rios (José Amador de los). *See* **Los Rios**.

Ripa (Cesare). Iconologia, overo descrittione d'imagini delle virtv', vitij, affetti, passioni humane, corpi celesti, mondo e sue parti. 16 p. l. 552 pp. 4°. *Padoua, P. P. Tozzi*, 1611.

——— The same. Iconologie. Tirée des recherches et des figures moralisées, par J. Bavdoin. 2 pts. in 1 v. 12 pl. 204 pp; 196 pp. fol. *Paris, M. Gvillemot*, 1644.

Risso (G. Antonio). Histoire naturelle des principales productions de l'Europe méridionale, et particulièrement de celles des environs de Nice et des Alpes maritimes. 4 v. 8°. *Paris, F. G. Levrault*, 1826. s.

Ritchie (Anna Cora Mowatt). The clergyman's wife, and other sketches. A collection of pen portraits and paintings. 384 pp. 12°. *New York, G. W. Carleton & Co.* 1867.

Ritchie (J. Ewing). Here and there in London. 228 pp. 16°. *London, W. Tweedie*, 1859.

Ritson (Joseph). Ancient songs, from the time of Henry the third, to the revolution. [With a preliminary dissertation. *anon.*] 1 p. l. lxxx, 332 pp. 12°. *London, J. Johnson*, 1790.

Ritson (Joseph). Robin Hood: a collection of all the ancient poems, songs, and ballads relative to that outlaw; with anecdotes of his life. xii, xxiv, 240 pp. 16°. *London, Longmans, etc.* 1820.

Ritter (Abraham). Philadelphia and her merchants, as constituted fifty and seventy years ago. 223 pp. 20 pl. 8°. *Philadelphia, author,* 1860.

Ritter (Carl). Comparative geography of Palestine and the Sinaitic peninsula. Translated and adapted to the use of biblical students by W. L. Gage. 4 v. 8°. *New York, Appletons, [printed at Edinburgh],* 1866.

——— Géographie générale comparée; ou, étude de la terre dans ses rapports avec la nature et avec l'histoire de l'homme. [Afrique]. Tr. de l'Allemand par E. Buret et Édouard Desor. 3 v. 8°. *Paris, Paulin,* 1836. S.

[No more published].

——— Die Stupa's (Topes); oder, die architectonischen denkmale an der indo-baktrischen königstrasse, und die colosse von Bamiyan. viii, 272 pp. atlas. 1 map. 8 pl. 8°. *Berlin, Nicolai,* 1838. S.

Rivarol (Antoine, *comte* de). Esprit de Rivarol. [Précédé d'une notice par F. J. M. Fayolle.] xli, 258 pp. 16°. *Paris, Perronneau,* 1808.

River (The) Plate as a field for emigration: its geography, agricultural capabilities, etc. [*anon.*] 35 pp. 8°. *London, Bates, Hendy & Co.* 1866.

Riverside (The) magazine for young people. An illustrated monthly. Jan. to Dec. 1867. v. 1. iv, 576 pp. 8°. *New York, Hurd & Houghton,* 1867.

Robbins (Thomas, *D.D.*) An historical view of the first planters of New England. x, 300 pp. 16°. *Hartford, Peter S. Gleason,* 1815.

——— A series of sermons on the divinity of Christ. 172 pp. 18°. *Hartford, Silas Andrus,* 1820.

Robert (A. C. M.) Fables inédits. *See* **La Fontaine** (Jean).

Robert (Louis Joseph Marie). Nouvel essai sur la mégalantropogénésie, ou l'art de faire des enfans d'esprit, qui deviennent des grands hommes; suivi des traits physiognomiques propres à les faire reconnoitre, décrits par Aristote, Porta, et Lavater, avec notes. 2e éd. 2 v. xxxvi, 47, 395 pp; 463 pp. 8°. *Paris, Le Normant,* 1803.

Robert (Louise Félicité Guinement de Kéralio). Collection des meilleurs ouvrages françois, composés par des femmes. 6 v. 8°. *Paris, l'auteur, et La Grange,* 1786–89.

Robert (Nicolas). Histoire particulière des oiseaux de la ménagerie du roi peints d'après nature, etc. S.

[*With* JONSTON (J.) Histoire naturelle des oiseaux. v. 1. 1773–74].

Robert (T.) Life of Rev. George Whitefield. 259 pp. 16°. *London,* [*n. d.*]

Robert-Dumesnil (Alexandre Pierre François). Le peintre-graveur français; ou, catalogue raisonné des estampes de l'école française, [etc.] ouvrage faisant suite au Peintre-graveur de M. Bartsch. 7 v. 8°. *Paris, G. Warée, etc.* 1835–44. S.

Roberts (David). Historical discourse on the life, deeds, and character of Mathew Cradock. 16 pp. 8°. *Salem, W. Ives,* 1856.

Roberts (Emma). Descriptions. *See* **Views in India**, China, etc. *London,* 1835.

Roberts (Lewis). The merchants' mappe of commerce: wherein the vniversall manner and matter of trade is compendiously handled. 7 p. l. 235 pp. 10 l. 262, 192 pp. 5 maps. fol. *London, R. Mabb,* 1638.

Robertson (*Rev.* Abram). Elements of plane and spherical trigonometry. S.

[*With* EUCLID. Elements, etc. by Robert Simson. *London,* 1834].

Robertson (T. *pseudon.*) Whole French language. *See* **Lafforgue** (P. C. T.)

Robertson (William). An historical disquisition concerning the knowledge which the ancients had of India; and the progress of trade with that country prior to the discovery of the cape of Good Hope, with appendix. 4th ed. viii, 369 pp. 18°. *London, T. Cadell, jr.* 1802.

——— The history of America; [with] the history of Virginia to 1688; and of New England to 1652. 2d ed. 2 v. 306 pp; 293 pp. 8°. *Philadelphia, S. Probasco,* 1821.

Robin (Charles Philippe). Des végétaux qui croissent sur l'homme et sur les animaux vivants. viii, 120 pp. 3 pl. 8°. *Paris, J. B. Baillière,* 1847. S.

Robin (——). New travels through North America, exhibiting the history of the campaign of the allied armies under general Washington and the count de Rochambeau, in 1781. 95 pp. 12°. *Boston, F. Battle,* 1784.

Robins (Benjamin). Mathematical tracts. Published by James Wilson. 2 v. xlvi, 341 pp. 2 pl; 380 pp. 1 pl. 8°. *London, J. Nourse,* 1761.

[Tracts on ordnance, gunnery, ammunition, etc.]

Robinson (Edward, *D.D.*) Biblical researches in Palestine, Mount Sinai, and Arabia Petræa. 3 v. 8°. *Boston, Crocker & Brewster,* 1841.

Robinson (Fayette). California and its gold regions, with a geographical and topographical view of the country, its mineral and agricultural resources. 137 pp. 1 map. 8°. *New York, Stringer & Townsend,* 1849.

Robinson (Horatio N.) Elements of geometry, plane and spherical trigonometry, and conic sections. 270, 65 pp. 12°. *Cincinnati, J. Ernst,* 1850. s.

——— Elements of natural philosophy. 287 pp. 12°. *Cincinnati, J. Ernst,* 1848. s.

——— Elements of plane and spherical trigonometry, with problems [and tables of logarithms]. pp. 243–383; 70 pp. *New York, Ivison & Co.* [1867].

——— The progressive primary arithmetic. 80 pp. 16°. *Boston, Sanborn & Carter,* 1858. s.

——— A treatise on astronomy, descriptive, physical, and practical. ix, 302, 53 pp. 8°. *Cincinnati, J. Ernst, etc.* 1849. s.

——— A new treatise on the elements of differential and integral calculus. Edited by J. F. Quimby. 472 pp. 8°. *New York, Ivison, Co.* 1868.

Robinson (J. H.) The Boston conspiracy; or, the royal police. A tale of 1773–75. 110 pp. 12°. *Boston, Dow & Jackson, and Gleason,* 1847.

Robinson (*Mrs.* Sara T. L.) Kansas; its interior and exterior life. ix, 366 pp. 2 pl. 12°. *Boston, Crosby, Nichols & Co.* 1856.

Robinson (Solon). Facts for farmers, also for the family circle, about domestic animals and domestic economy, farm buildings, orchards, and vineyards, etc. 2 v. in 1. 1050 pp. 22 pl. 8°. *New York, A. J. Johnson,* 1867.

——— The same. Thatsachen für landwirthe sowie für den familienkreis. Deutsch bearbeitet von H. Grube. 2 v. in 1. 996 pp. 22 pl. 8°. *New York, A. J. Johnson,* 1868.

Robinson (*Rev.* Stuart). Discourses of redemption; a popular method of exhibiting the "divers" revelations through patriarchs, prophets, Jesus, and his apostles. 488 pp. 8°. *New York, D. Appleton & Co.* 1866.

Robison (John). Anleitung zur verfertigung achromatischer fernröhre: aus dem Englischen von Dr. Friedrich Körner. viii, 221 pp. 5 pl. 12°. *Jena, A. Schmid,* 1828.

Roby (John). Seven weeks in Belgium, Switzerland, Lombardy, Piedmont and Savoy. 2 v. xi, 420 pp; viii, 424 pp. 12°. *London, Longman, Orme & Co.* 1838.

Robyn (Henry). Thorough description of the Braille system for the reading and writing of music; also, all characters of the English, French, and German language, cyphering, and algebra. 48, 8 pp. 8 pl. 12°. *St. Louis, A. Wiebusch & son,* 1867.

Rocha (Pio Bustamente). Compendio elemental de zoologia. 248 pp. 13 l. 13 pl. 16°. *Mexico, Munguia,* 1854. s.

Roche (Jean Antoine, *called* Antonin), *and* **Chasles** (Philarète). Histoire de France, depuis les temps les plus reculés. 2 v. vii, 604 pp; 447 pp. 8°. *Paris, Didot,* 1847.

Roche Flavin (Bernard de La). *See* **La Roche Flavin.**

Rochefort (César de). Histoire naturelle et morale des îles Antilles de l'Amérique. Avec vn vocabulaire caraïbe. 8 p. l. 527 pp. 6 l. 1 pl. 4°. *Rotterdam, Arnould Leers,* 1658.

[NOTE.—This work, though commonly attributed to Rochefort, or to L. de Poincy, was probably written by neither].

Rochester (*earl of*). *See* **Wilmot** (John).

Rochet, *known as* Rochet d'Héricourt, (Charles Xavier). Second voyage sur les deux rives de la Mer Rouge, dans le pays des Adels, et le royaume de Choa. xlviii, 406 pp. 12 pl. 8°. *Paris, A. Bertrand,* 1846. s.

Rockwell (*Rev.* Charles). The Catskill mountains and the region around. Their scenery, legends, and history: with sketches by Cooper and others. xii, 351 pp. 6 pl. 12°. *New York, Taintor, bros. & Co.* 1867.

Rodd (Thomas). Catalogue of books of voyages and travels in various parts of the world, including an extensive series relating to America. 95 pp. 8°. *London, Compton & Ritchie,* 1843.

Rodwell (James). The rat: its history and destructive character; [with hints on the management of poultry]. New ed. xii, 299 pp. 16°. *London, Routledge & Co.* 1858.

Roe (*Rev.* A. D. *and Mrs.* Marion H.) The months and seasons: a cantata, in four parts.

[*With* PALMER (H. R.) The song queen. pp. 71–96].

Roemer. *See* **Römer.**

Roeper. *See* **Röper.**

Rogeard (A.) Pauvre France! [poème, avec une préface]. xxvii, 104 pp. 16°. *Bruxelles, J. H. Briard,* 1865.

Roger de Hoveden. Annales. *In* **Savile** (*Sir* Henry). Rervm anglicarvm scriptores, etc. 1601.

Roger (Charles, *of Quebec*). The rise of Canada from barbarism to wealth and civilization. v. 1. viii, 412 pp. 8°. *Quebec, P. Sinclair,* 1856.

Rogers (*Rev.* Ammi). Memoirs. By himself. 3d ed. 268 pp. 16°. *Middlebury,* [*Vt.*] *J. W. Copeland,* 1830.

Rogers (George). Explanation of the painting by James Burns, of Washington crowned by three angels, emblematic of equality, fraternity, and liberty, etc. 16 pp. 8°. *New York, author,* 1850. s.

Rogers (Henry Darwin). First annual report of the state geologist [of Pennsylvania]. 32 pp. 8°. *Harrisburg, E. Guyer,* 1836. s.

——— Second annual report of the geological exploration of the state. 92 pp. 1 map. 8°. *Harrisburg, Packer, Barrett & Parker,* 1838. s.

[*With* the preceding].

——— Third annual report on the geological survey of the state. 118 pp. 8°. *Harrisburg, Boas & Coplan,* 1839. s.

[*With* the preceding].

——— Fourth annual report on the geological survey of the state. 215 pp. 8°. *Harrisburg, W. D. Boas,* 1840. s.

[*With* the preceding].

——— Fifth annual report on the geological survey of the commonwealth. 156 pp. 1 pl. 8°. *Harrisburg, Elliott & M'Curdy,* 1841. s.

[*With* the preceding].

Rogers (Samuel). Jacqueline: a tale. [*anon.*] 95, 128 pp. 18°. *London, J. Murray,* 1814.

[*With* BYRON. Lara. Ed. 1814].

Rogers (William B.) Report of the geological reconnoissance of the state of Virginia, made under the appointment of the board of public works. 52 pp. 1 pl. 4°. [*Richmond, public printer,* 1836]. s.

——— Report of the progress of the geological survey of Virginia for the years 1839–[40]. 2 v. in 1. 161 pp. 1 pl; 132 pp. 8°. *Richmond, S. Shepherd,* 1840–41. s.

Rogers (W. R. *M. D.*) An examination of the evidence relative to cow-pox, with letter from John Birch. pp. 105–133.

[*With* BIRCH (John). Vaccination. Cow-pox tracts. v. 3.]

Roggeween (Jakob). Dagverhaal der ontdekkings-reis met de schepen den Arend, Thienhoven, en de afrikaansche galei, 1721–22. 205, 23 pp. 1 map. 2 pl. 8°. *Middelburg, Abrahams,* 1838.

Rohde (Levin-Joergen). Système complet de signaux de jour et de nuit, à l'usage des navigateurs de toutes les nations. Traduction française de MM. C. Vilsoët et Meldola. xxviii, 245 pp. 8°. *Paris, Eberhart,* 1835. s.

——— The same. The universal sea language: a complete code of signals. Translated from the Danish by H. B. Dahlerup. 2d ed. xxviii, 174 pp. 8°. *London, A. W. Webster,* 1835. s.

Rohrer (Louis). Definitions and explanations of the science of book keeping; with commercial correspondence. Counting-house ed. 324 pp. 8°. *Philadelphia, J. B. Lippincott & Co.* 1867.

Roijaards. *See* **Royaards** (Herman Jan).

Rolevinck de Laer (Werner). Fasciculus temporum omnes antiquorum cronicas com plectens. [*anon.*] 9 p. l. 64 l. 4°. *Spirae, P. Drach,* 1477. s.

Rolfe (William J.) *and* **Gillet** (Joseph A.) The Cambridge course of elementary physics. Part 1. Cohesion, adhesion, chemical affinity, and electricity. viii, 324 pp. 12°. *Boston, Crosby & Ainsworth,* 1868.

Roll of honor. Names of soldiers who died in defence of the American union, interred in New Hampshire, Massachusetts, Connecticut, New Jersey, Ohio, Illinois, Wisconsin, Oregon, Maryland, South Carolina, Florida, Louisiana, Mississippi, Texas, Missouri, the military division of the Mississippi, and the territory of Dakota. 244 pp. 8°. *Washington, govt. printing office,* 1866.

——— The same. Names of soldiers, victims of the rebellion, buried in national cemeteries in Maine, Minnesota, Maryland, Pennsylvania, Rhode Island, Arkansas, Mississippi, Florida, Louisiana and Colorado. 138 pp. 8°. *Washington, govt. printing office,* 1866.

——— The same. Names of soldiers who died in defence of the American union, interred in Arkansas, California, Indiana, Michigan, Minnesota, and Nevada, and the territories of Arizona, Colorado, Idaho, New Mexico, and Mexico, 126 pp. 8°. *Washington, govt. printing offiee,* 1866.

——— The same. Interred in Wisconsin, New York, Pennsylvania, Iowa, Maryland, Missouri, North Carolina, Arkansas, Kansas and Dakota territory. 212 pp. 8°. *Washington, govt. printing office,* 1866.

——— The same. Interred at Fortress Monroe and Hampton, Va. 56 pp. 8°. *Washington, govt. printing office,* 1866.

——— The same. Interred in eastern district of Texas; central district of Texas; Rio Grande district, department of Texas; camp Ford, Tyler, Texas, and Corpus Christi, Texas. 35 pp. 8°. *Washington, govt. printing office,* 1866.

Roll of honor. Names of soldiers who died in defence of the American union. (No. xi). Interred in the national cemeteries at Chattanooga, Stone river, and Knoxville, Tenn. 442 pp. 8°. *Washington, govt. printing office,* 1866.

——— The same. (No. xiii). Interred in New York, Illinois, Virginia, West Virginia, Missouri, and the territories of Colorado and Utah, 135 pp. 8°. *Washington, govt. printing office,* 1867.

Rolle (Richard, *of Hampole).* English prose [religious] treatises. Edited from Robert Thornton's MS. (Cir. 1440 A. D.) by George G. Perry. xxxiii, 49 pp. 8°. *London, Trübner & Co.* 1866.

[Early English text society publications, No. 20].

Rollin (Charles). The ancient history of the Egyptians, Carthaginians, Assyrians, Babylonians, Medes, and Persians, Grecians and Macedonians. [With] life of the author by Rev. R. Lynam. Translated from the French. 8 v. 16°. *Hartford, Andrus & Judd,* 1833.

Rolt (Richard). Memoirs of the life of John Lindesay, earl of Crauford. [*anon.*] 336 pp. 16°. *London, T. Becket & Co.* 1769.

Roman des sept sages de Rome. *Paris,* 1838.

[*See* LOISELEUR DESLONGCHAMPS (A. L. A.) Essai sur les fables, etc.]

Romani (Giovanni). Dizionario generale de' sinonimi italiani. 3 v. 8°. *Milano, G. Silvestri,* 1825–26. s.

Romans (*Capt.* Bernard). Annals of the troubles in the Netherlands, from the accession of Charles V, emperor of Germany. 2 v. in 1. 3 p. l. cxx, 160; 243 pp. 12°. *Hartford, Watson & Goodwin,* 1778–82.

——— A concise natural history of east and west Florida. vol. i. viii, 342, lxxxix pp. 2 l. 1 map. 7 pl. 16°. *New York,* 1775.

[No more published].

Römer (Ferdinand). Die kreidebildungen von Texas und ihre organischen einschlüsse. Mit einem die beschriebung von versteinerungen aus paläozoischen und tertiären schichten enthaltenden anhange. viii, 100 pp. 11 pl. 4°. *Bonn, A. Marcus,* 1852. s.

——— Texas. Mit besonderer rücksicht auf deutsche auswanderung und die physischen verhältnisse des landes nach eigener beobachtung geschildert. 8°. *Bonn, A. Marcus,* 1849.

Römer (Friedrich Adolph). Synopsis der mineralogie und geognosie. xiv, 464 pp. 4 pl. 8°. *Hannover, Hahn,* 1853. s.

[*With* LEUNIS (J.) Synopsis der drei naturreiche. 3e theil].

——— Die versteinerungen des nord deutschen oolithen-gebirges. 218 pp. 16 pl. 4°. *Hannover, Hahn,* 1835–36. s.

Ronaldson (James). Specimen of printing type. 54 l. 8°. *Philadelphia,* 1822.

——— The same. 56 l. 8°. *Philadelphia,* 1822.

[*With* BRUCE (D. & G.) Specimen of printing types. 1820].

Ronge (Johannes). Reformation of the 19th century. Part i. Historical development, 1844–52. x, 93 pp. 16°. *London, Deutsch & Co.* 1852.

——— The same. Part ii. Religion of humanity: principles. vii, 93 pp. 16°. *Manchester, Oswald & Covacs,* 1852.

Rönne (Ludwig von). Das unterrichts-wesen des preussischen staates, etc. 2 v. xxviii, 967 pp; xx, 663 pp. 8°. *Berlin, Veit & Co.* 1854–55. s.

[Die Verfassung und verwaltung des preussischen staates. 8er theil. 2e band.]

CONTENTS.

v. 1. Allgemeiner theil. Privat-unterricht-volksschulwesen.

v. 2. Höhere schulen, universitäten, sonstige kulturanstalten.

Ronzelen (J. J. van). Beschreibung des baues des Bremer leuchtthurmes an der stelle der Bremerbaake in der Wesermündung. 52 pp. 2 pl. 1 map. 4°. *Bremerhaven, L. v. Vangerow,* 1857.

Roorbach (Orville A.) Supplement to the Bibliotheca americana: a list of books published in 1849. vii, 124 pp. 8°. *New York, G. P. Putnam,* 1850. s.

Root (Harmon Knox). The lover's marriage light-house: a series of sensible and scientific essays on marriage and free divorce, etc. 511 pp. 8°. *New York, author,* 1858. s.

Röper (Johannes August Christian). Enumeratio euphorbiarum quæ in Germania et Pannonia gignuntur. viii, 68 pp. 3 pl. 4°. *Göttingæ, C. E. Rosenbusch,* 1824.

——— Zur flora Mecklenburgs. 2 v. 160 pp; 296 pp. 8°. *Rostock, Adler's erben,* 1843–44.

Roscher (Albrecht). Ptolemæus und die handelsstrassen in Central-Afrika. viii, 114 pp. 2 maps. 8°. *Gotha, J. Perthes,* 1857. s.

Roscommon (*earl* of). *See* **Dillon** (Wentworth).

Rose (Gustav). Elemente der krystallographie, nebst einer tabellarischen uebersicht der mineralien nach den krystallformen. vi, 173 pp. 10 pl. 8°. *Berlin, E. S. Mittler,* 1833. s.

Rose (Heinrich). Ausführliches handbuch der analytischen chemie. 2 v. xiv, 968 pp; vi, 1,070 pp. 8°. *Braunschweig, Vieweg,* 1851. s.

CONTENTS.

v. 1. Qualitativen chemisch-analytischen untersuchungen.

v. 2. Quantitativen chemisch-analytischen untersuchungen.

Rose (Heinrich). Ausführliches handbuch der analytischen chemie. Traité pratique d'analyse chimique, suivi de tables, servant, dans les analyses, à calculer la quantité d'une substance d'après celle qui a été trouvée d'une autre substance. Traduit de l'Allemand, sur la 4e éd. par A. J. L. Jourdan, accompagnée de notes et additions, par E. Péligot. 2 v. viii, 664 pp; 792 pp. 8°. *Paris, J. B. Baillière*, 1843. s.

——— The same. A practical treatise of chemical analysis, including tables for calculations in analysis. Translated from the French and from the 4th German ed. with notes [etc.], by A. Normandy. 2 v. xvi, 746 pp; xxiv, 587 pp. 8°. *London, W. Tegg & Co.* 1848–9. s.

——— Nachtrag zu chemie. *See* **Weber** (R.)

——— *See, also,* **Normandy** (A.) Practical introduction, etc.

Rose (Philip), *and* **Evans** (John). Printer's job price book. iv, 65 pp. obl. sm. 4°. *Bristol, Philip Rose*, 1814.

Rosecrans (Sylvester H. *D. D.*) The divinity of Christ; together with thoughts on the passion of Jesus Christ. xx, 142 pp. 18°. *Cincinnati, J. P. Walsh*, 1866.

Rosell (Manuel). Apologia en defensa de la aparicion de San Isidro en la batalla de las Navas, [etc.] 123 pp. 12°. *Madrid, Imprenta real*, 1791. s.

Roselli (Antonio). Tractatus de ieiunijs. 6 l. sm. 4°. *Rome, Steffanus Planck*, 1486.

Rosen (Georg.) Elementa persica: narrationes persicae. xix, 199 pp. 12°. *Berolini, Veit*, 1843. s.

Rosenmüller (Johann Georg). Scholia in novum testamentum. [Ed. 6a cura E. F. C. Rosenmulleri]. 5 v. 8°. *Norimbergae, Felsecker*, 1815. s.

Ross (*Rev.* Arthur A.) Discourse embracing the civil and religious history of Rhode Island, delivered at Newport April 4, 1838, at the close of the second century from the first settlement of the island. 161 pp. 12°. *Providence, H. H. Brown*, 1838.

Ross (D. Barton). The rhetorical manual, or Southern fifth reader. 549 pp. 12°. *New Orleans, (La.) J. B. Steel*, 1853. s.

Ross *or* **Rouse** (John, *of Warwick*). Historia regum Angliæ. Descripsit, notisque et indice adornavit Tho. Hearnius. xxxvi, 236 pp. 2 pl. 8°. *Oxonii, J. Fletcher & J. Pote*, 1745.

Ross (*Sir* John). Explanation and answer to Mr. John Braithwaite's supplement to Captain Sir J. Ross's narrative of a second voyage in search of a northwest passage. iv, 26 pp. 8°. *London*, 1849.

[*With his* Observations on a work entitled "Voyages of discovery, etc." *London*, 1846].

——— Letter to John Barrow, on the late extraordinary and unexpected hyperborean discoveries. [*anon.*] 46 pp. 8°. *London, W. Pople*, 1826.

[*With his* Observations on a work, entitled "Voyage of discovery within the Arctic regions." *London*, 1846].

——— Observations on a work, entitled "Voyages of discovery and research in the Arctic regions," by Sir John Barrow. 62 pp. 8°. *London, Blackwood*, 1846.

——— A short treatise on the deviation of the mariner's compass. 39 pp. 1 pl. 8°. *London, Richardson*, 1849.

[*With his* Observations on a work, entitled "Voyages of discovery within the Arctic regions." *London*, 1846].

Ross (M.) Collieries in Northumberland, etc. *See* **Hair** (T. H.) *and* **Ross.**

Rossel (Élisabeth Paul Édouard de). Traité des calculs de l'astronomie nautique.

[*With* Biot (J. B.) Traité élémentaire d'astronomie, 1810–11].

Rossetti (William Michael). Swinburne's poems and ballads; a criticism. 80 pp. 16°. *London, J. C. Hotten*, 1866.

Rossi (Guglielmo, *prof. at Milan*). Prolusione ad un corso libero di letture, di scienza finanziaria, etc. 61 pp. 4°. *Milano, autore*, 1861. s.

Rossi (Pellegrino Luigi Odoardo). Cours d'économie politique. 2e éd. 2 v. ii, 464 pp; 448 pp. 8°. *Paris, Thorel, etc.* 1843. s.

Rossignon (Julio). Manuel del cultivo del añil y del nopal; ó sea extraccion del indigo, educacion y cosecha de la cochinilla. 309 pp. 18°. *Paris, Rosa & Bouret*, 1859.

[Encl. Hisp. Amer.]

——— Manuel del cultivo de la caña de azúcar, del laboreo del azúcar. 304 pp. 18°. *Paris, Rosa & Bouret*, 1857.

(Encl. Hisp. Amer.)

Rossmässler (Emil Adolf). Der naturgeschichtliche unterricht. Gedanken und vorschläge zu einer umgestaltung desselben. vi, 138 pp. 12°. *Leipzig, F. Brandsteller*, 1860. s.

——— Populare vorlesungen aus dem gebiete der natur. Mikroskopische blicke in den innern bau und das leben der gewächse. v. 1. ix, 100 pp. 15 col. pl. 12°. *Leipzig, H. Costenoble*, 1852. s.

——— Stirje letni casi. Predelal Ivan Tusek. vii, 255 pp. 8°. *Ljubljani, Matica slovenska*, 1867. s.

Rossmässler (Emil Adolf). Der wald. Den freunden und pflegern des waldes geschildert. xiv, 628 pp. 2 maps. 17 pl. 8°. *Leipzig, etc. C. F. Winter,* [1861]-63. s.

Roth von Schreckenstein (Carl Heinrich). Herr Walther von Geroldseck, bischof von Strassburg, (1261-1263). 76 pp. 8°. *Tübingen, H. Laupp,* 1857. s.

Rothe (A). Handbuch für angehenden landwirth. 2e aufl. xiv, 340 pp. 8°. *Leipzig, Veit & Co.* 1861. s.

Rother (Stanislaus, *M. D.*) Ueber echinococcen der leber. 32 pp. 8°. *Berlin, G. Lange,* 1867. s.

Rotteck (Carl Wenzel von), *and* **Welcker** (Carl Theodor). Das staats-lexikon. Encyclopädie der sämmtlichen staatswissenschaften für alle stände, [etc.] Neue auflage. 12 v. 8°. *Altona, J. F. Hammerich,* 1845-48.

Rouby (Jules). Bibliothèque de l'émigrant. Guide américain. 248 pp. 16°. *Paris, É. Blot,* 1859.

Rough sketch of modern Paris; or, letters on society, manners, public curiosities and amusements, in that capital, written 1801-2. [*anon.*] 8 p. l. 319 pp. 8°. *London, J. Johnson,* 1803.

Roulet (Jean Antoine). Recueil des mémoires sur la culture de la vigne. 188 pp. 8°. *Neuchatel, Fauche-Borel,* 1808. s.

Roullier (Auguste). Essai sur la philosophie médicale. xxii, 294 pp. 8°. *Paris, Croullebois,* 1815.

Round (The) table. July 28, 1866 to Dec. 1867. v. 4-6. sm. fol. *New York, J. A. Gray & Green,* 1866-67.

Rouse (*Sir* Charles William Broughton). Dissertation concerning the landed property of Bengal. 322 pp. 8°. *London, J. Stockdale,* 1791.

Rouse (John). *See* **Ross** (John, *of Warwick*).

Rouse (William). The doctrine of chances; or, the theory of gaming, made easy to every person. 350 pp. 8°. *London, Lackington,* 1814.

Rousseau (*baron* A.) Parnasse oriental; ou, dictionnaire historique et critique des meilleurs poètes, anciens et modernes, de l'Orient, etc. viii, 207 pp. 8°. *Alger, Brachet & Bastide,* 1841. s.

Rousseau (Jean Jacques.) Contrat social.
[Appended to TOROMBERT (C. L. H.) Principes, etc.]

Rousseau (Louis), *and* **Céran-Lemonnier** (——). Promenades au jardin des plantes. xxxi, 519 pp. 18°. *Paris, J. B. Baillière,* 1837.

Rousselot de Surgy (Jacques Philibert). Mélanges intéressans et curieux; ou, abrégé d'histoire naturelle, morale, civile, et politique de l'Asie, l'Afrique, l'Amérique, et des terres polaires. [*anon.*] v. 1-2. 12°. *Paris, Durand,* 1763. s.
[Wanting v. 3-10].

Roussillon (F. P. Vigo). *See* **Vigo-Roussillon.**

Roussin (Albin René, *baron*). Memoir on the navigation of the western coast of Africa from Cape Bojador to mount Souzos. [1817-18]. Translated by James Badgley. 68 pp. 4°. *London, Hydrographic office,* 1827. s.

Roux (Joseph). Recueil des principaux plans des ports et rades de la mer Mediterranée. 121 maps. obl. 18°. *Gènes, Gravier,* 1779.

Rover (A. *pseudon.*) *See* **Croquet**; its principles and rules.

Rovings in the Pacific, from 1837 to 1849; with a glance at California. By a merchant long resident at Tahiti. [*anon.*] 2 v. xi, 371 pp; xii, 351 pp. 4 pl. 12°. *London, Longman, Brown & Co.* 1851.

Rowe (*Mrs.* Elizabeth). Devout exercises of the heart. 4th ed. xviii, 148 pp. 18°. *Boston, Rogers and Fowle,* 1742.
[Imperfect].

Rowe (Nicholas). Poetical works. 8°. *Edinburgh,* 1793.
[Anderson's Brit. poets, v. 7].

Rowel (M.) Letters from hell. 2 v. vii, 336 pp; 328 pp. 12°. *London, Bentley,* 1866.

Rowlett (John). Tables of discount, or interest. 2d ed. 208 pp. 4°. *Philadelphia, J. Rowlett,* 1826.

Rowley (*Hon.* Hugh, *pseudon?*) Puniana; or, thoughts wise and other-wise. A new collection of the best riddles, conundrums, jokes, etc. Illustrated. xii, 258 pp. sm. 4°. *London, J. C. Hotten,* 1867.

Roxburghe (John Ker, 3*d duke of*). A catalogue of the library of the late duke, arranged by G. and W. Nicol, [etc.] which will be sold by auction, May, 1812, by R. H. Evans. 284 pp. 8°. *London, W. Bulmer & Co.* 1812. s.

——— A supplement to the catalogue, [etc.] iv. 21 pp. 8°. *London, W. Bulmer & Co.* 1812. s.
[*With* the preceding].

——— The prices of the Roxburghe library. 73 pp. 8°. *London, W. Bulmer & Co.* [1812.] s.
[*With* the preceding].

Royaards (Herman Jan). Hedendaagsch kerkregt bij de hervormden in Nederland. 2 v. xii, 261 pp; xii, 448 pp. 8°. *Utrecht, J. Altheer,* 1834.

Royal (The) family of the Stuarts vindicated from the false imputation of illegitimacy. [*anon.*] 44 pp. 12°.

[*With* ORLÉANS (P. J. d'). History of revolutions in England, 1603–90. 12°. *London*, 1711].

Royal geographical society. Journal. 1866. v. 36. 8°. *London, J. Murray*, [1867].

——— Proceedings. Sessions 1865–67. v. 10-11. 8°. *London, W. Clowes & sons*, 1866–67.

Royal institution of Great Britain. Catalogue of library, including a list of the Greek writers, by Charles Burney, with an index of authors by W. Harris. 8°. *London*, 1821. s.

Royal medical and chirurgical society, (*London*). Additions to the library during the years 1856–57–66. 9 v. 8°. *London, society*, 1856–66. s.

Royal (The) military chronicle; or, British officers' monthly register and mirror. [Supplements to v. 2, 3, 5, and 6, v. 1, new series, May to Nov. 1814]. 3v. 5 pl. 8°. *London, J. Davis*, 1811–14.

CONTENTS.

ANTHING (Friedrich). History of the campaigns of Suworow Rymnikski. v. 2.
Campaign of Moreau, in Germany, 1796. v. 1.
DEFOE (Daniel). Memoirs of Capt. Geo. Carleton. v. 1.
EUGENE (*of Savoy, prince*). Life of. v. 1.
GIRAUD (P. F. F. J.) Campaigns in France, 1813–14. v. 3.
VERTOT D'AUBEUF (R. A. de). History of the revolution in Portugal. v. 1.
VOLTAIRE (F. M. A. de). Life of Charles xii. v. 2.
——— Life of Peter the great. v. 2.

Royer (Charles Édouard). Notes économiques sur l'administration des richesses, et la statistique agricole de la France. xviii, 471 pp. 8°. *Paris, Pillet ainé*, 1843.

Royle (John Forbes, *M. D.*) Materia medica and therapeutics. Edited by Joseph Carson. 689 pp. 8°. *Philadelphia, Lea & Blanchard*, 1847. s.

Roys (Auren, *pseudon?*) Brief history of the town of Norfolk, [Conn.] from 1738 to 1844. 89 pp. 8°. *New York, Henry Ludwig*, 1847.

Rozy (H.) Étude sur les sociétés coopératives et leur constitution légale; précédée d'un coup d'œil sur les sociétés taisibles au moyen âge, et suivie d'une réponse à l'ouvrage de M. Cernuschi: illusions des sociétés coopératives. 212 pp. 8°. *Paris, Guillaumin*, 1866.

Rubek (Sennoia, *pseudon.*) *See* **Burke** (John).

Ruby (The): a token of friendship for 1849. [Tales and poetry]. 304 pp. 11 pl. 8°. *Philadelphia, Carey & Hart*, 1849. s.

Ruddiman (Thomas). Grammaticæ latinæ institutiones, ad puerorum captum perscriptæ. 10ª ed. 2 parts in 1 v. 128, 180 pp. 16°. *Edinburgi, Dickson & Elliot*, 1778.

——— Introduction to James Anderson's diplomata Scotiæ. [With] notes. New ed. 6 pl. 232 pp. 18°. *Edinburgh, P. Anderson*, 1782.

Rudge (E. J.) A short account of the history and antiquities of Evesham. vi, 145 pp. 5 pl. 16°. *Evesham, J. Agg*, 1820.

Rudolph (Ludwig). Die pflanzendecke der erde. viii, 416 pp. 8°. *Berlin, Nicolai*, 1853. s.

Rudolphi (Carl Asmund). Entozoorum, sive vermium intestinalium historia naturalis. 2 v. in 3. 8°. *Amstelædami, Tabernæ librariæ et artium*, 1808–10. s.

——— Entozoorum synopsis, cui accedunt mantissa duplex et indices locupletissimi. x, 811 pp. 3 pl. 8°. *Berolini, A. Rücker*, 1819. s.

Rue (De La). *See* **La Rue**.

Ruff (H.) History of Cheltenham. *See* **Dibdin** (T. F.)

Rufinianus (Julius). De figuris sententiarum. *See* **Rutilius** Lupus (P.)

Rufinus *antiochenus*. De metris comicis, et oratoriis numeris.

[*With* PRISCIANUS. Libri omnes. Ed. 1527].

Rufus (Sextus). *See* **Sextus** Rufus.

Rühl (Carl). Californien: ueber dessen bevölkerung und gesellschaftliche zustände, politische, religiöse, und schul-verhältnisse, handel, industrie, minen, ackerbau, u. s. w. Mit berücksichtigung der minen-regionen der benachbarten staaten, etc. Mit einer karte von Californien, Nevada, etc. viii, 283 pp. 2 col. maps. 8°. *New York, E. Steiger*, 1867. s.

Ruiz de Leon (Francisco). La Hernandia; triumphos de la fè, y gloria de las armas españolas: conquista de Mexico, etc. Poema heroyco. 10 p. l. 383 pp. sm. 4°. *Madrid, Viuda de Manuel Fernandez*, 1755.

Ruiz de Montoya (Antonio). La arte, vocabulario, catecismo, y tesoro de la lengua Guarani. Segunda parte: [vocabulario]. 4 p. l. 407 l. sm. 4°. *Madrid, Juan Sanchez*, 1639.

[Imperfect; p. l. wanting, title-page in ms.]

Rules and regulations for the government of racing, trotting, and betting, as adopted by the principal turf associations throughout the United States and Canada. Compiled at the office of "Wilkes' spirit of the times." 254 pp. 16°. *New York, M. B. Brown & Co.* [1866].

Rules and regulations for the management of the Philadelphia, Wilmington, and Baltimore, and the New Castle and Frenchtown railroads. 45 pp. 8°. *Philadelphia, J. H. Bryson*, 1854.

Rumohr (Carl Dietrich Ludwig Felix, *baron* von). Drey reisen nach Italien. viii, 327 pp. 16°. *Leipzig, F. A. Brockhaus,* 1832. s.

——— Italienische forschungen. [Zur theorie und geschichte neuerer kunstbestrebungen]. 3 v. 8°. *Berlin und Stettin, Nicolai,* 1827–31. s.

Rumph *or* **Rumpf** (Georg Eberhard). Thesaurus imaginum piscium testaceorum; quales sunt cancri, echini, echinometra, stellæ marinæ, etc. ut et cochlearum; quibus accedunt conchylia, ut nautilus, cornu Ammonis, etc. conchæ univalviæ et bivalviæ; denique mineralia. 2 p. l. 14 pp. 2, 60 pl. fol. *Lugduni Batavorum, P. Van der Aa,* 1739.

Rumsey (James). A plan wherein the power of steam is fully shown, by a new constructed machine for propelling boats or vessels against the most rapid streams or rivers. 20 pp. 8°. [*Philadelphia,* 1788].

[*With* FITCH (John). Original steamboat supported. 1788].

——— A short treatise on the application of steam, [showing] that steam may be applied to propel boats or vessels against rapid currents with great velocity. 26 pp. 8°. *Philadelphia, J. James,* 1788.

[Imperfect: pp. 17—24 wanting].

Runde (Christian Ludwig). Kurzgefasste oldenburgische chronik, bis zum tode des herzogs Peter Friedrich Ludwig fortgesetzt. 2^e ausg. xvii, 236 pp. 1 tab. 1 portrait. 8°. *Oldenburg, Schulze,* 1831. s.

Rundle (Thomas, *bishop of Derry*). Letters to Mrs. Barbara Sandys; with memoirs by James Dallaway. 2 v. in 1. clxxiv; 255 pp. 12°. *Glocester, T. Cadell,* 1789.

Rupertus, *abbas tuicensis* (*of* Deutz *or* Duytz). De diuinis officiis. 6 p. l. 187 pp. fol. *Coloniae, F. Birckman,* 1526.

Rupp (I. Daniel). History of Dauphin, Cumberland, Franklin, Bedford, Adams, and Perry counties, Pa. 606 pp. 4 pl. 8°. *Lancaster, Gilbert Hills,* 1846.

——— The same. [With Somerset, Cambria, and Indiana counties]. 660 pp. 10 pl. 8°. *Lancaster, Gilbert Hills,* 1846.

——— History of the counties of Berks and Lebanon, Pa. 512 pp. 2 pl. 8°. *Lancaster, Gilbert Hills,* 1844.

——— History of Northumberland, Huntingdon, Mifflin, Centre, Union, Columbia, Juniata, and Clinton counties, Pa. 568 pp. 3 pl. 8°. *Lancaster, Gilbert Hills,* 1847.

Rüppell (Wilhelm Peter Eduard). Atlas zu der reise im nördlichen Afrika. 5 v. fol. *Frankfurt am Main, Senkenbergische naturforschende gesellschaft,* 1826–31. s.

CONTENTS.

CRETZSCHMAR (Philipp J.) Säugethiere. 3 p. l. vii, 78 pp. 30 col. pl. 1826. Vögel, 1826.
HEYDEN (Carl Heinrich Georg von). Reptilien, 1827. 60 pp. 36 col. pl.
LEUCKART (Friedrich Sigismund), *and* RÜPPELL (W. P. E.) Neue wirbellose thiere des Rothen Meers. 1828.

——— Neue wirbelthiere zu der fauna von Abyssinien gehörig, entdeckt und beschrieben. 4 v. in 2. 4 p. l. 40 pp. 14 col pl; 116 pp. 42 col. pl. fol. *Frankfurt am Main, S. Schmerber,* 1835–40. s.

CONTENTS.

v. 1. Säugethiere.
v. 2. Vögel.
v. 3. Amphibien.
v. 4. Fische des Rothen Meeres.

Rural visiter; a literary and miscellaneous gazette. v. 1. 4°. *Burlington, (N. J.)* 1811.

Ruscelli (Girolamo). Expositioni et introdvttioni vniversali sopra tutta la geografia di Tolomeo. 27 l. sm. 4°. *Venetia, V. Valgrisi,* 1561.

[*With* PTOLEMÆUS (C.) Geografia. *Venetia,* 1561].

——— The same. sm. 4°. *Venetia, G. Zilletti* 1573.

[*With* PTOLEMÆUS (C.) Geografia, *Venetia,* 1574].

Rusden (Moses). A further discovery of bees. 12 p. l. 143 pp. 4 pl. 16°. *London, author,* 1679.

Rush (Benjamin *M. D.*) Considerations upon the present test-law of Pennsylvania. 23 pp. 16°. *Philadelphia,* 1785?

[Title wanting.]

Ruskin (John). Modern painters. By a graduate of Oxford. [*anon.*] 1st American from the 3d London ed. Pts. 1–3 in 2 v. lxvii, 422 pp; 222 pp. 12°. *New York, Wiley & Putnam,* 1847–48. s.

——— The stones of Venice. [v. 1.] The foundations. xvi, 435 pp. 21 pl. 8°. *New York, J. Wiley,* 1851. s.

Russel (George). Works. 2 v. xxx, 405 pp; 401 pp. 12°. *Cork, W. Flyn,* 1769.

Russell (Francis). A short history of the East India company; exhibiting their affairs, abroad and at home, political and commercial. [By] F. R. [*anon.*] 2d ed. 4 p. l. 95 pp. 4°. *London, J. Sewell,* 1793.

Russell (John). History of Greece and Rome, including Judea, Egypt, and Carthage. New ed. 266 pp. 2 pl. 12°. *Philadelphia, Lindsay & Blakiston,* 1854. s.

Russell (J. Rutherfurd, *M. D.*) Contribution to medical literature. viii, 053 pp. 8°. *London, Leath & Ross,* 1859.

Russell (John Scott). Modern system of naval architecture. v. 1. [Text]. xxxvii, 686 pp. 2 pl; v. 2–3. 165 pl. 3 v. fol. *London, Day & son,* 1865.

Russell (P.) *and* **Price** (Owen). England displayed: being a new, complete, and accurate description of the kingdom of England, and the principality of Wales. 2 v. viii, 392 pp; 314 pp. 51 maps. 79 pl. fol. *London, Adlard & Browne,* 1769.
[Imperfect, wanting map 1].

Russell (Richard, *M. D.*), *and* **Speed**, (J. *M. D.*) A dissertation on the use of sea-water in the diseases of the glands. [With] a commentary on sea-water. From the Latin, by an eminent physician. 3d ed. xii, 248 pp. 2 pl. 16°. *London, W. Owen,* 1755.

Russell (William Howard). The British expedition to the Crimea. Revised ed. vii, 629 pp. 4 maps. 10 pl. 8°. *London, etc. G. Routledge & Co.* 1858. s.

Russell (William S.) Pilgrim memorials, and guide to Plymouth. 3d ed. 229 pp. 1 map, 8 pl. 12°. *Boston, Crosby, Nichols, Lee & Co.* 1860.

Russia. Atlas économique et statistique de la Russie d'Europe, publié par le ministère des domaines de l'état, le département de d'économie rurale. 3e éd. 1 p. l. 10 col. maps. fol. Texte explicatif, viii, 164 pp. 8°. *St. Pétersbourg, Imprimerie de l'académie imp. des sciences,* 1857. s.

Ruthe (Johann Friedrich). *See* **Wiegmann** (Arend Friedrich August), *and others.*

Rutherforth *or* **Rutherford** (Thomas, *D.D.*) System of natural philosophy. 2 v. xi p. l. 1105 pp. 31 pl. 4°. *Cambridge, J. Bentham,* 1748.

Ruthven (A. S.) Proceedings of the grand lodge of Texas from its organization, A. D. 1837, to 1857. With an history of the origin, rise, and progress of the masonic order in Texas. 2 v. 640 pp; 308, 352 pp. 8°. *Galveston, Richardson & Co.* 1857.

Rutilius *or* **Roedelstein** (Johann). Epistolæ indicæ. De stvpendis et præclaris rebvs, quas diuina bonitas, in India et variis insulis per societatē nominis Iesv operari dignata est, in tam copiosa gentium ad fidem conuersione. 12 pl. 496 pp. 18°. *Lovanii, Rutgerus Velpius,* 1566.

Rutilius Lupus (P?) De figuris sententiarum et elocutionis libri duo. Recensuit David Ruhnkenius. Accedunt Aquilæ Romani et Julii Rufiniani de eodem argumento libri. c, 276 pp. 8 l. 8°. *Lugduni Batavorum, Luchtmans,* 1768.

Rütimeyer (Ludwig). Versuch einer natürlichen geschichte des rindes, in seinem beziehungen zu den wiederkauern im allgemeinen. Eine anatomisch-palæontologische monographie von Linné's genus *bos.* [Extract.] 175 pp. 6 pl. 4°. *Zürich, Schweiz-gesellschaft für gesammt. naturw.* 1867. s.

Rüxner (Georg). Thurnier buch. Von anfang, vrsachen, vrsprüng, vnd herkommen der thurnier im heyligen römischen reich teutscher nation, [etc.] 6 p. l. 243 l. 3 l. fol. *Franckfurt am Mayn,* 1566. s.

Rydqvist (Johan Erik). Svenska språckets lagar. Kritisk afhandling. v. i. 2 p. l. xlv, 304 pp. 8°. *Stockholm, S. Magnus,* 1850. s.

Ryland (John). The character of the Rev. James Hervey, with sixty-five of his original letters to the author. xv, xiv, 311, 99 pp. 1 pl. 8°. *London, Robarts,* 1791.

Ryssen (Leonhart van). Justa detestatio sceleratissimi libri Adriani Beverlandi De peccato originali. Accedit descriptio poëtica creationis et lapsus, versibus ex plerisque poetis concinnata. 2 p. l. 56 pp. 2 l. 13 pp. 16°. *Gorinchemi, C. Lever,* 1680.

Saadi. *See* **Sadi.**

Saalfeld (Jakob Christoph Friedrich). Geschichte des hollandischen kolonial-wesens in Ostindien. 2 v. xxiv, 352 pp; xvi, 264 pp. 3 tab. 12°. *Göttingen, H. Dieterich,* 1812–13. s.

Saavedra Faxardo (Diego de). The royal politician, represented in one hundred emblems. Done into English by Sir J. Astry. 2 v. 10 p. l. 376 pp; 2 p. l. 384 pp. 2 pl. 12°. *London, M. Gylliflower,* 1700.

Sabatier de Castres (Antoine, *l'abbé*). Apologie de Spinosa et du spinosisme contre les athéos, etc. 122 pp. 8°. *Altona,* 1805.

Sabau y Larroya (Pedro). Ilustracion de la ley fundamental de España, que establece la forma de suceder en la corona. 8°. *Madrid,* 1833.

Sabbath (The) at home. An illustrated religious magazine for the family. Jan. to Dec. 1867. v. 1. vi, 764 pp. 8°. *Boston, Am. tract soc.* [1867].

Sabbathier (François). Dictionnaire pour l'intelligence des auteurs classiques, grecs et latins, tants sacrés que profanes, contenant la géographie, l'histoire, la fable, et les antiquités. 37 v. 8°. *Paris,* 1760–1815. s.
[v. 36–37 wanting].

Sabin (Joseph, *editor*). Bibliotheca americana. A dictionary of books relating to America, from its discovery to the present time. Part i–v. A. to Barringer. 480 pp. 8°. *New York, J. Sabin,* 1867–68.

Sabine (Lorenzo). Biographical sketches of loyalists of the American revolution, with an historical essay. 2d ed. 2 v. xii, 608 pp; 600 pp. 8°. *Boston, Little, Brown & Co.* 1864.

Sabunde, Sebon, *or* **Sebeide** (Ramon). [Theologia naturalis, siue liber creaturarum]. 162 l. 4°. *Argentorati, Martin Flach,* 1501.
[Title and l. 7 wanting].

——— The same. Le creature; ampio libro dell' uomo. Rifusa ed accomodata agli studj della gioventù del secolo xix, da un sacerdote della compagnia di Gesù. 3 v. in 1. 12°. *Reggio, G. Davolio e figlio,* 1818. s.

CONTENTS.

v. 1. Delle creature e del creatore. 273 pp.
v. 2. Del mondo morale. 204 pp.
v. 3. Dell' intrinseca struttura del christianesimo. 187 pp.

Sacc (*Dr.* F.) Précis élémentaire de chimie agricole. 5 p. l. 420 pp. 12°. *Paris, librairie agricole,* 1848. s.

Sacerdos (Marcus Claudius). Artium grammaticarum libri duo.
[*With* EICHENFELD (J. von). Analecta grammatica. *Vindobonae,* 1837].

Sachtleben (Johann Heinrich). L'art d'économiser le bois; ou, dix procédés de feu économiques. Tr. de l'Allemand par J. Goy. 152 pp. 14 pl. 8°. *Paris, Valade,* 1792. s.

Sackville (Charles, *earl of Dorset*). Poetical works. 8°. *Edinburgh,* 1793.
[Anderson's Brit. poets. v. 6].

Sad tale of the courtship of the chevalier Henry Sly-fox Wikof. [A series of plates, without title]. 48 pp. obl. 16°. [*New York, about* 1855].

Saddharma pundarîka. Le lotus de la bonne loi, traduit du Sanscrit, accompagné d'un commentaire et de vingt et un mémoires relatifs au buddhisme, par M. E. Burnouf. 897 pp. 4°. *Paris, Imprimerie nationale,* 1852.

Sadeler *or* Sattler (Jan *and* Raphael). Trophævm vitæ solitariæ. [25 plates.] obl. fol. *Venetijs, J. & R. Sadeler,* 1598. s.
[*With* GALLE (Philippe). Acta apostolorum, etc.]

——— Oracvlvm anachoreticvm. [25 plates]. obl. fol. *Venetijs, J. & R. Sadeler,* 1600. s.
[*With* GALLE (Philippe). Acta apostolorum, etc.]

Sadeur (Jacques, *pseudon.*) *See* **Foigny** (Gabriel).

Sadi *or* Moslih-ed-dín Sadí Ben Abdallah. Gulistan. [Original text, with Persian-English vocabulary]. New ed. collated with original Mss. by E. B. Eastwick. 13, 127, 231 pp. 8°. *Hertford, Stephen Austin,* 1850.

——— Selections from the Bostân of Sadi. (Persian). By Forbes Falconer. iii, 107 pp. pp. 24°. *London, L. Schönberg,* 1838. s.

Sadler (Percy). Cours gradué de langue anglaise, (2e partie); ou, petit cours de versions, contenant un recueil d'anecdotes; et suivi d'un dictionnaire des mots. 12e éd. 288 pp. 18°. *Paris, J. H. Truchy,* 1858.

Saez (Liciniano). Demostracion histórica del verdadero valor de todas las monedas que corrian en Castilla durante el reynado del señor Enrique iv, y de su correspondencia con las del señor Carlos iv, [etc.] xx, 582 pp. 4°. *Madrid, Real academia de la historia,* 1805. s.

Safaríka (Pawl Josef). *See* **Schafarik.**

Safford (James M.) Geological reconnoissance of the state of Tennessee; first biennial report. 164 pp. 1 map. 8°. *Nashville, G. C. Torbett & Co.* 1856. s.

Sagard-Théodat (Gabriel). Histoire du Canada, et voyages que les frères mineurs recollects y ont faicts pour la conversion des infidèles, depuis l'an 1615 jusqu'en 1629. Nouv. éd. 4 v. 12°. *Paris, Tross,* 1865–66.

——— Le grand voyage du pays des Hurons situé en l'Amèrique vers la Mer Douce, ès derniers confins de la Nouvelle-France dite Canada. 2 p. l. xxv, 268 pp. 12°. *Paris, Tross,* 1865.

——— Dictionnaire de la langve huronne. Nouv. éd. 12 pp. 65 l. 12°.
[*With* SAGARD-THÉODAT (Gabriel). His oire du Canada, etc. v. 4. 12°. *Paris,* 1865].

——— The same.
[*With* SAGARD-THÉODAT (Gabriel). Le grand voyage du pays des Hurons. 12°. *Paris,* 1865].

Sâgean (Mathieu). Extrait de la relation des avantures et voyage de Mathieu Sâgean. 32 pp. 12°. *Nouvelle York, J. M. Shea,* 1863. s.

Sagen (Lyder Christian), *and* **Foss** (H.) Bergens beskrivelse. xxiii, 786 pp. 1 map. 12°. *Bergen, C. Dahl,* 1824. s.

Sailor's (The) companion; or, book of devotion for seamen in public and private. [*anon.*] 263 pp. 12°. *Philadelphia, Presbyterian board of publication,* 1858. s.

Saints (The) apologie; or, a vindication of the churches which endeavour after a pure communion, from the odious names of Brownists, and Separatists. [*anon.*] 2 p. l. 15 pp. sm. 4°. *London,* 1644.

Saint Anthony (*Minnesota*). Merwin's directory, 1867. 264 pp. 12°. *Minneapolis, H. Merwin,* 1867.

Saint Augustin (Marie Tranchepain de). *See* **Tranchepain** de St. Augustin.

Saint Croix and lake Superior railroad co. Acts of the legislature of Wisconsin, and of the congress of the United States, relative to the St. Croix and lake Superior railroad co. with the statement of the president and directors, and of the chief engineer of said company. 157 pp. 1 map. 8°. *New York, J. W. Amerman,* 1866.

Saint Fargeau. *See* **Le Pelletier** de Saint Fargeau.

Saint Foix (Germain François Poullain). *See* **Poullain de St. Foix.**

Saint-Génois (Jules, *baron* de). Inventaire analytique des chartes des comtes de Flandre [etc.] déposées au chateau de Rupelmonde, et conservées aujourd'hui aux archives de la Flandre-orientale, [etc.]; et suivi d'un glossaire, des notes, [etc.] x, xliv, 579 pp. 3 pl. 8°. *Gand, Vanryckegem Hovaere,* 1843–46. s.

Saint Germain (Claude Louis, *comte* de). Mémoires [militaires. Rédigés par l'abbé La Montagne et publiés par l'abbé Dubois]. xii, 320 pp. 16°. *Amsterdam, M. M. Rey,* 1779.

Saint Hilaire (Émile Marco de) *or* **Hilaire** (Marc). Histoire des conspirations et des exécutions politiques en France, en Angleterre, en Russie, et en Espagne depuis les temps les plus reculés jusqu'à nos jours. 4 v. 8°. *Paris, G. Havard,* 1849.

——— Mémoires et révélations d'un page de la cour impériale, de 1802 à 1815. [*anon.*] 2 v. 4, 380 pp; 375 pp. 8°. *Paris, C. Malot,* 1830.

Saint Hilaire (Geoffroy). *See* **Geoffroy** Saint Hilaire.

Saint John (Henry, *lord Bolingbroke*). Letters on the study and use of history. New ed. iv, 413 pp. 8°. *Paris, Theophilus Barrois, jr.* 1808.

Saint John (James Augustus). Egypt and Nubia, their scenery and their people. viii, 472 pp. 8°. *London, Chapman & Hall,* [1845].

Saint John (John R.) A true description of the lake Superior country, with an account of the copper mines. 118 pp. 2 maps. 16°. *New York, William H. Graham,* 1846.

Saint Jure (Jean Baptiste de). L'homme religievx. Livre i. Des règles et des voevx de la religion. 4 p. l. 571 pp. 32 l. 4°. *Paris, D. Bechet,* 1657.

Saint Louis. Guide book and pocket map; giving the early history, etc. By J. H. Cook. 44 pp. 1 map. 24°. *St. Louis, Clayton & Babington,* 1867.

Saint Marc (Girardin.) *See* **Girardin** (Saint Marc.)

St. Mark's library (*Venice*). Latina et italica D. Marci bibliotheca codicvm manvscriptorvm per titulos digesta. 2 p. l. 268 pp. 4 pl. fol. [*Venetiis*]. 1741. s.

——— Graeca D. Marci bibliotheca codicvm manvscriptorvm [etc.] xx, 323 pp. 2 pl. fol. [*Venetiis*], *S. Occhi,* 1740. s.
[*With* the preceding].

Saint Paul (*Minnesota*). McClung's St. Paul directory, and statistical record for 1866. 7 p. l. 284 pp. 8°. *St. Paul, J. W. McClung,* 1866.

——— Directory, for 1867. v. 3. 287 pp. 8°. *St. Paul, Bailey & Wolfe,* 1867.

St. Petersbourg. Catalogue des manuscrits et typographes orientaux de la bibliothèque impériale publique de St. Pétersbourg. xliv, 719 pp. 8°. *St. Pétersbourg, imprimerie de l'acad. imp. des sciences,* 1852. s.

——— Jardin botanique impérial de St. Pétersbourg. fol. *St. Pétersbourg, Fischer,* 1846–52. s.

CONTENTS.

Notice sur la construction d'une nouvelle serre de palmiers. (Par G. Tolstoy). 2 l. 1 pl.
Notice sur la serre des palmiers. (Par *baron* C. de Kuster). 2 l. 5 pl.
Sertum petropolitanum, seu icones et descriptiones plantarum quæ in hortu botanico floruerunt. 22 l. 20 pl.

Saint Pierre (Jacques Henri Bernardin de). Paul and Virginia. Illustrations by A. Hoppin. xxv, 149 pp. 6 pl. 16°. *New York, Hurd & Houghton,* 1867.

Saint Priest (Alexis Guignard, *comte* de). Études diplomatiques et littéraires. 2 v. 402 pp; 416 pp. 8°. *Paris, Amyot,* [1850].

Saint Réal (César Vichard de). The history of the conspiracy of the Spaniards against the republic of Venice, 1618. 135 pp. 24°. *Glasgow, R. & A. Foulis,* 1752.

Saint Victor (Jacques Maximilien Benjamin Bins de). Briefe über die Vereinigten Staaten von Nord Amerika. Geschrieben in 1832–33. Aus dem Französischen des herrn von J. M. B. de *****. [*anon.*] viii p. l. 293 pp; xii p. l. 372 pp. 2 v. 8°. *Berlin, F. Dümmler,* 1835.

Sainte-Beuve (Charles Augustin). Nouveaux lundis. 2e éd. v. 1–8. 16°. *Paris, Lévy,* 1864–67.

——— Volupté. 3e éd. [*anon.*] 422 pp. 16°. *Paris, Charpentier,* 1845.

Sainte Palaye (Jean Baptiste de La Curne de). Les amours du bon vieux tems. [*anon.*] 76 pp. 16°. *Vaucluse et Paris, Duchesne,* 1760.

Saintes (Amand). L'homme, sa haute antiquité, son origine, et le problème de l'unité de sa race. 114 pp. 8°. *Paris, Dentu,* 1867.

Saintine (Joseph Zavier Boniface, *dit.*) Picciola. [Translated].
[Masterpieces of foreign literature. pp. 281—339. *London,* 1866].

Sala (George Augustus). Looking at life; or, thoughts and things. vi, 473 pp. 12°. *London, Routledge, Warne & Routledge,* 1860.

Salem Athenæum. Catalogue of the library, with the by-laws and regulations. xvi, 171 pp. 8°. *Salem, Gazette office,* 1842. s.

——— The same. 8°. *Boston,* 1858. s.

Salerne (François). *See* **Ray** (John). L'histoire naturelle, etc.

Salford borough royal museum and library. Catalogue of the library: with rules, etc. xi, 238 pp. 8°. *Manchester, G. Falkner,* 1851. s.

——— First—fourth report of the executive committee, 1850–52. [With other documents.] 8°. *Manchester, (Eng.)* 1850–52. s.

——— Proceedings of the council, 1858, 1859, 1860. With abstracts of the treasurer's accounts. 6 v. in 3. 8°. *Salford, [corporation,]* 1858–60. s.

Salih Gelil *or* **Selah-ed-din-Kalil**? Anales de Egipto, en qve se trata de las cosas mas principales que han sucedido desde el principio del mundo hasta de cien años a esta parte. [Con sentencias filosoficas por Seaid.] Traducidos de lengua turca en Castellana por don Vicento Bratuti. 8 p. l. 358 pp. 2 l. sm. 4°. *Madrid, M. Alvarez,* 1678.

Salio (Pietro). Opuscula medica, continentia tractatum de febre pestilenti, curationes quorundam particularium morborum, etc: nec non annotationes in artem medicam, etc. à Donato Antonio ab Altomari conditam. Ed. nova. 4 p. l. 523 pp. 14 l. 16°. *Amstelodami, Boom,* 1681. s.

Salisbury, *Eng.* Proceedings at the inauguration of Blackmore museum, 4th and 5th September, 1867. 71 pp. 16°. *Salisbury, [Eng.] Wiltshire co. mirror,* [1867]. s.

Salisbury (Richard Anthony). The genera of plants. A fragment containing part of Liriogamæ. vi, 143 pp. 8°. *London, J. Van Voorst,* 1866. s.

Salius. *See* **Salio.**

Sallengre (Albert Henri). Éloge de l'ivresse. Nouv. éd. augmentée [par P. A. M. Miger]. 250 pp. 1 pl. 16°. *Paris, Michel,* 1798.

Salles (Eusèbe François de). Histoire génerale des races humaines; ou, philosophie ethnographique. viii, 385 pp. 12°. *Paris, B. Duprat,* 1849. s.

Sallustius (Caius Crispus). De bello jugurthino liber. Grammatisch, kritisch, und historisch erklärt von Christian G. Herzog. xx, 497 pp. 8°. *Leipzig, K. F. Köhler,* 1840. s.

Salmasius (Claudius). *See* **Saumaise** (Claude de).

Salmon (Thomas). A geographical and historical grammar, showing the present state of the kingdoms of the world. 6th ed. 640 pp. 8 l. 23 maps. 8°. *London, W. Johnston,* 1758.
[Imperfect; maps iv to xv, xvii to xx, and xxiii wanting].

——— The same. 7th ed. 640 pp. 8 l. 23 maps. 8°. *London, W. Johnston and others,* 1760.
[Imperfect; map ii wanting, map xviii imperfect].

——— The same. 9th ed. 605 pp. 9 l. 23 maps. 8°. *London, W. Johnston and others,* 1764.
[Imperfect; map iii wanting].

——— A short view of the families of the present Irish nobility. 2 p. l. 272 pp. 3 l. 16°. *London, William Owen,* 1759.

Salt Lake city directory; including business directory of towns in Utah territory. Compiled by G. Owens. 135 pp. 8°. [*New York*], 1867.

Salter (*Rev.* Henry George). Book of illustrations; or, scripture truths exhibited by the aid of similes. xxxii, 532 pp. 8°. *London, Hatchard & son,* 1840.

Salter (John William). Monograph of British trilobites. Parts 1–3. 4°. *London, Palæontographical society,* 1864–66.

——— *and* **Blanford** (H. F.) Palæontology of Niti in the northern Himalaya. 111 pp. 23 pl. 8°. *Calcutta, O. T. Cutter,* 1865. s.

Saltmarsh (*Rev.* John). Sparkles of glory; or, some beams of the morning star. [new ed.] 3 p. l. xx, 212 pp. 24°. *London, W. Pickering,* 1847.

Salverte (Anne Joseph Eusèbe). Romances et poésies érotiques. viii, 104 pp. 16°. *Paris, Hennert,* 1798. s.

Salvin (Osbert). Exotic ornithology. *See* **Sclater** (Philip S.), *and* **Salvin.**

Salvini (Salvino), *and* **Casaregi** (Giovanni Bartolommeo). Componimenti poetici toscani. [Pubb. per le cure di A. F. Gori.] xix, 56, 223 pp. 8°. *Firenze, G. Albizzini,* 1750.

Salzenberg (W.) Alt-christliche baudenkmale von Constantinopel vom v. bis xii jahrhundert. Im anhange des Silentarius Paulus beschreibung der heiligen Sophia und des Ambon. Metrisch übersetzt und mit anmerkungen versehen von Dr. C. W. Kortüm. 2 p. l. 40 pp. 1 l. xiv pp. 1 l, 40 pl. fol. *Berlin, k. ministerium für handel, gewerbe, und öffentliche arbeiten,* 1854. s.

Samson (George W. *D. D.*) Elements of art criticism, with a historic survey of the methods of art execution. 840 pp. 8°. *Philadelphia, J. B. Lippincott & Co.* 1867.

Samuels (Edward A.) Ornithology and oölogy of New England: full descriptions of the birds of N. E. and adjoining states and provinces, with a complete history of their habits, [etc.] vii, 583 pp. 27 pl. 8°. *Boston, Nichols & Noyes,* 1867.

Sanchez (Pedro Antonio). Discurso sobre la eloquencia sagrada en España. 3 p. l. 214 pp. 16°. *Madrid, Blas Roman,* 1778. s.

Sand (George, *pseudon.*) *See* **Dudevant** (A. L. A. Dupin).

Sandberg (J. G.), *and* **Grafström** (A.) Ett år i sverge. Taflor af svenska almogens klädedrägt, lefnadssätt och hemseder, samt de för landets historia märkvärdigaste orter; utgifne af C. Forssell. 2 p. l. 139 pp. 48 pl. 4°. *Stockholm, J. Hörberg,* 1827. s.

Sandeau (Léonard Sylvain Jules). Le docteur Herbeau. 2 v. in 1. 223 pp; 219 pp. 24°. *Paris, Paulin,* 1846.

——— Madeleine. 288 pp. 16°. *Paris, Charpentier,* 1856.

——— Marianna. 5e éd. 392 pp. 16°. *Paris, Charpentier,* 1855.

——— Nouvelles. 421 pp. 16°. *Paris, Lévy,* 1851.

——— Valcreuse. 3e éd. 383 pp. 16°. *Paris, Charpentier,* 1853.

Sandeman (Patrick). Monthly tables of daily means of meteorological elements, deduced from observations taken at the observatory, Georgetown, Demerara, 1846–56. 275 pp. 4°. *Greenock, Gov. Brit. Guiana,* 1857. s.

Sandeman (Robert). Letters on Theron and Aspasio. Addressed to the author of that work. [Rev. J. Hervey]. 4th ed. 2 v. xxviii, 400 pp; iv, 448 pp. 16 l. 8°. *London, J. Charter,* 1768.

Sander (Anton). Bibliotheca belgica manvscripta, [etc. v. i]. 6 p. l. 368 pp. 4°. *Insvlis, T. LeClercq,* 1641. s.

[Wanting, v. 2.]

Sander (Constantin). Geschichte des vierjährigen bürgerkrieges in den Vereinigten Staaten von America. xv, 587 pp. 3 maps. 8°. *Frankfurt am M. J. D. Sauerländer,* 1865.

Sandford (Daniel). Remains; including extracts from his diary and correspondence, and a selection from his unpublished sermons. [Edited] with a memoir, by J. Sandford. 2 v. 4 p. l. 384 pp; 2 p. l. 339 pp. 8°. *Glasgow, Waugh & Innes,* 1830.

Sandifort (Gerhard). Catalogus librorum cum medicorum, et chemiae, tum historiae natural. geogr. itin, litteraturae, historiae, item effigierum, nec non praeparatorum ad anatomem, etc. Quorum publica fiet auctio, [etc.] 326 pp. 8°. *Lugduni Batavorum, E. J. Brill,* 1849. s.

Sands (Robert C.) Yamoyden. *See* **Eastburn** (*Rev.* James Wallis) *and* **Sands.**

Sandys (*Sir* Edwin). Europae speculum; or, a view of the state of religion in the western parts of the world. 276 pp. 18°. *London, Bassett,* 1687.

Sandys (Edwin William). The subaltern officer and his duties; a practical guide to the junior officers of the army. viii, 105 pp. 16°. *London, W. Mitchell,* 1863.

Sandys (George). Travailes: containing a history of the original and present state of the Turkish empire; a description of Constantinople, of Greece, of Egypt, of the holy land; lastly, Italy described, and the islands adjoyning. 6th ed. 2 p. l. 240 pp. 1 map. 5 pl. sm. fol. *London, J. Sweeting,* 1658.

NOTE.—[Engr. title pages of London ed. 1652, and Amsterdam ed. 1665 prefixed; 4 pl. and several illustrations inserted from ed. of 1665, with pl. No. 241 from ROBERTS (David). Sketches in the holy land, Egypt, etc.]

San Francisco. Assaying and refining works. Tables of the value of gold and silver per ounce troy, at different degrees of fineness; also, tables showing the net returns from gold and silver of different fineness, [etc.] 28 l. 4°. *San Francisco, Towne & Bacon,* 1867.

——— Directory for 1867[-68]. 9th year. Compiled by H. G. Langley. xcvi, 698, 87 pp. 1 map. 8°. *San Francisco, H. G. Langley,* 1867.

——— Mercantile library. Catalogue of the library, with the constitution and list of members. 197, 46 pp. 8°. *San Francisco, daily evening news office,* 1854. s.

——— Municipal reports for the fiscal years 1865–66. Published by order of the board of supervisors. 8°. *San Francisco,* 1866.

Sanfuentes (Salvador). Ricardo i Lucia, o la destruccion de la imperial. v. 1. 344 pp. 8°. *Santiago, Ferrocarril,* 1857. s.

Sangermano (——, *barnabite father*). Description of the Burmese empire [from native authorities.] Translated from his ms. by W. Tandy. viii, 224 pp. 4°. *Rome,* 1833.

[Oriental translation fund publications].

San Joseph (Francisco). Arte y reglas de la lengva tagala. 8 p. l. 311 pp. 4 l. 4°. *Partido de Bataan, T. P. Tagalo,* 1610. s.

Sankey (Francis F. *M. D.*) Malta, considered with reference to its eligibility as a place of residence for invalids. 36 pp. 8°. *Malta, Izzo & Co.* 1843. s.

Sannazaro (Jacopo). Arcadia. Di nvovo ristampata, con le annotationi di Thomaso Porcacchi, et ripurgata per Borgarutio Borgarucci. Con la vita dell' avttore, descritta dal medesimo [T. Porcacchi]. 287 pp. 24°. *Venetia, Pietro Marinelli,* 1589.

——— Rime. Di nvovo ristampate per Borgarutio Borgarucci. 96 pp. 24°. *Venetia, Pietro Marinelli,* 1589.

[*With* SANNAZARO (J.) Arcadia. *Venetia,* 1589].

San Severino (Giulio Roberto). Les vies des hommes et des femmes illustres d'Italie, depuis le rétablissement des sciences et des beaux arts. [Trad. de l'Italien par d'Açarq]. 2 v. xi, 429 pp; 430 pp. 16°. *Paris, Vincent,* 1767.

Sanson (Nicolas). L'Amériqve en plvsievrs cartes, et en divers traittés de géographie et d'histoire. 42 l. 15 pl. 4°. *Paris, l'avthevr,* 1657.

——— [Collection of maps of the world]. 161 maps. fol. *Paris,* 1652–70. s.

——— Geographia sacra, ex veteri et nova testamento desvmpta, et in tabulas tres concinnata. 38 pp. 16 l. fol. *Lutetiæ Parisiorum, P. Mariette,* 1665. s.

[*With* the preceding.]

Santa Cruz de Marzenado (Alvaro de Navia Osorio, *marquis* de). Reflections, military and political. Translated into English by Capt. James Ogilvie. v. 1. 16 p. l. 510 pp. 8°. *London, G. Strahan and others,* 1737.

[v. 2 wanting].

Santos (Domingo de los). *See* **Los Santos** (Domingo de).

Sanuto (Marino). Itinerario per la terra ferma veneziano, 1483. 157, 64 pp. 4°. *Padova, Tipografia del seminario,* 1847. s.

Sappho. Odes, fragments, and epigrams. *See* **Anacreon**. Works. *London,* 1735.

——— The same. Translated [by F. Fawkes]. 8°. *Edinburgh,* [1792].

[ANDERSON'S British poets. v. 5].

——— Works. *See* **Anacreon**, Sappho, *and others. Lond.* 1768.

——— *See, also,* **Anacreon** *and* **Sappho**, Oeuvres. *Paris,* 1692.

Saratoga. A story of 1787. [*anon.* by Daniel Shepherd?] 400 pp. 12°. *New York, Fetridge & Co.* 1856.

Sargent (Epes). The life and public services of Henry Clay. 120 pp. 1 pl. 8°. *New York, Greeley & McElrath,* 1848.

——— (*editor*). The emerald. A collection of tales, poems, and essays, gleaned chiefly from fugitive literature of the 19th century. vi, 316 pp. 12°. *Boston, J. L. Shorey,* 1866.

——— ——— The sapphire. A collection of tales, poems, and essays, gleaned from fugitive literature of the 19th century. 319 pp. 12°. *Boston, J. L. Shorey,* 1867.

Sargent (F. W.) On bandaging, and other operations of surgery. 379 pp. 12°. *Philadelphia, Lea & Blanchard,* 1848. s.

Sargent (John). The mine: a dramatic poem. [With] two historic odes. 3d ed. xxvii, 122 pp. 5 pl. 18°. *London, T. Cadell,* 1796.

Sargent (*col.* Winthrop, *governor of Miss. territory*). Diary of Col. Winthrop Sargent, adjt. gen. U. S. A. during the campaign of MD.CC.XCI, [under major general St. Clair, against the western Indians]. 58 pp. 3 pl. 4°. *Wormsloe, (N. C.) privately printed,* 1851.

——— A journal of the general meeting of the Cincinnati, in 1784. Edited by Winthrop Sargent. 59 pp. 8°. *Philadelphia,* 1859.

Sargent (Winthrop). *See* **Loyalist** poetry of the revolution.

Sarles (*Rev.* John W.) Memorial of Mary E. Smalley, late the wife of John W. Sarles. vii, 217 pp. 1 pl. 12°. *New York, author,* 1867.

Sarmiento (Domingo F.) Arjiropolis, o la capital de los estados confederados del Rio de la Plata. 161 pp. 8°. *Santiago, J. Belin i Ca.* 1850.

——— Campaña en ejercito grande aliado de Sud America. 1ra entrega. 14, 254 pp. 8°. *Rio Janeiro, J. Villeneuve y C.* 1852. s.

——— Comentarios de la constitucion de la Confederacion Arjentina, con numerosos docmentos illustrativos del texto. xxii, 236 pp. 8°. *Santiago de Chile, J. Belin i Ca.* 1853. s.

——— Educacion comun. Memoria presentada al consejo universitario de Chile, sobre estas cuestiones: "1. Influencia de la instruccion primaria en las costumbres," [etc]; "2. Organizacion que convenga darla, atendidas las circunstancias del pais;" "3. Sistema que convenga adoptar para procurarla rentas con que costearla." 156 pp. 8°. *Buenos Aires, imprenta del Nacional,* 1855. s.

——— De la educacion popular 542 pp. 8°. *Santiago, J. Belin,* 1849.

Sarmiento (Domingo F.) Emigracion alemana al Rio de la Plata; memoria escrita en Alemania por D. F. Sarmiento, i enriquecida con notas sobre el Chaco, etc. por el Dr. [J. E.] Vappaüs, traducido por G. Hilliger. viii, 176 pp. 8°. *Santiago, J. Belin,* 1851.

——— Plan combinado de educacion comun, silvicultura, e industria pastoril, aplicable al estado de Buenos Aires. 96 pp. 12°. *Santiago, J. Belin y Ca.* 1855. s.

——— Recuerdos de provincia. viii, 211 pp. 1 tab. 8°. *Santiago, J. Belin y Ca.* 1850. s.

——— Viages en Europa, Africa i America. 1ª—2ª entrega. 2 v. xii, 486 pp; 486 pp. 8°. *Santiago, J. Belin i Ca.* 1849-51.

Sars (Michael). Om de i Norge forekommende fossile dryelevninger fra quartærperioden. viii, 134 pp. 4 pl. 4°. *Christiania, Brogger & Christie,* 1865.

——— Oversigt af Norges echinodermer. [Extract.] vi, 160 pp. 16 pl. 8°. *Christiania, Videnskabs-selskabet,* 1861. s.

Sartain (John). The American gallery of art, from the works of the best artists, with poetical and prose illustrations by distinguished American authors. 111 pp. 10 pl. 4°. *Philadelphia,* 1848.

Sartorius (C.) Mexiko. Landschaftsbilder und skizzen aus dem volksleben. viii, 364 pp. 25 pl. 8°. *Darmstadt, etc. G. G. Lange, etc.* 1855. s.

Saturday (The) review of politics, literature, science, and art. July, 1866 to Dec. 1867. v. 22-24. fol. *London,* [*D. Jones*], 1866-67.

Saubert (Johann). De sacrificiis vetervm. 20 p. l. 721 pp. 6 l. 18°. *Jenæ, M. Birckneri,* 1659.

Saugnier (——), *and* **Brisson** (Pierre Raymond de). Voyages to the coast of Africa, their shipwreck on different vessels, and slavery at Senegal and Galam. Translated from the French. viii, 500 pp. 1 map. 8°. *London, G. G. J. and J. Robinson,* 1792.

Saumaise (Claude de). Defensio regia pro Carolo i. 444 pp. 24°. [*n. p.*] 1649.

Saumery (—— de). L'heureux imposteur; ou, avantures du baron de Janzac. Par M. de Mirone. [*pseudon.*] x, 276 pp. 18°. *Utrecht, E. Néaulme,* 1740.

Saunders (Ann). Narrative of the shipwreck and sufferings of Miss Ann Saunders, a passenger on board ship Frances Mary, which foundered at sea on 5th Feb. 1826. 38 pp. 16°. *Providence, (R. I.)* 1827.

Saunders (Daniel, *jr.*) A journal of [his] travels and sufferings on the coast of Arabia. 104, 21 pp. 24°. *Leominster,* [*Mass.*] *Robert B. Thomas,* 1797.

Saunders (Simon M.) Domestic poultry; with instructions for breeding, etc. Illustrated. 104 pp. 1 pl. 16°. *New York, O. Judd,* 1865.

Sausseret (——). *See* **Mémoire** historique sur l'hospice de la maternité. *Paris,* 1808.

Saussure (Henri F. de). Hymenoptera, 1867. *See* **Wüllerstorf-Urbair** (B. von). Reise der Novara.

——— Mémoires pour servir à l'histoire naturelle du Mexique, des Antilles, et des États-Unis. 2 v. 4°. *Genève, J. G. Fick, etc.* 1858-64. s.

CONTENTS.

v. 1. Mémoire sur divers crustacés nouveaux de Mexique et des Antilles. 80 pp. 6 pl.
v. 2. Essai d'une faune des myriapodes du Mexique, etc. 135 pp. 7 pl.
v. 3-4 in 1. Orthoptères de l'Amérique moyenne. Blattides. 279 pp. 2 col. pl. 1864-65.

——— *and* **Sichel** (Jules, *M. D.*) Catalogus specierum generis *scolia* (sensu latiori), continens specierum diagnoses, descriptiones, synonymiamque. Catalogue des espèces de l'ancien genre *scolia,* contenant les diagnoses, les descriptions et la synonymie des espèces, [etc.] 2 p. l. 352 pp. 2 col. pl. 8°. *Genève, H. Georg,* 1864. s.

Saussure (Horace Bénedict de). Voyages dans les Alpes; précédés d'un essai sur l'histoire naturelle des environs de Genève. 4 v. 8°. *Neuchatel, S. Fauche,* 1779-96. s.

Sauval (Henri). Amours des rois de France. [*With* VANEL. Galanteries, etc. *Paris,* 1738. v. 2].

Savage (M. W.) Reuben Medlicott; or, the coming man. vii, 400 pp. 16°. *London, Chapman & Hall,* [1864].

Savage (Richard). Poetical works. 8°. *Edinburgh,* 1794.
[Anderson's Brit. poets, v. 8].

Savage (The). By Piomingo, a headman and warrior of the Muscogulgee nation. [*pseudon.*] 2 p. l. 311 pp. 12°. *Philadelphia, Thomas S. Manning,* 1810.

Savart (Nicolas Pierre Antoine). Cours élémentaire de fortification, etc. 1 v. in 2. xvi, 564 pp; atlas, 21 pl. 4°. *Paris, Magimel, Anselin & Pochard,* 1812. s.
[Atlas wanting].

Savary (Claude). Letters on Greece. Translated from the French. 407 pp. 4 l. 1 map. 8°. *London, G. & J. Robinson,* 1787.

——— The same. viii, 442 pp. 1 map. 8°. *London, Elliot & Kay,* 1788.

Savérien (Alexandre). Histoire des philosophes modernes. 7 v. 16°. *Paris, Brunet,* 1761-69. S.

CONTENTS.

v. 1. Métaphysiciens.
v. 2. Moralistes et législateurs.
v. 3-4. Restaurateurs des sciences.
v. 5. Mathématiciens.
v. 6. Physiciens.
v. 7. Chimistes et cosmologistes.

Savigny (Marie Jules César Lelorgne de). Mémoires sur les animaux sans vertèbres. 2 v. in 1. v, 117 pp. 8 pl; vi, 239 pp. 24 pl. 8°. *Paris, G. Dufour, Déterville,* 1816. S.

CONTENTS.

v. 1. Fasc. 1-2. La bouche des crustacés et des insectes.
v. 2. Fasc. 1-3. Ascidies.

Savile (*Rev.* Bourchier Wrey). Lyra sacra; a collection of hymns, ancient and modern, odes, etc. With preface. [1st ed.] xvi, 276 pp. 18°. *London, Longman, Green & Co.* 1861.

Savile (George, 1*st marquis of Halifax*). A character of king Charles ii, and miscellaneous thoughts and reflections. 4 p. l. 183 pp. 12°. *London, J. & R. Tonson,* 1750.

——— Miscellanies. 370 pp. 16°. *London,* 1700.

Savonarola (Raffaello). Universus terrarum orbis scriptorum calamo delineatus, quovis tempore et qualibet lingua auctores scripserunt, cvm anno, loco, et forma editionis. Studio et labore Alphonsi Lasor a Varea. [*anagram*]. 2 v. 5 p. l. 68, 536 pp. 2 pl; 687 pp. 48 pl. fol. *Patavii, J. B. Gonzatti,* 1713.

Sawaszkiewicz (L. L.) Le génie de l'Orient, commenté par ses monuments monétaires, [etc.] 2 p. l. 220 pp. 11 pl. 12°. *Bruxelles, A. Van Dale,* 1846. S.

Sawin (Thomas E.) Sawin; summary notes concerning John Sawin and his posterity. 48 pp. 8°. *Athol depot, (Mass.) Rufus Putnam,* 1866.

Saxby (Henry). The British customs; containing an historical and practical account of each branch of that revenue. xviii, 654 pp. 8°. *London, J. Nourse,* 1757.

Saxe *or* **Sachsen** (Hermann Moritz von, *comte* de). The art of war. Translated from the French. iv, 96 pp. 5 pl. 8°. *London, J. Davis,* 1811.

Saxe *or* **Saxius** (Christoph). Onomasticon literarivm, sive nomenclator historico-criticvs omnis aetatis scriptorvm. Item monvmentorvm maxime illvstrivm. Ed. altera. 8v. 8°. *Traiecti ad Rhenvm, Paddenburg,* 1775-1803. S.

Say (Jean Baptiste). Cours complet d'économie politique pratique. 2e éd. 2 v. vii, 676 pp; 628 pp. 8°. *Paris, Guillaumin,* 1840.

——— The same. 6e éd. vii, 640 pp. 8°. *Paris, Guillaumin,* 1841.

——— Traité d'économie politique. 4e éd. 2 v. lxxxvi, 477 pp; 509 pp. 8°. *Paris, Déterville,* 1819.

Say (Thomas). American conchology; or, description of the shells of North America. 125 l. 60 pl. 8°. *New Harmony, (Ind.)* 1830-32.

[Part 7 wanting].

——— American entomology; or, descriptions of the insects of North America. 3 v. 60 l; 72 l; 68 l. 54 pl. 8°. *Philadelphia, S. A. Mitchell,* 1824-28. S.

——— The complete writings of Thomas Say on the conchology of the United States. Edited by W. G. Binney. vi, 252 pp. 75 col. pl. 8°. *New York, H. Baillière,* 1858.

——— Glossary to Say's conchology. 25 pp. 8°. *New Harmony, (Ind.) R. Beck,* 1832.

[*With* his American conchology. 8°. 1830-32].

——— Conchyliologie américaine; ou, descriptions et figures des coquilles du nord de l'Amérique. Trad. de l'Anglais par J. C. Chenu. [Extract.] 64 pp. 17 pl. 8°. *Paris, Bibliothèque conchyliologique,* 1845. S.

Sayer (Abram). Report on the zoology of Michigan.

[*With* HOUGHTON (Douglass). Reports, etc. Doc. No. 1].

Scanlan (Michael). Love and land: poems. 262 pp. 16°. *Chicago, Western news co.* 1866.

Scarburgh (Edmond). Document enclosing col. Edmond Scarburgh's account of proceedings in an expedition from Virginia to Annamessecks and Manokin, in 1663. 16 pp. 8°. *Annapolis, J. Hughes,* 1833.

Scaruffi (Gasparo). Discorso sopra le monete.

[SCRITTORI class. ital. di econ. pol. v. 43].

Scenes at Washington; a story of the last generation. By a citizen of Baltimore. [*anon.*] 197 pp. 12°. *New York, Harpers,* 1848.

Schacht (*Dr.* Hermann). Die pflanzenzelle, der innere bau und das leben der gewächse. Nach microscopisch-chemischen untersuchungen. xvi, 472 pp. 20 pl. 8°. *Berlin, G. W. F. Müller,* 1852. S.

——— Das mikroskop und seine anwendung insbesondere für pflanzen-anatomie und physiologie. Mit sechs lithographirten tafeln. xv, 198 pp. 6 pl. 8°. *Berlin, G. W. F. Müller,* 1851. S.

Schafarik (Paul Josef, *editor*). Wybor z literatury ceské díl prwni od nejstarsích, casůw az pocátku xv století. xvi, 1295 pp. 8°. *Praze, Kronbergra i Riwnáce*, 1845. s.

——— *and* **Palacky** (Frantisek). Die ältesten denkmaler der böhmischen sprache. [Extract]. 233 pp. 6 l. 4°. *Prag, K. böhm. gesellschaft d. wiss.* 1840. s.

Schaff (Philip, *D.D.*) History of the christian church. v. 2–3. From Constantine the great to Gregory the great. A. D. 311—600. 2 v. xiv, 538 pp; viii, pp. 539—1037. 8°. *New York, C. Scribner & Co.* 1867.

Schäffer (Jakob Christian). Elementa ornithologica, iconibvs vivis coloribvs expressis illvstrata. 44 l. 70 col. pl. 4°. *Ratisbonæ, typis Weissianis*, 1774. s.

——— Mvsevm ornithologicvm, exhibens enumerationem et descriptionem avivm quas nova prorsvs ratione sibi paratas, in mvseo svo asservat. 2 p. l. 75 pp. 2 col. pl. 4°. *Ratisbonæ*, 1789. s.
[*With* the preceding].

Schafhäutl (Carl). Geognostische untersuchungen des südbayerischen Alpengebirges. xxxii, 212 pp. 8 tab. 44 pl. 8°. *München, Lit. artistische anstalt*, 1850.

Schalch (Edward Vernon). Arabic selections, with a vocabulary. 2 p. l. 43, 46 pp. 4°. [*Haileybury*], *East India college*, 1830. s.

Schanz (Martin). Beiträge zur vorsokratischen philosophie aus Plato. heft i: "Die sophisten." vii, 160 pp. 8°. *Göttingen, A. Rente*, 1867. s.

Scharff (Benjamin). Juniperi descriptio curiosa, variis medicamentis ac observationibus referta. 380, 12 pp. 5 pl. 16°. *Francofurti, C. Wolff*, 1679. s.

Schauer (L.) Encore le droit de visite. Revue administrative de la marine française. 2 p. l. 120 pp. 8°. *Paris*, 1842. s.

Schaufuss (L. W.) Monographie der scydmaeniden Central und Südamerika's. (Extract.) 103 pp. 4 pl. 4°. *Dresden, K. leopold. carol. akad. der nat.* 1866.

Schayes (Antoine Guillaume Bernard). Histoire de l'architecture en Belgique. 2e éd. 2 v. 12°. *Bruxelles*, 1853.

Schede *or* **Schedius** (Elias). De diis germanis, sive veteri Germanorvm, Gallorvm, Britannorvm, Vandalorvm religione. Notis illvstravit J. Jarkivs. Accedit J. G. Keysleri dissertatio de cvlto solis, Freji et Othini. 771 pp. 16°. *Halae*, 1728.

Schedel (Hartmann). [Liber] cronicarum cū figuris et ymagībus ab inicio mūdi. [*anon.*] 20 pl. 299 l. 1 l. fol. *Nuremberge, Koberger*, 1493.

Scheerer (Theodor). Lehrbuch der metallurgie, mit besonderer hinsicht auf chemische und physikalische principien. 2 v. 8°. *Braunschweig, Vieweg*, [1846–53]. s.
[v. 2 wanting].

——— Löthrohrbuch. Eine anleitung zum gebrauch des löthrohrs, nebst beschreibung der vorzüglichsten löthrohrgebläse. ix, 113 pp. 16°. *Braunschweig, F. Vieweg & sohn*, 1851. s.

——— Der paramorphismus und seine bedeutung in der chemie, mineralogie und geologie. xv, 128 pp. 8°. *Braunschweig, Vieweg*, 1854. s.

——— Über den norit, und die auf der insel Hitteröe in dieser gebirgsart vorkommenden mineralienreichen granitgange, 1844.
[*With* KEILHAU (B. M.) Gaea norvegica. v. ii].

Schefer (Gottlieb Leopold Immanuel). The layman's breviary; or, meditations for every day in the year. From the German, by C. T. Brooks. iv, 452 pp. 1 portrait. 12°. *Boston, Roberts Bros.* 1867.

Scheffer (Frederick, *pseudon.*) *See* **King** (William, *LL.D.*)

Scheffer (Johann). Lappland, das ist: neue und wahrhafftige beschreibung von Lappland und dessen einwohnern, [etc.] 7 p. l. 424 pp. 1 map. 4°. *Franckfurt am Mäyn, und Leipzig, M. Hallerwarden*, 1675.

——— Svecia literata. *See* **Moller** (Johann). Bibliotheca septentrionis.

Schele de Vere (Maximilian). Studies in English; or, glimpses of the inner life of our language. vi, 365 pp. 12°. *New York*, [*printed at Cambridge*], *C. Scribner & Co.* 1867.

——— Grammar of the French language. 2 v. in 1. 273 pp; 256 pp. 12°. *New York, Richardson & Co.* 1867.

Schelor (Jean Auguste Notalric). Commentaire sur l'Œdipe roi de Sophocle. xxxii, 246 pp. 12°. *Bruxelles, C. Muquardt*, 1843. s.

Schellen (*Dr.* H.) Der elektromagnetische telegraph. xii, 368 pp. 8°. *Braunschweig, Vieweg*, 1850. s.

——— The same. Nebst einer kurzen einleitung über die optische und akustische telegraphie, etc. 2e ausg. xii, 259 pp. 8°. *Braunschweig, Vieweg*, 1854. s.

Scheller (Carl Friedrich A.) Bücherkunde der sassisch-niederdeutschen sprache, hauptsächlich nach den schriftdenkmälern der herzogl. bibliothek zu Wolfenbüttel entworfen. xvi, 528 pp. 8°. *Braunschweig, H. Vogler*, 1826. s.

Fichte (T. G.) *and* **Schelling** (Friedrich Wilhelm Joseph von). Philosophischer briefwechsel. iv, 131 pp. 8°. *Stuttgart, T. G. Cotta,* 1856. s.

Schembri (Antonio). Quadro geografico-ornitologico, ossia quadro comparativo. Le ornitologie di Malta, Sicilia, Roma, Toscana, Liguria, Nizza, e la provincia di Gard. 2 p. l. 66 pp. 4°. *Malta,* 1843. s.

Schenck (*Rev.* W. E.) Nearing home. Comforts and counsels for the aged. Compiled [by W. E. S.] 464 pp. 12°. *Philadelphia, Presbyt. board of pub.* [1867].

Schenkel (Daniel). Character of Jesus portrayed; a biblical essay, with an appendix. Translated from the 3d German edition, with introduction and notes, by W. H. Furness. 2 v. xxvii, 279 pp; iv, 359 pp. 12°. *Boston, Little, Brown & Co.* 1866.

Scherb (——). *See* **Paic** *and* **Scherb.** Cèrnagora, 1851.

Scherer (Friedrich). Die zukunft der blinden. 2e aufl. 2 p. l. 239 pp. 8°. *Gotha, Stollberg,* 1858. s.

Scherzer (Carl von). Reise der oesterreichischen fregatte Novara um die erde, unter den befehlen des commodore B. von Wüllerstorf-Urbair. 1857–59. Beschreibender theil. *See* **Wüllerstorf-Urbair.**

Scheuchzer (Johann Jakob). Herbarium diluvianum collectum. Ed. novissima. 3 p. l. 119 pp. 15 pl. fol. *Lugduni Batavorvm, P. Van der Aa.* 1723. s.

——— Der natur-histori des Schweitzerlands. 3 v. 4°. *Zürich, Bodmer,* 1716–18. s.

CONTENTS.

v. 1. Helvetiæ stoicheiographia, orographia, et oreographia. Oder beschreibung der elementen, grenzen und bergen des Schweitzerlands. 3 p. l. 268, 2 l. 6 pl.
v. 2. Hydrographia helvetica. Beschreibung der seen, flüssen, brünnen, warmen und kalten böderen, und anderen mineral-wasseren des Schweitzerlands. 8 p. l. 480 pp. 4 l. 12 pl.
v. 3. Meteorologia et oryctographia helvetica. Oder beschreibung der lufft-beschichten steinen, metallen, und anderen mineralien des Schweitzerlands, [etc]. 8 p. l. 336 pp. 18 pl.

Schiebe (August). Auswahl deutscher handelsbriefe für handlungslehrlinge, mit einer französischen und englischen uebersetzung. Herausgegeben von Dr. Carl Gustav Odermann. 4e aufl. vi, 159 pp. 8°. *Leipzig, J. M. Gebhardt,* 1866. s.

——— Die lehre von der buchhaltung. 6e ausg. von Carl Gustav Odermann. xiv, 511 pp. 8°. *Grimma, J. M. Gebhardt,* 1861. s.

Schieffelin (Samuel B.) The foundations of history; a series of first things. xi, 264 pp. 11 pl. 18°. *New York, A. D. F. Randolph,* 1863. s.

Schiffner (Albert). Obersachsen und die Lausitz in physikalisch-geographischer beziehung. [*With* Geinitz (H. B.) Gäa von Sachsen].

Schiller (Johann Christoph Friedrich von). The Piccolomini, and Wallenstein. Translated by S. T. Coleridge. 8°. *London,* 1866. [*With* Masterpieces of foreign literature].

Schimmelpenninck (Mary Anne). Tour to Alet and La Grande Chartreuse, by Claude Lancelot; with some account of the monastery, and abbot reformer of La Trappe; also, biographical sketches, etc; and a brief view of Port Royal. 2d ed. 2 v. xxxii, 254 pp; viii, 338 pp. 8°. *London, J. & A. Arch,* 1816.

Schinz (C.) Die wärme-messkunst, und deren anwendung zur construction von apparaten für die industrie und für häusliche bedürfnisse. 8°. atlas. fol. *Stuttgart, Mäcken,* 1858. s.

Schinz (Heinrich Rudolph). Europäische fauna; oder, verzeichniss der wirbelthiere Europa's. 2v. xxiv, 448 pp; viii, 535 pp. 8°. *Stuttgart, E. Schweizerbart,* 1840. s.

Schirmbeck (Adam). Messis paraqvariensis a patribus societatis Jesv per sexennivm in Paraqvaria collecta, 1638-43. 5 p. l. 366 pp. 1l. 24°. *Monachii, Joannes Wagner,* 1649.

Schlabrendorf (Gustav von). Bonaparte and the French people under his consulate. Translated from the German. 3 p. l. 379 pp. 8°. *London, Tipper & Richards,* 1804.

Schlaepfer (Johann Georg). Dissertatio inauguralis medico-chirurgica, sistens experimenta de effectu liquidorum quorundam medicamentosorum ad vias aeriferas applicatorum in corpus animale. 60 pp. 8°. *Tubingae, auctor,* 1816. s.

Schlagintweit (Adolph *and* Hermann von). Neue untersuchungen über die physicalische geographie und die geologie der Alpen. xvi, 630 pp. 1 tab. 8°. *Leipzig, T. O. Weigel,* 1854. s.
[Wanting; atlas, 22 pl. fol.]

Schlechtendal (Diedrich Friedrich Ludwig von). De aseroës genere dissertatio. 12 pp. 1 col. pl. 4°. *Halae Saxonum, Gebauer,* 1847. s.

——— Flora berolinensis. 2 v. lxxii, 535 pp; xiv, 284 pp. 16°. *Berolini, F. Dümmler,* 1823–24. s.

Schlegel (Carl Wilhelm Friedrich von). Lectures on the history of literature, ancient and modern. xii, 420 pp. 12°. *London, Bell & Daldy,* 1865.

Schlegel (Hermann). Abhandlungen aus dem gebiete der zoologie und vergleichenden anatomie. 3 v. in 1. 15 pl. 4°. *Leiden, Arnz & Co.* 1841–51. s.

CONTENTS.

v. 1. Beiträge zur charakteristik der cetaceen. 2 p. l. 44 pp.
v. 2. Weitere beiträge zur naturgeschichte der cetaceen. 12 pp.
v. 3. Beschreibung einiger neuen grossen edelfalken, etc. 20 pp.

——— Die europäischen tag-raubvögel. Mit 44 tafeln von J. C. und E. E. Susemihl. [Extract.] Text, 100 pp; atlas, 44 col. pl. 8°. *Darmstadt, C. Susemihl & sohn*, [1847–52?] s.

——— Handleiding tot de beoefening der dierkunde. v. 1. 6 p. l. lii, 532 pp. 8°. *Breda, k. Akad. voor de zee en landmagt*, 1857. s.
[Wanting v. 2 and atlas, 34 pl. fol.]

——— Loxiens. *See* **Bonaparte** (C. L.) *and* **Schlegel.**

Schleicher (August). Compendium der vergleichenden grammatik der indogermanischen sprachen. 2 v. viii, 764 pp. 8°. *Weimar, H. Böhlau*, 1861–62. s.

CONTENTS.

v. 1. Kurzer abriss einer lautlehre der indogermanischen ursprache, des altindischen (sanskrit), alteranischen (altbaktrischen), altgriechischen, altitalischen (lateinischen, umbrischen, oskischen), altkeltischen (altirischen), altslawischen (altbulgarischen), litauischen und altdeutschen (gotischen). pp. 1–283.
v. 2. Kurzer abriss einer formelehre [derselben]. pp. 285–764.

Schleiermacher (Friedrich Ernst Daniel). Gelengentliche gedanken über universitäten im deutschen sinne. Nebst einem anhange über eine neu zu errichtende. viii, 176 pp. 16°. *Berlin, Realschulbuchhandlung*, 1808. s.

Schlemm (Friedrich). Operations-uebungen am cadaver. *See* **Ravoth** (F.) Grundriss der akiurgie.

Schlereth (Franz Anton von). Dispensatorium fuldense tripartitum, tam patriæ usibus quam sæculi moderni genio accommodatum. xvi, 327 pp. 1 pl. 8°. *Fuldæ, author*, 1787. s.

Schlömilch (Oskar). Compendium der höheren analysis. xvi, 549 pp. 8°. *Braunschweig, Vieweg*, 1853. s.

Schlossberger (Julius Eugen). Erster versuch einer allgemeinen und vergleichenden thier-chemie, v. 1. Die chemie der gewerbe des gesammten thierreichs. x, 344, 364 pp. 8°. *Leipzig, etc. C. F. Winter*, 1854–56. s.
[No more published].

Schlosser (Friedrich Christoph). Geschichte des achtzehnten jahrhunderts, und des neunzehnten bis zum sturz des französischen kaiserreichs. v. 1–3 in 4 v. 8°. *Heidelberg, J. C. B. Mohr*, 1836–43. s.
[v. 4—7 wanting].

Schmarda (Ludwig Carl). Die geographische verbreitung der thiere. 3 v. in 1. viii, 755 pp. 1 col. map. 8°. *Wien, Gerold*, 1853. s.

——— Neue wirbellose thiere beobachtet und gesammelt auf einer reise um die erde, 1853–57. v. i. Neue turbellarien, rotatorien, und anneliden beobachte, [etc.] 1 v. in 2. xviii, 66 pp. 15 col. pl; 3 p. l. 164 pp. 22 col. pl. (16–37). *Leipzig, W. Engelmann*, 1859–61. s.

Schmid (*Dr.* L.) Geschichte der pfalzgrafen von Tübingen. xxxii, 606, 293 pp. 8°. *Tübingen, L. F. Fues*, 1853.

Schmidt (Andreas Gottfried). Gallerie deutscher pseudonymer schriftsteller vorzüglich des letzen jahrzehents. viii, 253 pp. sq. 16°. *Grimma, Verlags-comptoir*, 1840. s.

Schmidt (Carl, *M. D.*) Das alphabeth der hieroglyphen enträthselt. 3er theil des werkes der zitterstoff. xcii, 231 pp. 8°. *Breslau, Verfasser*, 1805. s.

——— Der zitterstoff (*electrogen*) und seine wirkungen in der natur. xii, vi, xix, 229 pp. 8°. *Breslau, Verfasser*, 1803. s.

Schmidt (*Dr.* Carl). Zur vergleichenden physiologie der wirbellosen thiere. Eine physiologisch-chemische untersuchung. 79 pp. 8°. *Braunschweig, Vieweg*, 1845. s.

Schmidt (C. F.) Die gestüte des königs Wilhelm von Württemberg. *See* **Hugel** (J. von), *and* **Schmidt.**

Schmidt (Emil). Schilderungen aus der Schweiz. vi, 234 pp. 12°. *Leipzig, L. Fernau*, 1853.

Schmidt (Friedrich). La Suède sous Charles xiv Jean. 1e éd. viii, 392 pp. 8°. *Paris, Roret*, 1843. s.

Schmidt (W. Adolph). Geschichte der denk- und glaubens-freiheit im ersten jahrhundert der kaiserherrschaft und des christenthums. viii, 456 pp. 8°. *Berlin, Veit & Co.* 1847. s.

Schmieder (Benjamin Friedrich). Commentarivs in M. Accii Plavti qvae svpersvnt comoedias. 452 pp. 8°. *Gottingae, H. Dieterich*, 1804. s.

Schnaase (Carl). Geschichte der bildenden künste. v. 1–2. Geschichte der bildenden künste bei den alten. 2 v. xx, 457 pp; x, 534 pp. 8°. *Düsseldorf, J. Buddeus*, 1843. s.

CONTENTS.

v. 1. Die völker des Orients.
2. Griechen und Römer.

——— The same. v. 3. Geschichte der bildenden künste im mittelalter. v. 1. Altchristliche und muhamedanische kunst. xi, 555 pp. 8°. *Düsseldorf, J. Buddeus*, 1844. s.

Schneider (Johann Gottlob). Allgemeine naturgeschichte der schildkröten. xlviii, 364 pp. 2 pl. 8°. *Leipzig, J. G. Müller*, 1783. s.

——— Disputatio de veterum scriptorum hippopotamo. 4°. s.

[*With* ARTEDI (Peter). Synonymia piscium, etc. 4°. *Lipsiæ*, 1789. pp. 247–270].

Schneider (Leonhard). Unsterblichkeitslehre des Aristoteles. x, 141 pp. 8°. *Passau, Elsaesser et Waldbauer*, 1867. s.

Schneider (Wilhelm Gottlieb). Monographia generis *rhaphidiae* Linnaei. 2 p. l. 96 pp. 7 col. pl. 4°. *Vratislaviae, Grassii, Barthii et soc.* 1843. s.

——— Symbolae ad monographiam generis *chrysopae* Leach. 178 pp. 60 col. pl. 8°. *Vratislaviae, F. Hirt*, 1851. s.

Schneller (Joseph). Arzneimittellehre in ihrer anwendung auf die krankheiten des kindlichen alters. vii, 176 pp. 8°. *Wien, Sallmeyer & Co.* 1867. s.

Schnitzler (Johann Heinrich). De la création de la richesse; ou, des intérêts matériels en France. 2 v. xx, 394 pp; 459 pp. 8°. *Paris, H. Lebrun*, 1842. s.

——— Les institutions de la Russie depuis les réformes de l'empereur Alexandre ii. 2 v. xiii, 495 pp; 524 pp. 8°. *Paris, Berger Levrault*, 1866.

Schnütgen (Emil). Die visio beatifica, ihr wesen und ihre theologisch-philosophische berechtigung. Spekulativer theil. viii, 160 pp. 8°. *Würzburg, F. E. Thein*, 1867. s.

Schober (Hugo Emil). Encyclopädie der landwirthschaftswissenschaft. Nebst einer uebersicht über die neuere deutsche landwirthschaftliche literatur. x, 171 pp. 16°. *Dresden, Schönfeld*, 1856. s.

Schoefert (J. G.) Der preussische beamte; oder, die kenntniss der gesetze und verordnungen über die befähigung der höhern und niedern verwaltungs-, justiz-, bau-, und eisenbahn-beamten, etc. viii, 296 pp. 8°. *Glogau, C. Flemming*, 1852.

Schoelcher (Victor). Dangers to England of the alliance with the men of the coup d'état. iv, 194 pp. 16°. *London, Trübner*, 1854.

Schoen. *See* **Schön.**

Schoenhals. *See* **Schönhals.**

Schoenherr. *See* **Schönherr.**

Schoepflin. *See* **Schöpflin.**

Schoff (S. S.) *and* **Caswell** (B. S.) People's own book of recipes: and information for the million. Containing directions for the preservation of the health, treatment of the sick, [etc.] Also, 1000 useful recipes, embracing every department of domestic economy, [etc.] 408 pp. 16°. *Kenosha, (Wis.) Schoff & Winegar*, 1867.

Scholar's companion: parts 1 and 2, containing exercises in the orthography, derivation, and classification of English words. Revised ed. with introduction by R. W. Bailey. 159 pp. 12°. *Philadelphia, E. H. Butler & Co.* 1867.

Scholfield (Nathan). Higher geometry and trigonometry. 232 pp. 8°. *New York, Collins*, 1845. s.

——— Higher geometry and mensuration. 250, 10 pp. 8°. *New York, Collins*, 1845. s.

[*With* the preceding].

Scholz (Benjamin). Anfangsgründe der physik, als vorbereitung zum studium der chemie. 5e aufl. von Anton Schrötter. xvi, 776 pp. 5 pl. 8°. *Wien, J. G. Heubner*, 1837. s.

Schomberg (Isaac). Naval chronology, from the time of the Romans, to the treaty of peace, 1802, with an appendix. 5 v. 8°. *London, T. Egerton, [and others]*, 1802.

Schomburg (Carl). Briefwechsel und nachlass: mit biographischen andeutungen, herausgegeben von Dr. Karl Bernhardi. viii, 471 pp. 1 pl. 8°. *Krassel, J. J. Bohné*, 1845. s.

Schomburgk (Richard, *editor*). Reisen in Britisch Guiana, etc. v. 3. [or pp. 533–1260]. Versuch einer fauna und flora von Britisch-Guiana. Nach vorlagen von Johannes Müller, Ehrenberg, Erichson, Klotzsch, Troschel, Cabanis, und andern. 728 pp. 8°. *Leipzig, J. J. Weber*, 1848. s.

CONTENTS.

Die mikroskopischen leben. Von Ehrenberg.
Mollusca. Von F. H. Troschel.
Insecten. Von W. F. Erichson.
Fische. Von J. Müller und F. H. Troschel.
Amphibien. Von F. H. Troschel.
Voegel. Von J. Cabanis.
Saeugethiere. Von J. Cabanis.
Flora.

Schomburgk (*Sir* Robert Hermann). Reisen in Britisch-Guiana in den jahren, 1840–44. Im auftrag des königs von Preussen ausgeführt. *See* **Schomburgk** (Richard, *editor*).

——— Twelve views in the interior of Guiana: from drawings executed by Mr. Charles Bentley, after sketches taken during the expedition carried on in the years 1835–39. With descriptive letter press. 4 p. l. 38 pp. 1 map, 12 col. pl. fol. *London, Ackermann & Co.* 1841. s.

Schön (Friedrich Gotthold). De personarum in Euripidis Bacchabus habitu scenico commentatio. 166 pp. 8°. *Lipsiae, A. Lehnhold,* 1831. s.

Schön (Julius). Rifled infantry arms. A brief description of the modern system of small arms, as adopted in the various European armies. 2d ed. Dresden, 1855, tr. from the German by J. Gorgas. 4°. *Washington,* 1860.
[*With* MORDECAI (A.) Report, etc. 1860].

Schönberg (Anders). Historiska bref om det svenska regeringssättet, i äldre och nyare tider. Utgifna af Adolf Iwar Arwidsson. 3 v. 8°. *Stockholm, P. A. Norstedt & söner,* 1849–51. s.

Schoner (Johann). Orbis typvs. 65 l. sm. 4°. *Noribergæ, Joannes Stuchss,* 1515.

NOTE.—"This title is one of the forms under which Schoner's 'Luculentissima quaedā terrae totius descriptio' is sometimes found. HARRISSE.

Schönhals (Carl von). Erinnerungen eines österreichischen veteranen aus dem italienischen kriege, 1848–49. [*anon.*] 4e aufl. 2 v. viii, 236 pp; 314 pp. 8°. *Stuttgart, J. G. Cotta,* 1852. s.

Schönherr (Christoph Joseph). Curculionidum dispositio methodica, cum generum characteribus, descriptionibus atque observationibus variis, seu prodromus ad synonymiae insectorum partem iv. xi, 338 pp. 8°. *Lipsiae, F. Fleischer,* 1826. s.

——— Synonymia insectorum, oder versuch einer synonymie aller bisher bekannten insekten; nach Fabricii systema eleutheratorum etc. geordnet, [etc.] 3 v. 8°. *Stockholm, Nordstroem, etc.* 1806–17.
[Imperfect: v. 3 and title-page of v. 2 wanting].

Schön-Swaartz (Van, *pseudon.*) *See* **Beaunoir.**

Schoolcraft (Henry Rowe). A bibliographical catalogue of books, translations of the scriptures, and other publications in the Indian tongues of the United States, with critical notices. [*anon.*] 28 pp. 8°. *Washington, C. Alexander,* 1849.

——— Notes on the Iroquois; or, contributions to American history, antiquities, and general ethnology. xv, 498 pp. 2 col. portraits. 8°. *Albany, E. H. Pease & Co.* 1847. s.

——— Red race of America. 416 pp. 2 pl. 8°. *New York, Wm. H. Graham,* 1847.

Schoolcraft (*Mrs.* Mary Howard). The black gauntlet: a tale of plantation life in South Carolina. 569 pp. 16°. *Philadelphia, J. B. Lippincott & Co.* 1860.

Schoonebeeck (Adriaan). Heroicae tabulae. *See* **Smids** (Lodewick). Pictura loquens. *Amstelaedami,* 1695.

Schooten (Henry, *pseudon.*) The hairy giants; or, a description of two islands in the South sea, called Benganga and Coma. Englished [from the Dutch] by P. M. 3 p. l. 16 pp. 2 l. 1 map. sm. 4°. *London, John Watson,* 1671.

Schopenhauer (Arthur). Die beiden grundprobleme der ethik in zweiakade emischen preisschriften. 2e aufl. xliv, 276 pp. 8°. *Leipzig, Brockhaus,* 1860.

——— Parerga und paralipomena: kleine philosophische schriften. 2e aufl. Herausgegeben von J. Frauenstädt. 2 v. xii, 530 pp; iv, 698 pp. 8°. *Berlin, A. W. Hahn,* 1862.

——— Ueber die vierfache wurzel des satzes vom zureichenden g unde. Herausgegeben von J. Frauenstädt. 3e aufl. xvi, 160 pp. 1 pl. 8°. *Leipzig, F. A. Brockhaus,* 1864.

——— Die welt als wille und vorstellung. 3e aufl. 2 v. xxxii, 634 pp; vi, 740 pp. 8°. *Leipzig, F. A. Brockhaus,* 1859.

Schöpflin (Johann Daniel). Vindiciæ typographicæ. [With appendix: Documenta typographicarum originum ex argentinensibus tabulariis et bibliothecis nunc primum edita]. 3 p. l. 120 pp. 42 pp. 5 l. 7 pl. 4°. *Argentorati, J. G. Bauer,* 1760.

Schoppe *or* **Scioppius** (Caspar *conde de Clara Valle*). Arcana societatis Iesv publico bono vulgata, cum appendicibus utilissimis. 341 pp. 5 l. 16°. [*n. p.*] 1635.
[*With* CONTZEN (Adam). Disceptatio de secretis, etc.]

Schott (Arthur). Geology and botany.
[*With* EMORY (W. H.) Report on the U. S. and Mexican boundary survey].

Schott (Wilhelm, *prof. at Berlin*). Vocabularium sinicum. iv, 88 pp. 4°. *Berolini, officina academica,* 1844. s.

Schöttgen (Christian). Historie derer buchhändler, wie solche in alten und mittern zeiten gewesen, [etc.] 2e aufl. 20 pp. 4 portraits. sm. 4°. *Nürnberg, etc. J. D. Tauber's erben,* 1722. s.

Schouten (Willem Cornelisz). Diarivm vel descriptio laboriosissimi et molestissimi itineris, facti annis 1615–17, cum a parte australi freti magellanici novum ductum aut fretum in magnum mare australe detexit, totumq. orbem terrarum circumnavigavit. 4 p. l. 83 pp. 3 maps. 3 pl. sm. 4°. *Amsterdam, Petrus Kærius,* 1619.

——— The same. Jovrnal ov relation exacte dv voyage dans les Indes: par vn nouueau destroit, et par les grandes mers australes qu'il à descouuert, vers le pole antartique. [Redigé par Aris Classen]. 7 p. l. 232 pp. 4 maps. 4 pl. 16°. *Paris, Gobert,* 1619.

Schouw (Joakim Frederik). Dissertatio de sedibus plantarum originariis. 80 pp. 16°. *Havniæ, [auctor]*, 1816. s.

Schouwalof. *See* **Schuwalof.**

Schreber (Johann Christian Daniel von). Die säugthiere in abbildungen nach der natur, mit beschreibungen. Fortgesetzt von Johann Andreas Wagner. 5 v. with atlas. 51 col. pl. 4°. *Erlangen und Leipzig, Voss, etc.* 1840–55 s. [Atlas wanting, pl. 1–21].

CONTENTS.

v. 1. Die affen und flederthiere. xiv, vi, 551 pp.
v. 2. Die raubthiere. viii, 558 pp.
v. 3. Die beutelthiere und nager (1). xiv, 614 pp.
v. 4. Die nager (1), zahnlücker, einhufer dickhäuter, und wiederkäuer. xii, 523 pp.
v. 5. Die affen, zahnlücker, beutelthiere, hufthiere, insectenfresser, und handflügler. Ein zusammenstellung der neuesten entdeckungen auf dem gebiete der säugthierkunde. xxvi, 810 pp.

Schreckenstein (C. H. Roth von). *See* **Roth** von Schreckenstein.

Schreger (Christian Heinrich Theodor). Kurze beschreibung der chemischen geräthschaften älterer und neuerer zeit. Nebst einer vorrede des Friedrich Hildebrand. 3 v. 12°. *Fürth*, 1802. s.

Schreiber (Aloys Wilhelm), *and others*. Traditions populaires du Rhin, de la Forêt Noire, de la vallée du Nècre, de la Moselle, et du Taunus. 102 pp. 13 pl. 16°. *Heidelberg, J. Engelmann*, [1827].

Schreiber (Heinrich). Die älteste verfassungsurkunde der stadt Freiburg im Breisgau, zum erstenmal in ihrer ächten gestalt herausgegeben. 46 pp. 4°. *Freiburg im Breisgau, Albert Ludwig's universität*, 1833. s.

——— Matthæus Hummel im Bach, bevollmächtigter zur stiftung der universitat und erster rector derselben. 41 pp. 4°. *Freiburg, gebrüder Groos*, 1833. s.

Schrenk (Leopold von). Ideen zu einer hydrographie der landseen, mit besonderer rücksicht auf die seen der Alpen. 59 pp. 8°. *Dorpat, H. Loakman*, 1852. s.

Schreuder (Hans Paludan Smith). Grammatik for Zulu-sproget. Med fortale og anmærkninger af C. A. Holmboe. viii, 88 pp. 8°. *Christiania, W. C. Fabritius*, 1850. s.

Schrevel *or* **Schrevelius** (Cornelius). Lexicon manuale græco-latinum et latino-græcum; studio atque opera J. Hill, J. Entick, nec non G. Bowyer. Ed. 18ª emendatior. 365 l. 8°. *Edinburgi, C. Stewart*, 1805.

Schröter (Johann Samuel). Einleitung in die conchylien-kenntniss, nach Linné. 3 v. 8°. *Halle, J. J. Gebauer*, 1783–86. s.

Schröter (Johann Samuel). Versuch einer systematischen abhandlung über die erdkonchylien, [etc.] 240 pp. 16°. *Berlin, Bosse*, 1771. s.

——— Vollständige einleitung in die kenntniss und geschichte der steine und versteinerungen. 4 v. 4°. *Altenburg, Richter*, 1774–84. s.

Schryver (Cornelius). *See* **Goes** (Damião de). Legatio magni Indorvm imperatoris. *Anvers*, 1532.

Schubarth (F.) Repertorium der technischen literatur, 1823–53. xvi, 1049 pp. 8°. *Berlin, Decker'sche und geheime ober-hofbuchdruckerei*, 1856. s.

Schubert (Friedrich Theodor). Populäre astronomie. Neue ausg. 3 v. 8°. *Hamburg, Perthes & Besser*, 1834. s.

CONTENTS.

v. 1. Geschichte der astronomie und sphärische astronomie. xvi, 337 pp. 4 pl.
v. 2. Theoretische astronomie. xiv, 388 pp. 5 pl.
v. 3. Physische astronomie. xi, 391 pp. 5 pl.

Schubert (Friedrich Wilhelm). Handbuch der allgemeinen staatskunde von Europa. 6 v. 8°. *Königsberg, Bornträger*, 1835–46. s.

CONTENTS.

v. 1. Die allgemeine einleitung, und das russische reich.
v. 2. Frankreich und das britische reich.
v. 3. Spanien und Portugal.
v. 4. Die italienischen staaten.
v. 5. Oesterreich.
v. 6. Der preussische staat.

Schultze (Maximilian Johann Sigismund). Beiträge zur naturgeschichte der turbellarien. 1te abth. vi, 79 pp. 7 col. pl. 4°. *Greifswald, C. A. Koch*, 1851. s.

Schulze (Friedrich Gottlob). Nationalökonomie; oder, volkswirthschaftslehre, vornehmlich für land, forst, und staatswirthe. 2 v. in 1. xxx, 952 pp. 2 tab. 8°. *Leipzig, G. Wigand*, 1856. s.

Schulze (Gottlob Leberecht). Neue astronomische versinnlichungswerkzeuge und deren vielseitiger gebrauch. viii, 70 pp. 2 pl. 8°. *Leipzig, F. Fleischer*, 1823. s.

Schulze (Johannes Ludwig), **Knapp** (Georg Ludwig), *and* **Niemeyer** (August Hermann). Beschreibung des hallischen waisenhauses und der übrigen damit verbundenen frankischen stiftungen, nebst die geschichte ihres ersten jahrhunderts. xvi, 214 pp. 2 pl. 8°. *Halle, Waisenhaus*, 1779. s.

Schumann (G. D.) Chemische laboratorium für realschulen und zur selbstbelehrung. Mit einem vorworte von Fr. J. P. von Riecke. 2e aufl. xii, 355 pp. 4 pl. 8°. *Esslingen, C. Weychardt*, 1857. s.

Schumann (L.) Sachregister zum kayser'schen bücherlexicon. *See* **Kayser** (C. G.)

Schurz (Carl). Speeches. x, 392 pp. 12°. *Philadelphia, J. B. Lippincott & Co.* 1865.

Schütz (Ferdinand). Propagation des sciences européennes dans l'extrême orient. Nouveau syllabaire et alphabet chinois phonétique. [Extract.] 60, 25 pp. 8°. *Nancy, acad. de Stanislas,* 1856-57. s.

——— Simplification de l'étude des langues par la philosophie du langage et des signes graphiques de la pensée. Introduction. [Extract.] 124 pp. 8°. *Nancy, acad. de Stanislas,* 1855. s.

Schuwalof (Andrej, *de*). The antidote; or, an enquiry into the merits of a book entitled "a journey into Siberia," made in 1761, by the abbé Chappe D'Auteroche. By a lover of truth. [*anon.*] Translated into English by a lady. iv, 202 pp. 8°. *London, S. Leacroft,* 1772.

Schuyler (George L.) Correspondence and remarks upon Bancroft's history of the northern campaign of 1777, and the character of major gen. Philip Schuyler. 47 pp. 8°. *New York, D. G. Francis,* 1867.

Schwab (Gustav), *and* **Klüpfel** (Carl). Wegweiser durch die literatur der Deutschen. Ein handbuch für laien. 356 pp. 8°. *Leipzig, G. Mayer,* 1846. s.

——— The same. 3e aufl. vi, 196 pp. 8°. *Leipzig, G. Mayer,* 1861.

——— Literarischer wegweiser für gebildete laien. Nachträge 1—7 zu dem Schwab u. Klüpfel'schen wegweiser. 1847—1867. 7 v. 8°. *Leipzig, G. Mayer,* 1853-67.

Schwarz (Christian Gottlieb). Panegyricvs divo Carolo vi, imperatori, [with appendix]. Odae ii divi Caroli vi. in gloriosissimam obitvm, etc. 60 pp. 4 l. fol. *Norimbergae, F. Koengott,* 1741. s.

[*With* WILLEBRANDT (J. P.) Hansische chronick, etc. 1748].

——— Oratio panegyrica de Pomeranorvm et Rvgianorvm pristinis cvm Holsatia, belli pacisqve commerciis, [etc.] 26 pp. fol. *Gryphiswaldiae, J. & J. Struck,* 1743. s.

[*With* WILLEBRANDT (J. P.) Hansische chronick, etc. 1748].

Schwarz (Joseph). A descriptive geography and brief historical sketch of Palestine. Translated by Isaac Leeser. 519 pp. 2 maps, 13 pl. 8°. *Philadelphia, A. Hart,* 1850. s.

Schwarzwäller (Udo). Der praktische brennerei-verwalter. vii, 152 pp. 12°. *Leipzig, Reichenbach,* 1861. s.

Schweigger (Johann Salomo Christoph). Bruchstücke aus dem leben des als opfer seiner wissenschaft gefallenen, A. F. Schweigger. Nebst einem anhange über den an seinem grabe gestifteten verein zur ausführüng eines Leibnitzischen missionsplanes. 95 pp. 12°. *Halle, E. Anton,* 1830. s.

——— Einleitung in die mythologie auf dem standpunkte der naturwissenschaft. ix, 381 pp. 2 pl. 8°. *Halle, E. Anton,* 1836. s.

——— Über die älteste physik und den ursprung des heidenthums aus einer missverstandenen naturweisheit. [Extract]. viii, 120 pp. 12°. *Nürnberg, Jahrbuch der chemie, etc.* 1823. s.

——— Ueber stöchiometrische reihen im sinne Richter's. xxvi, 69 pp. 8°. *Halle, Schrödel & Simon,* 1853. s.

Schweinhart (William). The young crook's guide; or self-varying system for cutting garments. 7 pp. 4 pl. 8°. *Gettysburg,* [*Pa.*] *author,* 1851. s.

Schwenck (Conrad). Wörterbuch der deutschen sprache in beziehung auf abstammung und begriffsbildung. 2e ausg. iv, 750 pp. 8°. *Frankfurt am Main, J. D. Sauerländer,* 1836. s.

Schwerd (*Prof.* Fr. M.) Die beugungserscheinungen aus den fundimentalgesetzen der undulationstheorie analytisch entwickelt. xii, 143 pp. 5 l. 18 pl. 4°. *Mannheim, Schwan,* 1835. s.

Schwindel (Georg Jakob). Theophili Sinceri neue sammlung von lauter, alten und raren büchern. [*pseudon.*] 6 pts in 1 v. 4 p. l. 544 pp. 8 l. 1 pl. 8°. *Franckfurt und Leipzig, J. Stein,* 1733. s.

Scientific American (The). v. 7-14, Sept. 1852-June, 1859. New series, v. 1-13. July, 1859-Dec. 1865. 21 v. in 14. fol. *New York, Munn & Co.* 1852-65.

Scientific (The) art of lettering taught in one lesson; for the use of painters, gilders, [etc.] Also a collection of receipts for gilding, [etc.] 40 pp. 24 pl. obl. 24°. *St. Louis, J. M. Bagley & Co.* 1866.

Scilla (Agostino). De corporibus marinis lapidescentibus quae defossa reperiuntur. Addita dissertatione Fabii Columni de glossopetris. 3 p. l. 78 pp. 3 l. 28 pl. 4°. *Romae, A. de Rubeis,* 1747. s.

Scioppius (Caspar). *See* **Schoppe.**

Sckell (F. L. von). Beiträge zur bildenden gartenkünst für angehende gartenkünstler und gartenliebhaber. 2e aufl. xxviii, 280 pp. 6 pl. 8°. *München, C. T. F. Sauer,* 1825. s.

Sclater (Philip Lutley), *and* **Salvin** (Osbert). Exotic ornithology. Part 1-2. 4°. *London, B. Quaritch,* 1866-7.

Sclaverei (Ueber), sclaven-emancipation, und die einwanderung freier neger nach den colonieen. [*anon.*] 27 pp. 12°. *Bremen, J. G. Heyse,* 1861.

Scopoli (Giovanni Antonio). Bemerkungen aus der naturgeschichte. Erstes jahr, welches die vögel, etc. beschreibet. Aus dem lateinischen, von Friedrich Christian Günther. xxvii, 211 pp. 12°. *Leipzig, C. G. Hilscher,* 1770. S.

Scoresby (William, *D. D.*) The Franklin expedition; or, measures for the discovery and relief of our absent adventurers in the arctic regions. 99 pp. 2 maps. 8°. *London, Longman, Brown & Co.* 1850.

[Imperfect; maps wanting].

——— On the Greenland or polar ice. 78 pp. 8°. [*n. p.* 1815?]

Scot (A. *member of the university of Paris*). Rudiments and practical exercises for learning the French language. 7, 162 pp. 8°. *London, Longman & Cadell,* 1781.

Scot (*Sir* John). The staggering state of the Scots statesmen, from 1550 to 1650. xxxiv, 190 pp. 16°. *Edinburgh, W. Ruddiman, jr. & Co.* 1754.

Scot (*Rev.* William, *of Cupar*). An apologetical narration of the state and government of the kirk of Scotland since the reformation. [With] certaine records touching the estate of the kirk in M.D.CV and M.D.CVI, by John Forbes. [Edited by J. Anderson and D. Laing.] lxxxviii, 578 pp. 8°. *Edinburgh, Wodrow society,* 1846.

Scot (*Sir* William, *of Thirlestane*). Poemata.

[*With* PITCAIRN (Archibald, *and others*). Selecta poemata, 1727].

Scotland (*Church of*). The confession of faith, the larger and shorter catechisms, covenants, [etc.] of public authority in the church of Scotland, with the acts of assembly and parliament relative to and approbative of the same. 546 pp. 11 l. 12°. [*Edinburgh?*] 1768.

Scott (John, *D. D. canon of Windsor*). A sermon before the queen, 22d of May, 1692, on occasion of the late victory by the fleet over the French. 35 pp. sm. 4°. *London, Walter Kettilby,* 1692.

Scott (John, *major C. S. A. so-called*). Letters to an officer in the army, proposing constitutional reform in the confederate government after the close of the present war; a supplement to the "Lost principle." 82 pp. 8°. *Richmond, A. Morris,* 1864.

——— Partisan life with col. John S. Mosby. 492 pp. 3 pl. 1 map. 8°. *New York, Harpers,* 1867.

Scott (Joseph). A geographical description of the states of Maryland and Delaware. 191 pp. 18°. *Philadelphia, Kimber, Conrad & Co.* 1807.

Scott (*Rev.* Orange). Life: compiled from his personal narrative, correspondence, [etc.] By L. C. Matlack. 307 pp. portrait. 12°. *New York, C. Prindle & L. C. Matlack,* 1847. S.

Scott (*Mrs.* Sarah). The life of Théodore Agrippa d'Aubigné, containing an account of the civil wars of France, in the reigns of Charles IX, Henry III, Henry IV, and Lewis XII. 123 pp. [*anon.*] 8°. *Philadelphia, J. M. Campbell & Co.* 1843.

——— *See, also,* **Raymond** (H. A.)

Scott (*Mrs.* Sarah E.) Every-day cookery for every family, containing nearly 1,000 receipts. 288 pp. 16°. *Philadelphia, H. C. Davis & Co.* 1866.

Scott (Thomas, *B. D.*) Sir Walters Rawleigh's ghost; or, England's forewarner. [*anon.*] 2 p. l. 41 pp. 1 pl. 4°. *Utricht, J. Schellem,* 1626.

Scott (*Sir* Walter). The field of Waterloo. 48 pp. 24°. *Philadelphia, M. Thomas,* 1815.

——— The lay of the last minstrel. 203 pp. 18°. *New York, Elliot and Crissy,* 1811.

——— Halidon hill; a dramatic sketch. 108 pp. 16°. *Philadelphia, Carey & Lea,* 1822.

Scott (*Rev.* William). Epigrams of Martial, etc. with mottos from Horace, etc. translated, imitated, adapted, with notes. xxiv, 262 pp. 16°. *London, J. Wilkie,* 1773.

Scott (Winfield). Memoirs of lieut. general Scott, *LL. D.* Written by himself. 2 v. xxii, 653 pp. 2 portraits. 12°. *New York, Sheldon & Co.* 1864.

——— *See* **Taylor** and his generals.

Scott (*Rev. Dr.* ——). A sure guide to happiness and social love. *See* **Weems** (M. L.) Immortal mentor. pp. 133–321. 16°. *Phila.* 1796.

Scott. *See, also,* **Scot.**

Scotto (Andrea). Itinerario, overo nova descrittione de viaggi principali d'Italia. 3 pts. in 1. 5 p. l. 20 pp. 153 l; 112 l; 72 l. 1 map. 18 pl. 16°. *Padoua, Francesco Bolzetta,* 1628–29.

Scottoni (Giovanni). Dissertazione sopra il quesito: se in uno stato di terreno fertile, favorir debbasi maggiormente l'estrazione delle materie prime, ovvero quella delle manifatture.

[SCRITTORI class. ital. di econ. pol. v. 31].

Scoutetten (Henri). L'ozone; ou, recherches chimiques, météorologiques, physiologiques, et médicales sur l'oxygène électrisé. 273 pp. 6 tab. 1 pl. 12°. *Paris, V. Masson,* 1856. S.

Scoville (Joseph A.) The old merchants of New York city. By Walter Barrett, *clerk.* [*pseudon.*] 4th series. 255 pp. 12°. *New York, Carleton,* 1866.

Scribner (Theodore T.) Indiana's roll of honor. v. 2. 652 pp. 10 pl. 8°. *Indianapolis, (Ind.) A. D. Streight,* 1866.

Scribonius (Cornelius). *See* **Schryver.**

Scriptores rerum prussicarum. Die geschichtsquellen der preussischen vorzeit bis zum untergange der ordensherrschaft. Herausgegeben von Theodor Hirsch, Max Töppen, und Ernst Strehlke. 2 v. xiv, 818 pp; 866 pp. 8°. *Leipzig, S. Hirzel,* 1861–63. S.

Scrittori classici italiani di economica politica. [Collezione publicata per cura di Pietro Custodi]. Parte moderna, v. 1—41. Parte antica, v. 42—49. Indici, v. 50. 50 v. 8°. *Milano,* 1805–17.

CONTENTS.

ALGAROTTI (Francesco). Saggio sopra il comercio. v. 1.

ARCO (Giambattista Gherardo, *conte* d'). Dell' armonia politico-economica tra la città e il suo territorio: 1. Sulla populazione. 2. Dell' annona. v. 30.

——— Dell' influenza del comercio sopra i talenti e i costumi; risposta al quesito: se in uno stato di terreno fertile favorir debbasi maggiormente l'estrazione delle materie prime, ovvero quella delle manifatture; del diritto ai transiti. v. 31.

BANDINI (Salustio Antonio). Discorso economico; con elogio, scritto da G. Gorani. v. 1.

BECCARIA (Cesare). Elementi di economia pubblica, 2 v; della riduzione delle misure di lunghezza all' uniformità per lo stato di Milano. v. 11–12.

BELLONI (Girolamo). Dissertazione sopra il comercio. v. 2.

BRIGANTI (Filippo). Esame economico del sistema civile. v. 28–29.

BROGGIA (Carlo Antonio). Trattato de' tributi. Trattato delle monete. v. 45–46.

CANTALUPO (Gennaro di Domenico). Annona ossia piano economico di pubblica sussistenza. v. 40.

CARACCIOLI (Domenico, *marchese* di Villamaina). Riflessioni sull' economia e l'estrazione de' frumenti della Sicilia fatte in occasione della carestia dell' indizione iii, 1784 e 1785. v. 40.

CARLI (Gian. Rinaldo). Della moneta; relazione del censimento dello stato di Milano; breve ragionamento sopra i bilanci economici delle nazioni; del libero commercio de' grani. v. 13–14.

CORNIANI (Giambattista). Riflessioni sulle monete; della legislazione relativamente all' agricoltura. v. 39.

DAVANZATI (Bernardo). Lezione delle monete, con la notizia de' cambj. v. 43.

DELFICO (Melchiorre). Memoria sulla libertà del commercio. v. 39.

FILANGIERI (Gaetano). Delle leggi politiche ed economiche. v. 32.

GALIANI (Ferdinando). Della moneta; dialogues sur le commerce de blés; estrato del discorso sulla perfetta conservazione del grano. v. 3–6.

GENOVESI (Antonio). Lezioni di economia civile; opuscoli di economia politica. v. 7–10.

MENGOTTI (Francesco). Del commercio de' Romani dalla prima guerra punica a Costantino; il colbertismo, ossia, della libertà di commercio de' prodotti della terra. v. 36.

MONTANARI (Geminiano). Della moneta. v. 44.

NERI (Pompeo). Osservazioni sopra il prezzo legale delle monete, con documenti. Sopra la materia frumentaria: discorso. v. 47–49.

ORTES (Giammaria). Della economia nazionale. v. 21–23 and 49. Riflessioni sulla popolazione delle nazioni per rapporto all' economia nazionale; delle scienze utili e delle dilettevoli per rapporto alla felicità umana ragionamento; calcolo sopra il valore delle opinioni, e sopra i piaceri e i dolori della vita umana; lettere: v. 24 and 49. Errori popolari intorno all' economia nazionale considerati sulle presenti controversie tra i laici e i chierici in ordine al possedimento de' beni; Lettere sulla religione e il governo de' popoli: v. 25–26. Dei fidecommessi in proposito dei termine di mani-morte: v. 27.

PAGNINI (Gio. Francesco). Saggio sopra il giusto pregio delle cose; della moneta e sopra il commercio dei Romani. v. 2.

PALMIERI (Giuseppe). Riflessioni sulla pubblica felicità relativamente al regno di Napoli: v. 37. Osservazioni sulle tariffe; Della ricchezza nazionale: v. 38. Osservazioni sul lusso: v. 49.

PAOLETTI (Ferdinando). Estratto de' pensieri sopra l'agricoltura; I veri mezzi di render felici le società: dell' annona. v. 20.

RICCI (Lodovico). Riforma degl' istituti pii della città di Modena. v. 41.

SCARUFFI (Gasparo). Discorso sopra le monete, e delle vera proporzione tra l'oro e l'argento. v. 43.

SCOTTONI (Giovanni). Dissertazione sopra il quesito: se in uno stato di terreno fertile favorir debbasi maggiormente l'estrazione delle materie prime, ovvero quella delle manifatture. v. 31.

SCROFANI (Saverio). Memoria sulla libertà del commercio dei grani della Sicilia; Riflessioni sopra le sussistenze. v. 40.

SERRA (Antonio). Cause che possono far abbondare li regni d'oro e d'argento dove non sono miniere. v. 42.

SOLERA (Maurizio). Essai sur les valeurs. v. 39.

TURBOLO (Gian. Donato). Discorsi sulle monete del regno di Napoli. v. 42.

VASCO (Giambattista). Della moneta saggio politico; Delle università delle arti e mestieri dissertazione; Mémoire sur les causes de la mendicité et sur les moyens de la supprimer: v. 33. La felicità pubblica considerata nei coltivatori di terre proprie; L'usura libera: v. 34. Dell' indigenza cagionata da scarsezza di seta; Annunzj ed estratti sopra diversi oggetti di economia politica: v. 35.

VERRI (Pietro). Meditazioni sulla economia politica, con annotazioni di G. R. Carli, v. 15; 1. Sulle leggi vincolanti principalmente nel commercio de' grani; 2. Dialogo sul disordine delle monete nello stato di Milano nel 1762; 3. Estratto del progetto di una tariffa, v. 16; 1. Memorie storiche sulla economia pubblica dello stato di Milano; 2. Osservazioni sulla tortura; 3. Varj opuscoli di economia pubblica, v. 17.

ZANON (Antonio). Lettre scelte sull' agricoltura, sul commercio e sulle arti, v. 18; 1. Apologia della mercatura; 2. Estratto del trattato dell' utilità delle academie di agricoltura, arti, e commercio, v. 19.

Scrofani (Saverio). Memoria sulla libertà del commercio dei grani della Sicilia.
[SCRITTORI class. ital. di econ. pol. v. 40].

——— Riflessioni sopra le sussistenze desunte da' fatti osservati in Toscana.
[*With* the preceding.]

Scudder (John, *D. D. of the Madras mission*). A voice from the east to the young, in a series of letters to the children of the reformed protestant Dutch church of North America. 322 pp. 1 pl. 16°. *New York, Board of publication of the ref. prot. Dutch church,* 1856. S.

Scudder (John M. *M. D.*) Familiar treatise on medicine. 4th ed. 2 v. in 1. 594; 242 pp. 8°. *Cincinnati, Moore, Wilstach & Baldwin,* 1866.

——— On the use of medicated inhalations in the treatment of diseases of the respiratory organs. With an introduction by W. Abbotts Smith. 94 pp. 12°. *Cincinnati, Moore, Wilstach & Baldwin,* 1866.

Scudéry (Georges de). Curia politiæ: or, the apologies of several princes; justifying to the world their most eminent actions. Faithfully render'd into English. 8 p. l. 190 pp. 11 pl. fol. *London, R. Boulter*, 1673.

Scudéry (Madeleine de). Clelia, an excellent new romance. Written in French by Monsieur de Scudéry. [*pseudon.* Translated by J. Davies]. 4 p. l. 736 pp. 1 pl. fol. *London, H. Herringman*, 1678.

Scully (William). Brazil; its provinces and chief cities; agricultural, commercial, and other statistics. xv, 398 pp. 1 map. 16°. *London, Murray & Co.* 1866.

Sealsfield (Carl). Les émigrés français dans la Louisiane, 1800–1804. 194 pp. 16°. *Paris, Hachette & Cie.* 1853.

Seaman (Ezra C.) Essays on the progress of nations; [with statistics, etc.] viii, 455 pp. 8°. *Detroit, M. Geiger & Co.* 1846. S.

Search (John, *pseudon?*) Considerations on the law of libel, relating to publications on the subject of religion. [With appendix]. 88 pp. 8°. *London*, 1833.

Searle (E.) Agatha, and other poems. 152 pp. 16°. *Morrison, (Ill.)* 1867.

Sears (*Rev.* Edmund Hamilton). Athanasia; or, foregleams of immortality. 8th ed. xii, 340 pp. 16°. *Boston, Am. unit. assoc.* 1867.

——— Regeneration. 7th ed. 248 pp. 12°. *Boston, Am. unit. assoc.* 1866.

Sea-side pleasures. [*anon.*] 85 pp. 8 pl. 16°. *London, Soc. promot. christ. knowledge*, 1853.

Seasonable reflections on a late pamphlet, [by Abraham *or* Abednego Seller], entituled a history of passive obedience since the reformation. [*anon.*] 67 pp. 4°. *London, R. Clavell*, 1689.

Seat (*Rev.* W. H.) The confederate states of America in prophecy. 144 pp. 16°. *Nashville, (Tenn.)* 1861.

Seaton (Walter). A man in search of a wife. 100 pp. 8°. *New York, De Witt & Davenport.* 1853.

Secession; or, prose in rhyme; and East Tennessee, a poem. By an East Tennessean. [*anon.*] 64 pp. 16°. *Philadelphia, the author*, 1864.

Secchi (Angelo). Osservazioni e ricerche astronomiche sulla grande cometa del Giugno, 1861. [Extract]. 66 pp. 8°. *Roma, tipografia delle belle arti*, 1861. S.

Seckendorf (Veit Ludewig von). Commentarius historicus et apologeticus de lutheranismo, in quo ex Ludovici Maimburgii historia lutheranismi libri tres, ab anno 1517 ad annum 1546, latine versi exhibentur. 21 p. l. 319, 219 pp; 4 p. l. 700 pp. 72 l. 2 pl. fol. *Francofurti & Lipsiæ, J. F. Gleditsch*, 1692.

Secker (Thomas, *archbishop of Canterbury*). Works; [with] a review of his life and character, by B. Porteus. New ed. 6 v. 8°. *London, F. C. & J. Rivington*, 1811.

——— An answer to Dr. Mayhew's observations on the charter and conduct of the society for the propagation of the gospel in foreign parts. [*anon.*] 59 pp. 8°. *Boston, R. & S. Draper, etc.* 1764.

——— The same. *Boston*, 1764.

[*With* MAYHEW (Jonathan, *D. D.*) Observations on the charter of the soc. for the prop. of the gospel in foreign parts. *Boston*, 1763].

Secret (The) history of the calves-head club, complt.; or, the republican unmask'd. [*anon.* By Samuel Butler?] 5th ed. corrected. 72 pp. 12°. *London*, 1705.

Secretan (*optician*). Catalogue et prix des instruments d'optique, de physique, de chimie, de mathématiques, d'astronomie et de marine, etc. Chimie, galvanoplastie, mineralogie. 160 pp. 8°. *Paris*, 1862. S.

[*With* LEREBOURS *and* Secretan. Catalogue, etc. 1853].

Secretaria di Apollo; or, letters from Apollo, historical and political. By Trajano Boccalini. From the Italian. 2 v. 8 p. l. 304 pp; 4 p. l. 280 pp. 1 pl. 12°. *London, R. Smith*, 1704.

[*Note.*—Mazzuchelli decides that this composition is not Boccalini's].

Secrets merveilleux de la magie naturelle et cabalistique du petit Albert. Traduits sur l'original Latin, intitulé Alberti Parvi Lucii libellus. [*anon.*] 240 pp. 3 pl. 18°. *Lyon, Héritiers de Beringos fratres*, 1776.

Seddon (Thomas). Memoir and letters. [Being mainly reminiscences of eastern travel]. By his brother. viii, 208 pp. portrait. 16°. *London, J. Nisbet & Co.* 1858.

Sedgwick (*Rev.* Adam). A synopsis of the classification of the British palæozoic rocks. With a detailed systematic description of the British palæozoic fossils in the geological museum of the university of Cambridge. By Frederick McCoy. 4°. *Cambridge*, 1852–55. S.

Sedgwick (Catharine Maria). Redwood; a tale. [*anon.*] 2 v. 275 pp; 290 pp. 12°. *New York, Bliss & White*, 1824.

Sedlaczek (Ernest). Anleitung zum gebrauche einiger logarithmisch getheilter rechenschieber, (sliding-rule, règle-à-calcul,) etc. 2e aufl. xv, 124 pp. 8°. *Wien, W. Braumüller*, 1856. S.

Sedlaczek (Ernest). Kompendium der ebenen und sfärischen trigonometrie. xviii, 124 pp. 8°. *Wien, W. Braumüller*, 1856. s.

Sedulius (Coelius). Poemata sacra. Denuo recognita, collata et brevibus notis illustrata. Nec non prior ejusdem epistola ad Macedonium presbyterum. xvi, 109 pp. 2 l. 16°. *Edinburgi, A. Anderson*, 1701.

See (Henricus vom, *pseudon.*) Gedichte. xii, 237 pp. 12°. *Milwaukee, (Wis.) J. B. Hoeger & sohn*, 1866.

Seebach (Carl von). Der hannoversche Jura. 2 p. l. 160 pp. 1 map. 10 pl. 4°. *Berlin, W. Hertz*, 1864. s.

Seebohm (Benjamin). Memoirs of William Forster. 2 v. viii, 394 pp; v, 400 pp. 8°. *London, A. W. Bennett*, 1865.

Seelen (Johann Heinrich von). De Iano magistratvs imagine cogitata, [etc.] 2 l. fol. *Lvbecæ, J. N. Green*, 1742.
[*With* WILLEBRANDT (J. P.) Hansiche chronick].

——— De Iosepho Arimathæo senatore ad Marc. xv, 43; Lvc. xxiii, 50. 2 l. fol. *Lvbecæ, J. N. Green*, 1739. s.
[*With* the preceding].

——— De magistratibus λειτουργοις Θεου, ministris Dei, Rom. xiii, 6, emphatice appellatis ecloga, [etc.] 2 l. fol. *Lvbecæ, J. N. Green*, 1735.
[*With* the preceding].

——— De præcipvis nominibvs magistratvi honoris cavsa impositis philologema, [etc.] 2 l. fol. *Lubecæ, Koop*, 1728. s.
[*With* the preceding].

——— De probandis et improbandis in Platonis doctrina de republica disserit, [etc.] 2 l. fol. *Lvbecæ, J. N. Green*, 1738. s.
[*With* the preceding].

——— Paradoxon dippelianvm de magistratv in regno Christi non necessario falsitatis et iniqvitatis convictvm, [etc.] 2 l. fol. *Lvbecæ, J. N. Green*, 1743. s.
[*With* the preceding].

——— Pietatis vetervm christianorvm erga magistratvm civilem encomium, etc. 2 l. fol. *Lvbecæ, J. N. Green*, 1732. s.
[*With* the preceding].

Seeley (John Robert). Student's guide to the university of Cambridge. viii, 338 pp. 12°. *Cambridge, (England,) Deighton, Bell & Co.* 1863. s.

Seelye (Edward E. *D. D.*) Bible emblems. 222 pp. 12°. *New York, Amer. tract soc.* 1866.

Seemiller (Sebastian). Bibliothecæ academicæ ingolstadiensis incunabula typographica; seu libri ante annum 1500 impressi circiter mille et quadringenti. 4 v. in 1. 4°. *Ingolstadii, J. W. Krüll*, 1787.

Segnitz (Edmund). Dreissig bücher von der landwirthschaft; ein encyclopädisches handbuch. 3 v. 8°. *Dresden, Arnold*, 1847–50. s.

Segoing *or* **Ségoin** (Charles). Armorial vniversal, contenant les armes des principales maisons, estatz, et dignitez, [etc.] de l'Europe, [etc.] 9 p. l. 193 pl. 4°. *Paris, N. Berey*, 1654. s.

Ségur (Philippe Paul, *comte* de). Histoire de Napoléon et de la grande armée pendant l'année 1812. 10e éd. 2 v. 308 pp; 332 pp. 1 map. 7 pl. 8°. *Bruxelles, Lacrosse*, 1835.

——— The same. 4e éd. 410 pp. 1 map. 16°. *Paris, C. Gosselin*, 1841. s.

Seiler (Emma). The voice in singing. From the German, by a member of the American philosophical society. 178 pp. 12°. *Philadelphia, J. B. Lippincott & Co.* 1868.

Seingalt (Jacques Casanova de). *See* **Casanova** de Seingalt (Jacques).

Selden (D. J. *M. D.*) The American horse doctor. 128 pp. 16°. *Cleveland, Fairbanks & Co.* 1866.

Selden (John). Titles of honor. 3d ed. with additions. 17 p. l. 756 pp. 1 pl. sm. fol. *London, T. Dring*, 1672.
[Portrait wanting].

Select (A) collection of modern poems from the best authors. 16°. *Edinburgh, A. Donaldson*, 1758.

CONTENTS.

Hammond. Love-elegies.
Gray. Elegy in a country church-yard.
Hervey, *lord* John. Epistles in the manner of Ovid.
Akenside. Pleasures of imagination. Odes.
Armstrong. Art of preserving health.

Select essays from the batchelor; or, speculations of Jeoffry Wagstaffe, esq. [*pseudon.* Written by Jephson, Courtenay, Borroughs, etc.] 2 v. 7 p. l. 359, 60 pp. 16°. *Dublin, J. Hoey*, 1772.

Select letters taken from Fog's weekly journal. [*anon.*] 2 v. xii, 266 pp. 4 l; 290 pp. 4 l. 2 pl. 12°. *London*, 1732.

Select views in Sicily; accompanied by an historical and descriptive account. Translated from the original [of Achille Étienne Gigault de La Salle,] published at Paris, by J. F. d'Ostervald. 29 l. 22 col. pl. 4°. *London, J. Weale*, 1825.

Selection (A) of hymns for the use of social religious meetings. [*anon.*] 4th ed. 18°. *Baltimore, Armstrong & Plaskitt*, 1824.

Selections from the masquerade; a collection of enigmas, logogriphs, charades, rebuses, queries, and transpositions. [*anon.*] 2 p. l. 215 pp. 16°. *London, Baker & Fletcher*, 1826.

Selmi (Francesco). Nouveau manuel complet de dorure et d'argenture. Trad. de l'Italien par E. de Valicourt. xii, 173 pp. 18°. *Paris, Roret*, 1845. S.

Selys-Longchamps (Michel Edmond de), *and* **Hagen** (Hermann August). Monographie des caloptérygines. xi, 291 pp. 8°. *Bruxelles, C. Muquardt*, 1854. S.

——— Monographie des gomphines. viii, 460 pp. 23 pl. 8°. *Bruxelles, C. Muquardt*, 1858. S.

Semblanzas de los representantes que compusieron el congreso constituyente de 1836. [*anon.*] 45 pp. 18°. *México, M. R. Gallo*, 1837.

Semmedo *or* **Semedo** (Alvaro). The history of that great and renowned monarchy of China. Now put into English [from his "Imperio de la China y cultura evangelica en el, por los religiosos de la compañia de Jesus"], by a person of quality. 4 p. l. 248 pp. map. fol. *London, John Crook*, 1655.

Semple (Robert). Observations on a journey through Spain and Italy to Naples, and thence to Smyrna and Constantinople, [with] the Spanish post guide. 2d ed. 2 v. lxiv, 208 pp; 254 pp. 1 map. 12°. *London, C. & R. Baldwin*, 1808.

Sendel (Nathanael). Historia svccinorvm corpora aliena involventivm et natvrae opere pictorvm et caelatorvm, ex regiis Avgvstorvm cimeliis Dresdae conditis aeri inscvlptorvm conscripta. viii, 328 pp. 13 pl. fol. *Lipsiae, J. F. Gleditsch*, 1742.

Sendtner (Otto). Die vegetations-verhältnisse Südbayerns, nach den grundsätzen der pflanzengeographie und mit bezugnahme auf landescultur. xii, 910 pp. 9 pl. 1 map. 8°. *München, Literarisch-artistische anstalt*, 1854. S.

Senebier (Jean). Catalogue raisonné des manuscrits conservés dans la bibliothèque de la ville et république de Genève. iv, 478 pp. 8°. *Genève, B. Chirol*, 1779.

Seneca (Lucius Annæus). Epistles, with annotations by Thomas Morell. 2 v. xix, 308 pp; 368 pp. 4°. *London, W. Woodfall*, 1786.

——— Proverbia: de moribus.

[*With* ISOCRATES (Paræenesis). Ed. 1699].

——— *and* **Syrus** (Publius). Singulares sententiae, centum aliquot versibus ex codd. Pall. et Frising. auctæ et correctæ studio Jani Gruteri. Acced. nova versio græca Scaligeri. 12 p. l. 569 pp. 1 pl. 8°. *Lugduni-Batavorum, H. Teering*, 1727. S.

Senft (Ferdinand). Classification und beschreibung der felsarten. xxxii, 442 pp. 12 tab. 8°. *Breslau, W. G. Korn*, 1857. S.

Senoner (Adolph). Die sammlungen der k.-k. geologischen reichs-anstalt in Wien. 44 pp. 1 pl. 16°. *Wien, C. Gerold's sohn*, 1862. S.

Sentenze e detti memorabili d'antichi, e di moderni autori. 299 pp. 12°. *Bologna, Mobili e Comp.* 1826.

Senter (Isaac). The journal of Isaac Senter on a secret expedition against Quebec, under the command of col. Benedict Arnold, in September, 1775. 40 pp. 8°. *Philadelphia, Historical society of Pennsylvania*, 1846.

Serenius *or* **Sören** (Jacob). An English and Swedish dictionary. 2d ed. [of the author's Dictionarium anglo-svethico-latinum]. 4 p. l. 16 pp. 313 l. 4°. *Harg and Stenbro, P. Momma*, 1757. S.

Serious (A) address to such of the quakers on the continent of North America as profess scruples relative to the present government. By a native of Pennsylvania. 2d ed. [*anon.*] 48 pp. 8°. *Philadelphia, Styner & Cist*, 1778.

Sermini (Gentile). Novelle.

[*In* NOVELLE di autori senesi, v. 1. 18°. *Milano*, 1815].

Sermons delivered during the second plenary council of Baltimore, October, 1866, and pastoral letter; with the Papal rescript and letters of convocation. liv, 244 pp. 36 pl. 12°. *Baltimore, Kelly & Piet*, 1866.

Sermons by eminent living divines of the church of England. xxxiv, 326 pp. 16°. *Glasgow, Griffin & Co.* 1856.

Sermons preached at the church of St. Paul the apostle, New York, during the years 1865 and 1866. 440 pp. 12°. *New York, L. Kehoe*, 1867.

Serra (Antonio). Breve trattato delle cause che possono far abbondare li regni d'oro e d'argento dove non sono miniere.

[SCRITTORI class. ital. di econ. pol. v. 42].

Serres (Étienne Renaud Augustin). Anatomie comparée du cerveau, dans les quatres classes des animaux vertébrés. 2 v. cxii, 576 pp; vii, 795 pp. 8°. *Paris, Gabon et Cie.* 1827. S.

[Atlas of 16 pl. 4°. wanting].

Serville (Audinet). *See* **Audinet** Serville (Jean Guillaume).

Sestier (Félix). De la foudre, de ses formes, et de ses effets sur l'homme, les animaux, les végétaux et les corps bruts, des moyens de s'en préserver et des paratonnerres. Rédigé par C. Méhu. 2 v. xxxii, 480 pp; 632 pp. 8°. *Saint Germain, Baillière,* 1866.

Set (A) of plans and forts in America, reduced from actual surveys, 1763. [Engraved by P. Andrews. *anon.*] 29 pl. obl. 8°. *n. p.* 1763?

Seven days' battles in front of Richmond. Copied from the detailed accounts of the newspaper press. [*anon.*] 45 pp. 8°. *Richmond, West & Johnston,* 1862.

Severus (Sulpicius). Opera; ad mss. codices emendata, notisque, observationibus et dissertationibus illustrata studio et labore Hieronymi de Prato, veronensis. 2 v. 11 p. l. lxxxiii, 413 pp. 1 pl; li, 543 pp. 4°. *Veronae, typis seminarii,* 1741–54. S.

Sewall (Jonathan Mitchell). Miscellaneous poems, with several specimens from the author's manuscript version of the poems of Ossian. 304 pp. 18°. *Portsmouth, (N. H.) Treadwell & Co.* 1801.

Sewall (*Rev.* Joseph). Desires that Joshua's resolution may be revived, with other sermons. xii, 116 pp. 18°. *Boston, B. Green,* 1715.

Seward (*Miss* Anna). Monody on major Andrè, [with] letters addressed to her by Andrè in 1769. 2d ed. vi, 47 pp. 4°. *Lichfield, J. Jackson,* 1781.

Seward (Edward S.) Poems. 42 pp. 48°. *Baltimore, James Lucas,* 1847.

Seward (Theodore F. *joint author*). *See* **Temple** choir.

Sewel *or* **Sewell** (William). Die geschichte von dem ursprung, zunehmen, und fortgang des christlichen volcks, so quäcker genennet werden. Aus dem Englischen ins Hochdeutsche übersetzt. 5 p. l. 647 pp. 9 l. fol. [*Jena, Frommann*], 1742.

Sewell (Elizabeth Missing). Ivors; or, the two cousins. [*anon.*] New ed. 489 pp. 12°. *London, Longman, Brown & Co.* 1858.

——— Ursula; a tale of country life. [*anon.*] 544 pp. 12°. *London, Longman, Green & Co.* 1862.

Sextus *Empiricus.* Les hipotiposes; ou, institutions pirroniennes. Traduites du Grec, avec des notes. [Par Huart?] 16 p. l. 434 pp. 1 pl. 18°. [*Amsterdam?*] 1725.

——— Traduction d'une partie du livre vii. contre les mathématiciens et contre les logiciens [par G. M. M. Salvimeni di Castiglione].

[*With* CICERO. Livres académiques, par Castillon. v. 1].

Sextus Rufus, *or* **Rufus** Festus. De historia romana epitome.

[*With* FLORUS (L. A.) De gestis Romanorum, etc. 1532].

Seymour (C. A. E.) General English and German glossary; or, collection of words, phrases, names, customs, proverbs, etc. in English and Scotch poets, from the time of Chaucer. Revised by Dr. J. G. Flügel. x, 206 pp. 8°. *Leipzic, E. Fleischer,* 1835.

Seymour (Silas). Incidents of a trip through the great Platte valley, to the Rocky mountains and Laramie plains, in the fall of 1866; and an account of the Union Pacific railroad excursion. 129 pp. 12°. *New York, D. Van Nostrand,* 1867.

Shaffner (Taliaferro P.) The telegraph manual: a complete history and description of the semaphoric, electric, and magnetic telegraphs of Europe, Asia, Africa, and America, ancient and modern. 850 pp. 10 portraits. 8°. *New York, etc. Pudney & Russell,* 1859.

Shafton (Piers, *pseudon?*) Vagaries in quest of the wild and the whimsical. 3d ed. vi, 256 pp. 6 pl. 16°. *London, G. Cowie,* 1833.

Shakespear (John). A dictionary of Hindūstānī and English, etc. 3d ed. viii, 2212 pp. 4°. *London, Parbury, Allen & Co.* 1834. S.

Shakespeare (William). Comedies, histories, and tragedies. Published according to the true originall copies. A reproduction in exact fac-simile of the famous first folio, London, I. Iaggard and E. Blount, 1623, by photo lithography. Under the superintendence of H. Staunton. 9 p. l. 896 pp. fol. *London, Day & son,* 1866.

——— The same. Shakespeare as put forth in 1623. A reprint. 11 p. l. 399 pp. sm. 4°. *London, L. Booth,* 1864.

——— The same. Plays, from the text of Reed. 6 v. 24°. *Boston, C. Williams,* 1813.

——— The same. Dramatic works. With the corrections and illustrations of Johnson, Steevens, and others, revised by I. Reed. 10 v. 12°. *New York, Collins & Hannay,* 1821.

[First American stereotype ed.]

——— A supplement to the plays; comprising the seven dramas which have been ascribed to his pen, but which are not included with his writings in modern editions. Edited by W. G. Simms. 178 pp. 2 pl. 8°. *New York, Coolidge,* 1848. S.

——— Poetical works. 8°. *Edinburgh,* 1793.

[Anderson's British poets, v. 2].

Shakespeare (William). Poetical works. With illustrative remarks, [and] a sketch of the author's life [by W. C. Oulton]. 2 v. xlvi, 183 pp; 247 pp. 5 pl. 18°. *London, C. Chapple,* 1804.

——— Oeuvres complètes. François Victor Hugo traducteur. 18 v. 8°. *Paris, Pagnerre,* 1859–66.

CONTENTS.

v. 1. Les deux Hamlet; [essai].
Le premier Hamlet.
Le second Hamlet.
v. 2. Les féeries; [essai].
Le songe d'une nuit d'été.
La tempête.
v. 3. Les tyrans; [essai].
Macbeth.
Le roi Jean.
Richard iii.
v. 4. Les jaloux; [essai].
Troylus et Cressida.
Beaucoup de bruit pour rien.
Le conte d'hiver.
v. 5. Les jaloux; [essai].
Cymbeline.
Othello.
v. 6. Les comédies de l'amour; [essai].
La sauvage apprivoisée.
Tout est bien qui finit bien.
Peines d'amour perdues.
v. 7. Les amants tragiques; [essai].
Antoine et Cléopatre.
Roméo et Juliette.
v. 8. Les amis; [essai].
Les deux gentilshommes de Vérone.
Le marchand de Venise.
Comme il vous plaira.
v. 9. La famille; [essai].
Coriolan.
Le roi Lear.
v. 10. La société; [essai].
Mesure pour mesure.
Timon d'Athènes.
Jules César.
v. 11. La patrie; [essai].
Richard ii.
Henry iv, (1e partie).
Henry iv, (2e partie).
v. 12. La patrie; [essai].
Henry v.
Henry vi, (1e partie).
v. 13. La patrie; [essai].
Henry vi, (2e partie).
Henry vi, (3e partie).
Henry viii.
v. 14. Les farces; [essai].
Les joyeuses épouses de Windsor.
La comédie des erreurs.
Le soir des rois; ou, ce que vous voudrez.
v. 15. Préface de la nouvelle traduction, (par Victor Hugo). Sonnets; poëmes; testament.
v. 16. Les apocryphes; [essai].
Titus Andronicus.
Une tragédie dans l'Yorkshire.
Les deux nobles parents.
v. 17. Les apocryphes; [essai].
Périclès.
Édouard iii.
Arden de Feversham.
v. 18. Les apocryphes; [essai].
La tragédie de Locrine.
La vie et la mort de Thomas Lord Cromwell.
Le prodigue de Londres.
La puritaine; ou, la veuve de Watling Street.

Sham (The) patriot unmasked. [*anon.*] 143 pp. 24°. *Hudson, Sampson, Chittenden & Croswell,* 1802.

Sharland (George). Knapsack notes of Sherman's campaign through the state of Georgia. 68 pp. 8°. *Springfield, (Ill.) Johnson & Bradford,* 1865.

Sharland (Joseph B.) The grammar school chorus. *See* **Hullah** (John), *and* **Sharland** (J. B.)

Sharp (Granville). An account of the ancient division of the English nation into hundreds and tithings. 370 pp. 8°. *London, Galabin & Baker,* 1784.

——— The case of Saul, showing that his disorder was a real spiritual possession. [With] a short tract wherein the influence of demons [is] illustrated by remarks on 1 Timothy iv, 1–3. [2d ed.] iv, 187, xv pp. 16°. *London, Vernor & Hood, and others,* [1807].

——— A declaration of the people's natural right to a share in the legislature. 2d ed. xl, 279 pp. 12°. *London, B. White,* 1775.

——— Dissertation on the supreme divine dignity of the Messiah. 64 pp. 16°. *London, R. Edwards,* 1807.

[*With* SHARP (G.) The case of Saul. 1807].

——— Inquiry, whether the destruction of Babylon, in the 18th chapter of Revelations, agrees perfectly with Rome as a city. With appendix of notes. xxxiii, 69, 114; xxv pp. 16°. *London, W. Calvert,* 1805.

[*With his* REMARKS on the uses of the definitive article. 3d ed. *London,* 1803].

——— Remarks on the opinions of some of the most celebrated writers on crown law [on] the distinction between manslaughter and murder. xviii, 76 pp. 12°. *London, B. White & R. Horsfield,* 1773.

——— Remarks on several very important prophecies. In five parts. 2d ed. 271 pp. 12°. *London, B. White,* 1775.

——— Remarks on the uses of the definitive article in the Greek text of the new testament; containing many new proofs of the divinity of Christ. 3d ed. xxxviii, 148 pp. 16°. *London, Vernor & Hood, etc.* 1803.

——— The same. 1st Am. from 3d London ed. xxxvi, 150 pp. 12°. *Philadelphia, E. B. Hopkins & Co.* 1807.

——— Remarks on the two last petitions in the Lord's prayer. 25 pp. 16°. *London, Richard Edwards,* 1807.

[*With* SHARP (G.) The case of Saul. *London,* 1807].

——— Serious reflections on the slave trade and slavery. 46 pp. 16°. *London, W. Calvert,* 1805.

[*With* SHARP (G.) The case of Saul. 1807].

——— System of colonial law compared with the eternal laws of God, and with the principles of the English constitution. 30 pp. 16°. *London, Richard Edwards,* 1807.

[*With* SHARP (G.) The case of Saul. 1807].

Sharp (Granville). Three tracts on the syntax and pronunciation of the Hebrew tongue; with an appendix. 106, 32, 146, 36 pp. 16°. *London, W. Calvert, for Vernor & Hood, etc.* 1804.

——— Tract on duelling. 2d ed. xix, 75 pp. 16°. *London, B. White & son & C. Dilly,* 1790.

[*With* SHARP (G.) The case of Saul. *London,* 1807].

——— A tract on the law of nature and principles of action in man. 2d ed. 467 pp. 12°. *London, W. Calvert,* 1809.

——— Tracts concerning the ancient and only true legal means of national defence by a free militia. 3d ed. 141 pp. 12°. *London, Dilly, and others,* 1782.

Sharpe (Daniel). Description of the fossil remains of mollusca found in the chalk of England. Pts. 1–3. [Cephalopoda]. 2 p. l. 68 pp. 27 l. 27 pl. 4°. *London, Palæontographical society,* 1853–56. s.

[No more published].

Sharswood (George). Essay on professional ethics. 2d ed. liv, 158 pp. 12°. *Philadelphia, T. & J. W. Johnson & Co.* 1860.

Shattuck (Lemuel). Blank book forms for family registers, [etc.] 12 pp. 28 l. 4°. *Boston, author,* 1846. s.

Shaw (Elijah). A short sketch of his life by himself. 87 pp. 16°. *Rochester, Strong & Dawson,* 1843.

Shaw (James). Plans, elevations, and sections, with observations and explanations, of forcing-houses in gardening. 15 l. 11 pl. fol. *Whitby, T. Webster,* 1794.

Shaw (John, *lecturer on anatomy in London*). A manual for the student of anatomy; elementary views of anatomy, and their application to pathology and surgery. Revised, with notes by William Anderson, M. D. 1st Am. from last London ed. 355 pp. 2 pl. 12°. *Troy, J. Disturnell,* 1825. s.

Shaw (John Robert). A narrative of his life and travels, by himself. 180 pp. 5 pl. 8°. *Lexington, [Ky.] Daniel Bradford,* 1807.

Shaw (Thomas B.) Complete manual of English literature. Ed. with notes, by W. Smith, LL. D. With a sketch of American literature, by H. T. Tuckerman. 540 pp. 12°. *New York, Sheldon & Co.* 1867.

Shea (John Gilmary). Relations diverses sur la bataille du Malangueulé, gagné le 9 juillet, par les François sur les Anglois [sous le commandement du col. Braddock]. Recueillies par J. M. Shea. 51 pp. 8°. *Nouvelle York, Cramoisy press,* 1860. s.

Shecut (J. L. E. W.) Ish-noo-ju-lut-sche; or, the eagle of the Mohawks. 2 v. 234 pp; 284 pp. 18°. *New York, R. Price,* 1841.

Shedd (William Greenough Thayer, *D. D.*) Homiletics and pastoral theology. vi, 429 pp. 8°. *New York, C. Scribner & Co.* 1867.

Sheffield (John, *duke of Buckinghamshire*). Poetical works. 8°. *Edinburgh,* 1793.

[Anderson's Brit. poets, v. 7].

Sheldon (*Miss* Ann). Memoirs. *See* **Archer** (*Mrs.* Ann).

Sheldon (Henry Olcott). The Sheldon magazine; or, a genealogical list of the Sheldons in America, etc. 4 nos. in 1 v. 11 pp. 113 l. 8°. *Londonville, (Ohio),* 1855–57. s.

Shelley (Mary Wollstonecraft). The last man. [*anon.*] 2d ed. 3 v. 12°. *London, H. Colburn,* 1826.

Shelley (Percy Bysshe). Alastor; or, the spirit of solitude; and other poems. 16°. *London, Baldwin,* 1816.

——— The Cenci, a tragedy. xiv, 104 pp. 8°. *Italy, for C. & J. Ollier, London.*

[*With his* Rosalind and Helen. 1819 ed.]

——— Prometheus unbound, a lyrical drama; with other poems. 222 pp. 8°. *London, C. & J. Ollier,* 1820.

——— The revolt of Islam: a poem, in 12 cantos. xxxii, 271 pp. 8°. *London, C. & J. Ollier,* 1818.

——— Rosalind and Helen, a modern eclogue; with other poems. vii, 92 pp. 8°. *London, C. & J. Ollier,* 1819.

Shelly (A. Fishe, *pseudon.*) *See* **Gerhard** (J. W.)

Shenstone (William). Works, in verse and prose. With decorations. 3 v. 12°. *London, J. Dodsley,* 1777.

CONTENTS.

v. 1. Poetical works. Verses to Mr. Shenstone.
v. 2. Description of the Leasowes. Essays on men and manners.
v. 3. Letters.

——— Poetical works. 8°. *Edinburgh,* 1794.

[Anderson's Brit. poets, v. 9].

Shepard (*Rev.* Thomas, *of Cambridge, Mass.*) Autobiography, with notices of his life and character, by N. Adams. 129 pp. 18°. *Boston, Pierce & Parker,* 1832.

——— Certain select cases resolved, specially tending to the right ordering of the heart. 32 pp. 16°. *London, John Rothwel,* 1655.

[*With* SHEPARD (*Rev.* Thomas). Theses sabbaticæ. *London,* 1655].

——— The cleare sun-shine of the gospell, breaking forth upon the Indians in New-England. 3 p. l. 38 pp. sm. 4°. [*London,* 1648?]

[Imperfect; title page wanting].

Shepard (*Rev.* Thomas, (*of Cambridge, Mass.*) The first principles of the oracles of God. 17 pp. 16°. *London, John Rothwel,* 1655.

[*With* SHEPARD, (*Rev.* Thomas). Theses sabbaticæ. *London,* 1655].

——— The parable of the ten virgins. Opened and applied: being the substance of divers sermons. [2 pts. in 1 v.] 3 p. l. 232, 190 pp. 3 l. fol. *Reprinted, London,* 1695.

——— Select cases resolved; first principles of the oracles of God; and a private diary. With some account of the author. 176 pp. 18°. *Boston, Rogers & Fowle,* 1747.

——— Theses sabbaticæ, or the doctrine of the sabbath. xiv, 320 pp. 16°. *London, J. Rothwel,* 1655.

Shephard (Charles). Historical account of the island of Saint Vincent. 8°. *London,* 1831.

Shepherd (*Rev.* Edward John). The history of the church of Rome to the end of the episcopate of Damascus, A. D. 384. xi, 541 pp. 8°. *London, Longman, Brown & Co.* 1851.

Shepherd (*lady* Mary). Essay on the perception of an external universe, and other subjects connected with the doctrine of causation. xvi, 416 pp. 12°. *London, Hatchard & son,* 1827.

Sheppard (*Mrs.* Edwin). "Judge not"; or, Hester Powers' girlhood. 224 pp. 12°. *Boston, Loring,* 1868.

Sheppard (Furman). The constitutional text-book: a practical and familiar exposition of the constitution of the United States, and of portions of the public and administrative law of the federal government. 324 pp. 12°. *Philadelphia, Sower, Barnes & Potts,* [1855].

——— The first book of the constitution: a familiar exposition of the constitution of the United States. Revised ed. 210 pp. 12°. *Philadelphia, Sower, Barnes & Potts,* 1866.

Sheppard (W.) Notes on some of the plants of lower Canada.

[*With* QUEBEC. Lit. and hist. soc. transactions, v. 2. pp. 39–64.]

Sherburne (Andrew). Memoirs of A. S. a pensioner of the navy of the revolution. 262 pp. 16°. *Utica, W. Williams,* 1828. s.

Sherburne (Henry). The oriental philanthropist, or true republican. 215 pp. 16°. *Portsmouth, (N. H.) William Treadwell,* 1800.

Sherburne (John Henry). Life and character of the chevalier John Paul Jones. 364 pp. 1 portrait. 8°. *Washington, the author,* [*printed in N. Y.*] 1825.

Sherer (*major* Moyle). Notes and reflections during a ramble in Germany. [*anon.*] iv, 400 pp. 8°. *London, Longman & Co.* 1826.

——— Sketches of India. [*anon.*] 4th ed. iv, 297 pp. 8°. *London, Longman & Co.* 1826.

——— Recollections of the Peninsula. [*anon.*] 4th ed. 358 pp. 8°. *London, Longman & Co.* 1825.

Sheridan (Richard Brinsley). The duenna: a comic opera. New ed. [*anon.*] ii, 43 pp. 12°. *London, E. Johnson,* 1776.

Sheridan (Thomas, *D. D. father*). Essay upon the immortality of the soul. xxxix pp.

[*With* DAVIS (*Sir* John). Poem, etc. *Dublin,* 1733].

Sheridan (Thomas, *A. M. son*). A complete dictionary of the English language, to which is prefixed a prosodial grammar. 4th ed. 2 v. 12 p. l. cviii pp. 231 l; 302 l. 8°. *London, C. Dilly,* 1797.

Sheriff (D.) Cultivation of flax as a national advantage. 16 pp. 16°. *Sheffield, (England), Social science association,* 1865.

Sherlock (Thomas, *D. D. bishop of London*). Arguments against a repeal of the corporation and test acts. iv, 73 pp. 8°. *London, G. G. J. & J. Robinson,* 1787.

Sherman (John). A description of Trenton Falls, Oneida county, N. Y. 23 pp. 18°. *New York, W. H. Colyer,* 1847.

Sherwin (W. T.) Sherwin's political register, April 5th, 1817, to May 1, 1819. 4 v. 8°. *London, W. T. Sherwin,* 1819.

Sherwood (Adiel). A gazetteer of the state of Georgia, [with appendix of biographical sketches, etc.] 2d ed. 300 pp. map. 24°. *Philadelphia, J. W. Martin,* 1829.

Sherwood (Henry Hall, *M. D.*) Manual for magnetizing, with the vibrating magnetic machine, and for the magnetic or duodynamic treatment of diseases. 14th ed. 375 pp. 24°. *New York, Fowler & Wells,* 1850. s.

Sherwood (*Mrs.* Mary Martha Butt). The life of Mrs. Sherwood, abridged for the Presbyterian board of publication. 152 pp. 1 portrait. 12°. *Philadelphia, Presbyterian board of publication,* 1857. s.

Sherwood (William, *M. D.*) General pathology.

[*With* JONES (J. G.) American eclectic practice of medicine, v. 1, 1857].

Sherwood (William, *teacher of elocution*). Self-culture in reading, speaking, and conversation. 383 pp. 12°. *New York, A. S. Barnes & Co.* 1856. s.

Sheville (John), *and* **Gould** (James L.) Guide to the royal arch chapter: a complete monitor for royal arch masonry; [also] monitorial instructions in the order of high priesthood. 272 pp. 1 pl. 12°. *New York, Masonic pub. co.* 1867.

Shew (Joel, *M.D.*) The cholera; its causes, prevention, and cure, showing the inefficacy of drug-treatment, and the superiority of the water-cure. 98 pp. 16°. *New York, Fowlers & Wells*, 1848.

Shimeall (*Rev.* Richard Cunningham). Christ's second coming: is it pre-millenial or post-millenial? With a reply to prof. Shedd on "eschatology." 320, 153 pp. 8°. *New York, J. F. Trow*, 1865.

Shipley (Conway). Sketches in the Pacific. The South Sea islands. 18 l. 26 pl. fol. *London, McLean*, 1851.

Shipmaster's (The) medical directory. By an experienced physician. [*anon.*] xiv, 77 pp. 16°. *Boston, J. G. Nichols*, 1854. s.

Shippey (Josiah). Specimens; or, leisure hours poetically employed on various subjects. With notes. 238 pp. 16°. *New York, J. B. Allee*, 1841.

Shipping and commercial list [and New York price current]. v. 50–52. 1864–66. 3 v. fol. *New York, Autens & Bourne*, 1864–66.

Shirley (*pseudon.*) *See* **Nugae** criticae.

Shively (J. M.) Route and distances to Oregon and California, with a description of watering places, crossings, dangerous Indians, etc. 15 pp. 8°. *Washington, W. Greer*, 1846.

Shoberl (Frederick). Narrative of the most remarkable events which occurred in and near Leipzig, before, during, and subsequent to the engagement between the allied armies and the French, 14th to 19th Oct. 1813. 3d ed. xvi, 104 pp. 2 maps. 8°. *London, R. Ackermann*, 1814.

Shores of Vespucci; or, romance without fiction. [*anon.*] 244 pp. 16°. *Lexington, (Mass.) M. Tufts*, 1833.

Short catechism for the use of the Catholic church in the U. S. of America. 64 pp. 32°. *Baltimore, F. Lucas*, [1836]?

Short (A) collection of the most remarkable passages from the originall to the dissolution of the Virginia company. 20 pp. sm. 4°. *London, Edward Husband*, 1651.

[*With* SOMMER islands company. Copy of a petition. *London*, 1651].

Short (A) compendium of ancient and modern geography, translated from the French by Mr. de Lanségüe. viii, 478 pp. 8°. *London, Logographic press.* 1791.

[Imperfect: all after 478th page wanting].

Short (A) description of the Tennasee government, or the territory of the United States south of the river Ohio, to accompany and explain a map of that country. [*anon.*] 20 pp. 8°. *Philadelphia, M. Carey*, 1793.

[Imperfect; map wanting].

Shrimpton (Charles, *M. D.*) Cholera; its seat, nature, and treatment. viii, 109 pp. 1 pl. 8°. *London, Churchill & sons*, 1866.

Shrimpton (Charles). The black phantom; or, woman's endurance; a narrative [of] the early history of Canada and the American revolution. 358 pp. 12°. *New York, Crowen & Co.* 1867.

Shriver (James). An account of the surveys and examinations, with remarks and documents relative to the projected Chesapeake and Ohio, and Ohio and lake Erie canals. 116 pp. 8°. *Baltimore, F. Lucas, jr.* 1824. s.

Shrubs (The) of Parnassus. Poetical essays, moral and comic. By J. Copywell. [*pseudon.*] 21, 154 pp. 18°. *London, J. Newbery*, 1770.

Shuck (J. Lewis, *editor*). Portfolio chinensis; or, a collection of authentic Chinese state papers illustrative of the history of the present position of affairs in China. With a translation, notes, and introduction, [Chinese and English]. xvi, 194 pp. 8°. *Macao, F. F. De Cruz*, 1840. s.

Shuckard (William E.) British bees. 12°. *London, Reeve*, 1866.

Shumard (Benjamin Franklin). A catalogue of the palæozoic fossils of North America. [i. Echinodermata. Extract.] 75 pp. 8°. *St. Louis, Acad. of sciences*, 1865. s.

——— Local details of geological sections on the St. Peter's, Mississippi, Wisconsin, Barraboo, Snake, and Kettle rivers. s.

[*With* OWEN (D. D.) Report of a geological survey of Wisconsin, etc. 1852].

——— Geology of Kentucky. *See* **Yandell** (Lunsford P.) *and* **Shumard**.

Shute (Samuel M.) A manual of Anglo-Saxon for beginners; comprising a grammar, reader, and glossary, with notes. xxi, 195 pp. 12°. *New York, Leypoldt & Holt*, 1867.

Siber (Thaddæus). Grundlinien der experimental physik. x, 226 pp. 11 pl. 8°. *München, G. Franz*, 1837. s.

Sibley (John Langdon). A history of the town of Union, Lincoln co. Maine; with a family register of the settlers before the year 1800, and of their descendants. ix, 540 pp. 1 pl. 12°. *Boston, B. B. Mussey & Co.* 1851.

Sichel (Jules). Catalogus specierum generis scoliæ, etc. 1864. *See* **Saussure** (H. F. de), *and* **Sichel.**

——— Hymenoptera. 1867. *See* **Wüllerstorf-**Urbair (B. von). Reise der Novara.

——— Nouveau recueil de pierres sigillaires d'oculistes romains, pour la plupart inédites. (Extrait des Annales d'oculistique). 119 pp. 8°. *Paris, Victor Masson et fils*, 1866. s.

Siddons (Sarah Kemble). Siege of Mansoul, a drama. vi, 82 pp. 8°. *Bristol, W. Bulgins*, 1801.

——— Story of our first parents. *See* **Milton** (John).

Sidney, *or* **Sydney** (Algernon). Discourses concerning government, [with] the paper deliver'd to the sheriffs immediately before his death. 2d ed. 4 p. l. 424 pp. 24 l. 1 pl. fol. *London, T. Atkinson*, 1705.

——— Essence of Algernon Sydney's work on government, [with] his essay on love. By a student of the inner temple. xxii, 287 pp. 8°. *London, J. Johnson*, 1795.

Sidney (*Rev.* Edwin). The life and ministry of Rev. Samuel Walker. 2d ed. xx, 564 pp. 8°. *London, R. B. Seeley & W. Burnside*, 1838.

Sidney (*Sir* Philip). Aphorisms, with remarks by Miss [Jane] Porter. 2 v. xv, vi, 222 pp; vi, 225 pp. 2 pl. 18°. *London, Longmans*, 1807.

Siebold (Carl Theodor Ernst von). Die süsswasserfische von Mitteleuropa. viii, 431 pp. 2 col. pl. 8°. *Leipzig, W. Engelmann*, 1863. s.

——— On tape and cystic worms, with an introduction on the origin of intestinal worms. Translated by T. H. Huxley. 88 pp. 8°. *London, Sydenham society*, 1857.

[*With* KÜCHENMEISTER (F.) Animal and vegetable parasites. v. 2].

——— *and* **Stannius** (Friedrich Hermann). Nouveau manuel d'anatomie comparée. Trad. de l'Allemand par A. Spring et Th. Lacordaire. 2 v. in 3. 18°. *Paris, Roret*, 1850. s.

[Wanting v. 1, part 2].

Siemssen (Adolph Christian). Handbuch zur systematischen kenntniss der meklenburgischen land und wasservögel. viii, 272 pp. 16°. *Rostok, etc. C. C. Stiller*, 1794. s.

——— Die fische Meklenburgs. Zum behuf vaterländisch-akademischer vorlesungen systematisch verzeichnet. 112 pp. 16°. *Rostok, etc. C. C. Stiller*, 1794. s.

[*With his* Handbuch, etc. 1794].

Sierra Leone company. Substance of the report delivered by the court of directors to the general court of proprietors, 1794. 175 pp. 1 map. 12°. *London, J. Phillips*, 1794. s.

Signorelli. *See* **Napoli-Signorelli.**

Sigonio (Carlo). Historiarvm de occidentali imperio libri xx. [A. D. 284–565]. 358 pp. 9 l. fol. *Francofvrti, Haeredes A. Wecheli*, 1593. s.

Sikes (George). The life and death of Sir Henry Vane. [*anon.*] 162 pp. 1 l. sm. 4°. [*London*], 1662.

Silbernagl (Isidor). Albrecht iv, der weise, herzog von Bayern, und seine regierung. 109 pp. 8°. *München, J. Deschler*, 1857. s.

Silius Italicus (Caius). Punicorum libri septemdecim, [cum notis variorum]. Fr. Modii, Casp. Barthii, [Dan. et Nic. Heinsii], curante A. Drakenborch. 16 p. l. 880 pp. 13 l. 8 pl. 4°. *Trajecti ad Rhenum, G. Van de Water*, 1717.

Sill (Edward Rowland). The hermitage, and other poems. 152 pp. 16°. *New York, Leypoldt & Holt*, 1868.

Silliman (Benjamin). A journal of travels in England, Holland, and Scotland, and of two passages over the Atlantic, in the years 1805–6. 2 v. 347 pp; 372 pp. 8°. *New York, Ezra Sargeant*, 1810. s.

——— Outline of the course of geological lectures given at Yale college. 128 pp. 8°. *New Haven, H. Howe*, 1829. s.

[*With* BAKEWELL (R.) An introduction to geology. 1829].

Silliman (Benjamin, *jr.*) First principles of chemistry. 492 pp. 12°. *Philadelphia, Loomis & Peck*, 1847. s.

[**Silliman's**] American journal of science and arts. Conducted by B. Silliman, J. D. Dana, [and others]. Jan. to Nov. 1867. 2d series. v. 43–44. [Complete series, v. 93–94.] 8°. *New Haven, editors*, 1867.

Silva; or, the triumph of virtue. By the author of "Lorenzo." [*anon.*] Translated by a sister of charity. 212 pp. 1 pl. 16°. *Baltimore, J. Murphy & Co.* 1858. s.

Silva (Innocencio Francisco da). Diccionario bibliographico portuguez. Estudos applicaveis a Portugal e ao Brasil. 7 v. 8°. *Lisboa, Imprensa nacional*, 1858–62.

Silver (J. M. W.) Sketches of Japanese manners and customs. Illustrated by native drawings, reproduced in fac-simile. 4 p. l. 51 pp. 28 pl. 4°. *London, Day & son*, 1867.

Silver (Joseph S.) Philosophy of evil, showing its uses and its unavoidable necessity. [*anon.*] 183 pp. 1 pl. 16°. *Philadelphia, G. B. Zieber & Co.* 1845.

Silver (The) cup. [A story for children. *anon.*] 316 pp. 4 pl. 16°. *Philadelphia, Am. S. S. union,* [1865].

Silver (The) wreath; a choice collection of selected songs, ballads, etc. arranged with an accompaniment for the piano-forte. 216 pp. 4°. *Philadelphia, Lee & Walker,* 1866.

Silvermere annals. By C. E. B. [*anon.*] 109 pp. 18°. *London, John Morgan,* [*about* 1850].

Silvestre de Sacy (Antoine Isaac, *baron*). Anthologie grammaticale arabe; ou, morceaux choisis de divers grammairiens et scholiastes arabes, avec une traduction française et des notes; pouvant faire suite à la chrestomathie arabe. x, 521, 186 pp. 8°. *Paris, Imprimerie royale,* 1829.

CONTENTS.

Béidhawi; Hariri; Ebn-Héscham; Abou'l Fath Nasir Motarrézi; Zamakhschari; Ebn-Malec; Sibawaïh; Ebn-Khaldoun.

——— [Catalogue de sa] bibliothèque. v. 1. Imprimés: philosophie, théologie, sciences naturelles. v. 3. Manuscrits, tables générales. [Redigé par R. Merlin. Avec une notice historique sur la vie et les ouvrages de Silvestre de Sacy par M. Daunou.] 2 v. in 1. 12, liv, 436 pp; 4 p. l. 63 pp. 8°. *Paris, Imprimerie royale,* 1842. S.

——— Chrestomathie arabe; ou, extraits de divers écrivains arabes, tant en prose qu'en vers, avec une traduction française et des notes. 2e éd. corrigée. 3 v. 8°. [*Paris*], *Imprimerie royale,* 1826–27.

CONTENTS.

v. 1. Makrizi; Ebn-Khaldoun; Abd-Alkader.
v. 2. Khalil Dhahéri; Makrizi; Livres des Druzes; Ebn-Khaldoun; Schanfara; Nabéga Dhobyani; Ascha; Tantarani.
v. 3. Moténabbi; Abou'lala; Ebn-Faredh; Hariri; Hamadani; Lettres et pièces diplomatiques; Kazwini.

Simes (Thomas). New military, historical, and explanatory dictionary. 148 l. 12°. *Philadelphia, Humphreys, Bell & Aitken,* 1776.

Simms (William Gilmore). Donna Florida. A metrical tale. [*anon.*] 97 pp. 18°. *Charleston, Burges & James,* 1843.

——— Guy Rivers, the outlaw. 213 pp. 8°. *London,* 1841.

[Hazlitt's romancist and novelist's lib. v. 2].

——— The kinsmen; or, the black riders of Congaree: a tale. [*anon.*] 2 v. 241 pp; 275 pp. 12°. *Philadelphia, Lea & Blanchard,* 1841.

——— The life of Francis Marion. 8th ed. 347 pp. 12°. *New York, G. F. Cooledge,* 1846.

——— Lyrical and other poems. 198 pp. 3 l. 16°. *Charleston, Ellis & Neufville,* 1827.

——— The partisan: a tale of the revolution. [*anon.*] 2 v. 276 pp; 244 pp. 12°. *New York, Harpers,* 1835.

Simon (John). A physiological essay on the thymus gland. xvi, 100 pp. 4°. *London, H. Renshaw,* 1845. S.

——— On the comparative anatomy of the thyroid gland. [Extract.] 11 pp. 4°. *London, Royal soc.* 1844. S.

[*With his* Physiological essay, etc. 1845].

Simon (Jules François Simon **Suisse,** *dit*). Le travail. 420 pp. 8°. *Paris, Lacroix, Verboeckhoven & Cie.* 1866.

Simon (Richard). Critical inquiries into the various editions of the Bible, with animadversions upon a small treatise of Dr. Isaac Vossivs, concerning the oracles of the sibylls. Translated into English [from the Latin], by N. S. 8 p. l. 207 pp. 4°. *London, Tho. Braddyll,* 1684.

Simond (Louis). Journal of a tour and residence in Great Britain, 1810–11. [*anon.*] 2 v. xiii, 382 pp; 360 pp. 21 pl. 8°. *Edinburgh, Ramsay & Co.* 1815.

Simonds (William). Whistler; or, the manly boy. By Walter Aimwell. [*pseudon.*] 308 pp. 16°. *Boston, Gould & Lincoln,* 1856. S.

Simpson (*Sir* George). An overland journey round the world, during the years 1841 and 1842. 2 v. in 1. 273 pp; 230 pp. 8°. *Philadelphia, Lea & Blanchard,* 1847.

Simpson (Henry J.) Three weeks in the gold mines, or adventures with the gold diggers of California, in August, 1848. 30 pp. 1 map. 8°. *New York, Joyce & Co.* 1848.

Simpson (*Rev.* John, *of Baldock, Eng.*) Internal and presumptive evidence of christianity, considered separately, and as uniting to form one argument. xii, v, 635 pp. 8°. *Bath, R. Cruttwell,* 1801.

Simpson (Joseph Cairn). Horse portraiture; embracing breeding, rearing, [etc.] With an appendix containing the performances of Dexter. 458 pp. 1 pl. 12°. *New York, W. A. Townsend & Adams,* 1868.

Simpson (Stephen, *M. D.*) Practical view of homœopathy. xvii, 352 pp. 8°. *London, J. B. Baillière,* 1836. S.

Simpson (Stephen), *and* **Wise** (Edward). The readiest reckoner ever invented for finding the amount, at any given price, of any number from one to ten thousand. 18°. *London, Sharpe and Hailes,* 1811.

Simson (Robert). *See* **Euclides,** *Lond. ed.* 1834.

Simson. *See* **Symson.**

Sincerus (Theophilus, *pseudon.*) *See* **Schwindel** (G. J.)

Sinclair (Catherine). The lives of the Cæsars; or, the juvenile Plutarch. Translated into Gujarátí. 301 pp. 1 pl. 12°. *Bombay, Tract and book society,* 1852. s.

——— Shetland and the Shetlanders; or, the northern circuit. 2d ed. iv, 428 pp. 1 map. 12°. *Edinburgh, W. Whyte & Co.* 1840.

——— Sir Edward Graham; or, railway speculations. 208 pp. 8°. *N. York, Harpers,* 1850.

Singer (George John). Elemente der electricität und elektrochemie. Aus dem Englischen üb ersetzt mit anmerkungen von C. H. Müller. xxx, 502 pp. 4 pl. 8°. *Breslau, W. A. Holäufer,* 1819. s.

Singer (Samuel Weller). Some account of the book printed at Oxford in 1468, under the title of Exposicio Sancti Jeronimi in simbolo apostolorum. ii, 44 pp. 8°. *London, Ballintyne & Byworth,* 1812.

Single (A) gentleman. Designs by the author. By Timothy Thistle. [*pseudon.*] Illustrations by J. Hyde. 182 pp. 7 pl. 16°. *Boston, O. Ellsworth,* 1867.

Singleton (John). A general description of the West Indian islands, as far as relates to to the British, Dutch and Danish governments from Barbados to Saint Croix, in blank verse. 159 pp. 4°. *Barbados, Esmand & Walker,* 1767.

Sinnett (*Mrs.* Percy). Herdsmen and tillers of the ground; or, illustrations of early civilization. x, 150 pp. 4 pl. 16°. *London, Chapman & Hall,* 1847.

——— Hunters and fishers; or, sketches of primitive races in the lands beyond the sea. x, 146 pp. 4 col. pl. 16°. *London, Chapman & Hall,* 1846.

Siret (Adolphe). Dictionnaire historique des peintres de toutes les écoles, depuis l'origine de la peinture jusqu'à nos jours. 2e éd. 1155 pp. 8°. *Bruxelles, Lacroix, Verboeckhoven et Cie.* 1866.

Sirtema de Grovestins (C. F. *baron*). Histoire des luttes et rivalités politiques entre les puissances maritimes et la France durant la seconde moitié du xviie siècle. 8 v. 8°. *Paris, Amyot,* 1851–54.

Sirven (Alfred). Journaux et journalistes. La gazette de France. 4 p. l. 337 pp. 1 pl. 16°. *Paris, Cournol,* 1866.

——— ——— Le journal des débats. 2 p. l. 354 pp. 2 pl. 16°. *Paris, Cournol,* 1866.

——— ——— La presse. La liberté. 2 p. l. 5, 370 pp. 1 pl. 16°. *Paris, Cournol,* 1866.

——— ——— Le siècle. 2 p. l. 396 pp. 2 pl 16°. *Paris, Cournol,* 1866.

Sismonda (Eugenio). Elementi di storia naturale generale. v. 1. Regno inorganico. viii, 247 pp. 16°. *Torino, Stamperia reale,* 1853. s.

Sismondi (Jean Charles Léonard Simonde de). Histoire des républiques italiennes, du moyen age. 4e éd. 12 v. 8°. *Bruxelles, A. Wahlen,* 1826. s.

——— Julia Sévéra; ou, l'an quatre cent quatrevingt-douze. 3 v. 18°. *Paris, Treuttel et Würtz,* 1822.

Sivers (Jegór von). Ueber Madeira und die Antillen nach Mittellamerika. Reisedenkwürdigkeiten und forschungen. xii, 388 pp. 8°. *Leipzig, C. F. Fleischer,* 1861. s.

——— Cuba, die perle der Antillen. iv, 364 pp. 8°. *Leipzig, C. F. Fleischer,* 1861. s.

Six hundred dollars a year; a wife's effort at low living, under high prices. [*anon.*] vii, 183 pp. 18°. *Boston, Ticknor & Fields,* 1867.

Skene (William F. *editor*). Chronicles of the Picts, chronicles of the Scots, and other early memorials of Scottish history. cxcv, 499 pp. 2 pl. 8°. *Edinburgh, H. M. general register house,* 1867. s.

Sketch of a descriptive journey through Switzerland. [*anon.*] iv, 78 pp. 1 pl. 8°. *Berne, J. J. Burgdorfer,* 1816.

Sketch (A) of the life and public services of Wm. H. Harrison. [*anon.*] 36 pp. 8°. *Philadelphia,* 1836.

Sketch (A) of the politics, relations, and statistics of the western world, and of those characteristics of European policy which most immediately affect its interests. [*anon.*] 200 pp. 8°. *Philadelphia, R. H. Small,* 1827.

Sketch (A) of the reign of George the third, from 1780 to 1790. [*anon.*] 6th ed. 206 pp. 8°. *London, J. Debrett,* 1791.

[*With* HENDERSON (John). Letters and poems. *London,* 1786].

Sketch of the Seminole war, and sketches during a campaign. By a lieutenant of the left wing. [*anon.*] ix, 311 pp. 12°. *Charleston, (S. C.) D. J. Dowling,* 1836.

Sketches and recollections of Lynchburg, [Va.] By the oldest inhabitant. [*anon.*] 363 pp. 12°. *Richmond, C. H. Wynne,* 1858.

Sketches for the fireside; or, anecdotes for the family, selected from history and biography. By a clergyman. [*anon.*] Illustrated. 448 pp. 1 pl. 8°. *Hartford, Brainard & Sampson,* 1867.

Sketches from Cambridge. By a don. [*anon.*] 144 pp. 12°. *London, Macmillan & Co.* 1865.

Sketches in Greece and Turkey: with the present condition and future prospects of the Turkish empire. [*anon.*] vii, 266 pp. 8°. *London, J. Ridgway,* 1833.

Sketches of the city of Detroit. [*anon.*] 63 pp. 8°. *Detroit, R. F. Johnstone & Co.* 1855.

Sketches of the higher classes of colored society in Philadelphia. By a southerner. [*anon.*] 116 pp. 16°. *Philadelphia, Merrihew & Thompson,* 1841.

Sketches of the war between the United States and the British isles, from 1812 to 1815. [*anon.*] 2 v. in 1. iv, 496 pp. 8°. *Rutland, (Vt.) Fay & Davison,* 1815.

Sketches of the West; or, the home of the badgers: an early history of Wisconsin. [*anon.*] 48 pp. 1 map. 8°. *Milwaukie, J. A. Hopkins,* 1847.

Sketches of Yale college, with numerous anecdotes. [*anon.*] 192 pp. 3 pl. 16°. *New York, Saxton & Miles,* 1843.

Skinner (Andrew). Maps of the roads of Ireland. *See* **Taylor** (G.), *and* **Skinner** (A.)

Skinner (John). Amusements of leisure hours; or, poetical pieces, chiefly in the Scottish dialect. 144 pp. 16°. *Edinburgh, S. Cheyne,* 1809.

Skinner (J. E. Hilary). After the storm; or, Jonathan and his neighbours in 1865–6. 2 v. xv, 312 pp; v, 369 pp. 12°. *London, R. Bentley,* 1866

Skinner (John S.) Introductory remarks on the cow and the dairy. s.
[*With* GUÉNON (F.) Treatise on milch cows].

——— Supplement to Mason and Hind's popular system of farriery. 101 pp. 12°. *Philadelphia, Grigg, Elliot & Co.* 1848. s.
[*With* BELL (J). Farriery, 1848].

Slaughter (Philip). A history of Bristol parish, [Petersburg, Va.] 51 pp. 1 pl. 8°. *Richmond, B. B. Minor,* 1846.

Slave songs of the United States. [Compiled by W. F. Allen, C. P. Ware, and Lucy McK. Garrison]. xliv, 115 pp. 8°. *New York, A. Simpson & Co.* 1867.

Sleeper (Jacob S.) Mark Rowland; a tale of the sea. By Hawser Martingale. [*pseudon.*] 206 pp. 16°. *Boston, Loring,* 1867.

——— Tales of the ocean, and essays for the forecastle. By Hawser Martingale. [*pseudon.*] 130 pp. 8°. *New York, Samuel French,* [*about* 1840].

Slingsby (*Sir* Henry). Diary, [1638–48]; trial; his rare tract "A father's legacy," and extracts from family correspondence, with notices and a genealogical memoir by Rev. Daniel Parsons. xxiii, 441 pp. 8°. *London, Longman, etc.* 1836.

Sloan (Samuel). Homestead architecture; designs for villas, cottages, and farm houses; with essays on landscape gardening, furniture, etc. 2d ed. 355 pp. 53 pl. 8°. *Philadelphia, J. B. Lippincott & Co.* 1867.

Slobod (Daniel). Rostlinnictví, cili návod k snadnému urcení a pojmenování rostlin v Cechách, Moravě a Jinych zemích rakouského mocnárství domácích. xlviii, 733 pp. 12°. *Praze, F. Rivnáce,* 1852. s.
[Malá encyclopedie nauk, v. 8].

Sluyter (Peter). Journal of a voyage to New York, etc. in 1679–80. *See* **Dankers** (J.) *and* Sluyter (P.)

Smart (Benjamin Humphrey.) Beginnings of a new school of metaphysics. 2 p. l. 518 pp. 8°. *London, J. Richardson,* 1839.

Smeaton (John). Experimental enquiry concerning the natural powers of wind and water to turn mills and other machines depending on a circular motion, etc. iv, 110 pp. 5 pl. 8°. *London, I. & J. Taylor,* 1794. s.

——— The same.
[*With* TREDGOLD (T.) Tracts on hydraulics].

Smedley (*Rev.* Edward). Poems; with a selection from his correspondence, and memoir of his life. xx, 457 pp. 1 pl. 8°. *London, Baldwin & Cradock,* 1837.

Smedley (John). Practical hydropathy. Including plans of baths, and remarks on diet, clothing, and habits of life. 7th ed. 444 pp. 12°. *London, J. Caudwell,* 1864.

Smedley (*Miss* M. B.) Lays and ballads from English history, etc. By S. M. [*anon.*] New ed. 178 pp. 16°. *London, E. Lumley,* [1845].

Smee (Alfred). Elements of electro-biology, or the voltaic mechanism of man; of electro-pathology, especially of the nervous system; and of electro-therapeutics. xii, 264 pp. 2 tab. 8°. *London, Longman, etc.* 1849. s.

——— Elements of electro-metallurgy. 2d ed. xxx, 338 pp. 8°. *London, E. Palmer,* 1843. s.

——— The sources of physical science. An introduction to the study of physiology through physics. xx, 296 pp. 8°. *London, H. Renshaw,* 1843. s.

Smethurst (Gamaliel). A narrative of an escape out of the hands of the Indians, in the gulph of St. Lawrence; also, a providential escape after a shipwreck in said gulph. Likewise, a plan for reconciling the differences between Great Britain and her colonies. 48 pp. 4°. *London, J. Bew,* 1774.

Smids *or* **Smidt** (Ludolf, *or* Lodewick). Pictura loquens; sive heroicarum tabularum Hadriani Schoonebeeck enarratio et explicatio, e poetis latinis. 7 p. l. 240 pp. 8 l. 61 pl. 18°. *Amstelædami, H. Schoonebeeck,* 1695.

Smidth (Jens Hansen). Arboretum scandinavicum, fasc. i. 160 pp. 12°. [*Kjöbenhavn, Schubothe,* 1831.] S.

[Title wanting: no more published].

Smiles (Samuel). The huguenots: their settlements, churches, and industries in England and Ireland. With appendix relating to the huguenots in America. 448 pp. 12°. *New York, Harpers,* 1868.

Smiley, (Thomas T.) The new federal calculator; or, scholar's assistant, [etc]. 180 pp. 16°. *Philadelphia, Lippincott, Grambo & Co.* 1851. S.

Smith (Adam). Inquiry into the nature and causes of the wealth of nations. 7th ed. 3 v. x, 499 pp; vi, 521 pp; v, 465 pp. 25 l. 8°. *London, A. Strahan and T. Cadell,* 1793.

Smith (Albert). Wild oats and dead leaves. 2d ed. vi, 359 pp. 12°. *London, Chapman & Hall,* 1860.

Smith (Asa). An abridgment of Smith's illustrated astronomy, [etc.] 5th ed. 72 pp. 11 pl. 12°. *New York, Cady & Burgess,* 1850. S.

Smith (Buckingham). Documents in the Spanish and two of the early tongues of Florida, (Apalachian and Timmquan). 10 l. fol. *Washington,* 1860.

——— An inquiry into the authenticity of documents concerning a discovery in North America claimed to have been made by Verazzano. 31 pp. 1 map. 8°. *New York, J. F. Trow,* 1864.

——— The same. 4°.

Smith (*Col.* Charles Hamilton). The natural history of the human species. 464 pp. 35 pl. 12°. *Edinburgh, W. H. Lizars,* 1848. S.

Smith (David S. C. H.) Reptilia of Massachusetts. S.

[*With* HITCHCOCK (E.) Catalogue of animals, etc. of Massachusetts].

Smith (Denis E. *M. D.*) Leaves from a physician's journal. 336 pp. 12°. *New York, N. Y. publishing co.* 1867.

Smith (Edmund). Poetical works. 8°. *Edinburgh,* 1793.

[Anderson's British poets, v. 6].

Smith (Edward, *M. D.*) Account of a journey through northeastern Texas, in 1849, for the purposes of emigration. 188 pp. 2 maps. 12°. *London, Hamilton, Adams & Co.* 1849.

Smith (*Rev.* Elias, *of Portsmouth, N. H.*) Life, etc. 406 pp. 16°. *Portsmouth, (N. H.)* 1816.

[Imperfect; title-page and 12 leaves wanting].

Smith (Elisha). Cure of deism; or, the mediatorial scheme by Jesus Christ the only true religion, in answer to [Tindal, Shaftesbury, and Morgan. *anon.*] 2d ed. 2 v. 8 p. l. xxxii, 431 pp; 5 p. l. 352, 84 pp. 14 l. 12°. *London, Innys & Manby,* 1737.

Smith (*Rev.* Ethan). View of the Hebrews; or, the tribes of Israel in America. [In favour of the natives of America being the descendants of Israel.] 2d ed. 285 pp. 12°. *Poultney, (Vt.) Smith & Shute,* 1825.

Smith (Francis H.) My experience; or, footprints of a presbyterian to spiritualism. 232 pp. 12°. *Baltimore,* [*author*], 1860.

Smith (George, *upholsterer*). Collection of designs for household furniture and interior decoration. xiv, 33 pp. 158 pl. 4°. *London, J. Taylor,* 1808.

Smith (*Rev.* George Charles). Bob, the sailor boy. [In Cherokee.] Lawinv nugvwiyusadeginotsiyuganitohi. pp. 57-67. 24°.

[*With* RICHMOND (Legh). Dairyman's daughter. In Cherokee].

Smith (George Henry). Outlines of political economy. v, 70 pp. 8°. *London, Longmans,* 1866.

Smith (Goldwin). Three English statesmen [Pym, Cromwell, and Pitt]: a course of lectures on the political history of England. 112 pp. 8°. *Manchester, Macmillan & Co.* 1867.

——— The same. 298 pp. 12°. *New York, Harpers,* 1867.

Smith *or* **Schmidt** (H. I. *prof. in Penn. coll.*) Education. Part i. History. Part ii. Plan of culture based on christian principles. 340 pp. 18°. *New York, Harpers,* 1845.

[Harpers' family library, v. 158].

Smith (*Col.* James). Narrative of the most remarkable occurrences during his captivity among the Indians, 1755-59.

[*With* METCALF (Samuel S.) Collection, etc. 1821. pp. 163—257].

Smith (*Sir* James Edward). Sketch of a tour on the continent. 2d ed. 3 v. xxxi, 372 pp; iv, 445 pp; iv, 376 pp. 8°. *London, Longmans,* 1807.

Smith (Jerome Van Crowninshield). Fishes of Massachusetts. S.

[*With* HITCHCOCK (E.) Catalogue of animals, etc. of Massachusetts].

Smith (*Capt.* John). The generall historie of Virginia, New England, and the Summer isles; with the names of the adventurers, planters, and governours from their first beginning, 1584, to this present, 1624. Engraved title. 6 p. l. 248 pp. 4 maps. fol. *London, Michael Sparkes,* 1624.

——— True travels, adventvres, and observations in Europe, Asia, Affrica, and America, 1593—1629. Together with a continuation of of his generall history of Virginia, etc. since 1624, to 1629. 6 p. l. 60 pp. fol. *London, Thomas Slater,* 1630.

——— A true relation of Virginia. With an introduction and notes by Charles Deane. [Reprint of London ed. 1608.] xlvii, v, 88 pp. sm. 4°. *Boston, Wiggin & Lunt,* 1866.

[Virginia series, No. 1].

Smith (John, *M. D.*) The portrait of old age. A paraphrase upon the 12th chapter of Ecclesiastes. 3d ed. 4 p. l. 237 pp. 3 l. 16°. *London, E. Withers,* 1752.

Smith (John Gordon, *M. D.*) Analysis of medical evidence, and an appendix of professional testimony. xix, 386 pp. 8°. *London, T. & G. Underwood,* 1825.

Smith (John Jay, *editor*). Letters of Dr. Richard Hill and his children; or, the history of a family, as told by themselves. xlv, 466 pp. 9 pl. 8°. *Philadelphia, privately printed for the descendants,* 1854. s.

Smith (J. Lawrence). Minerals [of Chile].

[*With* GILLISS (J. M.) U. S. astronomical exped. v. 2].

Smith (John Russell). Bibliographical catalogue of books on angling.

[*With* BLAKEY (Robert). Historical sketches of the angling literature of all nations. pp. 293–335. *London,* 1856].

Smith (John Y.) History of Madison, Wisconsin. *See* **Madison** (Wis.) City directory for 1866, pp. 9–78.

Smith (Jonathan S.) The siege of Algiers; or, the downfal of Hadgi-Ali-Bashaw: a tragic comedy. 140 pp. 12°. *Philadelphia, J. Maxwell,* 1823.

Smith (Joshua Hett). An authentic narrative of the causes which led to the death of major André. 106 pp. 24°. *New York, Evert Duyckinck,* 1809.

Smith (Josiah W.) The divine law; or, the scriptural duty and happiness of man. xi, 256 pp. 18°. *London, Rivingtons,* 1866.

Smith (*Rev.* Matthew Hale). Universalism examined, renounced, exposed. 12th ed. 396 pp. 16°. *Boston, Tappan & Dennet,* 1844.

Smith (Moses, *of Huntington, L. I.*) History of adventures and sufferings in the Miranda expedition, etc. 1806–1811. 124 pp. 16°. *Brooklyn, Thomas Kirk,* 1812.

——— The same. 146 pp. 3 l. 16°. *Albany, Packard & Van Benthuysen,* 1814.

Smith (Nathan Ryno, *M. D.*) Treatment of fractures of the lower extremity by the use of the anterior suspensory apparatus. 70 pp. 8°. *Baltimore, Kelly & Piet,* 1867.

Smith (Noah). A speech delivered at Bennington, on the anniversary of the 16th of August, 1777. 8 pp. 12°. *Hartford, (Ct.) Watson & Goodwin,* 1779.

[pp. 5–6 imperfect].

Smith (Oliver, *A. M.*) Outlines of nature. 198 pp. 12°. *New York, [author],* 1847. s.

Smith (Richard, *esq. F. R. S. L.*) Notes made during a tour in Denmark, Prussia, Poland, [Germany], and France. ii, 504, xxiv pp. 8°. *London, C. & J. Rivington,* 1827.

Smith (Robert). Universal directory for taking alive and destroying rats, and all other kinds of four-footed and winged vermin, in a method hitherto unattempted. vii, 218 pp. 16°. *London, R. Smith,* 1768.

Smith (Roswell C.) New arithmetic. Arithmetic on the productive system, [etc.] 312 pp. 12°. *New York, Cady & Burgess,* 1850. s.

——— English grammar, on the productive system. 150th ed. 192 pp. 16°. *Philadelphia, Marshall & Co.* 1840.

——— The same. Stereotype ed. 16°. *Hartford, J. Paine,* 1842.

——— The same. New stereotype ed. 16°. *Philadelphia, Butler & Williams,* 1845.

——— Quarto, or second book of geography. A concise and practical system of geography. 84 pp. including 32 maps. 4°. *New York, D. Burgess & Co.* 1855. s.

Smith (*Rev.* Samuel Abbot). Christian lessons and a christian life: sermons. With a memoir by E. J. Young. lxi, 289 pp. 1 pl. 16°. *Boston, Nichols & Noyes,* 1866.

Smith (Samuel Harrison). History of the last session of Congress, [commencing] Dec. 7, 1801. 195 pp. 8°. *Washington, Samuel H. Smith,* 1802.

——— Memoir of the life, character, and writings of Thomas Jefferson; delivered before the Columbian institute, 6th Jan. 1827. 38 pp. 8°. *Washington, S. A. Elliot,* 1827.

Smith (*Mrs.* Spencer). First lessons in English composition. 131 pp. 12°. *Boston, Hickling, Swan & Co.* 1856. s.

Smith (*Rev.* Thomas, *of Falmouth, Me.*) Extract from [his] journals kept from 1720 to 1788, with an appendix. 164 pp. 2 l. 154 pp. 1 l. 12°. *Portland, Thomas Todd & Co. & A. Shirley*, 1821.

——— *and* Deane (Samuel, *D. D.*) Journals, with notes and biographical notices; and a summary history of Portland, by William Willis. 483 pp. 1 map. 3 pl. 8°. *Portland, Joseph S. Bailey*, 1849.

Smith (Thomas). Every man his own house painter and paper hanger. [*anon.*] 80 pp. 1 pl. 12°. *St. Louis, J. J. Daly*, 1866.

Smith (Truman, *senator of the U. S.*) Inquiry into the origin of modern anæsthesia. 165 pp. 1 pl. 8°. *Hartford, Brown & Gross*, 1867.

Smith (T. Marshall). Legends of the war of independence and of the earlier settlements in the west. 397 pp. 8°. *Louisville, (Ky.) J. F. Brennan*, 1855.

Smith (William, *chief justice of the province of New York*). The history of the province of New York, from the first discovery to the year 1732. 2d ed. 276 pp. 8°. *Philadelphia, Mathew Carey*, 1792.

——— The same. From its discovery to the appointment of gov. Colden in 1762. 2 v. xvi, 390 pp; 4 pl. 390 pp. 8°. *New York, Historical society*, 1830. S.

Smith (William, *LL. D. of the London university*). Dictionary of the Bible. American edition; revised and edited by prof. H. B. Hackett, D. D. [and] Ezra Abbot. Parts i—vii. A—Euphrates. vi, 784 pp. 8°. *New York, Hurd & Houghton*, 1867.

Smith (*Rev.* William, *F. L. S.*) A synopsis of the British diatomaceae; with remarks on their structure, functions, and distribution. The plates by Tuffen West. 2 v. xxxiv, 89 pp. 31 pl; xxx, 107 pp. 36 pl. 8°. *London, Smith & Beck*, 1853–56. S.

Smith (William W.) A complete etymology of the English language; containing the Anglo-Saxon, French, (etc.) roots, and the English words derived therefrom, accurately spelled, accented, and defined. 323 pp. 8°. *New York, A. S. Barnes & Co.* 1867.

——— The juvenile speller; or, speller's new manual. 168 pp. 12°. *New York, A. S. Barnes & Co.* 1858. S.

Smith. *See, also,* **Smyth.**

Smithers (Henry). Observations made during a residence in Brussels, and several tours through the Netherlands. 3d ed. 282 pp. 2 pl. 8°. [*Brussels,*] *Author*, [1819.]

Smithsonian institution (*Washington, D. C.*) Annual reports of the board of regents, 1853–67. 15 v. 8°. *Washington*, 1854–67.

——— Catalogue of publications of societies, and of periodical works belonging to the Smithsonian institution, Jan. 1, 1866. Deposited in the library of congress. iv, 591 pp. 8°. *Washington, Smithsonian inst.* 1866. S.

——— Smithsonian contributions to knowledge. v. 14. 4°. *Washington, Smithsonian inst.* 1865.

CONTENTS.

BACHE (A. D.) Discussion of the magnetic and meteorological observations made at Girard college in 1840–45. 3d sect. pts. vii–ix. Vertical force. (No. 175).

——— Same. 4th sect. pts. x, xii. Dip and total force. (No. 186).

DRAPER (H.) On the construction of a silvered glass telescope, 5½ in. aperture, and its use in celestial photography. (No. 180).

LEIDY (J.) Cretaceous reptiles of the United States. [No. 192).

MEEK (F. B.) *and* HAYDEN (F. V.) Palaeontology of the upper Missouri. Invertebrates. Part 1. (No. 172).

——— Smithsonian miscellaneous collections. v. 6. 8°. *Washington, Sm. inst.* 1867.

CONTENTS.

Art. 1–2. Monograph of the diptera of North America, by H. Löw. Parts 1–2, edited, with additions, by R. Osten-Sacken.
3. List of the coleoptera of North America. Part 1, March, 1863–April, 1866, by John L. Leconte.
4. New species of North American coleoptera, by John L. Leconte, March 1863–April 1866.

——— The same. v. 7. 8°. *Washington, Sm. inst.* 1867. S.

CONTENTS.

Art. 1. Monograph of the bats of North America, by H. Allen, June, 1864.
2. Land and fresh water shells of North America. Part ii. Pulmonata limnophila and thalassophila, by W. G. Binney.
3. The same. Part iii. Ampullaridæ, valvatidæ, viviparidæ, fresh-water rissoidæ, cyclophoridæ, truncatellidæ, fresh-water neritidæ, helicinidæ, by W. G. Binney.
4. Researches upon the hydrobiinae and allied forms, [etc.] by Wm. Stimpson.
5. Monograph of American corbiculadæ (recent and fossil), by Temple Prime.
6. Check list of the invertebrate fossils of North America, eocene and oligocene, by T. A. Conrad.
7. The same. Miocene, by F. B. Meek.
8. The same. Cretaceous and jurassic, by F. B. Meek.
9. Catalogue of minerals, with their formulas, etc. by T. Egleston.
10. A dictionary of the Chinook jargon, or trade language of Oregon, by George Gibbs.
11. Instructions for research relative to the ethnology and philology of North America, by George Gibbs.
12. List of works published by the Smithsonian institution.

Smollett (Tobias George). The history of England, from the revolution to the death of George ii. Designed as a continuation of Hume. [With life, by R. Anderson]. 5 v. 8°. *Edinburgh, Hill and Doig*, 1810.

——— The same.

[*With* HUME (D). The history of England. ed. 1832. pp. 821–1354].

Smuts (Jan). Dissertatio zoologica enumerationem mammalium capensium continens. vi, 108 pp. 3 col. pl. 4°. *Leidae, J. C. Cyfveer,* 1832. S.

Smyth (*Mrs.* A. Gillespie). The romance of diplomacy: historical memoir of queen Carolina Matilda of Denmark. With memoir and a selection from the correspondence of Sir Robert Murray Keith. 2 v. xvii, 493 pp; ix, 484 pp. 4 pl. 8°. *London, Hogg & sons,* 1861.

Smyth (David William). A short topographical description of Upper Canada, [with] a provincial gazetteer. 2d ed. 123 pp. 8°. *London, W. Faden,* 1813.

[*With* GRAY (H.) Letters from Canada, 1809].

Smyth (Thomas, *D. D.*) Calvin and his enemies. A memoir of the life, character, and principles of Calvin. New ed. 180 pp. 16°. *Philadelphia, Presbyterian board of publication,* 1856. S.

——— Obedience the life of missions. 170 pp. 18°. *Philadelphia, Presbyterian board of publication,* 1858. S.

Smyth (Warington W.) Treatise on coal and coal-mining. vi, 253 pp. 12°. *London, Virtue bros. & Co.* 1867.

Smyth (William, *prof. in Bowdoin college).* Elementary algebra, [etc.] 236 pp. 12°. *Portland, [Maine], Sanborn & Carter,* 1851. S.

——— The same. New elementary algebra. 312 pp. 12°. *Portland, Bailey & Noyes,* 1866.

Smyth (William, *prof. of modern history, Cambridge, Eng.*) Lectures on modern history, from the irruption of the northern nations to the close of the American revolution. 2 v. xx, 433 pp; 494 pp. 8°. *London, Pickering,* 1840.

——— Lectures on history. Second series, on the French revolution. 3 v. 374 pp; 448 pp; 431 pp. 8°. *London, Pickering,* 1840.

Smyth (William Henry, *admiral, R. N.*) Ædes hartwellianæ; or, notices of the manor and mansion of Hartwell: [its apartments, paintings, library, museum, numismata, and Egyptian antiquities]. vii, 414 pp. 13 pl. 4°. *London, printed for private circulation, by J. B. Nichols & son,* 1851. S.

——— Nautical observations on the port and maritime vicinity of Cardiff, with strictures on the 9th report of the Taff Vale railway directors, and some remarks on the commerce of Glamorganshire. viii, 100, 12 pp. 8°. *Cardiff, (Wales,) W. Bird,* 1840. S.

——— Sidereal chromatics: a reprint, with additions, from the "Bedford cycle of celestial objects" and its "Hartwell continuation," on the colors of multiple stars. 96 pp. 8°. *London, author,* 1864. S.

Smyth (William M.) Poems on several occasions, written in Pennsylvania. [*anon.*] 141 pp. 1 pl. 16°. *Philadelphia, Enoch Story,* 1786.

Smythe (Charles W.) Our own primary grammar for the use of beginners. 3d ed. 72 pp. 16°. *Raleigh, Sterling, Campbell, & Albright,* 1863.

Snelgrave (*Captain* William). A new account of Guinea and the slave trade. 12 p. l. 288 pp. 1 map. 8°. *London, J. Wren,* 1754.

Snellaert (Ferdinand Augustijn). Vlaemsche bibliographie, of lyst der nederduitsche boeken van 1830 tot 1855 in Belgie uitgegeven. [Nieuw uitg.] xiv, 230 pp. 16°. *Gent, E. Vanderhaeghen,* 1857.

[Uitgaven van het Willems'-fonds. Nr. 26].

Snow (Edwin M. *M.D.*) A report upon sundry documents relating to Asiatic cholera. 13 pp. 8°. *Providence (R. I.) City,* 1865. S.

Snow (The) angel; a tale of life-land and dream-land, by mistress [Frigida] Knutt. [*pseudon.*] 261 pp. 5 pl. 16°. *New York, J. Miller,* 1867.

Snowden (Richard). The American revolution; written in the style of ancient history. [*anon.*] 2 v. xii, 226 pp; 216 pp. 16°. *Philadelphia, Jones, Hoff & Derrick, etc.* 1793–94.

[Imperfect: v. 2 wanting table of contents].

——— The same; written in scriptural or ancient historical style. 6 p. l. 360 pp. 16°. *Baltimore, W. Pechin,* [*about* 1800].

——— Columbiad; or, a poem on the American war. 44 pp. 16°. *Baltimore, W. Pechin,* [*about* 1800].

[*With* SNOWDEN (Richard). American revolution. *Baltimore,* Ed. *about* 1800].

Snowe (Joseph). The Rhine, legends, traditions, history, from Cologne to Mainz. 2 v. xii, 511 pp; viii, 468 pp. 22 pl. 8°. *London, F. C. Westley,* 1839.

Sobieski (Jan, *king of Poland*). Lettres du roi de Pologne à la reine Marie Casimire, pendant la campagne de Vienne. Traduites par M. le comte Plater, et publiées par N. A. de Salvandy. xxvii, 224 pp. 1 pl. 8°. *Paris, Michaud,* 1826.

Socher (Georg). Grundriss der geschichte der philosophischen systeme von den Griechen bis auf Kant. 5 p. l. 339 pp. 8°. *München, J. Lentner,* 1802. S.

Social science: selections from John Cassell's prize essays, by working men and women. xix, 360 pp. 12°. *London, Cassell, Petter & Galpin,* 1861.

Social (The) and political dependence of women. [*anon.*] 2d ed. vii, 92 pp. 8°. *London, Longmans*, 1867.

Society (The) of arts, and of the institutions in union. Journal, Nov. 1865 to Nov. 1867. v. 14–15. 8°. *London, Bell & Daldy*, 1866–67.

Socinus *or* **Sozzini** (Fausto). Epistolæ ad amicos, in quibus variæ de rebus divinis quæstiones expediuntur. 695 pp. 3 l. 18°. *Racoviæ, Sebastian Sternac*, 1618.

——— Epistolæ ad Andream Dudithium, ex Italico in Latinum conversæ a M. R. H. 82 pp. 18°. *Racoviæ, S. Sternac*, 1635.
[*With* the preceding].

Socrates *Scholasticus*. Historia ecclesiastica.
[*With* HISTORIAE eccl. scriptores graeci. J. Christophorsono interprete, 1581 ed.]

——— The same. Versa ab Epiphanio.
[*With* AUCTORES hist. eccl. fol. *Basileae*, 1523].

——— The same. Ecclesiastical history, translated and abridged by [Samuel] Parker.
[*With* ECCLESIASTICAL histories, etc. 3d ed. 4°. *London*, 1729].

Soden (Theodore). Elements of the German language: a manual of reading, speaking, and composing. 319 pp. 1 pl. 12°. *Cincinnati, Applegate & Co.* 1856. s.

Soemmering. *See* **Sömmerring**.

Sohm (Rudolph). Die lehre vom subpignus. v, 152 pp. 8°. *Rostock, H. Schmidt*, 1864. s.

Sohncke (L. A.) Bibliotheca mathematica. Verzeichniss der bücher über die gesammten zweige der mathematik, welche in Deutschland und dem auslande, vom jahre 1830 bis mitte des jahres 1854 erschienen sind. Mit einem vollständigen materien register. xviii, 388 pp. 8°. *Leipzig, W. Engelmann*, 1854.

Soldier's (The) daughter. [*anon.*] 296 pp. 16°. *Boston, R. A. Ballou*, 1866.
[Prize series].

Solera (Maurizio). Essai sur les valeurs.
[SCRITTORI class. ital. di econ. pol. v. 39].

Solignac (Pierre Joseph de la Pimpie, *chevalier* de). Les amours d'Horace. [*anon.*] 18°. *Cologne, Marteau*, 1728.

Solinus (Caius Julius). De memoralibvs mvndi. 46 l. 4°. *Venetiis*, 1493. s.

——— The same. Liber de memorabilibus mūdi diligenter annotatus et indicio alphabetico prenotatus. 4, 44 l. 4°. *Spire, C*[*onra*]*d*, 1512. s.

Solis y Ribadeneyra (Antonio de). Historia de la conquista de Mexico, poblacion, y progressos de la America Septentrional, conocida por el nombre de Nueva España. 10 p. l. 151 l. 1 map. 12 pl. fol. *Brusselas, Francisco Foppens*, 1704.

Solly (Thomas). A syllabus of logic. x, 164 pp. 8°. *Cambridge, (Eng.) J. & J. J. Deighton*, 1839.

Some observations on the charge by hon. James De Lancey, chief justice of the province of New York, to the grand jury, January 15th, 1733. [*anon.*] 18 pp. fol. *New York, J. Peter Zenger*, 1733.

Some reasons that influenced the governor to take, and the councillors to administer, the oath required by the act of parliament, commonly called the stamp act. [*anon.*] 14 pp. 8°. *Hartford, Thomas Green*, [*about* 1766].

Some remarks on a pamphlet [by John Fletcher] entitled, A third check to antinomianism. [*anon.*] 16 pp. 8°. *London, Edward & Charles Dilly*, 1772.
[*With* HILL (*Sir* Richard). Apology for brotherly love. *London*, 1798].

Some transactions between the Indians and Friends in Pennsylvania, in 1791–92. [*anon.*] 14 pp. 12°. *London, James Phillips*, 1792.

Somerset (Edward, *earl of Glamorgan, and 2d marquis of Worcester*). A century of the names and scantlings of such inventions as I can call to mind to have tried and perfected. xxvii, 76 pp. 24°. *Glasgow, R. & A. Foulis*, 1767. s.

Somerville (*Mrs.* Mary). On the connexion of the physical sciences. 2d ed. xvi, 493 pp. 5 pl. 12°. *London, J. Murray*, 1835. s.

——— The same. 9th ed. xvi, 523 pp. 10 pl. 12°. *London, J. Murray*, 1858. s.

Somerville (Thomas). The history of political transactions, and of parties, from the restoration of king Charles ii. to the death of king William. xxviii, 755 pp. 8°. *Dublin, P. Byrne & others*, 1793.

Somerville (William). Poetical works. 8°. *Edinburgh*, 1793.
[Anderson's British poets, v. 8].

——— The chase. A poem. [*With* **Blane** (William). Cynegetica. *London*, 1781].

Sömmerring (Samuel Thomas von). Abbildungen des menschlichen auges. x, 110 pp. 16 pl. fol. *Frankfurt am Main, Varrentrapp & Werner*, 1801. s.

——— Abhandlung über die schnell und langsam tödtlichen krankheiten der harnblase und harnröhre bey männern im hohen alter. xiv, 146 pp. 4°. *Frankfurt am Main, Varrentrapp & Werner*, 1809. s.

——— Über das organ der seele. viii, 86 pp. 1 l. 2 pl. 4°. *Königsberg, Nicolovius*, 1796. s.

——— Über die wirkungen der schnürbrüste. Neue aufl. 844 pp. 1 pl. 8°. *Berlin, Voss*, 1793. s.

Sömmerring (Samuel Thomas von, *and* **Reisseisen** (Fr.) Über die structur, die verrichtung, und den gebrauch der lungen. Zwei preisschriften. iv, 126 pp. 8°. *Berlin, Voss,* 1808. s.

Sommers *or* **Summers** islands company. Orders and constitvtions; ordained by the gouvernour and company of the city of London, for the plantation of the Svmmer islands; for the better gouerning of the actions and affaires of the said company and plantation, 6 Febr. 1621. 83 pp. sm. 4°. *London, Felix Kyngston,* 1622.

Somner (William). The antiquities of Canterbvry; or, a svrvey of that ancient citie, with the svbvrbs and cathedrall. [1st ed.] 7 p. l. 516 pp. 7 l. 1 pl. sm. 4°. *London, R. Thrale,* 1640.

Songs of the free, and hymns of christian freedom. 227 pp. 16°. *Boston, I. Knapp,* 1836.

Sonnenkalb (Hugo). Anilin und anilinfarben in toxikologischer und medicinalpolizeilicher beziehung. v, 61 pp. 8°. *Leipzig, O. Wigand,* 1864. s.

——— Der strassenstaub in Leipzig. 31 pp. 8°. *Leipzig, A. Förstner,* 1861. s.

——— Statistische tabelle der in der stadt Leipzig vom anno 1595 angetrauten, getauften und gestorbenen, sowie der einwohner. sheet folded in 8°. *Leipzig, L. Rocca,* 1864. s.

Sonnini de Manoncour (Charles Nicolas Sigisbert). Travels in upper and lower Egypt. Undertaken by order of the old government of France. Translated from the French by H. Hunter. 3 v. 8°. *London, J. Stockdale,* 1799. s.

——— *and* **Latreille** (Pierre André). Histoire naturelle des reptiles, etc. 4 v. 18°. *Paris, Déterville,* 1799. s.

Sophocles. Tragedies; literally translated into English prose. 2d ed. 2 v. in 1. 278 pp; 187 pp. 8°. *Oxford, D. A. Talboys,* 1828.

——— The same. A new literal translation with copious notes. 345 pp. 12°. *Cambridge, (Eng.) J. Hall,* 1844.

Sophocles (Evangelinus Apostolides). A Romaic grammar, accompanied by a chrestomathy, with a vocabulary. x, 264 pp. 12°. *Hartford, H. Huntington, jr.* 1842. s.

Sopwith (Thomas). Description of a series of geological models, illustrating the nature of stratification, valleys of denudation, succession of coal fields in the Newcastle coal field, the effects produced by faults, [etc.] 84 pp. 12 pl. 16°. *Newcastle-on-Tyne, author,* 1841. s.

Sorbait (Paul). Consilium medicum, seu dialogus loimicus de peste viennensi. 3 p. l. 168 pp. 19 l. 24°. *Viennæ, J. Van Ghelen,* [1680]. s.

Sorel (Charles, *sieur* de Souvigny). De la connoissance des bons livres; ou, examen de plusieurs autheurs. [*anon.*] 5 p. l. 429 pp. 18°. *Paris, André Pralard,* 1671. s.

——— L'histoire comique de Francion. [*anon.*] Nouv. éd. 3 v. 24°. *Maestricht, J. Delessart,* 1714.

NOTE.—Other editions of this popular book bear the name of Nicolas de Moulinet (sieur du Parc). The work was never acknowledged by Sorel.

Sosare Itomeio (*pseudon.*) *See* **Imperiali** (Francesco).

Soter (Joannes). Epigrammata græca vetervm elegantissima, eademque latina ab utriusque lingua uiris doctissimis uersa. 366 pp. 16°. *Fribvrgi Brisgoioe, S. M. Grauius,* 1544.

Sotheby (Samuel Leigh). Specimen-notice for the disposal of Principia typographica, on the block-books issued in Holland, Flanders, and Germany during the 15th century. xvi, 12 l. 8 pl. 4°. [*London,* 1845].

——— The typography of the fifteenth century: being specimens of the productions of the early continental printers; fac-similes from one hundred works. 63 pp. 4°. *London, T. Rodd,* 1845.

——— Unpublished documents, marginal notes, and memoranda in the autograph of Philip Melancthon and of Martin Luther. With numerous fac-similes. 34 l. 35 pl. fol. *London, for the author,* 1840.

Soto (Hernando de). Letter to the magistrates in Santiago de Cuba, July 9, 1539. Translated from the Spanish by Buckingham Smith. 10 pp. 4°. *Washington, privately printed for G. W. Riggs, jr.* 1854.

Soubeiran (Eugène). Précis élémentaire de physique. 2e éd. 2 p. l. 420 pp. 13 pl. 8°. *Paris, Fortin, Masson & Cie.* 1844. s.

Souder (*Mrs.* Edmund A.) Leaves from the battle-field of Gettysburg; a series of letters from a field hospital; and national poems. 144 pp. 1 pl. 12°. *Philadelphia, C. Sherman, son & Co.* 1864.

Soulavie (Jean Louis Giraud). Historical memoirs and anecdotes of the court of France, during the favor of madame de Pompadour; from original papers preserved in the portfolio of madame la maréchale D'***. 2d ed. vii, 415, iv pp. 8°. *London, W. Lindsell,* 1811.

Soule (Richard, *jr.*) Memorial of the Sprague family; a poem, with the family genealogy and biographical sketches in notes. xii, 191 pp. 1 pl. 12°. *Boston, James Munroe & Co.* 1847.

Souligné (N. de). Old Rome and London compared. By a person of quality. [*anon.*] 2d ed. 2 p. l. 158 pp. 16°. *London, J. Harding*, 1710.

Sousa Farinha (Bento José de). Summario da bibliotheca luzitana. [*anon.*] 3 v. 18°. *Lisboa, A. Gomez*, 1786. s.

——— Bibliotheca luzitana escolhida. [v. 4 of preceding]. 18°. *Lisboa, A. Gomez*, 1786. s.

South Carolina. The debates which arose in the house of representatives of South Carolina on the constitution framed for the United States by a convention of delegates assembled at Philadelphia. 95 pp. 8°. *Charleston, A. E. Miller*, 1831.

——— The report of the committee of both houses of assembly, appointed to inquire into the causes of the disappointment of success in the late expedition against St. Augustine, under General Oglethorpe. 112 pp. 12°. *London, J. Roberts*, 1743.

South Carolina jockey club. [Racing memoranda from 1734 to 1857. Compiled by officers of the club—E. P. Milliken, J. C. Cochran, Henry C. King]. 211 pp. 8°. *Charleston, (S. C.) Russell & Jones*, 1857.

South Carolina legislative times; being the debates and proceedings in the legislature, at the session commencing November, 1855. 4°. *Columbia, (S. C.)* 1856.

South (The) Sea islander; containing interesting facts relative to the state of society in Otaheite. [*anon.*] 175 pp. 16°. *New York, W. B. Gilley*, 1820.

Southard (Lucian H.) Lyra Catholica. *See* **Wilcox** (J. H.) *and* **Southard** (L. H.)

Southard (Samuel L. *LL.D.*) An address before the societies of the College of New Jersey, 1837. 50 pp. 8°. *Princeton, R. E. Hornor*, 1837.

Southern (The) botanic journal, devoted to the Thomsonian system of medical practice. Edited by D. F. Nardin and J. L. Wood. v. 1 and 2. sm. fol. *Charleston, (S. C.)* 1838.

Southern (The) cultivator. A practical and scientific newspaper, for the plantation, the garden, and the family circle. Designed to improve the soil and the mind. D. Redmond, W. N. White, and J. Camak, editors. Jan. to Dec. 1867. v. 25. 8°. *Athens, (Ga.) W. N. White*, 1867.

Southey (Robert). The early naval history of England. 366 pp. 16°. *Philadelphia, Carey, Lea, & Blanchard*, 1835.

——— Letters written during a short residence in Spain and Portugal. With some account of Spanish and Portugueze poetry. xx, 551 pp. 8°. *Bristol, J. Cottle, [and others,]* 1797.

——— Madoc. 2 v. 258 pp; 320 pp. 8°. *Boston, Munroe and Francis*, 1806.

Southworth (*Mrs.* Emma D. E. Nevitte). The bride of Llewellyn. 550 pp. 12°. *Philadelphia, T. B. Peterson & bros.* 1866.

——— Retribution; or, the vale of shadows. 108 pp. 8°. *New York, Harpers*, 1849.

Souvenirs historiques. i. Correspondance secrète de Marie Antoinette avant et après le voyage de Varennes. Documens administratifs relatifs à l'adoption de la guillotine. Mélanges. 116 pp. 8°. *Leipzig, W. Zirges*, 1835. s.

Souvestre (Émile). Causeries historiques et littéraires. 3 v. 16°. *Paris, Lévy*, 1861.

——— *See* **Bretagne** pittoresque.

Sowerby (George Brettingham, *jr.*) Conchological illustrations. 200 pl. 8°. *London, Sowerby*, 1841. s.

CONTENTS.

Amphidesma. 2 pp. pl. 17-19.
Bulinus. 4 pp. pl. 21-23, 26-27, 30-31, 34-35, 137-146, 185-186.
Cancellaria. 8 pp. pl. 9-13.
Cardium. 8 pp. pl. 46-51, 149-150, 177-184.
Chilina. 2 pp. pl. 135-136.
Chiton and Chitonellus. } 8, 10 pp. pl. 38-45, 159-176.
Conus. 4 pp. pl. 24-25, 28-29, 32-33, 36-37, 54-57, 147-148, 151-158.
Cypræadæ. 20 pp. pl. 1-8, 101-131.
Eburna. 2 pp. pl. 20.
Erato. *See* Cypræadæ.
Eulima. 2 pp. pl. 52-53.
Fissurella. 10 pp. pl. 68-78, 80.
Margarita. 2 pp. pl. 132-134.
Monoceros. 2 pp. pl. 79, 81-83.
Murex. 12 pp. pl. 58-67, 187-199.
Neritina. 6 pp. pl. 86-89, 90-91, 94-100.
Nucula. 4 pp. pl. 14-16.
Ovulum. *See* Cypræadæ.
Ranella. 2 pp. pl. 84-85, 88-89, 92-93.
Typhis. 2 pp. pl. 200.

Sozomenus (Hermias). Historia ecclesiastica.

[HISTORIAE eccl. scriptores graeci. J. Christophorsono interprete, 1581 ed.]

——— The same. Versa ab Epiphanio.

[AUCTORES hist. eccl. fol. *Basileae*, 1523].

——— The same. Ecclesiastical history, translated and abridged by [Samuel] Parker.

[*With* ECCLESIASTICAL histories, etc. 3d ed. 4°. *London*, 1729].

Sozzini (Alessandro). Novelle.

[*With* NOVELLE di autori senesi. v. 2. 18°. *Milano*, 1815].

Sozzini (Fausto). *See* **Socinus.**

Spafford (Horatio Gates, *LL.D.*) A gazetteer of the state of New York. 334 pp. 1 map. 8°. *Albany, H. C. Southwick*, 1813.

——— A pocket guide for the tourist and traveller, along the line of the canals, and the interior commerce of New York. iv, 72 pp. 24°. *New York, F. & J. Swords*, 1824.

Spain. Estado militar de España é Indias. Año de 1852. 247 pp. 16°. *Madrid, Imprenta nacional,* [1852]. s.

[*With* MADRID. Guia de forasteros, 1852].

——— Indice de manuscritos de la biblioteca nacional. 90 l.

[Appendix to v. 2 of Gallardo (B. J.) Ensayo de una biblioteca española. *Madrid,* 1866].

——— *See* **Great Britain.** Convention with Spain at the Prado, 1739.

Spalding (Martin J. *D. D.*) Miscellanea; comprising reviews, etc. on historical, theological, and miscellaneous subjects. 4th ed. 2 v. v. 1. lxi, 807 pp. 8°. *Baltimore, J. Murphy & Co.* 1866.

Spanheim (Ezechiel). Epistolæ tres. *See* **Liebe** (Christian Sigismund). Gotha nvmaria. *Amstelædami,* 1730.

Spaniards' (The) cruelty and treachery to the English in time of peace and war discovered; being the council of a person of honour to king James, then upon treaty of peace with them, for to insist upon a free trade in the West Indies. With expedients for the subjecting of the Spaniard in America to the obedience of England. [*anon.*] 2. p. l. 56 pp. sm. 4°. *London, L. Lloyd,* 1656.

Sparrow (Anthony, *D. D. bishop of Exeter, and Norwich*). Collections of articles, injunctions, canons, orders, ordinances and constitutions ecclesiastical of the church of England. 3d ed. 7 p. l. 406 pp. sm. 4°. *London, Robert Pawlet,* 1675.

Spayth (*Rev.* Henry G.) History of the church of the united brethren in Christ. 1st ed. 344 pp. 1 pl. 12°. *Circleville, (O.) conference office un. brethren,* 1851.

Spear (*Mrs.* C. H.) Brief essay on the position of woman. 37 pp. 18°. *London, Trübner,* 1866.

Specimens of the British poets who flourished [from] Henry viii [to] George iii. 2 v. xiv, 456 pp; vi, 460 pp. 24°. *London, W. Suttaby,* 1809.

Speck-Sternburg (Maximilian von). Landswirthschaftliche beschreibung des rittergut Lützschena bei Leipzig, mit seinen gewerbszweigen. viii, 232 pp. 4 pl. 8°. *Leipzig, K. Tauchnitz,* 1842. s.

——— Zweites verzeichniss der gemälde sammlung, sowie der vorzüglichsten handzeichen, kupferstiche, kupferstichwerke, und plastichen gegenstände. Herausgegeben [etc.] vom besitzer. 3 p. l. 186 pp. 20 pl. 4°. *Leipzig, K. Tauchnitz,* 1837. s.

Spectateur (Le) militaire. Recueil de science, d'art, et d'histoire militaires. 40e–42e année. Juillet, 1865, Sept. 1867. 3e série. v. 1–9. 8°. *Paris,* [*E. Martinet*], 1865–67.

Speculum regale. Konungs-Skuggsjá. Konge-speilet; et philosophisk-didaktisk skrift, forfattet i Norge mod slutningen af det 12te aarhundrede. xxii, 204 pp. 2 col. pl. 8°. *Christiania, C. C. Werner & Co.* 1848. s.

Speed (John *M. D.*) Commentary on sea water. *See* **Russell** (Richard), *and* **Speed.**

Speed (John). The history of Great Britaine under the conquests of ye Romans, Saxons, Danes, and Normans. From Ivlivs Cæsar to king Iames. 3d ed. revised. 6 p. l. 155–921 pp. 25 l. fol. *London, G. Humble,* 1650.

——— A prospect of the most famovs parts of the world. 1 p. l. 48 pp. 22 maps. fol. *London, G. Humble,* 1631.

[*With* SPEED (John). Theatre of Great Britain, 1627].

——— The same. New ed. With description of his majesty's [American] dominions abroad. 1 p. l. 56 pp. 30 maps. fol. *London, T. Basset,* 1676.

[*With* SPEED (John). Theatre of Gt. Brit. 1676. Imperfect: 1 map wanting].

——— The theatre of the empire of Gt. Britaine. 7 p. l. 146 pp. 67 maps. fol. *London, G. Humble,* 1627.

——— The same. New ed. 7 p. l. 154 pp. 6 l. 67 maps. fol. *London, T. Basset,* 1676.

Spelman (*Sir* Henry). Archæologvs in modvm glossarii ad rem antiquam posteriorem: continentis, latino-barbara, peregrina, obsoleta, et novatæ significationis vocabvla, etc. [pars prima, A–L.] 3 p. l. 452 pp. fol. *Londini, J. Beale,* 1626.

Spence (William). Introduction to entomology. *See* **Kirby** (W.) *and* **Spence.**

Spencer (Albert J. *editor*). Book of comic speeches and humorous recitations. 192 pp. 16°. *New York, Dick & Fitzgerald,* [1867].

Spencer (Cornelia Phillips). Last ninety days of the war in North Carolina. 2d ed. 287 pp. 16°. *New York, Watchman pub. Co.* 1866.

Spencer (*Rev.* George, *called* father Ignatius, of St. Paul). Life of father Ignatius, of St. Paul, passionist. Compiled chiefly from his autobiography, journal, and letters. By the Rev. Father Pius. xxx, 525 pp. portrait. 12°. *Dublin, J. Duffy,* 1866.

Spencer (George). Latin lessons, with exercises in parsing. 2d ed. 196 pp. 12°. *New York, Pratt, Woodford & Co.* 1845. s.

Spencer (Herbert). Principles of biology. v. 2. 12°. *New York, Appleton,* 1867.

——— Education: intellectual, moral, and physical. 283 pp. 12°. *New York, Appleton,* 1861. s.

Spencer (*Rev.* Jesse Ames). The east: sketches of travel in Egypt and the holy land. xvi, 503 pp. 9 pl. 8°. *New York, G. P. Putnam,* 1850. S.

Spencer (Oliph Leigh). Life of Henry Chichelé, archbishop of Canterbury. xi, 232 pp. 8°. *London, J. Walter,* 1783.

Spencer (*Rev.* O. M.) Indian captivity: a true narrative. Written by himself. 160 pp. 16°. *New York, Lane & Tippett,* 1846.

Spencer (William Robert). Poems. viii, 240 pp. 1 pl. 8°. *London, T. Cadell & W. Davies,* 1811.

Spenser (Edmund). Poetical works. 8°. *Edinburgh,* 1792.

[Anderson's British poets, v. 2].

Sperry (J. Austin). Fothergill; or, the man of enterprise. 118 pp. 8°. *Cincinnati, "The great west" office,* 1849.

Spilbergen *or* **Spielberg** (Georg von). Specvlvm orientalis occidentalisqve Indiæ navigationvm; quarum una Georgii a Spilbergen, altera Jacobi Le Maire auspiciis imperioque directa [est], annis 1614–18. 175 pp. 25 pl. obl. 4°. *Lugduni Batauorum, N. a Geelkercken,* 1619.

Spiller (Philipp). Handbuch der physik. 2 v. 568 pp; 560 pp. 8°. *Berlin, L. Oehmigke,* 1865–66. S.

Spindler (Carl). Lenzblüthen. Erzählungen und novellen. 2 v. 390 pp; 368 pp. 18°. *Stuttgart, Hallberger,* 1834.

——— The jesuit: a picture of manners and character from the first quarter of the 18th century. Translated from the German. 2 v. 292 pp; 261 pp. 12°. *London, E. Bull,* 1839.

——— Schildereien. 2 v. in 1. 166 pp; 167 pp. 18°. *Stuttgart, Hallberger,* 1855. S.

Spinola (Massimiliano, *marchese*). Insectorum Liguriæ species novæ aut rariores. 2 v. in 1. xvii, 159 pp. 2 pl; ii, 262, v pp. 5 pl. 4°. *Genuæ, auctor,* 1806–08. S.

Spinoza (Baruch *or* Benedictus de). Opera qvæ svpersvnt omnia. Itervm edenda cvravit, præfationes, vitam avctoris, qvæ ad historiam scriptorvm pertinent addidit Henr. E. G. Pavlvs. 2 v. xxiv, 724 pp; xl, 680 pp. 8°. *Jenæ, in bibliopolio academico,* 1802–03.

CONTENTS.

v. 1. Principia philosophiæ cartesianæ.
Tractatus theologico-politicus.
Epistolæ.
v. 2. Ethice.
Tractatus politicus.
De intellectus emendatione.
Compendium grammatices linguæ Hebraeæ.
De vita Spinozæ.

——— Œuvres, traduites par Émile Saisset. 1re et 2e série. 2 v. viii, 436 pp; ccviii, 354 pp. 16°. *Paris, Charpentier,* 1842–43.

CONTENTS.

v. 1. Introduction.
Vie de Spinoza, (par Jean Coler).
Théologie de Spinoza.
v. 2. Éthique.
Réforme de l'entendement.
Correspondance.

Spirit (The) of the martyrs revived. [*anon.*] 4 p. l. 648 pp. 8°. *London, J. Sowle,* 1719.

Spirit (The) of Partridge; or, the astrologer's pocket companion and general magazine. [Aug. 5, 1824—Jan. 15, 1825. Nos. 1—xvii.] iii, 356 pp. 12°. *London, Astrological society,* 1825.

Spiritualist (The): being a short exposition of psychology based upon material truths, and of the faith to which it leads. By D. F. G. [*anon.*] xvi, 111 pp. sq. 16°. *London, L. Booth,* 1857.

Spirk (Anton). Geschichte und beschreibung der k. k. universitäts-bibliothek zu Prag. [Extract.] 109 pp. 1 pl. 8°. *Wien, Öst. blätter für lit. und kunst,* 1844. S.

Spix (Johann Baptist von), *and* **Martius** (Carl Friedrich Philipp von). Reise in Brasilien, 1817—1820. 3 v. 4°. *München, Verfasser,* 1823–31. S.

[Wanting 3 atlases].

Spofford (*Mrs.* Harriet Elizabeth Prescott). The amber gods and other stories. 432 pp. 16°. *Boston, Ticknor & Fields,* 1863.

——— Azarian: an episode. 251 pp. 16°. *Boston, Ticknor & Fields,* 1864.

Spofford (Jeremiah, *M.D.*) A family record of the descendants of John Spofford, and Elizabeth his wife, who came from England to America, and settled at Rowley, in 1638. 64 pp. 8°. *Haverhill, (Mass.) B. G. Frothingham,* 1851.

——— A gazetteer of Massachusetts. 348 pp. 1 map. 16°. *Newburyport, C. Whipple,* 1828.

Spon (Jacob). Tractatvs novi de potv caphé; de Chinensivm thé; et de chocolata. 3 p. l. 202 pp. 2 l. 2 pl. 18°. *Parisiis, P. Muguet,* 1685.

Spooner (Lucius H.) Suggestions on town sewerage and its application to land by gravitation. 30 pp. 8°. *London, R. Hardwicke,* 1865.

Spotswood *or* **Spottiswoode** (John, *abp. of of St. Andrews*). The history of the church of Scotland, beginning the year 203, and continued to the end of the reign of king James vi. 11 p. l. 546 pp. 6 l. fol. *London, R. Royston,* 1655.

Spottiswoode society publications, viz:

1. KEITH (*rt. rev.* Robert). History of the affairs of church and state in Scotland, from [1527] to 1568. With biographical sketch, [etc.] 3 v. 8°. *Edinburgh*, 1844–50.
2. SAGE (*rt. rev.* John). Works; with memoir and notes. 3 v. 8°. *Edinburgh*, 1844–46.
3. Spottiswoode miscellany: a collection of original papers and tracts, chiefly illustrative of the civil and ecclesiastical history of Scotland. 2 v. 8°. *Edinburgh*, 1844.

Sprague (Homer B.) History of the 13th infantry regiment of Connecticut volunteers, during the great rebellion. 353 pp. 12°. *Hartford, Case, Lockwood & Co.* 1867.

Sprat (Thomas, *D. D. bishop of Rochester*). Poetical works. 8°. *Edinburgh*, 1793.

[Anderson's British poets, v. 6].

——— Sermons on several occasions. 440 pp. 8°. *London*, 1722.

[Title wanting].

——— A true account and declaration of the horrid conspiracy against the late king, his present majesty, and the government. [The rye-house plot. *anon.*] 2 p. l. 167 pp. fol. *London, T. Newcomb*, 1685.

——— The same. 2d ed. 2 p. l. 167 pp. fol. *London, T. Newcomb*, 1685.

——— The same. 3d ed. 4 p. l. 221 pp. 16°. *London, T. Newcomb*, 1686.

Sprengel (Curt). Geschichte der botanik. 2 v. 4 p. l. 424 pp; 8 p. l. 396 pp. 8°. *Altenburg & Leipzig, F. A. Brockhaus*, 1817–18. s.

——— Versuch einer pragmatischen geschichte der arzneikunde. 2e aufl. 5 v. 8°. *Halle, J. S. Gebauer*, 1800–03. s.

Sprengel (Joachim Friedrich). Beschreibung der harzischen bergwerke nach ihrem ganzen umfange. 32 l. 110 pp. 16°. *Berlin, Buchhandlung der realschule*, 1753. s.

Sprenger (Aloys, *M. D.*) A catalogue of the Arabic, Persian and Hindústány manuscripts of the libraries of the king of Oudh. v. 1. Persian and Hindústány poetry. viii, 648 pp. 8°. *Calcutta, Govt. of India*, 1854. s.

Spring (Gardiner, *D. D.*) First things; lectures on the great facts and moral lessons first revealed to mankind. 2d ed. 2 v. 395 pp; 296 pp. 12°. *New York, M. W. Dodd*, 1851.

——— Memoirs of Rev. Samuél J. Mills. 247 pp. 8°. *New York, Evangelical miss. soc.* 1820.

——— A tribute to New England; sermon preached before the New England society of New York, Dec'r 22, 1820. 44 pp. 8°. *New York, L. & F. Lockwood*, 1821.

Sproat (P. W.) The savage beauty; a satirical and allegorical novel. 12°. *Philadelphia, S. Roberts*, 1822.

Spruner (Carl von). Atlas antiquus. Ed. 2a. 27 col. maps. obl. fol. *Gothae, J. Perthes*, 1855. s.

——— Historisch-geographischer hand-atlas zur geschichte der staaten Europa's vom anfang des mittelalters. 2e aufl. 73 col. maps. obl. fol. *Gotha, J. Perthes*, 1854. s.

——— The same. Erläuternde vorbemerkungen. [2e aufl.] 58 pp. 4°. [*Gotha, J. Perthes*, 1854]. s.

[Text of, and bound with the preceding].

——— Historisch-geographischer schul-atlas. 5 p. l. 22 maps. 4°. *Gotha, J. Perthes*, 1856. s.

Spurgeon (*Rev.* Charles Haddon). "The modern Whitfield." Sermons. With an introduction and sketch of his life, by E. L. Magoon. xxxvi, 320 pp. 1 pl. 12°. *New York, Sheldon, Blakeman & Co.* 1856.

Spurzheim (Johann Gaspar). Examination of the objections made in Britain against the doctrines of Gall and Spurzheim. 99 pp. 12°. *Boston, Marsh, Capen & Lyon*, 1833.

Squibb (Robert). Gardener's calendar for the states of North Carolina, South Carolina, and Georgia. With appendix. 4 p. l. 176 pp. 12°. *Charleston, (S. C.) P. Hoff*, 1827.

Squier (Ephraim George). Monograph of authors who have written on the languages of Central America, or composed works in the native dialects of that country. 90 pp. 4°. *New York, C. B. Richardson*, 1861. s.

——— The states of Central America, [etc]; and the Honduras inter-oceanic railway. 782 pp. 5 maps, 8 pl. 8°. *New York, Harper & brothers*, 1858. s.

Squier (Miles P. *D. D.*) Reason and the Bible; or, the truth of religion. 340 pp. 12°. *New York, C. Scribner*, 1860.

Squire (*Rev.* Francis). An answer to some late papers, entitled, The independent whig, so far as they relate to the church of England. xvi, 188 pp. 12°. *London, W. & J. Innys*, 1723.

Stabbert (Carl Ludvig Franz). De echinococco. 32 pp. 8°. *Berolini, G. Lange*, 1867. s.

Stabile (Giuseppe). Mollusques terrestres vivants du Piémont. 141 pp. 2 pl. 8°. *Milan, Bernardoni*, 1864. s.

Stacions of Rome, (in verse from MS. ab. 1370 A. D. and in prose from MS. ab. 1460–70 A. D.) and the Pilgrims sea-voyage; with Clene maydenhod (from MS. ab. 1370). A supplement to "Political, religious, and love poems," and "Hali meidenhad." Edited by F. J. Furnivall. xvi, 40, 8 pp. 8°. *London, N. Trübner & Co.* 1867.

[Early English text society publications, No. 25].

Stacke (Henry). The story of the American war, 1861-65. viii, 264 pp. 1 map. 18°. *London, Warne & Co.* 1866.

Stackhouse (*Rev.* Thomas). A new history of the holy Bible, from the beginning of the world, to the establishment of christianity. 2d ed. 2 v. lxviii, 1650 pp. 25 l. 5 maps. 31 pl. fol. *London, S. Austen,* 1742.

Stadnitski (Pieter). Voorafgaand bericht wegens eene negotiatie op landen in America. 37 pp. 12°. *Amsterdam,* 1792.

Staelin. *See* **Stälin.**

Stagg (John). Miscellaneous poems. vii, 256 pp. 16°. *Wigton, R. Hetherton,* 1808.

Stählberg (Georg). An history of the late revolution in Sweden, [of] the 19th Aug. 1772. By a gentleman who was a Swede. [*anon.*] xv, 370 pp. 8°. *Edinburgh,* 1776.

Stahr (Adolf Wilhelm Theodor). Life and works of Gotthold Ephraim Lessing. From the German, by E. P. Evans. 2 v. 12°. *Boston, Ticknor & Fields,* 1866.

Staiger (B.) Landwirthschaftlicher katechismus. 2e aufl. vi, 172 pp. 11 pl. 12°. *Augsburg, Verfasser,* 1861. s.

Stainton (Henry Tibbats, *and others*). Natural history of the tineina. vol. 9. 8°. *London, J. Van Voorst,* 1865.

Stälin (Christoph Friedrich). Zur geschichte und beschreibung alter und neuer büchersammlungen im königreich Würtemberg, [etc.] 96 pp. 16°. *Stuttgart, Cotta,* 1838. s.

Stallard (J. H.) The female casual and her lodging; with a scheme for the regulation of workhouse infirmaries. iv, 143 pp. 12°. *London, Saunders, Otley & Co.* 1866.

Stalsberg (F.) Udsigt over de væsentligste forbedringer ved ierntilvirkningen i de seneste decennier. xx, 213 pp. 8°. *Christiania, J. Dahl,* 1866. s.

Stamler (Johann). Dyalogvs de diversarvm gencivm sectis et mvndi religionibvs. 3 p. l. xxxi l. 2 l. folio. *Auguste, E. Oglin & Nadler,* 1508.

Stammer (Carl). Lehrbuch der physik. 2 v. in 1. xi, 279 pp; vi, 194 pp. 8°. *Lahr, M. Schauenburg & Co.* 1858-59. s.

Stanbury (George). Practical guide to lithography, and the various uses of the materials supplied by him. 8°. *London, Houlston,* 1851. s.

Standish (Frank Hall). The shores of the Mediterranean. xii, 339 pp. 8°. *London, C. Roworth & sons,* 1837.

Standish, the puritan. A tale of the American revolution. By Eldred Grayson, esq. [*pseudon.*] 320 pp. 12°. *New York, Harpers,* 1850. s.

Stanhope (Philip Dormer, *4th earl of Chesterfield*). The elements of polite education; selected from the letters of the late earl of Chesterfield, by G. Gregory, D.D. 6 p. l. 456 pp. 16°. *London, R. Phillips,* [1800?]

Stanhope (Philip Henry, *5th earl Stanhope, formerly lord Mahon*). History of England, from the peace of Utrecht to the peace of Versailles, 1713—1783. 3d ed. 7 v. 16°. *Boston, Little, Brown & Co.* 1853-54.

Stanley (Henry). Rouman anthology; or, selections of Rouman poetry, ancient and modern, in the original; with translation of some of the poems. xx, 226 pp. 8°. *Hertford, S. Austin,* 1866.

Stannius (Friedrich Hermann). Animaux vertèbrés.

[SIEBOLD (C. T. E. von), *and* STANNIUS. Nouveau manuel d'anatomie comparée, v. 2].

——— Das peripherische nervensystem der fische, anatomisch und physiologisch untersucht. iv, 156 pp. 5 pl. 4°. *Rostock, Stiller,* 1849. s.

Stanton (Robert Livingston, *D.D*). The church and the rebellion: a consideration of the rebellion; and the agency of the church, north and south, in relation thereto. xiv, 562 pp. 12°. *New York, Derby & Miller,* 1864.

Staples (William R.) The documentary history of the destruction of the Gaspee. Compiled for the Providence journal. 56 pp. 8°. *Providence, Knowles, Vose & Anthony,* 1845.

Starck (Johann Friedrich Christian Ekhardt). De hydrocephali paracentesi. 290, vii pp. 3 tab. 12°. *Rostochii, auctor,* 1841. s.

Staring (W. C. H.) De bodem van Nederland. De zamenstelling en het ontstaan der gronden in Nederland. v. 1. xii, 441 pp. 1 map. 7 pl. 8°. *Haarlem, A. C. Kruseman,* 1856. s.

Stark (Augustin). Beschreibung der meteorologischen instrumente, nebst einer einleitung zum gebrauche desselben bey den beobachtungen. 4 p. l. 79 pp. 5 pl. 4°. *Augsburg, Verfasser,* 1815. s.

Stark (John, *F. R. S. E.*) Elements of natural history. 2 v. vi, 527 pp. 4 pl; 515 pp. 4 pl. 8°. *Edinburgh, W. Blackwood,* 1828. s.

CONTENTS.

v. 1. Vertebrata.
v. 2. Invertebrata.

Starke (Mariana). Letters from Italy, 1792—1798. 2 v. in 1. xv, 383 pp; x, 409 pp. 8°. *London, R. Phillips,* 1800.

Starkey (Benjamin). Memoirs of his life. 14 pp. 1 pl. 8°. *Newcastle, W. Hall,* 1818.

Stars (The) and the earth; or, thoughts upon space, time, and eternity. [*anon.*] From the 3d English ed. [With preface by Thomas Hill]. 88 pp. 16°. *Boston, Crosby & Nichols,* 1849.

——— The same. 7th ed. 98 pp. 18°. *London, H. Baillière,* 1861.

Startling facts for native Americans called "know-nothings;" or, a vivid presentation of the dangers to American liberty to be apprehended from foreign influence. [*anon.*] 112 pp. 8°. *New York,* 1855.

State tracts: being a collection of several treatises relating to the government. [1671–81]. Privately printed in the reign of king Charles ii. ii, 468 pp. fol. *London,* 1689.

——— The same. Being a farther collection, 1660–1689. [v. 2]. 4 p. l. 499 pp. fol. *London, R. Baldwin,* 1692.

[*With* the preceding].

State (The) triumvirate: a political tale; and the epistles of brevet major Pindar Puff. [*pseudon.* With separate title-page: Dr. Busby's edition of the Bucktail bards. In part by Gulian C. Verplanck?] 215 pp. 18°. *New York, J. Seymour,* 1819.

States (The) and union [Washington daily]. Jan. 2, 1860, to Apr. 20, 1861. v. 1, no. 45—v. 2, no. 94. in 3 v. fol. *Washington, J. P. Heiss & J. S. Holland,* 1860–61.

Statesman's (The) year-book for 1867–68. A statistical, genealogical, and historical account of the states and sovereigns of the civilized world. By Frederick Martin. 2 v. 12°. *London, Macmillan,* 1867–68.

Statistical (A) account of the Schuylkill permanent bridge. [*anon.*] 84 pp. 1 pl. 8°. *Philadelphia, Jane Aitken,* 1807.

[*With* PHILADELPHIA society for promoting agriculture. Memoirs. v. 1. 1808].

Statistical illustrations of the territorial extent and population, commerce, taxation, consumption, insolvency, pauperism, and crime of the British empire. xx, 88, xi pp. 8°. *London, J. Miller,* 1825.

Statistical society of London. Journal. v. 29–30. For the years 1866–67. 8°. *London, E. Stanford,* 1866–67.

Statistical summary of the progress of the colony of Victoria to the year 1865. [*anon.*] 24 pp. 8°. *Melbourne, J. Ferres,* 1865. s.

Statistics of the British empire. [*anon.*] 3 pts. in 1 v. 415 pp. 4°. [*London, R. Wilkes,* 1832?]

CONTENTS.

Part 1. Account of the population in 6,000 towns and parishes, with the annual value of real property, 1801–31.
Part 2. Locality, relation, superficies, and population of each county, section, district, and colony, births and deaths, and the resources and condition of each, 1790–1831; with a like display for Europe, the United States, and China.
Part 3. Finances, navigation, and commerce, 1693–1831.

Statius (Publius Papinius). [Opera omnia], denuo ac serio emendata. 356 pp. 32°. *Amsterodami, Joannes Jansonius,* 1630.

——— The Thebaid. Translated into English verse, with notes and observations, by Wm. L. Lewis. 8°. *Edinburgh,* [1792].

[Anderson's Brit. poets, v. 1].

Staunton (Howard). Memorials of Shakespeare; comprising the poet's will, the indentures of conveyance and mortgage of [his] house in Blackfriars, and photographs of the Droeshout and Chandos portraits, with annotations. 11 pp. 2 pl. 5 facs. fol. *London, Day,* [1864].

Staunton (*Rev.* William). The book of common praise: a collection of music adapted to the book of common prayer, according to the use of the protestant episcopal church in the U. S. 336 pp. oblong 8°. *New York, F. J. Huntington & Co.* 1866.

Stearns (Charles). The national armories. A review of the systems of superintendence, civil and military, particularly with reference to economy and general management at the Springfield armory. [*anon.*] 3d ed. 82 pp. 1 pl. 8°. *Springfield, author,* 1853. s.

Stebbins (J. E.) Our departed friends; or, glory of the immortal life. Illustrated. 559 pp. 8°. *Hartford, L. Stebbins,* 1867.

Steczkowski (Jan Kant). Astronomija sposobem dla ka'zdego dostepnym wylo'zona. xv, 608 pp. 1 pl. 8°. *Kraków, D. E. Friedleina,* 1861. s.

——— Elementarny wyklad matematyki. 5 v. 8°. *w Krakowie, w drukorni c. k. uniwersytetu,* 1851–59. s.

CONTENTS.

Czesc 1. Arytmetyka. xvi, 321 pp. 1851.
Czesc 2. Algebra. 4 p. l. 327 pp. 1 pl. 1852.
Czesc 3. Geometryja.
(v. 1). Planimetryi z stereometryja. 5 p. l. 398 pp. 11 pl. 1858.
(v. 2). Trigonometryja prostokreslna i sferyczna. 4 p. l. 231 pp. 2 pl. 1858.
(v. 3). Geometryja analityczna wraz z linijami i powierzchniami krzywemi drugiego rzedu. 4 p. l. 484 pp. 10 pl. 1859.

Stedman (C.) The history of the origin, progress, and termination of the American war. 2 v. xi, 446 pp; xvii, 502 pp. 13 l. 8°. *Dublin, P. Wogan, etc.* 1794.

Steed (J. M.) Grammatical stenography; or, short-hand. 16 pp. 18°. *Washington, F. S. Myer,* 1828.

Steel (David). The shipmaster's assistant, and owner's manual. 10th ed. xvi, 450 pp. 8°. *London, P. Steel,* 1803.

——— Tables of the British custom and excise duties. 3d ed. 128, 40 pp. 8°. *London, P. Steel,* 1803.

[*With* STEEL (D.) Shipmaster's assistant. 1803].

Steele (J. Dorman). A fourteen weeks' course in chemistry. 264 pp. 16°. *New York, A. S. Barnes & Co.* 1867.

Steendam (Jacob). The praise of New Netherland.

[*With* MURPHY (Henry C.) Jacob Steendam, etc. 1861].

Steenstrup (Johan Japetus Smith). Hectocotyldannelsen has octopodslægterne argonauta og tremoctopus. [Extract]. 32 pp. 2 pl. 4°. *Kjöbenhavn, k. danske vid. selskabs,* 1856. s.

Steetz (William). Instruction nautique sur les passages à l'île de Cuba et au golfe du Mexique, par le canal de la Providence et le grand banc de Bahama. 64 pp. 2 maps. 8°. *Paris, Béchet,* 1825. s.

Steiger (Ernest). Volks-kalender für 1868. 120 pp. 16°. *New York, E. Steiger,* 1867.

Stein (Friedrich). Der organismus der infusionsthiere nach eigenen forschungen in systematischer reihenfolge bearbeitet. 1. Allgemeiner theil, und naturgeschichte der hypotrichen infusionsthiere. xii, 206 pp. 14 pl. 4°. *Leipzig, W. Engelmann,* 1859. s.

Steinbuch (Johann Georg). De taenia hydatigena anomala, adnexis cogitatis quibusdam de vermium visceralium physiologia. 4 p. l. x, 132 pp. 1 pl. 8°. *Erlangae, Hilpert,* 1801. s.

Steller (Georg Wilhelm). Reise von Kamtschatka nach Amerika mit dem commandeur-capitän Bering. 133 pp. 8°. *St. Petersburg, J. Z. Logan,* 1793. s.

Stellwag von Carion (Carl). Treatise on the diseases of the eye, including the anatomy of the organ. Translated from the German and edited, by C. E. Hackley and D. B. St. John Roosa. With an appendix. xiv, 774 pp. 3 pl. 8°. *New York, Wood & Co.* 1868.

Stendhal (—— de, *pseudon.*) *See* **Beyle** (H.)

Stephanus. *See* **Estienne.**

Stephens (*Mrs.* Ann S.) Myra: the child of adoption. A romance of real life. 120 pp. 1 pl. 18°. *New York, Beadle,* 1860.

——— *See* **Portland** sketch book. 12°. *Portland,* 1836.

Stephens (*prof.* George, *F. S. A.*) Förteckning öfver de förnämsta brittiska och fransyska handskrifterna, uti köngl. bibliotheket i Stockholm. xii, 204 pp. 8°. *Stockholm, P. A. Norstedt,* 1847. s.

——— The old northern runic monuments of Scandinavia and England. Part 1. 362 pp. fol. *London, J. R. Smith,* 1866. s.

Stephens (Henry.) The book of the farm. [with] notes by John S. Skinner. 2 v. 569 pp. 4 pl; xvii, 462 pp. 17 pl. 8°. *New York, Greeley & McElrath,* 1847. s.

[Farmers' library, v. 2-3].

Stephens (James). James Stephens, chief organizer of the Irish republic; embracing an account of the Fenian brotherhood; being a semi-biographical sketch. [*anon.*] 117 pp. 1 pl. 12°. *New York, Carleton,* 1866.

Stephens (John Langdon). Incidents of travel in Egypt, Arabia Petræa and the Holy Land. 3d ed. 2 v. 240; 286 pp. 1 map. 16 pl. 12°. *New York, Harpers,* 1838.

——— The same. 10th ed. With additions. [*anon.*] 2 v. 240, 286 pp. 1 map. 12°. *New York, Harpers,* 1848.

Stephens (William, *esq.*) Journal of the proceedings in Georgia, beginning October 20, 1737. To which is added, a state of that province, as attested upon oath in the court of Savannah, November 10, 1740. 2 v. 480 pp. 8 l; 508, 32 pp. 7 l. 8°. *London, W. Meadows,* 1742.

——— The same. Journal [in Georgia], received by the trustees for establishing the colony. Sept. 22 to Oct. 28, 1741. 22 l. 12°. *London, W. Meadows,* 1742.

Stephens. *See* **Stevens.**

Stephenson. *See* **Stevenson.**

Stepney (George). Poetical works. 8°. *Edinburgh,* 1793.

[Anderson's Brit. poets, v. 6].

Sterling (Richard). Southern orator; containing lectures for declamation and recitation. 544 pp. 12°. *New York, Owens & Agar,* 1867.

Sternburg (Max von Speck). *See* **Speck-Sternburg.**

Stetson (Isaac). Stenography, reduced to certain and fixed principles. 8 pp. 16°. *Philadelphia, Matthews & Bell,* 1834.

——— The universal writer; or, short-hand shortened. 2d ed. 49 pp. 18°. *New York, Dood & Manter,* 1824.

Steuart (*Sir* James). Works; political, metaphysical, and chronological. Collected by his son. [With] anecdotes of the author. 6 v. 8°. *London, Cadell & Davies,* 1805.

Steuart (*Sir* James). Works; political, metaphysical, and chronological.—*Continued.*

CONTENTS.

v. 1-4. Political economy.
v. 5. Principles of money, applied to the state of Bengal and German coin.
Considerations on the interest of Lanark.
Plan for uniformity of weights and measures.
v. 6. Observations on Dr. Beattie's essay on truth.
Remarks on a book entitled System of nature by M. de Mirabaud, [*baron* d'Holbach].
Motive of obedience to the laws of God.
Apologie du sentiment de Newton sur l'ancienne chronologie des Grecs.
Answer to Des Vignolles upon Newton's chronology.
Anecdotes of [his] life.

Stevens (Abel). Centenary of American methodism; a sketch of its history, theology, practical system, and success. With a statement of the plan of the centenary celebration of 1866, by John M'Clintock. 287 pp. 12°. *New York, Carlton & Porter,* 1866.

——— History of the methodist episcopal church in the United States. v. 3-4. 12°. *New York, Carlton & Porter,* 1867.

Stevens (Henry). An account of the proceedings at the dinner given by Mr. George Peabody, to the Americans connected with the great exhibition, at the London coffee house, Ludgate Hill, 27th October, 1851. 114 pp. 8°. *London, William Pickering,* 1851.

——— Catalogue of my English library. xi, 107 pp. 16°. *London, C. Whittingham,* 1853.

Stevens (*Capt.* John). A new collection of voyages and travels: with historical accounts of discoveries and conquests in all parts of the world, translated [1st ed.] 5 nos. in 1 vol. 4 maps. 1 pl. sm. 4°. *London, J. Knapton,* 1708-9.

[Imperfect].

CONTENTS.

ARGENSOLA (Bartolomé Leonardo de). Discovery and conquest of the Molucco and Philippine Islands.
CIEZA DE LEON (Pedro de). Seventeen years' travels through Peru, Cartagena, and Popayan.
LAWSON (John). New voyage to Carolina.
MOUETTE (Germain). Travels in the kingdoms of Fez and Morocco.

——— The royal treasury of England: or, an historical account of all taxes, from the con quest to the present year. [*anon.* 1st ed.] xxxi, 372 pp. 8°. *London, T. Jebb,* 1725.

Stevens (John Austin, *jr.*) Colonial New York. Sketches, biographical and historical, 1768—1784. 172 pp. 4 pl. 8°. *New York, J. F. Trow & Co.* 1867.

[*With* NEW YORK (*City of*). Chamber of commerce. Colonial records, 1867].

Stevens. *See, also,* **Stephens.**

Stevenson (Henry). The birds of Norfolk; with remarks on their habits, migration, and local distribution. v. 1. lxxii, 445 pp. 3 pl. 8°. *London, J. Van Voorst,* 1866.

Stevenson (*Rev.* John). Christ on the cross; an exposition of the twenty-second Psalm. 2d Am. from 10th Lond. ed. 345 pp. 12°. *New York, Robert Carter,* 1846.

Stevenson (Thomas). Lighthouse illumination: a description of the holophotal system, and of azimuthal-condensing, and apparent lights, etc. viii, 122 pp. 4 pl. 8°. *London, J. Weale,* 1859. s.

Stewart (Balfour). Elementary treatise on heat. xx, 392 pp. 16°. *Oxford, Clarendon press,* 1866. s.

Stewart (Dugald). Elements of the philosophy of the human mind. Abridged, with notes by F. Bowen. New ed. xi, 490 pp. 12°. *Boston, W. H. Dennet,* 1864.

Stewart (James). Steam engineering on sugar plantations, steamships, and locomotive engines. 138 pp. 16°. *New York, Russell,* 1867.

Stewart (Kensey Johns). The freemason's manual; a companion for the initiated through all the degrees of freemasonry, [etc.] 316 pp. 13 pl. 12°. *Philadelphia, E. H. Butler & Co.* 1851. s.

Stewart (Robert, *M. D.*) The American farmer's horse-book; embracing a full description of the diseases peculiar to the American horse, [etc.] Also, a treatise on stock raising, [etc.] 600 pp. 1 pl. 8°. *Cincinnati, C. F. Vent & Co.* 1867.

Stewart. *See, also,* **Stuart.**

Stielei (Adolf). Atlante scholastico per la geografia politica efisica. 1 p. l. 44 maps. 4°. *Gothas, Justus Perthes,* 1855.

Stieren (Eduard). Chemische fabrik; ein practisches handbuch zur fabrikmässigen darstellung chemischer präparate. Mit einer vorrede von G. C. Wittstein. vi, 621 pp. 8°. *München, J. Grubert,* 1865.

Stierlin (*Dr.* G.) Revision der europäischen otiorhynchus arten. 344 pp. 8°. *Berlin, Nicolai,* 1861. s.

Stillé (Alfred, *M. D.*) Elements of general pathology. 483 pp. 8°. *Philadelphia, Lindsay & Blakiston,* 1848.

——— Epidemic meningitis; or, cerebro-spinal meningitis. 178 pp. 8°. *Philadelphia, Lindsay & Blakiston,* 1867.

Stillfried-Rattonitz (Rudolph Maria Bernhard von, *conde* de Alcantara). Alterthümer und kunst Maria Bernhard denkmale des erlauchten hauses Hohenzollern. Neue folge. v. 1. fol. *Berlin, Ernst & Korn,* 1859. s.

Stillfried-Rattonitz. (Rudolph Maria von Bernhard, von *conde de* Alcantara), *and* **Märcker** (Traugott). Monumenta zollerana. Urkundenbuch zur geschichte des hauses Hohenzollern. v. 1–6. 4°. *Berlin, Ernst & Korn*, 1852–60. s.

CONTENTS.

v. 1. Urkunden der schwäbischen linie. A. D. 1095–1418. viii, 558 pp.
v. 6. Urkunden der fränkischen linie. A.D. 1235–1411.

Stillingfleet (Edward, *bishop of Worcester*). The doctrine of the trinity and transubstantiation compared, as to scripture and reason, in a dialogue between a protestant and papist. 40 pp. 8°. *Oxford*, 1825.

[*In* RANDOLPH (John, *bishop of London*). Enchiridion theologicum, v. 1).

——— Irenicum; or, the divine right of church government. 16 p. l. 557 pp. 12° *London, Henry Mortlock*, 1681.

——— The mysteries of the christian faith asserted and vindicated. 25 pp. 8°. *Oxford*, 1825.

[*In* RANDOLPH (John, *bishop of London*). Enchiridion theologicum. v. 1.)

Stillman (Samuel *D.D.*) Four sermons on important subjects. 87 pp. 16°. *Boston, E. Russell*, 1769.

Stimpson (William). Researches upon the hydrobiinae, and allied forms; chiefly made upon materials in the museum of the Smithsonian institution. iv, 59 pp. 8°. *Washington, Smithsonian inst.* 1865.

[Smithsonian miscel. coll. v. 7].

Stirry (Thomas). A rot among the bishops; or, a terrible tempest in the sea of Canterbury. 14 pp. 4 pl. 18°. *London*, 1641. [*Reprint, London*, 1838].

Stisser (Christian Friedrich). Friderich der gröste [etc]; in einer rede, welche wegen des [etc.] geschlossenen höchstglorwürdigen friedens, in dem grössern horsaal des k. akad. gymnasii zu Stettin, den 20 Jul. 1742, [etc] bewundert. 24 pp. fol. *Stettin, J. F. Spiegeln*, 1742. s.

[*With* WILLEBRANDT (J. P.) Hansische chronick].

Stisted (*Mrs.* Henry). Letters from the byeways of Italy, with illustrations, by Col. Stisted. xviii, 496 pp. 16 pl. 8°. *London, J. Murray*, 1845. s.

Stjerngranat (G. G. H.) Militär-statistik. Preussen. 1^{sta} afdelningen. 5 p. l. 274 pp. 8°. *Stockholm, P. A. Norstedt & söner*, 1840. s.

Stock (John Edmonds). Memoirs of the life of Thomas Beddoes, M. D. with an analytical account of his writings. v, 413, lxxi pp. 1 pl. 4°. *London, J. Murray*, 1811.

Stöckel (*Dr.* Gustave J.) Sacred music. [Hymns and tunes]. 165 pp. 8°. *New York, Taintor bros. & Co.* 1868.

Stockell (*Capt.* William). Eventful narrative of his travels and engagements in land and naval service of England and United States, and in the whale fishery. Revised by Edwin A. Atlee, M. D. 326 pp. 8°. *Cincinnati*, 1840.

Stockfleth (Nils Joachim Christian Vibe). Norsk-lappisk ordbog. iv, 892 pp. 8°. *Christiania, J. W. Cappeleus*, 1852.

Stöckhardt (Julius Adolph). Die schule der chemie; oder, erster unterricht in der chemie, versinnlicht durch einfache experimente. 8^e aufl. xiv, 706 pp. 12°. *Braunschweig, Vieweg*, 1855. s.

Stockholder (The). Monitor of finance and industry. [A weekly journal]. Nov. 1862 to Nov. 1867. v. 1–5. fol. *New York*, 1863–67.

Stoddard (*Mrs.* Elizabeth). Temple house. A novel. 347 pp. 12°. *New York, G. W. Carleton & Co.* [1867].

Stoddard (John F.) The practical arithmetic. 2 p. l. 292 pp. 12°. *New York, Cornish, Lamport & Co.* 1852. s.

——— *and* **Henkle** (W. D.) An algebra. 440 pp. 12°. *New York, Sheldon, Blakeman & Co.* 1857. s.

Stoddard (Richard Henry). The king's bell. [A poem.] With illustrations by Alfred Fredericks. 60 pp. 8 pl. 8°. *New York, Bunce & Huntington*, 1866.

——— The late English poets. [Selected poems.] xii, 539 pp. 16°. *New York, Bunce & Huntington*, 1865.

Stoeckel. *See* **Stöckel.**

Stoeckhardt. *See* **Stöckhardt.**

Stokes (William, *M. D.*) Lectures on physic. *See* **Bell** (John, *M. D.*) *and* **Stokes.**

Stoltz (J. L.) Manuel élémentaire du cultivateur alsacien. Elementar-handbuch des elsässischen ackerbauers. [Fr. and Ger. texts]. ii, 479 pp. 3 pl. 12°. *Strasbourg, F. C. Heitz*, 1842. s.

Stolze (Franz). Gabelsberger oder Stolze? Eine beleuchtung der streitschriften des geheimen regierungsraths Häpe in Dresden: die "stenographie als unterrichtsgegenstand," und des senators Dr. Eggers aus Rostock: "die stenographie in den schulen." ix, 187 pp. 13 pl. 8°. *Berlin, Mittler & sohn*, 1864. s.

Stone (*Rev.* Edwin Martin). Biography of Rev. Elhanan Winchester. 250 pp. 1 l. 12°. *Boston, H. B. Brewster*, 1836.

Stone (*Rev.* Edward Martin). Invasion of Canada in 1775; including the journal of Capt. Simeon Draper, describing the perils and sufferings of the army under Col. Benedict Arnold, in its march to Quebec. With notes and appendix. xxiv, 104 pp. 5 l. 2 pl. 1 map. 8°. *Providence, Knowles, Anthony & Co.* 1867.

Stone (John Seeley, *D. D.*) Christian sacraments; or, scriptural views of baptism and the Lord's supper. 631 pp. 8°. *New York, A. D. F. Randolph*, 1866.

——— The divine rest; or, scriptural views of the Sabbath. 304 pp. 12°. *New York, A. D. F. Randolph*, 1867.

Stone (*Rev.* Nathaniel). Rulers are a terror, not to good, but evil-workers. [Election] sermon, 1720. 22 pp. 1 l. 12°. *Boston, B. Green*, 1720.

[*With* WALLEY, (*Rev.* Thomas). Balm in Gilead. *Cambridge*, 1670].

Stone (Nicholas). Enchiridion of fortification; or, a handful of knowledge in martiall affaires. [*anon.* 2d ed.] 4 p. l. 70 pp. 8 l. 20 pl. 16°. *London, for the author*, 1669.

Stone (*Rev.* Samuel). A congregational church is a catholike visible church; or, an examination of M. Hudson, his vindication, etc. 4 p. l. 43 pp. sm. 4°. *London, Peter Cole*, 1652.

Stone (William Leet). The life and times of sir William Johnson, bart. 2 v. xv, 555 pp. 1 pl; xv, 544 pp. 8°. *Albany, J. Munsell*, 1865.

Stonehenge (*pseudon.*) *See* **Walsh** (J. H.)

Stoppani (Antonio). Les pétrifications d'Ésino; ou, description des fossiles appartenant au dépôt triassique supérieur des environs d'Ésino en Lombardie, comprenant les gastéropodes, les acéphales, les brachiopodes, les céphalopodes, les crinoïdes, les zoophytes, et les amorphozoaires. xi, 152 pp. 1 map. 31 pl. 4°. *Milan, J. Bernardoni*, 1858–60. s.

Stoppelaar (Jan Herman de). De zelandica gente de Huybert, ejusque meritis de re cum publica tum litteraria, et de partibus quas in publicis Belgii foederati rebus curandis egit Petrus de Huybert. 4 p. l. 171, xxviii pp. 1 tab. 8°. *Lugduni-Batavorum, J. Hazenberg*, 1852. s.

Storch (Heinrich Friedrich von), *and* **Adelung** (Friedrich von). Systematische uebersicht der literatur in Russland, während des 5 jähr. zeitraums von 1801 bis 1805. v. 1. Russische literatur. 12°. *St. Petersburg und Leipzig, Hartknoch*, 1811. s.

Storch (Johann). Theoretische und practische abhandlung von kinder-kranckheiten. 2 v. in 1. viii, 436 pp. 6 l. 4 pl; viii, 439 pp. 4 l. 12°. *Eisenach, M. G. Greissbach*, 1750. s.

Storer (James). History and antiquities of the cathedral churches of Great Britain. Illustrated with engravings. 4 v. 8°. *London, Rivingtons, etc.* 1814–19.

Stories and sketches by our best authors. [*anon.*] 307 pp. 12°. *Boston, Lee & Shepard*, 1867.

Storm (Theodor). Immen-see. From the German, by H. Clark. 77 pp. 16°. *Philadelphia, F. Leypoldt*, 1863.

Story of a Chinese boy. [*anon.*] 343 pp. 5 pl. 16°. *Philadelphia, Am. S. S. union*, [1867].

Story (The) of a penitent: Lola Montez. [*anon.*] 46 pp. 18°. *New York, Prot. episcopal soc. prom. evang. knowl.* 1867.

Story (The) of a stomach: an egotism. By a reformed dyspeptic. [R. D. *anon.*] 60 pp. 16°. *New York, Fowler & Wells*, 1867.

Story (Joseph, *LL. D.*) The power of solitude and other poems. New ed. 260 pp. 1 pl. 16°. *Salem, B. B. Macnulty*, 1804.

Stosch (Philipp von). Pierres antiques gravées, sur lesquelles les graveurs ont mis leurs noms. [Also, Latin title: Gemmæ antiquæ cælatæ]. Dessinées et gravées par Bernard Picart. Traduites en François par M. de Limiers. [Lat. et fr.] 3 p. l. xxi, 97 pp. 70 pl. fol. *Amsterdam, B. Picart*, 1723.

Stoughton (*Rev.* William, *lieut. gov. of Mass.*) New England's true interest not to lie. A sermon preached in Boston, April 19th, 1668, being the day of election. 40 pp. sm. 4°. *Cambridge, S. Green & M. Johnson*, 1670.

[Title page wanting].

Stout (*Capt.* Benjamin). Narrative of the loss of the ship Hercules on the coast of Caffraria; also, account of his travels through southern Africa to the Cape of Good Hope. With introductory address to John Adams, president of the continental congress of America. liii, 113 pp. 16°. *New York, J. Chevalier*, [1797].

Stow (John). Annales; or, a generall chronicle of England. Begun by John Stow; continued unto 1631, by Edmund Howes. 10 p. l. 1087 pp. 14 l. fol. *Londini, Richard Meighen*, 1632.

——— The survey of London. Enlarged and finished by A[nthony] M[unday], H[enry] D[yson], and others. 7 p. l. 939 pp. 14 l. fol. *London, E. Pvrslovv*, 1633.

Stowe (Calvin Ellis, *D. D.*) Origin and history of the books of the Bible, both the canonical and the apocryphal, [showing] what the Bible is not, what it is, and how to use it. The New Testament, illustrated. 8°. *Hartford, Publishing co.* 1867.

——— The right interpretation of the sacred scriptures; an inaugural discourse delivered at Andover, Sept. 1, 1852. 31 pp. 8°. *Andover, [Mass.] W. F. Draper*, 1853.

Stowe (Harriet Esther Beecher). Queer little people. Illustrated. 185 pp. sm. 4°. *Boston, Ticknor & Fields*, 1867.

——— Religious poems. With illustrations. iv, 107 pp. 16°. *Boston, Ticknor & Fields*, 1867.

Stowe (J. G.) A new guide to the sheet iron and boiler plate roller. *See* **Perkins** (C. H.) *and* **Stowe** (J. G.)

Stower (Charles). The printer's price-book; containing the master printer's charges to the trade for printing works of various descriptions, sizes, types, and pages. With specimen pages. iv pp. 1 l. 446 pp. 8°. *London, C. Cradock & W. Joy*, 1814.

Strabo. Geographia. De situ orbis libri xvii, a Guarino Veronensi et a Gregorio Thiphernio translati. 217 l. fol. [*Venetiis, per Vindelinum spirensem*], 1472.

Note.—The colophon ends thus;

[Strabonis] libellos
Nunc antenorei uident penates:
Impressos digitis uidelianis.

Strackerjan (Christian Friedrich). Beiträge zur geschichte der stadt Jever, [etc.] 192 pp. 8°. *Bremen, W. Kaiser*, 1836. s.

——— Beiträge zur geschichte des grossherzogthums Oldenburg. v. 1. 512 pp. 8°. *Bremen, W. Kaiser*, 1837. s.
[No more published].

——— Geschichte der buchdruckerei im herzogthum Oldenburg und der herrschaft Jever, [etc.] Ein festgabe, [etc.] 48 pp. 1 pl. 8°. *Oldenburg, Schulze*, 1840. s.

——— Oldenburg's fest-und jubelbuch. Ausführliche beschreibung aller feierlichkeiten am 27 Novbr. und 24 Decbr. 1838, als den jubelfesten, [etc.] des selbständigkeit des herzogthums Oldenburg und der neu organisirten landesbewaffnung, [etc.] stattgefunden, [etc.] 166 pp. 1 pl. 8°. *Oldenburg, Schulze*, 1839. s.

Strafford (H.) Herd book. *See* **Coates** (George).

Strahlenberg (Philipp Johann Tobbert von). Historico-geographical description of the north and eastern parts of Europe and Asia, particularly of Russia, Siberia, and Great Tartary, both in their ancient and modern state, with a polyglot table of dialects of 32 Tartarian nations. Translated into English. 8 p. l. 463 pp. 1 map. 4 pl. 4°. *London, Innys & Manby*, 1738.

Strain (Isaac G.) A paper on the history and prospects of interoceanic communication by the American isthmus. 27 pp. 8°. *New York, Vinten*, 1856.

Strang (John). Germany in 1831. 2 v. xxiv, 360 pp. 1 pl; xii, 456 pp. 1 pl. 8°. *London, J. Macrone*, 1836. s.

Strange (*Sir* Robert). An inquiry into the rise and establishment of the royal academy of arts. vi, 141 pp. 16°. *London, E. & C. Dilly*, 1775.

Stranger's (The) guide to Baltimore. By a Baltimorean. [*anon.*] 80 pp. 1 map. 11 pl. 24°. *Baltimore, Murphy & Co.* 1852. s.

Straparola (Giovanni Francesco da Caravaggia). Les facétieuses nuits de Straparole. Traduites [de l'Italien] par Jean Louveau et Pierre de Larivey. [*pseudon.*] 2 v. lxiii, 384 pp; 408 pp. 16°. *Paris, P. Jannet*, 1857.

Stratman (Francis Henry). A dictionary of the English language, of the xiii, xiv, and xv centuries. Parts i–vi. 576 pp. 8°. *Krefeld, Kramer & Baum*, 1864–67.

Stratton (R. B.) Captivity of the Oatman girls: an interesting narrative of life among the Apache and Mohave Indians. 231 pp. 1 map. 1 pl. 16°. *San Francisco, L. D. Oatman*, 1857.

Stratton (Thomas). Aureae sententiae: select sentences from eminent divines and other writers. [*anon.*] vii, 221 pp. 18°. *London*, 1768.

Strecker (Adolph). Kurzes lehrbuch der organischen chemie. xix, 417 pp. 12°. *Braunschweig, Vieweg*, 1853. s.
[REGNAULT (H. V.) Kurzes lehrbuch. v. 2].

Street (Alfred B.) Poems. 2 v. v, 302 pp; v, 338 pp. 16°. *New York, Hurd & Houghton*, 1867.

Strength in weakness. A sermon preached at the funeral of Mrs. Matilda Brooks, by J. C. [*anon.*] 2 p. l. 39 pp. sm. 4°. *London, John Hancock*, 1676.

Stretch (Richard H.) Annual report of the state mineralogist of the state of Nevada, for 1866. 151 pp. 8°. *Carson city, J. E. Eckley*, 1867. s.

Strickland (Agnes). Lives of the queens of England, from the Norman conquest. Abridged by the author. Revised and edited by Caroline G. Parker. 675 pp. 1 pl. 12°. *New York, Harper & bros.* 1867.

Strickland (Hugh Edwin). Ornithological synonyms. Edited by Mrs. H. E. Strickland and Sir W. Jardine. v. 1. Accipitres. xlvi, 222 pp. 8°. *London, J. Van Voorst,* 1855. s.
[No more published].

Stringfellow (*Rev.* T.) Two letters on cases of cure at Fauquier white sulphur springs, [and] mineral waters in general. 16 pp. 8°. *Washington, Union office,* 1851.

Ström (Hans). Physisk og œconomisk beskrivelse over fogderiet söndmör, beliggende i Bergens stift i Norge. 2 pts. in 2 v. 9 p. l. 572 pp. 4 pl. 1 map; 12 p. l. 509 pp. 4°. *Soröe, Rothe,* 1762–66.

Strombeck (Friedrich Carl von). Souvenirs d'un voyage en Suède en 1839. [Trad. de l'Allemand]. 266 pp. 8°. *Strasbourg, G. Silbermann,* 1840.

Strong (George A.) The song of Milgenwater, translated from the original Feejee, by Marc Antony Henderson. [*pseudon.*] 96 pp. 16°. *Cincinnati,* 1856.

Strong (Henry K. *chairman*). Report to the legislature of Pennsylvania, containing a description of the Swatara mining district. 61 pp. 8 pl. 8°. *Harrisburg, Boas & Coplan,* 1839. s.

Strong (James, *S. T. D.*) Cyclopædia, etc. *See* **McClintock** (John, *D. D.*) *and* **Strong.**

Strong (*Rev.* William). A treatise shewing the subordination of the will of man unto the will of God. 7 p. l. 335 pp. 6 l. 16°. *London, Francis Tyton,* 1657.

Strong (W. C.) Culture of the grape. xvi, 355 pp. 12°. *Boston, Tilton & Co.* 1866.

Strozzi (Carlo). Flore fossile italienne. *See* **Gaudin** (C. T.) *and* **Strozzi.**

Strutt (Elizabeth). Domestic residence in Switzerland. 2 v. 282 pp; 288 pp. 2 pl. 8°. *London, T. C. Newby,* 1842.

Struve (Burkhard Gotthilf.) Corpvs historiæ germanicæ a prima gentis origine ad annvm 1730. Præmittitur C. G. Bvderi bibliotheca scriptorvm rervm germanicarvm. 2 v. 8°. 974 pp; 622 pp. 8 pl. *Jenæ, J. F. Bielckii,* 1730.

Strype (John). Life and acts of Matthew Parker, first archbishop of Canterbury. xxvi, 544, 208 pp. 1 pl. fol. *London, J. Wyat,* 1711.

Stuart (Bernard). How to become a successful engineer. 2d ed. 127 pp. 16°. *Edinburgh, W. P. Nimmo,* 1866.

Stuart (Charles). A memoir of Granville Sharp. 156 pp. 12°. *New York, William S. Dorr,* 1836.

Stuart (John). Memoir of Indian wars, and other occurrences.
[VIRGINIA historical soc. collections. vol. i].

Stuart. *See, also,* **Stewart.**

Stubbe (Henry). A justification of the present war against the United Netherlands. By an English man. [*anon.*] 4 p. l. 80 pp. 5 pl. sm. 4°. *London, H. Hills,* 1672.

——— A further justification of the war against the United Netherlands. 12 p. l. 136 pp. 6 pl. sm. 4°. *London, H. Hills,* 1673.
[*With* the preceding].

Stucley *or* **Stukeley** (*Sir* Lewis). Humble petition and information touching his owne behaviour in the bringing up [to London] of Sir Walter Raleigh. 17 pp. sm. 4°. *London, Bonham Norton and John Bill,* 1618.

Student (The) and schoolmate. An illustrated monthly for all our boys and girls. Jan. 1866 to Dec. 1867. v. 17–20. 4 v. in 2. 8°. *Boston, J. H. Allen,* 1866–67.

Studer (Bernhard). Beyträge zu einer monographie der molasse, oder geognostische untersuchungen über die steinarten und petrefakten, die zwischen den Alpen und dem Jura gefunden werden. xxxviii, 427 pp. 2 pl. 8°. *Bern, C. A. Jenni,* 1825. s.

Stülpnagel (Fr. von), *and* **Bär** (J. C.) Karte von Europa in vier blättern entworfen und gezeichnet. 3e aufl. verbessert durch A. Petermann. 1 fol. in 4°. *Gotha, J. Perthes,* 1855. s.

Stumpf (Johann). Keyser Heinrychs des vierdten hertzogen historia. 10 p. l. cxxxvii l. fol. *Zürych, C. Froschouer,* 1556.

Sturgeon (William). Scientific researches, experimental and theoretical, in electricity, magnetism, galvanism, electro-magnetism, and electro-chemistry. viii, 566 pp. 18 pl. 4°. *London, Longmans,* 1852. s.

Sturges (John, *LL. D.*) Discourses, chiefly on the evidences of natural and revealed religion. xii, 454 pp. 8°. *London, T. Cadell,* 1792.

Sturm (Jacob). Abbildungen zu Karl Illiger's übersetzung von Olivier's entomologie, oder naturgeschichte der insecten; mit ihren gattungs und artmerkmalen, ihren beschreibung und synonymie. Käfer. 2 v. iv, 136 pp; 132 pp. 96 col. pl. 4°. *Nürmberg, Herausgeber,* 1802. s.

——— Catalog der kaefer-sammlung. xii, 386 pp. 6 pl. 8°. *Nürmberg, Verfasser,* 1843. s.

——— Deutschlands fauna in abbildungen nach der natur, mit beschreibungen. 5e abtheilung. Insekten. v. 1–4. civ pl. 18°. *Nürmberg,* 1805. s.
[Abth. ii, iii, v, & vi, vols. 5–7, wanting].

Sturtevant (S. T. *D. D.*) The preacher's manual: lectures on preaching; furnishing rules and examples for every kind of preaching. 4th ed. With an introductory essay on preaching, by Rev. A. M. Henderson. xl, 609 pp. 8°. *London, Reeves & Turner*, 1866.

Stüve (C. G. A.) Wesen und verfassung der landgemeinden und des ländlichen grundbesitzes in Niedersachsen und Westphalen. Geschichtliche und statistische untersuchungen mit unmittelbarer beziehung auf das königreich Hannover. xviii, 321 pp. 8°. *Jena, F. Frommann*, 1851. s.

Suarez *or* Soarez (José). Libertas evangelium Christi annunciandi et propagandi in imperio Sinarum, declarata 1692, et pro Europæorum notitia descripta. 175 pp. 18°. *Ultrajecti, W. Broedeleth*, 1699.

[*With* LEIBNITZ (G. W.) Novissima sinica. *Ultrajecti*, 1699].

Suasso Diaz de Fonseca (Antonio Lopez, *baron*). The theory of the infantry movements. New ed. 2 v. lxvi, 371 pp; viii, 392 pp. 8°. *London, Clowes*, 1846. s.

Subligny (——). La fausse Clélie, histoire françoise, galante et comique. [*anon.*] Éd. nouv. 3 p. l. 322 pp. 3 l. 1 pl. 24°. *Amsterdam, J. Waguenar*, 1672.

Succinct (A) view of the origin of our colonies, with their civil state, whereby the nature of the empire established in America, and the errors of various hypotheses formed thereupon may be clearly understood. [*anon.*] 46 pp. 12°. *London*, 1766.

Suchet (Louis Gabriel, *maréchal, duc d'Albufera*). Mémoires sur ses campagnes en Espagne. 1808–14. 2v. li, 376 pp; ix, 572 pp. 1 pl. 8°. *Paris, Didot*, 1828.

——— The same. 2 v. xlix, 366 pp; ix, 570 pp. 1 pl. 8°. *Paris et Londres, Colburn & Bossange*, 1828–29.

Suckling (*Sir* John). Poetical works. *Edinburgh*, 1793.

[Anderson's Brit. poets, v. 3].

Sudendorf (H.) Urkundenbuch zur geschichte der herzöge von Braunschweig und Lüneburg, und ihrer lande, gesammelt und herausgegeben. v. 1–4. 4°. *Hannover, C. Rümpler*, 1859–64. s.

CONTENTS.

v. 1. Bis zum jahre 1341. lxxxviii, 358 pp. 1 tab.
v. 2. Vom jahre 1343–1356. c, 315 pp.
v. 3. Vom jahre 1357–1369. clx, 299 pp.
v. 4. Vom jahre 1370–1373. clx, 270 pp.

Sue (Marie Joseph, *dit* Eugène). L'art de plaire. [Nouvelle]. 292 pp. 18°. *Bruxelles, Meline*, 1840.

——— Le colonel de Surville; histoire du temps de l'empire. 294 pp. 18°. *Bruxelles, Meline*, 1840.

——— L'hotel Lambert: histoire contemporaine. 2 v. in 1. 285 pp; 271 pp. 18°. *Bruxelles, Meline*, 1842.

——— Latréaumont. 2 v. 326 pp; 377 pp. 18°. *Bruxelles, Meline*, 1838.

——— Mathilde: mémoires d'une jeune femme. 5 v. 18°. *Bruxelles, Meline*, 1843.

——— Plik et Plok. [El gitano. Kernok le pirate]. 266 pp. 16°. *Paris, Paulin*, 1845.

——— La Salamandre. 2 v. in 1. 224 pp; 208 pp. 24°. *Paris, Paulin*, 1845.

——— Les secrets de l'oreiller. 6 v. 18°. *Naumbourg, L. Garcke*, 1858.

——— Thérèse Dunoyer. 2 v. 249 pp; 360 pp. 16°. *Bruxelles, Hauman et Cie.* 1842.

——— Mysteries of the people; or, the story of a plebeian family for 2000 years. Translated by Mary L. Booth. [1st series. The dragoon's helmet, The golden sickle, The brass bell, and The iron collar]. 177 pp. 8°. *New York, C. M. Clark*, 1867.

——— The negro's revenge; or, Brulart, the black pirate. iv, 49 pp. 8°. *London*, [1841?]

[HAZLITT's romancist and novelist's library. v. 5].

Sugenheim (Samuel). Geschichte der entstehung und ausbildung des kirchen-staates. Gekrönte preisschrift. viii, 439 pp. 8°. *Leipzig, Brockhaus*, 1854. s.

Suite de la vie du Pierre Joseph Marie Chaumonot, par un père de la compagnie [de Jésus], avec la manière d'oraison du vénérable père, écrite par lui même. [*anon.*] 66 pp. sm. 4°. *Nouvelle York, J. M. Shea*, 1858. s.

Sullivan (John L.) The answer of Mr. Sullivan to the letter and mis-statements of Cadwallader D. Colden, in his "brief exposition" of himself as the advocate of steamboat monopoly. 40 pp. 8°. *Troy, W. S. Parker*, 1823.

——— [Letter to Israel Cael on steamboat monopoly]. 20 pp. 8°. *Albany*, 1817.

[Imperfect: wanting title-page].

Sullivan (William, *LL.D.*) History of the United States of America, for the use of schools and families. [*anon.*] Stereotype ed. 276 pp. 16°. *Keene, (N. H.) John Prentiss*, 1822.

——— Moral class book, or the law of morals. x, 282 pp. 12°. *Boston, Richardson, Lord, and Holbrook*, 1831.

Sullivant (William S.) Mosses and liverworts.

[*With* GRAY (Asa). Manual of botany, etc.]

——— Musci alleghanienses, sive enumeratio muscorum atque hepaticarum. 86 pp. 8°. *Columbus (O.) printed at Cambridge, (Mass.) author*, 1846.

Sulpicia. Poetical works. Translated by J. Grainger. 8°. *Edinburgh*, 1792.
[ANDERSON'S British poets. v. 5].

Sulzer (Johann Georg). Allgemeine theorie der schönen künste in einzeln, nach alphabetischer ordnung der künst-wörter. v. 1–4, und register. 5 v. 8°. *Leipzig, Wiedmann*, 1799. S.

——— Discours sur l'allégorie.
[*With* WINCKELMANN (J. J. *and others*). De l'allégorie. v. 2.]

——— Illustrations of the theory and principles of taste, the fine arts, and literary composition. Translated from the German by E. A. de Brusasque. xxiii, 417 pp. 16°. *London, J. Mawman*, 1806.
[v. 1. No more published].

Summary (A) historical, geographical, and statistical view of the city of New York, with notices of Brooklyn, Williamsburgh, etc. [*anon.*] 46 pp. 18°. *New York, J. H. Colton*, 1836.

Summer (A) month; or, recollections of a visit to the falls of Niagara, and the lakes. [*anon.*] 248 pp. 12°. *Philadelphia, H. C. Carey & I. Lea*, 1823.

Summer islands company. *See* **Sommer** islands company.

Sumner (Charles). Speech on the cession of Russian America to the United States. 48 pp. 1 map. 8°. *Washington, Cong. globe office*, 1867.

Sumner (John Bird, *D. D. archbishop of Canterbury*). The evidence of christianity, derived from its nature and reception. xiii, 429 pp. 8°. *London, J. Hatchard & son*, 1824.

——— Treatise on the records of the creation and on the moral attributes of the creator; with particular reference to the Jewish history, and to the consistency of the principle of population with the wisdom and goodness of the deity. 4th ed. 2 v. xxviii, 390 pp; xi, 444 pp. 8°. *London, J. Hatchard & son*, 1825.

Sumner (William Hyslop). Memoir of Increase Sumner, governor of Massachusetts, with a genealogy of the Sumner family. 70 pp. 1 pl. 8°. *Boston, S. G. Drake*, 1854.

Sunday (The) school teacher. [A monthly magazine], devoted to the interests of Sunday schools. Jan. 1866, to Dec. 1867. v. 1–2. 8°. *Chicago, Adams, Blackmer & Lyon*, 1867.

Sunderland (La Roy). Pathetism, with practical instructions, illustrating those laws which induce somnambulism, second-sight, sleep, dreaming, trance, and clairvoyance. xvi, 247 pp. 16°. *New York, P. P. Good*, 1843.

Sundevall (Carl Johan). Conspectus avium picinarum. xiv, 116 pp. 8°. *Stockholmiae, Samson & Wallin*, 1866. S.

Sure guide to hell, by Beelzebub. [*anon.*] 62 pp? 12°. *London*, 1750.
[Imperfect; title-page, and leaves at the end wanting].

Surgy (Rousselot de). *See* **Rousselot** de Surgy (Jacques Philibert).

Surinaamsche koloniale bibliothek. Catalogus. vii, 59 pp. 2 l. 8°. *Gravenhage, M. Nijhoff*, 1859. S.

——— The same. 1862. viii, 56 pp. 8°. *Gravenhage, M. Nijhoff*, 1862. S.

Suringar (W. F. R.) De sarcina (*sarcina ventriculi* Goodsir) onderzoek naar de plantaardige natuur, den ligchaamsbouw en de ontwikkelingswelten van dit organisme. 4 p. l. 129 pp. 3 pl. 4°. *Leeuwarden, G. T. N. Suringar*, 1865. S.

Surius (Lorenz). Commentarivs brevis rervm in orbe gestarvm, 1500–1574. Nunc ad annum 1586 opera et studio Michaelis ab Isselt perductus. 48 p. l. 1199 pp. 16°. *Coloniae, G. Calenius et Quentelius*, 1586.

Surprising (The) life and death of Dr. John Faustus, D. D. [with] The necromancer, or harlequin doctor Faustus, as performed at the theatres. [*anon.*] 144 pp. 18°. *Worcester*, 1795.

Surville (Joseph Étienne, *marquis* de). Poésies de Marguerite Éléonore Clotilde de Vallon Chalys, depuis madame de Surville; poète français du 15ᵉ siècle. [*pseudon.*] Publiées par Ch. Vanderbourg. ci, 257 pp. 13 pl. 12°. *Paris, Didot*, 1804.

Sûrya-Siddhânta. Translation of the Sûrya-Siddhânta, a text-book of Hindu astronomy; with notes and an appendix. By Ebenezer Burgess. (Extract.) iv, 354 pp. 8°. *New Haven, Am. oriental soc.* 1860. S.

Suspiria vinctorum. Some account of the condition to which the protestant interest in this world is at this day reduced; and the duty to which all that would prove themselves true christians must count themselves obliged. [*anon.*] 22 pp. 18°. *Boston, T. Fleet*, 1726.

Sutherland (*Capt.* David). A tour up the straits, from Gibraltar to Constantinople; with leading events in the present war between the Austrians, Russians, and Turks, to 1789. xlvii, 372 pp. 8°. *London, J. Johnson*, 1790.

Sutherland (James). Biographical sketches of the members of the forty-first general assembly of Indiana, with that of the state officers and judiciary. 210 pp. 8°. *Indianapolis*, 1861.

Sutherland (J. W.) The science of horsemanship: a new method of training horses. [With] a treatise on lady equestrianship, and upon shoeing, [etc.] 119 pp. 16°. *Harvard, (Ill.) H. V. Reed & Co.* 1867.

Sutton (Thomas). Dictionary of photography. vii, 423 pp. 12°. *London, S. Low,* 1858. s.

Sutton (W. L. *M.D.*) History of the disease usually called typhoid fever, as it has appeared in Georgetown and its vicinity, etc. iv, 127 pp. 8°. *Louisville, Maxwell & Co.* 1850. s.

Swallow (George C.) Geological report of the country along the line of the southwestern branch of the Pacific railroad, Missouri. xvii, 93 pp. 1 map. 2 pl. 8°. *St. Louis, Knapp & Co.* 1859. s.

——— *and* **Hawn** (F.) Report of the geological survey of Miami county, Kansas. 24 pp. 8°. *Kansas city, (Mo.)* 1865. s.

Swallows on the wing o'er garden springs of delight; a medley of prose and verse. By Will de Grasse. [*pseudon.*] 81 pp. 12°. *New York, M. Doolady,* 1866.

Swan (William D.) The American comprehensive reader. 312 pp. 12°. *Boston, Hickling, Swan & Brown,* 1855. s.

Swartz (Olaf). Nova genera et species plantarum; seu, prodromus descriptionum vegetabilium maximam partem incognitorum quæ sub itinere in Indiam Occidentalem annis 1783–87 digessit. x, 152 pp. 8°. *Holmiæ, M. Sweder,* 1788. s.

——— Synopsis filicum, earum genera et species systematice complectens. Adjectis lycopodineis, etc. xviii, 445 pp. 5 pl. 8°. *Kiliæ, Imp. bibliop. novi acad.* 1806. s.

[*With* SWARTZ. Nova genera, etc. 1788].

Sweden. Recueil des exposés de l'administration du royaume de Suède présentés aux états généraux, depuis 1809 jusqu'à 1840; traduit par J. F. de Lundblad. xxiii, 366 pp. 8°. *Paris, Parent-Des Barres,* 1840. s.

Swedenborg (Emanuel). Dictionary of correspondences, representatives, and significatives, derived from the word of the Lord. Extracted from the writings of Swedenborg. [Abridged from G. Nicholson, by C. Bolles]. 3d ed. 453 pp. 12°. *Boston, O. Clapp,* 1860.

——— Heaven and its wonders, and hell. 453 pp. 8°. *Philadelphia, J. B. Lippincott & Co.* 1867.

——— The New Jerusalem, and its heavenly doctrine; with something concerning the new heaven and the new earth. A new translation, by T. B. Hayward. 104 pp. 18°. *Boston, T. H. Carter & son,* 1867.

——— A treatise on the nature of influx, or of the intercourse between the soul and body. Translated from the Latin, [by Thomas Hartley]. 3d ed. 16°. *London, R. Hindmarsh,* 1788.

——— *See* **White** (William).

Sweetser (William, *M.D.*) Human life; considered in its present condition and future developments, especially with reference to its duration. xvi, 322 pp. 12°. *New York, G. P. Putnam,* 1867.

——— Mental hygiene; or, an examination of the intellect and passions. 2d ed. 370 pp. 12°. *New York, G. P. Putnam,* 1850. s.

Swett (John). Common school readings; containing new selections for declamation, [etc.] 230 pp. 12°. *San Francisco, H. H. Bancroft, & Co.* 1867.

Swieten (Gerhard, *baron* van). The diseases incident to armies. With the method of cure. From the Latin. 44 pp. 8°. *Boston, M'Dougall,* 1777.

Swift (*Rev.* Elisha P.) A memoir of the Rev. Joseph W. Barr, late missionary under the direction of the western foreign missionary society, [etc.] 291 pp. 18°. *Pittsburgh, R. Patterson,* 1833. s.

Swift (Jonathan). An argument to prove that the abolishing of christianity in England, may, as things now stand, be attended with some inconveniences. [*anon.*] 38 pp. 16°. *London, T. Atkins,* 1717.

——— Gulliver's travels into several remote regions of the world. New ed. With notes and life of the author by John Francis Waller. Illustrated by T. Morten. xliv, 352 pp. 1 pl. 4°. *London, Cassell, Petter & Galpin,* [1865].

——— A modest inquiry into the reasons of the joy expressed by a certain sett of people, upon the report of her majesty's [Queen Anne] death. [*anon.*] 24 pp. 16°. *London, J. Morphew,* 1714.

[Imperfect, pp. 23–24 wanting.]

——— Poetical works. 8°. *Edinburgh,* 1794.

[Anderson's British poets. v. 9].

Swinburne (Algernon Charles). Chastelard; a tragedy. 178 pp. 16°. *New York, Hurd & Houghton,* 1866.

——— Notes on poems and reviews. 23 pp. 8°. *London, J. C. Hotten,* 1866.

——— A song of Italy. 47 pp. 18°. *Boston, Ticknor and Fields,* 1867.

Swinton (William). The twelve decisive battles of the war; a history of the eastern and western campaigns; 520 pp. 7 portraits. 7 maps. 8°. *New York, Dick & Fitzgerald,* 1867.

Sydney. *See* **Sidney.**

Sylvius (Jacobus). *See* **Dubois** (Jacques).

Symmes (Thomas). Lovewell lamented; or, a sermon occasioned by the battle of Piggwacket, [with an historical preface]. xii, 32 pp. 18°. *Boston, S. Gerrish*, 1725.

——— The same. Historical memoirs of the late fight at Piggwacket, with a sermon [on the death] of capt. John Lovewell. Pronounced at Bradford, May 16, 1725. 2d ed. corrected.

[*With* KIDDER (Frederic). Expeditions of Capt. John Lovewell. 4°. pp. 25–73. *Boston*, 1865].

Symons (Jelinger Cookson). Tactics for the times; as regards the condition and treatment of the dangerous classes. viii, 245 pp. 8°. *London, J. Ollivier*, 1849.

Sympathies (Les); ou, l'art de juger, par les traits du visage. Par Mme. de G. [*anon.*] 79 pp. 32 pl. 24°. *Paris, Saintin*, 1813.

Symson (Patrick). The historie of the church since the days of our Saviour, Jesus Christ, vntill this present age. [1st ed.] 8 p. l. 790 pp. sm. 4°. *London, J. Bellamie*, 1624.

Syracuse (*N. Y.*) Boyd's daily journal Syracuse directory, and Onondaga co. business directory, 1867–68. 295 pp. 8°. *Syracuse, Andrew Boyd*, 1867.

[Imperfect: wanting pp. 25–32].

Syrus (Publius). Singulares sententiae. *See* **Seneca** *and* **Syrus.**

System (A) of exercise and instruction of field artillery, including manœuvres for light or horse-artillery. [By a board of officers, U. S. A.] 78 pp. lvi pl. 16°. *Boston, Hilliard, Gray & Co.* 1833.

Szeredy (J.) Asiatic chiefs. [A historical, romantic tableau of the Hungarian Magyar nation]. 2 v. vii, 527, viii pp; 464 pp. 12°. *London, Longmans*, 1856.

Szerlecki (Ladislaus A.) Dizionario di terapeutica. Versione italiana per cura del Luigi Marieni, con tavole di ragguaglio de' principal pesi medici dell'Europa. xxiv, 651 pp. 8°. *Milano, Perelli e Mariani*, 1844. S.

Tabella cibaria. The bill of fare: a Latin poem, translated and explained in copious notes. [*anon.*] viii, 104 pp. 4°. *London, Sherwood & Co.* 1820.

Taber (Joseph, *and others*). Address to the people called quakers, concerning the manner in which they treated Timothy Davis, for writing and publishing a piece on taxation. 67 pp. 12°. *Boston, T. & J. Fleet*, 1784.

Tablet (The), or picture of real life; in a select set of essays. [*anon.*] xx, 371 pp. 8°. *London, Longman*, 1762.

Taché (J. C.) Canada at the universal exhibition of 1855. 463 pp. 1 map. 1 pl. 8°. *Toronto, J. Lovell*, 1856. S.

CONTENTS.

Sketch of Canada, its industrial condition and resources. pp. 67–144. 1 map.
Descriptive catalogue of the productions of Canada exhibited, etc. pp. 147–203. 8°. *Paris*, 1855.
Observations on the exhibition. pp. 206–409. 1 pl.
Sketch of the geology of Canada, etc. By W. E. Logan and T. Sterry Hunt. pp. 413–454. 8°. *Paris*, 1855.

Tacitus (Caius Cornelius). Opera quæ extant. 686 pp. 24°. *Parisiis, Broca*, 1736. S.

——— Cn. Julii Agricolæ vita. 36 pp. fol. *Parisiis, C. L. F. Panckoucke*, 1827. S.

——— Oeuvres, traduits par C. L. F. Panckoucke. (Lat. et fr.) 7 v. 8°. *Paris, C. L. F. Panckoucke*, 1843. S.

Taddei (Gioacchino). Saggio di ematalloscopia; o, ricerche chimiche e comparative sul sangue degli animali vertebrati. 134 pp. 2 l. 8°. *Firenze, Piatti*, 1844. S.

Tahçin-uddin. Les aventures de Kamrup. Publiées en Hindoustani, par Garcin de Tassy. 100 pp. 8°. *Paris, Imprimerie royale*, 1835.

——— The loves of Camarúpa and Cámalata, an ancient Indian tale. Translated from the Persian by William Francklin. [*anon.*] viii, 284 pp. 12°. *London, T. Cadell*, 1793.

Taillandier (René Gaspard Ernest, *dit* St. René). Maurice de Saxe: étude historique d'après les documents des archives de Dresde. vii, 430 pp. 8°. *Paris, Lévy*, 1865.

Tailor's (The) manual; or twenty years a New England tailor. [A system of accounts.] By one of the craft. [*anon*]. 39 pp. 8°. *Worcester, [Mass.] author*, 1856. S.

Taine (Hippolyte Adolphe). Essai sur Tite Live. viii, 348 pp. 16°. *Paris, L. Hachette et Cie.* 1856.

——— Le positivisme anglais: étude sur Stuart Mill. viii, 157 pp. 16°. *Paris, G. Baillière*, 1864.

——— Voyage en Italie. 2 v. 4 p. l. 528 pp; 2 p. l. 562 pp. 8°. *Paris, Hachette et Cie.* 1866.

——— Voyage aux Pyrénées. 3e éd. illustrée par Gustave Doré. vi, 554 pp. 8°. *Paris, L. Hachette & Cie.* 1860.

Taitbout de Marigny (E.) Plans de golfes, baies, ports et rades de la mer Noire et de la mer d'Azov. 2 p. l. 35 maps. obl. 4°. *Odessa, A. Braun*, 1830. S.

——— Portulan de la mer Noire et de la mer d'Azov, ou déscription des côtes de ces deux mers à l'usage des navigateurs. vii, 170 pp. 16°. *Odessa, Imprimerie de la ville*, 1830. S.

Talbot (*Mr.* ——). History of North America; comprising a geographical and statistical view of the United States, and of the British Canadian possessions. With plates and maps. [*anon.*] 2 v. iv, 498 pp. 3 pl. 1 map; 458 pp. 8°. *Leeds, (Eng.) Davies & Co.* 1820.

Talbott (John L.) New arithmetic: scholar's guide to the science of numbers. 212 pp. 12°. *Cincinnati, J. A. & U. P. James,* 1848. s.

Tales from "Bentley." 6 v. 16°. *London, R. Bentley,* 1865.

Tallack (William). Malta, under the Phenicians, Knights, and English. vi, 322 pp. 1 pl. 12°. *London, A. W. Bennett,* 1861.

Talleyrand-Perigord (Charles Maurice de). Rapport sur l'instruction publique fait au nom du comité de constitution à l'assemblée nationale, 1791. 216 pp. 8 tab. 4°. *Paris, Assemblée nationale,* 1791. s.
[Written by Guilhe, Desrenaudes, etc.]

Tamayo de Vargas (Tomas). Restavracion de la civdad del Salvador, ibaìa de Todos-Sanctos, en la provincia del Brasil. Por las armas de Philippe iv. 7 p. l. 178, 4 l. sm. 4°. *Madrid, Alonso Martin,* 1628.

Tannenberg (Constant Wurzbach von). *See* **Wurzbach** von Tannenberg.

Tanner (Henry S.) Memoir on the recent surveys, observations, and internal improvements in the U. S. To accompany his new map of the U. S. 108 pp. 16°. *Philadelphia, H. S. Tanner,* 1829.

Tansillo (Luigi). The nurse, a poem. Translated from the Italian by W. Roscoe. 3d ed. 31, 89; 34 pp. 18°. *Liverpool, Cadell & Davies,* 1800.

Tappan (David, *D. D.*) Two friendly letters from Toletus to Philalethes, [the Rev. Samuel Spring, *D. D.*] containing remarks on his dialogue on the nature of duty. 136 pp. 12°. *Newburyport, John Mycall,* 1785.

Tarbox (*Rev.* Increase Niles). Missionary patriots. Memoirs of James H. Schneider and Edward M. Schneider. 357 pp. 2 pl. 16°. *Boston, Mass. S. S. soc.* 1867.

Targioni-Tozzetti (Giovanni). Notizie sulla storia della scienze fisiche in Toscana, cavate da un manoscritto inedito. xxvii, 335 pp. 4°. *Firenze, Im. biblioteca palatina,* 1852. s.

Tarleton (*Lt. col.* Banastre). A history of the campaigns of 1780 and 1781, in the southern provinces of North America. vii, 533 pp. 8°. *Dublin, Colles and others,* 1787.

Taschereau (Jules Antoine). Histoire de la vie et des ouvrages de Molière. vi, 448 pp. 1 portrait. 8°. *Paris, Ponthieu,* 1825.

Tasistro (Louis Fitzgerald). Etiquette of Washington. 30 pp. 18°. *Washington, W. H. & O. H. Morrison,* 1866.

Tasso (Torquato). La Gervsalemme liberata. Con le annotationi di Scipion Gentili, e di Givlio Guastauini, et li argomenti di Oratio Ariosti. Figurata da Bernardo Castelli. [Ed. 4ª.] 8 p. l. 255, 71, 40 pp. 22 pl. sm. fol. *Genova, Givseppe Pauoni,* 1617.

—— The same. Con le figure di Bernardo Castelli, e le annotationi di Scipio Gentili e di Givlio Guastivini. Aggiuntovi la vita dell' autore scritta da Gio. Battista Manso. [Publicata da N. F. Haym]. 2 v. 12 p. l. 331 pp; 375, 122 pp. 3 l. 20 pl. 4°. *Londra, G. Tonson & G. Watts,* 1724.

Tastu (Sabine Casimire Amable Voïart, *madame*). Chroniques de France. 3ᵉ éd. 315 pp. 1 pl. 18°. *Paris, Didier,* 1839. s.

Tate (George). The ancient British sculptured rocks of Northumberland and the eastern borders, etc. 46 pp. 12 pl. 4°. *Alnwick, author,* 1865. s.

—— The history of the borough, castle, and barony of Alnwick, with notices of the antiquities, geology, botany, and zoology of the district. v. 1. vi, 484, iv pp. 9 pl. 8°. *Alnwick, H. H. Blair,* 1866. s.

Tate (Nahum). Version of the Psalms. *See* **Brady** (Nicholas), *and* **Tate.**

Tate (Thomas). Notes on a voyage to the Arctic seas in 1863. 50 pp. 16°. *Alnwick, [Eng.] H. H. Blair,* 1864. s.

Tatem (John H.) The monitor of the eastern star; containing the ritual of adoptive masonry, embraced in the eastern star degree, with forms, and rules of lodges. 88 pp. 1 pl. 24°. *Adrian, (Mich.) Holmes, Cook & Bonner,* [1867].

Tatham (William). Communications concerning the agriculture and commerce of America, with observations on the commerce of Spain with her American colonies in time of war. viii, 120 pp. 8°. *London, J. Ridgway,* 1800.

Tatnall (Edward). Catalogue of the phænogamous and filicoid plants of Newcastle county, Delaware. 112 pp. 8°. *Wilmington institute, [Philadelphia, Collins,]* 1860. s.

Tauler *or* **Thauler** (Johann). De vita et passione salvatoris nostri Jesu Christi piisima exercitia. Juxta primam versionem latinam denuo impressa. 461 pp. 24°. *Coloniæ, J. M. Heberle,* 1857.

Taunton (Mass.) directory, 1859. 234, 28 pp. 18°. *Taunton, (Mass.) S. O. Dunbar,* 1859.

Taverner (Richard). The garden of wysdome, conteynynge pleasaunt floures; that is to say, propre and quycke sayinges of princes, philosophers, [etc.] Drawē forth of good aucthours as well Grekes as Latyns. Newly recognised and augmented. 18°. *London, imprinted by Wyllyam Myddylton*, [1590].

Tawaststjerna (J. J.) *and* **Stähl** (Lorentz). Föreläsningar uti permanenta fortification, vid kongl. artilleri-läroverket på Marieberg. xxxi, 376 pp. 8°. *Stockholm, C. Deleen*, 1826. s.

Tayler (*Rev.* John James). A retrospect of the religious life of England; or, the church, puritanism, and free enquiry. xii, 563 pp. 8°. *London, J. Chapman*, 1845.

Taylor (Alfred Swaine). Medical jurisprudence. 3d Am. from 4th London ed. Edited, with additions, by Edward Hartshorne. 621 pp. 8°. *Philadelphia, Blanchard & Lea*, 1853. s.

Taylor (Bayard, *or* James Bayard). Colorado: a summer trip. 3 p. l. 185 pp. 12°. *New York, G. P. Putnam, & son*, 1867.

Taylor (Benjamin C.) Annals of the classis of Bergen, of the reformed Dutch church, and of the churches under its care; including the civil history of Bergen, N. J. 3d ed. 479 pp. 21 pl. 12°. *New York, board of publ. ref. Dutch ch.* [1857.]

Taylor (Charles Fayette). Infantile paralysis, and its attendant deformities. 119 pp. 12°. *Philadelphia, J. B. Lippincott & Co.* 1867.

Taylor (George, *of the bank of England*). The mental claims of the sexes relatively considered, with other poems. xi, 164 pp. 16°. *London, Adlard*, 1821.

Taylor (George), *and* **Skinner** (Andrew). Maps of the roads of Ireland, surveyed in 1777, and corrected down to 1783. 2d ed. 289 pp. of maps. 5 l. 2 maps. *London, T. Longman*, 1783.

Taylor (Isidore Justin Séverin, *baron*). Les Pyrénées. iv, 618 pp. 8°. *Paris, C. Gide*, 1843. s.

Taylor (*Rev.* James B.) Virginia baptist ministers. 2 v. 516 pp; 514 pp. 12°. *New York, Sheldon & Co.* 1860.

Taylor (*Mrs.* Jane). Wouldst know thyself! or, the outlines of human physiology. 65 pp. 12°. *New York, G. F. Cooledge*, 1858. s.

Taylor (*Mrs.* Janet). Lunar tables; by which the true distance is obtained from the apparent altitudes, [etc.] Likewise, a short treatise on the chronometer, [etc.] 3d ed. 20, 124 pp. 8°. *London, G. Taylor*, [1836]. s.

Taylor (Jeremy, *bishop of Down and Connor*). Discourse concerning prayer ex tempore; or, by pretence of the spirit. [*anon.*] 30 pp. sm. 4°. *London, R. Royston*, 1647.

[*With* TAYLOR (J.) Sermon preached in Saint Marie's church. *Oxford*, 1638].

——— Of the sacred order, and offices of episcopacy, by divine institution, apostolicall tradition, and catholike practice. 8 p. l. 386 pp. 1 pl. sm. 4°. *Oxford, L. Lichfield*, 1642.

[*With his* sermon in Saint Marie's church. *Oxford*, 1638].

——— Rules and advices to the clergy of [his] diocese. 20 pp. 8°. *Oxford*, 1825.

[*With* RANDOLPH (John, *bishop of London*). Enchiridion theologicum, v. 1].

——— Sermon preached in Saint Marie's church in Oxford, vpon the anniversary of the gunpowder treason. 5 p. l. 64 pp. sm. 4°. *Oxford, L. Lichfield*, 1638.

——— Theologia eklektike: a discourse of the liberty of prophesying. 48, 267 pp. sm. 4°. *London, R. Royston*, 1647.

[*With* TAYLOR (J.) Sermon preached in Saint Marie's church. *Oxford*, 1638].

Taylor (John). Pocket lacon; comprising nearly one thousand extracts from the best authors. 2 v. ii, 264; 252 pp. 18°. *Philadelphia, Lea & Blanchard*, 1839.

Taylor (John Edward). Michael Angelo, considered as a philosophic poet. With translations. iv, 139 pp. 16°. *London, Saunders & Otley*, 1840.

Taylor (Philip Meadows). Sketches of the Deccan. Drawn on stone by Weld Taylor, E. Morton, and G. Childs. 20 pl. fol. *London, Charles Tilt*, 1837.

Taylor (Richard Cowling). Two reports on the coal lands, mines, and improvements of the Dauphin and Susquehanna coal company, and of the geological examinations of the Stony creek coal estate, etc. iii, 74 pp. 5 maps. 8°. *Philadelphia, E. G. Dorsey*, 1840. s.

Taylor (William Cooke). Pictorial history of France and Normandy, to the present time. 512 pp. 8°. *Philadelphia, Thomas, Cowperthwait & Co.* 1848.

Taylor and his generals; a biography of major-general Zachary Taylor, and sketches of the lives of generals Worth, Wool, Twiggs, and Scott. [*anon.*] 318 pp. 16°. *Philadelphia, E. H. Butler & Co.* 1847.

Tchihatcheff, *or* **Tschihatscheff** (Pierre de). Coup d'oeil sur la constitution géologique des provinces méridionales du royaume de Naples. Suivi de quelques notions sur Nice et ses environs. 284 pp. 2 maps. 8°. *Berlin, S. Schropp & Co.* 1842. s.

Techener (Jacques Joseph, *editor*). *See* **Bulletin** du bibliophile, etc.

Tegg (Thomas). Chronology, or the historian's companion; being an authentic register of events, from the earliest period to the present time, with a list of eminent men. 7th ed. xxiv, 324 pp. 1 pl. 16°. *London, T. Tegg*, 1831.

Teichmeyer (Hermann Friedrich). Elementa anthropologiae; sive, theoria corporis hvmani. Ed. alt. 8 p. l. 286 pp. 9 l. 1 pl. 4°. *Ienae, J. F. Bielck*, 1739. s.

——— Elementa philosophiæ natvralis experimentalis. 4 p. l. 259 pp. 12 l. 5 pl. 4°. *Ienae, J. F. Bielck*, 1733. s.

——— Institvtiones materiae medicae, sive introitvs apertvs ad materiam medicam et methodvm medendi. 4 p. l. 234 pp. 7 l. 4°. *Ienae, J. A. Melchior*, 1737. s.

[*With* the preceding].

——— Institvtiones medicinae legalis vel forensis. Ed. 3[a]. 4 p. l. 256 pp. 12 l. 4°. *Ienae, J. F. Bielck*, 1740. s.

Teissier (Antoine). Catalogus avctorvm qui librorvm catalogos, indices, bibliothecas, virorum litteratorum elogia, vitas, aut orationes funebres, scriptis consignarunt. Cvm Philippi Labbæi bibliotheca nummaria, [etc.] 2 v. in 1. 4 p. l. 559 pp; 3 p. l. 368, 30 pp. 4°. *Genevae, S. de Tovrnes*, 1686–1705. s.

Telegraph secrets. [Nine tales.] By a stationmaster. [*anon.*] 122 pp. 16°. *London, C. H. Clarke*, [1866].

Temminck (Conrad Jacob). Observations sur la classification méthodique des oiseaux, et remarques sur l'Analyse d'une nouvelle ornithologie élémentaire par L. P. Vieillot. 60 pp. 8°. *Amsterdam, G. Dufour*, 1817. s.

——— *and* **Meiffren-Laugier**, *baron* de Chartrouse. Nouveau recueil de planches coloriées d'oiseaux, pour servir de suite et de complément aux planches enluminées de Buffon, d'après les dessins de Huet et Prêtre. 5 v. 4°. *Paris, etc. F. G. Levrault, etc.* [1820–38]. s.

CONTENTS.

v. 1. Rapaces.
v. 2. Rapaces, (continued); omnivores; insectivoræ.
v. 3. Insectivoræ, (continued); granivoræ; zygodactylæ.
v. 4. Zygodactylæ, (continued); anisodactylæ; alcyones; chelidones; columbæ.
v. 5. Gallinæ; alectorides; cursores; grallatores; pinnatipedes; palmipedes; inertes.

Temple (*Sir* William, *and others*). Letters, containing an account of the most important transactions that pass'd in christendom, 1665–1672. Published by Jonathan Swift. 2 v. in 1. 5 p. l. 520 pp; 360 pp. 12°. *London, J. Tonson*, 1700.

Temple (The) choir: a collection of sacred and secular music. By Theodore F. Seward, assisted by Dr. Lowell Mason and Wm. B. Bradbury. 384 pp. obl. 16°. *New York, Mason bros.* [1867].

Templeman (Thomas). A new survey of the globe; or, an accurate mensuration of all the empires, kingdoms, countries, etc. in the world. 2 p. l. x pp. 35 tab. obl. 4°. *London, T. Cole*, [1776]? s.

Tennent (*Rev.* Gilbert). The espousals; or, a passionate perswasive to a marriage with the lamb of God. 51 pp. 12°. *Boston, Thomas Fleet*, 1741.

[*With* WALLEY (*Rev.* Thomas). Balm in Gilead. *Cambridge*, 1670].

——— The necessity of holding fast the truth represented in three sermons on Rev. iii: 3. To which are added, a sermon on the priestly office of Christ, and another on the virtue of charity. vi, 110 pp. 16°. *Boston, S. Kneeland & T. Green*, 1743.

——— Sermons on important subjects, lately preached in Philadelphia. xxxvii, 429 pp. 16°. *Philadelphia, James Chattin*, 1758.

Tennessee. House journal. [1st] and 2d extra sessions of the 33d general assembly. 8°. *Nashville*, 1861.

[*With* SENATE journal].

——— The same. Appendix to House journal, 1865–66. 8°. *Nashville*, 1865–66.

——— The same. [1st] and 2d adjourned session of the 34th general assembly, 1865–67. 2 v. 8°. *Nashville, S. C. Mercer*, 1867.

——— Senate journal. [1st] and 2d extra sessions of the 33d general assembly. 2 v. 8°. *Nashville, J. O. Griffith & Co.* 1861.

——— The same. [1st] and 2d adjourned session of the [34th] general assembly, 1865–[67]. 2 v. 8°. *Nashville, S. C. Mercer*, 1867.

——— Report of the comptroller of the treasury to the 35th general assembly, Oct. 1867. 83 pp. 8°. *Nashville, S. C. Mercer*, 1867.

Tenore (Michele). Essai sur la géographie physique et botanique du royaume de Naples. 3 p. l. 130 pp. 2 maps. 8°. *Naples, Imprimerie française*, 1827. s.

Tenré (L.) Les états américains, leurs produits, leur commerce, en vue de l'exposition universelle de Paris. viii, 328 pp. 8°. *Paris, Plon*, 1867.

Tentzel (Wilhelm Ernst). Saxonia nvmismatica, oder medaillen-cabinet von bedächtniss-müntzen und schau-pfennigen, [etc.] sive nvmmophylacivm nvmismatvm mnemonicorvm et iconicorvm a serenissimis electoribvs dvcibvsqve Saxoniæ lineæ albertinæ collectvm, [etc.] 8 v. in 4. 4°. *Dressden, J. Rieldel,* 1705–12. S.

Terentius Afer (Publius). Comoediae, ex recensione Danielis Heinsii, cum italica versione. Recensuit, notasque antiquam artem comicam, et nonnulla antiquitatum romanarum monumenta illustrantes addidit Carolus Cocquelines. 2 v. 4 p. l. xxxxii, 254 pp; 252 pp. fol. *Romæ, N. Roisech,* 1767.

——— Fabvlae, anglicae factae opera R[ichardi] B[ernardi. Latin and English]. Ed. 2ª. 4 p. l. 455 pp. 8°. *Cantabrigiae, J. Legat,* 1607.

[Imperfect: wanting parts of pp. 33–34, and pp. 449–50].

Terhune (Mary Virginia Hawes). Sunnybank. [A novel]. By Marion Harland. [*pseudon.*] 12°. *New York, Sheldon & Co.* 1866.

Terme (Jean François). Des eaux potables à distribuer pour l'usage des particuliers et le service public; rapport présenté au conseil municipal de Lyon. 259 pp. 8°. *Paris,* 1844. S.

Ternaux-Compans (Henri). Archives des voyages; ou, collection d'anciennes relations inédites ou très-rares, de lettres, mémoires, itinéraires et autres documents relatifs à la géographie et aux voyages. 2 v. 477, iii pp; 474, vi pp. 8°. *Paris, A. Bertrand,* [1840–41].

Territorial company. Plan of association of the territorial company, established April, 1795. 21 pp. 8°. *Philadelphia, R. Aitken & son,* 1795.

Terry (*Rev.* Edward). Voyage to East India, within the empire of the great Mogul. Reprinted from the ed. of 1655. xix, 511 pp. 8°. *London, J. Wilkie,* 1777.

Terver (——). Catalogue des mollusques terrestres et fluviatiles observés dans les possessions françaises au nord de l'Afrique. 39 pp. 3 pl. 8°. *Paris, etc. J. B. Baillière, etc.* 1839. S.

Tesauro (Emanuele). Arte de cartas missivas; o, methodo general para redvcir al papel quantas materias pide el politico comercio, [etc]. Tradvce en Español M. Migliavaca. 8 p. l. 243 pp. 8°. *Valencia, J. de Baeza,* 1696. S.

——— Philosophia moral, derivada de la alta fvente del grande Aristoteles stagarita. Escribidla en Toscano. Traducela en español don Gomez de la Rocha y Figveroa. 11 p. l. 455 pp. 8°. *Barcelona, J. Llopis,* 1694. S.

Tessin (Carl Gustav, *count*). Museum tessinianum. Naturalie-samling. 4 p. l. 132 pp. 12 pl. fol. *Holmiæ,* [*auctor,*] 1753. S.

Test (The). [A political newspaper, published weekly]. No. 1–35. Nov. 6, 1756 to July 9, 1757. 204 pp. sm. fol. *London, S. Hooper,* 1756–57.

[*Note.* No more published].

Testaments (The) of the twelve patriarches, the sonnes of Jacob, translated out of Greek into Latine by Robert Grosthead, now Englished by A[rthur] G[olding]. 83 l. 18°. *London, Company of the stationers,* 1806.

[Imperfect: wanting all after leaf 83].

Tétot (*Archiviste*). Répertoire des traités de paix, de commerce, d'alliance, etc. conventions et autres actes conclus entre toutes les puissances du globe, principalement depuis la paix de Westphalie jusqu'à nos jours. Table générale des recueils de Dumont, Wenck, Martens, Samwer, etc. Partie chronologique, 1493–1866. 2 p. l. viii, 463 pp. 8°. *Paris, Amyot,* 1866.

Teufel (Albert). Life, adventures, and confessions of Albert Teufel, convicted of the murder of James Wiley, with his trial, etc. by Arrelsee [R. L. C.] 72, 32 pp. 8°. *Doylestown, (Pa.) W. W. H. Davis,* 1867.

Tewrdannkhs *or* **Theuerdannckhs.** *See* **Pfinzing** (Melchior). Die geüerlicheiten, etc.

Texas. Journal of the house of representatives. 11th legislature. 938, xliii pp. 8°. *Austin,* 1866.

——— Journal of the senate. 11th legislature. 657, xxix pp. 8°. *Austin,* 1866.

——— Report of joint select committee [on] the burning of Brenham. 54 pp. 8°. *Austin,* 1866.

[*With* TEXAS. Journal of the house of representatives. 11th legislature. 8°. *Austin,* 1866].

——— Report [on] state lunatic asylum, 1866. 76 pp. 8°. *Austin,* 1866.

[*With* TEXAS. Journal house of representatives. 11th legislature. 8°. *Austin,* 1866].

Texas, an English question. [*anon.*] 40 pp. 8°. *London, E. Wilson,* 1837.

Textor (Cajetan). Grundzüge zur lehre der chirurgischen operationen, welche mit bewaffneter hand unternommen werden. xix, 447 pp. 8°. *Würzburg, Stahel,* 1834–35. S.

Textor (Carl, *M. D.*) Versuch über das vorkommen der harnsteine in Ostfranken. viii, 88 pp. 4°. *Würzburg, F. E. Thein,* 1843. S.

Teyler van der Hulst (Pieter). Musée Teyler à Harlem. Catalogue de la bibliothèque. vi, 228 pp. 8°. *Harlem, Loosjes,* 1865. S.

Thaarup (Frederik). Faedrenclandsk nekrolog, eller efterretninger om de ved stilling og virksomhed udmærkede og ellers bekjendte afdöde, 1821–26. x, 520 pp. 8°. *Kjöbenhavn, Forfatter*, 1835–44. s.

Thackeray (William Makepeace). Early and late papers, hitherto uncollected. vi, 407 pp. 1 pl. 16°. *Boston, Ticknor & Fields*, 1867.

Thaer (Albrecht). The principles of agriculture. Translated by William Shaw and W. Johnson. 552 pp. 8°. *New York, Greeley & McElrath*, 1841. s.
[Farmer's library, v. 1].

Thalatta! or, the great commoner. A political romance. [*anon.*] vii, 371 pp. 16°. *London, Parker, son, & Bourn*, 1862.

Thalén (Robert). Spectralanalys, exposé och historik. [Extract.] 3 p. l. 68, 54 pp. 1 tab. 8°. *Upsala, Universitet*, 1866. s.

Thaxter (Thomas, *M. D.*) A narrative of the proceedings in the north parish of Hingham, from the time of Rev. Dr. Ware's leaving it, to the ordination of Rev. Joseph Richardson over the first church, and Mr. Henry Colman over the third church. [*anon.*] 84, 52 pp. 8°. *Salem, Joshua Cushing*, 1807.

Thayer (*Capt.* Simeon). Journal describing the perils and sufferings of the army under col. Benedict Arnold, in its march to Quebec.
[*With* STONE (Edwin M.) Invasion of Canada in 1775. pp. 1–45. *Providence*, 1867].

Thayer (William M.) Youth's history of the rebellion, [v. 1.] Sumter to Roanoke. 5th ed. xiii, 347 pp. 4 pl. 16°. *Boston, Walker, Wise & Co.* 1864.

Theocritus. Theocriti aliorvmqve poetarvm idyllia. Eiusdem epigrammata. Omnia cum interpretatione latina. In virgilianas et nas[onianas] imitatiões Theocriti obseruationes H. Stephani. 654 pp. 24°. [*n. p.*] *H. Stephanus*, 1579.

——— The same. Works. Translated by F. Fawkes. 8°. *Edinburgh*, 1792.
[ANDERSON'S British poets. v. 5].

Theoctistus. Sententiæ, etc.
[*With* ISOCRATES. Paræenesis. Ed. 1699].

Theodoretus. Historia ecclesiastica.
[*With* HISTORIAE eccl. scriptores graeci J. Christophorsono interprete, 1581 ed.]

——— The same. Versa ab Epiphanio.
[*With* AUCTORES hist. eccl. fol. *Basileae*, 1523.]

——— The same. Ecclesiastical history, translated and abridged by Mr. [Samuel] Parker.
[*With* ECCLESIASTICAL histories, etc. 3d ed. 4°. *London*, 1729].

Theognis. Gnomologici libri duo. [Græce et Latine].
[*With* NEANDER (Michael). Opus aureum, etc. *Lipsiae*, 1777].

Theophrastus. De historia plantarum libri decem græcè et latinè. Latinam Gazae versionem nova interpretatione, notis, item rariorum plantarum iconibus illustravit J. Bodaeus à Stapel. Accesserunt Julii Cæsaris Scaligeri animadversiones, et Roberti Constantini annotationes. 10 p. l. 1187 pp. 44 l. fol. *Amstelodami, H. Laurentius*, 1644. s.

——— The same. Emendavit, cum adnotatione critica edidit Fridericus Wimmer. xlviii, 348 pp. 8°. *Vratislaviæ, F. Hirt*, 1842. s.

Théry (Augustin François). Histoire de l'éducation en France depuis le cinquième siècle jusqu'à nos jours. 2e éd. 2 v. 412 pp; 528 pp. 16°. *Paris, Dezobry, Magdeleine et Cie.* 1861.

Thévenot (Melchisedech). The art of swimming. With advice for bathing. Done out of French. 3d ed. 11 p. l. 50 pp. 40 pl. 18°. *London, J. Lever*, 1789.

Thevet (André). Les singvlaritez de la France antarctiqve, avtrement nommée Amérique; et de plusieurs terres et isles découertes de nostre temps. 8 p. l. 166 pp. 2 l. sm. 4°. *Paris, les héritiers de Maurice de La Porte*, 1557.

Thiébault (Dieudonné). Original anecdotes of Frederick the Great, king of Prussia, and of his family, his court, his ministers, his academies, and his literary friends. From the French. 2 v. x, 433 pp; iv, 438 pp. 8°. *Philadelphia, for Robert Gray, Alexandria*, 1806.

Thiébault (Paul Charles François Adrien Henri Dieudonné, *baron* de). Manuel général du service des états-majors généraux et divisionnaires dans les armees. xvi, 592 pp. 1 tab. 8°. *Paris, Magimel*, 1813. s.

Thiébaut de Berneaud (Arsène). Voyage à Ermenonville, contenant des anecdotes inédites sur J. J. Rousseau. vii, 300 pp. 1 pl. 16°. *Paris, P. F. Dupont*, 1819.

Thieme (Friedrich Wilhelm). Anfangsgründe der theoretischen und praktischen chemie. viii, 232 pp. 5 pl. 12°. *Leipzig, G. Wigand*, 1839. s.

Thierry (Amédée Simon Dominique). Histoire d'Attila et de ses successeurs jusqu' à l'établissement des Hongrois en Europe. Suivie des légendes et traditions. 2 v. xv, 455 pp; 2 p. l. 463 pp. 8°. *Paris, Didier & Cie.* 1856.

——— Histoire des Gaulois, depuis les temps les plus reculés jusqu'à l'entière soumission de la Gaule à la domination romaine. 3e éd. 3 v. 8°. *Paris, J. Labitte*, 1845. s.

Thierry (Jacques Nicolas Augustin). Récits des temps mérovingiens; précédés de considérations sur l'histoire de France. 2e éd. 2 v. 463 pp; 448 pp. 8°. *Paris, J. Tessier,* 1842. s.

——— Histoire de la conquête de l'Angleterre, par les Normands, de ses causes et de ses suites jusqu'à nos jours. 6e éd. 4 v. 8°. Atlas, 1 p. l. 32 pp. 14 pl. obl. 4°. *Paris, J. Tessier,* 1843. s.

Thierry (Jean, *of Langres*). Homiliarius doctorum, qui omeliarius dici solet: in euangelia sacratissima dierum dominicalium ac seriatorum: qui pone pilares militantis ecclesie Hieronymum: Augustinum: Ambrosium: Gregorium: Origenem: Io. Chrysostomum: Bedam: et complures permagne litterature doctores affabre obseruabatur. Cum additis sanctorum sermonibus. 143, 63 l. fol. *Lugduni, Io. Clein,* 1516.

Thiers (Louis Adolphe). Histoire de la révolution française, annotée par Félix Wouters. 10 v. 8°. *Bruxelles, Wouters frères,* 1845–49.

——— The same. The history of the French revolution. Translated, with notes and illustrations, by Frederick Shoberl. 3d Am. ed. 4 v. in 2. 8°. *Philadelphia, Carey & Hart,* 1844.

——— Histoire du consulat et de l'empire, annotée par Félix Wouters. v. 1–11. 8°. *Bruxelles, Ve Wouters,* 1846–51.
[Imperfect; v. 10 wanting].

Thiersch (Bernhardt). Ueber das zeitalter und vaterland des Homer. 2e aufl. nebst der quaestio de diversa Iliadis et Odysseæ aetate. viii, 328 pp. 8°. *Halberstadt, F. A. Helm,* 1832. s.

Thiersch (Friedrich Wilhelm). Ueber gelehrte schulen, mit besonderer rücksicht auf Bayern. 2 v. 8°. *Stuttgart, J. G. Cotta,* 1826–27. s.
[V. ii, pt. i, and v. iii wanting].

Thilenius (Moriz Gerhard). Medicinische und chirurgische bemerkungen. 2 v. lxii, 334 pp. 1 tab. 1 pl; xxxii, 534 pp. 8°. *Frankfurt am Main, H. L. Brönner,* 1809–14. s.

Thilo (G.) Die preussische disziplinargesetzgebung für die unmittelbaren und mittelbaren staatsbeamten. viii, 187 pp. 8°. *Berlin, J. Guttentag,* 1864.

Thomas Aquinas. *See* **Aquino** (Tommaso d')

Thomas (*Rev.* Abel C.) Autobiography. 408 pp. 1 pl. 12°. *Boston, J. M. Usher,* 1852.

Thomas (Elizabeth). Pylades and Corinna; or, memoirs of the lives, amours, and writings of Richard Gwinnett and Mrs. Elizabeth Thomas; letters and miscellaneous pieces; [with] life of Corinna [by herself]. xi, lxxx, 287 pp. 8°. *London,* 1731.
[Imperfect: wanting 1 pl.]

Thomas (Frederick William). An autobiography of William Russell. [*anon.*] 119 pp. 8°. *Baltimore, Gobright, Thorne & Co.* 1852.

——— Howard Pinckney. 159 pp. 8°. *London,* 1841.
[Hazlitt's romancist and novelist's lib. v. 2].

——— Sketches of character, and tales founded on fact. 117 pp. 12°. *Louisville,* 1849.

Thomas (John J.) American fruit culturist. Illustrated. 511 pp. 12°. *New York, W. Wood & Co.* 1867.

——— Farm implements, and the principles of their construction and use, etc. 267 pp. 12°. *New York, Harpers,* 1854. s.

Thomas (Louis, *of Leipzig*). Das buch der welt. 3 v. in 1. 8°. *Leipzig, O. Spamer,* 1854–55.

CONTENTS.

v. 1. Wanderungen durch die ruinen der vergangenheit und die riesenwerke der gegenwart. Von Louis Thomas. viii, 192 pp. 5 pl.
v. 2, Abtheil. 1. Wanderungen nach nord und süd, ost und west, etc. Die alte welt, von Friedrich Körner. 2 p. l. 190 pp. 2 pl.
v. 2, Abtheil. 2. The same. Gesittetes und wildes leben in der neuen welt, von Julius Moritz. vi, 182 pp. 1 pl.

Thomas (R. *A. M.*) An authentic account of the most remarkable events: containing the lives of the most noted pirates, and piracies. Also, the most remarkable shipwrecks and disasters on the sea. 298, 360 pp. 25 pl. 16°. *New York, Ezra Strong,* 1837.

Thomas (Robert, *M. D.*) The modern practice of physic, exhibiting the characters, causes, etc. and method of treating the diseases of all climates. Abridged by W. Currie and D. F. Condie. vi, 515 pp. 8°. *Philadelphia, Dobson & son,* 1817.

Thomas (William). The historie of Italie, intreating of the astate of many and divers common weales. 7 p. l. 216 l. sm. 4°. *London, Thomas Berthelet,* 1549.

Thomassy (Marie Joseph Raymond). Jean Gerson et le grand schisme d'Occident. 2e éd. lxii, 375 pp. 16°. *Paris, Perisse,* 1852. s.

——— Les papes géographes, et la cartographie du Vatican. 140 pp. 8°. *Paris, A. Bertrand,* 1852. s.

Thomassy (R.) Géologie pratique de la Louisiane. lxviii, 264 pp. 6 maps. 4°. *Nouvelle-Orléans, (printed at Paris), auteur,* 1860. s.

Thomé de Gamond. *See* **Gamond.**

Thomé de Jésus, *born* **Andrade** (Thomé). Les souffrances de notre-seigneur Jésus Christ. En Français par le P. Alleaume. Nouv. éd. 3 v. 16°. *Lyon, J. B. Kindelem,* 1820.

Thomes (William H.) The bushrangers; a Yankee's adventures during his second visit to Australia. 480 pp. 12°. *Boston, Lee & Shepard,* 1866.

Thompson (Daniel Pierce). May Martin; or, the money diggers. 48 pp. 8°. *London,* 1841.
[HAZLITT's romancist and novelist's lib. v. 1].

Thompson (*Rev.* Edward). Popular lectures upon the differences between the church of England and the church of Rome. xx, 417 pp. 8°. *London, Hatchard & son,* 1845.

Thompson (Pishey). Collections for a topographical and historical account of Boston, and the hundred of Skirbeck, in the county of Lincoln. iv, 382, 84 pp. 5 pl. 1 tab. 8°. *London, Longman,* 1820. S.

Thompson (*General* Waddy). Recollections of Mexico. x, 304 pp. 8°. *New York, etc. Wiley & Putnam,* 1846. S.

Thompson (*Elder* Wilson). Autobiography. With a history of the old order of regular baptist churches. 497 pp. 1 pl. 12°. *Cincinnati, Moore, Wilstach & Baldwin,* 1867.

Thompson (Zadock). A gazetteer of the state of Vermont. 310 pp. 2 l. 1 map. 3 pl. 16°. *Montpelier, E. P. Walton,* 1824.

——— The Green Mountain repository for the year 1832. v. 1. 284 pp. 12°. *Burlington, (Vt.) Edward Smith,* 1832.

——— History of the state of Vermont to 1832. 252 pp. 16°. *Burlington, (Vt.) Edward Smith,* 1833.

——— History of Vermont, natural, civil, and statistical, in three parts. iv, 224, 224, 204 pp. 8°. *Burlington, author,* 1842. S.

Thomson (C. G.) Skandinaviens coleoptera synoptiskt bearbetade. 8 v. 8°. *Lund, Författare,* 1860–66. S.
[v. 1 wanting].

Thomson (James). Poetical works. 8°. *Edinburgh,* 1794.
[Anderson's British poets, v. 9].

Thomson (*Mrs.* Katherine Byerley). Memoirs of the life of Sir Walter Raleigh. 287 pp. 12°. *Philadelphia, Gihon & Smith,* 1846.

Thomson (William). Military memoirs, relating to campaigns, battles, and stratagems of war, antient and modern. xxiv, 588 pp. 8°. *London, J. Johnson,* 1804.

Thorburn (Grant). Forty years' residence in America, written by himself. 264 pp. 12°. *Boston, Russell, Odiorne & Metcalf,* 1834.

——— Men and manners in Britain, being notes from a journal in 1833–4. 187 pp. 12°. *New York, Wiley & Long,* 1834.

Thorley (*Rev.* John). Melisselogia; or the female monarchy, being an enquiry into the nature, order, and government of bees. xliii, 206 pp. 5 pl. 8°. *London, J. Thorley,* 1744.

Thorn (——, *gov. of the province of Luxembourg*). Exposé de la situation administrative de la province de Luxembourg, adressé à la ministère de l'intérieur. 131, viii pp. 31 tab. 8°. *Arlon,* 1834.

Thornthwaite (W. H.) A guide to photography, containing simple and concise directions for obtaining views, portraits, etc. and the method of taking stereoscopic pictures, etc. 15th ed. 2 p. l. 120 pp. 12°. *London, Simpkin, Marshall & Co.* 1858. S.

Thornton (John Wingate). The first records of Anglo-American colonization. 12 pp. 8°. *Boston, Gould & Lincoln,* 1859.

——— A genealogical memoir of the Gilbert family, in both old and New England. 23 pp. 1 pl. 8°. [*Boston, author,*] 1850.

Thornton (Robert John). The British flora; or, genera and species of British plants: arranged after the reformed sexual system, [etc.] 5 v. in 1. 8°. *London, author,* 1812. S.
[Wanting plates].

Thornton (William, *M.D.*) Cadmus; or, a treatise on the elements of written language. With an essay on teaching the deat and dumb to speak. 110 pp. 1 tab. 8°. *Philadelphia, R. Aitken,* 1793.

——— The same. 8°. *Philadelphia,* 1793. S.

——— Outlines of a constitution for United North and South Columbia. 14 pp. 8°. *Washington,* 1815. S.
[*With* THORNTON (W.) Cadmus.]

——— Political economy; founded in justice and humanity. By W. T. [*anon.*] 24 pp. 8°. *Washington, S. H. Smith,* 1804. S.
[*With* THORNTON (W.) Cadmus.]

Thorowgood (*Rev.* Thomas). Iewes in America; or, probabilities that the Americans are of that race. 20 p. l. 136 pp. 3 l. sm. 4°. *London, Tho. Slater,* 1650.

——— Jews in America; or, probabilities that those Indians are Judaical made more probable by some additionals to the former conjectures. [With a] discourse of John Elliot touching their origination, and the vindication of the planters. 5 p. l. 33 pp. 4 l. 28, 67 pp. sm. 4°. *London, Henry Brome,* 1660.

Thorpe (Benjamin). Analecta anglo-saxonica. A selection, in prose and verse, from Anglo-Saxon authors of various ages; with a glossary. xii, 268 pp. 8°. *London, J. & A. Arch,* 1834. S.

Thorvaldsen (Bertel). Den danske billedhugger Bertel Thorvaldsen og hans værker, ved J. M. Thiele. 2 v. xxiv, 174 pp; 196 pp. atlas, 2 v. 81 pl; 78 pl. 4°. *Kjöbenhavn, Thiele,* 1831–32. s.

——— The same. Thorvaldsen og hans værker. Texten forkortet efter Thiele, ved F. C. Hillerup. 2 v. 1 p. l. 44 pp. 2 tab. 79 pl; 1 p. l. 58 pp. 79 pl. [80—158.] 4°. *Kjöbenhavn, C. A. Reitzel,* 1842–43. s.

Thou (Jacques Auguste de). The history of the bloody massacres of the protestants in 1572, written in Latin, and translated into English. [By Edward Stephens]. 3 p. l. 66 pp. sm. 4°. *London, John Leigh,* 1674.

——— A true narration of that horrible conspiracy against king James and the whole parliament of England, commonly called the gun-powder treason, translated from Latin into English. [By Edward Stephens]. 24 pp. sm. 4°. *London, John Leigh,* 1674.

[*With* THOU (J. A. de). History of the bloody massacres. *London,* 1674].

Thoughts on the Canada bill now depending in parliament. [*anon.*] 50 pp. 8°. *London, J. Debrett,* 1791.

Thouvenel (Pierre). Mélanges d'histoire naturelle, de physique, et de chimie. Mémoires sur l'aérologie et l'électrologie. [*anon.*] 3 v. 8°. *Paris, Valade,* 1806. s.

Three ballads concerning the times: consisting of, i. The royal embassy. ii. A humoursom ditty to Dr. Sacheverell's back friends. iii. A cure for religious disputes. [*anon.*] 8 pp. 16°. *London,* [*about* 1710].

Three (The) holy kings. [*anon.*] 3 p. l. 31 pp. 6 photog. pl. 8°. *New York, Hurd & Houghton,* 1868.

Three letters to lord Brougham on the execution in Upper Canada of the traitors Lount and Matthews. By a British subject. [From the London Times. *anon.*] 18 pp. 8°. *London, John Murray,* [1838?]

Three (The) rivals; or Theodora, the Spanish widow. Translated from the French. [*anon.*] 26 pp. 8°. *London,* [1841?]

[Hazlitt's romancist and novelist's library, v. 5].

Three years among the working classes of the United States. By the author of "Autobiography of a beggar boy. [*anon.*] 12°. *London,* 1865.

Three years in field hospitals of the army of the Potomac. By Mrs. H. [*anon.*] 131 pp. 12°. *Philadelphia, J. B. Lippincott & Co.* 1867.

Throsby (John). New copper-plate magazine, containing select views of noblemen's and gentlemen's seats in England. From original drawings. 82 pl. obl. 4°. *London, Edwards,* [*about* 1795].

Thucydides. [De bello peloponnesiaco libri viii]. Cvm commentariis antiqvis et valde vtilibvs. [Græce; edente Ant. Francino]. 6 p. l. 159 pp. 1 l. fol. *Florentiæ, Bernardus Junta,* 1526.

——— The same. The history of the Peloponnesian war. Translated from the Greek, [with] preliminary discourses, by William Smith. New ed. 2 v. xxiv, lxxi, 427 pp; 2 p. l. 398 pp. 1 map. 1 pl. 8°. *London, J. Walker & others,* 1812.

——— The same. Histoire grecque; traduite en Français, par J. B. Gail. 3 v. in 2. 8°. *Paris, Imprimerie royale,* 1829. s.

Thuet (Melchior Jacob). Disquisitiones anatomicæ psittacorum. 36 pp. 2 pl. 4°. *Turici, Orelli, Fuesslini et soc.* 1838. s.

Thun (Johann Paul). Verzeichniss neuer bücher mit einschluss der landkarten und sonstiger im buchhandel vorkommender artikel zu finden bei Julius Klinkhardt. 4er 7er jahrgang. 16 v. in 4. 12°. *Leipzig, Klinkhardt,* 1846–49. s.

Thunberg (Carl Peter). Reise durch einen theil von Europa, Afrika, und Asien, hauptsächlich in Japan, 1770–79. Aus dem Schwedischen frei übersetzt von Chr. H. Groskurd. 2 v. 10 p. l. 266 pp. 5 pl; 6 p. l. xvi, 264 pp. 8°. *Berlin, Haude & Spener,* 1792–94.

Thurn (Wilhelm Friedrich). Beiträge zur geschichte und kritik des verfahrens bei freihandiger ausziehung des kindes. iv, 195 pp. 8°. *Friedberg, Bindernagel,* 1860. s.

Thurston (Elizabeth A.) The little wrinkled old man: a christmas extravaganza; and other trifles. 124 pp. 16°. *Boston, W. V. Spencer,* 1866.

Thurston (J.) Illustrations of Lord Byron's poem, The corsair. 2 p. l. 7 pl. 8°. *London, T. Tegg,* 1814.

[Miscellaneous pamphlets, v. 56].

Tibullus (Albius). Elegies. Translated from the Latin by James Grainger. 8°. *Edinburgh,* [1792].

[Anderson's British poets, v. 5].

Tickell (Thomas). Poetical works. 8°. *Edinburgh,* 1794.

[Anderson's British poets, v. 8].

Ticknor (Almon). A key to Ticknor's mensuration, [etc.] 132 pp. 12°. *Pottsville, (Pa.) B. Bannan,* 1850. s.

——— The youth's columbian calculator: being an introductory course on arithmetic. 96 pp. 12°. *Pottsville, Pa. B. Bannan,* 1848. s.

Ticozzi (Stefano). Dizionario dei pittori dal rinnovamento delle belle arti fino al 1800. 2 v. xv, 328 pp; 363 pp. 8°. *Milano, V. Ferrario,* 1818.

Tieck (Christian Friedrich). Verzeichniss von werken der Della Robbia, majolica, glasmalereien, u. s. w. welche in den neben-sälen der sculpturen-gallerie des königl. museums zu Berlin aufgestellt sind. vi, 139 pp. 8°. *Berlin, Druckerei der k. akad. der wissenschaften,* 1835. s.

Tieck (Johann Ludwig). La réconciliation: légende, traduction de É. de La Bédollierre. 20 pp. 12°. *Paris,* 1842.
[*Included in* PLÉIADE, (La)].

Tiedemann (Friedrich). Icones cerebri simiarum et quorundam mammalium rariorum. 55 pp. 10 pl. fol. *Heidelbergae, Mohr & Winter,* 1821. s.

——— Anatomy of the foetal brain; with a comparative account of its structure in animals. Translated by William Bennett. xviii, 324 pp. 14 pl. 12°. *Edinburgh, Carfrae,* 1826. s.

Tiffany (Joel). A treatise on government and constitutional law, being an inquiry into the source and limitation of governmental authority, according to the American theory. 398, 179 pp. 8°. *Albany, W. C. Little,* 1867.

Tilke (Samuel Westcott). An autobiographical memoir, and a full description of his mode of treating diseases. xl, 399 pp. 1 pl. 8°. *London, S. W. Tilke,* 1840.

Tillard (John). Future rewards and punishments believed by the ancients; particularly the philosophers. [With] an address to freethinkers. [*anon.*] ix, 230 pp. 8°. *London, M. Steen,* 1740.

Tillet (Matthieu). Histoire d'un insecte qui devore les grains de L'Angoumois). *See* **Duhamel** du Monceau, *and* **Tillet**.

Tillier (Rodolphe). Translation of a memorial of Rodolphe Tillier's justification of the administration of Castorland, N. Y. 16 pp. 8°. *Rome, (N. Y.) Thos. Walker,* 1800.

Tilton (Theodore). The sexton's tale, and other poems. 173 pp. 16°. *New York, Sheldon & Co.* 1867.

Timberlake (*Lieut.* Henry). Memoirs of travels to and from the Cherokee nation, with a description of the country, government, genius, and customs of that nation. viii, 160 pp. 1 map. 8°. *London, J. Ridley,* 1765.

Timbs (John). English eccentrics and eccentricities. 2 v. viii, 319 pp; vii, 320 pp. 12°. *London, R. Bentley,* 1866.

——— Year book of facts in science and art [for 1866 and 1867]. 2 v. 16°. *London, Lockwood Co.* 1866–67.

Times (The). [London daily]. Oct. 1866 to Dec. 1867. 5 v. fol. *London,* 1866–67.

"**Times**" (The London) on the American war; a historical study. By L. S. [*anon.*] 107 pp. 8°. *London, W. Ridgway,* 1865.

Timkovski, (Georj). Reise nach China durch die Mongoley in der jahren, 1820 und 1821. Aus dem Russischen übersetzt von J. A. E. Schmidt. 3 v. in 1. 8°. *Wien, Kaulfuss & Krammer,* 1826. s.

Timmins (Samuel). The resources, products, and industrial history of Birmingham, and the midland hardware district. xiii, 721 pp. 8°. *London, R. Hardwicke,* 1866.

Tingry (P. F.) Painter and varnisher's guide. xlii, 540 pp. 5 pl. 8°. *London, G. Kearsley,* 1804.

Tiraboschi (Girolamo). Storia della letteratura italiana. 2ª ed. modenese [con notizie della vita di Tiraboschi dall' ab. C. Ciocchi]. 9 v. in 10. 4°. *Modena, Societa tipografica,* 1787–94. s.

Tischendorff (Lobgott Friedrich Constantin). Prolegomena. Commentarius. Tabulae. *See* **Bible** (*Greek*). Bibliorum codex sinaiticus, 1862.

Titan Agonistes; the story of an outcast. [*anon.*] 544 pp. 12°. *New York, G. W. Carleton & Co.* 1867.

Tite (William, *architect*). A descriptive catalogue of the antiquities found in the excavations at the new royal exchange, preserved in the museum of the corporation of London, etc. With some particulars and suggestions relating to Roman London. xlv, 96 pp. 1 l. 1 pl. 8°. *London, Corporation,* 1848. s.

Titus (*Col.* Silas). Killing no murder; briefly discoursed in three questions. [3d ed.] 2 p. l. 27 pp. sm. 4°. *London,* 1689.

Tixier de Ravisi (Jean). Epitheta. Praepositi fuerunt de prosodia lib. iv. cum perpulchris G. Sabini præceptis de carminibus. 134 pp. 501 l. 16°. *Tolosæ, Vidua J. Colomeri,* 1606.

——— Theatrvm poeticvm atqve historicvm; siue officina, post Conr. Lycosthenis vigilias redacta: cum cornvcopiæ libello. 16 p. l. 942 pp. 35 l. 16°. *Basileae, C. Waldkirch,* 1610.

Tobold (Adelbert). Chronic diseases of the larynx, with special reference to laryngoscopic and local therapeutics. Translated from the German, and edited by G. M. Beard. With an introduction. xvii, 270 pp. 8°. *New York, Wood & Co.* 1868.

Tocqueville (Charles Alexis Henri Maurice Clérel de). Oeuvres complètes. 9 v. 8°. *Paris, Lévy,* 1864–66.

CONTENTS.

v. 1–3. De la démocratie en Amérique.
v. 4. L'ancien régime et la révolution.
v. 5–7. Correspondance et oeuvres posthumes.
v. 8. Mélanges: fragments historiques, et notes sur l'ancien régime, la révolution, et l'empire. Notes de voyages.
v. 9. Études économiques, politiques et littéraires.

——— Démocratie en Amérique. 2 v. xxviii, 413 pp; 509 pp. 18°. *Bruxelles, Hauman et Cie.* 1835.

——— The same. [7e éd.?] v. 3–4 in 1. 8°. *Paris, C. Gosselin,* 1840.

Tod (*Col.* James). Travels in western India; embracing a visit to the sacred mounts of the Jains, and the most celebrated shrines of Hindu faith, between Rajpootana and the Indus. lx, 518 pp. 9 pl. 4°. *London, Allen & Co.* 1839.

Todd (Henry John). Illustrations of the lives and writings of Gower and Chaucer. xlvii, 394 pp. 2 pl. 8°. *London, Rivington,* 1810.

——— Life of archbishop Cranmer. 2 v. xxiv, 394 pp; xi, 541 pp. 2 pl. 8°. *London, C. & F. Rivington,* 1831.

Todd (John, *D. D.*) Hints and thoughts for Christians. 260 pp. 12°. *New York, Am. tract society,* 1867.

Todd (S. Edwards). The young farmer's manual; or, how to make farming pay, giving details of farm management; with a chapter on soils, [etc.] v. 2. v, 418 pp. 1 portrait. 12°. *New York, G. W. Woodward,* 1867.

Todhunter (Isaac). History of the mathematical theory of probability, from the time of Pascal to that of Laplace. xvi, 624 pp. 8°. *Cambridge, Macmillan and Co.* 1865.

Toelken. *See* **Tölken.**

Toeppen. *See* **Töppen.**

Tolhausen (*Dr.* ——, *and* F.) *and* **Desnos-Gardissal** (C.) Technological dictionary in the English, French, and German languages, comprising the technical terms of arts and manufactures. 3 v. 12°. *Paris, Hennuyer,* 1854–5. S.

CONTENTS.

Part i. Français-anglois-allemand. xi, 402 pp.
ii. English, French and German. ix, 475 pp.
iii. Deutsch-englisch-französisch. xv, 658 pp.

Tölken (Ernst Heinrich). Erklärendes verzeichniss der antiken geschnittenen steine der königlich preussischen gemmensammlung. lxviii, 462 pp. 8°. *Berlin, Druckerei der k. akad. der wissenschaften,* 1835. S.

Toll (Jacob). Animadversionum criticarum ad Longinum gustus. 4 p. l. 36 pp. 24°. *Lugduni Batav. Daniel à Gaesbeeck,* 1677.
[*With* CICERO (M. T.) Oratio pro A. Licinio Archia. 24°. *Lugdun. Batav.* 1677].

Tolomeo. *See* **Ptolemæus** (C.)

Tolstoy (G). Notice sur la nouvelle serre de palmiers.
[*In* SAINT PÉTERSBOURG. Jardin botanique impérial de].

Tomes (Robert, *M. D.*) Battles of America, by sea and land. 3 v. 4°. *New York, Virtue & Co.* 1861. S.

——— The Champagne country. xv, 231 pp. 16°. *New York, Hurd & Houghton,* 1867.

——— The war with the South. A history of the late rebellion, with biographical sketches. Continued to the end of the war, by Benj. G. Smith. 3 v. 70 pl. 11 maps. 4°. *New York, Virtue & Yorston,* [1867].

——— The same. Krieg mit dem Süden, umfassende schilderung des ursprungs und verlaufs der rebellion. Nach dem Englischen, fortgeführt vom anfang des jahres 1864 bis zum schluss des krieges, von B. G. Smith. 2 v. 4°. *New York, Virtue & Yorston,* 1863–66.

Tomícek (Josef Slavomir). Lehrbuch der böhmischen sprache für Deutsche. 4 p. l. 299 pp. 8°. *Prag. J. G. Calve,* 1851. S.

Tomlin (John). Tales of the Caddo. 110 pp. 8°. *Cincinnati, Stratton & Barnard,* 1849.

Tomlinson (Charles). Rudimentary treatise on warming and ventilation. 2 p. l. 260 pp. 12°. *London, J. Weale,* 1850. S.

Tompson (Martin K.) Telegraph cipher for transmitting telegrams in a condensed form. 72 pp. 32°. [*New York*], 1867.

Tong (William). An account of the life and death of Matthew Henry. 283 pp. 18°. *London, M. Lawrence,* 1716.

Tonti (*le chevalier*). Dernières découvertes dans l'Amérique Septentrionale de M. de La Sale. 2 p. l. 333 pp. 10 l. 16°. *Paris, Jean Guignard,* 1687.

Tooke (Andrew). The pantheon; representing the fabulous histories of the heathen gods, and most illustrious heroes. 29th ed. 2 p. l. 359 pp. 16 l. 26 pp. 16°. *Dublin, P. Wogan,* 1792.

Tooke (John Horne). Epea pteroenta; or, the diversions of Purley. 1st Am. ed. 2 v. 5 p. l. 432 pp; 5 p. l. 463 pp. 14 l. 8°. *Philadelphia, Wm. Duane,* 1806–7.

Tooke (Thomas). An inquiry into the currency principle. 2d ed. viii, 165 pp. 8°. *London, Longman,* 1844.

Töpffer (Rodolphe). Nouvelles génevoises. Illustrées d'après les dessins de l'auteur. 4e éd. 372 pp. 37 pl. 16°. *Paris, Garnier,* 1855.

Toplady (*Rev.* Augustus Montague). The doctrine of absolute predestination stated and asserted: with a preliminary discourse on the divine attributes, translated in great measure from the Latin of Jerom Zanchius. 148 pp. 12°. *Wilmington, (Del.) Adams,* 1793.

Töppen (Maximilian). Historisch-comparative geographie von Preussen. xiv, 398 pp. 8°. *Gotha, J. Perthes,* 1858. S.
[Wanting atlas, 5 maps. fol.]

Torbuck (J.) A collection of Welsh travels, and memoirs of Wales. [*anon.*] viii, 111 pp. 16°. *London, J. Torbuck,* [1749].

Torfesen *or* **Torfæus** (Thormodur). Gronlandia antiqva, seu veteris Gronlandiæ descriptio. 64, 269 pp. 10 l. 5 maps. 16°. *Havniæ, ex typographeo regiæ majest.* 1706.
[*With his* Historia Vinlandiæ antiqvæ. 1705].

——— Historia Vinlandiæ antiqvæ, seu partis Americæ Septentrionalis. 26 p. l. 83 pp. 8 l. 16°. *Havniæ, ex typographeo regiæ majest.* 1705.

——— Historia Hrolfi Krakii inter potentissimos in ethnicismo Daniæ reges celeberrimi. 24 p. l. 179 pp. 7 l. 16°. *Havniæ, ex typographeo regiæ majest.* 1705.
[*With his* Historia Vinlandiæ antiquæ. 1705].

Tornberg (Carl Johan). Numi cufici regii numophylacii holmiensis, quos omnes in terra Sueciae repertos digessit et interpretatus est. 3 p. l. xxxviii, 316 pp. 14 pl. 4°. *Upsaliæ, Leffler & Sebell,* 1848. S.

Tornel (José Maria). Tejas y los Estados-Unidos de América, en sus relaciones con la república mexicana. 98 pp. 8°. *Mexico, J. Cumplido,* 1837.

Tornos (Alberto de). Combined Spanish method, a new system of learning the Castilian language, with vocabulary. xxiv, 470 pp. 12°. *New York, Appletons,* 1867.

Torombert (Charles Louis Honoré). Principes du droit politique mis en opposition avec le Contrat social de J. J. Rousseau. Avec la réfutation du [8e] chapitre, intitulé, de la religion civile, par Lanjuinais; suivis du texte entier du Contrat social. 382, cxxxvi pp. 8°. *Paris, Rey & Gravier,* 1825.

Toronto (University of). Annual examinations, 1855. 139 l. fol. [*Toronto, University,* 1855]. S.

Torquemada (Juan de). Expositio brevis et utilis super toto psalterio. 204 l. fol. *Rome, per Vdalricum Gallum de Bienna,* 1476. S.

——— Questiones super euangelia de tempore. 286 l. fol. *Nurmberge, F. Creussner,* 1478. S.

Torrens (Henry D.) Travels in Ladâk, Tartary, and Kashmir. iv, 367 pp. 1 map, 12 pl. 8°. *London, Saunders, Otley & Co.* 1862.

Torrens (*Col.* Robert). Colonization of South Australia. xv, 303, xxii pp. 1 map. 8°. *London, Longmans,* 1835.

——— Letter to lord John Russell, on the ministerial measure for establishing poor laws in Ireland. viii, 149 pp. 8°. *London, Longman, etc.* 1837.

Torrey (*Rev.* Charles Turner). Memoir of William Randall Saxton, of Lebanon, Conn. with the funeral sermon. 130 pp. 18°. *Salem, W. & S. B. Ives,* 1838.

Torrey (Jesse, *jr.*) The intellectual flambeau, demonstrating that national happiness, virtue, and temperance, exist, in a collateral ratio, with the dissemination of philosophy, science, and intelligence; with appendix and postscript. 143, 35 pp. 24°. *Washington, Daniel Rapine,* 1816.

Torrey (John, *M. D.*) Botany [of the Mexican boundary survey].
[*With* Emory (W. H.) Report on the U. S. and Mexican boundary survey. v. 2, pt. 1].

——— Botany.
[*With* Emory (W. H.) Notes of a military reconnoissance, etc. Appendix 2 and appendix 6].

——— Catalogue of North American genera of plants. *See* **Lindley** (John). Introduction, etc.

——— Catalogue of plants, etc.
[*With* Nicollet (J. N.) Report, etc. *Washington,* 1843].

——— Descriptions of some new genera and species of plants.
[*With* Frémont (J. C.) Report of the exploring expedition to Rocky mountains in 1842. *Washington,* 1845].

——— Reports on the botany of New York.
[*With* New York (*State of*). Geol. survey. v. 1 and 3].

Torrey (John W.) Interest tables, showing, at sight or by one addition, the interest on any number of dollars from $1 to $10,000; from 1 day to 136 days; and from 1 month to 12 months. 78 pp. 8°. *Philadelphia, J. B. Lippincott & Co.* 1857. S.

Torrey (*Rev.* Samuel, *of Weymouth, Mass.*) The exhortation unto reformation. A sermon preached May 27, 1674, being the day of election. 4 p. l. 44 pp. sm. 4°. *Cambridge, (Mass.) Marmaduke Johnson,* 1674.

——— A plea for the life of dying religion, from the word of the Lord. A sermon, May 16, 1683, the day of election. 4 p. l. 46 pp. sm. 4°. *Boston, Samuel Sewall,* 1683.
[pp. 45-6 imperfect].

——— The same. 4 p. l. 46 pp. sm. 4°. *Boston, Samuel Sewall,* 1683.
[Title-page wanting].

Torricelli (Evangelista). Opera geometrica. 2 v. in 1. 253; 151 pp. 8°. *Florentiæ, A. Masse & L. de Landis,* 1644. s.

Torsellini (Orazio). Epitome historiarvm libri x. 12 p. l. 640 pp. 34 l. 24°. *Lvgdvni, J. Cardon & P. Cavellat,* 1620. s.

——— The same. Ristretto dell'istorie del mondo. Col supplimento del sig. Lod. Aurelii, traduttore dell' opera. Accresciuto in questa editione della seconda parte dal sig. Bernardo Oldoini fino all' anno 1650. 2 pts. 11 p. l. 557 pp; 258 pp. 3 l. 1 pl. 18°. *Venetia, Francesco Baba,* 1653.

Tosh (Edmund G.) On the hæmatite pig irons of West Cumberland. 38 pp. 8°. *Gœttingen, E. A. Huth,* 1866. s.

Toswill (Edward B.) The American cambist; or, principles and practice of foreign exchanges; [with] tables of European arbitrations. 21 l. 4°. *New York, E. B. Clayton's sons,* 1867.

Totten (*Maj. Gen.* Joseph Gilbert). Report on the subject of national defences. 108 pp. 8°. *Washington, U. S. govt.* 1851.

Totze (Eobald). *See* **Toze** (Eobald).

Tourist (The); or, pocket manual for travellers on the Hudson river, the western and northern canals and railroads. [*anon.*] 6th ed. 108 pp. 1 map. 18°. *New York, Harpers,* 1838.

Tournachon (Félix). Mémoires du Géant [ballon]; à terre et en l'air. Par Nadar. [*pseudon.*] Avec introduction par M. Babinet. 2e éd. 452 pp. 12°. *Paris, Dentu,* 1865.

Tournefort (Joseph Pitton de). Élémens de botanique; ou, méthode pour connoître les plantes. 2 v. 10 p. l. 562 pp. 10 l; 235 pl. 8°. *Paris, Imprimerie royale,* 1694. s.

Toussaint (François Vincent). Les mœurs. Par Panage. [*pseudon.*] Nouv. éd. xl, 391 pp. 18°. *Amsterdam,* 1749.

——— The same. Manners. Translated from the French. [*anon.*] 3d ed. 9 p. l. vi, 251 pp. 16°. *London, W. Owen,* 1752.

——— The same. [With] a preliminary discourse on virtue. By Panages. [*pseudon.*] 5th ed. xx, 275 pp. 16°. *Glasgow, R. Urie,* 1770.

Toussenel (Alphonse). Le monde des oiseaux; ornithologie passionnelle. 2 v. [in 1]. 3 p. l. iii, 486 pp; viii, 413 pp. 8°. *Paris, Libr. phalanstérienne,* 1853. s.

Tower (David B.) Gradual lessons in grammar. 288 pp. 12°. *New York, Cady & Burgess,* 1850. s.

——— Intellectual algebra; or, oral exercises in algebra. 7th ed. 208 pp. 12°. *New York, Cady & Burgess,* 1850. s.

Towgood (*Rev.* Micaiah). The dissenting gentleman's answer to the Rev. Mr. White's three letters. [*anon.*] 2d ed. 40 pp. 8°. *London, R. Hett,* 1746.

——— Dissenting gentleman's second letter to Rev. Mr. White, in answer to his three letters. [*anon.*] 90 pp. 8°. *London, R. Hett,* 1747.
[*With* the preceding].

——— Dissenting gentleman's third and last letter to Rev. Mr. White, in answer to his two defences of his three letters. [*anon.*] 94 pp. 2d ed. corrected. 8°. *London, J. Noon & A. Tozer,* 1749.
[*With* the preceding].

——— The dissenting gentleman's answer to the Rev. Mr. White's three letters. 5th ed. 121 pp. 16°. *Boston, Rogers & Fowle,* 1748.

——— The same. Dissent from the church of England fully justified. Dissenting gentleman's three letters and postcript in answer to Mr. John White. [With] a letter to the bishop. 4th ed. xi, 322 pp. 16°. *Boston,* 1768.
[Title page imperfect].

Towler (John, *M. D.*) American photographic almanac for 1867. Being an annual appendix to Humphrey's journal of photography. 12°. *New York, J. H. Ladd,* 1867.

——— The negative and the print; or, photographer's guide in the gallery and field. 150 pp. 12°. *New York, J. H. Ladd,* 1866.

Town (Ithiel). School-house architecture. xii, 48 pp. 8°. *Hartford, Case, Tiffany & Burnham,* 1842.
[*With* CONNECTICUT. Reports of the commissioners of the school fund, 1818–19. 40 pp. 8°. 1839].

Town (Salem). Analysis of derivative words in the English language. 118 pp. 16°. *Auburn, H. Iverson & Co.* 1835.

Town (Thomas). The complete military tutor; a system of modern tactics, applicable to infantry. 377 pp. 16 pl. 8°. *Philadelphia, T. Town,* 1809.

Townley (James, *D.D.*) Illustrations of biblical literature. 2 v. 602 pp; 604 pp. 2 pl. 8°. *New York, Lane, Sandford & Tippett,* 1842–47.

——— An introduction to the literary history of the Bible. 2d Amer. ed. 16°. *New York, James Arthur,* 1833.

Townsend (*Rev.* George, *of Trinity college, Cambridge*). Poems. xxv, 448 pp. 8°. *London, Deighton,* [*and others*]. 1810.

Townsend (George Alfred). The real life of Abraham Lincoln. A talk with Mr. Herndon, his late law partner. 15 pp. 1 portrait. 8°. *New York, Publication office, bible house,* 1867.

Townsend (Howard). Glycogenic function of the liver. (Extract). 10 pp. 8°. *Albany, N. Y. state med. soc.* 1864. s.

Townsend (John Kirk). Sporting excursions in the Rocky mountains, including a journey to the Columbia river, and a visit to the Sandwich Islands, Chili, etc. 2 v. xii, 310; xi, 312 pp. 2 pl. 8°. *London, Henry Colburn,* 1840.

Townsend (*Rev.* Joseph). A journey through Spain in 1786–87, with remarks in passing through a part of France. 3 v. 8°. *London, C. Dilly,* 1791.

Townsend (*Mrs.* Mary E.) Reading at home for the holidays of the church. viii, 175 pp. 16°. *Dresden, E. Blochmann & son,* 1867.

Townsend (Virginia F.) Darryll Gap; or, whether it paid. 456 pp. 12°. *Boston, W. V. Spencer,* 1866.

——— Janet Strong. [A novel.] 314 pp. 12°. *Philadelphia, J. B. Lippincott & Co.* 1865.

Townson (Robert). Travels in Hungary, with a short account of Vienna, 1793. xviii, 506 pp. 1 map. 16 pl. 4°. *London, G. & J. Robinson,* 1797.

Toze (Eobald). Present state of Europe; [with] a discourse on the principles of polity and government. Translated from the German, by Thomas Nugent. 3 v. 8°. *London, J. Nourse,* 1770.

Traeger (Albrecht). Deutsche lieder in volkes herz und mund. xx, 233 pp. 8°. *Leipzig, C. F. Amelang,* 1864.

Trafford (F. G. *pseudon.*) *See* **Riddell** (*Mrs.* J. H.)

Traherne (Thomas). Roman forgeries; discovering the impostures and counterfeit antiquities of the church of Rome. [*anon.*] 17 p. l. 316 pp. 16°. *London, J. Edwin,* 1673.

Traill (*Mrs.* Catharine Parr). The backwoods of Canada: being letters from the wife of an emigrant officer. [*anon.*] 3d ed. viii, 351 pp. 16°. *London, C. Knight,* 1838.

Train (George Francis). Spread-eagleism. 177 pp. 12°. *New York, Derby & Jackson,* 1859.

Train (Joseph). Historical and statistical account of the Isle of Man, from the earliest times to the present date. 2 v. in 1. 400 pp. 2 pl. 1 map; 388 pp. 2 pl. 1 map 8°. *Douglas, Isle of Man, M. A. Quiggin,* 1845. s.

Traité sur les eaux minérales du duché de Nassau. Précédé d'une esquisse et d'une carte géologique du Taunus. Par une réunion de médecins de ces eaux. De l'Allemand, par H. Kaula. Avec une introduction du Dr. Aronssohn. [*anon.*] xii, 281 pp. 1 map. 8° *Wiesbade, C. G. Kreidel,* 1853. s.

Tranaltos (F. de). Histoire de la guerre civile américaine. *See* **Cortambert** (L.) *and* **Tranaltos.**

Tranchepain de St. Augustin (Marie). Relation du voyage des premières Ursulines à la Nouvelle Orléans, et de leur établissement en cette ville. 62 pp. 16°. *Nouvelle York, J. G. Shea,* 1859.

Transactions of the Loggerville literary society. [*anon.*] 168 pp. 8°. *London, J. R. Smith,* 1867.

Trask (John B.) Report on the geology of the Sierra Nevada, or California range. 30 pp. 8°. [*Sacramento, state printer,* 1853]. s.

——— Report on the geology of the Coast mountains, and part of the Sierra Nevada; embracing their industrial resources in agriculture and mining. 95 pp. 8°. [*Sacramento, California state printer,* 1854]. s.

Trauschenfels (Eugen von, *editor*). Deutsche fundgruben zur geschichte Siebenbürgens. (Neue folge). 3 p. l. 415 pp. 8°. *Kronstadt, J. Gött,* 1860.

Travels in North America. [*anon.*] 184 pp. 24°. *Dublin, C. Bentham,* 1822.

Travels of Hildebrand Bowman, esq. into Carnovirria, Taupiniera, Olfactaria, and Auditante in New Zealand; in the island of Bonhommica, and in the powerful kingdom of Luxo-volupto, on the great Southern continent. Written by himself. [*pseudon.*] xv, 400 pp. 8°. *London, Strahan & Cadell,* 1778.

Travels through Sicily and the Lipari islands, in Dec. 1824. By a naval officer. [*anon.*] Illustrated by L. Haghe. xvi, 367 pp. 13 pl. 8°. *London, T. Flint,* 1827.

Treadwell (Francis C.) Secession an absurdity, [with] treason defined, declaration of independence, and constitution of the United States. 16, 32 pp. 32°. *New York, Torry bros.* 1861.

Treat (Samuel). Oration illustrative of the revolutionary warfare in western New York, delivered before the people of the Genesee valley, August 20th, 1841. 121 pp. 18°. *Rochester, W. Alling,* 1842.

[*With* NOTICES of Sullivan's campaign, *Rochester,* 1842].

Treatise (A) on marriage. [*anon.* In Cherokee]. Ditsvsdi gesvi kanohesgi. 20 pp. 24°. [*With* POOR Sarah. 24°. 1843].

Treatise on tennis. By a member of the tennis club. [*anon.*] viii, 120 pp. 8°. *London, Rodwell & Martin,* 1822.

Tredgold (Thomas, *editor*). Tracts on hydraulics. 2d ed. ix, 219 pp. 7 pl. 8°. *London, M. Taylor,* 1836. S.

CONTENTS.

1. SMEATON (John). Experimental inquiry concerning the natural powers of water and wind to turn mills, etc. Experimental examination of the quantity and proportion of mechanical power necessary to be employed in giving different degrees of velocity to heavy bodies from a state of rest; fundamental experiments upon the collision of bodies.
2. VENTURI (Giovanni Battista). Experimental inquiries on the motion of fluids.
3. EYTELWEIN (Johann Albert). Summary of hydraulics; abridged by Thomas Young.

Treitschke (Johann Friedrich). Fortsetzung des ochsenheimer'schen Schmetterlinge von Europa.

[OCHSENHEIMER (F.) Schmetterlinge, etc. v. 5-10].

Treitzsaurwein von Erntreitz (Marcus). Der weiss kunig. Eine erzehlung von den thaten kaiser Maximilian des ersten. 8 p. l. 310 pp. 237 pl. fol. *Wien, J. Kurzböckens,* 1775. S.

Trembley (Abraham). Mémoires pour servir à l'histoire d'un genre de polypes d'eau douce. 2 v. xix, 310 pp. 10 pl; 351 pp. 10 pl. 12°. *Paris, Durand,* 1744. S.

Trench (Richard Chenevix). Select glossary of English words used formerly in senses different from their present. xi, 218 pp. 12°. *New York, Blakeman & Mason,* 1859. S.

Trenchard (John), *and* **Gordon** (Thomas). Cato's letters, [upon various publick and important subjects. *anon.*] 4 v. 16°. *London, W. Wilkins,* 1723-24.

Trenton (*N. J.*) city directory, 1857. Compiled by William H. Boyd. vi, 221 pp. 1 pl. 12°. *Trenton, C. Scott & Co.* 1857.

Tressan (Louis Élizabeth de La Vergne, *comte de*). Histoire de Robert, surnommé le brave. xii, 259 pp. 1 pl. 8°. *Londres, A. Dulau & Co.* 1800.

Treviranus (Gottfried Reinhold). Die erscheinungen und gesetze des organischen lebens. Neu dargestellt. 3 v. in 2. viii, 456 pp; 234, 196 pp. 8°. *Bremen, J. G. Heyse,* 1831-33. S.

——— (*and* Ludolf Christian). Vermischte schriften anatomischen und physiologischen inhalts. 4 v. in 3. 4°. *Göttingen, J. F. Römer, J. G. Heyse,* 1816-21. S.

Tribune (The) almanac and political register for 1864-68. 5 v. 12°. *New York, Tribune association,* 1864-68.

Tridace-Nafé-Théobrôme de Kaout't'Chouk. (*pseudon.*) *See* **Delmotte** (H. F.)

Trigault (Nicolas). De christianis apvd Japonios trivmphis; sive de gravissima ibidem contra Christi fidem persecvtione exorta, anno M.D.CXII vsq. ad annvm M.D.CXX libri qvinq. 8 p. l. 518 pp. sm. 4°. *Monachii,* 1623.

Trigueros (Candido Maria de). La Riada. Describese la terrible inundacion que molestò a Sevilla, 1783-84. xxvi, 115 pp. 8°. *Sevilla, Vazquez y comp.* 1784. S.

Trimmer (*Mrs.* Sarah Kirby). An essay on christian education. 4 p. l. 339 pp. 8°. *London, F. & J. Rivington,* 1812.

Trip (A) from Boston to Littleton, through the notch of the White Mountains. By B. K. Z. [*anon.*] 30 pp. 8°. *Washington, J. Gideon, jr.* 1836.

Tristan l'Hermite (François). *See* **L'Hermite** (François).

Trithemius *or* **Trittenheim** (Johann). Liber lugubris de statu et ruina monastici ordinis. 30 l. sm. 4°. [*Moguntiæ, Petrus Friedberg,* 1493].

Triumphant deaths of pious children. In the Choctaw language. By missionaries of the Am. board of foreign missions. [*anon.*] 54 pp. 18°. *Boston, Am. board for. miss.* 1835.

Troianski (J. K.) Ausführliches polnisch-deutsches handwörterbuch zum gebrauche für Deutsche und Polen. Neu ausgearbeitet 2 v. 1148 pp. 8°. *Posen, E. S. Mittler,* 1835-36. S.

Trollope (Anthony). The last chronicle of Barset. 2 v. 2 p. l. 384 pp; 2 p. l. 384 pp. 32 pl. 18°. *London, Smith, Elder & Co.* 1867.

——— North America. vii, 623 pp. 12°. *New York, Harpers,* 1862. S.

——— The warden. 288 pp. 16°. *New York, Dick & Fitzgerald,* 1862.

——— The West Indies and the Spanish main. 385 pp. 12°. *New York, Harpers,* 1860. S.

Trollope (Thomas Adolphus). Gemma. A novel. 443 pp. 12°. *Philadelphia, Peterson,* 1868.

Tröltsch (Anton von). Die krankheiten des ohres. 2e aufl. x, 262 pp. 8°. *Würzburg, Stahel,* 1862. S.

Troost (Gerard). Third [to eighth] geological reports to the 21st, [22d, 23d, 24th, 25th, and 26th] general assembly of the state of Tennessee. 8 v. in 1. 8°. *Nashville, State printers,* 1835-45. S.

[NOTE.—The first and second reports were never published].

Troschel (Franz Hermann). Das gebiss der schnecken, zur begründung einer natürlichen classification untersucht. v. 1-2. viii, 252 pp. 20 l. 20 pl; 96 pp. 8 pl. 8 l. 4°. *Berlin, G. Parthey,* 1856-68. S.

Troschel (Franz Hermann). System der asteriden. *See* **Müller** (Johannes), *and* **Troschel.**

Trotti (Alberto). Tractatus ieiunii. 22 l. 4°. *Norimbergæ, F. Creüssner*, 1477.

Trow (John F.) Specimens of type in [his] printing and stereotyping establishment. 8°. *New York, J. F. Trow*, 1851. s.

Troward (Richard). A collection of the statutes in force relative to elections down to the present time. 2d ed. 11 p. l. 357, c pp. 25 l. 8°. *London, J. Butterworth*, 1796.

——— The same. Continuation to the present time. 61 pp. 8°. *London, J. Butterworth*, 1802.

[*With* the preceding].

Trowbridge (J. T.) The ferry-boy and the financier. [*anon.*] 332 pp. 4 pl. 16°. *Boston, Walker, Wise & Co.* 1864.

——— Neighbors' wives. 318 pp. 12°. *Boston, Lee & Shepard*, 1867.

Troy, *(N. Y.)* Directory for 1867; including West Troy, Cohoes, Lansingburgh, and Green Island. Sampson, Davenport & Co. compilers. v. 39. 332 pp. 8°. *Troy, W. H. Young*, [1867].

Troy young men's association. Catalogue of the library. iv, 230 pp. 8°. *Troy, N. Y. association*, 1859. s.

——— The same. [With appendix.] Supplementary catalogue of books in the library. 2 v. in 1. iv, 230 pp; 2 p. l. 111 pp. 8°. *Troy, N. Y. association, etc.* 1859–66. s.

Troyon (Frédéric). Habitations lacustres des temps anciens et modernes. xii, 495 pp. 17 pl. 8°. *Lausanne, G. Bridel*, 1860. s.

Trübner (Nicolas). Bibliographical guide to American literature; being a classified list of books, (etc.) published in the United States during the last forty years. With an introduction (etc.) and an index. xxxii, 108 pp. 12°. *London, Trübner & Co.* 1855. s.

Trübner's American and oriental literary record. A monthly register of the most important works published, etc. March 1865 to Feb. 1868. 3 v. 8°. *London, Trübner & Co.* 1865–67.

True (A) and impartial narrative of arbitrary proceedings, by certain justices of the peace, and others, against innocent non-conformists in and near Bedford. With an account of the sudden death of the grand informer against these poor people. [*anon.*] 15 pp. sm. 4°. [*n. p.*] 1670.

True method of promoting perfect love. From debates in the New York preachers' meeting of the M. E. church. 3d ed. 136 pp. 16°. *New York, Foster & Palmer, jr.* 1867.

Trumbull (Benjamin, *D. D.*) A century sermon; or, sketches of the history of the eighteenth century. 36 pp. 8°. *Newhaven, Read & Morse*, 1801.

Trumbull (John). M'Fingal: a modern epic poem. 2d ed. vii, 136 pp. 9 pl. 8°. *New York, E. Low*, 1810.

——— The same. With explanatory notes. 184 pp. 18°. *Boston, John G. Scobie*, 1826.

Trussell (John). Continuation of the collection of the history of England. 4 p. l. 263 pp. sm. fol. *London, D. Pakeman*, 1641.

[*With* Daniel (Samuel). The collection of the history of England. 1650 ed.]

——— The same. [Richard II to Richard III. inclusive]. 4 p. l. 260 pp. sm. fol. *London, E. Dawson*, 1636].

[*With* Daniel (S.) Collection of the hist. of England. 1634].

Truth's advocate and monthly anti-Jackson expositor. [Jan–Oct. 1828.] 2 p. l. 400 pp. 8°. *Cincinnati, Lodge, L'Hommedieu, and Hammond*, 1828.

Truxtun (Thomas). Remarks, instructions, and examples relating to the latitude and longitude; [with] chart of the globe, and short account of winds, calms, and currents met in voyages, and appendix [relating] to the general duties of officers on ships of war. 3 p. l. 105, xxvi pp. 1 map. 1 pl. sm. fol. *Philadelphia, T. Dobson*, 1794.

Tschihatscheff. *See* **Tchihacheff.**

Tschitschagoff (Wassilji Jakowlewitsch, *Russian admiral).* Reise nach dem eismeer. 8°. *St. Petersburg, Logan*, 1793.

Tschudi (Friedrich von). Das thierleben der Alpenwelt. Naturansichten und thierzeichnungen aus dem schweizerischen gebirge. xvi, 560 pp. 8°. *Leipzig, Weber*, 1853. s.

Tschudi (Johann Jakob von). Die Kechua-sprache. 2 v. in 1. iv, 268 pp; vi, 110 pp. 8°. *Wien, k.- k. hof- und staatsdruckerei*, 1853. s.

——— Reisen durch Südamerika. 3 v. 8°. *Leipzig, F. A. Brockhaus*, 1866–67. s.

——— Untersuchungen über die fauna peruana. xxx, 316, 80, 35 pp. 54 pl. fol. *St. Gallen, Scheitlin & Zollikofer*, 1844–46. s.

Tucker (Benjamin). Sacred and profane history epitomized; with a continuation of modern history to the present time. 338 pp. 16°. *Philadelphia, J. Johnson*, 1806.

Tucker (*Rev.* H. H.) Happiness to be found only in the discharge of duty, a sermon.

[*With* Wake Forrest college. Commencement exercises, 1854].

Tucker (Henry St. George). A few lectures on natural law. 224 pp. 12°. *Charlottesville, (Va.) J. Alexander*, 1844. s.

Tucker (James, *M. D.*) Essay on the nature and treatment of cholera and fever, with remarks on the cattle plague. 40 pp. 8°. *Dublin, John Falconer*, 1865.

Tucker (Josiah, *D. D.*) Berufung auf die gerechtigkeit und den vortheil der groszbrittanischen nation in den gegenwärtigen streitigkeiten mit Amerika. 68 pp. 8°. *Braunschweig, F. Waisenhaus*, 1777.
[*With* REMER (J. A.) Americanisches archiv. v. 2].

——— Zweyte berufung auf die gerechtigkeit und den vortheil des volks, in absicht der maaszregeln gegen Amerika. 86 pp. 8°. *Braunschweig, F. Waisenhaus*, 1777.
[*With* REMER (J. A.) Americanisches archiv. v. 2]

——— Ein demüthige vorstellung an diejenigen verehrungswürdigen personen in Groszbrittanien und Ireland, welche geschicktesten sind zu urtheilen, und die tüchtigsten zu entscheiden, ob est für das beste der nation mit den amerikanischen colonien vereinight zu bleiben oder sich von ihnen zu trennen. 82 pp. 8°. *Braunschweig, Waisenhaus*, 1777.
[*With* REMER (J. A.) Amerikanisches archiv. v. 2].

Tucker (Mary E.) Poems. x, 216 pp. 2 portraits. 16°. *New York, M. Doolady*, 1867.

Tucker (N. Beverly, *prof. William and Mary coll. Va.*) George Balcombe. A novel. [*anon.*] 2 v. 282 pp; 319 pp. 12°. *New York, Harpers*, 1836.

Tucker (Pomeroy). Origin, rise, and progress of mormonism. Biography of its founders, and history of its church. Personal remembrances and historical collections hitherto unwritten. 302 pp. 4 pl. 12°. *New York, Appletons*, 1867.

Tuckerman (Edward). An enumeration of North American lichens, with a preliminary view of the structure and general history of these plants, and of the Friesian system. To which is prefixed, an essay on the natural systems of Oken, Fries, and Endlicher. vi, 59 pp. 8°. *Cambridge, (Mass.) J. Owen*, 1845. s.

——— A synopsis of the lichens of New England, the other northern states, and British America. v, 93 pp. 8°. *Cambridge, (Mass.) G. Nichols*, 1848. s.

Tuckerman (Henry Theodore). Book of the artists. American artist life; comprising biographical and critical sketches of American artists; preceded by an historical account of the rise and progress of art in America. With an appendix, containing an account of notable pictures and private collections. xi, 639 pp. 1 portrait. 8°. *New York, G. P. Putnam & son*, 1867.

——— Maga papers about Paris. 16°. *New York, G. P. Putnam & son*, 1867.

——— The sad bird of the Adriatic. 10 pp. 8°. *London*, 1841.
[Hazlitt's romancist and novelist's library. v. 2].

Tudor (William). Letters on the eastern states. [*anon.*] 356 pp. 8°. *New York, Kirk & Mercein*, 1820.

Tuel (John E.) St. Clair; or, the protegé; a tale of the federal city. viii, 142 pp. 8°. *Washington, W. Q. Force*, 1846.

Tukic (Francis). Zemljopis i poviestnica Bosne. Od Slavoljuba Bosnjaka. [*pseudon.*] 10 pp. 1 l. 164 pp. 8°. *Zagrebu, L. Gaja*, 1851.

Tulasne (Louis René *and* Charles). Fungi hypogæi. Histoire et monographie des champignons hypogées. xix, 222 pp. 21 pl. 4°. *Parisiis, F. Klincksieck*, 1851. s.

Tully (William, *M. D.*) Materia medica; or, pharmacology and therapeutics. v. i. (in 2 parts). xi, 1534, viii pp. 8°. *Springfield, (Mass.) J. Church*, 1857–58. s.
[No more published].

Tupper (Martin Farquhar). A hymn for all nations, 1851. Translated into thirty languages. 2d ed. 72 pp. 8°. *London, T. Brettell*, 1851.

Turba philosophorum. *See* **Morgenstern** (Philipp, *editor*).

Turbolo (Giovanni Donato). Discorsi sulle monete del regno di Napoli.
[SCRITTORI class. ital. di econ. pol. v. 42].

Turgenieff (Ivan Sergheïevitch). Father and sons; a novel. Translated by Eugene Schuyler. viii, 248 pp. 16°. *New York, Leypoldt & Holt*, 1867.

Turnbull (John). A voyage round the world in the years 1800 to 1804. 1st Amer. ed. 364 pp. 12°. *Philadelphia, B. & T. Kite*, 1810.

Turnbull (Robert J.) Visit to the Philadelphia prison. With observations on the impolicy of capital punishment. 93 pp. 8°. *London, James Phillips & son*, 1797.

Turnbull (William, *U. S. A.*) Drawings accompanying a report on the survey and construction of the Alexandria aqueduct. [35 pl. etc.] obl. fol. [*Washington,*] *Govt. printer*, 1838. s.

Turner (Daniel). A short history of the Westminster forum. [*anon.*] 2 v. in 1. 14 p. l. 422 pp; 2 p. l. 223 pp. 8°. *London, T. Cadell, etc.* 1781.

Turner (Jacob). Genealogy of the descendants of Humphrey Turner; with family records. In two parts. 63 pp. 8°. *Boston, David Turner,* 1852.

Turner (William). Journal of a tour in the Levant. [Illustrated.] 3 v. 2 maps. 8°. *London, J. Murray,* 1820.

Turpin (Pierre Jean François). Iconographie végétale; ou, organisation des végétaux illustrée au moyen de figures analytiques. Avec un texte explicatif et une notice biographique sur M. Turpin, par A. Richard. xii, 144 pp. 61 pl. 8°. *Paris, Panckoucke,* 1841. s.

Turrecremata (J. de). *See* **Torquemada.**

Turrell (*Rev.* Ebenezer). The life and character of Rev. Benjamin Colman. 9 p. l. 238 pp. 8°. *Boston, Rogers & Fowle, etc.* 1749.

Tursellinus. *See* **Torsellini.**

Turton (Thomas, *D. D. bishop of Ely*). A vindication of the literary character of the late professor [Richard] Porson, from the animadversions of Thomas Burgess, in various publications on 1 John, v. 7. By Crito Cantabrigiensis. [*pseudon.*] viii, 404 pp. 8°. *Cambridge, J. & J. Deighton,* 1827.

Turton (William). Conchylia [dithyra] insularum britannicarum. The [bivalve] shells of the British islands. xlvii, 279 pp. 20 pl. 4°. *London, M. A. Nattali,* 1822. s.

——— Manual of the land and fresh-water shells of the British islands. viii, 150 pp. 10 pl. 12°. *London, Longmans,* 1831. s.

——— The same. New ed. Enlarged by John Edward Gray. ix, 324 pp. 12 pl. 8°. *London, Longmans,* 1840. s.

Tustin (*Rev.* Josiah Phillip). A discourse delivered at the dedication of the new church edifice of the baptist church and society in Warren, (R. I.) May 8, 1845. 193 pp. 18°. *Providence, H. H. Brown,* 1845.

Twain (Mark, *pseud.*) *See* **Clemens** (Samuel).

Tweddell (John). Remains, being a selection of his correspondence, a republication of his Prolusiones juveniles, an appendix, etc. preceded by a memoir by Rev. R. Tweddell. [With] a vindication of the editor against the earl of Elgin and others. 2d ed. viii, 575, 179 pp. 12 pl. 4°. *London, J. Mawman,* 1816.

Twenty essays on literary and philosophical subjects. [*anon.*] 306 pp. 16°. *Dublin, R. White,* 1791.

Twice lost. A novel. By the author of Queen Isabel. [*anon.*] 323 pp. 12°. *London, Virtue bros. & Co.* 1863.

Twiggs (*Gen.* David Emanuel). *See* **Taylor** and his generals.

Twining (Elizabeth). Short lectures on plants, for schools and adult classes. xi, 369 pp. 16°. *London, D. Nutt,* 1858. s.

Twiss (Travers). Epitome of Niebuhr's history of Rome. *See* **Niebuhr** (B. G.)

Twisse (William, *D. D.*) A treatise of Mr. [John] Cotton's, clearing certaine doubts concerning predestination, with an examination thereof. [Also, a ms. sermon in stenograph by Benj. Woodbridge, dated 1656.] 4 p. l. 288 pp. 8 l. sm. 4°. *London, A. Crook,* 1646.

Tyas (Robert). Flowers and heraldry. xiv, 238 pp. 24 pl. 18°. *London, Houlston & Stoneman,* 1851.

——— Flowers from foreign lands: their history and botany. With groups of flowers, coloured by J. Andrews. ix, 198 pp. 12 pl. 16°. *London, Houlston & Stoneman,* 1853.

Tyers (Thomas). Dramatic conversations. [*anon.*] iv, 96 pp. 8°. *London, J. Nichols,* 1782.

[*With his* Political conferences, etc. *London,* 1781].

——— An historical essay on Mr. Addison. [*anon.*] viii, 92 pp. 8°. *London,* 1783.

[*With his* Political conferences, etc. *London,* 1781].

——— An historical rhapsody on Mr. Pope. 2d ed. xi, 143 pp. 8°. *London, T. Cadell,* 1782.

[*With his* Political conferences, etc. *London,* 1781].

——— Political conferences between several great men in the last and present century. 2d ed. 9 p. l. 192 pp. 8°. *London, T. Cadell,* 1781.

Tyler (Bennet, *D. D.*) Memoir of the life and character of Rev. Asahel Nettleton, D. D. 2d ed. 367 pp. 1 pl. 12°. *Hartford, Robins & Smith,* 1845.

Tyler (Edward Royall). The congregational catechism. A survey of the government and discipline of christian churches. 137 pp. 18°. *New Haven, A. H. Maltby,* 1844.

Tyler (William Seymour). The theology of the Greek poets. 365 pp. 12°. *Boston, Draper & Halliday,* 1867.

Tyndale (William). Doctrinal treatises and introductions to different portions of the holy scriptures. Edited by Rev. H. Walter. lxxvi, 532 pp. 8°. *Cambridge, Univ. press,* 1848. [Parker society publications].

CONTENTS.

Biographical notice; Pathway into the holy scripture; Parable of wicked mammon; Obedience of a christian man; Of the sacraments; Prologues to various books of the O. and N. T.

Tyndall (John). The glaciers of the Alps. xx, 446 pp. 1 pl. 12°. *Boston, Ticknor & Fields,* 1861. s.

Tyng (*Rev.* Stephen Higginson, *jr.*) Address at the installation of officers of the Prince of Orange lodge, No. 16, New York city, Dec. 29, 1866. 22 pp. 4°. *New York, Baldwin & Jones,* 1867.

Tyrrell (*Sir* James). Bibliotheca politica; or, an inquiry into the ancient constitution of the English government, in respect to regal power and the rights and liberties of the subject. In thirteen dialogues. [*anon.*] 6 p. l. 968 pp. 16 l. sm. 4°. *London, R. Baldwin,* 1694.

Tyson (Job R.) Discourse on the first anniversary of the Girard college for orphans. 42 pp. 8°. *Philadelphia, Crissy & Markley,* 1849.

——— Discourse on history, as a branch of the national literature. 53 pp. 8°. *Philadelphia, T. K. & P. G. Collins,* 1849.

Tyson (Philip T.) Information in relation to the geology and topography of California. 127, 37 pp. 6 maps. 8°. [*Washington, public printer,* 1850]. s.

——— Second report of the state agricultural chemist to the house of delegates of Maryland, 1862. 92 pp. 8°. *Annapolis, T. J. Wilson,* 1862. s.

Tzetzes (Joannes). Historiarum variarum chiliades, graece. Textum ad fidem duorum codicum monacensium recognovit, brevi adnotatione et vindicibus instruxit Theophilus Kiesslingius. xxiv, 568 pp. 8°. *Lipsiæ, F. C. W. Vogel,* 1826. s.

Udine (Leonardo da). Sermones aurei de sanctis. 359 l. unp. fol. *Colonie, J. Kolhof,* 1473.

——— The same. 313 l. unp. 4°. *Venetijs, Franciscus de Hailbrun et Nicolaus de Frāckfordia,* 1473. s.

Ukert (Friedrich August). Beiträge zur ältern litteratur, [etc.] *See* **Jacobs** (C. F. W.) *and* **Ukert.**

Ule (Otto). Die neuesten entdeckungen in Afrika, Australien, und der arktischen polarwelt, mit besonderer rücksicht auf die natur- und kulturverhältnisse der entdeckten länder. viii, 394 pp. 4 maps. 2 pl. 8°. *Halle, G. Schwetschke,* 1861. s.

Ulloa (Antonio de). Voyage historique de l'Amérique Méridionale, 1752. *See* **Juan** y Santacilia (Jorge) *and* **Ulloa** (Antonio de).

Umbreit (August Ernst). Die erfindung der buchdruckerkunst, [etc.] xxxiv, 244 pp. 8°. *Leipzig, W. Engelmann,* 1843.

Unanúe (Hipolito). Observaciones sobre el clima de Lima, y sus influencias en los seres organizados, en especial el hombre. 2ª ed. xxvi, 315 pp. 8°. *Madrid, De Sancha,* 1815.

Under the ban (Le maudit): a tale of the nineteenth century. Translated from the French of M. l'abbé***. [*anon.*] 247 pp. 8°. *New York, Harpers,* 1864.

Under two flags. A novel. By Ouida. [*pseudon.*] 652 pp. 12°. *Philadelphia, Lippincott,* 1867.

Underhill (Edward Bean). Letter addressed to hon. E. Cardwell, with illustrative documents on the condition of Jamaica. 3d [ed.] 92 pp. 8°. *London, A. Miall,* [1866].

Unger (Franz, *M. D.*) Ideal views of the primitive world. 2 p. l. 8 pp. 14 l. 14 phot. pl. 4°. *London, S. Highley,* [1855]. s.

——— Genera et species plantarum fossilium. xl, 627 pp. 8°. *Vindobonae, Acad. caes. scient.* 1850. s.

——— Synopsis plantarum fossilium. xviii, 330 pp. 12°. *Lipsiæ, L. Voss,* 1845. s.

Union theological seminary, *(Prince Edward, Va.)* Catalogue of the library. 107 pp. 8°. *Richmond, J. Macfarlan,* 1833. s.

United service magazine. *See* **Colburn's** united service magazine.

United States of America.

Colonial and revolutionary period.

——— Proceedings of the congress at New York, 1765. 28 pp. fol. *Annapolis, Jonas Green,* 1766.

——— Articles of confederation and perpetual union between the states of New Hampshire, Massachusetts, Rhode Island and Providence Plantations, Connecticut, New York, New Jersey, Pennsylvania, Delaware, Maryland, Virginia, North Carolina, South Carolina, and Georgia. 16 pp. fol. *Boston, John Gill,* 1777.

——— The same. [Authorized copy, certified by president Laurens]. 26 pp. fol. *Lancaster, (Pa.) Francis Bailey,* 1777.

——— Addresses and recommendations to the states by the United States in congress assembled, [upon revenue matters]. 91 pp. 8°. *London, J. Stockdale,* 1783.

——— Journals of congress from Sept. 5, 1774, to Dec. 31, 1776. 2 v. 310 pp. 6 l; 513 pp. 11 l. 8°. *Philadelphia, R. Aitken,* 1777.

——— Observations on the American revolution. Published according to a resolution of Congress, by their committee. 1 p. l. 122 pp. 8°. *Philadelphia, Styner & Cist,* 1779.

——— Recueil des loix constitutives des colonies angloises, confédérées sous la dénomination d'États Unis de l'Amérique Septentrionale. Traduit de l'Anglois. 6 p. l. 370 pp. 16°. *Paris, Cellot & Jombert,* 1778.

United States of America—*Continued.*

——— Statement of all sums of money borrowed from the treasury of the United States by individual states, or advanced to them during the late war. Transmitted to congress in letter dated 26 Sept. 1786, from the board of the treasury. With mss. notes by J. Nourse. 82 pp. fol. [*New York*, 1786]?

——— Statement of taxes required by congress; and of payments made by the several states, on account of their respective quotas on the requisitions for paper money; with the balances due thereon, 1785. 14 pp. fol. [*New York*, 1785]?

[*With* NORTH Carolina. Journal of the house of commons. 52 pp. fol. 1785].

Constitutions, etc.

——— The constitution, as reported by the convention of delegates begun at Philadelphia on the first Monday of May, 1787, and continued to the 17th day of September following. 16 pp. 12°. *Boston, Thomas & John Fleet,* [*about* 1787].

[Imperfect: wanting parts of pp. 7–10].

——— The same. [Another ed.] 16 pp. 12°. *Boston, Thomas & John Fleet,* [*about* 1787].

——— The same. 16 pp. 12°. *Portsmouth, (N. H.)* 1787.

——— The same. Together with the articles of amendment, adopted by the congress of said states, 1789. 23 pp. sm. 4°. *Windsor, (Vt.) Alden Spooner,* 1790.

——— A collection of the constitutions of the thirteen United States of North America. 257 pp. 12°. *Glasgow, John Bryce,* 1783.

——— The same. The constitutions of the United States, [with] the declaration of independence, the federal constitution, and the bill of rights of the state of Virginia. 334 pp. 8°. *Winchester, (Va.) J. Foster,* 1811.

Agricultural department.

——— Monthly report of the department of agriculture. Jan. 1866 to Dec. 1867. J. R. Dodge, editor. 2 v. 8°. *Washington, Govt. printing off.* 1866–67.

Navy department.

——— Astronomical observations made at the United States naval observatory during 1851–52. xxvii, 652 pp. 4°. *Washington, Govt. printing office,* 1867.

——— ——— The same. 1861 and 1864. 2 v. 4°. *Washington, Govt. printing office,* 1862–66.

——— Register of the officers of the navy, including the marine corps, etc. 1815, 1817–18, 1820–67. 59 v. 8°. 12°. and 16°. *Washington,* 1815–67.

Navy department.

——— Regulations for the government of the naval academy at Annapolis, Md. Prepared by a board of navy officers. 26 pp. 8°. *Washington, C. Alexander,* 1851.

——— ——— Regulations for the uniform and dress of the navy. 14 pp. 1 chart. 12°. [*Washington*], *J. & G. S. Gideon,* 1841.

——— ——— Sailing directions and nautical remarks: by officers of the U. S. naval expedition to Japan, under the command of Com. M. C. Perry. 21 pp. 1 map. 4°. *Washington, A. O. P. Nicholson,* 1857.

Treasury department.

——— Report of the special commissioner of the revenue, 1866. 233 pp. 8°. *Washington, Govt. printing office,* 1867.

[Title page wanting].

——— ——— The same: with form of a bill establishing rates of duty on goods, wares, and merchandise, imported into the United States, prepared by the special commissioner of the revenue. 233, 57 pp. 8°. *Washington, Govt. printing office,* 1867.

[Title page wanting].

——— ——— Reports of a commission appointed for a revision of the revenue system of the United States. D. A. Wells, S. Colwell, S. S. Hayes, commissioners. 483 pp. 8°. *Washington, Govt. printing office,* 1866.

——— ——— Tariff; or rates of duty payable, according to the existing laws and treasury decisions, July 1, 1828. 33, 111 pp. 4°. *Washington, De Krafft,* 1828.

War department.

——— *Army.* Abstract of infantry tactics; for the use of the militia. 138 pp. 30 pl. 16°. *Boston, Hilliard, Gray, & Co.* 1830.

——— ——— Cavalry tactics. 2 v. vii, 198 pp; x, 293 pp. 100 pl. 24°. *Philadelphia, Lippincott,* 1862.

——— ——— Instruction for field artillery, horse and foot. Compiled by a board of artillery officers. 166 pp. 69 pl. 12°. *Baltimore, J. Robinson,* 1845.

——— ——— General regulations for the army. xxxix, 236 pp. 12°. *Washington, F. P. Blair,* 1834.

——— ——— Meteorological register, 1826–30, from observations made at the military posts of the United States. Prepared under the direction of T. Lawson, surgeon, U. S. A. [With] meteorological register, 1822–25. 161 pp. 1 map. 8°. *Philadelphia, Haswell, Barrington & Haswell,* 1840.

——— ——— The same. 1831–42 inclusive. 324 pp. 8° *Washington, C. Alexander,* 1851.

United States of America—*Continued.*

War department.

——— Official register of the army for 1867. 178 pp. 2 tab. 12°. *Washington, Govt. print. office,* 1867.

——— ——— Report of experiments on gunpowder, made at Washington arsenal, in 1843 and 1844. By Capt. A. Mordecai. viii, 328 pp. 6 pl. 8°. *Washington, J. & G. Gideon,* 1845.

——— ——— Reports of experiments with small arms for the military service, by officers of the ordnance department, U. S. army. 117, 35 pp. 4 pl. 8°. *Washington, public printer,* 1836.

——— ——— *Army medical museum.* Catalogue of the surgical [and other] section[s] of the museum. 961 pp. 6 pl. 4°. *Washington, Govt. printing office,* 1866.

——— ——— The same. Catalogue of the medical section of the museum. 136 pp. 5 pl. 4°. *Washington, Govt. printing office,* 1867.

[*With* "catalogue of the surgical section").

——— ——— The same. Catalogue of the microscopical section of the museum. 161 pp. 1 pl. 4°. *Washington, Govt. printing office,* 1867.

[*With* "catalogue of the surgical section").

——— ——— The same. *Surgeon general's office,* 1867. Circular no. 5. Report on epidemic cholera in the army of the United States during the year 1866. [By J. J. Woodward, asst. surg. general U. S. A.] xviii, 65 pp. 4°. *Washington, Govt. printing office,* 1867.

——— ——— The same. Circular no. 6. Report showing the material available in the surgeon general's office for the publication of the medical and surgical history of the war. 4°. *Washington, Govt. printing office,* 1866.

——— ——— The same. Circular no. 7. A report on amputations at the hip-joint, in military surgery. 87 pp. 9 col. pl. 4°. *Washington, Govt. printing office,* 1867.

——— ——— The same. Statistical report on the sickness and mortality in the army of the United States, compiled from the records of the surgeon general's office, 1839–1855. Prepared by R. H. Coolidge. 703 pp. 1 map. 4°. *Washington, A. O. P. Nicholson,* 1856.

——— ——— *Bureau of refugees, freedmen and abandoned lands.* Fourth semi-annual report on schools for freedmen, July, 1867. By J.W. Alvord, general supt. 96 pp. 12°. *Washington, Govt. printing office,* 1867.

Miscellaneous documents.

——— Census of the United States. [Third.] 1810. 90 l. obl. fol. [*Washington,* 1812?]

——— ——— The same. Fifth census. 1830. [With] a schedule of the whole number of persons within the U. S. 1790–1820. 361 pp. fol. *Washington, D. Green,* 1832.

——— Congressional directory for the second session of the 40th Congress; compiled by B. P. Poore. 2d ed. 106 pp. 1 pl. 8°. *Washington, Govt. print. office,* 1868.

——— ——— Fac-simile of the original treaty with Japan, with the English version. 14, 2 pp. 4°.

[*With* UNITED STATES: sailing directions by officers of the Japan expedition].

——— Message of the president communicating information in relation to the heating and ventilation of the capitol extension, post office department, etc. 254 pp. 8°. *Washington, Senate,* 1860. S.

——— Statement on the part of the U. S. of the case, [relative to the northeastern boundary,] referred, in pursuance of the convention of 29th Sept. 1827, between the said states and Great Britain, to his majesty, the king of the Netherlands. 734 pp. fol. *Washington, off. U. S. Telegraph,* 1829.

——— Virginia revolutionary claims: bounty land and commutation pay. Report, no. 436, house of representatives, 26th congress, 1st session. [With] views of the minority of said committee. 135 pp. 8°. *Washington, Congress,* [1840].

United States agricultural society. Journal. 1853–59. 7 v. 20 pl. 8°. *Boston & Washington, Society,* 1854–59.

[Imperfect. Nos. 1–2, 1853; nos 1–4, 1855, and nos. 2, 3, 4. 1859, wanting].

United States (The) army and navy journal and gazette of the regular and volunteer forces. Aug. 1866, to Aug. 1867. v. 4. sm. fol. *New York,* [*W. C. & F. P. Church,* 1867].

United States consular regulations. A practical guide for consular officers, merchants, ship owners, and masters of American vessels in all their consular transactions. 3d ed. 683 pp. 8°. *Washington, French & Richardson,* 1868.

United States hotel guide and railway companion for 1867. [*anon.*] 1st ed. 165 pp. 16°. *Jas. Miller,* 1867.

United States (The) insurance almanac for the year 1858. v. 3. Edited by G. E. Currie. iv, 156 pp. 4 pl. 8°. *New York, G. E. Currie,* 1858. S.

United States (The) literary gazette. v. i, April, 1824, to April, 1825. 380 pp. 4°. *Boston, Cummings, Hilliard & Co.* 1825.

——— The same. Apr. 1, 1825. to Oct. 1, 1826. v. 2–4. 8°. *Boston, Cummings, Hilliard & Co.* [*etc.*] 1825–26.

United States (The) review and literary gazette, October 1, 1826, to September, 1827. v. 1-2. 3, 480 pp; 480 pp. 8°. *Boston, Bowles & Dearborn*, 1827.

[Title page of v. 2 wanting].

United States sanitary commission. Bulletin, [1863-1865]. 3 v. in 1: v. 1, Nos. 1 to 12, pp. xvi, 384; v. 2, Nos. 13 to 24, pp. xvi, 385 to 768; v. 3, Nos. 25 to 40, pp. xviii, 769 to 1280. 1 map. 8°. *New York*, 1866.

——— Documents. 2 v. v. 1, Nos. 1 to 60; v. 2, Nos. 61 to 95. 8°. *New York*, 1866.

Univercœlum (The) and spiritual philosopher. Edited by S. B. Brittan. v. 1. 8°. *New York, by an association*, 1848.

[Imperfect; Nos. 6, 12-15, 17-22, 24-26 wanting].

Universal (The) letter-writer; or, whole art of polite correspondence. [*anon.*] New ed. 124 pp. 1 pl. 16°. *Philadelphia, M. Carey*, 1810.

[Imperfect; pp. 9-10 wanting].

Universal suffrage. Female suffrage. By a republican, (not a "radical"). 116 pp. 12°. *Philadelphia, J. B. Lippincott & Co.* 1867.

Up the Elbe, and on to Norway. By Mr. Nihil. [*pseudon.*] 178 pp. 12°. *London, Cassell, Petter & Galpin*, [1867].

Up and down the Rhine for £5! How to do it. By B. A. [*anon.*] 32 pp. 18°. *London, J. W. Last*, 1866.

Updike (Wilkins). History of the episcopal church in Narragansett, Rhode Island; with an appendix, entitled "America dissected," by Rev. J. Macsparran, D. D. vii, xvi, 9—533 pp. 2 portraits. 8°. *New York, H. M. Onderdonk*, 1847.

Upham (Albert Gallatin, *M.D.*) Family history. Notices of the life of John Upham, the first inhabitant of New England who bore that name. xi, 92 pp. 16°. *Concord, (N. H.) A. McFarland*, 1845.

Upham (Charles Wentworth). Life, explorations, and public services of John C. Frémont. 30th thousand. 365 pp. 13 pl. 12°. *Boston, Ticknor & Fields*, 1856.

——— Salem witchcraft; with an account of Salem village, and a history of opinions on witchcraft and kindred subjects. 2 v. xl, 469 pp. 1 map. 1 pl; 553 pp. 3 pl. 12°. *Boston, Wiggin & Lunt*, 1867.

Upham (Thomas Cogswell, *D. D.*) American [poetical] sketches. vii, 120 pp. 18°. *New York, David Longworth*, 1819.

Upton (Emory). A new system of infantry tactics, double and single rank. 392 pp. 109 pl. 18°. *New York, D. Appleton & Co.* 1867.

Urcullu (José de). Grammática inglesa reducida á veinte y dos lecciones. Ed. 1ra amer. aumentada, por Fayette Robinson. 262 pp. 12°. *Filadelfia, Thomas, Cowperthwaite & Co.* 1848. s.

Ure (Andrew). Dictionary of arts, manufactures, and mines, containing a clear exposition of their principles and practice. Edited by R. Hunt. 6th ed. 3 v. 8°. *London, Longmans*, 1867.

Urlsperger (Samuel). Ausführliche nachricht von den saltzburgischen emigranten, die sich in America niedergelassen haben. 3 v. 2 maps. 2 pl. sm. 4°. *Halle, Wäysenhaus*, 1735-52.

Urquhart (David). Progress of Russia in the west, north, and south, by opening the sources of opinion and appropriating the channels of wealth and power. 3d ed. lxx, 438 pp. 1 map. 16°. *London, Trübner*, 1853.

——— Recent events in the east. viii, 311 pp. 16°. *London, Trübner & Co.* 1854.

Urrutia (Carlos de), *and* **Fonseca** (Fabian de). Historia general de real hacienda [en Nueva España]. 6 v. 8°. *Mexico, V. G. Torres*, 1845-53.

Ursini *or* **Orsini** (Fulvio). De Romanorum gentibus scriptores. *See* **Agustin** (Antonio), *and* **Orsini**.

Urstis, *or* **Wurstis** (Christian). *See* **Wursteisen.**

Use and abuse; a tale. By the author of wayfaring sketches among the Greeks and Turks. [*anon.*] viii, 445 pp. 8°. *London, F. & J. Rivington*, 1849.

Ussher, *or* **Usher** (James, *archbishop of Armagh*). Of the original and first institution of corbes, erenachs, and termon lands. Written 1609. 29 pp. 8°. *Dublin, T. Ewing*, 1774.

[VALLANCEY (C.) Collectanea de rebus hibernicis. v. 1, no. 2].

Utino (Leonardus de). *See* **Udine** (L. da).

Vaca (Alvar Nuñez, *surnamed* Cabeça de). *See* **Nuñez** (Alvar).

Vacher (L. *M.D.*) Étude médicale et statistique sur la mortalité à Paris, à Londres, à Vienne, et à New York en 1865. 180 pp. 1 pl. 8°. *Paris, F. Savy*, 1866.

Vacquerie (Auguste). Les miettes dé l'histoire. 4e éd. 495 pp. 8°. *Paris, Pagnerre*, 1863.

Vadianus. *See* **Watt** (Joachim de).

Vænius (Otho). *See* **Veen** (Octavius von der).

Vaillant (Auguste Nicolas). Voyage autour du monde pendant 1836–37, sur la corvette La Bonite. Physique par B. Darondeau et E. Chevalier. 4 v. 8°. *Paris, A. Bertrand,* 1840–46. s.

CONTENTS.

Observations magnétiques. 2 v. 386 pp. 1 l. 4 pl; 307 pp.
Observations météorologiques. 2 v, 2 p. l. 1, 336 pp; 2 p. l. 310 pp. 1 pl.

Vaillant (Jean Foy). Nummi antiqui familiarum romanarum perpetuis interpretationibus illustrati. 2 v. 10 p. l. 536 pp; 576 pp. 24 l. 152 pl. fol. *Amstelædami, G. Gallet,* 1703.

Vaillant (Sébastien). Botanicon parisiense; ou, dénombrement par ordre alphabétique des plantes, qui se trouvent aux environs de Paris. 25 p. l. 205 pp. 24 l. 1 map. 34 pl. fol. *Leide, J. & H. Verbeek,* 1727.

Valdés *or* **Valdesius** (Diego). De dignitate regvm regnorumque Hispaniæ. 5, 197, 5 l. fol. *Granatæ, F. Diaz á Montoya,* 1602. s.

Valdes (José Francisco). Vida de la gloriosisima madre de la madre de Dios, y abuela de Jesuchristo señora Santa Ana. 6 p. l. 208 pp. 1 l. 1 pl. 8°. *Mexico, herederos de F. de Zúñiga y Ontiveros,* 1794.

Valenciennes (Achille). Poissons. *See* **Cuvier** (G. L. C. F. D.) Règne animal.

Valentia (Pedro de). Les académiques; ou, des moyens de juger du vrai. s.

[*With* CICERO. Livres académiques, trad. par Castillon, v. 1].

Valentin (Gabriel Gustav). Grundriss der physiologie des menschen. 4e aufl. viii, 800 pp. 7 pl. 8°. *Braunschweig, Vieweg,* 1855. s.

——— Lehrbuch der physiologie des menschen. 2e aufl. 2 v. in 4. 8°. *Braunschweig, Vieweg,* 1849–50. s.

——— Nachträge zur zweiten auflage vom lehrbuche der physiologie des menschen. 101 pp. 8°. *Braunschweig, Vieweg,* 1851. s.

[*With his* Lehrbuch der physiologie. v. 1].

Valentine (David T.) *See* **New York** city. Manual of corporation.

Valentyn (François). Oud en nieuw Oost-Indien. 5 v. in 9. fol. *Dordrecht, J. Van Braam,* 1724–26. s.

CONTENTS.

v. 1. Nederlands mogentheid.
2. Moluccos; Molukse zaaken.
3. Amboina; Ambonsche zaaken.
4. Ambonsche zaaken, etc. cont'd. Boomen, planten, etc. van Amboina.
5. Banda, Macassaarsche zaaken, Borneo, Tonkin, Cambodia, Siam, Buli.
6. Java, Bantam, Batavia.
7. Godsdienst op het eyland Java; levens der groote Mogols; Tsjina; Tayouan of Formosa.
8. Choromandel, Pegu, Arrakan, Bengal, Mocha, Persien, Malakka, Sumatra, Ceylon.
9. Malabar, Japan, Kaap der Goede Hoope, Mauritius.

Valerius Maximus. Dictorvm et factorvm memorabilivm libri ix. 118 l. fol. [*Venetiis*], *Vindelinus,* 1471.

Valette (J. B. Philippe), *and* **Benat** Saint Marsy (Gustave). Traité de la confection des lois; ou, examen raisonné des règlements suivis par les assemblées législatives françaises, comparés aux formes palementaires de l'Angleterre, des États-Unis, de la Belgique, etc. 2e tirage. 400 pp. 18°. *Paris, Joubert,* 1839. s.

Valicourt (E. de). Nouveau manuel complet de photographie sur métal, sur papier et sur verre. Nouv. éd. xvi, 368 pp. 1 pl. 24°. *Paris, Roret,* 1851. s.

Vallancey (Charles, *LL. D.*) Collectanea de rebus hibernicis. v. 1–5. 8°. *Dublin,* 1774–90.

CONTENTS.

v. 1, No. 1. Piers: description of the county of West-Meath, 126 pp.
No. 2. Davis: letter to the earl of Salisbury, 44 pp.
Usher: original and first institution of corbes, erenachs, and termon lands, 29 pp.
Account of two ancient instruments lately discovered, 5 pp. 1 pl.
No. 3–4. Vallancey: on the ancient Irish laws called gavel-kind and thanistry, 414 pp.
No. 2. Part of the ancient Brehon laws of Ireland, 24 pp.
v. 2, No. 5. Vallancey: literature of the Irish in heathenish times, 5 pp; translation of fragment of Brehon laws, 21 pp; gavel law of the ancient Irish explained, 9 pp; literature of the Irish after the establishment of christianity, 16 pp; enquiry into the first inhabitants of Ireland, 16 pp.
No. 6. Ledwich: on the study of Irish antiquities, 32 pp; on the round towers in Ireland, 23 pp; memoirs of Dunamase and Shean castle, 12 pp.
No. 7. Beauford: druidism revived, characters and modes of writing of the ancient Irish, 56 pp; origin and language of the Irish, and the learning of the druids, 30 pp.
No. 8. Vallancey: on the antiquity of the Irish language, 2d ed. 123 pp.
No. 9. Ledwich: history and antiquities of Irishtown and Kilkenny, 212 pp.
v. 3, No. 10. Vallancey: continuation of the Brehon laws, 126 pp—[imperfect: pp. 119–22 wanting]; Chinese and Japonese languages collated with the Irish, 62 pp; on the round towers of Ireland, 4 pp.
Pownall: account of the ship temple near Dundalk, 10 pp. 1 pl.
O'Conor: history of Ireland during the times of heathenism, 22 pp.
Letter from Curio, with further explanation of the silver instrument described in No. 2. 3 pp.
No. 11. Beauford: ancient topography of Ireland, 173 pp.
Ledwich: on the ship temple near Dundalk, 12 pp.
No. 12. Vallancey: ancient history of Ireland vindicated, 173 pp; of all hallow eve, [and] of the gule or Lammasday of August, 68 pp; description of the banqueting hall of Tara, 31 pp. 1 pl; of the kiss of salutation, 10 pp; of a colony from Scythopolis, in Palestine, 3 pp; of the Phoenician and Thebaian dialects of the Irish, 74 pp; antient Etruscan collated with the Irish, 20 pp.
O'Conor: on the heathen state and ancient topography of Ireland, 28 pp.
v. 4, No. 13. O'Conor: third letter on the same, 27 pp.
Vallancey: on the ancient implements, etc. of the Irish, 106 pp. 14 pl.

Vallancey (Charles, *LL. D.*) Collectanea de rebus hibernicis.—*Continued.*

No. 14. Vallancey: vindication of the ancient history of Ireland; containing the descent of its old inhabitants from the Phoeno-Scythians; early skill of the Phoeno-Scythians in navigation, arts, and letters; [and] several accounts of the ancient Irish bards, 551 pp. 11 pl.—[imperfect: pp. 1-16, 465-480, wanting].

v. 5. Vallancey: Uraikeft, or, book of Oghams, translated and explained, 105 pp; on the origin of alphabetic writing, 96 pp. 12 pl; terms of the Brehon-Amhan laws explained, 82 pp; origin of the feudal system of government, 64 pp.

Walker: anecdotes of chess in Ireland, 4 pp.

Vallandigham (Clement L.) Record of hon. C. L. Vallandigham on abolition, the union, and the civil war. 248 pp. 1 pl. 8°. *Cincinnati, J. Walter & Co.* 1863.

Vallardi (Giuseppe). Manuale calcografico per l'artista, il mercante, e l'amatore. Manifesto. xvi pp. 8°. *Milano, P. e G. Vallardi,* 1832.

[*With* CICOGNARA (L. *conte*). Memoria della calcografia, 1831].

Valle (*Rev.* Enrico). A family of martyrs. A drama. Translated from the Italian, by Rev. F. P. Garesche. vii, 76 pp. 16°. *Cincinnati, J. P. Walsh,* 1864.

Valle (Guglielmo della). Stampe del duomo di Orvieto. 2 p. l. 38 pl. fol. *Roma,* 1791.

[Text wanting]. S.

Vallerange (Prosper). Le panlatinisme, confédération gallo-latine et celto-gauloise. Alliance fédérative de la France, la Belgique, l'Angleterre, l'Espagne, le Portugal, l'Italie, la Grèce, etc. Nouv. éd. (etc.) xxviii, 236 pp. 1 pl. 8°. *Paris, Passard,* [1862]. S.

Vallet de Viriville (Auguste). Histoire de l'instruction publique en Europe et principalement en France, depuis le christianisme jusqu'à nos jours. 2 p. l. 400 pp. 14 pl. 4°. *Paris, Administration du moyen age, etc.* 1849.

Vallière (Jean Florent, *marquis* de). The art of war. [Manœuvres of armies]. 4 p. l. pp. 145-264. 12°. *Philadelphia, R. Bell,* 1776.

[Imperfect; pp. 259--62 wanting]. S.

Vallière (Louise Françoise de La Baume Le Blanc, *duchesse* de La). *See* **La Vallière.**

Valori (Niccolò). La vie de Laurent de Médicis, traduite du Latin, [par Claude Pierre Gouge]. xxiv, 346 pp. 16°. *Paris, Nyon,* 1761.

Vámbery (Arminius). Travels in Central Asia; an account of a journey from Teheran to Khiva, Bokhara, and Samarcand, in the year 1863. 493 pp. 12 pl. 1 map. 8°. *New York, Harpers,* 1865.

Van Abkoude (Johannes). Naamregister van de bekendste en meest in gebruik zynde nederduitsche boeken, welke sedert het jaar 1600 tot het jar 1761 zyn uitgekomen; nu overzien, verbeterd en tot het jaar 1787 vermeerderd door Reinier Arrenberg. 2° druk. 2 v. 6 p. l. 598 pp. sm. 4°. *Rotterdam, G. A. Arrenberg,* 1788.

——— The same. Alphabetische naamlijst van boeken, welke 1790--1832, in Noord Nederland zijn uitgekomen; strekkende ten vervolge op het Naamregister van R. Arrenberg. [Door J. de Jong.] viii, 755, 159 pp. sm. 4°. *Gravenhage, gebroeders van Cleef,* 1835.

——— The same. Alphabetische naamlijst van boeken, plaat- en kaartwerken, wie 1833-49, in Nederland uitgegeven of herdrukt zijn; strekkende ten vervolge op de alphabetische naamlijst, 1790—1832, bewerkt door J. de Jong. Uitgegeven bij [C. L. Brinkman]. 3 p. l. 792 pp. sm. 4°. *Amsterdam, C. L. Brinkman,* 1858.

Van Cleef (Pieter). Alphabetische naamlijst van fondsartikelen, voorkomende in het naamregister van nederlandsche boeken, alsmede in de alphabetische naamlijst van boeken, achtervolgens uitgegeven bij R. Arrenberg en de gebroeders Van Cleef. xii, 122 pp. sm. 4°. *Gravenhage, gebroeders Van Cleef,* 1838.

Van den Bosch (Jan). Heemel geschiedenis naer de denkbeelden der poëten, der philosofen, en van Mozes. 2 v. 540 pp. 6 l; 25 p. l. 549 pp. 17 l. 24 pl. 18°. *Amsterdam, H. Boussiere,* 1743.

Van den Broecke (J. C.) *and* **De Man** (J. C.) De cholera asiatica in Zeeland, haar oorsprong en hare verspreiding gedurende de jaren 1832—1833, en 1848—1849. viii, 223 pp. 8°. *Middleburg, Abrahams,* 1850. S.

Van den Corput (———, *M. D.*) De l'organisation des écoles pratiques professionelles en Allemagne, en Suède, et en Russie; et en particulier des écoles des arts et métiers de Vienne et de Saint Pétersbourg. Extrait des annales du génie civil, Mars 1866. 19 pp. 8°. *Paris, Lacroix,* 1866.

Van der Aa (A. J.) Nieuw biografiesch, anthologiesch, en kritiesch woordenboek van nederlandsche dichters. 3 v. 8°. *Amsterdam, C. L. Van Langenhuysen,* 1864.

Van der Helle (———). Catalogue de [sa] bibliothèque. La vente 10 février, 1868. 253 pp. 8°. *Paris, Bachelin-Deflorenne,* 1868.

Vandermaelen (Philippe Marie Guillaume). Dictionnaire des hommes de lettres, des savans, et des artistes de la Belgique. [*anon.*] iv, 264 pp. 8°. *Bruxelles, Établissement géographique,* 1837.

Van der Putten (Hendrik). Epistolarum atticarum promulsis, in centvrias tres distribvta. 16°. *Coloniæ*, 1616.

Vane (*Sir* Henry). A healing question propounded and resolved upon occasion of the late publique and seasonable call to humiliation, in order to love and union amongst the honest party. 24 pp. 2 l. sm. 4°. *London, T. Brewster*, 1656.

Vane-Stewart (Charles William, 3*d marquess of Londonderry*). Story of the Peninsular war. New ed. ix, 396 pp. 1 map. 6 pl. 12°. *London, Willis & Sotheran*, 1856.

Vanel *or* **Vannel** (——). Galanteries des rois de France, depuis le commencement de la monarchie. Nouv. éd. augmentée des Amours des rois de France, par Henri Sauval. 2 v. 443 pp. 3 pl; 285 pp. 3 l. 1 pl. 16°. *Suivant la copie imprimée à Paris, C. Moette*, 1738. [*n. p. or d.*]

Van Evrie (John H. *M. D.*) White supremacy and negro subordination; or, negroes a subordinate race, and (so-called) slavery its normal condition. With an appendix, showing the past and present condition of the countries south of us. 339, 60 pp. 6 col. pl. 12°. *New York, Van Evrie, Horton & Co.* 1868.

Van Hennekeler (Gysbert). Verhandeling over de primitieve wortels van alle getallen, en hunne toepassing op de decimale breuken. xvii, 210 pp. 8°. *Leyden, E. J. Brill*, 1855. s.

Vanini (Giulio Cesare). Œuvres philosophiques. Traduites pour la première fois; par X. Rousselot. xvi, 321 pp. 16°. *Paris, C. Gosselin*, 1842.

CONTENTS.

[L'amphithéatre de l'éternelle providence. Dialogues sur la nature].

Vanmeter (*Rev.* Isaac N.) Pocket hymns, original and selected, for the use of the regular baptist church. iv, 314, 10 pp. 24°. *Galesburg, (Ill.) Register printing house*, 1867.

Van Nest (A. R. *D. D.*) Memoir of rev. Geo. W. Bethune, D. D. vi, 446 pp. 4 pl. 12°. *New York, Sheldon & Co.* 1867.

Vannier (Hippolyte). French pronunciation and spelling. 181 pp. 16°. *New York, Lockwood*, 1853. s.

Van Oelen (Abraham). Kort verhaal van het avontuurlijk wedervaren geschied in het jaar 1682, in die bekende hooge watervloed. En hoe hij in het selve jaar op een wonderlijke en nooijt gehoorde wijs by St. Anna Land een walvis gevangen heest. 51 pp. 6 pl. sm. 4°. [n. p.] 1683.

[*With* LA PEYRÈRE (I. de). Nauwkeurige beschrijvingh van Groenland. sm. 4°. 1678].

Van Oosterzee (J. J. *D. D.*) The epistle general of James. [A commentary]. *See* **Bible**, (*English*). Commentary, etc. by J. P. Lange, and others.

Van Rees (O.) Geschiedenis der Nederlandsche volkplantingen in Noord Amerika, beschouwd uit het oogpunt der koloniale politiek. 162 pp. 8°. *Tiel, H. Campagne*, 1855. s.

Vansleben. *See* **Wansleben.**

Vanuxem (Lardner). Reports on geology.

[NEW YORK (*State* of). Geological survey, annual reports. v. 2–5].

Vanvitelli (Luigi). Dichiarazione dei disegni del reale palazzo di Caserta. 3 p. l. xix pp. 14 pl. fol. *Napoli, nella regia stamperia*, 1756.

Van Zandt (Nicholas Biddle). Full description of the soil, water, timber and prairies of each lot or quarter section of the military lands between the Mississippi and Illinois rivers, and of Illinois and Missouri territories. iv, 127 pp. 8°. *Washington, P. Force*, 1818. s.

——— Tabular statistical views of the United States. *See* **Watterston** (George) *and* **Van Zandt.**

Vapereau (Louis Gustave). Dictionnaire universel des contemporains. 3e éd. 2 p. l. x, 1862 pp. 8°. *Paris, Hachette et Cie.* 1865.

Varchi (Benedetto). L'ercolano; dialogo delle lingue, ed in particolare della toscana e della fiorentina. Colla correzione ad esso fatta da Lodovico Castelvetro, e colla varchina di Girolamo Muzio. 2 v. in 1. xii, 370 pp; 169 pp. 12°. *Padova, G. Comino*, 1744.

——— Le terze rime. 1542.

[*With* BERNI (F.) Tutte le opere, etc.]

Varea (Lasor a, *anagram*). *See* **Savonarola** (Rafaello).

Varen *or* **Varenius** (Bernhard). Geographia generalis. 20 p. l. 784 pp. 24°. *Amstelodami, Elzeviri*, 1671. s.

——— The same. Compleat system of geography. Translated into English, by Mr. Dugdale: revised and corrected by Peter Shaw, M. D. 2d ed. 2 v. xxiv, 528 pp; xvi, 529–898 pp. 7 l. 12 pl. 8°. *London, Stephen Austen*, 1734.

Varennes de Mondasse (—— de). Lettres de M * * * à son ami. [*anon.*] 212 pp. 16°. *Amsterdam*, 1750.

Varet (Alexandre Louis). The christian education of children. Translated [from the French] into English. [*anon.*] 11 p. l. 412 pp. 16°. *London, H. Brome*, 1678.

Vargas (Juan de, *pseudon.*) Aventures, racontées par lui-même. Traduites de l'Espagnol sur le manuscrit inédit, par C. Navarin. 184 pp. 16°. *Paris, P. Jannet*, 1853.

Varillas (Antoine). History of William de Croy, [seigneur de Chièvres], governor to the emperor Charles V; being a pattern for the education of princes. Now made English. 20 p. l. 629 pp. 12°. *London, G. Welles*, 1687.

Varlo (C.) The floating ideas of nature, suited to the philosopher, farmer, and mechanic. 2 v. 318 pp. 1 l; 299 pp. 16°. *London*, 1796.

Varnhagen (F. A. de). Examen de quelques points de l'histoire géographique du Brésil, comprenant des éclaircissements sur le second voyage de Vespuce. 70 pp. map. 8°. *Paris, L. Martinet*, 1858.

——— Vespuce et son première voyage; ou notice d'une découverte et exploration primitive du golfe du Mexique et des côtes des États-Unis en 1497 et 1498, avec le texte de trois notes importantes de la main de Colomb. 31 pp. 8°. *Paris, L. Martinet*, 1858.

Varrerius (Caspar). *See* **Barreiros** *or* **Barros** (Caspar).

Varro (Marcus Terentius). De re rustica.
[*With* Libri de re rustica].

Vasari (Giorgio). Opere. 6 v. in 12. 18°. *Firenze, S. Audin e Co.* 1822–23. s.

CONTENTS.

v. 1. Dell'architettura, della scultura, della pittura, vite degli artefici, pittori, et scultori.
v. 2–10. Vite.
v. 11. Ragionamenti.
v. 12. Lettere.

Vasco (Giambattista). Della moneta saggio politico; Delle università delle arti e mestieri dissertazione; Mémoire sur les causes de la mendicité et sur les moyens de la supprimer, v. 33; La felicità pubblica considerata nei coltivatori di terre proprie; L'usura libera, v. 34; Dell'indigenza cagionata da scarsezza di seta; Annunzj ed estratti sopra diversi oggetti di economia politica, v. 35.
[Scrittori class. ital. di econ. pol. v. 33–35].

Vasquez *or* **Vazquez** (Gabriel). De cvltv adorationis libri tres. Accesserunt disputationes duæ contra errores Foelicis et Elipandi, de adoptione et seruitute Christi, in concilio francofordiensi damnatos, eodē autore. 8 p. l. 271 l. 35 l. 8°. *Compluti, ex officina J. Gratiani*, 1594. s.

Vasquez Gastelu (Antonio). Arte de lengua mexicana. 2 p. l. 50 l. sm. 4°. *Puebla, Diego Fernandez de Leon*, 1693.
[Imperfect; wanting l. 23, 48, 49, (supplied in Mss.) and part of l. 50].

Vater (Johann Severin). Litteratur der grammatiken, lexika, und wörter-sammlungen aller sprachen der erde. 2e ausgabe, von B. Jülg. xii, 592 pp, 2 l. 8°. *Berlin, Nicolai*, 1847.

Vattel (Emeric de). The law of nations; or, principles of the law of nature applied to the conduct of nations and sovereigns. From the French. New ed. corrected. xvi, 444 pp. 8°. *London, G. G. J. & J. Robinson, etc.* 1793.

Vattier (G.) Galerie des académiciens, portraits littéraires et artistiques. 3 v. 18°. *Paris, Amyot*, 1866.

CONTENTS.

v. 1. Sainte Beuve. Mérimée. Ponsard. Saint-Marc Girardin. Michelet. Ingres.
v. 2. A. de Vigny. Legouvé. Octave Feuillet. Beulé. Cousin. Dumont.
v. 3. De Sacy. De Montalembert. Sandeau. Viennet. Renan.

Vauban (Sébastien Leprêtre, *maréchal* de). Mémoire pour servir d'instruction dans la conduite des siéges et dans la défense des places. 4 p. l. 204 pp. 29 pl. 4°. *Leide, J. & H. Verbeek*, 1740. s.

——— First system of fortification; consisting of six drawings, with instructions giving the dimensions of every line and angle; preceded by a life of Vauban, etc. By Thomas Kimber. 3d ed. 56 pp. 6 col. pl. 8°. *London, Longman, etc.* 1861. s

——— The new method of fortification, with an explication of all terms appertaining to that art. Translated into English by Abel Swall. 8 p. l. 104 pp. 27 pl. 16°. *London, A. Swall*, 1693.

Vaucher (Jean Pierre Étienne). Histoire des conferves d'eau douce, etc. xv, 285 pp. 17 pl. 4°. *Genève, J. J. Paschoud*, 1803. s.

Vaughan (Daniel). A new system of vegetable physiology. 23 pp. 8°. *Cincinnati, author*, 1848. s.

——— Popular physical astronomy; or, an exposition of remarkable celestial phenomena. 144 pp. 8°. *Cincinnati, Truman & Spofford*, 1858. s.

——— Vegetation traced to natural causes. 16 pp. 8°. [*about* 1850]. s.

Vaughan (Rice). A discourse of coin and coinage: the first invention, use, etc. ancient and modern; with the advantages and disadvantages of the rise or fall thereof. Edited by H. Vaughan. 6 p. l. 248 pp. 2 l. 18°. *London, T. Basset*, 1675.

Vaughan (*Sir* William). The golden fleece; transported from Cambrioll Colchos, out of the southermost part of the iland commonly called the Newfoundland, by Orpheus iunior, for the generall and perpetuall good of Great Britaine. In three parts. 14 p. l. 149, 105, 96 pp. sm. 4°. *London, F. Williams*, 1626.

Vaughan (William, *Esq.*) The narrative of David Woodard and four seamen [among] the Malays, in the island of Celebes. xl, 252 pp. 1 pl. 8°. *London, J. Johnson,* 1804.

——— The same. 2d ed. xxxii, 236 pp. 8°. *London, J. Johnson,* 1805.

Vauhello. *See* **Le Saulnier** de Vauhello.

Vazquez (Gabriel). *See* **Vasquez.**

Veen (Otto van). Theatro moral de la vida humana en cien emblemas [de Horacio, con los discursos de Gomberville]; con el enchiridion de Epicteto, y la tabla de Cebes, philosofo platonico. 10 p. l. 207, 27, 50 pp. 1 pl. fol. *Amberes, H. y C. Verdussen,* 1701.

Veer (Gerard de). Tre navigationi, fatte dagli Olandesi, e Zelandesi, al settentrione nella Norvegia, Moscovia, e Tartaria, verso il Catai, e regno de'Sini, doue scopersero il mare di Veygatz, la Nvova Zembla, et vn paese nell'ottantesimo grado creduto la Groenlandia. Descritte in Latino, et nuouamente da Giouan Givnio Parisio tradotte nella lingua italiana. 4 p. l. 79 l. sm. 4°. *Venetia, Ieronimo Porro* [*or Ciotti,*] *& Co.* 1599.

Vega (Georg von). Logarithmisch-trigonometrisches handbuch. Vierzigste auflage. Bearbeitet von Dr. C. Bremiker. xxxii, 575 pp. 8°. *Berlin, Weidmann,* 1856. s.

——— Sammlung mathematischer tafeln. Als neue völlig umgearbeitete auflage. Grösseren logarithmisch-trigonometrischen tafeln herausgegeben von Dr. J. A. Hülsse. xxiii, 840 pp. 8°. *Leipzig, Weidmann,* 1849. s.

Veitia Linage (José de). The rule established in Spain for the trade in the West Indies, being a proper scheme for directing the trade to the South sea. Translated from the Spanish by Capt. John Stevens. 12 p. l. 368 pp. 4 l. 12°. *London, S. Crouch,* [*about* 1715].

Velasquez de La Cadena (Mariano). Elementos de la lengua inglesa. 432 pp. 8°. *Nueva-York, R. M'Dermut,* 1810. s.

——— Elementos de la lengua castellana. 3ª ed. 112 pp. 1 l. 16°. *Nueva-York, E. Grattan,* 1827. s.

Velloso (José Marianno da Conceição). Florae fluminensis icones nunc primo editae. Edidit Antonius da Arrabida, episcopus de Anemuria, [etc.] 11 v. fol. 1,676 pl. Text; 1 p. l. index methodicus, 21 pp; index alphabeticus, 14 pp. fol. *Parisiis, officina lith. Senefelder, curante E. Knecht,* 1827. s.

[v. 3, 4, 7, 8, 9, wanting: NOTE.—By Pretzel, this work is attributed to Joaquim Vellozo de Miranda, but the authority of the work itself, and of Silva's Dicc. bibl. Portuguez is preferred.

Velpeau (Alfred Armand Louis Marie). New elements of operative surgery. Translated by P. S. Townsend. With notes and observations by Valentine Mott. 3 v. 8°. atlas, 4°. *New York, S. S. & W. Wood,* 1847. s.

——— Surgical clinic of La Charité. Lessons upon the diagnosis and treatment of surgical diseases. Collected and edited by A. Regnard. Translated by W. C. B. Fifield, *M. D.* 103 pp. 16°. *Boston, J. Campbell,* 1866.

Venezia (Sigismondo da, *conventual name*). Bibliografia universale sacra e profana. 998 pp. 8°. *Venezia, G. B. Merlo,* 1842.

Venn (*Rev.* Henry). The life, and a selection from the letters of H. Venn. The life by H. Venn. Ed. by Rev. Henry Venn, B. D. 6th ed. xvii, 556 pp. 1 pl. 16°. *London, Hatchard & son,* 1839.

Venn (John). The logic of chance; an essay on the foundations and provinces of the theory of probability, with especial reference to moral and social science. xxvii, 370 pp. 16°. *London, Macmillan,* 1866.

Ventum (*Mrs.* Harriet). Tales for domestic instruction. 131 pp. 1 pl. 18°. *London, J. Harris,* 1806.

Venture de Paradis (Jean Michel). Grammaire et dictionnaire abrégés de la langue berbère. Revus par P. Amédée Jaubert. xxiii, 236 pp. 4°. *Paris, Soc. de géographie,* 1844. s.

Venturi (Giovanni Batista). Experimental inquiries on the motion of fluids.

[*With* TREDGOLD (T.) Tracts on hydraulics].

Venturoli (Giuseppe). Elementi di meccanica et d'idraulica. 3ª ed. 2 v. 6 p. l. 416 pp. 7 pl; 4 p. l. 397 pp. 7 pl. 8°. *Milano, P. E. Giusti,* 1817–18. s.

Verany (Jean Baptiste). Mollusques méditerranéens; observés, décrits, figurés et chromolithographiés d'après le vivant. 1re partie. Céphalopodes. xvi, 132 pp. 41 pl. 4°. *Gènes, Imp. des Sourds-muets,* 1851. s.

[Contains suppressed editions of pl. 38–39].

Verardi (Carlo), *and* **Colombo** (Cristoforo). In laudem serenissimi Ferdinandi Hispaniarum regis, Bethicæ et regni Granatæ obsidio, victoria et triũphus. Et de insulis in mari indico nuper inuentis epistola Christoferi Colom quam Aliander de Cosco ab hispano ideomate in latinum conuertit. 36 l. sm. 4°. [*Basileæ, Bergmann de Olpe,*] 1494.

Verbiest (Ferdinand). Voyages de l'empereur de la Chine [Khang-Hi] dans la Tartarie; ausquels on a joint une nouvelle découverte au Mexique. [*anon.*] 4 p. l. 110 pp. 24°. *Paris, E. Michallet,* 1685.

Verboquet (——, *pseudon.*) Les délices, ou discovrs ioyevx et récréatifs. Par Verboqvet le généreux. Dernière éd. 258 pp. 3 l. table. 18°. *Paris, Iean Martin*, 1630.

——— Les subtiles et facécievses rencontres de I. B. disciple du généreux Verboquet. [*pseudon.*] 71 pp. 18°. *Paris, I. Martin*, 1630.
[*With* the preceding].

Verdadas (Las) mas importantes al hombre, [etc.] por un hombre pio. [*anon.*] iv, 172 pp. 12°. *Barcelona, J. Verdaguer*, 1847. s.

Verdier (François, *painter*). La vie de Samson: Simpsonischer lebens-laüff. 39 pl. in 20 l. fol. *Augusta Vindelicorum, J. U. Krause*, [*about* 1700]. s.

Verelst (Harry). A view of the rise, progress, and present state of the English government in Bengal. 6 p. l. 148, 253 pp. 4°. *London, J. Nourse*, 1772.

Verhaal hoe de wal-vissen in Greenland gevangen werden. pp. 24–51. [*anon.*]
[*With* LA PEYRÈRE (I. de). Nauwkeurige beschrijvingh van Groenland. Een rijm. 8°. 1678].

Veritable (The) history of Mr. Bachelor Butterfly. [*anon.*] 65 pl. obl. 24°. *London, D. Bogue*, 1845.

Véritable (La) magie noire, ou le secret des secrets. Traduit de l'Hébreu, du mage Iroé-Grego. [*anon.*] 142 pp. 1 pl. 18°. *Rome, Garcia*, 1750.

Véritables (Les) clavicules de Salomon, trésor des sciences occultes. [*anon.*] 111 pp. 11 pl. 18°. *Memphis*, [*Paris ?*] *Alibeck*, 1827.

Vérité (La) défendue [en la cause des jésuites,] et prouvée par les faits, contre les calomnies anciennes et nouvelles. [*anon.* Par Jean Louis de Leissegues de Rozaven.] 2e éd. 344 pp. 12°. *Avignon, L. Aubanel*, 1825. s.

Verity (Robert, *pseudon ?*) Homœopathy examined; or, homœopathy in theory, allopathy in practice. 24 pp. 8°. *Paris, Galignani*, 1836. s.

Vermigli (Pietro Martire). In librvm Ivdicvm [etc.] commentarij doctissimi, etc. ed. 3a. 15 p. l. 195 pp. fol. *Tigri, C. Froschovervs*, 1571. s.

——— The common places. Translated by Anthonie Marten. 4 parts in 3 v. fol. [*London ?*] 1574.

——— Another collection of certeine diuine matters and doctrines, [with] the author's life, [by J. Simler]. Translated by Anthonie Marten. 2 p. l. 101–252 pp; 165 pp. 40 l. fol. [*London ?*] 1583.
[*With* his Common places. v. 3. Part 4. (*London ?*) 1574].

Vermont. Annual directory for the use of the general assembly, containing rules, constitutions, manual of parliamentary practice, and statistical information. 202 pp. 1 map. 2 diagrams. 16°. *Montpelier, Walton*, 1867.

——— The constitution of Vermont as established by the convention held at Windsor, July 2d, 1777. 24 pp. 12°. *Hartford, (Ct.) Watson & Goodwin*, [1777 ?]

——— ——— The constitution, as adopted by the convention holden at Windsor, July 4th, 1793. 29 pp. 12°. *Windsor, (Vt.) Alden Spooner*, 1793.

——— A copy of a remonstrance of the council of the state of Vermont against the resolutions of congress on the 5th of December last, which interfere with their internal police. 20 pp. 12°. *Hartford, Hudson & Goodwin*, 1783.

——— First, second, seventh and eighth registration reports, of births, deaths, and marriages, for 1857, 1858, 1863, and 1864. 4 v. 8°. *Middlebury and Montpelier, State*, 1859–66.

——— Journal of the senate and house of representatives, annual session, 1866. 2 v. 8°. *Montpelier, State*, 1867.

——— Legislative documents and official reports, annual session, 1866. 8°. *Montpelier, State*, 1866.

——— Report of the adjutant and inspector general, from Oct. 1, 1865, to Oct. 1, 1866. 8°. *Montpelier, State*, 1866.

Vermont, University of. Catalogue of the books belonging to the library. 94 pp. 8°. *Burlington, V. Harrington*, 1836. s.

——— The same. Supplement. 25 pp. 8°. [*Burlington*], 1842. s.
[*With* the preceding].

——— The same. Alphabetical and analytical catalogue of the library. iv, 164 pp. 8°. *Burlington, Free press office*, 1854. s.

Vermont (*Marquis* de), *and* **Darnley** (*Sir* Charles: *pseudonyms.*) London and Paris; or, comparative sketches. xvi, 293 pp. 8°. *London, Longmans*, 1823.

Verne (Jules). Voyages et aventures du capitaine Hatteras. Les Anglais au pôle nord—le désert de glace. 150 vignettes par Riou. 467 pp. 1 pl. sm. fol. *Paris, Hetzel*, 1867.

Vernois (A. G. Maxime). Traité pratique d'hygiène industrielle et administrative; comprenant l'étude des établissements insalubres, dangereux et incommodes. 2 v. xcii, 668 pp; 680 pp. 8°. *Paris, J. B. Baillière*, 1860.

Vernon (John). The compleat compting-house. 6 p. l. 146 pp. 18°. *Dublin, G. Grierson*, 1719.

Vernon (*Prof.* N.) Essay on the origin and structure of language. With a concise system of English grammar. 122 pp. 16°. *Frederick city, (Md.) D. Schley & T. Haller*, 1847. s.

Veron (John). A frvteful treatise of predestination, and of the deuyne prouidence of God, as far forth as the holy scriptures and word of God shall lead vs. 123 l. 24°. *London, J. Tisdale*, [1551].

Verreaux (Jules). Histoire nat. des oiseaux. *See* **Chenu** (J. C.) **Des Murs** (P. O.) *and* **Verreaux.**

Verri (Alessandro). Opere scelte. 2 v. lx, 276 pp; 386 pp. 1 pl. 8°. *Milano, [Soc. tipo. de classici italiani]*, 1822.

CONTENTS.

v. 1. Le avventure di Saffo.
La vita di Erostrato.
Vita di A. Verri da Giovanni A. Maggi.
v. 2. Le notti romane.

Verri (Pietro). Meditazioni sulla economia politica, con annotazioni di G. R. Carli, v. 15; 1. Sulle leggi vincolanti principalmente nel commercio de'grani; 2. Dialogo sul disordine delle monete nello stato Milano nel 1762; 3. Estratto del progetto di una tariffa, v. 16; 1. Memorie storiche sulla economia pubblica dello stato di Milano; 2. Osservazioni sulla tortura; 3. Varj opuscoli di economia pubblica, v. 17.

[SCRITTORI class. ital. di pol. econ. v. 15-17].

Verrier *or* **Le Verrier** (Jean). Histoire des Canaries. *Paris*, 1630. *See* **Bethencourt** (Jean de).

Vertot d'Aubeuf (René Aubert de). History of the revolutions that happened in the government of the Roman republic. Translated by [John] Ozell. 6th ed. 2 v. 8 p. l. xxii, 425 pp; 404 pp. 8°. *London, C. Bathurst and others*, 1770.

——— History of the revolutions in Sweden. Done into English by J. Mitchel. 6th ed. 12 p. l. 312 pp. 16°. *London, J. & J. Knapton*, 1729.

——— History of the revolution in Portugal. [in 1640]. xxiv, 53 pp. 8°. *London, J. Davis*, 1813.

[Royal military chronicle, v. 1].

Vertue (George). Catalogue of engravers. *See* **Walpole** (Horace).

Verwaerloosde Formosa, of waerachtig verhael, hoedanigh door verwaerloosinge der Nederlanders in Oost Indien, het eylant Formosa, van den Chinesen mandorijn, ende zeeroover Coxinja, [Tching-Tching-Koung, or Xoninga], overrompelt, vermeestert, ende ontweldight is geworden. Twee deelen. [*anon.*] 4 p. l. 45, 72, 38 pp. 7 pl. sm. 4°. *Amsterdam, Jan Claesz ten Hoorn*, 1675.

[*With* LA PEYRÈRE (I. de). Nauwkeerige beschrijvingh van Groenland. 1678].

Vesling (Johann). Paræneses ad rem herbariam; opobalsami veteribus cogniti vindiciæ. 4°. *Lugduni Bataovrum.*

[*With* ALPINO (P.) Historiae Aegypti naturalis, 1735].

Vespucci (Amerigo). De ora antarctica per regem Portugallie pridem inventa [per Albericum Vesputium]. 6 l. sm. 4°. *Argentine, Mathias Hupfuff*, 1505.

——— Navigatio. *See* **Novus** orbis. *Roterodami*, 1616.

——— Navigationes. *See* **Montalboddo.**

——— Quatvor navigationes. *See* **Cosmographiae** introdvctio. [Deodatæ]. 1507.

Vestiges of the natural history of creation. [*anon.*] 10th ed. xii, 325, lxvii pp. 8°. *London, J. Churchill*, 1853. s.

——— The same. Naturliche geschichte der schöpfung des weltalls, der erde, und der auf ihr befindlichen organismen. Nach der sechsten auflage, von Carl Vogt. vi, 322 pp. 8°. *Braunschweig, Vieweg*, 1851. s.

Vetromile (*Rev.* Eugene). The Abnakis and their history; or, historical notices on the aborigines of Acadia. 171 pp. 16°. *New York, J. B. Kirker*, 1866.

Vetvsta monvmenta: qvae ad rervm britannicarvm memoriam conservandam societas antiqvariorum Londini svmpto svo edenda cvravit. v. 1-4. fol. *London*, 1747-1815.

CONTENTS.

v. 1. 4 pp. 70 pl. 7 pp.
v. 2. 89 pp. 55 pl.
v. 3. 167 pp. 44 pl.
v 4. 28 pp. 52 pl.
[NOTE.—v. 3 contains an index to v. 1-3].
[v. 5-6 wanting].

Vibe (Andreas). Höhenmessengen in Norwegen, 1844-50. s.

[*With* KEILHAU (B. M.) Gaea Norvegica, v. 2].

Vicat (Louis Joseph). Résumé des connaissances positives actuelles sur les qualités, le choix, et la convenance réciproque des matériaux propres à la fabrication des mortiers et cements calcaires. xii, 149 pp. 16 tab. 4 pl. 4°. *Paris, F. Didot*, 1828. s.

Victor (*Mrs.* Metta Victoria Fuller). The dead letter; an American romance. By Seeley Register. [*pseudon.*] 120 pp. 8°. *New York, Beadle & Co.* 1866.

——— The same. 308 pp. 12°. *New York, Beadle and Co.* 1867.

——— Who was he? A story of two lives. 83 pp. 1 pl. 8°. *New York, Beadle & Co.* [1866.]

Victoria. Census of Victoria, 1861. Population tables. 8 v. in 2. fol. *Melbourne, J. Ferres,* 1861–64. s.

CONTENTS.

Part 1. Inhabitants and houses, showing the numbers and distribution of the people. xxxvi, 140 pp.
" 2. Occupations of the people. xvii, 370 pp.
" 3. Birthplaces of the people. vii, 119 pp.
" 4. Religions of the people. xi, 211 pp.
" 5. Ages of the people. ix, 81 pp.
" 6. Conjugal condition of the people. ix, 57 pp.
" 7. Education of the people. viii, 71 pp.
" 8. Health of the people. vii, 7 pp.

——— Reports of the mining surveyors and registrars—quarter[s] ending 31st March, 1864; 30th June, 1864; 30th September, 1864; and 30th June, 1865. 4 v. fol. *Melbourne, J. Ferres,* [1864–65].

——— Votes and proceedings of the legislative assembly, session 1851 [to 1866]. With copies of the various documents ordered by the assembly to be printed. 28 v. fol. *Melbourne, J. Ferres,* 1852–66.

——— The same. Papers presented to both houses of parliament by command of his excellency the governor. Session 1856–7 [to 1866.] Legislative assembly. 14 v. fol. *Melbourne, J. Ferres,* 1857–66.

CONTENTS OF "VOTES" AND "PAPERS."

Sess.	1851–2.	Votes.	1 v.		
"	1852–3.	"	2 v.		
"	1853–4.	"	3 v.		
"	1854–5.	"	3 v.		
"	1855–6.	"	2 v.		
"	1856–7.	"	v. 1–3.	Papers,	v. 4.
"	1857–8.	"	v. 1.	"	v. 2.
"	1858–9.	"	v. 1.	"	v. 2.
"	1859–60.	"	v. 1–2.	"	v. 3-4.
"	1860–1.	"	v. 1–2.	"	v. 3.
"	1861–2.	"	v. 1–2.	"	v. 3.
"	1862–3.	"	v. 1–2.	"	v. 3–4.
"	1864.	"	v. 1.	"	v. 2–3.
"	1864–5.	"	v. 1–2.	"	v. 3–4.
"	1866 (1st sess.)	"	v. 1.		
"	" (2d sess.)	"	v. 1.	"	v. 2.

Victoria (*Queen of Great Britain and Ireland*). The early years of his royal highness the prince consort. Compiled under the direction of her majesty the queen, by Hon. C. Grey. 3d ed. xxxi, 469 pp. 2 pl. 8°. *London, Smith, Elder & Co.* 1867.

——— The same. 371 pp. 2 pl. 12°. *New York, Harpers,* 1867.

——— Leaves from the journal of our life in the highlands, from 1848 to 1861. Edited by Arthur Helps. 287 pp. 2 pl. 12°. *New York, Harpers,* 1868.

Victory. [*anon.*] 304 pp. 16°. *Boston, R. A. Ballou,* 1866.
[The prize series].

Vicuña Mackenna (Benjamin). Introduccion à la historia de los diez años de la administracion Montt. Don Diego Portales. 2 v. 372 pp; 510 pp. 8°. *Valparaiso, Imprenta, del Mercurio,* 1863. s.

——— Historia de los diez años de la administracion de Don Manuel Montt. 5 v. 8°. *Santiago, Imprenta chilena,* 1862–63. s.

——— El ostracismo del general D. Bernardo O'Higgins. 576 pp. 6 pl. 8°. *Valparaiso, Imprenta del Mercurio,* 1866. s.

——— El ostracismo de los Carreras. Episodio de la independencia de Sud-América. 353 pp. 11 pl. 8°. *Santiago, Ferrocarril,* 1857. s.

——— Pájinas de mi diario durante tres años de viajes, 1853–55. California, Mejico, Estados Unidos, Canada, Islas Britanicas, Francia, Italia, Alemania, Paises-Bajos, Costas del Brasil, Provincias del Plata. 3 p. l. 454 pp. 1 map. 4°. *Santiago, Ferrocarril,* 1856. s.

Vida (Marco Girolamo). Art of poetry. Translated by C. Pitt.
[*With* PITT (C.) Poems. Anderson's British poets, v. 8].

Vidocq (Eugène François). Les vrais mystères de Paris. 9 v. 24°. *Bruxelles, A. Lebègue et Sacré fils,* 1844.
[NOTE.—Ascribed by Quérard to Alfred Lucas.]

Vieillard (——), *and* **Deplanche** (E.) Essais sur la Nouvelle Calédonie. Extrait de la Revue maritime et coloniale. 152 pp. 8°. *Paris, Challamel ainé,* 1863. s.

Vienna. K. k. hof- und staats druckerei in Wien. Album. 4 v. fol. Wien. *K. k. hof- und staats druckerei,* 1851. s.

Vieusseux (André). Italy and the Italians in the nineteenth century: with a treatise on modern Italian literature. 2 v. xvi, 308 pp; viii, 352 pp. 12°. *London, C. Knight,* 1824.

Views in India, China, and on the shores of the Red sea; drawn by Prout, etc. from original sketches by R. Elliott. With descriptions by Emma Roberts. 2 v. 68 pp; 64 pp. 63 pl. 4°. *London, H. & R. Fisher & P. Jackson,* [1835].

Vigne (Godfrey T.) Six months in America. 209 pp. 18°. *Philadelphia, T. T. Ash,* 1833.

Vigo (Giovanni da). The whole worke: newly corrected. [Translated by Bartholeme Traheron]. 10 p. l. 455 l. 12°. *London, Thomas East,* 1586.
[Imperfect: wanting l. 441–443.]

Vigo-Roussillon (F. P.) Puissance militaire des États Unis d'Amérique d'après la guerre de la sécession, 1861–65. 7 p. l. 468 pp. 1 pl. 3 maps. 8°. *Paris, Dumaine,* 1866.

Vila y Camps (Antonio). El vasallo instruido en las principales obligaciones que debe á su legitimo monarca, [etc.] 8 p. l. 215 pp. 8°. *Madrid, M. Gonzalez,* 1792. s.

Vilar. *See* **Villar.**

Villagra (Gaspar de). Historia de la Nveva Mexico. 24 p. l. 287 l. 1 pl. 16°. *Alcala, Luys Martinez Grande,* 1610.

Villani (Gio. Pietro Giacomo. *pseudon.*) *See* **Aprosio** (Angelico).

Villanova *or* **Villanuova** (Arnaldo di). *See* **Regimen** sanitatis salernitanū, etc.

Villar (Juan Gonzalez). Tratado de la sagrada luminaria en forma de disertacion, en el que se demuestra la antiguedad, y piedad de las velas y lamparas encedidas a honra de Dios, y en obsequio de las santas imagenes y reliquias. xxvii, 331 pp. 8°. *Madrid, Sancha,* 1798. s.

Villars (Louis Hector, *duc* de). Mémoires. [Depuis 1670 jusqu' en 1734; rédigés par l'abbé de Margon]. Nouv. éd. 3 v. 16°. *Londres,* [*La Haye*], *Jean Nourse,* 1739. s.

Villavicencio (Lorenzo de). De formandis sacris concionibvs, seu de interpretatione scripturarum populari, libri iii. 3 p. l. 236 pp. 16°. *Antverpiæ, Birckmann,* 1565. s.

——— De recte formando theologiæ studio, libri quatuor. 7 p. l. 576 pp. 16°. *Antverpiæ, J. Stelsius,* 1565. s.
[*With* the preceding].

Villedieu (Marie Catharine Hortense Desjardins, *Mad.* de). The secret history of the court of Augustus Cæsar. [*anon.*] 1 p. l. 235 pp. 12°. *London,* 1729.
[Imperfect: pt. iv wanting].

Villiers (George, 5*th duke of Buckingham*). Poems on several occasions. pp. 203–233 1 pl. 12°. [*London*], 1714.

Vincendon-Dumoulin (Clement Adrien). Portulan général, contenant les plans des ports, rades, baies, etc. du globe. Océan atlantique. 2 p. l. 24 pl. 4°. *Paris, Dépôt de la marine,* 1852. s.

——— The same. Océan atlantique. Côtes d'Afrique. 83 pl. 4°. *Paris, Dépôt de la marine,* 1852. s.

Vincent, *of Beauvais, or,* **Vincentius** *bellovacensis.* Speculum doctrinale. 10 p. l. 256 l. fol. *Uenetiis, H. Liechtenstein, coloniensis,* 1494. s.

——— Speculum morale. 266 l. fol. *Uenetiis, H. Liechtenstein, coloniensis,* 1493. s.
[*With* his Speculum doctrinale. Ed. 1494].

——— The same. v. 1. 262 l. fol. [*Argentorati, J. Mentelin,* 1473]. s.
[v. 2 wanting].

——— Speculum naturale. v. 1. 318 l. fol. [*Argentorati, J. Mentelin,* 1473]. s.
[v. 2 wanting].

Vincent (L.) Der wiesenbau, dessen theorie und praxis. 2e aufl. xiv, 228 pp. 12 pl. 8°. *Berlin, Veit & Co.* 1858. s.

Vincent (*Rev.* Marvin R.) Amusement a force in christian training. Four discourses. 140 pp. 12°. *Troy,* (*N. Y.*) *Wm. H. Young,* 1867.

Vincent (Thomas). An explicatory catechism; or, an explanation of the assemblies' shorter catechism. xii, 324 pp. 18°. *Glasgow, Bryce & Paterson,* 1752.

Vinci (Lionardo da). Trattato della pittura, colla vita dell'istesso autore, scritta da Rafaello [Trichet] Du Fresne. fol. *Napoli, Ricciardo,* 1733. s.
[Imperfect].

Vincke (—— *freiherr* von). *See* **Kiepert** (C. J. *editor*). Memoir über die karte von Kleinasien.

Vindication of the divine authority of rvling elders in the churches of Christ. Asserted by the ministers and elders, met together in a provincial assembly, November 2d, 1649. [*anon.*] 15 pp. 12°. *Boston, T. Fleet,* 1734.
[*With* WILLIAMS (*Rev.* John). Redeemed captive. *Boston,* 1734].

Vindication (A) of the bishop of Landaff's sermon from the gross misrepresentations contained in William Livingston's letter to his lordship. [*anon.*] viii, 82 pp. 12°. *New York, J. Holt,* 1768.

Vindication (A) of the royal martyr, king Charles I, wherein are laid open the republican mysteries of rebellion. Written by Samuel Butler, [?] 3 p. l. 64 pp. 12°. *London,* 1705.
[*With* SECRET history of the Calves-head club, London, 1705].

Vinet (Alexandre Rodolphe). Discours sur quelques sujets religieux. 5e éd. xiv, 479 pp. 8°. *Paris, Ch. Meyrueiset Cie.* 1853.

——— L'éducation, la famille et la société. vi, 552 pp. 8°. *Paris, Ch. Meyrueis et Cie.* 1855.

Vingut (Francisco Javier). *See* **Delmar** (E.) Guia en Español, etc.

Vinnassa (Eduard, *M. D.*) Dissertatio inauguralis, sistens observationes quasdam de arteriarum encephali in diversis mammalibus decursu. 20 pp. 4°. *Tubingæ, auctor, L. F. Fues,* 1821. s.

Vinton (John Adams). The Giles memorial. Genealogical memoirs of the families bearing the names of Giles, Gould, Holmes, Jennison, Leonard, Lindall, etc. With a history of Pemaquid, ancient and modern. viii, 600 pp. 2 pl. 8°. *Boston, author,* 1864.

——— Thomas Gyles and his neighbors, 1669–89: or the settlement of the lower Kennebec. First printed in the N. E. hist. and geneal. register. 13 pp. 8°. *Boston, D. Clapp & son,* 1867.

Vinton (John Adams). The Vinton memorial, comprising a genealogy of the descendants of John Vinton of Lynn, 1648: also, genealogical sketches of several allied families. With an appendix. xv, 534, 4 pp. 6 pl. 8°. *Boston, S. K. Whipple & Co.* 1858.

Vio (Tommaso da, *cardinale* Gaetano). Jentacula Noui Testamenti. Preclarissima sexagintaquatuor notabilium sententiarum Noui Testamenti liberalis expositio. 94 l. 18°. [*Lugduni, Joannes Crespin,* 1529].

——— Summula caietana. Perquam docta resoluta ac compendiosa de peccatis summula. 224 l. 18°. *Lugduni, Joannes Crespin,* 1529. [*With* the preceding].

Violet (Thomas). Proposals for the calling to a true and just accompt all persons that have been entrusted with the publick revenue; with reasons for the doing thereof; also, for the regulating of the manufacture of gold and silver thread and wyer; and for passing an act against transporting gold and silver; and likewise a narrative of the proceedings against the silver ships. 27 p. l. 79, 112 pp. 1 pl. fol. *London,* 1656.

Violette (J. Henri M.) *and* **Archambault** (P. J.) Dictionnaire des analyses chimiques. 2 v. vii, 528 pp; 446 pp. 8°. *Paris, J. B. Baillière,* 1851. s.

Viollet-le-duc (Eugène Emmanuel). Dictionnaire raisonné de l'architecture française du xie au xvie siècle. v. 7–8. 8°. *Paris, A. Morel,* 1864–66.

Virchow (Rudolph). Die cellularpathologie in ihrer begründung auf physiologische und pathologische gewebelehre. Vorlesungen. xvi, 440 pp. 8°. *Berlin, A. Hirschwald,* 1858. s.

——— Handbuch der speciellen pathologie und therapie, bearbeitet von Prof. Bamberger, Dr. Falck, Prof. N. Friedreich, Prof. Griesinger, Prof. Hasse, Prof. Hebra, Prof. Lebert, Prof. Pitha, Dr. Simon, Dr. Spielmann, Dr. Stiebel, Prof Veit, Prof. R. Virchow, Prof. J. Vogel, Prof. Wintrich. 6 v. in 10. 8°. *Erlangen, F. Enke,* 1854–65. s.
[Wanting v. 2, abth. 1; v. 3, lief 1, 2; v. 4, abth. 2; v. 5, abth. 1, lief 5].

——— Untersuchungen über die entwicklung des schädelgrundes im gesunden und kranken zustande, und über den einfluss derselben auf schädelform, gesichtsbildung und gehirnbau. 128 pp. 6 col. pl. 4°. *Berlin, G. Reimer,* 1857. s.

Virey (Julien Joseph). De la femme, sous ses rapports physiologique, moral et litteraire. 2e éd. viii, 424 pp. 8°. *Paris, Crochard,* 1825.

Virgilius Maro (Publius). Opera, cum integris commentariis Servii, Philargyrii, Pierii. Ad cod. ms. regium parisiensem recensuit Pancratius Masvicius [Van Maaswick]. 2 v. 123 p. l. 717 pp; 720 to 1308 pp. 96 l. 1 map. 4°. *Leovardiae, F. Halma,* 1717.

——— The same. Bucolica, Georgica, et Æneis, ab Antonio Ambrogi italico versu reddita; adnotationibus, et antiquissimi cod. vaticani picturis ære incisis, etc. illustrata. 3 v. fol. *Romæ, exc. J. Zembel, Venantii Monaldini sumtibus,* 1763–65.

——— The same. Opera. Cura Joannis Hunter. 2 v. 233 pp; xii, 252 pp. 16°. *Andreapoli, J. Morison,* 1799.

——— The same. Opera, in tironum gratiam perpetua annotatione illustrata a Chr. Gottl. Heyne; edidit E. C. F. Wunderlich. 2 v. lxxviii, 546 pp; 493 pp. 8°. *Lipsiæ, Hahn,* 1822. s.

——— The same. Opera, cum notis gallicis. vi, iii, 333 pp. 24°. *Parisiis, A. Delalain,* 1832. s.

——— The same. Opera; with notes, by Rev. J. G. Cooper. 5th ed. xvi, 615 pp. 8°. *New York, N. and J. White,* 1835.

——— The same. The whole genuine works, translated from the Latin, [into English verse, by John Dryden], with notes, memoirs of the life of Virgil, and dissertations on epic, heroic, didactic, and pastoral poetry. Revised by William Henry Melmoth. iv, 407 pp. 31 pl. 4°. *London, A. Hogg,* [*about* 1800].
[pp. 295–6 wanting].

——— The same. Works. Translated into English verse by John Dryden. 2 v. 270 pp; 290 pp. 1 pl. 24°. *Baltimore, Lucas & Maxwell,* 1818.

——— The same. A translation of the works of Virgil; partly original and partly altered from Dryden and Pitt. By John Ring. 2 v. lxv, 355 pp; 635 pp. 8°. *London, Longman, etc.* 1820.

——— The same. Œuvres, traduites en Français, le texte vis-a-vis la traduction, par l'abbé Des Fontaines. Nouv. éd. avec les remarques de M. de Martignac. 2 v. 36, 415 pp; 483 pp. 12°. *Amsterdam, Compagnie des libraires,* [*about* 1770]. s.

——— Spisy básnické. Z latiny prelozil Karol Vinaricky. iv, 144 pp. 8°. *Praze, Rivnáce,* 1851. s.

——— The Eclogues and Georgics. [Lat.] With notes and a metrical index. By Charles Anthon. l, 452 pp. 12°. *New York, Harpers,* 1846. s.

Virgilius Maro (Publius). The first book of the Æeneis: translated by George Sandys.
[*With* OVIDIUS Naso (Publius). Metamorphosis Englished. By G. S[andys]. fol. 1640].

——— The Eneis, books i and ii, rendered into English blank iambic, with new interpretations and illustrations, by James Henry. vi, 126 pp. 8°. *London, Taylor & Walton,* 1845. s.

——— The first six books of the Aeneid, together with the first, second, and fourth eclogues. [Lat.] With notes, by R. W. McFarland. viii, 231 pp. 12°. *Cincinnati, E. D. Truman,* 1849.

——— The Eneid: translated into English [octosyllabic] verse by John Conington. xxiv, 482 pp. 12°. *New York, W. J. Widdleton,* 1867.

——— Georgicorum libri quattuor. The georgicks; with an English [prose] translation and notes by John Martyn. 4th ed. xv, 421 pp. 13 l. 1 map. 10 pl. 8°. *Oxford, W. Baxter,* 1819.

——— Georgica hexaglotta: Georgica in quinque linguas conversa, hispanicam a J. de Guzman; germanicam a J. H. Voss; anglicam a G. Sotheby; italicam a F. Soave; gallicam a J. Delille. 3 p. l. 563 pp. fol. *Londini, Gul. Nicol,* 1827.

Virginia. Catalogue of the library of the state, [with] rules and regulations. 77 pp. 8°. *Richmond, S. Shepherd,* 1835.

——— The same. 8°. *Richmond, Colin, Baptist & Nowlan,* 1849. s.

——— The same. 370 pp. 8°. *Richmond, J. Nowlan,* 1856. s.

——— Communications from several states on the resolutions of the legislature of Virginia respecting the alien and sedition laws; also, instructions from the general assembly of Virginia to their senators in Congress, and the report of the committee to whom was committed the proceedings of sundry of the other states, in answer to the resolutions of the general assembly, 21st Dec. 1798. 194 pp. 16°. *Richmond, Meriwether Jones,* [1800?]

——— Debates in the house of delegates of Virginia upon the acts of Congress passed at their last session, commonly called the alien and sedition laws. 189 pp. 8°. *Richmond, T. Nicolson,* 1798.

——— Journal [and documents] of the house of delegates, session of 1866–67. 8°. *Richmond, Enquirer office,* 1866.

——— Journal [and documents] of the senate, [session of 1866–67]. 8°. *Richmond, J. E. Goode,* 1866.

——— Memorial and remonstrance presented to the general assembly of the state of Virginia, 1785, in consequence of a bill brought [in] for the establishment of religion by law. [*anon.*] 12 pp. 18°. *Worcester, Isaiah Thomas,* 1786.

Virginia historical and philosophical society. Collections. v. 1. [With] an address, Feb. 4th, 1833, by Jonathan P. Cushing. 87 pp. 8°. *Richmond,* 1833.

Virginia; or, the fatal patent. [*anon.*] 68 pp. 12°. *Washington, Davis & Force,* 1825.

Virginia richly valued, by the description of the maine land of Florida. By a Portugall gentleman of Eluas. *See* **Relaçam** verdadeira, etc.

Viriville (Auguste Vallet de). *See* **Vallet** de Viriville.

Virulus *or* **Monneken** (Carl *or* Karel). Epistolarum perutiles formule. 6 p. l. lxxxii l. 1 l. sm. 4°. [*n. p. about* 1488].

——— The same. lxix l. 5 l. sm. 4°. *Dauētrie, Jacobus de Breda,* 1496.

Visconti (Ennio Quirino). Osservazioni sopra un antico cammeo rappresentante Giove Egioco. 52 pp. 1 pl. 4°. *Padova, Stamperia del seminario,* 1793. s.

——— *and* **Visconti** (Giambattista). Il museo pio clementino illustrato e descritto. [Opere. Classe prima.] 7 v. 8°. *Milano, editore,* 1818–22. s.

——— *See* **Worsley** (*Sir* Richard).

Visconti (Filippo Aurelio), *and* **Guattani** (Giuseppe Antonio). Il museo Chiaramonti descritto e illustrato. xvi, 350 pp. 48 pl. 8°. *Milano, editori,* 1820. s.

Vishnu Purána (The): a system of Hindu mythology and tradition. Translated from the original Sanskrit, and illustrated by notes chiefly from other Purânas, by H. H. Wilson. Edited by Fitz Edward Hall. v. 1–3. 8°. *London, Trübner,* 1864–66.
[WILSON (Horace Hayman). Works. v. 6–8].

Visit to Belgrade. Translated by James Whittle. [*anon.*] 105 pp. 16°. *London, Chapman & Hall,* 1854.

Vitet (Louis *or* Ludovic). Monographie de l'église Notre-Dame de Noyon. Plans, [etc.] par D. Ramée. 4°. Atlas, fol. *Paris, Imprimerie royale,* 1845. s.

Vitruvius Pollio (Marcus). Di architettura, dal vero esemplare latino nella volgar lingua tradotto [da F. L. Durantino]. 12 p. l. cx l. fol. *Vinegia, Zoppino,* 1535.

——— The same. I dieci libri dell' architettvra. Tradotti i commentati da Daniel Barbaro. 4 p. l. 506 pp. sm. fol. *Venetia, A. de' Vecchi,* 1629.

Vitruvius Pollio (Marcus)—*Continued.* The architecture of Vitruvius, in ten books. Translated from the Latin by Joseph Gwilt. New ed. xxxv, 316 pp. 23 pl. 16°. *London, J. Weale,* 1860.

Vivenot (Rudolph von). Beiträge zur kenntniss der klimatischen evaporationskraft und deren beziehung zu temperatur, feuchtigkeit, luftströmungen und niederschlägen. vii, 103 pp. 1 pl. 8°. *Erlangen, F. Enke,* 1866. s.

Vivie *or* **Du Vivie** (Johannes). Beschryving van de beroemde, en van ouds vermaarde vrye keiserlyke ryks-en krooning-stad Aken, mitsgaders van alle desselfs fonteinen, en minerale wateren en baden, [etc.] 12 p. l. 232 pp. 18 pl. sm. 4°. *Leiden, J. du Vivie,* 1727. s.

Vivien (Alexandre François Auguste). Études administratives. 3e éd. 2 v. 354 pp; 426 pp. 16°. *Paris, Guillaumin,* 1859.

Vocabolario degli accademici della Crvsca. Con tre indici delle voci, locvzioni, etc. 11 p. l. 1024, 118 pp. fol. *Venetia,* 1697. s.

Vocabulary (A) of the English, Bugis, and Malay languages. [*anon.*] vi, 66 pp. 12°. *Singapore, Mission press,* 1833. s.

Vocabulary of the language of the Society Islands. [*anon.*]

[*With* COOK (James). Voyage towards the South Pole, etc. 1772–75. v. 2. pp. 317—363. 4°. *London,* 1784].

Vogdes (William). An elementary treatise on mensuration and practical geometry. 299 pp. 12°. *Philadelphia, E. C. & J. Biddle,* 1846. s.

Vogel (Ernst Gustav). Literatur früherer und noch bestehender europäischer öffentlicher und corporations-bibliotheken, zusammengestelt. xvi, 548 pp. 8°. *Leipzig, T. O. Weigel,* 1840. s.

Vogt (Carl). Lehrbuch der geologie und petrefactenkunde. 2e aufl. 2 v. xxxi, 672 pp. 2 pl; xxix, 641 pp. 16 pl. 8°. *Braunschweig, Vieweg,* 1854. s.

Vogt (Niklas). Rheinische geschichten und sagen. 2 v. xvi, 453 pp; iv, 409 pp. 8°. *Frankfurt-am-Main, Hermann,* 1817. s.

Voigt (Friedrich Siegmond). Die farben der organischen körper, wissenschaftlich bearbeitet. xvi, 228 pp. 18°. *Jena, Cröker,* 1816. s.

——— Lehrbuch der zoologie. 6 v. 8°. atlas, 4°. *Stuttgart, E. Schweizerbart,* 1835–40. s.

[Naturgeschichte, v. 7—13].

Voiture (Vincent). Works, translated by Dryden [and others]. 3d ed. 2 v. xxiv, 300 pp; xxiii, 287 pp. 1 pl. 16°. *London, A. Betteswortlı, etc.* 1736.

CONTENTS.

v. 1. Letters.
v. 2. Poems; letters; metamorphoses; Alcidalis and Zelida, a romance.

Voix (La) du proscrit, organe de la république universelle. Oct. 27, 1850 to Sept. 1, 1851. 372, 282, 16 pp. sm. fol. *Saint-Amand, C. Chotteau,* 1850–51.

Volcanoes, or burning mountains; containing a description of Mt. Vesuvius, the opinions of eminent philosophers on the causes of volcanoes, etc. [*anon.*] 24 pp. 1 pl. 8°. *Philadelphia, J. Coats, Jr.* 1833.

Volger (G. H. Otto). Untersuchungen über das phänomen der erdbeben in der Schweiz, und seine bedeutung fur die physiologie des erdorganismus. 3 v. in 1. 8°. *Gotha. J. Perthes,* 1857–58. s.

CONTENTS.

v. 1. Chronik der erdbeben in der Schweiz. 367 pp. 6 pl.
v. 2. Die geologie von Wallis. 283 pp. 1 pl.
v. 3. Die erdbeben in Wallis. 4 p. l. 524 pp, 1 map.

Volney (Constantin François Chasseboeuf, *comte* de). The law of nature, or principles of morality, deduced from the physical constitution of mankind and the universe. viii, 161 pp. 32°. *Philadelphia, T. Stephens,* 1796.

——— The ruins; or, a survey of the revolutions of empires. Translated from the French. 12th ed. 248 pp. 2 l. 2 maps. 16°. *Glasgow, W. Lang,* 1804.

[Imperfect; pp. 13–24 wanting].

Volpato (Giovanni), *and* **Morghen** (Raffaele). Principes du dessein tirés d'après les antiques statues. 2 p. l. v pp. 36 pl. fol. *Rome, Pagliarini,* 1786. s.

Voltaire, (François Marie Arouëet de). The history of Charles xii. king of Sweden. Translated from the last Paris edition. 275 pp. 16°. *Otsego, (N. Y.) H. & E. Phinney,* 1811.

——— The same. [*anon.*] 142 pp. 8°. *London, J. Davis,* 1812.

[Royal military chronicle. v. 2].

——— Life of Peter the great, emperor of Russia, including the history of Russia during his reign. Translated from the French. [*anon.*] 167 pp. 8°. *London, J. Davis,* 1812.

[Royal military chronicle. v. 2].

——— The same. 348 pp. 16°. *Frederick-town, (Md.) J. P. Thomson,* 1813.

——— Zadig; or, the book of fate. Translated from the French. 32 pp. 8°. *London,* 1841.

[HAZLITT'S romancist and novelist's library. v. 4].

Voltoire (——). Anciens proverbes basques et gascons. Remis au jour par [P.] G. B[runet]. 14 pp. 8°. *Paris, Techener,* 1845.

Vopiscus (Flavius). [Vitæ imperatorum Romanorum, viz:] Divvs Avrelianvs, Tacitvs, Florianvs, Probvs, Firmvs, Satvrninvs, Proculus et Bonosus, Carvs, Nvmerianvs, Carinvs. [*With* Varii hist. Rom. scriptores, v. iii.]

Voragine *or* **Varaggio** (Jacopo da). Legenda sanctorum. 1 p. l. ccccxx l. fol. [*Argentorati, about* 1476].

Vormeng (Carl). Die bandwürmer des menschen, nach den neuesten forschungen. 32 pp. 8°. *Berlin, G. Lange,* 1867. s.

Vortisch (Louis Christian Heinrich). Die jüngste katastrophe des erdballs, ein geologischer versuch. xiii, 172 pp. 8°. *Braunschweig, Vieweg,* 1852. s.

Vose (George L.) Orographic geology; or, the origin and structure of mountains. 134 pp. 8°. *Boston, Lee & Shepard,* 1866. s.

Voyage (A) to the South seas, 1740–41, by his majesty's ship Wager. [*anon.* By John Bulkley]. ii, 194 pp. 16°. *London, J. Twig,* 1743. [*With* OLD England forever. *London,* 1740].

Voyages and travels of the renowned captain Sir Francis Drake into the West Indies, and round the world. [*anon.*] 24 pp. 16°. *Coventry, (Eng.) J. Turner,* [*about* 1815].

Voyages de découverte au Canada, 1534 et 1542, par Jacques Quartier, le sieur de Roberval, Jean Alphonse de Xanctoigne, etc. iv, 130 pp. 2 pl. 8°. *Québec, W. Cowan et fils,* 1843.

Voyageur (Le) en Hollande, ou manuel pour ceux qui veulent visiter ce pays. [*anon.*] 60 pp. 16°. *Amsterdam, L. A. C. Hesse,* 1804.

Vrolik (Gerardus). Catalogue de la bibliothèque d'histoire naturelle, de médecine, et d'autres sciences de feu G. Vrolik, dont la vente se fera 3 Decembre, 1860 [etc.] par Frederik Müller. [Avec] notice biographique de G. Vrolik. viii, xvi, 154 pp. 8°. *Amsterdam, F. Müller,* 1860. s.

Vrolik (Willem, *M. D.*) Tabulae ad illustrandam embryogenesin hominis et mammalium, tam naturalem quam abnormem. [Dutch and Latin]. 7, 218 l. 100 pl. 4°. *Amstelodami, G. M. Londonck,* 1849. s.

——— Catalogue de la collection d'anatomie. *See* **Dusseau** (J. L.)

Vulpius (Christian August). Rinaldo Rinaldini, captain of banditti. A tale of the last century. Translated from the German. 4th ed. 136 pp. 8°. *London,* 1841. [HAZLITT's romancist and novelist's library, v. 1].

Waagen (Gustav Friedrich). Verzeichniss der gemälde-sammlung des königlichen museums zu Berlin. xvi, 394 pp. 1 pl. 16°. *Berlin, Druckerei der k. akademie der wissenschaften,* 1841. s.

——— The same. Königliche museen, verzeichniss der gemälder-sammlung. 11e aufl. xxxii, 451 pp. 16°. *Berlin, W. Moeser & Kühn,* 1851. s.

Waan, *or* **Wann** (Paul). Sermones de tempore. 266 l. fol. *Hagenaw, H. Gran,* 1499.

Wace (Robert *or* Mathieu). Illustrations of master Wace his chronicle of the Norman conquest, from the Roman de Rou. Translated by Edgar Taylor. 1 p. l. 50 col. pl. 8°. *London, W. Pickering,* 1837. s.

Wachenhusen (Hans). Skizzenbuch aus Neuenburg und der Schweiz. 288 pp. 12°. *Berlin, O. Janke,* 1857.

Wackerbarth (Athanasius Frans Didrik). Om planeten Neptunus. [Extract.] 2 p. l. 125 pp. 8°. *Upsala, universitets,* 1865. s.

Waddle (J. C.) *and* **Smith** (J. B.) Capon springs, Hampshire co. Va. 8 pp. 8°. *Baltimore, Hanzsche & Co.* 1859.

Wade (Henry). Halcyon: or, rod fishing with fly, minnow, and worm. [With] a short method of dressing flies. xvi, 212 pp. 12 pl. 12°. *London, Bell & Daldy,* 1861.

Wagener (W. L.) *See* **Kruger** (*Dr.* F.) First discovery of America.

Wagler (Johann Georg). Monographia psittacorum. [Extract.] 288 pp. 6 col. pl. 4°. [*München, Bayr. akad. der wissenschaften,* 1832]. s.

——— Natürliches system der amphibien, mit vorangehender classification der säugethiere und vögel. vi, 354 pp. 8°. *München und Stuttgart, Cotta,* 1830. s. [Wanting, 2 pl.]

Wagner (Johann Andreas). Geschichte der urwelt, mit besonderer berücksichtigung der menschenrassen und des mosaischen schöpfungsberichts. 2e aufl. 2 v. xvi, 550 pp; vi, 528 pp. 8°. *Leipzig, L. Voss,* 1857–58. s.

CONTENTS.

v. 1. Die erdveste nach ihrem felsbaue und ihrer schöpfungsgeschichte.
v 2. Das menschengeschlecht und das thier- und pflanzenreich der urwelt.

——— Die säugthiere in abbildungen nach der natur, mit beschreibungen. Mit atlas. 5 v. 4°. 1846–55. s.

[*See* SCHREBER (J. C. D. von). Die säugthiere, etc.]

Wagner (Rudolph, *editor*). Handwörterbuch der physiologie, mit rücksicht auf physiologische pathologie. In verbindung mit mehren gelehrten herausgegeben. 4 v. in 5. 8°. *Braunschweig, Vieweg,* 1842–53. s.

Wagner (Rudolph, *editor*). Neurologische untersuchungen. xvi, 244 pp. 2 pl. 8°. *Göttingen, G. H. Wigand*, 1854. s.

Wahl (Samuel Friedrich Günther). Allgemeine geschichte der morgenländischen sprachen und literatur, etc. Nebst einem anhang zur morgenländischen schriftgeschichte. viii, 648 pp. 6 l. 11 pl. 8°. *Leipzig, J. G. I. Breitkopf*, 1784. s.

Wailes (B. L. C.) Addresses delivered in the college chapel before the agricultural, horticultural, and botanical society of Jefferson college, Washington, Miss. 24 April, 1841, and 29 April, 1842. 29, 20 pp. 8°. *Natchez*, 1842. s.

[*With* JEFFERSON college, etc. charter, 1840].

Wailly (Joseph Noël, *dit* Natalis de). Éléments de paléographie. 2 v. xii, 716 pp; 2 p. l. iv, 452 pp. 37 pl. fol. *Paris, Imprimerie royale*, 1838. s.

Waistell (Charles). Designs for agricultural buildings, including labourers' cottages, farm houses and out-offices. xi, 115 pp. 12 pl. 4°. *London, Longman*, 1827.

Wake Forrest college, (*North Carolina*). Commencement exercises, 1854. 103 pp. 8°. *Philadelphia, C. Sherman*, 1854. s.

CONTENTS.

The true man. Oration by Rev. Tiberius Gracchus Jones. pp. 3--37.
Plea for colleges. Address by Rev. Basil Manly, jr. pp. 39--69.
Happiness to be found only in the discharge of duty. Sermon by Rev. H. H. Tucker. pp. 71--103.

Wake (Isaac). Rex platonicus: sive de potentissimi principis Jacobi [i.] Britanniarum regis, ad illustrissimam academiam oxoniensem adventu, Aug. 27, 1605, narratio. Ed 6a. 4 p. l. 239 pp. 24°. *Oxoniæ, G. West*, 1663.

Wakefield (Gilbert). Correspondence with Charles James Fox, 1796–1801, chiefly on subjects of classical literature. vi, 232 pp. 8°. *London, Cadell & Davies*, 1813.

Wakefield (S.) Deutsches choralbuch; eine sammlung von deutschen und englischen kirchenmelodien. 127 pp. obl. 18°. *Cincinnati, L. Swormstedt und A. Poe*, 1852. s.

Wakeley (Andrew). The mariner's compass rectified. With the description and use of in struments in use in navigation. Enlarged by J. Atkinson. Revised by W. Mountaine. 272 pp. 16°. *London, Mount & Page*, 1766.

Walckenaer (Charles Athanase, *baron*). Vies de plusieurs personnages célèbres des temps anciens et modernes. 2 v. 12, 376 pp; 442 pp. 8°. *Laon, Melleville*, 1830. s.

Walcott (James). The new pilgrim's progress; or, the pious Indian convert, Hattain Gelashmin, who was baptised by the name of George James. 316 pp. 16°. *London, M. Cooper*, 1748.

Waldie (*Miss* E. A.) Sketches descriptive of Italy in 1816–17. [*anon.*] 4 v. 16°. *London, J. Murray*, 1820.

Waldo (Loren P.) Early history of Tolland; an address at Tolland, Conn. Aug. 22, and Sept. 27, 1861. 148 pp. 8°. *Hartford, Case, Lockwood & Co.* 1861.

Waldo (Samuel, *of Boston*). A defence of the title of the late John Leverett, to a tract of land in Massachusetts bay, commonly called Muscongus lands. 41 pp. fol. [*Boston*], 1736.

Waldseemüller (Martin). *See* **Cosmographiae** introdvctio. [*Deodate*], 1507.

Walford (Edward). The handybook of the civil service. xiii, 207 pp. 16°. *London, Longman*, 1860.

——— Men of the time: a dictionary of contemporaries. Edited by G. H. Townsend. 7th ed. vii, 859 pp. 12°. *London, Routledge*, 1868.

Wali *or* Mohammed Wali Ullah. Les oeuvres. [Avec]une traduction et notes, par Garcin de Tassy. 2 v. in 1. xx, 144 pp. 1 pl; 68 pp. 4°. *Paris, Imprimerie royale*, 1834–36. s.

CONTENTS.

v. 1. Texte hindoustani.
v. 2. Traduction et notes.

Walker (A.) A complete system of stenography. 8 pp. 16°. *Philadelphia*, 1821.

Walker (Adam, *of London*). Ideas suggested on the spot in a late excursion through Flanders, Germany, France, and Italy. 2 p. l. 442 pp. 8°. *London, J. Robson*, 1790.

Walker (Adam, *of N. H.*) A journal of two campaigns of the 4th regiment of U. S. infantry in Michigan and Indiana territories, under Col. Boyd and Col. Miller, 1811–12. 143 pp. 12°. *Keene, (N. H.)* 1816.

Walker (*Sir* Hovenden). A journal; or, full account of the late expedition to Canada. 304 pp. 8°. *London, D. Brown*, 1720.

[*With* JOUTEL. Journal of voyage to Mexico. xxix, 205 pp. 12°. *London*, 1719].

Walker (*Rev.* James Barr). God revealed in the process of creation, and by the manifestation of Jesus Christ. 273 pp. 1 pl. 12°. *Boston, Gould & Lincoln*, 1855.

Walker (John, *philologist*). Critical pronouncing dictionary and expositor of the English language. 4th Phil. ed. 960 pp. 8°. *Philadelphia, Johnson & Warner, and others*, 1815.

——— The same, [with] key to the pronunciation of Greek, Latin, and scripture proper names. 609, 103 pp. 8°. *New York, Collins and Hannay*, 1819.

Walker (Joseph Cooper). Anecdotes of chess in Ireland.

[VALLANCEY (C.) Collectanea de rebus hibernicis. v. 5].

——— An historical and critical essay on the revival of the drama in Italy. xvi, 272, 38 pp. 8°. *Edinburgh, Mundell & son,* 1805.

Walker (Timothy, *LL. D.*) Elements of geometry. With elementary treatise on descriptive geometry, by E. Otis Kendall. 159 pp. 18 pl. 12°. *Philadelphia, E. H. Butler,* 1843. s.

Walker (W. *engineer*). Useful hints on ventilation. 131 pp. 1 pl. 12°. *Manchester, J. T. Parkes,* 1850. s.

Walker (William, *B. A.*) The royal grammar, commonly called Lilie's grammar, explained. 3d ed. 6 p. l. 504 pp. 18°. *London, E. Pawlet,* 1695.

Walker (William, *R. N.*) The magnetism of ships, and the mariner's compass. xx, 207 pp. 1 pl. 16°. *London, Piper bros. & Co.* 1853.

Walkington (*Rev.* Thomas). The optick glasse of humors, [etc.] or the philosopher's stone to make a golden temper, [etc.] By T. W. [*anon.*] 12 p. l. 168 pp. 2 pl. 16°. *London, I. D.* 1639.

Wallace (Horace Binney). Art, scenery, and philosophy in Europe. xxxvi, 346 pp. 12°. *Philadelphia, H. Hooker,* 1855.

Wallace (J. H.) American stud-book, being a compilation of the pedigrees of American and imported blood horses, with an appendix and supplement. v. i. 1017 pp. 17 pl. 8°. *New York, W. A. Townsend & Adams,* 1867.

Wallace (John M.) & Co. Telegraphic cypher, compiled for the exclusive use of their correspondents and themselves. 60 pp. 16°. *New York, Donogh & Black,* 1867.

Wallace (John William). An address at the celebration by the N. Y. historical society, May 20th, 1863, of the two-hundredth birth day of Mr. William Bradford. 114 pp. 3 pl. 8°. *Albany, J. Munsell,* 1863.

Wallace (William). Hindoo astronomy and mathematics, with an account of col. Lambton's trigonometrical surveys in India.

[*With* MURRAY (Hugh). Account of British India. v. 3. pp. 279--325. *New York,* 1833-36].

Wallace (William A.) The Great Eastern's log. Her first transatlantic voyage, and particulars of her American visit. By W. A. W. [*anon.*] 91 pp. 16°. *London, Bradbury & Evans,* 1860.

Wallenberg (Carl Friedrich Theodor Gideon von). De molluscis Lapponiae lulensis. Dissertatio inauguralis. 48 pp. 1 pl. 8°. *Berolini, auctor,* [1858]. s.

Waller (*Sir* William). Recollections of his times.

[*With* POETRY of Anna Matilda. Hannah Cowley. pp. 97—139. 1788].

Walley (*Rev.* Thomas). Balm in Gilead to heal all Zion's wounds: a sermon preached before the general court of the colony of New Plimouth, June 1, 1669, being the day of election there. 3 p. l. 20 pp. sm. 4°. *Cambridge, S. G[reen] & M. J[ohnson],* 1669.

——— The same. sm. 4°. *Cambridge, S. Green & M. Johnson,* 1670.

Wallingford (John). Chronica. fol. *Oxoniæ,* 1691.

[GALE (Thomas), *and* FELL (John). Rerum anglicarum scriptores veteres. *Oxoniæ,* 1684-91. v. 3].

Walpers (Gerard Wilhelm). Annales botanices systematicae, [for 1846-50]. 3 v. 8°. *Lipsiae, F. Hofmeister, A. Abel,* 1848-53. s.

——— Repertorium botanices systematicae. 6 v. 8°. *Lipsiae, F. Hofmeister,* 1842-47. s.

Walpole (Horace, *4th earl of Orford*). Works. [Illustrated. Edited by Robert Berry]. 5 v. 4°. *London, Robinson,* 1798.

CONTENTS.

v. 1. Fugitive pieces.
Catalogue of the royal and noble authors of England.

v. 2. The castle of Otranto.
An account of the giants lately discovered.
Historic doubts on the life and reign of Richard iii. with supplement, observations, etc.
Ædes walpolianæ.
Sermon on painting.
Nature will prevail: a moral entertainment.
Thoughts on tragedy.
Thoughts on comedy.
Detection of a late forgery, called Testament politique du chevalier Robert Walpoole.
Life of Rev. Thomas Baker.
Account of my conduct relative to the places I hold under government.
Letters to and from ministers.
Description of Strawberry Hill.
On modern gardening.
On the late dismission of a general officer.

v. 3. Anecdotes of painting [and the other fine arts].

v. 4. Catalogue of engravers, from the mss. of G. Vertue.
Life of G. Vertue, with list of works.
Appendix to anecdotes of painting.
Chatterton papers.
Narrative of the quarrel of Mr. David Hume and J. J. Rousseau, as far as Mr. Horace Walpole was concerned in it.
Letters between D. Hume and H. Walpole, relative to Rousseau.
Reminiscences, written in 1788.
Hieroglyphic tales.
Parody on Chesterfield's letters.
Criticism on Dr. Johnson's writings.
Strange occurrences: a continuation of Baker's chronicle.
Detached thoughts.
Miscellaneous verses.
Prologues and epilogues.
Epigrams.
Index to catalogue of engravers.

v. 5. Letters.

——— A catalogue of engravers who have been born or resided in England, from the mss. of George Vertue; [with] an account of the life and works of the latter. 230 pp. 17 pl. 12°, *London, J. Caulfield* [etc.], 1794. s.

Walpoole (George Augustus, *editor*). The new British traveller; or, a complete modern universal display of Great Britain and Ireland. With upwards of 150 views. 520 pp. 110 pl. fol. *London, A. Hogg*, [1784]. s.

Walsh (Francis). The antediluvian world; or, a new theory of the earth. 9 p. l. 308 pp. 30 l. 12°. *Dublin, S. Powell*, 1743.

Walsh (J. H.) The shot-gun and sporting rifle; and the dogs, ponies, ferrets, etc. used with them in the various kinds of shooting and trapping. By Stonehenge. [*pseudon.*] 2d ed. xvi, 496 pp. 20 pl. 8°. *London, Routledge, Warne & Routledge*, 1862. s.

——— (*and others*). Athletic sports and manly exercises. By "Stonehenge," J. G. Wood, etc. 477 pp. 24°. *London, Routledge, Warne & Routledge*, 1864.

Walsh (Michael McN.) The lawyer in the school-room; comprising the laws of all the states on important educational subjects. 161 pp. 12°. *New York, J. W. Schermerhorn & Co.* 1867.

Walsh (William). Poetical works. 8°. *Edinburgh*, 1793.

[Anderson's British poets, v. 6].

Walter *of Exeter*. The siege of Carlaverock in the xxviii. Edward i. A. D. mccc; with the arms of earls, barons, and knights who were present on the occasion. [*anon.*] With a translation, a history of the castle, and memoirs of the personages commemorated by the poet, by Sir Harris Nicolas. xxxii, 380 pp. 1 pl. 4°. *London, Nichols & son*, 1828.

Walter (Emile). What is free trade? An adaptation of F. Bastiat's "Sophismes économiques." 158 pp. 12°. *New York, G. P. Putnam & son*, 1867.

Walter (*Rev.* Richard). A voyage round the world, in the years 1740–44, by George, lord Anson. 5th ed. 10 p. l. 417 pp. 1 l. 4 maps. 39 pl. 4°. *London, J. & P. Knapton*, 1749.

[NOTE.—Said to have been written by Benjamin Robins].

Walther (Ph. A. F.) Systematisches repertorium über die schriften sämmtlicher historischer gesellschaften Deutschlands. xxx, 649 pp. 12°. *Darmstadt, Historische verein für Hessen*, 1845. s.

Waltl (Joseph). Reise durch Tyrol, Ober-Italien und Piemont nach dem südlichen Spanien. 2e ausg. 3 p. l. 247 pp. 16°. *Passau, Pustet*, 1839. s.

[APPENDED.—Ueber die thiere Andalusiens. 120 pp.]

Walton (George, *and others*). Observations upon the effects of certain late political suggestions. By the delegates of Georgia. 14 pp. 4°. *Privately printed, Worsmsloe* (*N. C.*) *G. Wymberley Jones*, 1847.

Walton (G. A.) Metric system of weights and measures. 24 pp. 16°. *Boston, Brewer & Tileston*, 1867.

Walton (Izaac). The complete angler; or, contemplative man's recreation. In two parts: the second by C. Cotton. With lives of the authors, and notes, by Sir John Hawkins and the present editor, [Henry Ellis. Designs by Wale, etc: engraved by Audinet]. 514 pp. x l. 12 pl. 8°. *London, S. Bagster*, 1815.

Walton (W. *land-surveyor*). An essay proving iron far superior to stone for breaking and grinding of corn, grain, and pulse; also, proving an hand engine upon an entire new construction. [With] appendix. 35 pp. 16°. *Lynn*, (*Eng.*) *R. Marshall*, 1788.

Walworth (*Rev.* Clarence). The gentle skeptic; or, essays and conversations of a country justice on the authenticity and truthfulness of the Old Testament records. 366 pp. 12°. *New York, D. Appleton & Co.* 1863.

Walworth (Reuben Hyde, *LL.D.*) Hyde genealogy; or, the descendants from William Hyde, of Norwich. 1 v. in 2. viii, 1446 pp. 23 pl. 8°. *Albany, J. Munsell*, 1864.

Wanderings (The) and adventures of Reuben Delano; a narrative of twelve years' life in a whale ship. 100 pp. 8°. [*New York*], *Greenfield, H. Long & brother*, 1846.

Wann (Paul). *See* **Waan** (Paul).

Wansleben (Johann Michael). Relazione dello stato presente dell'Egitto, [etc.] 16 p. l. 285 pp. 24°. *Parigi, A. Cramoisy*, 1671. s.

Wappäus (J. E.) Deutsche auswanderung und colonization. vi, 152 pp. 8°. *Leipzig, J. C. Hinrich*, 1846.

War life; illustrated by stories of the camp and field. Compiled by Tim. Tramp. [*pseudon.*] 144 pp. 12°. *New York, Calender, Perce & Welling*, 1862.

Warburton (Eliot). The conquest of Canada. 2 v. xxiii, 351 pp; 366 pp. 8°. *New York, Harpers*, 1850.

Ward (Edward). Writings. 2d ed. 2 v. ii, 439 pp; iii, 401 pp. 12°. *London, J. How*, 1704.

CONTENTS.

v. 1. The London spy, compleat.
v. 2. Poems and miscellanies.

Ward (George A.) Description of New Brighton, on Staten island, opposite the city of New York. 8 pp. 1 map. 1 pl. 12°. [*New York*, 1836].

Ward (Henry A.) Catalogue of casts of fossils, from the principal museums of Europe and America, etc. viii, 228 pp. 4 pl. 8°. *Rochester, Author,* 1866. s.

——— Notice of the Ward cabinets of mineralogy and geology lately presented to the university of Rochester. 44 pp. 1 pl. 8°. *Rochester, (N. Y.) University,* 1863. s.

Ward (Nathaniel). The simple cobler of Aggawam, in America, willing to help mend his native country, lamentably tattered, both in the upper leather and sole, with all the honest stitches he can take. By Theodore de La Guard. [*pseudon.*] 5th ed. 2 p. l. 100 pp. 24°. *Boston, Daniel Henchman,* 1713.

——— The same. vi, 96 pp. 12°. *Boston, James Munroe & Co.* 1843.

Ward (Thomas). England's reformation. A poem, in four cantos. 2 v. in 1. vii, 279 pp; 238 pp. 16°. *Dublin, R. Coyne,* 1814.

——— Errata of the protestant Bible. [*With*] the preface of Lingard, in answer to Ryan's "Analysis," and a vindication by Milner, in answer to Ryan's "Reply." 2 p. l. 24,118 pp. sm. fol. *New York, D. & J. Sadlier,* 1844.

Ward (William, *D. D.*) A view of the history, literature, and religion of the Hindoos; abridged. xi, 453 pp. 9 pl. 12°. *Hartford, H. Huntington,* 1824.

Wardell (James). Municipal history of the borough of Leeds, to 1836. With appendix. vii, 96, ccxix pp. 6 pl. 8°. *London, Longmans,* 1846.

Warder (John A. *M. D.*) American pomology. Apples. 744 pp. 12°. *New York, O. Judd & Co.* 1867.

Wardlaw (Ralph, *D. D.*) Discourses on the principal points of the socinian controversy. xii, 431 pp. 8°. *Andover, M. Newman,* 1815.

——— Lectures on female prostitution; its nature, extent, effects, guilt, causes, and remedy. xi, 163 pp. 12°. *Glasgow, J. Maclehose,* 1842.

Ware (Henry, *jr, D. D.*) The formation of the christian character, addressed to those seeking to lead a religious life; and Progress of the christian life; a sequel. 2d ed. viii, 176, 93 pp. 18°. *Boston, American unit. association,* 1867.

——— Two discourses containing the history of the Old North and New Brick churches, united as the Second church in Boston. 60 pp. 8°. *Boston, J. W. Burditt,* 1821.

Ware (*Mrs.* Mary G. Chandler). Death and life. 174 pp. 16°. *Boston, W. Carter & bro.* 1864.

Waring (George E. *jr.*) Draining for profit, and draining for health. Illustrated. 244 pp. 12°. *New York, O. Judd & Co.* [1867].

Warmholtz (Carl Gustaf). Bibliotheca historica sueo-gothica; eller, förteckning uppå så väl trykte som handskrifne böcker, tractater och skrifter, hvilka handla om svenska historien, eller därutinnan kunna gifva ljus, [etc.] 15 v. in 6. 8°. *Stockholm, etc. A. J. Nordström, etc.* 1782–1817. s.

Warner (Susan). Queechy. By Elizabeth Wetherell. [*pseudon.*] 410 pp; 396 pp. 12°. *New York, Putnam,* 1852.

——— The word. The house of Israel. [*anon.*] v, 504 pp. 16°. *New York, R. Carter & bros.* 1867.

Warnstedt (*Dr.* A. von). Die oldenburger und brandenburger erbansprüche auf die herzogthümer Schleswig-Holstein. ccccxli, 252 pp. 2 l. 1 pl. 8°. *Hannover, Schmorl & Von Seefeld,* 1865. s.

Warr (G. Finden). Dynamics, construction of machinery, equilibrium of structures, and the strength of materials. viii, 296 pp. 8°. *London, R. Baldwin,* 1851. s.

Warren (Charles). The Missouri harmony; or, a collection of psalm and hymn tunes, and anthems. 20, 268 pp. 1 l. obl. 18°. *Cincinnati,* 1850. s.

Warren (Emory F.) Sketches of the history of Chautauque county (N. Y). 159 pp. 18°. *Jamestown, (N. Y.) J. W. Fletcher,* 1846.

Warren (George). An impartial description of Surinam. 28 pp. sm. 4°. *London, Nathaniel Brooke,* 1667.

Warren (*Rev.* Israel Perkins). The wicked not annihilated: refutation of modern sadduceeism. Revised ed. 76 pp. 18°. *Boston, Am. tract society,* 1867.

Warren (John, *and others*). Constitutions of the fraternity of free and accepted masons; with history of masonry in Massachusetts. With songs, etc. 288 pp. 4°. *Worcester, Isaiah Thomas,* 1792.

Warren (John Collins, *M. D.*) Remarks on some fossil impressions in the sandstone rocks of Connecticut river. 54 pp. 1 phot. pl. 8°. *Boston, Ticknor & Fields,* 1854. s.

Warren (Jonathan Mason, *M. D.*) Surgical observations, with cases and operations. xv, 631 pp. 6 pl. 8°. *Boston, Ticknor & Fields,* 1867.

Warren (Nathan B.) Christmas in the olden time; its carols and customs: with the boar's head song. 58 pp. 1 pl. 8°. *Troy, (N. Y.) A. W. Scribner,* 1866.

Warren (S. Edward). General problems of shades and shadows; together with the theory of shading. 140 pp. 15 pl. 8°. *New York, J. Wiley & son,* 1867.

——— A manual of elementary geometrical drawing, involving three dimensions. 3d ed. ix, 121 pp. 17 pl. 12°. *New York, Wiley & son,* 1867.

——— Plane problems in elementary geometry; the point, straight line, and circle. 162 pp. 1 pl. 12°. *New York, J. Wiley & son,* 1867.

Warville (Catherine A.) The romance of Beauseincourt. An episode extracted from the retrospect of Miriam Monfort. By the author of "The household of Bouverie." [*anon.*] 456 pp. 12°. *New York, G. W. Carleton & Co.* 1857.

Washington (Bailey, *M. D.*) Observations on yellow fever. 36 pp. 8°. [*Washington, author, about* 1824]. s.

Washington (E. K.) Echoes of Europe; or, word pictures of travel. 697 pp. 8°. *Philadelphia, J. Challen & son,* 1860.

Washington (George). Epistles: domestic, confidential, and official. xiv, 303 pp. 1 pl. 8°. *New York, G. Robinson & J. Bull,* 1796.

——— The same. xvi, 303 pp. 8°. *London, F. & C. Rivington,* 1796.

——— Letters to the marquis de Chastellux. 35 pp. 8°. *Charleston, (S. C.) C. C. Sebring,* 1825.

——— Monuments of patriotism; a collection of documents connected with [his] military command and civil administration. 338 pp. 2 pl. 8°. *Philadelphia, J. Ormrod,* 1800.

——— Political legacies; [with] an appendix containing an account of his illness, death, and the national tributes of respect paid to his memory, with an outline of his life and character. 208, 14 pp. 8°. *Boston, John Russell & John West,* 1800.

Washingtoniana (The): containing a biographical sketch of George Washington, with various outlines of his character. viii, 298 pp. 3 l. 1 pl. 16°. *Baltimore, Samuel Sower,* 1800.

——— The same. Containing a sketch of the life and death of the late George Washington: with a collection of elegant eulogies, orations, poems, etc. sacred to his memory. Also, an appendix comprising all his most valuable public papers, [etc.] 411 pp. 1 portrait. 8°. *Lancaster, (Pa.) W. Hamilton,* 1802. s.

——— The same; or, memorials of the death of George Washington; giving an account of the funeral honors paid to his memory, with a list of tracts and volumes printed upon the occasion, and a catalogue of medals commemorating the event. By Franklin B. Hough. 2 v. 272 pp. 1 map. 1 portrait; 304 pp. 1 portrait. 4°. *Roxbury, W. E. Woodward, [printed in Albany by J. Munsell,]* 1865.

Washington's birth day: an historical poem. By a Washingtonian. [*anon.*] 64 pp. 1 pl. sm. 4°. *Albany, E. & E. Hosford,* 1812.

Washington (*D. C.*) The Washington directory. 22, 107 pp. 16°. *Washington, S. A. Elliot,* 1830.

——— Boyd's directory of Washington and Georgetown: with a business directory of Alexandria, Va. Compiled by W. H. Boyd, 1867. 669 pp. 1 map. 8°. *Washington, Boyd's directory co.* [1867].

——— Washington library. A catalogue of books. 75 pp. 16°. *Washington, Gales & Seaton,* 1835.

——— Washington metropolitan mechanics' institute. Record of the second and third exhibition, 1855, 1857. 2 v. in 1. 160 pp; vii, 152 pp. 8°. *Washington, H. Polkinhorn,* 1855–57. s.

Watelet (Claude Henri). Essai sur les jardins. 160 pp. 8°. *Paris, Prault,* 1764.

Waterhouse (Edward). A declaration of the state of the colony and affaires in Virginia. With a relation of the massacre by the native infidels vpon the English, the 22d of March last, etc. and a treatise by Henry Briggs, of the northwest passage by fretum Hudson. 3 p. l. 54 pp. sm. 4°. *London, Robert Mylbourne,* 1622.

Waterland (Daniel, *D. D.*) A vindication of Christ's divinity: being a defense of some queries relating to Dr. Clarke's scheme of the Trinity. In answer to [John Jackson]. 13 p. l. 494 pp. 12°. *Cambridge, (Eng.) C. Crownfield,* 1719.

Waterman (*Rev.* Elijah). A century sermon preached before the first church in Windham, [Ct.] December 10, 1800, containing facts relative to its settlement and progress. 42 pp. 8°. *Windham, (Ct.) John Byrne,* 1801.

Waterston. *See* **Watterston.**

Watson (Egbert P.) The modern practice of American machinists and engineers, including the construction, application, and use of drills, lathe tools, cutters for boring, etc. With workshop management, the steam-engine, etc. 276 pp. 12°. *Philadelphia, H. C. Baird,* 1867.

Watson (Henry C.) Lives of the presidents of the United States, to which is prefixed an introductory history of the United States, [etc]. 640 pp. 24 pl. 8°. *Boston, Kelley & brother*, 1853. s.

Watson (J. Madison). National fifth reader. *See* **Parker** (R. G.) *and* **Watson.**

Watson (Richard, *D. D. bishop of Llandaff*). An apology for the Bible, in a series of letters, addressed to Thomas Paine. 178 pp. 16°. *New York, T. and J. Swords*, 1796.

——— The same. 3d Phila. ed. 80 pp. 8°. *Philadelphia, J. Carey*, 1797.

[*With* PAINE, (Thomas). Works. v. 2. 1797 ed.]

Watson (Winslow C.) Pioneer history of the Champlain valley; being an account of the settlement of Willsborough by William Gilliland, with his journal and other papers, and a memoir and notes, by W. C. Watson. viii, 231 pp. 8°. *Albany, J. Munsell*, 1863.

Watt, *or* **Vadianus**, (Joachim de). Scolia. [*With* **Mela** (Pomponius). Libri de situ orbis. 1518].

Watterston (George). Gallery of American portraits. 123 pp. 16°. *Washington, P. Thompson*, 1830.

——— The same. 3d ed. 157 pp. 16°. *Washington, F. Taylor*, 1836.

——— The L * * * * family in Washington; or, a winter in the metropolis. [*anon.*] 159 pp. 12°. *Washington, Davis & Force*, 1822.

——— Letters from Washington on the constitution and laws; with sketches of prominent public characters. By a foreigner. [*anon.*] 139 pp. 12°. *Washington, J. Gideon, jr.* 1818.

——— A picture of Washington. 131 pp. 2 pl. 24°. *Washington, W. M. Morrison*, 1841.

——— The wanderer in Washington. [*anon.*] 226 pp. 12°. *Washington, J. Elliot & P. Thompson*, 1827.

——— *and* **Van Zandt** (Nicholas Biddle). Tabular statistical views of the population, commerce, navigation, public lands, etc. of the United States. 132 pp. obl. 4°. *Washington, J. Elliot*, 1828.

——— The same. Continuation for 1833. 210 pp. 8°. *Washington, Way & Gideon*, 1833.

Watts (Elizabeth). Fish, and how to cook it. 140 pp. 16°. *London, F. Warne & Co.* 1866.

Watts (*Rev.* George). A sermon before the trustees for establishing the colony of Georgia, in America, 1735. 27 pp. 4°. *London, M. Downing*, 1736.

Watts (Isaac, *D. D.*) Hymns and spiritual songs. 24th ed. xxiv, 304 pp. 18°. *Edinburgh, J. Gray*, 1772.

——— Poetical works. 8°. *Edinburgh*, 1794.

[Anderson's British poets, v. 9].

——— Psalms, carefully suited to the Christian worship in the United States of America, being an imitation of the Psalms of David, as improved by Mr. Barlow. 287 pp. 10 l. 24°. *Wilmington, Peter Brynberg*, 1797.

Watts (William). The seats of the nobility and gentry in England and Scotland; a collection of views, engraved by W. Watts. With descriptions. [*anon.*] 85 l. 84 pl. 4°. *London, William Lewis*, 1830.

Wauters (Pierre Engelbert.) Dispensatorium pharmaceuticum Belgii pauperibus congruum atque dicatum. 108 pp. 8°. *Gandavi, Vanryckegem-Hovaere*, 1831. s.

Waverley abbey. Annales waverlienses, [mlxvi—mccxci. *anon.*] fol. *Oxoniæ*, 1687.

[GALE (Thomas) *and* FELL (John). Rerum anglicarum scriptores veteres. *Oxoniæ*, 1684–91. v. 2].

Waverley (The) dramas, from the novels of Sir W. Scott. [*anon.*] 523 pp. 8 pl. 16°. *London, G. Routledge*, 1845.

CONTENTS.

Guy Mannering.	Antiquary.
Rob Roy.	Fortunes of Nigel.
Heart of Mid Lothian.	Peveril of the Peak.
Kenilworth.	Ivanhoe.

Wayland (Francis, *jr. and* H. L.) A memoir of the life and labors of Francis Wayland, D. D. LL.D. including selections from his personal reminiscences and correspondence. By his sons. 2 v. 429 pp. 1 portrait; 379 pp. 1 portrait. 12°. *New York, Sheldon & Co.* 1867.

Waylen (Edward). A history of Prince George's parish, Montgomery co. with a glance at the rise and establishment of the episcopal church in Maryland. 26 pp. 18°. *Rockville, J. W. Spates*, 1845.

Wayne (Henry C.) Exercise for the broadsword, sabre, cut and thrust, and stick. 43 pp. 12 pl. 12°. *Washington, Gideon & Co.* 1849.

[*With his* Sword exercise].

——— The sword exercise, arranged for military instruction. 62 pp. 11 pl. 12°. *Washington, Gideon & Co.* 1850.

Weale (John). Divers works of early masters in christian decoration; with the biography of Albert Durer, and a succinct account of painted and stained glass. 2 v. 52 pp. 66 col. pl. fol. *London, John Weale*, 1846.

Webb (A. C.) Historical companion, with geographical and historical notes: chronology, wars, etc. of the United States. Part 1. 4th ed. 104 pp. 12°. *Philadelphia, E. C. & J. Biddle,* 1858. s.

Webb (C. H.) Liffith Lank; or, lunacy. Illustrations by Sol. Eytinge, jr. Quotations by various authors. 48 pp. sq. 18°. *New York, Carleton,* 1866.

—— St. Twel'mo; or, the cuneiform cyclopedist of Chattanooga. Illustrations by Sol. Eytinge, jr. 60 pp. sq. 16°. *New York, C. H. Webb,* 1867.

Webb (Francis). Panharmonicon: the principles of harmony in the human frame, etc. 45 pp. 3 pl. 4°. [*London,* 1815].

Webb (James Watson). Altowan; or, incidents of life and adventure in the Rocky Mountains. 2 v. 12°. *New York, Harpers,* 1846. s.

Webb (*Rev.* John). Some plain and necessary directions to obtain eternal salvation, in six sermons. iv, 170 pp. 16°. [*n. p. about* 1729]. [Title-page wanting].

Webber (Samuel). Introduction to English grammar. viii, 116 pp. 12°. *Cambridge, (Mass.) Hilliard & Brown,* 1832. s.

Weber (Albrecht). Verzeichniss der sanskrit handschriften im königliche bibliothek zu Berlin. *See* **Berlin.**

Weber (*Dr.* C.) Der sonderbund und seine auflösung von dem standpunkte einer nationalen politik. iv, 108 pp. 8°. *St. Gallen, Scheitlin & Zollikofer,* 1848.

Weber (E.) Gewächse Esth-Liv-und Curland. *See* **Wiedemann** (F. J.) *and* **Weber.**

Weber (Friedrich Benedict). Handbibliothek der deutschen forstwirthschaftlichen literatur. 116 pp. 8°. *Berlin, H. Frolich,* 1803. s.
[WEBER'S handbuch der ökonomischen literatur, theil. i, band 2].

Weber (Rudolph). Atomgewichts-tabellen zur berechnung der bei analytisch-chemischen untersuchungen erhaltenen resultate. (Nachtrag zu dem handbuche der analytischen chemie von H. Rose). 4 p. l. 125 pp. 1 tab. 8°. *Braunschweig, Vieweg,* 1852. s.

Weber (Veit). Woman's revenge; or, the tribunal of blood. 42 pp. 8°. *London,* 1841.
[HAZLITT'S romancist and novelist's library. v. 3].

Weber (Wilhelm). *See* **Gauss** (C. F.) *and* **Weber.** Resultate aus den beobachtungen des magnetischen vereins.

Webster (Daniel). The constitutional text book: containing selections from his writings, the declaration of independence, etc. With indexes. 504 pp. 12°. *Boston, C. S. Francis & Co.* 1854.

Webster (Daniel). A discourse at Plymouth. Dec. 22, 1820. 104 pp. 8°. *Boston, Wells & Lilly,* 1821.

Webster (Noah). An American dictionary of the English language, etc. Stereotype ed. xxiv, 1011 pp. 8°. *New York, White & Sheffield,* 1839. s.

—— The same. Abridged from the American dictionary, for the use of primary schools and the counting house. 19th ed. 536 pp. sq. 16°. *New York, F. J. Huntington & Co.* 1840. s.

—— The same. Thoroughly revised, enlarged, and improved by C. A. Goodrich and Noah Porter. 4°. *Springfield, (Mass.) G. & C. Merriam,* 1867.

—— The same. A dictionary of the English language, with appendix. Mainly abridged from the quarto dictionary as revised by C. A. Goodrich and N. Porter. By W. A. Wheeler. Illustrated. xl, 1000 pp. 8°. *Springfield, (Mass.) G. & C. Merriam,* 1868.

—— A high school pronouncing dictionary of the English language, abridged from the American dictionary, etc. by William G. Webster. 360 pp. 12°. *New York, Huntington & Savage,* 1849. s.

—— An American selection of lessons in reading and speaking, being the third part of a grammatical institute of the English language. 12th ed. 240 pp. 12°. *Boston, Isaiah Thomas & E. T. Andrews,* 1800.

—— A grammatical institute of the English language. Part second. Containing a plain and comprehensive grammar. 3d Connecticut ed. 131 pp. 16°. *Hartford, Hudson & Goodwin,* 1792.

Webster (Pelatiah). Essay on money as a medium of commerce. By a citizen of the United States. [*anon.*] 2 pl. 60 pp. 24°. *Philadelphia, Young, Stewart & McCulloch,* 1786.

Webster (William). An essay on book-keeping by double entry. 3 p. l. 36, 15 pp. 18°. *Dublin, J. Grierson,* 1719.
[*With* VERNON (John). Complete compting house. 18°. *Dublin,* 1719].

Webster (William C.) The dulcedo: a choice collection of music, arranged to be sung by one, two, three, and four voices. obl. 18°. *Buffalo, O. G. Steele & Co.* 1853. s.

Wedel (Georg Wolfgang). Amœnitates materiæ medicæ. 7 p. l. 512 pp. 7 l. 4°. *Jenæ, J. Bielck,* 1704. s.

—— De medicamentorvm facultatibvs cognoscendis et applicandis, libri duo. Ed. 2ª. 10 p. l. 238 pp. 7 l. 4°. *Jenæ, J. Bielck,* 1696. s.
[*With* the preceding].

Wedel (Georg Wolfgang). Syllabus materiæ medicæ selectioris. 40 pp. 4°. *Jenæ, J. Bielck,* 1701. s.
[*With* the preceding].

Weekly (The) inspector, from Nov. 8, 1806, to Aug. 22, 1807. [Edited by Thomas Green Fessenden.] v. 1–2. 312 pp; 416 pp. 8°. *New York, Hopkins & Seymour,* 1807.

Weeks (Helen C.) Grandpa's house. 239 pp. 6 pl. 16°. *New York, Hurd & Houghton,* 1868.

Weeks (Robert K.) Poems. 142 pp. 16°. *New York, Leypoldt & Holt,* 1866.

Weems (*Rev.* Mason L. *editor*). The immortal mentor; or, man's unerring guide to a healthy, wealthy, and happy life. In 3 pts. By Lewis Cornaro, Dr. Franklin, and Dr. Scott. iv, 321 pp. 16°. *Philadelphia, M. L. Weems,* 1796.

——— The life of Benjamin Franklin, with many of his choice anecdotes and admirable sayings. 239 pp. 1 pl. 16°. *Philadelphia, Uriah Hunt,* 1829.

——— The life of William Penn. 208 pp. 1 pl. 12°. *Philadelphia, Uriah Hunt,* 1829.

——— The life of George Washington; with curious anecdotes. 228 pp. 16°. *Philadelphia, Joseph Allen,* 1838.

——— *and* **Horry** (*brig. gen.* P.) The life of gen. Francis Marion. 2d ed. 270 pp. 16°. *Baltimore, W. D. Bell & J. F. Cook,* 1814.

——— The same. 252 pp. 1 pl. 16°. *Philadelphia, J. Allen,* 1828.

Weerth (Ernst aus'm, *pseudon.*) Kunstdenkmäler des christlichen mittelalters in das Rheinlanden. 1 abth: Bildnerei. 2 v. in 1. vi, xxii, 45 pp; 145 pp. 4°. atlas, 20 p. l. 19 pl. fol. *Leipzig, S. O. Weigel,* 1857–60. s.

Weigand (Friedrich Ludwig Carl). Deutsches wörterbuch. *See* **Grimm** (Jacob L. K.)

Weigel (Johannes August Gottlieb). Apparatvs literarivs, sive index librorvm lectissimorvm qvos svo sibi aere coemtos emtvrientibvs offert. Cvm indice. 496 columns on 248 pp. 64 l. 66 pp. 4°. *Lipsiae, Weigel,* 1821. s.

Weigel (Rudolph). Kunstcatalog. 1e–14e abtheilung, nebst register. 2 v. 8°. *Leipzig, R. Weigel,* 1838–43.

——— Suppléments au Peintre-graveur de A. Bartsch. *See* **Bartsch** (Adam von).

Weinland (Christoph David Friedrich). Human cestoides. An essay on the tapeworms of man, [with] an appendix, containing a catalogue of all species of helminthes hitherto found in man. x, 93 pp. 8°. *Cambridge, (Mass.) Metcalf & Co.* 1858. s.

Weinmann (J. A.) Enumeratio stirpium in agro petropolitano sponte crescentium, secundum systema sexuale linneanum composita. iv, 320 pp. 8°. *Petropoli,* 1837. s.

Weisbach (Julius). Anleitung zum axonometrischen zeichnen. vi, 128 pp. 2 pl. 12°. *Freiburg, J. G. Engelhardt,* 1857. s.

——— Lehrbuch der ingenieur- und maschinenmechanik. Mit den nöthigen hülfslehren aus der analysis für den unterricht an technischen lehranstalten sowie zum gebrauche für techniker. 2e aufl. 1e–3e theile. 4 v. 8°. *Braunschweig, Vieweg,* 1851–59. s.

CONTENTS.

v. 1. Theoretische mechanik. xiv, 697 pp.
v. 2. Statik der bauwerke und mechanik der umtriebsmaschinen. viii, 712 pp.
v. 3–4. 3e theil. Die mechanik der zwischen- und arbeitsmaschinen. 1 v. in 2. xv, 1362 pp. S.

——— The same. 1er thiel: Lehrbuch der theoretischen mechanik. 4e aufl. xxxi, 1066 pp. 8°. *Braunschweig, Vieweg,* 1862–63. s.

Weiser (*Rev.* R.) Luther, by a Lutheran; or, a full-length portrait of the great reformer. 6th ed. ccccxliii pp. 12°. *Baltimore, T. N. Kurtz,* 1853.

Weishampel (J. F. *jr.*) The stranger in Baltimore; a new hand-book, containing sketches of the early history and present condition of Baltimore. 182 pp. 24°. *Baltimore, J. F. Weishampel, jr.* [1866].

Weiss (*Dr.* J. Joseph). Handbuch der wasserheilkunde. 2e aufl. iv, 508 pp. 12°. *Leipzig, F. Brandstetter,* 1847. s.

Weiss (Philipp Friedrich). Ueber den starrkrampf. viii, 92 pp. 12°. *Stuttgart,* 1824. s.

Weitenweber (Wilhelm Rudolph). Der arabische kaffee, in naturgeschichtlicher, chemischer, diätetischer und ärztlicher beziehung. 2e ausg. 130 pp. 1 pl. 12°. *Prag, Leitmeritz u. Teplitz,* 1837. s.

Welch (A. S.) Analysis of the English sentence. 264 pp. 12°. *New York, A. S. Barnes & Co.* 1855. s.

Welcker (Hermann). Ueber irradiation und einige andere erscheinungen des sehens. x, 198 pp. 8 pl. 8°. *Giessen, J. Ricker,* 1852. s.

Weld (Allen H.) English grammar. 234 pp. 12°. *Portland, (Me.) Sanborn & Carter,* 1849. s.

Weld (Charles Richard). Arctic expeditions; a lecture at the London institution, 1850. 48 pp. 1 map. 8°. *London, J. Murray,* 1850.

Welde (Thomas). A short story of the rise, reign, and ruin of the antinomians, familists, and libertines, that infected the churches of New England. 9 p. l. 66 pp. sm. 4°. *London, Ralph Smith,* 1644.

Well (Johann Jakob von). Methodische eintheilung mineralischer körper. 375 pp. 4 pl. 8°. *Wien, R. Gräffer*, 1786. s.

Wellcome (J. C.) *and* **Goud** (Clarkson). Christian baptism; its duty and object considered and enforced. With extracts from histories on immersion, etc. 81 pp. 12°. *Yarmouth, (Me.) author*, 1867.
[*With his* "Plan of redemption," etc.]

——— The plan of redemption by our Lord Jesus Christ; examined and argued. 328 pp. 12°. *Yarmouth, (Me.) authors*, 1867.

Weller (Emil). Die falschen und fingirten druckorte. Repertorium der seit erfindung der buchdruckerkunst unter falscher firma erschienenen deutschen, lateinischen, und französischen schriften. 2e aufl. 2 v. viii, 333 pp; v, 309 pp. 8°. *Leipzig, W. Engelmann*, 1864.

CONTENTS.

v. 1. Enthaltend die deutschen und lateinischen schriften.
v. 2. Enthaltend die französichen schriften. Dictionnaire des ouvrages français portant de fausses indications des lieux d'impression et des imprimeurs. Depuis le 16e siècle jusqu' aux temps modernes.

——— Index pseudonymorum. Wörterbuch der pseudonymen; oder, verzeichniss aller autoren, die sich falscher namen bedienten. 2e ausg. x, 391 pp. 8°. *Leipzig, G. Oehme*, 1862.
[v. 1 of Weller's "Die maskirte literatur der älteren und neueren sprachen"].

Wellesley (Arthur, *duke of Wellington*). General orders in Portugal, Spain, and France, 1809–14, and the Low Countries and France, 1815. Compiled by lieutenant colonel Gurwood. xxx, 460 pp. 8°. *London, W. Clowes*, 1832.

Wellesley (Henry, *D. D.*) Anthologia polyglotta: a selection of versions in various languages, chiefly from the Greek anthology. vii, 485 pp. 4°. *London, J. Murray*, 1849.

Wellesley (Richard Colley, *marquess Wellesley*). Despatches, minutes, and correspondence, during his administration in India. Edited by Montgomery Martin. 5 v. 3 pl. 2 maps. 8°. *London, W. H. Allen & Co.* 1836–7.

——— Despatches and correspondence, during his mission to Spain in 1809. Ed. by Montgomery Martin. lxix, 197 pp. 8°. *London, John Murray*, 1838.

Wellington (Arthur Wellesley, *duke of*). *See* **Wellesley** (Arthur).

Wells (Oliver), & Co. A specimen of printing types and ornaments, etc. 8°. *Cincinnati, O. Wells & Co.* 1829. s.

Wells (S. M.) The electropathic guide, prepared [for] home practice: containing hints on the care of the sick, the treatment of disease, and the use of electricity, with full directions for treating over 100 cases. 90 pp. 16°. *Chicago, Horton & Leonard*, 1867.

Welwood (James, *M. D.*) Memoirs of the most material transactions in England, for the last hundred years preceding the revolution in 1688. 11 p. l. 405 pp. 12°. *London, T. Goodwin*, 1700.

——— The same. New ed. 288 pp. 6 l. 16°. *Glasgow, Urie & Co.* 1744.

Wenig (Christian). Gedrängtes handwörterbuch der deutschen sprache. ix, 830 pp. 8°. *Erfurt, Keyser*, 1821. s.

Weninger (*Rev.* Francis Xavier, *S. J.*) Sacred heart mission book: a guide to christian perfection. 584 pp. 1 pl. 18°. *Cincinnati, J. P. Walsh*, 1864.

Wentworth (May, *pseudon?*) Poetry of the Pacific. Selections and original poems from the poets of the Pacific states. 415 pp. 12°. *San Francisco, Pacific pub. Co.* 1867.

Wentz (Sarah A.) Amy Denbrook. A life drama. [*anon.*] 482 pp. 12°. *New York, J. O'Kane*, [1867].

Werlauff (Erik Christian). Historiske efterretninger om det store kongelige bibliothek i Kiobenhavn. 2en udgave. x, 432 pp. 2 pl. 8°. *Kiobenhavn, Samfundet til den danske literaturs fremme*, 1844. s.

Werne (Ferdinand). Feldzug von Sennaar nach Taka, Basa, und Beni-Amer, mit besonderem hinblick auf die völker von Bellad-Sudan. 3 p. l. 272 pp. 3 pl. 1 map. 8°. *Stuttgart, Hofbuchdruckerei zu Guttenberg*, 1851. s.

Werth (John J.) A dissertation on the resources and policy of California. 87 pp. 12°. *Benicia, (Cal.) St. Clair & Pinkham*, 1851.

Wertheim (Guillaume). Mémoires de physique mécanique. [Extract.] 6 v. in 1. 8°. *Paris, [Annales de chimie, etc.]* 1842—1848. s.

CONTENTS.

Recherches sur l'élasticité. 114 pp. 1 pl. 1842.
Mémoire sur les sons produits par le courant électrique. 26 pp. 1848.
Note sur l'élasticité de verre; par E. Chevandier et G. Wertheim. 45 pp. 1845.
Mémoire sur la vitesse du son dans les liquides. 43 pp. 1 pl.
Mémoire sur les propriétés mécaniques du bois; par E. Chevandier et G. Wertheim. 135 pp. 2 p. l. 1848.
Mémoire sur l'élasticité et la cohésion des principaux tissus du corps humain. 30 pp. 1846.

Werz (H.) Der kleine rechner. 171 pp. 12°. *St. Louis, (Mo.) H. Werz, etc.* 1858. s.

Werzdorf (J. F. L. Th.) Geschichte der freimaurerlogen im herzogthume Oldenburg. 3 p. l. 154 pp. 8°. *Oldenburg, B. Berndt,* 1852. s.

Wesley (*Rev.* Charles). Charles Wesley seen in his finer and less familiar poems. [Ed. by F. M. Bird]. xvi, 398 pp. 16°. *New York, Hurd & Houghton,* 1867.

Wesley (*Rev.* John). A collection of hymns for the use of the people called methodists. 1st. Amer. from 18th London ed. iv, 152 pp. 4 l. 24°. *Baltimore, R. W. Pomeroy,* 1814.

——— The same. New ed. 552 pp. 24°. *Derby, (Eng.) H. Mozley,* 1820.

——— An extract of [his] journal, from his embarking for Georgia, [Oct. 14, 1735,] to [Oct. 24, 1790]. 21 nos. in 5 v. 12°. *London,* 1777–97.

——— Sermon on the death of Rev. George Whitefield. 32 pp. 12°. *London, J. and W. Oliver,* 1770.

West (Gilbert). A defence of the christian revelation; as contained in observations on the history and evidences of the resurrection of Jesus Christ. iv, 196 pp. 8°. *London, printed by subscription,* 1748.

——— Poetical works. 8°. *Edinburgh,* 1794.
[Anderson's Brit. poets, v. 9].

West (Hans). Bidrag til beskrivelse over St[e]. Croix, med en kort udsigt over St. Thomas, St. Jean, Tortola, Spanishtown og Crabeneiland. 3 p. l. 363 pp. 12°. *Kiöbenhavn, F. W. Thiele,* 1793.

West (Nathaniel, *D. D.*) Complete analysis of the holy bible. *See* **Bible** (*English*).

West (Thomas). A guide to the lakes, in Cumberland, Westmoreland, and Lancashire. [*anon.*] 6th ed. xii, 313 pp. 1 map. 2 pl. 8°. *London, W. Richardson,* 1796.

Westcott (James D.) Masonic address at the funeral of col. Abraham Bellamy. 29 pp. 8°. *Tallahassee, S. S. Sibley,* 1839.

Western (The) academician and journal of education and science. Edited by J. W. Picket. v. 1. iv, 704 pp. 8°. *Cincinnati, J. R. Allbach,* 1837–38.

Western (The) agriculturist, and practical farmer's guide. By the Hamilton co. (O.) agricultural society. xii, 367 pp. 4 pl. 16°. *Cincinnati, Robinson & Fairbank,* 1830.

Western literary institute and college of professional teachers. Transactions. Fourth to tenth annual meeting. 1834–1840. 6 v. 8°. *Cincinnati,* 1835–41.

Western (The) monthly magazine, a continuation of the Illinois monthly magazine. Conducted by James Hall. v. 1–3. 8°. *Cincinnati, Corey & Fairbank,* 1833–36.

Western (The) review and miscellaneous magazine. v. 1–4. Sept. 1819 to June, 1821. 4 v. 8°. *Lexington, (Ky.) W. G. Hunt,* 1820.

Westminster (The) review. Jan. 1866, to Oct. 1867. New series. v. 29–32. [Complete series, v. 85–88.] 8°. *London, Trübner & Co.* 1866–67.

Weston (Edward Payson). Bowdoin poets. 2d ed. 180 pp. 1 pl. 12°. *Brunswick, (Me.) J. Griffin,* 1849.

Weston (William). The complete merchant's clerk. 4 p. l. 284 pp. 8°. *London, C. Rivington,* 1754.

West Point. Register of the officers and graduates of the U. S. military academy, from March 16, 1802, to January 1, 1850. Compiled by George W. Cullum. 302 pp. 12°. *New York, J. F. Trow,* 1850. s.

Westwood (John Obadiah). Arcana entomologica; or, illustrations of new, rare, and interesting insects. 2 v. iv, 192 pp. 48 col. pl; 2 p. l. 192 pp. 49–95 col. pl. 8°. *London, Wm. Smith,* 1845. s.

——— Palæographia sacra pictoria; being a series of illustrations of the ancient versions of the Bible, copied from illuminated manuscripts, executed between the 4th and 16th centuries. xvii pp. 88 l. 50 col. pl. 4°. *London, W. Smith,* 1843–45.

Wetenhall (Edward, *bishop of Cork and Ross*). A short introduction to grammar, for the use of the college and academy in Philadelphia; being a new edition of Whittenhall's Latin grammar. 3d ed. v, 145 pp. 18°. *Philadelphia, J. Crukshank,* 1779.

Wetherell (Elizabeth, *pseudon.*) *See* **Warner** (Susan).

Wetmore (*Rev.* James). Quakerism, a judicial infatuation. vii, 69 pp. 18°. *New York, J. Peter Zenger,* (1730?)

Wharton (*Rev.* Francis). The silence of scripture. xii, 122 pp. 16°. *Boston, E. P. Dutton & Co.* 1867.

Whately (Richard, *abp. of Dublin*). Easy lessons on money matters for young people. [*anon.*] 86 pp. 24°. *London, J. W. Parker,* 1833.
[Society for promoting christian knowledge].

Wheat (M. T.) Progress and intelligence of Americans; collateral proof of slavery from Genesis; progress of slavery, through the acquisition of territory; advantages explained. 2d ed. 595, xx pp. 8°. *Louisville, (Ky.)* 1862.

Wheatley (Phillis). Poems on various subjects, religious and moral. 3 p. l. 124 pp. 1 pl. 16°. *London, A. Bell,* 1773.

Wheaton (Henry). Address at the opening of the New York Athenæum, 1824: [a retrospect of what the American mind has accomplished and may achieve]. 2d ed. 62 pp. 8°. *New York, J. W. Palmer & Co.* 1825.

Wheeler (David Hilton). Brigandage in South Italy. By David Hilton. [*pseudon.*] 2 v. xv, 328 pp; viii, 195 pp. 12°. *London, Sampson Low & Co.* 1864.

Wheeler (Gervase, *architect*). Homes for the people, in suburb and country; the villa, mansion, and cottage. With examples showing how to alter and remodel old buildings. Illustrated. 6th thousand. Revised ed. x, 441 pp. 11 pl. 12°. *New York, G. E. Woodward,* 1868.

——— Rural homes; or, sketches of houses suited to American country life, with original plans, designs, etc. Rev. ed. 298 pp. 8 pl. 12°. *New York, G. E. Woodward,* 1868.

Wheeler (James). Manchester, [England]: its political, social, and commercial history, ancient and modern. xi, 538 pp. 12°. *London, Whittaker & Co.* 1836. s.

Wheeler (*Capt.* Thomas). Narrative of an expedition to the Nipmuck country, and to Quaboag, now Brookfield, Mass.

[*With* FOOT (J. I.) Hist. address at West Brookfield, pp. 31-47. 1843].

Wheeler (William Adolphus). Appendix to Webster's dictionary; containing a glossary of Scottish words and phrases; a vocabulary of perfect and allowable rhymes; an account of the deities, etc. of Greek and Roman mythology, [etc. With] pictorial illustrations of terms defined in the dictionary. 8°. *Springfield, (Mass.) G. & C. Merriam,* 1868.

[*With* WEBSTER (Noah). Dictionary of the English language. 8°. ed. 1868. pp. 837—1000].

Wheeler. *See, also,* **Wheler.**

Wheeling, (*West Va.*) Directory for 1867-'8. [Also], a U. S. post office directory. Williams & Co. compilers. 3d issue. 248, 109 pp. 8°. *Wheeling, J. C. Orr & Co.* 1867.

——— Directory and advertiser. By J. B. Bowen. 18 p. l. 90 pp. 18°. *Wheeling, J. M. McCreary,* 1839.

Wheelwright (H. W.) Bush wanderings of a naturalist; or, notes on the field sports and fauna of Australia Felix. By an old bushman. [*anon.*] xv, 272 pp. 16°. *London, Routledge,* 1861.

——— Spring and summer in Lapland, with notes on the fauna of Luleä Lapmark. By an "old bushman." [*anon.*] viii, 407 pp. 12°. *London, Groombridge,* 1864.

Wheler (*Sir* George). A journey into Greece. 7 p. l. 483 pp. 1 map. 4 pl. fol. *London, W. Cademan,* 1682.

Where shall he find her? [*anon.*] Translated from the French, by J. D. A. 16°. *New York,* 1867.

[Library of light literature, no. 1].

Whewell (William). History of scientific ideas. 3d ed. 2 v. xvi, 386 pp; xv, 324 pp. 12°. *London, J. W. Parker,* 1858. s.

——— Indications of the creation. 86 pp. 12°. *Philadelphia, Carey & Hart,* 1845. s.

——— The mechanical Euclid; containing the elements of mechanics and hydrostatics, demonstrated after the manner of the elements of geometry. viii, 182 pp. 12° *Cambridge, (Eng.) J. W. Parker,* 1837. s.

——— Report on the recent progress and present state of mineralogy. 43 pp. 8°. *British assoc. advance. science,* 1832.

[*With* NAUMANN (C. F.) Table, etc. 1833].

Whisperer (The, a political weekly). 100 nos. Feb. 17, 1770—Jan. 11, 1772. [With a manuscript index, and several numbers of the North Briton, etc.] 634 pp. 4 l. *ms.* 1 pl. fol. *London, W. Moore,* 1770-72.

Whitaker (*Mrs.* Mary Scrimzeour). Poems. 300 pp. 12°. *Charleston, J. B. Nixon,* 1850.

Whitaker (William, *D. D.*) Disputation on holy scripture, against the papists, especially Bellarmine and Stapleton. Translated and edited by Rev. W. Fitzgerald. xii, 718 pp. 8°. *Cambridge, (Eng.) Univ. press,* 1849. [*Parker society publications*].

CONTENTS.

Number of the canonical books of scripture.
Authentic editions and versions of the scriptures.
Authority, perspicuity, interpretation and perfection of scripture against unwritten tradition.

Whitbourne (*Capt.* Richard). A discourse and discovery of Nevv-fovnd-land. 8 p. l. 69, iv pp. sm. 4°. *London, W. Barrer,* 1622.

——— The same. With invitation and certaine letters. 8 p. l. 107, v pp. sm. 4°. *London, William Barrer,* 1622.

[Imperfect. Title page in ms.]

Whitcher (*Mrs.* Frances M.) Widow Spriggins, Mary Elmer, and other sketches. Ed. with memoir, by Mrs. M. L. Ward Whitcher. With comic illustrations. 378 pp. 6 pl. 12°. *New York, G. W. Carleton & Co.* 1867.

White (Adam). A popular history of mammalia. viii, 362 pp. 16 pl. sq. 16°. *London, Reeve, Benham, & Reeve,* 1850. s.

White (Charles, *Col. British army*). Three years in Constantinople; or, domestic manners of the Turks in 1844. 3 v. 8°. *London, H. Colburn*, 1845.

White (Charles Abiathar), *and* **St. John**, (Orestes Henry). State geological survey of Iowa. Preliminary notice of new genera and species of fossils. 3 pp. 8°. [*Iowa city, State*], 1867. s.

White (*Rev.* Charles I. *D. D.*) Life of Mrs. Eliza A. Seton, foundress and first superior of the sisters or daughters of charity in the U. S. 2d ed. 462 pp. 1 portrait. 12°. *Baltimore, J. Murphy & Co.* 1856. s.

White (Christopher, *B. D.*) Of oathes, their object, forme, and bond: the punishment of perivrie, and the impietie of papal dispensations. Three sermons. 2 p. l. 55 pp. sm. 4°. *London, Ralph Mab*, 1627.

White (Daniel Appleton). New England congregationalism in its origin and purity; illustrated by the foundation and early records of the First church in Salem. 3 p. l. 319 pp. 8°. *Salem*, 1861.

White (Elijah). A concise view of Oregon territory, its colonial and Indian relations, together with the organic laws of the colony. 72 pp. 8°. *Washington, T. Barnard*, 1846.

White (George, *of Georgia*). An accurate account of the Yazoo fraud. 61 pp. 8°. *Marietta, (Ga.) advocate office*, 1852.

White (*Rev.* Gilbert). A naturalist's calendar, with observations in various branches of natural history. 175 pp. 1 col. pl. 8°. *London, B. & J. White*, 1795. s.

White (Henry, *Ph. D.*) A guide to the civil service; with directions for candidates, examination papers, standards of qualification, amount of salaries, etc. 8th ed. revised by A. C. Ewald. vi, 148 pp. 16°. *London, F. Warne & Co.* 1867.

White (*Rev.* John, *of Dorchester, Eng.*) The planter's plea; or the grovnds of plantations examined, and vsuall objections answered. [*anon.*] 85 pp. sm. 4°. *London, W. Jones*, 1630.

White (John, *lawyer, of London*). The first centvry of scandalous, malignant priests admitted to benefices by the prelates. A narration of the causes for which parliament hath ordered the sequestration of [their] benefices. 3 p. l. 51 pp. sm. 4°. *London, George Miller*, 1643.

White (*Rev.* John, *of Gloucester, Mass.*) New England's lamentations, under these three heads, the decay of the power of godliness; the danger of Arminian principles; the declining state of our church order, government, and discipline. 42 pp. 16°. *Boston, T. Fleet*, 1734.

[*With* WILLIAMS (*Rev.* John). Redeemed captive. *Boston*, 1734].

White (*Rev.* John, *of Philadelphia*). Art of measuring. 66 pp. 12°. *Philadelphia, Anderson and Meehan*, 1818.

[*With his* Practical system of mental arithmetic. *Philadelphia*, 1818].

——— Key to appendix in White's mental arithmetic, with key to White's self-instructor. 109 pp. 8°. *Philadelphia, D. Heartt*, 1818.

[*With his* Practical system of arithmetic. 1818 ed.]

——— Practical system of mental arithmetic. 118 pp. 8°. *Philadelphia, D. Heartt*, 1818.

——— Self-instructor, or a system of practical arithmetic. 71 pp. 8°. *Philadelphia, D. Heartt*, 1818.

[*With his* Practical system of mental arithmetic. *Philadelphia*, 1818].

White (John J.) Peace, and other poems. 126 pp. 12°. *Philadelphia, Lippincott*, 1867.

White (José Maria Blanco). Law of anti-religious libel reconsidered, in a letter to the editor of the Christian examiner, in answer to an article of that periodical against Search's considerations, etc. 106 pp. 8°. *Dublin, R. Milliken & Co.* 1834.

[*With* SEARCH (John). Considerations, etc].

——— Observations on heresy and orthodoxy. xvi, 120 pp. 8°. *London, J. Mardon*, 1835.

[*With* SEARCH (John). Considerations, etc.]

——— Practical and internal evidence against catholicism. 1st Am. ed. 315 pp. 12°. *Georgetown, (D. C.) James C. Dunn*, 1826.

White (Richard Grant). The adventures of Sir Lyon Bouse in America during the civil war. [*anon.*] 64 pp. 12°. *New York, Am. news co.* 1867.

——— The new gospel of peace according to St. Benjamin. [*anon.*] xxvi, 343 pp. 12°. *New York, Am. news co.* 1866.

White (Robert—*In continuation*). Appendix to ephemeris for 1836–37. [Edited by O. Gregory].

[*With* WAKELEY (A.) Mariner's compass rectified. 1766].

White (Seneca). Ki noh shuh, nr wen ne uh, na da wi sem nyo gurh. [Hymn book in the Seneca (?) language]. 45 pp. 32°. [*n. p.*] 1832.

White (Walter). Eastern England, from the Thames to the Humber. 2 v. 6 p. l. 304 pp; 6 p. l. 315 pp. 12°. *London, Chapman & Hall*, 1865.

——— A July holiday in Saxony, Bohemia, and Silesia. xiv, 305 pp. 12°. *London, Chapman & Hall*, 1857.

White (Walter). Papers on railway and electric communications, arctic and antarctic explorations, and the sanitary movement. (Extracts.) 12°. *Edinburgh,* [*Chambers,*] 1850–51. s.

White (William, *of Belfast, Me.*) A history of Belfast, (Maine,) with remarks on Acadia. 119 pp. 16°. *Belfast, E. E. Fellowes,* 1827.

White (William, *of London*). Emanuel Swedenborg: his life and writings. 2 v. xxiv, 604 pp; xix, 694 pp. 4 pl. 8°. *London, Simpkin, Marshall & Co.* 1867.

White (William Hale). Argument for an extension of the franchise. 19 pp. 8°. *London, F. Farrah,* 1866.

White (William Henry). General regulations for the government of the order of royal arch masons of England, established by the grand chapter. [*anon.*] 31 pp. 14 pl. 8°. *London, W. H. White,* 1852.

White (William S.) Sketches of the life of Capt. Hugh A. White, of the Stonewall brigage. By his father. 124 pp. 8°. *Columbia, (S.C.) South Carolinian steam press,* 1864.

White, Hagar, & Co. Specimens of modern and light face printing types and ornaments. 160 l. 8°. *New York,* [*White, Hagar, & Co.*] 1833.

White. *See, also,* **Whyte.**

White acre *vs.* black acre. A case at law, reported by J. G. Esq. [*anon.*] 16°. *Richmond, (Va.) J. W. Randolph,* 1856.

White Sulphur papers; or, life at the springs of western Virginia. By Mark Pencil. [*pseudon.*] 166 pp. 12°. *New York, Samuel Colman,* 1839.

Whitefield (George). An expostulatory letter addressed to Nicholas Lewis, count Zinzendorff. 3d ed. 15 pp. 12°. *Philadelphia, William Bradford,* 1753.

——— Indwelling of the spirit, the common privilege of all believers. Sermon. 22 pp. 12°. *London, W. Strahan,* 1739.

——— Journal: (bound together.)

Voyage from London to Savannah. 5th ed. 55 pp. 12°. *London, James Hutton,* 1739.

——— Continuation, from arrival at Savannah to return to London. 2d ed. 38 pp. 12°. *London, W. Strahan,* 1739.

——— The same. (Stay in England. Title-page wanting). iv, 115 pp. 12°. (*London, W. Strahan,* 1739) ?

——— The same, during the time he was detained in England by the embargo. 3d ed. iv, 40 pp. 12°. *London, W. Strahan,* 1739.

——— The same, from embarking after embargo to arrival at Savannah. 88 pp. 12°. *London, W. Strahan,* 1740.

——— The same, from arrival at Georgia to second return thither from Philadelphia. 58 pp. 12°. *London, W. Strahan,* 1741.

——— The same, from return to Georgia to arrival at Falmouth. 86 pp. 12°. *London, W. Strahan,* 1741

——— Letter to Gov. Wright, giving an account of the steps to convert the Georgia orphanhouse into a college, with plans. 30 pp. 8°. *London, J. Millan,* 1768.

——— The nature and necessity of our new birth in Christ Jesus, in order to salvation. A sermon. viii, 28 pp. 12°. *London, C. Rivington,* 1737.

——— The nature and necessity of society in general, and of religious society in particular. A sermon. 3d ed. viii, 30 pp. 12°. *London, W. Bowyer,* 1738.

——— Observations on some fatal mistakes in a book, intitled, The doctrine of grace, by B'p Warburton. 24 pp. 16°. *Boston, R. and S. Draper,* 1764.

——— The putting on the new man a certain mark of the real christian. A sermon. iv, 30 pp. 8°. *London, J. Towers,* [1771] ?

——— A sermon, being his last farewell to his friends, before his departure for Georgia. iv, 32 pp. 12°. *London, S. Bladon,* 1769.

——— Several discourses upon practical subjects. 2 p. l. 186 pp. 8°. *London, J. Hodges,* 1738.

——— A short account of God's dealings with Rev. Geo. Whitefield, written by himself. 76 pp. 16°. *London, W. Strahan,* 1740.

——— Thankfulness for mercies received a necessary duty. A sermon. 19 pp. 16°. *London, James Hutton,* 1738.

——— The two first parts of his life, with journals. 3 p. l. 446 pp. 18°. *London, W. Strahan,* 1756.

Whitefield. *See, also,* **Whitfield.**

Whitehead (George), *and* **Penn** (William). A serious apology for the principles and practices of the people called Quakers. 4 p. l. pp. 77–207. sm. 4°. [*n. p.*] 1671.

Whitelaw (Alexander, *editor*). The casquet of literary gems. [Illustrated]. 4 v. 12°. *Glasgow, Blackie & son,* 1836–39.

Whitelocke (*Sir* Bulstrode). The history of England; or, memorials of the English affairs, from the suppos'd expedition of Brute to the end of the reign of James i. Publish'd by W. Penn. [With] the author's life by J. Welwood. [2d ed.] 8 p. l. vii, 310 pp. 16 l. portrait. fol. *London, E. Curll,* 1713.

——— Memorials of the English affairs; or, an historical account of what passed from the beginning of the reign of Charles i. to Charles ii. his happy restauration. [1st ed. *anon.*] 4 p. l. 704 pp. 8 l. fol. *London, N. Ponder,* 1682.

[NOTE.—"Published by Arthur Annesley, earl of Anglesey, who took considerable liberties with the ms." Lowndes.]

Whitelocke (*Sir* Bulstrode). Notes uppon the king's writt for choosing members of parlement, xiii. Car. ii. being disquisitions on the government of England. Published by Charles Morton, M. D. 2 v. xlv, 518 pp; 2 p. l. 452 pp. 6 l. 4°. *London, A. Millar,* 1766.

Whitfield (Thomas). The doctrines of the Arminians and Pelagians stated and answered. 99 pp. sm. 4°. *London, John Bellamie,* 1652.

Whitfield (*Rev.* Henry). The light appearing more and more towards the perfect day; or, a farther discovery of the present state of the Indians in New England, concerning the progresse of the gospel amongst them. Manifested by letters from such as preacht to them there. 4 p. l. 46 pp. sm. 4°. *London, John Bartlett,* 1651.

——— Strength out of weakness; or, a glorious manifestation of the further progresse of the gospel amongst the Indians in New England. 6 p. l. 40 pp. sm. 4°. *London, John Blague,* 1652.

Whitfield. *See, also,* **Whitefield.**

Whiting (William). The war powers of the president, and the legislative powers of congress, in relation to rebellion, treason, and slavery. 7th ed. vi, 151 pp. 8°. *Boston, J. L. Shorey,* 1863. s.

Whitlock (George Clinton). Elements of geometry, theoretical and practical, etc. 324 pp. 8°. *New York, Pratt, Woodford & Co.* 1848. s.

Whitlocke (*Sir* Bulstrode). *See* **Whitelocke.**

Whitmarsh (*Miss* Caroline S. *compiler*). Prayers of the ages. xvii, 335 pp. 12°. *Boston, Ticknor & Fields,* 1868.

——— *and* **Guild** (A. E.) Hymns for mothers and children. [*anon.*] Second series. xi, 347 pp. sq. 12°. *Boston, Walker, Fuller & Co.* 1866.

Whitmore (William Henry). Memoranda of the Lane, Reyner, and Whipple families, Yorkshire and Massachusetts. 24 pp. 8°. *Boston, Henry W. Dutton,* 1857.

——— Register of families settled at the town of Medford, Mass. 96 pp. 11 pl. 8°. *Boston, J. Wilson & son,* 1855.

Whitney (Elisha). Address at a meeting of the Whittlesey family, which convened at Saybrook, Connecticut, September 20, 1855. 22 pp. 8°. *Washington,* 1855.

Whitney (George). Some account of the early history and present state of Quincy. 64 pp. 8°. *Quincy, (Mass.) S. B. Manning,* [*about* 1827].

Whitney (James Dwight). Report of a geological survey of the Upper Mississippi lead region. vi, pp. 75–455. 7 maps. 2 pl. 8°. *Albany,* 1862. s.

——— *See, also,* **California.** Geological survey.

Whitney (J. H. E.) The Hawkins zouaves. [Ninth N. Y. V.] Their battles and marches. 216 pp. 12°. *New York, author,* 1866.

Whitney (William Dwight). Language, and the study of language. Twelve lectures on the principles of linguistic science. xi, 489 pp. 12°. *New York, C. Scribner & Co.* 1867.

Whiton (John Milton, *D. D.*) Sketches of the history of New Hampshire, from its settlement in 1623 to 1833. 222 pp. 12°. *Concord, (N.H) Marsh, Capen & Lyon,* 1834.

Whittenhall (Edward). *See* **Wetenhall** (E.)

Whittier (John Greenleaf). Poetical works, complete. [Diamond edition]. xi, 410 pp. sq. 18°. *Boston, Ticknor & Fields,* 1867.

——— Maud Muller. With illustrations by W. J. Hennessy. v, 12 l. sm. 4°. *Boston, Ticknor & Fields,* 1867.

——— Snow-bound; a winter idyl. Illustrated. 65 pp. 8°. *Boston, Ticknor & Fields,* 1868.

——— The tent on the beach, and other poems. 16°. *Boston, Ticknor & Fields,* 1867.

Whittington (*Rev.* G. D.) An historical survey of the ecclesiastical antiquities of France; with a view to illustrate the rise and progress of gothic architecture in Europe. xv, 188 pp. 1 pl. 4°. *London, J. Taylor,* 1809.

[*With* DRUMMOND (*Sir* W.) *and* WALPOLE (*Rev.* R.) Herculanensia. *London,* 1810].

Whittlesey (*Col.* Charles). Early history of Cleveland, Ohio, and the adjacent country; with biographical notices of the pioneers and surveyors. 487 pp. 6 pl. 8°. *Cleveland, Fairbanks, Benedict & Co.* 1867.

——— Geographical report of that part of Wisconsin, south of Lake Superior, etc. s.

[*With* OWEN (D. D.) Report of a geological survey of Wisconsin, etc. 1852].

Whitty (Edward M.) The governing classes of Great Britain. Political portraits. 2 p. l. 218 pp. 16°. *London, Trübner,* 1854.

Whitworth (Charles, *lord*). Account of Russia as it was in the year 1710. [Edited by Horace Walpole]. xxiv, 159 pp. 12°. *Strawberry Hill,* [*Twickenham, Eng.*] 1758.

Who is the legitimate king of Portugal? A Portuguese question submitted to impartial men. By a Portuguese residing in London. [*anon.*] Translated from the Portuguese. 96 pp. 8°. *London,* 1828.

Whyte (Samuel, *teacher, in Dublin*). The shamrock; or, Hibernian cresses. A collection of poems, songs, etc. Latin as well as English, the production of Ireland. xviii, 515 pp. 4°. *Dublin, R. Marchbank,* 1772.

—— *and* (Edward A.) A miscellany, containing remarks on Boswell's Johnson; a critique on Bürger's Leonora, and an essay on the art of reading and speaking in public. viii, 188 pp. 12°. *Dublin, E. A. Whyte,* 1799.

Wicar (Jean Baptiste Joseph). Tableaux, statues, bas-reliefs et camées, de la galerie de Florence, et du palais Pitti. Dessinés par M. Wicar, peintre, et gravés sous la direction de M. Lacombe, peintre; avec les explications, par M. Mongez l'aîné. [v. 1.] 50 pl. fol. *Paris,* 1789. s.

Wickenden (Joseph Frederic). Seven days in Attica, in 1852. New ed. xi, 35 pp. 24 maps and pl. 8°. *London, Harrison,* 1857.

Widdup (John). An essay on the physical constitution of the celestial bodies, and the extraordinary coincidence of scripture with the most recent discoveries in science. viii, 146 pp. 1 pl. 8°. *London, Saunders & Otley,* 1858. s.

Wideburg (Friedrich). Friderico regi Porussiae [etc.] magno, felici, invicto, hostibvs pvlsis, provinciis pace firmatis, die 24 Ian. 1746, publice gratvlata est [etc.] academia fridericiana, interprete F. Widebvrgio, academiae oratore. xxx pp. fol. *Halae Magdebvrgicae, J. F. Grunert,* [1746]. s.

[*With* WILLEBRANDT (J. P.) Hansische chronick, etc.]

Widow (The) of the wood: an authentic narrative of a late remarkable transaction in Staffordshire. [*anon.*] 98 pp. 16°. *Dublin, S. Powell,* 1755.

[Imperfect].

Wiedemann (F. J.) *and* **Weber** (E.) Beschreibung der phanerogamischen gewächse Esth,-Liv,-und Curlands. cxxvi, 664 pp. 4 pl. 8°. *Reval, F. Kluge,* 1852. s.

Wied-Neuwied (Maximilian, *prinz* von). *See* **Maximilian** (Alexander Philipp).

Wiegmann (Arend Friedrich August), *and* **Ruthe** (Johann Friedrich). Handbuch der zoologie. 3e aufl. von Dr. F. H. Troschel und J. F. Ruthe. iv, 651 pp. 8°. *Berlin, C. G. Lüderitz,* 1848. s.

Wieland (Christoph Martin). Geschichte der Abderiten. Neue ausg. 2 v. 336 pp; 279 pp. 16°. *Frankfurt,* 1782. s.

Wieselgren (P.) Sveriges sköna litteratur, en öfverblick vid akademiska föreläsningar. 3 v. 8°. *Lund, C. W. K. Gleerup,* 1833. s.

CONTENTS.

v. 1. Kyrkans sköna litteratur. xxxii, 479 pp.
v. 2–3. Statens sköna litteratur. x, 541 pp; x, 531 pp.

Wietersheim (Eduard von). Geschichte der völkerwanderung. 4 v. 8°. *Leipzig, T. D. Weigel,* 1859–64.

Wigand (J. W. Albert). Der baum: betrachtungen über gestalt und lebensgeschichte der holzegewächse. xiv, 254 pp. 2 pl. 8°. *Braunschweig, Vieweg,* 1854. s.

—— Botanische untersuchungen. vi, 168 pp. 6 pl. 8°. *Braunschweig, Vieweg,* 1854. s.

—— Intercellular substanz und cuticula. Eine untersuchung über das wachsthum der vegetabilien. vi, 130 pp. 2 col. pl. 8°. *Braunschweig, Vieweg,* 1850. s.

Wiggers (Julius). Kirchengeschichte Mecklenburgs. xvi pp. 2 l. 248 pp. 8°. *Parchim, etc. Hintorff,* 1840. s.

Wigglesworth (Edward, *D. D.*) The blessedness of the dead who die in the Lord: a sermon preached upon the news of the death of Thomas Hollis. iv, 23 pp. 8°. *Boston, S. Gerrish,* 1731.

Wigglesworth (*Rev.* Michael). The day of doom; or, a poetical description of the great and last judgment. With other poems. From the 6th ed. 1715. 120 pp. 12°. *New York, Am. news Co.* 1867.

Wightman (Joseph M.) A catalogue of philosophical, astronomical, chemical, and electrical apparatus. 48, 36 pp. 12°. *Boston, S. N. Dickerson & Co.* 1846. s.

Wikes (Thomas). *See* **Wycke** (Thomas).

Wikoff (Henry). Napoleon Louis Bonaparte, first president of France. Biographical and personal sketches, [etc.] xii, 155 pp. 1 portrait. 12°. *New York, G. P. Putnam,* 1849. s.

Wikström (Johan Emanuel). Stockholms flora, eller korrt beskrifning af de vid Stockholm i vildt tillstand förekommande växter, med en öfversight af Stockholms-tractens natur-beskaffenhet. Förra delen. vi, 185, 423, 27 pp. 1 map. 8°. *Stockholm, Norstedt,* 1840.

[No more published]. s.

Wilbur (*Mrs.* Jennie Aurelia). Songs of the West. 300 pp. 12°. *Chicago,* [*C. E. Pomeroy,*] 1866.

Wild (Charles). Select examples of architectural grandeur in Belgium, Germany, and France: a series of 24 sketches. Etched under his direction, by J. Le Keux and other artists. 2 series in 1 v. each having 2 p. l. 8 pp. 12 pl. fol. *London, H. G. Bohn,* 1837.

Wild (*Dr.* H.) Die selbstregistrirenden meteorologischen instrumente der sternwarte in Bern. Aus dem ii. bande von Carl's repertorium. 41 pp. 9 pl. 8°. *München, R. Oldenbourg*, 1866. s.

Wilde (William R.) Narrative of a voyage to Madeira, Teneriffe, and along the shores of the Mediterranean. 2 v. xiv, 464 pp; viii, 495 pp. 2 pl. 8°. *Dublin, Curry & Co.* 1840.

Wilder (Samson V. Stoddard). Records from [his] life. 404 pp. portrait. 12°. *New York, Am. tract. society*, [1867].

Wiley & Putnam. Catalogue of English, French, and American books, in four divisions. 3 pts in 1 v. 8°. *New York*, [*about* 1851]. s.

[Wants part 3: Theological literature].

Wilford (John). Memorials and characters, with the lives of divers eminent and worthy persons, from 1600 to the present time, and appendix of monumental inscriptions in Latin and English. 8 p. l. 788, 42 pp. fol. *London, J. Wilford*, 1741.

Wilhelm (Gottlieb Tobias). Unterhaltungen aus der naturgeschichte. Die amphibien. 8 p. l. 328 pp. 40 pl. 12°. *Wien*, 1818. s.

Wilisch (Christian Gotthold). Arcana bibliothecae annaebergensis, in partes iii. divisa; epistolas lxxii. summorum quorundam principum clarissimorumque saeculi xvi. et xvii. virorum nondum editas, nec non annalium typograph. vsque ad MD specimen complexa. 2 p. l. 332 pp. 16°. *Lipsiae, sumtu heredum Lanckischianorum*, 1730. s.

Wilkes (Charles). United States exploring expedition, during the years 1838–42. v. 9. The races of man; and their geographical distribution. By Charles Pickering. 447 pp. 1 map. 12 col. pl. 4°. *Boston, Little & Brown*, 1848.

——— The same. v. 11. Meteorology. By Charles Wilkes. lviii, 1 col. map. 24 pl. 4°. *Philadelphia, C. Sherman*, 1851. s.

——— Voyage round the world, embracing the principal events of the narrative of the United States exploring expedition. xx, 668 pp. 8°. *Philadelphia, G. W. Gorton*, 1849. s.

Wilkes (John, *and others*). The North Briton. [*anon.*] 2 v. in 1. 1 p. l. 269 pp. 2 l. 16°. *London*, 1766.

——— The same, with tracts and papers relating to the North Briton, the proceedings against Mr. Wilkes, essay on women, election for Middlesex, etc. 4 v. 4 pl. 18°. *London*, 1772.

Wilkes (*Rev.* Wetenhall). Short history of the state of man, with regard to religion and morals, from the beginning of the world to the reformation. xxii, 376 pp. 8°. *London, T. Gardner*, 1746.

Wilkins (Alvan). United States directory for bankers and underwriters, for 1856–1857. 334 pp. 8°. *New York, A. Wilkins*, 1856. s.

Wilkins (Henry). Suite de vues pittoresques des ruines de Pompéii, et un précis historique de la ville. 5 p. l. 23 pp. 31 pl. obl. fol. *Rome*, 1819. s.

Wilkins (John, *bishop of Chester*). Mathematical and philosophical works. With the author's life, etc. 2 v. xv, 261 pp; vi, 260 pp. 8°. *London, Vernor & Hood*, 1802.

CONTENTS.

v. 1. That the moon may be a world; That the earth may be a planet.
v. 2. Mercury, or the secret and swift messenger; showing how a man may communicate with speed his thoughts to a friend at any distance; Mathematical magic, or mechanical geometry; Essay toward a real character, and a philosophical language.

——— Mathematicall magick; or, the wonders that may be performed by mechanicall geometry. 7 p. l. 294 pp. 18°. *London, S. Gellibrand*, 1648.

——— Mercury; or, the secret and swift messenger. Shewing how a man may with privacy and speed communicate his thoughts to a friend at any distance. 2d ed. 7 p. l. 172 pp. portrait. 16°. *London, R. Baldwin*, 1694.

Wilkinson (David), *and* **McAlpine** (W. J.) Description of the hydraulic power at the outlet of lake George, owned by Edward Ellice. 12 pp. 16°. [*n. p.* 1839].

Wilkinson (Robert, *D. D.*) The stripping of Joseph; or, the crueltie of brethren to a brother: a sermon. With a consolatorie epistle to the English East India company for their wrongs sustayned in Amboyna by the Dutch there. 2 p. l. 50 pp. 16°. *London, H. Holland and G. Gibbs*, 1625.

Will (Heinrich). Outlines of chemical analysis. Translated from the 3d German ed. by Daniel Breed and L. H. Steiner. xxxv, 297 pp. 8°. *Boston, J. Munroe & Co.* 1855. s.

Willard (David). History of Greenfield, [Massachusetts]. 180 pp. 18°. *Greenfield, Kneeland and Eastman*, 1838.

Willard (*Mrs.* Elizabeth Osgood Goodrich). Sexology as the philosophy of life; implying social organization and government. 483 pp. 8°. *Chicago, J. R. Walsh*, 1867.

Willard (*Mrs.* Emma Hart). Astronography; or, astronomical geography. 298 pp. 1 pl. 12°. *Troy, Merriam, Moore & Co.* 1854. s.

Willard (*Mrs.* Emma Hart). Morals for the young. 217 pp. 1 pl. 12°. *New York, A. S. Barnes & Co.* 1857.

Willard (Joseph). An address to the members of the bar of Worcester county, Massachusetts, October 2, 1829. 144 pp. 8°. *Lancaster, (Mass.) Carter, Andrews & Co.* 1830.

Willard (Samuel, *D.D.*) [Covenant keeping the way to blessedness. In several sermons. With] the necessity of sincerity, in renewing the covenant. 3 p. l. 150 pp. 24°. *Boston, S. Sewall*, 1682.

[Imperfect; title and 4 p. l. wanting].

——— The fountain opened; or, blessings dispensed at the national conversion of the Jews. 2d ed. 40 pp. 18°. *Boston, B. Green*, 1722.

Willard (Solomon, *architect*). Plans and sections of the obelisk on Bunker's Hill. With details of experiments made in quarrying the granite. 31 pp. 14 pl. fol. *Boston*, 1843.

Willcox (John H.) *and* **Southard** (L. H.) Lyra catholica: a collection of masses, hymns, [etc.] 272 pp. obl. 8°. *Boston, O. Ditson & Co.* [1866].

Willcox (Orlando B.) Shoepac recollections: a way-side glimpse of American life. By Walter March. [*pseudon.*] 360 pp. 12°. *New York, Bunce & bro.* 1856. s.

Willebrandt (Johann Peter). Hansische chronick aus beglaubten nachrichten zusammen getragen. 3 v. in 1. fol. *Lübeck, autor*, 1748. s.

Willem. *See* **William** ii, *(king of the Romans).*

Willement (Emily Elizabeth). A catechism of familiar things; their history, [etc.] With explanation of natural phenomena. 206 pp. 16°. *Philadelphia, Lindsay & Blakiston*, 1852.

Willems (Jean François). Oude vlaemsche liederen ten deele met de melodiën. 548, lx pp. 8°. *Gent, F. & E. Gyselynck*, 1848. s.

Willett (William M.) Herod Antipas; sequel to Herod the Great, with passages from the life of Jesus of Nazareth. 345 pp. 12°. *New York*, [*author*], 1866.

William ii, (*earl of Holland, king of the Romans*). Agalma religiosorum, sive meditationes circa mysteria passionis dominicæ. Vitam exposuit F. G. Otto. 127 pp. 24°. *Coloniæ, H. Lempertz*, 1849.

William, *of Malmesbury. See* **Malmesbury** (William *of*).

Williams (Aaron, *D.D.*) The harmony society, at Economy, Penn'a, founded by George Rapp in 1805. With an appendix [of mystical literature]. 182 pp. 8°. *Pittsburgh, W. S. Haven*, 1866.

Williams (*Mrs.* Catharine R.) Fall River; an authentic narrative [of Sarah Maria Cornell]. 198 pp. 18°. *Providence, Marshall Brown & Co.* 1834.

——— The neutral French; or, the exiles of Nova Scotia. 2d ed. 2 v. in 1. 238, 109 pp. 12°. *Providence, B. Cranston & Co.* [1841].

Williams (Charles). Old world scenes. xiii, 272 pp. 16°. *Pittsburgh, W. S. Haven*, 1867.

Williams (*Sir* Charles Hanbury). Odes. [Edited by Joseph Ritson]. 2 p. l. 133 pp. 18°. *London, S. Vandenburgh*, 1775.

[Imperfect; pp. 73—80 wanting].

Williams (*Mrs.* Charlotte). Letters between an English lady and her friend at Paris; in which are contained the memoirs of Mrs. Williams. New ed. 2 v. vi, 241 pp; 287 pp. 18°. *London, T. Becket & P. A. de Hondt*, 1771.

Williams (C. Greville). A hand-book of chemical manipulation. xv, 580 pp. 12°. *London, J. Van Voorst*, 1857. s.

Williams (*Rev.* David). Lectures on political principles: the subjects of eighteen books in Montesquieu's Spirit of laws. 4 p. l. 176 pp. 8°. *Merthyr Tydfil*, [*Wales*], *W. Williams*, 1817.

——— Letters on political liberty. [*anon.*] 2 p. l. 86 pp. 8°. *London, T. Evans*, 1782.

Williams (Edwin). The statesman's manual. The addresses and messages of the presidents of the United States, from 1789 to 1849, with a memoir of each, a history of their administrations, and a selection of important documents, [etc.] Reference ed. 3 v. 8°. *New York, E. Walker*, 1849. s.

CONTENTS.

v. 1. Washington to Adams.
v. 2. Jackson to Van Buren.
v. 3. Tyler to Taylor.

Williams (Folkestone, *or* Robert Folkestone). Mephistophiles in England; or, the confessions of a prime minister. [*anon.*] 3 v. 12°. *London, Longman*, 1835.

Williams (Griffith, *bishop of Ossory*). The true church: showed to all men that desire to be members of the same. 6 p. l. 933 pp. 12 l. fol. *London, N. Butter*, 1629.

Williams (John, *of London*). An authentic history of the professors of painting, sculpture, and architecture in Ireland, [with] memoirs of the royal academicians. By Anthony Pasquin. [*pseudon.*] 64, 148 pp. 1 pl. 8°. *London, H. D. Symonds*, 1794.

——— A critical guide to the exhibition at the royal academy, 1796–1797. 32 pp; 24 pp. 8°. *London, H. D. Symonds*, 1796–97.

[*With his* Authentic history of the professors of painting, etc. *London*, 1794].

Williams (John). The life of Alexander Hamilton. By Anthony Pasquin. [*pseudon.*] (*Boston,* 1804). Reprint. 60 pp. 8°. *New York, Hamilton club,* 1865.
(Hamilton club series, No. 1).

Williams (*Rev.* John, *of Deerfield, Mass.*) The redeemed captive returning to Zion. A faithful history of remarkable occurrences in [his] captivity and deliverance. [With] a sermon preached by him, upon his return, in Boston, December 5, 1706. With an appendix, containing an account of those taken captive at Deerfield, Feb. 29, 1703-4. 5th ed. 70 pp. 12°. *Boston, John Boyle,* 1774.

——— The same. [With] a biographical memoir of the author, [etc.] by Stephen W. Williams. 192 pp. 1 pl. 12°. *Northampton, Hopkins, Bridgman & Co.* 1853. s.

Williams (*Sir* John Bickerton). Memoirs of the life and character of Mrs. Sarah Savage, daughter of Rev. Philip Henry. 1st Am. ed. 240 pp. 18°. *Boston, S. T. Armstrong,* 1821.

Williams (*brig. gen.* Jonathan). Thermometrical navigation through the gulph stream. Extracted from the American philosophical transactions, v. 2 and 3, with additions and improvements. xii, 98 pp. 2l. 1 map. 8°. *Philadelphia, R. Aitken,* 1799.

——— The same. s.
[*With* SMEATON (J.) Experimental enquiry, etc.]

Williams (J. J.) El istmo de Tehuantepec. Resultado del reconocimiento que para la construction de un ferro-carril de comunicacion entre los oceanos Atlantico y Pacifico ejecutó la comision científica, bajo la direccion del sr. J. G. Barnard, [etc.] Ilustrado con varios grabados y mapas, [etc.] por J. J. Williams. Trad. al Castellano, por Francisco de Arrangoiz. 327 pp. 8°. *Mejico, V. G. Torres,* 1852. s.

Williams (L. S.) Family education and government; a discourse in the Choctaw language. 48 pp. 16°. *Boston, Am. board for. miss.* 1835.

Williams (Monier). A dictionary, English and Sanscrit. xii, 859 pp. 4°. *London, W. H. Allen & Co.* 1851. s.

Williams (Roger). The blovdy tenent of persecution, for cause of conscience, discussed in a conference between trvth and peace. 1644. [Reprint. Edited by Samuel L. Caldwell]. xiv, 425 pp. 4°. *Providence, (R. I.)* 1867.
[Narragansett club publications, v. 3].

——— Key into the language of America. Edited by J. H. Trumbull. 222 pp. 4°. *Providence, (R. I.)* 1866.
[Narragansett club publications, v. 1, pp. 61–282].

——— Mr. [John] Cotton's letter [on church-membership] lately printed, examined and answered. [Edited by R. A. Guild]. 84 pp. 4°. *Providence, (R. I.)* 1866.
[Narragansett club publications, v. 1. pp. 313-396].

——— Queries of the highest consideration, proposed to Mr. Tho. Goodwin [and others], and to the commissions from the generall assembly (so called) of the church of Scotland. Edited by R. E. Guild. 36 pp. 4°. *Providence, (R. I.)* 1867.
[Narragansett club publications, v. 2. pp. 241–276].

Williams (Stephen West, *M. D.*) A biographical memoir of the Rev. John Williams, first minister of Deerfield, Mass. With a slight sketch of ancient Deerfield, and an account of the Indian wars in that place. With the journal of Stephen Williams during his captivity. 127 pp. 16°. *Greenfield, (Mass.) C. J. J. Ingersoll,* 1837.

——— The same.
[*With* WILLIAMS (*Rev.* John). The redeemed captive, etc. *Northampton,* 1853].

Williams (W.) The traveller's and tourist's guide through the United States of America, Canada, etc. 216 pp. 1 map. 18°. *Philadelphia, Lippincott, Grambo & Co.* 1851. s.

Williams (W. Mattieu). Through Norway with a knapsack. 3d ed. xii, 340 pp. 6 pl. 1 map. 12°. *London, Smith, Elder & Co.* 1860.

Williams. *See, also,* **Willyams.**

Williamson (Hugh, *M.D.*) Observations on the climate in different parts of America; to which are added remarks on the different complexions of the human race; with some account of the aborigines of America. viii, 199 pp. 2 pl. 8°. *New York, T. & J. Swords,* 1811. s.

Willis (John R.) Carleton; or, duty and patriotism. 188 pp. 8°. *London,* 1841.
[HAZLITT'S romancist and novelist's library. v. 4.]

Willis (Nathaniel Parker). Life, here and there; or, sketches of society and adventure, [etc.] vii, 377 pp. 12°. *New York, C. Scribner,* 1853.

Willis (Robert, *prof. nat. phil. Camb. Eng*). Remarks on the architecture of the middle ages, especially of Italy. ix, 200 pp. 15 pl. 8°. *Cambridge, (Eng.) J. & J. J. Deighton,* 1835.

Willkomm (Moritz). Die halbinsel der Pyrenäen; eine geographisch-statistische monographie, [etc.] xiii, 594 pp. 2 tab. 8°. *Leipzig, G. Mayer,* 1855. s.

Willsford. *See* **Wilsford.**

Willson (Forceythe). The old sergeant, and other poems. 115 pp. 16°. *Boston, Ticknor & Fields,* 1867.

Willson (Marcius). Juvenile American history. 160 pp. 16°. *New York, M. H. Newman & Co.* 1847. s.

Willyams (*Rev.* Cooper). A selection of views in Egypt, Palestine, Italy, etc. with descriptions in English and French. 16 l. 30 pl. fol. *London, J. Hearne,* 1822.

Wilmington *(N. C.)* Proceedings of the safety committee for the town of Wilmington, N. C. in 1774, 1775, and 1776. Ed. by Thomas Loring. 76 pp. 8°. *Raleigh,* 1844.

Wilmot (John, *earl of Rochester*). Poetical works. 8°. *Edinburgh,* 1793.
[Anderson's British poets, v. 6].

Wilsford (Thomas). The art of building. 33 pp. 16°. *London, N. Brook,* 1659.
[*With his* Scales of commerce and trade. 16°. *London,* 1660].

——— The debitor and creditor; or, a perfect method of keeping merchant's accounts. 16°. *London, N. Brook,* 1659.
[*With his* Scales of commerce and trade. pp. 201–254. 16°. *London,* 1660].

——— Scales of commerce and trade. 13 p. l. 254 pp. 1 pl. 16°. *London, N. Brook,* 1660.

Wilson (Alexander, *ornithologist), and* **Bonaparte** (Charles Lucien). American ornithology; or, the natural history of the birds of the United States. Edited by Robert Jameson. [With a memoir of A. Wilson, by W. M. Hetherington]. 4 v. 16°. *Edinburgh, Constable & Co.* 1831. s.

Wilson (James, *F. R. S. E.*) An introduction to the natural history of fishes; being the article "Ichthyology," from the seventh edition of the Encyclopædia britannica. ix, 90 pp. 11 pl. 4°. *Edinburgh, A. & C. Black,* 1838. s.

——— Zoology of India.
[*With* MURRAY (Hugh). Account of British India. v 3. pp. 11–116. *New York,* 1833–36].

Wilson (James Grant). Love in letters; illustrated in the correspondence of eminent persons; with biographical sketches of the writers. By Allan Grant. [*pseudon.*] 336 pp. 12°. *New York, Carleton,* 1867.

——— Mr. secretary Pepys; with extracts from his diary. By Allan Grant. [*pseudon*]. 264 pp. 1 pl. 16°. *New York, J. Porteus,* 1867.

Wilson (John, *of Lincoln's Inn*). A discourse of monarchy, more particularly of the crowns of England, Scotland, and Ireland, with a close from the whole as it relates to the succession of James, duke of York. 8 p. l. 272 pp. 16°. *London, Joseph Hindmarsh,* 1684.

Wilson (John, *printer, of Boston*). The concessions of trinitarians. Being a selection of extracts from the writings of the most eminent biblical critics and commentators. x, 614 pp. 8°. *Boston, Munroe & Co.* 1845.

——— The same. Unitarian principles confirmed by trinitarians. 5th ed. xv, 504 pp. 12°. *Boston, Am. unit. assoc.* 1867.

Wilson (Joseph). A history of mountains, geographical and mineralogical. To accompany a picturesque view by R. A. Riddell. 3 v. 4°. *London, Nicol,* 1807–10.

Wilson (Oliver M.) Digest of parliamentary law; including the constitution of the United States and of Indiana. 132 pp. 8°. *Indianapolis, Douglass & Conner,* 1867.

Wilson (Samuel). An account of the province of Carolina, in America. 27 pp. 1 map. sm. 4°. *London, Francis Smith,* 1682.

Wilson (*Rev.* Thomas, *of St. George's, Canterbury*). A christian dictionary, opening the signification of the chief words of scripture. 5th ed. 256 l. fol. *London, W. Hope,* 1648.

Wilson (Thomas, *bishop of Sodor and Man*). Works, with life, compiled by C. Cruttwell. 3d ed. 4 v. 8°. *Bath, R. Cruttwell,* 1782.

CONTENTS.

v. 1. Life.
History of the Isle of Man.
v. 2. Instructions for better understanding the Lord's supper.
Sacra privata: private meditations and devotions.
v. 3. Knowledge and practice of christianity made easy.
Observations for reading the historical books of the Old Testament.
Private and family prayers, etc.
Form for consecrating churches, etc.
v. 4. Parochialia; or, instructions for the clergy.
Maxims of piety.
Forms of prayer for the herring fishery.
Instructions for youth. Catechism.

——— The knowledge and practice of christianity made easy; or, an essay towards an instruction for the Indians. 5th ed. 18°. *London, J. Osborne,* 1743.

——— The same. 9th ed. 328 pp. 18°. *London, B. Dod,* 1759.

——— The same. 12th ed. 3 p. l. xxiv, 280 pp. 18°. *London, J. Rivington,* 1776.

——— The same. 15th ed. 4 p. l. xxiv, 280 pp. 18°. *London, F. & C. Rivington,* 1782.

——— Sermons. 4th ed. 8°. *Bath, R. Cruttwell,* 1785.

Wilson (*Rev.* Thomas, *of Clitheroe*). Archæological dictionary; or, classical antiquities of the Jews, Greeks, and Romans. 2d ed. 6 p. l. 480 pp. 8°. *London, D. Ogilvy, etc.* 1793.

Wily (Thomas). Narrative of the military excursion of the Montreal volunteer militia rifles to Portland, Aug. 1858. 8°. *Montreal,* 1858. s.

Wimmer (Friedrich). Salices europaeæ. xcii, 286 pp. 8°. *Vratislaviæ, F. Hirt,* 1866. s.

Winchell (Alexander, *prof. in university of Michigan.*) Geology [of Michigan]. *See* **Michigan.** Geological survey.

——— Report on the geological and industrial resources of the counties of Antrim, Grand Traverse, Benzie, and Leelanaw, Michigan. 97 pp. 1 map. 8°. *Ann Arbor, (Mich.) Chase,* 1866. s.

Winchell (N. H.) Botany [of Michigan]. *See* **Michigan.** Geological survey.

Winchester (Elhanan). The divinity of Christ proved from the scriptures of the Old and New Testament. 39 pp. 8°. *Philadelphia,* [1784?]

[Title-page imperfect].

Winchester (George W.) Winchester's book-keeping; or, the teacher's guide. Containing the principles of double entry, [etc.] 92 pp. 4°. *Hartford, J. H. Mather & Co.* 1848. s.

Winckelmann (Johannes Joachim). Werke. Einzig rechtmässige original ausg. 2 v. 1. 586 pp. 1 portrait; viii, 676 pp. 24 pl. 8°. *Dresden, Walther,* 1839. s.

——— Lettres familières [traduites de l'Allemand par H. Jansen]. 2 v. xxxiv, 292 pp. 1 pl; 292 pp. 8°. *Amsterdam, Couturier fils,* 1781.

——— Recueil de lettres sur les découvertes faites à Herculanum, à Pompeii, à Stabia, à Caserte, et à Rome. Traduit de l'Allemand [par H. Jansen]. 330 pp. 8°. *Paris, Barrois,* 1784.

——— Recueil de différentes pièces sur les arts. Traduit de l'Allemand [par H. Jansen]. vi, 295 pp. 8°. *Paris, Barrois,* 1786.

CONTENTS.

Réflexions sur l'imitation des artistes grecs dans la peinture et la sculpture; Sur le sentiment du beau.

——— Remarques sur l'architecture des anciens. Traduites de l'Allemand [par Jansen]. xvi, 140 pp. 8°. *Paris, Barrois,* 1783.

——— (*and others.*) De l'allégorie; ou, traités sur cette matière [traduits par H. Jansen]. 2 v. vii, 429 pp; 475 pp. 8°. *Paris, H. J. Jansen,* 1799.

Windischmann (Friedrich). Mithra. Ein beitrag zur mythengeschichte des Orients. iv, 90 pp. 8°. *Leipzig, F. A. Brockhaus,* 1857. s.

Windt (John). The honest man's book of finance and politics, showing the cause and cure of artificial poverty, dearth of employment, and dullness of trade. [*anon.*] 287 pp. 18°. *New York, S. Tousey,* 1862.

Wing (Vincent). Astronomia britannica: in qua per novam concinnioremq. methodum, hi quinq. tractatus traduntur: i, logistica astronomica, etc. ii, trigonometria. iii, doctrina sphærica. iv, theoria planetarum. v, tabulæ novæ astronomicæ. 9 p. l. 244, 369 pp. fol. *Londini, G. Sawbridge,* 1669. s.

Wingfield (Edward Maria). A discourse of Virginia. Edited, with notes and an introduction, by Charles Deane. 45 pp. 4°. *Boston, John Wilson & son,* 1860.

[From the American antiquarian society's transactions, v. 4].

Winkelblech (Carl). Elemente der analytischen chemie. viii, 464 pp. 1 pl. 8°. *Marburg, N. G. Elwert,* 1840. s.

Winsem (Peter van). Historiarvm ab excessv Caroli v. Cæsaris; sive rerum sub Philippo ii. per Frisiam gestarum libri vii. 2 v. 8 p. l. 342 pp. 1 l; 8 p. l. 415 pp. 4°. *Leovardiæ et Franekeræ, Fontanus et Balck,* 1629–33. s.

Winslow (Charles Frederick, *M. D.*) Cosmography; or, philosophical views of the universe. iv pp. 2 p. l. 174 pp. 16°. *Boston, Crosby, Nichols & Co.* 1853. s.

[*With his* Preparation of the earth, etc. *Boston,* 1854].

——— The preparation of the earth for the intellectual races. 59 pp. 16°. *Boston, Crosby, Nichols & Co.* 1854. s.

Winslow (E. S.) Comprehensive mathematics; being an extensive cabinet of numerical, arithmetical, and mathematical facts, tables, [etc.] 6th ed. 52, 374 pp. 16°. *Boston, author,* 1867.

Winter (Christopher T.) Six months in British Burmah; or, India beyond the Ganges in 1857. xii, 288 pp. 4 pl. 12°. *London, R. Bentley,* 1858.

Winter (William H.) Route across the Rocky Mountains. 8°. *Lafayette,* 1846. *See* **Johnson** (Overton), *and* **Winter.**

Winter (A) at Woodlawn; or, the armor of light illustrated. By the author of "Four days in July." [*anon.*] 278 pp. 16°. *New York, Carlton & Porter,* 1857. s.

Winterbotham (William). An historical, geographical, and philosophical view of the Chinese empire; [with] account of Lord Macartney's embassy. 2 v. 2 p. l. 303 pp; 1 p. l. 322 pp. 2 l. 8°. *Philadelphia, R. Lee,* 1796.

Winterbottom (Thomas Masterman, *M. D.*) An account of the native Africans in the neighborhood of Sierra Leone; [with] an account of the present state of medicine among them. 2 v. xi, 362 pp. 11 l; 2 p. l. 283 pp. 6 l. 2 maps. 6 pl. 8°. *London, J. Hatchard,* 1803.

Winthrop (James, *LL. D. judge, of Mass.*) An attempt to translate the prophetic part of the apocalypse of Saint John into familiar language. 79 pp. 8°. *Boston, Belknap & Hall,* 1794.

——— A systematic arrangement of several scripture prophecies relating to antichrist; with their application to the course of history. 35 pp. 8°. *Boston, Thomas Hall,* 1795.
[*With* the preceding].

Winthrop (Robert Charles). Addresses and speeches, 1852–1867. xiii, 725 pp. 8°. *Boston, Little, Brown & Co.* 1867.

——— Life and letters of John Winthrop, governor of the Massachusetts Bay company at their emigration to New England. [v. 1 to] 1630. [v. 2], from 1630 to his death in 1649. 2 v. xiii, 452 pp. 3 fac-sim; xv, 483 pp. 1 pl. 1 fac-sim. 8°. *Boston, Ticknor & Fields,* 1864–67.

——— Oration on the occasion of laying the corner-stone of the national monument to the memory of Washington. With an introduction and appendix. 67 pp. 4°. *Washington, Nat. monument assoc.* 1848.

Winwood (*Sir* Ralph). Memorials of affairs of state in the reigns of queen Elizabeth and king James i. Collected from the original papers, by E. Sawyer. 2d ed. 3 v. fol. *London, T. Osborne,* 1727.

Wirt (E. W.) Flora's dictionary. 132, 96 pp. 7 pl. 4°. *Baltimore, Lucas bros.* [1855].

Wirt (William). The letters of the British spy. [*anon.*] 3d ed. 128 pp. 18°. *Richmond, S. Pleasants,* 1805.

——— The life of Patrick Henry. 4th ed. 443, 19 pp. 1 pl. 8°. *New York, M'Elrath & Bangs,* 1831.

——— The old bachelor. [*anon.*] 3d ed. 2 v. 263 pp; 240 pp. 24°. *Baltimore, F. Lucas,* 1818.

Wisconsin. Annual report of the adjutant general, with reports from the quartermaster general and surgeon general, for 1865. [With appendix]. 1 v. in 2. 1168 pp. 8°. *Madison, W. J. Park & Co.* 1866.

——— Annual report of the state superintendent of public instruction for 1856. [By A. Constantine Barry]. 208 pp. 8°. *Madison, Calkins & Proudfit,* 1857. s.

——— Governor's message and accompanying documents, 1855–58, 1860–65. 12 v. 8° and 12°. *Madison, state printer,* 1855–65.

——— Journals of the senate and assembly, 1855–56, 1858, 1860–65. 22 v. 8° and 12°. *Madison, state printer,* 1855–65.

Tenth and eleventh annual reports on the condition and improvement of the common schools and educational interests for 1858–59. By Lyman C. Draper. 2 v. 397 pp. 1 pl; 205 pp. 8°. *Madison, Atwood & Rublee,* 1858. s.

Wise (Henry Augustus). Los gringos; or, an inside view of Mexico and California, with wanderings in Peru, Chili, and Polynesia. xvi, 453 pp. 12°. *New York, Baker & Scribner,* 1849. s.

Wise (Isaac M. *Rabbi*). Divine service of American Israelites for the day of atonement. [In Hebrew, German, and English]. 307, 55 pp. 16°. *Cincinnati, Block & Co.* 1866.

——— Divine service of American Israelites for the new year. [In Hebrew, German, and English]. 212 pp. 16°. *Cincinnati, Block & Co.* 1866.

Wise (Thomas). A confutation of the reason and philosophy of atheism. An abridgement of Cudworth's Intellectual system of the universe. 2 v. xlviii, 143; 811 pp. 1 pl. sm. 4°. *London, A. & J. Churchill,* 1706.

Wislizenus (A. *M. D.*) Memoir of a tour to northern Mexico, connected with col. Doniphan's expedition, in 1846–7. With a botanical appendix, by George Engelmann, M. D. 141 pp. 3 maps. 8°. *Washington, Tippin & Streeper,* 1848.

With (Émile). Railroad accidents: their causes and the means of preventing them. With an introduction by Aug. Perdonnet. From the French by C. F. Barstow. xi, 152 pp. 12°. *Boston, Little, Brown & Co.* 1856.

Wither (George). Britain's remembrancer; containing a narration of the plagve lately past; a declaration of the mischiefs present; and a prediction of ivdgments to come. [1st ed.] 289 l. 1 pl. 24°. *London, J. Grismond,* 1628.
[Frontispiece wanting].

Withers (J. R.) Poems upon various subjects. viii, 183, viii pp. 16°. *Cambridge, (Eng.) C. W. Naylor,* 1854.

Witherspoon (John, *D. D.*) Miscellaneous works. 368 pp. 8°. *Philadelphia, William W. Woodward,* 1803.

——— A serious inquiry into the nature and effects of the stage. 154 pp. 16°. *New York, Whiting & Watson,* 1812.

Withington (*Rev.* Leonard). The puritan; a series of essays, critical, moral, and miscellaneous. By John Oldbug, esq. [*pseudon.*] 2 v. 248 pp; 268 pp. 16°. *Boston, Perkins & Marvin,* 1836.

Withington (William). Christian radicalism. 152 pp. 18°. *Boston, Perkins & Marvin,* 1836.

Witsen Geysbeek (P. G.) *See* **Geysbeek** (P. G. Witsen).

Wittenberg university. Bibliothecæ academiæ wittebergensis publicæ librorum [etc.] extantiores classiciqve ferè, [etc.] Editore A. Sennerto. 1 p. l. 54 pp. 4°. *Wittebergae, impensis editoris,* 1678. s.
[*With* SCHÖTTGEN (C.) Historie, etc.]

Witter (Conrad). Improved interest tables, from 1 cent to 1000 dollars, at 6 and at 10 per cent. from 1 day to 6 years. 24 l. 8°. *St. Louis, C. Witter,* 1858. s.

——— Ready calculator in dollars and cents; with tables for selling and purchasing; [also] an appendix containing the calculation of wages, [etc.] 168 pp. 32°. *St. Louis, (Mo.) C. Witter,* 1867.

Witting (Victor). Andelaga sånger för böneklass- och förlängda möten. Öfwersatta, urwalda och originella. Andra samlingen. 128 pp. 32°. *Chicago, Poe & Hitchcock,* 1867.

Wittman (Joseph, *M. D.*) Chronik der niedrigsten wasserstände des Rheins, 70–1858, und nachrichten über die im jahre 1857–58, im Rheinbette von der Schweiz bis nach Holland zu tage gekommenen alterthümer und merkwürdigkeiten, [etc.] 142 pp. 8°. *Mainz, Seifert,* 1859. s.

Wittman (William, *M. D.*) Travels in Turkey, Asia Minor, Syria, and across the desert into Egypt; also through Germany, Holland, etc. 1799–1801, [with] observations on the plague, and on the diseases prevalent in Turkey. xvi, 595 pp. 1 map. 22 pl. 4°. *London, R. Phillips,* 1803.

——— The same. 426 pp. 8°. *Philadelphia, J. Humphreys,* 1804. s.

Wittstein (G. C.) Vollständiges etymologisch-chemisches handwörterbuch, mit berücksichtigung der chemie. 2 v. vi, 926 pp; 992 pp. 8°. *München, J. Palm,* 1847. s.

——— The same. Drittes ergänzungsheft. 359 pp. 8°. *München, J. Palm,* 1858. s.
[Wanting; erg. 1–2].

Witzleben (Ferdinand August von). Arthur, herzog von Wellington, und seine zeit. 2e ausgabe. 8°. *Leipzig,* 1853. s.

Wocel (Jan Erazmi). Grundzüge der böhmischen alterthumskunde. xv, 238 pp. 8 pl. 8°. *Prag, Kronberger & Rziwnatz,* 1845. s.

Wodarch (Charles). Introduction to the study of conchology, describing the orders, genera, and species of shells. 2d ed. By J. Mawe. xv, 152 pp. 8 col. pl. 12°. *London, Longman,* 1822. s.

Wodenote (Theophilus). Hermes theologus; or, a divine mercurie dispatcht with a grave message of new descants upon old records. 1 pl. 155 pp. 18°. *London, R. Royston,* 1649.

Wöhler (Friedrich). Grundriss der chemie. Unorganische chemie. 5e aufl. x, 190 pp. 8°. *Berlin, Duncker & Humblot,* 1838. s.

——— Hand-book of inorganic analysis. Edited by A. W. Hoffman. viii, 249 pp. 12°. *London, Walton & Maberly,* 1854.

Wolf (Christian von). The real happiness of a people under a philosophical king. [Translated from the German]. vii, 96 pp. 12°. *London, M. Cooper,* 1750.

Wolf (Johann Christian). Monumenta typografica, qvae artis hujus praestantissimæ originem, laudem, et abusum posteris produnt. 2 v. 8 p. l. 1104 pp; 1232 pp. 46 l. 16°. *Hamburgi, C. Herold,* 1740. s.

Wolf (Johann Christoph). Historia lexicorvm hebraicorvm quae tam a judaeis quam a christianis edita sunt. 240 pp. 7 l. 16°. *Vitembergæ, C. T. Lvdovick,* 1705.
[*With* DANZ (J. A.) Interpres ebraeo-chaldaevs. Ed. 3a. 1715].

Wolf (Johann Wilhelm). Niederländische sagen. xxxviii, 708 pp. 1 pl. 8°. *Leipzig, F. A. Brockhaus,* 1843. s.

Wolf (Peter Philip). Allgemeine geschichte der jesuiten, von dem ursprunge ihres ordens bis auf gegenwärtige zeiten. 4 v. 16°. *Lissabon, Pombal & Co.* 1792. s.

Wolfe (James, *major general*). Instructions to young officers. 142 pp. 12°. *Philadelphia, Robert Bell,* 1778.
[*With* SIMES (Thomas). New military dictionary. *Philadelphia,* 1776].

Wolfe (Samuel M.) Helper's impending crisis dissected. 2 p. l. 223 pp. 12°. *Philadelphia, J. T. Lloyd,* 1860.

Wolff (Emil Th.) Quellen-literatur der theoretisch-organischen chemie. [1775–1844]. vii, 404 pp. 8°. *Halle, E. Anton,* 1845. s.

Wollaston (George). The life and history of a pilgrim. By G. W. [*anon.*] v, 540 pp. 12°. *Dublin, O. Nelson,* 1753.

Wollaston (Thomas Vernon). Insecta maderensia: account of the [coleopterous] insects of the islands of the Madeiran group. xliii, 634 pp. 13 col. pl. 4°. *London, J. Van Voorst,* 1854. s.

Wollaston (William). The religion of nature delineated. [*anon.*] 219 pp. 5 l. 4°. *London, Samuel Palmer,* 1726.

——— The same. Ébauche de la religion naturelle; traduite de l'Anglais, [par Garrigue] avec un supplément, etc. xx, 442 pp. 3 l. 4°. *La Haye, J. Swart,* 1726.

Wolowski (Louis François Michel Raymond). La banque d'Angleterre et les banques d'Écosse. xi, 560 pp. 8°. *Paris, Guillaumin*, 1867.

——— Enquête sur les principes et les faits généraux qui régissent la circulation monétaire et fiduciaire. [L'Institut de France:] séances des 21, 28, et 30 Nov. 1865. iv, 292 pp. fol. *Paris, Imprimerie impériale*, 1866.

——— La question des banques. 2 p. l. 592 pp. 8°. *Paris, Guillaumin & Cie.* 1864. s.

Wolseley (*Sir* Charles). The unreasonablenesse of atheism made manifest. [*anon.* 1st ed.] 197 pp. 16°. *London, N. Ponder*, 1669.

Women as they are. By one of them. By the author of "Margaret." [*anon.*] 2 v. iv, 334 pp; 296 pp. 16°. *London, R. Bentley*, 1854.

Wood (Anthony). Historia et antiquitates universitatis oxoniensis. [Latinitate donata R. Peers, et R. Reeve]. 2 v. in 1. 4 p. l. 414 pp. 1 pl; 447 pp. 3 l. 1 pl. fol. *Oxonii, e theatro sheldoniano*, 1674.

Wood (Edward J.) Curiosities of clocks and watches. x, 443 pp. 1 pl. 12°. *London, Bentley*, 1866.

Wood (Ephraim). Quakerism unveiled: truth prevalent. 379 pp. 8°. *Liverpool, H. Forshaw*, 1815.

Wood (George B. *M. D.*) A treatise on therapeutics and pharmacology, or materia medica. 3d ed. 2 v. xx, 838 pp; 990 pp. 8°. *Philadelphia, J. B. Lippincott & Co.* 1868.

Wood (*Rev.* John George). The common objects of the country. New ed. iv, 132 pp. 11 pl. 16°. *London, Routledge*, 1858. s.

——— Illustrated natural history. 3 v. 8°. *London, Routledge*, [1860]–63. s.

CONTENTS.

v. 1. Mammalia. vii, 800 pp. 1 pl.
v. 2. Birds. 786 pp. 1 pl.
v. 3. Reptiles, fishes, molluscs, etc. 810 pp. 1 pl.

——— Our garden friends and foes. viii, 438 pp. 8 pl. 12°. *London, Routledge*, 1864. s.

Wood (Searles Valentine). A monograph of the crag mollusca; or, descriptions of shells from the middle and upper tertiaries of the east of England. 2 v. 4°. *London, Palæontographical society*, 1848–50. s.

CONTENTS.

v. 1. Univalves. xii, 208 pp. 21 l. 21 pl.
v. 2. Bivalves. 342, 2 pp. 31 l. 31 pl.

——— A monograph of the eocene mollusca; or, descriptions of shells from the older tertiaries of England. Parts i, ii. 4°. *London, Palæontographical society*, 1861–64.

Wood (William, *secretary to the commissioners of customs*). A survey of trade, with considerations on our money and bullion. xiv, 373 pp. 12°. *London, John Walthoe*, 1722.

Wood (William, *F.R.S.*) Index testaceologicus; or, a catalogue of shells, British and foreign, arranged according to the Linnean system. xxxii, 190 pp. 38 col. pl. 8°. *London, W. Wood*, 1825. s.

——— Supplement. Index, etc. iv, 59 pp. 8 pl. 8 col. pl. 8°. *London, W. Wood*, 1828. s.

Wood (William). Manual of physical exercises; comprising gymnastics, rowing, [etc.] With rules for training, [etc.] Illustrated. 316 pp. 1 pl. 12°. *New York, Harpers*, 1867.

Woodard. *See* **Woodward.**

Woodbury (Augustus). Major general Ambrose E. Burnside and the ninth army corps: a narrative of campaigns in N. Carolina, etc. viii, 554 pp. 1 pl. 7 portraits. 8 maps. 8°. *Providence, S. S. Rider & bro.* 1867.

Woodford (O. P.) Domestic and social harp: a collection of tunes and hymns. vi p. l. 166 pp. 1 l. obl. 18°. *Hartford, D. R. Woodford & Co.* 1848. s.

Woodhouse (Robert). The principles of analytical calculation. 4 p. l. xxxiv, 219 pp. 4°. *Cambridge, (Eng.) University press*, 1803.

Woodman (David, *jr.*) Guide to Texas emigrants. 192 pp. 1 map. 12°. *Boston, M. Hawes*, 1835.

Woodruff (William T.) New York masonic code; containing the old charges, compiled in 1720; constitutions, decisions, etc. 126 pp. 18°. *New York, Masonic pub. and manuf. co.* 1866.

Woods (John). The history of London: illustrated by views in London and Westminster, engraved by J. W. Edited by W. G. Fearnside and T. Harral. iv, 203 pp. 30 pl. 8°. *London, Orr & Co.* 1838. s.

Woodward (Augustus B.) The presidency of the United States. 2d ed. 88 pp. 8°. *Fredericktown, (Md.) T. Taylor*, 1826. s.

Woodward (*Capt.* David). Narrative. 8°. *London*, 1805. *See* **Vaughan** (William).

Woodward (George E.) Architecture and rural art. Nos. 1–2, 1867–68. 2 v. 132 pp; 132 pp. 12°. *New York, G. E. Woodward*, 1868.

——— Record of horticulture for 1866. Edited by Andrew S. Fuller. 125 pp. 12°. *New York, Geo. E. & F. W. Woodward*, 1867.

Woodward (Joseph Janvier). Report on epidemic cholera in the army of the U. S. during 1866. *See* **United States.** *War Department. Surgeon general's Office, Circular No.* 5.

Woodward (Samuel). An outline of the geology of Norfolk. 2 p. l. 60 pp. 2 maps. 6 pl. 8°. *Norwich, J. Stacy,* 1833. s.

Woodward (Samuel P.) A manual of the mollusca; or, rudimentary treatise of recent and fossil shells. xvi, 486 pp. 1 map. 25 pl. 12°. *London, J. Weale,* 1851-56. s.

——— The same. 2d ed. xiv, 518 pp. 24 pl. 12°. *London, Virtue,* 1866.

Woodward (W. Elliot). Records of Salem witchcraft, copied from the original documents. 2 v. 279 pp; 287 pp. sm. 4°. *Roxbury, (Mass.) W. Elliot Woodward,* [*J. Munsell, Albany, print.*] 1864.

Woodworth (Samuel). Poems, odes, songs, and other metrical effusions. 288 pp. 1 pl. 12°. *New York, A. Asten & M. Lopez,* 1818.

——— The war. A faithful record of the transactions of the war between the United States of America, and the united kingdom of Great Britain and Ireland, declared 18th June, 1812. [June 27, 1812—Feb. 1817]. v. 1-3 in 1 v. 2 p. l. 214 pp; 206 pp; 71 pp. 4°. *New York, S. Woodworth & Co.* 1812-17.

Wool (*Gen.* John E.) *See* **Taylor** and his generals.

Woolman (John). The works of J. Woolman. 2 parts in 1 v. xiv, 436 pp. 8°. *Philadelphia, J. Crukshank,* 1774.

Worcester (Edward Somerset, 2*d marquess of Worcester*). *See* **Somerset** (Edward).

Worcester (Joseph Emerson). A comprehensive pronouncing and explanatory dictionary of the English language. 491 pp. 12°. *Boston, Jenks, Palmer & Co.* 1848. s.

——— A geographical dictionary, or universal gazetteer. 2d ed. 2 v. v, 972 pp; 960 pp. 8°. *Boston, Cummings & Hilliard,* 1823.

Worcester (Samuel Melanchthon, *D. D.*) A memorial of the old and new tabernacle, Salem, Mass. 1854-55. 84 pp. 12°. *Boston, Crocker & Brewster,* 1855. s.

Worcester, (*Mass.*) Directory for 1868. By H. J. Howland. 248, 59 pp. 9 l. 1 map. 8°. *Worcester, H. J. Howland,* 1868.

Worcester county, (*Mass.*) Directory for 1866-67. 204, 104 pp. 8°. *Boston, Briggs & Co.* 1866.

Word (A) without-doors concerning the bill for succession [to the crown of England]. By J. D. [*anon.*] 12 pp. sm. 4°. [*n. p.* 1675?]

Wordsworth (William). Poetical works. New ed. 6 v. 16°. *London, Moxon,* 1864.

CONTENTS.

v. 1. Poems written in youth; poems of childhood; of the affections; poems on the naming of places.

v. 2. Poems of the fancy; of the imagination; Peter Bell; miscellaneous sonnets.
v. 3. Tour in Scotland, 1803; tour in Scotland, 1814; poems dedicated to national independence and liberty; tour in Italy, 1837; river Duddon; sonnets; white doe of Rylstone.
v. 4. Ecclesiastical sonnets; Yarrow revisited, and other poems; evening voluntaries; tour of 1833; poems of sentiment and reflection; sonnets dedicated to liberty and order; sonnets upon the punishment of death; miscellaneous poems.
v. 5. Inscriptions; selections from Chaucer modernised; poems of old age; epitaphs and elegiac pieces; the prelude, or growth of a poet's mind.
v. 6. The excursion; prefaces, notes, etc.

World (The). By Adam Fitz Adam. [*pseudon.* By Edward Moore, R. O. Cambridge, Horace Walpole, lord Chesterfield, etc.] 6 v. 16°. *London, R. & J. Dodsley,* 1755-57.

World (The). [New York daily]. July 1866 to Dec. 1867. 3 v. fol. *New York,* 1866-67.

World (The) almanac, 1868. 108 pp. 16°. *New York,* [*World office*], 1868.

World's (The) mistake in Oliver Cromwell; or, a short political discourse, shewing that Cromwell's mal-administration layed the foundation of our present condition, in the decay of trade. [*anon.* Supposed to have been written by Sir Slingsby Bethel]. 21 pp. sm. 4°. *London,* 1668.

Worlidge (John). Apiarivm: or, a discourse of the government and ordering of bees. [*anon.*] 2d ed. 4 p. l. 42 pp. 16°. *London, T. Dring,* 1678.

[*With his* Vinetum britannicum, 1678].

——— Vinetum britannicum; or, a treatise of cider, and other wines and drinks from fruits growing in this kingdom. 2d ed. 11 p. l. 240 pp. 6 l. 2 pl. 16°. *London, T. Dring,* 1678.

Worlidge (Thomas). A select collection of drawings from curious antique gems, [etc.] etched after the manner of Rembrandt. 6 p. l. 48 pp. 1 portrait. 180 pl. 4°. *London, M. Worlidge,* 1768. s.

Worm (Olaus, *M. D.*) Museum wormianum; seu, historia rerum rariorum, tam naturalium, quam artificialium, tam domesticarum, quam exoticarum, in aedibus authoris. [Curante Wilhelmo Wormio]. 6 p. l. 392 pp. fol. *Lugduni-Batavorum, Elsevir,* 1655. s.

Worsaae (Jens Jacob Asmussen). Zur alterthumskunde des nordens. 1 p. l. ii, 130 pp. 20 pl. 4°. *Leipzig, L. Voss,* 1847. s.

Worsley (*Sir* Richard). Museo worslejano descritto e illustrato [da E. Q. Visconti]. xxxix, 192 pp. 78 pl. 8°. *Milano, Società tipogr. de' classici italiani,* 1834. s.

Worth (*Gen.* William J.) *See* **Taylor** and his generals.

Wrangell (Ferdinand Petrovich von). Narrative of an expedition to the polar sea in the years 1820–1823. Ed. by E. Sabine. cxxxvii, 413 pp. 1 map. 8°. *London, J. Madden & Co.* 1840. s.

Wraxall (Frederick Charles Lascelles). The fife and drum; or, would be a soldier. xvi, 277 pp. 8°. *London, S. O. Beeton,* 1863.

Wraxall (*Sir* Nathaniel William). A tour round the Baltic, thro' the northern countries of Europe. 4th ed. 452 pp. 8°. *London, Cadell & Davies,* 1807.

Wright (John, *M. D.*) Report on the botany of Michigan.

[*With* HOUGHTON (Douglass). Reports, etc. Doc. No. 2].

Wright (John F.) Sketches of the life and labors of James Quinn, [etc.] 324 pp. 1 pl. 12°. *Cincinnati, Methodist book concern,* 1851. s.

Wright (N. Hill). Monody on the death of brigadier general Zebulon Montgomery Pike, and other poems. 79 pp. 8°. *Middlebury, (Vt.) Slade & Ferguson,* 1814.

Wright (Robert). Memoir of general James Oglethorpe. xvi, 414 pp. 1 map. 8°. *London, Chapman & Hall,* 1867.

Wright (Robert W.) Vision of judgment; or, the South church. Ecclesiastical councils viewed from celestial and satanic stand-points. By Quevedo Redivivus, jr. [*pseudon.*] 176 pp. 12°. *New York, Van Evrie, Horton & Co.* 1867.

Wright (Thomas, *F. S. A; antiquary*). The history of the county of Lincoln. Illustrated. [*anon.*] 2 v. 5 p. l. 360 pp. 15 pl. 2 maps; 360 pp. 5 l. 25 pl. 4°. *London & Lincoln, J. Saunders, jr.* 1833–34.

Wright (Thomas, *M. D; F. R. S.*) Monograph on the British fossil echinodermata from the cretaceous formations. v. 1. part 1. 2 p. l. pp. 1—64. 11 l. pl. 1—11. 4°. *London,* 1864.
[Palæontographical society, 1864].

——— A monograph on the British fossil echinodermata of the oolitic formations. v. 1. x, 468 pp. 43 l. 43 pl. v. 2. 2 p. l. pp. 1—154, pl. 1–18. 4°. *London,* 1855–62.
[Palæontographical society].

Wright (*Rev.* William). Slavery at the Cape of Good Hope. vi, 107 pp. 8°. *London, Longmans, Rees & Co.* 1831.

[*With* POYNDER (J.) Human sacrifices in India].

Wright (William, *accountant*). National system of book-keeping; double entry. 166 pp. obl. 8°. *Philadelphia, J. B. Lippincott & Co.* 1866.

Wright (William). Grotesque architecture; or, rural amusement. Consisting of plans, elevations, and sections for huts, retreats, hermitages, [etc.] 14 pp. 29 pl. 8°. *London, H. Webley,* 1867.

Wright (William C.) The piano-forte manual. 84 pp. 12°. *New York, Mason & bros.* 1854. s.

Wüllerstorf-Urbair (Bernhard von). Reise der österreichischen fregatte Novara um die erde in den jahren 1857–59. s.

CONTENTS.

MÜLLER (*Dr.* Friedrich). Linguistischer theil. vii, 358 pp. 4°. *Wien, k-k. hof- und staatsdruckerei,* 1867.

SAUSSURE (Henri de). Hymenoptera. Nebst einem supplement von Dr. J. Sichel. 156 pp. 4 l. 4 col. pl. 1867.

SCHERZER (Carl von). Beschreibender theil. 3 v. 8°. *Wien, Hof- und staatsdruckerei,* 1861–62.

Wulffen (Carl von). Entwurf einer methodik zur berechnung der feldsysteme. [Extract.] x, 188 pp. 8°. *Berlin, Veit & Co.* 1847. s.

[*From the* Annalen des landes-oecon. coll.]

Wurffbain (Johann Paul). Salamandrologia: i. e. descriptio historico-philologico-philosophico-medica salamandrae quæ vulgo in igne vivere creditur. 3 p. l. 133 pp. 7 l. 5 pl. 4°. *Norimbergae, G. Scheurer,* 1683. s.

Wursteisen (Christian). Germaniæ historicorvm illustrium ab Henrico iv. ad annum 1400 tomus i–ii. [Ed. 2a]. 2 v. in 1. 6 p. l. 626 pp. 10 l; 182 pp. 5 l. fol. *Francofvrti ad Moenvm, J. G. Seyler,* 1670.

Wurzbach von Tannenberg (Constant). Bibliographisch-statistische übersicht der literatur des östreichischen kaiserstaates, 1854. Zweiter bericht. xxii, 686 pp. 8°. *Wien,* [*Pfautsch u. Voss*], 1856.

——— Das Schiller-buch. Festgabe zur ersten säcular-feier von Schiller's geburt. xxiv, 324 pp. 40 pl. 4°. *Wien, Gerold,* 1859.

Wuttke (Heinrich). Die entwickelung der öffentlichen verhältnisse Schlesiens, vornämlich unter den Habsburgern. 2 v. in 1. xii, 370 pp; viii, 452 pp. 8°. *Leipzig, W. Engelmann,* 1842–43. s.

——— The same. Abfertigung des Dr. Karl Gustav Kries's recension über Wuttke's Schlesien. 40 pp. 8°. *Leipzig, W. Engelmann,* 1843. s.

[*With* the preceding].

——— Die schlesischen stände; ihr wesen, ihr werken, und ihr werth in alter und neuer zeiten. 247 pp. 8°. *Leipzig, J. F. Hartknoch,* 1847. s.

Wycke *or* Wickes (Thomas). Chronicon salisburiensis monasterii, ab adventu conquestoris ad annum M.CCC.IIII. fol. *Oxoniæ*, 1687.

[GALE (Thomas), *and* FELL (John). Rerum anglicarum scriptores veteres. *Oxoniæ*, 1684–91. v. 2].

Wyman (Jeffries, *M. D.*) Fossil mammals [of Chile].

[*With* GILLISS (J. M.) U. S. astronom. exped. v. 2].

Wyman (Seth). Life and adventures. Written by himself. 310 pp. 12°. *Manchester, (N. H.) J. H. Cate*, 1843.

Wynkoop (J. M.) Anecdotes and incidents, comprising daring exploits of the army, and thrilling incidents of the Mexican war. 132 pp. 8°. *Pittsburg*, 1848.

Wynn (*Sir* John). The history of the Gwydir family, [with] memoirs of distinguished cotemporary Welshmen. 121 pp. 3 pl. 4°. *Ruthin, R. Jones*, 1827.

Wyth *or* **With** (John). Portraits to the life, and manners of the inhabitants of that province in America called Virginia. 39 l. 24 pl. 8°. *New York, J. & H. G. Langley*, 1841.

[Published as part i of GRAPHIC sketches, illustrating the costume of the aborigines, etc.]

Wythes (Joseph H. *M. D.*) The microscopist; or, a complete manual on the use of the microscope, [etc.] 191 pp. 1 pl. 12°. *Philadelphia, Lindsay & Blakiston*, 1851. s.

Wythes (William W.) A description of the cyclo-ellipto-pantograph. 4 pp. 6 pl. 8°. *Philadelphia, H. B. Ashmead*, 1858. s.

Xenophon. Anabasis. De Cyri expeditione libri septem. Ex recensione, et cum notis Thomæ Hutchinson. xx, 362, 34 pp. 8°. *Glasguæ, A. & J. Duncan*, 1817. s.

——— The same. Expedition of Cyrus, with English notes, etc. by Charles Dexter Cleveland. xv, 320 pp. 12°. *Boston, Hilliard, etc.* 1830. s.

——— The same. Expedition of Cyrus into Persia; and the retreat of the ten thousand Greeks. Translated from the Greek by Edward Spelman. vii, 143 pp. 1 map. 8°. *London, J. Davis*, 1812.

[*With* SAXE (M. *comte* de). Art of war. 8°. *London*, 1811].

——— Cyropædia. The institvtion and life of Cyrvs. Translated by Philemon Holland. 9 p.l. 213 pp. fol. *London, Robert Allot*, 1632.

——— The same. The first four books [translated] by F. Digby, the four last by John Norris. 8 p. l. 214, 190 pp. 16°. *London, M. Gilliflower & J. Norris*, 1685.

——— The same. From the Greek by Maurice Ashley [Cooper]. 367 pp. 15 l. 8°. *Philadelphia, Hopkins & Co.* 1810.

Xenophon. Memorabilia Socratis. Edidit G. H. Schaefer. xvi, 176 pp. 18°. *Lipsiæ, C. Tauchnitz*, 1811. s.

Ximeno (Vicente). Escritores del reyno de Valencia, desde el año 1238 hasta el de 1747. 2 v. 15 p. l. x, 368 pp. 4 l; 11 p. l. 385 pp. 26 l. fol. *Valencia, J. E. Dolz*, 1747–49.

Yago (Pedro Manuel). En el fondo. Aforismos caseros sobre varias cosas, fragmentos, articulos, etc. 211 pp. 18°. *Valencia, J. Rius*, 1863.

Yajurveda (The white). Edited by Albrecht Weber. 3 v. 4°. *Berlin, F. Dümmler*, 1849–59. s.

CONTENTS.

v. 1. The Vâjasaneyi-sanhita in the Mâdhyandina, and the Kânvaçâkhâ, with the commentary of Madîdhara. xcv, 989 pp.
v. 2. The Catapatha-Brâhmana in the Mâdhyandina-Câkhâ with extracts made from the commentaries of Sâyana, Harisvâmin, and Dvivedaganga. xiii, 1194 pp.
v. 3. The Crautasûtra of Kâtyâyana with extracts from the commentaries of Karka and Yâjnikadeva. xvi, 1114 pp. 3 l.

——— *See, also,* **Rig-veda.**

Yalden (Thomas). Poetical works. 8°. *Edinburgh*, 1794.

[ANDERSON'S British poets. v. 7].

Yale College. Catalogue of the library of the society of brothers in unity. 294 pp. 1 pl. 8°. *New Haven, T. J. Stafford*, 1851.

——— Catalogus senatus academici, [etc.] in collegio yalensi, [1862]. 170 pp. 8°. *Novi Portus, E. Hayes*, 1862.

——— The same. 178 pp. 8°. *Novi Portus, E. Hayes*, 1865.

——— Obituary record of graduates [for] the year ending July, 1866. (No. 7, printed series, and No. 25, of the whole record). pp. 189 to 222. 8°. [*New Haven*, 1866].

Yandell (Lunsford P.) *and* **Shumard** (Benjamin F.) Contributions to the geology of Kentucky. 36 pp. 1 pl. 8°. *Louisville, Prentice & Weissinger*, 1847.

Yankee doodle. 2 v. [Illustrated.] iv, 284 pp; iv, 256 pp. sm. fol. *New York, W. H. Graham*, 1846–47.

Yankee (The) slave driver; or, the black and white rivals. With illustrations. [By William White Smith?] 365 pp. 12°. *New York, H. Dayton*, 1860.

Yate (Walter Honywood). Political and historical arguments, proving the necessity of a parliamentary reform, and pointing out the means of effecting that important measure. 2 v. xxxiv, 312 pp; xiv, 340 pp. 8°. *London,* [*printed at Edinburgh, W. Balfour,*] 1812.

[NOTE.—Written by Capt. Thomas Ashe].

Yates (Edmund). Black sheep. A novel. 3 v. 12°. *London, Tinsley bros.* 1867.

——— The forlorn hope. A novel. New ed. 3 p. l. 426 pp. 12°. *London, Tinsley,* 1867.

Yates (Robert). Secret proceedings and debates of the convention for forming the constitution of the United States; with other documents. 308 pp. 8°. *Washington, (D. C.) G. Templeman,* 1836.

Yatman (John V.) Sterling exchange tables, showing the equivalent rates for currency as compared with gold. [*anon.*] 191 pp. 24°. *New York, E. B. Clayton's sons,* 1864.

Yeaman (George H.) Allegiance and citizenship. An inquiry into the claim of European governments to exact military service of naturalized citizens of the United States. 50 pp. 8°. *Copenhagen, F. Möller,* 1867.

Year (The) book and almanac for British North America, for 1867; political and trade statistics, etc. 161 pp. 8°. *Montreal, M. Longmoore & Co.* 1866.

——— The same. The year book and almanac of Canada for 1868; being an annual statistical abstract for the dominion, and a record of legislation and of public men in British North America. 169 pp. 1 map. 12°. *Montreal, Print. and pub. co.* [1867].

Yelverton (*Hon.* Theresa). Martyrs to circumstance. 7th ed. 377 pp. 16°. *London, R. Bentley,* 1861.

Yemeniz (N.) Catalogue de [sa] bibliothèque, précédé d'une notice par M. Le Roux de Lincy. lxiv, 780 pp. 8°. *Paris, Bachelin-Deflorenne,* 1867. s.

Yendys (Sydney, *pseudon.*) *See* **Dobell** (Sydney).

Yonge (Charlotte Mary). The daisy chain; or, aspirations. A family chronicle. [*anon.*] 9th ed. vi, 667 pp. 12°. *London, Macmillan,* 1867.

——— The Danvers papers: an invention. [*anon.*] 147 pp. 16°. *London, Macmillan,* 1867.

——— Dynevor terrace; or, the clue of life. [*anon.*] 2 v. 367 pp; 375 pp. 16°. *London, Parker & son,* 1857.

——— The heir of Redclyffe. [*anon.*] 16th ed. 524 pp. 12°. *London, Macmillan,* 1866.

——— Landmarks of history. Ancient history, from the earliest times to the Mahometan conquest. Revised by Edith L. Chase. 3d Am. ed. 240 pp. 12°. *New York, Leypoldt & Holt,* 1867.

——— The same. Middle ages; from the reign of Charlemagne to that of Charles v. Revised by Edith L. Chase. 1st Am. ed. viii, 252 pp. 12°. *Leypoldt & Holt,* 1867.

——— The young stepmother; or, a chronicle of mistakes. [*anon.*] 482 pp. 16°. *London, Parker, son & Bourn,* 1861.

Yorick turned trimmer; or, the gentleman's jester: and newest collection of songs. [*anon.*] 72 pp. 3 pl. 16°. *London, W. Nicoll,* 1789.

Yorke (James, *bishop of St. David's*). A sermon before the society for the propagation of the gospel in foreign parts, at their anniversary, 1779; with abstract of the proceedings of the society, 1778–9. 90 pp. sm. 4°. *London, T. Harrison,* 1779.

Yorke (Philip, 1*st earl* of Hardwicke). Speech March 19th, 1746, upon giving judgment against Simon, lord Lovat, on the impeachment of high treason. 8 pp. fol. *London, S. Billingsley,* 1747.

Yorke (Philip, *of Erthig*). Royal tribes of Wales. viii, 195 pp. 12 pl. 4°. *Wrexham, J. Painter,* [1799].

Youatt (William). The dog. Edited, with additions, by E. J. Lewis. 403 pp. 23 pl. 8°. *Philadelphia, Lea & Blanchard,* 1847. s.

——— *and* **Martin** (W. C. L.) Cattle: being a treatise on their breeds, management, and diseases. Edited by A. Stevens. 469 pp. 4 pl. 12°. *New York, C. M. Saxton,* 1851. s.

Youmans (Edward L. *M. D.*) Correlation and conservation of forces; a series of expositions by Profs. Grove, Helmholtz, Liebig, and Drs. Mayer, Faraday and Carpenter. With an introduction and brief biographical notices of the chief promoters of the new views. xlii, 438 pp. 12°. *New York, Appletons,* 1865.

——— The culture demanded by modern life: a series of addresses and arguments on the claims of scientific education. By Profs. Tyndall, Henfrey, Huxley, etc. With an introduction on mental discipline in education by E. L. Youmans. xii, 473 pp. 12°. *New York, D. Appleton & Co.* 1867.

——— Elementos de quimica, para uso de los colegios y escuelas. Traducido de la ult. ed. ingl. por Marco A. Rojas, D. M. 500 pp. 12°. *Nueva York, D. Appleton & Co.* 1867.

Young (Augustus). Unity of purpose; or, rational analysis: a treatise designed to disclose physical truths, and to detect and expose popular errors. 292 pp. 8°. *Boston, author,* 1846. s.

Young (David). Wonderful history of the Morristown ghost. v, 76 pp. 24°. *Newark, B. Olds,* 1826.

Young (Edward, *LL. D. rector of Wellwyn*). The last day; a poem. 124 pp. 16°. *Elizabethtown, S. Kollock*, 1797.

——— Night thoughts on life, death, and immortality. 227 pp. 32°. *Baltimore, Neal and Wills*, 1812.

Young (James Reynolds). Elementary treatise on algebra, theoretical and practical. xvi, 211 pp. 8°. *London, J. Souter*, 1827.

——— Elements of geometry, with notes. x, 208 pp. 8°. *London, J. Souter*, 1833. s.

——— The elements of analytical geometry. xxi, 312 pp. 12°. *London, J. Souter*, 1833. s.

——— Elements of plane and spherical trigonometry, with its applications to the principles of navigation and nautical astronomy. xii, 208 pp. 12°. *London, J. Souter*, 1836. s.

Young (John, *of Nova Scotia*). The letters of Agricola on the principles of vegetation and tillage. Written for Nova Scotia. 462 pp. 5 l. 8°. *Halifax, (N. S.) Holland & Co.* 1822.

Young (Thomas, *F. R. S.*) A course of lectures on natural philosophy and the mechanical arts. [With a catalogue of works relating to natural philosophy and the mechanical arts]. 2 v. xxiv, 796 pp. 43 pl; xii, 738 pp. 15 pl. 4°. *London, J. Johnson*, 1807.

Young (The) lady of pleasure. [Being letters on the formation of character. *anon.*] 316 pp. 12°. *New York, Am. tract soc.* 1865.

Yule (Henry). Cathay, and the way thither; being a collection of medieval notices of China. Translated and edited, with a preliminary essay on the intercourse between China and the western nations previous to the discovery of the Cape route. 2 v. ccliii, 250 pp; 596, xcviii pp. 2 maps. 8°. *London*, 1866.

[HAKLUYT society publications, v. 36–37].

CONTENTS.

v. 1. Travels of friar Odoric; Letters and reports of missionary friars.

v. 2. Cathay under the Mongols, extracted from Rashid-uddin; Pegolotti's notices of the land route to Cathay; Marignolli's eastern travel; Ibn Batuta's travels in Bengal and China; Journal of Benedict Goës from Agra to Cathay.

Zabarella (Francesco, *cardinal*). Lectura sup. clemētinis. 338 l. [with 1 l. MS. index]. fol. *Romæ, Georiū Laur. de Herbipoli*, 1477.

Zachariä (Justus Friedrich Wilhelm). Les quatre parties du jour, poëme traduit de l'Allemand [en prose, par Muller]. xx, 163 pp. 18°. *Amsterdam, D. J. Changuion*, 1769.

Zaddach (Gustav). Untersuchungen über die entwickelung und den bau der gliederthiere. i. Die entwickelung des phryganiden-eies. 2 p. l. 138 pp. 5 pl. 4°. *Berlin, G. Reimer*, 1854. s.

[No more published].

Zambelli (Andrea). Delle differenze politiche tra i popoli antichi ed i moderni. Parte prima: La guerra. Libri tre. 2 v. 253 pp; 319 pp. 8°. *Milano, Santo Bravetta*, 1839. s.

Zanon (Antonio). Lettre scelte sull' agricoltura, sul commercio, e sulle arti, v. 18. Apologia della mercatura; Estratto del trattato dell' utilità delle accademie di agricoltura, arti, e commercio, v. 19.

[SCRITTORI class. ital. di econ. pol. v. 18–19].

Zantedeschi (Francesco). Trattato del magnetismo e della elettricità. 2 v. 4 p. l. 389 pp. 2 l; 3 p. l. 546 pp. 3 l. 4 pl. 8°. *Venezia, Tipografia armena di S. Lazzaro*, 1844–45. s.

Zanth (Carl Ludwig). Architecture de la Sicile. *See* **Hittorf** (J. I.), *and* **Zanth**.

Zárate (Agustin de). Historia del descvbrimiento y conqvista de las provincias del Peru. 4 p. l. 117 l. 3 l. fol. *Sevilla, Alonso Escriuano*, 1577.

——— The same. Historie dello scoprimento et conqvista del Perv. Nvovamente tradotte dal S. Alfonso Vlloa. viii, 294 pp. 8°. *Vinegia, G. Giolito de' Ferrari*, 1563.

Zauschner (Johann Baptist Joseph). Dissertatio de sale a mineralogis haud descripto, acidularum coronariarum nomine insignito. 8 p.l. 184 pp. 12°. *Pragæ, J. J. Clauser*, 1768. s.

Zavala y Auñon (Miguel de). Representacion al rey Phelipe v. dirigida al mas seguro aumento del real erario, y conseguir la felicidad, mayor alivio, riqueza, y abundancia de su monarquia. 2 p. l. 180 pp. sm. fol. [*Madrid? J. O. de Zavala*], 1732.

Zeballos, *or* **Cevallos**, (Pedro Ordoñez de). *See* **Ordoñez** de Zeballos.

Zeiller (Martin). Collectanea; oder, nachdenckliche reden verwunderlich vnd seltzame geschichten vnd andere sonderbare sachen. 2 parts in 1 v. 18 p. l. 411 pp; 182 pp. 18°. *Ulm, G. Wildeisen*, 1658.

Zendavesta. Commentaire sur le yaçna, l'un des livres religieux des Parses; [attribué à Zoroastre]; ouvrage contenant le texte zend expliqué pour la prémière fois, et la version sanscrite inédite de Nériosengh. Par Eugène Burnouf. v. 1 in 2 v. cx, cvi, 592 pp. 4°. *Paris, Imprimerie royale*, 1833.

Zeno (Caterino). Dei commentarii del viaggio in Persia di Caterino Zeno, e delle guerre fatte nell' imperio persiano dal tempo di Vssuncassano in quà libri dve; et dello scoprimento dell' isole Frislanda, Eslanda, Engrouelanda (etc.) fatto sotto il polo artico, da due fratelli Zeni, Nicolo e Antonio, libro uno. 6 p. l. 53 pp. 18°. *Venetia, Francesco Marcolini*, 1558.

[Map wanting].

Zentner (L.) Une collection choisie de paysages; ou, un échantillon de chaqu'un des meilleurs anciens maitres. A select collection of landscapes from the best old masters, one of each, [with] portraits of the artists, and biographical accounts of each. [Fr. and Engl.] 55 pl. obl. 8°. *London, J. Thane,* 1791.

Zernikow (*Dr.* ——). Die theorie der dampfmaschinen. xii, 233 pp. 8°. *Braunschweig, Vieweg,* 1857. s.

Zestermann (A. Charles Adolphe). De basilicis libri iii. 179 pp. 7 pl. 4°. *Bruxellis, M. Hayez,* 1847. s.

Zetterstedt (Johan Wilhelm). Diptera Scandinaviæ disposita et descripta. 12 v. 8°. *Lundæ, Officina lundbergiana,* 1842–55. s.

Zetzsche (Carl Eduard). Die copirtelegraphen, die typendrucktelegraphen, und die doppeltelegraphie. vi, 198 pp. 8°. *Leipzig, B. G. Teubner,* 1865. s.

Ziegler (J. M.) Sammlung absoluter höhen der Schweiz und der angrenzenden gegenden der nachbarländer, als ergänzung der karte in reduction von 1: 380,000. (German and French). xiv, 398 pp. 1 map. 8°. *Zürich, Zürcher & Furrer,* 1853. s.

Ziemann (Julius Eduard). Comparatio columnæ vertebralis hominis cum eadem parte sceleti mammalium et terrestrium et maritimorum. 30 pp. 1 pl. 8°. *Halis, Heynemann,* 1848. s.

Zimmermann (Eberhard August Wilhelm von). Specimen zoologiae geographicae, quadrupedum domicilia et migrationes sistens. xxiv, 685 pp. 1 map. 4°. *Lugduni Batavorum,* 1777. s.

Zimmermann (Johann Georg von). Aphorisms and reflections on men, morals, and things. Translated from ms. with notes. 2 p. l. 356 pp. portrait. 16°. *London, Vernor & Hood,* 1800.

Zimmermann (R.) Abrégé de l'histoire de la Suisse. Traduit par Ch. Richon. 2e éd. 434 pp. 8°. *Lausanne, Pache-Simmen,* 1850.

Zimmerman (W. F. A.) Die wunder der welt; eine populäre darstellung der geschichte der schöpfung und des urzustandes unseres weltkörpers sowie der verschiedenen entwickelungsperioden seiner oberflächen, etc. 8e aufl. viii, 512 pp. 1 col. pl. 8°. *Berlin, G. Hempel,* 1855. s.

[Der ERDBALL und seine naturwunder. v. 3. Abtheil 1].

—— Les phénomènes de la nature, leurs lois et leurs applications aux arts et à l'industrie. 2 v. 515 pp; 1 col. pl. 3 maps. 584 pp. 1 col. pl. 8°. *Bruxelles, C. Muquardt,* 1858. s.

CONTENTS.

v. 1. Electricité, magnétismé, galvanisme.
v. 2. Mécanique, acoustique, optique, calorique.

Zinckgreff *or* **Zincgrefe** (Julius Wilhelm). Emblematum ethico-politicorum centuria. Editio ultima. 8 p. l. c pp. 3 l. sm. 4°. *Heidelbergæ, C. Ammonius,* 1666.

Zirkel (Ferdinand). Reise nach Island, 1860. *See* **Preyer** (W.) *and* **Zirkel.**

Zoller (Edmund). Die bibliothekwissenschaft im umrisse. vi, 72 pp. 1 pl. 16°. *Stuttgart, J. Weise,* 1846. s.

Zollickoffer (William, *M. D.*) A materia medica of the United States, systematically arranged. 2d ed. 245 pp. 8°. *Baltimore, J. Lovegrove,* 1827. s.

Zornlin (R. M.) Physical geography, for families and schools. Revised by W. L. Gage. xvi, 159 pp. 16°. *Boston, Munroe & Co.* 1855. s.

Zschokke (Johann Heinrich Daniel). Des Schweizerlands geschichte für das Schweizervolk. 2e auflage. 260 pp. 8°. *Aarau, H. R. Sauerländer,* 1824. s.

—— The history of the invasion of Switzerland by the French, and the destruction of the democratical republics Schwitz, Uri, and Unterwalden. Translated from the French. vii, 365 pp. 1 map. 8°. *London, J. Taylor,* 1803.

—— Stray leaves from the German; or, select essays from Zschokke. By W. B. Flower. 29, 168 pp. 8°. *London, Simpkin, Marshall & Co.* 1845.

Zschokke (Th.) Die wassermangel in einem theile der Schweiz, besonders im kanton Aargau im winter 1864–65. iv, 91 pp. 8°. *Aarau, Aargauische naturf. gesellschaft,* 1866. s.

Zuchold (Ernst Amandus). Bibliotheca chemica. Verzeichniss der auf dem gebiete der reinen, pharmaceutischen, physiologischen, und technischen chemie, 1840–58, in Deutschland und im auslande erschienenen schriften. vii, 342 pp. 8°. *Göttingen, Vandenhoeck & Ruprecht,* 1859. s.

—— Bibliotheca theologica. Verzeichniss der auf dem gebiete der evangelischen theologie, während der jahre 1830–62, in Deutschland erschienenen schriften. 1 v. in 2. vi, 1560 pp. 8°. *Göttingen, Vandenhoeck & Ruprecht,* 1864.

Zundel (John). The choral friend; a collection of new church music. 96 pp. 8°. *New York, A. S. Barnes & Co.* 1852. s.

Zürich. Catalog der bibliothek der cantonal lehranstalten. Bearbeitet von O. F. Fritzsche. viii, 932 pp. 8°. *Zürich, F. Walder & sohn,* 1859. s.

Zurla (Placido). Di Marco Polo e degli altri viaggiatori veneziani più illustri dissertazioni; con appendice sopra le antiche mappe lavorate in Venezia, e con quattro carte geografiche. 2 v. viii, 391 pp; 408 pp. 4 maps. 4°. *Venezia, Giacomo Fuchs,* 1818.

LAW BOOKS.

ABBOT (George, *archbishop of Canterbury*). Memorials touching the nullity between [Robert Devereux], earl of Essex, and his lady, [Frances Howard], pronounced Sept. 1613, at Lambeth. fol. *London, T. Wright,* 1779. [HARGRAVE'S state trials, v. 10].

ABBOTT (Benjamin V. *and* Austin). A digest of the reports of the United States courts, and of the acts of congress, from the organization of the government to the year 1867, comprising the reports of the United States supreme court, those of the circuit and district courts, and of the various territorial and local courts established by the United States; together with the leading provisions of the statutes at large, and important auxiliary information upon the national jurisprudence. v. 1—2. A—I. 8°. *New York, Diossy & Cockcroft,* 1867. [21 copies of v. 1; 20 copies of v. 2.)

——— Digest of New York statutes and reports, from July, 1863, to January, 1867, [v. 7.] 8°. *New York, Baker, Voorhis & Co.* 1867. (2 copies.)

——— Reports of practice cases in the state of New York. New series. v. 1—2. 8°. *New York, Diossy & Cockcroft,* 1866–67. (2 copies.)

ABINGTON (Edward), *and others*. Trial, at Westminster, for high treason, Sept. 1586. fol. *London, T. Wright,* 1776. [HARGRAVE'S state trials, v. 1].

ABRIDGMENT (An) of the laws in force and use in her majesty's plantations; (viz.) of Virginia, Jamaica, Barbadoes, Maryland, New England, New York, Carolina, etc. [*anon.*] 2 p. l. 475 pp. 8°. *London, J. Nicholson,* 1704.

ACCOLTI (Francesco). Cōmentaria super titulo de verbo. obliga. et de duobus reis. 156 l. unp. fol. *Piscie, impensis Sebastiani et Raphaelis frat. et fil. Ser Jacobi Gerardi de Orlādis,* 1486.

ACTON (William). Trial of, for the murder of T. Bliss, J. Bromfield, R. Newton, and J. Thompson, at Kingston upon Thames, Aug. 1729. fol. *London, T. Wright,* 1778. [HARGRAVE'S state trials, v. 9].

ADAIR (John). The law of costs, especially as administered in courts of equity. lii, 322 pp. 8°. *Dublin, Ponsonby,* 1865.

ALABAMA (*State of*). Laws, 1866. 8°. *Montgomery,* 1867.

——— Alabama reports. v. 37–38. By John W. Shepherd. 8°. *Montgomery, Barrett & Brown,* 1866–67.

ALLEN (Charles). Reports of cases in the supreme judicial court of Massachusetts. v. 10–12. 8°. *Boston, Houghton & Co.* 1867. (2 copies.)

AMERICAN law register. v. 14. 8°. *Philadelphia, Canfield & Co.* 1866.

AMERICAN law review, 1866–67. v. 1. 764 pp. 8°. *Boston, Little, Brown & Co.* 1867. (2 copies.)

AMES (Samuel). Law of private corporations. *See* **ANGELL** (Joseph K.) *and* **AMES**.

ANDERSON (Lionel), *and others*. Tryals and condemnation for high treason as Romish priests, Old-Baily, Jan. 1679. 1 p. l. 53 pp. fol. *London, T. Collins,* 1680. [TRIALS for treason, v. 3].

——— The same. fol. *London, T. Wright,* 1776. [HARGRAVE'S state trials, v. 2].

ANDERTON (William). Trial at the Old-Bailey, June, 1693, for high treason. fol. *London, T. Wright,* 1778. [HARGRAVE'S state trials, v. 8].

ANDREWE (Eusebius). Proceedings, examination, and trial, before the high court of justice, Aug. 1650, for high treason. fol. *London, T. Wright,* 1778. [HARGRAVE'S state trials, v. 7].

ANGELL (Joseph K.) *and* **AMES** (Samuel). Treatise on the law of private corporations aggregate. 8th ed. Revised, corrected, and enlarged, by John Lathrop. lviii, 843 pp. 8°. *Boston, Little, Brown & Co.* 1866.

ANGLESEY (Richard Annesley, *6th earl of*). *See* **ANNESLEY**.

ANNESLEY (James). Trial in ejectment. *See* **ANNESLEY** (Richard).

——— *and* **READING** (Joseph). Trial for the murder of T. Egglestone, Old-Bailey, July, 1742. fol. *London, T. Wright*, 1778.
[HARGRAVE'S state trials, v. 9].

ANNESLEY (Richard, *6th earl of Anglesey*). The trial in ejectment between Campbell Craig, lessee of James Annesley, and others, plaintiff; and Richard [Annesley], earl of Anglesey, defendant; court of exchequer in Ireland. Nov. 1743. 2 p. l. 259 pp. fol. *London, J. & P. Knapton*, 1744.

——— The same. fol. *London, T. Wright*, 1779.
[HARGRAVE'S state trials, v. 9].

——— *and others*. Trial, for an assault on Hon. James Annesley, [and others], Athy, Aug. 1744. fol. *London, T. Wright*, 1744.
[HARGRAVE'S state trials, v. 9].

ANTIGUA. The laws of the island of Antigua; consisting of the laws of the Leeward islands, commencing 8th November 1690, ending 21st April, 1798; and acts of Antigua, commencing 10th April 1668, ending 7th May 1804. 2 v. lxvii, 584; xx, 636 pp. 4°. *London, S. Bagster*, 1805.

ARCHBOLD (John Frederick). The practice of the new county courts, with forms, and the statutes and rules. 2d ed. xv, 278 pp. 1 map. 12°. *London, Shaw & sons*, 1847.

——— The joint stock companies acts, 19 and 20 Vict. cap. 47, and the amendment act, 20 and 21 Vict. cap. 14. xviii, 68 pp. 8°. *London, Shaw & sons*, 1857.

ARGYLL (Archibald Campbell, *marquess, and 8th earl of*). *See* **CAMPBELL** (Archibald).

ARGYLL (Archibald Campbell, *9th earl of*). *See* **CAMPBELL** (Archibald).

ARIZONA (*Territory of*). Laws. 1865 and 1866. 2 v. 8°. *Prescott*, 1866-67.

ARKANSAS (*State of*). Acts of Congress and of the state of Arkansas, on the subject of swamp and overflowed lands, from 1850 to 1857. 84 pp. 8°. *Little Rock, Johnson & Yerkes*, 1857.

——— Laws, 1823, (4 copies); 1829, 1831, 1833, 1837-38, 1842-43, 1844-45, 1854-55, 1860-61, 1862, (2 copies of each); and 1866-67, (4 copies). 26 v. 8°. *Little Rock*, 1824-67.

ARKANSAS (*State of*). Arkansas reports. v. 24. By L. E. Barber. 8°. *Little Rock, Woodruff & Blocher*, 1867. (2 copies).

ARMSTRONG (*Sir* Thomas). Proceedings against [him] in the king's bench, upon an outlawry for high treason, etc. As also an account of what passed at his execution, the 20th June, 1684. 8 pp. fol. *London, Havne & Co.* 1684.
[*With* BRADDON (Lawrence), *and* SPEKE (Hugh).

——— The same. fol. *London, T. Wright*, 1776.
[HARGRAVE'S state trials, v. 3].

ARNOLD (Edward). Trial for felony, (in maliciously shooting at and wounding the lord Onslow), Kingston-upon-Thames, March, 1724. fol. *London, T. Wright*, 1778.
[HARGRAVE'S state trials. v. 8].

ARUNDEL (Philip Howard, *earl of*). *See* **HOWARD**.

ASHBY (Mathew). Proceedings in the case of Ashby and White. *See* **WHITE** (William, *mayor of Aylesbury, Eng.*)

ASHTON (John). Trial for treason. *See* **GRAHAM** (Richard, *viscount Preston*), *and* **ASHTON**.

——— True copy of part of that paper left in a friend's hands; [with] a letter in which he sent it enclosed. fol. *London, T. Wright*, 1778.
[HARGRAVE'S state trials. v. 8].

ASPDEN (Matthias). Supreme court of the U. S. [Dec. term, 1851.] John A. Brown, adm'r of John Aspden, of London; Samuel Jackson, adm'r d. b. n. t. a. of John Aspden, of Lancashire; James McMurtrie and Rebecca, his wife, et al. appellants, *vs.* Matthias Aspden's adm'r d. b. n. c. t. a. et al. On appeal from the circuit court for the eastern district of Penn'a. vii, 1209 pp. 8°. [*Washington*], *J. Gideon*, [1852].

ATKINS (*Sir* Robert). A defence of the late lord Russell's innocency. By way of answer of an Antidote against poison. [By Sir B. Shower. With] two letters upon the subject of his lordship's trial. fol. *London, T. Wright*, 1776.
[HARGRAVE'S state trials, v. 3].

——— The same. 26 pp. fol. *London, T. Goodwin*, 1689.
[*With* RUSSELL (William, *Lord*, etc.) History of the whiggish plot].

——— The lord Russell's innocency further defended; in answer to the Magistracy and government of England further vindicated. [By Sir B. Shower.] fol. *London, T. Wright*, 1776.
[HARGRAVE'S state trials, v. 3].

ATKINS (Samuel). Account of his examination before the committee of lords appointed to examine after the murder of Sir Edmundbury Godfrey. fol. *London, T. Wright*, 1778.
[HARGRAVE'S state trials. v. 8].

ATKINS (Samuel). Trial for being accessary to the murder of Sir Edmundbury Godfrey, king's bench, Feb. 1679. fol. *London, T. Wright*, 1776.

[HARGRAVE'S state trials, v. 2].

ATKINS (William). Trial at Stafford for high treason, being a Romish priest, Aug. 1679. fol. *London, T. Wright*, 1776.

[HARGRAVE'S state trials, v. 2].

——— The same. *See* **BROMMICH** (A.) *and* **ATKINS** (W.)

ATTERBURY (Francis, *bishop of Rochester, and others*). Proceedings in parliament against [them], upon bills of pains and penalties for a treasonable conspiracy, May, 1723. fol. *London, T. Wright*, 1777.

[HARGRAVE'S state trials, v. 6].

AUBRY (Charles Marie Barbe Antoine), *and* **RAU** (Carl Heinrich). Cours de droit français d'après l'ouvrage allemand de Carl Salomon Zachariæ von Lingenthal. 3e éd. entièrement refondue et complétée. 6 v. 8°. *Paris, Coste*, 1856–58.

AUDISIO (Guglielmo). Droit public de l'église et des nations chrétiennes. Traduit de l'Italien avec approbation de l'auteur, par M. le chanoine Labis. 3 v. 8°. *Louvain, C. Peeters*, 1864–65.

——— Idée historique et rationelle de la diplomatie ecclésiastique. Traduite de l'Italien, avec approbation de l'auteur, par M. le chanoine Labis. 520 pp. 8°. *Louvain, C. Peeters*, 1865.

AUDLEY (Mervin Touchet, *earl of Castlehaven, baron*). *See* **TOUCHET**.

AURELIUS (J. R.) *See* **ROBERT** (Jean).

AUSTIN (John). Lectures on jurisprudence; being the sequel to "the province of jurisprudence determined." To which are added notes and fragments. v. 2 and 3. 8°. *London, John Murray*, 1863.

——— The province of jurisprudence determined. 2d ed. [v. 1.] 8°. *London, John Murray*, 1861.

AUSTIN (L. S.) *v.* Sandel (Mary). Argument in the supreme court of Louisiana upon the liability of debtors to pay the unpaid price of slaves. By J. H. Muse. 22 pp. 8°. [*n.p.* 1867].

AYCKBOURN (Hubert). The practice of the high court of chancery, as altered by recent statutes. 8th ed. By J. Napier Higgins. xlviii, 710 pp. 12°. *London, Wildy & sons*, 1866.

AZEGLIO (Luigi Taparelli d'). Essai théorique de droit naturel basé sur les faites. Traduit de l'Italien d'après la dernière éd. 4 v. 8°. *Paris, H. Casterman*, 1857.

BABINGTON (Anthony), *and others*. Proceedings against [them] at Westminster for high treason, Sept. 1586. fol. *London, T. Wright*, 1776.

[HARGRAVE'S state trials, v. 1].

BACON (A. O.) Digest of the decisions of the supreme court of Georgia, from vols. 21 to 30, inclusive. xii, 663 pp. 8°. *Macon, Burke & Co.* 1867.

BACON (Francis, *baron Verulam, viscount St. Alban's, lord chancellor of England*). Proceedings in parliament against [him], upon an impeachment for bribery and corruption in the execution of his office, March, 1620. fol. *London, T. Wright*, 1776.

[HARGRAVE'S state trials, v. 1].

BACON (John). Liber regis, vel thesaurus rerum ecclesiasticarum. xvii, 1391 pp. 4°. *London, J. Nichols*, 1786.

BACON (Matthew). Compleat arbitrator; or, the law of awards. 3d ed. xii, 310 pp. 21 l. 8°. *London, J. Worrall*, 1770.

——— New abridgment of the law. To which are added notes and references to American law and decisions, by John Bouvier. 10 v. 8°. *Philadelphia*, 1856.

BADELEY (Edward). The privilege of religious confessions in English courts of justice considered, in a letter to a friend. 79 pp. 8°. *London, Butterworths*, 1865.

BADEN (Gustav Ludvig). Forsog til et dansk-norsk juridisk ord- og sag-leksikon. iv, 348 pp. 16°. *Odense, S. Hempel*, 1814.

BAGLEY (William). The new practice of the courts of law at Westminster. xliv, 704 pp. 8°. *London, A. Maxwell*, 1840.

BAHAM (Alfred, John, *and* Marvin). Particulars of the murder of Nathan Adler, on the night of November 6th, 1842, in Venice, New York, including the whole testimony taken by the coroner and the inquisition, and arrest of the three Bahams. 69 pp. 8°. *Albany, Finn & Rockwell*, 1850.

BAILLIE (David). Proceedings before the lords of the council in Scotland against [him], Feb. 1704, for defaming [James Douglas], duke of Queensbury, and [William Johnstone], marquis of Anandale. fol. *London, T. Wright*, 1778.

[HARGRAVE'S state trials, v. 8].

BAILLIE (Robert). Trial in Scotland for high treason, Dec. 1684. fol. *London, T. Wright*, 1776.

[HARGRAVE'S state trials, v. 3].

BAKER (Thomas). The laws relating to salmon fisheries in Great Britain, including the Scotch bye-laws. vi, 206 pp. 12°. *London, Horace Cox,* 1866.

BALBO (J. P.) Constitutions républicaines du globe. France, États-Unis (amendée), Delaware (état), Saint-Domingue (revisée), Italie, Venise, Génes, St. Marin, Allemagne, (conf.) Bavière (état), Suisse, (conféd.) Vaud (canton). Texte officiel. 259 pp. 12°. *Paris, Bénard et Cie.* 1848.

BALMERINOCH (*Sir* James Elphinstone, *1st lord*). *See* **ELPHINSTONE**.

BALMERINOCH (*Sir* John Elphinstone, *2d lord*). *See* **ELPHINSTONE**.

BALTIMORE (Frederick Calvert, *7th baron*). *See* **CALVERT**.

BAMBRIDGE (Thomas), Several proceedings relative to the bailing of Mr. Bambridge, both at the king's-bench and the Old-Bailey, 1729, previous to his trial for felony. fol. *London, T. Wright,* 1778.
[HARGRAVE'S state trials, v. 9].

——— Trial for felony, Old-Bailey, Dec. 1729. fol. *London, T. Wright,* 1778.
[HARGRAVE'S state trials, v. 9].

——— Trial for the murder of Robert Castell, Old-Bailey, May, 1729. fol. *London, T. Wright,* 1778.
[HARGRAVE'S state trials, v. 9].

——— *and* **CORBETT** (Richard). Trial, at Guildhall, London, on an appeal, for the murder of Robert Castell, Jan. 1730. fol. *London, T. Wright,* 1778.
[HARGRAVE'S state trials, v. 9].

BANBURY (Charles Knollys, *claiming to be earl of*). *See* **KNOLLYS**.

BARBADOES. Acts of assembly from 1648 to 1732. [With] an abridgment. 484 pp. fol. *London, J. Baskett,* 1732.

BARBOSA (Manuel). Remissiones doctorum de officiis pvblicis, jvrisdictione, et ordine jvdiciario. Accessere castigationes et aditimenta ad remissiones libri quarti, et quinti ordin. reg. Rev. per Avgvstinvm Barbosa. 1 p. l. 480 pp. 36 l. 56 pp. 6 l. 4°. *Vlyssipone, Craesbeeck,* 1620.

BARBOT (John). Trial for the murder of Mathew Mills, at Basseterre, Island of St. Christopher, Jan. 1753. fol. *London, T. Wright,* 1779.
[HARGRAVE'S state trials, v. 10].

BARBOUR (Oliver L.) Reports of cases in law and equity in the supreme court of the state of New York. v. 45–48. 8°. *Albany, W. C. Little,* 1866–68. (2 copies.)

BARINETTE (Pietro). Diritto romano; parte generale. 1. Idee fondamentali intorno al diritto ed alle leggi. 2. Delle persone. 3. Delle cose. 4. Delle azioni. 6 p. l. 288 pp. 8°. *Milano, Vallardi,* 1864.

BARNARD (William). Trial, Old-Bailey, May, 1758, on the black act, for sending a letter in a fictitious name to Charles [Churchill], duke of Marlborough, demanding a genteel support for life. fol. *London, T. Wright,* 1799.
[HARGRAVE'S state trials, v. 10].

BARNARDISTON (*Sir* Samuel). Trial, at the Guild-Hall of London, for a misdemeanor, Feb. 1683. fol. *London, T. Wright,* 1776.
[HARGRAVE'S state trials, v. 3].

——— Proceedings in the court of king's bench, 1674. Parliamentary election case. *See* **Soame** (*Sir* William).

BARRY (William Whittaker). A treatise on the law and practice of benefit building societies; with rules and forms. xx, 189 pp. 12°. *London, Horace Cox,* 1866.

BARTHOLUS. *See* **BARTOLO**, *da Sasso Ferrato.*

BARTOLO, *da Sasso-ferrato.* In dvodecim libros codicis commentaria. Studio et opera Iac. Concenatii, [etc.] 28 p. l. 969 pp. fol. *Basileæ, Froben,* 1562. s.

——— In institutiones et authenticas commentaria. Eivsdem tractatvs xxxix. Stvdio et opera Iac. Concenatii, [etc.] 22 p. l. 758 pp. fol. *Basileæ, Froben,* 1562. s.

——— In ivs vniversvm civile commentaria. Stvdio et opera Iac. Concenatii, [etc.] 3 v. fol. *Basileæ, Froben,* 1562. s.

BAST (Louis Amédée de). Les galeries du palais de justice de Paris; mœurs, usages, coutumes, et traditions judiciaires, 1280–1780. 4 v. 8°. *Paris, Lévy frères,* 1851–54.

BASTWICK (John, *M. D.*) *and others.* Proceedings in the star-chamber against [them], for several libels, June, 1639. Wrote by their friends. fol. *London, T. Wright,* 1776.
[HARGRAVE'S state trials, v. 1].

BATEMAN (Charles, *surgeon*). Trial, at the Old-Bailey, for high treason, Dec. 1685. fol. *London, T. Wright,* 1777.
[HARGRAVE'S state trials, v. 4].

BATES (John). The case of impositions, on an information in the exchequer against [him], 1604. fol. *London, T. Wright,* 1781.
[HARGRAVE'S state trials, v. 11].

BATHURST (Charles). Proceedings in the house of peers and house of commons on [his] case, in Jan. 1703. fol. *London, T. Wright,* 1778.
[HARGRAVE'S state trials, v. 8].

BATTEN (Edmond Chisholm), *and* **LUDLOW** (Henry). A treatise on the jurisdiction, pleadings, and practice of the county courts, in equity. xlix, 524 pp. 8°. *London, William Amer*, 1866.

BATTRAGH (William). Trial for treason. *See* **CHADWICK** (Thomas), *and* **BATTRAGH.**

BAXTER (*Rev.* Richard). Proceedings against [him], for a seditious libel, intituled, A paraphrase on the testament, Guildhall, May, 1685. fol. *London, T. Wright*, 1779.
[HARGRAVE'S state trials, v. 10].

BAYARD (*Col.* Nicholas). Trial, in the pro vince of New York, for high treason, Feb. 1702. fol. *London, T. Wright*, 1777.
[HARGRAVE'S state trials, v. 5].

BAYNTON (Sarah), *and others.* Trials for forceably taking away Mrs. Pleasant Rawlins, and procuring her to be married to Haagen Swendsen. Queen's bench, Nov. 1702. fol. *London, T. Wright*, 1777.
[HARGRAVE'S state trials. v. 5].

BEAUFORT (F. L.) Digest of the criminal law of the presidency of Fort William, and guide to all criminal authorities therein. lxiii, 1000 pp. 4°. *Calcutta, R. C. Lepage*, 1850.

BEDDINGFIELD (Margery), *and* **RINGE** (Richard). Genuine trial, at the assizes held at Bury St. Edmund's, 21st March, 1763, for petty treason and murder. 44 pp. 8°. *London, Davis & Rymers*, 1763.

BEDFORD (Francis Russell, *4th earl of*). *See* **RUSSELL.**

BEDLOW *or* **BEDLOE** (*Capt.* William). Examination relating to the popish plot, taken in his last sickness by Sir F. North. [With] the narrative of Sir F. North at the council board, [etc.] 16 pp. fol. *London, assigns of J. Bill*, 1680.
[Trials for treason, v. 3].

——— The same. fol. *London, T. Wright*, 1778.
[HARGRAVE'S state trials, v. 8].

BELL (John). A copious and practical treatise on the game laws, including all the statutes connected therewith; and the law and practice of appeals against charges by surveyors of taxes; with a chapter on the property in animals feræ naturæ, and on forest lands. xxiii, 443 pp. 12°. *London, W. Crofts*, 1839.

BELL (William H.) Trial. *See* **HALL** (Lucian, *and others*). Trial.

BELLO (Andres). Principios de derecho internacional. 2ª ed. Aumentada y corregida por el autor. iv, 302 pp. 8°. *Paris, Garnier*, 1864.

BEMIS (George). American neutrality: its honorable past, its expedient future. A protest against the proposed repeal of the neutrality laws, and a plea for their improvement and consolidation. vii, 212 pp. 8°. *Boston, Little, Brown & Co.* 1866.

——— Hasty recognition of rebel belligerency, and our right to complain of it. ix, 57 pp. 8°. *Boston, Williams & Co.* [1865].

BENNETT (G. C.) *See* **STRONG** (D.)

BENTINCK (William, *1st earl of Portland*), *and others.* Proceedings in parliament against [them] upon an impeachment for high crimes and misdemeanors, 1701. fol. *London, T. Wright*, 1777.
[HARGRAVE'S state trials. v. 5].

BÉRAULT (Josias). La covstvme reformée dv pays et dvché de Normandie, anciens ressorts et enclaus d'iceluy. Avec les commentaires, annotations, et arrests donnez sur l'interprétation d'icelle. 2ᵉ éd. 8 p. l. 1064, 6 pp. 18 l. 4°. *Roven, D. dv Petit Val*, 1614.

BERNARDI (John), *and others.* The case, with the proceedings against [them] on account of the assassination plot, 1695. Wrote by J. Bernardi, after he had been thirty-three years a prisoner. fol. *London, T. Wright*, 1799.
[HARGRAVE'S state trials. v. 10].

BERWICK (John). Trial for high treason; Southwark, July, 1746. fol. *London, T. Wright*, 1778.
[HARGRAVE'S state trials. v. 9].

BEST (William Mawdesley) *and* **SMITH** (George James Philip). Report of cases in the court of queen's bench, and the court of exchequer chamber, on appeal from the court of queen's bench. v. 6. 8°. *London, H. Sweet*, 1867.

BETHEL (Slingsby). Trial for an assault and battery on Robert Mason, Southwark, Oct. 1681. fol. *London, T. Wright*, 1776.
[HARGRAVE'S state trials. v. 3].

BINGHAM (Anson). A treatise on the law of real property. xvi, 698 pp. 8°. *Albany, Author*, 1868.

BIOCHE (Charles Jules Armand). Traité des actions possessoires contenant l'exposé complet de la jurisprudence, l'opinion des auteurs, suivi de formules. xxiv, 452 pp. 8°. *Paris, A. Durand*, 1865.

BLACKSTONE (*Sir* William). Commentaries abridged. *See* **CURRY** (William).

BLAGUE *or* **BLAGG** (William). Trial at the Old Bailey for high treason, July, 1683. fol. *London, T. Wright*, 1776.
[HARGRAVE'S state trials, v. 3].

——— The same. *See* **WALCOT** (Thomas) *and others.* Trial, etc.

BLANDY (Mary). Trial for the murder of her father, Francis Blandy, Oxford, Feb. 1752. fol. *London, T. Wright,* 1779.
[HARGRAVE'S state trials, v. 10].

BLATCHFORD (Samuel). Reports of cases in prize, in the circuit and district courts of the United States, for the southern district of New York, 1861–65. viii, 729 pp. 8°. *New York, Baker, Voorhis & Co.* 1866.

BLOODGOOD (F.) *See* **VAN RENSSELAER** (S.)

BLUNT (*Sir* Christopher), *and others.* Trial for high treason; March, 1600. fol. *London, T. Wright,* 1776.
[HARGRAVE'S state trials, v. 1].

BLUNTSCHLI (Johann Caspar). Das moderne kriegsrecht der civilisirten staaten als rechtsbuch dargestellt. iv, 69 pp. 8°. *Nördlingen, Beck,* 1866.

BOEHMER (Justus Henning). Jus ecclesiasticum, usum modernum juris canonici juxta seriem decretalium ostendens. 3a ed. 5 v. 4°. *Halæ, Orphanotrophei,* 1730–36.

BOHUN (Edmund). Defence of Sir Robert Filmer against the mistakes and misrepresentations of Algernon Sidney; in a paper delivered by him to the sheriffs upon the scaffold on Tower Hill, December 17th, 1863, before his execution there. 16 pp. fol. *London, W. Kettilby,* 1684.
[*With* SIDNEY (Algernon). Arraignment, trial, etc. 1684].

BOLEYN (Anne, *queen of England*), **BOLEYN** (George), *viscount Rochford, and others.* Trials for high treason, May, 1536. fol. *London, T. Wright,* 1781.
[HARGRAVE'S state trials, v. 11].

BONNET (Stede), *and others.* Trials at Charles-town, in South Carolina, for piracy; Oct. 1718. fol. *London, T. Wright,* 1777.
[HARGRAVE'S state trials, v. 6].

BOOTH (Henry, *2d baron Delamere, 1st earl of Warrington*). The late lord Russel's case, with observations upon it. 1 p. l. 15 pp. fol. *London, A. Churchill,* 1689.
[Trials for treason, v. 5].

——— Tryal for high treason, Westminster Hall, Jan. 1685, [1686]. 2 p. l. 87 pp. fol. *London, D. Newman,* 1686.
[Trials for treason, v. 4].

——— The same.
[Trials for treason, v. 6].

——— The same. fol. *London, T. Wright,* 1777.
[HARGRAVE'S state trials, v. 4].

BORATZI. *See* **BOROSKY.**

BOROSKY *or* **BORATZI** (Carol Jerzy) *and others.* Trial at the Old Bailey, for the murder of Thomas Thynn, Feb. 1681. fol. *London, T. Wright,* 1776.
[HARGRAVE'S state trials, v. 3].

BOSTON (*City of*). A digest of decisions of municipal interest, of the supreme judicial court of Massachusetts, 1804–65. Published by order of the city council of Boston. [By James C. Davis]. viii, 157 pp. 8°. *Boston, Farwell & Co.* 1866.

BOTHWELL (James Hepburn, 4th *earl of*). *See* **HEPBURN.**

BOUCHER (James). Proceedings against [him], at the queen's bench, for high treason, Feb. 1704. fol. *London, T. Wright,* 1777.
[HARGRAVE'S state trials, v. 5].

——— Proceedings in the house of commons and house of lords, relative to [him]. fol. *London, T. Wright,* 1778.
[HARGRAVE'S state trials, v. 5].

BOUVIER (John). Law dictionary, adapted to the constitution and laws of the United States of America, and the several States of the Union. 11th ed. revised, improved and greatly enlarged. 2 v. xi, 692 pp; 827 pp. 8°. *Philadelphia, G. W. Childs,* 1866.

——— The same. 12th ed. Revised and greatly enlarged. 2 v. viii, 780 pp; 782 pp. 8°. *Philadelphia, G. W. Childs,* 1868.

BOYD (William, 4th *earl of Kilmarnock*) *and others.* The whole proceedings in the house of peers, upon the indictments against [them] for high treason, Aug. 1746. fol. *London, T. Wright,* 1778.
[HARGRAVE'S state trials, v. 9].

BRADDON (Laurence). The earl of Essex's [R. Devereux] innocency and honour vindicated. fol. *London, T. Wright,* 1776.
[HARGRAVE'S state trials, v. 3].

——— *and* **Speke** (Hugh). Tryal upon an information of high misdemeanour, subornation and spreading false reports. Thereby to raise a belief that the late earl of Essex did not murther himself in the tower. 2 p. l. 78 pp. fol. *London, B. Tooke,* 1684.

——— The same. 1684.
[Trials for treason, v. 4].

——— The same. fol. *London, T. Wright,* 1776.
[HARGRAVE'S state trials, v. 3].

BRADSHAW (James). Trial at Southwark, Oct. 1746, for high treason. fol. *London, T. Wright,* 1778.
[HARGRAVE'S state trials, v. 9].

BRAZIL. Constituição politica do imperio do Brasil, seguida da lei das reformas constitucionaes. 35 pp. 12°. *São Paulo, Garraux & Ca.* [1834].

BRETT (——, *of Drogheda*). The case of mixed money in Ireland, 1605. [Gilbert *vs.* Brett]. fol. *London, T. Wright,* 1781.
[HARGRAVE'S state trials, v. 11].

BREULIER (Adolphe), *and* **DESNOS-GARDISSAL** (Charles). Du régime de l'invention. Examen des améliorations proposées à la législation relative aux inventions, à propos du nouveau projet de loi sur les brévets. 160 pp. 8°. *Paris, A. Durand,* 1862.

BREWSTER (Thomas), *and others.* Trial for misdemeanors, Old Bailey, Feb. 1664. fol. *London, T. Wright,* 1776.
[HARGRAVE'S state trials, v. 2].

BRIGHTLY (Frederick C.) Analytical digest of the laws of the United States, 1857–65. v. 2. 8°. *Philadelphia, Kay & bro.* 1865. (2 copies).

—— Annual digest of the laws of Pennsylvania, 1862–67. 8°. *Philadelphia, Kay & bro.* 1867.

BRITTON (John). [Ancient pleas of the crown]. The French text carefully revised, with an English translation, introduction, and notes, by Francis Morgan Nichols. 2 v. lxv, 419 pp; 399 pp. 8°. *London, Macmillan & Co.* 1865.

BROADFOOT (Alexander). The case of pressing mariners, for his majesty's service, argued on [his] trial for murder, Bristol, Aug. 1743. fol. *London, T. Wright,* 1781.
[HARGRAVE'S state trials, v. 11].

BRODWAY (Giles). Trial for rape and sodomy. *See* **FITZPATRICK** (L.) *and* **BRODWAY**.

BROMMICH (Andrew). Trial at Stafford for high treason, being a Romish priest, Aug. 1679. fol. *London, T. Wright,* 1776.
[HARGRAVE'S state trials, v. 2].

—— *and* **ATKYNS** (William). The tryal and condemnation of two popish priests, A. Brommich and W. Atkyns, for high treason, Stafford, Aug. 1679. With an account of the equivocation of some witnesses there produced. [*anon.*] 8 pp. fol. *London, J. Amery,* 1679.
[Trials for treason, v. 1].

—— The same. [With] the tryal of Charles Kern, Hereford, 1679. 20 pp. fol. *London, R. Pawlett,* 1679.
[Trials for treason, v. 2].

BROOKE (Richard). A treatise on the office and practice of a notary of England, with a full collection of precedents. 3d ed. Edited by Leone Levi. xvi, 473 pp. 8°. *London, Stevens & sons,* 1867.

BROOM (Herbert). Constitutional law viewed in relation to common law, and exemplified by cases. xxviii, 1012 pp. 8°. *London, W. Maxwell,* 1866.

—— Selection of legal maxims, classified and illustrated. 5th Am. from the 3d London ed. with references to American cases. 8°. *Philadelphia,* 1864.

BROWN (William). Formulæ bene placitandi. A book of entries, containing variety of choice precedents. In two parts. 2d ed. 1 p. l. 375 pp. 10 l; 2 p. l. 295 pp. 6 l. fol. *London, Place, Basset & Place,* 1675.

BROWNE (G. Latham). A treatise on the companies act, 1862, with special reference to winding up, for the purposes of reconstruction or amalgamation, with forms and precedents. xl, 460 pp. 8°. *London, Stevens & Haynes,* 1867.

BRUCE (Alexander). Principia juris feudalis, institutionum imperialium methodo, (quantum materiæ feudalis ratio patitur,) disposita. xxiv, 352 pp. 12°. *Edinburgi, R. Freebairn,* 1713.

BRUCE (Michael). Trial of, 1816. *See* **WILSON** (*Sir* R. T. *etc.*)

BRUNNEMANN (Johann). Commentarivs in dvodecim libros codicis jvstineanei. Ed. novissima. 8 p. l. 684 pp. 43 l. fol. *Lugduni, Huguetan et Barbier,* 1669.

BUCKINGHAM (Edward de Stafford, 3*d duke of*). *See* **STAFFORD** (Edward).

BUDÆUS *or* **BUDÉ** (Guillaume). Annotationes in quatuor et viginti pandectarum libros, et annotationes reliquæ. 2 p. l. 381 pp. 9 l; 143 pp. 3 l. fol. *Paris, R. Stefanus,* 1535.

BULLETIN des arrêts de la cour de cassation rendus en matière civile. v. 67. Année 1865. 8°. *Paris, Imprimerie impériale,* 1866.

BULLETIN des arrêts de la cour de cassation rendus en matière criminelle. v. 70. Année 1865. 8°. *Paris, Imprimerie impériale,* 1866.

BULLINGBROOKE (Edward, *LL. D.*) The duty and authority of justices of the peace and parish officers for Ireland, revised by James Goddard Butler. xix, 911 pp. 10 l. 4°. *Dublin, George Grierson,* 1788.

BUNYAN (Charles John). The law of fire insurance. xii, 291 pp. 8°. *London, Charles & Edwin Layton,* 1867.

BURKE (Thomas). Trial of. *See* **FRASER** *and* **VANDERPOOL**.

BURNET (Gilbert, *bishop of Salisbury*). Speech in the house of lords on the first article of impeachment of Dr. Henry Sacheverell. 6 pp. fol. *London, J. Morphew,* 1710.
[*With* SACHEVERELL (Henry). Tryal, 1710].

BURTON (Henry, *B. D.*) Proceedings against, in the star-chamber, for libel, June 1639. *See* **BASTWICK** (John) *and others.*

BUSBY (George). Tryal and condemnation for high treason, as a Romish priest and jesuite, Derby, July, 1681. 1 p. l. 38 pp. fol. *London, R. Taylor,* 1681.
[Trials for treason, v. 3].

——— The same. fol. *London, T. Wright,* 1776.
[HARGRAVE'S state trials, v. 3].

BUTLER, *alias* **STRICKLAND** (Mary). Trial at the Old Bailey, for forging a bond of 40,000 l. in the name of R. Clayton, Oct. 1699. fol. *London, T. Wright,* 1777.
[HARGRAVE'S state trials, v. 5].

BYLES (*Sir* John Barnard). A treatise on the law of bills of exchange, promissory notes, bank notes, and checks. 5th Am. from the 9th Lond. ed. by George Sharswood. lxii, 760 pp. 8°. *Philadelphia, T. & J. W. Johnson & Co.* 1867.

BYNG (*admiral* John). Trial at a court-martial on board the St. George, in Portsmouth harbour, Dec. 1756, for an inquiry into his conduct while he commanded in the Mediterranean, [with] his defence; likewise an appendix. Taken in short-hand, by T. Cook. v, 595 pp. 8°. *London, J. Lacy,* 1757.

BYRON (William, *5th baron Byron*). Trial in the house of peers, for the murder of William Chaworth, April, 1765. fol. *London, T. Wright,* 1779.
[HARGRAVE'S state trials, v. 10].

CABRYE (E. D.) Du droit de rétention. (Droit romain. Ancien droit français. Droit actuel). 216 pp. 8°. *Paris, A. Durand,* 1860.

CALAS (Jean). Trial. *See* **VOLTAIRE.**

CALIFORNIA reports, v. 28–31. By C. A. Tuttle. 8°. *Sacramento, S. Whitney, etc.* 1866–67. (3 copies of v. 29–30).

CALLAN (John F.) Laws of the United States relating to the navy and marine corps, from the formation of the government to the end of the 38th congress, 1864–65. 464, 190 pp. 8°. *Baltimore, Murphy & Co.* 1866.

CALTHROP *or* **CALTHORP** (*Sir* Henry). Reports of speciall cases touching severall customs and liberties of the city of London. 3 p. l. 177 pp. 12°. *London, A. Roper,* 1655.

CALVERT (Frederick, *7th baron Baltimore*). The trial of . . . for a rape on the body of Sarah Woodcock; and of Eliz. Griffinburg, and Ann Harvey, otherwise Darby, as accessaries before the fact. Before the hon. sir Sydney Stafford Smythe, 26th March, 1768. 167 pp. 8°. *Edinburgh, John Balfour,* [1768].

CALVIN (Robert). The case of the postnati, or of the union of the realm of Scotland with England, 1607. fol. *London, T. Wright,* 1781.
[HARGRAVE'S state trials, v. 11].

CAMBRIDGE (University of). Proceedings in the case of Alban Francis, 1687. *See* **PEACHELL** (John, *vice-chancellor*), *and* **CAMBRIDGE** (University of).

CAMERON (Archibald, *M. D.*) Proceedings against, king's bench, May, 1753, on the bill of attainder, for being in the rebellion, 1745. fol. *London, T. Wright,* 1779.
[HARGRAVE'S state trials, v. 10].

CAMPBELL (Archibald, *marquess and 8th earl of Argyll*). Proceedings in Scotland against [him], 1661, for high treason. fol. *London, T. Wright,* 1776.
[HARGRAVE'S state trials, v. 2].

——— The same. fol. *London, T. Wright,* 1778.
[HARGRAVE'S state trials, v. 7].

CAMPBELL (Archibald, *9th earl of Argyll*). Trial, in Scotland, for treason, Nov. 1681. fol. *London, T. Wright,* 1776.
[HARGRAVE'S state trials, v. 3].

CAMUS (Armand Gaston). Profession d'avocat. Bibliothèque choisie des livres de droit qu'il est la plus utile d'acquérir et de connaitre. 5e éd. revue et augmentée. Par M. Dupin ainé. 2 v. xx, 740 pp; xvi, 879 pp. 8°. *Paris, A. Gobelet,* 1832.

CANADA. Statutes of the province of Canada, 1866. 8°. *Ottawa,* 1866.

CANADA, West. Reports of cases in the court of queen's bench, by C. Robinson. v. 25. 8°. *Toronto, H. Rowsell,* 1867.

CANNING (Elizabeth). Trial for wilful and corrupt perjury, Old Bailey, May, 1754. fol. *London, T. Wright,* 1779.
[HARGRAVE'S state trials, v. 10].

——— *See* **VOLTAIRE** (F. M. Arouet de).

CANOVAS DEL CASTILLO (Emilio). Diccionario de derecho español. *See* **COSGAYON** (Fernando).

CANTERBURY (George Abbot, *archbishop of*). *See* **ABBOT.**

CANTERBURY (William Laud, *archbishop of*). *See* **LAUD.**

CANTERBURY (William Sancroft, *archbishop of*). *See* **SANCROFT.**

CANTERBURY (Thomas Tenison, *archbishop of*). *See* **TENISON.**

CANTERBURY (William Wake, *archbishop of*). *See* **WAKE.**

CAPETOWN (William Long, *bishop of*). *See* **LONG.**

CAPMANI y MONTPALAU (Antonio de). Practica y estilo de celebrar cortes, en el reino de Aragon, principado de Cataluña y reino de Valencia, y una noticia de las de Castilla y Navarra. [Con reglamento de los comunes para discutir y votar]. 8°. *Madrid, José del Collado,* 1821.

CARETTE (Antoine Auguste). Recueil des lois et des arrêts. *See* **DEVILLENEUVE.**

CARNEGIE (James). Trial, at Edinburgh, July, 1728, for the murder of Charles [Lyon], earl of Strathmore. fol. *London, T. Wright,* 1778.
[HARGRAVE'S state trials, v. 9].

CARR (Frances, *born Howard, countess of Somerset*). *See* **HOWARD** (Frances).

CARR (Henry). Trial, at the Guild-Hall of London, for a libel, July, 1680. fol. *London, T. Wright,* 1776.
[HARGRAVE'S state trials, v. 3].

CARR (Robert, *viscount Rochester, earl of Somerset*). Trial for the murder of Sir Thomas Overbury, May, 1616. fol. *London, T. Wright,* 1776.
[HARGRAVE'S state trials, v. 1].

CARRINGTON (Nathan), *and others.* The case of seizure of papers, being an action of trespass by John Entick against N. Carrington and three others, messengers in ordinary to the king, in the court of common pleas, 1765. fol. *London, T. Wright,* 1781.
[HARGRAVE'S state trials, v. 11].

CASE (The) of the [London] bankers in the court of exchequer, and afterwards in the exchequer chamber and parliament, 1690–99. fol. *London, T. Wright,* 1781.
[HARGRAVE'S state trials, v. 11].

CASTLEHAVEN (Mervin Touchet, *2d earl of*). *See* **TOUCHET.**

CASTLEMAINE (Roger Palmer, *earl of*). *See* **PALMER.**

CAUSES célèbres et intéressantes, avec les jugemens qui les ont décidées. Rédigées de nouveau par M. [François] Richer. 22 v. 12°. *Amsterdam, M. Rhey,* 1772–88.

CAUSES célèbres, curieuses et intéressantes, de toutes les cours souveraines du royaume, avec les jugemens qui les ont décidées. [Par François Richer]. 180 v. in 61 v. 12°. *Paris, P. G. Simon,* 1773–89.

CAVENAGH (Maurice), *and others.* Trial, in Ireland, for felony, March, 1689. fol. *London, T. Wright,* 1777.
[HARGRAVE'S state trials, v. 4].

CAVENDISH (Mary, *countess of Shrewsbury*). Proceedings against [her], before a select council, for contempt in refusing to answer fully before the privy council, 1614. fol. *London, T. Wright,* 1781.
[HARGRAVE'S state trials, v. 11].

CAVENDISH (William, *1st duke and 4th earl of Devonshire*). [His] case, on an information in the king's bench, in 1687, for assaulting Col. Culpepper in the king's palace. fol. *London, T. Wright,* 1781.
[HARGRAVE'S state trials, v. 11].

CELLIER (Elizabeth). Malice defeated; or a brief relation of [her] accusation and deliverance. With an abstract of her arraignment and trial. 1 p. l. 48 pp. fol. *London, E. Cellier,* 1680.
[TRIALS for treason, v. 4].

——— Tryal and sentence, for writing, printing, and publishing a scandalous libel, call'd Malice defeated, etc. Old-Bailey, Sept. 1680. 39 pp. fol. *London, T. Collins,* 1680.
[TRIALS for treason, v. 3].

——— The same. fol. *London T. Wright,* 1776.
[HARGRAVE'S state trials, v. 3].

——— Trial, at the king's bench, for high treason, June 1680. fol. *London, T. Wright,* 1776.
[HARGRAVE'S state trials, v. 3].

CHADWICK (Thomas), *and* **BATTRAGH** (William). Trials for high treason, Southwark, July, 1746. fol. *London, T. Wright,* 1778.
[HARGRAVE'S state trials, v. 9].

CHAMBERS (Richard). Proceedings against [him], in the star chamber, for seditious speeches before the privy council, 1629. fol. *London, T. Wright,* 1781.
[HARGRAVE'S state trials, v. 11].

CHARLES I (*king of England*). Trial before the high court of justice for high treason, Jan. 1648. fol. *London, T. Wright,* 1776.
[HARGRAVE'S state trials, v. 1].

——— Journal of the high court of justice for [his] trial, as it was read in the house of commons, and attested under the hand of Phelps, clerk to that court; with additions by J. Nalson. fol. *London, T. Wright,* 1776.
[HARGRAVE'S state trials, v. 1].

CHARNOCK (Robert), *and others.* Trials at the Old Bailey, for high treason, March, 1695. fol. *London, T. Wright,* 1777.
[HARGRAVE'S state trials, v. 4].

CHAUVEAU (Adolphe), *and* **HÉLIE** (Faustin). Théorie du code pénal. 2e éd. 6 v. 8°. *Paris, E. Legrand,* 1843. S.

CHETWYND (William). Trial for the murder of Thomas Ricketts, Old Bailey, Oct. 1743. fol. *London, T. Wright,* 1778.
[HARGRAVE'S state trials, v. 9].

CHITTY (Joseph, *jr.*) Precedents in pleading; with copious notes on pleading, practice, and evidence. 3d ed. By Thomas Chitty, and by Leofric Temple and R. G. Williams. Part i. cii, 527 pp. 8°. *London, Butterworths,* 1867.

CHRISTIAN (Edward). Charges delivered to grand juries in the Isle of Ely, upon libels, vagrants, criminal law, religion, rebellious assemblies, etc. 2d ed. with large additions. v, 408 pp. 8°. *London, Clarke & sons,* 1819.

——— A dissertation, showing that the house of lords, in cases of judicature, are bound by the same rules of evidence that are observed by all other courts. 2d ed. With observations upon the subjects of law which have arisen in the bill of pains and penalties at present pending against the queen of England. 136 pp. 8°. *London, Clarke & sons,* 1820.
[*With* the preceding].

——— Notes to Blackstone's commentaries, [etc.] 4 v. in 1. 16°. *Boston, J. Thomas & E. T. Andrews, et al.* 1801. s.

——— A vindication of the right of the universities of Great Britain to a copy of every new publication. 2d ed. 159 pp. 8°. *London, Clarke & sons,* 1814.
[*With his* Charges to grand juries, 1819].

CHRISTIANSEN (*Dr.* J.) Institutionen des römischen rechts; oder, erste einleitung in das studium des römischen privatrechts. xviii, 788 pp. 8°. *Altona, J. F. Hammerich,* 1843.

CHUDLEIGH (Elizabeth, *duchess dowager of Kingston-upon-Hull*). Trial for bigamy, in Westminster Hall, April, 1776. fol. *London, T. Wright,* 1781.
[HARGRAVE'S state trials, v. 11].

CLARENDON (Edward Hyde, 1*st earl of*). *See* **HYDE.**

CLARK (Francis William). A treatise on the law of partnership and joint-stock companies, according to the law of Scotland. 1 v. in 2. lxviii, 1202 pp. 8°. *Edinburgh, T. & T. Clark,* 1866.

CLERK'S instructor in the ecclesiastical courts: consisting of a variety of the best precedents in English, now made use of in the practice of the civil law. [*anon.*] 548 pp. 8°. *London, Nutt & Gosling,* 1740.

CLIFFORD (Henry). Argument in the court of king's bench on a motion for an habeas corpus [in the case of B. Flower], and remarks on the judgment of that court. 80 pp. 8°. *London,* 1800.
[*With* FLOWER (Benj.) Proceedings in the house of lords for libel, 1800].

COBHAM (*Sir* John Oldcastle, *baron*). *See* **OLDCASTLE.**

COHEN (Jacob I.) *and* **LEE** (James Fenner). Digest of the Maryland reports, from the ninth to the twentieth volume, inclusive. xl, 529 pp. 8°. *Baltimore, Cushings & Bailey,* 1866. (2 copies).

COKE (Arundel). Trial for felony. *See* **WOODBURNE** (John) *and* **COKE.**

COLDWELL (Thomas H.) Reports of cases in the supreme court of Tennessee, 1860–61, and 1865–66. 2 v. 8°. *Nashville, S. C. Mercer,* 1867. (2 copies).

COLE (Henry Warwick). Our commons and open spaces. 34 pp. 8°. *London, Longmans, Green & Co.* 1866.

COLE (John). Trial at the Old Bailey, for the murder of Andrew Clenche, Sept. 1692. fol. *London, T. Wright,* 1776.
[HARGRAVE'S state trials, v. 4].

COLEMAN (Edward). Tryal for conspiring the death of the king, and the subversion of the government of England, and the protestant religion, king's bench, Westminster, Nov. 1678. 1 p. l. 104 pp. fol. *London, R. Pawlet,* 1678.
[TRIALS for treason, v. 1].

——— The same.
[TRIALS for treason, v. 2].

——— The same. fol. *London, T. Wright,* 1776.
[HARGRAVE'S state trials, v. 2].

——— The true manner of execution, behaviour and last words of E. Coleman at Tyburn, Dec. 3d, 1678. [*anon.*] 7 pp. sm. 4°. *London, R. G.* 1678.
[TRIALS for treason, v. 1].

COLLEDGE (Stephen). Trial at Oxford, for high treason, August, 1681. fol. *London, T. Wright,* 1776.
[HARGRAVE'S state trials, v. 3].

COLLIER (*Rev.* Jeremy), *and others.* Proceedings against [them] for publickly absolving Sir W. Perkins and Sir J. Friend, at Tyburn, 1696. fol. *London, T. Wright* 1779.
[HARGRAVE'S state trials, v. 10].

COLOMBA (Defendente). Delle lettere di cambio e dei biglietti all' ordine. 118 pp. 8°. *Torino, G. Favale e comp.* 1863.

COMPLEAT collection of remarkable tryals of the most notorious malefactors at the Old-Bailey. v. 4. 12°. *London,* 1721.

COMPTON (Henry, *bishop of London*). Proceedings against [him], at Whitehall, for not suspending John Sharp, rector of St. Giles's, Aug. 1686. fol. *London, T. Wright,* 1777.
[HARGRAVE'S state trials, v. 4].

CONFEDERATE States of America, (*so called*). Acts and resolutions of the first session of the provisional congress of the confederate states, 1861. 8°. *Montgomery, (Ala.) Barrett, Wimbish & Co.* 1861.

——— The same. The fourth session, 1861–62. 8°. *Richmond, Tyler, Wise, etc.* 1862.

——— Public laws of the confederate states of America, from the first session of the first congress, 1862, to the first session of the second congress, 1864. Edited by James M. Matthews. 2 v. 8°. *Richmond, R. M. Smith,* 1862–64.
[2 copies. 1 copy bound with the preceding vol.]

——— Statutes at large of the provisional government of the confederate states of America, from February 8, 1861, to February 18, 1862. Together with the constitution of the provisional government, and the permanent constitution of the confederate states, and the treaties concluded by the confederate states with Indian tribes. Edited by James M. Matthews. 8°. *Richmond, R. M. Smith,* 1864.

CONJUGIUM languens: or, the natural, civil, and religious mischiefs arising from conjugal infidelity and impunity. By Castamore.
[*In* select and curious cases of polygamy, etc. pp. 213–240. 12°. *London,* 1736].

CONNECTICUT (*Colony of*). Acts and laws [to 1728. With] the charter of Charles ii to the colony. 1 p. l. 6 pp. 1 l. vii, 356 pp. fol. *New London, T. Green,* 1715–28.

——— ——— The same. [To 1730]. 1 p. l. 6 pp. 7 l. 376 pp. fol. *New London, T. Green,* 1715–30.

——— The same. [To 1732]. 1 p. l. 392 pp. fol. *New London, T. Green,* 1715–32.
[Imperfect: table of contents, pp. 379–80, and leaves at the end, wanting].

——— ——— The same. [To 1750]. 2 p. l. 6 pp. 1 l. 258 pp. fol. *New London, T. Green,* 1750.

——— ——— The same.
[NOTE.—Imperfect: wants title-pages and pp. 5–6 of charter. The table of contents differs from that in the preceding vol. In all other respects the copies are similar].

——— ——— The same. [To 1786]. 4 p. l. [368] pp. fol. *Hartford, E. Babcock,* 1786.

——— Acts and laws of his majesty's English colony of Connecticut, in New England, in America [digested]. 8, 10, 406 pp. fol. *New London, T. Green,* 1769.

——— (*State of*). Public acts, May session, 1861; public and private acts, October session, 1861, and May session, 1862; and public and private acts, May session, 1866. 3 v. 8°. *Hartford and New Haven,* 1861–66.

CONNECTICUT (*Colony of*). Public and private acts of the state of Connecticut, May session, 1866. 8°. *New Haven,* 1866.

——— Laws, May session, 1867. 8°. *Hartford,* 1867. (2 copies.)

——— Connecticut reports. v. 32–33. By John Hooker. 8°. *Hartford, Case, Lockwood & Co.* 1866–67. (2 copies of v. 32.)

CONSIDERATIONS on criminal law. [*anon.*] xxxii, 434 pp. 8°. *London, T. Cadell,* 1772.

COOK (Peter). Trial at the Old Bailey, for high treason, May, 1696. fol. *London, T. Wright,* 1777.
[HARGRAVE'S state trials, v. 4].

COOLEY (Thomas M.) A digest of the reported cases contained in the Michigan reports. [*anon.*] xxviii, 73 pp. 8°. *Ann Arbor, by the compiler,* 1866. [2 copies].

COOPER (Anthony Ashley, 1*st earl of Shaftesbury*). Proceedings in [his] case, at the king's bench, June, 1677. fol. *London, T. Wright,* 1776.
[HARGRAVE'S state trials, v. 2].

——— Proceedings in the Old Baily, 24th Nov. 1681, upon the bill of indictment for high treason. 1 p. l. 48 pp. fol. *London, S. Mearne,* 1681.
[TRIALS for treason, v. 4].

——— The same. fol. *London, T. Wright,* 1776.
[HARGRAVE'S state trials, v. 3].

COOPER (C. D.) Trial. *See* **VAN RENSSELAER** (S.)

CORBETT (Richard). Trial for murder. *See* **BAMBRIDGE** (Thomas), *and* **CORBETT**.

CORNISH (Henry). Tryal for conspiring the death of the king, and raising a rebellion; and [of] J. Fernley, W. Ring, and E. Gaunt, for harbouring and maintaining rebels: Old Baily, Oct. 1685. 1 p. l. 42 pp. fol. *London, G. Croom,* 1685.
[TRIALS for treason, v. 5].

——— ——— The same.
[TRIALS for treason, v. 6].

CORNWALLIS (Charles, 3*d baron Cornwallis*). Trial at Westminster, for the mūrder of Robert Clerk, 1678. fol. *London, T. Wright,* 1776.
[HARGRAVE'S state trials, v. 2].

CORPUS juris civilis. *See* **JUSTINIANUS**.

CORSINI (*Brigadier* D. Luis). Las leyes de la guerra, segun las tradiciones y los adelantos de la civilizacion. viii, 264 pp. 12°. *Madrid, M. Rivadeneyra,* 1857.

CORYTON (John). A treatise on the law of letters-patent, for the sole use of inventions in the united kingdom of Great Britain and Ireland; with a summary of the patent laws in force in the principal foreign states. xxvii, 563 pp. 8°. *London, H. Sweet,* 1855.

COS-GAYON (Fernando), *and* **CÁNOVAS** Del Castillo (Emelio). Diccionario manual de derecho administrativo español, para uso de los funcionarios dependientes de los ministerios de gobernacion y fomento, y las alcaldes y ayuntamientos. viii, 992 pp. 8°. *Madrid, Herederos de Vallejo,* 1860.

COWPER (Spencer), *and others.* Trial at Hertford, for the murder of Mrs. Sarah Stout, July, 1699. fol. *London, T. Wright,* 1777.
[HARGRAVE'S state trials, v. 5].

——— [Their] case. Published by them. [With] the Hertford letter. A reply to the Hertford letter, [and] some observations on the trial. fol. *London, T. Wright,* 1778.
[HARGRAVE'S state trials, v. 8].

COX (Edward). Forms of practical proceedings in the chambers of the master of the rolls and the vice-chancellors. 3d ed. Revised and considerably enlarged. By John Biddle. xx, 687, 53 pp. 8°. *London, E. Cox,* 1863.

COX (Edward William). Reports of all the cases decided by the superior courts of law and equity, relating to the law of joint-stock companies; commencing Hilary term, 1864. v. i. xxxi, 704 pp. 8°. *London, Horace Cox,* 1867.

CRAIG (Richard Davis). Legal and equitable rights and liabilities as to trees and woods. xiii, 194 pp. 8°. *London, William Maxwell,* 1866.

CRANBURNE (Charles). Trial, for high-treason, king's bench, April, 1696. fol. *London, T. Wright,* 1777.
[HARGRAVE'S state trials, v. 4].

CREIGHTON (Robert, *lord Sanquhar*). *See* **CRICHTON.**

CRICHTON (Robert, *lord Sanquhar*). Arraignment and confession, at the king's-bench, June, 1612, for procuring the murder of John Turner. fol. *London, T. Wright,* 1778.
[HARGRAVE'S state trials, v. 7].

CRISENOY (J. de). Les ordonnances de Colbert, et l'inscription maritime. 24 pp. 8°. *Paris, Guillaumin et Cie.* 1862.

CROCKER (Uriel H.) Notes on common forms: a book of Massachusetts law. xvi, 235 pp. 8°. *Boston, Little, Brown & Co.* 1867.

CROMARTIE (George Mac Kenzie, 3*d earl of*). *See* **MAC KENZIE.**

CRONE (Mathew). Proceedings against [him] for high treason [London], May, 1690. fol. *London, T. Wright,* 1779.
[HARGRAVE'S state trials, v. 10].

CROOK (John), *and others.* Trial, [being] quakers, at the Old-Baily, for refusing to take the oaths of allegiance and supremacy, June, 1662. Related by J. Crook. fol. *London, T. Wright,* 1776.
[HARGRAVE'S state trials, v. 2].

CROSBY (Brass, *lord mayor of London*). [His] case, on a commitment by the house of commons. Court of common-pleas, 1771. fol. *London, T. Wright,* 1781.
[HARGRAVE'S state trials, v. 11].

CROSBY *alias* **PHILLIPS** (——). Case. [Trial for treason. 1695?] fol. *London, T. Wright,* 1779.
[HARGRAVE'S state trials, v. 10].

CUDDON (James). A succinct treatise on the copyhold acts, the practical working and effect thereof, and the mode of procedure under the same, for effecting enfranchisement. viii, 291 pp. 8°. *London, Stevens & sons,* 1865.

CURL *or* **CURLL** (Edmund). [His] case. 1727. That an obscene book is punishable as a libel. fol. *London, T. Wright,* 1779.
[HARGRAVE'S state trials, v. 10].

CURRY (William). The commentaries of Sir William Blackstone on the laws and constitution of England; carefully abridged, in a new manner, and continued down to the present time. 2d ed. xvi, 704 pp. 8°. *London, Clarke & sons,* 1809.

CURTIS (George Ticknor). A treatise on the law of patents for useful inventions, as enacted and administered in the United States of America. 3d ed. Revised and enlarged. xxxviii, 631 pp. 8°. *Boston, Little, Brown & Co.* 1867. (4 copies).

CURTIS (Jane). Trial, at Guildhall, for publishing a libel, entitled, An appeal from the country to the city, etc. 1679. fol. *London, T. Wright,* 1776.
[HARGRAVE'S state trials, v. 2].

DACRE (William, 3*d baron Dacre of Gillesland, of the North*). Trial for high treason, July, 1535. fol. *London, T. Wright,* 1781.
[HARGRAVE'S state trials, v. 11].

DALY (Charles P.) Reports of cases in the court of common pleas for the city and county of New York. v. 1. xii, 633 pp. 8°. *New York, Baker, Voorhis & Co.* 1866. (2 copies.)

DAMMAREE (Daniel), *and others.* Trials for high treason, in levying war in the kingdom, against the queen, under pretence of pulling down meeting houses; Old Bailey, 1710. fol. *London, T. Wright,* 1778.
[HARGRAVE'S state trials, v. 8].

DANA (Richard Henry, *jr.*) *See* **LAWRENCE** (William Beach).

DANBY (Thomas Osborne, 1*st earl of*). *See* **OSBORNE.**

DANGERFIELD (Thomas). Information [relative to the popish plot] delivered at the bar of the house of commons, 26th Oct. 1680. 15 pp. fol. *London, assigns of J. Bill,* 1680.
[Trials for treason, v. 3].

DANIELL (Edmund Robert). Forms and precedents of pleadings and proceeding in the high court of chancery, with practical notes and observations, and references to the fourth ed. of Daniell's chancery practice; and also incorporating the forms in Braithwaite's record and writ practice. By Leonard Field and Edward Clennell Dunn, and John Biddle. Part I. xii, 1068 pp. 8°. *London, Stevens & sons,* 1867.

DARESTE de LA **CHAVANNE** (Rodolphe Madeleine Cléophas). Code des pensions civiles, contenant la loi de 9 juin, 1855, le décret du novembre suivant, et tous les règlements antérieurs, avec commentaires. 4e éd. 247, vi pp. 12°. *Paris, Paul Dupont et Cie.* 1862.

DARNEL (*Sir* Thomas), *and others.* Proceedings on the habeas corpus, brought by [them], Nov. 1627, at the king's bench. [The case of forced loans]. fol. *London, T. Wright,* 1778.
[HARGRAVE'S state trials, v. 7].

DAVIS (Edwin A.) Collection of the laws of Indiana, for the use of merchants, manufacturers, bankers, and all business men, as well as for members of the legal profession. 44 pp. 8°. *Indianapolis, Downey & Brouse,* 1867. (2 copies).

DAVISON (William). Arraignment in the star chamber, March, 1587, for misprision and contempt. fol. *London, T. Wright,* 1778.
[HARGRAVE'S state trials, v. 7].

DAWSON (Joseph), *and others.* Trial at the Old Bailey for felony and piracy, Oct. 1696. fol. *London, T. Wright,* 1777.
[HARGRAVE'S state trials, v. 5].

DEACON (Thomas Theodorus). Trial for high treason, Southwark, July, 1746. fol. *London, T. Wright,* 1778.
[HARGRAVE'S state trials, v. 9].

DEGGE (*Sir* Simon). The parson's counsellor; with the law of tithes or tithing. 7th ed. With additions, by Charles Ellis. xix, 543 pp. 8°. *London, C. Hunter,* 1820.

DEINSE (A. J. van). De algemeene beginselen van strafregt, ontwikkeld en in verband beschouwd, met de algemeene bepalingen der nederlandsche strafwetgeving. xxviii, 466 pp. 8°. *Middleburg, J. C. & W. Altorfer,* 1852. s.

DELAMERE (Henry Booth, 2*d baron*). *See* **BOOTH.**

DE LANCEY (James, *chief justice, N. Y.*) Charge to the grand jury for the city and county of New York, Tuesday, January 15th, 1733. 6 pp. fol. *New York, William Bradford,* 1733.

DELAWARE (*State of*). Laws of Delaware, 1845 to 1865. [v. 10-12]. 8°. *Dover,* 1845-65.

——— The same, 1865 and 1866. 8°. *Dover,* 1865-66.
[2 copies].

——— Revised statutes of the state of Delaware, 1852. xliii, 574 pp. 8°. *Dover, S. Kimmey,* 1852.

DEMOLOMBE (Jean Charles Florent). Cours de code Napoléon. v. 22-23. 8°. *Paris, A. Durand,* 1865-66.

DENEW (Nathaniel), *and others.* Trial, at the queen's bench, for an assault and conspiracy, with an intent to wound and beat, etc. William Colepepper, Feb. 1704. fol. *London, T. Wright,* 1778.
[HARGRAVE'S state trials, v. 8].

DERWENTWATER (James Radcliffe, 3*d earl of*). *See* **RADCLIFFE.**

DESNOS-GARDISSAL (Charles). Régime del' invention. *See* **BRDULIER** (Adolphe).

DEVEREUX (Robert, 2*d earl of Essex*), *and* **WRIOTHESLEY** (Henry, 3*d earl of Southampton*). Trial, at Westminster, for high treason, Feb. 1600. fol. *London, T. Wright,* 1776.
[HARGRAVE'S state trials, v. 1].

DEVEREUX (Robert, 3*d earl of Essex*). Proceedings between the lady Frances Howard, countess of Essex, and Robert, earl of Essex, her husband, in a cause of divorce, 1613. fol. *London, T. Wright,* 1613.
[HARGRAVE'S state trials, v. 1].

DEVILLENEUVE (Jean Esprit Marie Pierre Lemoine), *and* **CARETTE** (Antoine Auguste). Recueil général des lois et des arrêts. Fondé par J. B. Sirey. 2e série. Ans 1864-66. 3 v. 4°. *Paris,* 1864-66.

DEVONSHIRE (William Cavendish, 1*st duke and* 4*th earl of*). *See* **CAVENDISH.**

DISNEY (William). Trial, at Southwark, June 1685, for high treason. fol. *London, T. Wright,* 1778.
[HARGRAVE'S state trials, v. 7].

DIXON (Joseph). A treatise on the law of partnership. xviii, 563 pp. 8°. *London, Butterworths,* 1866.

DONNALL (Robert Sawle). The trial of, for the wilful murder, by poison, of Mrs. Elizabeth Downing, at the assize of Launceston, March 31, 1817. By Alexander Frazer. xv, 179 pp. 8°. *Falmouth, J. Lake,* 1817.

DONOSO (Justo). Instituciones de derecho canónico americano. 2 v. 8°. *Valparaiso,* 1848–49.

DORR (Thomas Wilson). Report of his trial for treason against the state of Rhode Island, containing the arguments of counsel and the charge of chief justice Durfee. By Joseph S. Pitman. 132 pp. 8°. *Boston, Tappan & Dennet,* 1844.

DREWRY (Charles Stewart), *and* **SMALE** (J. Jackson). Reports of cases in the high court of chancery, 1862–65. v. 2. 8°. *London, Stevens & sons,* 1867.

DUCROCQ (Théophile). Cours de droit administratif, contenant l'exposé des principes, le résumé de la législation administrative dans son dernier état, l'analyse ou la reproduction des principaux textes dans un ordre méthodique. 2e éd. xii, 624 pp. 8°. *Paris, A. Durand,* 1863.

——— Traités des édifices publics, d'après la législation civile, administrative, et criminelle; des ventes domaniales avant et depuis la loi du 1er juin, 1864; des partages de biens communaux et sectionnaires. xxv, 126, 194, 118 pp. 8°. *Paris, Cotillon,* 1865.

DUDLEY (Edmund). Trial for treason. *See* **EMPSON** (*Sir* Richard), *and* **DUDLEY**.

DUDLEY (John, *duke of Northumberland*), *and others.* Trial for high treason, Westminster, Aug. 1553. fol. *London, T. Wright,* 1781.

[HARGRAVE'S state trials. v. 11].

DUMOLLAND (Martin). A full account of his trial and conviction. 32 pp. 8°. *New York, "National Police Gazette" office,* 1862.

DUPIN (André Marie Jean Jacques). Bibliothèque choisie des livres de droit. *See* **CAMUS** (A. G.)

DUTCHER (Andrew). Reports of cases in the supreme court of New Jersey. v. 5. 8°. *Trenton, Phillips & Boswell,* 1863.

DUVALL (Alvin). Reports of cases in the court of appeals of Kentucky. v. 1—2. 8°. *Frankfort, Kentucky Yeoman office,* 1865–67.

DYER (*Sir* James). Les reports des divers select matters et resolutions des reverend judges et sages del ley, en le several reignes de les roys Hen. 8, et Edw. 6, et les reignes Mar. et Eliz. [6e éd. par Georges Treby, écuyer]. 7 p. l. 378 pp. 27 l. fol. *London, S. Keble,* 1688.

DYING speeches and behaviour of the several state prisoners that have been executed the last 300 years. With their several characters from the best historians, as Cambden, Spotswood, Clarendon, Sprat, Burnet, etc. [*anon.*] 9 p. l. 495 pp. 8°. *London, Brotherton & Meadows,* 1720.

EARES (Teodosio). Lecciones de derecho administrativo. 8°. *Mexico,* 1852.

EAST INDIA Co. Case of monopolies, 1683. *See* **SANDYS** (Thomas).

EGAN (Charles). A handy book on the law relative to the sale and purchase of horses. xii, 60 pp. *London, Thomas Day,* 1862.

ELIOT (*Sir* John), *and others.* Proceedings against [them], for seditious speeches in parliament, in banc. reg. 1629. fol. *London, T. Wright,* 1778.

[HARGRAVE'S state trials, v. 7].

ELIOT (Thomas Dawes) *and* **STETSON** (T. M.) Circuit court of the U. S.; Mass. dist. Hetty H. Robinson, in equity, *vs.* Thomas Mandell *et al.* Arguments for respondents. Reported by J. M. W. Yerrinton. 216 pp. 8°. *Boston, A. Mudge & son,* 1867.

ELLES *or* Ellis (Richard). The king against [him], upon an information, in the nature of a quo warranto, to show by what authority he claims to be mayor of the town and port of New Romney, at Maidstone, Aug. 1734. fol. *London, T. Wright,* 1779.

[HARGRAVE'S state trials, v. 10].

ELLIS (Thomas Flower, *and* Francis). Reports of cases in the court of king's bench, and the court of exchequer chamber, on error from the court of queen's bench, 1860 and 1861. v. 3. 8°. *London, H. Sweet,* 1867.

ELOY (Henry). De la codification des lois criminelles concernant les matières non réglées par le code pénal, et d'un projet de code des pénalités. xii, 158 pp. 8°. *Paris, A. Durand,* 1865.

——— De la responsibilité des notaires, d'après les lois, la doctrine, la jurisprudence, et les circulaires ministérielles. 2 v. xvi, 510 pp; 539 pp. 8°. *Paris, A. Durand,* 1863.

ELPHINSTONE (Arthur, *6th lord Balmerinoch*). Trial for treason, 1646. *See* **BOYD** (William, *4th earl of Kilmarnock*).

ELPHINSTONE (*Sir* James, *1st lord Balmerinoch*). Trial, at St. Andrews, March, 1609, for high treason. fol. *London, T. Wright*, 1778.
[HARGRAVE'S state trials, v. 7].

ELPHINSTONE (*Sir* John, *2d lord Balmerinoch*). Trial, in Scotland, for a libel, Dec. 1634. fol. *London, T. Wright*, 1776.
[HARGRAVE'S state trials, v. 1].

ELWES *or* **ELVIS** (*Sir* Jervis). Trial, at the Guild Hall of London, for the murder of Sir Thomas Overbury, Nov. 1615. fol. *London, T. Wright*, 1776.
[HARGRAVE'S state trials, v. 1].

EMPSON (*Sir* Richard), *and* **DUDLEY** (Edmund). Trial for high treason, Guild Hall, 1509. fol. *London, T. Wright*, 1781.
[HARGRAVE'S state trials, v. 11].

ENGLAND. Statutes of the realm. Printed by command of his majesty king George the third. In pursuance of an address of the house of commons of Great Britain. From original records and authentic manuscripts. [From magna charta to the end of the reign of Q. Anne.] 9 v. fol. *London*, 1810–24.

——— The same. The alphabetical index to the statutes of the realm. fol. *London*, 1824.

——— The same. The chronological index to the statutes of the realm. fol. *London*, 1833.

——— Statutes of the United kingdom of Great Britain and Ireland. By George Kettilby Rickards. 1865 and 1866. v. 27. 4°. *London*, 1866.

——— Statutes of. *See, also*, **LAW REPORTS**.

ENTICK (John). The case of seizure of papers. *See* **CARRINGTON** (Nathan), *and others*.

ESSEX (Robert Devereux, *earl of*). *See* **DEVEREUX**.

ESSEX (Frances Howard, *countess of*). *See* **HOWARD** (Frances, *countess of Somerset*).

EVERARD (Edmund). Depositions and examinations concerning the horrid popish plot. 2 p. l. 16 pp. fol. *London, D. Newman*, 1679.
[Trials for treason, v. 1].

EVERY MAN his own lawyer; or, a summary of the laws of England in a new and instructive method. [*anon.*] 8th ed. vi, 538 pp. 8°. *London, Strahan, Rivington & sons*, 1779.

FABRIGAS (Anthony). Proceedings in an action for false imprisonment, etc. *See* **MOSTYN** (*Lieut. gen.* John).

FAGG (*Sir* John). Proceedings in the house of commons, on an appeal being brought in the house of lords, by Thomas Shirley, against Sir John Fagg and others, their members, May, 1675. fol. *London, T. Wright*, 1778.
[HARGRAVE'S state trials, v. 7].

FANSHAWE (*Sir* Thomas). The practice of the exchequer court, with its severall offices and officers. [*anon.*] By S. T. F. 1 p. l. 160 pp. 4 l. 12°. *London, Twyford & Place*, 1698.

FARREN (George). Common forms and rules for drawing and answering an original bill in chancery, as directed and suggested by the new orders of court, and reported cases; with notes and references to American and other authorities, by Richard Stone; also, rules of practice for the courts of equity of the United States, etc. by John J. McKinnon. 247 pp. 8°. *Chicago, Myers & Chandler*, 1866.

FAULCONER *or* **FALCONER** (Richard). Trial, at the king's bench, 1652, for perjury. fol. *London, T. Wright*, 1778.
[HARGRAVE'S state trials, v. 7].

FAWKES (Guy). Trial for treason. *See* **WINTER** (Robert), *and others*.

FELICI (Ettore). Tractatus de communione, seu societate. x, 504 pp. 34 l. 4°. *Francofurti, W. Richter*, 1608.

FENWICK (*Sir* John). The proceedings against [him], upon a bill of attainder for high treason. 348 pp. 5 l. 12°. [*n. p.*] 1698.

——— The same. fol. *London, T. Wright*, 1777.
[HARGRAVE'S state trials, v. 5].

FERGUSON (Grace R.) *v.* **FERGUSON** (James). Great divorce case. Most remarkable trial on record. Suit for divorce, on the ground of adultery. New York superior court. 100 pp. 12°. [*New York*, 1851].

FERNLEY (John), *and others*. Tryals for harbouring rebels. fol. *London*, 1685.
[*With* CORNISH (Henry). Tryal, 1685, for treason, v. 5.

——— The same. fol. *London, T. Wright*, 1777.
[HARGRAVE'S state trials, v. 4].

FERRERS (Laurence Shirley, *4th earl*). *See* **SHIRLEY**.

FERRO (Marco). Dizionario del diritto commune e veneto. 2ª ed. 2 v. xxiii, 783 pp; 855 pp. 8°. *Venezia, A. Santini e figlio*, 1845–47.

FIELDING (Robert). Trial at the Old Bailey for bigamy, in marrying the duchess of Cleveland [Barbara Villiers], his former wife being then living, Dec. 1706. fol. *London, T. Wright*, 1777.
[HARGRAVE'S state trials, v. 5].

FIENNES (*Col.* Nathanael). Trial, Dec. 1643, before a council of war at St. Alban's, for cowardly surrendering the city and castle of Bristol, 24 July 1643. Out of the account given by Prynn and Walker. fol. *London, T. Wright*, 1776.
[HARGRAVE'S state trials, v. 1].

FINCH (*Sir* John, *baron Finch of Fordwich*). Proceedings in parliament against [him], for high treason, 1640. fol. *London, T. Wright*, 1778.
[HARGRAVE'S state trials, v. 7].

FISHER (John, *bishop of Rochester*). Trial, for high treason, at Westminster, 1535. fol. *London, T. Wright*, 1781.
[HARGRAVE'S state trials, v. 11].

FISHER (R. A.) A digest of all the reported decisions in the house of lords, privy council, common law, equity, divorce, probate, admiralty, bankruptcy, and ecclesiastical courts. 1866–67. 8°. *London, H. Sweet*, 1867.

FITZ-HARRIS (Edward). An answer to the protestation of the nineteen lords against the rejecting the impeachment of [E.] Fitz-Harris. [*anon.*] 7 pp. fol. *London, C. Pulleyn*, 1681.
[TRIALS for treason, v. 4].

——— Arraignment [for high treason], and plea, king's bench, 1681. 2 p. l. 66 pp. fol. *London, F. Tyton*, 1681.
[TRIALS for treason, v. 3. 2 copies].

——— The same.
[TRIALS for treason, v. 4].

——— The same. fol. *London, T. Wright*, 1776.
[HARGRAVE'S state trials, v. 3].

——— Confession, July 1st, 1681, [with] his last speech. 7 pp. fol. *London, S. Carr*, 1681.
[TRIALS for treason, v. 4].

——— Examination relating to the popish plot, 10th of March, 1681. 18 pp. fol. *London, T. Fox*, 1681.
[TRIALS for treason, v. 3].

——— Proceedings in parliament against [him] upon an impeachment for high treason, March, 1681. fol. *London, T. Wright*, 1776.
[HARGRAVE'S state trials, v. 3].

——— Trial at the king's-bench, for high treason, June, 1681. fol. *London, T. Wright*, 1776.
[HARGRAVE'S state trials, v. 3].

FITZ-HERBERT (Anthony). The new Natura brevium; corrected and revised. By William Rastall. 35 p. l. 668 pp. 12°. *London, Streater & Co.* 1666.

FITZ-PATRICK (Lawrence), *and* **BRODWAY** (Giles). Trial at the king's bench for a rape and sodomy, June, 1631. fol *London, T. Wright*, 1776.
[HARGRAVE'S state trials, v. 1].

FLETCHER (George). Trial for high treason, Southwark, July, 1746. fol. *London, T. Wright*, 1778.
[HARGRAVE'S state trials, v. 9].

FLINTOFF (Owen). The rise and progress of the laws of England and Wales; with an account of the origin, history, and customs—warlike, domestic, and legal—of the several nations, Britons, Saxons, Danes, and Normans, who now compose the British nation. 238 pp. 8°. *London, Richards & Co.* 1840.

FLORIDA reports, v. 7, no. 1; v. 8–11, 1857–67. 8°. *Tallahassee*, 1857–67.

——— Index to the decisions of the supreme court of Florida, reported in Florida reports, from v. 1, to 1st number of v. 11 inclusive. By John B. Galbraith. xxiv, 252 pp. 8°. *Tallahassee, Dyke & Sparhawk*, 1866.

FLOWER (Benjamin). The proceedings of the house of lords in [his] case, for a supposed libel on the bishop of Llandaff [R. Watson]; with animadversions on the writings of the bishop, Rev. R. Ramsden, and Rev. Robert Hall. [Also], the argument in the court of king's bench on a motion for habeas corpus. 213 pp. 8°. *Cambridge, B. Flower*, 1800.

FORD (T.) An account of the behaviour of William [Boyd], late earl of Kilmarnock, and Arthur [Elphinstone], late lord Balmerinock, from the time of their being delivered into the custody of the sheriffs, to the time of their execution [1746]. fol. *London, T. Wright*, 1779.
[HARGRAVE'S state trials, v. 10].

FORSYTH (William). A treatise on the law relating to composition and arrangements with creditors. 3d ed. xxiv, 310 pp. 8°. *London, Benning & Co.* 1854.

FORTESCUE (*Sir* John). The case between Sir Francis Goodwin and Sir John Fortescue, 1604, as it stands upon the journals of the house of commons. [Parliamentary election case]. fol. *London, T. Wright*, 1778.
[HARGRAVE'S state trials, v. 7].

FORTI (Francesco). Libri due delle istituzioni di diritto civile accommodate all' uso del foro. v. 1—2. xxxii, 611 pp; 616 pp. 8°. *Firenze, E. e F. Cammeli*, 1863.

——— Raccolta di conclusioni criminali. Ordinati e annotate dall avvocato Baldassare Paoli. v. 5. 345 pp. 8°. *Firenze, E. e F. Cammeli*, 1864.

FORTI (Francesco). Scritti varii. v. 4. xxxi, 764 pp. 8°. *Firenze, E. e F. Cammeli,* 1865.

——— Trattati inediti di giurisprudenza. v. 3. xxvi, 894 pp. 8°. *Firenze, E. e F. Cammeli,* 1864.

FOSTER (James). An account of the behaviour of [William Boyd] earl of Kilmarnock, after his sentence, and on the day of his execution, Aug. 1746. fol. *London, T. Wright,* 1779.
[HARGRAVE'S state trials, v. 10].

FOSTER (T. Campbell), *and* **FINLASON** (W. F.) Reports of cases at nisi prius and at the crown side of circuit; with select decisions at chambers, 1863–67. v. 4. 8°. *London, Stevens & sons,* 1867.

FOUQUIER (Armand). Causes célèbres de tous les peuples. Éd. illustrée. v. 6–7. 4°. *Paris, Lebrun et Cie.* 1864–67.

FOWLIS (*Sir* David), *and others.* Proceedings in the star chamber against [them] on a charge of opposing the king's service, and traducing his officers of state, 1633. fol. *London, T. Wright,* 1781.
[HARGRAVE'S state trials, v. 11].

FRANCE. Bulletin des lois de l'empire français, janvier 1, 1865, jusqu' au 31 décembre, 1866. 8 v. 8°. *Paris,* 1865–67.

——— Les cinq codes, Napoléon, de procédure civile, de commerce, d'instruction criminelle, et pénal. Éd. soignée par T. D. 2 p. l. 645 pp. 8°. *Paris, Janet, etc.* 1811. S.

——— Code formulaire du possesseur de chiens et d'animaux domestiques nuisibles ou incommodes. 61 pp. 8°. *Grenoble, Prudhomme,* 1855.

——— Code formulaire de la taxe sur les chiens, contenant la loi et le décret relatifs à cette taxe. 6e éd. 33 pp. 8°. *Grenoble, Prudhomme,* 1857.

——— Collection complète des lois, décrets, ordonnances, règlements et avis du conseil d'état. Années 1865–66. 2 v. 8°. *Paris,* 1865–66.

——— Corps législatif. Constitutions de l'empire. Lois et décrets. 452 pp. 12°. *Paris, Poupart, Davyl et Cie.* 1865.

——— Législation de la propriété minière. Erreurs générales d'un demi-siècle, impossibilité actuelle d'exécuter la loi du 24 avril, 1810, sur les mines, et nécesssité d'une révision de cette loi. 40 pp. 8°. *Paris, E. Lacroix,* 1865.

——— Loi relative à l'établissement d'un impôt sur les voitures et les chevaux. Extrait de la loi de finances du 2 juillet, 1862. 28 pp. 8°. *Paris,* [1862].

——— Nouveau code des patentes, contenant le projet de loi, les modifications à apporter aux tarif et tableaux concernant les patentes annexées aux lois des 25 avril, 1844, et 19 mai, 1850, le rapport de la commission, la discussion au corps législatif, les amendemens proposées, le texte de la loi du 4 juin, 1858. 343 pp. 8°. *Paris, Paul Dupont,* 1858.

FRANCES *or* **FRANCIS** (Robert). Trial for the murder of Thomas Dangerfield, at the Old Bailey, July, 1685. fol. *London, T. Wright,* 1779.
[HARGRAVE'S state trials, v. 10].

FRANCIA (Francis). Trial at the Old Bailey, for high treason, Jan. 1716. fol. *London, T. Wright,* 1777.
[HARGRAVE'S state trials, v. 6].

FRANCIS (Philip). The law of charities; comprising the charitable trusts act, 1853, with explanatory notes. xii, xxxvi, 268 pp. 12°. *London, John Crockford,* 1854.

FRANCKLIN (Richard). Trial, for printing and publishing a letter from the Hague, in the Country journal, or Craftsman, of the 2d of Jan. 1730, at the king's bench, Dec. 1731. fol. *London, T. Wright,* 1778.
[HARGRAVE'S state trials, v. 9].

FRANKLIN (James). Trial, at the king's bench, for the murder of Sir Thomas Overbury, Nov. 1615. fol. *London, T. Wright,* 1776.
[HARGRAVE'S state trials, v. 1].

FRANQUET y BERTRAN (Cirilo). Ensayo sobre el origen, espiritu y progressos de la legislacion de los aguas, seguido de los elementos de hidronomia pública, del proyecto de ley general presentado al senado, de la legislacion general y foral, y de la jurisprudencia civil y administrativa. 2 v. 495 pp; 848 pp. 8°. *Madrid, José M. Ducazcal,* 1864.

FRASER (Ishmael), *and* **VANDERPOOL** (George). The confessions of .... under sentence of death, for arson; with some account of Thomas Burge, for the murder of his wife, sentenced to be executed on Friday, 19th Jan. 1816. 16 pp. 8°. *New York,* 1816.

FRASER (Patrick). A treatise on the law of Scotland relative to parent and child, and guardian and ward. 2d ed. by Hugh Cowan. xxxvi, 683 pp. 8°. *Edinburgh, T. & T. Clark,* 1866.

FRASER (Simon, *13th baron Fraser of Lovat*). The whole proceedings upon his impeachment for high-treason, Westminster-Hall, March 1746–7. fol. *London, T. Wright,* 1778.
[HARGRAVE'S state trials, v. 9].

——— Several proceedings relating to [him], with an account of his behaviour in the Tower. fol. *London, T. Wright,* 1779.
[HARGRAVE'S state trials, v. 10].

FREIND (*Sir* John). Trial, at the Old-Baily, for high treason, March, 1695. fol. *London, T. Wright,* 1777.

[HARGRAVE'S state trials, v. 4].

FRESNEAU (Armand). De la constitution politique des états de l'église. 232 pp. 8°. *Paris, A. Vaton,* 1860.

FRY (Danby P.) The lodging-houses acts; and the labouring classes dwelling acts; with notes. 3d ed. 132 pp. 16°. *London, Knight & Co.* 1866.

FULLER (William). Trial, at the Guild-hall of London, for a cheat and imposter, May, 1702. fol. *London, T. Wright,* 1777.

[HARGRAVE'S state trials, v. 5].

FUSTEL de Coulanges, (——). La cité antique; étude sur le culte, le droit, les institutions de la Grèce et de Rome. 2e éd. 323 pp. 8°. *Paris, L. Hachette et Cie.* 1866.

GAIL *or* **GAILL** (Andreas). Practicarvm observationvm libri ii. De pace publica et proscriptis sive bannitis imperii libri ii. De pignorationibus liber singularis. De manuum iniectionibus, sive arrestis imperii tractatus. Ed. postrema. 55 p. l. 623, 280 pp. 4 l. 4°. *Coloniæ Agrippinæ, A. Hieratus,* 1634.

GAMBIER (*Captain* James). Trial of captain G——, for crim. con. with Ad—l K[nowle]s's lady; which was tried in the court of king's bench, at Guildhall, by a special jury, on Saturday, the 11th of June, 1757. 5th ed. 52 pp. 8°. *London, H. Owen,* 1759.

GARCIA. *See* **GARSIAS**.

GARNET (Henry, *superior of the jesuits*). Trial at the Guild-hall, of London, for high treason, being a conspirator in the gunpowder plot, 1606. fol. *London, T. Wright,* 1776.

[HARGRAVE'S state trials, v. 1].

GARREL (A.) Manuel des pensions de l' armée de terre; ou, collection générale des lois, règlements, modèles, formules, etc. xi, 484 pp. 12°. *Paris, J. Dumaine,* 1858.

GARSIAS *or* **GARZIA** (Gallecus), *and* **GARSIAS** de Saavedra (Juan). Tractatvs de expēsis et meliorationibus, [etc.] Accesserunt tractatus alij de donatione remvneratoria, de tacito fidei commisso, de hypotheca post contractvm, de conivgali acqvaestv, [etc.] 23 p. l. 278 l. 58, 8 l. fol. *Pintiæ, Martinus à Cordova,* 1592. s.

GARZIA. *See* **GARSIAS**.

GASCOIGNE (*Sir* Thomas). An abstract of the accusation of R. Bolron and L. Maybury against [him] for high treason, with his tryal and acquittal, Feb. 1680. 2 p. l. 12 pp. fol. [*London*], *C. R.* 1680.

[TRIALS for treason, v. 4].

——Trial at the king's bench for high treason, Feb. 1679. fol. *London, T. Wright,* 1776.

[HARGRAVE'S state trials, v. 3].

GATTESCHI (Domenico). Manuale di diritto pubblico e privato ottomano, contenente le principali capitolazioni e trattati di commercio della porta colle potenze cristiane e relativi regolamenti; un estratto de diritto civile musulmano, disposto secondo l'ordine del codice napoleone, con i luoghi paralleli della legge romane; la legislazione commerciale ottomana, e varie leggi ed ordinanze. Seguito dei trattati ed atti diplomatici risguardenti l'Egitto e dei regolamenti in esso vigenti. Edito per cura dei sigg. Castelnuovo e Leoncavallo. lxxxii, 570 pp. 4°. *Alessandria di Egitto, V. Minasi e C.* 1865.

GAUTIEZ (François). Trial. *See* **HEAMAN** (Peter).

GEORGIA (*State of*). Session laws, 1820 to 1825. 2 v. 8°. *Milledgville,* 1821–26.

GERARD *or* **GERHARD** (John). A true and impartial relation of [his] death [and dying speech], July 10, 1654. fol. *London, T. Wright,* 1778.

[HARGRAVE'S state trials, v. 8].

—— *and others.* Trial before the high court of justice for high treason, in conspiring to murder the lord protector, June, 1654. fol. *London, T. Wright,* 1776.

[HARGRAVE'S state trials, v. 2].

GERMAINE (John). The trial between Henry [Howard], duke of Norfolk, plaintiff, and John Germaine, defendant, in an action of trespass on the case, at the court of king's-bench, Nov. 1692. fol. *London, T. Wright,* 1778.

[HARGRAVE'S state trials, v. 8].

GERRALD (Joseph). Defence on a charge of sedition, before the high court of justiciary, at Edinburgh. 296 pp. 8°. *London, J. Robertson,* 1794.

GESSNER (Ludwig). Le droit des neutres sur mer. xiv, 438 pp. 8°. *Berlin, Stilke & Van Muyden,* 1865.

GHOLSON (William Y.) and **OKEY** (J. W.) Digest of the Ohio reports; embracing the twenty volumes of Ohio reports, and fifteen volumes of the Ohio state reports. xx, 677, 181 pp. 8°. *Cincinnati, R. Clarke & Co.* 1867. (3 copies.)

GIBBON (John). The king against J. Gibbon. Upon an information, in the nature of a quo warranto, to show by what authority he claims to be a freeman of the town and port of New Romney. Maidstone, Aug. 1734. fol. *London, T. Wright,* 1779.
[HARGRAVE'S state trials, v. 10].

GIBBONS (Henry Frederick), *and* **HARVEY** (William Charles). Equity of the county court; being a treatise of the equitable jurisdiction conferred upon the county courts by stat. 28 and 29 Vict. cap. 99. xxii, 315 pp. 12°. *London, Horace Cox,* 1866.

GIBBONS (John). Trial, before the high court of justice, for high treason, July, 1651. fol. *London, T. Wright,* 1776.
[HARGRAVE'S state trials, v. 2].

GIBELIN (E.) Études sur le droit civil des Hindous; recherches de législation comparée sur les lois de l'Inde, les lois d'Athènes et de Rome, et les coutumes des Germains. 2 v. cxx, 336 pp; xcvi, 376 pp. 8°. *Pondichéry, A. Toutin,* 1846–47.

GIBSON (William Sidney). A letter on the reform of the bankruptcy law of England, addressed to the right hon. the lord chancellor. 34 pp. 12°. *London, Butterworths,* 1866.

GIFFORD (John). English lawyer; or, every man his own lawyer; containing a summary of the constitution of England; its laws and statutes. Also, a supplement containing the insurance laws. 11th ed. iv, 688, 148 pp. 8°. *London, A. Wheeler,* 1825.

GILBERT (——, *of London*). Case of mixed money in Ireland. *See* **BRETT** (——, *of Drogheda*).

GILBERT (Jeffery, *lord chief baron of the exchequer, Ireland*), *and others.* Proceedings of the house of lords in Ireland against [them], for issuing process in the cause of Annesley and Sherlock, in opposition to an order of that house, July, 1719. fol. *London, T. Wright,* 1777.
[HARGRAVE'S state trials, v. 6].

GILES (John). Tryal in the Old Bayly, July, 1680, for a barbarous attempt to assassinate and murther John Arnold. 58 pp. fol. *London, R. Taylor,* 1681.
[TRIALS for treason, v. 3].

——— The same. fol. *London, T. Wright,* 1776.
[HARGRAVE'S state trials, v. 3].

GODEFROY (Jacques). *See* **GOTHOFREDUS.**

GOLDING (John), *and others.* Proceedings before the lords of the council, and the admiralty, in relation to [their] trials as pirates, though acting under king James II's commission, Sept. 1693. fol. *London, T. Wright,* 1778.
[HARGRAVE'S state trials, v. 8].

GOMEZ DE LA SERNA (Pedro). Prolegomenos del derecho. 4ª ed. corregida y aumentada. 191 pp. 8°. *Madrid, Sanchez,* 1863.

GOODERE (Samuel), *and others.* Trials, for the murder of Sir John D. Goodere, at Bristol, March, 1740–41. fol. *London, T. Wright,* 1777.
[HARGRAVE'S state trials, v. 6].

GOODWIN (*Sir* Francis). Parliamentary election case, 1604. *See* **FORTESCUE** (*Sir* John).

GORDON (William, *6th viscount Kenmure*). Trial for treason. *See* **RADCLIFFE** (James, *3d earl of Derwentwater*), *and others.*

——— True copy of a letter written to a certain nobleman the day before his execution, 1715. fol. *London, T. Wright,* 1779.
[HARGRAVE'S state trials, v. 10].

GOTHOFREDUS (Jacobus), *or* **GODEFROY** (Jacques). Manuale juris; ubi quatuor sequentia continentur: i. Juris romani historia; ii. Biblioteca; iii. Florilegium sententiarum ex corpore justinianeo desumptarum; iv. Series librorum et titulorum in institutionibus digestis, et in codice. x, 525 pp. 12°. *Genevæ, S. de Tournes,* 1695.

GOURNOT (Achille). Du principe des droits d'auteur et de la perpétuité. 48 pp. 8°. *Paris, E. Dentu,* 1862.

GOWRIE (John Ruthven, *3d earl of*). *See* **RUTHVEN.**

GRADY (Standish Grove). The law of fixtures, with reference to real property and chattels of a personal nature. [With] the law of dilapidations, ecclesiastical and lay. xxi, 418 pp. 16°. *London, O. Richards,* 1845.

——— The same. 2d ed. xxvii, 511 pp. 12°. *London, Wildy & sons,* 1866.

GRÁGÁS *or* **GRAAGAAS.** Codex juris Islandorum antiqvissimus qvi nominatur grágás. Præmissa commentatione historica et critica, ab J. F. G. Schlegel conscripta. 2 v. clxix, 505 pp. 1 col. pl; 410, 133 pp. 2 tab. 4°. *Havniæ, sumptibus legati Arnæi Magnæani,* 1829–30. S.

GRAHAM (*Sir* Richard, *1st viscount Preston*), *and* **ASHTON** (John). Trials at the Old Bailey, for high treason, Jan. 1690. fol. *London, T. Wright,* 1777.
[HARGRAVE'S state trials. v. 4].

GRANEY (Leonard Grey, *viscount*). *See* **GREY.**

GRATIANUS *or* **GRAZIANO.** Decretum aureum. 45 p. l. cccccccxci pp. 1 l. 4°. *Lutecie, vidua Thielmanni Keruer,* 1542.

GRATTAN (Peachy R.) Reports of cases in the supreme court of appeals of Virginia. v. 15–16. 8°. *Richmond,* 1860–67. (2 copies of v. 15. 3 copies of v. 16).

GRAY (John). The country solicitor's practice in the high court of chancery. 4th ed. xx, 431 pp. 12°. *London, Edmund Lumley,* 1845.

GRAYDON (William). An abridgement of the laws of the United States; or, a digest of all such acts of congress as concern the U. S. at large. [With] an appendix. liii, 476, 163 pp. 8 l. 8°. *Harrisburgh, J. Wyeth,* 1803. (2 copies).

GREAT BRITAIN. An act for preventing frauds and regulating abuses in the plantation trade, 1695. 8 pp. fol. *Boston, B. Green & J. Allen,* 1696.
[*With* MASSACHUSETTS. Acts and laws, 1693–1700].

——— Informations and examinations, taken upon oath before a committee of the house of lords appointed to inspect who were the advisers and prosecutors of the murders of [William], lord Russell, [Algernon] Sidney, Sir T. Armstrong, and others, Dec. 1689. fol. *London, T. Wright,* 1778.
[HARGRAVE'S state trials, v. 8].

——— Method of proceedings upon the trial of a peer. fol. *London, T. Wright,* 1778.
[HARGRAVE'S state trials, v. 8].

——— Minutes of the proceedings of the committee appointed to inquire into the state of the gaols, touching a charge against Sir R. Eyre, chief justice of the common pleas, for personally visiting T. Bambridge, whilst a prisoner in Newgate, under a commitment of the house of commons, 1729. fol. *London, T. Wright,* 1778.
[HARGRAVE'S state trials, v. 9].

——— Proceedings of the committee appointed by the house of commons to enquire into the state of the gaols of this kingdom, as far as relates to J. Huggins and J. Bambridge, wardens of the fleet, and of R. Corbet and W. Acton, 1729. fol. *London, T. Wright,* 1778.
[HARGRAVE'S state trials, v. 9].

——— The report of the committee of the house of commons appointed to examine the proceedings of the judges [in the case of William Howard, viscount Stafford], made Dec. 1680. fol. *London, T. Wright,* 1776.
[HARGRAVE'S state trials. v. 3].

——— The report from the committee of the commons to consider the petition of Richard Thompson, and to examine complaints against him; and the resolution of the commons upon this report, for his impeachment of high crimes and misdemeanors, Dec. 1680. fol. *London, T. Wright,* 1778.
[HARGRAVE'S state trials, v. 7].

——— Report of the capital punishment commission, together with the minutes of evidence. Presented to both houses of parliament by command of her majesty. liv, 672 pp. 8°. *London, Eyre & Spottiswoode,* 1866.

——— Resolutions of the house of lords on several books, 1701–02. fol. *London, T. Wright,* 1778.
[HARGRAVE'S state trials, v. 8].

GREEN (Charles Ewing). Reports of cases in the high court of chancery, the prerogative court, and, on appeal, in the court of errors and appeals of the state of New Jersey, 1862–64. 599 pp. 8°. *Trenton, Hough & Gillespy,* 1867.

GREEN (*Rev.* John C.) *v.* **PIERCE** (John). Trial of, together with the speech of James M. Smith, jr. and a synopsis of John Graham's speech, reported by Cyril V. Gray. 87 pp. 8°. *New York,* 1850.

GREEN (Robert), *and others.* Tryals for the murder of Sir Edmond-bury Godfrey, king's bench, Westminster, Feb. 1679. 2 p. l. 92 pp. fol. *London, R. Pawlet,* 1679.
[TRIALS for treason, v. 1].

——— The same.
[TRIALS for treason, v. 2].

——— The same.
[TRIALS for treason, v. 3].

——— The same. fol. *London, T. Wright,* 1776.
[HARGRAVE'S state trials, v. 2].

GREEN (*Capt.* Thomas), *and others.* Trial, at Edinburgh, for piracy, March, 1705. fol. *London, T. Wright,* 1777.
[HARGRAVE'S state trials, v. 5].

GREENLEAF (Simon). Treatise on the law of evidence. 12th ed. carefully revised, with large additions, by Isaac F. Redfield. 3 v. 8°. *Boston, Little, Brown & Co.* 1866–67. (3 copies).

GREGG (William). Proceedings against [him] at the Old-Bailey, Jan. 1708, for high treason. fol. *London, T. Wright,* 1779.
[HARGRAVE'S state trials, v. 10].

GREGORIAN code. *See* **THEODOSIUS II,** (*emperor*).

GREGORY (A. F. L.) Specimen juris civilis de ratihabitione. xiv, 291 pp. 8°. *Hagæ Comitis, M. Nijhoff,* 1864.

GREY (Ford, *3d baron Grey, of Werke, earl of Tankerville*), *and others*. Trial at the king's bench for a misdemeanor, in debauching the lady Henrietta Berkeley, Nov. 1682. fol. *London, T. Wright*, 1776.

[HARGRAVE'S state trials, v. 3].

GREY (Leonard, *viscount Graney*). Trial at Westminster for high treason, June, 1540. fol. *London, T. Wright*, 1781.

[HARGRAVE'S state trials, v. 11].

GREY (Richard). A system of English ecclesiastical law. Extracted from the Codex juris ecclesiastici anglicani of [Edmund Gibson], the bishop of London. xiv, 448 pp. 38 l. 8°. *London, Nutt & Gosling*, 1730.

GRIFFINBURG (Elizabeth). *See* **CALVERT** (Frederick). Trial of.

GRIFFITH (Wm. Downes), *and* **HOLMES** (Charles Arbuthnot). The law and practice of bankruptcy; with an appendix of statutes, orders, and forms, partly founded on the 11th ed. of Mr. Archbold's treatise. 1 v. in 2. lxxii, 1559 pp. 8°. *London, H. Sweet*, 1867.

GRIMKE (John F.) South Carolina justice of the peace; to which is added a great variety of warrants, indictments, and other precedents. 3d ed. [*anon.*] vii, 504 pp. 8°. *New York, F. & J. Swords*, 1810.

GUERRAND (J.) Recueil de jurisprudence commerciale et maritime du Havre. v. 10–12. Années 1864–66. 8°. *Havre, Cazavan et Cie.* 1864–66.

GUILFORD (Francis North, *baron*). *See* **NORTH.**

GUIPUZCOA. Nveva recopilacion de los fver^s, priuilegios, buenos vsos, y costumbres, leyes, y orden^s, de la muy N.^e y muy L. prouincia de Guipuzcoa. 22 p. l. 361 pp. 50 l. fol. *Tolosa, Bernardo de Vgarte*, 1696.

HAAS (C. P. Marie). Administration de la France, histoire et mécanisme des grands pouvoirs de l'état, fonctions publiques, conditions d'admission et d'avancement dans toutes les carrières, privilèges et immunités. 2e éd. 4 v. 8°. *Paris, Cosse et Marchal*, 1861.

HALES (*Sir* Edward). Trial, for neglecting to take the oaths of supremacy and allegiance, with his plea thereto, upon the king's dispensing with the statute, and the opinion of the judges thereupon, 1686. fol. *London, T. Wright*, 1778.

[HARGRAVE'S state trials, v. 7].

HALES (William). Trial, for [obtaining money on false tokens, and for forging], 1729. fol. *London, T. Wright*, 1778.

[HARGRAVE'S state trials, v. 9].

——— Trial, for forging a promissory note in the name of T. Gibson, at the Old-Bailey, Dec. 1728. fol. *London, T. Wright*, 1779.

[HARGRAVE'S state trials, v. 10].

——— *and* **KINNERSLEY** (Thomas). Trials for forging promissory notes, 1729. fol. *London, T. Wright*, 1778.

[HARGRAVE'S state trials, v. 9].

HALL (John E.) American law journal and miscellaneous repertory. v. 1–3. 8°. *Philadelphia*, 1808–10.

HALL (Lucian), *and others*. Minute and correct account of the trial of Lucian Hall, Bethuel Roberts, and William H. Bell, for murder, at the Middlesex superior court, Connecticut, February term, 1844. 40 pp. 8°. *Middletown, C. H. Pelton*, 1844.

HAMBDEN (John). Tryal for conspiring the death of the king, and raising a rebellion in this kingdom, Old-Bayly, Dec. 1685. 1 p. l. 4 pp. fol. *London, E. Mallet*, 1685.

[TRIALS for treason, v. 6].

——— The same. fol. *London, T. Wright*, 1777.

[HARGRAVE'S state trials, v. 4].

——— Tryal and conviction upon an indictment of high misdemeanour, for contriving to disturb the peace of the king, [etc.] 1 p. l. 56 pp. fol. *London, B. Tooke*, 1684.

[TRIALS for treason, v. 6].

——— The same. fol. *London, T. Wright*, 1776.

[HARGRAVE'S state trials, v. 3].

HAMILTON (James, *1st duke and 3d marquess of Hamilton*). Trial, before the high court of justice, for high treason, Feb. 1648. fol. *London, T. Wright*, 1776.

[HARGRAVE'S state trials, v. 2].

HAMPDEN (John, *M. P.*) Proceedings in the case of ship-money, between the king and John Hampden, in the exchequer, 1637. fol. *London, T. Wright*, 1776.

[HARGRAVE'S state trials, v. 1].

HAMPDEN. *See, also,* **HAMBDEN.**

HARE (J. I. Clark), *and* **WALLACE** (Horace Binney.) American leading cases. 4th ed. enlarged and improved. With additional notes and references to American decisions. 2 v. xii, 778 pp; xxxi, 829 pp. 8°. *Philadelphia, T. & J. Johnson & Co.* 1857.

HARGRAVE (Francis). A complete collection of state trials, and proceedings for high treason, and other crimes and misdemeanours; commencing with the year [1388], and ending with the year [1777]. With two alphabetical tables to the whole. 4th ed. 11 v. in 5. fol. *London, T. Wright*, 1776–81.

HARGRAVE (Francis). A complete collection of state trials, and proceedings for high treason, etc.—*Continued.*

CONTENTS.

HARGRAVE (Francis). A complete collection of state trials, and proceedings for high treason, etc.—*Continued.*

Howard, Thomas, 3d duke of Norfolk, v. 11.
Howard, Thomas, 4th duke of Norfolk, v. 1.
Howard, William, viscount Stafford, v. 3.
Huggins, John, v. 9.
Hurly, Patrick, v. 5.
Hyde, Edward, 1st earl of Clarendon, v. 2, v. 8.
Ireland, William, and others, v. 2.
Ivy, Theodosia, v. 7.
Jackson, William, and others, v. 9.
James, John, v. 2.
Jenkes, Francis, v. 7.
Johnson, Samuel, v. 7.
Keach, Benjamin, v. 2.
Kendall, Thomas, and Roe, Richard, v. 4.
Kern, Charles, v. 2.
Kidd, Capt. William, and others v. 5.
Kinlock, Alexander and James, v. 9.
Kirkby, Richard, and others, v. 5.
Knevet, Sir Edmund, v. 11.
Knightley, Alexander, v. 4.
Knightly, Sir Richard, and others, v. 7.
Knollys, or Knowles, Charles, claiming to be earl of Banbury, v. 8.
Knox, Thomas, and Lane, John, v. 2.
Lalor, Robert, v. 11.
Langhorn, Richard, v. 2.
Laud, William, archbishop of Canterbury, v. 1.
Layer, Christopher, v. 6.
Lee, Capt. Thomas, v. 7.
Leech, Benjamin, v. 10.
Leighton, Alexander, v. 11.
Lewis, David, v. 2.
Lilburne, Col. John, v. 2, v. 7.
——— and Wharton, John, v. 7.
Lindsay, David, v. 5.
Lisle, Alice, v. 4.
Lloyd, William, bishop of Worcester, and Lloyd, ——, his son, v. 8.
Logan, Robert, v. 7.
London, city of, v. 3.
Love, Christopher, v. 2.
Lowick, Robert, v. 4.
Macdonald, Æneas, alias Angus, v. 9.
Mac Growther, Alexander, v. 9.
Mac Kenzie, George, 3d earl of Cromartie, v. 9, v. 10.
Magdalen college, Oxford, v. 4.
Maguire, Connor, baron Maguire, v. 1.
Maitland, Charles, v. 8.
Markham, Sir Griffin, and others, v. 7.
Mary, queen of Scots, v. 1.
Matthews, John, v. 9.
Messenger, Peter, and others, v. 2.
Mitchel, James, v. 2.
Moders, alias Stedman, Mary, v. 2.
Mohun, Charles, 5th baron Mohun, v. 4, v. 5.
Money, John, and others, v. 11.
Monson, Sir Thomas, v. 1.
Mordaunt, John, viscount Mordaunt, v. 2.
Mordaunt, Mary, duchess of Norfolk, v. 8, v. 5.
More, Sir Thomas, v. 1.
Morgan, David, v. 9.
Morris, Col. John, v. 7.
Morris, alias Poyntz, John, and others, v. 7.
Mostyn, lieut. gen. John, v. 11.
Murphy, Timothy, v. 10.
Nairn, Katharine, and Ogilvie, Patrick, v. 10.
Nayler, James, v. 2.
Nevill, Alexander, archbishop of York, and others, v. 1.
Noble, Richard, and others, v. 9.
Norkott, Arthur, and others, v. 10.
Oates, Titus, v. 3, v. 4.
Ogilvie, John, v. 7.
O'Key, John, and others, v. 8.
Oldcastle, Sir John, baron Cobham, v. 1.
Oneby, John, v. 9.
Osborne, Thomas, 1st earl of Danby, v. 2.
Owen, William, v. 10.
Palmer, Roger, earl of Castlemaine, v. 3, v. 4.
Papillon, Thomas, v. 3.
Parker, Thomas, 1st earl of Macclesfield, v. 6.
Parker, Thomas, 6th baron Morley, v. 7.
Parkyns, Sir William, v. 4.
Parry, William, v. 1.
Peachell, John, vice chancellor, and the university of Cambridge, v. 4.
Pemberton, Sir Francis, and Jones, Sir Thomas, v. 8.
Penn, William, and Mead, William, v. 2.
Penruddock, Col. John, v. 2.
Perrot, Sir John, v. 1.
Pilkington, Thomas, and others, v. 3.
Plunket, Oliver, D. D. v. 3.
Plunkett, John, and others, v. 6.
Pordage, Rev. John, v. 2.
Porteous, Capt. John, v. 6.
Powrie, William, and others, v. 8.
Price, John, and others, v. 4.
Priest, William, v. 11.
Prynne, William, v. 1, v. 8.
Purchase, George, v. 8.
Quelch, John, and others, v. 8.
Radcliffe, Charles, assumed earl of Derwentwater, v. 9.
Radcliffe, James, 3d earl of Derwentwater, and others, v. 6.
Raleigh, Sir Walter, v. 1, v. 8.
Ramsey, David, v. 11.
Reading, Nathaniel, v. 2.
Reason, Hugh, and Tranter, Robert, v. 6.
Regicides, v. 2.
Rich, Edward, 6th earl of Warwick, 3d earl of Holland, v. 5.
Rookwood, Ambrose, v. 4.
Rosewell, Thomas, v. 3.
Rouse, John, v. 3.
Russell, Francis, 4th earl of Bedford, v. 11.
Russell, William, lord Russell, v. 3.
Ruthven, John, 4th earl of Gowrie, v. 7.
Sacheverell, Henry, D. D. v. 5, v. 8.
Sacheverell, William, and others, v. 3.
St. John, Oliver, v. 11.
Sancroft, William, archbishop of Canterbury, and others, v. 4.
Sandys, Thomas, v. 7.
Scroggs, Sir William, and others, v. 7.
Seton, George, 5th earl of Wintoun, v. 6.
Seymour, Edward, 1st duke of Somerset, v. 7.
Seymour, Sir Thomas, baron Seymour of Sudley, v. 7.
Sherfield, Henry, v. 1.
Shirley, Laurence, 4th earl Ferrers, v. 10.
Sidney, Algernon, v. 3.
Sindercome, alias Fish, Miles, v. 7.
Slingsby, Sir Henry, v. 2.
Smith, Francis, v. 2.
Soame, Sir William, v. 7.
Sommersett, James, v. 11.
Spotiswood, Sir Robert, v. 1.
Sprat, Thomas, bishop of Rochester, v. 8.
Sprot, George, v. 1.
Stafford, Edward de, 3d duke of Buckingham, v. 11.
Standsfield, Philip, v. 4.
Stanley, Sir William, v. 11.
Stapleton, Sir Miles, v. 3.
Stayley, William, v. 2.
Stevenson, John, v. 10.
Stewart, Archibald, v. 9.
Stewart, James, of Appin, v. 10.
Stewart, Sir James, lord Ochiltrie, v. 7.
Stirling, James, and others, v. 5.
Streater, John, v. 2.
Stroud, William, and others, v. 7.
Swan, John, and Jefferys, Elizabeth, v. 10.
Swendsen, Haagen, v. 5.
Talbot, William, v. 11.
Tasborough, John, and, Price, Ann, v. 2.
Thompson, Nathaniel, and others, v. 3.
Thorpe, William, v. 1.
Throckmorton, Sir Nicholas, v. 1.
Thwing, Thomas, and Pressicks, Mary, v. 3.
Tonge, Thomas, and others, v. 2.
Tooke, John Horne, v. 11.
Touchet, Mervin, baron Audley, earl of Castlehaven, v. 1.
Townley, Francis, v. 9.
Turner, Anne, v. 1.
Turner, James, and others, v. 2.
Tutchin, John, v. 5.
Twyn, John, v. 2.
Udall, Rev. John, v. 1.
Vane, Sir Henry, v. 2.
Vaughan, Thomas, v. 5.
Wakeman, Sir George, and others, v. 2.
Walcott, Thomas, and others, v. 3.
Walters, Rowland, and others, v. 7.
Ward, Sir Patience, v. 3.
Wedderburn, Sir John, v. 9.
Wentworth, Sir Thomas, 1st earl of Strafford, v. 1.

HARGRAVE (Francis). A complete collection of state trials, and proceedings for high treason, etc.—*Continued.*

Weston, Richard, v. 1.
White, alias Whitebread, Thomas, and others, v. 2.
White, William, mayor of Aylesbury, England, v. 8.
Whitelock, James, v. 11.
Wiat, or Wyatt, Sir Thomas, v. 8.
Wilkes, John, v. 11.
Willis, Francis, v. 8.
Winter, Robert, and others, v. 1.
Woodburne, John, and Coke, Arundel, v. 6.
Wraynham, ——, v. 7.
Zenger, John Peter, v. 9.

HARLEY (Robert, 1*st earl of Oxford*). Proceedings against [him], before the house of lords, upon an impeachment for high treason, etc. June, 1717. fol. *London, T. Wright,* 1777.
[HARGRAVE'S state trials, v. 6].

HARMON (Henry C.) Manual of the pension laws of the United States of America, embracing all the laws under which pensions, bounties, and bounty lands are now granted, with forms, etc. x, 397 pp. 8°. *Washington, W. H. & O. H. Morrison,* 1867.

HARRIS (Benjamin). A short but just account of [his] tryal, for printing and vending a late seditious book called An appeal from the country to the city, [etc.] 8 pp. fol. *London,* 1679.
[TRIALS for treason, v. 2].

——— The same. fol. *London, T. Wright,* 1776.
[HARGRAVE'S state trials, v. 2].

HARRIS (George). Principia pıima legum; or, an enunciation and analysis of the elementary principles of law, in its several departments. Part i. xxxv, 235 pp. 8°. *London, Stevens & sons,* 1866.

HARRISON (Henry). Trial, at the Old-Bailey, for the murder of Andrew Clenche, April, 1692. fol. *London, T. Wright,* 1777.
[HARGRAVE'S state trials, v. 4].

HARRISON (Thomas). Trial, at the king's bench, for a misdemeanour, in speaking reflecting words of judge Hutton, 1638. fol. *London, T. Wright,* 1776.
[HARGRAVE'S state trials, v. 1].

HARVEY (Ann). *See* **CALVERT** (Frederick). Trial of.

HARWOOD (A. A.) The law and practice of United States naval courts-martial. 325 pp. 8°. *New York, D. Van Nostrand,* 1867.

HASTINGS, (*county of Sussex, England*). Henry Moore, plaintiff, against the mayor, jurats, and commonalty of the town and port of Hastings, defendants. Tried, July, 1736, at the King's-bench, on a mandamus admitting the plaintiff to be a freeman of Hastings, in pursuance of a custom there. fol. *London, T. Wright,* 1779.
[HARGRAVE'S state trials, v. 10].

HATHAWAY (Richard). Trial, at Surry assizes, for a cheat and impostor, March 1702. fol. *London, T. Wright,* 1777.
[HARGRAVE'S state trials, v. 5].

——— *and others.* Trial, at Surrey assizes, March 1702, for a riot and assault. fol. *London, T. Wright,* 1777.
[HARGRAVE'S state trials, v. 5].

HAURÉAU (Jean Barthélemy). Catalogue chronologique des œuvres imprimées et manuscrites de J. B. Gerbier, que possède la bibliothèque des avocats á la cour impériale de Paris. 92 pp. 8°. *Paris, Durand,* 1863.

HAWAIIAN, *or* **SANDWICH** islands. Ke Kumu kanawai, a me na kanawai o ko Hawaii pae aina. [Constitution and laws of Hawaii]. iv, 156 pp. 16°. *Honolulu, Oahu,* 1841.

HAWKINS (Francis, *D. D.*) A narrative of what discourse passed between [himself] and E. Fitz-Harys, late prisoner in the tower; with the manner of taking his confession. 1 p. l. 10 pp. fol. *London, S. Carr,* 1681.
[TRIALS for treason, v. 3].

——— The same.
[TRIALS for treason, v. 4].

HAWKINS (*Rev.* Robert). Trial, at Ailesbury, for felony, March 1668. Wrote by himself. fol. *London, T. Wright,* 1776.
[HARGRAVE'S state trials, v. 2].

HAWLES (John). Remarks upon the tryals of E. Fitzharris, S. Colledge, count Coningsmark, lord Russell, collonel [Algernon] Sidney, H. Cornish, and C. Bateman. As also on the earl of Shaftsbury's grand jury, Wilmore's homine replegiando, and the award of execution against Sir Thomas Armstrong. 104 pp. fol. *London, J. Tonson,* 1689.

——— The same.
[TRIALS for treason, v. 5].

——— The same. fol. *London, T. Wright,* 1777.
[HARGRAVE'S state trials, v. 4].

HAYES (Joseph). Trial, at the king's bench, for high treason in corresponding with Sir T. Armstrong, an outlaw for high treason, Nov. 1684. fol. *London, T. Wright,* 1776.
[HARGRAVE'S state trials, v. 3].

HEAD (John W.) Reports of cases in the supreme court of Tennessee. v. 3. 8°. *Nashville, S. C. Mercer,* 1866. (2 copies).

HEAMAN (Peter), *and* **GAUTIEZ** (François). Trial of.... before the high court of admiralty, at Edinburgh, 26th November, 1821, for piracy and murder. 72 pp. 12°. *Leith, W. Reed,* 1821.

HEATH (*Mrs.* Mary). Trial, for perjury (in the cause of Annesley *vs.* Annesley), at the king's bench in Ireland, Feb. 1744. fol. *London, T. Wright,* 1778.
[HARGRAVE'S state trials, v. 9].

HÉLIE (Faustin). Théorie du code pénal, 1843. *See* **CHAUVEAU** (A.) *and* **HÉLIE.**

HENDLEY (*Rev.* William), *and others.* Trial for preaching a charity sermon at Chislehurst, in Kent, for the charity children of St. Ann's, London, and for collecting money for the same; at Rochester, July, 1719. fol. *London, T. Wright,* 1779.
[HARGRAVE'S state trials, v. 10].

HENING (William Waller). The new Virginia justice, comprising the office and authority of a justice of the peace in Virginia. With a variety of useful precedents, [and] an appendix. 6 p. l. 539 pp. 8°. *Richmond, A. Davis,* 1799.

HENNEN (William D.) Digest of the reported decisions of the supreme court of the late territory of Orleans; the late court of errors and appeals; and the supreme court of the state of Louisiana; contained in the sixty-five volumes of reports, from first Martin to fifteenth Louisiana annual. 2 v. 963 pp; 1,946 pp. 8°. *Boston, H. O. Houghton,* 1861. (2 copies).

HEPBURN (James, *4th earl of Bothwell*). Trial for the murder of Henry [Stewart], lord Darnley, Edinburgh, April, 1567. fol. *London, T. Wright,* 1776.
[HARGRAVE'S state trials, v. 1].

HEPP (Edgar). De la correspondence privée postale ou télégraphique, dans ses rapports avec le droit civil, le droit commercial, le droit administratif, et le droit pénal. viii, 143 pp. 8°. *Paris, A. Durand,* 1864.

HERBERT (Philip, *7th earl of Pembroke, 4th earl of Montgomery*). Tryal [for the murder of N. Cony], Westminster hall, April, 1678. 1 p. l. 28 pp. fol. [*London*], 1679.
[TRIALS for treason, v. 1].

——— The same. fol. *London, T. Wright,* 1776.
[HARGRAVE'S state trials, v. 2].

HERMOGENIAN code. *See* **THEODOSIUS II** (*emperor*).

HEROLD (Ferdinand). Sur la perpétuité de la propriété littéraire. 45 pp.. 8°. *Paris, A. Marescq,* 1862.

HERTY (Thomas). A digest of the laws of the United States of America, (alphabetically arranged). From the commencement of the federal government, to March, 1799. 562 pp. 8°. *Baltimore, editor,* 1800.

HEWET (John, *D. D.*) Trial before the high court of justice for high treason, June, 1658. fol. *London, T. Wright,* 1776.
[HARGRAVE'S state trials, v. 2].

HEYL (Lewis). Digest of the statutes of the United States, prescribing the rates of duties on imports in force October 1, 1866. 53 pp. 8°. [*Washington,* 1867].

HICKERINGILL (*Rev.* Edmund). The test or tryal of the goodness and value of spiritual courts. 2 p. l. 22, 18 pp. fol. *London, assigns of the author,* 1683.
[TRIALS for treason, v. 5].

HICKES (George, *D. D.*) Ravillac redivivus: being a narrative of the late tryal of James Mitchel, a conventicle preacher, who was executed Jan. 18, 1677, for an attempt on the sacred person of [James Sharp], the archbishop of St. Andrews. [With] the tryal of Thomas Weir. [*anon.*] 2d ed. 2 p. l. 54 pp. fol. *London, W. Kettilby,* 1682.

HICKFORD (Robert). Trial for high treason, queen's bench, Feb. 1571. fol. *London, T. Wright,* 1776.
[HARGRAVE'S state trials, v. 1].

HIGGINS (G.) Trial for high treason. *See* **SMITH** (John), *and* **HIGGINS.**

HIGHMORE (Anthony). Treatise on the law of idiocy and lunacy. 1st Amer. ed. with selection of American cases. 8°. *Exeter, (N. H.)* 1822.

HILDENBRAND (Carl). De bona fide rei propriæ debitori ad temporis praescriptionem haud necessaria. 58 pp. 8°. *Monachii, Literarisch art. anstalt,* 1843. S.

HILL (John W.) A manual of the law of fixtures. 64 pp. 8°. *New York, Baker, Voorhis & Co.* 1867.

HILL (Lawrence). An account of the writing, [together] with the writing itself, that was found in the pocket of L. Hill, at the time he and [Robert] Green were executed. 3 pp. fol. *London, R. Pawlet,* 1679.
[Trials for treason, v. 1].

——— The same. fol. *London, T. Wright,* 1778.
[HARGRAVE'S state trials, v. 8].

——— *See* **GREEN** (Robert).

HILLIARD (Francis). The law of torts; or, private wrongs. xlvii, 595 pp. 8°. *Boston, Little, Brown & Co.* 1867.

HOFFMAN (David). Circular address to students of law in the United States. 15 pp. 8°. *Baltimore, J. D. Toy,* 1824. S.

——— A lecture introductory to a course of lectures now delivering in the university of Maryland. 77 pp. 8°. *Baltimore, J. D. Toy,* 1823. S.
[*With* his Circular address, etc.]

HOFFMAN (David). A lecture, being the second [and third] of a series of lectures introductory to a course of lectures now delivering in the university of Maryland. 50 pp; 62 pp. 8°. *Baltimore, J. D. Toy*, 1825–26. s.
[*With* his Circular, etc.]

——— Syllabus of a course of lectures on law; proposed to be delivered in the university of Maryland, [etc.] xii, 92 pp. 8°. *Baltimore, E. J. Coale*, 1821. s.
[*With* his Circular, etc.]

HOLLAND (Edward Rich, 3*d earl of*). *See* **RICH** (Edward).

HOLLIS (*Sir* John), *and others*. Proceedings against [them] in the star chamber, for traducing public justice, Nov. 1615. fol. *London, T. Wright*, 1776.
[HARGRAVE'S state trials, v. 1].

HOLLOWAY (James). Free and voluntary confession and narrative [concerning the whig conspiracy]; also, the proceedings against him in the king's bench. [With] a discourse at his execution. 16 pp. fol. *London, R. Horn*, 1684.
[Trials for treason, v. 4].

——— The same.
[Trials for treason, v. 5].

——— Proceedings against [him] in the king's bench, on an outlawry for high treason, April, 1684. fol. *London, T. Wright*, 1776.
[HARGRAVE'S state trials, v. 3].

HONE (William, *laborer*). Trial at the Old Bailey, for high treason, July, 1683. fol. *London, T. Wright*, 1776.
[HARGRAVE'S state trials. v. 3].

——— The same. *See* **WALCOT** (Thomas).

HONE (William, *bookseller*). The third trial of William Hone, on an ex-officio information, for publishing a parody on the Athanasian creed, entitled "The sinecurist's creed." 4th ed. 2 p. l. iv, 34 pp. 8°. *London, W. Hone*, 1818. s.

HORNE (Andrew). The mirrour of justices; [with] the diversity of courts and their jurisdiction. Translated from old French into English by William Hughes. New ed. 299 pp. 2 l. 1 pl. 24°. *Manchester, (Eng.) William Willis*, 1840.

HORNE (John). *See* **TOOKE** (John Horne).

HOUCK (Louis). A treatise on the mechanics' lien law in the United States. xxix, 256 pp. 8°. *Chicago, Callaghan & Cutler*, 1867.

HOUSTON (John). A treatise on the law of stoppage in transitu, and incidentally of retention and delivery. xvi, 253 pp. 8°. *London, W. Maxwell*, 1866.

HOUSTON (John W.) Reports of cases in the superior court, and the court of errors and appeals of the state of Delaware. v. 1. vi, 660 pp. 8°. *Philadelphia, Johnsons*, 1866. (2 copies).

HOWARD (Frances, *countess of Essex, afterwards countess of Somerset*). Proceedings, in a cause of divorce. *See* **DEVEREUX** (Robert, 3*d earl of Essex*).

——— Trial for the murder of Sir Thomas Overbury, May, 1616. fol. *London, T. Wright*, 1776.
[HARGRAVE'S state trials, v. 1].

HOWARD (Henry, *earl of Surrey*). Trial for high treason, at the Guildhall, London, Dec. 1546. With the proceedings against his father, Thomas [Howard, 3d] duke of Norfolk, for the same crime. fol. *London, T. Wright*, 1781.
[HARGRAVE'S state trials, v. 11].

HOWARD (Henry, 7*th duke of Norfolk*). Proceedings in divorce, 1700. *See* **MORDAUNT** (*lady* Mary).

——— Trial in an action of trespass on the case. *See* **GERMAINE** (John).

HOWARD (Nathan, *jr.*) Practice reports in the supreme court, and court of appeals of the state of New York. v. 31–33. 8°. *Albany, W. Gould & son*, 1866–67. (2 copies of v. 32–33).

HOWARD (Philip, *earl of Arundel*). Trial, before the lords, for high treason, April, 1589. fol. *London, T. Wright*, 1776.
[HARGRAVE'S state trials, v. 1].

——— The same. fol. *London, T. Wright*, 1781.
[HARGRAVE'S state trials, v. 11].

HOWARD (Thomas, 3*d duke of Norfolk*). Proceedings against him for treason. *See* **HOWARD** (Henry, *earl of Surrey*).

HOWARD (Thomas, 4*th duke of Norfolk*). Tryal of Thomas, duke of Norfolk, by his peers, for high treason against the queen, on the 16th day of January, 1571; for attempting to marry Mary, queen of Scots, without the consent and approbation of the said queen Elizabeth. 11 p. l. 150 pp. 8°. *London, J. Morphew*, 1709.

——— The same. fol. *London, T. Wright*, 1776.
[HARGRAVE'S state trials, v. 1].

——— [His] indictment for high treason, 1571. fol. *London, T. Wright*, 1778.
[HARGRAVE'S state trials, v. 8].

HOWARD (William, *viscount Stafford*). Speech on the scaffold, before his execution, Dec. 29, 1680. 1 p. l. 6 pp. fol. *London, W. Bailey*, 1680.
[TRIALS for treason, v. 5].

HOWARD (William, *viscount Stafford*). Tryal for high treason, Westminster hall, Nov. 30th–Dec. 7th, 1680. 1 p. l. 218 pp. fol. *London, assigns of J. Bills*, 1681.
[TRIALS for treason, v. 4].

——— The same.
[TRIALS for treason, v. 5].

——— The same. fol. *London, T. Wright*, 1776.
[HARGRAVE'S state trials, v. 3].

HOWISON (Robert R.) Reports of criminal trials in the circuit, state, and United States courts, held in Richmond, Virginia. 120 pp. 8°. *Richmond, West & brother*, 1851.

HUGGINS (John). Trial for the murder of Edward Arne, at the Old Bailey, May, 1729. fol. *London, T. Wright*, 1778.
[HARGRAVE'S state trials, v. 9].

HUGHES (*Dr.* John W.) Trial of... for the murder of Miss Tamzen Parsons; with a sketch of his life, as related by himself. A record of love, bigamy, and murder, unparalleled in the annals of crime. 58 pp. 8°. *Cleveland, Steller and Co.* 1866.

HUGHES (William). The practice of conveyancing. 2 v. vi, 482 pp; xii, pp. 483–1066. 12°. *London, John Crockford*, 1856–57.

——— The practice of sales of real property, with precedents of forms. 2d ed. enlarged. 2 v. xv, 564 pp; xx, 360, cclvi pp. 12°. *London, John Crockford*, 1849–50.

HUNT (Arthur Joseph). The law of boundaries and fences. xiv, 266 pp. 8°. *London, Butterworths*, 1866.

HUNTER (Robert, *M. D.*) *v.* **PALL MALL** gazette. *See* **PALL MALL** gazette.

HUNTINGTON (Samuel H.) Reports U. S. court of claims. *See* **NOTT** (Charles C.) *and* **HUNTINGTON.**

HURLY (Patrick). Trial, at the king's-bench in Ireland, for perjury, and [also] for conspiring with D. Hicky, etc. to cheat the popish inhabitants of the county of Clare, etc. May, 1701. fol. *London, T. Wright*, 1777.
[HARGRAVE'S state trials, v. 5].

HUSSON (Jean Christophe Armand). Traité de la législation des travaux publics et de la voirie en France. 2 v. xvi, 447 pp; viii, 549 pp. 8°. *Paris, L. Hachette*, 1841.

HYDE (Edward, 1*st earl of Clarendon*). Proceedings in parliament against [him], for high treason, etc. July, 1663. fol. *London, T. Wright*, 1776.
[HARGRAVE'S state trials, v. 2].

——— Vindication of himself against the articles of treason exhibited against him in parliament [1663]. fol. *London, T. Wright*, 1778.
[HARGRAVE'S state trials, v. 8].

ILLINOIS (*State of*). Reports. v. 33–38. By N. L. Freeman. 8°. *Chicago, Myers & Chandler*, 1866–67. (2 copies).

IMPARTIAL (The) lawyer; containing variety of matter. [*anon.*] 4 p. l. 255 pp. 12°. *London, J. Walthoe*, 1709.

INDERWICK (F. A.) The law of wills, as administered in the court of probate in England. xvi, 187 pp. 8°. *London, W. Maxwell*, 1866.

INDIANA (*State of*). Laws, at the called session, 1858, (2 copies;) 1861, (2 copies;) 1863, (3 copies;) 1865, (3 copies;) called session, 1865, (3 copies;) 1867, (3 copies.) 16 v. 8°. *Indianapolis, J. J. Bingham, etc.* 1858–67.

——— Indiana reports. v. 23 and 25. By B. Harrison. 8°. *Indianapolis, Douglass & Conner*, 1865–66. (2 copies of v. 25.)

IOWA (*State of*). Reports. v. 18–20. By T. F. Withrow. 8°. *Des Moines, by the reporter*, 1866. (3 copies.)

IRELAND (William), *and* **GROVE** (J.) The confessions and execution of the two jesuits, drawn, hang'd, and quartered at Tyburn, Jan. 24th. 1679, viz. W. Ireland and J. Grove. 1 p. l. 6 pp. sm. 4°. *London, R. G.* 1679.

——— *and others.* Tryals for conspiring to murder the king [Charles ii]; Old Baily, Dec. 1678. 2 p. l. 84 pp. fol. *London, R. Pawlet*, 1678.
[TRIALS for treason, v. 1].

——— The same.
[TRIALS for treason, v. 2].

——— The same. fol. *London, T. Wright*, 1776.
[HARGRAVE'S state trials, v. 2].

IRISH chancery reports. v. 12, and 14–17. 8°. *Dublin, Hodges, Smith & Co.* 1862–67.

IRISH common law reports. v. 12, and 14–17. 8°. *Dublin, Hodges, Smith & Co.* 1862–67.

IVY (*lady* Theodosia Bryan). Trial of the lady Ivy's claim to great part of Shadwell, in the county of Middlesex, June, 1684. Elam Mossam, plaintiff; *vs.* Theodosia Ivy, defendant. fol. *London, T. Wright*, 1778.
[HARGRAVE'S state trials, v. 7].

JACKSON (William), *and others.* Trials, at Chichester, Jan. 1749, for the murder of William Gally, and Daniel Chater. fol. *London, T. Wright*, 1778.
[HARGRAVE'S state trials, v. 9].

JAMES II (*king of Gt. Britain*). Writ of inquiry of damages between James, duke of York, and Titus Otes. *See* **OATES** (T.)

JAMES (Edwin). Bankrupt law of the United States, 1867. With notes, and a collection of American and English decisions upon the principles and practice of the law of bankruptcy. v, 325 pp. 8°. *New York, Harper & bros.* 1867.

JAMES (John). Trial, at the king's-bench, for high-treason, Nov. 1662. Wrote by his friends. fol. *London, T. Wright,* 1776.
[HARGRAVE'S state trials, v. 2].

JAMES (Thomas Henry). A handy book of the law of merchant shipping. Abridged from the large treatise by Maude and Pollock. xii, 142 pp. 12°. *London, Henry Sweet,* 1866.

JARVIS (*Mrs.* Sarah M.) *v.* **JARVIS** (*Rev.* Samuel Farmar). Report of the proceedings on the petition of Mrs. Sarah M. Jarvis, for a divorce from her husband, Rev. Samuel F. Jarvis, before a committee of the legislature of Connecticut. 2d ed. 116 pp. 8°. *Hartford, Review press,* 1839.

JEANNE d'Arc. *See* **JOAN** of Arc.

JEFFERYS (Elizabeth). Case for murder. *See* **SWAN** (J.) *and* **JEFFERYS.**

JENKES (Francis). Proceedings against [him], for a speech made by him on the hustings, at Guildhall, on midsummer-day, 1676. [Published by his friends]. fol. *London, T. Wright,* 1778.
[HARGRAVE'S state trials, v. 7].

JENKINS (Elisha), *v.* **VAN RENSSELAER** (Solomon). Report of the trials of the causes of Elisha Jenkins *v.* Solomon Van Rensselaer, *v.* John Tayler; the same, *v.* Charles D. Cooper, and the same, *v.* Francis Bloodgood. Before arbitrators, at Albany, August 16–18, 1808. 80 pp. 1 pl. 8°. *Albany, Croswell & Frary,* 1808.

JERVIS (*Sir* John). On the office and duties of coroners; with forms and precedents. By W. N. Welsby. 3d ed. By C. W. Lovesy. xx, 456 pp. 12° *London, H. Sweet, etc.* 1866.

JEVERLAND, (*Oldenburg*). Verzeichniss und summarischer inhalt der in den jeverschen wochenblättern von 1791–1813 bekannt gemachten landesherrlichen verordnungen und obrigkeitlichen verfügungen, [etc.] 144 pp. 8°. *Jever, C. L. Mettcker,* 1836. s.

JOAN of ARC, *or* **JEANNE DARC.** Procès de condamnation et de réhabilitation de Jeanne d'Arc. Par Jules Quicherat. 5 v. 8°. *Paris, J. Renouard, et Cie.* 1841–49.

JOHNSON (*Rev.* Samuel). The proceedings against [him], at the king's-bench, for high misdemeanours, [for] writing and publishing two scandalous libels against the government; June 21, 1686. fol. *London, T. Wright,* 1778.
[HARGRAVE'S state trials, v. 7].

JONES (Hamilton C.) Reports of cases in law in the supreme court of North Carolina. v. 7–8. 8°. *Salisbury, J. J. Bruner,* 1860–62.

JONES (*Sir* Thomas). Defence of judgment given [in the case of Jay *vs.* Topham]. *See* **PEMBERTON** (*Sir* Francis), *and* **JONES.**

JOURNAL du palais, 1865 and 1866. v. 76–77. 8°. *Paris, Bureaux de l'administration,* 1865–66.

JURIST (The). V. 12. Parts i and ii. 2 v. 8°. *London, H. Sweet,* 1867.

JUSTICE (Alexander). A general treatise of the dominion and laws of the sea. [With] discourses about the jurisdiction and manner of proceeding in the admiralty of England, both in criminal and civil matters, and adjudg'd cases concerning trade and navigation. 6 p. l. vi, 660, 40 pp. 4 l. 2 pl. sm. 4°. *London, S. & J. Sprint,* 1705.

JUSTINIANUS I. (Flavius Anicius, *Roman emperor*). Corpus juris civilis academicum parisiense, in quo Justiniani institutiones, digesta sive pandecta, codex, authenticæ seu novellæ constitutiones, et edicta comprehenduntur, etc. Opera et cura C. M. Gallisset. 7ª ed. 1268 pp. 4°. *Paris, A. Cotelle,* 1862.

——— Codex de tortis. 318 l. fol. *Uenetijs, Baptista de tortis,* [n. d.] s.
[Imperfect. Wanting l. 318].

——— Digestum uetus de tortis. 355 l. fol. *Uenetijs, Baptista de tortis,* 1498. s.

——— Infortiatum de tortis. 270 l. fol. *Uenetijs, Baptista de tortis,* 1497. s.

——— Instituta de tortis 198, 8 l. fol. *Uenetijs, Baptista de tortis,* 1498. s.
[Imperfect: wanting l. 1].

——— The same. Institutiones imperiales. 8 p. l. 139 l. sm. 4°. *Parisiis, Thielman Kerver,* 1511.

——— Novellarvm constitvtionvm, [etc.] qvae extant, et ut exstant volumen. Appositi sunt item canones sanctorũ apostolorũ per Clementem in unũ congesti, [Gr. Lat.] Gregorio Haloandro interprete. 12 p. l. 224, 266 pp. fol. *Norembergæ, Io. Petreius,* 1531. s.

——— Volvmen legvm parvvm qvod vocant, in qvo hæc insvnt, tres posteriores lib. cod. [etc.] græcæ leges, [etc.] authenticæ seu novellæ constitutiones eiusdem principis, [etc.] Omnia commentariis [Contii] illustrata. 1 p. l. 162, 144 l. fol. *Lvgdvni,* 1584. s.

——— The institutes of Justinian, with English introduction, translation, and notes. By Thomas Collett Sandars. 3d ed. vi, 606 pp. 8°. *London, Longmans, Green & Co.* 1865.

KEACH (Benjamin). Trial at Ailsbury for a libel, Oct. 1664. fol. *London, T. Wright,* 1776.

[HARGRAVE'S state trials, v. 2].

KEELE (William Conway). Provincial justice; or, magistrate's manual: being a complete digest of the criminal law of Canada, and a compendious and general view of the provincial law of Upper Canada. 2d ed. x, 652 pp. 8°. *Toronto, H. & W. Rowsell,* 1843.

KENDALL (Thomas), *and* **ROE** (Richard). Proceedings between the king and T. Kendall and R. Roe, in the king's bench, on an habeas corpus upon a commitment for high treason, Oct. 1695. fol. *London, T. Wright,* 1777.

[HARGRAVE'S state trials, v. 4].

KENMURE (William Gordon, *6th viscount*). *See* **GORDON**.

KENT (James). Commentaries on American law. 11th ed. Edited by George F. Comstock. 4 v. 8°. *Boston, Little, Brown & Co.* 1866.

——— On international law, revised, with notes and cases, brought down to the present time. Edited by J. T. Abdy. xxi, 484 pp. 8°. *Cambridge, Deighton, Bell & Co.* 1866. (2 copies).

KENTUCKY (*State of*). Code of practice in civil and criminal cases for the state of Kentucky. Prepared by M. C. Johnson, James Harlan, and J. W. Stevenson, commissioners, with all amendments made prior to Jan. 1, 1867. Edited by Harvey Myers. xii, 809 pp. 8°. *Cincinnati, R. Clarke & Co.* 1867. (2 copies).

——— A digest of the general law of Kentucky, Dec. 4, 1859, to 4th June, 1865, and session of 1865–66; with notes of the decisions of the court of appeals. By Harvey Myers. xvi, 796 pp. 8°. *Cincinnati, R. Clarke & Co.* 1866.

KERN (Charles). Tryal for being a Romish priest. fol. *London,* 1679.

[*With* BROMMICH (A.), *and* ATKINS (W.) Tryal. pp. 13–20. *London,* 1679].

——— The same. fol. *London, T. Wright,* 1776.

[HARGRAVE'S state trials, v. 2].

KERR (*Col.* Lewis). Trial. *See* **WORKMAN** (James), *and* **KERR**.

KERR (R. Malcolm). A digest of the law: how attainable. 31 pp. 8°. *London, Butterworths,* 1866.

KERR (William Williamson). A treatise on the law and practice of injunctions in equity. lvi, 710 pp. 8°. *London, Maxwell & son,* 1867.

KID (John), *and* **KING** (John). Spirit of popery, speaking out of the mouths of phanatical protestants; or, the last speeches of Mr. John Kid and Mr. John King, two presbyterian ministers, who were executed for high treason and rebellion, at Edinburgh, August 14th, 1679. 5 p. l. 73 pp. 3 l. fol. *London, W. Kittleby,* 1680.

KIDD (*Capt.* William), *and others.* Trial at the Old-Bailey for murder and piracy upon the high seas, May, 1701. fol. *London, T. Wright,* 1777.

[HARGRAVE'S state trials, v. 5].

KILMARNOCK (William Boyd, *4th earl of*). *See* **BOYD**.

KING (John). Last speech. *See* **KID** (John), *and* **KING**.

KINGSTON-UPON-HULL (Elizabeth Chudleigh, *duchess dowager of*). *See* **CHUDLEIGH**.

KINLOCH (Alexander), *and* **KINLOCH** (James). Proceedings, at Southwark, 1746, relating to their plea of being born in Scotland, and [that they] ought to be tried according to the laws of that kingdom, etc. fol. *London, T. Wright,* 1778.

[HARGRAVE'S state trials, v. 9].

KINNE (Asa). Questions and answers on law. 2d ed. 616 pp. 8°. *New York, Collins, Keese & Co.* 1840. s.

KINNERSLEY (Thomas). Trial for forgery. *See* **HALES** (William), *and* **KINNERSLEY**.

KIRKBY (*Col.* Richard), *and others.* Trials, at a court-martial in Jamaica, for offences against the articles of war, Oct. 1702. fol. *London, T. Wright,* 1777.

[HARGRAVE'S state trials, v. 5].

KNEVET (*Sir* Edmund). Trial, at Greenwich, for striking a person within the king's palace there, June, 1541. fol. *London, T. Wright,* 1781.

[HARGRAVE'S state trials, v. 11].

KNIGHTLEY (Alexander). Trial, at the king's-bench, for high treason, May, 1696. fol. *London, T. Wright,* 1777.

[HARGRAVE'S state trials, v. 4].

KNIGHTLY (*Sir* Richard), *and others.* Arraignment, in the star-chamber, for maintaining seditious persons, books, and libels, Feb. 1588. fol. *London, T. Wright,* 1778.

[HARGRAVE'S state trials, v. 7].

KNOLLYS *or* **KNOWLES** (Charles, *claiming to be earl of Banbury*). Proceedings against [him] for the murder of Philip Lawson, 1693. fol. *London, T. Wright,* 1778.

[HARGRAVE'S state trials, v. 8].

KNOX (Thomas), *and* **LANE** (John). Tryal and conviction, for a conspiracy, to defame and scandalize Dr. Oates and Mr. Bedloe; thereby to discredit their evidence about the horrid popish plot: king's-bench, Nov. 1679. 1 p. l. 68 pp. fol. *London, R. Pawlett,* 1680.
[TRIALS for treason, v. 3].

——— The same.
[TRIALS for treason, v. 4].

——— The same. fol. *London, T. Wright,* 1776.
[HARGRAVE'S state trials, v. 2].

LABATT (Henry J.) *and* **WALKER** (A.) Bankrupt law. *See* **UNITED STATES.**

LALOR (Robert, *priest*). The case of præmunire in Ireland, or [his] conviction and attainder, being indicted on the statute of the 16 R. ii. 1607. fol. *London, T. Wright,* 1781.
[HARGRAVE'S state trials, v. 11].

LAMÉ-FLEURY (Ernest Jules F.) De la législation minérale sous l'ancienne monarchie; ou, recueil méthodique et chronologique des lettres patentes, édits, ordonnances, déclarations, arrêts du conseil d'état du roi, du parlement, et de la cour des monnaies de Paris, etc. xvi, 224 pp. 8°. *Paris, A. Durand,* 1857.

LANE (John). Tryal for conspiracy. *See* **KNOX** (T.) *and* **LANE** (J.)

LANGHORN (Richard). Tryal for conspiring the death of the king, subversion of the government and protestant religion, Old Bayley, June, 1679. 68 pp. 1 l. fol. *London, H. Hills,* 1679.
[TRIALS for treason, v. 2].

——— The same. fol. *London, T. Wright,* 1776.
[HARGRAVE'S state trials, v. 2].

LASSIME (——). Traité de la contrainte par corps. 352 pp. 8°. *Paris, A. Durand,* 1863.

LASTARRIA (J. V.) Elementos de derecho publico constitucional teorico, positivo i politico. 3ª ed. xvii, 510 pp. 12°. *Gante, E. Vanderhaeghen,* 1865.

LATHAM (Francis Law). A treatise on the law of window lights. xvii, 254 pp. 12°. *London, Butterworths,* 1867.

LAUD (William, *archbishop of Canterbury*). Trial, for high treason, 1643. Wrote by himself. fol. *London, T. Wright,* 1776.
[HARGRAVE'S state trials, v. 1].

LAURENT (F.) Histoire du droit des gens et des relations internationales. 2ᵉ éd. corrigée. 12 v. 8°. *Bruxelles, A. Lacroix, Verboeckhoven et Cie.* 1863–66. (2 copies of v. 4–12).

LAW (The) relating to India and the East India company; with notes. 2d ed. viii, 758 pp. 4°. *London, W. H. Allen & Co.* 1841.

LAW journal; comprising reports of cases in the courts of chancery, king's bench, common pleas, exchequer of pleas, and exchequer chamber, and cases connected with the duties and office of magistrates, 1823–30. 9 v. 4°. *London, J. W. Paget and others,* 1823–31.

LAW journal reports. New series: comprising reports of cases in the house of lords, and in the courts of chancery and appeal in bankruptcy, probate, divorce and matrimonial causes, admiralty, queen's bench and the bail court, common pleas, exchequer, exchequer chamber, and crown cases reserved. Edited by Montague Chambers, Francis Towers Streeten, Freeman Oliver Haynes, and others. 35 v. in 92. 4°. *London, E. B. Ince and others,* 1832–66.

——— The same. An analytical digest of the cases published in the new series of the Law journal reports and other reports in the courts of common law and equity, and appeal in bankruptcy, in the house of lords, the privy council, in the court of probate, the court for divorce and matrimonial causes, and in the high court of admiralty. By F. T. Streeten and others. 8 v. 4°. *London, J. W. Paget and others,* 1831–63.

LAW list for 1867, by W. W. Dalbiac. 12°. *London, Stevens & sons,* 1867.

LAW magazine, August, 1866, to August, 1867. v. 22–23. 8°. *London, Butterworths,* 1867.

LAW reports. Chancery appeal cases, including bankruptcy and lunacy cases, before the lord chancellor and the court of appeal in chancery, 1865–67. Edited by G. W. Hemming. v. 1–2. 8°. *London, for the council of law reporting,* 1866–67. (2 copies).

——— Court of common pleas, 1865–67. Reported by John Scott and Henry Bompas. Edited by James Redfoord Bulwer. v. 1–2. 8°. *London,* 1866–67. (2 copies).

——— Court of exchequer, 1865–67. Reported by James Anstie and Arthur Charles. Edited by James Redfoord Bulwer. v. 1–2. 8°. *London,* 1866–67. (2 copies).

——— Court of queen's bench, 1865–67. Reported by William Mills and Henry Holroyd, and in the bail court by E. A. C. Schalch. Edited by James Redfoord Bulwer. v. 1–2. 8°. *London,* 1866–67. (2 copies).

——— English and Irish appeal cases and claims of peerage before the house of lords, 1866–67. Reported by Charles Clark. v. 1–2. 8°. *London,* 1866–67. (2 copies).

LAW reports. Equity cases before the master of the rolls and the vice-chancellors, 1865–67. Edited by G. W. Hemming. v. 1–4. 8°. *London*, 1866–67. (2 copies).

——— High court of admiralty and ecclesiastical courts, 1865–67. Reported by Ernst Browning. Edited by James Redfoord Bulwer. v. 1. 8°. *London*, 1867. (2 copies).

——— Privy council appeals. Cases heard and determined in the judicial committee and the lords of her majesty's most honourable privy council, 1865–67. Reported by Edmund F. Moore. v. 1. 8°. *London*, 1867. (2 copies).

——— Public general statutes, with a list of the local and private acts, 1866–67. v. 1–2. 8°. *London*, 1866–67. (2 copies).

LAW times and journal of property, from April, 1843, to March, 1851. 16 v. fol. *London, Law times office*, 1843–51.

——— The same. The journal and record of the law and the lawyers, from April, 1851, to November, 1866. v. 18–41. fol. *London*, 1851–64.

[v. 17 wanting].

LAW times reports, containing all the cases argued and determined in the house of lords, the privy council, the court of appeals in chancery, the rolls court, v. c. Kindersley's court, v. c. Stuart's court, v. c. Wood's court, the court of queen's bench, the court of common bench, the court of exchequer, the bail court, the exchequer chamber, the court of criminal appeal, the probate court, the court for divorce and matrimonial causes, the admiralty court, the bankruptcy courts, at nisi prius, maritime law cases. Together with a selection of cases of universal application, decided in the superior courts in Ireland and in Scotland. New series. March, 1860, to March, 1866. v. 2–13. 8°. *London*, 1860–66.

LAW (Stephen D.) Copyright and patent laws of the United States, 1790 to 1868, with notes of judicial decisions thereunder. 2d ed. 264 pp. 12°. *New York, Baker, Voorhis & Co.* 1867.

LAWRENCE (William Beach), *v.* **DANA** (Richard H. *jr.*) Circuit court of the United States, district of Massachusetts, ss. Bill in equity. Complainant's affidavits. B. R. Curtis and J. J. Storrow for complainant. 98, 6 pp. 8°. *Boston, Mudge & son*, 1866. (2 copies).

LAYER (Christopher). Trial at the king's bench for high treason, Nov. 1722. fol. *London, T. Wright*, 1777.

[HARGRAVE'S state trials, v. 6].

LEACH (Dryden). Proceedings in an action of false imprisonment, 1765. *See* **MONEY** (John), *and others*.

LEAKE (Stephen Martin). The elements of the law of contracts. lvi, 697 pp. 8°. *London, Stevens & sons*, 1867.

LE CARON (P. L.) Code des émigrès, ou recueil des dispositions législatives, concernant les impositions, le séquestre, la confiscation, la régle et la vente des biens des anciens propriétaires appelés à recueillir l'indemnité, de 1789 à 1825. 1 p. l. 438 pp. 8°. *Paris, Bossange*, 1825.

LECERF (Pierre Louis). Tableau général et raisonné de la législation française, [etc.] pour servir de préparation à l'étude du droit, [etc.] 4 p. l. viii, 476 pp. 8°. *Paris, G. Thorel*, 1841. s.

LEE (*Capt.* Thomas). Arraignment and judgment, at [London], Feb. 1600, for high treason. fol. *London, T. Wright*, 1778.

[HARGRAVE'S state trials, v. 7].

LEECH (Benjamin). Proceedings against [him] at the Old-Bailey, Oct. 1682, for a contempt, in offering a frivolous plea to the court. fol. *London, T. Wright*, 1779.

[HARGRAVE'S state trials, v. 10].

LE GENTIL (Charles). Origines du droit. Essai historique sur les preuves, sous les législations juive, égyptienne, indienne, grecque et romaine, avec quelques notes touchant les lois barbares et le vieux droit français. xv, 420 pp. 4°. *Paris, A. Durand*, 1863.

LEGISLACION de la propiedad literaria. [*anon.*] 270 pp. 8°. *Madrid, Moya y Plaza*, 1863.

LEICESTER (*Eng.*) *county of.* Rules and orders of the court of general quarter sessions of the peace for the county of Leicester. vii. 80 pp. 8°. *Leicester, J. Brown*, 1808.

LEIGHTON (Alexander, *D. D.*) Proceedings in the star chamber against [him] for a libel, June, 1630. fol. *London, T. Wright*, 1781.

[HARGRAVE'S state trials. v. 11].

LÉVÊQUE (B. A.) Vérification des écritures. 136 pp. 8°. *Agen, P. Noubel*, 1840.

LEWIS (David). Trial at Monmouth, for high treason, March, 1679. Wrote by himself. fol. *London, T. Wright*, 1776.

(HARGRAVE'S state trials, v. 2].

LEWIS (Hubert). Principles of equity drafting; with an appendix of forms. xi, 378 pp. 12°. *London, Butterworths*, 1865.

LEX ROMANA Visigothorum. Ad lxxvi librorum manu scriptorum fidem recognovit, septem eius antiquis epitomis, quæ præter duas adhuc ineditæ sunt, titulorum explanatione auxit, annotatione, appendicibus, prolegomenis instruxit Gustavus Haenel. cx, 468 pp. 2 pl. 4°. *Lipsiæ, B. G. Teubner,* 1848.

LEY (The) hipotecaria of Spain; or, law on the inscription of titles to immovable property, deeds and preventive annotations affecting the same; decrees respecting legal incapacity; absent parties, etc. and also provisions for giving effect in Spain to deeds executed in foreign countries, and to the judgments of foreign courts; with a glossary of Spanish terms therein used. Translated and edited by William Grain. ix, 150 pp. 8°. *London, H. Sweet,* 1867.

LIBER placitandi. A book of special pleading; containing precedents. 1 p. l. 460 pp. 14 l. fol. *London, Place & Basset,* 1674.

[NOTE. Sometimes cited as Thompson's entries].

LILBURNE (*Col.* John). Trial at the Guildhall of London, for high treason, Oct. 1649. [With] the examination of [his] jury, 1653. fol. *London, T. Wright,* 1776.

[HARGRAVE'S state trials, v. 2].

——— Trial in the Old Bailey, July, 1653, for returning into England, being banished by act of parliament. [Written (the chief part) by himself]. fol. *London, T. Wright,* 1778.

[HARGRAVE'S state trials, v. 7].

——— *and* **WHARTON** (John). Trial for printing and publishing seditious books. In the star chamber, Feb. 1637. fol. *London, T. Wright,* 1778.

[HARGRAVE'S state trials, v. 7].

LINCOLN (William Wake, *bishop of*). *See* **WAKE**.

LINDSAY (David). Trial at the Old Bailey, for high treason, April, 1704. fol. *London, T. Wright,* 1777.

[HARGRAVE'S state trials, v. 5].

LIPENIUS *or* **LIPEN** (Martin). Bibliotheca realis ivridica post Friderici Gottlieb Strvvii et Gottlob Avgvsti Jenichenii cvras emendata, mvltis accessionibvs avcta et locvpletata. 2 v. in 1. x, 860 pp; 476, 351 pp. fol. *Lipsiæ, J. Wendlervs,* 1757.

——— The same. Svpplementa ac emendationes. Collegit et digessit Avgvstvs Fridericvs Schott. [v. 1.] fol. *Lipsiæ,* 1775.

——— The same. Svpplementorvm ac emendationvm [libri]. Collegit et digessit Renatvs Carolus de Senkenberg. v. 2. fol. *Lipsiæ,* 1789.

——— The same. Auctore Lvd. God. Madihn. v. 3. fol. *Vratislaviæ,* 1816.

[Incomplete; v. 4 wanting].

LISLE (*lady* Alice). Trial, at Winton, for high treason, Aug. 1685. fol. *London, T. Wright,* 1777.

[HARGRAVE'S state trials, v. 4].

LITHUANIA. Zbior praw litewskich, 1389–1529. Tudziez' rozprawy sejmowe o tychze prawach, 1544–1563. 2 p. l. iv, 542 pp. 12 pl. 4°. *Poznan, Garbarach,* 1841. s.

LIVES, behaviour, and dying words of the most remarkable criminals who have been executed for the highway, street-robberies, piracy, rapes, murder, etc. [*anon.*] v. 2. 12°. *London, J. Osborn,* 1740.

LLANDAFF (Richard Watson, *bishop of*). *See* **WATSON**.

LLOYD (William, *bishop of Worcester*), *and* **LLOYD** (———, *his son*). The evidence given at the bar of the house of commons, upon the complaint of Sir John Pakington against [them. With] the proceedings of the house thereupon, 1702. fol. *London, T. Wright,* 1778.

[HARGRAVE'S state trials, v. 8].

LOGAN (Robert). Process and trial, for high treason, in conspiring with John [Ruthven], earl of Gowrie, to murder king James i, June, 1609. fol. *London, T. Wright,* 1778.

[HARGRAVE'S state trials, v. 7].

LOIR (J. N.) De l'état civil des nouveaux-nés, au point de vue de l'histoire, de l'hygiène et de la loi. Présentation de l'enfant sans déplacement. xv, 462 pp. 1 pl. 8°. *Paris, A. Durand,* 1865.

LONDON. The laws and customs, rights, liberties, and privileges of the city of London. xix, xii, 315 pp. 8°. *London, R. Witby,* 1765.

——— Proceedings between the king and the city of London, on an information in nature of a quo warranto, in the king's bench, 1683. fol. *London, T. Wright,* 1776.

[HARGRAVE'S state trials, v. 3].

LONDON (Henry Compton, *bishop of*). *See* **COMPTON.**

LONG (*Rev.* William), *v.* **GRAY**, (*Rt. Rev.* Robert, *bishop of Capetown*). The case of, embracing the opinions of the judges of the colonial court, hitherto unpublished, together with the decision of the privy council, and preliminary observations by the editor. 166 pp. 8°. *London, Butterworths,* 1866.

LOUIS XVI. Proceedings of the French national convention on the trial of Louis xvi, king of France and Navarre; to which are added several interesting occurrences and particulars attending the treatment, sentence, and execution of the ill-fated monarch. By Joseph Trapp. xii, 214 pp. 8°. *London, Murray & Co.* 1793.

LOUISIANA (*State of*). Laws, 1864 to 1867. 4 v. 8°. *New Orleans*, 1865–67.

——— Louisiana annual reports, 1860. v. 15. By A. N. Ogden. 8°. *New Orleans, Office of the Price Current*, 1861. (2 copies).

——— The same. v. 17–18, (1865—1866.) By S. F. Glenn. 8°. *New Orleans, Bloomfield & Steel*, 1866–67. (2 copies of v. 18.)

LOVAT (Simon Fraser, *13th baron Fraser of*). *See* **FRASER.**

LOVE (Christopher). Trial, before the high court of justice, for high treason, June, 1651. fol. *London, T. Wright*, 1776.
[HARGRAVE'S state trials, v. 2].

LOWELL, (*Mass.*) Charter and ordinances, etc. iv, 141 pp. 8°. *Lowell, J. Taylor*, 1846.

LOWICK (Robert). Trial, for high treason, April, 1696. fol. *London, T. Wright*, 1777.
[HARGRAVE'S state trials, v. 4].

LOWNDES (Richard). The admiralty law of collisions at sea. xx, 234 pp. 8°. *London, Stevens & sons*, 1867. (3 copies).

LUDLOW (Henry). *See* **BATTEN** (E. C.)

LUDWELL (Wilhelm). Synopsis juris feudalis. Ed. 3a. xiv, 423 pp. 19 l. 12°. *Altdorfi Noricorum, H. Meyer*, 1696.

LUSHINGTON (Godfrey). A manual of naval prize law. xviii, 130 pp. 8°. *London, Butterworths*, 1866. (4 copies).

MACAREL (Louis Antoine). Cours de droit administratif professé à la faculté de droit de Paris, (1842–43). 3 v. 8°. *Paris, G. Thorel*, 1844–46.
[Wanting v. 4].

CONTENTS.

v. 1, 2. Organisation et attributions des autorités administratives. vii, 679 pp; 956 pp.
v. 3. Principes généraux des matières administratives. vii, 488 pp.

——— Élémens de jurisprudence administrative; extraits des décisions rendues, par le conseil d'état, en matière contentieuse. Édition augmentée de la législation belge. xi, 347 pp. 8°. *Bruxelles, A. Wahlen et Cie.* 1837. S.

——— Législation et jurisprudence des ateliers dangereux, insalubres et incommodes. lxviii, 306 pp. 18°. *Paris, Roret*, 1828. S.

——— Des tribunaux administratifs, ou introduction à l'Étude de la jurisprudence administrative, [etc.] xii, 581 pp. 8°. *Paris, J. P. Roret*, 1828. S.

McCARTER (Thomas N.) Reports of cases in the court of chancery, the prerogative court, and the court of errors and appeals of New Jersey. v. 2. 8°. *Trenton, Hough & Gillespy*, 1867. (2 copies).

MACCLESFIELD (Thomas Parker, *1st earl of*). *See* **PARKER.**

McDANIEL (Stephen), *and others*. Trial, at the Old Bailey, for being accessaries before a felony committed by P. Kelly and J. Ellis, in the county of Kent. fol. *London, T. Wright*, 1779.
[HARGRAVE'S state trials, v. 10].

MACDONALD (Æneas *alias* Angus). Proceedings against [him], at Southwark, Dec. 1747, [for treason], and at the king's bench [for treason]. fol. *London, T. Wright*, 1778.
[HARGRAVE'S state trials, v. 9].

MAC GROWTHER (Alexander). Trial, at [Southwark], July, 1746, for high treason. fol. *London, T. Wright*, 1778.
[HARGRAVE'S state trials, v. 9].

MACGUIRE. *See* **MAGUIRE.**

MACKAY (*Sir* Donald, *1st baron Reay*). Proceedings on an appeal of high treason, 1631. *See* **RAMSEY** (David).

MACKENZIE (George, *3d earl of Cromartie*). [His] case, as printed in 1746. fol. *London, T. Wright*, 1779.
[HARGRAVE'S state trials, v. 10].

——— Indictment for high treason. *See* **BOYD** (William, *4th earl of Kilmarnock*), *and others.*

MACPHERSON (William). Procedure of the civil courts of the East India company in the presidency of Fort William, in regular suits. 523, lvii pp. 8°. *Calcutta, Lepage & Co.* 1850.

MACRORY (Edmund). Reports of cases relating to letters patent for inventions; decided in the courts of law and equity, and before the judicial committee of the privy council; with notes of application for amendments, leave to enter disclaimers, etc. 1852–54. Parts 1 and 2. ii, 256 pp. 2 pl. 8°. *London, Benning and Co.* 1855.

MADRE (*Madame de* ——). Formulaire pour contrats de mariage. 4e éd. revue et augmentée. xxiv, 112 pp. 4°. *Paris, Cosse et Marchal*, 1867.

——— Formulaire pour inventaires. 2e éd. viii, 96 pp. 4°. *Paris, Cosse et Marchal*, 1861.

MAFFA (Sebastiano). Commentaria in l. Si is qvi pro emptore; De vsvcapionibvs. Vna cvm paradoxis et argumentis doctissimi uiri D. Thomae Simeontii. 20 l. 191 l. 18°. *Venetiis, Marcus Amadorus*, 1572.

MAGDALEN college (*Oxford*). Proceedings against St. Mary Magdalen college in Oxon. for not electing Anthony Farmer president of the said college, June, 1687. fol. *London, T. Wright*, 1777.
[HARGRAVE'S state trials, v. 4].

MAGER von SCHOENBERG (Martin). De advocatia armata, siue clientelari patronorvm jvre et potestate, clientvmqve officio. 21 p. l. 826 pp. 56 l. fol. *Francofvrti, E. Emmelius,* 1626.

MAGUIRE (Connor, *baron Maguire*). Trial at the king's bench for high treason, in being concerned in the Irish massacre, Feb. 1644. fol. *London, T. Wright,* 1776.
[HARGRAVE's state trials, v. 1].

MAI (Angelo, *cardinal*). Vaticana juris romani fragmenta, Romæ nuper detecta et edita. xiv, 92 pp. 8°. *Paris, Fanjat,* 1823.

MAILLART (Adrien). Coutumes générales d'Artois, avec des notes. 8 p. l. 1016 pp. 4°. *Paris, N. Gosselin,* 1704.

MAINE (*State of*). Laws, 1866, 1867. 2 v. 8°. *Augusta,* 1866–67.

——— Maine reports. v. 52–53. By W. Wirt Virgin. 8°. *Hallowell, Masters, Smith & Co.* 1866–67. (3 copies).

MAISONNEUVE (T. Richard). Exposé de droit pénal et d'instruction criminelle. 2e éd. xi, 330 pp. 8°. *Paris, A. Durand,* 1865.

MAITLAND (Charles). The proceedings before the lords of the articles, etc. against [him] for perjury, in having given a false testimony at the trial of James Mitchel, [Edinburgh, 1681]. fol. *London, T. Wright,* 1778.
[HARGRAVE's state trials, v. 8].

MALLEIN (Jules). Considérations sur l'enseignement du droit administratif. xi, 417 pp. 8°. *Paris, H. Plon,* 1857.

——— Faut-il codifier les lois administratives? Examen de cette question. 54 pp. 8°. *Grenoble, Maisonville et fils, et Jourdan,* 1860.

MALLET (*Sir* John). Concerning penal laws; a discourse, or charge at sessions in Bridgewater, July, 1680. 20 pp. fol. *London, T. Cockeril,* 1680.
[TRIALS for treason, v. 5].

MALLORY (John). Quare impedit; in two parts. Part 1, containing an abridgement of the law concerning the patronages of the churches, etc. Part 2, containing precedents of pleadings. ix, 253 pp. 19 l. 150 pp. 8 l. fol. *London, Nutt & Gosling,* 1737.

MARIE (*sister, Benedictine nun*). Note pour la soeur Marie, remise a M. le procureur du roi et au tribunal [etc.] à la suite d'une communication officieuse d'une consultation en faveur de ses adversaires, [etc.] 8 pp. 8°. *Bayeux, Durant,* 1847. s.

——— Observations pour la soeur Marie sur les observations de ses adversaires. 17 pp. 8°. *Caen, B. de Laporte,* 1847. s.
[*With* the preceding].

——— Soeur sainte Marie, bénédictine. Récits, par elle-même, [etc.] 426 pp. 8°. *Caen, B. de Laporte,* 1846. s.
[*With* the preceding].

MARIE-ANTOINETTE. Procès de Marie-Antoinette ci-devant reine des Français; ou, recueil exact de tous ses interrogatoires, réponses, dépositions des témoins. 136 pp. 12°. *Paris, Alcan-Lévy,* 1865.

MARKHAM (*Sir* Griffin, *or* Griffith), *and others.* Trial for high treason, at Winchester, Nov. 1603. fol. *London, T. Wright,* 1778.
[HARGRAVE's state trials, v. 7].

MARRIOTT (W. T.) Clerical disabilities: a short account of the law upon the subject, and some remarks thereon. 31 pp. 8°. *London, Longmans,* 1865.

MARSHALL (Samuel). A treatise on the law of insurance. 2d ed. 2 v. xxviii, 484 pp; 912 pp. 8°. *London, J. Butterworth,* 1808.

MARTIN (François Xavier). A collection of the private acts of the general assembly of North Carolina. 3 p. l. 249 pp. 2 l. 4°. *Newbern, F. X. Martin,* 1794.

——— A collection of the statutes of the parliament of England, in force in North Carolina. xxvi, 426 pp. 4°. *Newbern, editor,* 1792.

MARY (*queen of Scots*). Proceedings against [her], at Fotheringay-castle, Oct. 1586, for being concerned in a conspiracy against queen Elizabeth. fol. *London, T. Wright,* 1776.
[HARGRAVE's state trials, v. 1].

MARYLAND (*Province of*). Laws, 1727 to 1731. 1 p. l. 176 pp. fol. *Annapolis, M. Parks,* 1727–31.
[Imperfect].

——— (*State of*). Laws, 1777–79. 4 v. in 1. fol. *Annapolis, F. Green,* [1777–79].
[*With* MARYLAND. Votes and proceedings of the senate, 1777].

——— The same. 1785–89. [With Ms. index of the laws from 1785–96]. 5 v. in 1. 51 pp. Ms. fol. *Annapolis, F. Green,* [1786–90].

——— Laws, 1867. 8°. *Annapolis,* 1867. (2 copies.)

——— Digest of the decisions construing the statutes of Maryland, of which the code of public general laws is composed, with specification of the acts of assembly. By Lewis Mayer. vii, 728 pp. 8°. *Baltimore, Murphy & Co.* 1866.

——— Supplement to the Maryland code, containing the acts of 1864 and 1865. v. 2–3. By Lewis Mayer. 8°. *Baltimore, Murphy & Co.* 1865.

MARYLAND reports. v. 21. By Nicholas Brewer. 8°. *Annapolis*, 1866–67. (2 copies).

MASSACHUSETTS (*Colony of*). [The generall laws of the colony. With] supplemental laws, 1672, 1674, and 1675. 170 pp. 14 l. 40 pp. fol. [*Cambridge, S. Green*, 1672].

[Imperfect; wants title-page, and pp. 1–4.

——— The same. Acts and laws, [1692–1700. With] the charter granted by William [iii]. 2 v. in 1. 1 p. l. 15 pp. 1 l; 192 pp. 2 l. fol. *Boston, B. Green & J. Allen*, 1699–1700.

——— The same. [1692–1705]. 15 pp. 1 l. 289 pp. 2 l. fol. *Boston, B. Green & J. Allen*, 1699–1705.

[Imperfect; wants title-page, and pp. 1–5 of charter].

——— The same. [1692–1719]. 3 p. l. 326 pp. fol. [*Boston, B. Green*, 1714–19].

[Imperfect. title-page, and pp. 1–4, 17–20 wanting; pp. 240–1, 325–6 imperfect].

——— The same. [1692–May, 1735. With] charter of William iii and George i. 1 pl. 14, 17 pp. 1 l. 549 pp. fol. *Boston, B. Green & J. Draper*, 1726–35.

——— The same. [1692–March, 1736. With Ms. notes of law cases]. 1 p. l. 14, 16 pp. 1 l. 560 pp. 39 pp. Ms. fol. *Boston, B. Green & J. Draper*, 1726–36.

[Imperfect. p. 17 of table wanting; pp. 359–60 imperfect].

——— The same. [1692–1738]. 1 p. l. 14, 17 pp. 1 l. 684 pp. fol. *Boston, B. Green & J. Draper*, 1726–39.

——— The same. [1692–1747. With] the charter. 14, 28 pp; 1 l. 380 pp. fol. *Boston, S. Kneeland & T. Green*, 1742–47.

[Wants title-page of charter].

——— The same. Temporary acts and laws, [1736–50]. 1 p. l. 3, 315 pp. fol. *Boston, S. Kneeland & T. Green*, 1742–50.

——— The same. 1692–March, 1761. With the charter. 1 p. l. 14, 24 pp. 1 l. 403 pp. fol. *Boston, S. Kneeland*, 1759–61.

——— The same. [1692–May, 1761]. 1 p. l. 14, 24 pp. 1 l. 409 pp. fol. *Boston, S. Kneeland*, 1759–61.

——— The same. [1692–1765]. 1 p. l. 14, 24 pp. 1 l. 497 pp. fol. *Boston, S. Kneeland and R. & S. Draper*, 1759–65.

[Imperfect: pp. 427–32, 459–62 wanting; pp. 1–2 of charter, and title-page, and pp. 1–2, 123–4, 351–2, 359–60, 397–8, 411–12, 415–16, 419–20, 433–8, 441–2, 445–6, 451–2, 457–8, 463–4, 480–1, 491–2, imperfect].

——— The same. Temporary acts and laws. 1 p. l. x, viii, 190 pp. fol. *Boston, Green & Russell*, 1763.

——— (*State of*). Resolves of the general court. [With] the governor's messages. 1796–1800. 5 v. in 1. fol. *Boston, Young & Minns*, 1796–1800.

[Imperfect: all after p. 68 in Resolves of 1800 wanting].

——— The same. 1810–12. 409 pp. 2 l. 8°. *Boston, Adams, Rhoades & Co.* 1810–12.

——— The same. Resolves respecting the sale of eastern lands, with the reports of the committees appointed to sell said lands, 1781–1803. 287 pp. 8°. *Boston, Young & Minns*, 1803.

MATA (Pedro). Tratado de medicina y cirurgia legal, teorica y practica, seguido de un compendio de toxicologia. 4ª ed. 3 v. 8°. *Madrid, Carlos Bailly-Baillière*, 1866–67.

MATTHEWS (John). Trial, for high treason, for printing a libel, entitled Ex ore tuo te judico; Vox populi vox Dei; at the Old-Bailey, Oct. 1719. fol. *London, T. Wright*, 1778.

[HARGRAVE'S state trials, v. 9].

MAUGER (N. J. B.) L'officier de l'état civil; ouvrage contenant un traité complet des actes de l'état civil. 234 pp. 8°. *Saintes, Fontanier*, 1865.

MAYER (Lewis). Maryland digest. *See* **MARYLAND**.

MEAD (William). Trial, for a tumultuous assemblage. *See* **PENN** (William), *and* **MEAD**.

MEIER (Moritz Hermann Eduard), *and* **SCHÖMANN** (Georg Friedrich). Der attische process; vier bücher. xxii, 794 pp. 8°. *Halle, Gebauer*, 1825. s.

MELLISH (Mary), *v.* **RANKIN** (Eliza). The whole proceedings on the trial of an ejectment, between John Doe on the several demises of Mary Mellish and others, against Eliza Rankin, in the court of common pleas, 10th and 11th May, 1786. By Joseph Gurney. 259 pp. 8°. *London, J. Debrett*, 1786.

MESSENGER (Peter), *and others*. Trials, at the Old-Bailey, for high treason, in tumultuously assembling themselves in Moorfields and other places, under color of pulling down bawdy-houses, April, 1668. fol. *London, T. Wright*, 1776.

[HARGRAVE'S state trials, v. 2].

MICHAEL (W. H.) The sanitary acts, comprising the sewage utilization act, 1865, and the sanitary act, 1866, and various sections of other acts incorporated therewith. xii, 132 pp. 12°. *London, H. Sweet*, 1867.

MICHAUD (J.) Le droit d'asile en Europe et en Angleterre. 48 pp. 8°. *Paris, Amyot*, 1858.

MICHAUX (Alexandre). Traité pratique des testaments notariés, olographes, mystiques et autres, et des actes qui en sont la conséquence. vi, 558 pp. 8°. *Paris, Cosse, Marchal et Cie.* 1865.

MICHELET (Jules). Procès des templiers. 2 v. viii, 681 pp; viii, 540 pp. 4°. *Paris, Imprimerie royale,* 1841.

[DOCUMENTS inédits sur l'histoire de France].

MICHIGAN (*State of*). Laws, 1867. 8°. *Lansing,* 1867. (2 copies.)

——— Michigan reports. v. 14. By W. Jennison. 8°. *Detroit, Throop & Co.* 1867. (2 copies).

MILAN. Atti del municipio di Milano, 1859–1865. 7 v. 8°. *Milano, L. de Giacomo Pirola,* 1859–65. S.

MILLIGAN (Lambdin P. *ex parte*). Decision of the U. S. supreme court on military commissions, delivered at December term, 1866. 23 pp. 8°. *Washington,* 1867.

MINGHETTI (——). De l'organisation administrative du royaume d'Italie. Traduction et préface d'Alexandre Mickiewicz. Avec introduction d'Armand Lévy. xx, 212 pp. 8°. *Paris, E. Dentu,* 1862.

MINNESOTA (*State of*). Reports. v. 10. By W. A. Spencer. 8°. *Chicago, Myers & Chandler,* 1866.

MISSISSIPPI (*State of*). Laws, called session, Oct. 1866, and January, 1867. 8°. *Jackson,* 1867. (2 copies).

——— Mississippi reports. v. 39. By James Z. George. 8°. *Philadelphia, Johnson & Co.* 1867. (2 copies).

——— The same. v. 40. By R. O. Reynolds. 8°. *New York,* 1867.

MISSOURI (*State of*). Laws, 1860–61, 1862–63, 1863–64, 1864–65, 1865–66, and 1867. 6 v. 8°. *Jefferson City,* 1861–67. (2 copies).

——— General statutes of the state of Missouri; revised by a committee appointed by the 23d general assembly, under a joint resolution of February 20, 1865, amended by the legislature, and passed March 20, 1866. A. F. Denny, commissioner appointed by the governor. xvi, 1012 pp. 8°. *City of Jefferson,* 1866. (2 copies).

——— Missouri reports. 1860–62. v. 31. 8°. *St. Louis,* 1862.

——— The same, 1862 to 1866. v. 32–39. By C. C. Whittelsey. 8°. *St. Louis, Knapp & Co.* 1863–66. (2 copies.)

MITCHEL (James). Trial, in Scotland, for attempting the murder of James Sharp, archbishop of St. Andrews, and wounding the bishop of Orkney [Murdoch Mackenzie], Jan. 1678. fol. *London, T. Wright,* 1776.

[HARGRAVE'S state trials, v. 2].

MODERS *alias* **STEDMAN** (Mary). Trial, at the Old Baily, for bigamy, June, 1663. fol. *London, T. Wright,* 1776.

[HARGRAVE'S state trials, v. 2].

MOHUN (Charles, *5th baron Mohun*). Trial, at Westminster, for the murder of William Mountford, Jan. 1692. fol. *London, T. Wright,*

[HARGRAVE'S state trials, v. 4].

——— Trial, before the house of lords, for the murder of Richard Coote, March, 1699. fol. *London, T. Wright,* 1777.

[HARGRAVE'S state trials, v. 5].

MOLITOR (J. B.) Les obligations en droit romain, avec l'indication des rapports entre la législation romaine et le droit français. 2e éd. revue et corrigée. 2 v. viii, 730 pp; 696 pp. 8°. *Paris, A. Durand,* 1866–67.

MOLLOY (Neale). Trial of, and of Vere Molloy, his wife, at a commission of oyer and terminer, for the city of Dublin, 10th December, 1762. 59 pp. 8°. *Dublin, B. Grierson,* 1763.

MONEY (John), *and others.* Proceedings on error in an action of false imprisonment by Dryden Leach, against John Money, [and others], kings messengers, [at the] king's bench, 1765. fol. *London, T. Wright,* 1781.

[HARGRAVE'S state trials, v. 11].

MONSON (*Sir* Thomas). Arraignment at the Guildhall, London, for the murder of Sir Thomas Overbury, Dec. 1615. fol. *London, T. Wright,* 1776.

[HARGRAVE'S state trials, v. 1].

MOORE (Edmund F.) Cases in the privy council on appeal from the East Indies, 1863–66. v. 10. 8°. *London, Stevens & sons,* 1867.

——— Reports of cases in the judicial committee and the lords of the privy council. New series. v. 3. 8°. *London, Stevens & sons,* 1867.

MOORE (Henry). Case on a mandamus admitting the plaintiff to be a freeman of the town of Hastings. *See* **HASTINGS** (*county of Sussex, England*).

MORDAUNT (John, *1st viscount Mordaunt of Avalon*). Trial before the high court of justice for high treason, June, 1658. fol. *London, T. Wright,* 1776.

[HARGRAVE'S state trials, v. 2].

MORDAUNT (Mary Howard, *duchess of Norfolk, called lady*). Proceedings before the house of lords, 1691, between [Henry Howard the 7th] duke and the duchess of Norfolk, upon the duke's bill, intituled an act to dissolve the marriage, etc. fol. *London, T. Wright,* 1778.
[HARGRAVE'S state trials, v. 8].

——— The proceedings in parliament upon the bill of divorce between [Henry Howard, 7th] duke of Norfolk, and the lady Mary Mordant, Feb. and March, 1699. fol. *London, T. Wright,* 1777.
[HARGRAVE'S state trials, v. 5].

MORE (*Sir* Thomas, *lord chancellor of England*). Trial for high treason, in denying the king's supremacy, May, 1535. fol. *London, T. Wright,* 1776.
[HARGRAVE'S state trials, v. 1].

MORGAN (David). Trial for high treason, Southwark, July, 1746. fol. *London, T. Wright,* 1778.
[HARGRAVE'S state trials, v. 9].

MORILLOT (Léon). De la condition des enfants nés hors mariage en Europe et specialement en France, dans l'antiquité, du moyen âge, et de nos jours. 491 pp. 8°. *Paris, A. Durand,* 1865.

MORLEY (Thomas Parker, *6th baron*). *See* **PARKER**.

MORRIS (*Col.* John). Trial, at York, Aug. 1649, for high treason. fol. *London, T. Wright,* 1778.
[HARGRAVE'S state trials, v. 7].

MORRIS *alias* **POYNTZ** (John), *and others.* Two judgments of the lords assembled in parliament, in 1647, against [them], for forging, framing, and publishing a copy of a pretended act of parliament. fol. *London, T. Wright,* 1778.
[HARGRAVE'S state trials, v. 7].

MOSSAM (Elam). Trial of lady Ivy's claim to great part of Shadwell parish. *See* **IVY** (*lady* Theodosia).

MOSTYN (*Lieut. Gen.* John). Proceedings in an action by Anthony Fabrigas, against lieut. gen. Mostyn, governor of Minorca, for false imprisonment and banishment; in the common pleas and king's bench, 1773–74. fol. *London, T. Wright,* 1781.
[HARGRAVE'S state trials, v. 11].

MOZZONI (A. Maria). La donna, e i suoi rapporti sociali in occasione della revisione del codice civile italiano. xxvi, 244 pp. 8°. *Milano, (proprietà dell' autrice,)* 1864.

MUELEN. *See* **VANDERMUELEN**.

MUIR (Thomas). Account of the trial of T. Muir, the younger, of Hunter's Hill, before the high court of justiciary, at Edinburgh, 30–31 August, 1793, for sedition. Robertson's ed. 160 pp. 8°. *Edinburgh, J. Robertson,* [1793].

MUNKS (James). The confession of J. M. who was executed at Bellefonte, Pennsylvania, January 23, 1819, for the murder of Reuben Guild. 8 pp. 8°. *New York,* 1819.

MURELL *or* **MURRELL** (John A.) History of the detection and trial of John A. Murel, the great western land pirate; together with a biographical sketch of Mr. Virgil A. Stewart. 8°. [*n. p.* 1834].

MURPHY (Timothy). Trial for felony and forgery, Old Bailey, Jan. 1753. fol. *London, T. Wright,* 1779.
[HARGRAVE'S state trials, v. 10].

MUYART DE VOUGLANS (Pierre François). Institutes au droit criminel; ou, principes généraux sur ces matières, suivant le droit civil, canonique, et la jurisprudence du royaume; avec un traité particulier des crimes. xx, 728 pp. 4°. *Paris, L. Cellot,* 1757.

MYERS (Harvey). Kentucky digest. *See* **KENTUCKY**.

MYERS (W. R.) Authenticated report of the trial of Myers and others, for the murder of Dudley Marvin Hoyt. Drawn up by the editor of the Richmond southern standard. 8°. *New York,* 1846.

NAIRN (Katharine), *and* **OGILVIE** (Patrick). Trial, for the crimes of incest and murder, before the high court of justiciary in Scotland, Aug. 1765. fol. *London, T. Wright,* 1779.
[HARGRAVE'S state trials, v. 10].

NALSON (John). A true copy of the journal of the high court of justice for the tryal of k. Charles i. 4 p. l. lxx, 128 pp. 3 l. 3 pl. fol. *London, T. Dring,* 1684.

NAVARRE. Fueros del reyno Navarra, desde su creacion, hasta su feliz union con el de Castilla. 24 pp; 299 pp. 1 pl. fol. *Pamplona, P. Longas,* 1815.

——— The same. Diccionario para facilitar la intelligencia de estos fueros, dispuesto por Felipe Baraiban de Haro. 39 pp. fol. *Pamplona, P. Longas,* 1815.
[*With* the preceding].

——— Qvaderno de las leyes, ordenanzas, provisiones, y agravios reparados, a svplicacion de los tres estados deste reyno de Navarra, en las cortes de los años 1652, 1653, y 1654. 126 pp. 7 l. fol. *Pamplona, Labayen y Zaula,* 1654.

NAYLER (James). Proceedings in the house of commons against [him] for blasphemy, etc. Dec. 1656. fol. *London, T. Wright*, 1776.
[HARGRAVE's state trials, v. 2].

NELSON (William). Lex maneriorum; or, the laws and customs of England, relating to manors and lords of manors, their stewards, deputies, tenants, and others. 2d ed. xiv, 280 pp; 176 pp. 8°. *London, Nutt & Gosling*, 1728.

NEOSTADIUS *or* **NEUSTADT** (Cornelis van). Utriusque Hollandiæ, Zelandiæ, Frisiæque curiæ decisiones. Item tractatus de feudi hollandici, frisicique occidentalis origine et successione. Accedunt observationes rerum judicatarum de pactis antenuptialibus. 3 v. 4 p. l. 311 pp. 28 l; 4 p. l. 170 pp. 14 l; 72 pp. 12 l. 4°. *Hagæ-Comitis, Steuckerii*, 1667. s.
[NOTE.—The "tractatus" and "observationes" have independent title-pages].

NEUFBOURG (J. F. Philippe de). De la loi naturelle. 3e éd. corrigée et augmentée. 398 pp. 8°. *Paris, A. Durand*, 1862.

NEVADA (*Territory of*). Laws, 1861. 8°. *San Francisco*, 1862.

——— (*State of*). Laws, special session, 1867, and 1867. 2 v. 8°. *Carson City*, 1867. (2 copies of 1867).

——— Nevada reports. v. 2. By Alfred Helm. 8°. *San Francisco*, 1867. (2 copies).

NEVILL *or* **NEVILLE** (Alexander, *archbishop of York*), *and others*. Proceedings in parliament against [them] for high treason, Feb. 1388. fol. *London, T. Wright*, 1776.
[HARGRAVE's state trials, v. 1].

NEW HAMPSHIRE (*Colony of*). Acts and laws. With sundry acts of parliament. 331, xii pp. fol. *Portsmouth, D. & R. Fowle*, 1771.
[NOTE. Title page in ms. Wants pp. 1–2 of commissions of Curtiss and Wentworth].

——— The same. vi, 186 pp. fol. *Exeter*, 1780.

——— (*State of*). New Hampshire reports. v. 46. By Amos Hadley. 8°. *Concord, G. P. Lyon*, 1867.

NEW JERSEY (*State of*). Laws, 1864–67. 4 v. 8°. *Newark & Paterson*, 1864–67. (2 copies of 1864–66).

NEW PLYMOUTH. *See* **PLYMOUTH**.

NEW YORK (*Colony of*). Laws from 1691 to 1751. Collected by W. Livingston and W. Smith. 6 p. l. 488 pp. fol. *New York, J. Parker*, 1752.

——— (*State of*). The code of procedure of the state of New York, as amended to 1867. With the rules of the courts. Edited by John Townshend. 9th ed. 292 pp. 12°. *New York, Baker, Voorhis & Co.* 1867.

——— The code of procedure; or, the new and old modes of proceeding compared; showing the necessity of restoring the forms of actions and pleadings in cases at common law. 100 pp. 8°. *Buffalo, Matthews & Warren*, 1867.

——— Laws of the state of New York, revised and passed at the 36th session of the legislature. With marginal notes and references, by W. P. Van Ness and John Woodworth. 2 v. vii, 592 pp; 570 l. 50 pp. 8°. *Albany, Southwick & Co.* 1813.

——— Laws, [session] 1812, 1814, 1823, 1862, 1865, and 1867. 7 v. 8°. *Albany*, 1812–67. (2 copies of 1867).

——— Private laws. 1810. 8°. *Albany*, 1810.

——— New York reports. v. 34–36. By Joel Tiffany. [v. 7–9 of Tiffany's reports]. 8°. *Albany, W. C. Little*, 1867–68. (2 copies).

——— Opinions of the judges [Yates, Thompson, Kent], of the supreme court, in the cause of R. R. Livingston and R. Fulton, *vs.* Van Ingen and twenty others. 47 pp. 8°. *Albany, S. Southwick*, 1812.

NEW YORK (*City of*). Ordinances of the mayor, aldermen, and commonalty of the city of New York. Revised A. D. 1859, by D. T. Valentine. xvi, 617 pp. 8°. *New York, C. W. Baker*, 1859.

NOBLE (Richard), *and others*. Trial for the murder of John Sayer, at Kingston-upon-Thames, March, 1713. fol. *London, T. Wright*, 1778.
[HARGRAVE's state trials, v. 9].

NORFOLK (Howard, *dukes of*). *See* **HOWARD**.

NORFOLK (Mary Mordaunt, *duchess of*). *See* **MORDAUNT**.

NORKOTT (Arthur), *and others*. Trial for the murder of Mary Norkott, 1628. From the papers of Sir John Maynard. fol. *London, T. Wright*, 1779.
[HARGRAVE's state trials, v. 10].

NORTH (Francis, *baron Guilford*). Narrative at the council board; and letter to secretary Jenkins, relating to [Bedlow's] examination. fol. *London*, 1680.
[*With* BEDLOW (*Capt.* W.) Examination relating to the popish plot. pp. 8–16. 1680. TRIALS for treason, v. 3].

——— The same. fol. *London, T. Wright*, 1778.
[HARGRAVE's state trials, v. 8].

NORTH CAROLINA (*State of*). Laws, 1866–67. 8°. *Raleigh*, 1867.

NORTHUMBERLAND (John Dudley, *duke of*). *See* **DUDLEY**.

NORTHWEST territory. Laws passed at the first session of the general assembly, Cincinnati, Sept. 16th, 1799; also certain laws enacted by the governor and judges, from the commencement of the government to Dec. 1792; with an appendix. v. 1. 248 pp. 8°. *Cincinnati, Carpenter & Findlay*, 1800.
[NOTE.—pp. 227-248 imperfect, also all after p. 248 wanting].

NORWICH (Charles Trimnell, *bishop of*). *See* **TRIMNELL.**

NOTARIES' and commissioners' hand-book, containing all the necessary forms, fees allowed, etc. 31 pp. 8°. *New York, Baker, Voorhis & Co.* 1867.

NOTT (Charles C.) *and* **HUNTINGTON** (Samuel H.) Cases decided in the court of claims of the United States, at the terms for 1863-1866, with the rules of practice and the acts of congress relating to the court. v. 1-2. xxxix, 427 pp; xi, 646 pp. 8°. *Washington, W. H. & O. H. Morrison, and Gov. printing office*, 1867-68. (2 copies).

NOVA SCOTIA. Statutes of Nova Scotia, 1866. 8°. *Halifax*, 1866.

OATES (Titus, *D. D.*) The account of the manner of executing a writ of inquiry of damages, between James, duke of York, and Titus Otes, king's bench, June, 1684. 1 p. l. 31 pp. fol. *London, B. Tooke*, 1684.
[TRIALS for treason, v. 4].

——— The same. fol. *London, T. Wright*, 1776.
[HARGRAVE'S state trials, v. 3].

——— Tryals, convictions, and sentence, upon two indictments for perjury, king's bench, May, 1685. 2 p. l. 94, 60 pp. fol. *London, R. Sare*, 1685.
[TRIALS for treason, v. 6].

——— The same. fol. *London, T. Wright*, 1777.
[HARGRAVE'S state trials, v. 4].

OCHILTRIE (*Sir* James Stewart, *lord*). *See* **STEWART.**

OCHINO (Bernardino). Dialogues of polygamy, and on divorce. *See* **SELECT** and curious cases of polygamy, etc. *London*, 1736.

O'COIGLY *or* **QUIGLEY** (James), *and others.* Trial for high treason, at Maidstone, in Kent, May, 1798. Taken in short-hand by J. Gurney. 539, iv pp. 8°. *London, M. Gurney*, 1798.

OFFICIAL (An) report of the trials of sundry negroes, charged with an attempt to raise an insurrection in the state of South Carolina; and a report of the trials of four white persons, on indictments for attempting to excite the slaves to insurrection. By Lionel H. Kennedy and Thomas Parker. xv, 188, x, 4 pp. 8°. *Charleston, James R. Schenck*, 1822.

OGILVIE (John). Proceedings against [him], for high treason, Feb. 1615, at Glasgow. fol. *London, T. Wright*, 1778.
[HARGRAVE'S state trials, v. 7].

OGILVIE (Patrick). Trial for incest and murder. *See* **NAIRN** (Katharine), *and* **OGILVIE.**

OHIO (*State of*). Laws, 1867. 8°. *Columbus*, 1868.

——— *See* **NORTHWEST** territory.

OHIO reports. New series, v. 16, by L. J. Critchfield. 8°. *Columbus, Nevins & Myers*, 1867. (2 copies).

OKEY (Charles Henry). A concise digest of the law, usage, and custom, affecting the commercial intercourse of the subjects of Great Britain and France. 6th ed. xviii, 338 pp. 8°. *Paris, Galignani & Co.* 1842.

OKEY (John), *and others.* Trials, [as regicides,] behaviour, and dying speeches, April, 1662. fol. *London, T. Wright*, 1778.
[HARGRAVE'S state trials, v. 8].

OLD BAILEY experience. Criminal jurisprudence, and the actual working of our penal code of laws. Also, an essay of prison discipline; to which is added, a history of the crimes committed by offenders in the present day. xi, 447 pp. 1 pl. 8°. *London, J. Fraser*, [1832?]

OLDCASTLE (*Sir* John, *baron Cobham*). Trial and examination, for heresy, before the archbishop of Canterbury, Sept. 1413. Collected by J. Bale. fol. *London, T. Wright*, 1776.
[HARGRAVE'S state trials, v. 1].

ONEBY (John). Trial, at the Old Bailey, March, 1726, for the murder of William Gower. fol. *London, T. Wright*, 1778.
[HARGRAVE'S state trials, v. 9].

OREGON (*State of*). Laws, 1866. 8°. *Salem, (Oregon)*, 1866. (4 copies).

O'REILLY (Antonio Bernal). Practica consular de España. Formulario de cancillerias consulares y coleccion de decretos, reales ordenes y documentos diversos. 3 p. l. 292 pp. 3 pl. 4°. *Havre, Alfonso Lemale*, 1864.

ORLANDO (Diego). Un codice di leggi e diplomi siciliani del medio evo. 211 pp. 8°. *Palermo, Fratelli Redone Lauriei*, 1857.

OSBORNE (Thomas, 1*st earl of Danby*, 1*st duke of Leeds*). An account of [his] argument at the king's bench upon his motion for bail, May, 1682. 2d ed. 1 p. l. 28 pp. fol. *London C. Mearne*, 1682.
[TRIALS for treason, v. 5].

OSBORNE (Thomas, *1st earl of Danby, 1st duke of Leeds*). Memoirs relating to his impeachment, in the year 1678. iv, 234, 110 pp. 8°. *London, John Morphew*, 1710.

——— Proceedings in parliament against [him], upon an impeachment of high treason, etc. Dec. 1678. fol. *London, T. Wright*, 1776.
[HARGRAVE'S state trials, v. 2].

OWEN (William). Trial, for printing and publishing a libel, intitled, "The case of Alexander Murray," at Guildhall, London, July, 1752. fol. *London, T. Wright*, 1779.
[HARGRAVE'S state trials, v. 10].

OXFORD (Robert Harley, *1st earl of*). *See* **HARLEY.**

OXFORD (Robert de Vere, *duke of Ireland, 9th earl of*). *See* **VERE.**

OXFORD (William Talbot, *bishop of*). *See* **TALBOT.**

PAINE (Thomas). Trial of, for a libel contained in the second part of Rights of man, at Guildhall, London, Dec. 18, 1792, before lord Kenyon and a special jury; together with the speeches at large of the attorney general and Mr. Erskine, and authentic copies of Mr. Paine's letters to the attorney general and others, on the subject of the prosecution. 2d ed. corrected. Taken in short-hand, by E. Hodgson. 143 pp. 8°. *London, J. S. Jordan*, 1793.

PAKINGTON *or* **PACKINGTON** (*Sir* John). Evidence at the bar of the house of commons, upon his complaint against William [Lloyd], bishop of Worcester. *See* **LLOYD** (William).

PALAA (G.) Dictionnaire législatif et réglementaire des chemins de fer. xvi, 736 pp. 8°. *Paris, Cosse et Marchal*, 1864.

——— The same. Supplément pour 1865 et 1866. 1 p. l. 244 pp. 8°. *Paris, Cosse, Marchal et Cie*. 1867.

PALL MALL gazette. Hunter (Robert, *M. D.*) *v.* Pall Mall gazette. Being a verbatim report of the medical evidence given by Dr. Williams, Dr. R. Bennett, Dr. O. Markham, Dr. G. Johnson, Dr. Cotton, Dr. R. Quain, and Dr. Odling: showing their opinions on the nature, causes, and cure of consumption, with explanatory remarks by Dr. Hunter. 404 pp. 8°. *London, C. Mitchell & Co.* 1867.

PALMER (Roger, *earl of Castlemain*). Trial at the king's bench for high treason, [meal-tub plot] June, 1680. fol. *London, T. Wright*, 1776.
[HARGRAVE'S state trials, v. 3].

——— Proceedings in the house of commons against [him] for high treason, in going ambassador to Rome, Oct. 1689. fol. *London, T. Wright*, 1777.
[HARGRAVE'S state trials, v. 4].

PALMER (William). Illustrated and unabridged edition of the Times' report of the trial of W. P. for poisoning John Parsons Cook, at Rugeley. 184 pp. numerous pl. 8°. *London, Ward & Lock*, 1850.

PANDO (José Maria de). Elementos del derecho internacional. 2ª ed. xvi, 700 pp. 8°. *Madrid, J. Martin Alegria*, 1852.

PAPILLON (Thomas). The trial between Sir William Pritchard, plaintiff, and Thomas Papillon, defendant, at the Guildhall of London, in an action upon the case for false arrest, Nov. 1684. fol. *London, T. Wright*, 1776.
[HARGRAVE'S state trials, v. 3].

PARDESSUS (Jean Marie). Cours de droit commercial. 5ᵉ éd. 6 v. 8°. *Paris, Nève*, 1841–42. s.

——— Traité des servitudes, ou services foncier. 8ᵉ édition, corrigée et considérablement augmentée en ce qui concerne principalement les actions possessoires, les chemins, les cours d' eaux, les usages, le voisinage et la compétence des juges de paix, d'après la loi du 25 mai 1838. 2 v. 8°. *Paris, Nève*, 1838. s.

PARIS. Bibliothèque des avocats. Catalogue des livres imprimés de la bibliothèque des avocats à la cour impériale de Paris. v. 1. 520 pp. 8°. *Paris, A. Durand*, 1866.

PARKER (Thomas, *6th baron Morley*). Trial for murder, April, 1666, before the house of lords. fol. *London, T. Wright*, 1778.

PARKER (Thomas, *1st earl of Macclesfield, lord high chancellor of Great Britain*). Trial before the house of lords, for high crimes and misdemeanours in the execution of his office, May, 1725. fol. *London, T. Wright*, 1777.
[HARGRAVE'S state trials, v. 6].

PARKER (Thomas, *barrister*). The laws of shipping and insurance, with a digest of adjudged cases; containing the acts of parliament relative to shipping, insurance, and navigation; together with the laws for the government of the navy, and an account of the jurisdiction of the admiralty courts. xxv, 584 pp. 4°. *London, Strahan & Woodfall*. 1775.

PARKYNS (*Sir* William). Trial, at the Old Baily, for high treason, March, 1695. fol. *London, T. Wright*, 1777.
[HARGRAVE'S state trials, v. 4].

PARRY (William). Trial, for high treason, Westminster, Feb. 1584. fol. *London, T. Wright,* 1776.
[HARGRAVE'S state trials, v. 1].

PARSONS (Theophilus). Law of contracts. 5th ed. 2 v. 8°. *Boston, Little, Brown & Co.* 1866. (4 copies).

——— Treatise on maritime law; including the law of shipping, the law of marine insurance, and the law and practice of admiralty. 2 v. xlv, 780 pp; xlviii, 871 pp. 8°. *Boston, Little, Brown & Co.* 1859. (4 copies).

——— Treatise on the law of partnership. liv, 654 pp. 8°. *Boston, Little, Brown & Co.* 1867. (3 copies).

PASCHAL (George W.) Texas digest. *See* **TEXAS**.

PASCHALIS *or* **PASQUALE** (Filippo). Tractatvs de viribvs patriæ potestatis. 21 p. l. lvi, 439 pp. 24 l. fol. [*Venetiis,* 1658?]

PATERSON (J.) **MACNAMARA** (H.) *and* **MARSHALL** (W.) The new practice of the common law. 1 v. in 2. lxxxvi, 1424 pp. 12°. *London, John Crockford,* 1857.

PATON (Thomas S.) Treatise on the law of stoppage in transitu. With appendix, containing English judgments, etc. xv, 257 pp. 8°. *Edinburgh, Bell & Bradfute,* 1859.

PEACHELL (John, *D. D. vice chancellor*), *and the university of Cambridge.* Proceedings against [them], for not admitting Alban Francis, a benedictine monk, to the degree of master of arts, April and May, 1687. fol. *London, T. Wright,* 1777.
[HARGRAVE'S state trials, v. 4].

PEMBERTON (*Sir* Francis), *and* **JONES** (*Sir* Thomas). Proceedings in parliament upon the case of Jay and Topham; and the defence made by Sir F. Pemberton and Sir T. Jones for their judgment given therein, 1689. fol. *London, T. Wright,* 1778.
[HARGRAVE'S state trials, v. 8].

PEMBERTON (Loftus Leigh). The practice in equity by way of revivor and supplement. viii, 201 pp. 8°. *London, Stevens & Haynes,* 1867.

PEMBROKE (Philip Herbert, *4th earl of Montgomery, 7th earl of*). *See* **HERBERT** (Philip).

PENN (William), *and* **MEAD** (William). Trial, at the Old Baily, for a tumultuous assembly, Sept. 1670. Wrote by themselves. fol. *London, T. Wright,* 1776.
[HARGRAVE'S state trials, v. 2].

PENNSYLVANIA (*Province of*). Laws, now in force, collected into one volumn. 3 p. l. 3 l. ms. 352 pp. 1 l. fol. *Philadelphia, A. Bradford,* 1728.

——— (*State of*). Laws, 1867. *Harrisburg,* 1867.

——— Pennsylvania state reports. v. 51–52. By P. Frazer Smith. 8°. *Philadelphia, Kay & bro.* 1867. (2 copies).

PENRUDDOCK (*Col.* John). Trial, at Exon [Exeter], for high treason, April, 1655. Wrote by himself. fol. *London, T. Wright,* 1776.
[HARGRAVE'S state trials, v. 2].

PERROT (*Sir* John, *lord deputy of Ireland*). Trial, at Westminster, for high treason, April, 1592. fol. *London, T. Wright,* 1776.
[HARGRAVE'S state trials, v. 1].

PERU. Código penal del Perú. Ed. oficial. 111 pp. 8°. *Lima, Imprenta calle de La Rifa,* 1863.

PETERS (Richard). Copyright case. *See* **WHEATON** (Henry).

PHILLIPS (Samuel March), *and* **ARNOLD** (Thomas James). A treatise on the law of evidence. 10th Eng. ed. 5th Am. ed. with Cowen and Hill's notes, and with additional notes and references to the English and American cases, to the present time, by Isaac Edwards. 3 v. 8°. *New York, Banks & brothers,* 1868. (2 copies).

PHILLIPS (Willard). A treatise on the law of insurance. 5th ed. 2 v. xcii, 708 pp; vii, 744 pp. 8°. *New York, Hurd & Houghton,* 1867. (2 copies).

PIERCE (John). *See* **GREEN** (*Rev.* John).

PILKINGTON (Thomas), *and others.* Tryal for the riot at Guildhall, midsommer-day, 1682, being the day for election of sheriffs. 2 p. l. 58 pp. fol. *London, D. Dring,* 1683.
[TRIALS for treason, v. 6].

——— The same. fol. *London, T. Wright,* 1776.
[HARGRAVE'S state trials, v. 3].

PIPON (*Col.* J. K.) *and* **COLLIER** (J. F.) Manual of military law for all ranks of the army, militia, and volunteer services; comprising an account of the constitution, composition, and procedure of courts-martial. 3d ed. revised. xvi, 473 pp. 12°. *London, W. H. Allen & Co.* 1863.

PISO (Taddeo). Variarvm resolvtionvm libri sex; in qvibvs vltimarvm volvntatvm et præsertim de testamentis, institvtione hered. codicillis, donat. cavsa mortis, bonorvm possessionis svitate, transmissione ivre accrescendi qvestiones in jvre dvbiæ, oppido et practicabiles resoluuntur, ac dilucide explicantur. 279 pp. 16 l. fol. *Hanoviæ, Wechel,* [*n. d.*]
[*With* ROBERT (Jean). Sententiarum jvris, libri iv.]

PLUNKET (Oliver, *D. D. titular primate of Ireland*). Trial at the king's bench for high treason, June, 1681. fol. *London, T. Wright*, 1776.
[HARGRAVE's state trials, v. 3].

PLUNKETT (John), *and others*. Proceedings in parliament against [them] upon bills of pains and penalties for a treasonable conspiracy, May, 1723. fol. *London, T. Wright*, 1777.
[HARGRAVE's state trials, v. 6].

PLYMOUTH (*N. E.*) The book of the general laws of the inhabitants of the jurisdiction of New Plymouth, collected out of the records of the general court, and lately revised. [With several laws of Mass. enacted 1686, in ms.] 3 p. l. 75 pp. 5 l. 7 ms. l. sm. fol. *Boston, S. Green*, 1685.

POL DE GUY (——). Le droit pour tous; ou, explication des lois civiles et commerciales; renfermant le code napoléon, le code de commerce, le code pénal, le code rural, le tarif général, des frais due aux notaires, huissiers, greffiers, etc. 1 p. l. 451 pp. 12°. *Paris, E. Rome*, 1866.

PONT (Paul). Explication théorique et pratique du code napoléon. Commentaire-traité des petits contrats, et de la contrainte par corps. v. 2. 8°. *Paris*, 1863–1867.

PORDAGE (*Rev.* John). The proceedings of the commissioners of Berks for ejecting scandalous and insufficient ministers, against him, Sept. 1654. Wrote by himself. fol. *London, T. Wright*, 1776.
[HARGRAVE's state trials, v. 2].

PORTEOUS (*Capt.* John). Proceedings in his trial for murder, [Edinburgh, 1736]. Published by order of the house of lords. fol. *London, T. Wright*, 1777.
[HARGRAVE's state trials, v. 6].

PORTLAND (William Bentinck, 1*st earl of*). *See* **BENTINCK**.

POSTNATI (The case of the). *See* **CALVIN** (Robert).

POWRIE (William), *and others*. Examinations and depositions, concerning the murder of the king [Henry Stewart, lord Darnley], queen Mary's husband; with their trial and sentence, 1567. fol. *London, T. Wright*, 1778.
[HARGRAVE's state trials, v. 8].

PRECERUTTI (Enrico). Elementi di diritto civile patrio. 2ª ed. 2 v. 400 pp; 460 pp. 8°. *Torino, G. Speirani e figli*, 1861.

PRESSICKS (Mary). Trial for treason. *See* **THWING** (Thomas), *and* **PRESSICKS**.

PRESTON (*Sir* Richard Graham, 1*st viscount*). *See* **GRAHAM**.

PRICE (Ann). Tryal for subornation of perjury. *See* **TASBOROUGH** (John), *and* **PRICE**.

PRICE (John), *and others*. Proceedings against them at Wicklow, in Ireland, for high treason against king James, March, 1689. fol. *London, T. Wright*, 1777.
[HARGRAVE's state trials, v. 4].

PRIEST (William). The case of duels; or, proceedings in the star chamber against him for writing and sending a challenge, and [against] Richard Wright for carrying it, Jan. 1615. fol. *London, T. Wright*, 1781.
[HARGRAVE's state trials, v. 11].

PRITCHARD (*Sir* William). Trial between Sir W. Pritchard and T. Papillon for false arrest. *See* **PAPILLON** (Thomas).

PRITCHARD (W. T.) Analytical digest of all the reported cases determined by the high court of admiralty of England. With notes. 8°. *Philadelphia*, 1854. (2 copies).

PROCEEDINGS (The) at the sessions for London and Middlesex, holden at the Old Bailey, July 16th, 1679. 4 pp. fol. *London*, 1679.
[TRIALS for treason, v. 1].

PROCEEDINGS against various persons in the reign of Henry viii. for treason, in denying the king's supremacy, and other capital crimes, principally relating to religion. fol. *London, T. Wright*, 1781.
[HARGRAVE's state trials, v. 11].

PROCEEDINGS on the case concerning the king's prerogative in respect to the education and marriage of the royal family, 1717. fol. *London, T. Wright*, 1781.
[HARGRAVE's state trials, v. 11].

PRUGNAUD (Eugène). Législation et administration de la marine; ou, résolution des questions présentées, sous le titre iv. du programme d'examen, en date du 15 mai, 1853, pour l'admission du grade d'aide-commissaire de la marine. 3ᵉ éd. avec un supplément. 3 v. 8°. *Rochefort, A. Mercier*, 1858.

PRYNNE (William). Argument in the case of Connor Magwire [lord Maguire], against whom he was assigned counsel by parliament. fol. *London, T. Wright*, 1778.
[HARGRAVE's state trials, v. 8].

—— Proceedings against [him] for several libels. *See* **BASTWICK** (John, *M. D.*) *and others*.

—— *and others*. Proceedings against them; in the star-chamber, for writing, publishing, printing, and licensing, a book intituled, "Histrio-mastix; or, a scourge for stage players." fol. *London, T. Wright*, 1776.
[HARGRAVE's state trials, v. 1].

PUCCIONI (Giuseppe). Saggio di diritto penale teorico-pratico. 1 p. l. 612 pp. 8°. *Firenze, Luigi Niccolai,* 1858.

PURCHASE (George). Trial, for high treason, in levying war against her majesty, under pretence of pulling down meeting-houses, 1710. fol. *London, T. Wright,* 1778.
[HARGRAVE'S state trials, v. 8].

PUTERBAUGH (Sabin D.) Illinois pleading and practice. A practical treatise on the forms of common law actions, pleading, and practice, now in use in the state of Illinois. 2d ed. revised and enlarged. 899 pp. 8°. *Chicago, Callaghan & Cutler,* 1867.

QUELCH (John), *and others.* Trial and condemnation, for sundry piracies, robberies, and murders, committed upon the subjects of the king of Portugal, at the court-house in Boston, [New England], June, 1704. fol. *London, T. Wright,* 1778.
[HARGRAVE'S state trials, v. 8].

QUICHERAT (Jules Étienne Joseph). Aperçus nouveaux sur l'histoire de Jeanne d'Arc. ii, 168 pp. 8°. *Paris, J. Renouard et Cie.* 1850.

QUIGLEY (James). *See* **O'COIGLY.**

RADCLIFFE (Charles, *assumed earl of Derwentwater*). Proceedings, at Westminster, Nov. 1746, against him, on a conviction and attainder of high-treason, in May, 1716. fol. *London, T. Wright,* 1778.
[HARGRAVE'S state trials, v. 9].

RADCLIFFE (James, *3d earl of Derwentwater*), *and others.* Proceedings in parliament against them, upon an impeachment for high treason, Feb. 1715. fol. *London, T. Wright,* 1777.
[HARGRAVE'S state trials, v. 6].

RALEIGH (*Sir* Walter). Trial, at Winton, for high treason, Nov. 1603. fol. *London, T. Wright,* 1776.
[HARGRAVE'S state trials, v. 1].

——— The same. The bringing of Sir W. Raleigh to execution, after his sentence had lain dormant so many years considered. fol. *London, T. Wright,* 1778.
[HARGRAVE'S state trials, v. 8].

RAMSEY (David). Proceedings in the court of chivalry, on an appeal of high treason, by Donald [Mackay], lord Rea, against David Ramsey, 1631. fol. *London, T. Wright,* 1781.
[HARGRAVE'S state trials, v. 11].

RANKIN (Eliza). Trial. *See* **MELLISH** (Mary).

RATCLIFFE. *See* **RADCLIFFE.**

READING (Joseph). Trial for murder. *See* **ANNESLEY** (James), *and* **READING.**

READING (Nathaniel). Tryal for attempting to stifle the king's evidence as to the horrid [popish] plot; king's bench, Westminster, April, 1679. 2 p. l. 71 pp. fol. *London, R. Pawlet,* 1679.
[TRIALS for treason, v. 1].

——— The same.
[TRIALS for treason, v. 2].

——— The same. fol. *London, T. Wright,* 1776.
[HARGRAVE'S state trials, v. 2].

REASON (Hugh), *and* **TRANTER** (Robert). Trial, at the king's bench, for the murder of Edward Lutterell, Feb. 1721. fol. *London, T. Wright,* 1777.
[HARGRAVE'S state trials, v. 6].

REAY (*Sir* Donald Mackay, *1st baron*). *See* **MACKAY.**

REDDING. *See* **READING.**

REDFIELD (Isaac Fletcher). The law of railways. 3d ed. greatly enlarged. 2 v. lxxx, 664 pp; lxxvi, 853 pp. 8°. *Boston, Little, Brown & Co.* 1867. (2 copies).

REGICIDES. The trial of twenty-nine regicides, at the Old Baily, for high treason, which began 9th of Oct. 1660. fol. *London, T. Wright,* 1776.
[HARGRAVE'S state trials, v. 2].

REID (James W.) Index to the amended laws of Michigan. 122 pp. 8°. *Lansing, Kerr & Co.* 1867.

REIFFENBERG (Frédéric Guillaume Émeric Cuno Marsilius, *baron* de). Administration militaire. Étude sur les services généraux de la guerre. 160 pp. 8°. *Paris, C. Tanera,* 1865.

REMARKS on the trial of John Peter Zenger, printer of the New York weekly journal, who was lately tried and acquitted, for printing and publishing two libels against the government of that province. By Anglo-Americanus and Indus Britannicus. [*pseudon.*] fol. *London, T. Wright,* 1778.
[HARGRAVE'S state trials, v. 9].

REPORTS of cases in the English courts of common law. v. 114–115. James Parsons, editor. 8°. *Philadelphia, T. & J. W. Johnson & Co.* 1866–68.

REVUE critique de législation et de jurisprudence. v. 26–29. 8°. *Paris, Cotillon,* 1865–66.

RICE (Clinton). Manual of the U. S. bankruptcy act, 1867, with the rules, orders, and forms of proceedings thereunder, conveniently annotated, classified, and arranged. 442 pp. 4°. *Washington, (D. C.) Philp & Solomons,* 1867.

RICH (Edward, *6th earl of Warwick, 3d earl of Holland*). Trial, before the house of lords, for the murder ot Richard Coote, March, 1699. fol. *London, T. Wright,* 1777.

[HARGRAVE'S state trials, v. 5].

RICHELMANN (Heinrich). Der einfluss des irrthums auf verträge. Ein civilistischer versuch. vi, 162 pp. 8°. *Hannover, Helwing,* 1837. s.

RINGE (Richard). Genuine trial for treason, 1761. *See* **BEDDINGFIELD** (Margery), *and* **RINGE.**

RITTIEZ (F.) Histoire du palais de justice de Paris, et du parlement, 860—1789. Mœurs, coutumes, institutions judiciaires, procès divers, progrès légal. iv, 392 pp. 8°. *Paris, Schlesinger frères,* 1863.

——— L'Hotel de ville et la bourgeoisie de Paris; origines, mœurs, coutumes, institutions municipales, depuis les temps les plus reculés jusqu'à 1789. iv,408 pp. 8°. *Paris, Schlesinger frères,* 1863.

——— Science des droits; ou, idéologie politique. xl, 356 pp. 8°. *Paris, Pagnerre,* 1844.

ROAD [Hill] murder [by Constance Kent]; being a complete report and analysis of the various examinations and opinions of the press on this mysterious tragedy. By a barrister-at-law. 63 pp. 8°. *London,* [1860].

ROBBERY of the bank of Pennsylvania, in 1798. The trial, in the supreme court, [etc.] Reported from notes by T. Lloyd. Upon which the president, [etc.] were sentenced to pay Patrick Lyon 12,000 dollars damages, [etc.] 2 p. l. 184 pp. 8°. *Philadelphia, publishers,* 1808.

ROBERT (Jean). Sententiarum juris libri iv. 300 pp. fol. *Parisiis, Vascosan,* 1557.

ROBERTS (Bethuel). Trial. *See* **HALL** (Lucian), *and others.*

ROBERTSON (Anthony L.) Reports of cases in the superior court of the city of New York. v. 1-2. 8°. *Albany, W. C. Little,* 1867. (2 copies).

ROCHESTER (Francis Atterbury, *bishop of*). *See* **ATTERBURY.**

ROCHESTER (Robert Carr, *viscount*). *See* **CARR.**

ROCHESTER (John Fisher, *bishop of*). *See* **FISHER.**

ROCHESTER (Thomas Sprat, *bishop of*). *See* **SPRAT.**

ROCHFORD (George Boleyn, *viscount*). *See* **BOLEYN.**

RŒDER (Ole Munch). Jury institutionen i Starbritanien, Canada og de forenede stater af Amerika. 3 v. 8°. *Christiania, Forfatter,* 1850-52. s.

ROESSLER. *See* **RÖSSLER.**

ROGUET (——). Législation de l'étranger aux États Unis. 92 pp. 8°. *Paris, Marescq et Dujardin,* 1857.

ROLLIT (A. K.) A course of reading for the final examination of the incorporated law society. A lecture delivered before the Hull law student's society. 32 pp. 8°. *London, Horace Cox,* 1866.

ROMO (Judas José). Discurso canónico acerca de la congrua del clero y de las fabricas. 277 pp. 8°. *Madrid, E. Aguado,* 1846. s.

ROOKWOOD (Ambrose). Trial for high treason, April, 1696, at the king's bench. fol. *London, T. Wright,* 1777.

[HARGRAVE'S state trials, v. 4].

ROSCOE (Henry). Digest of the law of evidence in criminal cases. By David Power. 6th Am. from the 6th Lond. ed. with notes and references to American cases, by George Sharswood. xl, 947 pp. 8°. *Philadelphia. T. and J. W. Johnson & Co.* 1866.

ROSE (U. M.) Digest of the Arkansas reports. lvi, 972 pp. 8°. *Little Rock, John E. Reardon,* 1867.

ROSEWELL (Thomas). Trial, at the king's bench, for high treason, Nov. 1684. fol. *London, T. Wright,* 1776.

[HARGRAVE'S state trials. v. 3].

ROSS (George). Leading cases in the commercial law of England and Scotland. v. 3. 982 pp. 8°. *Edinburgh, Constable & Co.* 1857.

RÖSSLER (Emil Franz). Deutsche rechtsdenkmäler aus Böhmen und Mähren, [etc.] v. 1. Das altprager stadtrecht aus dem xiv. jahrhunderte, [etc.] Mit einer vorrede von Jacob Grimm. ciiv, xl, 210 pp. 8°. *Prag, J. G. Calve,* 1845. s.

[v. 2, 1852, wanting].

ROUSE *or* **ROUS** (John). Rouse, his case, written with his own hand in Newgate, two days before his execution. [With] a letter to his wife. 1 p. l. 16 pp. fol. *London, J. Grantham,* 1683.

[TRIALS for treason, v. 4].

——— The same.

[TRIALS for treason, v. 5].

——— Trial at the Old Baily, for high treason, July, 1662. fol. *London, T. Wright,* 1776.

[HARGRAVE'S state trials, v. 3].

——— The same. *See* **WALCOT** (Thomas), *and others.*

RUMSEY (Almarie). A chart of family inheritance, according to orthodox Moohummudan law, with an explanatory treatise. vii, 37 pp. 8°. *London, William Amer*, 1866.

RUSSELL (Francis, *4th earl of Bedford*), *and others*. Proceedings against [them] in the star chamber, May, 1630, for publishing a seditious and scandalous writing. fol. *London, T. Wright*, 1781.
[HARGRAVE'S state trials, v. 11].

RUSSELL (William, *lord Russell*). Tryal for high treason. fol. *London*, 1683.
[*With* WALCOT (Thomas) *and others*. Trials, 1682].

——— The same. fol. *London, T. Wright*, 1776.
[HARGRAVE'S state trials, v. 3].

——— The case of William [Russell], lord Russell. [Criticism of arguments at the trial]. fol. *London, T. Wright*, 1776.
[HARGRAVE'S state trials, v. 3].

——— *and others*. History of the whiggish plot; or, a brief historical account of the charge and defence of William, lord Russel, capt. Tho. Walcot, John Rouse, William Hone, captain Blague, Algernon Sidney, sir Samuel Barnardiston, etc. 1 p. l. 71 pp. fol. *London, R. Taylor*, 1684.

RUTGERS (Elizabeth), *v.* **WADDINGTON** (Joshua). Case of, determined in the mayor's court, in the city of New York, August 7, 1786; with an historical introduction, by Henry B. Dawson. xlvi, 47 pp. 8°. *Morrisania (N. Y.) Bradstreet press*, 1866.

RUTHVEN (John, *3d earl of Gowrie*), *and others*. Proceedings in parliament against them for high treason, Nov. 1600, at Edinburgh. fol. *London, T. Wright*, 1778.
[HARGRAVE'S state trials, v. 7].

SAAVEDRA. *See* **GARSIAS** de Saavedra.

SACHEVERELL (Henry, *D. D.*) An account of what passed most remarkable in the sessions of parliament, 1709, in the house of commons, relating to his case. fol. *London, T. Wright*, 1778.
[HARGRAVE'S state trials, v. 8].

——— The same. 16 pp. 1 portrait. fol. *London, J. Tonson*, 1710.
[*With his* tryal before the peers, etc.]

——— The same. fol. *London, T. Wright*, 1777.
[HARGRAVE'S state trials, v. 5].

——— Tryal before the house of peers, for high crimes and misdemeanors, Feb.-March. 1710. 327 pp. fol. *London, J. Tonson*, 1710.

SACHEVERELL (William), *and others*. Trial at the king's bench, for a riot committed at Nottingham, May 1684. fol. *London, T. Wright*, 1776.
[HARGRAVE'S state trials, v. 3].

SAINT ALBANS (Francis Bacon, *viscount*). *See* **BACON** (Francis).

SAINT-JOHN (Oliver). His case, on an information *ore tenus*, in the star-chamber, April, 1615, for writing and publishing a paper against a benevolence, collected under letters of the privy council. fol. *London, T. Wright*, 1781.
[HARGRAVE'S state trials, v. 11].

SAINT-JOSEPH (Antoine de). Concordance entre les codes de commerce étrangers, et le code de commerce français. [Avec] Codes de commerce étrangers et lois commerciales étrangères non compris dans la concordance. xlvii, 425 pp. 4°. *Paris, Videcoq*, 1844. S.

SALA (Juan). Ilustracion del derecho real de España. 2ª ed. 2 v. in 1. xiv, 404 pp; 348 pp. sm. 4°. *Madrid, José del Collado*, 1820.

——— Sala adicionado, o ilustracion del derecho español, añadidas todas las novedades que se han introducido hasta el dia en la legislacion española, con apèndices de las de Chile, Méjico, y Venezuela, por dos jurisconsultos españoles. 2 v. 444 pp; 608 pp. 12°. *Paris, Garnier hermanos*, 1867.

SALEM *(Mass.)* The charter and ordinances of the city of Salem, together with the acts of the legislature relating to the city; collated and revised, [etc.] by J. B. F. Osgood. xi, 320 pp. 8°. *Salem, Ives & Pease*, 1853. S.

SALISBURY (Gilbert Burnet, *bishop of*). *See* **BURNET**.

SANCROFT (William, *archbishop of Canterbury*), *and others*. Proceedings and tryal, king's bench, June, 1688. 3 p. l. 140 pp. fol. *London, T. Basset*, 1689.
[TRIALS for treason, v. 5].

——— The same. fol. *London, T. Wright*, 1777.
[HARGRAVE'S state trials, v. 4].

SANDYS (Thomas). The great case of monopolies, between the East India company, plaintiff, and Thomas Sandys, defendant: Whether their patent for trading to the East Indies, exclusive of all others, is good? 1683. fol. *London, T. Wright*, 1778.
[HARGRAVE'S state trials, v. 7].

SANQUHAR (Robert Crichton, *lord*). *See* **CRICHTON**.

SARDINIA. Code civil pour les états [etc.] augmenté des lettres-patentes en date [etc. 1837–38]; de l'édit royal [etc.] et du manifeste de la chambre [etc.] 1838. 2 p. l. 420 pp. 12°. *Turin, hérétiers Bianco & Cie.* 1838. S.

SAVIGNY (Friedrich Carl von). Traité de la possession en droit romain. 7e éd. publiée d'après les notes laissées par l'auteur, et augmentée d'une appendice sur l'état actuel de la doctrine, par A. F. Rudorff. Traduit de l'Allemand par Henri Staedtler. xxxi, 783 pp. 8°. *Paris, A. Durand,* 1866.

SCHÜLLER (Christian Ludwig). Dissertatio juridico-inauguralis de necessitudine, cum morali tum civili, inter patronum et libertum. 5 p. l. 128 pp. 8°. *Trajecti ad Rhenum, L. E. Bosch,* 1838. S.

SCOTLAND. The acts of the parliaments of Scotland, 1124 to 1707. 11 v. fol. *Edinburgh,* 1814-24.

[NOTE.—The first vol. published in 1844, was edited by Thomas Thomson and Cosmo Innes].

——— Laws and acts of parliament made by king James the first, second, third, fourth, fifth, queen Mary, king James the sixth, Charles the first, Charles the second, kings and queen of Scotland. Collected and extracted from the public records of the said kingdom by Sir Thomas Murray. 2 v. 5 p. l. 521, 198 pp; 2 l. 11, 45 pp. 22 l. 8 pl. fol. *Edinburgh, D. Lindsay,* 1681.

SCRIBNER (Charles H.) A treatise on the law of dower. v. 2. xl, 806 pp. 8°. *Philadelphia, T. & J. W. Johnson & Co.* 1867.

SCROGGS (*Sir* William, *lord chief justice of the king's bench*). Articles of high misdemeanours, humbly offered to the consideration of his majesty, against him; exhibited by [Titus] Oates, and [William] Bedlow, 1679. fol. *London, T. Wright,* 1778.

[HARGRAVE'S state trials, v. 7].

——— Speech, the first day of Michaelmas-term, 1679, occasioned by many libellous pamphlets which are published against law, to the scandal of the government, and publick justice. fol. *London, T. Wright,* 1778.

[HARGRAVE'S state trials, v. 8].

——— *and others.* Proceedings against them, in parliament, 1680. fol. *London, T. Wright,* 1778.

[HARGRAVE'S state trials, v. 7].

SELECT and curious cases of polygamy, concubinage, adultery, divorce, etc. seriously and learnedly discussed: being a complete collection of all the remarkable tryals and tracts which have been written on those important subjects, particularly the famous Bernardino Ochino. With some memoirs and testimonies of his life and writings. lviii, 240 pp. 12°. *London, O. Payne,* 1736.

CONTENTS.

OCHINO (Bernardino). Dialogue: 21, on polygamy; 22, on divorce. Translated by F. Ozborn, with memorials and testimonies of Ochino. lviii, 106 pp.

WOLSELEY (*Sir* Charles). The case of divorce, and remarriage thereupon, discussed. pp. 107-126.

TREATISE concerning adultery and divorce. pp. 127-211.

CONJUGIUM LANGUENS; or, the natural, civil, and religious mischiefs arising from conjugal infidelity and impunity. By Castamore. pp. 213-240.

SELECT and impartial account of the lives, behaviour, and dying words of the most remarkable convicts, from the year 1700 down to the present time. [*anon.*] v. 1. vi, 3 l. 336 pp. 12°. *London, J. Hodges,* 1740.

SERRIGNY (Denis). Droit public et administratif romain; ou, institutions politiques, administratives, économiques, et sociales de l'empire romain du ive au vie siècle (de Constantin á Justinien). 2 v. 464 pp; 540 pp. 8°. *Paris, A. Durand,* 1862.

[v. 1 imperfect].

SESSION cases. Cases in the court of sessions, teind court, etc. and house of lords, July, 1865, to July, 1866. 3d series. v. 4. 8°. *Edinburgh, T. & T. Clark,* 1866.

SETON (George, 5*th earl of Wintoun*). Trial before the house of lords upon an impeachment for high treason, March, 1715. fol. *London, T. Wright,* 1777.

[HARGRAVE'S state trials, v. 6].

SEYMOUR (Edward, 1*st duke of Somerset, lord protector*). Proceedings against him in parliament, for misdemeanours and high treason, Feb. 1549, and Jan. 1550. fol. *London, T. Wright,* 1778.

[HARGRAVE'S state trials, v. 7].

——— Proceedings against [him], for high treason and felony, Dec. 1551, at Westminster. fol. *London, T. Wright,* 1778.

[HARGRAVE'S state trials, v. 7].

SEYMOUR (*Sir* Thomas, *baron Seymour, of Sudley*). Proceedings in parliament against him for high treason, Feb. 1549. fol. *London, T. Wright,* 1778.

[HARGRAVE'S state trials, v. 7].

SEYS (*Rev.* John). Extraordinary trial of, for an alleged assault and battery on Mrs. Elizabeth Cram. 3d ed. 15 pp. 8°. *New York, Camp & Wilkes,* 1847.

SHAFTESBURY (Anthony Ashley Cooper, 1*st earl of*). *See* **COOPER.**

SHEPPARD (William). Of corporations, fraternities, and guilds, with forms and precedents of charters of corporation. 2 p. l. 187 pp. 12°. *London, Twiford, Dring & Place,* 1659.

SHERFIELD (Henry, *recorder of Sarum*). Proceedings in the star-chamber against him, for breaking [altering] a painted glass window in the church of St. Edmonds, [Salisbury], Feb. 1632. fol. *London, T. Wright,* 1776.
[HARGRAVE'S state trials, v. 1].

SHERWOOD (Grace). Record of Grace Sherwood's trial for witchcraft, in 1705, in Princess Anne co. Va.
[VIRGINIA hist. and philos. soc. collections, v. 1].

SHERWOOD (Scott R.) Manual of legal study. For the use of students. 28 pp. 8°. *New York, Baker, Voorhis & Co.* 1867.

SHIRLEY (Laurence, *4th earl Ferrers*). His case, April, 1760, with an account of his behaviour, as published by authority of the sheriffs. fol. *London, T. Wright,* 1779.
[HARGRAVE'S state trials, v. 10].

——— Trial for the murder of John Johnson, before the house of peers, April, 1760. fol. *London, T. Wright,* 1779.
[HARGRAVE'S state trials, v. 10].

SHIRLEY (*Dr.* Thomas). Proceedings in the house of commons, on an appeal being brought in the house of lords, against Sir J. Fagg and others, their members. *See* **FAGG** (*Sir* John).

SHOWER (*Sir* Bartholomew). An antidote against poison; composed of some remarks upon the paper printed by the direction of the lady Russell, and mentioned to have been delivered by the lord Russell to the sheriffs at the place of his execution. 7 pp. fol. *London, C. Mearne,* 1683.
[HARGRAVE'S state trials, v. 8].

——— The same. [*anon.*] fol. *London, T. Wright,* 1778.
[*With* the preceding].

——— The magistracy and government of England vindicated. fol. *London, T. Wright,* 1776.
[HARGRAVE'S state trials, v. 3].

SHREWSBURY (Mary Cavendish, *countess of*). *See* **CAVENDISH.**

SIDNEY (Algernon). Arraignment, tryal, and condemnation of, for high treason, for conspiring the death of the king, and intending to raise a rebellion in this kingdom. At the court of king's bench, 7th–27th November, 1683. 67 pp. fol. *London, B. Tooke,* 1684.

——— The same. 67 pp. fol. [*London,* 1684].
[Title-page wanting. TRIALS for treason, v. 3].

——— The same. fol. *London, T. Wright,* 1776.
[HARGRAVE'S state trials, v. 3].

SIMONS (Henry). Case of Ashley and Simons the Jew, 1751. fol. *London, T. Wright,* 1779.
[HARGRAVE'S state trials, v. 10].

SINDERCOME *alias* **FISH** (Miles). Trial, Westminster, Feb. 1656, for high treason. fol. *London, T. Wright,* 1778.
[HARGRAVE'S state trials, v. 7].

SKENE (*Sir* John). Regiam maiestatem Scotiæ, veteres leges et constitvtiones, ex archivis pvblicis, et antiqvis libris mss. collectæ, recognitæ, et notis, jvris ciuilis, canonici, nortmannici auctoritate confirmatis, illustratæ, opera et studio Joannis Skenaei. 10 p. l. 172, 123 pp. fol. *London, J. Bill,* 1613.

SLADEN (Henry Mainwaring). The county courts' equitable jurisdiction act, 28 and 29 Vict. cap. 99, with the orders, rules, and forms. xvi, 132 pp. 12°. *London, Wildy & sons,* 1865.

SLINGSBY (*Sir* Henry). Trial, before the high court of justice, for high treason, May, 1658. fol. *London, T. Wright,* 1776.
[HARGRAVE'S state trials, v. 2].

SMITH (Francis). Trial, at the Guild-Hall of London, for publishing a libel, Feb. 1699. fol. *London, T. Wright,* 1776.
[HARGRAVE'S state trials, v. 2].

SMITH (George James Philip). Reports of cases in the court of queen's bench. *See* **BEST** (W. M.)

SMITH (George W.) Journal of proceedings of the senate [of New York] in the matter of George W. Smith, judge of Oneida county, in relation to charges submitted to the senate by the governor. 580 pp. 8°. *Albany, Van Benthuysen,* 1866.

SMITH (John, *of Walworth, England*). No faith or credit to be given to papists. With reflections on the perjury of Will. [Howard], viscount Stafford, in relation to S. Dugdale and W. Turbervill. 2 p. l. 32 pp. fol. *London, T. Cockerill,* 1681.
[TRALS for treason, v. 4].

SMITH (John, *of London, bookseller*). Trial of, before lord Kenyon, in the court of king's bench, December 6, 1796, for selling a work entitled, "A summary of the duties of citizenship." viii, 35 pp. 8°. *London, Mrs. Smith,* [1797].

——— *and* **Higgins** (George). Assassination of the king; the conspirators exposed; or, an account of the apprehension, treatment in prison, and repeated examinations before the privy council, of John Smith and George Higgins, on a charge of high treason. 82 pp. 8°. *London, J. Smith,* 1795.

SMITH (John William). Selection of leading cases, on various branches of the law. 6th Am. ed. from the last Eng. ed. by Willes, Keating, Maud, and Chilly. With additional notes, and references to American decisions, by J. I. Clark Hare and J. W. Wallace. 2 v. in 3. 8°. *Philadelphia, T. & J. W. Johnson & Co.* 1866. (4 copies).

SOACIUS. *See* **PISO** (Taddeo).

SOAME (*Sir* William). The proceedings in the court of king's bench, exchequer, and house of peers, in the case of Sir Samuel Barnardiston, against Sir William Soame, sheriff of Suffolk, concerning the election of members to parliament, 1674. fol. *London, T. Wright,* 1778.
[HARGRAVE'S state trials, v. 7].

SOME observations upon the late trials of Sir George Wakeman, Corker, and Marshal, Benedictine monks, 1679. [By Tom Ticklefoot, the taborer, late clerk to justice Clodpate. *pseudon.*] fol. *London, T. Wright,* 1778.
[HARGRAVE'S state trials, v. 8].

SOMERSET (Robert Carr, *earl of*). *See* **CARR.**

SOMERSET (Frances Howard, *countess of*). *See* **HOWARD.**

SOMERSET (Edward Seymour, 1*st duke of*). *See* **SEYMOUR.**

SOMMERSETT (James). The case of James Sommersett, a negro, on a habeas corpus, king's bench, 1771–72. fol. *London, T. Wright,* 1781.
[HARGRAVE'S state trials, v. 11].

SOUTHAMPTON (Henry Wriothesley, 3*d earl of*). *See* **WRIOTHESLEY.**

SOUTH CAROLINA (*State of*). Laws and regulations for the militia of the state of South Carolina. 188 pp. 2 l. 8 pl. 8°. *Charleston, Timothy & Mason,* 1794.

——— Public laws, from its first establishment as a British province to 1790. By J. F. Grimke. lxxvii, 504, 43 pp. 27 l. 4°. *Philadelphia, Aitken & son,* 1790.

SPAIN. Coleccion legislativa de España. [Reales ordenes]. Ed. oficial, 1864–1866. v. 91–96. sm. 4°. *Madrid, Imprenta del ministerio de gracia y justicia,* 1864–66.

——— Sentencias del consejo de estado, 1864–1866. 3 v. 8°. *Madrid,* 1864–66.

——— Sentencias del tribunal supremo de justicia, 1864 y 1865. 4 v. 8°. *Madrid,* 1865–66.

SPEKE (Hugh). Tryal. *See* **BRADDON** (L.) *and* **SPEKE** (H.)

SPENCER (John). De legibus Hebræorum ritualibus et earum rationibus, libri tres. 6 p. l. 1051 pp. fol. *Cantabrigiæ, R. Chiswel,* 1685.
[Imperfect: pp. 1039–1042 are in MS.]

SPOTISWOOD (*Sir* Robert). Trial, for high treason, in the parliament held at St. Andrews, Nov. Dec. and Jan. 1645. fol. *London, T. Wright,* 1776.
[HARGRAVE'S state trials, v. 1].

SPRAT (Thomas, *bishop of Rochester*). Proceedings against him, before the privy council, 1692, in relation to a plot to restore king James ii. Written by himself. fol. *London, T. Wright,* 1778.
[HARGRAVE'S state trials, v. 8].

SPROT (George). Trial, for high treason, in conspiring with John [Ruthven], earl of Gowrie, to murder king James i. Aug. 1608. fol. *London, T. Wright,* 1776.
[HARGRAVE'S state trials, v. 1].

STAFFORD (Edward de, 3*d duke of Buckingham*). Trial, for high treason, in the court of the lord high steward of England, May, 1522. fol. *London, T. Wright,* 1781.
[HARGRAVE'S state trials, v. 11].

STALEY (William). *See* **STAYLEY.**

STANDSFIELD (Philip). Tryal for the murther of his father, and other crimes, [Edinburgh], Feb. 1688. 2 p. l. 36 pp. fol. *Edinburgh, heir of A. Anderson,* 1688.
[TRIALS for treason, v. 5].

——— The same. fol. *London, T. Wright,* 1777.
[HARGRAVE'S state trials, v. 4].

STANLEY (*Sir* William). Trial, for high treason, 1494–5. fol. *London, T. Wright,* 1781.
[HARGRAVE'S state trials, v. 11].

STAPLETON (*Sir* Miles). Trial, at York, for high treason, June, 1681. fol. *London, T. Wright,* 1776.
[HARGRAVE'S state trials, v. 3].

STATEMENT (A) of the penal laws, which aggrieve the catholics of Ireland; with commentaries. [*anon.*] Part 1. xvi, 370 pp. 8°. *Dublin, H. Fitzpatrick,* 1812. s.
[Part ii wanting].

STAYLEY *or* **STALEY** (William). An account of the digging up of the quarters of W. Stayley, lately executed for high treason. Broadside. fol. *London, R. Pawlet,* 1678.
[TRIALS for treason, v. 1].

——— The same.
[Inperfect. TRIALS for treason, v. 2].

——— The same. fol. *London, T. Wright,* 1778.
[HARGRAVE'S state trials, v. 8].

——— Trial for speaking treasonable words against his majesty, [Charles ii.]; king's bench, Nov. 1678. 10, 12 pp. fol. *London, R. Pawlet,* 1678.
[TRIALS for treason, v. 1].

STAYLEY *or* **STALEY** (William). Trial for speaking treasonable words against his majesty, [Charles ii.]; king's bench, Nov. 1678. 10, 12 pp. fol. *London, R. Powlet*, 1678.
[TRIALS for treason, v. 2].

——— The same.
[TRIALS for treason, v. 5].

——— The same. fol. *London, T. Wright*, 1776.
[HARGRAVE'S state trials, v. 2].

STEPHEN (Henry John). Treatise on the principles of pleading in civil actions: comprising a summary view of the whole proceedings in a suit at law. 9th Am. ed. with notes; and additions from the London editions. By Franklin Fiske Heard. xxvii, 457, clxxvi pp. 8°. *Philadelphia, Kay and brother*, 1867.

STEPHEN (James Fitzjames). The definition of murder considered in relation to the report of the capital punishment commissioners. 57 pp. 8°. *London, Longmans*, 1866.

STEPHENSEN (Magnus). Commentatio de legibus, qvæ jus islandicum hodiernum efficiant, deqve emendationibus nonnullis, qvas hæ leges desiderare videantur. 1 p. l. viii, 189 pp. 16°. *Havniæ, P. D. Kiöpping*, 1819. S.

STETSON (T. M.) Arguments for respondents, Robinson *vs.* Mandell *et al.* *See* **ELIOT** (T. D.) *and* **STETSON**.

STEVENSON (John). Trial, at Chester, April 1759, for the murder of Francis Elcock. fol. *London, T. Wright*, 1779.
[HARGRAVE'S state trials, v. 10].

STEWART (Archibald, *lord provost of Edinburgh*). Trial, before the high court of justiciary in Scotland, June, 1747, for neglect of duty and misbehaviour in office, before and at the time the rebels got possession of that city, in Sept. 1745. fol. *London, T. Wright*, 1778.
[HARGRAVE'S state trials, v. 9].

STEWART (*Mrs.* Emilie J.) *v.* **STEWART** (*Rev.* Hart L.) The Stewart divorce case, tried at the supreme court of Chicago, January term, 1867. Full report of the trial. vii, 130 pp. 8°. *Chicago, P. L. Hanscom*, 1867.

STEWART (*Sir* James, *lord Ochiltrie*). Trial for calumnies and slanderous speeches against James [Hamilton, 3d] marquis of Hamilton, [and others], tending to the sowing of sedition between his majesty and the said noblemen, at Edinburgh, Nov. 1631. fol. *London, T. Wright*, 1778.
[HARGRAVE'S state trials, v. 7].

STEWART (James, *of Appin*). Trial for the murder of Colin Campbell, of Glenure, Inverary, Sept. 1752. fol. *London, T. Wright*, 1779.
[HARGRAVE'S state trials, v. 10].

STIRLING (James), *and others*. Trials for high treason, [Edinburgh], Nov. 1708. fol. *London, T. Wright*, 1777.
[HARGRAVE'S state trials, v. 5].

STORY (Joseph). Commentaries on the conflict of laws. 6th ed. carefully revised and considerably enlarged. xxxvi, 868 pp. 8°. *Boston, Little, Brown & Co.* 1865. (3 copies).

——— Commentaries on the constitution of the United States. 3d ed. 2 v. 8°. *Boston, Little, Brown & Co.* 1858. (6 copies).

——— Commentaries on equity pleadings, and the incidents thereto. 6th ed. carefully revised, with large additions, by Isaac F. Redfield, xxxiii, 802 pp. 8°. *Boston, Little, Brown & Co.* 1865. (2 copies).

——— Commentaries on equity jurisprudence, as administered in England and America. 9th ed. carefully revised, with extensive additions, by Isaac F. Redfield. 2 v. lxxxiv, 767 pp; 853 pp. 8°. *Boston, Little, Brown & Co.* 1866. (3 copies).

——— Commentaries on the law of agency, as a branch of commercial and maritime jurisprudence, with occasional illustrations from the civil and foreign law. 6th ed. revised, corrected, and enlarged, by Edmund H. Bennett. xxxv, 658 pp. 8°. *Boston, Little, Brown & Co.* 1863. (2 copies).

——— Commentaries on the law of bailments. 7th ed. revised and enlarged, by Edmund H. Bennett. xlviii, 623 pp. 8°. *Boston, Little, Brown & Co.* 1863. (2 copies).

——— Commentaries on the law of bills of exchange, foreign and inland, as administered in England and America. 4th ed. revised, corrected, and enlarged. xxx, 642 pp. 8°. *Boston, Little, Brown & Co.* 1860. (2 copies).

——— Commentaries on the law of partnership. 5th ed. xxix, 754 pp. 8°. *Boston, Little, Brown & Co.* 1859. (2 copies).

——— Commentaries on the law of promissory notes. 5th ed. xxxvi, 703 pp. 8°. *Boston, Little, Brown & Co.* 1859. (2 copies).

STORY (William W.) Treatise on the law of contracts. 4th ed. revised and greatly enlarged. 2 v. cxi, 782 pp; viii, 820 pp. 8°. *Boston, Little, Brown & Co.* 1856.

STRAFFORD (*Sir* Thomas Wentworth, 1*st earl of*). *See* **WENTWORTH**.

STRANG (Jesse). Trial of, for the murder of John Whipple, at a special court of oyer and terminer, holden in Albany, in July, 1827. 35 pp. 8°. *Albany, D. M'Glashan*, 1827.

STREATER (John). [His] case, on an habeas corpus, Westminster hall, Nov. 1653. fol. *London, T. Wright,* 1776.
[HARGRAVE'S state trials, v. 2].

STRICKLAND (Mary). *See* **BUTLER** *alias* **STRICKLAND** (Mary).

STRONG (Demas) *v.* **BENNETT** (G. C.) The Strong-Bennett libel suit. Senator Demas Strong *v.* G. C. Bennett, proprietor Brooklyn daily times. Supreme court, King's county, June term, 1866. Before Hon. J. F. Barnard. 151 pp. 8°. *Brooklyn,* 1866.

STROUD (William), *and others.* Proceedings against [them] on an habeas corpus, in banco regis, 1629. fol. *London, T. Wright,* 1778.
[HARGRAVE'S state trials, v. 7].

SUGDEN (Edward Burtenshaw, *baron St. Leonards*). A series of letters, to a man of property, on the sale, purchase, lease, settlement, and devise of estates. viii, 127 pp. 8°. *Philadelphia, Tarrand & Nicholas,* 1811. s.

SUGDEN (Henry). An essay on the law of wills, as altered by the i. Victoria, c. 26. xix, 252 pp. 8°. *London, S. Sweet,* 1837.

SULIVAN (Richard Joseph). Thoughts on martial law, with a mode for conducting the proceedings of general courts martial. 2d ed. viii, 104 pp. 12°. *London, T. Becket,* 1784.
[*With* ADYE (S. P.) Treatise on courts martial. 1797].

SURREY (Henry Howard, *earl of*). *See* **HOWARD.**

SWAN (John), *and* **JEFFERYS** (Elizabeth). Case, for the murder of Joseph Jefferys. Chelmsford, March, 1752. fol. *London, T. Wright,* 1779.
[HARGRAVE'S state trials, v. 10].

SWENDSEN (Haagen). Trial, at the queen's bench, for forceably taking away and marrying Mrs. Pleasant Rawlins, Nov. 1702. fol. *London, T. Wright,* 1777.
[HARGRAVE'S state trials, v. 5].

SWINBURNE (Henry). A treatise of spousals, or matrimonial contracts; wherein all the questions relating to that subject are resolved. 8 p. l. 240 pp. 4°. *London, R. Clavell,* 1686.

SYDNEY (Algernon). *See* **SIDNEY.**

SYNOPSIS of contemporary reports in equity and at common law. [4] pp. 8°. [*London,* 1867].

TALBOT (William, *bishop of Oxford*). Speech in the house of lords on the first article of impeachment of Dr. Henry Sacheverell. 7-11 pp. fol. *London, J. Morphew,* 1710.
[*With* SACHEVERELL (Henry). Tryal, 1710].

TALBOT (William). [His] case, on an information *ore tenus,* in the star chamber, for maintaining a power in the pope to depose and kill kings. fol. *London, T. Wright,* 1781.
[HARGRAVE'S state trials, v. 11].

TANKERVILLE (Ford Grey, 3*d baron Grey of Werke, earl of*). *See* **GREY.**

TASBOROUGH (John), *and* **PRICE** (Ann). Tryal and conviction for subornation of per jury, in endeavoring to perswade S. Dugdale to retract his evidence about the horrid popish plot, king's bench, Feb. 1680. 1 p. l. 59 pp. fol. *London, R. Pawlett,* 1680.
[TRIALS for treason, v. 3].

——— The same. fol. *London, T. Wright,* 1776.
[HARGRAVE'S state trials, v. 2].

TAYLER (John). Trial. *See* **JENKINS** (Elisha) *v.* **VAN RENSSELAER.**

TAYLER (Thomas). A law glossary of the Latin, Greek, Norman, French, and other languages, interspersed in the Commentaries by Sir W. Blackstone, and various law treatises upon each branch of the profession: translated into English. iv, 220 pp. 8°. *London, Clarke & sons,* 1819.

——— The same. 7th ed. revised and enlarged. 580 pp. 8°. *New York, J. S. Voorhies,* 1865. (2 copies).

TAYLOR (George). The law of appeals to the superior courts of law by appeal case: including appeals from justices, appeals from county courts, appeals from revising barristers, and similar appeals. xxviii, 270 pp. 12°. *London, Horace Cox,* 1865.

TENISON (Thomas, *archbishop of Canterbury*), *and others.* Address to queen Anne, respecting the expulsion of William Whiston from the university of Cambridge, for heresy, April, 1711. With the opinion of the judges thereon. fol. *London, T. Wright,* 1778.
[HARGRAVE'S state trials, v. 8].

TENNESSEE (*State of*). Laws, 1865-66, and 1866-67. 2 v. 8°. *Nashville,* 1866-67. (3 copies of 1866-67).

——— Tennessee reports. *See* **CALDWELL** (Thomas H).

TERRANOVA (Francis). Account of the trial and execution of F. Terranova, an American seaman, belonging to the ship Emily, inhumanly strangled upon a cross by the Chinese people, at Canton, Sunday, October 27th, 1821. 8 pp. 8°. [*n. p.* 1822].

TEXAS (*State of*). The constitution as amended, and ordinances of the convention of 1866, together with the proclamation of the governor declaring the ratification of the amendments to the constitution, and the general laws of the regular session of the eleventh legislature of the state of Texas, [1866]. 8°. *Austin*, 1866.

—— Digest of the laws of Texas; containing laws in force, and the repealed laws on which rights rest. Carefully annotated, by George W. Paschal. lxxiv, 1080 pp. 8°. *New York Banks & bros.* 1866. (2 copies).

—— General laws of the 8th legislature, 1859–60, and extra session, 1861; general laws of the 9th legislature, 1861–62, and extra session, 1863; general laws of the 10th legislature, 1863–64, and called session, with the provisional and permanent constitution of the confederate states, and of Texas, 1864; second extra session, 1864. 8°. *Austin*, 1860–65.

TEXAS reports. v. 26 and 27. By C. L. Robards and A. M. Jackson. 8°. *Austin, J. Walker*, 1867. (2 copies).

THEODOSIUS II. (*emperor*). Codices gregorianus, hermogenianus, theodosianus; et supplementum. Edidit Gustavus Haenel. 2 v. x, 1716; xxxviii, 480, 28 pp. 4°. *Bonnæ, A. Marcus*, 1842–44.

THIMUS (F. G. J.) Traité de droit public; ou, exposition méthodique des principes du droit public de la Belgique, etc. 3 v. 8°. *Liége, H. Dessain*, 1844–48.

THOMPSON (Isaac Grant). The law and practice of provisional remedies, with forms. viii, 712 pp. 8°. *Albany, Little, Gould & son*, 1867.

THOMPSON (Nathaniel), *and others*. Trial at the Guildhall of London, for writing, printing, and publishing letters importing that Sir Edmundbury Godfrey murdered himself, June, 1682. fol. *London, T. Wright*, 1776.
[HARGRAVE'S state trials, v. 3].

THOMPSON'S entries. *See* **LIBER** placitandi.

THOMSON (Henry Byerley). Institutes of the laws of Ceylon. 2 v. xxi, 647 pp; xx. 713, 71 pp. 8°. *London, Trübner & Co.* 1866.

THORIN (Ernest). Répertoire bibliographique des ouvrages de législation, de droit, et de jurisprudence en matière civile, administrative, commerciale et criminelle, publiés spécialement en France depuis 1789, jusqu'à la fin de novembre, 1865. Nouv. éd. corrigée et considérablement augmentée. 2 p. l. 324 pp. 8°. *Paris, Durand*, 1866.

66

THORPE (William). Trial and examination for heresye, before Thomas Arundel, archbishop of Canterbury, July, 1407. Written by himself. fol. *London, T. Wright*, 1776.
[HARGRAVE'S state trials, v. 1].

THROCKMORTON (*Sir* Nicholas). Trial in the Guildhall of London, for high treason, April, 1554. With the proceedings against his jury. fol. *London, T. Wright*, 1776.
[HARGRAVE'S state trials, v. 1].

THWING (Thomas), *and* **PRESSICKS** (Mary). Trial at York for high treason, July, 1680. fol. *London, T. Wright*, 1776.
[HARGRAVE'S state trials, v. 3].

TILLARD (Léon). Des actes dissolutifs de communauté, ou des actes de partage et de licitation, et de leurs variétés. 240 pp. 8°. *Paris, Durand*, 1851. s.

TONGE (Thomas), *and others*. Trial at the Old Baily for high treason, Dec. 1662. fol. *London, T. Wright*, 1776.
[HARGRAVE'S state trials, v. 2].

TOOKE (John Horne). Proceedings against him on an information in the king's bench for a libel, Nov. 1777, fol. *London, T. Wright*, 1781.
[HARGRAVE'S state trials, v. 11].

—— Trial, for high treason, Old Bailey, Nov. 1794. Taken in short-hand by J. Gurney. 2 v. 464 pp; 437 pp. 6 l. 8°. *London, M. Gurney*, 1795.

TOUCHET (Mervin, *baron Audley, earl of Castlehaven*). Trial, for a rape and sodomy, April, 1651. fol. *London, T. Wright*, 1776.
[HARGRAVE'S state trials, v. 1].

TOWNLEY (Francis). Trial, for high treason, Southwark, July, 1746. fol. *London, T. Wright*, 1778.
[HARGRAVE'S state trials, v. 9].

TRANTER (Robert). Trial for murder. *See* **REASON** (Hugh), *and* **TRANTER**.

TREATISE (A) concerning adultery and divorce.
[*In* SELECT and curious cases of polygamy, etc. pp. 177–211. 12°. *London*, 1736].

TRÉBUTIEN (E.) Cours élémentaire de droit criminel, comprenant l'exposé et le commentaire des deux premiers livres du code pénal, du code d'instruction criminelle en entier, et des lois et décrets qui sont venus modifier ces codes, jusques et y compris les lois qui viennent d'etre adoptés par le corps législatif dans la session de 1853, notamment les lois de 4 juin, 1853, sur la composition du juri, du 9 juin sur la majorité exigée pour la déclaration du juri, du 10 juin, sur les pourvois en matière criminelle, du 10 juin, sur les attentats contre la famille impériale. 2 v. vi, 472 pp; 704 pp. 8°. *Paris, A. Durand*, 1854.

TRIAL by jury, the birthright of the people of England. [*anon.*] 8°. *London, R. Hardwicke*, 1865.

TRIMNELL (Charles, *bishop of Norwich*). Speech in the house of lords, at the opening of the second article of the impeachment against Dr. Sacheverell. pp. 10–12. fol. *London, J. Morphew*, 1710.

[*With* SACHEVERELL (Henry). Tryal, 1710].

TROUBAT (F. J. *and* **HALEY** (W. W.) Practice in civil actions, and proceedings in the supreme court of Pennsylvania, in the district court, and court of common pleas for the city and county of Philadelphia, and in the courts of the United States. 4th ed. enlarged and rewritten, by A. J. Fish. v. 1, parts i and ii. cx, 1238 pp. 8°. *Philadelphia, Kay and brother*, 1867.

TROWER (Charles Francis). The law of the building of churches, parsonages, and schools; and of the divisions of parishes and places. xvi, 231 pp. 12°. *London, Butterworths*, 1867.

TURNER (Anne). Trial, at the king's bench, for the murder of Sir Thomas Overbury, Nov. 1615. fol. *London, T. Wright*, 1776.

[HARGRAVE'S state trials, v. 1].

TURNER (James), *and others*. Trial, at the Old Bailey, for felony and burglary, Jan. 1663. fol. *London, T. Wright*, 1776.

[HARGRAVE'S state trials, v. 2].

——— Speech and deportment at his execution, Jan. 1662. fol. *London, T. Wright*, 1778.

[HARGRAVE'S state trials, v. 8].

TUTCHIN (John). Trial at the Guildhall of of London, for a libel, entitled, "The observator," Nov. 1704. fol. *London, T. Wright*, 1777.

[HARGRAVE'S state trials, v. 5].

TWYN (John). Trial, for high treason, Old Bailey, Feb. 1664. fol. *London, T. Wright*, 1776.

[HARGRAVE'S state trials, v. 2].

UDALL (*Rev.* John). Trial, at Croydon, for felony, July, 1590. [Wrote by himself]. fol. *London, T. Wright*, 1776.

[HARGRAVE'S state trials, v. 1].

UNDERDOWN (E. M.) The law of art copyright. The engraving, sculpture, and designs acts, the international copyright act, and the art copyright act, 1862. With an introduction and notes. 211 pp. 12°. *London, John Crockford*, 1863.

UNITED STATES of America. The bankrupt law of the United States, 1841. With English and American decisions and notes. 21 pp. 8°. *Rochester, (N. Y.) Benton & Andrews*, 1867.

——— The United States bankrupt law, entitled, "An act to establish a uniform system of bankruptcy throughout the United States," passed at the 2d session of the 39th congress, March, 1867. With the household and homestead exemption laws of the several states. By Clinton Rice. 40 pp. 8°. *New York, Russell*, 1867. (2 copies).

——— The same. The bankrupt law, being "An act to establish a uniform system of bankruptcy throughout the United States," passed March 4, 1867. By Henry J. Labatt and Alex. Walker. 54 pp. 8°. *New Orleans, L. Graham*, 1867.

——— Laws. 1st to 30th congress, March 4, 1789, to March 3, 1849. 29 v. 8°. *Philadelphia and Washington*, 1849.

——— Laws and regulations for the government of the post office department. viii, 114, 93, 28 pp. 8°. *Washington, C. Alexander*, 1852.

——— Laws relating to the direct and excise taxes, passed during the 1st and 2d sessions of the 37th congress. 115 pp. 8°. *Washington, Government printing office*, 1862.

——— Laws, treaties, and other documents, having operation and respect to the public lands. xxvii, 356 pp. 8°. *Washington, R. C. Weightman*, 1811.

[Imperfect: pp. 25–28, 31–42, 55–60, and pp. 5–87 of appendix wanting. pp. 131–34, 241–2 imperfect].

——— The same. xxvii, 455 pp. 8°. *Washington, J. Gales*, [1811].

[Imperfect title-page].

——— The same. 439 pp.

[Imperfect: pp. i–xxvii; 5–28 wanting. pp. 241–2 imperfect].

——— United States digest. v. 17. Annual digest for 1863. By H. Farnham Smith. 8°. *Boston, Little, Brown & Co.* 1867. (3 copies).

VANDERMUELEN (Willem). Costumen, usantien, policien ende styl van procederen der stadt, jurisdicte ende vryheid van Utrecht. 6 p. l. 456 pp. 3 l. 2 pl. fol. *Utrecht, W. Broedelet*, 1709.

VANDERPOOL (George). Trial. *See* **FRASER** *and* **VANDERPOOL.**

VANE (*Sir* Henry). The tryal of Sir Henry Vane at the king's bench, Westminster, June the 2d and 6th, 1662. 134 pp. 1 l. sm. 4°. [*n. p.*] 1662.

[Imperfect: p. l. 3–4 wanting].

——— The same. Trial, at the king's bench, for high treason, June, 1662. Wrote by himself. fol. *London, T. Wright*, 1776.

[HARGRAVE'S state trials, v. 2].

VAN PATTON (John F.) The trial and life and confessions of, who was tried and convicted of the murder of Mrs. Maria Schermerhorn, and sentenced to be executed on the 25th February, 1825. 16 pp. 8°. *New York*, 1825.

VAN RENSSELEAR (Solomon) *v.* **JENKINS** *and v.* **COOPER.** *See* **JENKINS** (Elisha).

VAUGHAN (Thomas). Trial, at the Old Baily, for high treason on the high seas, Nov. 1696. fol. *London, T. Wright*, 1777.
[HARGRAVE'S state trials, v. 5].

VERE (Robert de, *duke of Ireland, 9th earl of Oxford*). Trial for treason, 1388. *See* **NEVILL** (Alexander, *archbishop of York*), *and others*.

VERMONT (*State of*). Laws, 1866. 8°. *Montpelier*, 1866.

——— Vermont reports. v. 38–39. By W. G. Veazey. 8°. *Rutland, Tuttle & Co.* 1867. (2 copies).

VESEY (Denmark). Trial. *See* **OFFICIAL** (An) report, etc.

VICTORIA, (*Australia.*) Acts of parliament of Victoria. 22–25 Victoria, 1859–61. 2 v. in 1. 7 p. l. 251 pp; 128 pp. fol. *Melbourne, Govt. printer*, 1860–61.

VIRGINIA (*Colony of*). Acts of assembly, 1662 [to 1715]. xxiv, 391 pp. fol. *London, J. Baskett*, 1728.

——— Abridgment of the public laws of Virginia, in force and use, June 10, 1720. By William Beverly. 2d ed. [*anon.*] 12°. *London, J. Clarke*, 1728.

——— (*State of*). Code of Virginia. 2d ed. including legislation to the year 1860. 8°. *Richmond, Ritchie, Dunnavant & Co.* 1860.

——— Laws of the state of Virginia, 1865–66, and 1866–67. 2 v. 8°. *Richmond*, 1866–67.

VITRIARIUS (Philipp Reinhard). Vitriarius illustratus, seu institutiones juris publici romano-germanici. Revisæ et auctæ a J. F. Pfeffingero. Ed. 3ª. 4 v. 4°. *Gothæ*, 1774.

VOIGT (Moritz). Die lex maenia de dote vom jahre dlxviii der stadt. 2 p. l. 84 pp. 4°. *Weimar, Landes industrie-comptoir*, 1866. s.

VOLTAIRE (François Marie Arouët de). Histoire d'Elizabeth Canning, et de Jean Calas. Mémoire de Donat Calas pour son père, sa mère, et son frère. Declaration de Pierre Calas. Avec les pièces originales, concernant la mort des Srs. Calas, et le jugement rendu à Toulouse. 59 pp. 8°. *Londres, J. Nourse*, 1762.

VOYSIN DE GARTEMPE (A.) Tables chronologique et alphabétique des lois et ordonnances d'un intéret public et général. Depuis 1789 jusqu'en 1860. 3ᵉ éd. 248 pp. 12°. *Guéret, Dugenest*, 1860.

VROOM (Peter D.) Reports of cases in the supreme court, and the court of errors and appeals of the state of New Jersey. v. 1–2. 608 pp. 8°. *Trenton, Hough & Yard, and Hough & Gillespy*, 1866–67. (2 copies of v. 1.)

WADDINGTON (J.) *See* **RUTGERS.**

WAIT (William). The law and practice in civil actions and proceedings in justices' courts and of appeals to the county courts in the state of New York. 2d ed. 2 v. lxxix, 1186 pp; xliii, 1253 pp. 8°. *Albany, Weed, Parsons & Co.* 1867.

WAKE (William, *archbishop of Canterbury*). Speech in the house of lords, at the opening of the second article of the impeachment against Dr. Sacheverell. 9 pp. fol. *London, J. Morphew*, 1710.
[*With* SACHEVERELL (Henry). Tryal, 1710].

WAKEMAN (*Sir* George, *M. D.*) *and others*. Tryals for high treason, for conspiring the death of the king, subversion of the government, and protestant religion, Old Baily, July, 1679. 1 p. l. 84 pp. fol. *London, H. Hills*, 1679.
[TRIALS for treason, v. 1].

——— The same.
[TRIALS for treason, v. 2].

——— The same. fol. *London, T. Wright*, 1776.
[HARGRAVE'S state trials, v. 2].

WALCOT (Thomas), *and others*. Tryals of Thomas Walcot, William Hone, William lord Russell, John Rous, and William Blagg, for high treason; at the Old Baily, July 12–14, 1683. 81, 14 pp. fol. *London, R. Royston & Co.* 1683.

——— The same. Tryals for high treason, for conspiring the death of the king, and raising a rebellion, Old Baily, July, 1683. 1 p. l. 81 pp. fol. *London, R. Royston*, 1683.
[TRIALS for treason, v. 6].

——— The same. fol. *London, T. Wright*, 1776.
[HARGRAVE'S state trials, v. 3].

WALLACE (John William). Cases argued and adjudged in the supreme court of the United States, December term, 1863–65. v. 1–3. 8°. *Washington, W. H. & O. H. Morrison*, 1866–68.

——— The same. December term, 1865 and 1866. v. 3, 4, and 5. 8°. *Washington, (D.C.) W. H. & O. H. Morrison*, 1866–67. (22 copies of v. 4; 20 copies of v. 5).

WALTERS (Rowland), *and others*. Trial, [for murdering Sir Charles Pymm], at the Old Bailey, June 1, 1688. fol. *London, T. Wright*, 1778.

[HARGRAVE'S state trials, v. 7].

WARD (*Sir* Patience). Trial, at the king's bench, for perjury, May, 1683. fol. *London, T. Wright*, 1776.

[HARGRAVE'S state trials, v. 3].

WARREN (Samuel). The moral, social, and professional duties of attorneys and solicitors. xii, 448 pp. 12°. *London, Blackwood & sons*, 1848.

WARWICK (Edward Rich, 3*d earl of Holland*, 6*th earl of*). *See* **RICH.**

WASHBURN (Emory). A treatise on the American law of easements and servitudes. 2d ed. xxxv, 744 pp. 8°. *Boston, Little, Brown & Co.* 1867.

WASHBURN (Peter T.) Laws of the United States, now in force, relating to copy-rights, with notes, etc. 4°. *Claremont, (N. H.)* [*n. d.*]

[*With* BLAKE (Alex. V.) American bookseller's trade list, etc. pp. 227-232].

WATSON (Richard, *bishop of Llandaff*). Proceedings of the house of lords in the case of B. Flower for libel. *See* **FLOWER** (Benj.)

WATTEVILLE de Grabe (Adolphe, *baron* de). Législation charitable; ou, recueil des lois, arrêtés, décrets, ordonnances royales, avis du conseil d'état, [etc.] qui régissent les établissements de bienfaisance, mise en ordre et annotée, avec une préface. xv, 711 pp. 8°. *Paris, A. Heois*, 1843. s.

WEDDERBURN (*Sir* John). Trial, at Southwark, Nov. 1746, for high treason. fol. *London, T. Wright*, 1778.

[HARGRAVE'S state trials, v. 9].

WEDGWOOD (William B.) *and* **HOMANS** (J. Smith). A manual for notaries public and bankers, including a summary of the law and principles of commercial paper. viii, 779 pp. 8°. *New York, Bankers' magazine office*, 1867.

WEIR (*Major* Thomas). Trial of. *See* **MITCHEL** (James).

WELLS (John C.) Every man his own lawyer and business form book. A complete guide in all matters of law and business regulations, for every state in the Union. 650 pp. 8°. *New York, B. W. Hitchcock*, 1867.

——— The same. Jedermann sein eigener anwalt und formularbuch. 449 pp. 8°. *New York, B. W. Hitchcock*, 1867.

WENTWORTH (*Sir* Thomas, 1*st earl of Strafford*). Trial, for high treason, March, 1640. fol. *London, T. Wright*, 1776.

[HARGRAVE'S state trials, v. 1].

WESTON (Richard). Trial, at the Guild Hall of London, for the murder of Sir Thomas Overbury, Oct. 1615. fol. *London, T. Wright*, 1776.

[HARGRAVE'S state trials, v. 1].

WEST VIRGINIA (*State of*). Ordinances and acts of the restored government of Virginia, prior to the formation of the state of West Virginia; with the constitution and laws of the state of West Virginia, to March 2d. 1866. 8°. *Wheeling, J. Frew*, 1866. (3 copies).

——— Laws, 1867. 8°. *Wheeling*, 1867.

——— [West Virginia reports]. Reports of cases in the supreme court of appeals of West Virginia. To which is prefixed, a brief sketch of the erection and formation of the state of West Virginia from the territory of Virginia. By John Marshall Hagans. From August, 1863, to January, 1866. v. 1. 8°. *Morgantown, Morgan & Hoffman*, 1866. (2 copies).

WHARTON (John). Trial for printing seditious books. *See* **LILBURN** (John), *and* **WHARTON.**

WHEATON (Henry). Elements of international law. 8th ed. Edited, with notes, by Richard Henry Dana, jr. 8°. *Boston, Little, Brown & Co.* 1866. (3 copies).

——— Report of the coyyright case of Wheaton *v.* Peters. Decided in the supreme court of the United States. 176 pp. 8°. *New York, J. Van Norden*, 1834.

WHITE *alias* **WHITEBREAD** (Thomas), *and others*. The speeches of the five jesuits executed at Tyburn, June 20th, 1679. 4 pp. fol. [*London*, 1679].

[Title-page wanting. TRIALS for treason, v. 1].

——— The same. [With observations]. 8 pp. fol. [*London*, 1679].

[Title-page wanting. TRIALS for treason, v. 1].

——— The same. With animadversions thereupon. [By D. Clarkson]. 1 p. l. 8, 24 pp. fol. *London, H. Hills*, 1679.

[TRIALS for treason, v. 1].

——— The same.

[TRIALS for treason, v. 3].

——— Tryals and condemnation, for high treason, in conspiring the death of the king, the subversion of the government, and the protestant religion, Old Bailey, June, 1679. 1 p. l. 95 pp. fol. *London, H. Hills*, 1679.

[TRIALS for treason, v. 1].

WHITE *alias* **WHITEBREAD** (Thomas), *and others.* The same. Tryals and condemnation, etc.
[TRIALS for treason, v. 2].

——— The same.
[TRIALS for treason, v. 3].

——— The same. fol. *London, T. Wright,* 1776.
[HARGRAVE'S state trials, v. 2].

WHITE (William, *mayor of Aylesbury, England*). Proceedings in the house of commons, house of peers, and the king's bench, in the case of Ashby and White, 1703–04. Whether an action lies at common law for an elector, who is denied his vote for members of parliament? fol. *London, T. Wright,* 1778.
[HARGRAVE'S state trials, v. 8].

WHITELOCKE (*Sir* Bulstrode). Speech in the house of commons upon the question, whether James Naylor should be punished with death? 1656. fol. *London, T. Wright,* 1776.
[HARGRAVE'S state trials, v. 2].

WHITELOCKE (James). Proceedings against him, in the star-chamber, June, 1613, for a contempt of the king's prerogative. fol. *London, T. Wright,* 1781.
[HARGRAVE'S state trials, v. 11].

WHITING (William). War powers under the constitution of the United States. 10th ed. xvii, 342 pp. 8°. *Boston, Little, Brown & Co.* 1864.

WHITTAKER (Henry). Analysis of recent decisions on practice and pleading, 1863–67; supplementary to Whittaker's practice, 3d ed. and to the annotated codes. 8°. *New York, Diosey and Cockcroft,* 1867.

WIAT. *See* **WYATT.**

WILKES (John). His case, on an habeas corpus, court of common pleas, 1763. fol. *London, T. Wright,* 1781.
[HARGRAVE'S state trials, v. 11].

——— Proceedings in his case, on two informations for libels, king's bench, 1764–1770. fol. *London, T. Wright,* 1781.
[HARGRAVE'S state trials, v. 11].

WILLIAMS (*Sir* Edward Vaughan). A treatise on the law of executors and administrators. 6th ed. 2 v. cxxiii, 853 pp; 855 pp. 8°. *London, Stevens & sons,* 1867.

WILLIAMS (Joshua). Principles of the law of personal property. American editors, Benjamin Gerhard and Samuel Wetherill. 3d Am. from the 5th Lond. ed. With notes and references by Samuel Wetherill. ciii, 570 pp. 8°. *Philadelphia, T. and J. W. Johnson & Co.* 1866.

——— Principles of the law of real property. 3d Am. from the 7th Eng. ed. by William Henry Rawle, and additional notes and references by James T. Mitchell. xxiv, 469 pp. 8°. *Philadelphia, T. and J. W. Johnson & Co.* 1866.

WILLIAMS (Thomas Walter). A compendious and comprehensive law dictionary; elucidating the terms and general principles of law and equity. 498 l. 8°. *London, Gale and Fenner,* 1816.

WILLIS (Francis). Trial, for high treason, in levying open war against her majesty, under pretence of pulling down meeting-houses, 1710. fol. *London, T. Wright,* 1778.
[HARGRAVE'S state trials, v. 8].

WILLS (William). An essay on the principles of circumstantial evidence. Illustrated by numerous cases. 4th ed. Edited by his son. xv, 324 pp. 8°. *London, Butterworths,* 1862.

WILSON (*Sir* Robert Thomas), **HUTCHINSON** (*Capt.* John Hely), *and* **BRUCE** (Michael). Trial of, before the court of assizes, at Paris. 112 pp. 8°. *Paris, Mouzou,* 1816.

WINTER (Robert), *and others.* Trials at Westminster for high treason, being conspirators in the gunpowder-plot, Jan. 1605. fol. *London, T. Wright,* 1776.
[HARGRAVE'S state trials, v. 1].

WINTOUN (George Seton, *5th earl of*). *See* **SETON.**

WISCONSIN reports. v. 18–20. By O. M. Conover. 8°. *Madison,* 1866. (2 copies of v. 19 and 20.)

WODON (Léon). Traité théorique et pratique de la possession et des actions possessoires. 2 v, 432 pp; 439 pp. 8°. *Bruxelles, Bruylant, Christophe et Cie.* 1866.

WOLSELEY (*Sir* Charles). The case of divorce, and re-marriage thereupon, discussed. Occasioned by the late act of parliament for the divorce of the lord Roos.
[*In* SELECT and curious cases of polygamy, etc. pp. 107–176. 12°. *London,* 1736].

WOODBURNE (John), *and* **COKE** (Arundel). Trial at Suffolk, for felony, in wilfully slitting the nose of Edward Crispe, March, 1721. fol. *London, T. Wright,* 1777.
[HARGRAVE'S state trials, v. 6].

WOODFALL (William). Law of landlord and tenant; with a full collection of precedents and forms of procedure. 9th ed. By W. R. Cole. lxviii, 1148 pp. 8°. *London, Henry Sweet,* 1867.

WOOLRYCH (Humphry W.) Remarks on the rank of queen's sergeant. 16 pp. 12°. *London, Stevens & sons,* 1866.

WORCESTER (William Lloyd, *bishop of*). *See* **LLOYD.**

WORKMAN (James), *and* **KERR** (Lewis). The trials of, before the United States court for the Orleans district on a charge of high misdemeanor, in planning and setting on foot within the United States an expedition for the conquest and emancipation of Mexico. 180 pp. 8°. *New Orleans, Bradford & Anderson,* 1807.

WRAYNHAM (——). Proceedings against him in the star chamber for slandering the lord chancellor [Francis] Bacon, of injustice, 1618. fol. *London, T. Wright,* 1776.
[HARGRAVE'S state trials, v. 7].

WRIGHT (Richard). Trial for carrying a challenge. *See* **PRIEST** (William). The case of duels.

WRIOTHESLEY (Henry, 3*d earl of Southampton*). Trial for treason. *See* **DEVEREUX** (Robert, 2*d earl of Essex*).

WYATT *or* **WIAT** (*Sir* Thomas). Arraignement [for high treason], Westminster, March, 1554. fol. *London, T. Wright,* 1778.
[HARGRAVE'S state trials, v. 8].

YEAR books of the reign of king Edward the first; years xx–xxxiii. Edited and translated by Alfred J. Harwood. v. 1–3. 8°. *London, Longmans,* 1863–66.

YORK (Alexander Nevill, *archbishop of*). *See* **NEVILL.**

YORK (Frederick, *duke of*). A circumstantial report of the evidence and proceedings upon the charges preferred against the duke of York, in the capacity of commander-in-chief, in February, 1809. By G. L. Wardle. 700 pp. 8°. *London, Albion press,* 1809.

YORK (Alexander Nevill, *archbishop of*). *See* **NEVILL.**

YOUNG lawyer's recreation; being a choice collection of several pleasant cases, passages, and customs in the law. [*anon.*] 7 p. l. 206 pp. 12°. *London, S. Briscoe,* 1694.

ZACHARIAE von LINGENTHAL (Carl Salomon). Cours de droit français. *See* **AUBRY** (C. M. B. A.) *and* **RAU** (C. H.)

ZENGER (John Peter). Trial for printing and publishing a libel against the government, at New York, Aug. 1735. fol. *London, T. Wright,* 1778.
[HARGRAVE'S state trials, v. 9].

www.ingramcontent.com/pod-product-compliance
Lightning Source LLC
LaVergne TN
LVHW021304110826
845150LV00003B/470

* 9 7 8 1 4 2 5 5 6 0 8 5 0 *